Get connected to the power of the Internet

McDougal Littell's online resources for teachers provide time-saving planning, instruction, and assessment support.

classzone.com

- Links correlated to the text
- Web Research Guide
- Self-scoring quizzes
- Interactive games and activities
- Links to current events
- Test practice
- Teacher Center

You have immediate access to *ClassZone's* teacher resources.

MCD3P9T4LV47R

Use this code to create your own username and password.

easyPlanner Plus ONLINE

- Customizable lesson plans
- Trackable state standards correlated to each lesson

Visit classzone.com for purchasing information and free demos

eEdition Plus ONLINE

- Online version of the text
- Interactive features to explore world history

eTest Plus ONLINE

- Customizable assessment tool
- Automatically grades tests
- Generates reports correlated to national and state standards

Now it all clicks!™

CLASSZONE.COM

 McDougal Littell

McDougal Littell

World History

Ancient Civilizations

Senior Consultants

Douglas Carnine
Professor of Education
University of Oregon

Carlos E. Cortés
Professor Emeritus of History
University of California,
Riverside

Kenneth R. Curtis
Professor of History and
Liberal Studies
California State University,
Long Beach

Anita T. Robinson
Los Angeles Unified
School District

Reading Consultant

MaryEllen Vogt
California State University,
Long Beach

English Learners Consultants

Mary Lou McCloskey
2002–2003 President
of TESOL

Lydia Stack
San Francisco Unified
School District

Content Consultants

Beverly Bossler
University of California
Davis, California

Philip Cunningham
Boston College
Chestnut Hill, Massachusetts

Susan L. Douglass
Council on Islamic Education
Fountain Valley, California

Joël DuBois
California State University
Sacramento, California

Vincent Farenga
University of Southern
California
Los Angeles, California

Claudio Fogu
University of Southern
California
Los Angeles, California

Charles L. Geshekter
California State University
Chico, California

Charles Hallisey
University of Wisconsin
Madison, Wisconsin

Dakota L. Hamilton
Humboldt State University
Arcata, California

Charles C. Haynes
First Amendment Center
Arlington, Virginia

Geoffrey Koziol
University of California
Berkeley, California

John Wolte Infong Lee
University of California
Santa Barbara, California

Maritere Lopez
California State University
Fresno, California

Shabbir Mansuri
Council on Islamic Education
Fountain Valley, California

Jacob Meskin
Hebrew College
Newton, Massachusetts

Robert Patch
University of California
Riverside, California

David D. Phillips
University of California
Los Angeles, California

Swami Tyagananda
Hindu Chaplain
Harvard University
Cambridge, Massachusetts

Kenneth Baxter Wolf
Pomona College
Claremont, California

R. Bin Wong
University of California
Los Angeles, California

Teacher Consultants

Yusuff Allahyah
Berendo Middle School
Los Angeles, California

Laura Carroll
Castillero Middle School
San Jose, California

Neal Cates
Hoover Middle School
Lakewood, California

Jeff Davis
Tioga Middle School
Fresno, California

Michele de Masi
Sinaloa Middle School
Simi Valley, California

Merrell Frankel
Berendo Middle School
Los Angeles, California

Dan Green
Goleta Valley Junior
High School
Goleta, California

Kim Maruyama
Castillero Middle School
San Jose, California

Lisa Meyers
La Paz Intermediate School
Mission Viejo, California

Randal Mitchell
Chaboya Middle School
San Jose, California

Rebecca O'Connor
Castillero Middle School
San Jose, California

Betty Parsons
Dartmouth Middle School
San Jose, California

Sally Reimers
Sinaloa Middle School
Simi Valley, California

Brenda Riddlesprigger
Kastner Intermediate School
Fresno, California

Teresa Sadler
Shirakawa School
San Jose, California

Joseph Staub
Thomas Starr King
Middle School
Los Angeles, California

Susan Tracy
Black Mountain
Middle School
San Diego, California

Chris Watson
Foothills Farms Junior High
Sacramento, California

Rhonda Weltz
Bret Harte Middle School
San Jose, California

History-Social Science Content Standards for California Public Schools reproduced by permission, California Department of Education, CDE Press, 1430 N Street, Suite 3207, Sacramento, CA 95814.

Maps on pages A2–A33 © Rand McNally & Company. All rights reserved.

Acknowledgments begin on page R110.

ISBN 0-618-53127-0

Printed in the United States of America
1 2 3 4 5 6 7 8 9-DWO-08 07 06 05

World History
Ancient Civilizations

McDougal Littell
The California Standard

Contents

Starting with a Story

THE DEATH OF RAMSES II

CALIFORNIA STANDARDS
Reading 1.1 Read aloud narrative and expository text fluently and accurately and with appropriate pacing, intonation, and expression.

Background: Egypt was one of the longest-lasting world empires. For almost 3,000 years, kings called pharaohs ruled the land. One of the most dazzling of all was Ramses II (RAM•SEEZ), who reigned from about 1279 to 1213 B.C. At a time when few Egyptians lived beyond the age of 40, Ramses II was in charge for 66 years!

Now he has finally died, and Egypt prepares for his funeral. Imagine you are there as the leader of Egypt's golden age is laid to rest.

Statue of Ramses II ▶

You are a profe
funerals. In th
but never a ph
spent hours preparing

No one remembe
your grandparents w
forever. Now he's dea
The ceremony began
foot statues of Rams
priests preserved the

Next, a royal barg
the pharaoh's mumm
Hundreds of importa

It's time to begin
behind a group of sla
There is his sword! C
fought Egypt's enemy

Tearing your hair
"Great lord of our em
reach for the sun! Do

Sometimes you fa
word. Trembling with

What do you
will be like?

R

1. **READIN**
benefit m
and expre

2. **WRITIN**
Ramses'
Write a b
fears for

CALIFORNIA ST
Write narrat

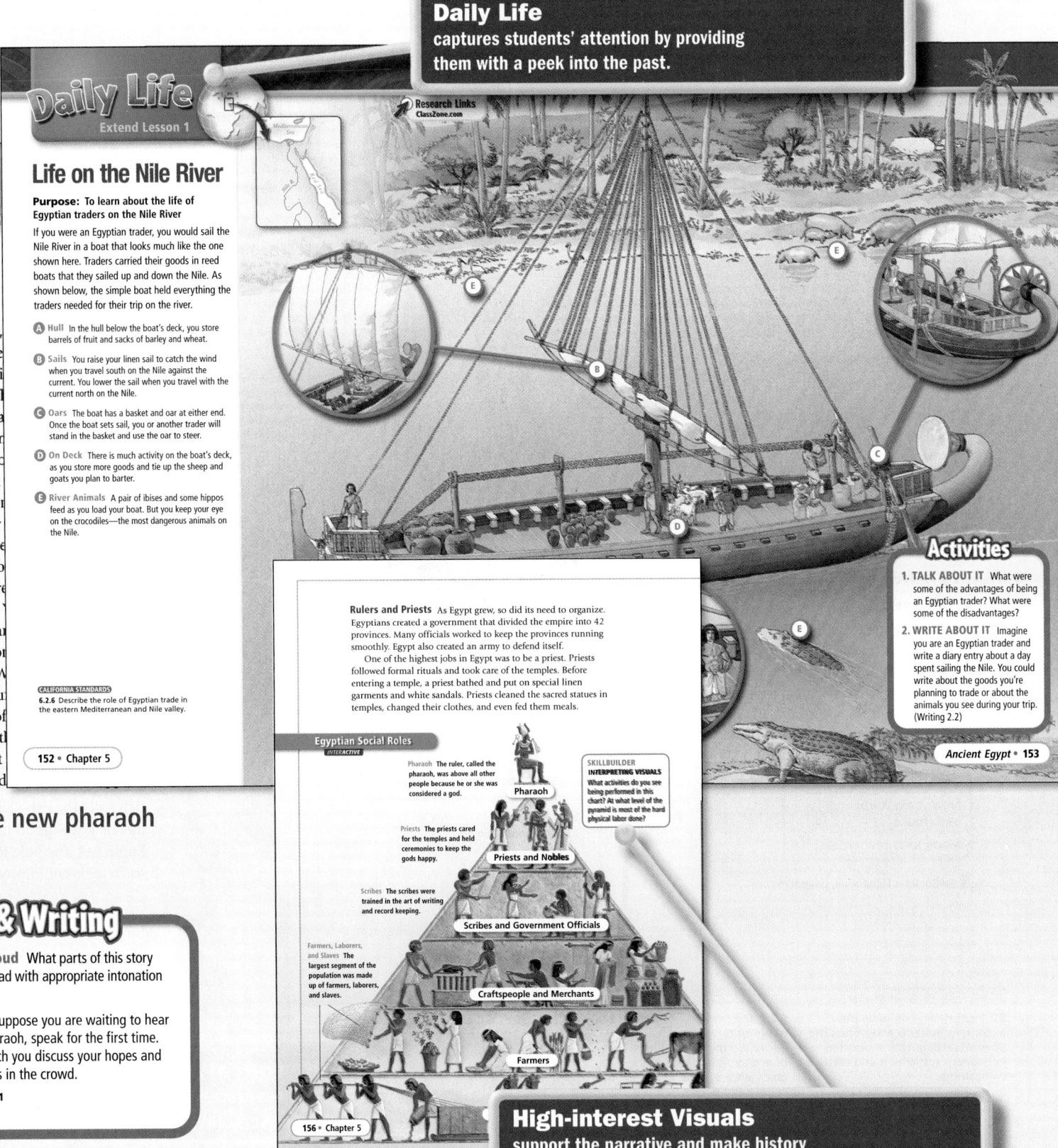

Daily Life
captures students' attention by providing them with a peek into the past.

Daily Life
Extend Lesson 1

Research Links ClassZone.com

Life on the Nile River

Purpose: To learn about the life of Egyptian traders on the Nile River

If you were an Egyptian trader, you would sail the Nile River in a boat that looks much like the one shown here. Traders carried their goods in reed boats that they sailed up and down the Nile. As shown below, the simple boat held everything the traders needed for their trip on the river.

A Hull In the hull below the boat's deck, you store barrels of fruit and sacks of barley and wheat.

B Sails You raise your linen sail to catch the wind when you travel south on the Nile against the current. You lower the sail when you travel with the current north on the Nile.

C Oars The boat has a basket and oar at either end. Once the boat sets sail, you or another trader will stand in the basket and use the oar to steer.

D On Deck There is much activity on the boat's deck, as you store more goods and tie up the sheep and goats you plan to barter.

E River Animals A pair of ibises and some hippos feed as you load your boat. But you keep your eye on the crocodiles—the most dangerous animals on the Nile.

CALIFORNIA STANDARDS
6.2.6 Describe the role of Egyptian trade in the eastern Mediterranean and Nile valley.

152 • Chapter 5

Activities

1. **TALK ABOUT IT** What were some of the advantages of being an Egyptian trader? What were some of the disadvantages?

2. **WRITE ABOUT IT** Imagine you are an Egyptian trader and write a diary entry about a day spent sailing the Nile. You could write about the goods you're planning to trade or about the animals you see during your trip. (Writing 2.2)

Ancient Egypt • 153

Rulers and Priests As Egypt grew, so did its need to organize. Egyptians created a government that divided the empire into 42 provinces. Many officials worked to keep the provinces running smoothly. Egypt also created an army to defend itself.

One of the highest jobs in Egypt was to be a priest. Priests followed formal rituals and took care of the temples. Before entering a temple, a priest bathed and put on special linen garments and white sandals. Priests cleaned the sacred statues in temples, changed their clothes, and even fed them meals.

Egyptian Social Roles
INTERACTIVE

Pharaoh The ruler, called the pharaoh, was above all other people because he or she was considered a god.
Pharaoh

**SKILLBUILDER
INTERPRETING VISUALS**
What activities do you see being performed in this chart? At what level of the pyramid is most of the hard physical labor done?

Priests The priests cared for the temples and held ceremonies to keep the gods happy.
Priests and Nobles

Scribes The scribes were trained in the art of writing and record keeping.
Scribes and Government Officials

Farmers, Laborers, and Slaves The largest segment of the population was made up of farmers, laborers, and slaves.
Craftspeople and Merchants

Farmers

156 • Chapter 5

High-interest Visuals
support the narrative and make history accessible to all students.

...he new pharaoh

...g & Writing

...Aloud What parts of this story ...g read with appropriate intonation

... Suppose you are waiting to hear ...pharaoh, speak for the first time. ...which you discuss your hopes and ...hers in the crowd.

...g 2.1

145

CA5

Research-Based Instruction

Lesson 1

MAIN IDEAS

1. **Geography** The Nile River helped Egypt develop a civilization.

2. **Economics** The fertile land provided everything Egyptians needed.

3. **Economics** The Nile and other resources influenced Egypt's economy.

TAKING NOTES

Reading Skill:
Understanding Cause and Effect

Following causes and effects will help you understand the main ideas in this lesson. In Lesson 1, look for the effects of each event listed in the chart. Record them on a chart of your own.

Causes	Effects
Floods	
New agricultural techniques	
Many land resources	

 Skillbuilder Handbook, page R26

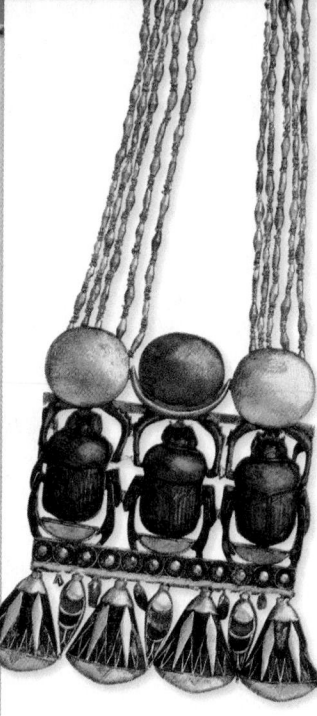

▲ **Lotus Pendants** This necklace once belonged to an Egyptian king. The pendants at the bottom are lotus buds. The lotus, a water lily that grows in the Nile River, is a symbol of Egypt.

Gift o

Build on What You K
that was very importan
The Nile River was so i
ago, an ancient Greek l
the Nile."

Geography of A

1 **ESSENTIAL QUESTION** \

The Greek historian kn
Nile River fed Egyptian

The Longest River T
world's longest river. It
flows north to the Med
with cataracts. A **catara**
the sea the Nile branch
a river's mouth where t
In the delta, the Nile di
The river is called th
lower Nile in the north.
caused the Nile to flood
rich soil along the Nile's
means it was good for g
Euphrates, the Nile Rive
so farmers could predict

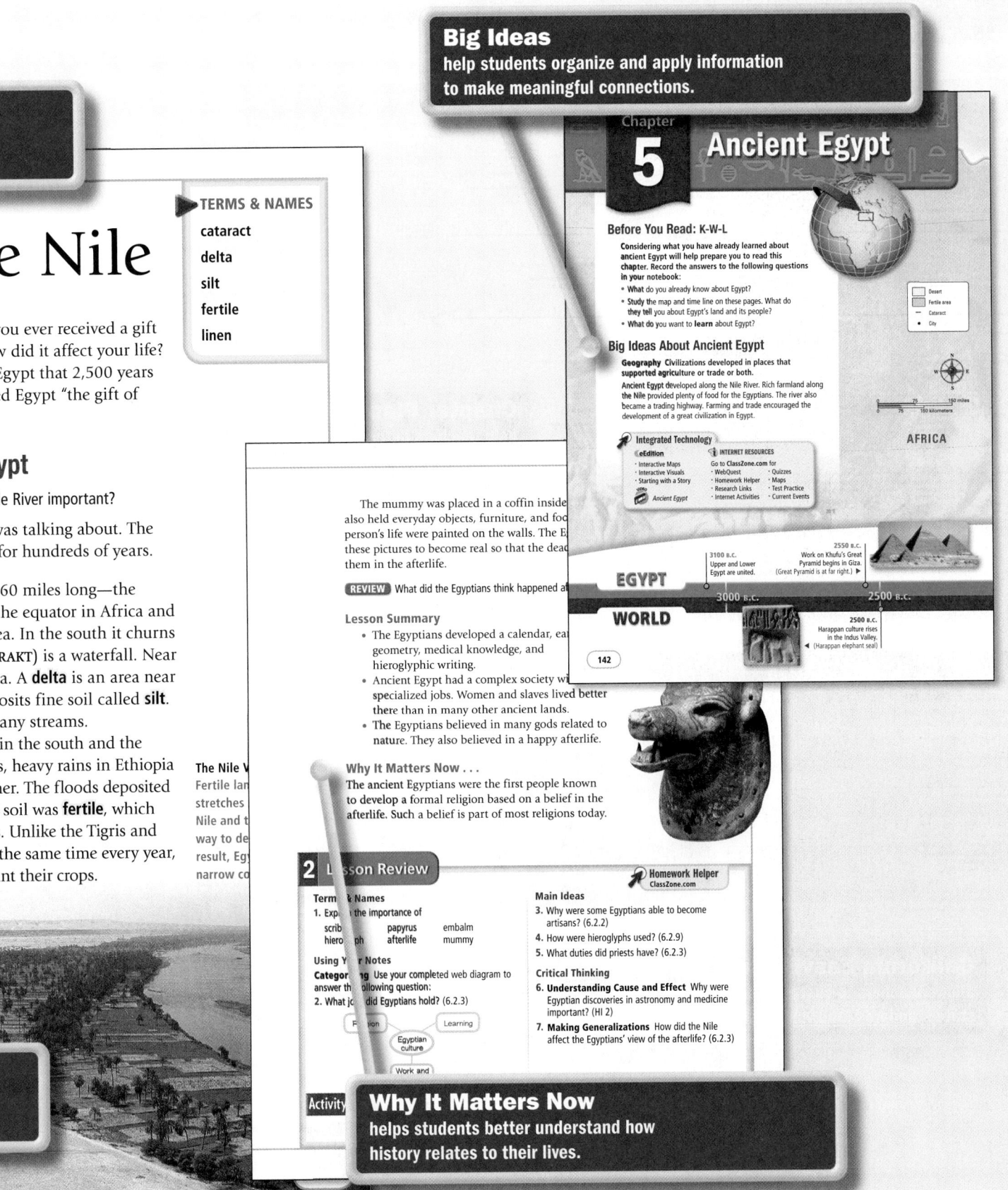

Chapter 5 — Ancient Egypt

Before You Read: K-W-L

Considering what you have already learned about ancient Egypt will help prepare you to read this chapter. Record the answers to the following questions in your notebook:

- **What** do you already know about Egypt?
- **Study** the map and time line on these pages. What do they **tell** you about Egypt's land and its people?
- **What** do you want to **learn** about Egypt?

Big Ideas About Ancient Egypt

Geography Civilizations developed in places that supported agriculture or trade or both.

Ancient Egypt developed along the Nile River. Rich farmland along the Nile provided plenty of food for the Egyptians. The river also became a trading highway. Farming and trade encouraged the development of a great civilization in Egypt.

Integrated Technology

eEdition
- Interactive Maps
- Interactive Visuals
- Starting with a Story

Ancient Egypt

INTERNET RESOURCES
Go to ClassZone.com for
- WebQuest
- Homework Helper
- Research Links
- Internet Activities
- Quizzes
- Maps
- Test Practice
- Current Events

Desert
Fertile area
Cataract
City

AFRICA

3100 B.C.
Upper and Lower Egypt are united.

2550 B.C.
Work on Khufu's Great Pyramid begins in Giza.
(Great Pyramid is at far right.) ▶

EGYPT
WORLD

3000 B.C.   2500 B.C.

2500 B.C.
Harappan culture rises in the Indus Valley.
◀ (Harappan elephant seal)

142

Nile (left page)

TERMS & NAMES
- cataract
- delta
- silt
- fertile
- linen

... you ever received a gift
... ow did it affect your life?
... Egypt that 2,500 years
... ed Egypt "the gift of

...gypt

...Nile River important?

... was talking about. The
... for hundreds of years.

...,160 miles long—the
... the equator in Africa and
...Sea. In the south it churns
...•RAKT) is a waterfall. Near
...lta. A **delta** is an area near
...posits fine soil called **silt**.
...many streams.
... in the south and the
...es, heavy rains in Ethiopia
...mer. The floods deposited
...is soil was **fertile**, which
...s. Unlike the Tigris and
...t the same time every year,
...lant their crops.

The Nile V...
Fertile lan...
stretches...
Nile and t...
way to de...
result, Eg...
narrow co...

The mummy was placed in a coffin inside
also held everyday objects, furniture, and foo
person's life were painted on the walls. The E...
these pictures to become real so that the dead
them in the afterlife.

REVIEW What did the Egyptians think happened a...

Lesson Summary

- The Egyptians developed a calendar, ea...
  geometry, medical knowledge, and
  hieroglyphic writing.
- Ancient Egypt had a complex society wi...
  specialized jobs. Women and slaves lived better
  there than in many other ancient lands.
- The Egyptians believed in many gods related to
  nature. They also believed in a happy afterlife.

Why It Matters Now . . .

The ancient Egyptians were the first people known
to **develop a** formal religion based on a belief in the
afterlife. Such a belief is part of most religions today.

---

2 Lesson Review

Homework Helper
ClassZone.com

Terms & Names
1. Expl... the importance of

scrib...   papyrus   embalm
hiero...ph   afterlife   mummy

Using Y... Notes
Categor...ng Use your completed web diagram to
answer th... ollowing question:
2. What jo... did Egyptians hold? (6.2.3)

R...ion   Learning
Egyptian culture
Work and...

Main Ideas
3. Why were some Egyptians able to become artisans? (6.2.2)
4. How were hieroglyphs used? (6.2.9)
5. What duties did priests have? (6.2.3)

Critical Thinking
6. **Understanding Cause and Effect** Why were Egyptian discoveries in astronomy and medicine important? (HI 2)
7. **Making Generalizations** How did the Nile affect the Egyptians' view of the afterlife? (6.2.3)

Activity

Time-Saving Resources

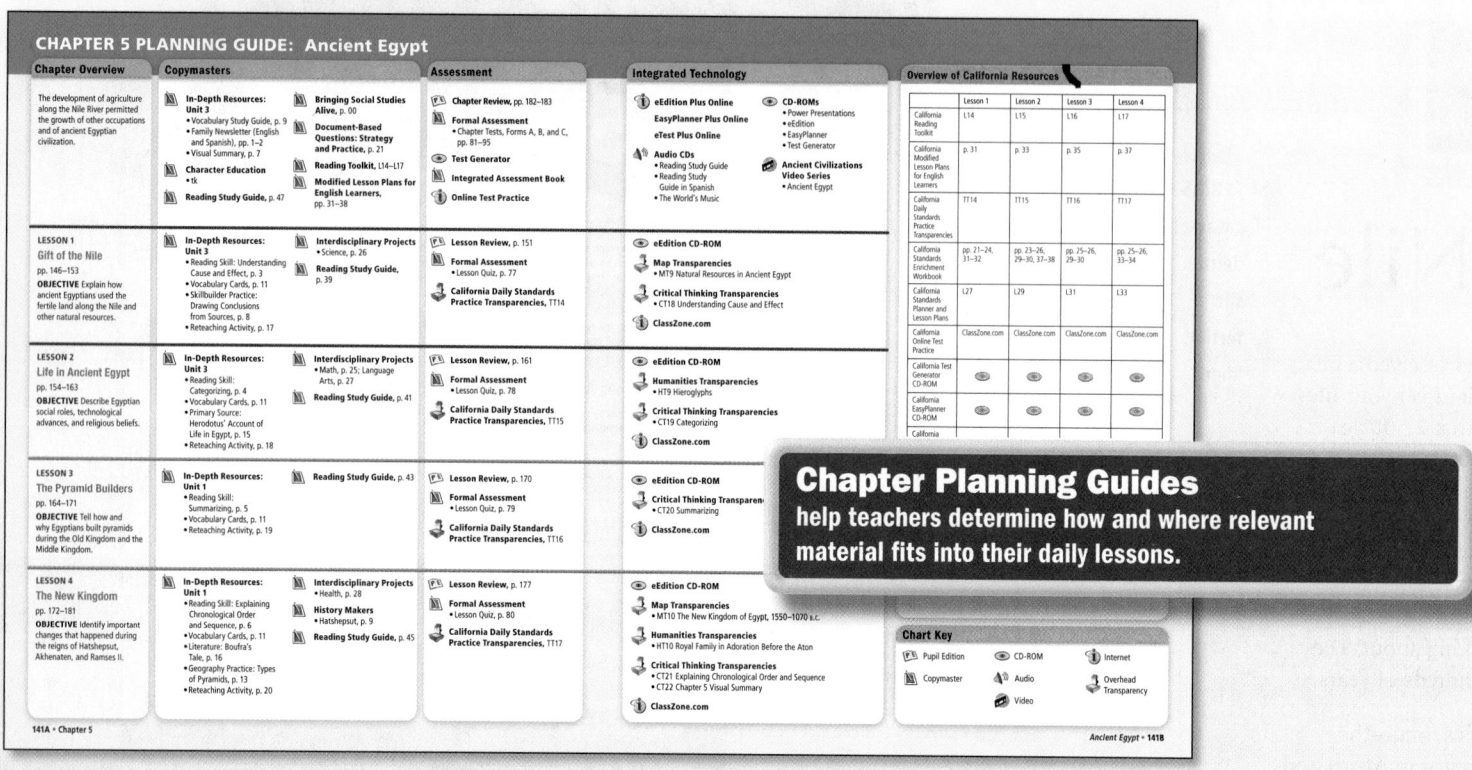

CHAPTER 5 PLANNING GUIDE: Ancient Egypt

Chapter Planning Guides
help teachers determine how and where relevant material fits into their daily lessons.

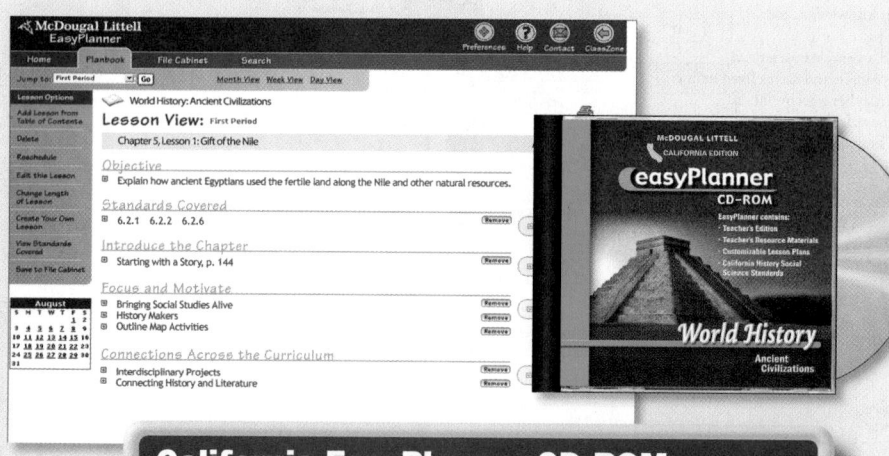

California EasyPlanner CD-ROM
allows teachers to customize lesson plans, track state standards, and view and print resources.

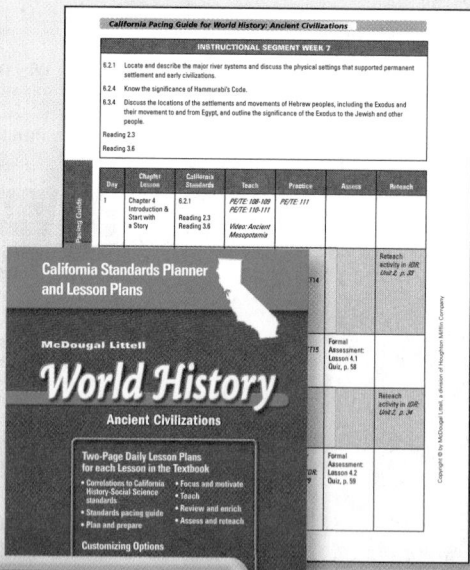

California Standards Planner and Lesson Plans
provides lesson plans and daily pacing guides covering the California History–Social Science Standards.

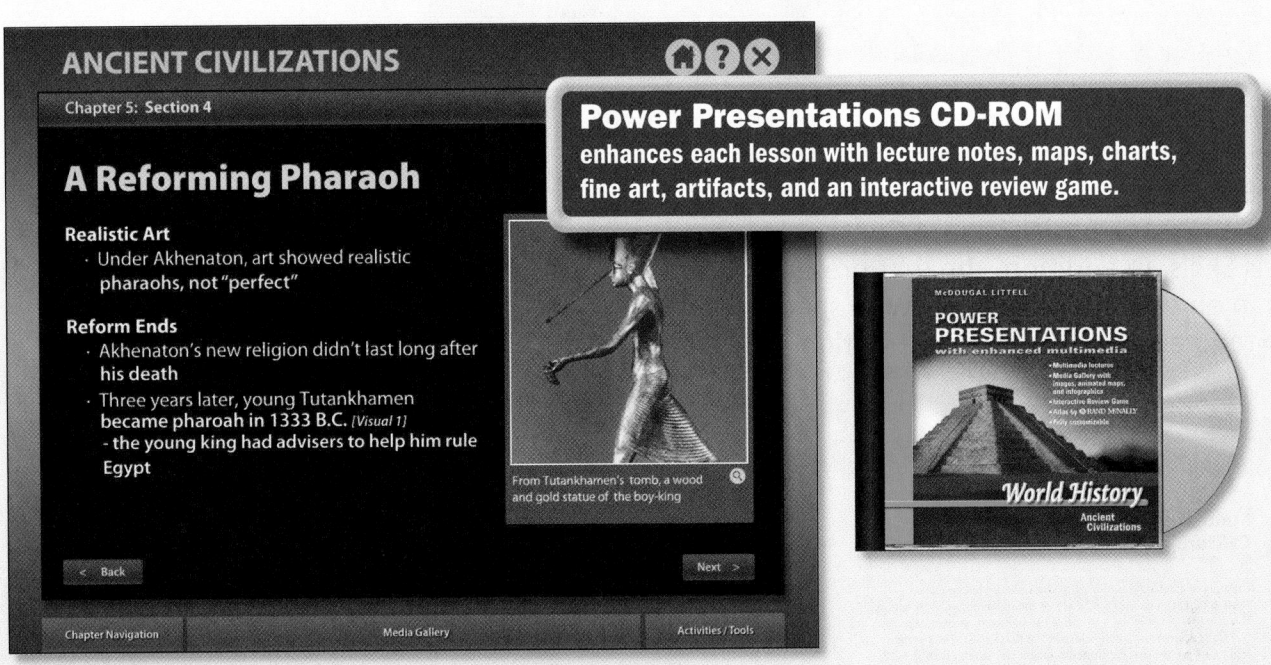

Power Presentations CD-ROM

enhances each lesson with lecture notes, maps, charts, fine art, artifacts, and an interactive review game.

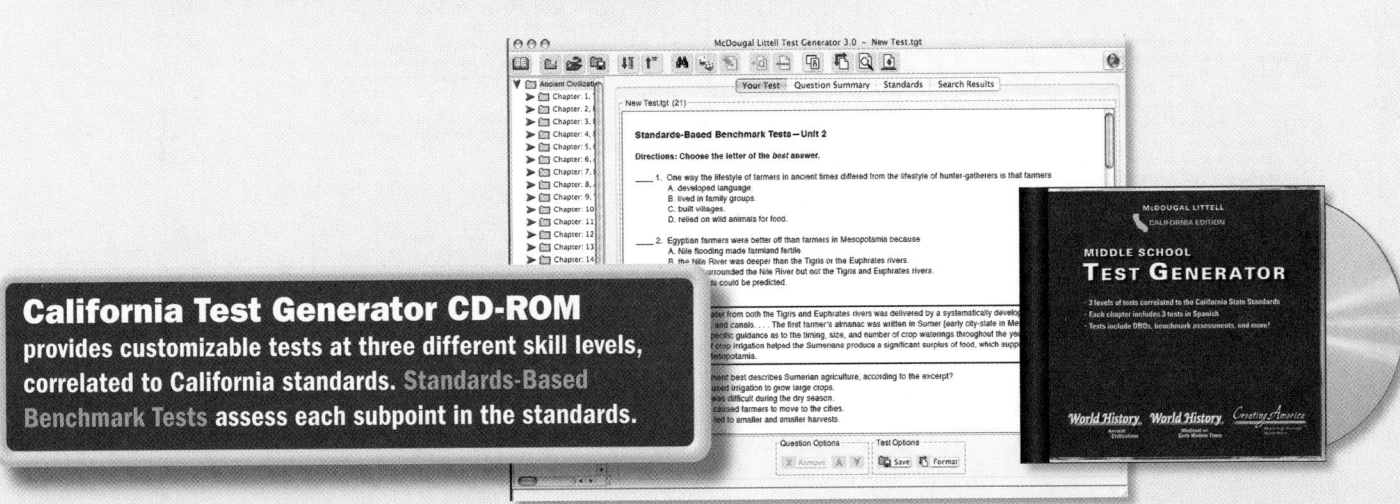

California Test Generator CD-ROM

provides customizable tests at three different skill levels, correlated to California standards. Standards-Based Benchmark Tests assess each subpoint in the standards.

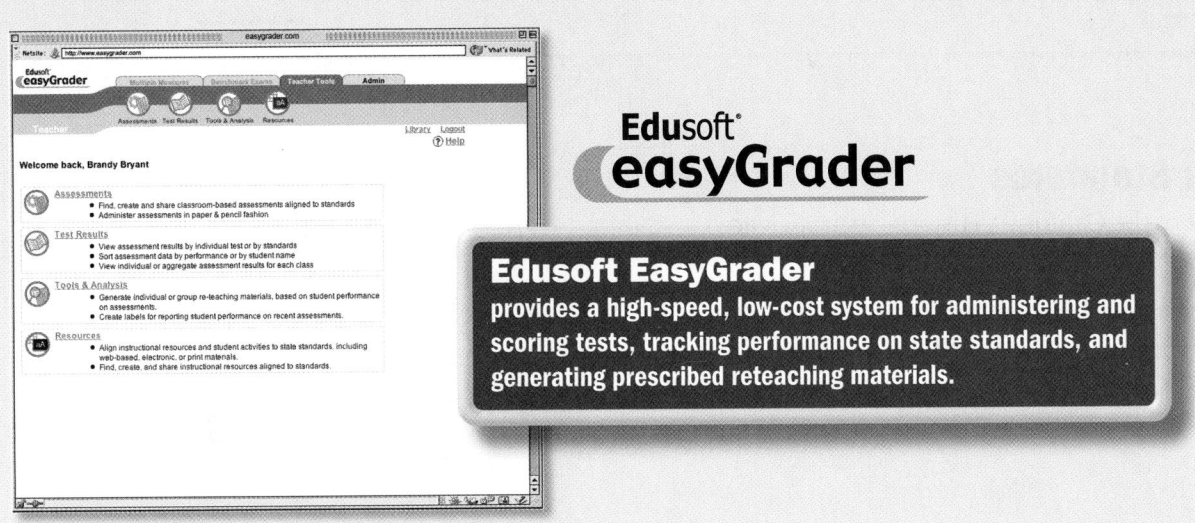

Edusoft EasyGrader

provides a high-speed, low-cost system for administering and scoring tests, tracking performance on state standards, and generating prescribed reteaching materials.

Standards-Based Pupil's Edition

World History: Ancient Civilizations is designed to meet the needs of California students and teachers. The Pupil's Edition provides comprehensive coverage of the California History–Social Science Content Standards and Analysis Skills. In addition, the text presents historical events in an engaging narrative with special features that extend and enhance the instruction.

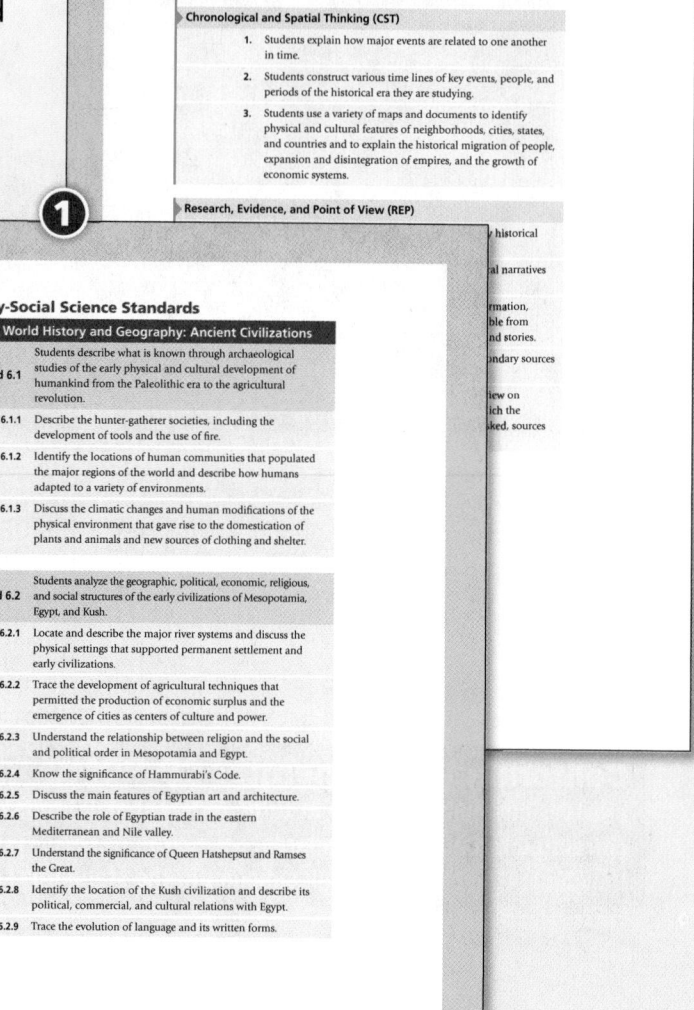

① California Standards

A complete list of the California History–Social Science Content Standards for Grade 6 and Analysis Skills standards is provided in the early pages of the Pupil's Edition. Students and their parents can become familiar with the standards that guide the content in the textbook.

Strategies for Taking Tests

World History: Ancient Civilizations includes a special section titled Strategies for Taking Tests. It offers students information on study skills and test-taking strategies that will help them to improve their performance on standards-based assessments.

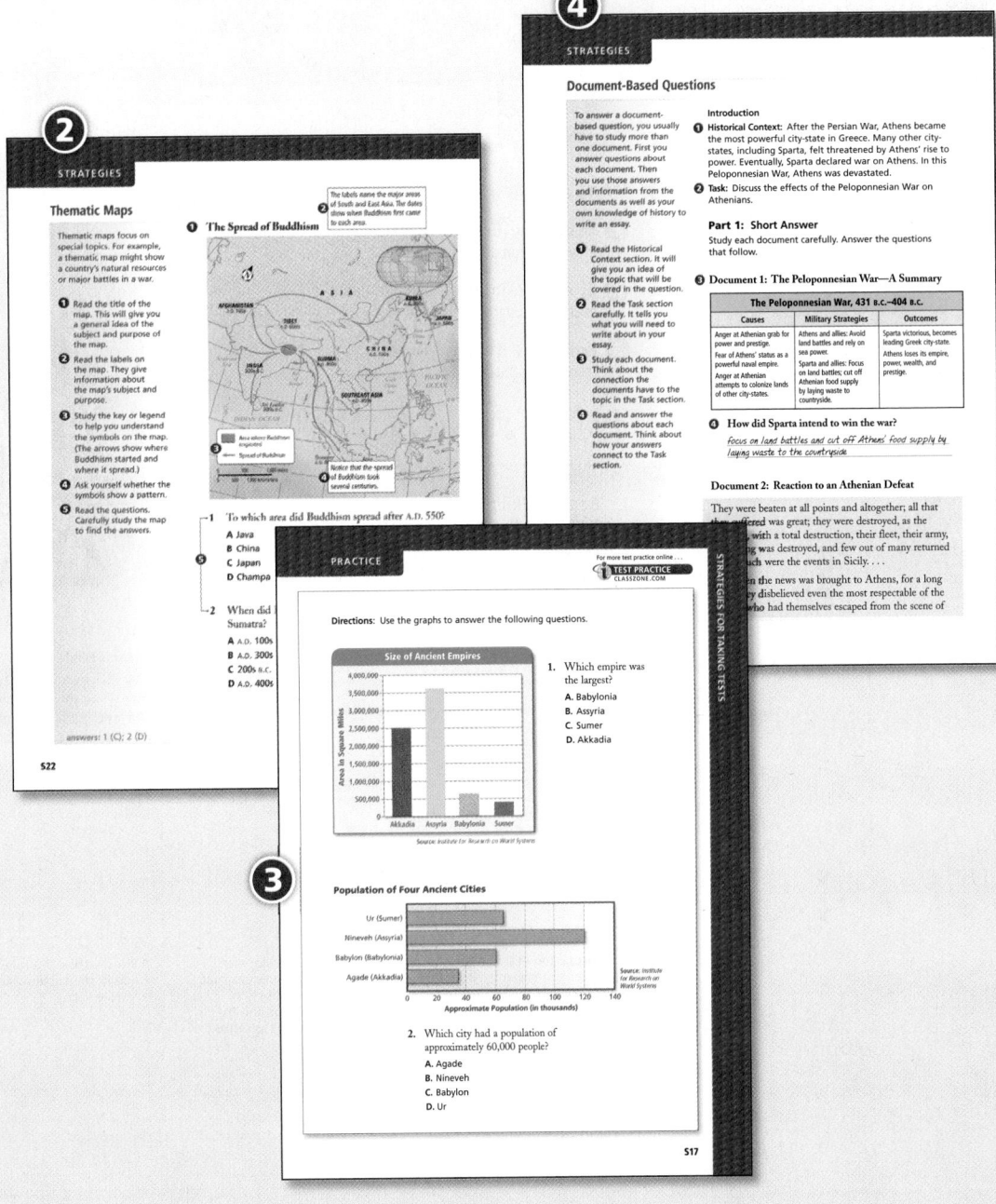

② Strategies

These pages offer students strategies for handling the various items they will find in tests that they take. For every type of item, strategies are presented in step-by-step format. Item types include multiple-choice, constructed-response, extended-response, primary and secondary sources, political cartoons, charts and graphs, maps, and time lines.

③ Practice

Each strategy page is followed by a practice page, where students can apply the strategies they have learned to a set of practice items.

④ Document-Based Questions

This section ends with strategies and practice for document-based questions. In these items, students analyze a variety of historical documents, including primary and secondary sources, charts and graphs, political cartoons, posters, and maps. They then write an essay.

Standards-Based Pupil's Edition

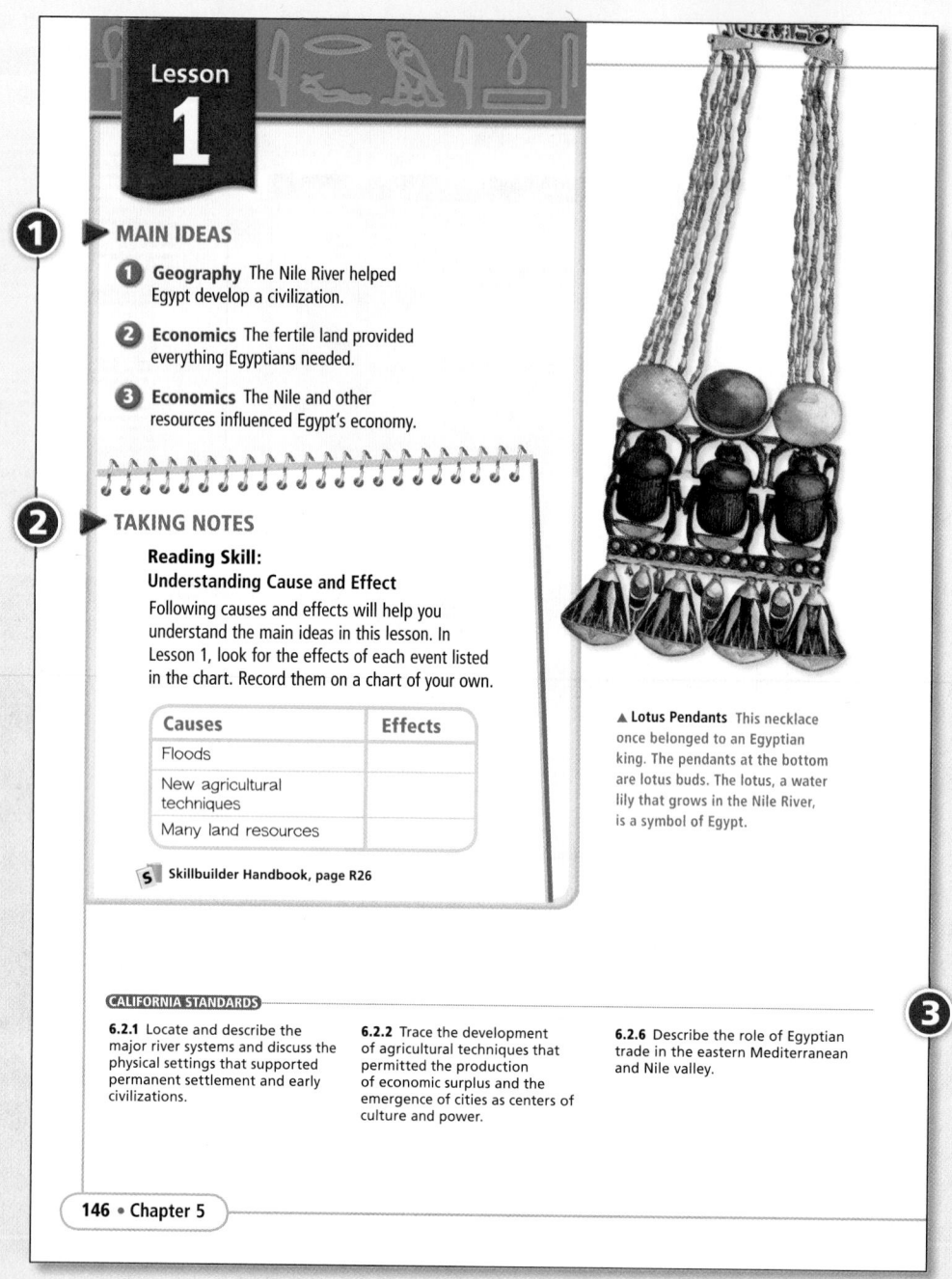

Lesson 1

1 ▶ MAIN IDEAS

1 Geography The Nile River helped Egypt develop a civilization.

2 Economics The fertile land provided everything Egyptians needed.

3 Economics The Nile and other resources influenced Egypt's economy.

2 ▶ TAKING NOTES

Reading Skill:
Understanding Cause and Effect
Following causes and effects will help you understand the main ideas in this lesson. In Lesson 1, look for the effects of each event listed in the chart. Record them on a chart of your own.

Causes	Effects
Floods	
New agricultural techniques	
Many land resources	

S Skillbuilder Handbook, page R26

▲ **Lotus Pendants** This necklace once belonged to an Egyptian king. The pendants at the bottom are lotus buds. The lotus, a water lily that grows in the Nile River, is a symbol of Egypt.

CALIFORNIA STANDARDS

6.2.1 Locate and describe the major river systems and discuss the physical settings that supported permanent settlement and early civilizations.

6.2.2 Trace the development of agricultural techniques that permitted the production of economic surplus and the emergence of cities as centers of culture and power.

6.2.6 Describe the role of Egyptian trade in the eastern Mediterranean and Nile valley.

3

146 • Chapter 5

---

1 Main Ideas

The key ideas for each lesson are identified on the lesson opener. These Main Ideas are drawn from six strands—Economics, Science and Technology, Belief Systems, Government, Culture, and Geography. Each Main Idea corresponds to a prominent heading and section of narrative in the lesson.

2 Reading Skills

Students learn to use a variety of reading skills to analyze information and take notes as they read. These skills include comparing and contrasting, cause and effect, sequencing, and categorizing. Students are asked to use their notes to answer a question in the Lesson Review that follows each lesson.

3 California Standards

Each lesson opener includes the full text of the content and skills standards covered in that lesson. These standards are covered in the narrative for the lesson, in special features that accompany the lesson, and in the Lesson Review questions.

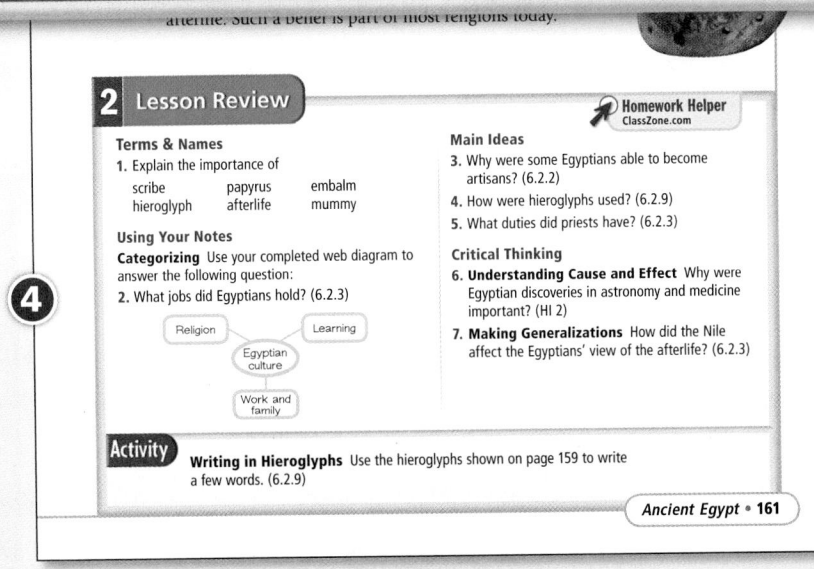

2 Lesson Review

Homework Helper
ClassZone.com

Terms & Names

1. Explain the importance of

scribe   papyrus   embalm
hieroglyph   afterlife   mummy

Using Your Notes

Categorizing Use your completed web diagram to answer the following question:

2. What jobs did Egyptians hold? (6.2.3)

- Religion
- Learning
- Egyptian culture
- Work and family

Main Ideas

3. Why were some Egyptians able to become artisans? (6.2.2)

4. How were hieroglyphs used? (6.2.9)

5. What duties did priests have? (6.2.3)

Critical Thinking

6. **Understanding Cause and Effect** Why were Egyptian discoveries in astronomy and medicine important? (HI 2)

7. **Making Generalizations** How did the Nile affect the Egyptians' view of the afterlife? (6.2.3)

Activity **Writing in Hieroglyphs** Use the hieroglyphs shown on page 159 to write a few words. (6.2.9)

Ancient Egypt • **161**

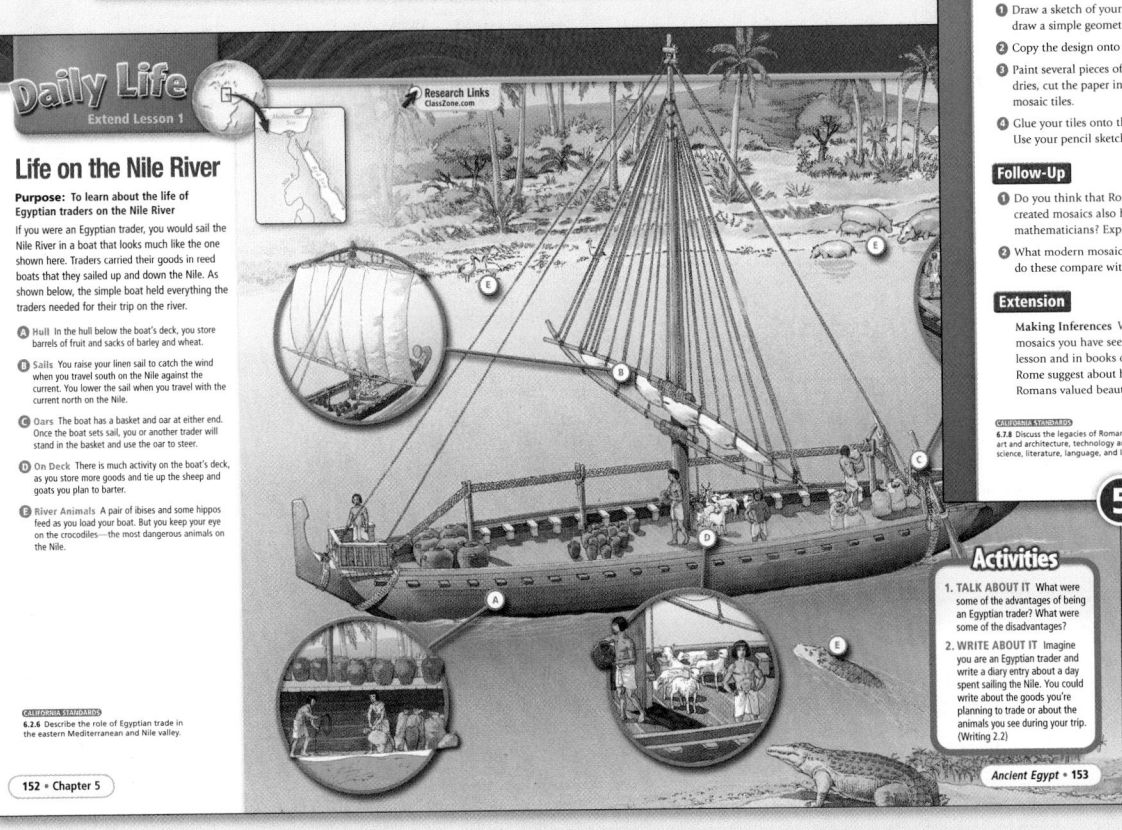

Daily Life
Extend Lesson 1

Research Links
ClassZone.com

Life on the Nile River

Purpose: To learn about the life of Egyptian traders on the Nile River

If you were an Egyptian trader, you would sail the Nile River in a boat that looks much like the one shown here. Traders carried their goods in reed boats that they sailed up and down the Nile. As shown below, the simple boat held everything the traders needed for their trip on the river.

A Hull In the hull below the boat's deck, you store barrels of fruit and sacks of barley and wheat.

B Sails You raise your linen sail to catch the wind when you travel south on the Nile against the current. You lower the sail when you travel with the current north on the Nile.

C Oars The boat has a basket and oar at either end. Once the boat sets sail, you or another trader will stand in the basket and use the oar to steer.

D On Deck There is much activity on the boat's deck, as you store more goods and tie up the sheep and goats you plan to barter.

E River Animals A pair of ibises and some hippos feed as you load your boat. But you keep your eye on the crocodiles—the most dangerous animals on the Nile.

CALIFORNIA STANDARDS
6.2.6 Describe the role of Egyptian trade in the eastern Mediterranean and Nile valley.

152 • Chapter 5

Activities

1. **TALK ABOUT IT** What were some of the advantages of being an Egyptian trader? What were some of the disadvantages?

2. **WRITE ABOUT IT** Imagine you are an Egyptian trader and write a diary entry about a day spent sailing the Nile. You could write about the goods you're planning to trade or about the animals you see during your trip. (Writing 2.2)

Ancient Egypt • **153**

Activity **Extend Lesson 4**

Make a Mosaic

Goal: To create a mosaic, a picture made of small colored tiles, that celebrates the legacy of Roman art

Materials & Supplies
- paper and pencil
- poster board
- paint and paintbrush
- scissors
- glue or paste

Prepare

1. Study the mosaic on page 452.

2. Look at Roman mosaics in books on ancient Rome.

Do the Activity

1. Draw a sketch of your design on a piece of paper. You might draw a simple geometric design or an animal or a flower.

2. Copy the design onto a piece of poster board.

3. Paint several pieces of paper in different colors. After the paint dries, cut the paper into small pieces. These will be your mosaic tiles.

4. Glue your tiles onto the design on your poster board. Use your pencil sketch as a guide. Let your mosaic dry.

Follow-Up

1. Do you think that Roman artists who created mosaics also had to be skilled mathematicians? Explain.

2. What modern mosaics have you seen? How do these compare with the one you made?

Extension

Making Inferences What do the mosaics you have seen in this lesson and in books on ancient Rome suggest about how Romans valued beauty?

CALIFORNIA STANDARDS
6.7.8 Discuss the legacies of Roman art and architecture, technology and science, literature, language, and law.

459

4 Lesson and Chapter Reviews

A range of questions, including Main Idea and Critical Thinking questions, are provided in the Lesson Reviews and Chapter Reviews. Each question addresses a California content or skills standard, which is identified in parentheses after the question.

5 Special Features

A collection of special features that accompany the lessons extend the instruction in the text. Longer features—including Daily Life, Connect to Today, Skillbuilders, and Activities—display the California standard addressed in the feature.

Standards-Based Teacher's Edition

The Teacher's Edition of *World History: Ancient Civilizations* provides the information teachers need to coordinate their teaching with the California History–Social Science Content Standards and Analysis Skills. In addition, a variety of teaching tips, informational notes, critical thinking questions, and resource listings make it possible to customize instruction for all student populations.

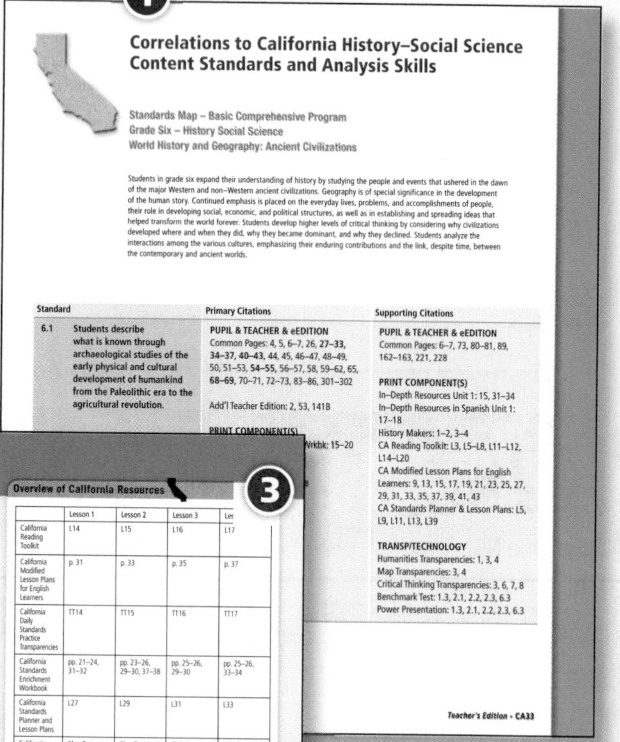

①

Correlations to California History–Social Science Content Standards and Analysis Skills

Standards Map – Basic Comprehensive Program
Grade Six – History Social Science
World History and Geography: Ancient Civilizations

Students in grade six expand their understanding of history by studying the people and events that ushered in the dawn of the major Western and non-Western ancient civilizations. Geography is of special significance in the development of the human story. Continued emphasis is placed on the everyday lives, problems, and accomplishments of people, their role in developing social, economic, and political structures, as well as in establishing and spreading ideas that helped transform the world forever. Students develop higher levels of critical thinking by considering why civilizations developed where and when they did, why they became dominant, and why they declined. Students analyze the interactions among the various cultures, emphasizing their enduring contributions and the link, despite time, between the contemporary and ancient worlds.

Standard	Primary Citations	Supporting Citations
6.1 Students describe what is known through archaeological studies of the early physical and cultural development of humankind from the Paleolithic era to the agricultural revolution.	**PUPIL & TEACHER & eEDITION** Common Pages: 4, 5, 6–7, 26, 27–33, 34–37, 40–43, 44, 45, 46–47, 48–49, 50, 51–53, 54–55, 56–57, 58, 59–62, 65, 68–69, 70–71, 72–73, 83–86, 301–302 Add'l Teacher Edition: 2, 53, 141B **PRINT COMPONENT(S)**	**PUPIL & TEACHER & eEDITION** Common Pages: 6–7, 73, 80–81, 89, 162–163, 221, 228 **PRINT COMPONENT(S)** In-Depth Resources Unit 1: 15, 31–34 In-Depth Resources in Spanish Unit 1: 17–18 History Makers: 1–2, 3–4 CA Reading Toolkit: L3, L5–L8, L11–L12, L14–L20 CA Modified Lesson Plans for English Learners: 9, 13, 15, 17, 19, 21, 23, 25, 27, 29, 31, 33, 35, 37, 39, 41, 43 CA Standards Planner & Lesson Plans: L5, L9, L11, L13, L39 **TRANSP/TECHNOLOGY** Humanities Transparencies: 1, 3, 4 Map Transparencies: 3, 4 Critical Thinking Transparencies: 3, 6, 7, 8 Benchmark Test: 1.3, 2.1, 2.2, 2.3, 6.3 Power Presentation: 1.3, 2.1, 2.2, 2.3, 6.3

Teacher's Edition • CA33

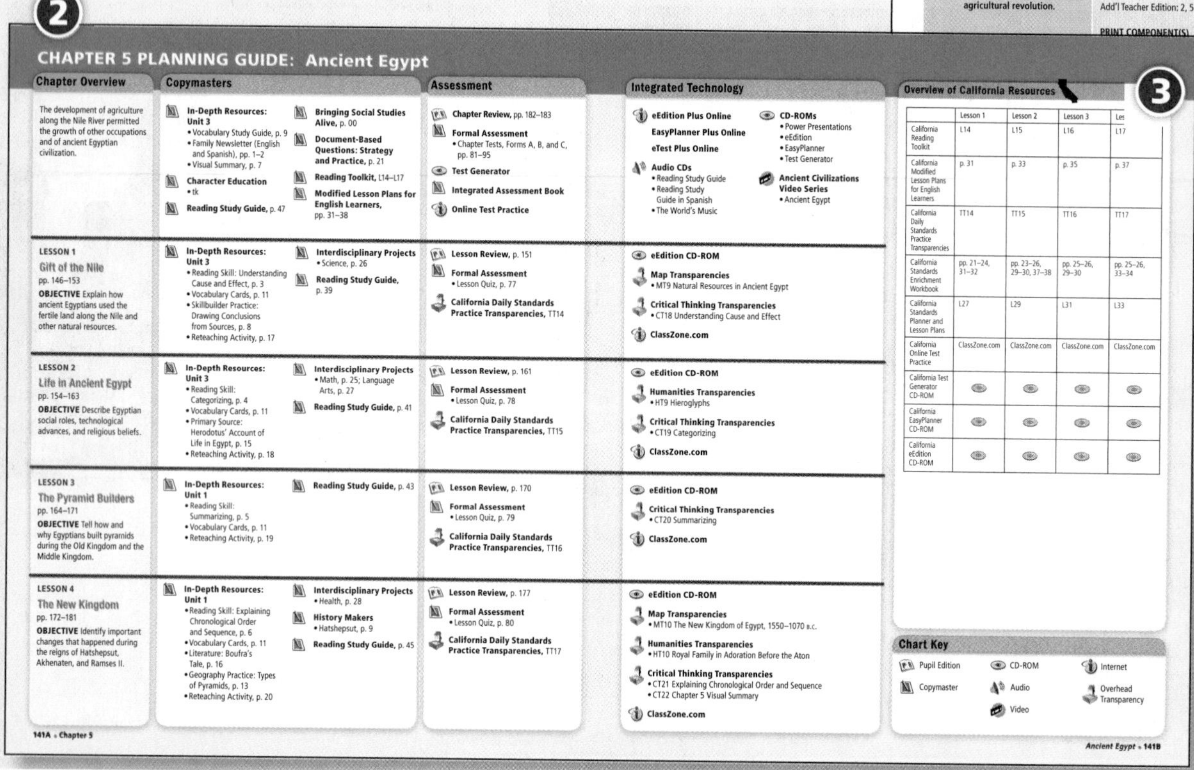

②

CHAPTER 5 PLANNING GUIDE: Ancient Egypt

Chapter Overview	Copymasters	Assessment	Integrated Technology	Overview of California Resources

The development of agriculture along the Nile River permitted the growth of other occupations and of ancient Egyptian civilization.

In-Depth Resources: Unit 3
• Vocabulary Study Guide, p. 9
• Family Newsletter (English and Spanish), pp. 1–2
• Visual Summary, p. 7

Character Education
• tk

Reading Study Guide, p. 47

Bringing Social Studies Alive, p. 00

Document-Based Questions: Strategy and Practice, p. 21

Modified Lesson Plans for English Learners, pp. 31–38

Chapter Review, pp. 182–183

Formal Assessment
• Chapter Tests, Forms A, B, and C, pp. 81–95

Test Generator

Integrated Assessment Book

Online Test Practice

eEdition Plus Online
EasyPlanner Plus Online
eTest Plus Online

Audio CDs
• Reading Study Guide
• Reading Study Guide in Spanish
• The World's Music

CD-ROMs
• Power Presentations
• eEdition
• EasyPlanner
• Test Generator

Ancient Civilizations Video Series
• Ancient Egypt

	Lesson 1	Lesson 2	Lesson 3	Les
California Reading Toolkit	L14	L15	L16	L17
California Modified Lesson Plans for English Learners	p. 31	p. 33	p. 35	p. 37
California Daily Standards Practice Transparencies	TT14	TT15	TT16	TT17
California Standards Enrichment Workbook	pp. 21–24, 31–32	pp. 23–26, 29–30, 37–38	pp. 25–26, 29–30	pp. 25–26, 33–34
California Standards Planner and Lesson Plans	L27	L29	L31	L33
California Online Test Practice	ClassZone.com	ClassZone.com	ClassZone.com	ClassZone.com
California Test Generator CD-ROM	💿	💿	💿	💿
California EasyPlanner CD-ROM	💿	💿	💿	💿
California eEdition CD-ROM	💿	💿	💿	💿

LESSON 1
Gift of the Nile
pp. 146–153

OBJECTIVE Explain how ancient Egyptians used the fertile land along the Nile and other natural resources.

In-Depth Resources: Unit 3
• Reading Skill: Understanding Cause and Effect, p. 3
• Vocabulary Cards, p. 11
• Skillbuilder Practice: Drawing Conclusions from Sources, p. 8
• Reteaching Activity, p. 17

Interdisciplinary Projects
• Science, p. 26

Reading Study Guide, p. 39

Lesson Review, p. 151

Formal Assessment
• Lesson Quiz, p. 77

California Daily Standards Practice Transparencies, TT14

eEdition CD-ROM

Map Transparencies
• MT9 Natural Resources in Ancient Egypt

Critical Thinking Transparencies
• CT18 Understanding Cause and Effect

ClassZone.com

LESSON 2
Life in Ancient Egypt
pp. 154–163

OBJECTIVE Describe Egyptian social roles, technological advances, and religious beliefs.

In-Depth Resources: Unit 3
• Reading Skill: Categorizing, p. 4
• Vocabulary Cards, p. 11
• Primary Source: Herodotus' Account of Life in Egypt, p. 15
• Reteaching Activity, p. 18

Interdisciplinary Projects
• Math, p. 25; Language Arts, p. 27

Reading Study Guide, p. 41

Lesson Review, p. 161

Formal Assessment
• Lesson Quiz, p. 78

California Daily Standards Practice Transparencies, TT15

eEdition CD-ROM

Humanities Transparencies
• HT9 Hieroglyphs

Critical Thinking Transparencies
• CT19 Categorizing

ClassZone.com

LESSON 3
The Pyramid Builders
pp. 164–171

OBJECTIVE Tell how and why Egyptians built pyramids during the Old Kingdom and the Middle Kingdom.

In-Depth Resources: Unit 1
• Reading Skill: Summarizing, p. 5
• Vocabulary Cards, p. 11
• Reteaching Activity, p. 19

Reading Study Guide, p. 43

Lesson Review, p. 170

Formal Assessment
• Lesson Quiz, p. 79

California Daily Standards Practice Transparencies, TT16

eEdition CD-ROM

Critical Thinking Transparencies
• CT20 Summarizing

ClassZone.com

LESSON 4
The New Kingdom
pp. 172–181

OBJECTIVE Identify important changes that happened during the reigns of Hatshepsut, Akhenaten, and Ramses II.

In-Depth Resources: Unit 1
• Reading Skill: Explaining Chronological Order and Sequence, p. 6
• Vocabulary Cards, p. 11
• Literature: Boufra's Tale, p. 16
• Geography Practice: Types of Pyramids, p. 13
• Reteaching Activity, p. 20

Interdisciplinary Projects
• Health, p. 28

History Makers
• Hatshepsut, p. 9

Reading Study Guide, p. 45

Lesson Review, p. 177

Formal Assessment
• Lesson Quiz, p. 80

California Daily Standards Practice Transparencies, TT117

eEdition CD-ROM

Map Transparencies
• MT10 The New Kingdom of Egypt, 1550–1070 B.C.

Humanities Transparencies
• HT10 Royal Family in Adoration Before the Aton

Critical Thinking Transparencies
• CT21 Explaining Chronological Order and Sequence
• CT22 Chapter 5 Visual Summary

ClassZone.com

Chart Key

📖 Pupil Edition	💿 CD-ROM	🖥 Internet
📄 Copymaster	🔊 Audio	Overhead Transparency
	📹 Video	

141A • Chapter 5

Ancient Egypt • 141B

③

---

① Correlation to California Standards

An easy-to-read chart correlates the text with the California content and skills standards for Grade 6. This correlation provides specific page references to the Pupil's Edition, Teacher's Edition, and selected ancillaries, with the strongest references shown in boldfaced type.

② Chapter Planning Guide

The Chapter Planning Guide gives complete listings of reproducible materials for the chapter as a whole and for each lesson. The listings reveal the depth of available resource materials.

③ California Chapter Resources

The Chapter Planning Guide provides a chart of California resources for each lesson. These resources include the *California Standards Enrichment Workbook,* the *California Standards Planner and Lesson Plans,* and the *California EasyPlanner CD-ROM.* This information is also provided at the lesson level.

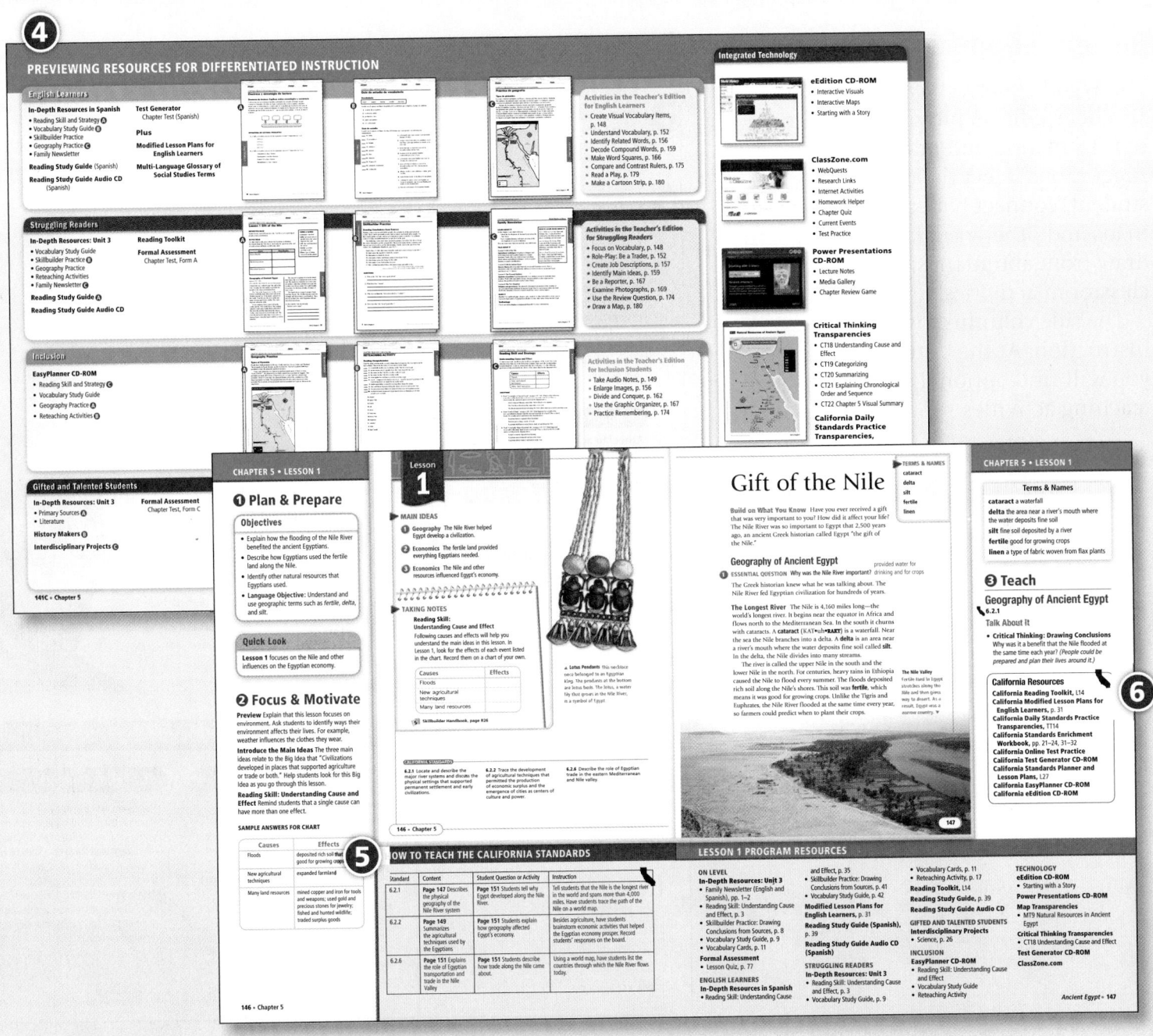

④ Resources for Differentiated Instruction

Each planning guide includes a listing of resources for teaching various student populations: English learners, struggling readers, gifted and talented students, and students included in the mainstream classroom. "Thumbnails" preview materials that support differentiation. Teacher's Edition activities for differentiation are also highlighted.

⑤ How to Teach the California Standards

California standards are listed at the beginning of each lesson. A chart immediately below lists each standard covered in the lesson, with a description of where instruction on the standard appears in the lesson and where the student completes an activity involving that standard. The chart also offers a teaching tip for each standard.

⑥ California Lesson Resources

A list of California resources available for each lesson is provided in the side column of the lesson opener.

Standards-Based Teacher's Edition

Lesson Support

The *World History: Ancient Civilizations* Teacher's Edition provides a wealth of information and practical teaching suggestions. Meet the needs of each student, connect history to today, use maps and other visuals effectively, and draw from abundant suggestions for classroom activities.

The side columns focus on core instruction. At the bottom of the pages, you will find optional suggestions and teaching activities.

---

1 **In-Depth Resources: Unit 5**
- Reading Skill: Finding Main Ideas, p. 39
- Skillbuilder Practice: Assessing Credibility of Sources, p. 44

2 **History Makers**

Pericles
Pericles did not rule Athens alone. He and nine other generals ran the military affairs of Athens. What set Pericles apart was his charisma. *Charisma* is a word of Greek origin that means the power or quality of attracting, personal magnetism or charm. It comes from the Greek root *kharis*, which means "favor." Pericles' vision of democracy combined with his charisma made him stand out from other men of his time.

Comparisons Across Cultures

Athenian and U.S. Democracy
Ask students to review the chart on page 395 and summarize the information it presents. (*It shows characteristics of direct and representative democracies and what they have in common.*)
According to the chart, what are the differences in the citizens in each democracy? (*Citizens in Athens were male, 18, and children of citizens. Citizens in the United States are male and female. They are people born in this country as well as immigrants who have become citizens.*)
Have students compare each point and discuss the differences between the two forms of democracy.

394 • Chapter 12

Paid Public Officials To spread power more evenly, Pericles changed the rule for holding public office. Most public officials were unpaid before he came to power. This meant that only wealthy people could afford to serve in government in Athens. Pericles increased the number of public officials who were paid. Now even poor citizens could hold a public office if elected or chosen randomly. However, to be a citizen an individual had to be a free male, over 18, and the son of Athenian-born parents.

Direct Democracy The form of democracy practiced in Athens was not the kind practiced in the United States today. The form used in Athens was called **direct democracy**. In a direct democracy all citizens participate in running the government. For example, all citizens in Athens could propose and vote directly on laws. By comparison, the United States has representative democracy, or a republic. U.S. citizens—male and female—elect representatives to take care of government business. These representatives propose and vote on laws. Study the chart on page 395 to find other differences.

REVIEW How is direct democracy different from representative democracy?
In direct democracy all citizens participate in government activities. In a representative democracy selected individuals do this task.

History Makers

Pericles (495–429 B.C.)
Pericles' speaking skills set him apart from other Athenians. He was so skilled that most regarded him as the best speaker of the time. Some people said that when he spoke, his words were like thunder and lightning.
Once, Pericles and another Athenian were involved in a wrestling match. Pericles lost. But his powers of speech were so great that he actually convinced the spectators that he won the match, even though they saw him lose!
His ability to speak so well made it possible for him to persuade Athenian citizens to back his reforms. These reforms brought about major changes in Athenian life. Unfortunately, toward the end of his life, Pericles was involved in several political scandals. As a result, he briefly stepped down from his position of leadership but later was reinstated. He is still thought of as one of the greatest leaders of Greece.

394 • Chapter 12

3 **DIFFERENTIATING INSTRUCTION**

English Learners

Preview the Text
Demonstrate how to turn headings and subheadings into *who, what, when, where, why, how* questions. The first heading can become "How did Pericles lead Athens?" Write the question on a chart. Help students skim the text to find a response to the question. Have student pairs work to turn headings into questions and chart them. Then have students scan the text to find responses. For more support, see *Modified Lesson Plans for English Learners*, p. 84.

Struggling Readers

Focus on Vocabulary
Have partners list the subsection headings of the section "Pericles Leads Athens" as main ideas and leave two lines to write details. As students read, have them discuss the section with a partner and agree on the details to be included under each subsection head. Have pairs share their details with another pair and explain the subsection in their own words.

---

1 Resource References at Point of Use

Throughout the Teacher's Edition, references to the program resources at their point of use will help you plan and teach every lesson.

2 History Makers

Short features in the Pupil's Edition are supplemented with additional information and suggested activities.

3 Differentiating Instruction

The *World History: Ancient Civilizations* Teacher's Edition provides several options at the bottom of pages. These options include activities for teaching struggling readers, English learners, gifted and talented students, and students included in the mainstream classroom.

Comparisons Across Cultures
Athenian and U.S. Democracy

Athenian Democracy
Direct Democracy
- Citizenship: male; 18 years old; born of citizen parents
- Assembly of all citizens votes on laws.
- Leader is selected randomly or elected.
- Council of Five Hundred prepares business for the assembly.
- As many as 500 jurors could serve.

Both
- Political power is held by all citizens.
- Government has three branches.
- Law-making branch passes laws.
- Executive branch carries out laws.
- Judicial branch holds trials.

U.S. Democracy
Representative Democracy
- Citizenship: born in United States or completed citizenship process
- Representatives are elected to law-making body.
- Leader is elected.
- Executive branch has elected and appointed officials.
- Juries usually have 12 jurors.

Expanding the Empire

② **ESSENTIAL QUESTION** How did Athens become more powerful?
Pericles took funds from the Delian League to build a huge navy. Greek wealth depended on overseas trade. Athens was determined to protect its overseas trade and its homeland. At the end of the Persian War, the Greek city-states formed a league for mutual protection. It was called the **Delian League**.

Delian League Athens helped to organize this league. It was called the Delian League because its headquarters and treasury were located at first on the island of Delos. Pericles used money from the league's treasury to build a strong navy. The naval fleet was made up of at least 300 warships.

Athens Dominates the Delian League The fleet of Athens was the strongest in the Mediterranean region. Because Athens now had a superior navy, it took over leadership of the Delian League. In 454 **B.C.**, the Delian League's treasury was moved to Athens. The transfer of the Delian League's treasury helped to strengthen Athens' power. Athens started treating the other members of the league as if they were conquered people, not allies. Eventually, Athens dominated all of the city-states to such an extent that they became part of an Athenian empire.

REVIEW How did the power of Athens expand?
Pericles used the Delian League's money to build a strong naval fleet for Athens. Then Athens dominated the other city-states.

Classical Greece • 395

DIFFERENTIATING INSTRUCTION

Inclusion
Conduct an Acropolis Tour Guide
Give students a layout map of the buildings on the Acropolis and provide one detail about each building. Then have them conduct a pretend tour of the Acropolis, using the details to point out the buildings.

Gifted and Talented Students
Compare Architecture
Have groups research various buildings in the United States that have been influenced by ancient Greek architecture. Have each group select a building, describe its construction, and connect it to Greek architectural styles. Present the buildings to the class.

Teach

Expanding the Empire
6.4

Talk About It
- What was the Delian League? *(an organization of Greek city-states formed to give mutual protection after the Persian War)*
- How did the league help Pericles build a navy? *(He used money from the league's treasury to build a fleet of at least 300 warships.)*
- What was the result of the Delian League's treasury being moved to Athens from Delos? *(Athens became leader of the league and gained more power; it started treating other members of the league like conquered people instead of allies.)*

④ • **Critical Thinking: Making Inferences**
What problems might have resulted from Athens' treatment of league members as conquered people? *(Possible answers: Members would be resentful and rebel, possibly taking control of Athens; they would probably not help Athens to face other enemies.)*

⑤ **More About . . .**

The Delian League
The Delian League was formed by Sparta, Athens, Greek cities in Asia Minor, and other Greek and island city-states to protect each other from Persia. Each city-state had one vote. The Persians were a constant threat, especially to the cities in Asia Minor. The league waged war to regain cities in Asia Minor. This democratic alliance was weakened by Athens becoming a superior force and exercising its authority above the will of other league members.

Classical Greece • 395

Teacher's Edition notes also include:
- Assessment Suggestions
- Time Line Discussions
- Recommendations for books, videos, and software
- Motivation Activities

---

④  # Critical Thinking
Critical Thinking questions focus on the main points students need to understand in order to meet specific lesson objectives.

⑤ # More About . . .
These terrific nuggets of information occur often to supplement the text.

Interdisciplinary Activities
In addition to suggestions for differentiating instruction, the bottom section of the Teacher's Edition offers Interdisciplinary Activities that link to math, science, language arts, music, art, and health.

Standards-Based Assessment

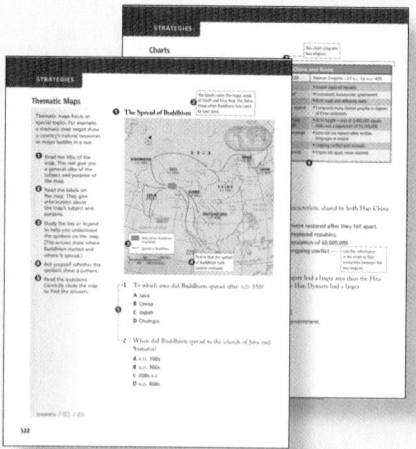

Strategies for Taking Tests

This innovative section of the Pupil's Edition includes strategies for answering multiple-choice, constructed-response, extended-response, and document-based questions, plus guidelines for analyzing primary and secondary sources.

Formal Assessment

The Formal Assessment book includes lesson quizzes, three levels of chapter tests with maps, and unit tests.

Integrated Assessment

Cooperative learning, role playing, and rubrics for alternative lesson support allow teachers to address a wide variety of student needs.

California Standards Enrichment Workbook

This ancillary provides teachers and students with a tool to reinforce learning of the California History–Social Science standards. The book includes a pre-test on content covered by the standards, content review and practice items in standardized-test format, and a post-test to measure student improvement.

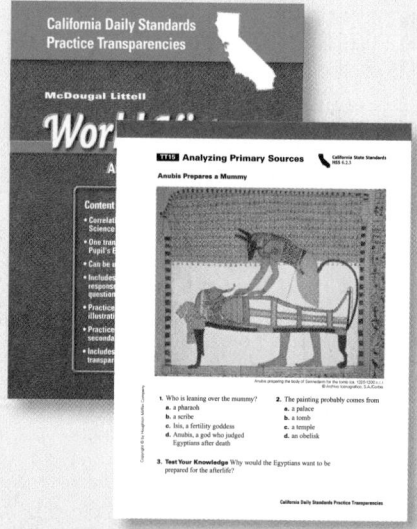

California Daily Standards Practice Transparencies

This book provides one transparency for each lesson in the textbook that familiarizes students with a variety of testing items. Each transparency is correlated to the California standards.

Document-Based Questions: Strategies and Practice

Constructed response and essay questions for each unit allow students to practice test-taking strategies using primary sources.

Edusoft® easyGrader

With this high-speed, low-cost testing system, teachers can

- print social studies tests correlated to the California standards
- build answer sheets that avoid the use of scan cards
- score tests automatically using a standard, inexpensive scanner
- generate individual or group reports to help identify each student's needs
- customize results by state standard and identify at-risk students and standards immediately
- use McDougal Littell resources to reteach concepts
- develop individual student instructional plans

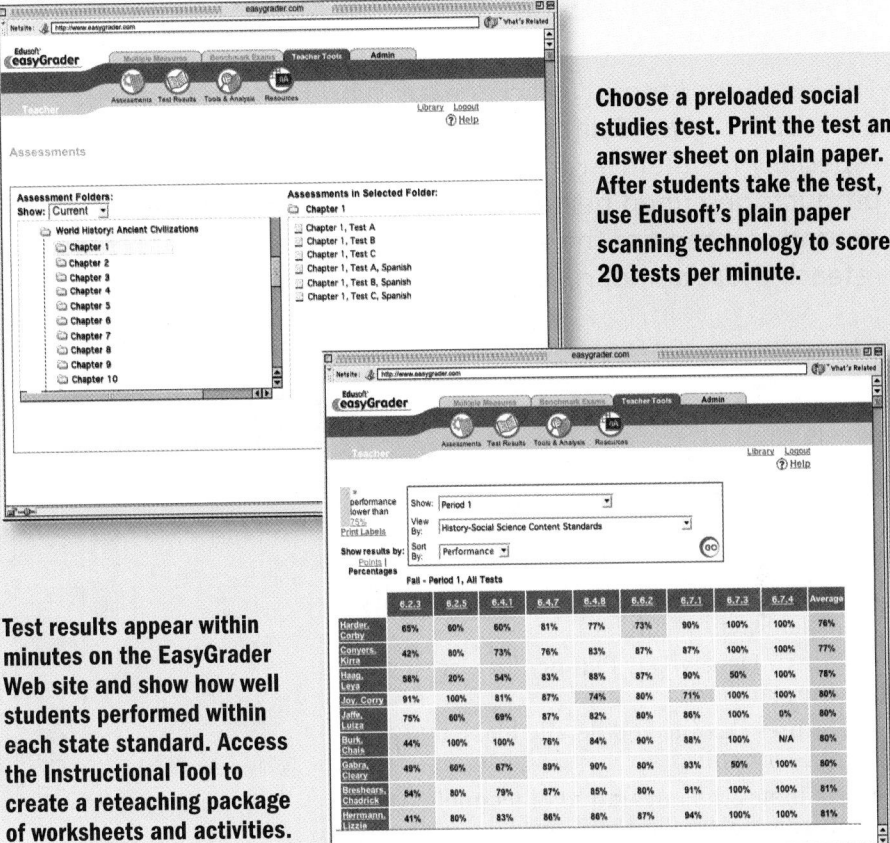

Choose a preloaded social studies test. Print the test and answer sheet on plain paper. After students take the test, use Edusoft's plain paper scanning technology to score 20 tests per minute.

Test results appear within minutes on the EasyGrader Web site and show how well students performed within each state standard. Access the Instructional Tool to create a reteaching package of worksheets and activities.

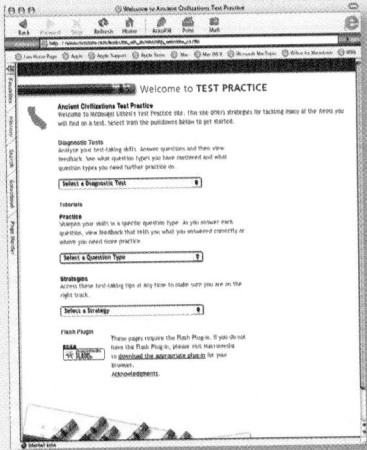

California Online Test Practice
Online student test practice, accessible through the *ClassZone* Web site, includes test-taking tips, diagnostic tests, skills-based tutorials, and skills and strategies help.

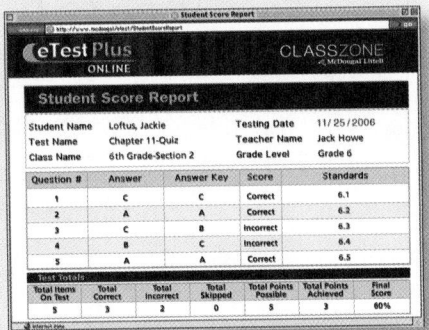

eTest Plus Online
This customizable assessment tool allows teachers to publish tests from the *Test Generator*. Students take the tests online, with results graded automatically. Individual and group score reports can be viewed, printed, and correlated to state and national standards.

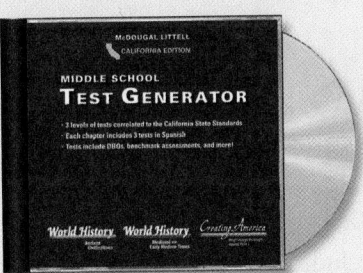

California Test Generator CD-ROM
Pre-made, customizable tests with three levels of questions, including document-based questions, are correlated to California state standards. Chapter tests are also available in Spanish. **Standards-Based Benchmark Tests** assess each subpoint in the California History–Social Science Standards for Grade 6.

Complete Instructional Support

The Teacher's Resource Package for *World History: Ancient Civilizations* gives California teachers resource materials developed especially for them—correlated to the California standards. The five products described below make it possible to plan each day's lesson around coverage of the social studies standards, and to teach and reteach those standards in the classroom every day.

Plan

California Standards Planner and Lesson Plans

- Provides correlations to California History–Social Science Standards

- Gives a Day-by-Day Planner for teaching all state standards

- Features flexible and detailed lesson plans for every unit

- Facilitates the integration of technology and other supplemental tools into daily lessons

- Enhances teaching, reteaching, tailored instruction, and assessment

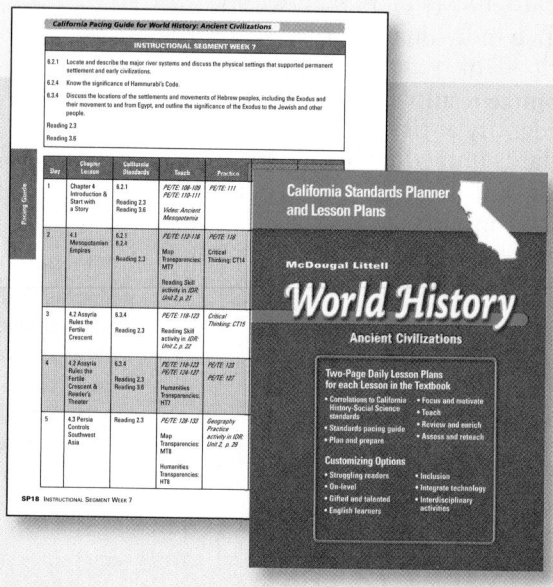

Teach/Reteach

California Standards Enrichment Workbook

- Reinforces learning of the California History–Social Science Standards

- Includes a unit-by-unit listing of the standards covered

- Provides a Pre-Test in standardized test format on standards covered

- Offers content review with graphic organizers and practice items for reteaching

- Ends with a Post-Test of the standards that provides a measure of student improvement

Teach/Reteach

California Daily Standards Practice Transparencies

- Provides one transparency per lesson
- Correlates transparencies with California standards
- Includes multiple-choice and other item formats
- Uses maps, charts, graphs, and time lines
- Uses primary sources and secondary sources

California Reading Toolkit for Social Studies

- Explains how to teach 30 reading strategies
- Correlates lesson-by-lesson plans to California standards
- Includes overhead transparencies for each strategy
- Includes articles by experts on teaching reading skills and building vocabulary in the social studies classroom

California Modified Lesson Plans for English Learners

- Provides 41 strategies to help students learning English
- Correlates lesson-by-lesson plans to California standards
- Provides research support for teaching English learners in the social studies classroom

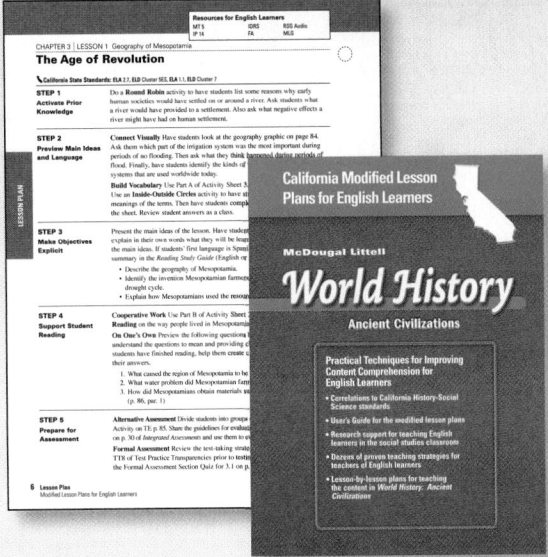

Complete Instructional Support

In-Depth Resources

Includes one booklet for each unit, organized by chapter and lesson, featuring:

- Reading Skill and Strategy
- Skillbuilder Practice
- Vocabulary Study Guide
- Vocabulary Cards
- Geography Practice
- Primary Sources
- Literature
- Reteaching Activities
- Family Newsletter

In-Depth Resources in Spanish

Provides Spanish translations of selected *In-Depth Resources* plus strategies for teaching English learners.

History Makers

Includes biographies of important individuals in history, plus comprehension and critical thinking questions.

Interdisciplinary Projects

Provides chapter-based activities and teaching strategies that involve additional math, science, and language arts skills that help connect history with other disciplines in the classroom.

Connecting History and Literature

Features activities and suggestions of relevant literature selections for each unit.

Reading Study Guide

Provides lesson summaries, main idea questions, and vocabulary activities to support less-proficient readers. Also available in Spanish.

Outline Map Activities

Features geographical, political, and historical maps for additional information.

Multi-Language Glossary of Social Studies Terms

Includes key terms from the text and other commonly used social studies terms defined in English with simple translations in Spanish, Chinese, Vietnamese, Khmer, Laotian, Arabic, Portuguese, Russian, Haitian Creole, and Hmong.

Document-Based Questions: Strategies and Practice

Constructed response and essay questions for each unit allow students to practice test-taking strategies using primary sources.

Character Education

Assists teachers in educating students about civic participation and other values and beliefs as demonstrated through the actions of historical individuals.

Bringing Social Studies Alive

Features hands-on activities and projects to further enhance students' understanding of historical events and time periods.

Formal Assessment

Includes lesson quizzes, three levels of chapter tests with maps, and unit tests.

Integrated Assessment

Includes cooperative learning, role playing, and rubrics for alternative lesson support.

Writing Research Reports for Social Studies

Offers support for writing research papers, historical narratives, essays, interviews, oral histories, book reviews, and short reports.

Workbook

Develops reading skills using essential content from each lesson.

Humanities Transparencies

Integrates fine art, photographs, and other historical artifacts into each chapter.

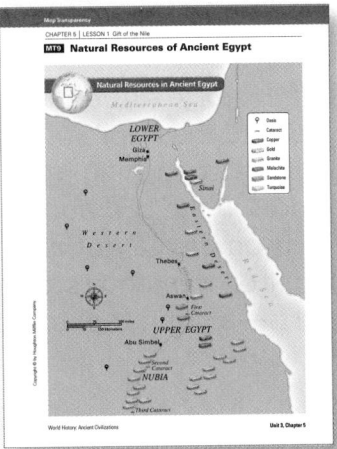

Map Transparencies

Includes maps to provide additional background and support.

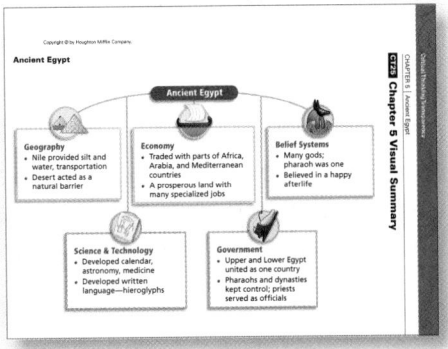

Critical Thinking Transparencies

Provides graphic organizers and visual summaries for each chapter.

Martin Luther King Jr.: His Life & Contributions

Provides a biography of civil rights leader Martin Luther King, Jr., with historical, cultural, and economic contexts for his life and work. Includes an illustrated time line, as well as five detailed lesson plans for each grade, from Grade Six through Grade Eleven. Each lesson plan explicitly connects King to historical topics required by California History-Social Science Content Standards.

Cesar Chavez: His Life & Contributions

Provides a biography of the labor leader Cesar Chavez, with historical, cultural, and economic contexts for his life and work. Includes an illustrated time line, as well as five lesson plans for each grade, from Grade Six through Grade Eleven. Each lesson plan explicitly connects Chavez's contributions to historical topics required by California History-Social Science Content Standards.

Integrated Technology

The technology resources that accompany *World History: Ancient Civilizations* enhance and extend the content beyond the Pupil's Edition. Each of the products shown here supports the teaching of the California standards, from the standards references in the *eEdition CD-ROM* to the Standards-Based Benchmark Tests on the *California Test Generator CD-ROM*. And the new EasyGrader conveniently scores standards-based tests and generates score reports—a great tool to help teachers monitor student peformance.

Plan

California EasyPlanner CD-ROM

- Customize lesson plans using all teacher resources.
- Plan a lesson, or plan the whole year.
- Access, view, and print all teacher resources.
- Print plans in daily, weekly, or monthly views.
- Track state standards correlated to each lesson.

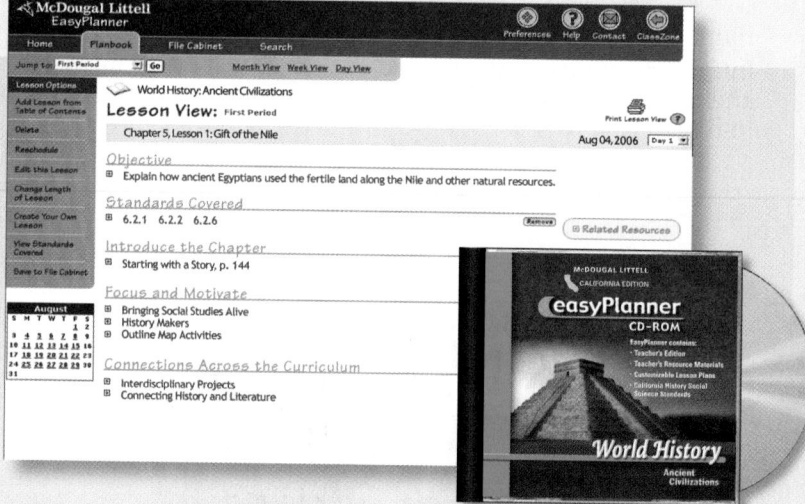

Teach

California eEdition CD-ROM

- Access all features of the student textbook.
- Engage learning with animated maps and infographics.
- Access activities, research links, and current events through ClassZone.
- Listen to lively recordings of Starting with a Story.

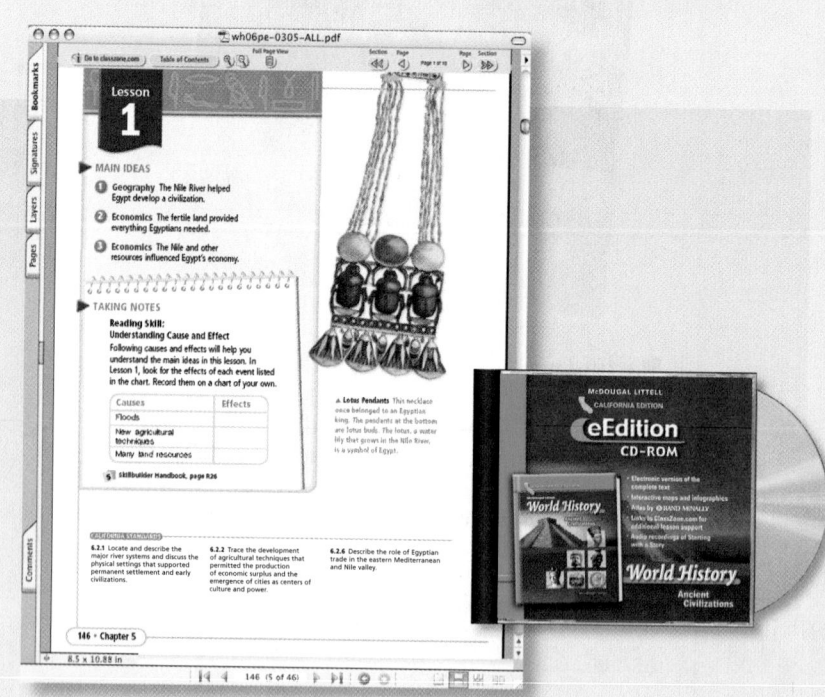

Assess

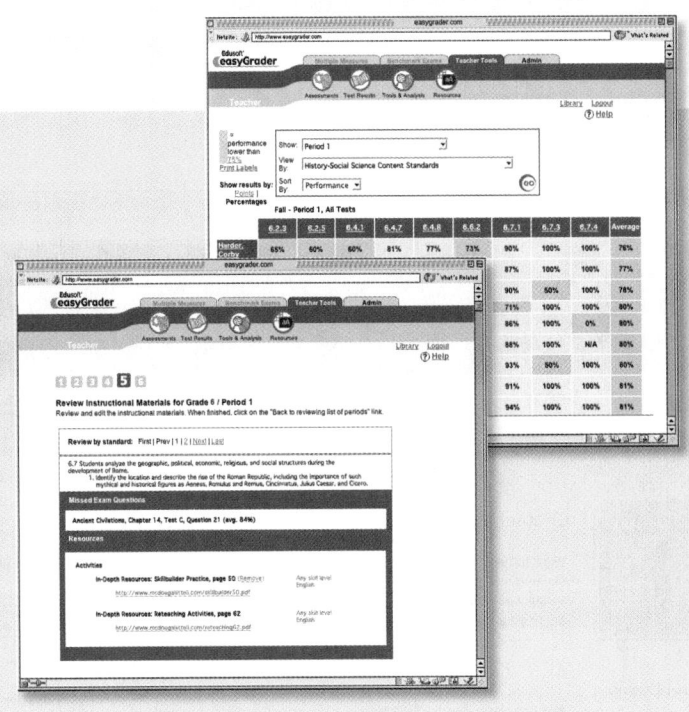

Edusoft EasyGrader

- Access tests that have been aligned to California State Standards.
- Print tests and answer keys on plain paper.
- Score tests quickly using a standard scanner.
- Read test results within minutes by individual test or by standards.
- Identify at-risk students and standards.
- Generate a customized package of reteaching materials that are aligned to test results.
- Track performance over time to measure and monitor improvement.

California Test Generator CD-ROM

with Standards-Based Benchmark Tests

- Three levels of tests are correlated to the California State Standards.
- Each chapter includes three tests in Spanish.
- Tests include DBQs, constructed-response, and extended-response questions.
- Each unit has Standards-Based Benchmark Tests to assess each subpoint in the California History–Social Science Standards for Grade 6.

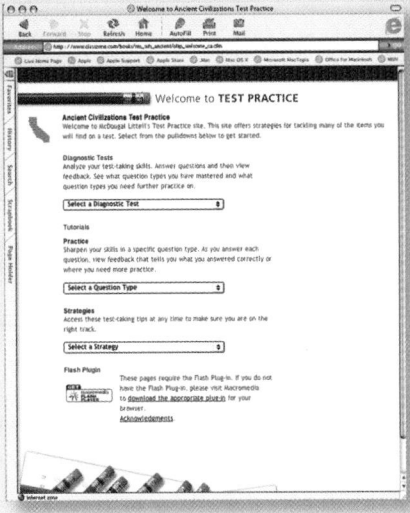

California Online Test Practice

- Take diagnostic tests.
- Get skill-based tutorials.
- Learn test-taking strategies.
- Tailored to California state standards.

Integrated Technology

CLASSZONE.COM

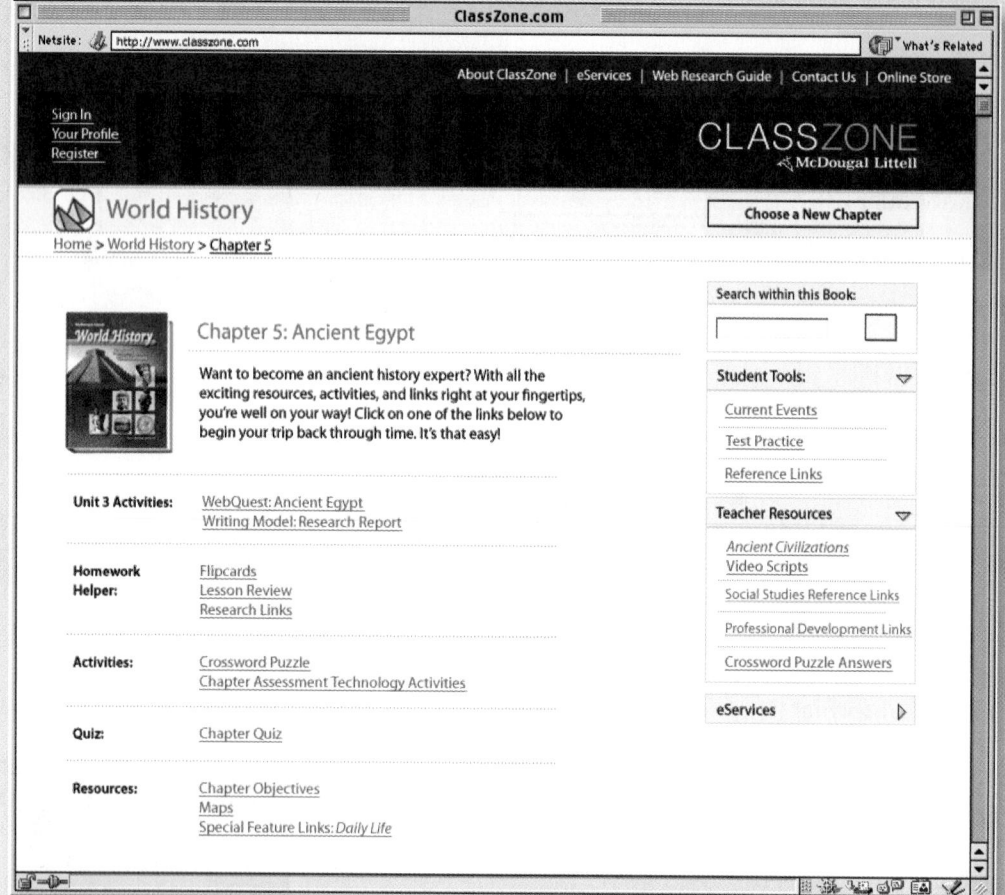

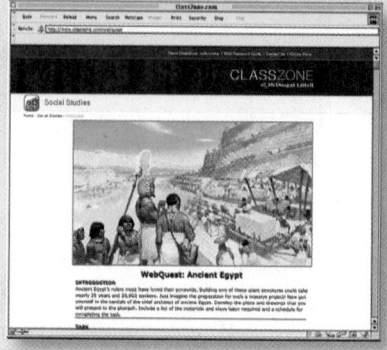

WebQuest
Prompt in-depth research and critical thinking on six world history topics.

ClassZone
Your online guide to *World History: Ancient Civilizations* offers

- WebQuests
- Writing Models
- Homework Helper
- Research Links
- Internet Activities
- Quizzes
- Maps
- Test Practice
- Current Events

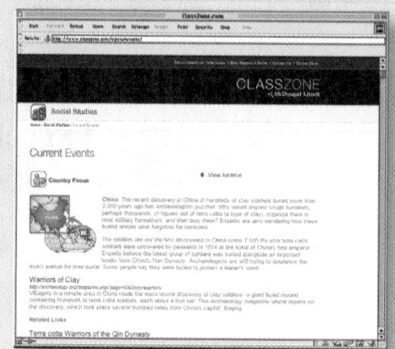

Current Events
Create real-world connections with links to current events.

Homework Helper
Reinforce lesson content with flipcards, research links to Web sites, and outlines.

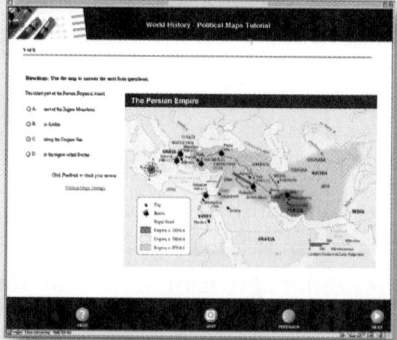

Test Practice
Support students with test-taking tips and skill-based tutorials.

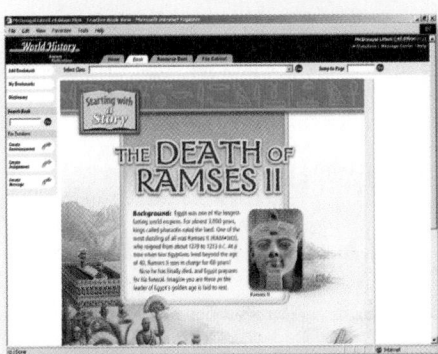

eEdition Plus Online

The online edition of the textbook features animated maps and infographics, and the capability to post assignments and announcements through an online message center.

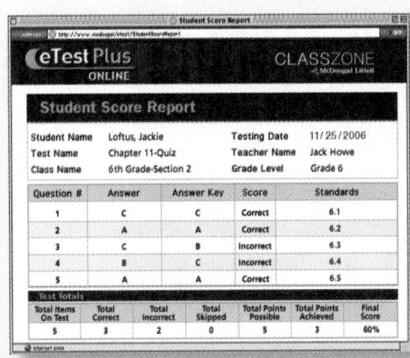

eTest Plus Online

Customizable assessment tool allows teachers to publish tests from the *Test Generator*. Students take the tests online, with results graded automatically. Individual and group score reports can be viewed, printed, and correlated to state and national standards.

World History: Ancient Civilizations Video Series

Integrated with the text, these selected video programs examine the religion, culture, and political systems of ancient civilizations. Each program uses illustrated maps, time lines, artifacts, and architectural overlays to teach history. Closed captions.

- Ancient Mesopotamia
- Ancient Egypt
- Ancient China
- Ancient Maya
- Ancient Greece
- Ancient Rome

The World's Music Audio CDs

A variety of recordings gives students the opportunity to hear music from many cultures.

Power Presentations CD-ROM

This multimedia presentation tool augments lectures and allows teachers to create presentations. Detailed lecture notes are enhanced by maps, charts, fine art, artifacts, and an interactive review game.

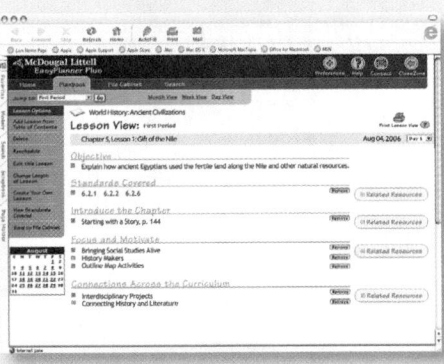

EasyPlanner Plus Online

This online planning tool allows teachers to customize lesson plans and track state standards correlated to each lesson. All teacher resources, plus PDF files of the Teacher's Edition pages, are available to view and print.

Differentiated Instruction

Multi-Language Glossary of Social Studies Terms

Key terms from the text and other commonly used social studies terms are defined in English with simple translations in Spanish, Chinese, Vietnamese, Khmer, Laotian, Arabic, Portuguese, Russian, Haitian Creole, and Hmong.

California Modified Lesson Plans for English Learners

Resourceful tips on adapting lessons and activities accompany lesson-by-lesson plans for teaching the content of *World History*. Proven strategies for teaching English learners are included with clear explanations of how they should be applied. Correlated to California History–Social Science Content Standards and English Language Development/English Language Arts Standards.

California Reading Toolkit for Social Studies

This classroom-tested reading support guide provides specific lesson plans correlated to before-, during-, and after-reading strategies, overhead transparencies, and vocabulary practice. Correlated to California History–Social Science Content Standards and English Language Development/English Language Arts Standards.

Reading Study Guide

Main idea questions, vocabulary activities, and lesson summaries written below grade level provide support for less-proficient readers. Also available in Spanish.

Reading Study Guide Audio CDs

Reading Study Guide lesson summaries on audio CD support struggling readers. Also available in Spanish.

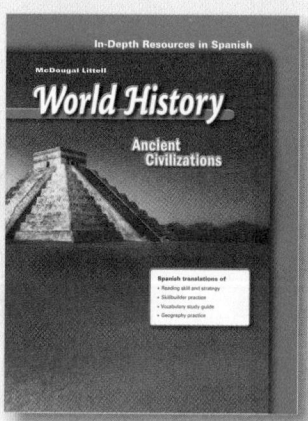

In-Depth Resources in Spanish

Spanish translations of selected *In-Depth Resources* are augmented with focused strategies for teaching English learners.

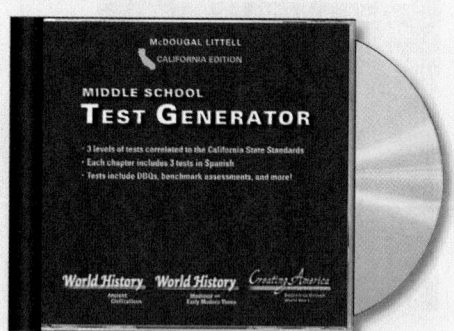

California Test Generator CD-ROM

Pre-made, customizable tests with three levels of questions translated into Spanish.

Teaching English Learners

NANCY SIDDENS
Consulting Editor, English for Speakers of Other Languages, McDougal Littell

McDougal Littell recognizes the challenges that English learners and their teachers face in the mainstream classroom. The trend to use English instruction in content classes (with less support in students' primary languages) and the federal legislation (No Child Left Behind) requiring instruction in content simultaneously with instruction in English, have driven the need for comprehensive, flexible support materials for teaching in English to English learners.

McDougal Littell's *World History: Ancient Civilizations* provides a wide range of support for these students and their teachers. This support gives teachers the tools needed to employ research-based principles for teaching standards-based curriculum to English learners while they learn the English language in meaningful historical contexts.

Research on facilitating the learning of content by students acquiring English has determined that effective instruction is built on these three principles:

- **Increase comprehension**
- **Enhance student interaction**
- **Improve thinking and study skills**

These principles, identified as effective through research by the Center for Applied Linguistics (Jameson), have guided McDougal Littell's approach to developing materials for teaching social studies and language to English learners.

Principle 1: Increase comprehension

Providing understandable information to the English learner is crucial for accessing both language and content. *World History: Ancient Civilizations* provides materials that enable teachers to employ practical strategies for increasing student comprehension. Verbal as well as nonverbal support is provided to make history more accessible to the English learner. The role of visual and experiential clues is especially important to beginning and intermediate language learners. Examples of nonverbal instruction include:

- A strong visual component in the Pupil's Edition, including vivid images, large maps, a variety of graphic organizers, charts, graphs, and time lines
- Complete audiovisual support through the *World History: Ancient Civilizations* video series, audio *Reading Study Guides*, multimedia presentations, and extensive online services
- A transparency program that includes *Map Transparencies*, *Critical Thinking Transparencies*, and *Humanities Transparencies*

Examples of verbal and print support include:

- The *Reading Study Guide* in both English and Spanish, chapter summaries written below grade level accompanied by comprehension questions
- The *Multi-Language Glossary of Social Studies Terms*, a compilation of translations of the key terms from the Pupil's Edition in nine languages
- *In-Depth Resources in Spanish*, Spanish translations of selected ancillary support pages

Principle 2: Enhance student interaction

Research shows that language is learned through communication with others—negotiating meaning to accomplish real purposes (Long and Porter). Participants in a discussion restate, question, explain, and clarify in order to come to a common understanding. This process helps students learn social studies as well as language. *World History: Ancient Civilizations*—and

(continues)

(continued)

Modified Lesson Plans for English Learners, which accompanies it—provide opportunities to increase interaction in the classroom in a variety of ways, including:

- Pair activities, in which students work in pairs to compare their own experiences relating to a particular lesson or topic
- Group work such as "jigsaw" reading, in which each student takes on responsibility for presenting one part of a lesson to a small group
- Class activities such as debates, unit projects, or games
- Opportunities for family involvement

Principle 3: Improve thinking and study skills

Explicit teaching of academic skills helps develop thinking skills and "thinking language" for English learners (Chamot and O'Malley). *World History: Ancient Civilizations* provides materials that focus instruction on performing higher-order thinking tasks, asking critical-thinking questions, assessing learning in a manner and language consistent with instruction, and reinforcing study and test-taking skills.

In the Pupil's Edition of *World History: Ancient Civilizations*, support for developing thinking and study skills includes:

- An emphasis on the main ideas of each lesson before reading begins
- Graphic organizers for note-taking practice in each lesson
- Highlighted vocabulary terms
- Main Idea comprehension questions that reinforce important content
- Skillbuilder questions accompanying large visuals such as maps and charts
- Lesson and chapter reviews that provide leveled questions from Main Idea to Critical Thinking
- A skills strand woven throughout the lesson and chapter reviews and reinforced in the Skillbuilder Handbook
- Test practice opportunities such as the 32-page "Strategies for Taking Tests" in the front of the book and Standards-Based Assessment practice in the chapter reviews

The Teacher's Edition and ancillaries for *World History: Ancient Civilizations* provide additional support for developing students' skills through activities for differentiated instruction, Reading Skill and Strategy pages, and Skillbuilder Practice pages.

World History: Ancient Civilizations provides teachers with the comprehensive support they need for teaching English learners. The program provides verbal and nonverbal support to increase understanding, promotes increased interaction and opportunities for communication, and encourages the development of academic thinking and study skills. Each of these areas has been identified, through research, as crucial for promoting the success of the English learner in acquiring content knowledge as well as language.

For more information:

Chamot, A.U. and O'Malley, J.M. (1994). *The CALLA Handbook: Implementing the Cognitive Academic Language Learning Approach.* Addison-Wesley: Reading, MA.

Jameson, J. (1998). "Three Principles for Success: English Language Learners in Mainstream Content Classes," From *Theory to Practice* 6, Center for Applied Linguistics: Region XIV Comprehensive Center.

Long, M. and Porter, P.A. (1985). "Group Work, Interlanguage Talk, and Second Language Acquisition," in *TESOL Quarterly* 19: 207–227.

Helping Students Read History

DONNA M. OGLE

Professor, Reading and Language, National-Louis University, Evanston, Illinois; Past President, International Reading Association

The best learners are active and engaged readers. Successful readers connect what they are reading with what they already know. These readers:

- build associations among ideas
- create visual images of what they are reading
- continually revise their interpretations as they gather more information.

Supporting Readers

World History: Ancient Civilizations uses many strategies to help students become active and engaged readers.

Various Learning Styles *World History: Ancient Civilizations* addresses various learning styles by including a variety of activity options, posing problems, providing graphic organizers to help students take notes, and asking thought-provoking questions for discussion.

Visual Information Many readers rely on visual information when reading unfamiliar material. In *World History: Ancient Civilizations*, photos and artifacts create a context for new ideas; maps help readers associate and compare ideas. In addition, charts of ideas and events summarize and clarify information. A visual summary at the end of each chapter provides another way of remembering ideas and events.

Personal Connections Personal stories and human connections can help to bring a subject such as history alive. *World History: Ancient Civilizations* uses historical stories and primary sources throughout to engage students' interest.

Primary Source

Whoever has walked with truth generates life.

Tell a lie and then tell the truth; it will be considered a lie!

He acquires many things; he must keep close watch over them.

Possessions are sparrows in flight which can find no place to alight.

from *Sumerian Proverbs*

VISUAL SUMMARY

Classical Greece

Culture (6.4)
- Developed the basis of western philosophy
- Established rules for the writing of history
- Set out rules of logic

Arts (6.4.8)
- Created drama
- Used the ideal as the basis for the arts
- Set artistic standards for art and architecture

Science & Technology (6.4.8)
- Made important discoveries about Earth and the planets
- Devised new mathematics
- Developed inventions such as compound pulley and water lifting devices

Government (6.4.3)
- Created and used direct democracy
- Expanded citizen participation in government
- Alexander built an enormous empire including land in Asia, Africa, and Europe

(continues)

(continued)

Vocabulary Two types of outer-column vocabulary notes help students read the text. Vocabulary Strategy notes offer proven vocabulary-building methods, such as analysis of prefixes, suffixes, root words, and compound words. Visual Vocabulary notes provide images to help students learn terms such as *pyramid* and *pictograph*.

English Learners Second-language learners need to have information and ideas presented to them in multiple ways. Being able to "see" history helps make it real for them. *World History: Ancient Civilizations* uses illustrations and visuals to present information to students in a variety of ways.

Evolving Forms of Reading

Students today need to be able to read in new ways.

Nonlinear Materials Today's students must:

- gather ideas from multiple sources— resource books, magazines, computerized databases, CD-ROMs, the Internet

- find their way through nonlinear materials, such as by deciding which area of a computer screen contains the information they want.

Graphic Layouts Today's readers must deal with informational materials that come in various formats.

- varying columns of text with many pictures, graphs, and maps, such as the three-dimensional graphic shown below

- single-column texts with large marginal areas used for illustrations, highlighted information, and thought-provoking ideas

World History: Ancient Civilizations familiarizes students with these multiple text formats and teaches students reading strategies for effectively obtaining information from each format.

Geography

Ancient Irrigation

The model below shows how an ancient irrigation system worked.

1 Gates controlled how much water flowed from the river.

2 Main canals led from the river. They sloped gently downward to keep the water flowing.

3 Medium-sized branch canals led away from the main canals.

4 Small feeder canals led water directly to the fields.

GEOGRAPHY SKILLBUILDER

INTERPRETING VISUALS

Human-Environment Interaction Why do you think it was important to control how much water flowed from the river?

Correlations to
California History–Social Science
Content Standards and Analysis Skills

World History
Ancient Civilizations

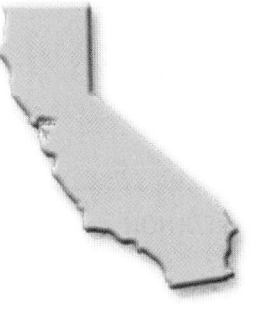

Correlations to California History–Social Science Content Standards and Analysis Skills

Standards Map – Basic Comprehensive Program
Grade Six – History Social Science
World History and Geography: Ancient Civilizations

Students in grade six expand their understanding of history by studying the people and events that ushered in the dawn of the major Western and non–Western ancient civilizations. Geography is of special significance in the development of the human story. Continued emphasis is placed on the everyday lives, problems, and accomplishments of people, their role in developing social, economic, and political structures, as well as in establishing and spreading ideas that helped transform the world forever. Students develop higher levels of critical thinking by considering why civilizations developed where and when they did, why they became dominant, and why they declined. Students analyze the interactions among the various cultures, emphasizing their enduring contributions and the link, despite time, between the contemporary and ancient worlds.

Standard	Primary Citations	Supporting Citations
6.1 Students describe what is known through archaeological studies of the early physical and cultural development of humankind from the Paleolithic era to the agricultural revolution.	**PUPIL & TEACHER & eEDITION** Common Pages: 4, 5, 6–7, 26, **27–33, 34–37, 40–43,** 44, 45, 46–47, 48–49, 50, 51–53, **54–55,** 56–57, 58, 59–62, 65, **68–69,** 70–71, 72–73, 83–86, 301–302 Add'l Teacher's Edition: 2, 53, 141B **PRINT COMPONENT(S)** CA Standards Enrichment Wrkbk: 15–20 **TRANSPARENCIES/TECHNOLOGY** CA Daily Standards Practice Transparencies: 3, 5, 6, 7	**PUPIL & TEACHER & eEDITION** Common Pages: 6–7, 73, 80–81, 89, 162–163, 221, 228 **PRINT COMPONENT(S)** In–Depth Resources Unit 1: 15, 31–34 In–Depth Resources in Spanish Unit 1: 17–18 History Makers: 1–2, 3–4 CA Reading Toolkit: L3, L5–L8, L11–L12, L14–L20 CA Modified Lesson Plans for English Learners: 9, 13, 15, 17, 19, 21, 23, 25, 27, 29, 31, 33, 35, 37, 39, 41, 43 CA Standards Planner & Lesson Plans: L5, L9, L11, L13, L39 **TRANSPARENCIES/TECHNOLOGY** Humanities Transparencies: 1, 3, 4 Map Transparencies: 3, 4 Critical Thinking Transparencies: 3, 6, 7, 8 Benchmark Tests: 1.3, 2.1, 2.2, 2.3, 6.3 Power Presentations: 1.3, 2.1, 2.2, 2.3, 6.3

Correlations to California History–Social Science Content Standards and Analysis Skills

Standard	Primary Citations	Supporting Citations
6.1.1 Describe the hunter–gatherer societies, including the development of tools and the use of fire.	**PUPIL & TEACHER & eEDITION** Common Pages: 26, 32, 46–47, 48–49, **50, 51–55,** 56, **57,** 58, **59–62,** 72–73, 83–86, R36 Add'l Teacher's Edition: 53 **PRINT COMPONENT(S)** CA Standards Enrichment Wrkbk: **15–16** **TRANSPARENCIES/TECHNOLOGY** CA Daily Standards Practice Transparencies: 5, 6	**PUPIL & TEACHER & eEDITION** Common Pages: 80–81 **PRINT COMPONENT(S)** In–Depth Resources Unit 1: 34 CA Reading Toolkit: L3, L5 CA Modified Lesson Plans for English Learners: 9, 13 CA Standards Planner & Lesson Plans: L5, L9 **TRANSPARENCIES/TECHNOLOGY** Humanities Transparencies: 1, 3, 4 Map Transparencies: 3 Critical Thinking Transparencies: 6 Benchmark Tests: 1.3, 2.1 Power Presentations: 1.3, 2.1
6.1.2 Identify the locations of human communities that populated the major regions of the world and describe how humans adapted to a variety of environments.	**PUPIL & TEACHER & eEDITION** Common Pages: 6–7, 28–31, 32–33, 34–37, 44–45, **46–47,** 48–49, 50, **51–53,** 54–55, 56–57, 58, **59–62,** 64, 65, 66, 67, **68–69, 70–71,** 72–73, 83–86, 202, 203, 205, 206, 207, 208 **PRINT COMPONENT(S)** CA Standards Enrichment Wrkbk: 17–18 **TRANSPARENCIES/TECHNOLOGY** CA Daily Standards Practice Transparencies: 5, 6	**PUPIL & TEACHER & eEDITION** Common Pages: 80–81 **PRINT COMPONENT(S)** In–Depth Resources Unit 1: 31–32 In–Depth Resources in Spanish Unit 1: 17–18 CA Reading Toolkit: L5, L6, L7, L20 CA Modified Lesson Plans for English Learners: 13, 15, 17, 43 CA Standards Planner & Lesson Plans: L11, L13, L39 **TRANSPARENCIES/TECHNOLOGY** Humanities Transparencies: 4 Map Transparencies: 4 Critical Thinking Transparencies: 7 Benchmark Tests: 2.2, 2.3, 6.3 Power Presentations: 2.2, 2.3, 6.3

Standard	Primary Citations	Supporting Citations
6.1.3 Discuss the climatic changes and human modifications of the physical environment that gave rise to the domestication of plants and animals and new sources of clothing and shelter.	**PUPIL & TEACHER & eEDITION** Common Pages: 30, 32–33, 44, **46–47, 51–55,** 56–57, 58, **59–62,** 64, **65–69, 70–71,** 72–73, 83–86 **PRINT COMPONENT(S)** CA Standards Enrichment Wrkbk: 19–20 **TRANSPARENCIES/TECHNOLOGY** CA Daily Standards Practice Transparencies: 7	**PUPIL & TEACHER & eEDITION** Common Pages: 80–81 **PRINT COMPONENT(S)** In–Depth Resources Unit 1: 31–33 In–Depth Resources in Spanish Unit 1: 17–18 History Makers: 3–4 CA Reading Toolkit: L6, L7 CA Modified Lesson Plans for English Learners: 15, 43 CA Standards Planner & Lesson Plans: L11, L13 **TRANSPARENCIES/TECHNOLOGY** Map Transparencies: 4 Critical Thinking Transparencies: 8 Benchmark Tests: 2.2, 2.3 Power Presentations: 2.2, 2.3

Correlations to California History–Social Science Content Standards and Analysis Skills

Standard	Primary Citations	Supporting Citations
6.2 Students analyze the geographic, political, economic, religious, and social structures of the early civilizations of Mesopotamia, Egypt, and Kush.	**PUPIL & TEACHER & eEDITION** Common Pages: 41, 47, 54, 59–62, 65–69, 70–71, 72–73, 76–77, 78–79, **80–81**, 82–86, 87, 88, 89–95, 96–97, 98, **99–103**, 104–105, 106–107, 108–109, 110–111, 114, 112–116, 117, 118–123, 124–127, 136–137, 140–141, 142–143, 144–145, 146–151, 152–153, 154–161, 162–163, 164–170, 171, 172–177, 178–181, 182–183, 184–185, 188–193, 194–195, 200, 206, 208–209, 221–224, 253–254, 255, 257, 282, 310, 358–359, 489, 516, 523 Add'l Teacher's Edition: 76, 141B, 150 **PRINT COMPONENT(S)** CA Standards Enrichment Wrkbk: 20–38, 45–46 **TRANSPARENCIES/TECHNOLOGY** CA Daily Standards Practice Transparencies: 11, 12, 14, 15, 16, 17, 18	**PUPIL & TEACHER & eEDITION** Common Pages: 92, 114, 142, 143, 182, 214, 252, 257, 282 **PRINT COMPONENT(S)** In–Depth Resources Unit 2: 1–7, 11, 15–17, 31; Unit 3: 13–14, 31–32 In–Depth Resources in Spanish Unit 2: 19–23, 25–26; Unit 3: 43–44, 51–52 History Makers: 7–8, 9–10 CA Reading Toolkit: L12 CA Modified Lesson Plans for English Learners: 21, 23, 25, 27, 33, 31, 33, 35, 37, 39, 41 CA Standards Planner & Lesson Plans: L9, 15, L17, L19, L21, L23, L27, L29, L31, L33, L35, L37 **TRANSPARENCIES/TECHNOLOGY** Humanities Transparencies: 7, 9, 10, 11 Map Transparencies: 7, 9, 10, 11 Critical Thinking Transparencies: 15, 18, 19, 20, 23 Benchmark Tests: 2.1, 3.1, 3.2, 3.3, 4.1, 4.2, 5.1, 5.2, 5.3, 5.4, 6.1, 6.2 Power Presentations: 2.1, 3.1, 3.2, 3.3, 4.1, 4.2, 5.1, 5.2, 5.3, 5.4, 6.1, 6.2
6.2.1 Locate and describe the major river systems and discuss the physical settings that supported permanent settlement and early civilizations.	**PUPIL & TEACHER & eEDITION** Common Pages: 78–79, 80–81, 82–86, 87, 92, 96–97, 106–107, 112, 114, 136, 142–143, 146–151, **152–153**, 182–183, 188, 189, 193, 197, 199–200, 208–209, **221–224**, 252, **253–254**, 257, 282 Add'l Teacher's Edition: 141B **PRINT COMPONENT(S)** CA Standards Enrichment Wrkbk: 21–22 **TRANSPARENCIES/TECHNOLOGY** CA Daily Standards Practice Transparencies: 14	**PRINT COMPONENT(S)** In–Depth Resources Unit 2: 1–3, 7, 11, 15 In–Depth Resources in Spanish Unit 2: 19, 23, 25–26 CA Reading Toolkit: L8, L11, L14, L18 CA Modified Lesson Plans for English Learners: 19, 25, 29, 31, 39 CA Standards Planner & Lesson Plans: L9, L15, L21, L27, L35 **TRANSPARENCIES/TECHNOLOGY** Map Transparencies: 9 Benchmark Tests: 2.1, 3.1, 4.1, 5.1, 6.1 Power Presentations: 2.1, 3.1, 4.1, 5.1, 6.1

Standard	Primary Citations	Supporting Citations
6.2.2 Trace the development of agricultural techniques that permitted the production of economic surplus and the emergence of cities as centers of culture and power.	**PUPIL & TEACHER & eEDITION** Common Pages: 47, **59–62, 65–69, 70–71,** 72–73, 78–79, 80–81, 82–86, 87, 88, 89–92, 98, 100–101, 104, 106–107, 113, 142–143, 146–149, 151, 154, 155, 161, 182–183, 221, 253–254 Add'l Teacher's Edition: 141B **PRINT COMPONENT(S)** CA Standards Enrichment Wrkbk: 23–24 **TRANSPARENCIES/TECHNOLOGY** CA Daily Standards Practice Transparencies: 11	**PUPIL & TEACHER & eEDITION** Common Pages: 92, 114, 142, 182, 252, 257, 282 **PRINT COMPONENT(S)** In–Depth Resources Unit 2: 1–4, 11, 16 In–Depth Resources in Spanish Unit 2: 19–20, 25–26 CA Reading Toolkit: L8, L9, L10, L14, L15 CA Modified Lesson Plans for English Learners: 19, 21, 23, 31 CA Standards Planner & Lesson Plans: L15, L17, L19, L27, L29 **TRANSPARENCIES/TECHNOLOGY** Critical Thinking Transparencies: 18 Benchmark Tests: 3.1, 3.3, 5.1, 5.2 Power Presentations: 3.1, 3.3, 5.1, 5.2
6.2.3 Understand the relationship between religion and the social and political order in Mesopotamia and Egypt.	**PUPIL & TEACHER & eEDITION** Common Pages: **88–95,** 98–103, 106–107, 108–109, 110–111, 112–116, 117, 118–123, 124–127, 128–133, 136, 140–141, 142–143, 144–145, 152–153, 154–161, 162–163, 164–170, 171, 172–177, 178–181, 182–183, R39 Add'l Teacher's Edition: 141B **PRINT COMPONENT(S)** CA Standards Enrichment Wrkbk: 25–26 **TRANSPARENCIES/TECHNOLOGY** CA Daily Standards Practice Transparencies: 15	**PRINT COMPONENT(S)** In–Depth Resources Unit 3: 15 CA Reading Toolkit: L9, L10, L15, L16, L17 CA Modified Lesson Plans for English Learners: 21, 23, 33, 35, 37 **PRINT COMPONENT(S)** CA Standards Planner & Lesson Plans: L17, L19, L29, L31, L33 **TRANSPARENCIES/TECHNOLOGY** Humanities Transparencies: 10 Critical Thinking Transparencies: 19 Benchmark Tests: 3.2, 3.3, 5.2, 5.3, 5.4 Power Presentations: 3.2, 3.3, 5.2, 5.3, 5.4

Correlations to California History–Social Science Content Standards and Analysis Skills

Standard	Primary Citations	Supporting Citations
6.2.4 Know the significance of Hammurabi's Code.	**PUPIL & TEACHER & eEDITION** Common Pages: 108, **110–111**, **112**, 114, **115–116**, **117**, **136–137**, R38 Add'l Teacher's Edition: 76 **PRINT COMPONENT(S)** CA Standards Enrichment Wrkbk: 27–28	**PUPIL & TEACHER & eEDITION** Common Pages: 143 **PRINT COMPONENT(S)** In–Depth Resources Unit 2: 31 History Makers: 7–8 CA Reading Toolkit: L11 CA Modified Lesson Plans for English Learners: 25 CA Standards Planner & Lesson Plans: L21 **TRANSPARENCIES/TECHNOLOGY** Benchmark Tests: 4.1 Power Presentations: 4.1
6.2.5 Discuss the main features of Egyptian art and architecture.	**PUPIL & TEACHER & eEDITION** Common Pages: 38, 140–141, 142–143, 144–145, **146–151**, 152–153, 154–161, 162–163, **164–170**, **171**, 172–177, 182, 183, 310 Add'l Teacher's Edition: 141B **PRINT COMPONENT(S)** CA Standards Enrichment Wrkbk: 29–30 **TRANSPARENCIES/TECHNOLOGY** CA Daily Standards Practice Transparencies: 16	**PRINT COMPONENT(S)** In–Depth Resources Unit 3: 13–14 In–Depth Resources in Spanish Unit 3: 43–44 CA Reading Toolkit: L15, L16 CA Modified Lesson Plans for English Learners: 33, 35 CA Standards Planner & Lesson Plans: L29, L31 **TRANSPARENCIES/TECHNOLOGY** Critical Thinking Transparencies: 20 Benchmark Tests: 5.2, 5.3 Power Presentations: 5.2, 5.3
6.2.6 Describe the role of Egyptian trade in the eastern Mediterranean and Nile valley.	**PUPIL & TEACHER & eEDITION** Common Pages: 146, 150, **151**, **152–153**, 155, 172, **173–174**, **178–181**, **182**, 190 Add'l Teacher's Edition: 141B, 150 **PRINT COMPONENT(S)** CA Standards Enrichment Wrkbk: 31–32	**PUPIL & TEACHER & eEDITION** Common Pages: 198 **PRINT COMPONENT(S)** CA Reading Toolkit: L14 CA Modified Lesson Plans for English Learners: 31 CA Standards Planner & Lesson Plans: L27 **TRANSPARENCIES/TECHNOLOGY** Benchmark Tests: 5.1 Power Presentations: 5.1

Standard	Primary Citations	Supporting Citations
6.2.7 Understand the significance of Queen Hatshepsut and Ramses the Great.	**PUPIL & TEACHER & eEDITION** Common Pages: 143, **144–145, 172–174, 175–177, 178–181, 182–183** Add'l Teacher's Edition: 141B **PRINT COMPONENT(S)** CA Standards Enrichment Wrkbk: 33–34 **TRANSPARENCIES/TECHNOLOGY** CA Daily Standards Practice Transparencies: 17	**PUPIL & TEACHER & eEDITION** Common Pages: 214 **PRINT COMPONENT(S)** CA Reading Toolkit: L17 CA Modified Lesson Plans for English Learners: 37 History Makers: 9–10 CA Standards Planner & Lesson Plans: L33 **TRANSPARENCIES/TECHNOLOGY** Map Transparencies: 10 Benchmark Tests: 5.4 Power Presentations: 5.4
6.2.8 Identify the location of the Kush civilization and describe its political, commercial, and cultural relations with Egypt.	**PUPIL & TEACHER & eEDITION** Common Pages: **184–185**, 186–187, **188, 189–193, 194–195**, 196–200, 201, **208–209** **PRINT COMPONENT(S)** CA Standards Enrichment Wrkbk: 35–36 **TRANSPARENCIES/TECHNOLOGY** CA Daily Standards Practice Transparencies: 18	**PRINT COMPONENT(S)** In–Depth Resources Unit 3: 31–32 In–Depth Resources in Spanish Unit 3: 51–52 CA Reading Toolkit: L18, L19 CA Modified Lesson Plans for English Learners: 39, 41 CA Standards Planner & Lesson Plans: L35, L37 **TRANSPARENCIES/TECHNOLOGY** Humanities Transparencies: 11 Map Transparencies: 11 Critical Thinking Transparencies: 23 Benchmark Tests: 6.1, 6.2 Power Presentations: 6.1, 6.2
6.2.9 Trace the evolution of language and its written forms.	**PUPIL & TEACHER & eEDITION** Common Pages: **41**, 54, 79, 88, 96–97, 98, **101–103, 106–107**, 115, 136, 154, **156–159**, 161, 182, 190, 191, 193, 200, 206, 208–209, 222, 255, 310, **358–359**, 489, 516, 523, R40 **PRINT COMPONENT(S)** CA Standards Enrichment Wrkbk: 37–38	**PRINT COMPONENT(S)** CA Reading Toolkit: L9, L10, L15 CA Modified Lesson Plans for English Learners: 21, 23, 33, 41 CA Standards Planner & Lesson Plans: L17, L19, L29 **TRANSPARENCIES/TECHNOLOGY** Humanities Transparencies: 9 Benchmark Tests: 3.2, 3.3, 5.2 Power Presentations: 3.2, 3.3, 5.2

Correlations to California History–Social Science Content Standards and Analysis Skills

Standard	Primary Citations	Supporting Citations
6.3 **Students analyze the geographic, political, economic, religious, and social structures of the Ancient Hebrews.**	**PUPIL & TEACHER & eEDITION** Common Pages: 318–319, 320–321, 322–323, 324, **325–329, 330–333,** 334, **335–339,** 340–341, 342, **343–346, 348–349,** R45–R50 Add'l Teacher's Edition: 320 **PRINT COMPONENT(S)** CA Standards Enrichment Wrkbk: 39–40, 41–42, 43–44, 45–46 **TRANSPARENCIES/TECHNOLOGY** CA Daily Standards Practice Transparencies: 33, 34, 35	**PRINT COMPONENT(S)** In–Depth Resources Unit 5: 11–14 In–Depth Resources in Spanish Unit 5: 89–90 History Makers: 19–20 CA Reading Toolkit: L12, L13, L33, L34, L35 CA Modified Lesson Plans for English Learners: 69, 71, 73 CA Standards Planner & Lesson Plans: L23, L25, L65, L67, L69 **TRANSPARENCIES/TECHNOLOGY** Humanities Transparencies: 19, 20 Map Transparencies: 19 Critical Thinking Transparencies: 42–43 Benchmark Tests: 4.2, 4.3, 10.1, 10.2, 10.3 Power Presentations: 4.2, 4.3, 10.1, 10.2, 10.3
6.3.1 Describe the origins and significance of Judaism as the first monotheistic religion based on the concept of one God who sets down moral laws for humanity.	**PUPIL & TEACHER & eEDITION** Common Pages: **322–323,** 324–325, **326–327,** 328–329, **330–333, 345–346, 348–349,** R45–R50 Add'l Teacher's Edition: 320 **PRINT COMPONENT(S)** CA Standards Enrichment Wrkbk: 39–40 **TRANSPARENCIES/TECHNOLOGY** CA Daily Standards Practice Transparencies: 33	**PRINT COMPONENT(S)** In–Depth Resources Unit 5: 14 In–Depth Resources in Spanish Unit 5: 90 CA Reading Toolkit: L33 CA Modified Lesson Plans for English Learners: 69 CA Standards Planner & Lesson Plans: L65 **TRANSPARENCIES/TECHNOLOGY** Benchmark Tests: 10.1 Power Presentations: 10.1

Standard	Primary Citations	Supporting Citations
6.3.2 Identify the sources of the ethical teachings and central beliefs of Judaism (the Hebrew Bible, the Commentaries): belief in God, observance of law, practice of the concepts of righteousness and justice, and importance of study; and describe how the ideas of the Hebrew traditions are reflected in the moral and ethical traditions of Western civilization.	**PUPIL & TEACHER & eEDITION** Common Pages: **322–323**, 324, **325–329**, **330–333**, 334, 338, 342, **343–346**, **348–349**, 466–467, R45–R50 Add'l Teacher's Edition: 320 **PRINT COMPONENT(S)** CA Standards Enrichment Wrkbk: 41–42 **TRANSPARENCIES/TECHNOLOGY** CA Daily Standards Practice Transparencies: 34	**PRINT COMPONENT(S)** In–Depth Resources Unit 5: 14 CA Reading Toolkit: L33, L34, L35 CA Modified Lesson Plans for English Learners: 69, 71, 73 CA Standards Planner & Lesson Plans: L65, L67, L69 **TRANSPARENCIES/TECHNOLOGY** Benchmark Tests: 10.1, 10.2, 10.3 Power Presentations: 10.1, 10.2, 10.3
6.3.3 Explain the significance of Abraham, Moses, Naomi, Ruth, David, and Yohanan ben Zaccai in the development of the Jewish religion.	**PUPIL & TEACHER & eEDITION** Common Pages: **322–323**, 324, **325–327**, 329, **330–333**, 334, 335, 336, 339, 341, 342, 344, **345–346**, **348–349** Add'l Teacher's Edition: 320 **PRINT COMPONENT(S)** CA Standards Enrichment Wrkbk: 43–44	**PRINT COMPONENT(S)** In–Depth Resources Unit 5: 11–13 In–Depth Resources in Spanish Unit 5: 89–90 History Makers: 19–20 CA Reading Toolkit: L33, L34, L35 CA Modified Lesson Plans for English Learners: 69, 71, 73 CA Standards Planner & Lesson Plans: L65, L67, L69 **TRANSPARENCIES/TECHNOLOGY** Humanities Transparencies: 19, 20 Map Transparencies: 19 Critical Thinking Transparencies: 42, 43 Benchmark Tests: 10.1, 10.2, 10.3 Power Presentations: 10.1, 10.2, 10.3

Correlations to California History–Social Science Content Standards and Analysis Skills

Standard	Primary Citations	Supporting Citations
6.3.4 Discuss the locations of the settlements and movements of Hebrew peoples, including the Exodus and their movement to and from Egypt, and outline the significance of the Exodus to the Jewish and other people.	**PUPIL & TEACHER & eEDITION** Common Pages: 118, 120, 122, 128, 129, 130, 131, 133, 318–319, 320–321, 322–323, 324, **325–329, 330–333,** 334, **335–339,** 340–341, 342, **343–346,** 348–349 **PRINT COMPONENT(S)** CA Standards Enrichment Wrkbk: 45–46	**PRINT COMPONENT(S)** In–Depth Resources Unit 5: 11–12 In–Depth Resources in Spanish Unit 5: 89–90 CA Reading Toolkit: L12, L13, L33, L34 CA Modified Lesson Plans for English Learners: 69, 71 CA Standards Planner & Lesson Plans: L23, L25, L65, L67, L69 **TRANSPARENCIES/TECHNOLOGY** Map Transparencies: 19 Critical Thinking Transparencies: 42 Benchmark Tests: 4.2, 4.3, 10.1, 10.2, 10.3 Power Presentations: 4.2, 4.3, 10.1, 10.2, 10.3
6.3.5 Discuss how Judaism survived and developed despite the continuing dispersion of much of the Jewish population from Jerusalem and the rest of Israel after the destruction of the second Temple in A.D. 70.	**PUPIL & TEACHER & eEDITION** Common Pages: 342, **345–346,** 347, 348, 483 **TRANSPARENCIES/TECHNOLOGY** CA Daily Standards Practice Transparencies: 35	**PRINT COMPONENT(S)** CA Reading Toolkit: L35 CA Modified Lesson Plans for English Learners: 73 **TRANSPARENCIES/TECHNOLOGY** Map Transparencies: 20 Critical Thinking Transparencies: 44 Benchmark Tests: 10.1, 10.2, 10.3, 11.1, 11.2 Power Presentations: 10.1, 10.2, 10.3, 11.1, 11.2

Standard	Primary Citations	Supporting Citations
6.4 Students analyze the geographic, political, economic, religious, and social structures of the early civilizations of Ancient Greece.	**PUPIL & TEACHER & eEDITION** Common Pages: 123, 128, 129–233, 134–135, 136, 137, 350–351, 352–353, 354, **355–359**, 360, **361–365**, 366–369, 370, **371–376**, 377, 378, **379–383**, 384–385, 386–387, 388–389, 390–391, 392, **393–397**, 398, 399–402, 404, 405–409, 410–417, 418–419, 420–421 Add'l Teacher's Edition: 350B **PRINT COMPONENT(S)** CA Standards Enrichment Wrkbk: 49–50, 51–52, 53–54, 55–56, 57–58, 59–60, 61–62, 63–64 **TRANSPARENCIES/TECHNOLOGY** CA Daily Standards Practice Transparencies: 12	**PUPIL & TEACHER & eEDITION** Common Pages: 177, 215, 338, 340, 341, 352–353, 382, 383 **PRINT COMPONENT(S)** In–Depth Resources Unit 2: 29–30, 32; Unit 5: 18–25, 29–36 In–Depth Resources in Spanish Unit 2: 33–34; Unit 5: 91–95, 97, 99–100 CA Reading Toolkit: L13, L36, L37, L38, L39, L40, L41, L42 CA Modified Lesson Plans for English Learners: 29, 75, 77, 79, 81, 83, 85, 87, 89 CA Standards Planner & Lesson Plans: L25, L71, L73, L75, L77, L79, L81, L83, L85 **TRANSPARENCIES/TECHNOLOGY** Benchmark Tests: 11.1, 11.2, 11.3, 11.4, 12.1, 12.3, 12.4 Power Presentations: 11.1, 11.2, 11.3, 11.4, 12.1, 12.3, 12.4
6.4.1 Discuss the connections between geography and the development of city–states in the region of the Aegean Sea, including patterns of trade and commerce among Greek city–states and within the wider Mediterranean region.	**PUPIL & TEACHER & eEDITION** Common Pages: **351**, 354, **355–359**, 370, **371–372**, 376, 378, **379**, 386–387, **389**, 392, 393–397, 398, 399–402 Add'l Teacher's Edition: 350B **PRINT COMPONENT(S)** CA Standards Enrichment Wrkbk: 49–50	**PRINT COMPONENT(S)** In–Depth Resources Unit 5: 18–20, 25, 29–30, 33 In–Depth Resources in Spanish Unit 5: 91, 97, 99–100 CA Reading Toolkit: L36, L38 CA Modified Lesson Plans for English Learners: 75, 79 CA Standards Planner & Lesson Plans: L71, L75 **TRANSPARENCIES/TECHNOLOGY** Benchmark Tests: 11.1, 11.3 Power Presentations: 11.1, 11.3

Correlations to California History–Social Science Content Standards and Analysis Skills

Standard	Primary Citations	Supporting Citations
6.4.2 Trace the transition from tyranny and oligarchy to early democratic forms of government and back to dictatorship in ancient Greece, including the significance of the invention of the idea of citizenship (e.g., from *Pericles' Funeral Oration*).	**PUPIL & TEACHER & eEDITION** Common Pages: 350, 370, **371–376**, 378, 379, **381**, 386–387, **390–391**, 392, **393–395**, 397, 398, 400, 402, 404, **405–406**, 407–409, 414, 419, 420–421 Add'l Teacher's Edition: 350B **PRINT COMPONENT(S)** CA Standards Enrichment Wrkbk: 51–52	**PRINT COMPONENT(S)** In–Depth Resources Unit 5: 18–19, 22, 35 In–Depth Resources in Spanish Unit 5: 93 CA Reading Toolkit: L38, L40, L41, L42 CA Modified Lesson Plans for English Learners: 79, 83, 85, 87 CA Standards Planner & Lesson Plans: L75, L79, L81, L83 **TRANSPARENCIES/TECHNOLOGY** Benchmark Tests: 11.3, 12.1, 12.3 Power Presentations: 11.3, 12.1, 12.3
6.4.3 State the key differences between Athenian, or direct, democracy and representative democracy.	**PUPIL & TEACHER & eEDITION** Common Pages: 370, **374–376**, 378, **379**, **381**, 383, 386, **390–391**, 392, **393–395**, 397, 398, 400, 404, 414, 420–421 Add'l Teacher's Edition: 350B **PRINT COMPONENT(S)** CA Standards Enrichment Wrkbk: 53–54	**PRINT COMPONENT(S)** In–Depth Resources Unit 5: 35 CA Reading Toolkit: L38, L39, L40 CA Modified Lesson Plans for English Learners: 79, 81, 83 CA Standards Planner & Lesson Plans: L75, L77, L79 **TRANSPARENCIES/TECHNOLOGY** Benchmark Tests: 11.3, 11.4, 12.1 Power Presentations: 11.3, 11.4, 12.1
6.4.4 Explain the significance of Greek mythology to the everyday life of people in the region and how Greek literature continues to permeate our literature and language today, drawing from Greek mythology and epics, such as Homer's *Iliad* and *Odyssey*, and from *Aesop's Fables*.	**PUPIL & TEACHER & eEDITION** Common Pages: **360–365**, **366–369**, 378, 383, 386–387, 396–397, 398, 410, **411–412**, **414–415**, 417, **420**, R51–R56 Add'l Teacher's Edition: 350B **PRINT COMPONENT(S)** CA Standards Enrichment Wrkbk: 55–56	**PRINT COMPONENT(S)** In–Depth Resources Unit 5: 18–19, 21, 32, 34 In–Depth Resources in Spanish Unit 5: 92 CA Reading Toolkit: L37 CA Modified Lesson Plans for English Learners: 77 CA Standards Planner & Lesson Plans: L73 **TRANSPARENCIES/TECHNOLOGY** Benchmark Tests: 11.2 Power Presentations: 11.2

Standard		Primary Citations	Supporting Citations
6.4.5	Outline the founding, expansion, and political organization of the Persian Empire.	**PUPIL & TEACHER & eEDITION** Common Pages: 123, 128, **129–133, 134–135, 136, 137** **PRINT COMPONENT(S)** CA Standards Enrichment Wrkbk: 57–58 **TRANSPARENCIES/TECHNOLOGY** CA Daily Standards Practice Transparencies: 12	**PUPIL & TEACHER & eEDITION** Common Pages: 338, 340, 341, 352–353, 382, 383 **PRINT COMPONENT(S)** In–Depth Resources Unit 2: 29–30, 32 In–Depth Resources in Spanish Unit 2: 33–34 CA Reading Toolkit: L13 CA Modified Lesson Plans for English Learners: 29 CA Standards Planner & Lesson Plans: L25 **TRANSPARENCIES/TECHNOLOGY** Humanities Transparencies: 8 Map Transparencies: 8 Critical Thinking Transparencies: 16 Benchmark Tests: 4.3 Power Presentations: 4.3
6.4.6	Compare and contrast life in Athens and Sparta, with emphasis on their roles in the Persian and Peloponnesian Wars.	**PUPIL & TEACHER & eEDITION** Common Pages: 352–353, 378, **379–383**, 384, **386–387**, 398, **399–402**, 403, 404, 411–417, 420, R56 Add'l Teacher's Edition: 350B **PRINT COMPONENT(S)** CA Standards Enrichment Wrkbk: 59–60	**PRINT COMPONENT(S)** In–Depth Resources Unit 5: 23, 36 In–Depth Resources in Spanish Unit 5: 94 CA Reading Toolkit: L39, L41 CA Modified Lesson Plans for English Learners: 81, 85 CA Standards Planner & Lesson Plans: L81 **TRANSPARENCIES/TECHNOLOGY** Benchmark Tests: 11.4 Power Presentations: 11.4
6.4.7	Trace the rise of Alexander the Great and the spread of Greek culture eastward and into Egypt.	**PUPIL & TEACHER & eEDITION** Common Pages: 389, 404, **405–409, 420–421** Add'l Teacher's Edition: 350B **PRINT COMPONENT(S)** CA Standards Enrichment Wrkbk: 61–62	**PUPIL & TEACHER & eEDITION** Common Pages: 177, 215 **PRINT COMPONENT(S)** CA Reading Toolkit: L42 CA Modified Lesson Plans for English Learners: 87 CA Standards Planner & Lesson Plans: L85 **TRANSPARENCIES/TECHNOLOGY** Benchmark Tests: 12.3 Power Presentations: 12.3

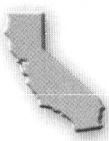

Correlations to California History–Social Science Content Standards and Analysis Skills

Standard	Primary Citations	Supporting Citations
6.4.8 Describe the enduring contributions of important Greek figures in the arts and sciences (e.g., Hypatia, Socrates, Plato, Aristotle, Euclid, Thucydides).	**PUPIL & TEACHER & eEDITION** Common Pages: **364–365,** 410, **411–412, 414–415, 416–417,** 420–421, R51–R53 Add'l Teacher's Edition: 350B **PRINT COMPONENT(S)** CA Standards Enrichment Wrkbk: 63–64	**PRINT COMPONENT(S)** In–Depth Resources Unit 5: 31 CA Reading Toolkit: L43 CA Modified Lesson Plans for English Learners: 89 CA Standards Planner & Lesson Plans: L85 **TRANSPARENCIES/TECHNOLOGY** Benchmark Tests: 12.4 Power Presentations: 12.4
6.5 **Students analyze the geographic, political, economic, religious, and social structures of the early civilizations of India.**	**PUPIL & TEACHER & eEDITION** Common Pages: **212–213,** 214–215, 216–217, 218, **219–224,** 226, **227–231,** 232, **233–239,** 240, **241–243,** 244–245, 246–247 Add'l Teacher's Edition: 226 **PRINT COMPONENT(S)** CA Standards Enrichment Wrkbk: 65–66, 67–68, 69–70, 71–72, 73–74, 75–76, 77–78	**PUPIL & TEACHER & eEDITION** Common Pages: 462, R62–R63 **PRINT COMPONENT(S)** In–Depth Resources Unit 4: 1–8, 13–20, 53, 61–62 In–Depth Resources in Spanish Unit 4: 53–57, 59, 61–62 CA Reading Toolkit: L21, L22, L23, L24 CA Modified Lesson Plans for English Learners: 45, 47, 49, 51 CA Standards Planner & Lesson Plans: L41, L43, L45, L47 **TRANSPARENCIES/TECHNOLOGY** Benchmark Tests: 7.1, 7.2, 7.3, 7.4 Power Presentations: 7.1, 7.2, 7.3, 7.4
6.5.1 Locate and describe the major river system and discuss the physical setting that supported the rise of this civilization.	**PUPIL & TEACHER & eEDITION** Common Pages: 215, **216–217,** 218, **219–221,** 222, 224, 225, 237, 244, 246 **PRINT COMPONENT(S)** CA Standards Enrichment Wrkbk: 65–66	**PRINT COMPONENT(S)** In–Depth Resources Unit 4: 3, 13–14, 17 In–Depth Resources in Spanish Unit 4: 53, 61–62 CA Reading Toolkit: L21 CA Modified Lesson Plans for English Learners: 45 CA Standards Planner & Lesson Plans: L41 **TRANSPARENCIES/TECHNOLOGY** Benchmark Tests: 7.1 Power Presentations: 7.1

Standard	Primary Citations	Supporting Citations
6.5.2 Discuss the significance of the Aryan invasions.	**PUPIL & TEACHER & eEDITION** Common Pages: **214, 226, 227–229, 231, 246–247** **PRINT COMPONENT(S)** CA Standards Enrichment Wrkbk: 67–68	**PRINT COMPONENT(S)** In–Depth Resources Unit 4: 8, 18 In–Depth Resources in Spanish Unit 4: 59 CA Reading Toolkit: L22 CA Modified Lesson Plans for English Learners: 47 CA Standards Planner & Lesson Plans: L43 **TRANSPARENCIES/TECHNOLOGY** Benchmark Tests: 7.2 Power Presentations: 7.2
6.5.3 Explain the major beliefs and practices of Brahmanism in India and how they evolved into early Hinduism.	**PUPIL & TEACHER & eEDITION** Common Pages: 226, **228–229,** 231, 246 **PRINT COMPONENT(S)** CA Standards Enrichment Wrkbk: 69–70	**PRINT COMPONENT(S)** In–Depth Resources Unit 4: 1–2, 4, 18 In–Depth Resources in Spanish Unit 4: 54 CA Reading Toolkit: L22 CA Modified Lesson Plans for English Learners: 47 CA Standards Planner & Lesson Plans: L43 **TRANSPARENCIES/TECHNOLOGY** Benchmark Tests: 7.2 Power Presentations: 7.2
6.5.4 Outline the social structure of the caste system.	**PUPIL & TEACHER & eEDITION** Common Pages: 214, 226, **228–229,** 231, 246–247 **PRINT COMPONENT(S)** CA Standards Enrichment Wrkbk: 71–72	**PRINT COMPONENT(S)** In–Depth Resources Unit 4: 1–2, 18 CA Reading Toolkit: L22 CA Modified Lesson Plans for English Learners: 47 CA Standards Planner & Lesson Plans: L43 **TRANSPARENCIES/TECHNOLOGY** Benchmark Tests: 7.2 Power Presentations: 7.2

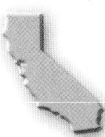

Correlations to California History–Social Science Content Standards and Analysis Skills

Standard	Primary Citations	Supporting Citations
6.5.5 Know the life and moral teachings of Buddha and how Buddhism spread in India, Ceylon, and Central Asia.	**PUPIL & TEACHER & eEDITION** Common Pages: **212–213**, 215, 232, **233–236**, 239, **241–242**, 246, **247** **PRINT COMPONENT(S)** CA Standards Enrichment Wrkbk: 73–74	**PUPIL & TEACHER & eEDITION** Common Pages: 462, R62–R63 **PRINT COMPONENT(S)** In–Depth Resources Unit 4: 1–2, 15, 19 CA Reading Toolkit: L23 CA Modified Lesson Plans for English Learners: 49 CA Standards Planner & Lesson Plans: L45 **TRANSPARENCIES/TECHNOLOGY** Benchmark Tests: 7.3 Power Presentations: 7.3
6.5.6 Describe the growth of the Maurya empire and the political and moral achievements of the emperor Asoka.	**PUPIL & TEACHER & eEDITION** Common Pages: 215, 232, **235–236**, **237**, 239, 246 **PRINT COMPONENT(S)** CA Standards Enrichment Wrkbk: 75–76	**PRINT COMPONENT(S)** In–Depth Resources Unit 4: 5, 19 In–Depth Resources in Spanish Unit 4: 55 CA Reading Toolkit: L23 CA Modified Lesson Plans for English Learners: 49 CA Standards Planner & Lesson Plans: L45 **TRANSPARENCIES/TECHNOLOGY** Benchmark Tests: 7.3 Power Presentations: 7.3
6.5.7 Discuss important aesthetic and intellectual traditions (e.g., Sanskrit literature, including the Bhagavad Gita; medicine; metallurgy; and mathematics, including Hindu–Arabic numerals and the zero).	**PUPIL & TEACHER & eEDITION** Common Pages: 212–213, 226, **229–230**, **231**, 232, **236**, 237, **238–239**, 240, **241–243**, **244–245**, 246–247, R41 Add'l Teacher's Edition: 226 **PRINT COMPONENT(S)** CA Standards Enrichment Wrkbk: 77–78	**PRINT COMPONENT(S)** In–Depth Resources Unit 4: 16 CA Reading Toolkit: L22, L23, L24 CA Modified Lesson Plans for English Learners: 49, 51 CA Standards Planner & Lesson Plans: L43, L45, L47 **TRANSPARENCIES/TECHNOLOGY** Benchmark Tests: 7.2, 7.3, 7.4 Power Presentations: 7.2, 7.3, 7.4

Standard		Primary Citations	Supporting Citations
6.6	**Students analyze the geographic, political, economic, religious, and social structures of the early civilizations of China.**	**PUPIL & TEACHER & eEDITION** Common Pages: 248–249, 250–251, 252, **253–257**, 258, **259–263**, 264–265, 266, **267–271**, 272–275, 276, **277–280**, 281, 282–283 Add'l Teacher's Edition: 248, 256 **PRINT COMPONENT(S)** CA Standards Enrichment Wrkbk: 79–80, 81–82, 83–84, 85–86, 87–88, 89–90, 91–92, 93–94	**PRINT COMPONENT(S)** In–Depth Resources Unit 4: 24, 25, 26, 35, 36 In–Depth Resources in Spanish Unit 4: 63, 64, 65 CA Reading Toolkit: L25, L26, L27, L28 CA Modified Lesson Plans for English Learners: 53, 55, 57, 59 CA Standards Planner & Lesson Plans: L49, L51, L53, L55 **TRANSPARENCIES/TECHNOLOGY** Humanities Transparencies: 16 Map Transparencies: 15, 16 Critical Thinking Transparencies: 32, 34 Benchmark Tests: 8.1, 8.2, 8.3, 8.4 Power Presentations: 8.1, 8.2, 8.3, 8.4
6.6.1	Locate and describe the origins of Chinese civilization in the Huang–He Valley during the Shang Dynasty.	**PUPIL & TEACHER & eEDITION** Common Pages: **248–249, 252**, 253, **254–255**, 257, 282 Add'l Teacher's Edition: 256	**PRINT COMPONENT(S)** In–Depth Resources Unit 4: 24 In–Depth Resources in Spanish Unit 4: 63 CA Reading Toolkit: L25 CA Modified Lesson Plans for English Learners: 53 **TRANSPARENCIES/TECHNOLOGY** Humanities Transparencies: 16 Map Transparencies: 15 Critical Thinking Transparencies: 32 Benchmark Tests: 8.1 Power Presentations: 8.1
6.6.2	Explain the geographic features of China that made governance and the spread of ideas and goods difficult and served to isolate the country from the rest of the world.	**PUPIL & TEACHER & eEDITION** Common Pages: 249, 252, **253–257**, **267–270**, **277–279**, **281**, 282 **PRINT COMPONENT(S)** CA Standards Enrichment Wrkbk: 81–82	**PRINT COMPONENT(S)** In–Depth Resources Unit 4: 24 In–Depth Resources in Spanish Unit 4: 63 CA Reading Toolkit: L25 CA Modified Lesson Plans for English Learners: 53 CA Standards Planner & Lesson Plans: L49 **TRANSPARENCIES/TECHNOLOGY** Benchmark Tests: 8.1 Power Presentations: 8.1

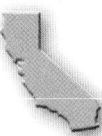
Standard	Primary Citations	Supporting Citations
6.6.3 Know about the life of Confucius and the fundamental teachings of Confucianism and Taoism.	**PUPIL & TEACHER & eEDITION** Common Pages: 248–249, **250–251, 258, 259–263, 264–265,** 276, **278,** 280, 282, 283, R42–R43 **PRINT COMPONENT(S)** CA Standards Enrichment Wrkbk: 83–84, 91–92, 93–94	**PRINT COMPONENT(S)** In–Depth Resources Unit 4: 25, 35, 36 In–Depth Resources in Spanish Unit 4: 64 CA Reading Toolkit: L26, L28 CA Modified Lesson Plans for English Learners: 55, 59 CA Standards Planner & Lesson Plans: L51, L55 **TRANSPARENCIES/TECHNOLOGY** Benchmark Tests: 8.2, 8.4 Power Presentations: 8.2, 8.4
6.6.4 Identify the political and cultural problems prevalent in the time of Confucius and how he sought to solve them.	**PUPIL & TEACHER & eEDITION** Common Pages: 249, **250–251, 258, 259–263, 264–265,** 282, 283, R42 **PRINT COMPONENT(S)** CA Standards Enrichment Wrkbk: 83–84, 85–86	**PRINT COMPONENT(S)** CA Reading Toolkit: L26 CA Standards Planner & Lesson Plans: L51 **TRANSPARENCIES/TECHNOLOGY** Benchmark Tests: 8.2 Power Presentations: 8.2
6.6.5 List the policies and achievements of the emperor Shi Huangdi in unifying northern China under the Qin Dynasty.	**PUPIL & TEACHER & eEDITION** Common Pages: **266, 267–268, 271, 272–275,** 282, **283** Add'l Teacher's Edition: 248 **PRINT COMPONENT(S)** CA Standards Enrichment Wrkbk: 87–88	**PRINT COMPONENT(S)** In–Depth Resources Unit 4: 26 In–Depth Resources in Spanish Unit 4: 65 CA Reading Toolkit: L27 CA Modified Lesson Plans for English Learners: 57 CA Standards Planner & Lesson Plans: L53 **TRANSPARENCIES/TECHNOLOGY** Benchmark Tests: 8.3 Power Presentations: 8.3

Standard		Primary Citations	Supporting Citations
6.6.6	Detail the political contributions of the Han Dynasty to the development of the imperial bureaucratic state and the expansion of the empire.	**PUPIL & TEACHER & eEDITION** Common Pages: 266, **269–271, 282** Add'l Teacher's Edition: 248 **PRINT COMPONENT(S)** CA Standards Enrichment Wrkbk: 89–90	**PRINT COMPONENT(S)** In–Depth Resources Unit 4: 26 In–Depth Resources in Spanish Unit 4: 65 CA Reading Toolkit: L27 CA Modified Lesson Plans for English Learners: 57 CA Standards Planner & Lesson Plans: L53 **TRANSPARENCIES/TECHNOLOGY** Humanities Transparencies: 16 Map Transparencies: 16 Critical Thinking Transparencies: 34 Benchmark Tests: 8.3 Power Presentations: 8.3
6.6.7	Cite the significance of the trans–Eurasian "silk roads" in the period of the Han Dynasty and Roman Empire and their locations.	**PUPIL & TEACHER & eEDITION** Common Pages: **276, 277–279, 280, 281, 282** **PRINT COMPONENT(S)** CA Standards Enrichment Wrkbk: 91–92	**PRINT COMPONENT(S)** CA Reading Toolkit: L28 CA Modified Lesson Plans for English Learners: 59 CA Standards Planner & Lesson Plans: L55 **TRANSPARENCIES/TECHNOLOGY** Benchmark Tests: 8.4 Power Presentations: 8.4
6.6.8	Describe the diffusion of Buddhism northward to China during the Han Dynasty.	**PUPIL & TEACHER & eEDITION** Common Pages: 276, **277–278**, 280, 282 **PRINT COMPONENT(S)** CA Standards Enrichment Wrkbk: 93–94	**PRINT COMPONENT(S)** CA Reading Toolkit: L28 CA Modified Lesson Plans for English Learners: 59 CA Standards Planner & Lesson Plans: L55 **TRANSPARENCIES/TECHNOLOGY** Benchmark Tests: 8.4 Power Presentations: 8.4

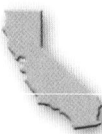

Correlations to California History–Social Science Content Standards and Analysis Skills

Standard	Primary Citations	Supporting Citations
6.7 Students analyze the geographic, political, economic, religious, and social structures during the development of Rome.	**PUPIL & TEACHER & eEDITION** Common Pages: 342, 344–346, 424–425, 426–427, 428–429, 430, **431–435, 436–441**, 442, **443–449**, 450–451, 452, **453–458**, 459, 460–461, 462–463, 464–465, 466, 467–468, 470, 472, 476–482, 483–486, 488–489, 490–491, 492–493, 494–498, 499, 500–505, 511–512, 514–519, 520–521, 522–523 Add'l Teacher's Edition: 320, 426, 430, 436, 442, 468 **PRINT COMPONENT(S)** CA Standards Enrichment Wrkbk: 95–96, 97–98, 99–100, 101–102, 103–104, 105–106, 107–108, 109–110, 111–112	**PUPIL & TEACHER & eEDITION** Common Pages: 516 **PRINT COMPONENT(S)** In–Depth Resources Unit 6: 13–14, 15, 16, 31–34, 43 In–Depth Resources in Spanish Unit 6: 119–120, 127–128 History Makers: 25–26, 27–28 CA Reading Toolkit: L35, L44, L45, L46, L47, L48, L49, L50, L54 CA Modified Lesson Plans for English Learners: 73, 91, 93, 95, 97, 99, 101, 103, 111 CA Standards Planner & Lesson Plans: L69, L87, L89, L91, L93, L95, L97, L99, L101, L107
	TRANSPARENCIES/TECHNOLOGY CA Daily Standards Practice Transparencies: 44, 45, 46, 47, 48, 49, 50	**TRANSPARENCIES/TECHNOLOGY** Humanities Transparencies: 27, 28 Map Transparencies: 16, 25, 26, 27, 28, 29 Critical Thinking Transparencies: 57, 59, 61, 62, 63 Benchmark Tests: 10.3, 13.1, 13.2, 13.3, 13.4, 14.1, 14.2, 14.3, 15.1, 15.4 Power Presentations: 10.3, 13.1, 13.2, 13.3, 13.4, 14.1, 14.2, 14.3, 15.1, 15.4
6.7.1 Identify the location and describe the rise of the Roman Republic, including the importance of such mythical and historical figures as Aeneas, Romulus and Remus, Cincinnatus, Julius Caesar, and Cicero.	**PUPIL & TEACHER & eEDITION** Common Pages: 426–427, **428–429**, 430, **431–435**, 436–441, 442, **443–449**, 460–461 **PRINT COMPONENT(S)** CA Standards Enrichment Wrkbk: 95–96 **TRANSPARENCIES/TECHNOLOGY** CA Daily Standards Practice Transparencies: 45	**PUPIL & TEACHER & eEDITION** Common Pages: 516 **PRINT COMPONENT(S)** In–Depth Resources Unit 6: 13–14, 15, 16 In–Depth Resources in Spanish Unit 6: 119–120 CA Reading Toolkit: L44, L45, L46 CA Modified Lesson Plans for English Learners: 91, 93, 95 CA Standards Planner & Lesson Plans: L87, L89, L91 **TRANSPARENCIES/TECHNOLOGY** Critical Thinking Transparencies: 56 Benchmark Tests: 13.1, 13.2, 13.3 Power Presentations: 13.1, 13.2, 13.3

Standard		Primary Citations	Supporting Citations
6.7.2	Describe the government of the Roman Republic and its significance (e.g., written constitution and tripartite government, checks and balances, civic duty).	**PUPIL & TEACHER & eEDITION** Common Pages: **428–429**, 436, **437–439**, 441, 460, 461 Add'l Teacher's Edition: 426 **PRINT COMPONENT(S)** CA Standards Enrichment Wrkbk: 97–98	**PRINT COMPONENT(S)** CA Reading Toolkit: L45 CA Modified Lesson Plans for English Learners: 93 CA Standards Planner & Lesson Plans: L89 **TRANSPARENCIES/TECHNOLOGY** Benchmark Tests: 13.2 Power Presentations: 13.2
6.7.3	Identify the location of and the political and geographic reasons for the growth of Roman territories and expansion of the empire, including how the empire fostered economic growth through the use of currency and trade routes.	**PUPIL & TEACHER & eEDITION** Common Pages: **426–427**, 430, 434, 435, 436, **440–441**, 442, **443–449**, **450–451**, **460–461** **PRINT COMPONENT(S)** CA Standards Enrichment Wrkbk: 99–100 **TRANSPARENCIES/TECHNOLOGY** CA Daily Standards Practice Transparencies: 44	**PRINT COMPONENT(S)** CA Reading Toolkit: L44, L45, L46 CA Modified Lesson Plans for English Learners: 91, 93, 95 CA Standards Planner & Lesson Plans: L87, L89, L91 **TRANSPARENCIES/TECHNOLOGY** Map Transparencies: 25, 26 Critical Thinking Transparencies: 57 Benchmark Tests: 13.1, 13.2, 13.3 Power Presentations: 13.1, 13.2, 13.3
6.7.4	Discuss the influence of Julius Caesar and Augustus in Rome's transition from republic to empire.	**PUPIL & TEACHER & eEDITION** Common Pages: 427, **428–429**, 442, **444–448**, 449, **460–461** Add'l Teacher's Edition: 426 **PRINT COMPONENT(S)** CA Standards Enrichment Wrkbk: 101–102 **TRANSPARENCIES/TECHNOLOGY** CA Daily Standards Practice Transparencies: 46	**PRINT COMPONENT(S)** CA Reading Toolkit: L46 CA Modified Lesson Plans for English Learners: 95 History Makers: 25–26 CA Standards Planner & Lesson Plans: L91 **TRANSPARENCIES/TECHNOLOGY** Benchmark Tests: 13.3 Power Presentations: 13.3
6.7.5	Trace the migration of Jews around the Mediterranean region and the effects of their conflict with the Romans, including the Romans' restrictions on their right to live in Jerusalem.	**PUPIL & TEACHER & eEDITION** Common Pages: 342, **344–346**, 466, **467–468**, 478, 488 Add'l Teacher's Edition: 320 **PRINT COMPONENT(S)** CA Standards Enrichment Wrkbk: 103–104	**PRINT COMPONENT(S)** CA Reading Toolkit: L35 CA Modified Lesson Plans for English Learners: 73 CA Standards Planner & Lesson Plans: L69 **TRANSPARENCIES/TECHNOLOGY** Benchmark Tests: 10.3 Power Presentations: 10.3

Correlations to California History–Social Science Content Standards and Analysis Skills

Standard	Primary Citations	Supporting Citations
6.7.6 Note the origins of Christianity in the Jewish Messianic prophecies, the life and teachings of Jesus of Nazareth as described in the New Testament, and the contribution of St. Paul the Apostle to the definition and spread of Christian beliefs (e.g., belief in the Trinity, resurrection, salvation).	**PUPIL & TEACHER & eEDITION** Common Pages: **462, 466, 467–481, 483–486,** 488, 489 **PRINT COMPONENT(S)** CA Standards Enrichment Wrkbk: 105–106 **TRANSPARENCIES/TECHNOLOGY** CA Daily Standards Practice Transparencies: 48, 49	**PRINT COMPONENT(S)** In–Depth Resources Unit 6: 31–34 In–Depth Resources in Spanish Unit 6: 127–128 History Makers: 27–28 CA Reading Toolkit: L48, L49, L50 CA Modified Lesson Plans for English Learners: 99, 101, 103 CA Standards Planner & Lesson Plans: L95, L97, L99 **TRANSPARENCIES/TECHNOLOGY** Humanities Transparencies: 27, 28 Map Transparencies: 27 Critical Thinking Transparencies: 61, 62 Benchmark Tests: 14.1. 14.2. 14.3 Power Presentations: 14.1. 14.2. 14.3
6.7.7 Describe the circumstances that led to the spread of Christianity in Europe and other Roman territories.	**PUPIL & TEACHER & eEDITION** Common Pages: **462–463,** 464–465, 466, **467–471,** 472–475, 476, 477–481, 482, **483–486,** 487, 488–489, **511–512,** 513, **518–519,** 521, 522–523 **PRINT COMPONENT(S)** CA Standards Enrichment Wrkbk: 107–108 **TRANSPARENCIES/TECHNOLOGY** CA Daily Standards Practice Transparencies: 50	**PRINT COMPONENT(S)** In–Depth Resources Unit 6: 127 CA Reading Toolkit: L49, L50 CA Modified Lesson Plans for English Learners: 101, 103 CA Standards Planner & Lesson Plans: L97, L99 **TRANSPARENCIES/TECHNOLOGY** Critical Thinking Transparencies: 63 Map Transparencies: 28 Benchmark Tests: 14.2, 14.3 Power Presentations: 14.2, 14.3
6.7.8 Discuss the legacies of Roman art and architecture, technology and science, literature, language, and law.	**PUPIL & TEACHER & eEDITION** Common Pages: 431, 433, 437, **439, 441,** 443, 446, 452, 453, 456, 458, 459, 460, 461, 514, **515–519, 520–521, 522–523** Add'l Teacher's Edition: 430, 436, 442 **PRINT COMPONENT(S)** CA Standards Enrichment Wrkbk: 109–110 **TRANSPARENCIES/TECHNOLOGY** CA Daily Standards Practice Transparencies: 47	**PRINT COMPONENT(S)** In–Depth Resources Unit 6: 43 CA Reading Toolkit: L47, L54 CA Modified Lesson Plans for English Learners: 97, 111 CA Standards Planner & Lesson Plans: L93, L107 **TRANSPARENCIES/TECHNOLOGY** Map Transparencies: 16, 29 Critical Thinking Transparencies: 59 Benchmark Tests: 13.4 Power Presentations: 13.4

Standard	Primary Citations	Supporting Citations
7.1 Students analyze the causes and effects of the vast expansion and ultimate disintegration of the Roman Empire.	**PUPIL & TEACHER & eEDITION** Common Pages: 314, 426–427, 428–429, 430, 436, 437–441, 442, **443–449, 450–451, 460–461**, 482, 484–486, 488–489, 490–491, 492–493, 494–498, 499, **500–505, 506–507**, 508, 509–513, 514, 522–523 Add'l Teacher's Edition: 426, 462 **PRINT COMPONENT(S)** CA Standards Enrichment Wrkbk: 111–112 **TRANSPARENCIES/TECHNOLOGY** CA Daily Standards Practice Transparencies: 29, 30, 45, 47	**PRINT COMPONENT(S)** CA Reading Toolkit: L45, L46, L47, L50, L51, L52, L53, L54 CA Modified Lesson Plans for English Learners: 93, 95, 97, 103, 105, 107, 109, 111 CA Standards Planner & Lesson Plans: L89, L91, L93, L99, L101, L103, L105, L107 **TRANSPARENCIES/TECHNOLOGY** Humanities Transparencies: 26 Map Transparencies: 25, 26 Critical Thinking Transparencies: 37, 38, 39, 57, 59 Benchmark Tests: 13.2, 13.3, 13.4, 14.3, 15.1, 15.2, 15.3, 15.4 Power Presentations: 13.2, 13.3, 13.4, 14.3, 15.1, 15.2, 15.3, 15.4
7.1.1 Study the early strengths and lasting contributions of Rome (e.g., significance of Roman citizenship; rights under Roman law; Roman art, architecture, engineering, and philosophy; preservation and transmission of Christianity) and its ultimate internal weaknesses (e.g., rise of autonomous military powers within the empire, undermining of citizenship by the growth of corruption and slavery, lack of education, and distribution of news).	**PUPIL & TEACHER & eEDITION** Common Pages: 428–429, 430, 436, **437–441**, 442, **443–449**, 452, 456, 458, 490–491, 494, **495–498**, 499, 500, **501–505**, 506–507, 514, **515–519**, 520–521, 522–523 Add'l Teacher's Edition: 426, 462 **PRINT COMPONENT(S)** CA Standards Enrichment Wrkbk: 111–112 **TRANSPARENCIES/TECHNOLOGY** CA Daily Standards Practice Transparencies: 45, 47	**PRINT COMPONENT(S)** CA Reading Toolkit: L45, L47, L51, L52, L54 CA Modified Lesson Plans for English Learners: 93, 97, 105, 107, 111 CA Standards Planner & Lesson Plans: L89, L93, L101, L103, L107 **TRANSPARENCIES/TECHNOLOGY** Humanities Transparencies: 26 Critical Thinking Transparencies: 57, 59 Benchmark Tests: 13.2, 13.4, 15.1, 15.2, 15.4 Power Presentations: 13.2, 13.4, 15.1, 15.2, 15.4

Correlations to California History–Social Science Content Standards and Analysis Skills

Standard		Primary Citations	Supporting Citations
7.1.2	Discuss the geographic borders of the empire at its height and the factors that threatened its territorial cohesion.	**PUPIL & TEACHER & eEDITION** Common Pages: **427**, 442, 443, **448**, 449, 461, **490–491**, 494, 498, 500, 505, 522 **PRINT COMPONENT(S)** CA Standards Enrichment Wrkbk: 111–112	**PRINT COMPONENT(S)** CA Reading Toolkit: L46, L51, L52 CA Modified Lesson Plans for English Learners: 95, 105, 107 CA Standards Planner & Lesson Plans: L91, L101, L103, L105 **TRANSPARENCIES/TECHNOLOGY** Map Transparencies: 25, 26 Critical Thinking Transparencies: 37, 38, 39 Benchmark Tests: 13.3, 15.1, 15.2 Power Presentations: 13.3, 15.1, 15.2
7.1.3	Describe the establishment by Constantine of the new capital in Constantinople and the development of the Byzantine Empire, with an emphasis on the consequences of the development of two distinct European civilizations, Eastern Orthodox and Roman Catholic, and their two distinct views on church–state relations.	**PUPIL & TEACHER & eEDITION** Common Pages: 482, **484–486**, 488–489, 494, **497–498**, 501, 508, **509–513**, 514, 522–523 Add'l Teacher's Edition: 462 **PRINT COMPONENT(S)** CA Standards Enrichment Wrkbk: 111–112	**PRINT COMPONENT(S)** CA Reading Toolkit: L50, L51, L53 CA Modified Lesson Plans for English Learners: 103, 105, 109 CA Standards Planner & Lesson Plans: L99, L101 **TRANSPARENCIES/TECHNOLOGY** Benchmark Tests: 14.3, 15.1, 15.3 Power Presentations: 14.3, 15.1, 15.3
7.7	Students compare and contrast the geographic, political, economic, religious, and social structures of the Meso–American and Andean civilizations.	**PUPIL & TEACHER & eEDITION** Common Pages: **284–285**, 286–287, 288, **289–293**, 294, **295–299**, 300, **301–304**, 305, 306, **307–311**, 312–313, 314–315 Add'l Teacher's Edition: 284, 288, 292, 294, 300, 312 **PRINT COMPONENT(S)** CA Standards Enrichment Wrkbk: 113–114 **TRANSPARENCIES/TECHNOLOGY** CA Daily Standards Practice Transparencies: 29, 30, 32, 45, 47	**PRINT COMPONENT(S)** In–Depth Resources Unit 4: 53–54, 55, 56 In–Depth Resources in Spanish Unit 4: 81–82 History Makers: 17–18 CA Reading Toolkit: L29, L30, L31, L32, L45, L47, L51, L52, L54 CA Modified Lesson Plans for English Learners: 61, 63, 65, 67, 93, 97, 105, 107, 111 CA Standards Planner & Lesson Plans: L57, L59, L61, L63 **TRANSPARENCIES/TECHNOLOGY** Humanities Transparencies: 18, 26 Map Transparencies: 17, 18, 25, 26 Critical Thinking Transparencies: 37, 38, 39, 40, 57, 59 Benchmark Tests: 9.1, 9.2, 9.3, 9.4 Power Presentations: 9.1, 9.2, 9.3, 9.4

Standard	Primary Citations	Supporting Citations
7.7.1 Study the locations, landforms, and climates of Mexico, Central America, and South America and their effects on Mayan, Aztec, and Incan economies, trade, and development of urban societies.	**PUPIL & TEACHER & eEDITION** Common Pages: 284–285, 288, **289–293, 296–299, 301–302**, 304, 306, 307–311, 314, 315, 441, 460, 461 Add'l Teacher's Edition: 284 **PRINT COMPONENT(S)** CA Standards Enrichment Wrkbk: 113–114	**PRINT COMPONENT(S)** In–Depth Resources Unit 4: 53–54 In–Depth Resources in Spanish Unit 4: 81–82 CA Reading Toolkit: L29, L32 CA Modified Lesson Plans for English Learners: 61, 67 CA Standards Planner & Lesson Plans: L57, L63 **TRANSPARENCIES/TECHNOLOGY** Map Transparencies: 17 Benchmark Tests: 9.1, 9.4 Power Presentations: 9.1, 9.4
7.7.2 Study the roles of people in each society, including class structures, family life, warfare, religious beliefs and practices, and slavery.	**PUPIL & TEACHER & eEDITION** Common Pages: **286–287, 295–296**, 298–299, **302–303**, 304, 306, **307–311, 312–313**, 314, 315 Add'l Teacher's Edition: 288, 294, 300, 312 **PRINT COMPONENT(S)** CA Standards Enrichment Wrkbk: 113–114	**PRINT COMPONENT(S)** In–Depth Resources Unit 4: 55, 56 History Makers: 17–18 CA Reading Toolkit: L32 CA Modified Lesson Plans for English Learners: 67 CA Standards Planner & Lesson Plans: L63 **TRANSPARENCIES/TECHNOLOGY** Humanities Transparencies: 18 Map Transparencies: 18 Benchmark Tests: 9.4 Power Presentations: 9.4
7.7.3 Explain how and where each empire arose and how the Aztec and Incan empires were defeated by the Spanish.	**PUPIL & TEACHER & eEDITION** Common Pages: **284–285**, 286–287, 288, **289–293**, 294, **295–299**, 300, **301–304**, 305, 306, **307–311**, 312–313, 314–315 **PRINT COMPONENT(S)** CA Standards Enrichment Wrkbk: 113–114	**PRINT COMPONENT(S)** CA Reading Toolkit: L32 CA Modified Lesson Plans for English Learners: 67 CA Standards Planner & Lesson Plans: L63 **TRANSPARENCIES/TECHNOLOGY** Critical Thinking Transparencies: 40 Benchmark Tests: 9.4 Power Presentations: 9.4

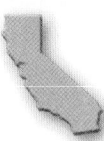

Correlations to California History–Social Science Content Standards and Analysis Skills

Standard	Primary Citations	Supporting Citations
7.7.4 Describe the artistic and oral traditions and architecture in the three civilizations.	**PUPIL & TEACHER & eEDITION** Common Pages: 285, **286–287**, 294, **295–296**, **297**, 298, 299, 300, **302–304**, 306, **309–310**, 311, **312–313**, 314, R44 Add'l Teacher's Edition: 288, 294, 300, 312 **PRINT COMPONENT(S)** CA Standards Enrichment Wrkbk: 113–114 **TRANSPARENCIES/TECHNOLOGY** CA Daily Standards Practice Transparencies: 32, 45, 47	**PRINT COMPONENT(S)** In–Depth Resources Unit 4: 55, 56 CA Reading Toolkit: L32 CA Modified Lesson Plans for English Learners: 67 CA Standards Planner & Lesson Plans: L63 **TRANSPARENCIES/TECHNOLOGY** Humanities Transparencies: 26 Map Transparencies: 18 Critical Thinking Transparencies: 57, 59 Benchmark Tests: 9.4 Power Presentations: 9.4
7.7.5 Describe the Meso–American achievements in astronomy and mathematics, including the development of the calendar and the Meso–American knowledge of seasonal changes to the civilizations' agricultural systems.	**PUPIL & TEACHER & eEDITION** Common Pages: 293, **296–298**, **302–303**, 306, **308–309**, **310–311**, 314, **315** Add'l Teacher's Edition: 292 **PRINT COMPONENT(S)** CA Standards Enrichment Wrkbk: 113–114	**PRINT COMPONENT(S)** CA Reading Toolkit: L32, L45, L47, L51, L52, L54 CA Modified Lesson Plans for English Learners: 67, 93, 97, 105, 107, 111 CA Standards Planner & Lesson Plans: L63 **TRANSPARENCIES/TECHNOLOGY** Map Transparencies: 25, 26 Benchmark Tests: 9.4 Power Presentations: 9.4

Correlations to California Historical and Social Sciences Analysis Skills Grades 6–8

The intellectual skills noted below are to be learned through, and applied to, the content standards for grades six through eight. They are to be assessed only in conjunction with the content standards in grades six through eight.

In addition to the standards for grades six through eight, students demonstrate the following intellectual reasoning, reflection, and research skills:

Standard	Primary Citations	Supporting Citations
CHRONOLOGICAL AND SPATIAL THINKING		
CST(1) Students explain how major events are related to one another in time.	**PUPIL & TEACHER & eEDITION** Common Pages: 1, 8, 14, 22, 24–25, 96, **104–105**, 162–163, 164, 170, 172, 177, 188, 193, 202, 203, 205, 206, 207, 240, 241, 242, 243, 244–245, 288, 290, 293, 294, **334**, 339, **340–341**, 418–419, 421, 442, 449, 466, 471, 486, 500, 505, 520–521, R14, R15 Add'l Teacher's Edition: 4, 29, 32, **46**, 78, 108, 142, 184, 190, 214, 237, 240, 284, 350, 388, 426, 462, 468 **PRINT COMPONENT(S)** CA Standards Enrichment Wrkbk: 1–14	**PRINT COMPONENT(S)** CA Reading Toolkit: L1, L2, L16, L20, L23, L24, L33, L52 CA Modified Lesson Plans for English Learners: 9, 85, 87, 103 CA Standards Planner & Lesson Plans: L1, L3, L7 **TRANSPARENCIES/TECHNOLOGY** Benchmark Tests: 1.2, 1.4 Power Presentations: 1.2, 1.4
CST(2) Students construct various time lines of key events, people, and periods of the historical era they are studying.	**PUPIL & TEACHER & eEDITION** Common Pages: **172, 177**, 188, 193, **334**, 339, **340–341**, 421, 442, 446, 449, 466, 471, 486, 500, 505, R14, R15 Add'l Teacher's Edition: 32, 190, 237, 468 **PRINT COMPONENT(S)** CA Standards Enrichment Wrkbk: 1–14	**PRINT COMPONENT(S)** In–Depth Resources Unit 4: 8 In–Depth Resources in Spanish Unit 4: 59 CA Reading Toolkit: L3, L17, L18, L25, L42, L51 CA Modified Lesson Plans for English Learners: 9, 95 CA Standards Planner & Lesson Plans: L1, L3, L7 **TRANSPARENCIES/TECHNOLOGY** Benchmark Tests: 1.2, 1.4 Power Presentations: 1.2, 1.4

Correlations to California Historical and Social Sciences Analysis Skills

Standard	Primary Citations	Supporting Citations
CST(3) Students use a variety of maps and documents to identify physical and cultural features of neighborhoods, cities, states, and countries and to explain the historical migration of people, expansion and disintegration of empires, and the growth of economic systems.	**PUPIL & TEACHER & eEDITION** Common Pages: 8, 12, 13, 14, 15, 19, 20, 21, 22, 23, 40–41, 45, 50, 52, **56–57**, 58, 59, 60, 65, 64, 68, 94, **96–97**, 102, 115, 120, 128, 130, 133, 148, 159, 169, 174, 188, 190, **194–195**, 196, 197, 198, 199, 200, 206, 208, 209, 218, 224, 228, 230, 231, 237, 239, 247, 261, 269, **278–279**, 283, 290, 291, 292, 295, 296, 299, 301, 303, 308, 315, 327, 329, 337, 340, 345, 349, 254, 356, 359, 365, 377, 380, 382, 387, 400, 401, 407, 409, 432, 440, 445, 448, 466, 468, 469, 471, 476, 478, 481, 486, 503, **506–507**, 511, 523, R9–R10, R19, R24, R25 Add'l Teacher's Edition: 16, 17, 18, 22, 220, 256, 331, 406 **PRINT COMPONENT(S)** CA Standards Enrichment Wrkbk: 1–14	**PRINT COMPONENT(S)** In–Depth Resources Unit 2: 11–12, 25–26; Unit 4: 13–14; Unit 5: 29–30 In–Depth Resources in Spanish Unit 2: 25–26; Unit 4: 61–62; Unit 5: 99–100 CA Reading Toolkit: L1, L2, L5, L7, L17, L18, L19, L21, L27, L28, L29, L30, L35, L36, L39, L41 CA Modified Lesson Plans for English Learners: 3, 7, 17, 45, 57, 61, 71, 73 CA Standards Planner & Lesson Plans: L1, L3, L7 **TRANSPARENCIES/TECHNOLOGY** Benchmark Tests: 1.2, 1.4 Power Presentations: 1.2, 1.4

RESEARCH, EVIDENCE, AND POINT OF VIEW

Standard	Primary Citations	Supporting Citations
REP(1) Students frame questions that can be answered by historical study and research.	**PUPIL & TEACHER & eEDITION** Common Pages: 38, **40**, 44, 45, 210–211, 218, 224, **519**, **524–525**, **R18** **PRINT COMPONENT(S)** CA Standards Enrichment Wrkbk: 1–14	**PRINT COMPONENT(S)** In–Depth Resources Unit 2: 21 In–Depth Resources in Spanish Unit 2: 11 CA Reading Toolkit: L4, L21 CA Standards Planner & Lesson Plans: L1, L3, L7 **TRANSPARENCIES/TECHNOLOGY** Benchmark Tests: 1.2, 1.4 Power Presentations: 1.2, 1.4
REP(2) Students distinguish fact from opinion in historical narratives and stories.	**PUPIL & TEACHER & eEDITION** Common Pages: 38, **42**, **43**, 74–75, 207, 297, 301, 417, 499, 504, **R22** **PRINT COMPONENT(S)** CA Standards Enrichment Wrkbk: 1–14	**PRINT COMPONENT(S)** In–Depth Resources Unit 2: 14; Unit 2: 22 In–Depth Resources in Spanish Unit 2: 28 CA Reading Toolkit: L4, L12, L30 CA Standards Planner & Lesson Plans: L1, L3, L7 **TRANSPARENCIES/TECHNOLOGY** Benchmark Tests: 1.2, 1.4 Power Presentations: 1.2, 1.4

Standard	Primary Citations	Supporting Citations
REP(3) Students distinguish relevant from irrelevant information, essential from incidental information, and verifiable from unverifiable information in historical narratives and stories.	**PUPIL & TEACHER & eEDITION** Common Pages: 8, **44**, 56–58, **170**, 231, 239, **314**, 360, 365, 481, R2, R22, **R23** **PRINT COMPONENT(S)** CA Standards Enrichment Wrkbk: 1–14	**PRINT COMPONENT(S)** In–Depth Resources Unit 2: 7, 23 In–Depth Resources in Spanish Unit 2: 23, 29 CA Reading Toolkit: L12, L16, L34, L35, L37, L39, L40, L49, L54 CA Standards Planner & Lesson Plans: L1, L3, L7 **TRANSPARENCIES/TECHNOLOGY** Benchmark Tests: 1.2, 1.4 Power Presentations: 1.2, 1.4
REP(4) Students assess the credibility of primary and secondary sources and draw sound conclusions from them.	**PUPIL & TEACHER & eEDITION** Common Pages: 40–41, **42–43**, 101, 170, 224, 231, 239, **263–264**, 314, 360, 365, 481, R22, **R23, R24, R25** **PRINT COMPONENT(S)** CA Standards Enrichment Wrkbk: 1–14	**PRINT COMPONENT(S)** In–Depth Resources Unit 2: 13; Unit 4: 15–16; Unit 5: 31–32 CA Reading Toolkit: L19, L31, L37, L46, L48 CA Modified Lesson Plans for English Learners: 11 CA Standards Planner & Lesson Plans: L1, L3, L7 **TRANSPARENCIES/TECHNOLOGY** Benchmark Tests: 1.2, 1.4 Power Presentations: 1.2, 1.4
REP(5) Students detect the different historical points of view on historical events and determine the context in which the historical statements were made (the questions asked, sources used, author's perspectives).	**PUPIL & TEACHER & eEDITION** Common Pages: **44, 231**, R19, R20, R31 **PRINT COMPONENT(S)** CA Standards Enrichment Wrkbk: 1–14	**PRINT COMPONENT(S)** In–Depth Resources Unit 2: 13; Unit 4: 15; Unit 5: 31 CA Standards Planner & Lesson Plans: L1, L3, L7 **TRANSPARENCIES/TECHNOLOGY** Benchmark Tests: 1.2, 1.4 Power Presentations: 1.2, 1.4

Correlations to California Historical and Social Sciences Analysis Skills

Standard	Primary Citations	Supporting Citations
HISTORICAL INTERPRETATION		
HI(1) Students explain the central issues and problems from the past, placing people and events in a matrix of time and place.	**PUPIL & TEACHER & eEDITION** Common Pages: 56–58, 96, 112, 113, 114, 118, 120, 121, 136, 138–139, 172, 177, 188, 193, **194–195**, 196, 197, 200, 202, 203, 205, 206, 207, 208, 243, 264–265, 334, 339, **340–341**, 342, 343, 348, 349, 398, 402, 410, 414, 417, 420, 421, 442, 449, 466, 470, 471, 473, 486, 499, 500, 505, **506–507**, 508, **524–525**, 713, R2, R14, R15, R27, R28, R30 Add'l Teacher's Edition: 4, 46, 78, 108, 142, 184, 214, 240, 284, 350, 388, 426, 462 **PRINT COMPONENT(S)** CA Standards Enrichment Wrkbk: 1–14	**PRINT COMPONENT(S)** In–Depth Resources Unit 2: 1–5, 15–17, 21; Unit 4: 1–4, 17–20; Unit 5: 18–19, 21, 25, 33–36 In–Depth Resources in Spanish Unit 2: 11, 19–22; Unit 4: 53–54; Unit 5: 92, 97 CA Reading Toolkit: L6, L9, L11, L13, L19, L20, L41, L43, L48, L53 CA Modified Lesson Plans for English Learners: 25, 27, 49, 53, 63, 65, 73, 97 CA Standards Planner & Lesson Plans: L1, L3, L7 **TRANSPARENCIES/TECHNOLOGY** Benchmark Tests: 1.2, 1.4 Power Presentations: 1.2, 1.4
HI(2) Students understand and distinguish cause, effect, sequence, and correlation in historical events, including the long– and short–term causal relations.	**PUPIL & TEACHER & eEDITION** Common Pages: 8, 14, 22, 24, **58, 62,** 82, 84, 88, 93, 118, 119, 146, 154, 161, 172, 177, 183, 188, 193, **209**, 243, 300, 303, 304, 314, 324, 334, 339, **340–341**, 354, 359, 370, 376, 378, 383, 398, 399, 402, 404, 408, 409, 421, 430, 432, 435, 436, 442, 449, 466, 471, 481, 486, 494, 500, 505, R14, R15, **R26** Add'l Teacher's Edition: 4, 46, 78, 108, 142, 184, 204, 214, 240, 284, 350, 388, 407, 426, 462 **PRINT COMPONENT(S)** CA Standards Enrichment Wrkbk: 1–14	**PRINT COMPONENT(S)** In–Depth Resources Unit 2: 1–2, 22; Unit 4: 1–2, 7, 20; Unit 5: 18–20 In–Depth Resources in Spanish Unit 2: 28; Unit 4: 57; Unit 5: 91 CA Reading Toolkit: L1, L2, L7, L8, L9, L10, L12, L17, L20, L26, L29, L36, L38, L39, L40, L41, L42, L44, L49, L50, L52 CA Modified Lesson Plans for English Learners: 15, 19, 23, 29, 31, 35, 43, 51, 59, 69, 75, 85, 87, 91 CA Standards Planner & Lesson Plans: L1, L3, L7 **TRANSPARENCIES/TECHNOLOGY** Benchmark Tests: 1.2, 1.4 Power Presentations: 1.2, 1.4

Standard		Primary Citations	Supporting Citations
HI(3)	Students explain the sources of historical continuity and how the combination of ideas and events explains the emergence of new patterns.	**PUPIL & TEACHER & eEDITION** Common Pages: 11, 13, **24–25**, 33, 44, 56–58, 59, 62, 74–75, 83, 85, 95, **104–105**, 107, 118, 121, 128, 130, 132, 133, 137, 146, 149, 162–163, 167, 183, 189, 191, 194–195, 209, 231, 234, 235, 244–245, 246, 260, 262, **264–265**, 271, 277, 281, 300, 311, 314, **316–317**, 324, 335, 336, 354, 358, 363, 387, **390–391**, 393, 394, 404, 408, 409, 417, 418–419, 420, 434, 436, 441, 443, 447, 458, 460, 467, 483, 485, 494, 501, 505, 508, 510, 513, 520–521, R26, R27, R29 Add'l Teacher's Edition: 4, 46, 78, 108, 142, 184, 214, 240, 284, 350, 388, 426, 462 **PRINT COMPONENT(S)** CA Standards Enrichment Wrkbk: 1–14	**PRINT COMPONENT(S)** In–Depth Resources Unit 2: 23 In–Depth Resources in Spanish Unit 2: 29 CA Reading Toolkit: L13 CA Modified Lesson Plans for English Learners: 21, 25, 33, 41, 47, 79, 83, 93, 99, 107 CA Standards Planner & Lesson Plans: L1, L3, L7 **TRANSPARENCIES/TECHNOLOGY** Benchmark Tests: 1.2, 1.4 Power Presentations: 1.2, 1.4
HI(4)	Students recognize the role of chance, oversight, and error in history.	**PUPIL & TEACHER & eEDITION** Common Pages: **42–43**, **44**, **231**, 410, 416, 417, **R19**, **R20**, **R31** **PRINT COMPONENT(S)** CA Standards Enrichment Wrkbk: 1–14	**PRINT COMPONENT(S)** CA Standards Planner & Lesson Plans: L1, L3, L7 **TRANSPARENCIES/TECHNOLOGY** Benchmark Tests: 1.2, 1.4 Power Presentations: 1.2, 1.4
HI(5)	Students recognize that interpretations of history are subject to change as new information is uncovered.	**PUPIL & TEACHER & eEDITION** Common Pages: 26, 29, 34, 38, 39, 40, 42, **44**, **231**, 294, 295, 299, 3300, 301, 304, 305, 314, 500, 505, **R19**, **R20**, **R31** Add'l Teacher's Edition: 350B **PRINT COMPONENT(S)** CA Standards Enrichment Wrkbk: 1–14	CA Reading Toolkit: L3, L30 CA Modified Lesson Plans for English Learners: 45 CA Standards Planner & Lesson Plans: L1, L3, L7 **TRANSPARENCIES/TECHNOLOGY** Benchmark Tests: 1.2, 1.4 Power Presentations: 1.2, 1.4

Correlations to California Historical and Social Sciences Analysis Skills

Standard	Primary Citations	Supporting Citations
HI(6) Students interpret basic indicators of economic performance and conduct cost–benefit analyses of economic and political issues.	**PUPIL & TEACHER & eEDITION** Common Pages: **217, 498, 499, 506–507, 523, R30** **PRINT COMPONENT(S)** CA Standards Enrichment Wrkbk: 1–14	**PRINT COMPONENT(S)** In–Depth Resources Unit 2: 1–5, 15–17, 21; Unit 4: 1–4, 17–20; Unit 5: 18–19, 21, 25, 33–36 In–Depth Resources in Spanish Unit 2: 11, 19–22; Unit 4: 53–54; Unit 5: 92, 97 CA Reading Toolkit: L11, L19, L20, L41, L43, L48, L53 CA Modified Lesson Plans for English Learners: 25, 27, 49, 53, 63, 65, 73, 97 CA Standards Planner & Lesson Plans: L1, L3, L7 **TRANSPARENCIES/TECHNOLOGY** Benchmark Tests: 1.2, 1.4 Power Presentations: 1.2, 1.4

World History
Ancient Civilizations

McDougal Littell
A DIVISION OF HOUGHTON MIFFLIN COMPANY

Nefertiti

The Buddha

African Mask

Athena

Olmec head

Caesar Augustus

World History
Ancient Civilizations

McDougal Littell
A DIVISION OF HOUGHTON MIFFLIN COMPANY

Douglas Carnine

Douglas Carnine is Professor of Education and Director of the National Center for Improving the Tools of Educators at the University of Oregon. He is the author of seven books and more than 100 other scholarly publications, primarily in the areas of instructional design and effective instructional strategies for diverse learners. Dr. Carnine is a member of the National Institute for Literacy Advisory Board.

Carlos E. Cortés

Carlos E. Cortés is Professor Emeritus of History at the University of California, Riverside. He has edited three major book series on Latinos in the United States. He has many other books, articles, documentaries, and educational materials to his credit. Fluent in Portuguese and Spanish, he often focuses on issues of multiculturalism, diversity, and media representation. Dr. Cortés has served on the summer faculty of the Harvard Institutes for Higher Education since 1990 and on the faculty of the Summer Institute for Intercultural Communication since 1995.

Kenneth R. Curtis

Kenneth R. Curtis is Professor of History and Liberal Studies at California State University, Long Beach, where he is Faculty Advisor to the California History/Social Science Project. He has been closely involved with the College Board's course and examination in Advanced Placement World History, serving as Chief Reader and as a member of the Test Development Committee. Dr. Curtis has co-authored a number of college-level world history texts.

Anita T. Robinson

Anita T. Robinson is Program Director for a Teaching American History/Department of Education grant. She served as a Master Lead Teacher and Social Studies Specialist in the Los Angeles Unified School District. Mrs. Robinson is an expert professional development presenter. Her topics include standards-based instruction, engaging English learners, literacy support, technology, visual literacy, and "big ideas."

Copyright © 2006 by McDougal Littell, a division of Houghton Mifflin Company. All rights reserved.
Maps on pages A1–A33 © Rand McNally & Company. All rights reserved.

Warning: No part of this work may be reproduced or transmitted in any form or by any means, electronic or mechanical, including photocopying and recording, or by any information storage or retrieval system without the prior written permission of McDougal Littell unless such copying is expressly permitted by federal copyright law. With the exception of not-for-profit transcription in Braille, McDougal Littell is not authorized to grant permission for further uses of copyrighted selections reprinted in this text without the permission of their owners. Permission must be obtained from the individual copyright owners as identified herein. Address inquiries to Supervisor, Rights and Permissions, McDougal Littell, P.O. Box 1667, Evanston, IL 60204.

Acknowledgments begin on page R109.
ISBN 0-618-53124-6

Printed in the United States of America.
1 2 3 4 5 6 7 8 9–DWO–09 08 07 06 05 04

Content Consultants

The content consultants reviewed the text for historical depth and accuracy and for clarity of presentation.

Beverly Bossler
Department of History
University of California, Davis
Davis, California

Philip Cunningham
Boston College
Chestnut Hill, Massachusetts

Susan L. Douglass
Council on Islamic Education
Fountain Valley, California

Joël DuBois
Humanities and Religious
   Studies Department
California State University,
   Sacramento
Sacramento, California

Vincent Farenga
Department of Comparative
   Literature
University of Southern
   California
Los Angeles, California

Claudio Fogu
Department of History
University of Southern
   California
Los Angeles, California

Charles L. Geshekter
Department of History
California State University,
   Chico
Chico, California

Charles Hallisey
University of Wisconsin
Madison, Wisconsin

Dakota L. Hamilton
Department of History
Humboldt State University
Arcata, California

Charles C. Haynes
First Amendment Center
Arlington, Virginia

Geoffrey Koziol
Department of History
University of California,
   Berkeley
Berkeley, California

John Wolte Infong Lee
Department of History
University of California,
   Santa Barbara
Santa Barbara, California

Maritere Lopez
Department of History
California State University,
   Fresno
Fresno, California

Shabbir Mansuri
Council on Islamic Education
Fountain Valley, California

Jacob Meskin
Shoolman Graduate School of
   Jewish Education
Hebrew College
Newton, Massachusetts

Robert Patch
Department of History
University of California,
   Riverside
Riverside, California

David D. Phillips
Department of History
University of California,
   Los Angeles
Los Angeles, California

Swami Tyagananda
Hindu Chaplain
Harvard University
Cambridge, Massachusetts

Kenneth Baxter Wolf
Department of History
Pomona College
Claremont, California

R. Bin Wong
Department of History
University of California,
   Los Angeles
Los Angeles, California

Teacher Consultants

The following educators provided ongoing review during the development of the program.

Yusuff Allahyah
Berendo Middle School
Los Angeles, California

Laura Carroll
Castillero Middle School
San Jose, California

Neal Cates
Hoover Middle School
Lakewood, California

Jeff Davis
Tioga Middle School
Fresno, California

Michele de Masi
Sinaloa Middle School
Simi Valley, California

Merrell Frankel
Berendo Middle School
Los Angeles, California
2003 CCSS Middle Level
   Teacher of the Year
2004 NCSS Middle Level
   Teacher of the Year

Dan Green
Goleta Valley Junior
   High School
Goleta, California

Kim Maruyama
Castillero Middle School
San Jose, California

Lisa Meyers
La Paz Intermediate School
Mission Viejo, California

Randal Mitchell
Chaboya Middle School
San Jose, California

Rebecca O'Connor
Castillero Middle School
San Jose, California

Betty Parsons
Dartmouth Middle School
San Jose, California

Sally Reimers
Sinaloa Middle School
Simi Valley, California

Brenda Riddlesprigger
Kastner Intermediate School
Fresno, California

Teresa Sadler
Shirakawa School
San Jose, California

Joseph Staub
Thomas Starr King
   Middle School
Los Angeles, California

Susan Tracy
Black Mountain
   Middle School
San Diego, California

Chris Watson
Foothills Farms Junior High
Sacramento, California

Rhonda Weltz
Bret Harte Middle School
San Jose, California

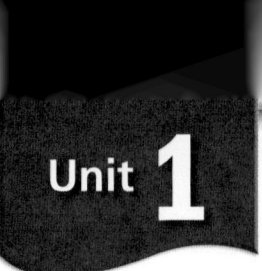

Introduction to World History

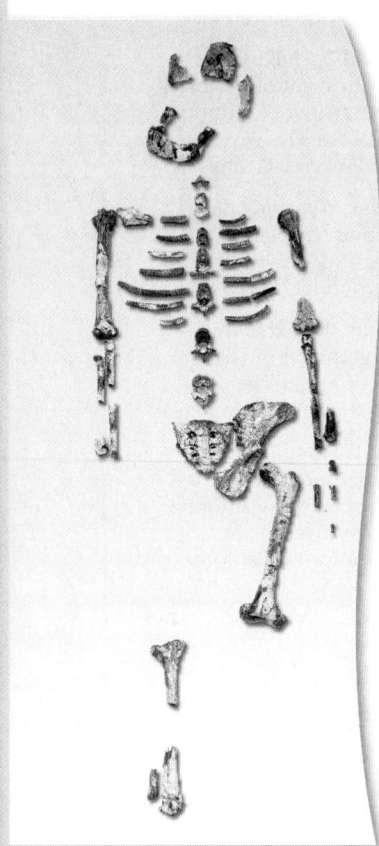

▲ Lucy (p. 31)

▲ Spear Thrower (p. 50)

Unit 2   Early Civilizations of Southwest Asia

Technology
For more on
Southwest Asia . . .
ClassZone.com

▲ **Sumerian
Pottery** (p. 98)

▲ **Detail from Ishtar
Gate** (p. 123)

Iranian Valley
(p. 129) ▼

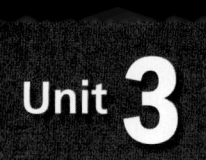

Unit 3   Ancient Africa

Technology
For more on ancient Africa . . .
ClassZone.com

▲ **Double Crown of Egypt** (p. 166)

▲ **Kuba Mask** (p. 207)

▼ **Pyramids** (p. 165)

▲ **The God Shiva** (p. 226)

▲ **Terra Cotta Army** (p. 267)

▲ **Olmec Head** (p. 302)

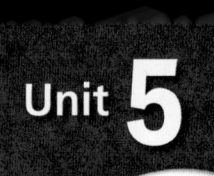

Unit 5

The Roots of Western Ideas

Technology
For more on the roots of western ideas . . .
ClassZone.com

▲ Fortress of Masada (p. 344)

▲ Greek Vase (p. 360)

▲ Alexander the Great
   (p. 406)

Technology
For more on the world of ancient Rome . . .
ClassZone.com

Unit 6 The World of Ancient Rome

▲ **Brutus** (p. 436)

▲ **Byzantine Cross** (p. 466)

▲ **Aqueducts** (p. 517)

SKILLBUILDER HANDBOOK   R1

PRIMARY SOURCE HANDBOOK   R34

WORLD RELIGIONS AND ETHICAL SYSTEMS   R60

GLOSSARY and GLOSSARY IN SPANISH   R78

Reading & Writing Support

Before You Read Strategies

Reading Activities

Writing Activities

Writing About History

Visual Vocabulary

Visual Vocabulary

Minted coins is a term for coins that are issued by the government and are official money.

Vocabulary Strategies

▲ **Abraham and Family** This painting shows Abraham and his family during their journey to Canaan.

Judaism and Monotheism Throughout the ancient world, people were polytheists (*poly* means "many"). This means that they worshiped many gods. The Hebrews believed that God spoke to Abraham and gave him important teachings. Abraham taught the belief in one all-powerful God who established moral laws for humanity. This belief is called **monotheism** (*mono* means "one"). **Judaism** today is descended from the religion of the ancient Hebrews. The name comes from the tribe of Judah, one of the 12 tribes descended from Abraham.

According to the Torah, during troubled times the Hebrews held to their belief that they were God's chosen people. They believed that a covenant (KUHV•uh•nuhnt), or a binding agreement, existed between God and Abraham and his descendants. They took courage from God's pledge to give a homeland to Abraham's descendants if they followed the laws of their faith and practiced righteousness and justice.

REVIEW How was Judaism different from other religions?

Canaan to Egypt and Back

❷ **ESSENTIAL QUESTION** Why did the Hebrews go to Egypt?

Over time, the Hebrews in Canaan took a new name—the Israelites. Their name came from Abraham's grandson Jacob. According to the Torah, he was given the name *Israel*. Jacob had 12 sons. Ten of these sons and two grandsons were the fathers of the 12 tribes.

Moses Leads the Israelites The Torah tells of a terrible famine in Canaan. The starving Israelites went to Egypt, where Jacob's son Joseph served as top adviser to Egypt's pharaoh.

In time, a new pharaoh came to power. He enslaved the Israelites and forced them to work on his building projects. The Torah tells how **Moses** helped the Israelites leave Egypt. The migration of the Israelites from Egypt is known as the **Exodus**.

The Ten Commandments After leaving Egypt, the Israelites wandered in the Sinai desert for 40 years, living as nomads. According to the Torah, Moses climbed to the top of Mount Sinai, where God spoke to him. When Moses came down the mountain, he carried two stone tablets that contained the **Ten Commandments**. These commandments became the basis for the laws of the Israelites. The commandments later became an important part of the moral and ethical traditions of Western civilization.

Vocabulary Strategy

The word *exodus* comes from the Greek word *exodos*. It combines the **root** *hodos*, which means "way" or "journey," with the **prefix** *ex-*, which means "out."

Primary Source

Background: According to the Torah, the Ten Commandments are the ten laws given by God to Moses on Mount Sinai. These orders serve as the basis for the moral laws of the Hebrews.

▲ **Moses with tablets of Ten Commandments**

The Ten Commandments*

1. I am the Lord thy God. . . . Thou shalt have no other gods before me.
2. Thou shalt not make unto thee any graven image. . . .
3. Thou shalt not take the name of the Lord thy God in vain. . . .
4. Remember the Sabbath day to keep it holy.
5. Honor thy father and thy mother. . . .
6. Thou shalt not kill.
7. Thou shalt not commit adultery.
8. Thou shalt not steal.
9. Thou shalt not bear false witness against thy neighbor.
10. Thou shalt not covet . . . any thing that is thy neighbor's.

Exodus 20:2–17

* Jews and some Christians word the commandments in ways slightly different from this version.

DOCUMENT-BASED QUESTIONS
1. What are the first four commandments concerned with?
2. What do the last six commandments have in common that makes them different from the first four?

Features

Comparisons Across Cultures

Geography

Geography

Ancient Irrigation

The model below shows how an ancient irrigation system worked.

1 Gates controlled how much water flowed from the river.

2 Main canals led from the river. They sloped gently downward to keep the water flowing.

3 Medium-sized branch canals led away from the main canals.

4 Small feeder canals led water directly to the fields.

GEOGRAPHY SKILLBUILDER
INTERPRETING VISUALS
Human-Environment Interaction Why do you think it was important to control how much water flowed from the river?

History Makers

Primary Source

Features

Skillbuilders

Starting with a Story

Daily Life

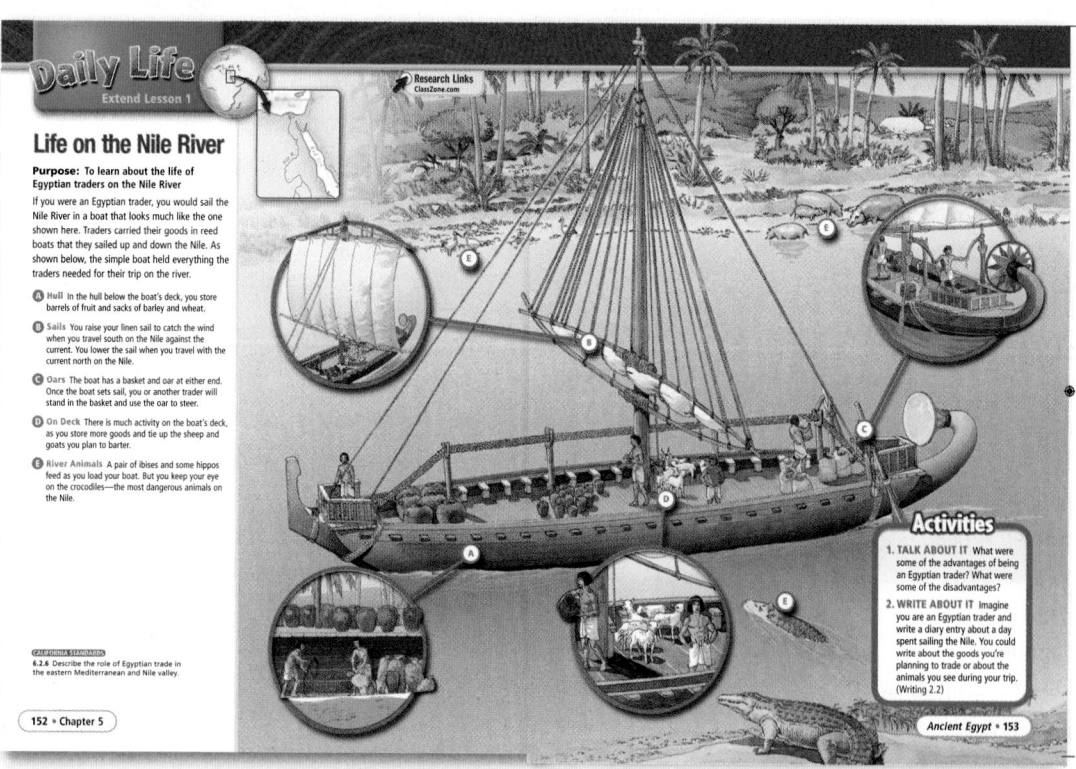

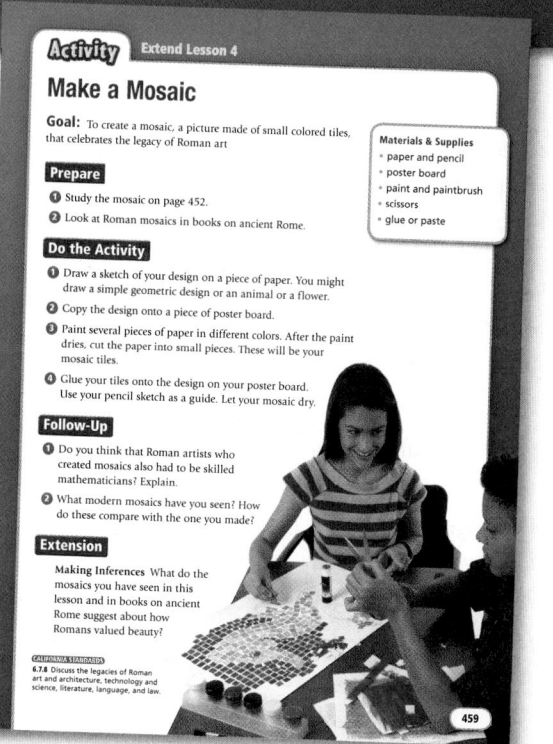

Activity   Extend Lesson 4

Make a Mosaic

Goal: To create a mosaic, a picture made of small colored tiles, that celebrates the legacy of Roman art

Materials & Supplies
- paper and pencil
- poster board
- paint and paintbrush
- scissors
- glue or paste

Prepare

1. Study the mosaic on page 452.
2. Look at Roman mosaics in books on ancient Rome.

Do the Activity

1. Draw a sketch of your design on a piece of paper. You might draw a simple geometric design or an animal or a flower.
2. Copy the design onto a piece of poster board.
3. Paint several pieces of paper in different colors. After the paint dries, cut the paper into small pieces. These will be your mosaic tiles.
4. Glue your tiles onto the design on your poster board. Use your pencil sketch as a guide. Let your mosaic dry.

Follow-Up

1. Do you think that Roman artists who created mosaics also had to be skilled mathematicians? Explain.
2. What modern mosaics have you seen? How do these compare with the one you made?

Extension

Making Inferences What do the mosaics you have seen in this lesson and in books on ancient Rome suggest about how Romans valued beauty?

CALIFORNIA STANDARDS
6.7.8 Discuss the legacies of Roman art and architecture, technology and science, literature, language, and law.

459

Infographics & Interactives

Infographics

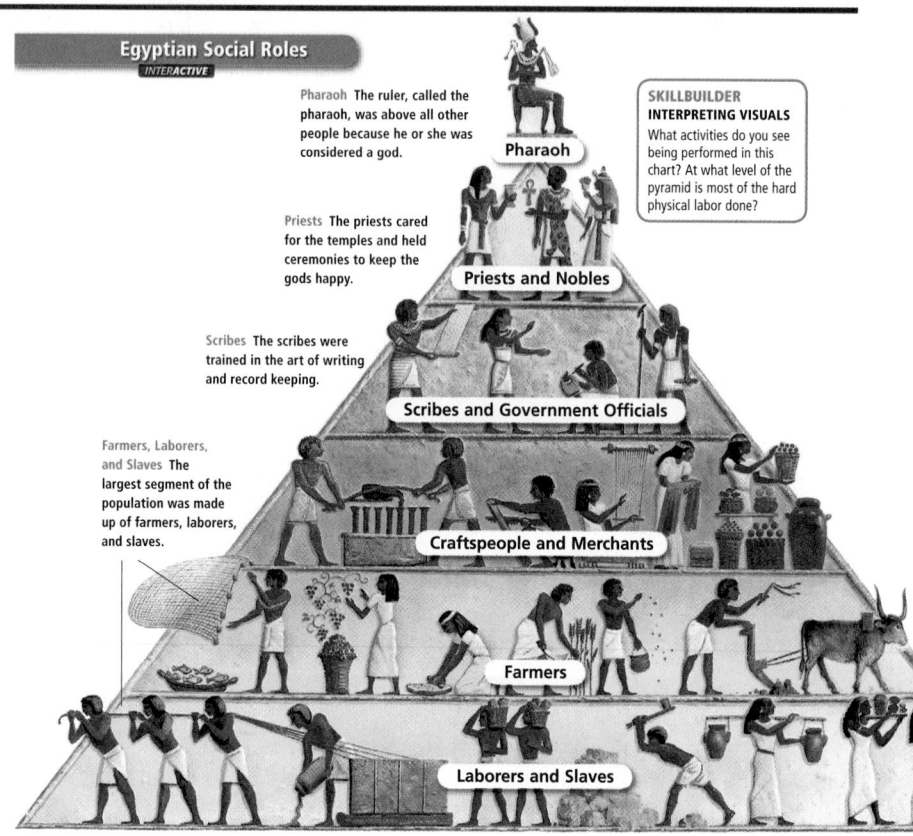

Egyptian Social Roles
INTERACTIVE

Pharaoh The ruler, called the pharaoh, was above all other people because he or she was considered a god.

Pharaoh

Priests The priests cared for the temples and held ceremonies to keep the gods happy.

Priests and Nobles

Scribes The scribes were trained in the art of writing and record keeping.

Scribes and Government Officials

Farmers, Laborers, and Slaves The largest segment of the population was made up of farmers, laborers, and slaves.

Craftspeople and Merchants

Farmers

Laborers and Slaves

SKILLBUILDER
INTERPRETING VISUALS
What activities do you see being performed in this chart? At what level of the pyramid is most of the hard physical labor done?

INTERACTIVE Maps and Visuals

Maps

Visuals

Maps

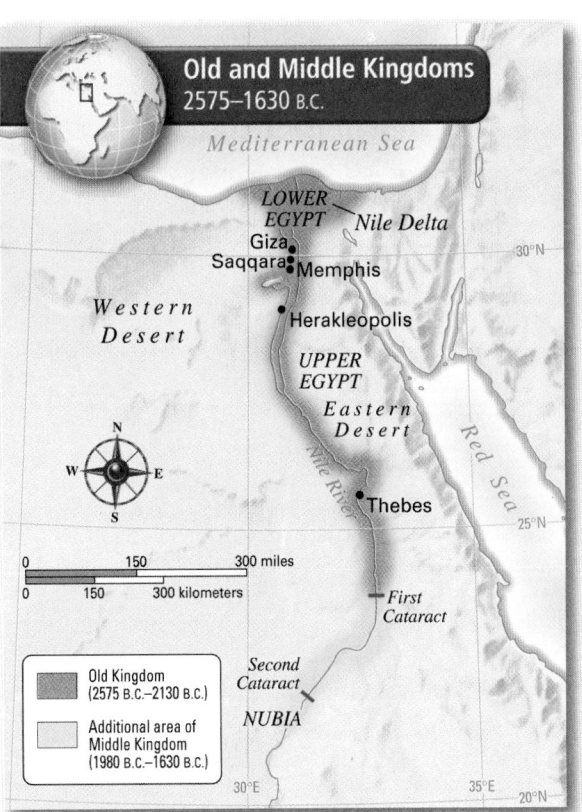

Old and Middle Kingdoms
2575–1630 B.C.

Maps

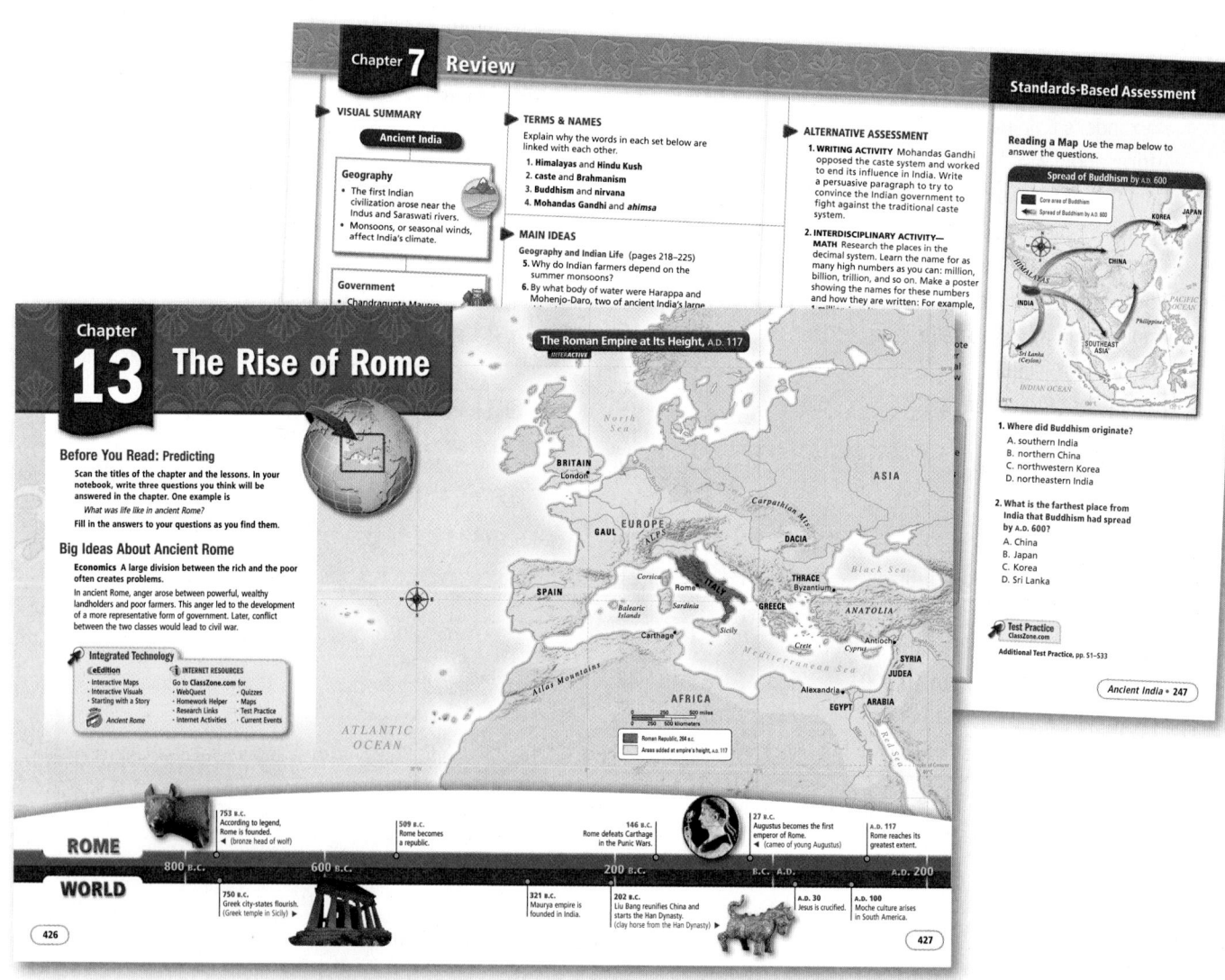

Charts & Time Lines

Charts

Time Lines

Jupiter This statue of Jupiter shows the god riding an eagle—his symbol—and throwing a lightning bolt. ▼

Greek and Roman Gods		
Description	**Greek**	**Roman**
Supreme god	Zeus	Jupiter
Supreme goddess	Hera (wife of Zeus)	Juno (wife of Jupiter)
God of the sea	Poseidon	Neptune
God of music and poetry	Apollo	Apollo
Goddess of love and beauty	Aphrodite	Venus
God of war	Ares	Mars

SKILLBUILDER
INTERPRETING VISUALS
Why do you think the Romans were so deeply influenced by Greek religion?

Student Guide to the California State Standards for Grade 6

The state of California has developed standards that guide the content taught in its public schools. At the beginning of every lesson in this book, you will see a listing of the California content standards and skills standards that are addressed in that lesson. The standards begin with a code that combines numbers and letters (such as 6.2.3 or HI 2), followed by the statement of the standard. These standards describe the knowledge and skills you are expected to have learned by the end of specific grades.

Standards that use numbers only (such as 6.2.3) are content standards, which describe the actual historical people and events that you will study in this book. Standards that combine letters and numbers (such as HI 2 or CST 3) refer to standards that cover the Historical and Social Sciences Analysis Skills that you will apply to the content standards for Grade 6.

The following charts contain the complete wording of the content and skills standards for Grade 6. These charts will help you keep track of what you learn throughout the year.

History-Social Science Standards

Grade 6 World History and Geography: Ancient Civilizations

Standard 6.1 Students describe what is known through archaeological studies of the early physical and cultural development of humankind from the Paleolithic era to the agricultural revolution.

6.1.1 Describe the hunter-gatherer societies, including the development of tools and the use of fire.

6.1.2 Identify the locations of human communities that populated the major regions of the world and describe how humans adapted to a variety of environments.

6.1.3 Discuss the climatic changes and human modifications of the physical environment that gave rise to the domestication of plants and animals and new sources of clothing and shelter.

Standard 6.2 Students analyze the geographic, political, economic, religious, and social structures of the early civilizations of Mesopotamia, Egypt, and Kush.

6.2.1 Locate and describe the major river systems and discuss the physical settings that supported permanent settlement and early civilizations.

6.2.2 Trace the development of agricultural techniques that permitted the production of economic surplus and the emergence of cities as centers of culture and power.

6.2.3 Understand the relationship between religion and the social and political order in Mesopotamia and Egypt.

6.2.4 Know the significance of Hammurabi's Code.

6.2.5 Discuss the main features of Egyptian art and architecture.

6.2.6 Describe the role of Egyptian trade in the eastern Mediterranean and Nile valley.

6.2.7 Understand the significance of Queen Hatshepsut and Ramses the Great.

6.2.8 Identify the location of the Kush civilization and describe its political, commercial, and cultural relations with Egypt.

6.2.9 Trace the evolution of language and its written forms.

Standard 6.3	Students analyze the geographic, political, economic, religious, and social structures of the Ancient Hebrews.
6.3.1	Describe the origins and significance of Judaism as the first monotheistic religion based on the concept of one God who sets down moral laws for humanity.
6.3.2	Identify the sources of the ethical teachings and central beliefs of Judaism (the Hebrew Bible, the Commentaries): belief in God, observance of law, practice of the concepts of righteousness and justice, and importance of study; and describe how the ideas of the Hebrew traditions are reflected in the moral and ethical traditions of Western civilization.
6.3.3	Explain the significance of Abraham, Moses, Naomi, Ruth, David, and Yohanan ben Zaccai in the development of the Jewish religion.
6.3.4	Discuss the locations of the settlements and movements of Hebrew peoples, including the Exodus and their movement to and from Egypt, and outline the significance of the Exodus to the Jewish and other people.
6.3.5	Discuss how Judaism survived and developed despite the continuing dispersion of much of the Jewish population from Jerusalem and the rest of Israel after the destruction of the second Temple in A.D. 70.

Standard 6.4	Students analyze the geographic, political, economic, religious, and social structures of the early civilizations of Ancient Greece.
6.4.1	Discuss the connections between geography and the development of city-states in the region of the Aegean Sea, including patterns of trade and commerce among Greek city-states and within the wider Mediterranean region.
6.4.2	Trace the transition from tyranny and oligarchy to early democratic forms of government and back to dictatorship in ancient Greece, including the significance of the invention of the idea of citizenship (e.g., from *Pericles' Funeral Oration*).
6.4.3	State the key differences between Athenian, or direct, democracy and representative democracy.
6.4.4	Explain the significance of Greek mythology to the everyday life of people in the region and how Greek literature continues to permeate our literature and language today, drawing from Greek mythology and epics, such as Homer's *Iliad* and *Odyssey*, and from *Aesop's Fables*.

6.4.5 Outline the founding, expansion, and political organization of the Persian Empire.

6.4.6 Compare and contrast life in Athens and Sparta, with emphasis on their roles in the Persian and Peloponnesian Wars.

6.4.7 Trace the rise of Alexander the Great and the spread of Greek culture eastward and into Egypt.

6.4.8 Describe the enduring contributions of important Greek figures in the arts and sciences (e.g., Hypatia, Socrates, Plato, Aristotle, Euclid, Thucydides).

Standard 6.5 Students analyze the geographic, political, economic, religious, and social structures of the early civilizations of India.

6.5.1 Locate and describe the major river system and discuss the physical setting that supported the rise of this civilization.

6.5.2 Discuss the significance of the Aryan invasions.

6.5.3 Explain the major beliefs and practices of Brahmanism in India and how they evolved into early Hinduism.

6.5.4 Outline the social structure of the caste system.

6.5.5 Know the life and moral teachings of the Buddha and how Buddhism spread in India, Ceylon, and Central Asia.

6.5.6 Describe the growth of the Maurya empire and the political and moral achievements of the emperor Asoka.

6.5.7 Discuss important aesthetic and intellectual traditions (e.g., Sanskrit literature, including the *Bhagavad Gita*; medicine; metallurgy; and mathematics, including Hindu-Arabic numerals and the zero).

Standard 6.6 Students analyze the geographic, political, economic, religious, and social structures of the early civilizations of China.

6.6.1 Locate and describe the origins of Chinese civilization in the Huang-He Valley during the Shang Dynasty.

6.6.2 Explain the geographic features of China that made governance and the spread of ideas and goods difficult and served to isolate the country from the rest of the world.

6.6.3 Know about the life of Confucius and the fundamental teachings of Confucianism and Daoism.

6.6.4 Identify the political and cultural problems prevalent in the time of Confucius and how he sought to solve them.

6.6.5	List the policies and achievements of the emperor Shi Huangdi in unifying northern China under the Qin Dynasty.
6.6.6	Detail the political contributions of the Han Dynasty to the development of the imperial bureaucratic state and the expansion of the empire.
6.6.7	Cite the significance of the trans-Eurasian "silk roads" in the period of the Han Dynasty and Roman Empire and their locations.
6.6.8	Describe the diffusion of Buddhism northward to China during the Han Dynasty.

▶ **Standard 6.7** — Students analyze the geographic, political, economic, religious, and social structures during the development of Rome.

6.7.1	Identify the location and describe the rise of the Roman Republic, including the importance of such mythical and historical figures as Aeneas, Romulus and Remus, Cincinnatus, Julius Caesar, and Cicero.
6.7.2	Describe the government of the Roman Republic and its significance (e.g., written constitution and tripartite government, checks and balances, civic duty).
6.7.3	Identify the location of and the political and geographic reasons for the growth of Roman territories and expansion of the empire, including how the empire fostered economic growth through the use of currency and trade routes.
6.7.4	Discuss the influence of Julius Caesar and Augustus in Rome's transition from republic to empire.
6.7.5	Trace the migration of Jews around the Mediterranean region and the effects of their conflict with the Romans, including the Romans' restrictions on their right to live in Jerusalem.
6.7.6	Note the origins of Christianity in the Jewish Messianic prophecies, the life and teachings of Jesus of Nazareth as described in the New Testament, and the contribution of St. Paul the Apostle to the definition and spread of Christian beliefs (e.g., belief in the Trinity, resurrection, salvation).
6.7.7	Describe the circumstances that led to the spread of Christianity in Europe and other Roman territories.
6.7.8	Discuss the legacies of Roman art and architecture, technology and science, literature, language, and law.

Local Option: Your school district may also include the following 7th-grade standards in your world history course.

▶ **Standard 7.1**	Students analyze the causes and effects of the vast expansion and ultimate disintegration of the Roman Empire.

7.1.1 Study the early strengths and lasting contributions of Rome (e.g., significance of Roman citizenship; rights under Roman law; Roman art, architecture, engineering, and philosophy; preservation and transmission of Christianity) and its ultimate internal weaknesses (e.g., rise of autonomous military powers within the empire, undermining of citizenship by the growth of corruption and slavery, lack of education, and distribution of news).

7.1.2 Discuss the geographic borders of the empire at its height and the factors that threatened its territorial cohesion.

7.1.3 Describe the establishment by Constantine of the new capital in Constantinople and the development of the Byzantine Empire, with an emphasis on the consequences of the development of two distinct European civilizations, Eastern Orthodox and Roman Catholic, and their two distinct views on church-state relations.

▶ **Standard 7.7**	Students compare and contrast the geographic, political, economic, religious, and social structures of the Meso-American and Andean civilizations.

7.7.1 Study the locations, landforms, and climates of Mexico, Central America, and South America and their effects on Mayan, Aztec, and Incan economies, trade, and development of urban societies.

7.7.2 Study the roles of people in each society, including class structures, family life, warfare, religious beliefs and practices, and slavery.

7.7.3 Explain how and where each empire arose and how the Aztec and Incan empires were defeated by the Spanish.

7.7.4 Describe the artistic and oral traditions and architecture in the three civilizations.

7.7.5 Describe the Meso-American achievements in astronomy and mathematics, including the development of the calendar and the Meso-American knowledge of seasonal changes to the civilizations' agricultural systems.

Grades 6 Through 8 Historical and Social Sciences Analysis Skills

Chronological and Spatial Thinking (CST)

1. Students explain how major events are related to one another in time.

2. Students construct various time lines of key events, people, and periods of the historical era they are studying.

3. Students use a variety of maps and documents to identify physical and cultural features of neighborhoods, cities, states, and countries and to explain the historical migration of people, expansion and disintegration of empires, and the growth of economic systems.

Research, Evidence, and Point of View (REP)

1. Students frame questions that can be answered by historical study and research.

2. Students distinguish fact from opinion in historical narratives and stories.

3. Students distinguish relevant from irrelevant information, essential from incidental information, and verifiable from unverifiable information in historical narratives and stories.

4. Students assess the credibility of primary and secondary sources and draw sound conclusions from them.

5. Students detect the different historical points of view on historical events and determine the context in which the historical statements were made (the questions asked, sources used, author's perspectives).

Historical Interpretation (HI)

1. Students explain the central issues and problems from the past, placing people and events in a matrix of time and place.

2. Students understand and distinguish cause, effect, sequence, and correlation in historical events, including the long- and short-term causal relations.

3. Students explain the sources of historical continuity and how the combination of ideas and events explains the emergence of new patterns.

4. Students recognize the role of chance, oversight, and error in history.

5. Students recognize that interpretations of history are subject to change as new information is uncovered.

6. Students interpret basic indicators of economic performance and conduct cost-benefit analyses of economic and political issues.

Beginning with Your Own Experience

Welcome to the study of world history. It is a big topic—the story of the most important things that ever happened to human beings. This book covers more than 5,000 years of that history.

You may be wondering how you will learn all the facts about such a long period of time. The best way is to sort the information into categories (similar groupings). The broad categories are called themes. This opening section of the book will introduce you to six major themes of history.

Let's begin with your life. Although you may not know it, you have already had many experiences that will help you to understand the themes. Consider the questions below and discuss your answers with your classmates.

Geography Is your town or city near a lake, an ocean, or mountains? What is the weather like? How do the landscape and the weather affect the way you live?

Culture Have you ever met someone from another place—another country, another state, or another city? In what ways did that person act differently from you? In what ways did he or she act like you?

Economics Are you always able to buy all the things you want? How do you decide what to buy when you don't have enough money for everything?

Government In your school, what would happen if every student could come to class at whatever time he or she wanted? Leave class whenever he or she wanted? Talk out loud anytime, even during tests?

Belief Systems When you were growing up, how did you learn what were the right and wrong ways of behaving? What people or groups taught you those things?

Science & Technology Think about a time when you wanted to share important news with a friend or relative who lived in another city or state. How did you share your news with them?

Understanding Historical Themes

As you and your classmates shared your answers, you probably discovered you had many different experiences. But you probably also found that you had things in common too.

For example, some people who live near the ocean like to surf, while others prefer fishing. Still others play beach volleyball. Some people who live directly on the coast build sea walls to protect their homes. Each of those activities is a different response to living by the ocean. Yet, what these people have in common is that the place where they live affects their lives.

Once you understand what a group of facts has in common, you are ready to talk about themes. The six themes of this history program are described below. As you read this book, you will notice that many statements and questions are labeled by one of these themes.

Geography

Geography refers to the characteristics of a physical place, the ways that environment affects human life, and the ways that humans change the environment. It also refers to the movement of people, goods, and ideas from place to place.

Culture

Culture is the way of life that a society or group shares. It includes the way people act, the way they express themselves, and the way they are organized.

Economics

Economics includes the ways that people use their limited resources to satisfy their needs and desires. It also refers to the ways that societies produce wealth and how they organize labor.

Government

Government refers to the system of laws and authority that a society uses to guide or control its members.

Belief Systems

Belief systems are often religions, which are beliefs in a god or gods. Belief systems may also be systems of ethics, or principles of right and wrong.

Science & Technology

The theme of science and technology includes discoveries, inventions, and improved methods of doing things.

Looking for Big Ideas

As you read this book, you will begin to notice that certain patterns occur over and over in history. Different societies go through similar stages, make similar choices, or organize themselves in similar ways. We call those patterns the **Big Ideas** of history.

For example, many of the ancient societies that you will study began in river valleys because such places were good for farming and transportation. Therefore, one of the Big Ideas in this book is:

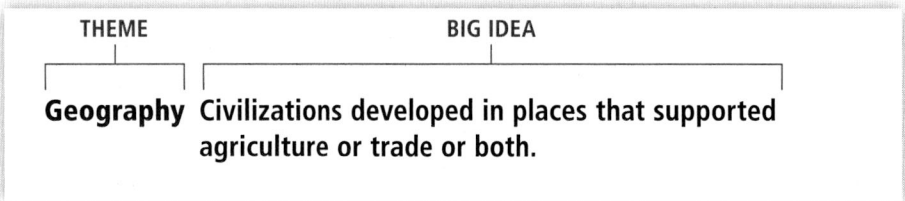

THEME	BIG IDEA
Geography	Civilizations developed in places that supported agriculture or trade or both.

As you can see from that example, the Big Idea is a statement of the historical pattern. The first page of every chapter lists a Big Idea, which introduces a pattern that occurs in the chapter. Each Big Idea starts with a theme, as shown above. Think about the Big Idea before you start to read. It will help you know what to focus on as you study.

In this book, you will encounter 12 different Big Ideas, two for each theme:

Big Ideas are Patterns in History		
Geography	Civilizations developed in places that supported agriculture or trade or both.	Migration, trade, warfare, and the action of missionaries spread ideas and beliefs.
Culture	Ways of living change as humans interact with each other.	Many societies rely on family roles and social classes to keep order.
Economics	Societies trade the surplus goods that they produce to obtain goods they lack.	Nomadic peoples often attacked settlements to gain the goods that civilizations produce.
Government	Governments create law codes and political bodies to organize a society.	New ideas and beliefs can challenge a government's authority, leading to change.
Belief Systems	Many religions and belief systems start with the ideas of a teacher or prophet.	Belief systems and religions may shape governments and societies.
Science & Technology	New scientific discoveries change human understanding of the world.	New inventions and techniques change the way humans live their daily lives.

Asking Historical Questions

You can use themes and Big Ideas to ask questions about historic periods and people. As you read this book, ask yourself questions that you will try to answer as you read. This approach will help you understand the importance of various facts and will help you remember them.

Sample Historical Questions

Geography How has the place where people lived been important in influencing how they lived? What effect does landscape and weather have on human life?

Culture Throughout history, what have cultures learned about each other? How have they learned it, and how have they borrowed from other cultures to change themselves?

Economics Have societies always been able to acquire what they needed or wanted? When societies are limited in what they can acquire, how do they choose what to do without?

Government Throughout history, how have societies developed laws to guide the behavior of their members? How did those laws affect the way people lived together?

Belief Systems Throughout history, how have societies developed ideas of right and wrong? How do different belief systems compare?

Science & Technology In different time periods, how have people solved the problem of spreading information over long distances? What other problems of daily life have people solved by using inventions, discoveries, or new techniques?

To help guide your reading, we have included historical questions in every lesson of this book. They appear at the beginning of each section and are labeled **ESSENTIAL QUESTIONS**. By looking for the answers to these questions as you read, you will focus on the most important information in each lesson.

Be careful when you ask historical questions. Don't assume that life in the past was the same as life today. For example, consider this question: In the past, how did people get rid of a ruler they didn't like?

Because we have frequent elections in the United States, we can vote officials out of office. However, in the past, most societies were ruled by a monarch who controlled the army. It was difficult to replace such powerful rulers.

In conclusion, as you study world history, remember these three tips:

- Consider how facts and details relate to the six themes.
- Look for the patterns explained in the Big Ideas.
- Ask and answer historical questions.

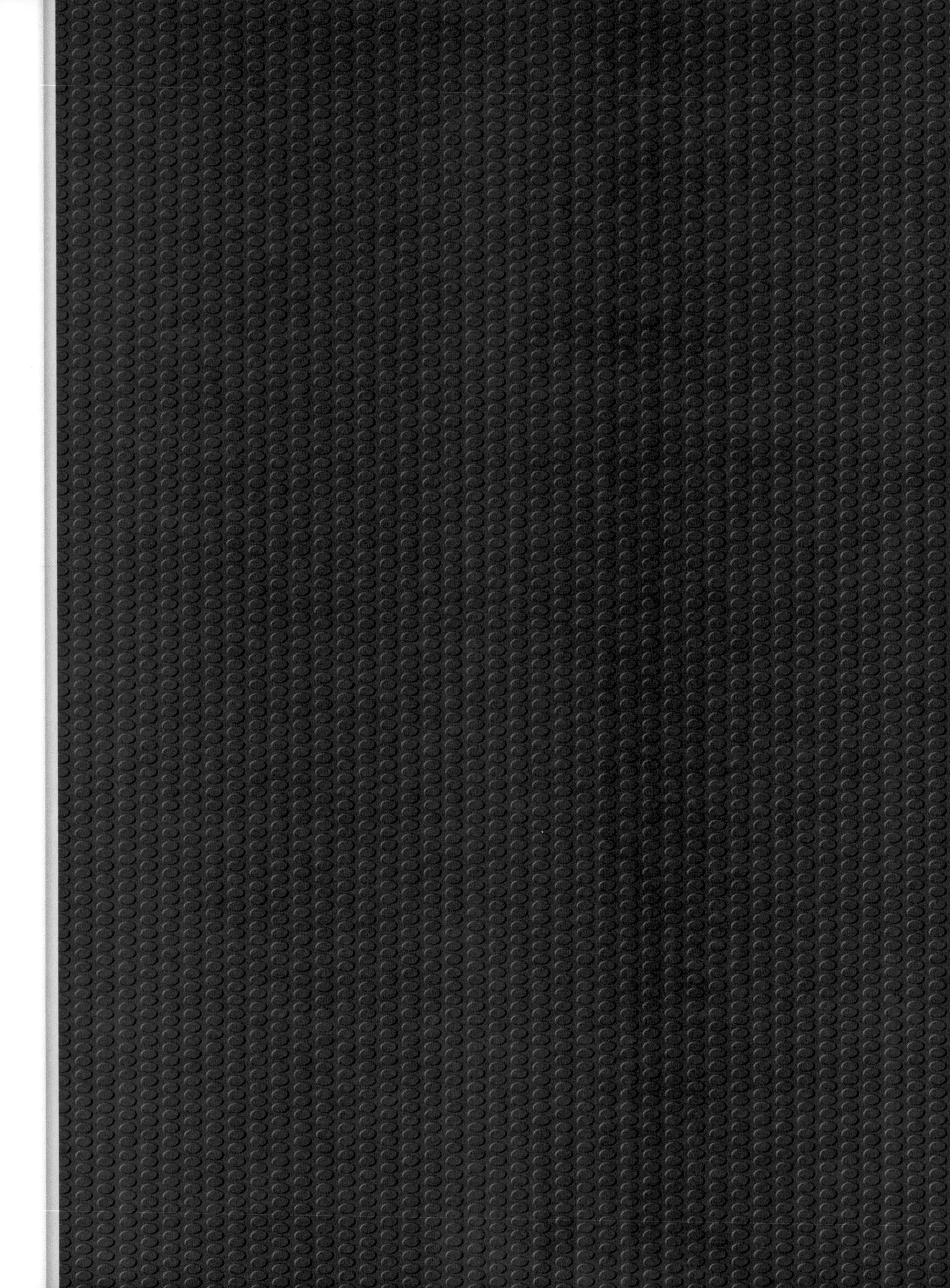

STRATEGIES for TAKING TESTS

This section will help you develop and practice the skills you need to study history and to take tests. Part 1, **Strategies for Studying History,** shows you the features of this book. It also shows you how to improve your reading and study skills.

Part 2, **Test-Taking Strategies and Practice,** gives you strategies to help you answer the different kinds of questions that appear on tests. Each strategy is followed by a set of questions you can use for practice.

CONTENTS

Part 1: Strategies for Studying History

Reading is the central skill in the effective study of history or any other subject. You can improve your reading skills by using helpful techniques and by practicing. The better your reading skills, the more you will remember what you read. The next four pages show how some of the features of *World History: Ancient Civilizations* can help you learn and understand history.

Preview Chapters Before You Read

Each chapter begins with a two-page chapter opener. Study these pages to help you get ready to read.

1 Read the chapter title for clues to what will be covered in the chapter.

2 Study the **Before You Read** section. The activities in this section will help to guide your reading.

3 Preview the time line and note the years covered in the chapter. Consider the important events that took place during this time period. Study the map to get an idea of where these events took place.

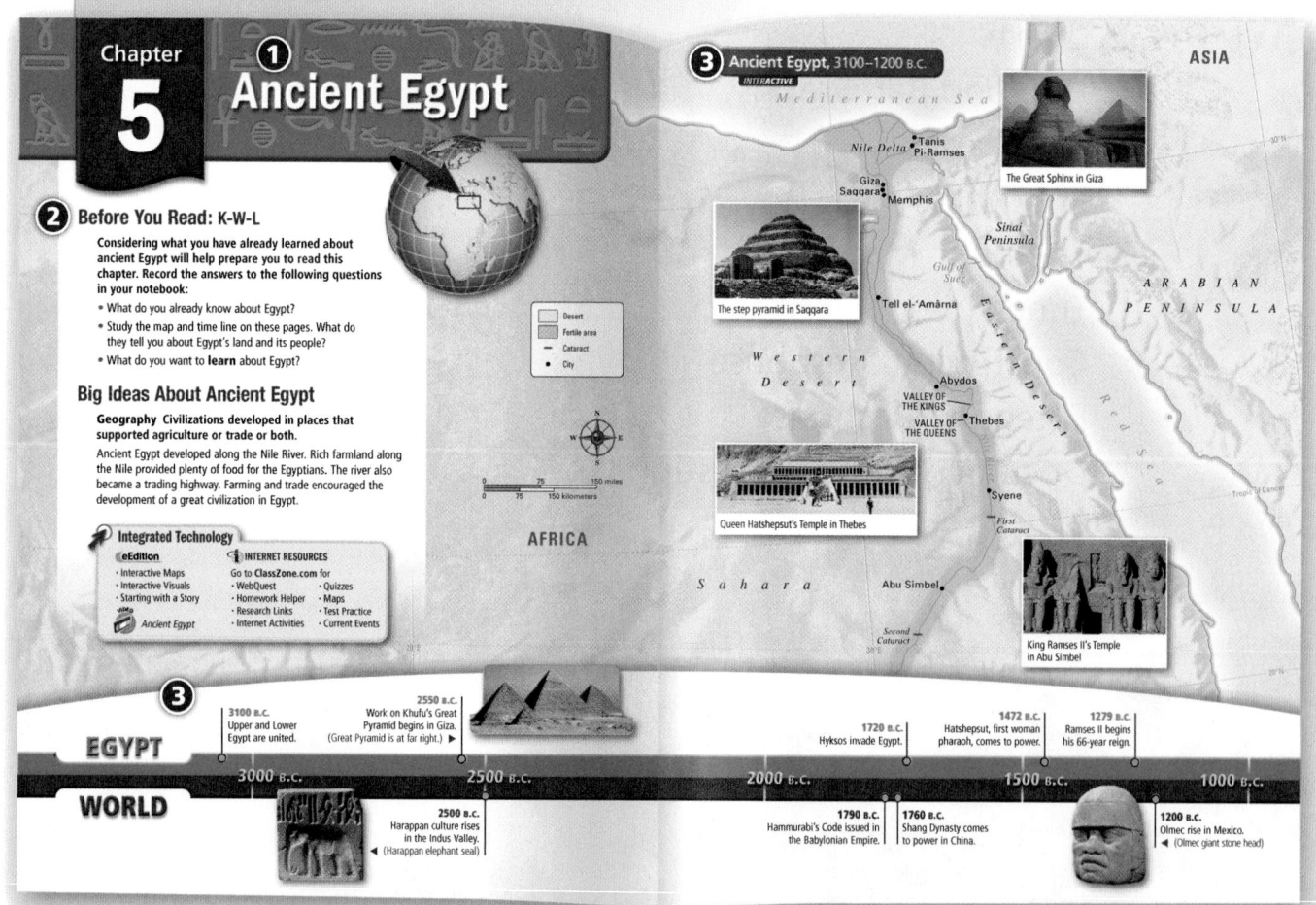

Preview Lessons Before You Read

Each chapter consists of either three or four lessons. These lessons focus on specific time periods or on particular historical themes.

1. Study the information under the heading **Main Ideas.** It tells you what is important in the material you are about to read.

2. Preview the **Terms & Names** list. This list tells you the topics that will be covered in the lesson.

3. Read the paragraph under the heading **Build on What You Know.** This relates the lesson to your experience or to subjects you've already studied.

4. Notice the structure of the lesson. Red headings label the major topics; run-in headings signal smaller topics.

5. Each lesson opener lists the standards covered in that lesson.

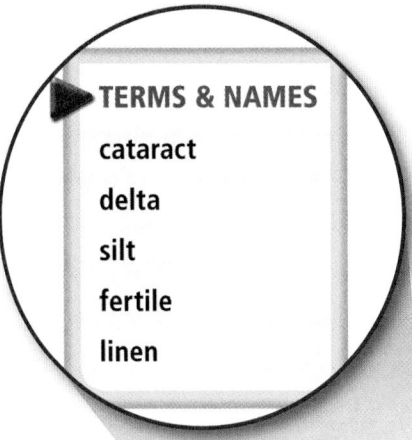

TERMS & NAMES

cataract

delta

silt

fertile

linen

Lesson 1

MAIN IDEAS

1. **Geography** The Nile River helped Egypt develop a civilization.

2. **Economics** The fertile land provided everything Egyptians needed.

3. **Economics** The Nile and other resources influenced Egypt's economy.

TAKING NOTES

Reading Skill:
Understanding Cause and Effect

Following causes and effects will help you understand the main ideas in this lesson. In Lesson 1, look for the effects of each event listed in the chart. Record them on a chart of your own.

Causes	Effects
Floods	
New agricultural techniques	
Many land resources	

S Skillbuilder Handbook, page R26

CALIFORNIA STANDARDS

6.2.1 Locate and describe the major river systems and discuss the physical settings that supported permanent settlement and early civilizations.

6.2.2 Trace the development of agricultural techniques that permitted the production of economic surplus and the emergence of cities as centers of culture and power.

6.2.6 Describe the role of Egyptian trade in the eastern Mediterranean and Nile valley.

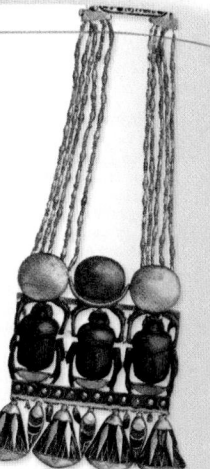

▲ **Lotus Pendants** This necklace once belonged to an Egyptian king. The pendants at the bottom are lotus buds. The lotus, a water lily that grows in the Nile River, is a symbol of Egypt.

Gift of the Nile

TERMS & NAMES

cataract
delta
silt
fertile
linen

Build on What You Know Have you ever received a gift that was very important to you? How did it affect your life? The Nile River was so important to Egypt that 2,500 years ago, an ancient Greek historian called Egypt "the gift of the Nile."

Geography of Ancient Egypt

ESSENTIAL QUESTION Why was the Nile River important?

The Greek historian knew what he was talking about. The Nile River fed Egyptian civilization for hundreds of years.

The Longest River The Nile is 4,160 miles long—the world's longest river. It begins near the equator in Africa and flows north to the Mediterranean Sea. In the south it churns with cataracts. A **cataract** (KAT•uh•RAKT) is a waterfall. Near the sea the Nile branches into a delta. A **delta** is an area near a river's mouth where the water deposits fine soil called **silt.** In the delta, the Nile divides into many streams.

The river is called the upper Nile in the south and the lower Nile in the north. For centuries, heavy rains in Ethiopia caused the Nile to flood every summer. The floods deposited rich soil along the Nile's shores. This soil was **fertile,** which means it was good for growing crops. Unlike the Tigris and Euphrates, the Nile River flooded at the same time every year, so farmers could predict when to plant their crops.

The Nile Valley Fertile land in Egypt stretches along the Nile and then gives way to desert. As a result, Egypt was a narrow country. ▼

Use Active Reading Strategies as You Read

Now you're ready to read the chapter. Read one lesson at a time, from beginning to end.

1 Ask and answer questions as you read. Look for the **Essential Question** under each main heading. Finding the answer to this question will help guide your reading.

2 Look for the story behind the events. Study the captions and any boxed features for additional information and interesting sidelights on the lesson content.

3 Try to visualize the people, places, and events you read about. Studying the pictures, maps, and other illustrations will help you do this.

4 Read to build your vocabulary. Use the **Vocabulary Strategy** in the margin to find the meaning of unfamiliar words.

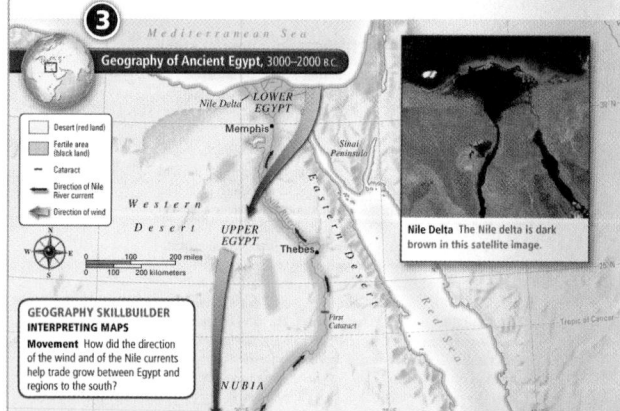

Red Land, Black Land The ancient Egyptians lived in narrow bands of land on each side of the Nile. They called this region the black land because of the fertile soil that the floods deposited. The red land was the barren desert beyond the fertile region.

Weather in Egypt was almost always the same. Eight months of the year were sunny and hot. The four months of winter were sunny but cooler. Most of the region received only an inch of rain a year. The parts of Egypt not near the Nile were a desert.

Isolation The harsh desert acted as a barrier to keep out enemies. The Mediterranean coast was swampy and lacked good harbors. For these reasons, early Egyptians stayed close to home.

REVIEW What did the floods of the Nile River provide for farmers?

Land of Plenty

2 ESSENTIAL QUESTION How did Egyptians use the land around the Nile? **1**

Each year, Egyptian farmers watched for white birds called ibises (EYE•bihs•uhz), which flew up from the south. When the birds

Geography of Ancient Egypt, 3000–2000 B.C. **3**

Desert (red land)
Fertile area (black land)
Cataract
Direction of Nile River current
Direction of wind

Mediterranean Sea

Nile Delta — LOWER EGYPT
Memphis
Sinai Peninsula
Western Desert
UPPER EGYPT
Thebes
Eastern Desert
Red Sea
First Cataract
NUBIA

100   200 miles
100   200 kilometers

Nile Delta The Nile delta is dark brown in this satellite image.

GEOGRAPHY SKILLBUILDER
INTERPRETING MAPS
Movement How did the direction of the wind and of the Nile currents help trade grow between Egypt and regions to the south?

arrived, the annual flood waters would soon follow. After the waters drained away, farmers could plant seeds in the fertile soil.

Agricultural Techniques By about 2400 B.C., farmers used technology to expand their farmland. Working together, they dug irrigation canals that carried river water to dry areas. Then they used a tool called a shaduf (shah•DOOF) to spread the water across the fields. These innovative, or new, techniques gave them more farmland.

 **3**

Egyptian Crops Ancient Egyptians grew a large variety of foods. They were the first to grind wheat into flour and to mix the flour with yeast and water to make dough rise into bread. They grew vegetables such as lettuce, radishes, asparagus, and cucumbers. Fruits included dates, figs, grapes, and watermelons.

Egyptians also grew the materials for their clothes. They were the first to weave fibers from flax plants into a fabric called **linen**. Lightweight linen cloth was perfect for hot Egyptian days. Men wore linen wraps around their waists. Women wore loose, sleeveless dresses. Egyptians also wove marsh grasses into sandals.

Egyptian Houses Egyptians built houses using bricks made of mud from the Nile mixed with chopped straw. They placed narrow windows high in the walls to reduce bright sunlight. Egyptians often painted walls white to reflect the blazing heat. They wove sticks and palm trees to make roofs. Inside, woven reed mats covered the dirt floor. Most Egyptians slept on mats covered with linen sheets. Wealthy citizens enjoyed bed frames and cushions.

Egyptian nobles had fancier homes with tree-lined courtyards for shade. Some had a pool filled with lotus blossoms and fish. Poorer Egyptians simply went to the roof to cool off after sunset. They often cooked, ate, and even slept outside.

REVIEW What agricultural techniques did ancient Egyptians use?

Connect to Today
▲ **Shaduf** A shaduf is a bucket on a lever. It was used to lift water from the Nile or canals. Some Egyptians still use shadufs today. **2**

Vocabulary Strategy **4**
The word *linen* has **multiple meanings.** Sheets and tablecloths are often called linens because they used to only be made from linen cloth.

Vocabulary Strategy

The word *linen* has **multiple meanings.** Sheets and tablecloths are often called linens because they used to only be made from linen cloth.

Review and Summarize What You Have Read

When you finish reading a lesson, review and summarize what you have read. If necessary, go back and reread information that was not clear the first time through.

1 Answer the **Review** questions at the end of each section of the lesson.

2 Reread the main headings and the run-in headings for a quick summary of the major points covered in the lesson.

3 Study any charts, graphs, or maps in the lesson. These visual materials usually provide a condensed version of the information in the lesson.

4 Complete all of the questions in the **Lesson Review.** This will help you think critically about what you have just read. Note that each question is labeled with a standard.

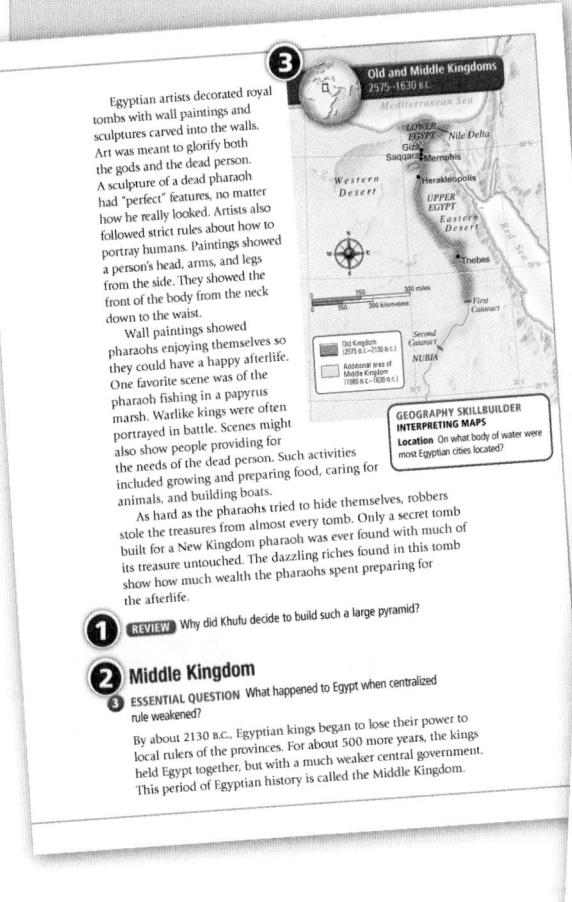

Egyptian artists decorated royal tombs with wall paintings and sculptures carved into the walls. Art was meant to glorify both the gods and the dead person. A sculpture of a dead pharaoh had "perfect" features, no matter how he really looked. Artists also followed strict rules about how to portray humans. Paintings showed a person's head, arms, and legs from the side. They showed the front of the body from the neck down to the waist.

Wall paintings showed pharaohs enjoying themselves so they could have a happy afterlife. One favorite scene was of the pharaoh fishing in a papyrus marsh. Warlike kings were often portrayed in battle. Scenes might also show people providing for the needs of the dead person. Such activities included growing and preparing food, caring for animals, and building boats.

As hard as the pharaohs tried to hide themselves, robbers stole the treasures from almost every tomb. Only a secret tomb built for a New Kingdom pharaoh was ever found with much of its treasure untouched. The dazzling riches found in this tomb show how much wealth the pharaohs spent preparing for the afterlife.

1 **REVIEW** Why did Khufu decide to build such a large pyramid?

2 ## Middle Kingdom

3 **ESSENTIAL QUESTION** What happened to Egypt when centralized rule weakened?

By about 2130 B.C., Egyptian kings began to lose their power to local rulers of the provinces. For about 500 more years, the kings held Egypt together, but with a much weaker central government. This period of Egyptian history is called the Middle Kingdom.

Old and Middle Kingdoms
2575–1630 B.C.

GEOGRAPHY SKILLBUILDER
INTERPRETING MAPS
Location On what body of water were most Egyptian cities located?

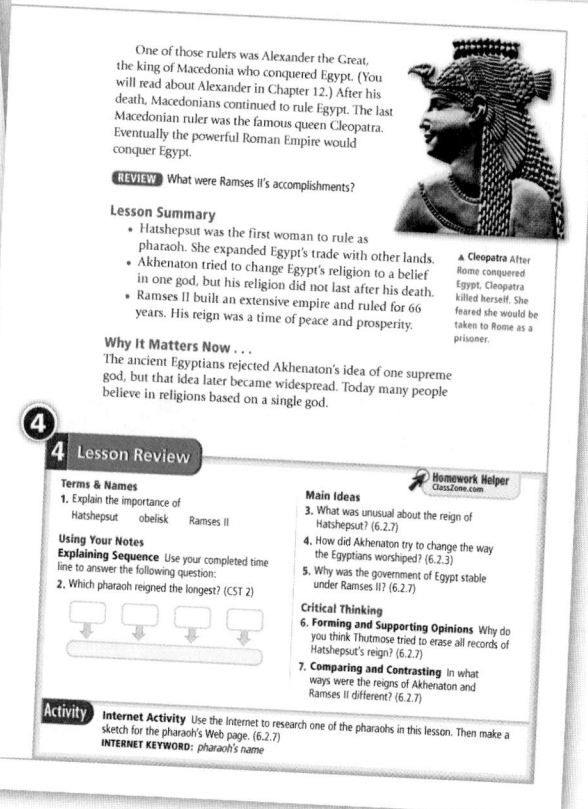

One of those rulers was Alexander the Great, the king of Macedonia who conquered Egypt. (You will read about Alexander in Chapter 12.) After his death, Macedonians continued to rule Egypt. The last Macedonian ruler was the famous queen Cleopatra. Eventually the powerful Roman Empire would conquer Egypt.

REVIEW What were Ramses II's accomplishments?

▲ **Cleopatra** After Rome conquered Egypt, Cleopatra killed herself. She feared she would be taken to Rome as a prisoner.

Lesson Summary
- Hatshepsut was the first woman to rule as pharaoh. She expanded Egypt's trade with other lands.
- Akhenaton tried to change Egypt's religion to a belief in one god, but his religion did not last after his death.
- Ramses II built an extensive empire and ruled for 66 years. His reign was a time of peace and prosperity.

Why It Matters Now . . .
The ancient Egyptians rejected Akhenaton's idea of one supreme god, but that idea later became widespread. Today many people believe in religions based on a single god.

4 ## Lesson Review

Homework Helper
ClassZone.com

Terms & Names
1. Explain the importance of
   Hatshepsut   obelisk   Ramses II

Using Your Notes
Explaining Sequence Use your completed time line to answer the following question:
2. Which pharaoh reigned the longest? (CST 2)

Main Ideas
3. What was unusual about the reign of Hatshepsut? (6.2.7)
4. How did Akhenaton try to change the way the Egyptians worshiped? (6.2.3)
5. Why was the government of Egypt stable under Ramses II? (6.2.7)

Critical Thinking
6. **Forming and Supporting Opinions** Why do you think Thutmose tried to erase all records of Hatshepsut's reign? (6.2.7)
7. **Comparing and Contrasting** In what ways were the reigns of Akhenaton and Ramses II different? (6.2.7)

Activity **Internet Activity** Use the Internet to research one of the pharaohs in this lesson. Then make a sketch for the pharaoh's Web page. (6.2.7)
INTERNET KEYWORD: pharaoh's name

Using Strategies For...

Multiple Choice Explain to students that they will do best on test questions by thinking them through carefully and by applying test-taking strategies such as the following:

1. In question 1, one of the possible answers is "all of the above." In questions that have this option, you know that if even one answer is incorrect you can eliminate that choice. Since the Andes do run through Colombia, Ecuador, and Peru, (D) is the correct answer.

2. Knowing that the prefix *pale-* means "ancient," "prehistoric," or "early" will help you to answer this question. The major work of the paleontologist is studying prehistoric plants and animals, so (C), fossils, is the correct answer.

3. Pay close attention to modifiers such as the word *essential*. This word affects the meaning of the question and can provide clues to help you narrow your choices.

4. Your general knowledge should tell you that Buddhism is connected to such countries as India, China, and Japan. Therefore, the correct answer is (A), Asia.

General Test-Taking Tips

Share these tips with your students.

- The night before a test, make sure you get at least eight hours of sleep.

- Have a healthy breakfast or lunch before taking your test.

- Wear clothes that make you comfortable.

- Relax and enjoy the challenge!

Part 2: Test-Taking Strategies and Practice

Use the strategies in this section to improve your test-taking skills. First read the tips on the left page. Then use them to help you with the practice items on the right page.

Multiple Choice

A multiple-choice question is a question or incomplete sentence and a set of choices. One of the choices correctly answers the question or completes the sentence.

1 Read the question or incomplete sentence carefully. Try to answer the question or complete the sentence before looking at the choices.

2 Look for key words in the question. They may help you figure out the correct answer.

3 Read each choice with the question. Don't decide on your final answer until you have read all of the choices.

4 Rule out any choices that you know are wrong.

5 Sometimes the last choice is *all of the above*. Make sure that the other choices are all correct if you pick this answer.

1 1. The Andes mountains run through
   A. Colombia.
   B. Ecuador. — **3** choices
   C. Peru.
   D. all of the above — **5** Before selecting *all of the above*, make sure that all of the choices are, indeed, correct.

2. Paleontologists study
   A. cultures.
   B. modern societies.
   C. fossils.
   D. ancient art.

3. Which is an (essential) characteristic — **2** The word *essential* is key here. All of the choices are characteristics of some civilizations, but record keeping is essential to all.
   of a civilization?
   A. warfare
   B. record keeping
   C. pyramids
   D. machines — **4** You can eliminate *D* because you know many civilizations lacked machines.

4. Where did Buddhism originate?
   A. Asia
   B. Africa
   C. Europe
   D. North America

answers: 1 (D); 2 (C); 3 (B); 4 (A)

Activity Options

Individual Needs: English Learners

Word Meaning Make sure students understand the following terms and concepts on these pages.

Strategy Page:

Question 2 *fossils:* remains of plant or animal life preserved in rock
Question 3 *essential:* absolutely necessary
   civilization: a group of people that have achieved a certain level of cultural development
   pyramids: structures with a square base and triangular sides

Question 4 *Buddhism:* one of the major religions of the world

Practice Page:

Question 1 *government:* rules and systems for ruling people
Question 4 *bronze:* a type of metal made mainly from copper and tin

For more test practice online . . .

TEST PRACTICE
CLASSZONE.COM

Directions: Read the following questions and choose the *best* answer from the four choices.

1. Which of the following is *not* a form of government?
   A. aristocracy
   B. monarchy
   C. oligarchy
   D. philosophy

2. In 431 B.C., Sparta and Athens fought the
   A. Trojan War.
   B. Peloponnesian War.
   C. Persian War.
   D. Civil War.

3. Olmec civilization developed in
   A. China.
   B. western Africa.
   C. Beringia.
   D. Meso-America.

4. Which of the following was invented during China's Han Dynasty?
   A. paper
   B. bronze
   C. steel
   D. silk

Practice Questions

Thinking It Through Share the following explanations with students as they discuss the strategies they used to answer the practice questions.

1. This item is an example of a *not* question. Look for the answer that is *not* a correct response to the question. You can recognize that philosophy is the study of systems of knowledge and not a type of government. Therefore, (D) is the correct answer.

2. In this question, you can quickly recognize that choice (D) is clearly false and can be eliminated. To choose from among the remaining options, you must call upon your knowledge of history. In this case, the correct answer is (B).

3. This question also requires you to use your knowledge of social studies to identify the correct answer. You can determine that no civilizations lived on Beringia, the strip of land that in prehistoric times linked Asia and North America. You should also recall that the Olmec were a Meso-American culture, meaning the correct answer must be (D).

4. Once again, use your knowledge of history to answer this question. You may recall that the Chinese are remembered for inventing paper. The correct answer is (A).

California Standards and Skills

STRATEGY ITEMS		PRACTICE ITEMS	
Item Number	Skill/Standard Tested	Item Number	Skill/Standard Tested
1. 3.	HI1 Students explain the central issues and problems of the past.	1. 3.	HI1 Students explain the central issues and problems of the past.
2.	6.1 Students describe what is known through archaeological studies of the early physical and cultural development of human kind.	2.	6.4.6 Compare and contrast life in Athens and Sparta.
4.	6.5.5 Know the life and moral teachings of Buddha and how Buddhism spread in India	4.	6.6.6 Detail the political contributions of the Han Dynasty.

CST = Chronological and Spatial Thinking, **HI** = Historical Interpretation, **REP** = Research, Evidence, and Point of View

Using Strategies For...

Primary Sources Students can learn about the past by studying primary sources. As students read the primary source, have them try to answer the following questions: Who is it about? What does it describe? When did it happen? Where did it happen? Why did it happen?

Explain to students that they will do best on test questions by thinking them through carefully and by applying test-taking strategies such as the following:

1. Question 1 asks you to identify the type of natural disaster the passage is describing. This is factual material that is available directly from the passage itself. The correct answer is (C).

2. The key word in question 2 is *best*. Recognize that in this type of question, several answers may seem to be correct in some way. You must look for the choice that represents the *whole* passage. The answer that best represents the whole passage is (A).

General Test-Taking Tips

Share these tips with your students.

- Read the directions carefully before you begin to answer the questions.

- Budget the time you are given to take the test, so you don't spend too much time on any one question.

- Check your answers to make sure you've made no obvious mistakes.

- Believe in yourself!

Primary Sources

Sometimes you will need to look at a document to answer a question. Some documents are primary sources. Primary sources are written or made by people who either saw an event or were actually part of the event. A primary source can be a photograph, letter, diary, speech, or autobiography.

1 Look at the source line to learn about the document and its author. Consider how reliable the information might be.

2 Skim the article to get an idea of what it is about. As you read, look for the main idea. The main idea is the writer's most important point. Sometimes it is not directly stated.

3 Note any special punctuation. For example, ellipses (. . .) mean that words and sentences have been left out.

4 Ask yourself questions about the document as you read.

5 Review the questions. This will give your reading a purpose and also help you find the answers more easily. Then reread the document.

answers: 1 (C); 2 (A)

The Eruption of Mount Vesuvius, A.D. 79

My mother now began to beg, urge, and command me to escape as best I could. . . . I replied that I would not be saved without her. Taking her by the hand, I hurried her along. (. . .) And now came the ashes, but at **3** first sparsely. I turned around. Behind us, an ominous thick smoke, spreading over the earth like a flood, followed us. . . . To be heard were only the shrill cries of women, the wailing of children, the shouting of men. Some were calling to their parents, others to their children, others to their wives—knowing one another only by voice.

1—Pliny the Younger, from letters written to the historian Tacitus

This text is from a personal letter.

1. Pliny is describing a
   A. flood.
   B. tidal wave.
   C. volcanic eruption.
   D. war.

2. Which sentence *best* expresses the idea of this passage?
   A. People were very frightened.
   B. Pliny disagreed with his mother.
   C. Thick smoke spread over the earth like a flood.
   D. Pliny got separated from his mother.

Activity Options

Individual Needs: English Learners

Word Meaning Make sure students understand the following terms and concepts on these pages.

Strategy Page: Primary Source
eruption: the shooting forth of ashes, hot gas, lava, and rock from an active volcano
ominous: promising a bad result
shrill: loud, piercing noise

Practice Page: Primary Source
fancies: favorite ideas or beliefs
enquiry: question
laborious: hard, time-consuming
eye-witnesses: the people who see an event directly

Directions: Use the passage to answer the following questions.

He [the historian] must not be misled by the exaggerated fancies of the poets, or by the tales of chroniclers who seek to please the ear rather than speak the truth. . . . At such a distance of time he must make up his mind to be satisfied with conclusions resting upon the clearest evidence which can be had. . . . Of the events of the war I have not ventured to speak from any chance information, nor according to any notion of my own; I have described nothing but what I either saw myself, or learned from others of whom I made the most careful and particular enquiry. The task was a laborious one, because eye-witnesses of the same occurrences gave different accounts of them, as they remembered or were interested in the actions of one side or the other.

—Thucydides, *The Peloponnesian War*

1. What does Thucydides think of poets?

   A. They are reliable.
   B. They are good storytellers.
   C. They exaggerate.
   D. They lie.

2. The task of writing the history of the war was difficult because

   A. eyewitnesses gave different accounts of the same events.
   B. the poets exaggerated.
   C. Thucydides did not see any of the events himself.
   D. the soldiers lied to Thucydides.

Practice Questions

Thinking It Through Share the following explanations with students as they discuss the strategies they used to answer the practice questions.

1. To answer this question, skim the passage to find the part where the author talks about poets. Read the sentence in which the word appears, then compare this passage to the available answers. You should observe that Thucydides refers to the "exaggerated fancies of the poets"; the correct answer is (C).

2. To answer this question, pay special attention to the portion of the passage where Thucydides describes the difficulties of his task. Compare his description of these difficulties with the options presented among the answers. The correct answer is (A).

California Standards and Skills

STRATEGY ITEMS		PRACTICE ITEMS	
Item Number	Skill Tested	Item Number	Skill Tested
1. 2.	REP4 Students assess the credibility of primary and secondary sources and draw sound conclusions from them.	1. 2.	REP4 Students assess the credibility of primary and secondary sources and draw sound conclusions from them.

CST = Chronological and Spatial Thinking, **HI** = Historical Interpretation, **REP** = Research, Evidence, and Point of View

Using Strategies For...

Secondary Sources Explain to students that they will do best on test questions by thinking them through carefully and by applying test-taking strategies such as the following:

1. Question 1 requires you to review the secondary source using the list of possible answers to see which is correct. Note that (D) is "all of the above." In fact, (A), (B), and (C) were among the foods eaten by Romans for breakfast. The correct answer is (D).

2. To answer this question, evaluate each of the answers to determine which is an opinion and which is fact. Recall that facts are statements or information that are either true or false. For example, it is not a matter of opinion whether people ate with their fingers. The only answer that qualifies as an opinion is (A).

General Test-Taking Tips

Share these tips with your students.

- Glance over the test to determine the types and numbers of questions.

- Estimate the amount of time you can spend on each type of question.

Secondary Sources

A secondary source is an account of events by a person who did not actually experience them. The author often uses information from several primary sources to write about a person or event. Biographies, many newspaper articles, and history books are examples of secondary sources.

❶ Read the title to get an idea of what the passage is about. (The title here indicates that the passage is about what and how the Romans ate.)

❷ Skim the paragraphs to find the main idea of the passage.

❸ Look for words that help you understand the order in which events happen.

❹ Ask yourself questions as you read. (You might ask yourself, Why were Roman dinner parties dignified or disgusting?)

❺ Review the questions to see what information you will need to find. Then reread the passage.

❶ Roman Eating Habits

The ordinary Roman was not a great eater of meat. . . . At home, porridge and bread were the staple food of most Romans, many of whom in the city had to rely on [government distribution of] corn . . . for their needs. . . .

In the well-to-do homes the regimen was different. [Breakfast], for those who wanted it, might be bread dipped in wine, or with cheese, dried fruits, or honey. The equivalent of lunch was . . . again a light meal, often consisting of leftovers from the previous day. The main meal of the **❸** day . . . was eaten in the middle of the afternoon, after work and the bath, and could, and often did, go on for hours. **❷** Dinner-parties were elaborate, and could be dignified or **❹** disgusting affairs, depending on the . . . host and his choice of guests. Overindulgence was the rule rather than the exception. Cicero wrote to his friend Atticus that when Julius Caesar stopped overnight at his country villa . . . in 45 B.C. . . . Caesar "had a bath at about one . . . oiled his body, and came to dinner. He [ate and drank] to excess, with obvious enjoyment." . . . Dinner guests reclined on their left elbow at an angle of about 45 degrees from the table, on couches set against three sides of it, and ate with their fingers.

—Antony Kamm, *The Romans: An Introduction*

❺ **1.** Which was a food eaten by Romans for breakfast?
   A. bread
   B. honey
   C. dried fruits
   D. all of the above

> Remember that an opinion is a statement that cannot be proved. A fact is a statement that can be proved.

2. Which of the following statements about Roman dinner parties is an opinion?
   A. They were disgusting affairs.
   B. They were eaten in the middle of the afternoon.
   C. They were eaten after work.
   D. Guests ate with their fingers.

answers: 1 (D); 2 (A)

S10

Activity Options

Individual Needs: English Learners

Word Meaning Make sure students understand the following terms and concepts on these pages.

Strategy Page: Secondary Source

porridge: a soft cereal made by boiling oatmeal or another meal in water or milk
regimen: standard routine
equivalent: something that is equal to something else
elaborate: complicated, involving many features
dignified: proud, worthy of respect
overindulgence: doing too much of something, such as eating or drinking

Practice Page: Secondary Source

generations: all the people living at about the same time
frontier: the edge of human settlement or exploration
colonizing: establishing colonies on or in
archipelagoes: chains of islands
embodied: giving a body or physical being to an idea or concept
stability: balance

Directions: Use the passage to answer the following questions.

Polynesian Canoes

The Polynesian voyaging canoe, one of the great ocean-going craft of the ancient world, was the means by which generations of adventurous voyagers were able to extend the human frontier far out into the Pacific, discovering and colonizing a vast realm of Oceanic islands. By 1000 B.C., when Mediterranean sailors were sailing in their land-locked sea, the immediate ancestors of the Polynesians had reached the previously uninhabited archipelagoes of Fiji, Tonga, and Samoa, in the middle of the Pacific Ocean. Their descendants went on from there to settle all of the habitable islands in a huge triangular section of the ocean bounded by the Hawaiian archipelago, tiny Easter Island, and the massive islands of New Zealand—an area equivalent to most of Europe and Asia combined.

The canoes in which people spread into the Pacific were not only humankind's first truly ocean-going craft, but also embodied a unique way of gaining the stability needed to carry sail in rough, open ocean waters. . . [This involved] adding outrigger floats to one or both sides of a single canoe hull, or by joining two hulls together by means of crossbeams and coconut-fiber lashings to make the so-called double canoe.

—Ben Finney, "The Polynesian Voyaging Canoe." From
*New World and Pacific Civilizations: Cultures of America,
Asia, and the Pacific,* edited by Goran Burenhult.

1. The Polynesians used voyaging canoes to colonize

   A. a small area of the Pacific.
   B. a large area of the Pacific.
   C. most of Europe and Asia.
   D. Australia and New Guinea.

2. The Polynesians gave their canoes the stability needed to handle the rough ocean waters by adding

   A. outrigger floats.
   B. more sails.
   C. ballasted hulls.
   D. wooden keels.

S11

Practice Questions

Thinking It Through Share the following explanations with students as they discuss the strategies they used to answer the practice questions.

1. This question requires you to review the secondary source and find the answer that best summarizes the content. First, identify the part of the world that the passage discusses. This should help you eliminate choice (C). Then, find the words used in the passage to describe the extent of Polynesian exploration ("a vast realm...."). The correct answer is (B).

2. The key word in this question is *stability*. To answer it, find the part of the passage in which this word appears. Read about the method used to provide stability for the canoes. You can see that this involved adding outrigger floats and joining two hulls together. The only answer that includes this information is (A), which is correct.

California Standards and Skills

STRATEGY ITEMS		PRACTICE ITEMS	
Item Number	**Skill/Standard Tested**	**Item Number**	**Skill/Standard Tested**
1. 2.	6.7 Students analyze the geographic, political, economic, religious, and social structures during the development of Rome.	1. 2.	**REP3** Students distinguish relevant from irrelevant information. **CST1** Students explain how major events are related to one another in time.

CST = Chronological and Spatial Thinking, **HI** = Historical Interpretation, **REP** = Research, Evidence, and Point of View

Using Strategies For...

Political Cartoons Political cartoons are a type of primary source. Remind students to study the political cartoon before reading the questions. They should try to identify the subject, note any important symbols and details, interpret the message, and analyze the point of view. Then they can read the questions to identify the information they need to find.

Explain to students that they will do best on test questions by thinking them through carefully and by applying test-taking strategies such as the following:

1. The correct answer is (B). The swastika is the symbol of Nazi Germany.
2. To answer question 2, analyze the cartoonist's message. Look at how he exaggerates the main object. The swastika, which represents Nazi Germany, is huge and appears to be turning like a wheel that is about to roll over Poland and crush it. The label "Poland" tells which country is the subject of the cartoon's title, "Next!" Therefore, (A) is the correct answer.

General Test-Taking Tips

Share these tips with your students.

- Ask any questions you have before the test begins.
- Know how to fill in the answer sheet before you start.
- Read and listen to directions carefully.

Political Cartoons

Cartoonists who draw political cartoons use both words and art to express opinions about political issues.

1. Try to figure out what the cartoon is about. Titles and captions may give clues.
2. Use labels to help identify the people, places, and events represented in the cartoon.
3. Note when and where the cartoon was published.
4. Look for symbols—that is, people, places, or objects that stand for something else.
5. The cartoonist often exaggerates the physical features of people and objects. This technique will give you clues as to how the cartoonist feels about the subject.
6. Try to figure out the cartoonist's message and summarize it in a sentence.

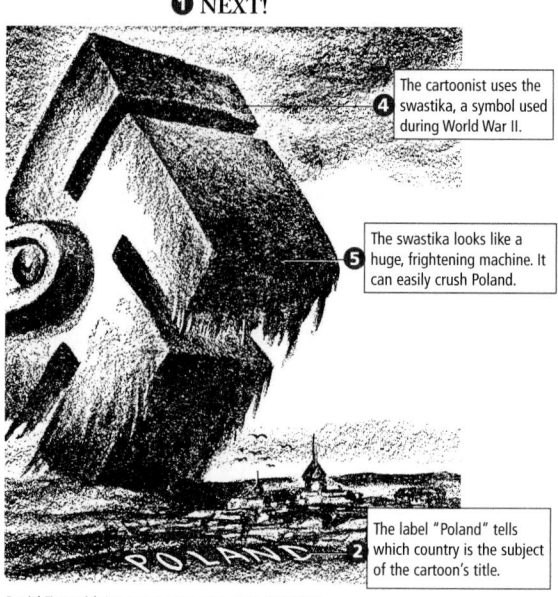

❶ NEXT!

❹ The cartoonist uses the swastika, a symbol used during World War II.

❺ The swastika looks like a huge, frightening machine. It can easily crush Poland.

❷ The label "Poland" tells which country is the subject of the cartoon's title.

Daniel Fitzpatrick / *St. Louis Post-Dispatch*, August 24, 1939.

❸ The date is a clue that the cartoon refers to the beginning of World War II.

1. What does the swastika in the cartoon stand for?
   - **A.** the Soviet Union
   - **B.** Nazi Germany
   - **C.** the Polish army
   - **D.** Great Britain

❻ 2. Which sentence *best* summarizes the cartoonist's message?
   - **A.** Germany will attack Poland next.
   - **B.** Poland should stop Germany.
   - **C.** Germany will lose this battle.
   - **D.** Poland will fight a civil war.

answers: 1 (B); 2 (A)

Activity Options

Individual Needs: English Learners

Word Meaning Make sure students understand the following terms and concepts on these pages.

Strategy Page: Political Cartoon
swastika: symbol used by the National Socialist German Workers Party, or Nazi Party

Practice Page: Political Cartoon
join: come together

Directions: Use the cartoon to answer the following questions.

The Granger Collection, New York

Benjamin Franklin (1754)

1. What do the sections of the snake in the cartoon represent?

   A. army units
   B. states
   C. Native American groups
   D. colonies

2. Which phrase *best* states the message of the cartoon?

   A. "East is East, and West is West, and never the twain shall meet."
   B. "Taxation without representation is tyranny."
   C. "United we stand, divided we fall."
   D. "Out of many, one."

Practice Questions

Thinking It Through Share the following explanations with students as they discuss the strategies they used to answer the practice questions.

1. Question 1 asks you to identify the meaning of the different sections of snake. Notice that the sections are labeled with letters, which you may recognize as the names of states or colonies. This can help you eliminate (A) and (C) as possible answers. Another clue is the date 1754, which was when the cartoon was created. This date indicates that the sections must represent colonies. Therefore, the correct answer is (D).

2. A key word in this question is the word *best*. Compare each possible answer to the cartoon to see which makes sense. By doing this, you can immediately eliminate answers (A) and (B). Of the two answers that remain, (C) seems to most closely match the caption, which urges the colonies to "join." The correct answer is (C).

S13

California Standards and Skills

STRATEGY ITEMS		PRACTICE ITEMS	
Item Number	**Skill/Standard Tested**	**Item Number**	**Skill/Standard Tested**
1. 2.	**HI1** Students explain central issues and problems of the past. **REP4** Students assess the credibility of primary and secondary sources and draw sound conclusions from them.	1. 2.	**REP4** Students assess the credibility of primary and secondary sources and draw sound conclusions from them.

CST = Chronological and Spatial Thinking, **HI** = Historical Interpretation, **REP** = Research, Evidence, and Point of View

Using Strategies For...

Charts Explain to students that they will do best on test questions by thinking them through carefully and by applying test-taking strategies such as the following:

1. Question 1 requires you to find in the chart an example of a characteristic that was shared by the Roman Empire and the Han Dynasty. Note that the chart contains two columns. By reading across the two columns, you can compare the characteristics of the Han Dynasty and the Roman Empire. (D) is the correct answer.

2. To answer this question, you will need to again compare the Han Dynasty to the Roman Empire. Look in the Han Dynasty column for the "categories" represented by choices. When you find each category, read across to the information in the Roman Empire column. You will find that the Han Dynasty had a larger population than the Roman Empire. Therefore, the correct answer is (A).

General Test-Taking Tips

Share these tips with your students.

- Use practice tests, such as the one you are taking now, to learn about your test-taking habits and weaknesses.

- Use this information to practice strategies that will help make you a successful test taker.

Charts

Charts present facts in a visual form. History textbooks use several different types of charts. The chart that is most often found on tests is the table. A table organizes information in columns and rows.

❶ Read the title of the chart to find out what information is represented.

❷ Read the column and row headings. Sometimes further information on headings is provided in footnotes.

❸ Notice how the information in the chart is organized.

❹ Compare the information from column to column and row to row.

❺ Try to draw conclusions from the information in the chart.

❻ Read the questions and then study the chart again.

❸ *This chart compares two empires.*

❶ Two Great Empires: Han China and Rome	
❷ Han Dynasty—202 B.C. to A.D. 220	Roman Empire—27 B.C. to A.D. 476
• Empire replaced rival kingdoms	• Empire replaced republic
• Centralized, bureaucratic government	• Centralized, bureaucratic government
• Built roads and defensive walls	• Built roads and defensive walls
• Conquered many diverse peoples in regions bordering China	• Conquered many diverse peoples in regions of three continents
• At its height—area of 1,500,000 square miles and a population of 60,000,000	• At its height—area of 1,300,000 square miles and a population of 54,000,000
• Chinese became common written language throughout empire	• Latin did not replace other written languages in empire
• Ongoing conflict with nomads	• Ongoing conflict with nomads
• Empire fell apart; restored by Sui Dynasty after 581	• Empire fell apart; never restored

❺

❹

The two empires shared some of the same features.

❻

1. Which was a characteristic shared by both Han China and Rome?

   A. Both empires were restored after they fell apart.

   B. Both empires replaced republics.

   C. Both had a population of 60,000,000.

   D. Both had an ongoing conflict with nomads.

   Use the information in the chart to find similarities between the two empires.

2. The Han Dynasty exceeded the Roman Empire in

   A. population.

   B. army.

   C. completed building projects.

   D. government agencies.

answers: 1 (D); 2 (A)

S14

Activity Options

Individual Needs: English Learners

Word Meaning Make sure students understand the following terms and concepts on these pages.

Strategy Page: Chart

centralized: concentrated in a central place
bureaucratic: governed by many different offices and agencies
diverse: made up of many different parts or types
nomad: person who does not live in one location and moves frequently

Practice Page: Chart

oracle-bone reading: interpreting messages from animal bones
specialized: having and practicing a certain, specific skill
institutions: established laws, practices, or customs
pictographic: picture writing
papyrus: a tall reed used to make a paper-like material
hieroglyphic: a picture or symbol representing a word
cuneiform: a type of writing featuring wedge shapes
scribes: people who write down records

For more test practice online . . .
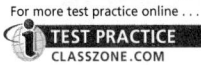
TEST PRACTICE
CLASSZONE.COM

Directions: Use the chart to answer the following questions.

Ancient Civilizations				
Feature	China	Egypt	Indus Valley	Mesopotamia
Location	River valley	River valley	River valley	River valley
Period	2000 B.C.–400 B.C.	3100 B.C.–600 B.C.	2500 B.C.–1500 B.C.	3500 B.C.–2000 B.C.
Specialized workers	Priests; government workers, soldiers; crafts people in bronze and silk; farmers	Priests; government workers, scribes, soldiers; workers in pottery, stone; farmers	Priests; government officials; workers in pottery, bricks; farmers	Priests; government officials, scribes, soldiers; workers in pottery, textiles; farmers
Institutions	Walled cities; oracle-bone reading	Ruling class of priests and nobles; education system	Strong central government	Ruling class of priests and nobles; education for scribes
Record keeping	Pictographic writing	Hieroglyphic writing	Pictographic writing	Cuneiform writing
Advanced technology and artifacts	Writing; making bronze and silk; irrigation systems	Papyrus; mathematics; astronomy; engineering; pyramids; mummification; medicine	Irrigation systems; indoor plumbing; seals	Wheel; plow; sailboat; bronze weapons

1. Which civilization appeared first?
   A. China
   B. Egypt
   C. Indus Valley
   D. Mesopotamia

2. The Indus Valley civilization did *not* have
   A. irrigation systems.
   B. walled cities.
   C. government officials.
   D. indoor plumbing.

Practice Questions

Thinking It Through Share the following explanations with students as they discuss the strategies they used to answer the practice questions.

1. The key word in this question is *first*. Read across the row with the heading "period" to find 3500 B.C., the earliest date that a civilization first appeared. Next, move your eyes to the top of the column and find the name of the civilization. The correct answer is (D).

2. Be careful with this question because it has the phrase *did not*. You need to find the three features that the Indus Valley civilization did have. The remaining feature in the choices will then be the correct answer. Look at the column with the heading "Indus Valley." Find the three features listed as choices. Since the Indus Valley civilization had an irrigation system, government officials, and indoor plumbing, (A), (C), and (D) are things the civilization did have. So the correct answer is (B).

S15

California Standards and Skills

STRATEGY ITEMS		PRACTICE ITEMS	
Item Number	Skill/Standard Tested	Item Number	Skill/Standard Tested
1. 2.	6.6 Students analyze the geographic, political, economic, religious, and social structures of the early civilizations of China. 6.7 Students analyze the geographic, political, economic, religious, and social structures during the development of Rome.	1. 2.	6.2 Students analyze the geographic, political, economic, religious, and social structures of the early civilizations of Mesopotamia, Egypt, and Kush. 6.5 Students analyze the geographic, political, economic, religious, and social structures of the early civilizations of India. 6.6 Students analyze the geographic, political, economic, religious, and social structures of the early civilizations of China.

CST = Chronological and Spatial Thinking, **HI** = Historical Interpretation, **REP** = Research, Evidence, and Point of View

Using Strategies For...

Line and Bar Graphs Remind students that line and bar graphs have a vertical (up-and-down) axis, which is normally on the left side of the graph; and a horizontal (left-to-right) axis, which is usually along the bottom of the graph.

Explain to students that they will do best on test questions by thinking them through carefully and by applying test-taking strategies such as the following:

1. To answer question 1, you will need to follow several steps. First, recognize that you will only need the graph on temperature to answer the question. Then, read the graph to find the point when the temperature was the lowest (20,000 years ago). This gives you (D), which is the correct answer.

2. To answer question 2, look at the population graph. Notice that the part of the graph representing the Agricultural Revolution is almost vertical, indicating a rapid rise in population. The correct answer is (A).

General Test-Taking Tips

Share these tips with your students.

- Do not spend too much time on one question.

- Skip any question you are having problems with. Go back to it later if you have the time.

- If you skip a question, be sure to skip the answer space for the same number on your answer sheet.

Line and Bar Graphs

Graphs show numbers in visual form. Line graphs are useful for showing changes over time. Bar graphs make it easy to compare numbers.

1 Read the title of the graph to find out what information is represented.

2 Study the labels on the graph.

3 Look at the source line that tells where the graph is from. Decide whether you can depend on the source to provide reliable information.

4 See if you can make any generalizations about the information in the graph. For example, you might note that the Agricultural Revolution began when global temperatures rose.

5 Read the questions carefully and then study the graph again.

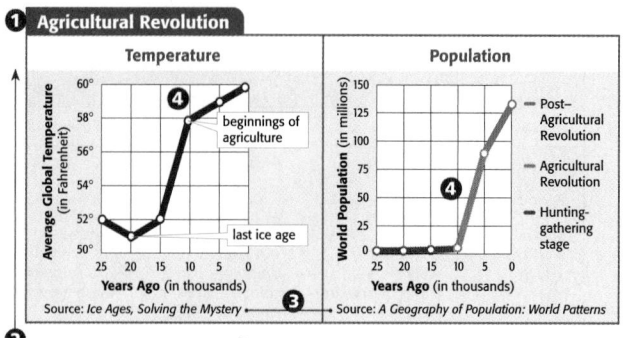

1. When was the world coldest?

A. 1,000 years ago

B. 5,000 years ago

C. 25,000 years ago

D. 20,000 years ago

2. During the Agricultural Revolution, world population

A. rose rapidly.

B. declined rapidly.

C. rose slightly.

D. declined slightly.

answers: 1 (D); 2 (A)

Activity Options

Individual Needs: English Learners

Word Meaning Make sure students understand the following terms and concepts on these pages.

Strategy Page: Temperature Graph
global: of or by the whole world
Fahrenheit: a temperature scale
Population Graph
revolution: a major change or development
hunting-gathering: a way of life in which food is obtained from hunting and gathering wild foods.

Practice Page:
Question 2 *approximately:* roughly, about

For more test practice online . . .

TEST PRACTICE
CLASSZONE.COM

Directions: Use the graphs to answer the following questions.

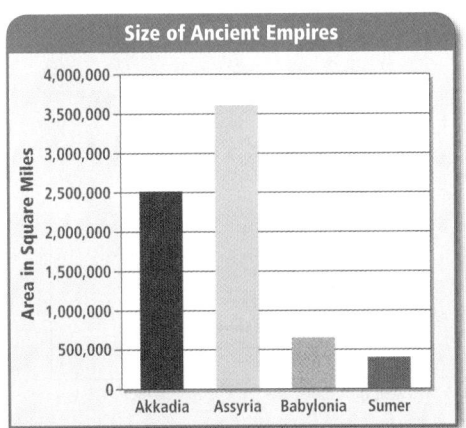

Size of Ancient Empires

Source: *Institute for Research on World Systems*

1. Which empire was the largest?
   A. Babylonia
   B. Assyria
   C. Sumer
   D. Akkadia

Population of Four Ancient Cities

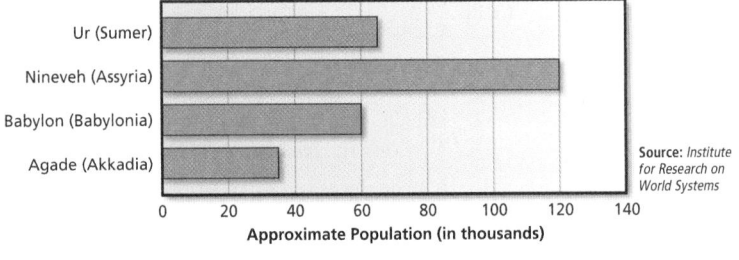

Source: *Institute for Research on World Systems*

2. Which city had a population of approximately 60,000 people?
   A. Agade
   B. Nineveh
   C. Babylon
   D. Ur

S17

Practice Questions

Thinking It Through Share the following explanations with students as they discuss the strategies they used to answer the practice questions.

1. To answer this question, study the top bar graph. Note that the bars represent the area of different empires. The tallest bar, which represents the empire with the largest area, is Assyria. The correct answer is (B).

2. To answer this question, you must use the bottom bar graph to determine which city had a specific population. First, study the horizontal axis. Then, find the point on the axis that marks 60,000. Read up the graph to find the city that corresponds to that point. The correct answer is (C).

California Standards and Skills

STRATEGY ITEMS		PRACTICE ITEMS	
Item Number	**Skill/Standard Tested**	**Item Number**	**Skill/Standard Tested**
1. 2.	**HI2** Students understand and distinguish cause, effect, and sequence, and correlation in historical events. **6.1.3** Discuss the climatic changes and human modifications of the physical environment that gave rise to the domestication of plants and animals.	1. 2.	**6.2** Students analyze the geographic, political, economic, religious, and social structures of the early civilizations of Mesopotamia, Egypt, and Kush.

CST = Chronological and Spatial Thinking, **HI** = Historical Interpretation, **REP** = Research, Evidence, and Point of View

Using Strategies For...

Pie Graphs Explain to students that they will do best on test questions by thinking them through carefully and by applying test-taking strategies such as the following:

1. For question 1, remember that pie graphs represent the whole and the way that whole is divided into parts. Understand that the key word in this question is *majority*, which means a portion that is more than half of the whole. In this case the portion represents citizens. The correct answer is (C).

2. To answer this question, compare the two graphs and how each portion of the graphs change in size. Look back and forth between the two graphs one category at a time. You can see that the only population groups whose percentages grew were metics and male slaves. Since male slaves increased the most, the correct answer is (A).

General Test-Taking Tips

Share these tips with your students.

- Read the question and each answer choice before answering.

- Many items include choices that may seem right at first glance but are actually wrong. Choose your answers carefully.

Pie Graphs

A pie, or circle, graph shows the relationship among parts of a whole. These parts look like slices of a pie. Each slice is shown as a percentage of the whole pie.

❶ Read the title of the chart to find out what information is represented.

❷ The graph may provide a legend, or key, that tells you what different slices represent.

❸ The size of the slice is related to the percentage. The larger the percentage, the larger the slice.

❹ Look at the source line that tells where the graph is from. Ask yourself if you can depend on this source to provide reliable information.

❺ Read the questions carefully, and study the graph again.

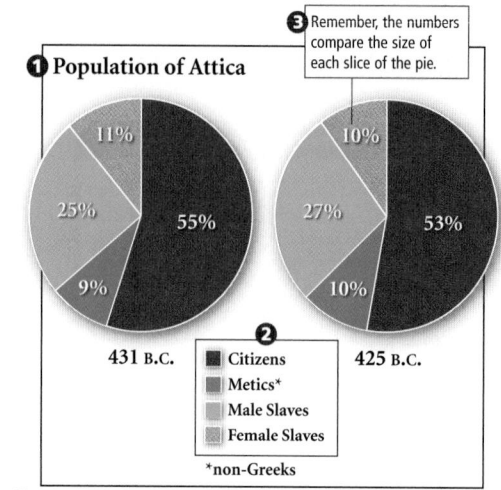

❸ Remember, the numbers compare the size of each slice of the pie.

❶ **Population of Attica**

431 B.C. — 11%, 25%, 9%, 55%

425 B.C. — 10%, 27%, 10%, 53%

❷ Legend:
- Citizens
- Metics*
- Male Slaves
- Female Slaves

*non-Greeks

❹ Source: A. W. Gomme, *The Population of Athens in the Fifth and Fourth Centuries* B.C.

❺

→1. Which group made up the majority of Attica's population in both years?

A. female slaves

B. male slaves

C. citizens

D. metics

→2. Which group's percentage of the population increased the *most* between 431 B.C. and 425 B.C.?

A. male slaves

B. female slaves

C. citizens

D. metics

answers: 1 (C); 2 (A)

Activity Options

Individual Needs: English Learners

Word Meaning Make sure students understand the following terms and concepts on these pages.

Strategy Page

Question 2 *percentage:* the amount of something expressed in hundredths; for example, 25 percent means 25 hundredths

Practice Page

affiliation: membership in, or belonging to, a certain group

Directions: Use the graph to answer the following questions.

World Population's Religious Affiliations

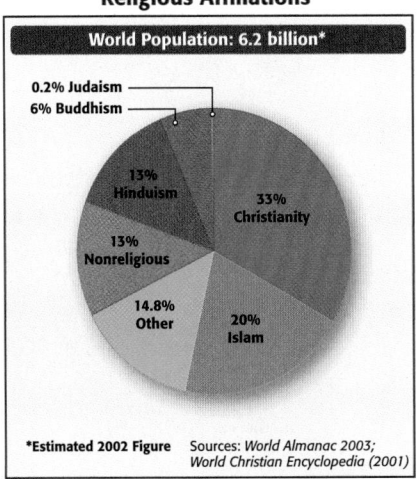

World Population: 6.2 billion*

- 0.2% Judaism
- 6% Buddhism
- 13% Hinduism
- 33% Christianity
- 13% Nonreligious
- 14.8% Other
- 20% Islam

*Estimated 2002 Figure

Sources: *World Almanac 2003; World Christian Encyclopedia (2001)*

1. To which religion does the largest number of people belong?
   - **A.** Islam
   - **B.** Christianity
   - **C.** Judaism
   - **D.** Hinduism

2. The religion that has the smallest percentage of followers worldwide is
   - **A.** Judaism
   - **B.** Buddhism
   - **C.** Other
   - **D.** Christianity

Practice Questions

Thinking It Through Share the following explanations with students as they discuss the strategies they used to answer the practice questions.

1. Remember that pie graphs show the whole—in this case, the world's population—and the way that the whole is divided into different parts. In this case, the parts represent membership in certain religions. The largest piece of the pie graph represents the group with the largest number of followers. The largest piece here is labeled "Christianity." The correct answer is (B).

2. This question requires you to consider the four possible answers and determine which one represents the smallest piece of the pie relative to the others. Start by looking at (A), Judaism, and noting its size. Next compare Judaism to (B), Buddhism. Then compare the smaller of the two to (C), and the smaller of these two to (D), Christianity. Whichever of these is smallest will represent the correct answer, which is (A).

California Standards and Skills

STRATEGY ITEMS		PRACTICE ITEMS	
Item Number	**Skill/Standard Tested**	**Item Number**	**Skill/Standard Tested**
1. 2.	**6.4** Students analyze the geographic, political, economic, religious, and social structures of the early civilizations of Ancient Greece.	1. 2.	**CST3** Students use a variety of maps and documents to identify physical and cultural features.

CST = Chronological and Spatial Thinking, **HI** = Historical Interpretation, **REP** = Research, Evidence, and Point of View

Using Strategies For...

Political Maps Explain to students that they will do best on test questions by thinking them through carefully and by applying test-taking strategies such as the following:

1. To answer this question, locate the four "answers" on the map and select the one that lies farthest to west. To ensure you arrive at the correct answer, use the North arrow. Note that if the top of the map represents north, the western part of the map is on the left side. This means the correct answer will be the one that extends farthest to the left. The answer is (B).

2. To answer question 2, use the scale that appears on the bottom left corner of the map. Use a slip of paper or a ruler to identify the distance on the map that represents 500 miles. Then measure how many times that distance "fits" between Vancouver and the western edge of the Great Lakes. The answer is (B).

General Test-Taking Tips

Share these tips with your students.

- Try to answer every question on the test.
- If you are not sure of an answer, make an educated guess.
- Eliminate the choices you are sure are *not* correct first. Then, choose your answer from the choices that remain.

Political Maps

Political maps show the divisions within countries. A country may be divided into states, provinces, and so on. The maps also show where major cities are. They may also show mountains, oceans, seas, lakes, and rivers.

1 Read the title of the map. This will give you the subject and purpose of the map.

2 Read the labels on the map. They also give information about the map's subject and purpose.

3 Study the key or legend to help you understand the symbols and colors on the map.

4 Use the scale to estimate distances between places shown on the map. Maps usually show the distance in both miles and kilometers.

5 Use the North arrow to figure out the direction of places on the map.

6 Read the questions. Carefully study the map to find the answers.

1 Canada and Its Provinces

The legend gives symbols for Canada's boundaries and major cities.

The labels identify Canada's provinces.

1. Which province or territory is the farthest west?

A. Northwest Territories

B. Yukon Territory

C. British Columbia

D. Alberta

2. About how many miles is the United States-Canada border from the Great Lakes west to Vancouver on the Pacific Ocean?

A. 1,000

B. 1,500

C. 2,000

D. 2,500

answers: 1 (B); 2 (B)

S20

Activity Options

Individual Needs: English Learners

Word Meaning Make sure students understand the following terms and concepts on these pages.

Strategy Page: Political Map

political maps: maps showing borders of countries and states
province: a political division of a country
Strategies 4 *estimate:* to make an educated guess about distance, amount, or some other measure

kilometer: a measure of distance in the metric system equal to 1000 meters, or roughly three-fifths of a mile

Practice Page: Political Map

Make sure students have studied the following empires:
Eastern Roman Empire
Western Roman Empire

Directions: Use the map to answer the following questions.

The Roman Empire, A.D. 400

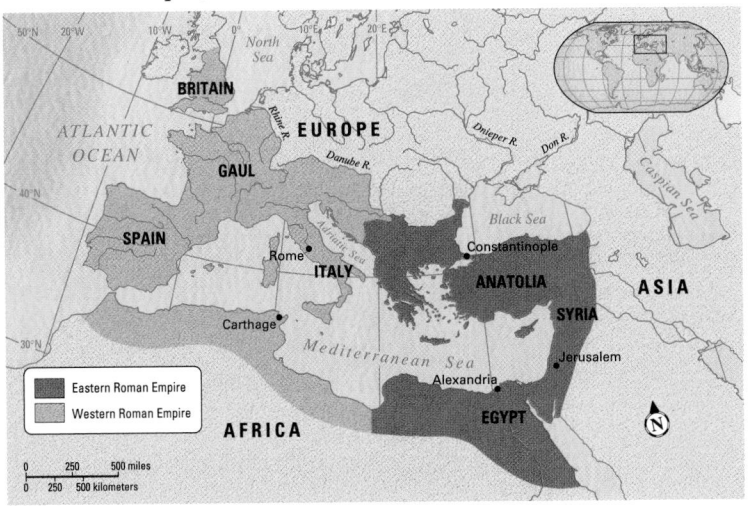

1. On which body of water was Syria located?

   A. Atlantic Ocean
   B. Mediterranean Sea
   C. Caspian Sea
   D. North Sea

2. The southernmost country in the Eastern Roman Empire was

   A. Syria.
   B. Gaul.
   C. Spain.
   D. Egypt.

S21

Practice Questions

Thinking It Through Share the following explanations with students as they discuss the strategies they used to answer the practice questions.

1. Question 1 requires you to first locate Syria on the map. Once you have found Syria, observe the large body of water on which it lies. The correct answer is (B).

2. To answer this question, first identify which part of the map represents the Eastern Roman Empire. Use the key to find which color shading corresponds to the Eastern Roman Empire. Then use the North arrow to determine which direction is south. You can determine that Egypt is the most southern country of the Eastern Roman Empire. Therefore, the correct answer is (D).

California Standards and Skills

STRATEGY ITEMS		PRACTICE ITEMS	
Item Number	Skill/Standard Tested	Item Number	Skill/Standard Tested
1. 2.	CST3 Students use a variety of maps and documents to identify physical and cultural features.	1. 2.	CST3 Students use a variety of maps and documents to identify physical and cultural features.
			6.7.3 Identify the location and the political and geographic reasons for the growth of Roman territories and the expansion of the empire.

CST = Chronological and Spatial Thinking, HI = Historical Interpretation, REP = Research, Evidence, and Point of View

Using Strategies For...

Thematic Maps Explain to students that they will do best on test questions by thinking them through carefully and by applying test-taking strategies such as the following:

1. Answering question 1 starts with identifying and reading the key. The shaded area represents the place where Buddhism originated. You can also see that the arrows represent the direction of Buddhism's spread. Then, on the map, places are labeled with dates indicating the approximate time when Buddhism arrived in the area. This information will enable you to see that Buddhism spread to Tibet after A.D. 550. The correct answer is (D).

2. To answer this question, locate Java and Sumatra on the map. The question provides a clue by telling you that these places are islands. Once you have found these islands, you can easily read the label that indicates when Buddhism reached these areas. The correct answer is (D).

General Test-Taking Tips

Share these tips with your students.

- Think positively.
- Tell yourself that you can do it!
- Know that if you have studied for the test, you are prepared to succeed.

Thematic Maps

Thematic maps focus on special topics. For example, a thematic map might show a country's natural resources or major battles in a war.

1 Read the title of the map. This will give you a general idea of the subject and purpose of the map.

2 Read the labels on the map. They also give information about the map's subject and purpose.

3 Study the key or legend to help you understand the symbols on the map. (The arrows show where Buddhism spread.)

4 Ask yourself whether the symbols show a pattern.

5 Read the questions. Carefully study the map to find the answers.

1 The Spread of Buddhism

2 The labels name the major areas of South Asia and East Asia. The dates show when Buddhism first came to each area.

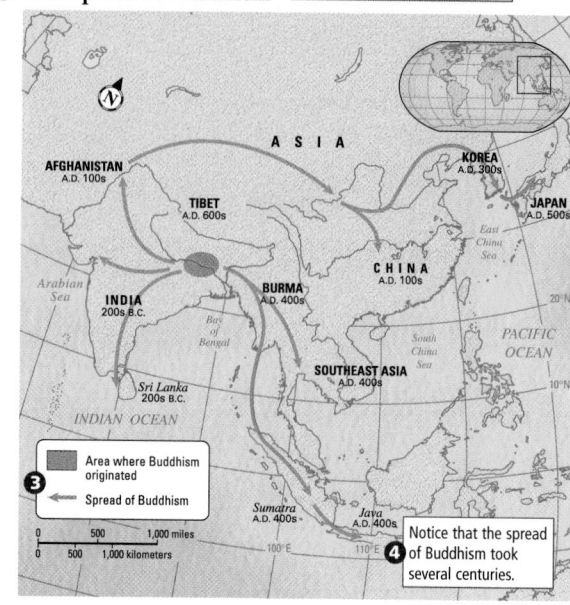

Notice that the spread of Buddhism took several centuries.

1. To which area did Buddhism spread after A.D. 550?
   - A. Java
   - B. China
   - C. Japan
   - D. Tibet

2. When did Buddhism spread to the islands of Java and Sumatra?
   - A. A.D. 100s
   - B. A.D. 300s
   - C. 200s B.C.
   - D. A.D. 400s

answers: 1 (D); 2 (D)

Activity Options

Individual Needs: English Learners

Word Meaning Make sure students understand the following terms and concepts on these pages.

Strategy Page: Thematic Map
thematic: focused on a major idea or subject
originated: began, came into being

Practice Page: Thematic Map
conquest: the conquering, or military defeat of, an area
Question 1 *easternmost:* lying farthest to the east

Directions: Use the map to answer the following questions.

The Christian Conquest of Muslim Spain

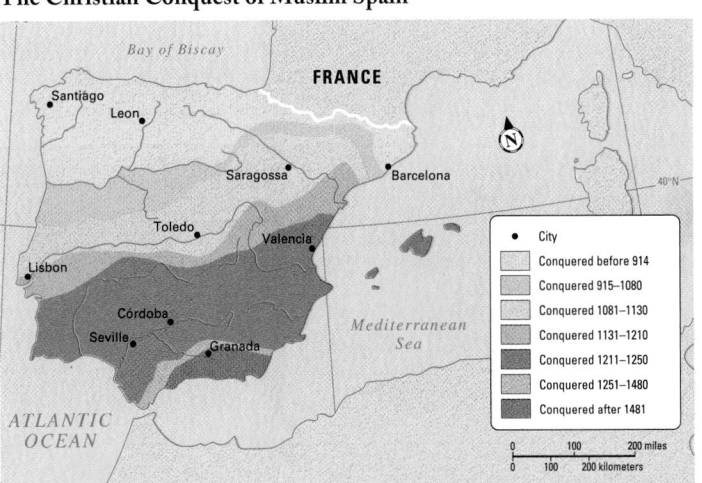

1. When did Christians conquer the easternmost city shown on the map?

   A. before 914
   B. between 1081 and 1130
   C. between 1211 and 1250
   D. after 1481

2. By 1480, how much of Spain did Christians control?

   A. only a small portion
   B. about one-third
   C. about one-half
   D. almost all of the land

S23

Practice Questions

Thinking It Through Share the following explanations with students as they discuss the strategy they used to answer the practice questions.

1. To answer question 1, use the North arrow to identify which direction is east on the map (to the right). Now find Barcelona, the city that lies farthest to the right. Next, note the color of the shaded area in which Barcelona lies on this map. On the key, find the time period that corresponds to that color. Here you will find that the correct answer is (A), before 914.

2. Question 2 asks you to examine the map for information about the year 1480. By examining the map and key, you can see that Spain had been almost completely reconquered by 1480. This means that the correct answer is (D).

California Standards and Skills

STRATEGY ITEMS		PRACTICE ITEMS	
Item Number	**Skill/Standard Tested**	**Item Number**	**Skill/Standard Tested**
1. 2.	**CST3** Students use a variety of maps and documents to identify physical and cultural features. **HI1** Students explain central issues and problems of the past. **6.5.5** Know the life and moral teachings of Buddha and how Buddhism spread.	1. 2.	**CST3** Students use a variety of maps and documents to identify physical and cultural features.

CST = Chronological and Spatial Thinking, **HI** = Historical Interpretation, **REP** = Research, Evidence, and Point of View

Using Strategies For…

Time Lines Explain to students that they will do best on test questions by thinking them through carefully and by applying test-taking strategies such as the following:

1. To answer question 1, look at the time line to find the dates mentioned (6000 B.C. and 2000 B.C.). Count the number of entries between these dates. The correct answer is (B).
2. To answer question 2, start at the top of the time line and read down until you reach the date of the second animal to be domesticated. The correct answer is (A), pig.

General Test-Taking Tips

Share these tips with your students.

- Relax during the test.
- Several times during the test, take a few seconds to breathe deeply. Occasional deep breaths will help relieve anxiety and keep you focused.

Time Lines

A time line is a chart that lists events in the order in which they occurred. Time lines can be vertical or horizontal.

❶ Read the title to learn what subject the time line covers.

❷ Note the dates when the time line begins and ends.

❸ Read the events in the order they occurred.

❹ Think about what else was going on in the world on these dates. Try to make connections.

❺ Read the questions. Then carefully study the time line to find the answers.

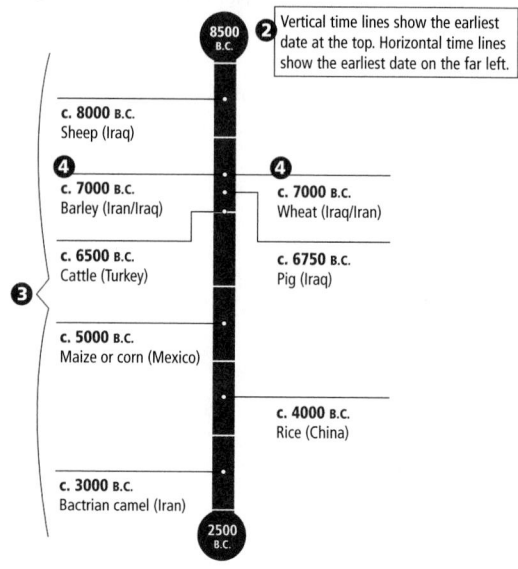

❶ **Domestication of Plants and Animals**

❷ Vertical time lines show the earliest date at the top. Horizontal time lines show the earliest date on the far left.

8500 B.C.

c. 8000 B.C. Sheep (Iraq)

❹ c. 7000 B.C. Barley (Iran/Iraq)

❹ c. 7000 B.C. Wheat (Iraq/Iran)

❸ c. 6500 B.C. Cattle (Turkey)

c. 6750 B.C. Pig (Iraq)

c. 5000 B.C. Maize or corn (Mexico)

c. 4000 B.C. Rice (China)

c. 3000 B.C. Bactrian camel (Iran)

2500 B.C.

❺
1. How many plants and animals were domesticated between 6000 B.C. and 2000 B.C.?
   A. 2
   B. 3
   C. 4
   D. 6

2. Which animal was the second to be domesticated?
   A. pig
   B. sheep
   C. Bactrian camel
   D. cattle

answers: 1 (B); 2 (A)

S24

Activity Options

Individual Needs: English Learners

Word Meaning Make sure students understand the following terms and concepts on these pages.

Strategy Page: Time Line

barley: a kind of cereal used in beverages and breakfast foods
Bactrian camel: a camel with two humps
vertical: up-and-down
horizontal: side-to-side
Question 1 *domesticated:* to tame animals or adapt wild foods for use by people

Practice Page: Time Line

expand: to increase
succcessor: someone who follows someone else to a throne or office

For more test practice online . . .

TEST PRACTICE
CLASSZONE.COM

STRATEGIES FOR TAKING TESTS

Directions: Use the time line to answer the following questions.

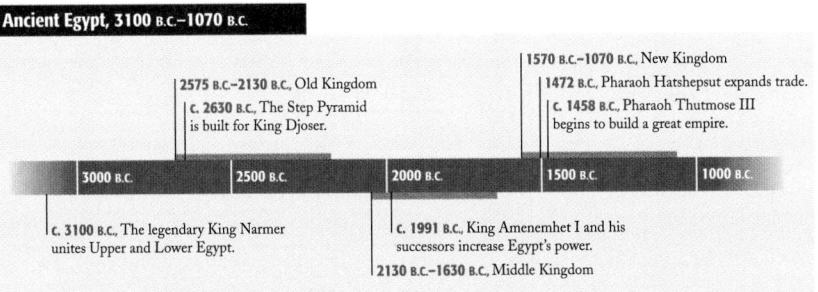

Ancient Egypt, 3100 B.C.–1070 B.C.

2575 B.C.–2130 B.C., Old Kingdom
c. 2630 B.C., The Step Pyramid is built for King Djoser.

1570 B.C.–1070 B.C., New Kingdom
1472 B.C., Pharaoh Hatshepsut expands trade.
c. 1458 B.C., Pharaoh Thutmose III begins to build a great empire.

3000 B.C.   2500 B.C.   2000 B.C.   1500 B.C.   1000 B.C.

c. 3100 B.C., The legendary King Narmer unites Upper and Lower Egypt.

c. 1991 B.C., King Amenemhet I and his successors increase Egypt's power.

2130 B.C.–1630 B.C., Middle Kingdom

1. When did Pharaoh Hatshepsut expand trade?
   A. c. 1458
   B. c. 1472
   C. c. 2630
   D. c. 3100

2. What happened after Pharaoh Hatshepsut expanded trade?
   A. The Step Pyramid was built.
   B. King Amenemhet I and his successors increased Egypt's power.
   C. The Middle Kingdom began.
   D. Pharaoh Thutmose III began to build a great empire.

Practice Questions

Thinking It Through Share the following explanations with students as they discuss the strategies they used to answer the practice questions.

1. Read across the time line from left to right until you find the date when Pharaoh Hatsheput increased trade. The correct answer is (B).

2. *After* is the keyword in this question. Look for the next event on the time line after Pharaoh Hatsheput expanded trade. The correct answer is (D), Pharaoh Thutmose III built a great empire.

S25

California Standards and Skills

STRATEGY ITEMS		PRACTICE ITEMS	
Item Number	**Skill/Standard Tested**	**Item Number**	**Skill/Standard Tested**
1. 2.	**CST1** Students explain how major events are related to one another in time. **HI2** Students understand and distinguish sequence in historical events. **6.1.3** Discuss the climatic changes and human modifications that gave rise to the domestication of plants and animals.	1. 2.	**HI2** Students understand and distinguish sequence in historical events. **6.2** Students analyze the geographic, political, economic, religious, and social structures of the early civilizations of Mesopotamia, Egypt, and Kush.

CST = Chronological and Spatial Thinking, **HI** = Historical Interpretation, **REP** = Research, Evidence, and Point of View

Using Strategies For...

Constructed Response Remind students of the following:

1. In the constructed-response questions on this page, you need to use the document and your knowledge of history to answer the questions.
2. Some constructed-response questions do not include a document. Instead, the questions may require you to use only your knowledge of history or social studies.
3. Sometimes, constructed response questions start with short-answer questions and build up to a short essay. The short answers may help you write the essay, so try to answer the questions in the order in which they are asked. When your responses are scored, each part will be worth points, but the short essay will probably be worth more than the short-answer questions.
4. Useful information may be found in a title, a caption, or a source line as well as in the document itself.

General Test-Taking Tips

Share these tips with your students.

- Be sure to answer all parts of constructed-response questions. Each part is worth points.
- As you answer each question, make sure that the number of the answer and the number of the question are the same.

Constructed Response

Constructed-response questions focus on a document, such as a photograph, cartoon, chart, graph, or time line. Instead of picking one answer from a set of choices, you write a short response. Sometimes you can find the answer in the document. Other times you will use what you already know about a subject to answer the question.

1. Read the title of the document to get an idea of what it is about.
2. Study the document.
3. Read the questions carefully. Study the document again to find the answers.
4. Write your answers. You don't need to use complete sentences unless the directions say so.

1

Determining the Age of Archaeological Finds		
Method	**Age Range**	**Process**
Written records	Up to about 5,000 years ago	Use written records of known age to date artifacts found along with them.
Tree-ring dating	Up to about 11,000 years ago	Match the pattern in a wooden object to a master tree-ring pattern; count the rings.
Radiocarbon dating	From about 300 to 45,000 years ago	Measure the amount of radioactive carbon remaining in the object (used to date the remains of plants and animals).
Potassium-argon dating	More than 1,000,000 years ago	Compare the amounts of potassium and argon present in volcanic rock (used to date bones and tools found in the rock).

2

Constructed-response questions use a wide range of documents. These include short passages, cartoons, charts, graphs, maps, time lines, posters, and other visual materials. This document is a chart of archaeological procedures.

1. What are two methods of dating artifacts?
   4 *radiocarbon dating and potassium-argon dating*

2. Which dating method would be best to use on burned grain found at an archaeological site?
   radiocarbon dating, because it is used on plants

3. How could written records found in the remains of an ancient Roman city be used to date other artifacts from the same site?
   Written records can be used to date mateials up to 5,000 years old. If the records were dated, they could be used to find the age of artifacts buried with them.

Activity Options

Individual Needs: English Learners

Word Meaning Make sure students understand the following terms and concepts on these pages.

Strategies Page: Document
radioactive: giving off certain kinds of powerful energy
argon: a colorless gas found in the air
potassium: a soft, silver-white metallic element often found in minerals
dating: determining the age of something
artifacts: objects left behind by ancient humans

Practice Page: Document
intruder: a person who is unwelcome in an area
ritual: a significant behavior that is repeated, such as for religious purposes
preliterate: of, or relating to, cultures that do not have a written language
divinities: gods
indigenous: native to a place

For more test practice online . . .

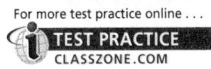
TEST PRACTICE
CLASSZONE.COM

Directions: Read the following passage from an art history book. Then answer the questions that follow.

The Meaning of Cave Paintings

Because [the cave paintings] were hidden away in order to protect them from intruders, they must have been considered important. There can be little doubt that they were made as part of a ritual. But of what kind? The standard explanation, based on "preliterate" societies of modern times, is that they are a form of hunting magic. According to this theory, in "killing" the image of an animal, people of the Late Stone Age thought they had killed its vital spirit. . . .

There is growing agreement that cave paintings must embody a very early form of religion. If so, the creatures found in them have a spiritual meaning that makes them the distant ancestors of the animal divinities and their half-human, half-animal cousins [of Ancient Egypt and Minoan civilizations]. . . . Such an approach accords with animism—the belief that nature is filled with spirits—which was found the world over in the indigenous societies that survived intact until recently.

—H. W. and Anthony F. Janson, *History of Art: The Western Tradition* (2004)

1. Why were the cave paintings hidden away?

2. What is the standard explanation for cave paintings?

3. Many scientists believe that the cave paintings are evidence of an early form of religion. If this is true, what is also true about the animals in the paintings?

S27

Practice Questions

Thinking It Through Share the following explanations with students as they discuss the strategies they used to answer the practice questions.

1. Read the question and then study the passage again. The answer is in the opening line: Cave paintings were hidden to protect them from intruders.

2. To answer this question, scan the passage for the words *standard explanation*. When you find them, read the text that follows. This will help provide the answer: The standard explanation for cave paintings is that they are a form of hunting magic.

3. To answer this question, you need to make assumptions and inferences about what the text has said. Read the portion that discusses the possible role of cave paintings in early religion. What does it say about the animals found in those paintings? Use this information to come up with your answer, which should include the idea that the animals may have represented gods.

California Standards and Skills

STRATEGY ITEMS		PRACTICE ITEMS	
Item Number	Skill/Standard Tested	Item Number	Skill/Standard Tested
1. 2. 3.	6.1 Students describe what is known through archaeological studies of the early physical and cultural development of humankind.	1. 2. 3.	REP4 Students assess the credibility of primary and secondary sources and draw sound conclusions from them.

CST = Chronological and Spatial Thinking, **HI** = Historical Interpretation, **REP** = Research, Evidence, and Point of View

Using Strategies For…

Extended Response Remind students of the following:

1. Sometimes, extended-response questions contain more than one part. Read all the extended-response questions that go with a document before beginning to develop an answer. Look for words that tell you how to organize your answers.

2. In this case, the extended-response question includes only one part: Write an essay about Hammurabi's Code.

3. It is a good idea to organize the information you collect from the source before beginning to write your essay. For example, you might make an outline in which you note (I) whether you believe "an eye for an eye" is an accurate description of the Code; and (II) examples from the Code that support your belief.

General Test-Taking Tips

Share these tips with your students.

- Write in complete sentences whenever appropriate. Extended-response essays require complete sentences.

- Use correct grammar, punctuation, and spelling to help ensure the scorer understands your answer.

- Remember, neatness counts! If the scorer cannot read your answer, you will not get credit for it.

Extended Response

Extended-response questions, like constructed-response questions, focus on a document of some kind. However, they are more complicated and require more time to complete. Some extended-response questions ask you to present the information in the document in a different form. For example, you might be asked to present the information in a chart or graph form. Other questions ask you to complete a document such as a chart or graph. Still others require you to apply your knowledge to information in the document to write an essay.

1 Read the title of the document to get an idea of what it is about.

2 Carefully read directions and questions.

3 Study the document.

4 Sometimes the question may give you part of the answer.

5 The question may require you to write an essay. Write down some ideas to use in an outline. Then use your outline to write the essay. (A good essay will contain the ideas shown in the rubric to the right.)

1 Hammurabi's Code

If a son has struck his father, they shall cut off his hand.

If a [noble] has destroyed the eye of a [noble], they shall destroy his eye.

3 If he has broken another [noble's] bone, they shall break his bone.

If he has destroyed the eye of a commoner or broken the bone of a commoner, he shall pay one mina of silver.

If he has destroyed the eye of a [noble's] slave or broken the bone of a [noble's] slave, he shall pay one-half [the slave's] value.

If a [noble] has knocked out the tooth of a [noble], they shall knock out his tooth.

If he has knocked out a commoner's tooth, he shall pay one-third mina of silver.

2 Hammurabi's Code is often described as "an eye for an eye." Is this an accurate description of the code? Is the code applied equally to all people? Explain your answer. **4**

> The question gives you an idea of what people think about Hammurabi's Code.

5 **Essay Rubric:** The best essays will point out that the strict "eye for an eye" rule only applies in some situations, such as when a noble destroys the eye of another noble. The description is accurate for nobles losing an eye, but not entirely accurate for other crimes that involve people who are not nobles. If someone wrongs a commoner by destroying his eye or breaking his bone, the commoner will receive a payment of one mina of silver. In this case, the wrongdoer would not lose an eye or have a bone broken. If a noble knocks a commoner's tooth out, he has to pay the commoner, but if a noble knocks another noble's tooth out, he gets his own tooth knocked out. The code does not seem to apply equally to all people. The code implies that a noble who harmed another noble was dealt with more harshly than a noble who harmed a commoner.

Activity Options

Individual Needs: English Learners

Word Meaning Make sure that students understand the following terms and concepts on these pages.

Strategies Page: Document

commoner: a person of a low economic or social class
mina: a measure of money

Practice Page: Document

mastery: control, skill
breakthrough: a significant invention or development
surplus: more than the minimal, needed amount

Directions: Complete the chart. Then use the information in the chart to answer the following question.

The Development of Civilization	
Key Achievements	Impact
• Invention of Tools	•
• Mastery over fire	• People were able to keep warm and cook food.
• Development of language	•
• Breakthroughs in farming technology	•
• Domestication of animals	• Animals could be bred for certain traits. Animals became more dependable.
• Food surpluses	• More people could live in one place, and there were fewer food shortages.
• Specialized workers	•
• Record keeping	•
• Advanced technology	•

1. Which achievements do you think had the most influence on the development of civilization? Why?

Practice Questions

Thinking It Through Share the following explanations with students as they discuss the strategies they used to answer the practice questions.

1. In this question you are asked to complete a chart. You need to use your knowledge of ancient history to complete this chart.

2. Once you have completed the chart, you can use the information in it to help you answer Question 1.

3. Chart, possible answers
   impact of tools—ability to farm, build up surplus food
   development of language—permitted communication and the organization of society into larger groups
   breakthroughs of farming technology—allowed farming in formerly unproductive areas, more surplus food
   specialized workers—richer culture, more trade
   record keeping—development of mathematics, writing
   advanced technology—greater ability to produce food, to conquer enemies

4. The best essays will:
   • Have a clear introduction, which lays out the basic argument you will be making.
   • Identify several examples of achievements that have influenced the development of civilization.
   • Provide a persuasive explanation for why those achievements were so influential.
   • Have a conclusion that restates the main point of the essay.

S29

California Standards and Skills

STRATEGY ITEMS		PRACTICE ITEMS	
Item Number	Skill/Standard Tested	Item Number	Skill/Standard Tested
1.	**REP4** Students assess the credibility of primary and secondary sources and draw sound conclusions from them. **6.2.4** Know the significance of Hammurabi's Code.	1.	**HI2** Students understand and distinguish cause, effect, sequence, and correlation in historical events. **6.1** Students describe what is known through archaeological studies of the early physical and cultural development of humankind.

CST = Chronological and Spatial Thinking, **HI** = Historical Interpretation, **REP** = Research, Evidence, and Point of View

Using Strategies For...

Document-Based Questions Remind students of the following:

1. Document-based questions are designed to help you work like a historian. You are given several documents from a variety of sources that you must analyze, evaluate, and synthesize in order to write an essay, much in the same way a historian would proceed.

2. Use information in the "Introduction" to help you organize your essay. The "Historical Context" gives you the focus of the document-based questions. The document-based questions shown here focus on events taking place in Ancient Greece.

3. Use the information in the "Task" section to help you make a graphic organizer to organize the information for your essay. For example, in this document-based question, "Task" instructs you to discuss the effects of the Peloponnesian War on Athenians. Make a web diagram on a piece of paper with the center circle marked "Peloponnesian War: Effect on Athenians."

4. As you answer the short-answer questions, also complete the web diagram.

5. Use the documents, the answers to the short-answer questions, the notes in your graphic organizer, and your knowledge of history to write the essay.

General Test-Taking Tips

Share these tips with your students.

- Write legibly.

- Answer sheets are scanned for scoring purposes. If your writing is not dark enough, they will not be readable.

Document-Based Questions

To answer a document-based question, you usually have to study more than one document. First you answer questions about each document. Then you use those answers and information from the documents as well as your own knowledge of history to write an essay.

❶ Read the Historical Context section. It will give you an idea of the topic that will be covered in the question.

❷ Read the Task section carefully. It tells you what you will need to write about in your essay.

❸ Study each document. Think about the connection the documents have to the topic in the Task section.

❹ Read and answer the questions about each document. Think about how your answers connect to the Task section.

Introduction

❶ **Historical Context:** After the Persian War, Athens became the most powerful city-state in Greece. Many other city-states, including Sparta, felt threatened by Athens' rise to power. Eventually, Sparta declared war on Athens. In this Peloponnesian War, Athens was devastated.

❷ **Task:** Discuss the effects of the Peloponnesian War on Athenians.

Part 1: Short Answer

Study each document carefully. Answer the questions that follow.

❸ **Document 1: The Peloponnesian War—A Summary**

The Peloponnesian War, 431 B.C.–404 B.C.		
Causes	**Military Strategies**	**Outcomes**
Anger at Athenian grab for power and prestige. Fear of Athens' status as a powerful naval empire. Anger at Athenian attempts to colonize lands of other city-states.	Athens and allies: Avoid land battles and rely on sea power. Sparta and allies: Focus on land battles; cut off Athenian food supply by laying waste to countryside.	Sparta victorious, becomes leading Greek city-state. Athens loses its empire, power, wealth, and prestige.

❹ **How did Sparta intend to win the war?**

focus on land battles and cut off Athens' food supply by laying waste to the countryside

Document 2: Reaction to an Athenian Defeat

They were beaten at all points and altogether; all that they suffered was great; they were destroyed, as the saying is, with a total destruction, their fleet, their army, everything was destroyed, and few out of many returned home. Such were the events in Sicily. . . .

When the news was brought to Athens, for a long while they disbelieved even the most respectable of the soldiers who had themselves escaped from the scene of

Activity Options

Individual Needs: English Learners

Word Meaning Make sure students understand the following terms and concepts on these pages.

Strategy Pages:

Historical Context *Peloponnesian War:* The war takes its name from the Peloponnesus, the southern section of Greece where Sparta and most of the other city-states that opposed Athens were located.

Document 1 *allies:* groups or countries that are united, especially by treaty during wartime

Document 2 *consternation:* paralyzing fear, dread

Question 2 *Syracuse:* a Greek colony, allied with Sparta, on the Mediterranean island of Sicily

action and clearly reported the matter, a destruction so complete not being thought credible. . . . Already distressed at all points and in all quarters, after what had now happened, they were seized by a fear and consternation quite without example. . . . [T]hey began to despair of salvation.

—Thucydides, *The Peloponnesian War*

This passage deals with the Athenian defeat at Syracuse. How did Athenians react to this loss?

with utter disbelief and then with fear, dismay, and despair

Document 3: The Cost of the Peloponnesian War

The economic consequences of the war were grave. Commerce by land and sea was disrupted. . . . Agriculture suffered in most of Greece. . . . A good deal of territory was [ruined], and livestock and farming implements destroyed as well as growing vines and olive trees. . . .

In Athens, as many as fifty thousand people had probably died of the plague. . . . War casualties seem to have included at least five thousand . . . soldiers and twelve thousand sailors. . . . Probably the number of adult male citizens in 403 was half what it had been in 431.

—Sarah B. Pomeroy and others, *A Brief History of Ancient Greece*

What was the human cost of the Peloponnesian War to Athens?

some 17,000 war casualties and as many as 50,000 from the plague, perhaps as much as half of the population of adult male citizens

❺ Part 2: Essay

Write an essay describing the Peloponnesian War's effect on Athens. Use information from the documents, your short answers, and your knowledge of history. ❻

❺ Read the essay question carefully. Then write a brief outline for your essay.

❻ Write your essay. The first paragraph should introduce your topic. The middle paragraphs should explain it. The closing paragraph should restate the topic and your conclusion. Support your ideas with quotations or details from the documents. Add other supporting facts or details from your knowledge of world history.

❼ A good essay will contain the ideas in the rubric below.

❼ Essay Rubric: The best essays will state that Athens was devastated. It lost its empire, power, wealth, and prestige (Document 1). Its economy was destroyed, and the human losses it suffered were immense (Document 3). Further, Athenians suffered a huge psychological blow because they could not believe that they could have been so thoroughly defeated (Document 2). This made them fear greatly for the future.

S31

Rubric for DBQ Essay

The following is a sample rubric that might be used to score a DBQ essay.

To score a 5, the DBQ essay:
- thoroughly answers all parts of Task.
- uses information from all the documents.
- is supported with relevant facts and details.
- is well developed and organized.
- has a strong introduction and conclusion.

To score a 4, the DBQ essay:
- answers all parts of the Task.
- uses information from most of the documents.
- is supported with relevant facts and details.
- is well developed and organized.
- has a good introduction and conclusion.

To score a 3, the DBQ essay:
- answers most parts of the Task.
- uses information from some documents.
- is supported with some relevant facts and details.
- is satisfactorily developed and organized.
- has a limited introduction or conclusion.

To score a 2, the DBQ essay:
- answers some or all parts of the Task in a limited way.
- uses limited information from the documents.
- uses few facts and details to support the essay.
- is poorly organized.
- has a limited or missing introduction or conclusion.

To score a 1, the DBQ essay:
- shows limited understanding of the Task.
- uses limited information from the documents.
- uses no facts or supporting details.
- is poorly organized.
- has a limited or missing introduction or conclusion.

To score a 0, the DBQ essay:
- does not answer the Task.
- is illegible.
- is blank or missing.

California Standards and Skills

STRATEGY ITEMS	
Item Number	**Skill/Standard Tested**
Part 1: Short Answer	
Document 1	6.4.6 Compare and contrast life in Athens and Sparta, with emphasis on their roles in the Peloponnesian War.
Document 2, 3	REP4 Students assess the credibility of primary and secondary sources and draw sound conclusions from them.
Part 2: Essay	6.4.6 Compare and contrast life in Athens and Sparta, with emphasis on their roles in the Peloponnesian War.

CST = Chronological and Spatial Thinking, **HI** = Historical Interpretation, **REP** = Research, Evidence, and Point of View

Practice Questions

Thinking It Through Share the following explanations with students as they discuss the strategies they used to answer the practice questions.

Part 1: Short Answers

Document 1. Analyze the picture and the information that accompanies it, then answer the question. The painting shows that elite dinner parties featured a small number of well-dressed people who ate and enjoyed the festivities.

Document 2. Read through the primary source in order to answer the question: The schoolboy is surrounded by family and those who serve him and try to make him comfortable, while the slaves seem to exist only to serve the schoolboy.

Document 3. Read through the primary source to answer the question: The fires would sweep quickly through the poorly constructed and maintained buildings.

Part 2: Essay.

Share the sample rubric on page S31 with students so they know the criteria they must meet to earn the maximum amount of points for this essay. Tell students the following.

1. Use the information in the "Introduction" to help you organize your essay. Jot down things you know about the time period or theme of the question. Use the information in the "Task" to help you make a graphic organizer, such as a T-chart with the headings "Lives of the Elite" and "Lives of the Poor and the Slaves." As you answer the questions, also complete this chart.
2. Use the documents, the answers to the questions, the notes in your graphic organizer, and your knowledge of history to help you write the essay.

Activity Options

Individual Needs: English Learners

Word Meaning Make sure students understand the following terms and concepts on these pages.

Practice Pages

Introduction *social status:* rank in the community
  elite: wealthy, powerful
  humble: homely, not grand

Document 2 *tunic:* a loose fitting type of shirt
  cloak: a type of overcoat
  attendant: someone who attends to, or serves, another

Document 3 *planks:* wooden boards

Introduction

Historical Context: By the time Rome was an empire, wealth and social status made a huge difference in the way people lived. Roman society was divided into three main social classes: the elite, the "more humble," and the slaves.

Task: Discuss how the life of an elite Roman would have been different from that of a "more humble" person or a slave.

Part 1: Short Answers

Study each document carefully. Answer the questions that follow.

Document 1: Roman Dinner Party

This painting found at Pompeii shows some elite Romans being entertained at a dinner party. What were elite dinner parties like?

S32

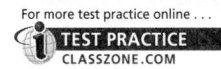
Document 2: A Schoolboy's Life

> Before it is light I wake up, and, sitting on the edge of my bed, I put on my shoes and leg-wraps because it is cold. . . . Taking off my nightshirt I put on my tunic and belt; I put oil on my hair, comb it, wrap a scarf around my neck and put on my white cloak. Followed by my school attendant and my nurse I go to say good morning to daddy and mummy and I kiss them both. I find my writing things and exercise book and give them to a slave. I set off to school followed by my school attendant. . . .
>
> I go into the schoolroom and say "Good morning master." He kisses me and returns my greeting. The slave gives me my wax tablets, my writing things and ruler. . . . When I finish learning my lesson I ask the master to let me go home to lunch. . . . Reaching home I change, take some white bread, olives, cheese, dried figs, and nuts and drink some cold water. After lunch I go back to school where the master is beginning to read. He says, "Let's begin work."
>
> —A Roman schoolboy, quoted by F. R. Cowell,
> *Everyday Life in Ancient Rome*

How did the schoolboy's day differ from his slave's?

Document 3: Poorer Neighborhoods

> But here we inhabit a city supported for the most part by [planks]: for that is how the [landlord] holds up the tottering house, patches up gaping cracks in the old wall, bidding the [tenants] sleep at ease under a roof ready to tumble about their ears. No, no, I must live where there are no fires, no nightly alarms.
>
> —Juvenal, *Satires III*

What is housing like in the poorer neighborhoods?

Part 2: Essay

Write an essay describing the differences between the lives of elite Romans, poor Romans, and slaves. Use information from the documents, your short answers, and your knowledge of history to write your essay.

S33

Rubric for Essay

The best essays will address the differences in the lives of all three groups—the elite, the poor Romans, and the slaves.

The Elite

- Enjoyed great luxury and abundance (Document 1)
- Had their needs attended to by slaves (Document 2)
- Had much more wealth than the poor (outside knowledge)

The Poor Romans

- Often lived in substandard housing (Document 3)
- Had little hope of improving their economic status (outside knowledge)

The Slaves

- Existed only to serve the elite (Document 2)
- Had little opportunity to change their economic status (outside knowledge)
- Sometimes suffered terrible abuse (outside knowledge)

California Standards and Skills

STRATEGY ITEMS	
Item Number	**Skill/Standard Tested**
Part 1: Short Answer	
Document 1, 2, 3	**REP4** Students assess the credibility of primary and secondary sources and draw sound conclusions from them.
Part 2: Essay	**6.7:** Students analyze the geographic, political, economic, religious, and social structures during the development of Rome.

CST = Chronological and Spatial Thinking, **HI** = Historical Interpretation, **REP** = Research, Evidence, and Point of View

RAND McNALLY

World Atlas

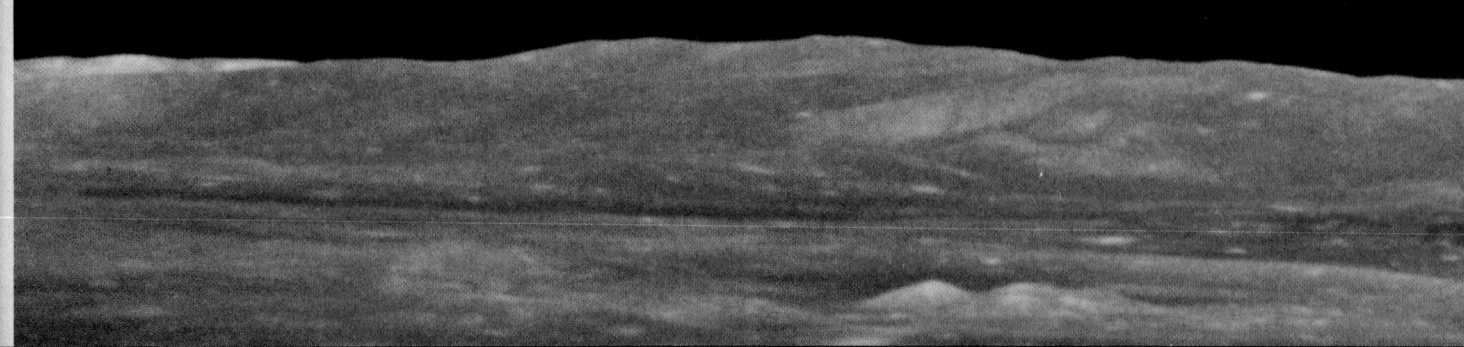

Contents

Complete Legend for Physical and Political Maps

Symbols

 Lake

 Seasonal Lake

 River

\ Waterfall

—— Canal

▲ Mountain Peak

Cities

■ Los Angeles — City over 1,000,000 population

▣ Calgary — City under 1,000,000 population

✹ Paris — National Capital

Boundaries

 International Boundary

 Secondary Boundary

Type Styles Used to Name Features

CHINA — Country

O N T A R I O — State, Province, or Territory

PUERTO RICO (U.S.) — Possession

A T L A N T I C O C E A N — Ocean or Sea

A l p s — Physical Feature

Borneo — Island

Land Elevation and Water Depths

Land Elevation

Meters		Feet
3,000 and over		9,840 and over
2,000 - 3,000		6,560 - 9,840
500 - 2,000		1,640 - 6,560
200 - 500		656 - 1,640
0 - 200		0 - 656

Water Depth

Less than 200		Less than 656
200 - 2,000		656 - 6,560
Over 2,000		Over 6,560

ARCTIC OCEAN

ATLANTIC
OCEAN

EUROPE

Alps

Pyrenees

Caucasus

Black Sea

Caspian Sea

Aral Sea

Coppa Nevigata

Troy

Catal Huyuk

Mersin

Anau

MEDITERRANEAN

Judeidah

Hassuna

Hissar

Knossos

Jarmo

Sialk

SEA

Jericho

Al-Ubaid

Susa

Eridu

Bakun

Merimde

Kul

Atlas Mountains

SAHARA

Badari
Naqada
Kharga

Red Sea

ARABIAN

PENINSULA

AFRICA

N

Judeidah Early Agricultural Communities

  Civilized areas in Third Millennium B.C.

  Civilized areas in Second Millennium B.C.

  Civilization 1000 B.C. - 200 A.D.

| 0 | 200 | 400 | 600 | 800 Miles |

| 0 | 300 | 600 | 900 | 1200 Kilometers |

Copyright by Rand McNally & Co.
Goodes Projection

RAND McNALLY

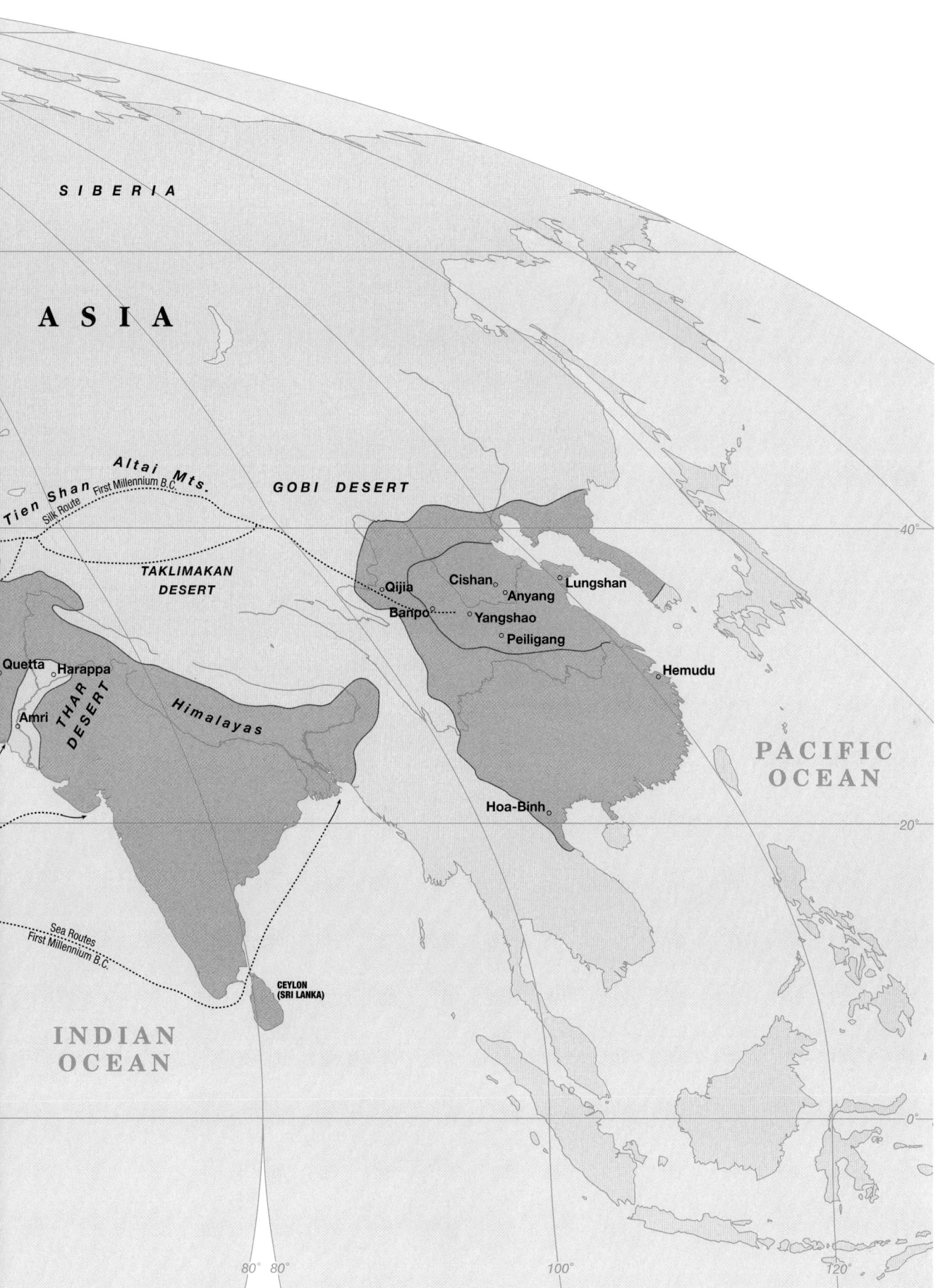

SIBERIA

A S I A

Tien Shan *Altai Mts.* *GOBI DESERT*

Silk Route
First Millennium B.C.

TAKLIMAKAN DESERT

Qijia

Cishan
Anyang
Lungshan

Banpo
Yangshao

Peiligang

Hemudu

Quetta   Harappa

THAR DESERT   *Himalayas*

Amri

Hoa-Binh

PACIFIC
OCEAN

Sea Routes
First Millennium B.C.

CEYLON
(SRI LANKA)

INDIAN
OCEAN

40°

20°

0°

80°   80°   100°   120°

RAND M^cNALLY

ARCTIC OCEAN

GREENLAND
(Den.)

Baffin
Bay

Arctic Circle

ICELAND

RUSSIA

ALASKA
Yukon (U.S.)

FAROE IS.
(Den.)

UNITED
KINGDO

IRELAND

Aleutian Islands

CANADA

Hudson
Bay

Newfoundland

London

FRAN

Missouri

Montréal

Ottawa *

Chicago

New York

UNITED STATES

* Washington D.C.

Azores
(Port.)

PORTUGAL

SPAI

Los Angeles *

Colorado

Houston

Mississippi

MIDWAY IS.
(U.S.)

Gulf of Mexico

ATLANTIC

Canary
Islands
(Sp.)

MOROCCO

Tropic of Cancer

Hawaiian
Islands
(U.S)

MEXICO

BAHAMAS

W. SAHARA

Mexico City *

CUBA

DOM. REP.

MAURITANIA

MA

BELIZE

HAITI

PUERTO RICO (U.S.)

CAPE VERDE

PACIFIC

GUAT.

HOND.

JAMAICA

Caribbean
Sea

SENEGAL

Niger

BUR

FAS

EL SAL.

NIC.

THE GAMBIA

GUINEA-BISSAU

GUINEA

COSTA
RICA

Caracas *

TRINIDAD AND TOBAGO

SIERRA LEONE

COTE
D'IVOIRE

PANAMA

VENEZUELA

GUYANA

LIBERIA

COLOMBIA

SURINAME
FRENCH GUIANA

Galapagos Islands
(Ecuador)

ECUADOR

Amazon

OCEAN

OCEAN

Equator

KIRIBATI

PERU

BRAZIL

ST. HELENA
(U.K.)

SAMOA

OCEAN

AMERICAN
SAMOA

COOK
ISLANDS
(N.Z.)

TONGA

BOLIVIA

FRENCH POLYNESIA

PARAGUAY

Rio de Janeiro

Tropic of Capricorn

Easter Island
(Chile)

ARGENTINA

URUGUAY

Buenos
Aires

CHILE

FALKLAND IS.
(U.K.)

South
Georgia
(U.K.)

0   1000   2000 Miles

0   1000   2000   3000 Kilometers

Copyright by Rand McNally & Co.
Robinson Projection

South
Orkney Is.
(U.K.)

Antarctic Circle

South
Shetland Is.
(U.K.)

Weddell
Sea

N

ARCTIC OCEAN

Spitsbergen
(Nor.)

Franz Josef
Land

Novaya
Zemlya

NORWAY
SWEDEN
FINLAND
DEN.
EST.
LAT.
LITH.
BELARUS
GERMANY
POLAND
UKRAINE
CZ.
SLK.
AUS.
HUNG.
ROM.
MOLD.
SWITZ.
ITALY
CRO.
BOS.
SERB.
BUL.
ALB.
MA.
Rome
GREECE
TURKEY
CYPRUS
LEB.
SYRIA
ISRAEL
JORDAN
IRAQ
KUWAIT
IRAN
Cairo
EGYPT
SAUDI
ARABIA
QATAR
U.A.E.
OMAN
YEMEN

RUSSIA

Volga
Moscow

Ob'

Yenisey

Lena

Bering
Sea

Sea of Okhotsk

KAZAKHSTAN

UZBEKISTAN
KYRG.
TAJIK.
TURKMENISTAN
AFGHANISTAN
PAKISTAN

MONGOLIA

CHINA

Beijing

NORTH
KOREA
SOUTH
KOREA
Sea of Japan
JAPAN
Tokyo

GEO.
ARM.
AZER.
Black Sea

Chang Jiang
Yangtze
Shanghai

PACIFIC

NEPAL
BHU.
Ganges
Kolkata
(Calcutta)
BNGL.
MYANMAR
LAOS
THAILAND
VIETNAM
CAMBODIA
TAIWAN

Tropic of Cancer

Mumbai
(Bombay)
INDIA

Arabian
Sea

Bay of
Bengal

Bangkok

South China
Sea

NORTHERN
MARIANA ISLANDS
(U.S.)

WAKE ISLAND
(U.S.)

GUAM (U.S.)

OCEAN

PHILIPPINES

PALAU

SRI LANKA

BRUNEI
MALAYSIA
SINGAPORE

FED. STATES OF
MICRONESIA

MARSHALL
ISLANDS

MALDIVES

Borneo

New Guinea

Equator

SEYCHELLES

Sumatra
Jakarta
Java

INDONESIA

EAST TIMOR

PAPUA
NEW GUINEA

SOLOMON
ISLANDS

INDIAN

COMOROS

MADAGASCAR
MAURITIUS
REUNION
(Fr.)

OCEAN

Coral Sea

VANUATU

NEW CALEDONIA
(Fr.)

FIJI

AUSTRALIA

Tropic of Capricorn

Darling
Sydney

Kerguelen
Islands
(Fr.)

Tasmania

NEW ZEALAND

SOUTHERN OCEAN

Antarctic Circle

ANTARCTICA

LIBYA
NIGER
CHAD
SUDAN
NIGERIA
Lagos
CENTRAL
AFRICAN
REPUBLIC
ETHIOPIA
Addis
Ababa
DJIBOUTI
ERITREA
SOMALIA
CAMEROON
EQ. GUIN.
GABON
REP. OF
CONGO
DEM. REP.
OF CONGO
RWANDA
BURUNDI
UGANDA
KENYA
TANZANIA
ANGOLA
ZAMBIA
ZIMBABWE
MOZAMBIQUE
MALAWI
NAMIBIA
BOTSWANA
SWAZILAND
SOUTH
AFRICA
LESOTHO
Cape Town

ALGERIA
TUNISIA
Crete
Mediterranean Sea
Nile
Red Sea
Congo

ARCTIC OCEAN

Baffin
Island

Baffin
Bay

Greenland

Jan Maye

Arctic Circle

Iceland

Mt. McKinley ▲
20,320 Ft.
6,194m

Yukon

Mackenzie

Canadian Shield

Hudson
Bay

Faroe Is.

British
Is

Aleutian Islands

NORTH

Newfoundland

London

Rocky Mountains

Great Plains

AMERICA

St. Lawrence

Mississippi

Appalachian Mts.

✷ Washington D.C.

Azores

Iberian
Peninsu

Los Angeles

Colorado

Cape Hatteras

ATLANTIC

Atlas
Mts

Midway Is.

Baja
California

Gulf of Mexico

Canary
Islands

Tropic of Cancer

Hawaiian Islands

Yucatan
Peninsula

Cuba

Hispaniola

Puerto Rico

Cape
Verde
Islands

PACIFIC

Jamaica

Caribbean
Sea

Cape Verde

Niger

Trinidad

OCEAN

Orinoco

Palmyra

Galapagos Islands

Amazon

Amazon

SOUTH

Equator

Kiribati

OCEAN

Basin

AMERICA

St. Helena

Marquesas Is.

Samoa Islands

Andes

Mato Grosso
Plateau

Tonga
Is.

Cook
Islands

Tahiti

Rio de Janeiro

Tropic of Capricorn

Easter Island

Andes

Paraná

Chatham Is.

▲ Mt. Aconcagua
22,881 Ft.
6,959m

✷ Buenos Aires

N

0   1000   2000 Miles

0   1000   2000   3000 Kilometers

Copyright by Rand McNally & Co.
Robinson Projection

Patagonia

Falkland Is.

South
Georgia

Tierra del Fuego

South
Sandwich Is.

Cape Horn

South
Orkney Is.

South
Shetland Is.

Antarctic
Peninsula

Weddell
Sea

Antarctic Circle

Ross
Sea

Marie
Byrd
Land

▲ Vinson Massif
16,066 Ft.
4,897m

ARCTIC OCEAN

Spitsbergen
Franz Josef Land
North Cape
Novaya Zemlya
Scandinavian Peninsula
Siberia
Yenisey
Lena
Bering Sea

EUROPE
Volga
*Moscow
Ural Mts.
Ob'
Amur
Sakhalin
Kamchatka Peninsula
Sea of Okhotsk

Alps
Don
Caucasus
Mt. Elbrus 18,510 Ft. 5,642m
Aral
A S I A
Altai Mts.
Gobi Desert
Beijing *
Huang
Hokkaidō
Honshū
Sea of Japan

Balkan Peninsula
Black Sea
Sardinia
Sicily
Crete
Cyprus
Zagros Mts.
Indus
Plateau of Tibet
Himalayas
▲Mt. Everest 29,035 Ft. 8,850m
Chang
East China Sea
Kyūshū
PACIFIC

Cairo *
Sahara
Arabian Peninsula
Ganges
Mekong
Taiwan
Tropic of Cancer

AFRICA
Nile
Red Sea
Mumbai (Bombay)
Deccan Plateau
Bay of Bengal
Hainan Island
South China Sea
Luzon
Mariana Islands
Wake Island
O C E A N

Sahel
Arabian Sea
Socotra
Lakshadweep
Sri Lanka
Malay Peninsula
Mindanao
Palau Islands
Caroline Islands
Marshall Islands

Gulf of Guinea
Ethiopian Plateau
Maldive Islands
Borneo
Celebes
Guam

Congo
Congo Basin
Rift Valley
▲Kilimanjaro 19,340 Ft. 5,895m
Seychelles
Sumatra
Java
Timor
New Guinea
Solomon Islands
Equator

I N D I A N
Cocos Island
New Hebrides

Zambezi
Madagascar
Mauritius
Reunion
Coral Sea
New Caledonia
Fiji Is.

Kalahari Desert
O C E A N
Great Sandy Desert
AUSTRALIA
Tropic of Capricorn

*Cape Town
Cape of Good Hope
Cape Leeuwin
Darling
Great Dividing Range
Sydney
North Island

Tasmania
Aoraki (Mt. Cook) 12,316 Ft. 3,754m▲
South Island

Kerguelen Islands

S O U T H E R N   O C E A N
Antarctic Circle

Queen Maud Land
Enderby Land
Wilkes Land
Victoria Land

A N T A R C T I C A

Land Elevation		
Meters		**Feet**
3,000		9,840
2,000		6,560
500		1,640
200		656
0		0

Water Depth		
0		0
200		656
2,000		6,560

RAND McNALLY

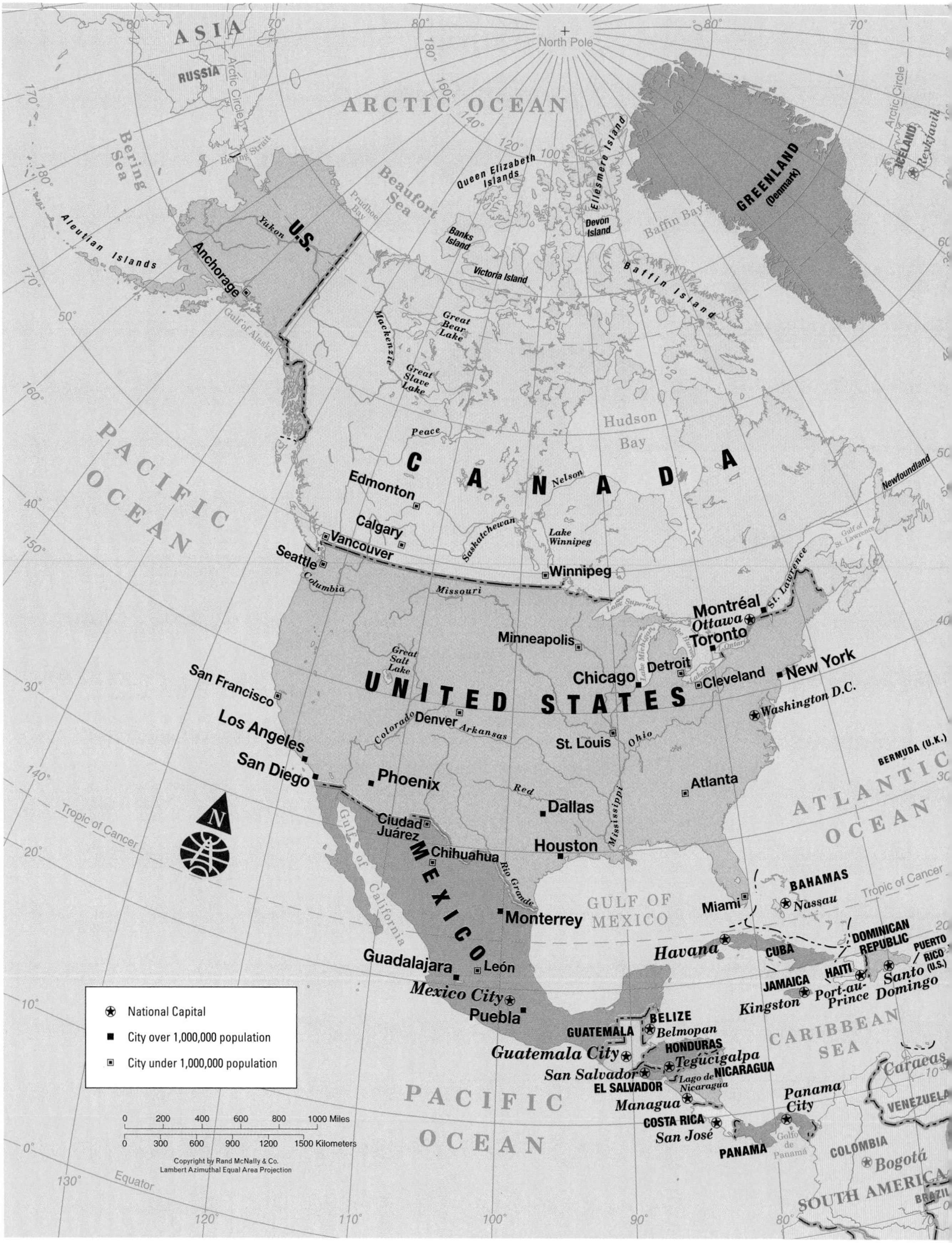

ASIA

RUSSIA

ARCTIC OCEAN

North Pole

Bering Strait

Arctic Circle

Beaufort Sea

Queen Elizabeth Islands

Ellesmere Island

Devon Island

Banks Island

Baffin Bay

GREENLAND (Denmark)

ICELAND

Reykjavik

Arctic Circle

Victoria Island

Baffin Island

Aleutian Islands

U.S.

Anchorage

Yukon

Prudhoe Bay

Gulf of Alaska

Mackenzie

Great Bear Lake

Great Slave Lake

Hudson Bay

Newfoundland

PACIFIC OCEAN

Peace

C A N A D A

Nelson

Gulf of St. Lawrence

Edmonton

Calgary

Vancouver

Seattle

Winnipeg

Saskatchewan

Lake Winnipeg

Columbia

Missouri

Montréal

Ottawa

Toronto

St. Lawrence

Minneapolis

Lake Superior

Lake Michigan

Lake Huron

Detroit

Lake Ontario

Lake Erie

New York

San Francisco

Great Salt Lake

UNITED STATES

Chicago

Cleveland

Washington D.C.

Los Angeles

Denver

Colorado

Arkansas

St. Louis

Ohio

Atlanta

BERMUDA (U.K.)

ATLANTIC OCEAN

San Diego

Phoenix

Red

Dallas

Mississippi

Tropic of Cancer

N

Ciudad Juárez

M E X I C O

Chihuahua

Rio Grande

Houston

Monterrey

GULF OF MEXICO

Miami

BAHAMAS

Nassau

Tropic of Cancer

Gulf of California

Guadalajara

León

Havana

CUBA

DOMINICAN REPUBLIC

PUERTO RICO (U.S.)

Mexico City

Puebla

BELIZE

Belmopan

JAMAICA

HAITI

Kingston

Port-au-Prince

Santo Domingo

GUATEMALA

Guatemala City

HONDURAS

Tegucigalpa

NICARAGUA

CARIBBEAN SEA

Caracas

San Salvador

Lago de Nicaragua

EL SALVADOR

Managua

COSTA RICA

Panama City

VENEZUELA

San José

PANAMA

Golfo de Panamá

COLOMBIA

Bogotá

PACIFIC OCEAN

SOUTH AMERICA

BRAZIL

Equator

Legend:
- ✪ National Capital
- ■ City over 1,000,000 population
- ▫ City under 1,000,000 population

| 0 | 200 | 400 | 600 | 800 | 1000 Miles |

| 0 | 300 | 600 | 900 | 1200 | 1500 Kilometers |

Copyright by Rand McNally & Co.
Lambert Azimuthal Equal Area Projection

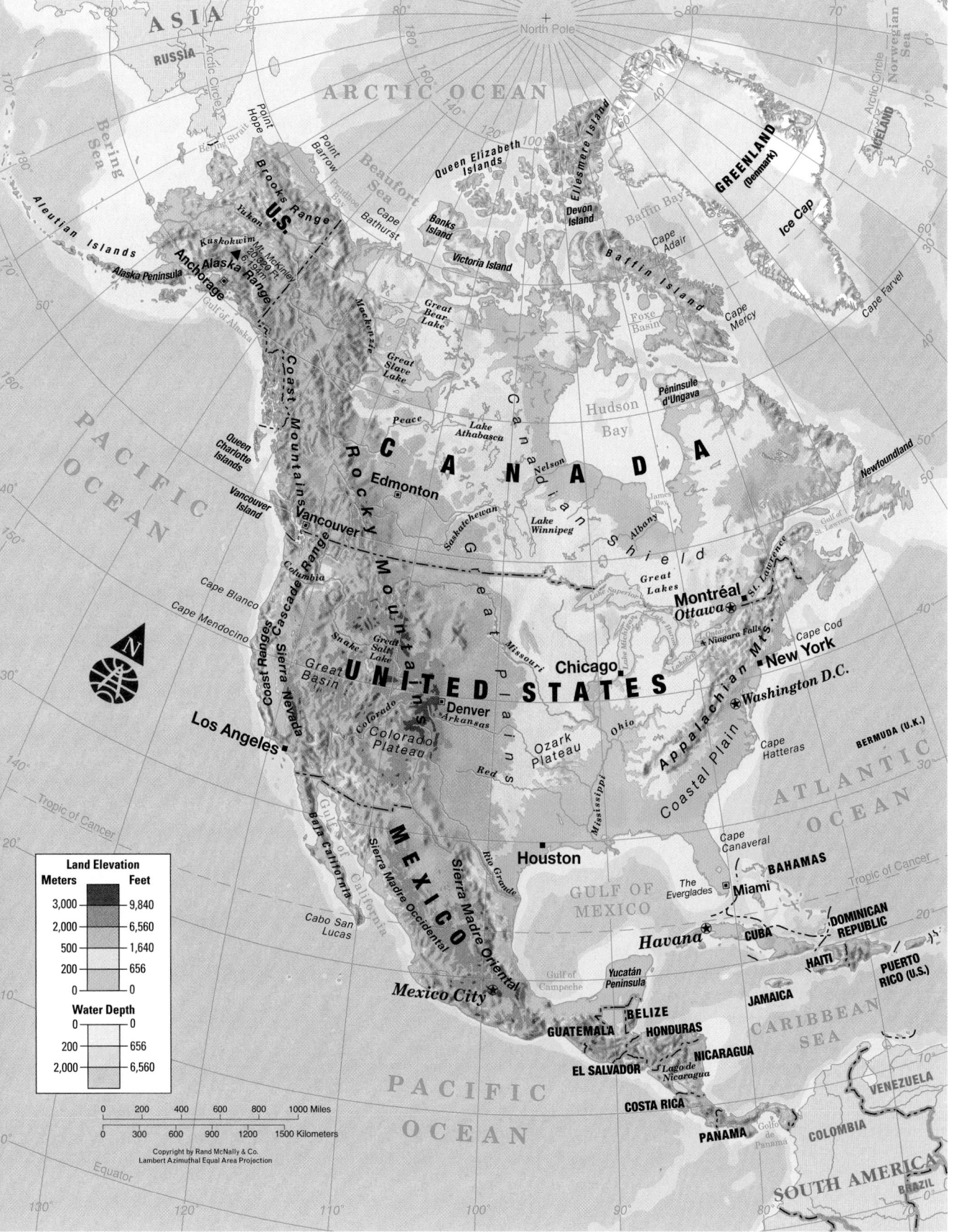

Land Elevation

Meters		Feet
3,000		9,840
2,000		6,560
500		1,640
200		656
0		0

Water Depth

0		0
200		656
2,000		6,560

0 200 400 600 800 1000 Miles

0 300 600 900 1200 1500 Kilometers

Copyright by Rand McNally & Co.
Lambert Azimuthal Equal Area Projection

RAND McNALLY

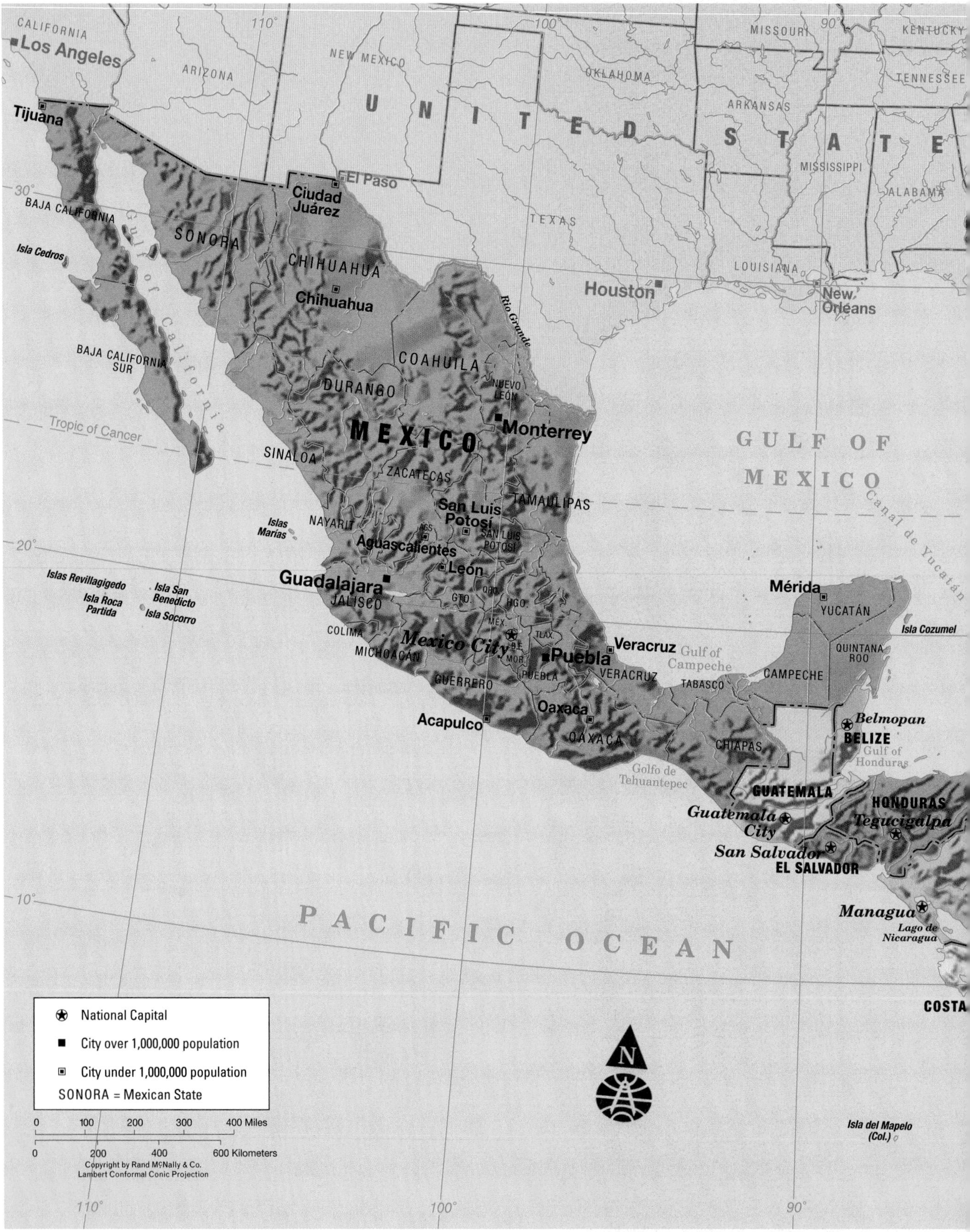

Map Labels

CALIFORNIA
Los Angeles
Tijuana
ARIZONA
NEW MEXICO
110°
El Paso
Ciudad Juárez
BAJA CALIFORNIA
SONORA
CHIHUAHUA
Chihuahua
Isla Cedros
BAJA CALIFORNIA SUR
Gulf of California
Tropic of Cancer
DURANGO
COAHUILA
NUEVO LEÓN
MEXICO
Monterrey
SINALOA
ZACATECAS
TAMAULIPAS
Islas Marías
NAYARIT
San Luis Potosí
SAN LUIS POTOSÍ
Aguascalientes
AGS.
León
QRO.
Islas Revillagigedo
Isla San Benedicto
Isla Roca Partida
Isla Socorro
Guadalajara
JALISCO
GTO.
HGO.
Mérida
YUCATÁN
Isla Cozumel
COLIMA
MEX.
TLAX.
Mexico City
D.F.
MOR.
Puebla
PUEBLA
Veracruz
VERACRUZ
Gulf of Campeche
QUINTANA ROO
CAMPECHE
MICHOACÁN
GUERRERO
Oaxaca
TABASCO
Acapulco
OAXACA
CHIAPAS
Golfo de Tehuantepec
Gulf of Honduras
Belmopan
BELIZE
GUATEMALA
Guatemala City
HONDURAS
Tegucigalpa
San Salvador
EL SALVADOR
Managua
Lago de Nicaragua
PACIFIC OCEAN

UNITED STATES
MISSOURI
KENTUCKY
OKLAHOMA
ARKANSAS
TENNESSEE
TEXAS
MISSISSIPPI
ALABAMA
LOUISIANA
Houston
New Orleans
Rio Grande
GULF OF MEXICO
Canal de Yucatán

COSTA

Isla del Mapelo (Col.)

Legend

⍟ National Capital

■ City over 1,000,000 population

▣ City under 1,000,000 population

SONORA = Mexican State

| 0 | 100 | 200 | 300 | 400 Miles |

| 0 | 200 | 400 | 600 Kilometers |

Copyright by Rand McNally & Co.
Lambert Conformal Conic Projection

N

RAND MCNALLY

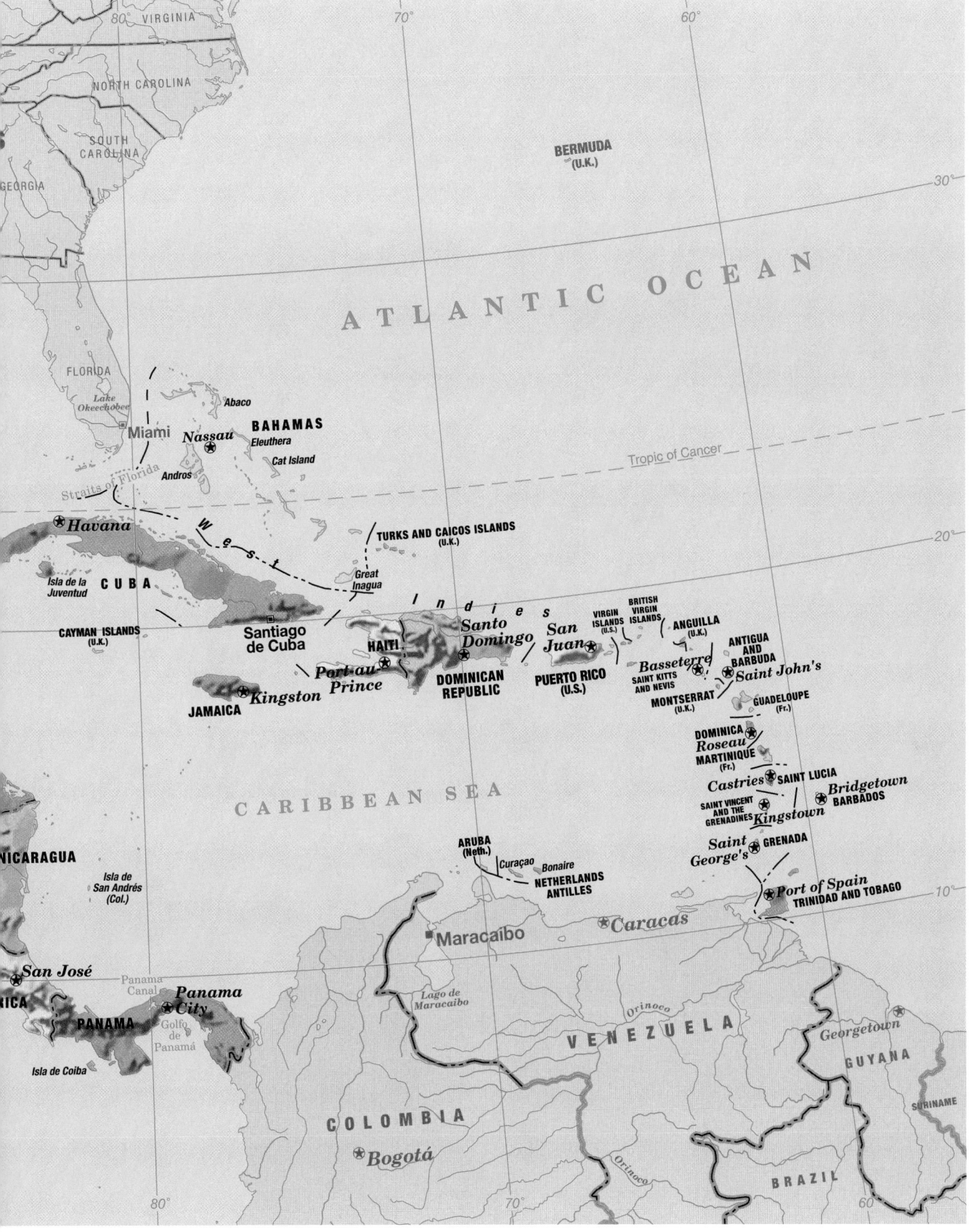

ATLANTIC OCEAN

VIRGINIA

NORTH CAROLINA

SOUTH CAROLINA

GEORGIA

FLORIDA

Lake Okeechobee

Miami

Straits of Florida

*Havana

Isla de la Juventud

CUBA

CAYMAN ISLANDS (U.K.)

Santiago de Cuba

JAMAICA

*Kingston

BERMUDA (U.K.)

Tropic of Cancer

Abaco

BAHAMAS

Nassau

Eleuthera

Cat Island

Andros

West Indies

TURKS AND CAICOS ISLANDS (U.K.)

Great Inagua

Santo Domingo

HAITI

Port-au-Prince

DOMINICAN REPUBLIC

San Juan

PUERTO RICO (U.S.)

VIRGIN ISLANDS (U.S.)

BRITISH VIRGIN ISLANDS

ANGUILLA (U.K.)

ANTIGUA AND BARBUDA

Basseterre

SAINT KITTS AND NEVIS

MONTSERRAT (U.K.)

Saint John's

GUADELOUPE (Fr.)

DOMINICA

Roseau

MARTINIQUE (Fr.)

Castries

SAINT LUCIA

SAINT VINCENT AND THE GRENADINES

Kingstown

Bridgetown

BARBADOS

Saint George's

GRENADA

CARIBBEAN SEA

NICARAGUA

Isla de San Andrés (Col.)

San José

RICA

Panama Canal

Panama City

PANAMA

Golfo de Panamá

Isla de Coiba

ARUBA (Neth.)

Curaçao

Bonaire

NETHERLANDS ANTILLES

*Caracas

Maracaibo

Lago de Maracaibo

VENEZUELA

Port of Spain

TRINIDAD AND TOBAGO

Orinoco

Georgetown

GUYANA

SURINAME

COLOMBIA

*Bogotá

Orinoco

BRAZIL

GULF OF MEXICO

Havana

CUBA

HAITI DOMINICAN REPUBLIC

NORTH AMERICA

JAMAICA

PUERTO RICO (U.S.)

MEXICO BELIZE
HONDURAS
GUATEMALA
EL SALVADOR NICARAGUA

CARIBBEAN SEA

Lesser Antilles

ATLANTIC OCEAN

COSTA RICA

PANAMA

Barranquilla Maracaibo Caracas

TRINIDAD AND TOBAGO

Orinoco

VENEZUELA

Georgetown Paramaribo

GUYANA SURINAM Cayenne FRENCH GUIANA

Medellín

Magdalena

Bogotá
COLOMBIA

Cali

Galapagos Islands (Ec.)

Quito
ECUADOR

Guayaquil

Putumayo

Japurá

Negro

Amazon

Manaus

Belém

Equator

Amazon

Juruá

Madeira

Tapajós

Tocantins

B R A Z I L

Fortaleza

PERU

Recife

Ucayali

Lima

Lake Titicaca

BOLIVIA

La Paz

Salvador

Goiânia

Brasília

Sucre

Belo Horizonte

PARAGUAY

Paraná

Rio de Janeiro

São Paulo

Tropic of Capricorn

Isla San Ambrosio (Chile)

Isla San Félix (Chile)

Asunción

Curitiba

Pôrto Alegre

Archipiélago Juan Fernández (Chile)

Córdoba

Rosario

Santiago

Buenos Aires

URUGUAY

Montevideo

Paraná

Río de la Plata

Concepción

A R G E N T I N A

C H I L E

PACIFIC OCEAN

N

Chiloé

Archipiélago de los Chonos

ATLANTIC OCEAN

★ National Capital

■ City over 1,000,000 population

▫ City under 1,000,000 population

FALKLAND ISLANDS (U.K.)

West Falkland

East Falkland

Strait of Magellan

Tierra del Fuego

South Georgia (U.K.)

0 200 400 600 800 1000 Miles

0 300 600 900 1200 1500 Kilometers

Copyright by Rand McNally & Co.
Lambert Azimuthal Equal Area Projection

Drake Passage

South Shetland Islands (U.K.)

South Orkney Islands (U.K.)

South Sandwich Islands (U.K.)

GULF OF MEXICO

NORTH AMERICA

MEXICO
BELIZE
GUATEMALA
HONDURAS
EL SALVADOR
NICARAGUA
COSTA RICA
PANAMA

Gulf of Honduras
Gulf of Panama

CUBA
Greater Antilles
JAMAICA
HAITI
DOMINICAN REPUBLIC
PUERTO RICO (U.S.)
Lesser Antilles

CARIBBEAN SEA

ATLANTIC OCEAN

TRINIDAD AND TOBAGO

Caracas

Llanos
Orinoco
VENEZUELA
GUYANA
SURINAM
FRENCH GUIANA
Cape Orange

Bogotá
COLOMBIA

Galapagos Islands (Ec.)

ECUADOR

Japurá
Putumayo
Negro
Amazon
Amazon
Manaus
Ilha de Marajó
Belém
Equator

Amazon Basin

Selvas

Juruá
Madeira
Tapajós
Tocantins

BRAZIL

Ucayali

Andes

PERU

Lima

Lake Titicaca

Cordillera Oriental

BOLIVIA

Mato Grosso Plateau

São Francisco

Recife

Brasília

Brazilian Highlands

Gran Chaco

PARAGUAY

Paraná

São Paulo

Rio de Janeiro

Tropic of Capricorn

Isla San Ambrosio (Chile)

Isla San Felix (Chile)

Atacama Desert

Andes

ARGENTINA

Paraná

URUGUAY

PACIFIC OCEAN

Archipiélago Juan Fernández (Chile)

Santiago

CHILE

Mt. Aconcagua 22,831 Ft. 6,959m

Buenos Aires

Río de la Plata

Pampas

N

Chiloé

San Matías Gulf
Península Valdés

ATLANTIC OCEAN

Patagonia

San Jorge Gulf

Point Medanoso

Grand Bay
Strait of Magellan
West Falkland
East Falkland

FALKLAND ISLANDS (U.K.)

Tierra del Fuego
Cape Horn

South Georgia (U.K.)

Drake Passage

South Shetland Islands (U.K.)
South Orkney Islands (U.K.)

South Sandwich Islands (U.K.)

Land Elevation

Meters	Feet
3,000	9,840
2,000	6,560
500	1,640
200	656
0	0

Water Depth

0	0
200	656
2,000	6,560

0 200 400 600 800 1000 Miles

0 300 600 900 1200 1500 Kilometers

Copyright by Rand McNally & Co.
Lambert Azimuthal Equal Area Projection

RAND MCNALLY

Europe: Political

ICELAND
⊛ Reykjavik

ATLANTIC OCEAN

FAROE ISLANDS (Den.)

NORWEGIAN SEA

NORWAY SWEDEN
⊛ Oslo
Stockholm ⊛

Vänern Vättern
Göteborg ⊡

Skagerrak

Gulf of Bothnia

BALTIC SEA

DENMARK
Copenhagen ⊛

LITHUANIA
Kaliningrad RUSSIA

SCOTLAND
Glasgow ⊡
UNITED
Edinburgh ⊡

NORTH SEA

Hamburg ■
Berlin ⊛
GERMANY
POLAND
Warsaw ⊛
Łódź ⊡
Wrocław ⊡

NORTHERN IRELAND
Belfast ⊡
KINGDOM

Dublin ⊛
IRELAND
Irish Sea
Liverpool ⊡ ■ Manchester
WALES
Birmingham ■ ENGLAND
Thames
Amsterdam ⊛
NETHERLANDS
The Hague ⊛
London ⊛

St. George's Channel

National Capital ⊛
City over 1,000,000 population ■
City under 1,000,000 population ⊡

Strait of Dover

English Channel

Brussels ⊛ ■ Cologne
BELGIUM
Luxembourg ⊛ LUX.
■ Frankfurt

Rhine
Elbe
Oder
Wisła

⊛ Prague
CZECH REPUBLIC
Kraków ⊡

SLOVAKIA

0 100 200 300 400 Miles
0 200 400 600 Kilometers
Copyright by Rand McNally & Co.
Lambert Conformal Conic Projection

⊛ Paris
FRANCE
Loire
Seine

Munich ■

Danube

Vienna ⊛ ⊛ Bratislava
AUSTRIA
Budapest ■
HUNGARY

Bordeaux ⊡

Lyon ⊡

Bern ⊛ ⊡ LIECH.
SWITZERLAND
SLOVENIA Ljubljana ⊛
■ Milan Zagreb ⊛ Belgrade ⊛

Toulouse ⊡

Rhône

Genoa ⊡
Po
CROATIA
SAN MARINO

ADRIATIC SEA

Bay of Biscay

Ebro

ANDORRA

Marseille ⊡

MONACO

Corsica (Fr.)

BOSNIA AND HERZEGOVINA
Sarajevo ⊛
SERBIA AND MONTENEGRO

PORTUGAL
Lisbon ⊛
Tagus
Madrid ⊛
SPAIN
■ Barcelona
Valencia ⊡
Seville ⊡

Rome ⊛
VATICAN CITY
ITALY

Naples ■

Skopje ⊛
ALBANIA MACEDONIA
Tiranë ⊛

Strait of Gibraltar
GIBRALTAR (U.K.)

Sardinia (It.)

Rabat ⊛

Algiers ⊛

AFRICA
MOROCCO ALGERIA

Tunis ⊛
TUNISIA

TYRRHENIAN SEA

Palermo ⊡
Sicily

MEDITERRANEAN

IONIAN SEA

Valletta ⊛ MALTA

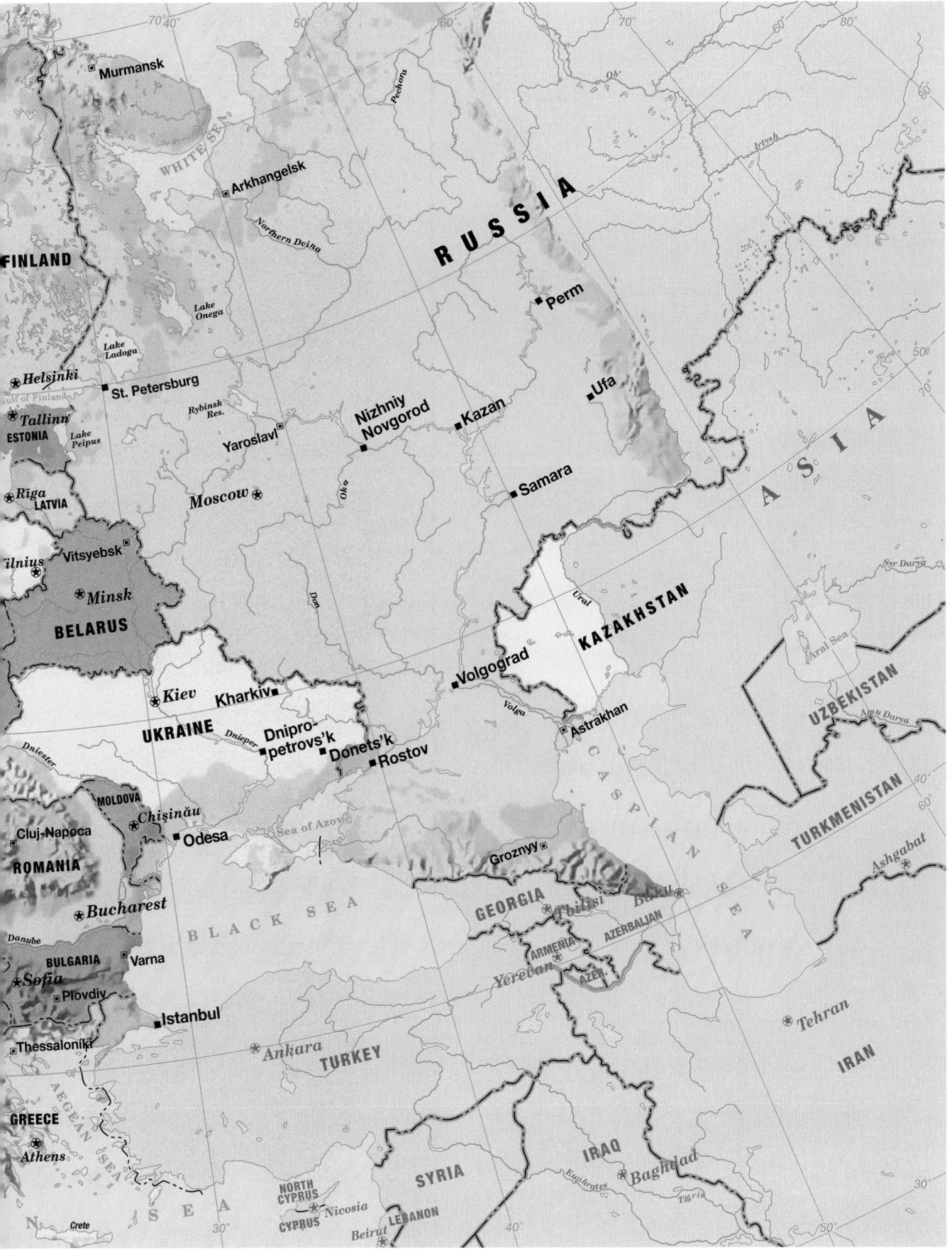

□ Murmansk

WHITE SEA

FINLAND

■ Arkhangelsk

Northern Dvina

R U S S I A

Pechora

Ob'

Irtysh

Lake
Onega

Lake
Ladoga

Helsinki

St. Petersburg

Rybinsk
Res.

Tallinn
ESTONIA

Lake
Peipus

Yaroslavl □

Gulf of Finland

Perm ■

Ufa ■

Nizhniy
Novgorod

Kazan ■

A S I A

Samara ■

Riga
LATVIA

Moscow ✪

Oka

Vilnius

Vitsyebsk □

Minsk

BELARUS

Don

Ural

KAZAKHSTAN

Aral Sea

Syr Darya

Volgograd ■

Kiev ✪

Kharkiv ■

Volga

UZBEKISTAN

UKRAINE

Dnieper

Dnipro-
petrovs'k

Donets'k ■

Astrakhan ■

Amu Darya

Dniester

Rostov ■

C A S P I A N

TURKMENISTAN

MOLDOVA

Chişinău ✪

Sea of Azov

Cluj-Napoca ■

Odesa ■

S E A

Ashgabat ✪

ROMANIA

Groznyy ■

Bucharest ✪

BLACK SEA

GEORGIA

Tbilisi ✪

Baku ✪

Danube

Yerevan

ARMENIA

AZERBAIJAN

BULGARIA

Varna ■

AZER.

Sofia ✪

Tehran ✪

Plovdiv □

Yerevan ✪

Istanbul ■

Ankara ✪

IRAN

Thessaloniki ■

TURKEY

AEGEAN SEA

GREECE

Athens ✪

Crete

NORTH
CYPRUS

Nicosia

SYRIA

IRAQ

Baghdad ✪

Euphrates

CYPRUS

LEBANON

Beirut ✪

Tigris

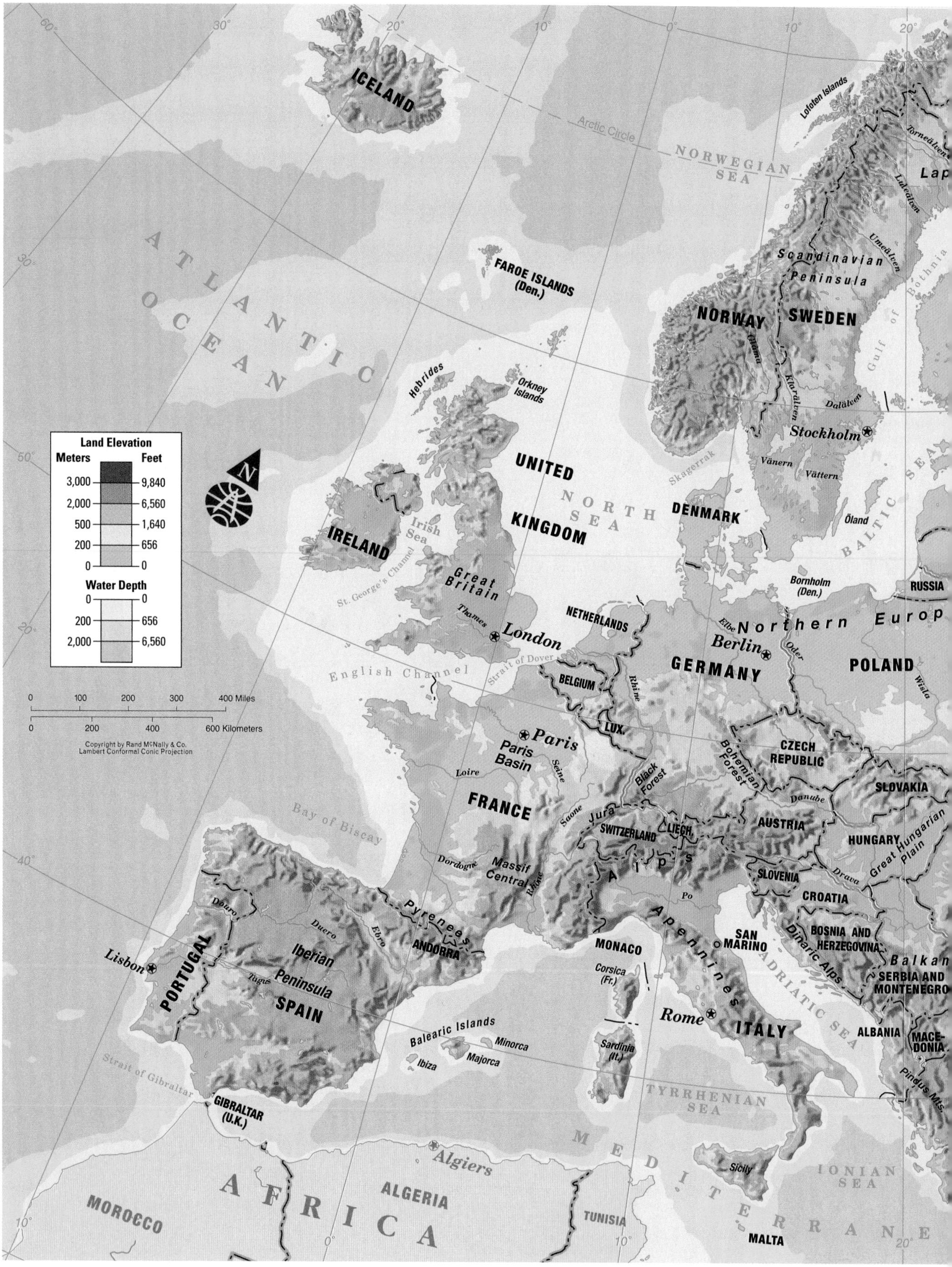

ICELAND

Arctic Circle

NORWEGIAN SEA

Lofoten Islands

Lap

FAROE ISLANDS (Den.)

ATLANTIC OCEAN

Scandinavian Peninsula

NORWAY SWEDEN

Gulf of Bothnia

Hebrides

Orkney Islands

UNITED KINGDOM

NORTH SEA

Skagerrak

DENMARK

Vänern Vättern

Stockholm

Land Elevation

Meters		Feet
3,000		9,840
2,000		6,560
500		1,640
200		656
0		0

Water Depth

0		0
200		656
2,000		6,560

IRELAND

Irish Sea

Great Britain

St. George's Channel

Thames

London

NETHERLANDS

BELGIUM

Rhine

LUX.

Öland

Bornholm (Den.)

BALTIC SEA

RUSSIA

Northern Europ

Berlin

Elbe

Oder

GERMANY

POLAND

Wisła

English Channel

Strait of Dover

N 0 100 200 300 400 Miles

0 200 400 600 Kilometers

Copyright by Rand McNally & Co.
Lambert Conformal Conic Projection

Paris

Paris Basin

Seine

Loire

FRANCE

Bay of Biscay

Saone

Black Forest

Jura

Danube

CZECH REPUBLIC

Bohemian Forest

SLOVAKIA

SWITZERLAND

LIECH

AUSTRIA

HUNGARY

Great Hungarian Plain

Rhône

A l p s

Massif Central

Dordogne

Pyrenees

ANDORRA

Ebro

Douro

Duero

Iberian Peninsula

PORTUGAL

Lisbon

Tagus

SPAIN

SLOVENIA

Po

Drava

CROATIA

SAN MARINO

Apennines

Dinaric Alps

Balkan

BOSNIA AND HERZEGOVINA

SERBIA AND MONTENEGRO

MONACO

Corsica (Fr.)

Rome

ITALY

ADRIATIC SEA

ALBANIA

MACE-DONIA

Balearic Islands

Minorca

Majorca

Ibiza

Sardinia (It.)

Pindus Mts.

Strait of Gibraltar

GIBRALTAR (U.K.)

Algiers

TYRRHENIAN SEA

Sicily

IONIAN SEA

MEDITERRANE

MOROCCO

AFRICA

ALGERIA

TUNISIA

MALTA

Murmansk

Kola
Peninsula
Ponoy

Mezen

Pechora

WHITE SEA

Northern Dvina

Ural Mountains

Ob'

Irtysh

FINLAND

Onega

Sukhona

Kama

A S I A

Lake
Onega

R U S S I A

Helsinki

Lake
Ladoga

Rybinsk
Res.

Gulf of Finland

ESTONIA

Lake
Peipus

Oka

* Moscow

LATVIA

Central
Russian
Upland

Khopër

Ural

KAZAKHSTAN

LITHUANIA

Plain

Don

Caspian Depression

BELARUS

Aral Sea

Neman

Pripyat

Volga

UZBEKISTAN

Kiev *

UKRAINE

Dnieper

Amu Darya

Syr Darya

Dniester

C A S P I A N

MOLDOVA

Carpathian Mts.

Sea of Azov

S E A

ROMANIA

Crimean
Peninsula

TURKMENISTAN

Transylvanian Alps

C a u c a s u s

Mt. Elbrus
18,510 Ft.
5,642m

Baku

Danube

GEORGIA

Peninsula

B L A C K   S E A

AZERBAIJAN

BULGARIA

ARMENIA

AZER.

* Tehran

Istanbul

IRAN

Mt. Olympus
9,570 Ft.
2,917m

TURKEY

GREECE

Euphrates

IRAQ

AEGEAN SEA

SYRIA

Tigris

Rhodes

NORTH
CYPRUS

Crete

CYPRUS

LEBANON

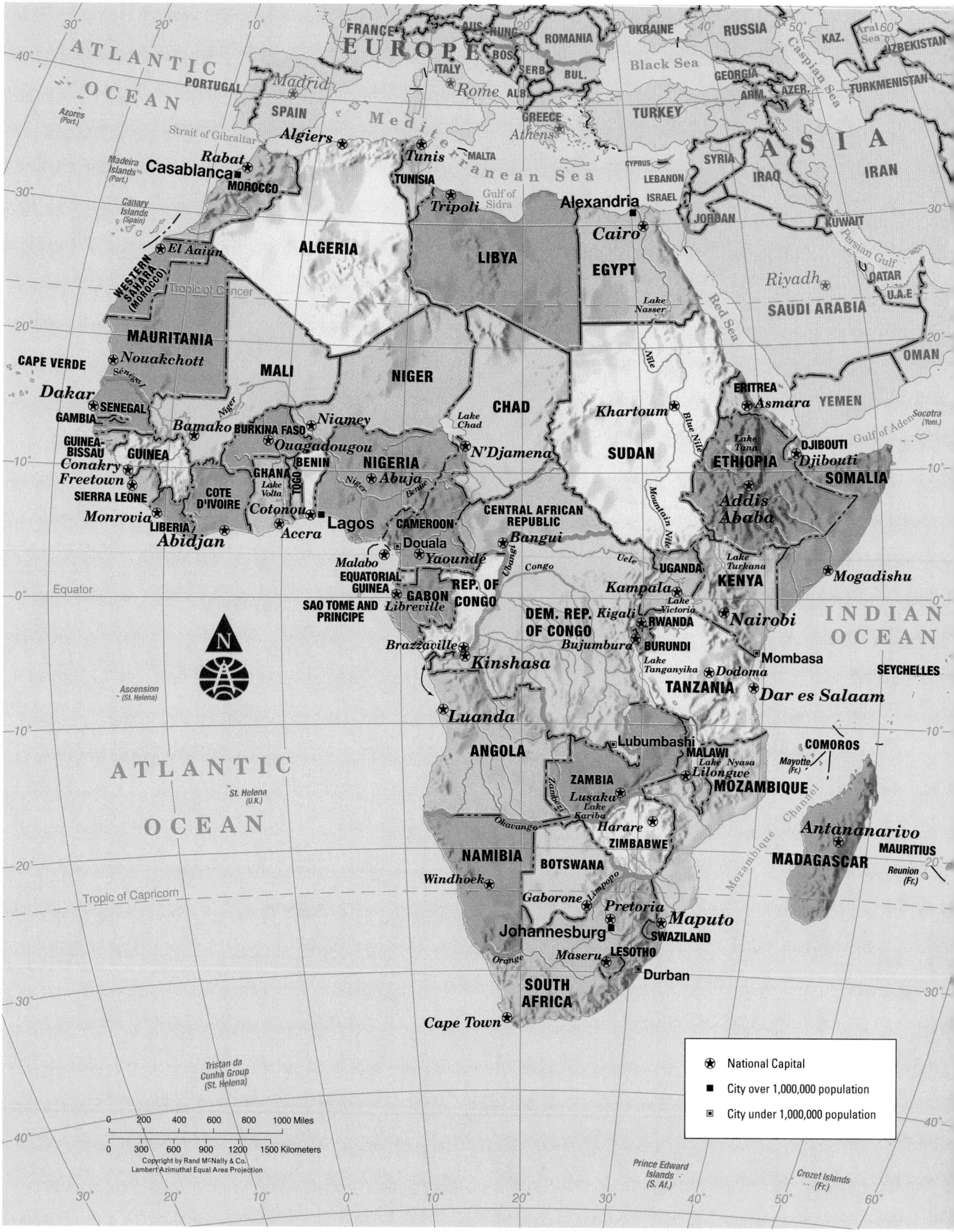

ATLANTIC OCEAN

PORTUGAL
Madrid
SPAIN
Strait of Gibraltar
Azores (Port.)

EUROPE
FRANCE
AUS. HUNG. ROMANIA UKRAINE RUSSIA KAZ.
ITALY BOS. SERB. BUL. Aral Sea UZBEKISTAN
Rome ALB. Black Sea GEORGIA TURKMENISTAN
GREECE ARM. AZER. Caspian Sea
Athens TURKEY
MALTA CYPRUS SYRIA ASIA
LEBANON IRAQ IRAN
ISRAEL
JORDAN KUWAIT

Algiers
Tunis
TUNISIA
Rabat
Casablanca
MOROCCO
Tripoli
Gulf of Sidra
Alexandria
Cairo
Riyadh
QATAR
U.A.E.
SAUDI ARABIA
OMAN

Madeira Islands (Port.)
Canary Islands (Spain)
El Aaiún
WESTERN SAHARA (MOROCCO)
Tropic of Cancer

ALGERIA
LIBYA
EGYPT
Lake Nasser
Red Sea
Nile

CAPE VERDE
Nouakchott
MAURITANIA
MALI
NIGER
CHAD
Khartoum
SUDAN
Lake Tana
ERITREA
Asmara
YEMEN
Gulf of Aden
Socotra (Yem.)
DJIBOUTI
Djibouti

Dakar
Senegal
SENEGAL
GAMBIA
GUINEA-BISSAU
Conakry
Freetown
SIERRA LEONE
Monrovia
LIBERIA
GUINEA
Bamako
BURKINA FASO
Niamey
Ouagadougou
GHANA
Lake Volta
COTE D'IVOIRE
TOGO
BENIN
Cotonou
Accra
Abidjan
Lagos
Niger
NIGERIA
Abuja
Benue
CAMEROON
Douala
Yaoundé
Malabo
EQUATORIAL GUINEA
SAO TOME AND PRINCIPE
GABON
Libreville
N'Djamena
Lake Chad
CENTRAL AFRICAN REPUBLIC
Bangui
Ubangi
REP. OF CONGO
Congo
Uele
DEM. REP. OF CONGO
Kinshasa
Brazzaville
Mountain Nile
ETHIOPIA
Addis Ababa
SOMALIA
Mogadishu
UGANDA
Kampala
Lake Turkana
Lake Victoria
Kigali
RWANDA
Bujumbura
BURUNDI
KENYA
Nairobi
Mombasa
Blue Nile

Equator

N

Ascension (St. Helena)

ATLANTIC OCEAN

St. Helena (U.K.)

Luanda
ANGOLA
Lake Tanganyika
Dodoma
TANZANIA
Dar es Salaam
SEYCHELLES
Lubumbashi
MALAWI
Lilongwe
ZAMBIA
Lake Nyasa
COMOROS
Mayotte (Fr.)
Lusaka
Lake Kariba
Zambezi
Okavango
Harare
ZIMBABWE
MOZAMBIQUE
INDIAN OCEAN
Antananarivo
MAURITIUS
MADAGASCAR
Mozambique Channel
Reunion (Fr.)

NAMIBIA
BOTSWANA
Windhoek
Gaborone
Limpopo
Pretoria
Maputo
Johannesburg
SWAZILAND
Maseru
LESOTHO
Durban
Orange
SOUTH AFRICA
Cape Town

Tropic of Capricorn

Tristan da Cunha Group (St. Helena)

	200	400	600	800	1000 Miles
0					
0	300	600	900	1200	1500 Kilometers

Copyright by Rand McNally & Co.
Lambert Azimuthal Equal Area Projection

Prince Edward Islands (S. Af.)
Crozet Islands (Fr.)

⊛ National Capital
■ City over 1,000,000 population
▫ City under 1,000,000 population

RAND MCNALLY

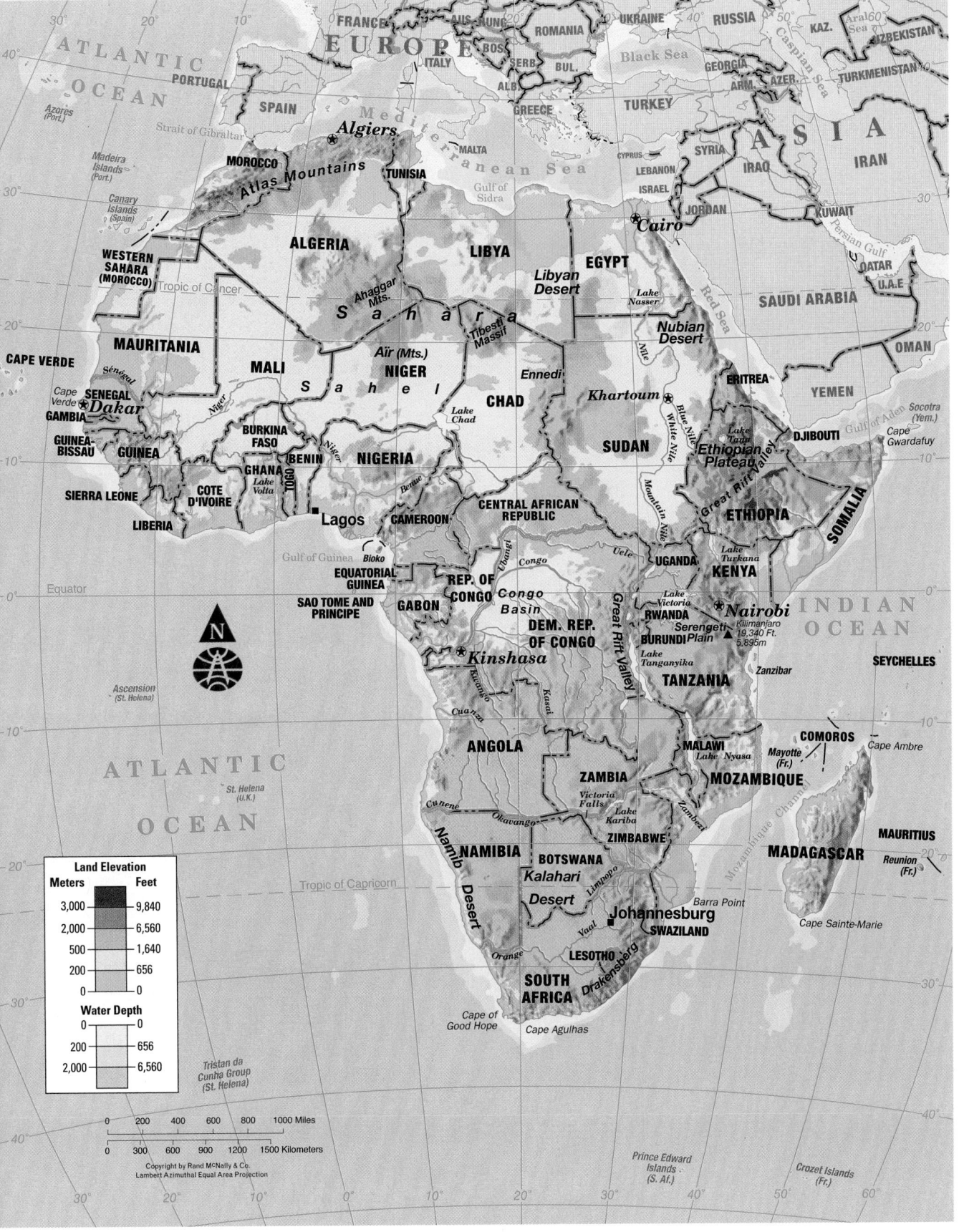

ATLANTIC
OCEAN

Azores
(Port.)

Madeira
Islands
(Port.)

Canary
Islands
(Spain)

Strait of Gibraltar

PORTUGAL

SPAIN

FRANCE

EUROPE

ITALY

AUS. HUNG.
BOS.
SERB.
ALB.

ROMANIA

UKRAINE

RUSSIA

Black Sea

BUL.

GREECE

MALTA

TURKEY

CYPRUS

GEORGIA

AZER.
ARM.

RUSSIA

KAZ.

Aral
Sea

Caspian Sea

UZBEKISTAN

TURKMENISTAN

ASIA

IRAN

SYRIA

LEBANON
ISRAEL

IRAQ

JORDAN

KUWAIT

Persian Gulf

QATAR
U.A.E.

OMAN

Mediterranean Sea

Gulf of
Sidra

Algiers

MOROCCO

Atlas Mountains

TUNISIA

ALGERIA

LIBYA

EGYPT

Cairo

WESTERN
SAHARA
(MOROCCO)

Tropic of Cancer

Sahara

Ahaggar
Mts.

Libyan
Desert

Lake
Nasser

SAUDI ARABIA

Red Sea

Nubian
Desert

Nile

CAPE VERDE

MAURITANIA

MALI

Sahel

Air (Mts.)

Tibesti
Massif

Ennedi

NIGER

Khartoum

ERITREA

YEMEN

Socotra
(Yem.)

Cape
Gwardafuy

Gulf of Aden

DJIBOUTI

Senegal

Cape
Verde

Dakar

SENEGAL

GAMBIA

GUINEA-
BISSAU

GUINEA

Niger

CHAD

SUDAN

Lake
Chad

White Nile

Blue Nile

Lake
Tana

Ethiopian
Plateau

BURKINA
FASO

BENIN

NIGERIA

GHANA

TOGO

Lake
Volta

SIERRA LEONE

COTE
D'IVOIRE

Niger

Benue

CENTRAL AFRICAN
REPUBLIC

Mountain Nile

ETHIOPIA

Great Rift Valley

SOMALIA

LIBERIA

Lagos

CAMEROON

Gulf of Guinea

Bioko

EQUATORIAL
GUINEA

SAO TOME AND
PRINCIPE

REP. OF
CONGO

GABON

Ubangi

Congo

Uele

Congo
Basin

UGANDA

Lake
Turkana

KENYA

Nairobi

Lake
Victoria

Equator

N

Ascension
(St. Helena)

Kinshasa

Kwango

Kasai

DEM. REP.
OF CONGO

Great Rift Valley

RWANDA

BURUNDI

Serengeti
Plain

Kilimanjaro
19,340 Ft.
5,895m

INDIAN
OCEAN

SEYCHELLES

Cuanza

Lake
Tanganyika

TANZANIA

Zanzibar

ATLANTIC

St. Helena
(U.K.)

Kwanza

ANGOLA

MALAWI

Lake
Nyasa

COMOROS

Mayotte
(Fr.)

Cape Ambre

OCEAN

Cunene

Okavango

ZAMBIA

Victoria
Falls

Lake
Kariba

Zambezi

MOZAMBIQUE

MAURITIUS

Reunion
(Fr.)

Namib
Desert

NAMIBIA

BOTSWANA

Kalahari
Desert

ZIMBABWE

Limpopo

MADAGASCAR

Mozambique Channel

Tropic of Capricorn

Orange

Vaal

Johannesburg

SWAZILAND

Barra Point

Cape Sainte-Marie

LESOTHO

Drakensberg

SOUTH
AFRICA

Cape of
Good Hope

Cape Agulhas

Tristan da
Cunha Group
(St. Helena)

Prince Edward
Islands
(S. Af.)

Crozet Islands
(Fr.)

Land Elevation

Meters		Feet
3,000		9,840
2,000		6,560
500		1,640
200		656
0		0

Water Depth

0		0
200		656
2,000		6,560

0	200	400	600	800	1000 Miles

0	300	600	900	1200	1500 Kilometers

Copyright by Rand McNally & Co.
Lambert Azimuthal Equal Area Projection

RAND McNALLY

ATLANTIC OCEAN

ARCTIC OCEAN

ICELAND

FAROE ISLANDS (Den.)

SVALBARD (Nor.)

Spitsbergen (Nor.)

Franz Josef Land

Severnaya Zemlya

Novaya Zemlya

Barents Sea

Kara Sea

Arctic Circle

Norwegian Sea

NORWAY

SWEDEN

FINLAND

UNITED KINGDOM

IRELAND

London

Paris

PORTUGAL

SPAIN

FRANCE

DENMARK

GERMANY

NETH.

BEL.

LUX.

SWITZ.

AUSTRIA

CZECH

SLOVAKIA

POLAND

ESTONIA

LATVIA

LITH.

BELARUS

Moscow

Kiev

UKRAINE

MOLDOVA

ROMANIA

HUNGARY

CROATIA

SLOVENIA

ITALY

BOS.

SERB.

MONT.

ALBANIA

MACEDONIA

BULGARIA

GREECE

Danube

Adriatic Sea

MONACO

ANDORRA

GIBRALTAR (U.K.)

MOROCCO

ALGERIA

TUNISIA

LIBYA

Mediterranean Sea

Volga

Ob'

Irtysh

Ishim

Ob'

Yenisey

Pechora

R U S S I A

Yekaterinburg

Chelyabinsk

Novosibirsk

Omsk

Astana

KAZAKHSTAN

Aral Sea

Syr Darya

Lake Balkhash

Almaty

Bishkek

KYRGYZSTAN

Tashkent

UZBEKISTAN

TURKMENISTAN

Ashgabat

Dushanbe

TAJIKISTAN

Caspian Sea

Black Sea

İstanbul

İzmir

Ankara

TURKEY

Yerevan

Tbilisi

GEORGIA

ARM.

AZER.

Baku

N. CYPRUS

CYPRUS

LEBANON

SYRIA

Damascus

Jerusalem

ISRAEL

Amman

JORDAN

Cairo

EGYPT

Nile

CHAD

SUDAN

Nile

Red Sea

Blue Nile

ERITREA

DJIBOUTI

ETHIOPIA

SOMALIA

Gulf of Aden

Socotra (Yem.)

YEMEN

SAUDI ARABIA

Riyadh

Jiddah

Mecca

BAHRAIN

QATAR

Abu Dhabi

U.A.E.

Muscat

OMAN

Gulf of Oman

Persian Gulf

KUWAIT

Kuwait

IRAQ

Baghdad

Euphrates

Tigris

Tabriz

Tehran

Eşfahān

IRAN

Mashhad

Kabul

AFGHANISTAN

Islamabad

Lahore

PAKISTAN

Karachi

Indus

Delhi

New Delhi

NEPAL

Kathmandu

Brahmaputra

Ganges

Ganges

Godavari

INDIA

Ahmadābād

Mumbai (Bombay)

Hyderābād

Bangalore

Kolkata (Calcutta)

Bay of Bengal

Chennai (Madras)

Lakshadweep (India)

Arabian Sea

MALDIVES

SRI LANKA

Colombo

INDIAN OCEAN

DEM. REP. OF THE CONGO (ZAIRE)

UGANDA

RWANDA

BURUNDI

KENYA

TANZANIA

ZAMBIA

MALAWI

MOZAMBIQUE

N

0   200   400   600   800 Miles

0   200 400 600 800 1000 Kilometers

Copyright by Rand McNally & Co.
Lambert Azimuthal Equal Area Projection

National Capital

■ City over 1,000,000 population

▫ City under 1,000,000 population

PACIFIC OCEAN

Bering Sea

ALEUTIAN ISLANDS (U.S.)

Kamchatka Peninsula

Petropavlovsk-Kamchatskiy

Sea of Okhotsk

Sakhalin

Kuril Islands

Tropic of Cancer

Hokkaido

Honshu

Tokyo

JAPAN

Osaka

Shikoku

Kyushu

Sea of Japan

Vladivostok

NORTH KOREA

Pyongyang

Seoul

SOUTH KOREA

Pusan

Harbin

Changchun

Shenyang

Beijing

Tianjin

Yellow Sea

Shanghai

East China Sea

NORTHERN MARIANA ISLANDS (U.S.)

A S I A

Angara

Kraynoyarsk

Irkutsk

Lena

Ulaanbaatar

MONGOLIA

Lake Baikal

Amur

Yana

New Siberian Islands

East Siberian Sea

Laptev Sea

Lena

Lanzhou

Huang

Huang

Xi'an

Nanjing

Wuhan

CHINA

Chengdu

Chang (Yangtze)

Chongqing

Taipei

TAIWAN

Guangzhou

Hong Kong

Luzon Strait

Luzon

PHILIPPINES

Samar

Mindanao

Philippine Sea

GUAM (U.S.)

FEDERATED STATES OF MICRONESIA

PALAU

Equator

BHUTAN

BNGL.

Dhaka

Chittagong

MYANMAR

Brahmaputra

LAOS

Hanoi

Hainan Island

Gulf of Tonkin

South China Sea

Manila

Vientiane

Yangon

THAILAND

Bangkok

Mekong

CAMBODIA

VIETNAM

Phnom Penh

Ho Chi Minh City

Sulu Sea

Celebes Sea

New Guinea

PAPUA NEW GUINEA

Andaman Islands (India)

Andaman Sea

Gulf of Thailand

Nicobar Islands (India)

MALAYSIA

Medan

Kuala Lumpur

Singapore

Sumatra

Bandar Seri Begawan

BRUNEI

MALAYSIA

Borneo

Celebes

Ceram

Banda Sea

INDONESIA

Arafura Sea

Gulf of Carpentaria

AUSTRALIA

Coral Sea

Jakarta

Bandung

Java

Java Sea

Dili

EAST TIMOR

Timor

Timor Sea

ATLANTIC OCEAN

ARCTIC OCEAN

ICELAND
IRELAND
London
UNITED KINGDOM
FAROE ISLANDS (Den.)
Arctic Circle
Barents Sea
Severnaya Zemlya

PORTUGAL
SPAIN
GIBRALTAR (U.K.)
MOROCCO
ANDORRA
Monaco
FRANCE
NETH.
BEL.
LUX.
DENMARK
NORWAY
SWEDEN
FINLAND
North Sea
ESTONIA
LATVIA
LITH.
Moscow
Novaya Zemlya
Kara Sea
Yamal Pen.

ALGERIA
ITALY
GERMANY
CZECH
AUSTRIA
SWITZ.
SLOVAKIA
POLAND
BELARUS
UKRAINE
Volga
Ural Mountains
Ob
Ishim
West Siberian Lowland
Yenisey

TUNISIA
HUNGARY
SLO.
CRO.
BOS.
SERB.
ALB. MAC.
ROMANIA
BULGARIA
GREECE
Black Sea
Caspian Depression
Astana
Irtysh
KAZAKHSTAN
Novosibirsk
Ob

LIBYA
Mediterranean Sea
Ankara
TURKEY
GEORGIA
Caucasus
ARM.
AZER.
Caspian Sea
Aral Sea
Syr Darya
Lake Balkhash
Tian Shan

N. CYPRUS
CYPRUS
LEBANON
SYRIA
ISRAEL
Cairo
Nile
Sinai Pen.
JORDAN
IRAQ
Tigris
Euphrates
Tehran
Dasht-e Kavir
IRAN
Zagros Mts.
UZBEKISTAN
TURKMENISTAN
Amu Darya
KYRGYZSTAN
TAJIKISTAN
Pamirs
Tarim Basin
Altun Sh.
Kunlun Mts.

EGYPT
An-Nafud
SAUDI ARABIA
KUWAIT
Persian Gulf
BAHRAIN
QATAR
AFGHANISTAN
Hindu Kush
PAKISTAN
Indus
HIMALAYAS

CHAD
SUDAN
Red Sea
Arabian Peninsula
U.A.E.
Gulf of Oman
New Delhi
Thar Desert
Ganges
NEPAL
Mt. Everest 29,035 Ft. 8,850m

ERITREA
Rub Al-Khali
OMAN
INDIA

YEMEN
DJIBOUTI
ETHIOPIA
Gulf of Aden
Mumbai (Bombay)
Godavari
Deccan Plateau
Western Ghats
Eastern Ghats
Bay of Bengal

DEM. REP. OF THE CONGO (ZAIRE)
UGANDA
KENYA
SOMALIA
Socotra (Yem.)
Arabian Sea

RWANDA
BURUNDI
N

TANZANIA

ZAMBIA
MALAWI
MOZAMBIQUE

Lakshadweep (India)
SRI LANKA

MALDIVES

INDIAN OCEAN

0 200 400 600 800 Miles
0 200 400 600 800 1000 Kilometers
Copyright by Rand McNally & Co.
Lambert Azimuthal Equal Area Projection

RAND McNALLY

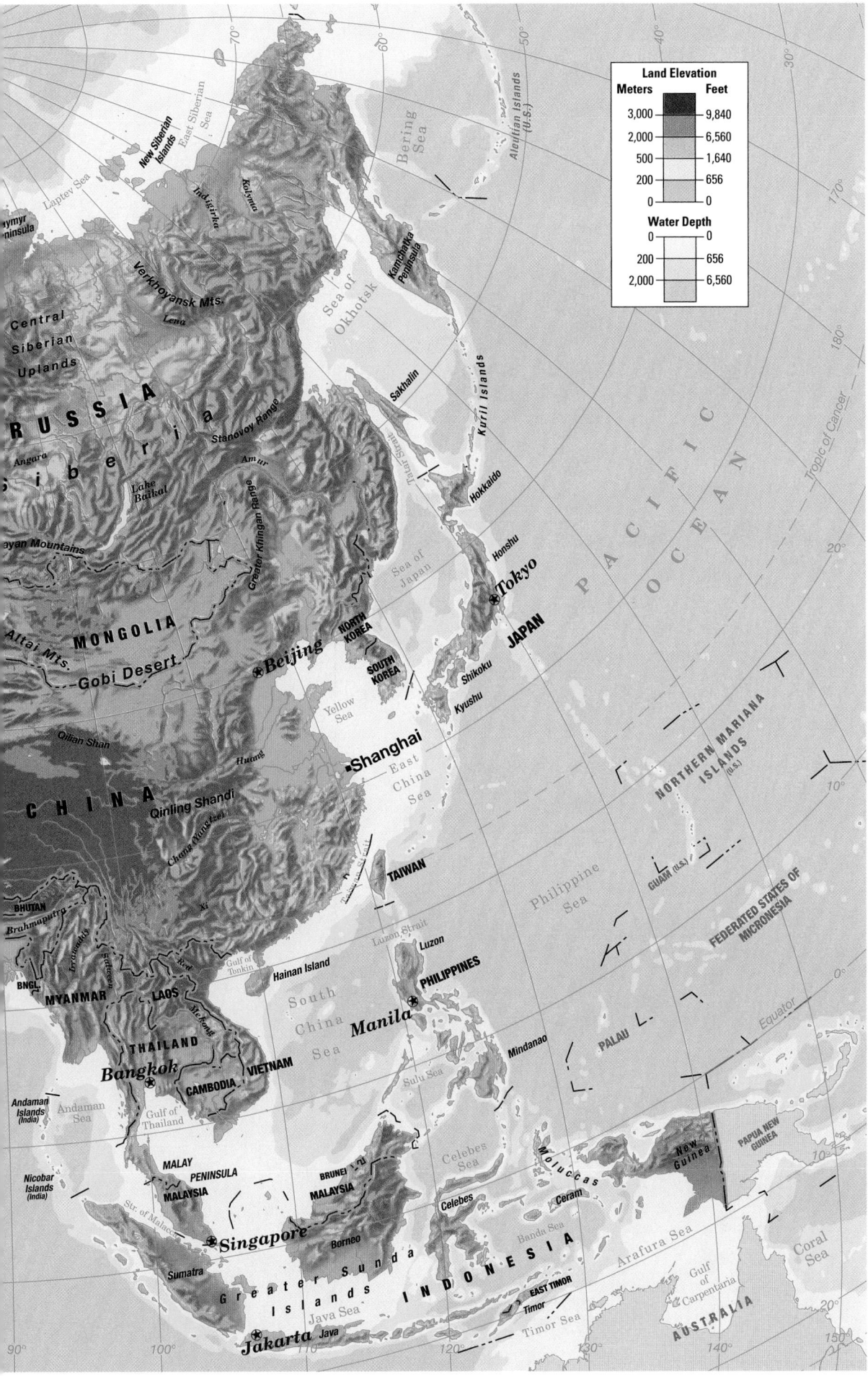

Land Elevation

Meters		Feet
3,000		9,840
2,000		6,560
500		1,640
200		656
0		0

Water Depth

0		0
200		656
2,000		6,560

New Siberian Islands
East Siberian Sea
Laptev Sea
Indigirka
Taymyr Peninsula
Kolyma
Kamchatka Peninsula
Central Siberian Uplands
Verkhoyansk Mts.
Lena
Sea of Okhotsk
Aleutian Islands (U.S.)
Bering Sea

RUSSIA
Siberia
Angara
Stanovoy Range
Amur
Lake Baikal
Sakhalin
Kuril Islands
Tatar Strait
Hokkaido
PACIFIC OCEAN

ayan Mountains
Greater Khingan Range
Sea of Japan
Honshu
Tokyo
JAPAN

Altai Mts.
MONGOLIA
Gobi Desert
Beijing
NORTH KOREA
SOUTH KOREA
Shikoku
Kyushu

Qilian Shan
Yellow Sea
Shanghai
East China Sea

CHINA
Qinling Shandi
Huang
Chang (Yangtze)

NORTHERN MARIANA ISLANDS (U.S.)

Tropic of Cancer

GUAM (U.S.)

FEDERATED STATES OF MICRONESIA

BHUTAN
Brahmaputra
TAIWAN
Philippine Sea

BNGL.
MYANMAR
Irrawaddy
Salween
LAOS
Red
Xi
Gulf of Tonkin
Hainan Island
Luzon Strait
Luzon
PHILIPPINES
PALAU

THAILAND
Mekong
VIETNAM
South China Sea
Manila
Mindanao
Equator

Bangkok
CAMBODIA
Sulu Sea

Andaman Islands (India)
Andaman Sea
Gulf of Thailand

Nicobar Islands (India)
MALAY PENINSULA
MALAYSIA
Str. of Malacca
BRUNEI
MALAYSIA
Celebes Sea
Moluccas
New Guinea
PAPUA NEW GUINEA
Ceram

Singapore
Borneo
Celebes
Banda Sea
Arafura Sea
Coral Sea

Sumatra
Greater Sunda Islands
INDONESIA
Gulf of Carpentaria

Jakarta
Java
Java Sea
EAST TIMOR
Timor
Timor Sea
AUSTRALIA

Australia and Oceania

CHINA

Taipei
TAIWAN

Luzon Strait

Luzon

Manila
PHILIPPINES

Mindoro

Mindanao

South China Sea

Sulu Sea

Celebes Sea

Celebes

Halmahera

Moluccas

Ceram

INDONESIA

Banda Sea

Timor

EAST TIMOR

Timor Sea

Philippine Sea

GUAM
(U.S.)

NORTHERN MARIANA ISLANDS
(U.S.)

PALAU

FEDERATED STATES OF MICRONESIA

M I C R O N E S I A

MARSHALL ISLANDS

NAURU

KIRIBATI

TUVALU

SOLOMON ISLANDS

M E L A N E S I A

Bismarck Sea

New Guinea

▲ Mount Wilhelm 14,793 Ft. 4,509m

PAPUA NEW GUINEA
⊛ *Port Moresby*

Solomon Sea

VANUATU

NEW CALEDONIA
(FR.)

New Caledonia

Coral Sea

Torres Strait

Cape York Peninsula

Gulf of Carpentaria

Arafura Sea

NORFOLK ISLAND
(Aust.)

P A C I F I C

O C E A N

P O L Y N E S I A

Hawaiian Islands

Hawaii

Tropic of Cancer

Equator

Line Islands

Kiritimati

TOKELAU (N.Z.)

SAMOA

AMERICAN SAMOA

WALLIS AND FUTUNA
(FR.)

FIJI

TONGA

Koro Sea

Marquesas Is.

FRENCH POLYNESIA

Tuamotu Archipelago

Tahiti

Society Islands

Austral Is.

Tropic of Capricorn

PITCAIRN
(U.K.)

Northern Cook Islands

COOK ISLANDS
(N.Z.)

Southern Cook Islands

NIUE
(N.Z.)

Kermadec Islands
(N.Z.)

Chatham Islands

North Island

NEW ZEALAND
⊛ *Wellington*

South Island

Tasman Sea

AUSTRALIA

GREAT DIVIDING RANGE

Great Barrier Reef

■ Brisbane

■ Sydney
⊛ Canberra

■ Melbourne

Tasmania

Bass Strait

Murray

Darling

GREAT VICTORIA DESERT

Great Sandy Desert

Gibson Desert

Kimberley Plateau

Great Australian Bight

International Date Line

N

Land Elevation

Meters	Feet
3,000	9,840
2,000	6,560
500	1,640
200	656
0	0

Water Depth

0	0
200	656
2,000	6,560

⊛ National Capital
■ City over 1,000,000 population
□ City under 1,000,000 population

0   200   400   600   800 Miles
0   200 400 600 800 1000 Kilometers
Copyright by Rand McNally & Co.
Lambert Azimuthal Equal Area Projection

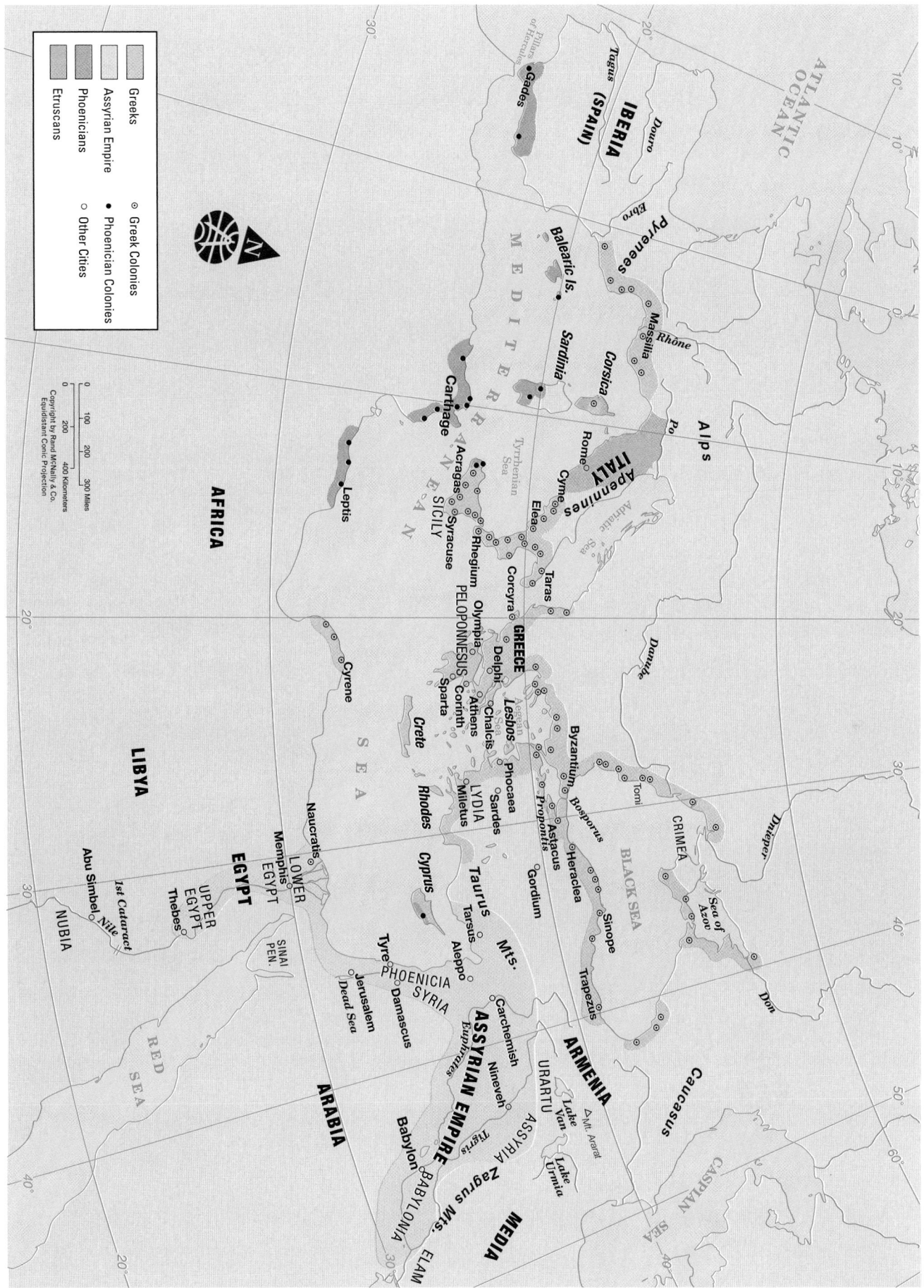

Greeks
Assyrian Empire
Phoenicians
Etruscans

⊙ Greek Colonies
● Phoenician Colonies
○ Other Cities

Copyright by Rand McNally & Co.
Equidistant Conic Projection

0   100   200   300 Miles
0   200   400 Kilometers

ATLANTIC OCEAN

Pillars of Hercules
Gades
IBERIA (SPAIN)
Tagus
Douro
Ebro
Pyrenees
Balearic Is.
Sardinia
Corsica
Massilia
Rhône
Alps
Po
Rome
ITALY
Apennines
Cyme
Elea
Adriatic Sea
Danube
MEDITERRANEAN SEA
Tyrrhenian Sea
Carthage
Acragas
SICILY
Syracuse
Rhegium
Leptis
Taras
Corcyra
Olympia
PELOPONNESUS
Delphi
Sparta Corinth
Athens
Chalcis
GREECE
Lesbos
Aegean Sea
Phocaea
Byzantium
Propontis
Bosporus
Astacus
Heraclea
Sinope
Trapezus
BLACK SEA
CRIMEA
Sea of Azov
Don
Dnieper
Tomi
Danube
AFRICA
LIBYA
Cyrene
Crete
Rhodes
Miletus
LYDIA
Sardes
Gordium
Taurus Mts.
Tarsus
Cyprus
Carchemish
Nineveh
ASSYRIA
URARTU
ARMENIA
Lake Van
Lake Urmia
△ Mt. Ararat
Caucasus
CASPIAN SEA
Naucratis
Memphis
LOWER EGYPT
EGYPT
UPPER EGYPT
Thebes
1st Cataract
Abu Simbel
Nile
NUBIA
SINAI PEN.
Jerusalem
Dead Sea
Tyre
PHOENICIA
Damascus
SYRIA
Aleppo
ASSYRIAN EMPIRE
Babylon
BABYLONIA
Euphrates
Tigris
Zagros Mts.
ELAM
MEDIA
ARABIA
RED SEA
N

RAND McNALLY

Adriatic
Sea

ILLYRIS

Strymon

Axius

Philippi

Pella

MACEDON

CHALCIDICE

Haliacmon

Mt. Olympus

EPIRUS

HESTIAEOTIS

Corcyra

THESSALY

Sciathus

Icus

Peparethus

DOLOPIANS

THESSALIOTIS

Ionian
Sea

Leucas

ACARNANIA

MALIS

Thermopylae

LOCRIS

EUBOEA

AETOLIA

DORIS

Cephallenia

Ithaca

OZOLIAN
LOCRIS

PHOCIS

Delphi

BOEOTIA

Thebes

Chalcis

Delium

Gulf of
Corinth

Plataea

ATTICA

Marathon

ACHAEA

MEGARIS

Megara

Athens

Piraeus

ELIS

Olympia

Zacynthus

ARCADIA

Mycenae

Tiryns

ARGOLIS

Elon

Corinth

Troezen

Salamis

Aegina

Ceos

Cythnos

Hydrea

Megalopolis

MESSENIA

CYNURIA

Myrtoan
Sea

Melos

Sparta

LACONIA

MEDITERRANEAN

Cythera

N

0   25   50   75   100 Miles

0   50   100 Kilometers

Copyright by Rand McNally & Co.
Lambert Comformal Conic Projection

THRACE

Hebrus

Thasos

Samothrace

Imbros

Myrina

Lemnos

Tenedos

Abydus

TROAS

HELLESPONTINE
PHRYGIA

Hellespont

Black Sea

Byzantium **Chalcedon**

Bosporus

Propontis

BITHYNIA

Sangarius

Cyzicus

Rhyndacus

**Heraclea
Pontica**

40°

*Aegean
Sea*

Lesbos

Scyros

Chios

AEOLIS

Pergamum

LYDIA

Phocaea

Smyrna

Sardes

PHRYGIA

Andros

IONIA

Samos

Ephesus **Tralles**

Maeander

PISIDIA

Tenos

Icaria

Samos

CARIA

Miletus

Mylasa

PAMPHYLLIA

Myconos

Delos

Leros

…*riphos*

Paros

Naxos

Calymnos

Siphnos

Cos

Cimolos

Polyaegos

Amorgos

Nisyros

Ios

LYCIA

Thera

Astypalaea

Telos

Rhodes

Anaphe

Camirus

Lindus

Rhodes

36°

SPORADES

CYCLADES

Cretan Sea

Carpathos

Knossos

CRETE

SEA

26°

28°

30°

26°

28°

MEDITERRANEAN
SEA

Salamis

CYPRUS

Paphos

35°

34°

30°

RAND McNALLY

Alexander's Empire, 336–323 B.C.

Dnieper

Don

Volga

Ural

Adriatic Sea

Danube

THRACE

Black Sea

Sea of Azov

Caspian

CAUCASUS MOUNTAINS

MACEDON

PAPHLAGONIA

Sinope

Trapezus

Byzantium

Nicomedia

BITHYNIA

Ancyra

CAPPADOCIA

ARMENIA

Corcyra

EPIRUS

THESSALY

Pella

Lemnos

Pergamum

Lesbos

Cyzicus

PHRYGIA

Ionian Sea

Delphi

Thebes

Chios

Smyrna

Sardes

TAURUS MTS.

LYCAONIA

CILICIA

MEDIA

Athens

Ephesus

PISIDIA

Tarsus

Ecbatana

PELOPONNESUS

Corinth

Miletus

CARIA

ASSYRIA

ZAGROS MTS.

Megalopolis

Sparta

Antioch

MESOPOTAMIA

Tigris

Rhodes

Cyprus

Salamis

SYRIA

Palmyra

Euphrates

Babylon

Crete

Byblos

Damascus

MEDITERRANEAN SEA

Tyre

PHOENICIA

BABYLONIA

Cyrene

PALESTINE

CYRENAICA

Gaza

Jerusalem

Alexandria

Memphis

Alexander

SINAI

ARABIA

Route of Alexander

Oasis of Siwah

Nile

Red Sea

LIBYA

Thebes

Berenice

	Allied Territory
	Subject Territory
	Independent States
....	Route of Alexander

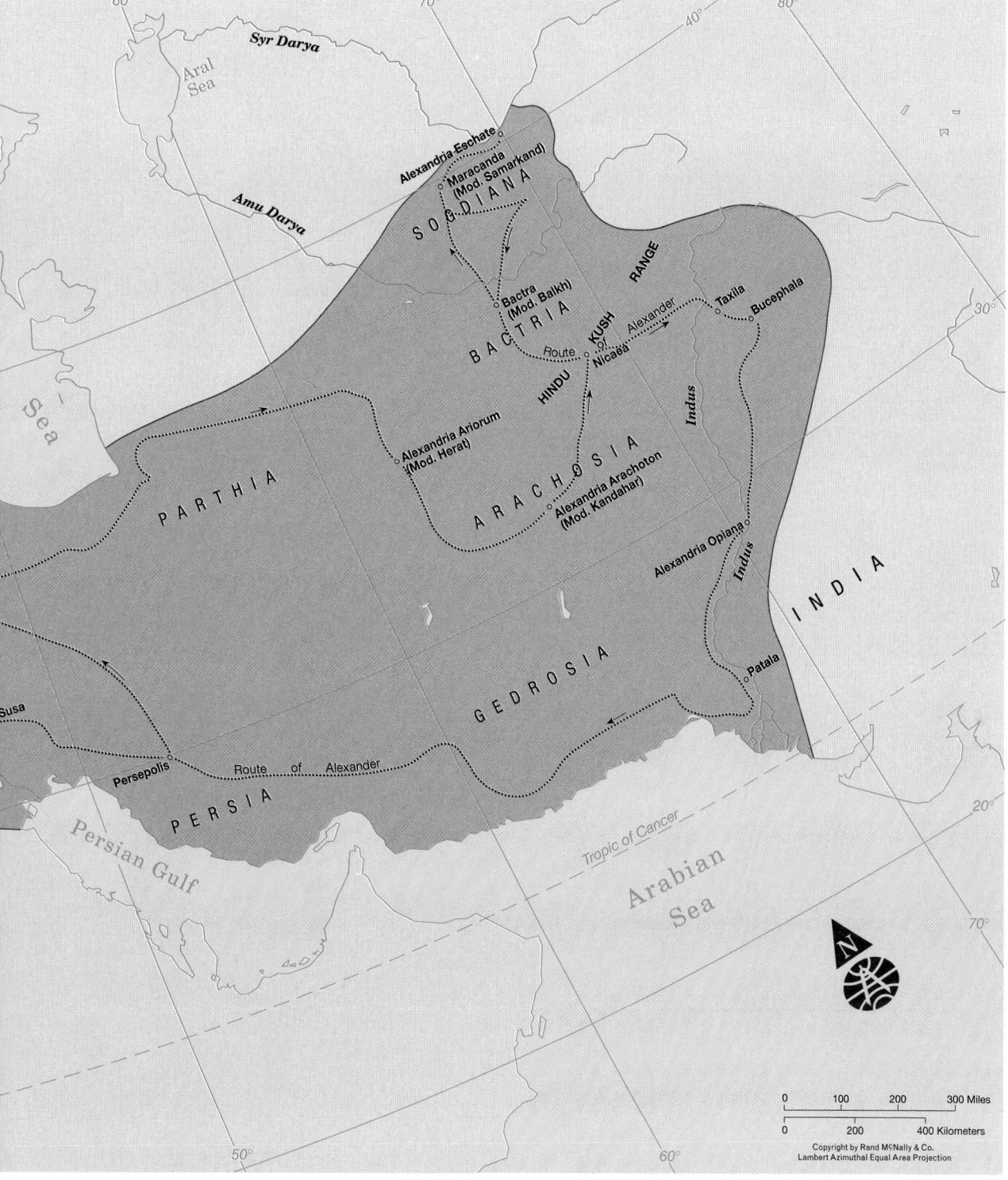

Aral Sea

Syr Darya

Amu Darya

Alexandria Eschate

Maracanda
(Mod. Samarkand)

SOGDIANA

Bactra
(Mod. Balkh)

BACTRIA

HINDU KUSH RANGE

Route of Alexander

Nicaea

Taxila

Bucephala

Alexandria Ariorum
(Mod. Herat)

Indus

ARACHOSIA

Alexandria Arachoton
(Mod. Kandahar)

PARTHIA

Sea

Alexandria Opiana

Indus

INDIA

GEDROSIA

Patala

Susa

Persepolis   Route   of   Alexander

PERSIA

Persian Gulf

Tropic of Cancer

Arabian
Sea

N

| 0 | 100 | 200 | 300 Miles |

| 0 | 200 | 400 Kilometers |

Copyright by Rand McNally & Co.
Lambert Azimuthal Equal Area Projection

60° 70° 40° 80° 30° 20° 70° 50° 60°

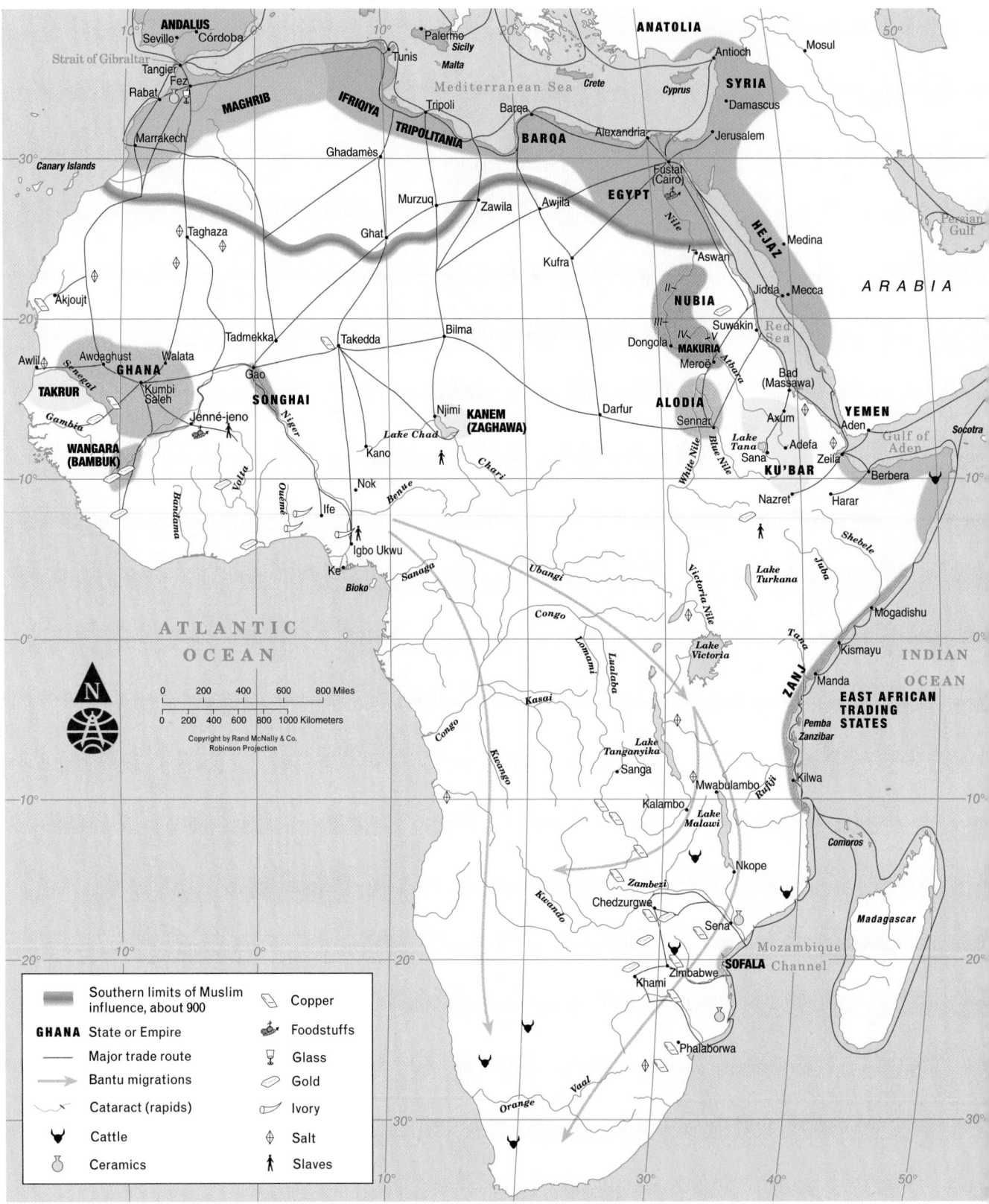

ANDALUS
Seville • Córdoba •
Strait of Gibraltar
Tangier
Fez
Rabat
Marrakech •
MAGHRIB
IFRIQIYA
Ghadamès •
TRIPOLITANIA
Canary Islands
Taghaza •
Ghat •
Murzuq •
Zawila •
Awjila •
Kufra •

ANATOLIA
• Mosul
• Antioch
SYRIA
• Damascus
Palermo •
Sicily
Malta
Mediterranean Sea
Crete
Cyprus
Jerusalem •
Tunis •
Tripoli •
Barqa •
BARQA
Alexandria •
Fustat (Cairo)
EGYPT
Nile
HEJAZ
• Medina
Aswan
• Jidda • Mecca
ARABIA
Persian Gulf

Akjoujt •
Awlil •
Senegal
GHANA
Awdaghust •
Walata •
TAKRUR
Kumbi Saleh
WANGARA (BAMBUK)
Gambia
Jenné-jeno •
SONGHAI
Gao •
Tadmekka •
Takedda •
Bilma •
NUBIA
Suwakin •
MAKURIA
Dongola •
Meroë •
Red Sea
Bad (Massawa)
YEMEN
Aden •
Socotra
Gulf of Aden

Njimi •
KANEM (ZAGHAWA)
Lake Chad
Kano •
Nok •
Ife •
Igbo Ukwu
Ke •
Bioko
Darfur •
ALODIA
Sennar •
Axum •
Adefa •
KU'BAR
Sana •
Nazret •
Harar •
Zeila •
Berbera •
Lake Tana

ATLANTIC OCEAN
Niger
Volta
Bandama
Oueme
Benue
Sanaga
Ubangi
Congo
Chari

White Nile
Blue Nile
Atbara

Shebele
Juba
Lake Turkana
Mogadishu •
Kismayu •
INDIAN OCEAN
Victoria Nile
Lake Victoria
Congo
Lomami
Lualaba
Kasai
Kwango
Lake Tanganyika
Sanga •
ZANJ
Manda •
EAST AFRICAN TRADING STATES
Pemba
Zanzibar
Tana
Kilwa •
Mwabulambo •
Rufiji
Kalambo •
Lake Malawi
Nkope •
Comoros
Zambezi
Chedzurgwe •
Sena •
Madagascar
Kwando
Zimbabwe •
Khami •
SOFALA
Mozambique Channel
Orange
Vaal
Phalaborwa •

Copyright by Rand McNally & Co.
Robinson Projection

0 200 400 600 800 Miles
0 200 400 600 800 1000 Kilometers

	Southern limits of Muslim influence, about 900		Copper
GHANA	State or Empire		Foodstuffs
	Major trade route		Glass
	Bantu migrations		Gold
	Cataract (rapids)		Ivory
	Cattle		Salt
	Ceramics		Slaves

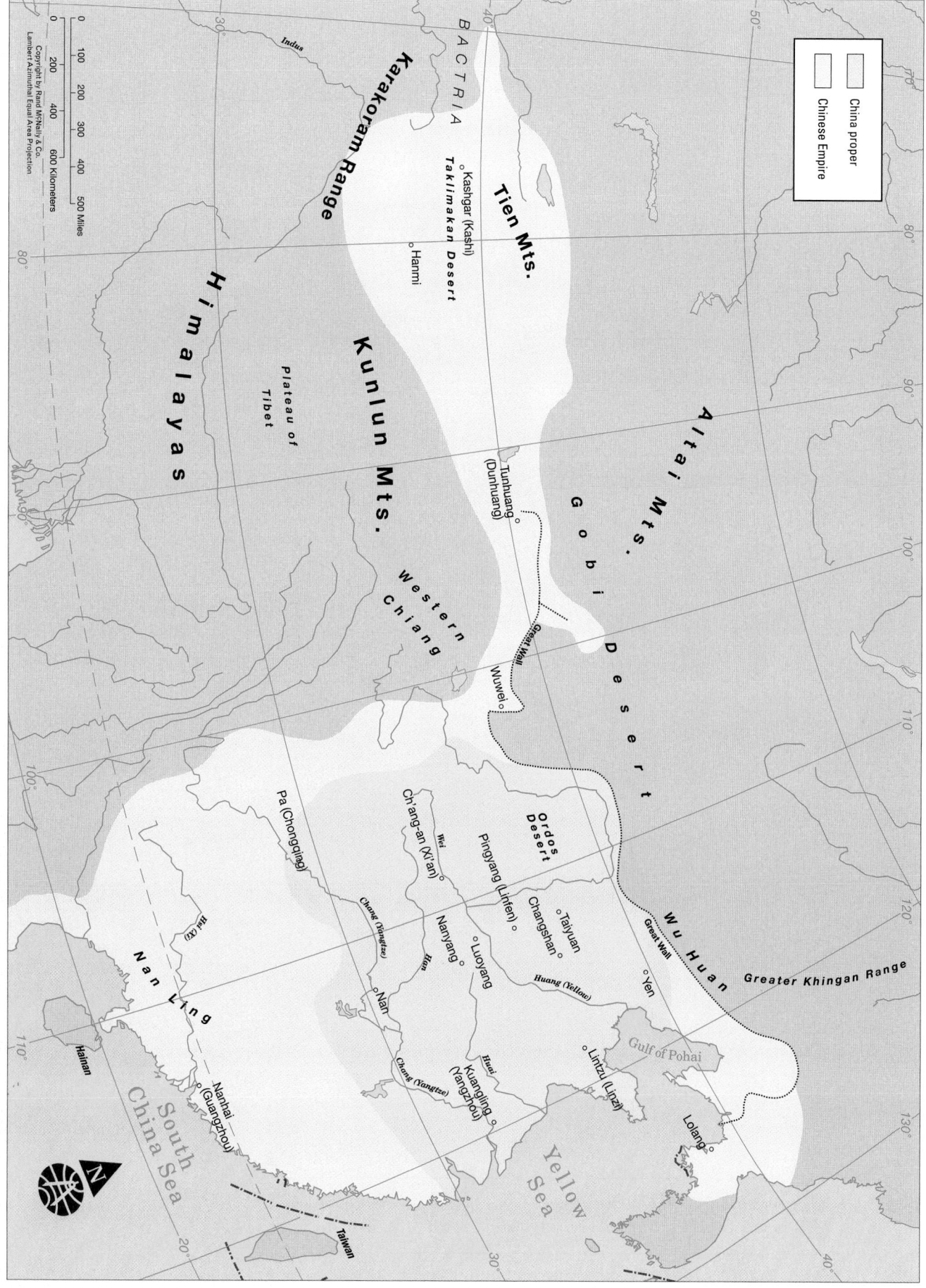

China proper
Chinese Empire

BACTRIA

Karakoram Range

Tien Mts.

Kashgar (Kashi)
Taklimakan Desert
Hami

Himalayas

Kunlun Mts.

Plateau of Tibet

Western Chiang

Altai Mts.

Gobi Desert

Tunhuang (Dunhuang)

Great Wall

Wuwei

Ordos Desert

Ch'ang-an (Xi'an)
Wei
Pingyang (Linfen)
Changshan
Taiyuan
Nanyang
Luoyang
Han
Chang (Yangtze)
Nan
Hsi (Xi)
Pa (Chongqing)

Nan Ling

Huang (Yellow)

Yen

Great Wall

Greater Khingan Range

Wu Huan

Huai
Kuangling (Yangzhou)
Chang (Yangtze)
Lintzu (Linzi)
Gulf of Pohai
Lolang

Yellow Sea

Hainan

Nanhai (Guangzhou)

South China Sea

Taiwan

Indus

N

Copyright by Rand McNally & Co.
Lambert Azimuthal Equal Area Projection

0   100 200 300 400 500 Miles
0 100 200 400 600 Kilometers

RAND McNALLY

ATLANTIC OCEAN

IRELAND

North Sea

Baltic Sea

BRITAIN
Wall of Antoninus
Wall of Hadrian
Eburacum
BRITAIN
Londinium

English Channel

Elbe

(Lost in 9 A.D.)

Vistula

LOWER GERMANY
Colonia Agrippina

GERMANY

Lutetia
LUGDUNENSIS
BELGICA

Loire

Rhine

GAUL
AQUITANIA
Lugdunum

Seine

Carpathians

UPPER GERMANY

Rhône

Alps
RHAETIA
NORICUM
Vindobona
Danube
Aquincum

Mediolanum
PANNONIA

Garonne
TARRACONENSIS
Douro
Numantia
Salmantica
Caesar Augusta
Pyrenees
Tolosa
NARBONENSIS
ALPINE PROVS.
Po
Patavium
ILLYRICUM

Olisipo
LUSITANIA
SPAIN
Ebro
Massilia
Ravenna
DACIA

Tagus
Toletum
Tarraco
ITALY
Rome
Adriatic Sea
DALMATIA

Guadiana
Corduba
BAETICA
Valentia
CORSICA AND SARDINIA
Ostia

Gades
Balearic Islands
Pompeii
MACEDONIA

New Carthage
MEDITERRANEAN
Carales
Tyrrhenian Sea
Corcyra
Ionian Sea
EPIRUS
Thessalonic

MAURETANIA
SICILY
Syracuse
Corinth
ACHAIA
Athen

Atlas Mountains
Carthage
SEA

AFRICA

GAETULIA

Crete

NUMIDIA

Cyrene

CYRENAICA

AFRICA

| Roman Empire | Parthian Empire | —— Provincial Boundary |
| Armenia | Temporarily held by Rome | BRITAIN Roman Province |

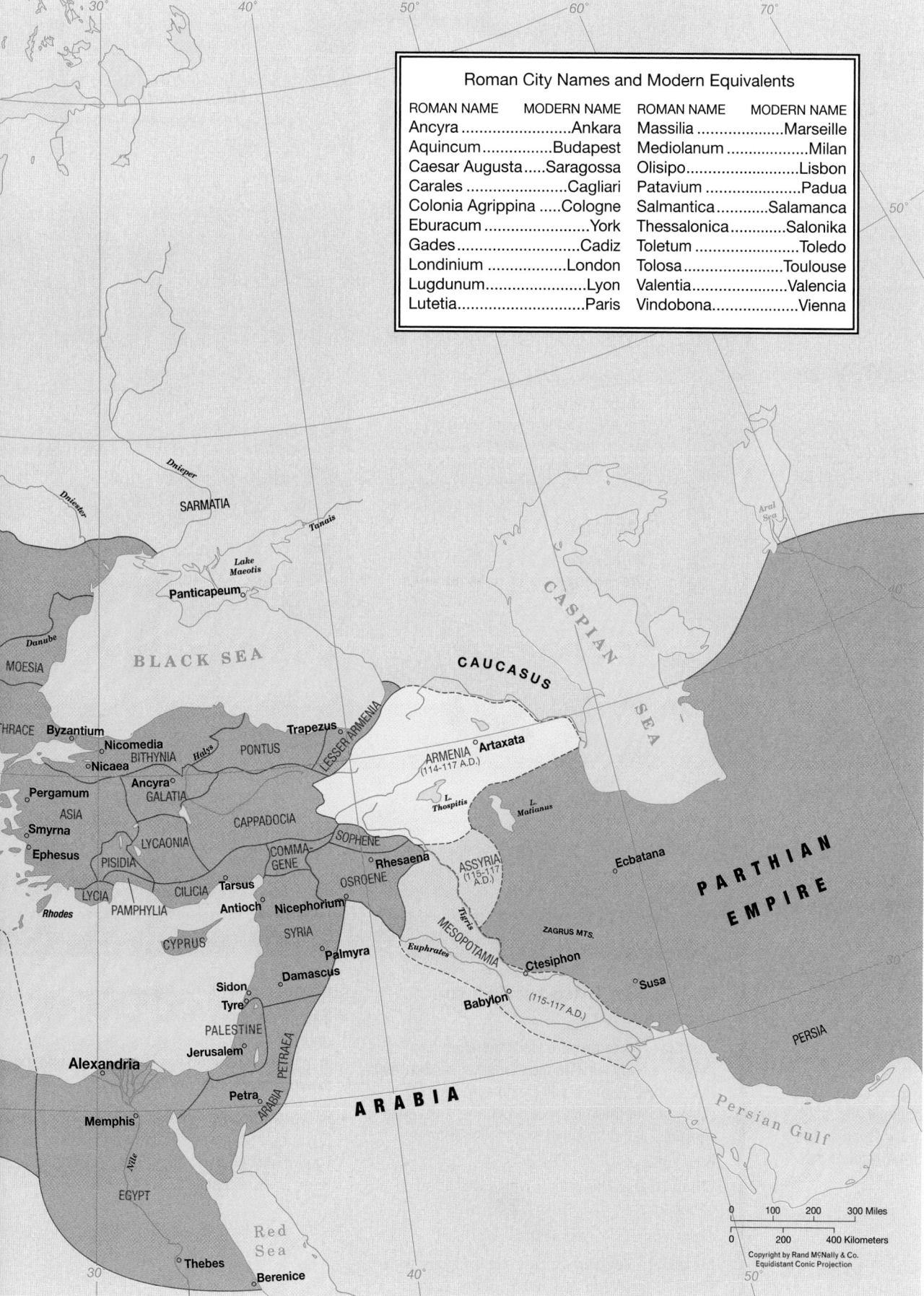

Roman City Names and Modern Equivalents

ROMAN NAME	MODERN NAME	ROMAN NAME	MODERN NAME
Ancyra	Ankara	Massilia	Marseille
Aquincum	Budapest	Mediolanum	Milan
Caesar Augusta	Saragossa	Olisipo	Lisbon
Carales	Cagliari	Patavium	Padua
Colonia Agrippina	Cologne	Salmantica	Salamanca
Eburacum	York	Thessalonica	Salonika
Gades	Cadiz	Toletum	Toledo
Londinium	London	Tolosa	Toulouse
Lugdunum	Lyon	Valentia	Valencia
Lutetia	Paris	Vindobona	Vienna

SARMATIA

Dnieper

Dniester

Tanais

Lake Maeotis

Panticapeum

Aral Sea

Danube

MOESIA

BLACK SEA

CAUCASUS

CASPIAN SEA

THRACE Byzantium

Nicomedia

Nicaea

BITHYNIA

PONTUS

Halys

Trapezus

LESSER ARMENIA

ARMENIA
(114-117 A.D.)

Artaxata

Pergamum

Ancyra

GALATIA

ASIA

CAPPADOCIA

L. Thospitis

L. Matianus

Smyrna

LYCAONIA

Ephesus

PISIDIA

COMMA-
GENE

SOPHENE

Rhesaena

ASSYRIA
(115-117 A.D.)

Ecbatana

PARTHIAN

EMPIRE

LYCIA

CILICIA

Tarsus

OSROENE

Rhodes

PAMPHYLIA

Antioch

Nicephorium

MESOPOTAMIA

Tigris

ZAGRUS MTS.

CYPRUS

SYRIA

Palmyra

Euphrates

Ctesiphon

Susa

Damascus

Sidon

Babylon (115-117 A.D.)

Tyre

PALESTINE

PERSIA

Jerusalem

PETRAEA

Alexandria

ARABIA

Petra

ARABIA

Persian Gulf

Memphis

Nile

EGYPT

Red
Sea

Thebes

Berenice

0   100   200   300 Miles

0   200   400 Kilometers

Copyright by Rand McNally & Co.
Equidistant Conic Projection

RAND McNALLY

Begin the Unit

Quick Look

Chapter 1 explores the major tools and skills that scholars and students use to understand the world and its history.

Chapter 2 explores significant events in the development of the earliest human societies.

Interact with History ▶

Purpose

To help students connect with the wonder and awe that come from exploring mysteries of the ancient world—such as Stonehenge

Visual Learning

Ask a student volunteer to read the text and questions aloud. Point out to students that the text and the three questions on these pages will help them answer the main question on page 2. Discuss the three questions before discussing the main one.

Interact ANSWERS

- What purpose do you think Stonehenge might have served? *(Stonehenge may have been used to keep track of time and seasons, or it may have been used to predict eclipses of the moon.)*

- What does the use of these tools suggest about the builders? *(They were ingenious; they shaped the material they had at hand for a specific use.)*

- Why would ancient societies want to use a calendar to divide time into days, months, and seasons? *(to keep track of planting and harvest times; to keep track of religious holidays)*

- What conclusions can you draw about what Stonehenge meant to the people who built it? *(The labor required to build Stonehenge suggests that it was very important to the people who built it.)*

UNIT **1**

Introduction to World History

Interact with History ▶

Visiting Stonehenge, about 1500 B.C.
For years, you have heard about the ancient monument that stands here in a large, open plain. Now you have traveled to see it for yourself. It's as beautiful and mysterious as people say. But you wonder what it is used for.

What purpose do you think Stonehenge might have served?

WebQuest ClassZone.com

Stonehenge was built in three phases. The first phase began around 3000 B.C. with the digging of a large ditch. Workers used deer antlers to break up the ground. They used the shoulder blades of oxen to shovel the dirt and stones.

What does the use of these tools suggest about the builders?

2

TECHNOLOGY

WebQuest: Introduction to World History

Visit **ClassZone.com** to lead your students through a WebQuest on the monuments of ancient civilizations. Students will create a museum exhibit about these ancient structures, answering questions about how and why they may have been built.

When to Use This project works well as an end-of-unit activity.

Class Time Two class periods

Materials Needed At least one computer with access to the World Wide Web, printer, word processor, graphics software (optional), poster board, pens

Customizing for Your Classroom

- If computer time is limited, have small groups rotate through stations, using encyclopedias, library books, and other sources of information to supplement students' Web searching.

- Encourage Spanish speakers to use the textbook's Spanish glossary or an English-Spanish dictionary to help them understand key terms and concepts.

Some of the stones line up with the rising and setting sun. Many people believe that Stonehenge was used to serve as a calendar or to predict eclipses of the moon.

Why would ancient societies want to use a calendar to divide time into days, months, and seasons?

The outer ring of stones was built during the third phase, around 2500 B.C. Some of the stones weighed as much as 50 tons. For years, people believed that only giants could have built Stonehenge.

What conclusions can you draw about what Stonehenge meant to the people who built it?

3

Correcting Misconceptions

Ask students what they know about prehistoric people, their tools and skills, and their knowledge about the world. When students have finished the unit, have them write down two ways in which their image of prehistoric people was inaccurate.

More About . . .

Studying Stonehenge
We have no records about who built Stonehenge and why they did so. In addition, much of the site is now in ruins, with many stones missing or fallen. Only in the 1800s did scholars discover the relationship of Stonehenge to the rising and setting sun. This discovery has influenced modern studies of Stonehenge and the monument's possible astronomical uses.

WHY STUDY WORLD HISTORY?

- The tools and skills we develop for understanding the past can be useful for understanding the present.

- What we discover about the geography of the world can inform our understanding of the modern world and modern societies.

- Archaeologists, researchers, and anthropologists work to discover evidence about how prehistoric people lived.

- Historians look for patterns as they try to understand how and why events happened. These patterns help historians understand human nature.

- Studying early human societies and examining historical events involves studying cultures, religions, politics, and economics.

Chapter Overview

Scholars and students use many tools to understand the world and its history.

Copymasters

In-Depth Resources: Unit 1
- Family Newsletter (English and Spanish), pp. 1–2
- Visual Summary, p. 7
- Vocabulary Study Guide, p. 9

Character Education

Reading Study Guide, p. 13

Bringing Social Studies Alive, Chapter 1

Document-Based Questions: Strategy and Practice

Reading Toolkit, L1–L4

Modified Lesson Plans for English Learners, pp. 3–12

Assessment

Chapter Review, pp. 44–45

Formal Assessment
- Chapter Tests, Forms A, B, and C, pp. 9–20

Test Generator

Integrated Assessment Book

Online Test Practice

LESSON 1
The World's Geography
pp. 8–13
OBJECTIVE Analyze the science of geography.

In-Depth Resources: Unit 1
- Reading Skill: Summarizing, p. 3
- Vocabulary Cards, p. 11
- Literature: The Origins of Continents and Oceans by Alfred Wegener, p. 16
- Skillbuilder Practice: Summarizing, p. 8
- Reteaching Activity, p. 17

Interdisciplinary Projects
- Math, p. 1

Reading Study Guide, p. 5

Lesson Review, p. 12

Formal Assessment
- Lesson Quiz, p. 5

California Daily Standards Practice Transparencies, TT1

LESSON 2
How Maps Help Us Study History
pp. 14–25
OBJECTIVE Analyze the tools used by geographers to learn about the world and its history.

In-Depth Resources: Unit 1
- Reading Skill: Comparing and Contrasting, p. 4
- Vocabulary Cards, p. 11
- Reteaching Activity, p. 18

Reading Study Guide, p. 7

Lesson Review, p. 23

Formal Assessment
- Lesson Quiz, p. 6

California Daily Standards Practice Transparencies, TT2

LESSON 3
How Archaeologists Study the Past
pp. 26–37
OBJECTIVE Identify the tools of archaeologists and some of their findings.

In-Depth Resources: Unit 1
- Reading Skill: Finding Main Ideas, p. 5
- Vocabulary Cards, p. 11
- Geography Practice: Archaeological Sites in the United States, p. 13
- Primary Source: Lucy, p. 15
- Reteaching Activity, p. 19

History Makers
- Louis Leakey, p. 1

Interdisciplinary Projects
- Science, p. 2; Art, p. 4

Reading Study Guide, p. 9

Lesson Review, p. 33

Formal Assessment
- Lesson Quiz, p. 7

California Daily Standards Practice Transparencies, TT3

LESSON 4
How Historians Study the Past
pp. 38–43
OBJECTIVE Learn why people study history and what tools historians use to study the past.

In-Depth Resources: Unit 1
- Reading Skill: Categorizing p. 6
- Vocabulary Cards, p. 11
- Reteaching Activity, p. 20

Interdisciplinary Projects
- Language Arts, p. 3

Reading Study Guide, p. 11

Lesson Review, p. 43

Formal Assessment
- Lesson Quiz, p. 8

California Daily Standards Practice Transparencies, TT4

Integrated Technology

 eEdition Plus Online

EasyPlanner Plus Online

eTest Plus Online

 Audio CDs
- Reading Study Guide
- Reading Study Guide in Spanish
- The World's Music

  **CD-ROMs**
- Power Presentations
- eEdition
- EasyPlanner
- Test Generator

---

 eEdition CD-ROM

 Map Transparencies
- MT1 Earth's Plates

 Critical Thinking Transparencies
- CT1 Summarizing

 ClassZone.com

---

 eEdition CD-ROM

 Map Transparencies
- MT2 The World According to Ptolemy, A.D. 150

 Critical Thinking Transparencies
- CT2 Comparing and Contrasting

 ClassZone.com

---

 eEdition CD-ROM

 Humanities Transparencies
- HT1 Stone Hammer Head

 Critical Thinking Transparencies
- CT3 Finding Main Ideas

 ClassZone.com

---

 eEdition CD-ROM

 Humanities Transparencies
- HT2 Stonehenge

 Critical Thinking Transparencies
- CT4 Categorizing
- CT5 Chapter 1 Visual Summary

 ClassZone.com

Overview of California Resources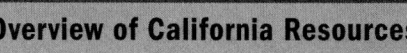

	Lesson 1	Lesson 2	Lesson 3	Lesson 4
California Reading Toolkit	L1	L2	L3	L4
California Modified Lesson Plans for English Learners	p. 3	p. 7	p. 9	p. 11
California Daily Standards Practice Transparencies	TT1	TT2	TT3	TT4
California Standards Enrichment Workbook	pp. 1–14	pp. 1–14	pp. 15–16	pp. 1–14
California Standards Planner and Lesson Plans	L1	L3	L5	L7
California Online Test Practice	ClassZone.com	ClassZone.com	ClassZone.com	ClassZone.com
California Test Generator CD-ROM				
California EasyPlanner CD-ROM				
California eEdition CD-ROM				

Chart Key

PE	Pupil Edition		CD-ROM		Internet
	Copymaster		Audio		Overhead Transparency
			Video		

REVIEWING RESOURCES FOR DIFFERENTIATED INSTRUCTION

English Learners

In-Depth Resources in Spanish
- Reading Skill and Strategy Ⓐ
- Skillbuilder Practice
- Geography Practice Ⓒ
- Vocabulary Study Guide Ⓑ

In-Depth Resources: Unit 1
- Family Newsletter (English and Spanish)

Reading Study Guide (Spanish)

Reading Study Guide Audio CD (Spanish)

Test Generator
Chapter Test (Spanish)

Plus

Modified Lesson Plans for English Learners

Multi-Language Glossary of Social Studies Terms

Struggling Readers

In-Depth Resources: Unit 1
- Vocabulary Study Guide
- Skillbuilder Practice Ⓑ
- Geography Practice
- Reteaching Activities
- Family Newsletter Ⓒ

Reading Study Guide Ⓐ

Reading Study Guide Audio CD

Reading Toolkit

Formal Assessment
Chapter Test, Form A

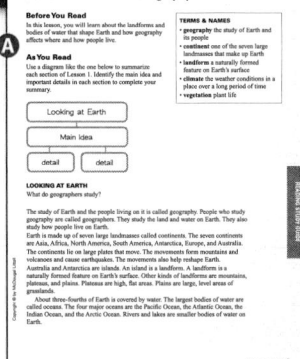

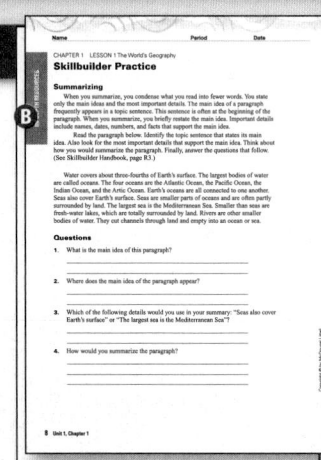

Inclusion

EasyPlanner CD-ROM
- Reading Skill and Strategy Ⓐ
- Vocabulary Study Guide Ⓑ
- Geography Practice Ⓒ
- Reteaching Activities

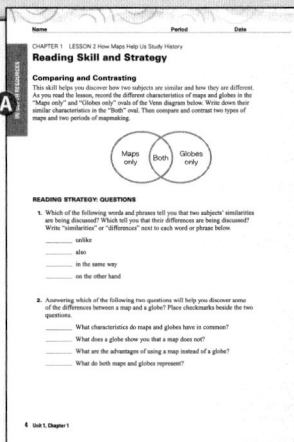

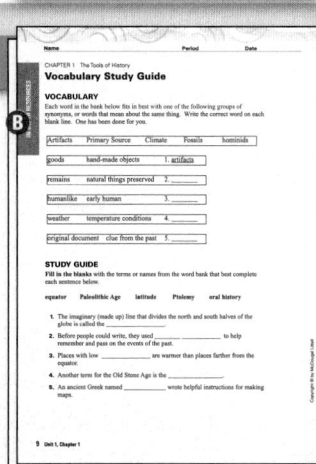

Gifted and Talented Students

In-Depth Resources: Unit 1
- Primary Source Ⓐ
- Literature

History Makers Ⓑ

Interdisciplinary Projects Ⓒ

Formal Assessment
Chapter Test, Form C

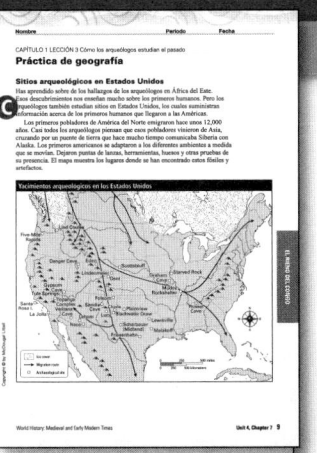

Activities in the Teacher's Edition for English Learners

- Describe the Five Themes, p. 10
- Make a Chart of Cognates, p. 20
- Discuss Navigation, p. 24
- Define Words in Context, p. 28
- Record Story Elements, p. 36
- Model Sources, p. 41

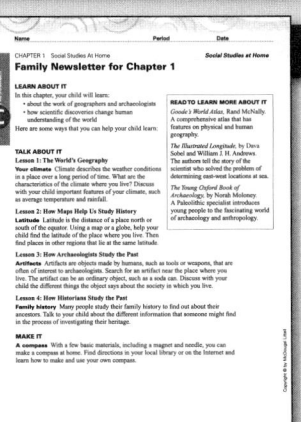

Activities in the Teacher's Edition for Struggling Readers

- Review the Names of the Continents and Oceans, p. 10
- Make Concept Flash Cards, p. 18
- Create a Map Web Diagram, p. 21
- Compare and Contrast, p. 24
- Divide and Conquer, p. 32
- Illustrate the Scene, p. 35
- Record an Oral History, p. 40

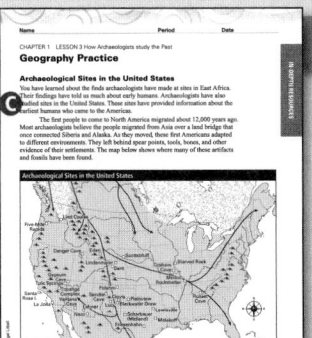

Activities in the Teacher's Edition for Inclusion Students

- Prepare and Give a Five-Themes Quiz, p. 11
- Write and Administer Map Quizzes, p. 20
- Analyze the Time Line, p. 29
- Act Out the Scene, p. 35
- Take Notes on Audiotape, p. 41

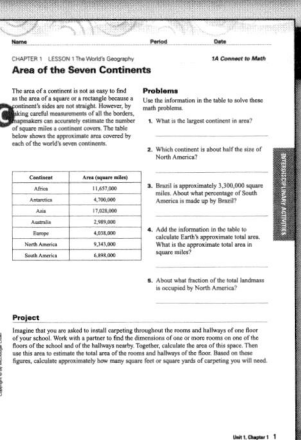

Activities in the Teacher's Edition for Gifted and Talented Students

- Perform a Five-Theme Analysis, p. 11
- Locate Places in Your Community, p. 18
- Making Physical and Political Maps, p. 21
- Trace the History of a Hominid, p. 29
- Make a Stone Age Time Line, p. 32
- Write Excavation Instructions, p. 36
- Identify Strengths and Weaknesses of Primary and Secondary Sources, p. 40

Integrated Technology

eEdition CD-ROM

- Interactive Visuals
- Interactive Maps
- Starting with a Story

ClassZone.com

- WebQuests
- Research Links
- Internet Activities
- Homework Helper
- Chapter Quiz
- Current Events
- Test Practice

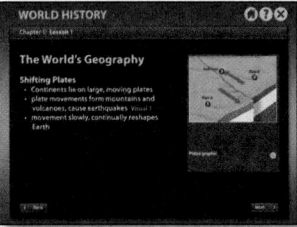

Power Presentations CD-ROM

- Lecture Notes
- Media Gallery
- Chapter Review Game

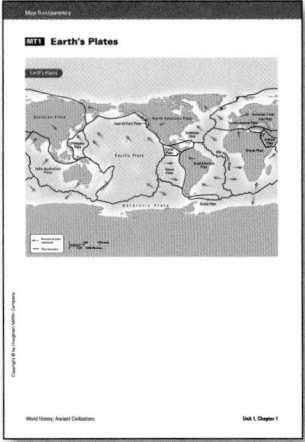

Critical Thinking Transparencies

- CT1 Summarizing
- CT2 Comparing and Contrasting
- CT3 Finding Main Ideas
- CT4 Categorizing
- CT5 Chapter 1 Visual Summary

California Daily Standards Practice Transparencies, TT1–TT4

Map Transparencies

- MT1 Earth's Plates
- MT2 The World According to Ptolemy, A.D. 150

Humanities Transparencies

- HT1 Stone Hammer Head
- HT2 Stonehenge

Test Generator CD-ROM

EasyPlanner CD-ROM

Begin the Chapter

Objective

Identify the tools and skills geographers, archaeologists, historians, and other scholars use to explore and learn about the past.

Quick Look

Lesson 1 introduces the key concepts geographers use to help us understand our planet and our relationship to it.

Lesson 2 introduces the tools, such as maps and globes, geographers have developed to help us interpret our planet and our relationship to it.

Lesson 3 explores the skills and tools archaeologists use to help us examine the past.

Lesson 4 describes the methods and techniques historians use to help us analyze and learn from the past.

Before You Read: Knowledge Rating

Understanding key terms and vocabulary is central to understanding content. Knowledge rating is a strategy that helps students identify words and terms they should look for as they read. It provides students with an opportunity to look up the meanings of words they need to know to fully understand the section content.

Have students follow these steps:

- Read the "Before You Read" instructions and copy the list of terms on a sheet of paper.
- Use a dictionary to look up the meanings of words that you rated 2 or 1. With this information, write sentences in which the words are used properly.
- When you come to these words in your reading, review what you learned about their definitions.

Chapter 1 The Tools of History

Before You Read: Knowledge Rating

Recognizing what you already know about each of these terms can help you understand the chapter.

    hominid   artifact   fossil

In your notebook, rate how well you know each term.

  3 = I know what this word means.
  2 = I've seen this word before, but I don't know what it means.
  1 = I've never seen this word before.

Define each term in your notebook as you read.

Big Ideas About the Tools of History

Science and Technology New scientific discoveries change human understanding of the world.

Geographers look for new ways to help us understand our place in the world. Archaeologists make discoveries that tell us about our earliest ancestors. Their findings answer questions about the past and provide insight into our lives today.

Integrated Technology

eEdition	INTERNET RESOURCES
· Interactive Maps	Go to **ClassZone.com** for
· Interactive Visuals	· WebQuest · Quizzes
· Starting with a Story	· Homework Helper · Maps
	· Research Links · Test Practice
	· Internet Activities · Current Events

German scientist Alfred Wegener proposed the continental drift theory in 1912. He claimed that more than 200 million years ago Earth was a single mass of land called Pangaea, meaning "all Earth." Eventually, the mass split apart, and its pieces have been moving ever since. You'll learn how this movement has affected Earth and its people in Chapter 1.

4.5 million B.C.
First hominids appear.
◄ (footprint of a hominid)

1.6 million B.C.
Homo erectus appears.

WORLD   5,000,000 B.C.   1,000,000 B.C.

2.5 million B.C.
Paleolithic Age begins.
◄ (Paleolithic hand ax)

(4)

TIME LINE DISCUSSION

Use the time line to help students gain an understanding of current scientific thinking on the history of humanlike creatures on Earth.

- When did the first hominids appear on Earth? *(about 4.5 million B.C.)*
- About how many years passed between the beginning of the Paleolithic Age and the appearance of *Homo erectus*? *(almost 1 million years)*

- According to the time line, when did Cro-Magnons appear? *(around 40,000 B.C.)*
- About how many years after the appearance of Cro-Magnons did the Neolithic Age begin? *(32,000 years)*

Continental Drift Theory
INTERACTIVE

200 million years ago
Earth was a single mass of land surrounded by water.

P A N G A E A
Tethys Sea
PANTHALASSA OCEAN

65 million years ago
The mass split apart, and the parts moved in different directions.

NORTH AMERICA
ASIA
SOUTH AMERICA
AFRICA
INDIA
AUSTRALIA
ANTARCTICA

Today
The continents continue to drift apart.

Eurasian Plate
NORTH AMERICA
EUROPE
ASIA
American Plate
AFRICA
African Plate
Pacific Plate
Pacific Plate
SOUTH AMERICA
Indo-Australian Plate
AUSTRALIA
Antarctic Plate
ANTARCTICA

200,000 B.C.
Neanderthals appear.

8000 B.C.
Neolithic Age begins.
◀ (Neolithic clay mask)

500,000 B.C.   100,000 B.C.   5000 B.C.

40,000 B.C.
Cro-Magnons appear.
◀ (Cro-Magnon skull)

(5)

Introduce the Big Ideas
Read aloud the text about the Big Ideas. Have students think about scientific discoveries or technological developments that have made the news in recent years. For example, students may recall explorations of Mars and other parts of outer space. Ask students how those developments have changed their views about the world and the universe.

Here are some other Big Ideas that you may want to emphasize in this chapter.

Geography
Many geographic features influenced history.

Culture
Humans want to understand the past to help them make decisions about the present.

Talk About It
Interpreting Maps
Ask students to look at the three maps on this page and read the title and captions that go with them. Ask what has happened to the land on Earth over the last 200 million years. *(It has broken into smaller masses, which have moved in different directions.)* How might the process shown in the maps affect Earth in the future? *(The landmasses will continue to drift.)*

INTERACTIVE

An interactive version of these maps are available on the eEdition and Power Presentations CD-ROMs.

Find Out More
How might the movement of Earth's landmasses have affected the history of life on the planet? Have students use library reference books or Internet resources to learn more about continental drift and the ways it has shaped our history.

RECOMMENDED RESOURCES

Books for the Teacher
De Blij, H. J., and Peter O. Muller. *Geography: Realms, Regions, and Concepts,* 10th ed. New York: Wiley, 2002. A leading textbook in the study of geography.

Morell, Virginia. *Ancestral Passions: The Leakey Family and the Quest for Humankind's Beginnings.* New York: Simon, 1995. Traces the history of the "first family" in the study of hominids.

Videos
Odyssey: Other People's Garbage. 60 minutes. Boston, Public Broadcasting Assoc., 1980. Account of archaeological findings at sites in the United States and what archaeologists have learned from them.

DVDs
The Standard Deviants— Learn World Geography. 90 minutes. Falls Church: Cerebellum, 2002. Provides an overview of world geography,

including basic concepts and terminology.

Internet
To access these sites, visit the Research Links for this chapter at **ClassZone.com.**

The Archaeology Channel. This online resource includes a wide variety of online videos on archaeological topics.

The United States Geological Service. Includes general information about geography as well as maps and other resources.

Objective

Describe the excitement involved in a major archaeological discovery.

Introducing the Story

Protecting the Lascaux Cave Paintings

The cave paintings at Lascaux are among the world's greatest prehistoric treasures. The location of the paintings deep within the cave, protected from the elements for thousands of years, explains their remarkable preservation. However, the paintings' discovery in 1940 led to their exposure to people and environmental factors that threatened to permanently harm them. For this reason, the French government closed the cavern to the public in 1963.

Vocabulary Preview

vertical in an up-and-down direction

cavern a cave

Reading the Story Aloud

1. **The teacher as reader:** Read the story aloud with expression, so that students hear the drama and understand the emotional impact of the events.

2. **The students as readers:** Give students a few minutes to read the story to themselves before reading it aloud to the class.

Starting with a Story

Students can also follow along as they listen to the story on the eEdition and Power Presentations CD-ROM.

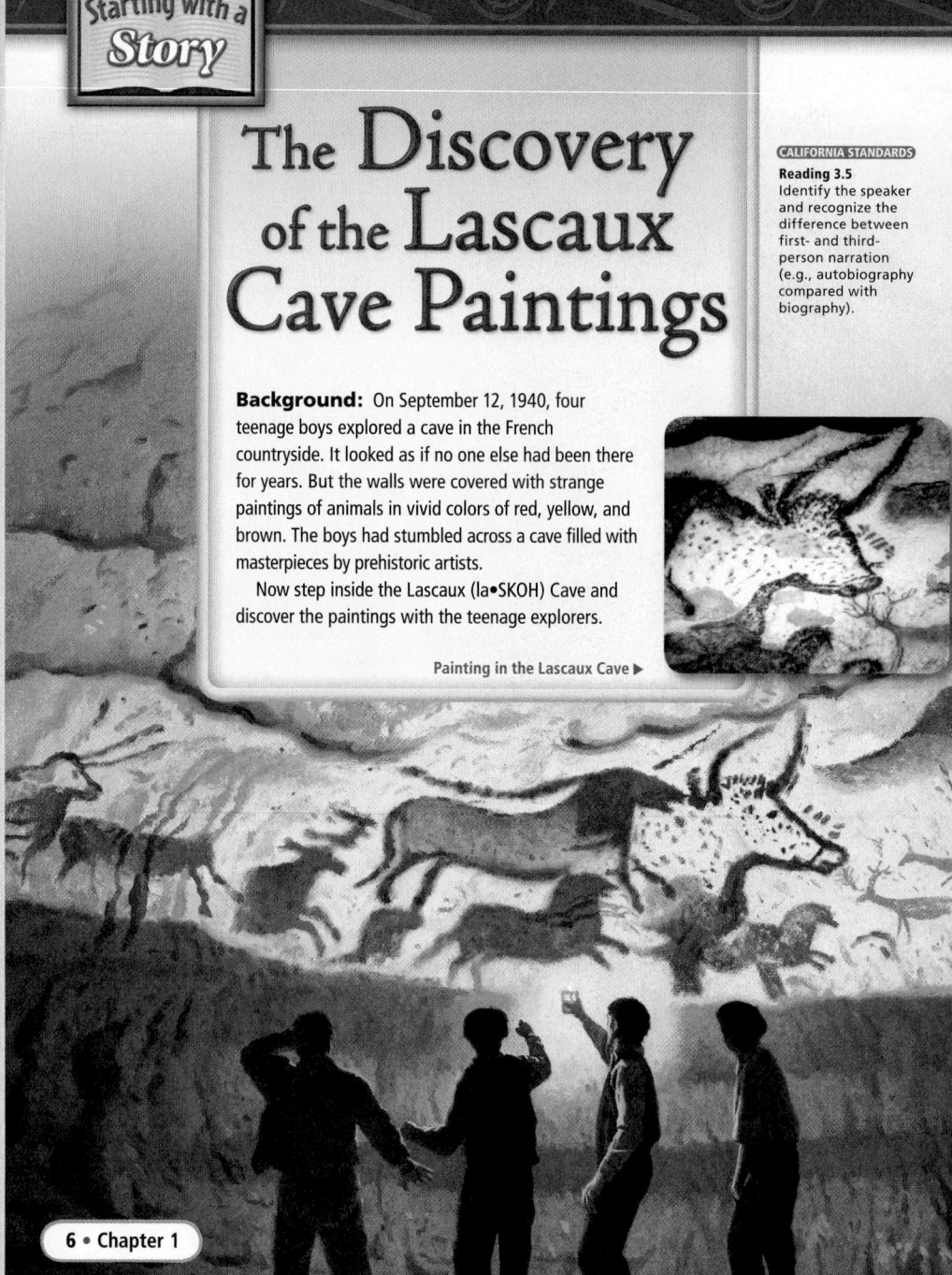

Starting with a Story

The Discovery of the Lascaux Cave Paintings

CALIFORNIA STANDARDS
Reading 3.5
Identify the speaker and recognize the difference between first- and third-person narration (e.g., autobiography compared with biography).

Background: On September 12, 1940, four teenage boys explored a cave in the French countryside. It looked as if no one else had been there for years. But the walls were covered with strange paintings of animals in vivid colors of red, yellow, and brown. The boys had stumbled across a cave filled with masterpieces by prehistoric artists.

Now step inside the Lascaux (la•SKOH) Cave and discover the paintings with the teenage explorers.

Painting in the Lascaux Cave ▶

6 • Chapter 1

ADDITIONAL RESOURCES

Books for the Student

Angeletti, Roberta. *The Cave Painter of Lascaux.* New York: Oxford UP, 1999. Fictionalized account of a young person's tour of Lascaux Cave.

Patent, Dorothy Hinshaw. *Mystery of the Lascaux Cave.* New York: Benchmark, 1998. Summarizes what is known and not known about the Lascaux art.

Videos

Lascaux Revisited. 35 minutes. Glenview: Crystal Productions, 1994. A video tour of the cave, set to the music of Beethoven.

Starting with a Story
eEdition

On September 8, Marcel went on a treasure hunt. For years, people had talked about a secret underground passage in the countryside around their French village. They said that the passage led to hidden treasure. The French teenager thought he had found it when he discovered the opening to a long vertical shaft. Four days later, on September 12, Marcel and three of his friends returned to explore it.

This time, Marcel brought an oil lamp to light the way. One after the other, the boys wriggled down the long passageway. Finally, they tumbled into a huge cavern, and Marcel held up the lamp. By its flickering light, they noticed a narrow, high passage. The friends entered the passage, and Marcel shone the light on its walls. What the French teenagers saw amazed them.

Herds of horses, oxen, and deer stampeded across the curving cave wall. The colorful animals seemed to leap off the walls. Excitedly, the teenagers ran through the cave and found room after room of paintings. They had found the real treasure of Lascaux.

At first the four teenagers promised to keep their great discovery a secret. But this secret was too hard to keep. They told their teacher, who contacted an expert. The expert said that the boys were probably the first modern people to lay eyes on this art. The paintings had been sealed in the Lascaux Cave for at least 17,000 years.

The cave walls are covered with more than 1,500 pictures of animals. Many of the animals include those that the early people of Lascaux hunted. Historians believe that the people told stories about the animals and sang as the artists painted them. But these oral stories are lost forever.

What do these cave paintings tell you about the people who painted them?

Reading & Writing

1. **READING: Speaker** This story is told by a third-person narrator. How would the story be different if Marcel or one of his friends told it?

2. **WRITING: Explanation** Research to find out what has happened to the Lascaux Cave, and write a paragraph explaining your findings.

   CALIFORNIA STANDARDS Writing 2.2
   Write expository compositions.

7

Talk About It

Ask students the following questions to begin the discussion:

- Why did the four teenagers in the story set out on a "treasure hunt"? *(because they had heard local legends about a secret underground passage in their area)*

- What was the real treasure that the teenagers found? *(prehistoric cave paintings)*

- Why do you think the discoverers decided to tell their teacher about what they had found? *(Possible answer: They realized they had made an important discovery that experts should know about.)*

What do these cave paintings tell you about the people who painted them?

Possible answer: The people appreciated and understood how to produce great art.

Making Personal Connections

Connect the discussion to today by asking about how we protect valuable, one-of-a-kind treasures in museums and national parks. Students may say that museums often try to protect items from human contact and that parks may limit access to places and buildings.

READING & WRITING ACTIVITIES

1. **READING** Possible answers: First-person narration would add more detail and suspense to the story. Information about the paintings, the cave, and the prehistoric people of Lascaux would be left out.

2. **WRITING** Students should discover that the paintings were damaged after the French government opened the cave to the public. As a result, measures were put in place to prevent people from touching and breathing on the paintings. Viewing times were also limited. The cave was eventually closed to the public, and a replica was built.

2. Writing Rubric

	Historical Details	Spelling and Punctuation	Writing Style
4	complete and accurate	no errors	lively and interesting
3	accurate but missing details	one or two errors	interesting
2	minor inaccuracies and missing details	three or four errors	mainly factual in style
1	major inaccuracies and few details	more than four errors	disorganized

❶ Plan & Prepare

Objectives

- Describe the key features of Earth's surface.
- Explain the five themes of geography.
- Summarize how humans are affected by their environment.
- **Language Objective:** Use personal experiences to gain a deeper understanding of the five themes of geography.

Quick Look

Lesson 1 introduces key concepts and vocabulary in the study of geography.

❷ Focus & Motivate

Preview Explain that this lesson focuses on some of the basic questions and concepts of the science of geography—the study of Earth and its people. Ask students why they think understanding geography will be important to the study of history. *(Possible answer: Geography will help explain how some civilizations rose and fell.)*

Introduce the Main Ideas The three main ideas help develop the Big Idea "New scientific discoveries change human understanding of the world." Help students identify parts of the lesson that show how our understanding of the world is expanding.

Reading Skill: Summarizing Remind students that summarizing involves repeating only the main points and details.

SAMPLE ANSWERS FOR DIAGRAM

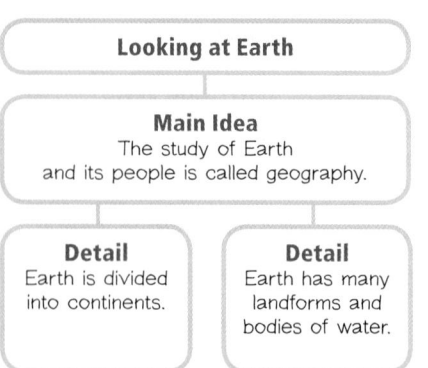

Looking at Earth

Main Idea
The study of Earth and its people is called geography.

Detail
Earth is divided into continents.

Detail
Earth has many landforms and bodies of water.

Lesson 1

▶ **MAIN IDEAS**

❶ Geography Continents, landforms, and bodies of water shape our planet.

❷ Geography Geographers organize information into five themes.

❸ Geography Where people live has an impact on how they live.

▶ **TAKING NOTES**

Reading Skill: Summarizing

When you summarize, you supply only main ideas and important details. Identify the main ideas and important details in each section of Lesson 1. Then put them in your own words and record them in a diagram like the one below.

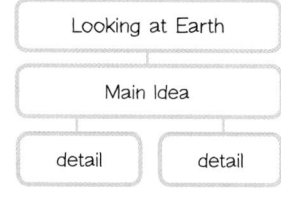

Looking at Earth

Main Idea

detail | detail

⬛ Skillbuilder Handbook, page R3

▲ **Earth** This "blue marble" image of Earth was put together using a collection of satellite pictures taken in 2001. It is the most detailed true-color image ever produced of Earth.

CALIFORNIA STANDARDS

FRAMEWORK In studying the ancient world, students should come to appreciate the special significance of geographic place in the development of the human story.

CST 1 Students explain how major events are related to one another in time.

CST 3 Students use a variety of maps and documents to identify physical and cultural features of neighborhoods, cities, states, and countries and to explain the historical migration of people, expansion and disintegration of empires, and the growth of economic systems.

HI 2 Students understand and distinguish cause, effect, sequence, and correlation in historical events, including the long- and short-term causal relations.

HOW TO TEACH THE CALIFORNIA STANDARDS

Standard	Content	Student Question or Activity	Instruction
CST 1	**Page 12** Defines the conditions of the weather over a long period of time	**Page 12** Students predict the result if the climate of a region suddenly turned colder.	Have a volunteer describe the weather outside. Have another volunteer describe the climate. Discuss the difference between the two concepts.
CST 3	**Page 9** Outlines Earth's main geographic features	**Page 12** Students identify Earth's main geographic features.	Have students examine a physical map of the United States. Ask volunteers to identify major geographic features located in or bordering the state of California.
HI 2	**Page 10** Describes how plate movements cause earthquakes	**Page 10** Students describe some of the effects of earthquakes.	Practice a class earthquake drill. Discuss the importance of earthquake drills, especially for residents of California.

The World's Geography

TERMS & NAMES
geography
continent
landform
climate
vegetation

Build on What You Know How would you describe your town? Is the land flat or hilly? Does a river run nearby? Who lives in your town? When you answer these questions, you describe your town's geography. Your town is part of the world's geography.

Looking at Earth

1 ESSENTIAL QUESTION What do geographers study? Earth and its people

Scientists study the land and water that cover Earth. They also study how people live on Earth. The study of Earth and its people is called **geography**.

Continents Earth is divided into seven large landmasses called **continents**. You can see the continents on the map below. From largest to smallest, the continents are Asia, Africa, North America, South America, Antarctica, Europe, and Australia.

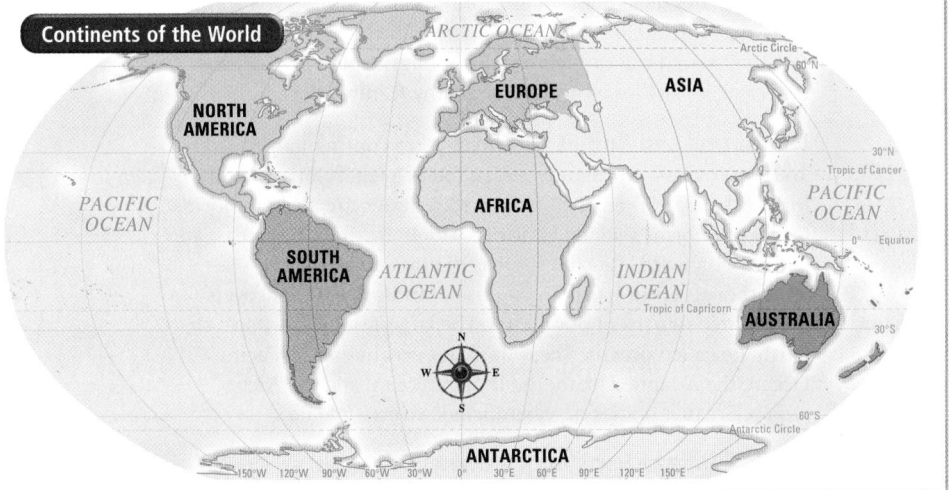

Continents of the World

The Tools of History • 9

Geography Handbook

Terms & Names

geography the study of Earth and its people

continent one of the seven large landmasses of Earth

landform a naturally formed feature of Earth's land surface

climate the pattern of weather conditions in a certain location over a long period of time

vegetation the plant life of an area

❸ Teach

Looking at Earth

❮ CST 3

Talk About It

• **Critical Thinking: Drawing Conclusions** Why do you think geographers divide Earth into different units, such as continents, for study? *(Possible answer: These units represent places where the land, water, and people have certain basic features in common.)*

LESSON 1 PROGRAM RESOURCES

ON LEVEL

In-Depth Resources: Unit 1
• Family Newsletter (English and Spanish), pp. 1–2
• Reading Skill: Summarizing, p. 3
• Skillbuilder Practice: Summarizing, p. 8
• Vocabulary Study Guide, p. 9
• Vocabulary Cards, p. 11

Formal Assessment
• Lesson Quiz, p. 5

ENGLISH LEARNERS

In-Depth Resources in Spanish
• Reading Skill: Summarizing, p. 2

Modified Lesson Plans for English Learners, p. 3

Reading Study Guide (Spanish), p. 5

Reading Study Guide Audio CD (Spanish)

STRUGGLING READERS

In-Depth Resources: Unit 1
• Reading Skill: Summarizing, p. 3
• Vocabulary Study Guide, p. 9
• Vocabulary Cards, p. 11
• Reteaching Activity, p. 17

Reading Toolkit, L1

Reading Study Guide, p. 5

Reading Study Guide Audio CD

GIFTED AND TALENTED STUDENTS

In-Depth Resources: Unit 1
• Literature: The Origins of Continents and Oceans, p. 16

Interdisciplinary Projects
• Math, p. 1

INCLUSION

EasyPlanner CD-ROM
• Reading Skill: Summarizing
• Vocabulary Study Guide
• Reteaching Activity

TECHNOLOGY

eEdition CD-ROM
• Starting with a Story

Power Presentations CD-ROM

Map Transparencies
• MT1 Earth's Plates

Critical Thinking Transparencies
• CT1 Summarizing

Test Generator CD-ROM

ClassZone.com

In-Depth Resources: Unit 1
• Reading Skill: Summarizing, p. 3
• Skillbuilder Practice: Summarizing, p. 8
• Literature: The Origins of Continents and Oceans, p. 16

More About . . .

Plate Tectonics
The theory of how plates shift to form continents, mountains, and other features is called plate tectonics. According to this theory, Earth's plates are set in motion by heat generated by radioactivity deep beneath Earth's surface.

The movement of Earth's plates is complex. At some places, called mid-ocean ridges, new plate material, or lithosphere, is formed as hot rock rises from deep inside Earth. Several inches of new plate may be formed each year. As plates spread out in opposite directions from these mid-ocean ridges, they plow into and rub up against other plates. These collisions can produce earthquakes and mountain ranges.

Map Transparencies
• MT1 Earth's Plates

History from Visuals

Interpreting Visuals
Ask students to view the photograph on this page. Point out that damage like that pictured in this photograph occurred over a wide area of San Francisco.

• What can you tell about the amount of energy released in an earthquake? *(Possible answer: It would take a great deal of energy to cause buildings to move and collapse like those in the picture.)*

GEOGRAPHY SKILLBUILDER ANSWER
Earthquakes are powerful enough to severely damage or even destroy buildings over a wide area. People trapped in these buildings could be injured or killed.

Geography

Earthquakes

At about 5:12 A.M. on April 18, 1906, the ground shook along the west coast of the United States. The earthquake was centered around San Francisco and destroyed much of the city, as shown in the photograph on the upper right.

The San Francisco earthquake was caused by plates sliding along a fault line, or break in Earth's crust. The diagram on the lower right shows their movement.

1 Plate A slides in one direction.

2 Plate B slides in the opposite direction.

3 The plates move past each other at the fault line, causing an earthquake.

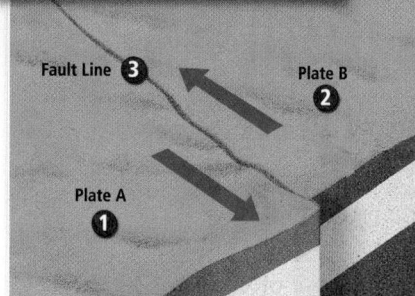
Fault Line **3**   Plate B **2**   Plate A **1**

> **GEOGRAPHY SKILLBUILDER**
> **INTERPRETING VISUALS** Human-Environment Interaction Based on the photograph above, what are some of the effects of earthquakes?

Shifting Plates Scientists believe that the continents lie on large moving plates. Plate movements form mountains and volcanoes and cause earthquakes. The movements slowly but continually reshape Earth. (You can learn more about the plate movements that cause earthquakes in the Geography feature above.)

Landforms and Bodies of Water Two continents—Australia and Antarctica—are islands. An island is a **landform**, or naturally formed feature on Earth's surface. Mountains are also landforms. Other landforms include plateaus, which are high, flat areas, and plains, which are large, level areas of grassland.

Although Earth has many kinds of landforms, water covers about three-fourths of our planet. The largest bodies of water on Earth are called oceans. The four major oceans are the Pacific Ocean, the Atlantic Ocean, the Indian Ocean, and the Arctic Ocean. Smaller bodies of water include rivers and lakes.

REVIEW What are Earth's largest landmasses and bodies of water called?
continents and oceans

DIFFERENTIATING INSTRUCTION

Struggling Readers

Review the Names of the Continents and Oceans
Have students draw, from memory, maps of the world on blank sheets of paper. Then have students label their maps with the names of the seven continents and four oceans. Students can check the accuracy of their work by looking at the map on page 9.

English Learners

Describe the Five Themes
Guide students as they describe the five themes of geography for their school community.
Location: Where is the school located?
Place: What language(s) do students speak?
Region: Discuss similarities/differences between two schools.
Movement: How do students get to school?
Human-Environment Interaction: Describe school's seasonal activities.

Themes of Geography

② **ESSENTIAL QUESTION** What are the five themes of geography?

Answer location, place, region, movement, human-environment interaction

Geographers use five themes of geography to describe Earth. The five themes help us understand our world and how we fit into it.

- **Location** The geographic question, Where is it? refers to location. Location can identify a precise spot or tell where one place is in relation to another.
- **Place** The question, What is it like? refers to place. Place includes physical characteristics as well as human ones, like language, religion, and politics.
- **Region** The question, How are places similar or different? refers to region. Region compares physical and human characteristics.
- **Movement** The question, How do people, goods, and ideas move from one location to another? refers to movement.
- **Human-Environment Interaction** The question, How do people relate to the physical world? refers to human-environment interaction. People learn to use and change what the environment offers them.

REVIEW Which two geographic themes are most concerned with people? movement and human-environment interaction

How Environment Affects People

affects how and where they live

③ **ESSENTIAL QUESTION** How does climate affect people's lives?

You probably wear a coat in cold weather and dress in light clothing in warmer weather. Of course, different people may develop different ways of adapting to the same area. But your environment—particularly its climate—has a big impact on the way you live.

Connect to Today

Hurricanes Natural disasters have a great impact on people and their homes. This photograph shows people fleeing during a 1998 hurricane in Florida. ▼

11

Geography Handbook

Teach

Themes of Geography

CST 1, CST 3

Talk About It

- What is the purpose of the five themes? *(Possible answer: to help geographers organize information and describe Earth)*
- What kinds of features can be included in a geographer's description of place? *(physical features and human features of a location)*
- **Critical Thinking: Categorizing** A study of how builders in earthquake-prone parts of the world develop special building methods to ensure that buildings survive frequent or severe earthquakes is an example of which theme? *(human-environment interaction)*

Teach

How Environment Affects People

HI 2

Talk About It

- Give two examples from the text of ways in which environment can affect people. *(It can affect where people live and what kind of vegetation grows there.)*
- How does climate differ from weather? *(Weather describes the conditions at a particular time; climate is a pattern of weather over time)*
- **Critical Thinking: Making Inferences** Why do you think the possibility that many places on Earth are in the midst of significant climate change concerns some scientists? *(Possible answer: Changes in climate would likely have a big impact on all people and may require major changes in the way people live.)*

DIFFERENTIATING INSTRUCTION

Inclusion

Prepare and Give a Five-Themes Quiz
Have students who have difficulty remembering details form pairs, then work together to prepare short multiple-choice quizzes on the five themes. Each pair should write 5–10 questions about the meanings and definitions of the themes. They should also prepare an answer key. After students have finished their quizzes, have teams exchange quizzes and test each other.

Gifted and Talented Students

Perform a Five-Theme Analysis
Have students select places they would like to learn more about. Then have each student write a brief report about one of those places that provides information related to each of the five themes.

④ Assess & Reteach

Assess Divide the class into small groups, and have each group answer the review questions. Then ask the groups to take turns presenting answers to the class. Discuss any differences in the answers provided by different groups.

 Formal Assessment
- Lesson Quiz, p. 5

Reteach Have students create outlines of this lesson. Tell them to list the major section headings on their papers, leaving plenty of room between the headings. Then have them write down at least two details from each section that help describe and explain that section.

 In-Depth Resources: Unit 1
- Vocabulary Cards, p. 11
- Reteaching Activity, p. 17

Homework Helper
Visit **ClassZone.com** for a lesson review, flip-card activities, and links to related Web sites.

Climate Weather refers to the temperature and conditions in a particular place at a particular time. **Climate**, on the other hand, describes the weather conditions in a place over a long period of time. Climate can influence where people live. For example, the harsh conditions of a cold, wet climate may prevent people from settling in that region.

Climate also has a big impact on the type of **vegetation**, or plant life, that grows in a location. For instance, thick jungle vegetation grows well in a tropical climate with heavy rainfall, while crops may be difficult to grow in a hot, dry climate.

REVIEW How does environment affect people?
affects where they live, what they wear, what they grow and eat

Lesson Summary
- Earth's largest landmasses, called continents, are surrounded by oceans.
- The five themes of geography help us explain our place in the world.
- Climate can affect how and where people live.

Why It Matters Now . . .
Geography helps us learn more about our neighbors and the ways we affect the world we share.

1 Lesson Review

Homework Helper
ClassZone.com

Terms & Names
1. Explain the importance of

| geography | landform | vegetation |
| continent | climate | |

Using Your Notes
Summarizing Use your completed diagram to answer the following question:
2. What are Earth's main geographic features? (CST 3)

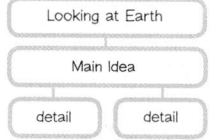

Looking at Earth

Main Idea

detail   detail

Main Ideas
3. Name three examples of landforms and three examples of bodies of water. (CST 3)
4. How do the five themes of geography help geographers? (CST 3)
5. How does the climate where you live affect your life? (CST 3)

Critical Thinking
6. **Understanding Cause and Effect** What might be the result if the climate of a region suddenly became much colder? (CST 1, HI 2)
7. **Making Inferences** Since more people live on Asia than on any other continent, what can you infer about Asia's environment? (CST 3)

Activity
Planning a Mural Work with a group of classmates to plan a mural that represents the physical features, climate, and vegetation in your town. (CST 3)

12 • Chapter 1

---

1 Lesson Review Answers

Terms & Names
1. • geography, p. 9
   • continent, p. 9
   • landform, p. 10
   • climate, p. 12
   • vegetation, p. 12

Using Your Notes
See page 8 for an example of a completed diagram.
2. continents, landforms, and bodies of water

Main Ideas
3. Possible answers: islands, mountains, plains; oceans, lakes, rivers

4. The themes help geographers describe and understand Earth and its inhabitants.
5. Possible answer: Cold and hot weather requires two different sets of seasonal clothes.

Critical Thinking
6. Possible answers: People might move away from the area; the vegetation would undergo change.
7. Possible answer: Asia has physical features, climate, and vegetation that encourage habitation.

Activity Rubric

	Ideas in Mural	Execution
4	has several examples of physical features, climate, and vegetation	very neat and clear
3	has at least one example of physical features, climate, and vegetation	mostly neat
2	missing an example from one category	unclear illustrations
1	missing examples from two or more categories	sloppy and unclear

Make a Geography Themes Poster

Goal: To understand that the five themes of geography relate to people's everyday lives

Materials & Supplies
• poster board
• magazines
• scissors
• tape or glue
• pen or pencil

Prepare

1 Reread "The Five Themes of Geography" on page 11.

2 Think about pictures that would illustrate each theme's question.

Do the Activity

1 Get together with a group of four other classmates. Each member should choose a different geography theme.

2 Look through magazines and cut out a picture that illustrates your theme. Note that the group member who selects region will need to find and compare two pictures to illustrate the theme.

3 After all members of the group have found their pictures, arrange all five illustrations on a poster.

4 Label each picture with its theme. Write a caption explaining how the picture answers the theme's question.

Follow-Up

1 What does the picture illustrating movement show?

2 What similarities and differences do the pictures illustrating region show?

Extension

Making a Brochure Use the five themes of geography to make a brochure about your community. Find or draw pictures that illustrate the themes.

CALIFORNIA STANDARDS
CST 3 Students use a variety of maps and documents to identify physical and cultural features of neighborhoods, cities, states, and countries and to explain the historical migration of people, expansion and disintegration of empires, and the growth of economic systems.

13

ACTIVITY: THEMES POSTER

Objective

Explain the five themes of geography by selecting and displaying representative photographs.

Suggestions for Completing the Activity

• Provide students with a wide range of newspapers and magazines in which to find pictures. Students can also use the Internet if they have access to a printer.

• Encourage students to be creative in thinking about possible pictures for their themes.

• Remind students to make sure their captions clearly explain the links between the pictures and the themes.

Follow-Up Activity

• Ask each team to share their movement pictures with the class.

• Make sure students clearly understand how each team's poster illustrates region.

ACTIVITY ANSWERS

Follow-Up Answers
1. movement of people, goods, or ideas
2. Possible answer: The pictures show similarities and differences in climate, landforms, and vegetation.

Extension Rubric

	Understanding of Five Themes	Required Elements
4	fully demonstrates understanding of five themes	includes at least one illustration for each theme and clear, accurate captions
3	reasonably demonstrates understanding of five themes	includes illustrations of all themes but is missing one or two captions
2	demonstrates understanding of all but one or two themes	missing as many as two pictures of themes and two captions
1	demonstrates understanding of only two or fewer themes	includes no more than two pictures and two captions

❶ Plan & Prepare

Objectives

- Describe the tools used by geographers to study Earth.
- Describe the different types of maps geographers use.
- Trace how maps have changed.
- **Language Objective:** Explore cognates to acquire information and make the text more comprehensible.

Quick Look

Lesson 2 introduces readers to maps and globes.

❷ Focus & Motivate

Preview Tell students that this lesson focuses on the tools used by geographers to study places—globes and maps. Ask students to think about how they might use maps to understand a place they were going to visit for the first time. (*Possible answer: They might use maps to identify places they'd like to visit to learn how to get to these places.*)

Introduce the Main Ideas The three main ideas for "How Maps Help Us Study History" bring together the Big Ideas about the tools geographers use.

Reading Skill: Comparing and Contrasting Remind students that comparing and contrasting involves identifying both similarities and differences between two or more things or ideas.

SAMPLE RESPONSES FOR DIAGRAM

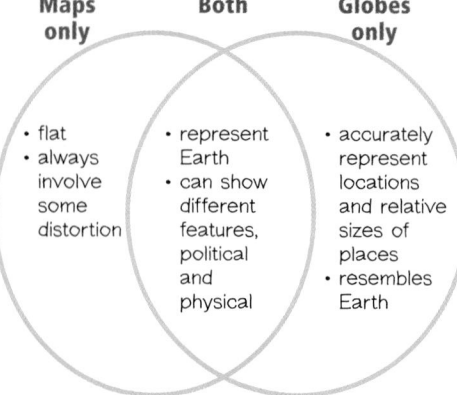

Maps only
- flat
- always involve some distortion

Both
- represent Earth
- can show different features, political and physical

Globes only
- accurately represent locations and relative sizes of places
- resembles Earth

Lesson 2

▶ **MAIN IDEAS**

❶ **Geography** Geographers use maps and globes to measure and describe Earth.

❷ **Geography** We use maps to see natural and human-made features and to understand patterns.

❸ **Geography** Maps have changed over time to reflect people's increasing understanding of the world.

▶ **TAKING NOTES**

Reading Skill: Comparing and Contrasting
When you compare and contrast two things, you look for ways in which they are similar and different. In Lesson 2, compare maps and globes, two types of maps, and two periods of mapmaking. Record their similarities and differences in a Venn diagram like the one below.

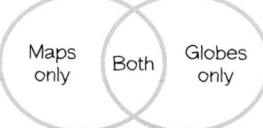

Maps only / Both / Globes only

S **Skillbuilder Handbook, page R4**

▲ **Compass** Early navigators used compasses, like this early Chinese one, to figure out where they were. Invented by the Chinese, the compass opened up the world to exploration and helped geographers make more accurate maps.

CALIFORNIA STANDARDS

FRAMEWORK In studying the ancient world, students should come to appreciate the special significance of geographic place in the development of the human story.

CST 1 Students explain how major events are related to one another in time.

CST 3 Students use a variety of maps and documents to identify physical and cultural features of neighborhoods, cities, states, and countries and to explain the historical migration of people, expansion and disintegration of empires, and the growth of economic systems.

HI 2 Students understand and distinguish cause, effect, sequence, and correlation in historical events, including the long- and short-term causal relations.

HOW TO TEACH THE CALIFORNIA STANDARDS

Standard	Content	Student Question or Activity	Instruction
CST 1	**Page 22** Traces the ways maps have changed over time	**Page 23** Students explain why maps in the Middle Ages were inaccurate.	Have students predict the next step in map technology. Ask what features they would like to see on maps in the future.
CST 3	**Page 19** Describes the three types of maps	**Page 23** Students describe the three types of maps.	After students read the lesson, have them explain how they could gain information about a culture from all three types of maps.
HI 2	**Page 23** Describes how the Mercator projection helped explorers	**Page 23** Students tell the effects of improved mapmaking on explorers.	Have students take notes about major improvements in mapmaking as they read the lesson.

How Maps Help Us Study History

▶ **TERMS & NAMES**

longitude

latitude

hemisphere

political map

physical map

thematic map

Build on What You Know You probably use maps when you visit the mall, get on a bus, or take a trip with your family. The skills you use to read those maps can be applied to read any map.

The Geographer's Tools

① **ESSENTIAL QUESTION** What are the geographer's tools? maps and globes

Geographers use both globes and maps to represent Earth. Both tools have advantages and disadvantages.

Globes One advantage of a globe is that it looks more like Earth, since both are round. A globe shows the viewer exactly how continents and oceans appear on Earth's curved surface. A globe also shows the true shapes, locations, and relative sizes of Earth's landforms and bodies of water.

Maps A map, on the other hand, is a flat representation of Earth's surface. It can be drawn to any size. No flat map can ever be as accurate as a globe. That is because Earth's surface is distorted somewhat when it is flattened to create a map. In other words, a map can alter how Earth really looks. But most people prefer to use maps because they do have several advantages. For one thing, a map lets you measure distances much more easily. For another, a map lets you see the world at a glance. Most important, it's much easier to carry a map because you can fold it up!

Globes One disadvantage of using a globe is that you can view only half of Earth at a time. This globe shows parts of North and South America. ▼

The Tools of History • 15

Geography Handbook

Terms & Names

longitude imaginary lines that measure distances east and west of the prime meridian

latitude imaginary lines that measure distances north and south of the equator

hemisphere an equal half of the globe

political map a map showing features people have created

physical map a map showing landforms and bodies of water

thematic map a map showing a distribution or pattern

❸ Teach

The Geographer's Tools

⬖ **CST 3**

Talk About It

- **Critical Thinking: Summarizing** What are some of the advantages of maps? *(see more details of Earth, easier to measure and carry)*

California Resources

California Reading Toolkit, L2

California Modified Lesson Plans for English Learners, p. 7

California Daily Standards Practice Transparencies, TT2

California Standards Enrichment Workbook, pp. 1–14

California Online Test Practice

California Test Generator CD-ROM

California Standards Planner and Lesson Plans, L3

California EasyPlanner CD-ROM

California eEdition CD-ROM

LESSON 2 PROGRAM RESOURCES

ON LEVEL

In-Depth Resources: Unit 1
- Reading Skill: Comparing and Contrasting, p. 4
- Vocabulary Study Guide, p. 9
- Vocabulary Cards, p. 11

Formal Assessment
- Lesson Quiz, p. 6

ENGLISH LEARNERS

In-Depth Resources in Spanish
- Reading Skill: Comparing and Contrasting, p. 3

Modified Lesson Plans for English Learners, p. 7

Reading Study Guide (Spanish), p. 7

Reading Study Guide Audio CD (Spanish)

STRUGGLING READERS

In-Depth Resources: Unit 1
- Reading Skill: Comparing and Contrasting, p. 4
- Vocabulary Cards, p. 11
- Reteaching Activity, p. 18

Reading Toolkit, L2

Reading Study Guide, p. 7

Reading Study Guide Audio CD

GIFTED AND TALENTED STUDENTS

Map Transparencies
- MT2 The World According to Ptolemy, A.D. 150

INCLUSION

EasyPlanner CD-ROM
- Reading Skill: Comparing and Contrasting
- Vocabulary Study Guide
- Reteaching Activity

TECHNOLOGY

eEdition CD-ROM

Power Presentations CD-ROM

Map Transparencies
- MT2 The World According to Ptolemy, A.D. 150

Critical Thinking Transparencies
- CT2 Comparing and Contrasting

Test Generator CD-ROM

ClassZone.com

In-Depth Resources: Unit 1
• Reading Skill: Comparing and Contrasting, p. 4

More About . . .

Map Projections

Because they present a curved surface as flat, all maps present distorted views of Earth's surface. The distortions may affect distance, direction, scale, area, or other factors. Different projections have different types of distortions. Some projections achieve less distortion in one aspect, such as scale or area, by allowing greater distortion in other aspects. Other projections attempt to achieve the least possible distortion of all factors.

History from Visuals

Interpreting Maps

Have students examine the map of Australia on this page. After they have reviewed the different features of the map, have them practice reading the content of the map.

• According to the map, what parts of Australia get the most rainfall? *(coastal areas, particularly the eastern coast)*

• What pattern can you see in the locations of the major cities shown on the map? *(Most cities are located in the wetter parts of the country.)*

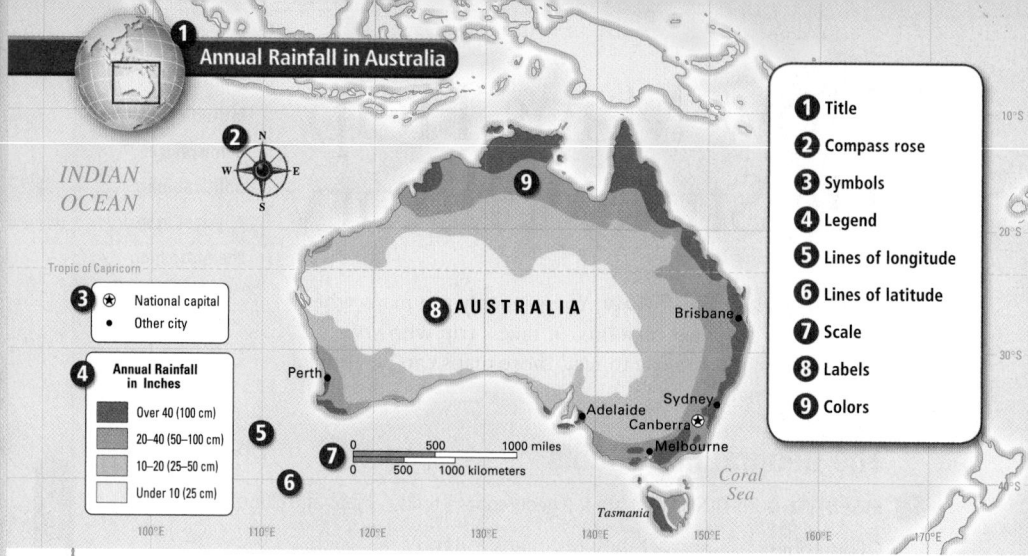

Reading a Map Most maps have nine features, as shown in the map above. These features, described below, help you read and understand maps.

• **Title** The title tells the subject of the map and gives you an idea of what information is shown.
• **Compass rose** The compass rose shows directions: north, south, east, and west.
• **Symbols** Symbols represent such items as capital cities and natural resources. The map legend explains what the symbols mean.
• **Legend** The legend, or key, lists and explains the symbols and colors used on the map.
• **Lines of longitude** These are imaginary lines that measure distances east and west of the prime meridian.
• **Lines of latitude** These are imaginary lines that measure distances north and south of the equator.
• **Scale** A scale can be used to figure out the distance between two locations on a map.
• **Labels** Labels indicate the names of cities, landforms, and bodies of water.
• **Colors** Colors represent a variety of information on a map. The map legend explains what the colors mean.

16 • Chapter 1

INTERDISCIPLINARY ACTIVITIES

Science

Research Different Projections

Have students use Internet or library resources to find examples of three different types of map projections of a similar area, such as the United States or North America. Instruct students to make copies of the maps and record the type of projection used for each map. Have students display their findings on a poster. Invite students to share and compare their findings.

Art

Create a Map

Have students create maps of a familiar place—their school or their neighborhood, for example—that contain the features described on this page. (Student maps need not indicate latitude and longitude.) Suggest that students use graph paper in order to make the measurement of distances easier. Students should label each feature correctly.

Map Projections As you have already learned, flat maps distort Earth's surface. Mapmakers try to control this distortion by using different projections. A projection is a way of showing the curved surface of Earth on a flat map. Compare the three common projections shown below.

Mercator Projection The Mercator (muhr•KAY•tuhr) projection shows most of the continents as they look on a globe. However, the projection stretches out the lands near the north and south poles. For example, the island of Greenland is actually one-eighth the size of South America.

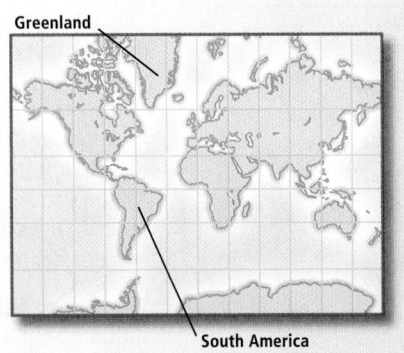

Greenland

South America

Homolosine Projection The homolosine (hoh•MAHL•uh•SYN) projection divides the oceans. This projection fairly accurately shows the sizes of landmasses. But distances on the map are not correct.

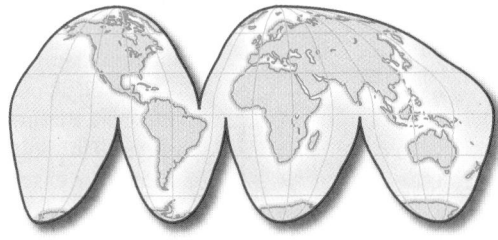

Robinson Projection The Robinson projection is often used in textbooks. It shows all of Earth with nearly the true sizes and shapes of the continents and oceans. However, the shapes of the landforms near the poles appear flat.

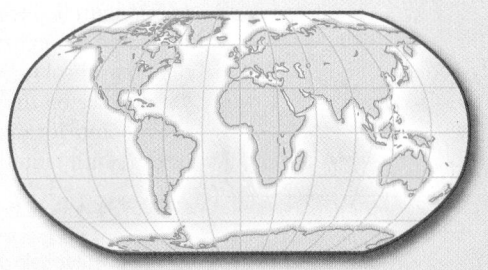

Geography Handbook

History from Visuals

Interpreting Maps
Make sure students recognize that each map shown has benefits and drawbacks. That is, presents some aspect accurately, such as the relative size of landmasses, while distorting something else, such as the distance between places. Remind students that globes do not distort Earth's surface.

More About . . .

The Politics of Map Projections
According to some geographers, distortions in maps shape the ways people view the world and each other. For example, the widely used Mercator world map exaggerates the sizes of North America and Europe in comparison with lands in the Southern Hemisphere. The island of Greenland appears as large as South America, when in fact it is less than one-eighth South America's size. Some observers have wondered whether such inaccuracies contribute to an undervaluing of the developing world.

The Tools of History • 17

INTERDISCIPLINARY ACTIVITIES

Art

Draw Maps from Different Perspectives
Have students use maps in the atlas at the front of this book as sources and draw their own maps of the world in which the center, or focal point, is not the equator. (For example, a map may focus on South America or Australia.) Have students compare their maps to see how different perspectives affect views of the world.

Math

Calculate Ratios
Have students use the Mercator projection shown above and library or Internet resources to conduct the following experiment: Select two landmasses on the map—for example, Greenland and Australia. Find the actual area of each landmass, and compare them. Then examine the map to see how their sizes compare. Have students write brief reports about their findings and share them with the class.

More About . . .

Finding Absolute Location
The distance represented by each degree of latitude is nearly 70 miles. (The distances represented by degrees of longitude get progressively smaller as one approaches the poles.) Therefore, the area represented by a given set of coordinates in whole degrees can be quite large, especially near the equator. For more precise expressions of location, degrees of latitude and longitude can be divided: there are 60 minutes in each degree of latitude or longitude and 60 seconds in each minute.

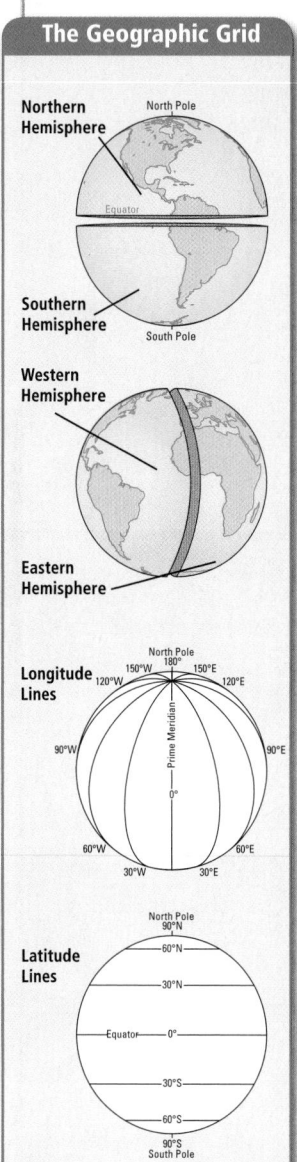

The Geographic Grid

Northern Hemisphere — North Pole — Equator
Southern Hemisphere — South Pole

Western Hemisphere
Eastern Hemisphere

Longitude Lines — North Pole — 180° — 150°W — 150°E — 120°W — 120°E — 90°W — 90°E — Prime Meridian — 0° — 60°W — 60°E — 30°W — 30°E

Latitude Lines — North Pole — 90°N — 60°N — 30°N — Equator — 0° — 30°S — 60°S — 90°S — South Pole

Hemispheres To study Earth, geographers divide the globe into equal halves. Each half is called a **hemisphere**. An imaginary line called the equator divides the globe into north and south halves. The half of Earth north of the equator is called the Northern Hemisphere. The half south of the equator is called the Southern Hemisphere.

Geographers use another imaginary line to divide Earth east from west. This line is called the prime meridian. The half of Earth west of the prime meridian is called the Western Hemisphere. The half east of the prime meridian is called the Eastern Hemisphere. As you can see in the diagram on the left, the United States is located in the northern and western hemispheres.

The Geographic Grid The diagram also shows two globes marked with lines of latitude and longitude. As you have already learned, latitude lines lie to the north and south of the equator. Longitude lines go around Earth over the poles. These lines run east and west of the prime meridian.

Geographers use a grid system to find the point where a latitude line and a longitude line cross. This point identifies an absolute location—the exact place on Earth where a city or other geographic feature can be found. Remember that location is one of the themes geographers use to describe Earth.

Absolute location is expressed using the coordinates, or set of numbers, of the latitude and longitude lines. These coordinates are measured in degrees. Every place on Earth has only one absolute location. For example, as you can see on the map on the following page, the absolute location of Rio de Janeiro, Brazil, is 23° south latitude, 43° west longitude.

REVIEW How do the latitude and longitude lines on a map help geographers?
They help geographers find the absolute locations of geographic features.

DIFFERENTIATING INSTRUCTION

Gifted and Talented Students

Locate Places in Your Community
Have students use library or Internet resources to find the absolute locations of key buildings or spots in their community. Students should also research the proper way to indicate latitude and longitude measurements. Have students record their information on a map they create of their community.

Struggling Readers

Make Concept Flash Cards
Have students work in pairs to create flash cards for the many terms and concepts mentioned in this section—*equator, prime meridian, geographic grid,* and so on. On one side of each card, students should write a term; on the other side, they should record the definition and an illustration. When students have finished the cards, have them take turns quizzing each other.

Different Maps for Different Purposes

2 **ESSENTIAL QUESTION** What different maps do we use to see natural and human-made features and to understand patterns? *physical, political, and thematic maps*

Different maps help us see different things. The three basic types of maps are political maps, physical maps, and thematic maps. You have probably used all of these different types of maps.

Political Maps **Political maps** show the features people have created, such as cities, states, provinces, territories, and countries. State and country boundaries can also be outlined on these types of maps. A political map of a smaller area, such as a state, often shows county boundaries.

Here are some of the questions the features of a political map, like the one below, might help you answer:
- Where on Earth's surface is this area located?
- What is the size and shape of the area? How might its size or shape affect its people?
- Who are the area's neighbors?
- How populated does the area seem to be?

Political Map: Brazil

GEOGRAPHY SKILLBUILDER
INTERPRETING MAPS
Location In what part of Brazil is Rio de Janeiro located?

INTERDISCIPLINARY ACTIVITIES

Science

Collect Data for a Political Map
Have students use library and Internet resources to collect data for a political map of their state. Students should find the following information:
- county names
- major cities
- state capital
- neighboring states

Math

Measure Distances
Have students use the scale on the map above to measure the following distances:
- Recife to Brasília *(about 1,000 miles or 1,600 kilometers)*
- Brasília to Rio de Janeiro *(about 600 miles or 1,000 kilometers)*
- Rio de Janeiro to Pôrto Alegre *(about 800 miles or 1,200 kilometers)*

Teach

Different Maps for Different Purposes

CST 3
Talk About It

- What are the three basic types of maps? *(physical, political, and thematic)*

- Give an example of how different types of maps can be combined. *(Possible answer: A map may include both political and physical information or both political and thematic information.)*

- **Critical Thinking: Categorizing** What kind of map would you look for if you wanted to learn about the practice of different religions in a particular region or country? *(Possible answer: a map that includes both thematic information and political information)*

History from Visuals

Interpreting Maps
Remind students that a map can sometimes include more than one type of information— for example, both political and physical information.

- Identify two different categories of information presented on this map. *(political information, such as the boundaries of countries, and physical information, such as the locations of mountains)*

GEOGRAPHY SKILLBUILDER ANSWER
It is located on the southeastern coast of Brazil.

History from Visuals

Interpreting Maps

Direct students' attention to the key in the upper right-hand corner of the map. Help them recognize the way colors are used to show differences in elevation.

- What is the approximate elevation of Brazil's capital? *(between 1,600 and 6,800 feet, or 500 and 2,000 meters)*

GEOGRAPHY SKILLBUILDER ANSWER

mainly between sea level and 650 feet (200 meters)

More About . . .

Brazil's Population Centers

As the political map of Brazil suggests, the nation has been most heavily settled along the coast. The historical capital city of the country was Rio de Janeiro. However, Brazilians long dreamed of establishing a new capital in the interior of the country. This would provide a secure location and, it was hoped, promote settlement of Brazil's interior.

In the 1950s, the Brazilian government began the task of building an entirely new city in what was then a completely remote location. There were no railroads or even roads in the area. Nevertheless, the new capital—called Brasília—was built. Today it is a thriving city.

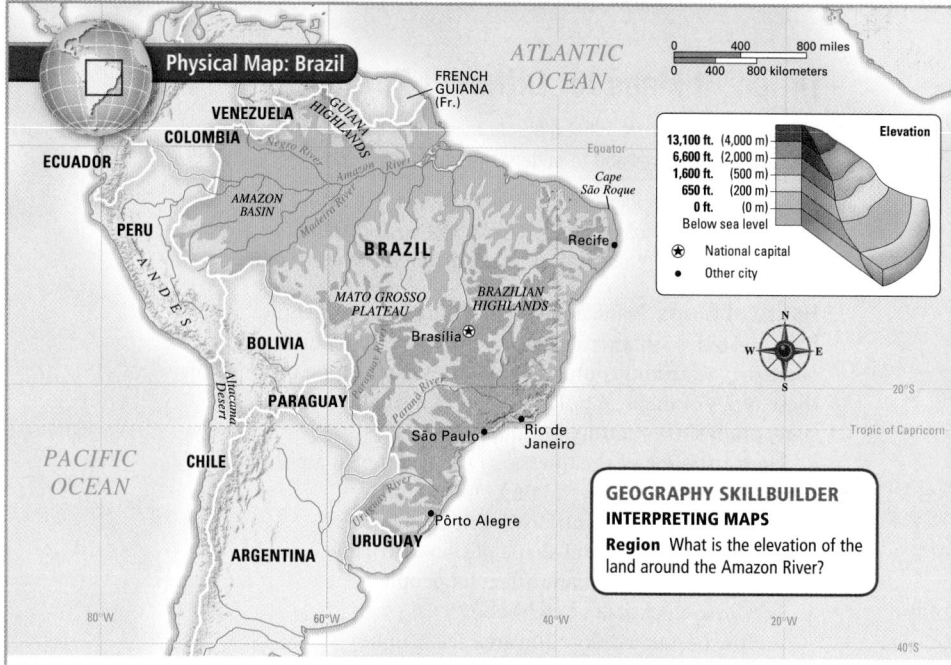

Physical Maps On a physical map, you can see what Earth's surface might look like from space. **Physical maps** show the landforms and bodies of water found in particular areas. Colors are often used to show elevations. On the map above, for example, brown indicates higher, more mountainous areas. Green shows areas that are relatively flat.

Political and physical features are often shown on one map. When this information is combined, you can use it to help you better understand the region. For instance, find the cities shown on the physical map of Brazil above. Notice that many of these cities are located near the coast.

Like political maps, physical maps can help you understand specific characteristics of places. Here are some questions the features of a physical map might help you answer:

- Are there mountains or plateaus in the area?
- Near what physical features do most people live?
- What is the area's range of elevation? How might higher and lower elevations affect people's lives?
- In which direction do the rivers flow? How might this affect travel and transportation in the area?

DIFFERENTIATING INSTRUCTION

English Learners

Make a Chart of Cognates

Explain that most cognates are words in English and Spanish that have similar spellings and pronunciations, and whose meanings are the same. Ask students to find words in the text that remind them of words in Spanish. Use an English/Spanish dictionary to find a definition that relates to the context of the lesson. Then make a chart of the cognates.

For more support, see *Modified Lesson Plans for English Learners*, p. 7.

Inclusion

Write and Administer Map Quizzes

Have students work in pairs, with each pair writing five questions about different types of maps. Pair more able readers with less able readers. (For example, students might write, "To find out the capital of a country, you would need a _____ map.") Each pair should also write an answer key for their questions. When the pairs have finished, have them exchange their quizzes. Have the pairs take turns quizzing each other and correcting the quizzes.

Thematic Maps A **thematic map** includes certain information about a place or region. For example, the thematic map on this page shows the climates in Brazil.

Thematic maps can use colors, symbols, lines, or dots to help you see patterns. The map's title and legend will help you understand the theme and the information presented. In this textbook, you will find thematic maps on such topics as historical events, vegetation, and population density.

In fact, a thematic map can show just about any kind of information you can imagine. Here are just a few of the questions different thematic maps can help you answer:

- Where in the world do people speak Spanish?
- What are the natural resources of Africa?
- What is the best route for sailing across the Atlantic?
- Where and when did key battles take place during World War II?
- Where were the major trade routes in Asia in ancient times?

REVIEW Which type of map might help you find the highest mountain in Brazil? physical map

Vocabulary Strategy

Thematic and *theme* belong to the same **word family.** Both words refer to a topic.

Geography Handbook

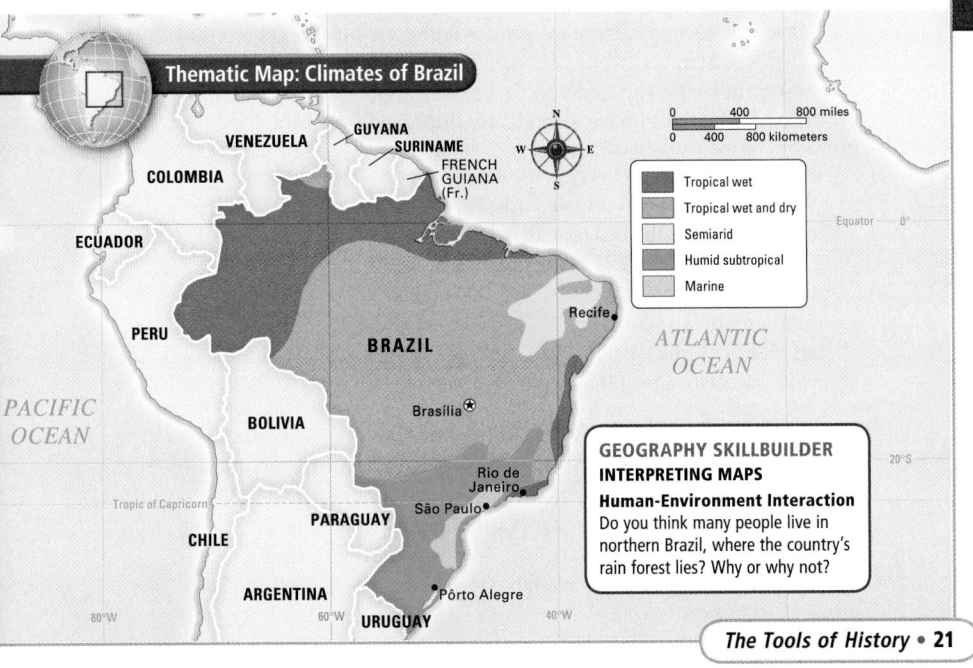

Thematic Map: Climates of Brazil

VENEZUELA
GUYANA
SURINAME
FRENCH GUIANA (Fr.)
COLOMBIA
ECUADOR
PERU
BRAZIL
Recife
ATLANTIC OCEAN
PACIFIC OCEAN
BOLIVIA
Brasília
Rio de Janeiro
São Paulo
Tropic of Capricorn
PARAGUAY
CHILE
ARGENTINA
Pôrto Alegre
URUGUAY

Equator 0°
20°S
80°W 60°W 40°W

- Tropical wet
- Tropical wet and dry
- Semiarid
- Humid subtropical
- Marine

0 400 800 miles
0 400 800 kilometers

GEOGRAPHY SKILLBUILDER
INTERPRETING MAPS
Human-Environment Interaction
Do you think many people live in northern Brazil, where the country's rain forest lies? Why or why not?

The Tools of History • 21

CHAPTER 1 • LESSON 2

Vocabulary Strategy

Word Families
Tell students that recognizing the family to which a word belongs can help them guess the word's meaning. Have students find some other words in this lesson that are parts of word families. Have them list other words in those families. One example is *physical*, which is in the same family as *physician* and *physics.*

History from Visuals

Interpreting Maps
Direct students' attention to the key in the upper right-hand corner of the map. Help them recognize the way colors are used to communicate information about the theme of this map—the climates of Brazil.

- What climate is found in the largest portion of Brazil? *(tropical wet and dry)*

Extension Ask students to compare this thematic map with the physical map of Brazil. Ask students what physical features might explain the large area of tropical wet climate in the north of Brazil. *(the Amazon River system and the low elevation)*

GEOGRAPHY SKILLBUILDER ANSWER
Possible answer: No, the thick vegetation and hot, humid climate probably make life difficult.

DIFFERENTIATING INSTRUCTION

Struggling Readers

Create a Map Web Diagram
Have students create web diagrams to describe the different types of maps and their key features. Each student should take a sheet of paper, draw a circle in the center, and write the word *map* in it. Then students should add circles for the three kinds of maps discussed in the lesson. In these circles, students can write the names and key features of these types of maps.

Gifted and Talented Students

Make Physical and Political Maps
Instruct students to create physical and political maps of their neighborhood. The political map can show the boundaries of properties. The physical map can show major natural features, such as streams.

Teach

How Maps Change

CST 1, CST 3, HI 2

Talk About It

- Why have the nature and quality of maps changed over history? *(Maps have become more accurate and detailed as people learn more about the world.)*

- What knowledge enabled Arab and Chinese mapmakers to create accurate maps? *(mathematics and astronomy)*

- What is one example in this section of a technology that has improved the quality of maps in recent years? *(the Global Positioning System)*

- **Critical Thinking: Compare and Contrast** How are the other maps you've seen in this lesson similar to and different from the map shown on this page? *(Possible answer: The modern maps show areas accurately, while the 1570 map reflects how little was known about the continents at the time.)*

More About . . .

Ptolemy's *Geography*
In addition to providing instructions for making maps, Ptolemy's *Geography* provided the latitudes and longitudes of thousands of places. Its translation into Latin in the 1400s helped spread its popularity in Europe. Among its readers was Christopher Columbus. Some experts think Ptolemy's information about Asia—he believed it extended much farther to the east—encouraged Columbus to attempt the journey on which he reached the Americas.

 Map Transparencies
- MT2 The World According to Ptolemy, A.D. 150

▲ **Map from the Past** This map of North and South America was drawn by European mapmakers in 1570. As you can see, the mapmakers had only a rough idea of what the two continents looked like.

How Maps Change

3 ESSENTIAL QUESTION How have maps changed to reflect people's increasing understanding of the world? They have become more accurate.

Have you ever made a map to show someone how to get to your house? A map you would draw today would probably be much better than one you made in first grade. Maps showing different parts of the world have also greatly improved over time.

Earliest Maps The very earliest maps were probably scratched on the ground or drawn on tree bark. The oldest surviving maps were carved on clay tablets by the Babylonians around 2300 B.C.

The ancient Greeks made great advances in developing maps. In the second century A.D., a Greek astronomer and mathematician named Ptolemy (TAHL•uh•mee) produced an eight-volume work called *Geography.* This work contained valuable instruction on preparing maps.

Maps in the Middle Ages In the Middle Ages, Arab and Chinese mapmakers used their knowledge of astronomy and mathematics to draw accurate maps of parts of the world. By contrast, European mapmakers filled empty spaces on their maps with pictures or warnings. This was partly because Ptolemy's work was not available to Europeans until about 1405.

INTERDISCIPLINARY ACTIVITIES

Art

Make an Old-Fashioned Map
Instruct students to study the map on this page. Students should note that the mapmakers used pictures of ships to decorate the map. Have students design their own maps of their community, including pictures or symbols that are meaningful in their area.

Science

Report on Ptolemy's Life
Have students research and report on the life of Ptolemy. Students should report on the many fields of study in which Ptolemy excelled, including mathematics and astronomy.

European maps greatly improved after 1569, when a Flemish mapmaker named Gerhardus Mercator showed the curved surface of Earth on a flat map. His Mercator projection, which you learned about on page 17, helped explorers plot straight routes on maps.

Today's Maps Many modern maps are made with the help of the satellites of the Global Positioning System (GPS). You will learn more about this system in the Connect to Today feature on page 24.

REVIEW What were some of the results as maps improved?
Improved maps aided exploration, and people learned more about Earth.

Lesson Summary

- Maps and globes have different advantages as tools used to measure and describe Earth.
- Political, physical, and thematic maps show us different things about the world and our place in it.
- Over time, maps have become more accurate.

Why It Matters Now . . .

We still use maps to find our way around and to learn more about familiar and unfamiliar places.

▲ **Ptolemy** Ptolemy's *Geography* remained one of the most important geographical works until 1496, when explorers began to prove some of his statements wrong.

Geography Handbook

---

2 Lesson Review

Homework Helper
ClassZone.com

Terms & Names

1. Explain the importance of

longitude hemisphere physical map
latitude political map thematic map

Using Your Notes

Comparing and Contrasting Use your completed Venn diagram to answer the following question:

2. How are maps and globes similar? (CST 3)

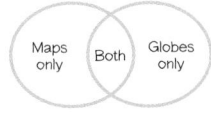

Maps only | Both | Globes only

Main Ideas

3. Would you use a map or a globe to see a continent's exact shape? Explain why. (CST 3)

4. Describe the three types of maps. (CST 3)

5. Why were European maps in the Middle Ages so inaccurate? (CST 1)

Critical Thinking

6. Drawing Conclusions Why did European mapmakers in the Middle Ages sometimes leave empty spots on their maps? (HI 2)

7. Making Inferences What impact do you think improved mapmaking had on explorers? (HI 2)

Activity **Making a Map** Create a thematic map of your neighborhood or school, showing, for example, populations, buildings, or numbers of people who own pets. Be sure to include a legend to explain any colors or symbols on your map. (CST 3)

The Tools of History • 23

---

❹ Assess & Reteach

Assess Have students work on their own to answer the questions. Then have the class come together to discuss answers together.

 **Formal Assessment**
- Lesson Quiz, p. 6

Reteach Have students review each of the maps and visuals in this lesson. Instruct students to write a caption for each, explaining the significance of the illustration to the whole lesson.

In-Depth Resources: Unit 1
- Vocabulary Cards, p. 11
- Reteaching Activity, p. 18

Homework Helper

Visit **ClassZone.com** for a lesson review, flip-card activities, and links to related Web sites.

---

2 Lesson Review Answers

Terms & Names

1.
- longitude, p. 16
- latitude, p. 16
- hemisphere, p. 18
- political map, p. 19
- physical map, p. 20
- thematic map, p. 21

Using Your Notes

See page 14 for an example of a completed diagram.

2. Possible answers: They both represent Earth's surface; they both show Earth's landforms and bodies of water; they both include lines of latitude and longitude.

Main Ideas

3. a globe, because it is round like Earth

4. Political maps show human creations, such as cities and roads; physical maps show landforms and bodies of water; thematic maps show specific information, such as climate, or historical events.

5. because people did not yet have the knowledge of astronomy and mathematics necessary to determine locations on Earth by the stars and their experience of travel was limited

Critical Thinking

6. Possible answer: They didn't know anything about the lands in some areas of the world.

7. Possible answers: helped them locate land, return home, steer clear of obstacles

Activity Rubric

	Features of Map	Clarity of Theme
4	includes most features of a map	clear, specific theme with detailed information
3	includes many features of a map	clear, specific theme
2	includes some features of a map	vague theme
1	includes few features of a map	no theme

The Tools of History • 23

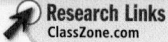
Research Links
ClassZone.com

Objectives

- Describe the historical challenge of navigating and determining location.
- Describe the navigation aids used by early explorers.
- Summarize key features of the Global Positioning System.

❶ Focus & Motivate

Preview Discuss with students that for as long as people have explored, they have faced the challenge of how to determine locations and stay on course for distant destinations. Explain that these two pages describe historical and modern solutions to this challenge.

❷ Teach

Talk About It

- What is one disadvantage of relying on a sextant for navigation? *(You cannot take measurements on cloudy nights because you cannot see the stars.)*

- Why are GPS devices able to work even in bad weather? *(They rely on radio waves rather than sight.)*

- **Critical Thinking: Making Inferences** Why do you think it is necessary to have 24 satellites in the GPS system? *(Possible answer: It takes that many satellites to monitor all areas of Earth.)*

Navigation and the Global Positioning System

CALIFORNIA STANDARDS
HI 2 Students understand and distinguish cause, effect, sequence, and correlation in historical events, including the long- and short-term causal relations.

Purpose: To learn about Global Positioning System, which is used to determine locations on Earth

Throughout history, people have tried to figure out where they were and how they could find their way to another place. The earliest explorers and sailors navigated by the stars. However, this method wasn't much use on a cloudy night. Today, navigators still look to the sky to find their location. But now they are guided by the orbiting satellites of the Global Positioning System, or GPS. These satellites can pinpoint any spot on Earth in any weather.

Past

The Sextant For several hundred years, sailors used sextants, like the one shown below, to navigate. A sextant is a device that measures the angle between two objects. A navigator used the mirrors on a sextant to sight the horizon and the sun or a star. The angle between the two appeared on the sextant's scale. The navigator in the illustration at the right is using a sextant.

DIFFERENTIATING INSTRUCTION

English Learners

Discuss Navigation
Invite students to imagine themselves on a ship crossing the ocean. Ask, "Would you want to navigate your ship by using the stars, using a sextant, or using GPS? Why?"

Struggling Readers

Compare and Contrast
Have students create a Venn diagram to compare and contrast the sextant and the Global Positioning System.

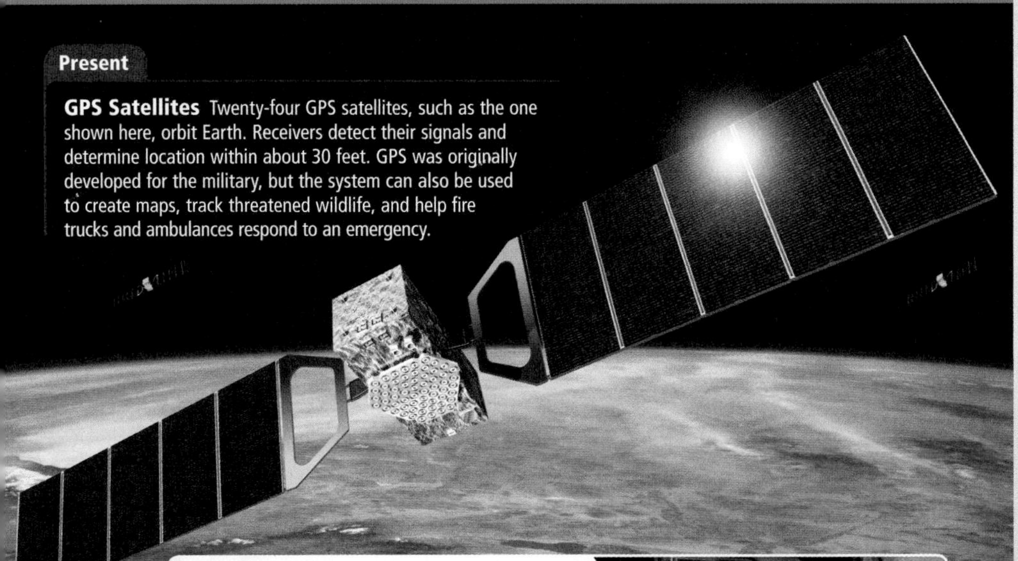

Present

GPS Satellites Twenty-four GPS satellites, such as the one shown here, orbit Earth. Receivers detect their signals and determine location within about 30 feet. GPS was originally developed for the military, but the system can also be used to create maps, track threatened wildlife, and help fire trucks and ambulances respond to an emergency.

Tracking Vehicles Monitoring the locations of cars is one of the fastest-growing GPS applications. Drivers can also use GPS map displays to plan trips.

Tracking Children Receivers mounted on watches help parents keep track of wandering children. The system finds a child and shows his or her location on a detailed map.

Activities

1. **TALK ABOUT IT** What uses for GPS can you think of?

2. **WRITE ABOUT IT** Write a dialogue in which a modern navigator explains the uses and benefits of GPS technology to an early explorer. (Writing 2.2)

The Tools of History • 25

Research Links
Visit **ClassZone.com** for editor-approved, age-appropriate Web sites related to this topic.

More About . . .

How Sextants Work
A sextant provides an easy, accurate way to measure latitude. For example, in the Northern Hemisphere, a sailor can determine latitude simply by measuring the angle between the horizon and Polaris, the North Star. This angle is precisely equal to the latitude. A sailor who knows the latitude of the port of departure has a reasonable chance of returning home safely by sailing north or south to the port's line of latitude and then following that line home.

The problem of determining longitude required the development of accurate methods for keeping time at sea. This problem was solved in the 1700s.

More About . . .

The Global Positioning System
The GPS system includes 24 satellites positioned about 11,000 miles above Earth's surface. In addition, the system includes a series of ground stations located around the world. The master control station is located in Colorado. These stations monitor the satellites, analyze data from them, and then return data to the satellites. The data are then transmitted to users of the GPS system. A GPS receiver uses data from four satellites to establish location, direction, and speed.

ACTIVITY ANSWERS

1. **TALK ABOUT IT** Possible answers: locating a missing pet; finding the exact location of a store or house; tracking speed and distance for athletic activities, such as running or biking

2. **WRITE ABOUT IT**

2. Writing Rubric

	Explanation of GPS System	Uses and Benefits of GPS	Errors in Mechanics
4	very accurate	identifies known uses and two benefits	two or fewer
3	includes only one or two errors	identifies known uses and one benefit	between three and five
2	includes several errors	identifies only known uses	between five and ten
1	largely inaccurate	identifies no uses	more than ten

❶ Plan & Prepare

Objectives

- Describe the tools used by archaeologists to study and understand human history.
- Summarize current knowledge about the history of humanlike beings.
- Summarize the current knowledge about the Stone Age.
- **Language Objective:** Use structural and context clues to define words to gain a deeper understanding of the information.

Quick Look

Lesson 3 explores the science of archaeology and discusses findings that add to our understanding of early people.

❷ Focus & Motivate

Preview Tell students that this lesson focuses on the tools of archaeology and some important findings in this field. Ask students to think about what a scientist studying the site of their home thousands of years in the future might be able to tell about their life. *(Possible answer: He or she might be able to tell what hobbies I pursued and what my family life was like.)*

Introduce the Main Ideas "How Archaeologists Study the Past" brings together the Big Ideas about science and technology and culture.

Reading Skill: Finding Main Ideas Have students use graphic organizers like the one below to help them find main ideas in each section as they read.

SAMPLE ANSWERS FOR DIAGRAM

```
┌─────────────────────────────────┐
│     FInding Clues to the Past    │
└─────────────────────────────────┘
                 │
┌─────────────────────────────────┐
│            Main Idea             │
│  Archaeologists are scientists who learn │
│       about early people.        │
└─────────────────────────────────┘
         │                │
┌──────────────┐   ┌──────────────┐
│    detail    │   │    detail    │
│ They work with│   │  They study  │
│ other scientists│  │   fossils.   │
│ to examine what│   │              │
│ they find in  │   │              │
│ the ground.   │   │              │
└──────────────┘   └──────────────┘
```

Lesson 3

▶ MAIN IDEAS

❶ **Science and Technology** Archaeologists are scientists who work to uncover the story of early people.

❷ **Science and Technology** Archaeologists have found evidence that tells us a great deal about early humans.

❸ **Culture** Human culture developed during the prehistoric period known as the Stone Age.

▶ TAKING NOTES

Reading Skill: Finding Main Ideas

The main idea of a passage is a sentence that sums up its most important point. Details in the passage help support the main idea. As you read Lesson 3, use a diagram like the one below to identify the main idea of each section.

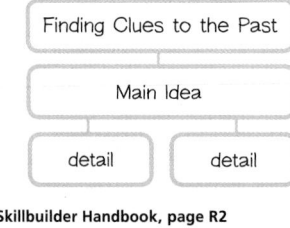

```
┌─────────────────────────────────┐
│    Finding Clues to the Past     │
└─────────────────────────────────┘
                 │
┌─────────────────────────────────┐
│            Main Idea             │
└─────────────────────────────────┘
         │                │
┌──────────────┐   ┌──────────────┐
│    detail    │   │    detail    │
└──────────────┘   └──────────────┘
```

Ⓢ Skillbuilder Handbook, page R2

▲ **Footprint** This footprint was made by a humanlike being about 3.6 million years ago. Footprints and other remains are the kind of evidence archaeologists study to learn about the past.

HOW TO TEACH THE CALIFORNIA STANDARDS

Standard	Content	Student Question or Activity	Instruction
6.1	**Page 29** Describes what is known about early humankind as far back as the Paleolithic era	**Page 33** Students tell what archaeologists have learned about early hominids.	Explain that archaeologists who discovered an early hominid named her Lucy after the Beatles' song "Lucy in the Sky with Diamonds." Have students listen to the song and discuss why scientists chose to name her Lucy.
6.1.1	**Page 32** Explains Stone Age achievements such as the development of tools and the mastery of fire	**Page 33** Students describe how people lived during the Paleolithic and Mesolithic ages.	Ask students to speculate how early people may have discovered fire and what steps they may have taken in an effort to use and control it.
HI 5	**Page 28** Describes how scientists make new discoveries and figure out how prehistoric people lived	**Page 33** Students tell why studying early people is difficult.	Have students think of questions about early hominids that they hope to find answers to in the lesson. If the answers can't be found in the lesson, have students research their questions on the Internet.

How Archaeologists Study the Past

TERMS & NAMES
artifact
fossil
hominid
Paleolithic Age
Mesolithic Age
Neolithic Age

CHAPTER 1 • LESSON 3

Terms & Names

artifact a human-made object

fossil a preserved remain of early life

hominid a human or human-like creature that walks on two feet

Paleolithic Age an era lasting from about 2.5 million to 8000 B.C.

Mesolithic Age an era lasting from about 10,000 to 6000 B.C.

Neolithic Age an era lasting from about 8000 to 3000 B.C.

Build on What You Know When you read a detective story, you use clues in the story to try to solve the mystery. Now you will find out how people solve the mysteries of the past without any written clues.

Finding Clues to the Past

1 ESSENTIAL QUESTION How do archaeologists uncover the story of early peoples? *by searching for and studying artifacts and fossils*

When you think about most researchers at work, you probably imagine them in libraries and book-lined studies. A day at the office for an archaeologist, on the other hand, often means sifting through the dirt in a small plot of land. Archaeologists are scientists who learn about early people by digging up and studying the traces of early settlements. On archaeological digs, these scientists search for bones and other evidence that might tell them about life long ago.

Archaeologists The archaeologists at this dig site use small shovels and brushes to carefully unearth and examine their findings. ▼

❸ Teach

Finding Clues to the Past

6.1, HI 5

Talk About It

- **Critical Thinking: Comparing and Contrasting** How are archaeology and anthropology similar? *(Both study human culture and try to connect the past and present.)*

California Resources

California Reading Toolkit, L3
California Modified Lesson Plans for English Learners, p. 9
California Daily Standards Practice Transparencies, TT3
California Standards Enrichment Workbook, pp. 15–16
California Online Test Practice
California Test Generator CD-ROM
California Standards Planner and Lesson Plans, L5
California EasyPlanner CD-ROM
California eEdition CD-ROM

27

LESSON 3 PROGRAM RESOURCES

ON LEVEL

In-Depth Resources: Unit 1
- Reading Skill: Finding Main Ideas, p. 5
- Vocabulary Study Guide, p. 9
- Vocabulary Cards, p. 11
- Geography Practice: Archaeological Sites in the United States, p. 13

Formal Assessment
- Lesson Quiz, p. 7

ENGLISH LEARNERS

In-Depth Resources in Spanish
- Reading Skill: Finding Main Ideas, p. 4

Modified Lesson Plans for English Learners, p. 9
Reading Study Guide (Spanish), p. 9
Reading Study Guide Audio CD (Spanish)

STRUGGLING READERS

In-Depth Resources: Unit 1
- Vocabulary Cards, p. 11
- Reteaching Activity, p. 19

Reading Toolkit, L3
Reading Study Guide, p. 9
Reading Study Guide Audio CD

GIFTED AND TALENTED STUDENTS

In-Depth Resources: Unit 1
- Primary Source: Lucy, p. 15

Interdisciplinary Projects
- Science, p. 2
- Art, p. 4

History Makers
- Louis Leakey, p. 1

INCLUSION

EasyPlanner CD-ROM
- Reading Skill: Finding Main Ideas
- Vocabulary Study Guide
- Reteaching Activity

TECHNOLOGY

eEdition CD-ROM

Power Presentations CD-ROM

Humanities Transparencies
- HT1 Stone Hammer Head

Critical Thinking Transparencies
- CT3 Finding Main Ideas

Test Generator CD-ROM

ClassZone.com

In-Depth Resources: Unit 1
• Reading Skill: Finding Main Ideas, p. 5

More About . . .

Dating of Artifacts and Fossils

Accurate dating of fossils and artifacts is important to the work of archaeologists. Scientists have developed various techniques for measuring the ages of objects found in the ground. For example, scientists can determine the relative ages of items by comparing the layers of dirt in which the objects are found. Layers nearer the surface were deposited after layers far below.

Scientists have also developed methods for determining absolute ages of objects. One example is radiocarbon dating, which measures the amount of radioactive carbon remaining in an object. Because scientists know the rate at which radioactive carbon decays, they can accurately determine the object's age.

Humanities Transparencies
• HT1 Stone Hammer Head

History from Visuals

Interpreting Time Lines

Have students examine the time line of hominid development.

• According to the illustrations that accompany the time line, what physical features changed as hominids developed? *(The shape of the head and the size of the brain changed.)*

• Which hominid existed for the longest time? *(australopithecines)*

Working Together Archaeologists work with teams of other researchers and scientists to make new discoveries about how prehistoric people lived. Some of the other scientists help archaeologists figure out when **artifacts**, or human-made objects, were made and what they might mean. The artifacts can help archaeologists answer old questions and lead them to ask new ones.

Scientists called anthropologists often work with archaeologists too. Anthropologists study culture, which is the way of life of a group of people. Culture includes a people's beliefs, common language, and shared ways of doing things. The information collected by anthropologists helps archaeologists make connections between the past and present.

Studying Fossils Evidence of early people can be found in **fossils**, remains of early life preserved in the ground. Human fossils often consist of small pieces of teeth, skulls, and other bones. Figuring out the approximate age of fossils is one of the archaeologist's greatest challenges. Archaeologists use complicated techniques to calculate the ages of ancient fossil remains and artifacts.

REVIEW What do archaeologists do?
excavate and study the traces of early human settlements

Hominid Development

This time line is based on the findings of archaeologists.

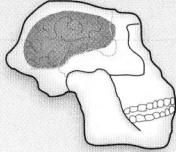

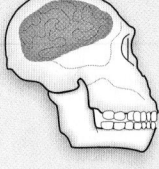

Australopithecine
• lived from about 4.5 million to 1 million B.C.
• found in southern and eastern Africa
• first humanlike creature to walk upright

Homo habilis
• lived from about 2.5 million to 1.5 million B.C.
• found in East Africa
• first to make stone tools

4 million B.C.

3 million B.C.

Homo habilis

Australopithecine

28 • Chapter 1

DIFFERENTIATING INSTRUCTION

English Learners

Define Words in Context

Help students understand the meanings of the key terms. Guide students to negotiate the words' definitions in the context of the lesson. Have students use the following sentence pattern for the vocabulary words: Fossils are remains of early life found in rocks, such as small pieces of teeth, skulls, and bone fragments.

The Search for Early Humans

 ESSENTIAL QUESTION What have archaeologists learned about early humans from the evidence they have found?

The search for our earliest ancestors has taken archaeologists to Africa, where most scientists believe that humans began. There, they have answered many questions about the first humans.

Earliest Humans Some of the earliest humanlike beings that archaeologists have found are called australopithecines (aw•STRAY•loh•PIHTH•ih•SYNZ). These beings and other creatures that walk on two feet—including humans—are called **hominids**. Most scientists believe that australopithecines learned to walk on East African grasslands about 4.5 million years ago.

About 2.5 million years ago, a hominid called *Homo habilis* (HOH•moh HAB•uh•luhs), which means "man of skill," also appeared in East Africa. Archaeologists believe that these hominids used stone tools to cut meat and crack open bones.

Most scientists believe that *Homo erectus* (HOH•moh ih•REHK•tuhs), or "upright man," first appeared about 1.6 million years ago. Scientists think this hominid may have gradually developed into our own large-brained species, *Homo sapiens* (HOH•moh SAY•pee•uhnz), or "wise man."

They have learned where and how early humans lived, what they were like, and how they developed.

Vocabulary Strategy

Hominid comes from the Latin **root word** *homo*, meaning "man." The names of human species, such as *Homo sapiens*, all derive from this root word.

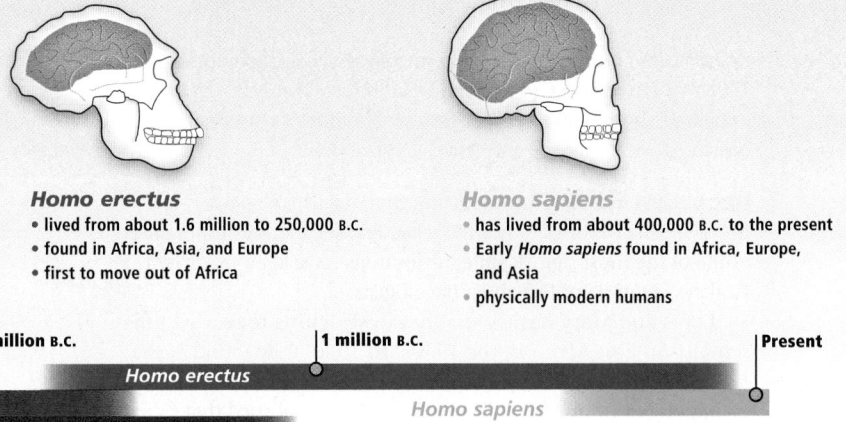

Homo erectus
- lived from about 1.6 million to 250,000 B.C.
- found in Africa, Asia, and Europe
- first to move out of Africa

Homo sapiens
- has lived from about 400,000 B.C. to the present
- Early *Homo sapiens* found in Africa, Europe, and Asia
- physically modern humans

2 million B.C.   1 million B.C.   Present

Homo erectus

Homo sapiens

The Tools of History • 29

Teach

The Search for Early Humans

6.1, HI 5

Talk About It

- What feature sets hominids apart from many other creatures? *(They walk on two feet.)*
- Which is the first known hominid? *(australopithecine)*
- According to what archaeologists have discovered so far, when did hominids first appear on Earth? *(about 4.5 million years ago)*
- **Critical Thinking: Explaining Geographic Patterns** What does the history of hominids suggest about where humanlike creatures first emerged? *(They probably first appeared in Africa and then spread to different parts of the world.)*

Vocabulary Strategy

Root Word
Have students review the names of hominids that appear in the time line and in the text under the heading "Earliest Humans." Ask students to observe how the Latin root word *homo* is used along with other words to create new terms.

DIFFERENTIATING INSTRUCTION

Inclusion

Analyze the Time Line
Students who have trouble putting ideas in sequence may benefit from examining a particular hominid in relationship to the other hominids. Divide the class into groups of two to three students. Assign each group one of the four hominids to examine. Each group should focus on the features of their assigned hominid and the ways it was related to those hominids that appeared before or after it. Ask a respresentative from each group to present the group's findings.

Gifted and Talented Students

Trace the History of a Hominid
Invite students to select one of the hominids and use library or Internet resources to research what is known about the fate of that creature. Students should write brief reports summarizing the latest scientific theories about their chosen hominids.

History from Visuals

Interpreting Maps

Have students study the map on this page, paying special attention to the locations of the important archaeological finds shown on the map.

- What does the map show that may help explain why the rift valley to the west of Lake Victoria has not yielded as many important discoveries? *(Much of the valley is underwater.)*

INTERACTIVE

An interactive version of this map is available on the eEdition and Power Presentations CD-ROMs.

More About . . .

Archaeology in the Great Rift Valley

There are a number of reasons why the Great Rift Valley is such fertile ground for archaeological study. One important factor is that this area is and has been the scene of much volcanic and earthquake activity. This has led to the exposure of once deeply buried layers of soil. In addition, the dry climate means that there is no significant vegetation to protect the land from wind erosion. This has left many fossils exposed for relatively easy discovery. Finally, the volcanic activity in the area has aided in the dating of archaeological finds.

Archaeological Finds in East Africa, 1960–1993

INTERACTIVE

0   250   500 miles
0   250   500 kilometers

Red Sea

INDIAN OCEAN

RIFT VALLEY

Lake Victoria

Present-day border
Rift valley

Archaeological Sites

■ **1960** Louis and Mary Leakey find *Homo habilis* fossils. (Olduvai Gorge, Tanzania)
■ **1974** Donald Johanson finds Lucy. (Hadar, Ethiopia)
□ **1978** Mary Leakey finds hominid footprints. (Laetoli, Tanzania)
■ **1984** Richard Leakey finds an almost complete *Homo erectus* skeleton. (West Turkana, Kenya)
■ **1992–1993** Tim White finds fossils of a new species. (Aramis, Ethiopia)

Modern Humans Human culture developed significantly with the appearance of *Homo sapiens*. Early *Homo sapiens* buried their dead, created cave paintings, and made sharper tools. In time, these humans began to farm, developed writing systems, and built complex villages. Some physically modern *Homo sapiens*, called Cro-Magnons (kroh•MAG•nuhnz), first appeared about 35,000 years ago. Cro-Magnons migrated from North Africa to Europe and Asia.

Important Finds Our understanding of early people is based on the findings of many archaeologists and anthropologists. Some of the most significant contributions have been made by the Leakeys, a family of British archaeologists.

Louis and Mary Leakey first began searching for early human remains in East Africa in the 1930s. In 1960, they found *Homo habilis* fossils in East Africa. Their discoveries showed that human evolution began in Africa. The Leakeys also established that *Homo habilis* was our ancestor.

▲ **Rift Valleys** Many archaeological digs have been carried out in East Africa's rift valleys. These valleys average 30 to 40 miles wide. They were formed as continental plates pulled apart over millions of years.

30 • Chapter 1

INTERDISCIPLINARY ACTIVITIES

Science

Diagram the Great Rift Valley

To connect the discussion of archaeology with what students have learned about the movement of plates in the shaping of Earth's surface, have students use Internet or library resources to research the Great Rift Valley. Students should create a diagram of how scientists believe the valley was formed.

Language Arts

Report on an Archaeological Finding

Have students write imaginary news reports about the significant archaeological findings discussed in this lesson. Each article should answer the basic journalistic questions *who, what, where, when, why,* and *how.*

In 1974, American archaeologist Donald Johanson discovered an unusually complete skeleton of an australopithecine. He and his team named the hominid Lucy. You will learn more about Lucy in the History Makers feature below. In 1978, Mary Leakey uncovered more information about australopithecines. She also became the first to discover a set of footprints made by these hominids. You can see a photograph of one of these footprints on page 26.

The Leakeys' son, Richard, also became an important archaeologist. He and his team found a 1.6-million-year-old skeleton of a *Homo erectus* in 1984. It is one of the most complete skeletons ever found.

More recent findings have added to our understanding of early humans. In the early 1990s, American anthropologist Tim White found apelike fossils that led to the naming of a new hominid species. In 2002, a team of archaeologists found a hominid skull in Chad. The 6- to 7-million-year-old skull belongs to our earliest human ancestor so far discovered. (You can read an excerpt from a novel about archaeologists and their discoveries in the Literature Connection on page 34.)

REVIEW What are the names of some early hominids?
australopithecines, Homo habilis, Homo erectus

History Makers

Lucy (lived around 3.5 million B.C.)

On November 30, 1974, Professor Donald Johanson and his student Tom Gray were searching the hot, dry ground of Hadar, Ethiopia. There they discovered a tiny piece of an arm bone. Several other bones lay nearby. They belonged to a type of australopithecine Johanson had never seen before.

Excited by the find, members of the expedition went back and retrieved 40 percent of the creature's skeleton, which is shown here. The pelvis indicated that she was female, and the archaeologists named her Lucy, after the Beatles' song "Lucy in the Sky with Diamonds."

At about 3.5 million years old, Lucy was older than any hominid discovered up to that time. She had a smallish brain, like a chimp's, and very long arms. But she walked upright. Lucy challenged the theory that a bigger brain had led to walking.

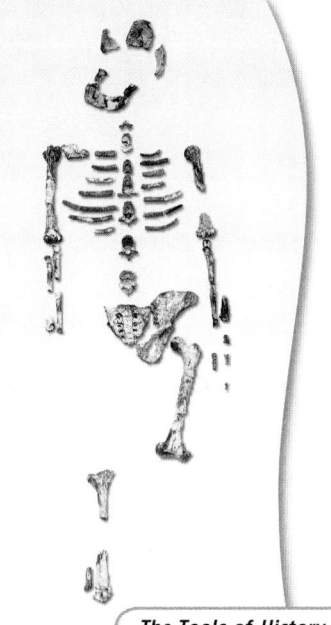

The Tools of History • 31

INTERDISCIPLINARY ACTIVITIES

Art

Draw a Portrait of Lucy

Ask students to create pictures of what they think Lucy may have looked like. Students may wish to use Internet or library resources to learn more about what is known about Lucy and other australopithecines.

Science

Diagram How People Walk

The ability to walk upright is one feature that helps make humans different from other creatures. Have students use Internet or library resources to learn about the skill of walking. Students should use their research to create diagrams of how people walk.

Teach

The Stone Age

▶ **6.1.1**

Talk About It

- What are three key achievements in human history that occurred during the Stone Age? *(Possible answer: invention of tools, mastery over fire, development of language)*

- How did the nature of tools change from the Paleolithic Age to the Mesolithic Age? *(The tools became more complex, and there were more types of tools.)*

- How did Mesolithic people learn to be more efficient hunters? *(They became more specialized hunters.)*

- **Critical Thinking: Making Inferences** Why do you think the development of farming made the settlement of communities possible? *(Possible answer: With farming, people no longer needed to travel and move in search of food. They could create their own food supplies right where they lived.)*

More About . . .

The First Farmers

Many scientists believe people first began to farm in the part of the world we refer to today as the Middle East. There they began to cultivate a type of wheat that their hunter-gatherer predecessors had once collected from the wild.

Scientists also believe that one reason for the development of farming may have been climate changes that occurred toward the end of the last ice age. These changes, which brought much drier weather to this region, may have made it harder for people to gather food from wild sources and led some to begin cultivation.

The Stone Age

Homo habilis, Homo erectus, and *Homo sapiens* lived during this period. They invented tools, mastered fire, and developed language and farming

③ ESSENTIAL QUESTION Who lived and what happened during the prehistoric period known as the Stone Age?

The invention of tools, the mastery of fire, and the development of language and farming are some of humankind's most important achievements. Scientists believe that these advances took place during the prehistoric period known as the Stone Age. This period dawned when hominids made and used the first stone tools.

The Stone Age is often divided into three phases: the Old Stone Age, the Middle Stone Age, and the New Stone Age. The Old Stone Age, also called the **Paleolithic** (PAY•lee•uh•LIHTH•ihk) **Age**, lasted from about 2.5 million to 8000 B.C. The Middle Stone Age, also called the **Mesolithic** (MEHZ•uh•LIHTH•ihk) **Age**, occurred roughly between 10,000 and 6000 B.C. This period served as a sort of bridge between the Old and New Stone Age. The New Stone Age, or **Neolithic** (NEE•uh•LIHTH•ihk) **Age**, began about 8000 B.C. and ended as early as 3000 B.C. You can compare the characteristics of the three periods in the chart below.

The Stone Age		
Period	**Dates**	**Characteristics**
Paleolithic Age	2.5 million–8000 B.C.	• *Homo habilis, Homo erectus,* and *Homo sapiens* lived during this period. • Early humans lived as hunters and gatherers. • People used simple stone tools with single sharp edges to cut and chop.
Mesolithic Age	10,000–6000 B.C.	• Mesolithic peoples developed needles and thread, harpoons, and spear throwers. • They began to control fire and develop language. • In some places, people specialized in hunting particular animals. • Gatherers developed grindstones to prepare the vegetables they collected.
Neolithic Age	8000–3000 B.C.	• Only *Homo sapiens* lived during this period. • People learned to polish stone tools and make pottery. • They began to grow crops, raise animals, and settle in villages.

Paleolithic Age figure ▶

Neolithic Age figure ▶

DIFFERENTIATING INSTRUCTION

Struggling Readers

Divide and Conquer

Divide the class into small groups. Have each group discuss a single one of the Stone Age phases discussed above. When groups have completed their discussions, bring the class together and have each group report on their findings.

Gifted and Talented Students

Make a Stone Age Time Line

Ask students to use the information from their text and from Internet and library resources to create an illustrated time line of the Stone Age.

The development of farming in the Neolithic Age greatly changed people's lives. Instead of wandering from place to place, people began to settle down and build communities. As time passed, these early humans' skills and tools for surviving and adapting to the environment became more sophisticated. You will learn more about these early people and their communities in Chapter 2.

REVIEW What achievements occurred during the Stone Age?

Lesson Summary use of tools, control of fire, development of language, raising of crops and animals

- Studying ancient artifacts and fossils helps reveal early human history.
- The first humanlike creatures developed in Africa.
- During the Stone Age, people began to use tools, control fire, speak, grow crops, and raise animals.

Why It Matters Now . . .
Learning about our common beginnings can help people see that our similarities outweigh our differences.

Australopithecine Skull
These hominids had small brains, but their thumbs could cross their palms. This meant that they could pick up small objects and use tools. ▼

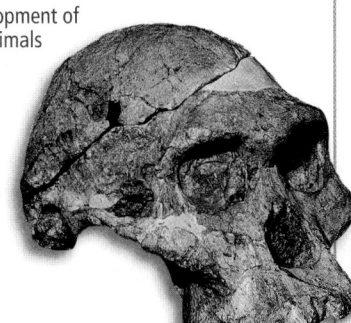

3 Lesson Review

 Homework Helper
ClassZone.com

Terms & Names
1. Explain the importance of
   - artifact
   - hominid
   - Mesolithic Age
   - fossil
   - Paleolithic Age
   - Neolithic Age

Using Your Notes
Finding Main Ideas Use your completed diagram to answer the following question:
2. What is the main idea of the section "The Search for Early Humans"? (6.1)

```
Finding Clues to the Past

Main Idea

detail        detail
```

Main Ideas
3. What can archaeologists learn by studying artifacts and fossils? (6.1)
4. What have archaeologists learned about early hominids? (6.1)
5. How did people live during the Paleolithic and Mesolithic ages? (6.1.1)

Critical Thinking
6. **Understanding Continuity and Change** What kinds of changes probably encouraged the development of early hominid societies? (6.1.1)
7. **Identifying Issues and Problems** Why is studying early people so hard? (HI 5)

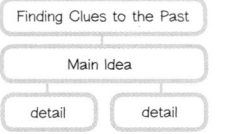 **Activity** **Internet Activity** Use the Internet to research one of the archaeologists named in this lesson. Present your findings, including pictures and maps, on a poster you can share with the class. (6.1)
INTERNET KEYWORD: *archaeologist's name*

The Tools of History • 33

❹ Assess & Reteach

Assess Have students work in pairs to answer the questions. Ask them to note the locations of the answers within the lesson.

 Formal Assessment
- Lesson Quiz, p. 7

Reteach Divide the class into teams of three. Each team member should prepare a brief oral presentation on one of the major sections of this lesson. Have team members present their reports to one another.

📝 **In-Depth Resources: Unit 1**
- Vocabulary Cards, p. 11
- Reteaching Activity, p. 19

🔎 **Homework Helper**
Visit **ClassZone.com** for a lesson review, flip-card activities, and links to related Web sites.

3 Lesson Review Answers

Terms & Names
1. • artifact, p. 28
   • fossil, p. 28
   • hominid, p. 29
   • Paleolithic Age, p. 32
   • Mesolithic Age, p. 32
   • Neolithic Age, p. 32

Using Your Notes
See page 26 for an example of a completed diagram.
2. Archaeologists have made important findings that tell us about early hominids.

Main Ideas
3. Possible answers: how long ago early people lived; how they lived; what they looked like

4. Possible answers: what tools they used, that they used fire, that they gradually became more sophisticated
5. They lived as hunters and gatherers.

Critical Thinking
6. Possible answers: increasing ability to use and refine tools, organizing hunting and gathering activities
7. Possible answer: They left behind no written records, so we must speculate about the meanings of the things they did leave.

Activity Rubric

	Required Elements	Content of Poster
4	includes all required elements	complete, accurate
3	includes all but one required element	nearly complete, accurate
2	includes all but two required elements	nearly complete, some inaccuracies
1	missing most or all required elements	incomplete and inaccurate

The Tools of History • 33

Objective

Describe the excitement created by a major scientific and historical discovery.

❶ Focus & Motivate

Connect to the Big Idea

Science and Technology Our knowledge of our own history depends on the work of skilled and dedicated scientists. Their discoveries have changed our understanding of the past.

Connect to Prior Knowledge

Ask students to recall what they have learned in Lesson 3 about what archaeologists do. *(They search for artifacts that can teach us about the distant past. They study fossils and other evidence to learn about the people who lived in ancient times.)*

More About . . .

Archaeology Techniques
Trained archaeologists bring great knowledge to their jobs. But much of the work they do is painstaking labor carried out with simple tools.

When an archaeological team identifies an area for study, they divide it into small sections for excavation. Often, archaeologists will work on a section that is only a few feet square. Within these sections, they carefully begin removing the dirt level by level. It is important to remove one layer at a time, because knowing the depths at which items are found is important to understanding the items' meaning. Archaeologists make a detailed record of each layer of each section. The dirt they remove is also studied for tiny objects they may have missed, such as seeds.

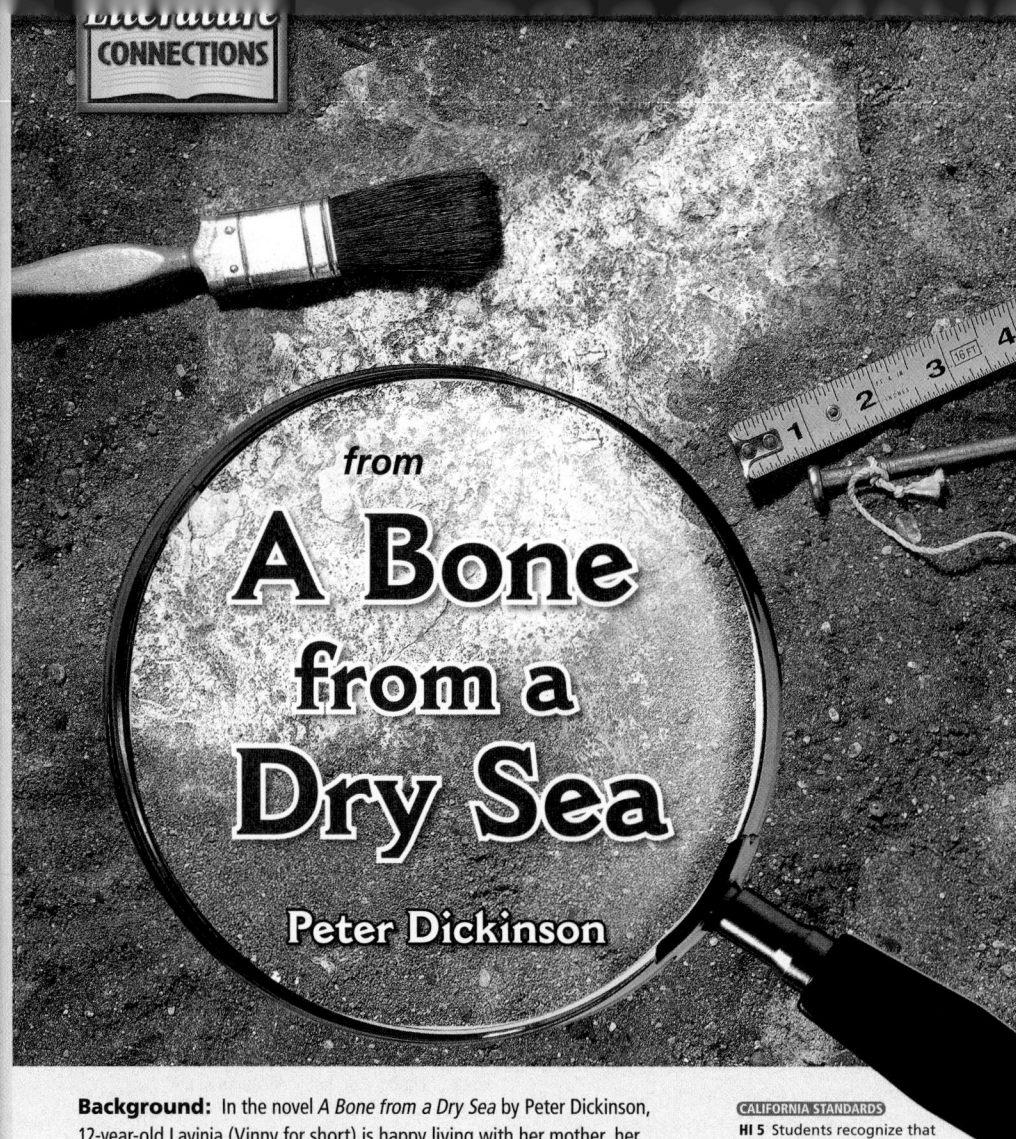

from

A Bone from a Dry Sea

Peter Dickinson

Background: In the novel *A Bone from a Dry Sea* by Peter Dickinson, 12-year-old Lavinia (Vinny for short) is happy living with her mother, her stepfather Colin, and her half-brothers in England. But she misses her father, Sam, an archaeologist. So Vinny asks to join her father in Africa, where he is part of a team searching for hominid fossils.

One day, Vinny goes to explore a site with the team leader, Dr. Joe Hamiska. And then Vinny makes her own discovery.

CALIFORNIA STANDARDS

HI 5 Students recognize that interpretations of history are subject to change as new information is uncovered.

Reading 3.2 Analyze the effect of the qualities of the character (e.g., courage or cowardice, ambition or laziness) on the plot and the resolution of the conflict.

34 • Chapter 1

ADDITIONAL RESOURCES

Books for the Student

Cork, Barbara, and Struan Reid. *The Young Scientist Book of Archaeology.* Tulsa: EDC, 1984. Thorough review of how archaeologists work to uncover the past.

Moloney, Norah. *The Young Oxford Book of Archaeology.* Oxford: Oxford UP, 1997. Reference book about the science of archaeology.

Panchyk, Richard. *Archaeology for Kids: Uncovering the Mysteries of Our Past.* Chicago: Chicago Review, 2001. Basic overview of the field of archaeology and some of its findings.

Videos

Mysteries of Mankind. 60 minutes. Washington: National Geographic Soc., 1988. Exploration of the origins and evolution of humans.

It seemed to be thin and flat and to lie almost level in the hill so that its left edge actually broke through the sloping line of tuff.[1] The outer edge had been snapped off where it reached the surface, and the right corner, about half a square inch, was cracked and loose from the main bit. [Vinny] was working not down but sideways into the hill, digging out a hollow like a miniature quarry[2] with the bone as its floor. Dr. Hamiska's boots crunched on the rock above her. She rose to let him see what she'd been doing.

"That's great," he said. "We'll have to employ you full-time."

"What is it? Do you know?"

"A fragment of scapula, I think. Shoulder blade to you, Vinny. Some fair-sized beast. Don't try and lever it out or you'll break it—you'll have to undercut it first. Look how the sequence[3] runs at the back there—that's beautiful."

"Do you think it was killed in the eruption?"

"Could be, could be. Your father's here to answer questions like that. The ash would have been soft, mind you, so the creature could have died after the eruption and then the bones partly embedded themselves. Lend me your trowel, will you? I could get a column of the sequence out there—something to show them on Thursday. Blind them with science, eh?"

Still chuckling, he forced the blade vertically down at the back of Vinny's quarry, as if he were cutting the first slice out of a birthday cake. The slice broke in two when he eased it out but he fitted the pieces together and laid them carefully out on the slope.

"Now if you'll ask Jane for a bag and a label," he said, "and then we'll—Hold it! Hold everything!"

▲ **Trowel** Archaeologists use trowels, or small shovels, to carefully dig for bones and artifacts.

---

1. **tuff:** a layer of fossilized ash from a volcanic eruption.
2. **quarry:** hole in the ground.
3. **sequence:** layers of earth.

The Tools of History • **35**

❷ Teach

Talk About It

- Have students read the story aloud, giving a dramatic presentation of the events.
- Ask student volunteers to play the roles of the narrator and the different characters in the story.
- What are Vinny and Dr. Hamiska doing when they make their important discovery? *(They're removing the bone of an animal.)*
- **Critical Thinking: Making Inferences** What do you think that Dr. Hamiska has noticed? *(Possible answers: another bone fragment; something more interesting in the ground)*

More About . . .

Multiple-Meaning Words
Point out to students that two of the vocabulary words on this page—*quarry* and *sequence*—have multiple meanings. Ask students if they can think of any other meanings of *quarry* and *sequence*. *(Students might know that* quarry *can also refer to an animal that is being hunted, and* sequence *also means "the order in which items or ideas appear.")* Have students use a dictionary to look up the multiple meanings of these words.

DIFFERENTIATING INSTRUCTION

Struggling Readers

Illustrate the Scene
Instruct students to review the text on this page and then draw a picture of the scene described. Encourage students to be careful to note all the details mentioned by the author.

Inclusion

Act Out the Scene
Students who have difficulty with reading comprehension may find dramatizing the story helpful. Divide the class into teams. Have each team stage a scene based on the story, in which they assume the different roles and act out the events described in the story.

Teach

Talk About It

- To what does the author compare Dr. Hamiska and Mrs. Hamiska as they examine the bone? *(to terriers at a rabbit hole)*

- Why do you think Dr. Hamiska is so excited by the find? *(Possible answer: He believes he has made a significant find.)*

- **Critical Thinking: Making Inferences** What can you infer from Mrs. Hamiska's statement that Dr. Hamiska is "too excited" to continue excavating the object? *(Possible answer: It is important to be extremely careful when working at archaeological sites.)*

History from Visuals

Interpreting Visuals
Direct students' attention to the picture on this page. Point out that archaeologists often find only parts of bones and skeletons. They must use their knowledge of how bodies work to draw conclusions from tiny bits of bone.

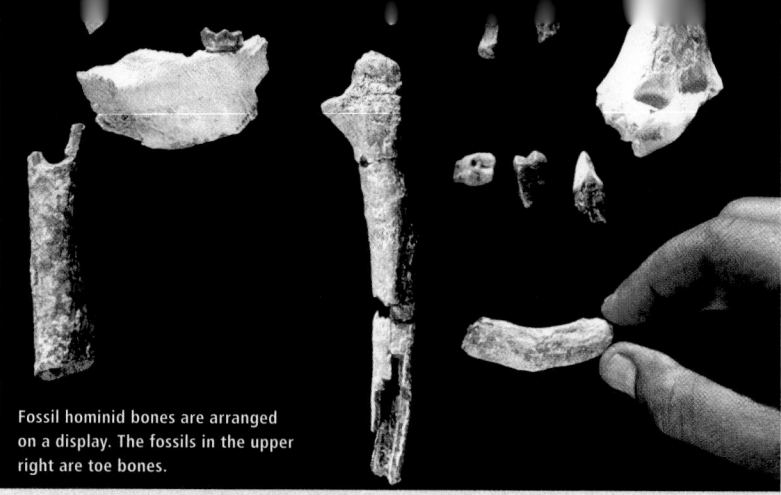

Fossil hominid bones are arranged on a display. The fossils in the upper right are toe bones.

He pushed his sunglasses onto his forehead and stared into the slice-shaped cut he had made. His breath hissed between closed teeth. With Vinny's brush he swept the loose bits from a pale lump which had been exposed on one side of the cut, just above the tuff. He took a magnifying glass from his shirt pocket and gazed intently through it.

"Jane," he called. "Come here a moment."

He'd changed. A moment before he'd been the friendly old professor showing off to the visitor. Now he'd forgotten she was there. Mrs. Hamiska came and crouched beside him. Every line of their bodies expressed enthralled[4] excitement. Two terriers at the same rabbit hole.

"Oh, yes," said Mrs. Hamiska. "I think so. I really do think so."

"Whoopee!" bellowed Dr. Hamiska, standing and flinging his cap into the air. It landed halfway down the hillside.

"Let me have a go," said Mrs. Hamiska. "You're a bit too excited."

REVIEW Why do you think Dr. Hamiska is so excited?
Vinny has made an important discovery.

Without waiting for an answer she started to chip the clay away from the other side of the cut. Vinny fetched Dr. Hamiska's cap, and then helped him measure and peg out an area around the find. Standing on the rock he began to draw a sketch map. By now Mrs. Hamiska had opened the cut enough for Vinny to see that the fossil was a stubby cylindrical[5] bone with a bulge at each end.

"Is it part of someone's hand?" she said.

_____
4. **enthralled:** absorbed with interest.
5. **cylindrical:** circular, in the shape of a cylinder.

DIFFERENTIATING INSTRUCTION

English Learners

Record Story Elements
Explain to students that the main elements of story structure are characters (the main people in a story), setting (the story's time and place), plot (the story events, which usually include a problem), and conclusion (how the story ends or the solution to the problem). Have students use index cards to record these elements. Then have groups share their note cards.

Gifted and Talented Students

Write Excavation Instructions
Have students use library or Internet resources to find out more about the excavation techniques of archaeologists. Then have them use the information to write instructions for the removal of the bone that Vinny and the Hamiskas have found in this story.

"Their foot, Vinny, their foot!" crowed Dr. Hamiska. "It's a distal phalanx—a toe bone to you, Vinny. You are looking at the left big toe of a creature that walked on its hind legs five million years ago! It's going to be datable by the tuff! And either my name's not Joseph Seton Hamiska or the rest of the skeleton is all there, right under our feet! The oldest fossil hominid yet found! I knew it! I knew it! I knew the moment I woke up that this was my day, and this was going to be the place! Whoopee!"

You could have heard his shouts a mile across the plain. Mrs. Hamiska straightened and watched him, like Mom watching Colin and the boys let the sea run into the moat[6] of their sandcastle, yelling with triumph as it swirled around their ramparts.[7]

"I think you'd better get Sam out here, darling," she said.

"Yes, yes, of course. And Fred and the others—as many witnesses as we can. . . . I'll call them up."

He charged down the hill toward the jeep, where he'd left the two-way radio, but halfway down he stopped and turned.

"Vinny!" he shouted. "Didn't I tell you, the moment I set eyes on you, you were going to bring us luck!"

REVIEW What does Vinny's discovery lead Dr. Hamiska to find?
a toe bone–according to Dr. Hamiska, part of the oldest fossil hominid yet found
_____
6. **moat**: water-filled ditch around a castle.
7. **ramparts**: defense barriers around a castle.

Reading & Writing

1. **READING: Character** What impact does Dr. Hamiska's personality have on the story?

2. **WRITING: Narration** What do you think will happen next? Write a scene in which Dr. Hamiska and Vinny present their find to the rest of the team. (Writing 2.1)

The Tools of History • 37

READING & WRITING ANSWERS

1. **READING** *Possible answer:* His personality adds excitement, tension, and interest.

2. **WRITING**

2. Writing Rubric

	Dramatic Quality	Number of Errors
4	interesting and realistic	few or none
3	realistic	some
2	confusing	many
1	incoherent	many major errors

Teach

Talk About It

- What is Dr. Hamiska able to determine about the bone he and Vinny have found? (*He can tell what kind of bone it is and that the individual from which it came walked on two feet.*)

- How does Dr. Hamiska know the age of the bone? (*He knows the age of the material in which the bone was found, so he thinks that the bone must be of a similar age.*)

- **Critical Thinking: Making Inferences** Why do you think Dr. Hamiska wants to get more witnesses to their find? (*Possible answer: He wants witnesses to help substantiate the facts of the nature, place, and circumstances of the find.*)

❶ Plan & Prepare

Objectives

- Analyze the reasons why people study history.
- Describe the tools historians use to study the past.
- Explain how our understanding of history is always subject to change.
- **Language Objective:** Determine whether scenarios presented constitute a primary source, secondary source, or oral history.

Quick Look

Lesson 4 explores the challenges and questions that historians face and the tools they use to pursue their studies.

❷ Focus & Motivate

Preview Tell students that this lesson focuses on the goals and tools of historians. Ask students to think about how they may draw on lessons learned in the past when making decisions about their lives today. For example, students might recall learning about the dangers of bees, then using what they learned to avoid being stung.

Introduce the Main Ideas This lesson touches on the Big Ideas of culture and science and technology.

Reading Skill: Categorizing Have students use graphic organizers like the one below to help them categorize the jobs of the historian.

SAMPLE ANSWERS FOR DIAGRAM

Asking questions
- How have groups interacted?
- What have been the results?

Using tools
- primary sources
- secondary sources

Historian's Job

Examining evidence
- evaluating sources
- testing theories

Lesson 4

▶ **MAIN IDEAS**

① **Culture** Historians often ask questions about the past in order to understand the present.

② **Culture** Historians use a variety of methods to help them answer questions about what happened in the past.

③ **Culture** Historians examine evidence and draw conclusions as they answer historical questions.

▶ **TAKING NOTES**

Reading Skill: Categorizing

When you categorize information, you organize similar kinds of information into groups. In Lesson 4, you will read about the three main jobs of a historian. Record what you learn in a web diagram like the one below.

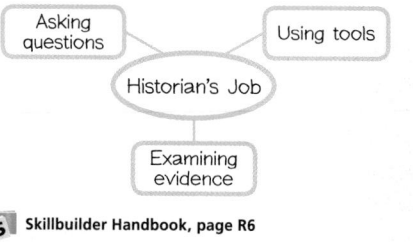

S **Skillbuilder Handbook, page R6**

▲ **Cave Paintings** Caves throughout the world have ancient paintings of human hands. These hand paintings were found in a cave in Argentina. Historians believe that the hands marked territorial ownership or served as the artists' signature.

CALIFORNIA STANDARDS

REP 1 Students frame questions that can be answered by historical study and research.

REP 2 Students distinguish fact from opinion in historical narratives and stories.

HI 5 Students recognize that interpretations of history are subject to change as new information is uncovered.

HOW TO TEACH THE CALIFORNIA STANDARDS

Standard	Content	Student Question or Activity	Instruction
REP 1	**Page 40** Lists types of questions that historians ask when conducting research	**Page 41** Students frame questions that the Rosetta Stone helped historians answer.	Have students brainstorm questions that a historian might ask about an unknown society at the beginning of a project. Compare the class list with the sample questions found in the lesson.
REP 2	**Page 42** Contrasts fact and fiction in historical evidence and in primary and secondary sources	**Page 43** Students list facts and opinions about Stonehenge.	Write facts from the lesson on the board and have volunteers read a fact aloud, then turn it into an opinion. Discuss why it's important for historians to be able to differentiate between fact and opinion.
HI 5	**Page 42** Describes how new discoveries can prove existing theories false	**Page 43** Students describe how historians sort through evidence and draw conclusions about unknown events in history.	Discuss a currently unsolved mystery, such as the Loch Ness Monster, Bigfoot, or the Bermuda Triangle. Ask students to make conjectures about the futures of these mysteries.

How Historians Study the Past

► TERMS & NAMES

primary source

secondary source

oral history

Build on What You Know You may know where your parents or ancestors came from and some of the stories about them. Relatives and their stories help people understand their family history. Now learn what historians use to help them understand the past.

Understanding the Past

① ESSENTIAL QUESTION What questions do historians ask to help them understand the past? *They ask questions that help them compare different societies.*

People investigate their family history to find out about their ancestors. In the process, however, they also find out about themselves. We study world history for the same reasons.

Why Study History? What has already happened to a person, a family, or a society affects what will occur today and in the future. But history is much more than simply recounting and studying past events. Examining a historical event also involves studying a society's culture, religion, politics, and economics.

When historians examine past events, they try to find patterns. They look for causes and effects that explain how and why events happened. They also try to understand why some ideas and traditions last and why others die out. Just as important, historians attempt to see the past through the eyes of the people who lived it. By doing so, historians gain greater insight into human nature and answer important historical questions.

Storyteller This West African griot, or storyteller, memorizes and tells the stories that make up his village's history. ▼

39

Terms & Names

primary source something written or created by a person who witnessed a historical event

secondary source an account of a historical event written by someone who did not witness the event

oral history an unwritten account of an event

❸ Teach

Understanding the Past

HI 5

Talk About It

- **Critical Thinking: Comparing and Contrasting** What do you think historians learn by comparing and contrasting different societies? *(Possible answer: a point of reference and helps them draw conclusions)*

California Resources

California Reading Toolkit, L4

California Modified Lesson Plans for English Learners, p. 11

California Daily Standards Practice Transparencies, TT4

California Standards Enrichment Workbook, pp. 1–14

California Online Test Practice

California Test Generator CD-ROM

California Standards Planner and Lesson Plans, L7

California EasyPlanner CD-ROM

California eEdition CD-ROM

LESSON 4 PROGRAM RESOURCES

ON LEVEL

In-Depth Resources: Unit 1
- Reading Skill: Categorizing, p. 6
- Vocabulary Study Guide, p. 9
- Vocabulary Cards, p. 11

Formal Assessment
- Lesson Quiz, p. 8

ENGLISH LEARNERS

In-Depth Resources in Spanish
- Reading Skill: Categorizing, p. 5

Modified Lesson Plans for English Learners, p. 11

Reading Study Guide (Spanish), p. 11

Reading Study Guide Audio CD (Spanish)

STRUGGLING READERS

In-Depth Resources: Unit 1
- Reading Skill: Categorizing, p. 6
- Vocabulary Cards, p. 11
- Reteaching Activity, p. 20

Reading Toolkit, L4

Reading Study Guide, p. 11

Reading Study Guide Audio CD

GIFTED AND TALENTED STUDENTS

Interdisciplinary Projects
- Language Arts, p. 3

INCLUSION

EasyPlanner CD-ROM
- Reading Skill: Categorizing
- Vocabulary Study Guide
- Reteaching Activity

TECHNOLOGY

eEdition CD-ROM

Power Presentations CD-ROM

Humanities Transparencies
- HT2 Stonehenge

Critical Thinking Transparencies
- CT4 Categorizing
- CT5 Chapter 1 Visual Summary

Test Generator CD-ROM

ClassZone.com

In-Depth Resources: Unit 1
• Reading Skill: Categorizing, p. 6

Teach

The Historian's Tools

REP 1, HI 5

Talk About It

• What kind of source would you call an artifact, such as a tool? *(a primary source)*

• What does it mean to say that a secondary source is an indirect link to an event? *(It means that the source was not produced by someone directly connected to the event.)*

• What are some examples of oral history? *(Possible answer: songs, stories, and customs that are passed down orally)*

• **Critical Thinking: Categorizing** If you were looking for a source that included several different points of view in an analysis of an event, what kind of source would you be looking for? *(You would be looking for a secondary source.)*

History from Visuals

Interpreting Artifacts
Direct students to examine the artifacts in the illustrations and note the progression in quality from the Paleolithic Age tool to the Bronze Age tool.

• From these pictures, what conclusions can you draw about early humans' ability to create tools? *(Possible answer: Humans developed more refined techniques for making tools and developed new materials for making tools.)*

Asking Historical Questions As historians study the past, they ask themselves questions like those below. These questions help historians compare different societies and draw conclusions about the past.

• How have groups or societies interacted, and what have been the results?
• How have leaders governed societies?
• How have belief systems developed and changed?
• How have societies dealt with differences among their people?
• How have societies tried to protect people's security?
• How are societies similar and different?

REVIEW Why do we study history?
to learn about the past and how it affects us today

The Historian's Tools

 ESSENTIAL QUESTION What methods do historians use to help them answer questions about what happened in the past? They consult written, oral, and human-made sources.

When you hang up a picture, you use a hammer to pound in the nail. Historians also use tools to do their job. These tools include primary sources, secondary sources, and oral history.

Primary Sources A **primary source** is something written or created by a person who witnessed a historical event. You will learn about an ancient primary source on the next page. Primary sources include letters, diaries, eyewitness articles, videotapes, speeches, and photographs. Artifacts, such as the human-made tools below, are also primary sources.

Artifacts

These ax heads from different prehistoric periods show historians how early peoples' toolmaking ability advanced over time.

  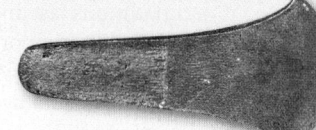

▲ 200,000 B.C. In the Paleolithic Age, humans made tools by chipping stone.

▲ 3000 B.C. In the Neolithic Age, humans learned to polish tools.

▲ 600 B.C. By the Bronze Age, humans had learned to shape a thin ax head.

40 • Chapter 1

DIFFERENTIATING INSTRUCTION

Struggling Readers

Record an Oral History
Have students identify subjects—for example, neighbors, parents, or teachers—and conduct oral-history interviews with the people about their school experiences. Have students use an audio or video recorder to record their subjects' recollections.

Gifted and Talented Students

Identify Strengths and Weaknesses of Primary and Secondary Sources
Have each student write a paragraph on primary sources and a paragraph on secondary sources, explaining the strengths and weaknesses of these tools. What does each offer the historian? What is each unable to provide in terms of insight and information?

Primary Source

The Rosetta Stone

The Rosetta Stone is a primary source from ancient Egypt that dates back to 196 B.C. Historians found the stone in 1799. They know now that the three different kinds of writing on the stone record the deeds of a young Egyptian ruler. The first writing is shown in the top inset. The other two writings are shown in the bottom inset. But no one could read much of the first two writings until 1822, when a French scholar cracked their code. The Rosetta Stone provided important information about the writing system of the ancient Egyptians.

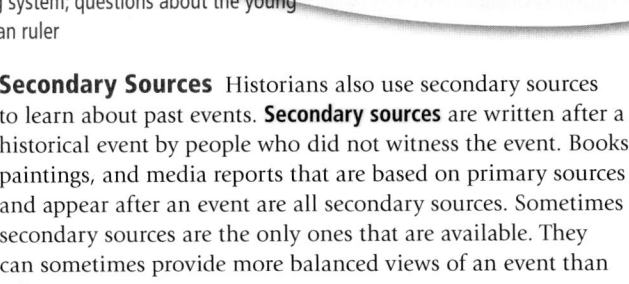

DOCUMENT–BASED QUESTION
What questions did the Rosetta Stone help historians answer?

Possible answer: questions about Egypt's writing system; questions about the young Egyptian ruler

Secondary Sources Historians also use secondary sources to learn about past events. **Secondary sources** are written after a historical event by people who did not witness the event. Books, paintings, and media reports that are based on primary sources and appear after an event are all secondary sources. Sometimes secondary sources are the only ones that are available. They can sometimes provide more balanced views of an event than primary sources.

Oral History When cultures have no written records, historians rely on oral history as a resource. **Oral history** is made up of all the unwritten verbal accounts of events. It includes the stories, customs, and songs that a culture has told and passed from generation to generation. For example, West African storytellers, like the one shown on page 39, have memorized and told family histories and the traditions and stories of their villages for hundreds of years.

REVIEW What tools do historians use to learn about the past?
primary sources, secondary sources, oral histories

The Tools of History • 41

Interpreting Primary Sources

- What factor made the Rosetta Stone a valuable source of information about ancient languages? (*It contains three different kinds of writing.*)
- What enabled historians to finally figure out what the writing on the stone said? (*A French scholar cracked the code.*)

DOCUMENT–BASED QUESTION ANSWER
The Rosetta Stone helped historians answer questions about the Egyptian writing system and about the young Egyptian ruler.

More About . . .

The Rosetta Stone
The Rosetta Stone contains writing in Greek as well as two forms of Egyptian writing. One is called demotic, and the other is hieroglyphics, a type of writing that was used for important ceremonial documents. When the Rosetta Stone was found in the late 1700s, knowledge of how to read hieroglyphics had been lost to the world.

The Greek writing on the stone was quickly translated. The demotic was soon unraveled too, in large part because it had a relationship to Coptic writing, which some European scholars knew. The last code to be cracked was the hieroglyphics.

DIFFERENTIATING INSTRUCTION

Inclusion

Take Notes on Audiotape
Have students who are visually impaired take oral notes on audiotape with a classmate. After finishing the lesson in class, have the pair review what they have learned and tape it. Encourage them to use written notes and to record not only main ideas but supporting details as well.

English Learners

Model Sources
Have students work in small groups to explain the difference between primary sources, secondary sources, and oral history. Use a graphic to record their findings. Guide students as they create a scenario that models a primary source, a secondary source, or oral history.

Teach

How Knowledge of the Past Changes

 6.2.5, REP 2 , HI 5

Talk About It

- What happens when a historian has more information than he or she can use in answering a historical question? *(The historian must sift through the evidence to choose only that which is necessary and trustworthy.)*

- How did historians disprove the myth of the mummy's curse? *(by examining the facts and figuring out a much more likely explanation for the deaths)*

- What are some of the different conclusions historians have reached about Stonehenge? *(that it was a temple for priests who practiced magic and that it was a temple for some other sort of worship, such as sun worship)*

- **Critical Thinking: Making Inferences** What can you infer from the fact that historians sometimes draw different conclusions from examining the same sources? *(Possible answer: Historians often must work with sources that do not provide definitive answers.)*

Humanities Transparencies
- HT2 Stonehenge

More About . . .

The Mummy's Curse
The myth of the mummy's curse was supported by some colorful details. These included the deaths not only of Lord Carnarvon but also of his dog—supposedly at the same instant as his master died. There were several other untimely deaths among those with some connection to the expedition, such as relatives or employees of leading figures. However, apart from Lord Carnarvon, the "curse" apparently skipped those who actually entered the tomb and worked with the mummy.

How Knowledge of the Past Changes

③ ESSENTIAL QUESTION What steps do historians take as they answer historical questions? They sort through information and choose what's most trustworthy as evidence.

Detectives use fingerprints and other evidence to solve crimes. Historians act as detectives too. They use evidence from primary, secondary, and oral sources.

Fact or Fiction? Historical evidence isn't always as simple as a bloodstain at a crime scene. Historians sometimes have more information than they can use when they try to answer a question. They must sort through all of the information and choose what's most important and most trustworthy as evidence.

In addition, sometimes what historians thought was true turns out to be false. For instance, one historian proved that the so-called mummy's curse was false. According to legend, the curse would kill anyone who entered the tomb of an ancient Egyptian ruler.

Many people believed the curse had caused the death of English archaeologist Lord Carnarvon. He died suddenly in 1923, shortly after entering the tomb of ancient Egyptian ruler "King Tut." People believed that the other archaeologists who had entered the tomb between 1923 and 1926 would also die as a result of the curse. However, a historian later examined the archaeologists' death records. Their average age at death was 70 years. The evidence did not support the existence of the mummy's curse.

Drawing Conclusions The mummy's curse was easy to disprove. But not all historical questions are so easily answered. Sometimes different historians arrive at different conclusions based on the same facts.

▲ **King Tut's Tomb** This photograph shows the interior of King Tut's tomb. Some people believed that exposure to the tomb killed Lord Carnarvon.

INTERDISCIPLINARY ACTIVITIES

Language Arts

Write a Legend
Have students identify a historical legend. (It could be a local legend or one involving Stonehenge or the mummy's curse.) Have students write accounts of the legend, conveying the mystery surrounding the events and adding details that support different theories.

Art

Create an Encoded Warning
The idea of a mummy's curse was based in part on the fact that the entrances to some mummies' tombs in Egypt bear messages warning outsiders not to enter. Have students create codes from numbers, symbols, or a combination of both. (Library and Internet sources can help students with codes.) Then have each student write a coded warning for the entrance to a private place—a room, a locker, or something similar.

On pages 2–3, you learned that Stonehenge was built out of stones dragged from faraway quarries. Most historians agree that the monument was begun around 3000 B.C. as a place of worship. Earlier theories held that it was built as a temple for a group of priests who practiced magic. However, later experts realized that the monument was finished long before these priests lived in the area. Today some historians suggest that the builders of Stonehenge were sun worshipers. But other experts maintain that Stonehenge will never reveal all its secrets.

REVIEW How are historians like detectives?
They both sift through evidence and draw conclusions from it.

Lesson Summary
- Asking historical questions can help solve mysteries about the past.
- A historian's most important tools are primary sources, secondary sources, and oral histories.
- Examining evidence can lead to a new answer to a question or deepen a mystery.

Why It Matters Now . . .
The answers to historical questions can help people as they respond to today's events and challenges.

---

4 Lesson Review

 Homework Helper
ClassZone.com

Terms & Names
1. Explain the importance of
   primary source   secondary source   oral history

Using Your Notes
Categorizing Use your completed web diagram to answer the following question:
2. What is the difference between primary and secondary sources? (REP 1)

Main Ideas
3. Name two of the questions historians ask themselves when they study the past. (REP 1)
4. What resources do historians particularly rely on when a society does not have a written history? (REP 1)
5. What do historians do when they sort through evidence, such as that involving the "curse" of King Tut's tomb? (HI 5)

Critical Thinking
6. **Distinguishing Fact from Opinion** List two facts and two opinions about Stonehenge. (REP 2)
7. **Comparing and Contrasting** Compare a historian's job with that of an archaeologist. (HI 5)

Activity
Recording an Oral History Interview an older relative about a historical event that occurred in his or her lifetime. Use the interview to write down what you learned about the event. (REP 1)

The Tools of History • 43

---

❹ Assess & Reteach

Review Have students work on their own to answer the questions and then meet in groups to discuss their answers.

📝 **Formal Assessment**
- Lesson Quiz, p. 8

Reteach Direct students' attention to the Lesson Summary. For each bulleted item, have students review the lesson for supporting information and then write a sentence that supports the item.

📝 **In-Depth Resources: Unit 1**
- Vocabulary Cards, p. 11
- Reteaching Activity, p. 20

🔍 **Homework Helper**
Visit **ClassZone.com** for a lesson review, flip-card activities, and links to related Web sites.

---

4 Lesson Review Answers

Terms & Names
1. • primary source, p. 40
   • secondary source, p. 41
   • oral history, p. 41

Using Your Notes
See page 38 for an example of a completed diagram.
2. A primary source is something written or created by someone who witnessed a historical event. A secondary source is derived from primary sources but is produced by someone who was not present at the event.

Main Ideas
3. Possible answers: How have leaders governed societies? How are societies similar and different?

4. oral history
5. They choose what is most important and figure out which evidence to believe.

Critical Thinking
6. Possible answers: Facts—Stones used to build Stonehenge were dragged from faraway quarries; Stonehenge was begun around 3000 B.C. Opinions: The builders of Stonehenge were sun worshipers; Stonehenge will never reveal all its secrets.
7. Possible answer: Archaeologists use unwritten evidence to answer their questions, while historians use both written and unwritten resources.

Activity Rubric

	Interview Questions	Content of Report
4	detailed, thorough	complete, accurate
3	thorough	nearly complete, accurate
2	general	nearly complete, some inaccuracies
1	superficial	incomplete and inaccurate

The Tools of History • **43**

Terms & Names

1. A region's *vegetation* depends on its *climate*.

2. These two measurements define a place's location; *latitude* lines measure distances north and south of the equator; *longitude* lines measure distances east and west of the prime meridian.

3. These are two phases of the Stone Age. Early humans were hunter-gatherers during the *Paleolithic Age;* more modern humans began to be farmers during the *Neolithic Age.*

4. These are two types of evidence historians use to answer questions about past events. *Primary sources* are created by people who witnessed events; *secondary sources* are created by people who were not present at the events.

Main Ideas

The World's Geography
(pages 8–13)

5. Earth and its people

6. Possible answer: It might affect how I dress, what natural disasters might occur in the area, and what plants grow in the area.

How Maps Help Us Study History
(pages 14–25)

7. They show features people have made, such as cities and boundaries.

8. They've changed as people's understanding of the world has increased.

How Archaeologists Study
the Past
(pages 26–37)

9. artifacts and fossils

10. *Homo erectus*

How Historians Study the Past
(pages 38–43)

11. Historians ask questions that help them compare different societies and draw conclusions about what caused events in the past.

12. Possible answers: letters, diaries, eyewitness articles, videotapes, speeches, photographs, artifacts

The Tools of History

Geography (CST 3)
• Earth is shaped by continents, landforms, and bodies of water.
• Physical features, climate, and vegetation affect where people live.
• People use political, physical, and thematic maps to learn about the world.

Culture (6.1, 6.1.1)
• Primary and secondary sources and oral histories answer questions about the past.
• Our earliest human ancestors first lived in Africa.
• Tools, use of fire, language, and farming developed during the Stone Age.

Science & Technology (HI 5)
• Fossils and artifacts reveal much about human development.
• Dating methods help determine a fossil's age.

► **TERMS & NAMES**

Explain why the words in each set below are linked with each other.

1. **climate** and **vegetation**
2. **longitude** and **latitude**
3. **Paleolithic Age** and **Neolithic Age**
4. **primary source** and **secondary source**

► **MAIN IDEAS**

The World's Geography (pages 8–13)
5. What do geographers study? (CST 3)
6. How might the climate where you live affect your life? (CST 3)

How Maps Help Us Study History (pages 14–25)
7. What do political maps show? (CST 3)
8. Why have maps changed throughout history? (HI 2)

How Archaeologists Study the Past (pages 26–37)
9. What do archaeologists study to learn about early humans? (6.1)
10. According to scientists, which hominid developed into *Homo sapiens?* (6.1.1)

How Historians Study the Past (pages 38–43)
11. What kinds of questions do historians ask when they study the past? (REP 1)
12. What are three examples of primary sources? (REP 1)

► **CRITICAL THINKING**
Big Ideas: Science and Technology

13. **EXPLAINING HISTORICAL PATTERNS** What does the continuing effort to develop and improve maps throughout history tell us about people and their place in the world? (HI 2)

14. **RECOGNIZING CHANGING INTERPRETATIONS OF HISTORY** Why is our understanding of the lives of early hominids subject to change? (HI 5)

15. **EVALUATING INFORMATION** What does the steady development of tools in the hunter-gatherer societies suggest about early humans' intelligence? (6.1)

ALTERNATIVE ASSESSMENT RUBRICS

1. Writing Rubric

	Clarity of Answer	Number of Errors
4	insightful, well supported	few or no errors
3	well supported	some errors
2	not well supported	many errors
1	unclear or completely unsupported	many major errors

2. Science Rubric

	Clarity of Diagrams	Accuracy of Diagrams
4	clear, accurate	detailed diagrams
3	adequate	less detailed diagrams
2	vague or incomplete	incomplete diagrams
1	inaccurate	inaccurate diagrams

ALTERNATIVE ASSESSMENT

1. WRITING ACTIVITY Apply one of the historical questions listed on page 40 to your city or state. Write a paragraph in which you answer the question. (REP 1)

2. INTERDISCIPLINARY ACTIVITY— SCIENCE Learn more about the movements of continental plates. Draw a series of diagrams demonstrating the different types of plate movement. (CST 3)

3. STARTING WITH A STORY

 Use the composition you wrote about the Lascaux Cave to create a dialogue between the four teenage explorers. Express their reactions to the cave's fate. (Writing 2.1)

Technology Activity

4. CREATING A VIRTUAL MUSEUM
Use the Internet or library to learn more about one of the early hominids discussed in this chapter. Then work with a group of classmates to create a virtual museum exhibit on how early humans lived. (6.1.1)

• Provide information about where these early hominids lived, what they ate, what tools and skills they used, and how they survived.

• Use maps, visuals, and sounds to engage your viewers' interest.

• Include documentation of your sources.

Research Links
ClassZone.com

Reading Maps Use the map below to answer the questions. (CST 3)

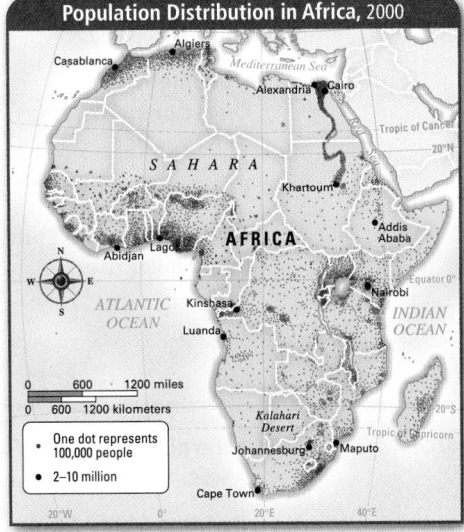

Population Distribution in Africa, 2000

One dot represents 100,000 people • 2–10 million

1. Where do most people live in Africa?
A. along the continent's coasts, rivers, and lakes
B. in the southwestern part of the continent
C. in the deserts
D. along the equator

2. Why do you think most Africans live in these areas?
A. to be near the deserts
B. to live in Africa's interior
C. to be near water sources
D. to live in a warm climate

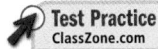
Test Practice
ClassZone.com

Additional Test Practice, pp. S1–S33

Critical Thinking

Big Ideas: Science and Technology

13. Possible answers: People want to determine exactly where they are in the world; people are curious about the world.

14. Possible answer: Our understanding may change as archaeologists and anthropologists uncover new information.

15. Possible answers: They understood that tools would help them accomplish tasks; they had the intelligence to discover ways to improve and refine tools.

Standards-Based Assessment

1. The correct answer is A. Nearly all major population centers are located near water.

2. The correct answer is C. Water is the common factor in the location of population centers.

 Research Links

Visit **ClassZone.com** for links to Web sites that can be resources for the virtual museum exhibit.

Test Practice

Visit **ClassZone.com** to access strategies and tutorials for taking standardized tests.

Formal Assessment
• Chapter Test, Forms A, B, and C, pp. 9–20

Test Generator
• Chapter Test, Forms A, B, and C (English and Spanish)

ALTERNATIVE ASSESSMENT RUBRICS

3. Starting with a Story Rubric

	Dialogue	Number of Errors
4	correct points of view, insightful, well supported	few or no errors
3	correct points of view, well supported	some errors
2	inconsistent points of view, not well supported	many errors
1	incorrect points of view, unclear or completely unsupported	many major errors

4. Technology Activity Rubric

	Required Elements	Organization
4	includes all	clear
3	includes most	reasonably clear
2	includes some	unclear
1	includes few or none	no organization

CHAPTER 2 PLANNING GUIDE: The Earliest Human Societies

Chapter Overview

Early humans initially hunted animals and gathered plants for food, but eventually started using tools and learning how to farm, setting the stage for the development of the first communities.

Copymasters

 In-Depth Resources: Unit 1
- Family Newsletter (English and Spanish), pp. 21–22
- Visual Summary, p. 26
- Vocabulary Study Guide, p. 28

 Character Education

Reading Study Guide, p. 21

 Bringing Social Studies Alive, Chapter 2

 Document-Based Questions: Strategy and Practice

Reading Toolkit, L5–L7

 Modified Lesson Plans for English Learners, pp. 13–18

Assessment

 Chapter Review, pp. 72–73

 Formal Assessment
- Chapter Tests, Forms A, B, and C, pp. 24–35

 Test Generator

 Integrated Assessment Book

 Online Test Practice

LESSON 1

Hunters and Gatherers
pp. 50–57

OBJECTIVE Trace the ways that the earliest human societies lived.

 In-Depth Resources: Unit 1
- Reading Skill: Summarizing, p. 23
- Vocabulary Cards, p. 29
- Literature: Cave Paintings, by Margaret W. Conkey, p. 33
- Reteaching Activity, p. 35

 Interdisciplinary Projects
- Science, p. 8; Art, p. 10

 Reading Study Guide, p. 15

 Lesson Review, p. 55

 Formal Assessment
- Lesson Quiz, p. 21

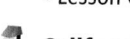 **California Daily Standards Practice Transparencies,** TT5

LESSON 2

Learning to Farm and Raise Animals
pp. 58–63

OBJECTIVE Analyze the development of agriculture and its impact on early peoples.

 In-Depth Resources: Unit 1
- Reading Skill: Understanding Cause and Effect, p. 24
- Vocabulary Cards, p. 29
- Skillbuilder Practice: Making Inferences, p. 27
- Reteaching Activity, p. 36

 Interdisciplinary Projects
- Language Arts, p. 9

 Reading Study Guide, p. 17

 Lesson Review, p. 62

 Formal Assessment
- Lesson Quiz, p. 22

 California Daily Standards Practice Transparencies, TT6

LESSON 3

The First Communities
pp. 64–71

OBJECTIVE Study the emergence of complex communities

 In-Depth Resources: Unit 1
- Reading Skill: Categorizing, p. 25
- Vocabulary Cards, p. 29
- Geography Practice: Early Farming Communities, p. 31
- Primary Source: Catal Huyuk, by William Carl Eichman, p. 34
- Reteaching Activity, p. 37

 History Makers
- Sophie of Catal Huyuk, p. 3

 Interdisciplinary Projects
- Math, p. 7

 Reading Study Guide, p. 19

 Lesson Review, p. 69

 Formal Assessment
- Lesson Quiz, p. 23

 California Daily Standards Practice Transparencies, TT7

Integrated Technology

 eEedition Plus Online

EasyPlanner Plus Online

eTest Plus Online

 Audio CDs
- Reading Study Guide
- Reading Study Guide in Spanish
- The World's Music

 CD-ROMs
- Power Presentations
- eEdition
- EasyPlanner
- Test Generator

---

 eEdition CD-ROM

 **Humanities Transparencies**
- HT3 Prehistoric Antler Pick

 Humanities Transparencies
- HT4 Cave Painting from Zimbabwe

 Map Transparencies
- MT3 Cave Art (Sites of the Upper Paleolithic)

 Critical Thinking Transparencies
- CT6 Summarizing

 ClassZone.com

---

 eEdition CD-ROM

 Critical Thinking Transparencies
- CT7 Understanding Cause and Effect

 ClassZone.com

---

 eEdition CD-ROM

 Map Transparencies
- MT4 Annual Rainfall in Southwest Asia

 Critical Thinking Transparencies
- CT8 Categorizing
- CT9 Chapter 2 Visual Summary

 ClassZone.com

Overview of California Resources

	Lesson 1	Lesson 2	Lesson 3
California Reading Toolkit	L5	L6	L7
California Modified Lesson Plans for English Learners	p. 13	p. 15	p. 17
California Daily Standards Practice Transparencies	TT5	TT6	TT7
California Standards Enrichment Workbook	pp. 15–16, 21–22	pp. 17–20	pp. 17–20
California Standards Planner and Lesson Plans	L9	L11	L13
California Online Test Practice	ClassZone.com	ClassZone.com	ClassZone.com
California Test Generator CD-ROM			
California EasyPlanner CD-ROM			
California eEdition CD-ROM			

Chart Key

 **P E** Pupil Edition

 Copymaster

CD-ROM

Audio

Video

Internet

Overhead Transparency

PREVIEWING RESOURCES FOR DIFFERENTIATED INSTRUCTION

English Learners

In-Depth Resources in Spanish
- Reading Skill and Strategy Ⓐ
- Skillbuilder Practice Ⓑ
- Geography Practice
- Vocabulary Study Guide

In-Depth Resources: Unit 1
- Family Newsletter (English and Spanish) Ⓒ

Reading Study Guide (Spanish)

Reading Study Guide Audio CD
(Spanish)

Test Generator
Chapter Test (Spanish)

Plus

Modified Lesson Plans for English Learners

Multi-Language Glossary of Social Studies Terms

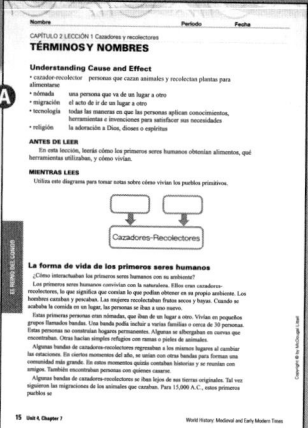
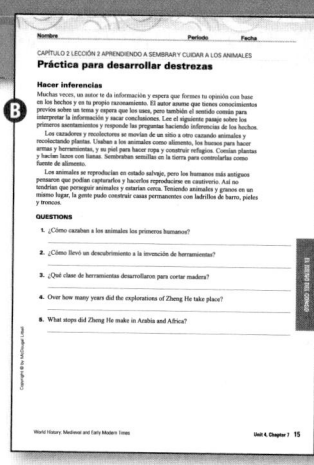

Struggling Readers

In-Depth Resources: Unit 1
- Vocabulary Study Guide Ⓑ
- Skillbuilder Practice Ⓒ
- Geography Practice
- Reteaching Activities Ⓐ
- Family Newsletter

Reading Study Guide

Reading Study Guide Audio CD

Reading Toolkit

Formal Assessment
Chapter Test, Form A

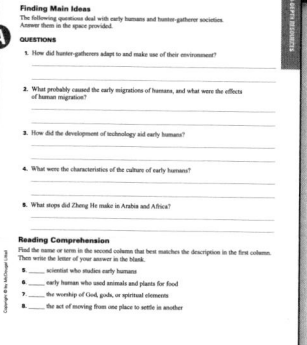
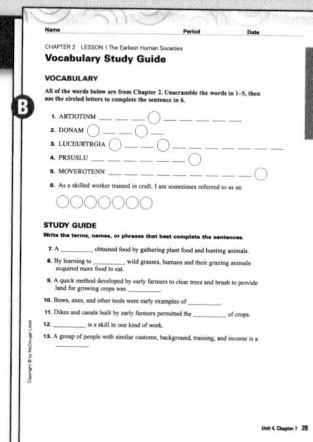

Inclusion

EasyPlanner CD-ROM
- Reading Skill and Strategy Ⓒ
- Vocabulary Study Guide Ⓐ
- Geography Practice
- Reteaching Activities Ⓑ

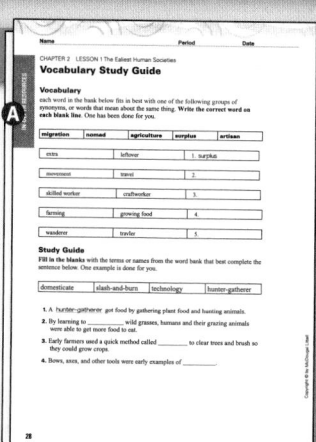
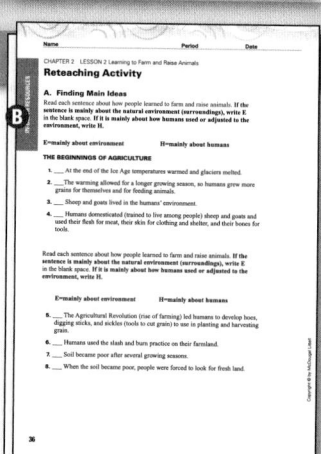

Gifted and Talented Students

In-Depth Resources: Unit 1
- Primary Source
- Literature Ⓐ

History Makers Ⓑ

Interdisciplinary Projects Ⓒ

Formal Assessment
Chapter Test, Form C

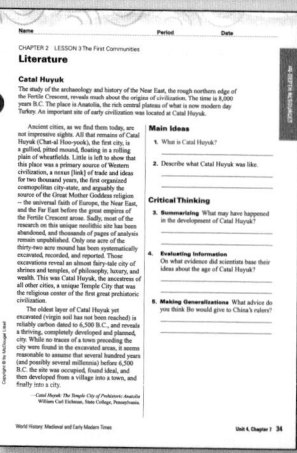

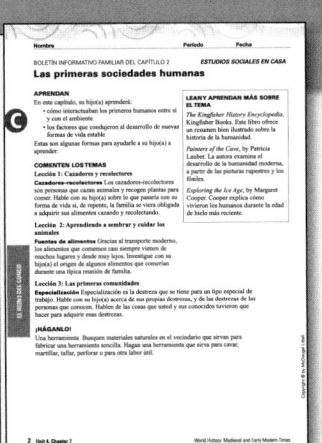

Activities in the Teacher's Edition for English Learners

- Cause and Effect, p. 52
- Main Ideas and Supporting Details, p. 56
- Make a Mural, p. 60
- Sentence Completion, p. 67
- Describe Illustration Detail, p. 70

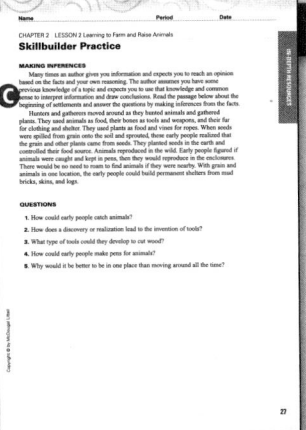

Activities in the Teacher's Edition for Struggling Readers

- Write a Hunter-Gatherer's Diary, p. 52
- Make Summary Sentences, p. 56
- Identify Pros and Cons, p. 61
- Summarize Paragraphs, p. 66
- Divide and Conquer, p. 70

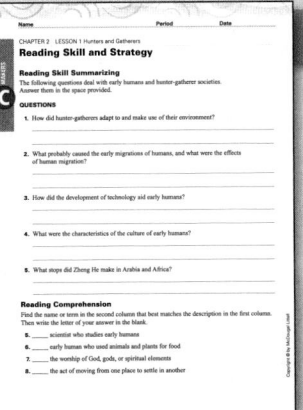

Activities in the Teacher's Edition for Inclusion Students

- Create a Sequence Diagram, p. 53
- Student Teachers, p. 61
- Divide and Conquer, p. 66

Activities in the Teacher's Edition for Gifted and Talented Students

- Design a Tool, p. 53
- Research an Early Farm Animal, p. 60
- Diagram a Complex Village, p. 67

Integrated Technology

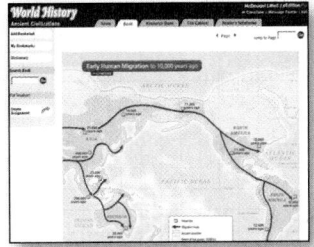

eEdition CD-ROM

- Interactive Visuals
- Interactive Maps
- Starting with a Story

ClassZone.com

- WebQuests
- Research Links
- Internet Activities
- Homework Helper
- Chapter Quiz
- Current Events
- Test Practice

Power Presentations CD-ROM

- Lecture Notes
- Media Gallery
- Chapter Review Game

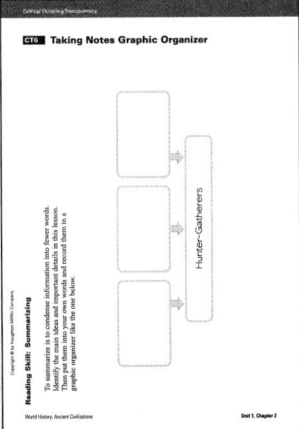

Critical Thinking Transparencies

- CT6 Summarizing
- CT7 Understanding Cause and Effect
- CT8 Categorizing
- CT9 Chapter 2 Visual Summary

California Daily Standards Practice Transparencies, TT5–TT7

Map Transparencies

- MT3 Cave Art (Sites of the Upper Paleolithic)
- MT4 Annual Rainfall in Southwest Asia

Humanities Transparencies

- HT3 Prehistoric Antler Pick
- HT4 Cave Painting from Zimbabwe

Test Generator CD-ROM

EasyPlanner CD-ROM

Begin the Chapter

Objective

Summarize the key points in the development of the earliest human societies.

Quick Look

Lesson 1 describes the ways of life for the earliest hunter-gatherer societies, including the development of tools, language, art and religion.

Lesson 2 explores the development, spread, and impact of agriculture.

Lesson 3 describes the emergence of the first significant communities.

Before You Read: K-W-L

K-W-L is a strategy that helps students set a purpose for reading. Students are asked to stop and think about what they already know, then about what they want to know. This process motivates students and helps them focus on material to come.

Tell students that to use K-W-L effectively, they should follow these steps:

• Think about what you already know about the earliest human beings. Perhaps you have seen television programs or read books about prehistoric people or places. Maybe you have seen prehistoric artifacts at a museum.

• Think next about what you would like to learn about the earliest people. What would you like to ask a prehistoric human if you had the chance?

• At the end of the chapter, think about what you have learned about the earliest human societies. Are there more things that you would like to learn?

Chapter 2 — The Earliest Human Societies

Before You Read: K-W-L

K-W-L stands for what you know, what you want to know, and what you have learned.

• What do you already know about early human societies?

• Study the map and the time line. What do they tell you about where early humans lived?

• What do you want to learn about the earliest human societies?

Big Ideas About the Earliest Human Societies

Culture Ways of living change as humans interact with one another.

The first humans hunted animals and gathered plants for food. Then, as they interacted with one another, they developed tools and weapons to aid them in these activities. New, more settled ways of living developed as people shared ideas.

 Integrated Technology

eEdition
• Interactive Maps
• Interactive Visuals
• Starting with a Story

INTERNET RESOURCES
Go to **ClassZone.com** for
• WebQuest
• Homework Helper
• Research Links
• Internet Activities
• Quizzes
• Maps
• Test Practice
• Current Events

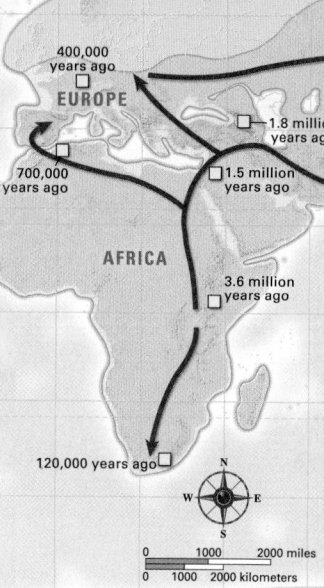

400,000 years ago
EUROPE
700,000 years ago
1.8 million years ago
1.5 million years ago
AFRICA
3.6 million years ago
120,000 years ago

0   1000   2000 miles
0   1000   2000 kilometers

20°W   0°   20°E   40°E   60°E

500,000 B.C.
Early humans learn how to control fire. (19th-century lithograph) ▶

WORLD   500,000 B.C.

40,000 B.C.
Cro-Magnons appear.

TIME LINE DISCUSSION

Use the time line to help students develop an understanding of the scope of human history and when key developments in human society took place.

• About how long before the appearance of Cro-Magnons did early humans gain control of fire? *(about 460,000 years)*

• What event on the time line occurs just before the domestication of animals and the development of agriculture? *(the end of the last ice age)*

• What event on the time line is described as a result of improved farming m ethods? *(the emergence of larger settlements such as Catal Huyuk)*

• About how many years passed between the introduction of agriculture and the development of the first cities? *(about 3,000 years)*

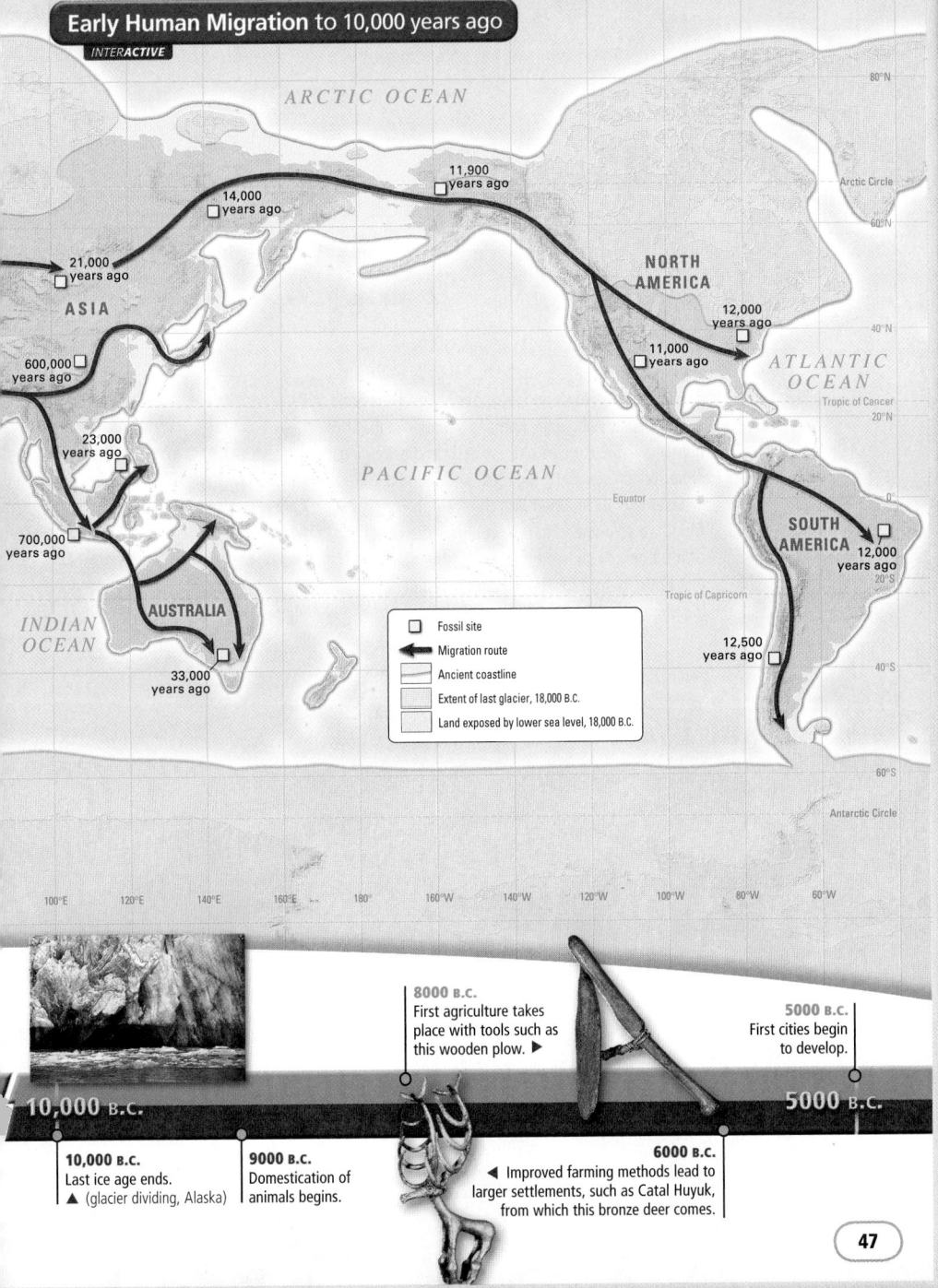

Early Human Migration to 10,000 years ago

INTERACTIVE

ARCTIC OCEAN

ASIA

NORTH AMERICA

PACIFIC OCEAN

ATLANTIC OCEAN

INDIAN OCEAN

AUSTRALIA

SOUTH AMERICA

600,000 years ago

700,000 years ago

23,000 years ago

21,000 years ago

14,000 years ago

11,900 years ago

33,000 years ago

12,000 years ago

11,000 years ago

12,000 years ago

12,000 years ago

12,500 years ago

Arctic Circle

Tropic of Cancer

Equator

Tropic of Capricorn

Antarctic Circle

☐ Fossil site
← Migration route
Ancient coastline
Extent of last glacier, 18,000 B.C.
Land exposed by lower sea level, 18,000 B.C.

10,000 B.C.

10,000 B.C.
Last ice age ends.
▲ (glacier dividing, Alaska)

9000 B.C.
Domestication of animals begins.

8000 B.C.
First agriculture takes place with tools such as this wooden plow. ▶

6000 B.C.
◀ Improved farming methods lead to larger settlements, such as Catal Huyuk, from which this bronze deer comes.

5000 B.C.

5000 B.C.
First cities begin to develop.

47

Introduce the Big Ideas

Read aloud the text about the Big Ideas. Have students think about their own culture and how their interactions with their classmates, friends, parents, and others affect their beliefs and practices. How are new ideas, fashions, and trends introduced and accepted? How do such changes affect them?

Here are some other Big Ideas that you may want to emphasize in this chapter:

Science and Technology
New technologies help the earliest humans gain control over their environment and change their ways of living.

Economics
The ability to produce goods helps shape the development of human society.

Government
The growth of settlements challenges early people to maintain order.

Talk About It

Interpreting Maps
Ask students to look at the map on these pages. What part of the earth was the last to be reached by human migration? *(North America)* What factors helped make possible the migration of people from Asia to North America? *(the lower sea level that existed around 18,000 B.C.)*

INTERACTIVE

An interactive version of this map is available on the eEdition and Power Presentations CD-ROMs.

Find Out More

Have students look at the map of the world on pages 46–47 to see how the landmasses have changed with the rise in sea levels since the end of the last ice age.

RECOMMENDED RESOURCES

Books for the Teacher
Feder, Kenneth L. *The Past in Perspective.* New York: McGraw-Hill Humanities, 2003. Overview of the physical and cultural development of humans.

Klein, Richard G. *The Dawn of Human Culture.* New York: Wiley, 2002. Traces the development of human culture.

Videos
Ancient Graves. 60 minutes. National Geographic Video/ Warner Home Video, 1998. An investigation of how ancient peoples lived and died.

Internet
To access these sites, visit the Research Links for this chapter at **ClassZone.com.**

The British Museum: World Cultures. Includes information on the history of human cultures from around the world.

The National Park Service: Bering Land Bridge National Preserve. Provides background on the conditions that made possible the migration of humans to North America.

Objective

Summarize how scientists have reconstructed the probable last moments of the hunter of the Alps to help increase understanding of prehistoric life.

Introducing the Story

The Hunter of the Alps

This story is based on a real event—the discovery of the body of a 5,300-year-old man literally frozen in time. The remarkable condition of the corpse provides scientists with a tremendous amount of information about how early humans lived—and died. The story represents a reconstruction of the events leading up to the hunter's death.

Vocabulary Preview

quiver a container for arrows

awl a sharp, pointed tool for making holes in leather or other materials

Reading the Story Aloud

1. **The teacher as reader:** Read the story at a smooth, even pace, so students can more easily understand the information given.
2. **The students as readers:** Ask student readers to read a section of the story to a partner, who can provide feedback to encourage evenly paced reading.

Starting with a Story

Students can also follow along as they listen to the story on the eEdition or Power Presentations CD-ROMs.

The Hunter OF THE Alps

CALIFORNIA STANDARDS
Reading 1.1
Read aloud narrative and expository text fluently and accurately and with appropriate pacing, intonation, and expression.

Background: In 1991, a couple hiking in the Alps in Europe discovered the frozen body of a man. Ancient-looking tools and weapons lay near the body. A scientist studying early humans announced that this hunter was 5,300 years old. His body and belongings were well preserved by the cold.

Scientists nicknamed him the Iceman. They found an arrowhead in his shoulder. The contents of his stomach showed that his last meal, eaten just hours before his death, had included deer, barley, and wheat.

The hunter's body found in the Alps ▶

48

ADDITIONAL RESOURCES

Books for the Student
Patent, Dorothy Hinshaw. *Secrets of the Ice Man.* New York: Benchmark Books, 1998. Traces the scientific studies of the hunter of the Alps.

Getz, David, and Peter McCarty. *Frozen Man.* New York: Henry Holt and Company, 2001. A recounting of the story of the discovery and examination of the hunter.

Videos
NOVA: Ice Mummies—Return of the Ice man. 60 minutes. Boston: WGBH Boston Video, 1998.

The hunter had been walking since dawn. The air in the Alps was cold, but the morning fog had cleared up during the course of the day. He was glad of his warm fur hat, goatskin clothes, and grass cloak.

He had spent most of his life walking in these mountains. He had worn out many pairs of deerskin shoes. The ones he was wearing had soles of bearskin.

On this day, the mountain seemed steeper than usual. It might have been his age. The hunter was over 40, one of the oldest people in his community. But he could still easily carry everything he needed. His leather quiver contained a bow, arrow shafts, and arrows with flint heads. He was also carrying a flint dagger and an ax made of wood from a yew tree, with a copper blade. His belt pouch held three flint tools, a bone awl, and a piece of tinder. He also carried a medicine kit in case he became sick or injured.

Suddenly a man lunged toward him. The hunter struggled with him in an attempt to escape. He managed to free himself from the man's grasp and knock the ax out of his hand. He bounded away across the icy landscape. As he looked back, he saw that others had joined the pursuit.

As the hunter turned to run, he felt a searing pain in his shoulder. He'd been shot from behind with an arrow. With his last bit of strength, he struggled farther up the mountain. He found a narrow cave in the ice and managed to hide from his enemies. As night approached, it turned very cold, and snow began to fall. Snow covered the dying hunter, and his body remained undisturbed for more than 5,000 years. He was discovered by hikers in 1991, when an unusually warm year caused the ice to thaw. His body then was studied by scientists, revealing much about how prehistoric people lived.

What do you think life was like for early humans?

Reading & Writing

1. **READING: Reading Aloud** One way to read text fluently and accurately is to rehearse it. With a partner, read the text aloud. Practice those parts that give you trouble to gain the full dramatic effect.

2. **WRITING: Description** Imagine that you are going to make a documentary film about the hunter. Write a brief description of the film.

CALIFORNIA STANDARDS Writing 2.2
Write expository compositions.

49

Talk About It

Ask students the following questions to begin the discussion:

- How can you tell that people who lived during the hunter's era did not live as long as they do today? *(He was over 40 and considered one of the oldest people in his community.)*

- What information supports the idea that someone had attacked the hunter? *(the arrowhead in his shoulder)*

- Which details in this story may have been made up by the writers? *(Possible answers: the weather on the day of the hunter's death, his feelings about his clothing, the details of his fight with his attacker.)*

What do you think life was like for early humans?

Possible answer: It was probably much more difficult to find food or shelter than it is today.

Making Personal Connections

Connect the discussion to today by asking students what kind of story someone would write about their lives if they were suddenly frozen in time—dressed as they are today and with the objects they carry on a daily basis.

READING & WRITING ACTIVITIES

1. **READING** Students should read fluently, accurately, and with expression.
2. **WRITING**

2. Writing Rubric

	Factual Details	Historical Interpretation	Style of Description
4	complete and accurate	rich and believable interpretation	lively and interesting
3	accurate but missing details	somewhat believable interpretation	interesting
2	minor inaccuracies and missing details	unrealistic interpretation	mainly factual in style
1	major inaccuracies and few details	no historical interpretation	disorganized

❶ Plan & Prepare

Objectives

- Describe the way of life of the hunter-gatherer.
- Trace the evolution of the earliest types of tools used by prehistoric peoples.
- Summarize the development of key cultural features among prehistoric peoples.
- **Language Objective:** Complete cause and effect chains to derive the meaning of the text in the lesson.

Quick Look

Lesson 1 describes basic features of the earliest human societies and some of the technological and cultural changes that marked their development.

❷ Focus & Motivate

Preview Explain that this lesson focuses on the ways that the first human beings lived their lives—how they obtained food and interacted with the world around them. Ask students to think about how their lives today are similar to—and different from—those of prehistoric people. *(Possible answers: They are similar in that humans today, as then, focus on how to survive. They are different in that people today have advanced tools and technology and more options for how to survive.)*

Introduce the Main Ideas The three main ideas relate to the Big Idea that "Ways of living change as humans interact with one another." Help students look for this Big Idea as you go through the lesson.

Reading Skill: Summarizing Remind students that summarizing involves repeating only the main points and details.

SAMPLE ANSWERS FOR DIAGRAM

Detail 1: gathered plants and hunted animals for food	Detail 2: moved when food became scarce

Hunter-Gatherers

Lesson 1

▶ **MAIN IDEAS**

❶ Geography Early humans adapted to the natural environment.

❷ Culture Humans created tools to ensure survival and to improve life.

❸ Culture Early humans developed language, religion, and art.

▶ **TAKING NOTES**

Reading Skill: Summarizing
To summarize is to condense information into fewer words. Identify the main ideas and important details in this lesson. Then put them into your own words and record them in a graphic organizer like the one below.

Hunter-Gatherers

S **Skillbuilder Handbook, page R3**

▲ **Spear Thrower**
Prehistoric hunters used spear throwers to throw spears faster and farther. These devices greatly improved their ability to hunt animals.

CALIFORNIA STANDARDS

Framework These studies also should focus on early peoples' attempts to explain the universe through cave art.

6.1.1 Describe the hunter-gatherer societies, including the development of tools and the use of fire.

6.1.2 Identify the locations of human communities that populated the major regions of the world and describe how humans adapted to a variety of environments.

CST 3 Students use a variety of maps and documents to identify physical and cultural features of neighborhoods, cities, states, and countries and to explain the historical migration of people, expansion and disintegration of empires, and the growth of economic systems.

HOW TO TEACH THE CALIFORNIA STANDARDS

Standard	Content	Student Question or Activity	Instruction
6.1.1	**Page 53** Summarizes how early humans developed tools and learned to make and control fire	**Page 55** Students summarize how hunter-gatherers lived.	Find out what students know about the early development of tools. Explain that the use of tools was the earliest form of technology for humankind.
6.1.2	**Page 51** Describes how early humans depended on the natural environment for food and shelter	**Page 53** Students explain why hunter-gatherers moved often.	Ask students to share advantages and disadvantages of living in a hunter-gatherer society.
CST 3	**Page 54** Describes cultural features that explain the historical migration of people	**Page 55** Students use a map to create an outline map of the world on which they mark the locations of hunter-gatherer groups.	Explain that the culture of the first human societies centered around language, art, and religion. Discuss why these three aspects still dominate present-day human culture.

Hunters and Gatherers

▶ TERMS & NAMES

hunter-gatherer
nomad
migration
technology
religion

CHAPTER 2 • LESSON 1

Build on What You Know Have you ever gone camping? How would you survive if you got lost in the woods? Where would you find food and water? In this chapter, you will learn how early humans got food to eat, how they lived, and what tools they used.

Early Humans' Way of Life

❶ ESSENTIAL QUESTION How did early humans interact with the environment? hunting animals and gathering plant food

Like early humans, you interact with the natural environment every day, often without thinking about it. You interact with the weather by wearing boots in the snow or sunglasses in the sunshine. Even your food is a product of the environment.

Hunter-Gatherers Adapt to Environments Early humans were **hunter-gatherers**. They hunted animals and gathered plants for food. When hunter-gatherers no longer had enough to eat, they moved to another location.

Early humans also depended on the natural environment for shelter. Some groups lived in caves and rock shelters. People who lived on plains or in desert areas may have made shelters out of branches, plant fibers, or animal skins.

African Savannah This photograph shows the kind of landscape over which the first hunter-gatherers roamed. Savannahs cover 40 percent of the African continent. ▼

The Earliest Human Societies • 51

Terms & Names

hunter-gatherer person who obtains food by hunting animals and gathering plants, and moves when food becomes scarce

nomad a person who moves from place to place

migration the act of moving from one place to settle in another

technology the ways people apply knowledge and tools to meet their needs

religion the worship of God, gods, or spiritual elements

❸ Teach

Early Humans' Way of Life

6.1.1, 6.1.2

Talk About It

• **Critical Thinking: Finding Main Ideas** Why might one group of hunter-gatherers be threatened by another that moved into its area? *(Possible answer: There might not be enough food to support the existing group.)*

California Resources

California Reading Toolkit, L5
California Modified Lesson Plans for English Learners, p. 13
California Daily Standards Practice Transparencies, TT5
California Standards Enrichment Workbook, pp. 15–16, 21–22
California Online Test Practice
California Test Generator CD-ROM
California Standards Planner and Lesson Plans, L9
California EasyPlanner CD-ROM
California eEdition CD-ROM

LESSON 1 PROGRAM RESOURCES

ON LEVEL

In-Depth Resources: Unit 1
• Family Newsletter (English and Spanish), pp. 21–22
• Reading Skill: Summarizing, p. 23
• Vocabulary Study Guide, p. 28
• Vocabulary Cards, p. 29

Formal Assessment
• Lesson Quiz, p. 21

ENGLISH LEARNERS

In-Depth Resources in Spanish
• Reading Skill: Summarizing, p. 11
• Vocabulary Study Guide, p. 16

Modified Lesson Plans for English Learners, p. 13

Reading Study Guide (Spanish), p. 15

Reading Study Guide Audio CD (Spanish)

STRUGGLING READERS

In-Depth Resources: Unit 1
• Reading Skill: Summarizing, p. 23
• Vocabulary Study Guide, p. 28
• Vocabulary Cards, p. 29
• Reteaching Activity, p. 35

Reading Toolkit, L5

Reading Study Guide, p. 15

Reading Study Guide Audio CD

GIFTED AND TALENTED STUDENTS

In-Depth Resources: Unit 1
• Primary Source: Cave Paintings by Margaret W. Conkey, p. 33

Interdisciplinary Projects
• Science, p. 8
• Art, p. 10

INCLUSION

EasyPlanner CD-ROM
• Reading Skill: Summarizing
• Vocabulary Study Guide
• Reteaching Activity

TECHNOLOGY

eEdition CD-ROM
• Starting with a Story
Power Presentations CD-ROM
Map Transparencies
• MT3 Cave Art (Sites of the Upper Paleolithic)
Critical Thinking Transparencies
• CT6 Summarizing
Humanities Transparencies
• HT3 Prehistoric Antler Pick
• HT4 Cave Paintings from Zimbabwe
Test Generator CD-ROM
ClassZone.com

The Earliest Human Societies • 51

In-Depth Resources: Unit 1
• Reading Skill: Summarizing, p. 23

More About . . .

Humans on the Move

Many scientists believe that about 13,000 years ago, humans crossed from Asia to North America. Their path was believed to have been a strip of land that once connected the two continents. This land, the Bering Land Bridge, now lies under the waters of the Bering Strait. Long ago, however, vast global glaciation held so much water in the form of ice that sea levels were about 300 feet lower than they are today. The lower sea level left this wide strip of land that animals and hunters may have crossed.

History from Visuals

Interpreting Maps

Ask students to view the maps on this page, pointing out that they show the change in the distribution of hunter-gatherer populations over time.

• What can you infer from the map about hunter-gatherers in the modern world? *(Possible answer: They still exist today, but are much more scattered than in the past.)*

GEOGRAPHY SKILLBUILDER ANSWER

They covered less and less territory and were reduced to more isolated groups.

INTERACTIVE

An interactive version of this map is available on the eEdition and Power Presentations CD-ROMs.

Small Bands Hunter-gatherers lived together in small bands, each made up of several families. The size of a group—probably around 30 people—reflected the number of people who could live off the plants and animals in a given region. Men hunted and fished. Women gathered foods, such as berries and nuts from plants that grew wild. They cared for the children, who also worked.

Early Humans on the Move Hunter-gatherers were **nomads**, people who move from place to place. Movement often was limited. Groups returned to the same places with the changes of seasons. At certain times of the year, these early bands joined together, forming larger communities. There was probably time for storytelling, meeting friends, and finding marriage partners.

Early humans also moved to new and distant lands. The act of moving from one place to settle in another is called **migration**. Migrations may have been the result of people's following animals to hunt. By around 15,000 B.C., hunter-gatherers had migrated throughout much of the world. They even traveled across a land bridge connecting Siberia and Alaska. In this way, they entered the Americas.

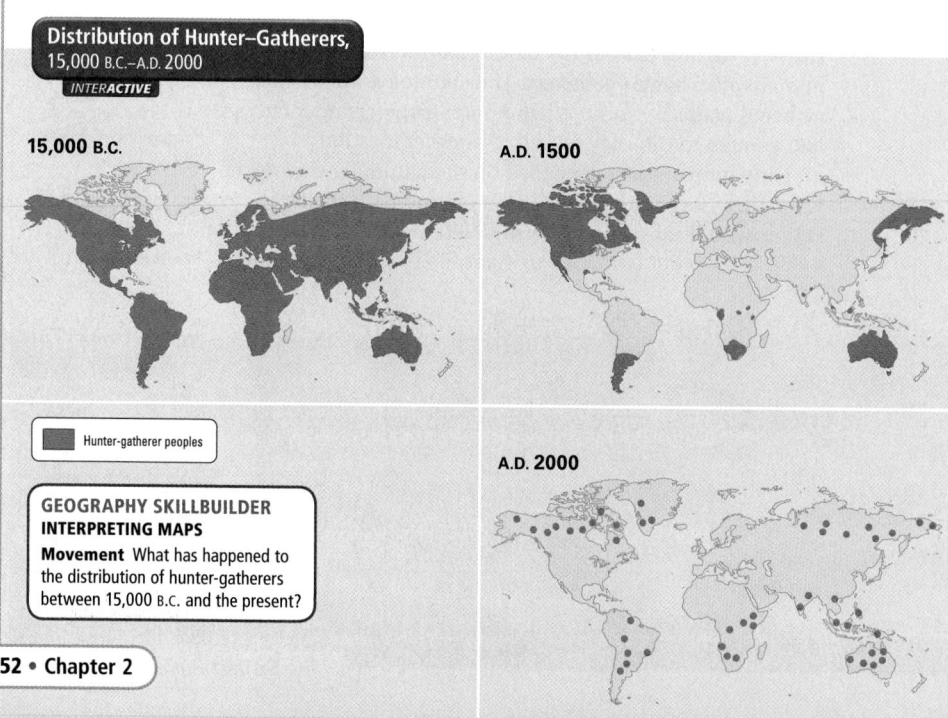

Distribution of Hunter–Gatherers, 15,000 B.C.–A.D. 2000
INTERACTIVE

15,000 B.C.

A.D. 1500

A.D. 2000

■ Hunter-gatherer peoples

GEOGRAPHY SKILLBUILDER
INTERPRETING MAPS
Movement What has happened to the distribution of hunter-gatherers between 15,000 B.C. and the present?

DIFFERENTIATING INSTRUCTION

Struggling Readers

Write a Hunter-Gatherer's Diary
Help students clarify their understanding of hunter-gatherers by writing a diary entry from the perspective of a nomadic group. The entry should include references to the kind of work a hunter-gatherer might do and some of the challenges a hunter-gatherer band may face.

English Learners

Complete a Cause and Effect Chain
Remind students that a *cause* tells why an event happened. An *effect* is the event that happened. Have students use the text to complete the following cause and effect chain. Demonstrate for students how key words signal a cause or effect.

Cause	Effect
As a result of having to work together to gather and share food,	people developed human language.

The arrival of a migrating group in the territory of another people could lead to both good and bad outcomes. Everyone benefited when knowledge and tools were shared. However, people sometimes turned violent when they felt threatened by newcomers. They feared that the newcomers might try to take their territory. Sometimes they may have feared them just because they were different.

REVIEW Why did hunter-gatherers move often? They moved in search of food, both plants and animals.

The Development of Tools

2 **ESSENTIAL QUESTION** What were some tools created by early humans?

carrying bags, axes, awls, drills, bows, spearheads

Imagine that you are planning a camping trip. Think about what tools you will take to make sure your trip is safe and enjoyable. Like you, early humans relied on tools.

The Use of Fire Around 500,000 years ago, early humans learned to make and control fire. Fire provided heat and light, and it enabled people to cook food. A good fire offered protection from animals. Early humans also used fire to temper, or harden, tools made of metal.

The Development of Technology **Technology** consists of all of the ways in which people apply knowledge, tools, and inventions to meet their needs. Technology dates back to early humans. At least 2 million years ago, people made stone tools for cutting. Early humans also made carrying bags, stone hand axes, awls (tools for piercing holes in leather or wood), and drills.

In time, humans developed more complex tools, such as hunting bows made of wood. They learned to make flint spearheads and metal tools. Early humans used tools to hunt and butcher animals and to construct simple forms of shelter. Technology—these new tools—gave humans more control over their environment. These tools also set the stage for a more settled way of life.

REVIEW How did early humans use fire? They used fire for heat, light, cooking, and protection and in the making of metal tools.

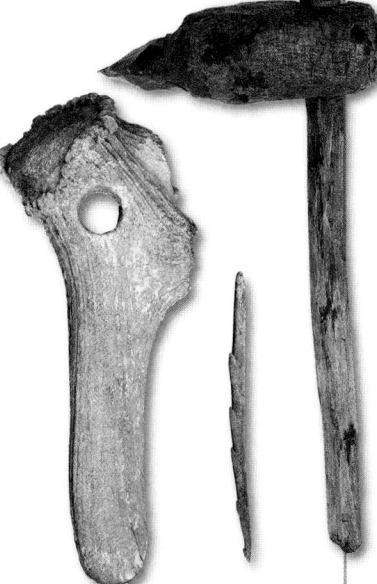

▲ **Early Tools** Among the tools used by early humans were the mattock (a digging tool), the harpoon, and the ax.

Vocabulary Strategy
You can figure out what *technology* means from its **root** and **suffix**. The Greek root *techn* means "craft" or "skill." The suffix *-logy* means "study of." *Technology* means "the study and application of crafts or skills."

The Earliest Human Societies • 53

Roots
Tell students that many roots and suffixes appear repeatedly in the English language. For example:

- The root *techn* also appears in such words as *technical* and *technician*.

- The suffix *-logy* is also part of *archaeology*, a word that students have already studied.

Teach

The Development of Tools

 6.1.1, 6.1.2

Talk About It

- How did the ability to control fire affect early humans? *(Fire helped make their lives more comfortable and safer.)*

- What is the earliest example of a tool mentioned in the text? *(stone tools for cutting)*

- **Critical Thinking: Finding Main Ideas** The text says that technology "gave humans more control over their environment." What do you think this means? *(Possible answers: Tools enabled people to use the materials around them, to work more efficiently, and to achieve more with less effort. They helped make people more comfortable and safe.)*

Humanities Transparencies
- HT3 Prehistoric Antler Pick

DIFFERENTIATING INSTRUCTION

Inclusion

Create a Sequence Diagram
Have students who have difficulty reading take a blank sheet of paper. Holding it lengthwise, have them draw three large boxes from left to right and connect the boxes with arrows. Then have students go through the text and write down the sequence in which tools were developed.

Gifted and Talented Students

Design a Tool
Early humans had to make everything they needed from the world around them. Have students create a plan for producing a useful tool. The plan should explain the purpose of the tool, what materials are needed to make it, and how it is constructed.

Teach

Early Human Culture

✎ **6.1.2, CST 3**

Talk About It

- What three examples of human culture are discussed in this section? *(language, religion, and art)*

- How might language have helped make hunters more effective? *(Possible answer: Language would make it easier for people to work together and cooperate, which could increase the success of the hunt.)*

- **Critical Thinking: Evaluating Information** How were religion and art connected for early people? *(Possible answer: Art was often part of religious expression. It was a way for early people to communicate their spiritual beliefs.)*

 In-Depth Resources: Unit 1
- Primary Source: Cave Paintings, p. 33

 Humanities Transparencies
- HT4 Cave Paintings from Zimbabwe

 Map Transparencies
- MT3 Cave Art (Sites of the Upper Paleolithic)

History from Visuals

Comparisons Across Cultures
Remind students that they have read earlier in this book about cave paintings—the cave paintings at Lascaux. Point out that such paintings are found in many parts of the world.

- Why do you think prehistoric artists painted in caves? *(Possible answers: They wanted their work to last, caves may have been considered holy places.)*

SKILLBUILDER ANSWER
These examples show that religion had an important role in early art. Even in widely separated cultures, religion was an important source of inspiration for early artists.

Early Human Culture

③ ESSENTIAL QUESTION What kind of culture did early humans create? *language, religion, art*

What sets humans apart from other creatures? Art, language, and religion are special to humans and help create their culture.

Language Human language probably developed as a result of the need for people to work together. One theory suggests that the need for cooperation during the hunt spurred language development. Hunters needed to be able to talk to one another in order to outsmart, trap, and kill animals for food. Another theory suggests that the cooperation needed to gather and share food led to the development of language.

Religion Religion is the worship of God, gods, or spirits. Early humans probably believed that everything in nature, including rocks, trees, and animals, had a spirit. Some archaeologists believe that early cave paintings of animals were made to honor the spirits of animals killed for food.

Comparisons Across Cultures

Prehistoric Cave Art

Prehistoric people in different parts of the world painted scenes on cave walls. Such rock paintings are among the oldest art in the world.

The cave art on the top was done by a Native American artist in Utah. The painting shows a holy man holding a snake. Snakes were seen as links between the human and underground worlds.

The painting at the bottom was done by an Australian Aboriginal artist. It shows a dreamtime spirit. Dreamtime is a supernatural past in which ancestor spirits shaped the natural world.

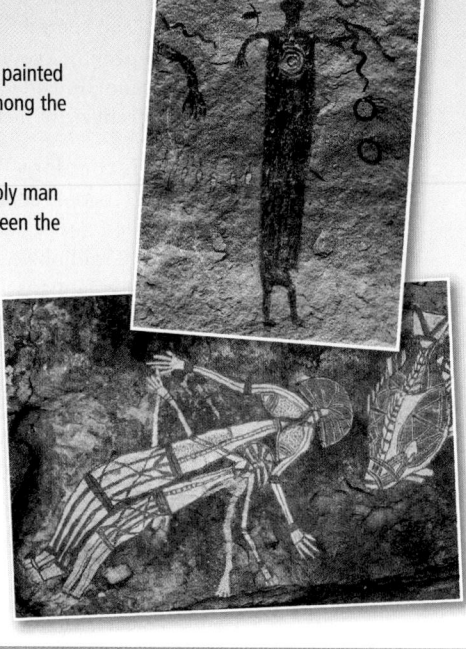

SKILLBUILDER
INTERPRETING VISUALS
Making Inferences What do these examples tell you about early human art? On the basis of their art, how important does religion seem to have been in the lives of prehistoric peoples?

54 • Chapter 2

INTERDISCIPLINARY ACTIVITIES

Art

Create Cave Paintings
Invite students to create paintings on a sheet of paper that might look like artwork found on cave walls. You may want to show students additional cave paintings to help them gain ideas for their art.

Language Arts

Communicate Without Words
Have groups of four students play a game of charades, in which one student tries to act out a familiar phrase or title of a book or movie without using words while the other teammates try to guess the phrase or title. After each student has played, have the class discuss what they learned about the importance of language.

Art Prehistoric art gives us insights into humans' daily life and shared beliefs. Early humans created art in caves and rock shelters. They also created art they could carry with them.

More than 200 sites of early cave art have been discovered in France and Spain. Cave paintings thousands of years old show lively images of bulls, stallions, and bison. Prehistoric art exists in Africa, Asia, Europe, Australia, and the Americas.

Jewelry and figurines are examples of portable art. Early humans may have worn these items. Other items may have had religious meaning. Art also included music, dance, and stories—art that could be performed anywhere.

Antler Headdress This red-deer antler headdress, which is about 9,500 years old, may have been used as a disguise in hunting or worn in hunting ceremonies. ▼

 REVIEW What were the main elements of prehistoric culture?
language, religion, and art

Lesson Summary

- Hunter-gatherers were nomads.
- Fire and tools improved lives.
- Early humans created language, religion, and art.

Why It Matters Now . . .
Early humans created the first tools. Today technology continues to improve our lives and help us survive.

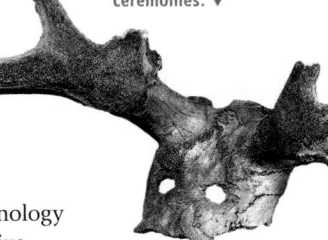

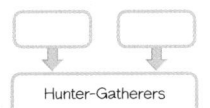 **Lesson Review**

 Homework Helper
ClassZone.com

Terms & Names

1. Explain the importance of

    hunter-gatherer   migration   religion
    nomad   technology

Using Your Notes

Summarizing Use your completed graphic organizer to answer the following question:

2. How did hunter-gatherers live? (6.1.1)

Hunter-Gatherers

Main Ideas

3. How did prehistoric people use available natural resources for food, housing, and clothing? (6.1.1)

4. How did the development of tools change the life of early humans? (6.1.2)

5. Where are some of the places that prehistoric art has been found? (6.1.2)

Critical Thinking

6. **Comparing and Contrasting** How was cave art different from other kinds of art created by early humans? (6.1.2)

7. **Drawing Conclusions** What does their art tell us about early humans? (6.1.2)

Activity **Making a Map** Use the map on pages A6-A7 of the Atlas to sketch a world outline map. You will add to this map in later units. Use the map on page 52 to mark the location of the hunter-gatherer group closest to where you live. (CST 3)

The Earliest Human Societies • 55

---

❹ Assess & Reteach

Assess Have students work in pairs on the questions and note the location of the answers.

📝 **Formal Assessment**
- Lesson Quiz, p. 21

Reteach Have students create an outline of this lesson. Tell them to write the major section headings on a sheet of paper, leaving plenty of room between each heading. Then, have them write down at least two details from each section that help describe and explain that section.

📝 **In-Depth Resources: Unit 1**
- Vocabulary Cards, p. 29
- Reteaching Activity, p. 35

🔎 **Homework Helper**

Visit **ClassZone.com** for a lesson review, a flip-card activity, and links to related Web sites.

---

1 Lesson Review Answers

Terms & Names

1. • hunter-gatherer, p. 51
   • nomad, p. 52
   • migration, p. 52
   • technology, p. 53
   • religion, p. 54

Using Your Notes

See page 50 for an example of a completed chart.

2. They lived by hunting animals and gathering plants that grew in the wild.

Main Ideas

3. They hunted animals and gathered plants. They used animal skins for clothing. They used caves, rock shelters, branches, plant fiber, and animal skins for shelter.

4. Tools helped them to hunt and gather, clothe themselves, and make shelter for themselves.

5. Africa, Asia, Europe, Australia, and the Americas

Critical Thinking

6. Jewelry and figurines could be carried around, where cave art had to stay where it was created.

7. Possible answer: Early art shows that humans had a spiritual life and that they shared certain beliefs about their world.

Activity Rubric

	Style of Map	**Accuracy of Locator**
4	accurate details	accurate location
3	reasonably accurate details	nearly accurate location
2	missing details	inaccurate location
1	many inaccuracies	no location given

The Earliest Human Societies • 55

Objectives

- Demonstrate the skill of finding the main idea in a passage of text.
- **Language Objective:** Discuss supporting details to determine the main ideas of the lesson.

❶ Focus & Motivate

Preview Tell students that finding the main idea is a reading skill that will enable them to study more effectively and efficiently, not just in social studies but in every subject.

❷ Teach

Talk About It

- What does the title of the passage on page 57 tell you about the topic? *(It tells that the passage is about hunter-gatherers.)*

- In which sentences are you most likely to find clues about the main idea? *(in the first and last sentences of the paragraph)*

- What appears to be the main idea of the first paragraph? *(Hunter-gatherers often enjoyed a good quality of life.)*

- What are some details that support this main idea? *(Their environments supported their needs, they had a variety of foods, they could meet their needs with a reasonable amount of effort.)*

- **Critical Thinking: Finding Main Ideas** Write one sentence that you think summarizes the main idea in the excerpt on page 57. *(Possible answer: Hunter-gatherers faced some difficult challenges, but they often enjoyed a decent quality of life.)*

Skillbuilder   Extend Lesson 1

Finding Main Ideas

Goal: To identify the main idea of a passage in order to better understand hunter-gatherer societies

CALIFORNIA STANDARDS
6.1.1 Describe the hunter-gatherer societies, including the development of tools and the use of fire.

Learn the Skill

A main idea is the most important point in a paragraph or a passage. A main idea may or may not be stated in so many words. In the example to the right, the main idea is not stated. To find the main idea of a passage, identify the topic. Then, as you read, ask yourself this question: What main idea do the details and examples support?

[S] See the Skillbuilder Handbook, page R2.

Practice the Skill

❶ Ask yourself what the passage at right, titled "Hunter-Gatherer Societies," is about. Identify the topic by first looking at the title. The title tells you this passage is about what hunter-gatherer societies were like.

❷ Look at the first and last sentences of each paragraph. These sentences often give clues to the main idea. See if any one sentence sums up the point of the whole passage. In this passage the main idea comes from combining the ideas in these sentences.

❸ Read the entire passage. Look for details about the topic. What main idea do they explain or support? This passage contains details about both the good and the bad parts of hunter-gatherers' lives.

❹ Use a chart like the one below to state the topic and list the supporting details. Use the information you record to help you state the main idea. This chart is based on the passage you just read.

Example:

❹ Topic: Hunter-Gatherer Societies

Detail	Detail	Detail	Detail	Detail	Detail
Enough food, varied diet	Didn't have to work too hard	Time to relax and play	Required a lot of land	Hard to settle down	Limited group size

Main Idea: Hunter-gatherers had a good life but had a hard time feeding lots of people.

DIFFERENTIATING INSTRUCTION

Struggling Readers

Make Summary Sentences
Pair students, and have them review the two paragraphs about hunter-gatherers on page 57. Have student pairs read the paragraphs aloud. Then, have each student write a one-sentence summary of each paragraph and read it to his or her partner. Students should take turns evaluating each other's summaries.

English Learners

Review Main Ideas and Supporting Details
Explain that details are facts that support or explain the main idea. The main idea is the most important point in the paragraph or passage and is often expressed in the topic or title. Guide students as they review the text to note three details or facts about the use of fire by early humans. Write the students' details on a chart.

Secondary Source

Ideas about life in hunter-gatherer societies have changed since the 1960s. Until then, most scholars thought that ancient peoples' lives were very hard. Now many scholars have changed their minds. They have based their ideas on studies of hunter-gatherers in the modern world—groups who still live by hunting animals and gathering plants for food.

❶ *Hunter-Gatherer Societies*

❷ Many scholars now believe that the lives of most hunter-gatherers were quite good. Their environment gave them all the kinds of food they needed. They had a varied diet of meat, fish, fruit, and wild plants. This diet was healthy and balanced. Usually, hunting and gathering did not require too much time and energy. People had time to relax, visit with friends, and play games. ❷

❸ ❷ Yet there were limits to the hunter-gatherer way of life. A lot of land was required to support a group of people. The group needed to roam across 7 to 500 square miles per person to get enough food. It was hard to settle in villages because people needed to move often to find food. They owned only what they could carry, and their houses had to be very simple. The groups had to be small, probably no more than about 30 people. As groups consumed the food in various areas, it became harder for societies to feed their people just by hunting and gathering. ❷

▲ **Game Animals** This rock painting in Tanzania shows the possible favorite game animals of hunters.

Apply the Skill

Turn to Chapter 1, Lesson 2, pages 17–19. Read "Different Maps for Different Purposes." Make a chart like the one at left to help you find the main ideas. Identify the topic, the most important details, and the main idea of the passage.

The Earliest Human Societies • 57

More About . . .

Hunter-Gatherer Diets
The modern human species evolved eating a hunter-gatherer diet. In addition, many of the most serious and widespread health problems plaguing our society today, such as heart disease and diabetes, are closely linked to diet. Some scientists have begun exploring how modern diets compare to those of hunter-gatherers and how differences might affect human health. There are even some experts who have proposed modern diets based on what is thought to be the eating patterns of early hunter-gatherers.

APPLY THE SKILL

SAMPLE ANSWER FOR CHART

Topic — Different Types of Maps

Detail Political maps—show cities, provinces, states, territories, and countries

Detail Physical maps—show landforms and bodies of water

Detail Thematic maps—show various information about a place

Main Idea — Different types of maps help us see unique features of a place.

❶ Plan & Prepare

Objectives

- Describe the development and spread of agriculture among humans.
- Trace the impact of farming on the development of settlements among early peoples.
- **Language Objective:** Describe the occupations of people in the first communities.

Quick Look

Lesson 2 describes the events and factors that helped promote the development of agriculture and its impact on humans.

❷ Focus & Motivate

Preview Tell students that this lesson focuses on a far-reaching shift in the way human beings met their needs for food. Ask students how much they depend on farmers to supply them with the food they eat. *(Students should recognize that most people depend almost entirely on farm-raised food.)*

Introduce the Main Ideas The three main ideas relate to the Big Idea that "Ways of living change as humans interact with one another." Help students look for this Big Idea as you go through the lesson.

Reading Skill: Understanding Cause and Effect Have students use the chart to identify and record the effects of different causes as they read.

SAMPLE ANSWERS FOR DIAGRAM

Cause	Effects
Agricultural revolution causes changes in tools for growing and harvesting grain.	Farmers develop new tools, such as hoes.
	Farmers improve their efficiency as tools improve.
	Improved efficiency allows farmers to move less often.

Lesson 2

▶ **MAIN IDEAS**

❶ **Science and Technology** New technologies supported an agricultural revolution.

❷ **Culture** Agriculture made a big change in how people lived.

❸ **Geography** Farming developed independently in many areas of the world.

▶ **TAKING NOTES**

Reading Skill: Understanding Cause and Effect
Identifying causes and effects will help you understand the relationships among events in this lesson. In Lesson 2, look for the effects of the cause listed in the chart below. Record them in a chart of your own.

Cause	Effects
Agricultural revolution causes changes in tools for growing and harvesting grain.	1.
	2.
	3.

 **Skillbuilder Handbook, page R26**

▲ **Pottery** This pottery figure from Hungary is holding a sickle, a farming tool. The figure represents a deity, or god, and dates back to about 4500 B.C.

CALIFORNIA STANDARDS

6.1.2 Identify the locations of human communities that populated the major regions of the world and describe how humans adapted to a variety of environments.

6.1.3 Discuss the climatic changes and human modifications of the physical environment that gave rise to the domestication of plants and animals and new sources of clothing and shelter.

CST 3 Students use a variety of maps and documents to identify physical and cultural features of neighborhoods, cities, states, and countries and to explain the historical migration of people, expansion and disintegration of empires, and the growth of economic systems.

HOW TO TEACH THE CALIFORNIA STANDARDS

Standard	Content	Student Question or Activity	Instruction
6.1.2	**Page 61** Identifies the locations of human communities in Asia and Africa	**Page 62** Students compare and contrast the areas in which farming developed in Asia and Africa with those in the Americas.	Discuss ways that humans adapt to the weather and climate in order to survive—in the past as well as the present.
6.1.3	**Page 60** Describes how humans learned to domesticate animals and plant seeds to raise crops	**Page 62** Students explain how the end of the last Ice Age affected how people lived.	Explain that during the last Ice Age, agriculture was difficult or impossible in many areas. Ask students to list ways that people obtained food before they practiced agriculture.
CST 3	**Page 61** Illustrates the settlement of people and the growth of agricultural and economic systems	**Page 62** Students list the geographical regions in which farming developed in Asia, Africa, and the Americas.	Have a volunteer locate the Nile and Huang He rivers on a world map. Discuss reasons why agriculture began in these two areas.

Learning to Farm and Raise Animals

► TERMS & NAMES
domesticate
agriculture
slash-and-burn
irrigation

Terms & Names

domesticate to grow and tend wild plants or animals

agriculture planting of seeds to grow crops

slash-and-burn the clearing of land for farming by cutting and burning vegetation

irrigation the watering of crops

Build on What You Know In the United States today, few people are farmers. However, in early human societies, almost everyone was a farmer. Today, because of technology, one farmer can raise enough food to feed many people.

The Beginnings of Agriculture

1 ESSENTIAL QUESTION What new farming tools and methods did early farmers invent? planting seeds; hoes, digging sticks, sickles; slash-and-burn

Early humans were nomadic. They moved around in search of food. By around 8000 B.C., though, they had learned to modify the environment by growing plants and raising animals.

Climate Changes Global warming resulted in the retreat of the Ice Age glaciers. This retreat meant that early humans could move into new areas. As temperatures rose, the growing season became longer. Wild grasses spread and were **domesticated** by humans—that is, humans learned to grow and tend the grasses. This skill provided humans and grazing animals with more grain to eat.

Connect to Today

Peru A shepherd tends her sheep in the Andes Mountains of Peru. Sheep were among the first animals that humans learned to domesticate. ▼

59

3 Teach

The Beginnings of Agriculture

✎ **6.1.3, CST 3**

Talk About It

• **Critical Thinking: Making Inferences** What can you infer from the fact that the introduction of agriculture is referred to as a "revolution"? *(Possible answer: The introduction of agriculture had an enormous impact on human culture.)*

California Resources

California Reading Toolkit, L6
California Modified Lesson Plans for English Learners, p. 15
California Daily Standards Practice Transparencies, TT6
California Standards Enrichment Workbook, pp. 17–20
California Online Test Practice
California Test Generator CD-ROM
California Standards Planner and Lesson Plans, L11
California EasyPlanner CD-ROM
California eEdition CD-ROM

LESSON 2 PROGRAM RESOURCES

ON-LEVEL

In-Depth Resources: Unit 1
• Reading Skill: Understanding Cause and Effect, p. 24
• Vocabulary Study Guide, p. 28
• Vocabulary Cards, p. 29
• Skillbuilder Practice: Making Inferences, p. 27

Formal Assessment
• Lesson Quiz, p. 22

ENGLISH LEARNERS

In-Depth Resources in Spanish
• Reading Skill: Understanding Cause and Effect, p. 12

• Skillbuilder Practice: Making Inferences, p. 15

Modified Lesson Plans for English Learners, p. 15

Reading Study Guide (Spanish), p. 17

Reading Study Guide Audio CD (Spanish)

STRUGGLING READERS

In-Depth Resources: Unit 1
• Reading Skill: Understanding Cause and Effect, p. 24
• Vocabulary Cards, p. 29
• Reteaching Activity, p. 36

Reading Toolkit, L6
Reading Study Guide, p. 17
Reading Study Guide Audio CD

GIFTED AND TALENTED STUDENTS

Interdisciplinary Projects
• Language Arts, p. 9

INCLUSION

EasyPlanner CD-ROM
• Reading Skill: Understanding Cause and Effect
• Vocabulary Study Guide
• Reteaching Activity

TECHNOLOGY

eEdition CD-ROM

Power Presentations CD-ROM

Critical Thinking Transparencies
• CT7 Understanding Cause and Effect

Test Generator CD-ROM

ClassZone.com

In-Depth Resources: Unit 1
- Reading Skill: Understanding Cause and Effect, p. 24
- Skillbuilder Practice: Making Inferences, p. 27

More About . . .

Domestication of Animals

In addition to providing food, clothing, and materials for shelters, some domesticated animals provided labor for early peoples. For example, dogs were among the first domesticated animals. They helped with hunting and with herding other domesticated animals. Other animals that were domesticated mainly for labor were horses and donkeys. Some of the first animals that were domesticated for food include sheep, goats, and pigs.

Teach

Settlements Begin

6.1.3

Talk About It

- Early farmers discovered that land was especially rich in which kind of location? *(river valleys)*

- What factors encouraged the settlement of villages? *(access to the best land, access to more food, greater safety in numbers from attack)*

- **Critical Thinking: Understanding Cause and Effect** How might the settlement of communities have affected the development of human culture? *(Possible answer: Settlement in larger communities would have promoted the development of language, as large numbers of people faced the need to work closely together for the common good.)*

The Domestication of Animals Early humans learned to domesticate animals such as sheep and goats around 9000 B.C. People raised them for food and clothing.

Domesticated animals offered a reliable source of meat and milk products. After people killed an animal, they used its skin to make clothing and shelters. They made harpoons, needles, and other tools from the bones.

The Agricultural Revolution Food gatherers noticed that grain sprouted from spilled seed. Around 8000 B.C., people got the idea of **agriculture**—planting seeds to raise crops.

Agricultural revolution is the name given to the shift from food gathering to food raising. The agricultural revolution brought about changes in tools and technology. People made hoes to loosen the soil, sticks to dig holes, and sickles to harvest grain.

Early farmers practiced **slash-and-burn** agriculture. They cut and then burned trees and brush to clear land for crops. After a number of growing seasons, soil often became poor. People then moved on to a new location.

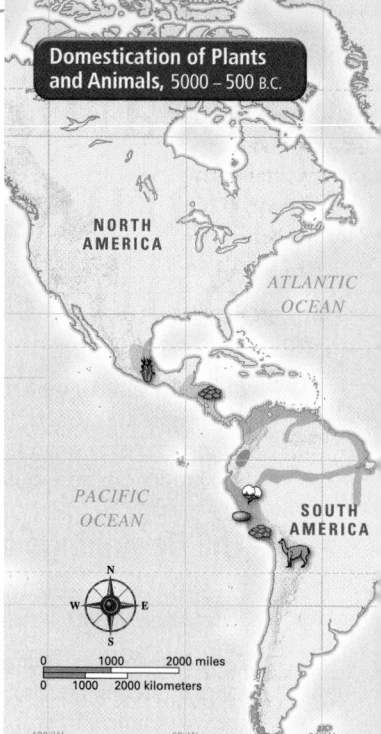

Domestication of Plants and Animals, 5000 – 500 B.C.

REVIEW What was the impact of new tools on early humans?
The new tools enabled people to raise crops and animals and have better nutrition.

Settlements Begin

 ESSENTIAL QUESTION Why did villages develop?

People remained in the same area to take advantage of fertile soil to grow crops; farmers settled in villages to be close to the fields

People learned to be better farmers as their tools improved. Groups often remained in the same areas instead of moving around every few years. They began to develop permanent settlements.

Farming Villages Develop Fertile soil produced bigger and better crops. This attracted farmers. River valleys had soil that was especially rich. Their soil was better than that in fields that had been cleared by slashing and burning. Farmers settled in villages and went out to the fields to work. Villages grew to hold several thousand people. People lived in shelters made of mud, bricks, logs, and hides.

DIFFERENTIATING INSTRUCTION

Gifted and Talented Students

Research an Early Farm Animal
Invite students to use library or Internet resources to learn about the domestication of a farm animal, such as a goat, sheep, pig, llama, or horse. Students should write a brief report about where the animal was domesticated and what its uses were.

English Learners

Make a Mural
Have students work with a partner to create a farming village mural showing crops and animals that were raised by early farmers. Have students draw and label food, clothing, tools and technology that became available as a result of the agricultural revolution. Have students explain their murals to their classmates. Post murals in classroom.

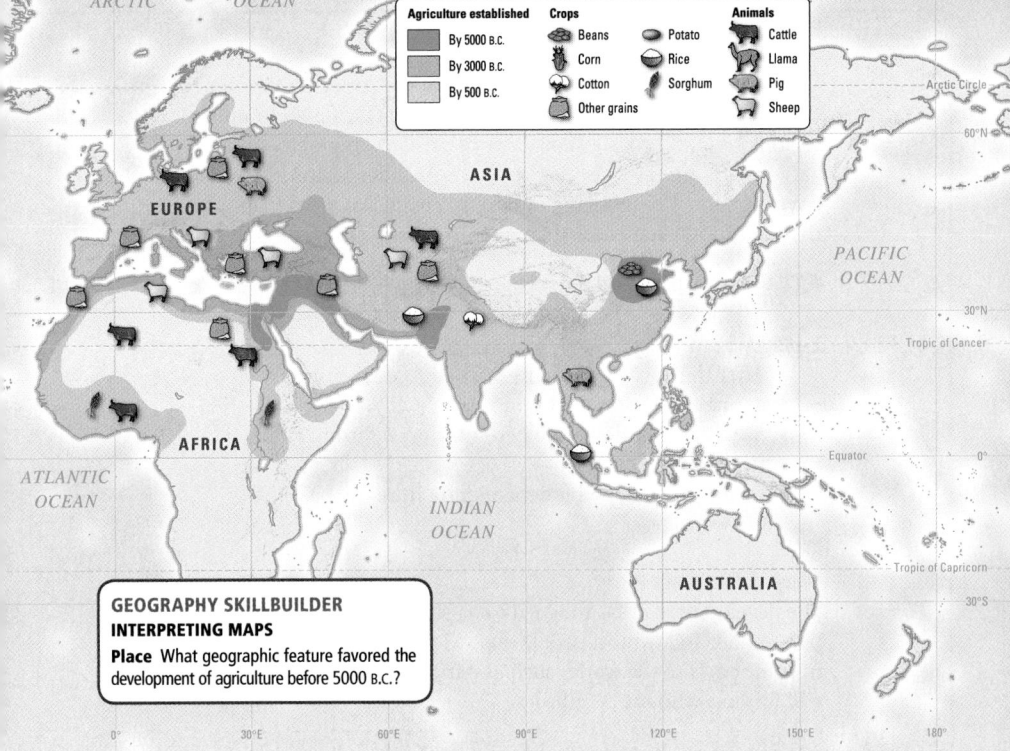

Agriculture established
- By 5000 B.C.
- By 3000 B.C.
- By 500 B.C.

Crops
- Beans
- Corn
- Cotton
- Other grains
- Potato
- Rice
- Sorghum

Animals
- Cattle
- Llama
- Pig
- Sheep

GEOGRAPHY SKILLBUILDER
INTERPRETING MAPS
Place What geographic feature favored the development of agriculture before 5000 B.C.?

Teach

Farming Develops in Many Places
6.1.2, CST 3

Talk About It

- What are two rivers mentioned in the text that were the scene of early farming development? *(the Huang He in China and the Nile in Africa)*

- What is one example of how farmers in the Americas adapted their practices to the environment? *(Possible answer: They terraced the land.)*

- **Critical Thinking: Making Inferences** What are two reasons referred to in the text that may help explain why farming first developed in river valleys? *(Possible answers: The rivers helped make the soil more fertile; the rivers provided water for irrigation.)*

Village life provided many advantages. Food was more plentiful. People living in larger groups could more easily withstand attacks by nomadic bands. Village life also had disadvantages, including the risks of fire, disease, and flood.

REVIEW How did farming change the way people lived?
People began to settle and live in villages permanently.

Farming Develops in Many Places

3 ESSENTIAL QUESTION Where did farming develop? *river valleys such as Huang He in China and Nile in Africa*

About 8000 B.C., people in different parts of the world began to develop farming. Early farmers invented new methods of farming.

River Valleys in Africa and Asia Early farming developed in areas where water was available, such as in river valleys. These included the Huang He in China and the Nile in Africa. African farmers along the Nile were among the first to use **irrigation**—the watering of crops. They built irrigation systems of dikes and canals.

The Earliest Human Societies • 61

DIFFERENTIATING INSTRUCTION

Inclusion

Assign Student Teachers
Have students who have difficulty reading pair up in teams of two. Then, have each student take turns reading the sections and asking the review questions that follow. Have the student teachers help their partners find the correct answers in the text.

Struggling Readers

Identify Pros and Cons
Have students make a T-chart on a blank sheet of paper. On the top of the left column, have them write the word *pro;* on the right, have them write *con*. Then have students go through the section "Settlements Begin" and write down the pros and cons of village life for early peoples.

④ Assess & Reteach

Assess Divide students into small groups and have them answer the review questions. Then ask groups to take turns presenting their answers to the class. Invite other groups to comment on the answers—pointing out errors, incomplete answers, or alternative answers.

 Formal Assessment
• Lesson Quiz, p. 22

Reteach On a blank sheet of paper, have students work individually to write each of the section headings in the form of a question. Then, have the students find information from each section that answers their own questions.

 In-Depth Resources: Unit 1
• Vocabulary Cards, p. 29
• Reteaching Activity, p. 36

 **Homework Helper**

Visit **ClassZone.com** for a lesson review, a flip-card activity, and links to related Web sites.

Uplands in the Americas Farming in the Americas developed later than in the rest of the world. It developed mainly in upland regions—plateaus and other flat areas at fairly high elevations. Farmers in the Americas developed techniques suited to the environment. The terracing of land to create flat areas helped adapt the land for raising crops such as corn, beans, potatoes, and squash.

REVIEW What crops did early farmers raise in the Americas?
The crops were corn, beans, potatoes, and squash.

Lesson Summary
• After the Ice Age, humans learned to domesticate animals and plant crops.
• As people learned to be better farmers, farming villages developed.
• Farming developed independently in many parts of the world.

Why It Matters Now . . .
The development of farming led to a great increase in human population. Today most people depend on agriculture for their food. In some parts of the world, such as Africa and India, most people are still farmers who live in villages.

2 Lesson Review

 Homework Helper
ClassZone.com

Terms & Names
1. Explain the importance of
   domesticate   slash-and-burn
   agriculture   irrigation

Using Your Notes
Understanding Cause and Effect Use your completed chart to answer the following question:
2. What new technologies developed for growing and harvesting grain? (6.1.3)

Cause	Effects
Agricultural revolution causes changes in tools for growing and harvesting grain	1.
	2.
	3.

Main Ideas
3. What farming techniques were part of the agricultural revolution? (6.1.2)
4. How did agriculture change the way people lived together? (6.1.3)
5. In what geographical regions did farming develop in Asia, Africa, and the Americas? (CST 3)

Critical Thinking
6. **Cause and Effect** How did the end of the Ice Age affect the way people lived? (6.1.3)
7. **Comparing and Contrasting** Compare the areas in which farming developed in Asia and Africa with those in which farming developed in the Americas. How were they different and similar? (6.1.2)

Activity **Internet Activity** Use the Internet to research farming techniques used by early farmers. Design one scene or panel of a mural on a blank sheet of paper. (6.1.3)
INTERNET KEYWORD: *prehistoric farming tools*

---

2 Lesson Review Answers

Terms & Names
1. • domesticate, p. 59
   • agriculture, p. 60
   • slash-and-burn, p. 60
   • irrigation, p. 61

Using Your Notes
See page 58 for an example of a completed chart.
2. Possible answers: hoes, digging sticks, and sickles

Main Ideas
3. loosening soil with hoes, digging holes with sticks, harvesting grain with sickles, and slashing and burning trees and brush to clear land for crops

4. Instead of moving around, people tended to settle and live in one place.
5. Asia and Africa—river valleys; Americas—upland regions

Critical Thinking
6. Possible answers: Global warming lengthened the growing season; the domestication of wild grasses provided humans and grazing animals with more food.
7. Possible answers: Farming in Asia and Africa developed in river valleys; farming in the Americas developed in uplands. Farmers in Africa developed irrigation systems; farmers in the Americas developed terracing.

Activity Rubric

	Detail of Content	**Style of Presentation**
4	clear, detailed	neat, attractive
3	reasonably well-detailed	neat
2	few details	a bit sloppy
1	vague, no details	sloppy

Grow a Plant

Goal: To understand the development of agriculture

Prepare

Your teacher will assign you to work in a group. He or she will recommend some fast-growing seeds. For each type of seed, you will learn about the effects of soil, light, and water.

Soil	potting soil	sand	subsoil
Sunlight	full sunlight	partial sunlight	minimal or no sunlight
Water	daily	every 3 days	every 5 days

Do the Activity

1. Attach a label to each of the pots being used. Fill each pot with soil and moisten the soil. Plant two seeds in each pot. Cover each pot with plastic wrap, secured by a rubber band.

2. Once shoots appear, remove the plastic wrap. Pots being used to test for sunlight should be placed in locations that get different amounts of light. The amount of sunlight for all other pots should remain constant.

3. Record your observations over 4–6 weeks. Observations should include plant height, number of leaves, and greenness.

Follow-Up

1. At the end of the period, which plant was healthiest? What challenges do your observations suggest early farmers faced?

2. How have technological advances helped farmers?

Extension

Making a Presentation Each group should display its plants. As a class, discuss the ideal conditions for growing seeds.

Materials & Supplies
- plant pots, paper cups, or milk cartons
- potting soil
- sand
- subsoil (found 50–60 cm beneath topsoil)
- water
- three types of fast-growing seeds
- plastic wrap
- rubber bands

CALIFORNIA STANDARDS
6.1.3 Discuss the climatic changes and human modifications of the physical environment that gave rise to the domestication of plants and animals and new sources of clothing and shelter.

63

ACTIVITY: GROW A PLANT

Objective

Demonstrate an understanding of how different factors affect plant growth.

Suggestions for Completing the Activity

- Suggest that students pick seeds that grow quickly, such as rye or another kind of grass, radish, marigold, or mustard. The labels of seed packets may also have information about germination time.

- Make sure students understand they need 27 pots because they will be testing the 3 different seed types using the 9 different variables shown in the chart.

- Be sure to label each pot with the type of seed it contains and the variable for which it is being tested.

- To test the soil variable, use potting soil in one pot, sand in a second, and subsoil in a third. (All the other pots will have topsoil.)

- Make sure students understand how the other variables will be tested: For example, the three pots (of each plant type) to be tested for sunlight will be placed as instructed; the remaining six (of each type) will all be in the same sun conditions.

ACTIVITIES ANSWERS

Follow-Up Answers

1. Health is to be determined by height, leaves, and greenness. Possible answer: Farmers faced challenges of different soil types and variations in climate conditions.

2. Possible answer: Technology has helped farmers overcome the effects of certain variables, such as lack of water.

Extension Rubric

	Style of Presentation	Understanding of Concepts
4	attractive, well-organized presentation	demonstrates thorough, accurate understanding
3	clear presentation	demonstrates accurate understanding
2	disorganized presentation	some inaccuracies in understanding
1	no organization to presentation	little or no understanding

❶ Plan & Prepare

Objectives

- Describe the processes by which the first significant communities in human history emerged.
- Describe what life was like in these early complex villages.
- **Language Objective:** Describe the occupations of people in the first communities.

Quick Look

Lesson 3 examines the changes in human culture that led to the development of complex communities.

❷ Focus & Motivate

Preview Tell students that this lesson explores the development of complex communities. Ask students what they think makes cities and towns interesting and exciting places to be. *(Students may mention the wide availability of goods and services and the richness and variety of cultural expression.)*

Introduce the Main Ideas The three main ideas relate to the Big Idea that "Ways of living change as humans interact with one another." Help students look for this Big Idea as you go through the lesson.

Reading Skill: Categorizing Have students use the graphic organizer to identify different categories of information discussed in this lesson and to record examples of each.

SAMPLE RESPONSES FOR ORGANIZER

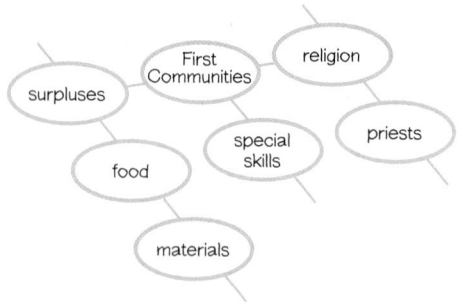

Lesson 3

▶ **MAIN IDEAS**

❶ **Culture** Some simple farming villages expanded and developed into more complex villages.

❷ **Culture** A cultural pattern involving early forms of government, specialized workers, and social classes began to develop in complex villages.

❸ **Culture** The way of life in a complex village was different from that in a simple farming village.

▶ **TAKING NOTES**

Reading Skill: Categorizing

Sorting information into groups helps you understand differences among the groups. In Lesson 3, look for the following three categories of information about the first communities. Record examples or details for each category in a web diagram.

S Skillbuilder Handbook, page R6

▲ **Brooch** This prehistoric brooch was used for fastening a cloak at the neck. It was found on the bank of the Thames River in England.

CALIFORNIA STANDARDS

6.1.2 Identify the locations of human communities that populated the major regions of the world and describe how humans adapted to a variety of environments.

6.1.3 Discuss the climatic changes and human modifications of the physical environment that gave rise to the domestication of plants and animals and new sources of clothing and shelter.

CST 3 Students use a variety of maps and documents to identify physical and cultural features of neighborhoods, cities, states, and countries and to explain the historical migration of people, expansion and disintegration of empires, and the growth of economic systems.

HOW TO TEACH THE CALIFORNIA STANDARDS

Standard	Content	Student Question or Activity	Instruction
6.1.2	**Page 67** Lists characteristics of complex villages	**Page 69** Students describe the basic characteristics of a complex village.	Explain that while villages grew more complex, technology was still advancing slowly. Tell students to look for new types of technology in this lesson.
6.1.3	**Page 66** Describes how villagers settled in one place	**Page 66** Students explain how surpluses affected village life.	Ask students what new sources of clothing and shelter would be available in complex villages that weren't available in a hunter-gatherer society.
CST 3	**Page 67** Explains how workers became more specialized, expanding the growth of the economic system	**Page 69** Students tell how the inhabitants' way of life shows that Catal Huyk was a complex village.	Discuss basic goods and services that early villages would need. Ask students what service they would provide or what good they would produce if they lived in an early complex village.

The First Communities

TERMS & NAMES

surplus

specialization

artisan

social class

government

Build on What You Know Do you live in the country, a small town, a city, or a suburb? In the distant past, simple farming villages developed, over hundreds of years, into more complex villages and eventually into cities.

Villages Around the World

① **ESSENTIAL QUESTION** How did farming villages develop?

When villages prospered, they were able to support more people. Their populations grew. People's skills became more specialized. Village economies became more varied.

Surpluses Boost Development As agricultural techniques improved, farmers sometimes produced surpluses—more than what they needed to survive. For example, farmers might grow more grain than their families or village could use. The extra was an economic surplus.

Surpluses in early farming villages were not limited to food. Surpluses also included materials for making cloth and other products. Sheep raisers, for example, may have had surplus wool. Surpluses of food and other materials in good seasons helped villages survive bad seasons.

farming villages produced surpluses that allowed for specialization of skills; village economies became more varied

Moroccan Village
This modern village in the Atlas Mountains of Morocco in North Africa continues a way of life that has lasted for thousands of years. ▼

Terms & Names

surplus an amount of a good that is in excess of what is needed for survival

specialization a skill in a particular work

artisan a person trained and skilled in a craft

social class group of people with similar customs, background, training, and income

government ways of creating order and offering leadership

❸ Teach

Villages Around the World

6.1.2, CST 3

Talk About It

- **Critical Thinking: Understanding Cause and Effect** How did surpluses contribute to the development of religion? *(Possible answer: One of the specializations that emerged was that of a priest.)*

California Resources

California Reading Toolkit, L7

California Modified Lesson Plans for English Learners, p. 17

California Daily Standards Practice Transparencies, TT7

California Standards Enrichment Workbook, pp. 17–20

California Online Test Practice

California Test Generator CD-ROM

California Standards Planner and Lesson Plans, L13

California EasyPlanner CD-ROM

California eEdition CD-ROM

65

LESSON 3 PROGRAM RESOURCES

ON LEVEL

In-Depth Resources: Unit 1
- Reading Skill: Categorizing, p. 25
- Vocabulary Study Guide, p. 28
- Vocabulary Cards, p. 29
- Geography Practice: Early Farming Communities, p. 31

Formal Assessment
- Lesson Quiz, p. 23

ENGLISH LEARNERS

In-Depth Resources in Spanish
- Reading Skill: Categorizing, p. 13
- Chapter 2 Visual Summary, p. 14
- Geography Practice: Early Farming Communities, p. 17

Modified Lesson Plans for English Learners, p. 17

Reading Study Guide (Spanish), p. 19

Reading Study Guide Audio CD (Spanish)

STRUGGLING READERS

In-Depth Resources: Unit 1
- Reading Skill: Categorizing, p. 25
- Vocabulary Cards, p. 29
- Reteaching Activity, p. 37

Reading Toolkit, L7

Reading Study Guide, p. 19

Reading Study Guide

Audio CD

GIFTED AND TALENTED STUDENTS

In-Depth Resources: Unit 1
- Literature: Catal Huyuk by William Carl Eichman, p. 34

History Makers
- Sophie of Catal Huyuk, p. 3

Interdisciplinary Projects
- Math, p. 7

INCLUSION

EasyPlanner CD-ROM
- Reading Skill: Categorizing
- Vocabulary Study Guide

- Reteaching Activity

TECHNOLOGY

eEdition CD-ROM

Power Presentations CD-ROM

Map Transparencies
- MT4 Annual Rainfall in Southwest Asia

Critical Thinking Transparencies
- CT8 Categorizing
- CT9 Chapter 2 Visual Smmmary

Test Generator CD-ROM

ClassZone.com

In-Depth Resources: Unit 1
• Reading Skill: Categorizing, p. 25
• Geography Practice: Early Farming Communities, p. 31

More About . . .

Early Civilization
One early civilization in Southwest Asia was the Canaanite civilization. Its first small cities emerged sometime around 8,000 B.C. Canaan was eventually conquered and became the biblical land of Israel. In the Bible, Canaanite civilization is noted for its great cities and also for its religion, which featured several gods. Canaanite civilization also produced notable art.

Teach

Simple Villages Grow More Complex

6.1.2, 6.1.3

Talk About It

• What were some examples of the kinds of artisans found in complex villages? *(carpenters, toolmakers, potters, and cloth makers)*

• How did specialization and the development of different trades lead to the development of social classes? *(People developed into classes based on their work, which led to the development of social classes.)*

• What fact of village life led to the need for government? *(Possible answer: When larger groups settled in the same area, the need for leadership and order increased.)*

• **Critical Thinking: Making Inferences** What do you think the text means when it says that complex village life was more "complicated"? *(Possible answer: The goals and needs of the people living in the village were not all the same. This probably led to conflict or confusion.)*

People Develop Different Skills As farmers began producing surpluses, not everyone had to raise food. People began specializing in other kinds of work. A **specialization** is a skill in one kind of work.

Potters and weavers probably were among the first to specialize. They made products that everyone could use. Potters made vessels for carrying and storing water and food. Weavers created cloth from spun cotton, wool, and flax—the plant from which linen is made. Potters and weavers traded their products for food.

Certain people in a community were regarded as holy. These holy people, or shamans, interpreted natural events such as rain or fire. They explained the meaning of a good or bad harvest. They were also healers. They were thought to be in contact with the spiritual world. Such people evolved into the priests of the first cities.

The way of life in a village was new and very different. Hunter-gatherers led a nomadic life, moving from place to place. Villagers settled in one place and no longer depended on hunting and gathering for food. Instead, farmers worked to raise enough food for everyone in the village. Work became more specialized, with nonfarmers trading their goods and services for food.

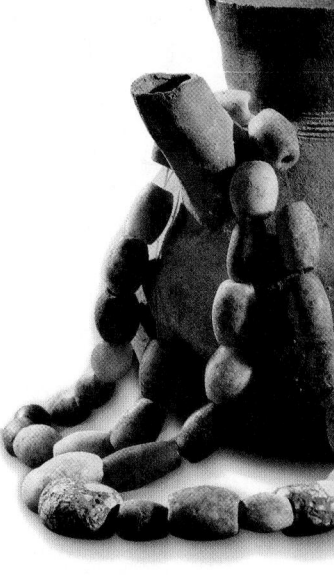

▲ **Necklace and Pottery** People with special skills made different objects. The pottery jar was made about 1800 B.C. The necklace is roughly the same age. Both were produced by early civilizations in Southwest Asia.

REVIEW How did surpluses affect village life?
Surpluses meant that not everyone had to raise food; people could specialize and develop other skills.

Simple Villages Grow More Complex

2 ESSENTIAL QUESTION How did life in villages become more complex?

Surpluses and specialization led to the growth of villages. Life became more complex in certain villages as they developed.

A Changing Way of Life Extra food and other supplies meant that more people could live together. In this way, surpluses encouraged the growth of villages and populations. Surpluses also led to increased trade. People in one village might trade their surplus food for the surplus tools in another village.

Surpluses and special skills led to increased trade and a more complicated social structure; as workers became more specialized and social classes became more complicated, government developed.

DIFFERENTIATING INSTRUCTION

Struggling Readers

Summarize Paragraphs

Put students together in pairs. Have them read the section titled "Simple Villages Grow More Complex" together. Then, have one partner summarize the first paragraph while the other comments on the accuracy of the summary. Have the pair switch roles for the next paragraph, then continue the process for the rest of the section.

Inclusion

Divide and Conquer

Pair up students who do not read well with more accomplished readers. Assign each pair one of the paragraphs under "Simple Villages Grow More Complex" to analyze. When teams have finished studying their paragraphs, bring groups together, and invite one team member from each team to share what they learned from its paragraph.

Workers became more specialized. Potters, weavers, and other craftspeople often spent years learning their skills. People trained in skills or crafts are called **artisans**. Carpenters, toolmakers, cloth makers, and potters are all artisans. People with similar skills developed into occupational classes. In this way, specialization led to the development of social classes. A **social class** is a group of people with similar customs, background, training, and income, such as farmers, craftspeople, priests, or rulers.

As ancient communities grew into larger villages, people felt the need for laws and leadership to keep order and settle disputes. People developed early forms of **government**—that is, ways of creating order and providing leadership. Early humans made laws to make their communities both safer and more stable.

From Simple to Complex Villages A complex village had a larger population than a simple village, with people living closer together. The larger population had a greater supply of skills, ideas, and needs. As a result, life in a complex village was more varied and complicated than that in a simple village.

> **REVIEW** What are some examples of specialized labor?
> potters, weavers, and other craftspeople

Life in a Complex Village

3 **ESSENTIAL QUESTION** How did life in a complex village compare with that in a simple village?

Complex villages were not like the cities of today. Although one of these villages may have had as many as 5,000 people, it would be quite small by today's standards. However, thousands of years ago, a village with a population of 5,000 would have been very large.

Technology was still in its early stages. Electricity, rapid transit, sewer systems, and concrete buildings support today's huge city populations. In ancient times, these tools and technologies had not yet been invented. Most farming villages had only a few hundred inhabitants.

Vocabulary Strategy

Artisan means "a skilled worker or craftsperson." Its **antonym,** or opposite, is *unskilled worker.* The movement from unskilled to skilled workers represented an important change.

Characteristics of Complex Villages	
Larger populations	thousands of people
Beginnings of government	leaders; laws or other means of settling disputes
Public buildings	shrines and other accommodations for gatherings of people
Specialized workers	artisans and other skilled workers
Social classes	groups with similar trainings and incomes
Trade	exchange of surplus goods

The Earliest Human Societies • 67

Vocabulary Strategy

Antonyms
Tell students that the use of antonyms can signal an important historical development, such as the one described in the shift from unskilled to skilled workers. Have students look for an example of such a shift signaled by antonyms elsewhere on this page. (*simple* to *complex* villages)

Teach

Life in a Complex Village

6.1.2, CST 3

Talk About It

- About how many people lived in the early complex villages? (*up to 5,000 people*)

- How do we know so much about life at Catal Huyuk? (*Archaeologists have been studying it since 1961.*)

- **Critical Thinking: Making Inferences** What evidence supports the notion that the people of Catal Huyuk had a religious life? (*Archaeologists have found special buildings designed for religious purposes. These buildings have religious art in them and show evidence of religious ceremonies.*)

History from Visuals

Interpreting Tables
Direct students' attention to the table on this page that describes the characteristics of complex villages. Help them see that the left column lists the characteristics and the right column gives details.

DIFFERENTIATING INSTRUCTION

English Learners

Complete the Sentence
Tell students that since everyone in the first communities couldn't be a farmer, people soon started doing other types of work. Have students listen for other types of jobs that were available in the community as you read the passage. Have students complete the following sentence pattern for different occupations and share out loud with classmates.

_____ specialized in_____ such as
_____ .

Gifted and Talented Students

Diagram a Complex Village
Have students use the information presented in this lesson to create a diagram of a complex village. The village should reflect the various features of life in a complex village.

Interpreting Primary Sources

Artifacts

- How do you think a seal might be used to show ownership? *(The owner of an object would use the seal to mark the object with his or her seal.)*

- What details support the belief that a seal was used as described? *(None of the designs is repeated on the many seals that have been found.)*

- What detail suggests that a dagger had a ceremonial purpose? *(Possible answer: the carved handle)*

DOCUMENT–BASED QUESTION ANSWER

They traded with people from distant lands, had many possessions, and had a rich artistic life.

More About . . .

Catal Huyuk

Initial archaeological study of Catal Huyuk began in 1961 but was halted in 1965, when the archaeologist who did this early work was forced to leave Turkey. Work did not begin again at the site until the 1990s. Archaeologists expect the excavation of Catal Huyuk to continue into the second decade of the twenty-first century. The archaeological team is made up of people from many different countries, including the United States.

In-Depth Resources: Unit 1
- Literature: Catal Huyuk by William Carl Eichman, p. 34

Map Transparencies
- MT4 Annual Rainfall in Southwest Asia

Artifacts

Primary sources include artifacts, or objects, from the past. Artifacts include tools, weapons, sculptures, and jewelry made by human beings. These objects can tell us much about ancient peoples and cultures.

- The seal at the top was found in a burial site in Catal Huyuk. (chah•TAHL hoo•YOOK) It was used as a stamp to show ownership. None of the designs is repeated on the many seals that have been found.

- The dagger at the bottom was also found in Catal Huyuk. It has a snake handle. The blade is made of flint imported from Syria. It was probably used in religious ceremonies or rituals.

> **DOCUMENT–BASED QUESTION**
> What conclusions can you draw about the life of the people in Catal Huyuk by looking at these artifacts?

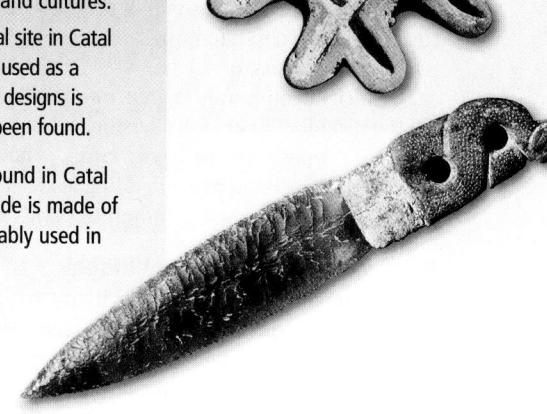

Catal Huyuk Catal Huyuk is an example of a complex village. Its ruins are at least 8,000 years old, and it had a population of about 5,000. Archaeologists began unearthing and studying Catal Huyuk in 1961.

Catal Huyuk is located in Turkey, where agriculture developed fairly early. (See map on page 61.) The bones of many water birds found at Catal Huyuk suggest that the village was built in a marshy area. Farming probably took place in outlying areas.

A Village Develops Although Catal Huyuk had a small population, its site has yielded evidence of the complex life of its dwellers. The layout of the village shows that people lived in clusters of permanent buildings. Houses had similar floor plans, although the bricks used to build them varied in size.

Other buildings served as shrines, where religious ceremonies took place. Wall paintings in the shrines have religious meaning. Small amounts of charred grain and other offerings to the gods show that these buildings were sacred sites.

INTERDISCIPLINARY ACTIVITIES

Language Arts

Give a Speech

An archaeological dig such as the one at Catal Huyuk is very expensive. Have students write and deliver a speech in which they appeal to the public to provide funds for the project. The speech should explain what is being studied and why it is important.

Language Arts

Translate Turkish

The name "Catal Huyuk" comes from the Turkish language. The village is located in Turkey. Have students use library and Internet resources to learn what Catal Huyuk means in Turkish and report back to the class on what they find.

The people of Catal Huyuk developed special skills, such as making tools. Artisans also created luxury items, such as mirrors and metal beads. They produced cloth, wooden vessels, and simple pottery. Artists created murals on the clay walls of many buildings. Specialization established Catal Huyuk as a center of trade, culture, and influence.

REVIEW What characteristics of Catal Huyuk identify it as a complex village?

permanent buildings, wall paintings, shrines, specialized labor, trade

▲ **Wall Painting**
This painting shows a red bull surrounded by humans. It was painted on the inside wall of a shrine in the village of Catal Huyuk.

Lesson Summary
- Improved farming techniques enabled village farmers to grow surplus food.
- Simple villages sometimes grew into complex villages.
- Catal Huyuk is the site of an early complex village.

Why It Matters Now . . .
The development of complex villages was an important step in the change from simple villages to cities.

---

❹ Assess & Reteach

Assess Have students work on their own to answer the questions, then meet in groups to discuss their answers.

 Formal Assessment
- Lesson Quiz, p. 23

Reteach Have students review the lesson summary that appears at the end of the lesson. For each bulleted item, have students write a second sentence using information from the text to provide additional details or information on the summary topic. Have students share their additional sentences with the class.

 In-Depth Resources: Unit 1
- Vocabulary Cards, p. 29
- Reteaching Activity, p. 37

 **Homework Helper**

Visit **ClassZone.com** for a lesson review, a flip-card activity, and links to related Web sites.

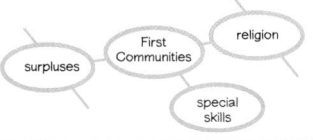

3 Lesson Review

Homework Helper
ClassZone.com

Terms & Names
1. Explain the importance of

surplus   artisan   government
specialization   social class

Using Your Notes
Categorizing Use your completed web diagram to answer the following question:

2. Why were pottery and weaving among the first skills to be developed? (6.1.3)

[web diagram: First Communities — surpluses, religion, special skills]

Main Ideas
3. Why did surpluses lead to the growth of trade? (6.1.3)

4. What are the basic characteristics of a complex village? (6.1.2)

5. How does its inhabitants' way of life indicate that Catal Huyuk was a complex village? (CST 3)

Critical Thinking
6. **Comparing and Contrasting** What would be the pros and cons of living as a nomad? in a simple village? in a complex village? (6.1.2)

7. **Making Inferences** How did specialization help to establish social classes? (6.1.3)

Activity **Planning a Museum Display** Plan a museum display showing specializations that people practiced in early villages. On a poster, make a two-column chart. List the display items on the left. Opposite each item, write a brief description. (6.1.3)

The Earliest Human Societies • 69

---

3 Lesson Review Answers

Terms & Names
1.
- surplus, p. 65
- specialization, p. 66
- artisan, p. 67
- social class, p. 67
- government, p. 67

Using Your Notes
See page 64 for an example of a completed chart.
2. Potters and weavers made items that everyone could use.

Main Ideas
3. Because with extra food and other goods—such as wool—available, villages could trade these surplus goods for surplus goods from other villages.
4. Their shrines, specialized skills, and trade all suggest a complex village.
5. Planned layouts, public religious buildings, specialized labor, and trade all suggest a complex village.

Critical Thinking
6. Possible answers: Nomadic life would involve frequent changes of scene. Simple village life might be stable and secure but somewhat dull.

Complex village life would be more varied, with a bigger pool of skills, ideas, and needs.
7. Possible answer: Potters, weavers, and other craftspeople spent years learning their skills. This led them to have common ideas and values. A social class is a group of people with such similar backgrounds and training.

Activity Rubric

	Content of Chart	Style of Presentation
4	clear, detailed	neat, attractive
3	reasonably well-detailed	neat
2	few details	a bit sloppy
1	vague, no details	sloppy

Objectives

- Describe the way of life in an early complex village.
- Analyze and interpret information from an infographic.
- **Language Objective:** Interpret the information from an illustration that supports the text and makes the content more comprehensible.

❶ Focus & Motivate

Preview Explain that this feature will help students visualize what life might have been like for a resident of Catal Huyuk or another complex village.

❷ Teach

Talk About It

- Why did people travel on the rooftops of buildings? *(There were no streets or alleys to separate the houses and to allow travel between them.)*
- What evidence is there of religious life in Catal Huyuk? *(There were shrines, which featured known religious symbols such as bulls' heads and horns.)*
- **Critical Thinking: Categorizing** How do you think the living conditions of Catal Huyuk affected the people living there? *(Possible answer: It helped produce a strong sense of community; it created tensions among people living in such close proximity.)*

Daily Life

Extend Lesson 3

Research Links
ClassZone.com

Living in a Complex Village

Purpose: To learn about life in a village around 7000 B.C.

Catal Huyuk was located on a river in a plain that was well suited for growing crops. As the settlement prospered, permanent homes were built of mud brick. Around 7000 B.C., perhaps as many as 5,000 or 6,000 people lived in the town, which contained more than a thousand houses. Many different activities were part of daily life in the town.

Ⓐ **House Interiors** The houses had windows and doors. Within the houses, people attended to their daily chores, including the preparation of food. The clay hearths and ovens were built in and had curbs around them to prevent embers from spreading.

Ⓑ **Shrines** Shrines contained bulls' heads and horns. These were common religious symbols in the village.

Ⓒ **Houses with Ladders** Over a thousand houses were packed together. No streets or alleys separated the houses. For security, people used ladders to enter the village.

Ⓓ **Rooftops** People used the rooftops for a variety of purposes. They traveled across roofs. They slept on the roofs in hot weather. They also used the roofs to dry their crops in the sun.

CALIFORNIA STANDARDS

6.1.2 Identify the locations of human communities that populated the major regions of the world and describe how humans adapted to a variety of environments.

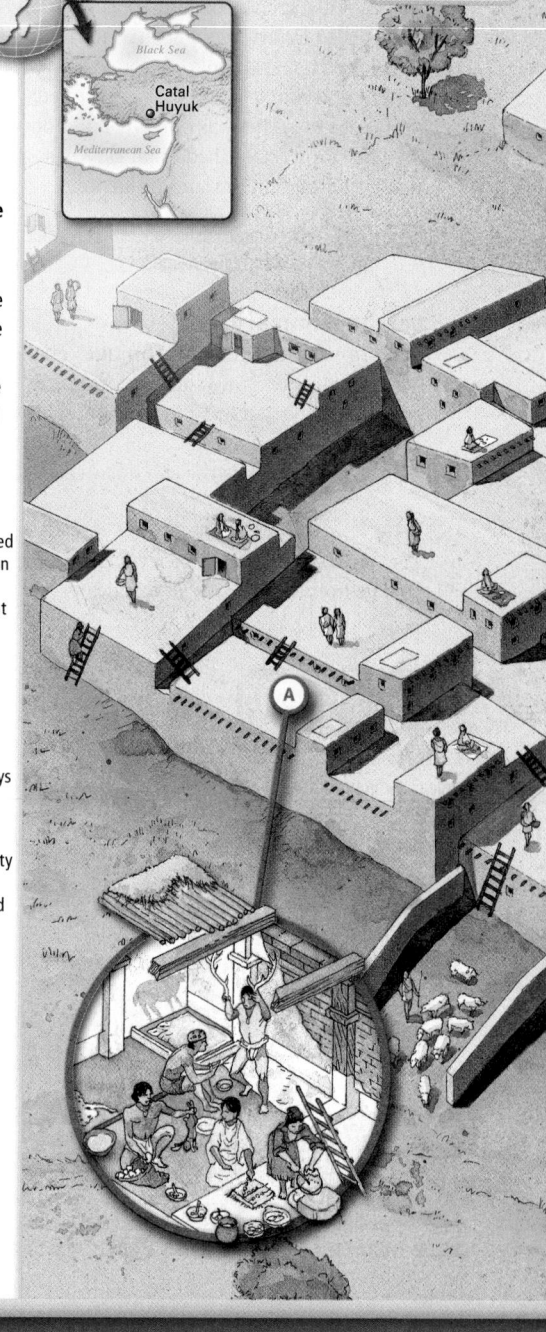

DIFFERENTIATING INSTRUCTION

English Learners

Describe Illustration Detail
Tell students that studying the details of the illustration will help them gain a deeper understanding of the text. Have students describe some of the details in the illustration. Discuss how the details in the captions are illustrated in the scenes. Have students discuss what they would like or not like about living in this village.

Struggling Readers

Divide and Conquer
To help students who have a difficult time reading, divide and conquer the blocks of text on this page. Divide the group into teams of two, and assign each pair one of the text blocks to read together. When students have had a few moments to work through the meaning of their text, bring the group together, and ask each pair to summarize the meaning of its text block.

Research Links

Visit **ClassZone.com** for editor-approved, age-appropriate Web sites related to this topic.

More About . . .

Burial Practices at Catal Huyuk
One of the more interesting features of life at Catal Huyuk was the burial of the dead. Archaeologists have found that bodies were placed in the fetal position in pits, many under raised platforms in the living areas of homes. The burial platforms were covered for ordinary household purposes, such as for sleeping.

Activities

1. **TALK ABOUT IT** What were some of the advantages of living in a village like Catal Huyuk?

2. **WRITE ABOUT IT** This illustration shows a variety of scenes in an early village. Choose one of the scenes and write a brief story about it. (Writing 2.1)

The Earliest Human Societies • **71**

ACTIVITIES ANSWERS

1. **TALK ABOUT IT** Possible answer: Advantages may include security and having a sense of community.

2. **WRITE ABOUT IT**

2. Writing Rubric

	Level of Creativity	Understanding of Concepts	Number of Errors
4	highly creative and imaginative	demonstrates thorough, accurate understanding	zero or one
3	creative	demonstrates accurate understanding	between two and four
2	not very creative	some inaccuracies in understanding	between five and seven
1	unimaginative	little or no understanding	more than seven

Terms & Names

1. *Hunter-gatherers* are *nomads*—people who moved frequently in search of food.

2. Both *irrigation* and *slash-and-burn* refer to techniques used by farmers to prepare or care for fields.

3. *Artisans* are an example of the kind of *specialization* that took place in early human communities.

Main Ideas

Hunters and Gatherers
(pages 50–57)

4. They collected food from naturally occurring sources (plants and animals), and when the food was gone they moved to another area.

5. Technology enabled early humans to collect food more efficiently. This enabled many humans to settle in one place rather than moving all the time.

Learning to Farm and Raise
Animals (pages 58–63)

6. Domestication helped produce a more stable food supply.

7. Early farms were generally located in places such as river valleys, where the soil was rich and water plentiful.

The First Communities
(pages 64–71)

8. Villages grew larger, helping to bring together a larger variety of ideas, skills, and needs.

9. Possible answers: It was large, with about 5,000 residents. It had specialization of skills and religious worship.

▶ VISUAL SUMMARY

The Earliest Human Societies

Geography (6.1.2)
- Early humans adapted to their environment.
- Hunter-gatherers lived a nomadic life in pursuit of animals.
- Farming developed in many parts of the world.

Science & Technology (6.1.1)
- Humans desire to explore the world and solve problems.
- Weapons and tools helped hunter-gatherers to survive.
- New technologies developed to support the agricultural revolution.

Culture (6.1.3)
- Early humans developed language, religion, and art.
- Agriculture caused a change in how people lived.
- Simple farming villages developed into complex villages.

▶ TERMS & NAMES

Explain why the words in each pair below are linked with each other.

1. **hunter-gatherer** and **nomad**
2. **irrigation** and **slash-and-burn**
3. **specialization** and **artisan**

▶ MAIN IDEAS

Hunters and Gatherers (pages 50–57)
4. How did hunter-gatherers interact with the environment? (6.1.1)
5. Why was the development of technology important to early humans? (6.1.2)

Learning to Farm and Raise Animals (pages 58–63)
6. How did the domestication of animals affect people's lives? (6.1.2)
7. How did environmental conditions influence the locations of early farms? (6.1.2)

The First Communities (pages 64–71)
8. What factors caused simple villages to develop into complex villages? (6.1.2)
9. In what ways was life in Catal Huyuk more complex than life in a simple farming village? (6.1.3)

▶ CRITICAL THINKING
Big Ideas: Culture

10. **FINDING MAIN IDEAS** As early communities grew larger, how did village life change? (6.1.2)

11. **UNDERSTANDING CAUSE AND EFFECT** How did the development of tools affect agriculture? (6.1.1)

12. **UNDERSTANDING CONTINUITY AND CHANGE** What were some of the changes that occurred in the way people lived as they changed from a nomadic to a settled way of life? (6.1.2)

ALTERNATIVE ASSESSMENT RUBRICS

1. Writing Rubric

	Level of Creativity	Number of Errors
4	very creative	few or none
3	somewhat creative	some
2	not very creative	many
1	dull and uninteresting	many major

2. Science Rubric

	Clarity of Charts	Number of Components
4	clear, accurate	includes all required components
3	adequate	includes two required components
2	vague or incomplete	includes only one required component
1	inaccurate	includes no required components

ALTERNATIVE ASSESSMENT

1. WRITING ACTIVITY Choose one of the examples of early art shown in this chapter. Write one or two paragraphs about an event that might have inspired the work of art or about a story that the art is attempting to tell. (Writing 2.1)

2. INTERDISCIPLINARY ACTIVITY— SCIENCE Make a chart comparing early farming in the Americas with that in African and Asian river valleys. Include the following factors: type of terrain, crops grown, and farming techniques. Use books and the Internet to find information. (6.1.2)

3. STARTING WITH A STORY Review the description you wrote of your documentary. Create a storyboard with simple sketches of the scenes you will include. Write a brief caption for each. (6.1.1)

Technology Activity

4. CREATING A MULTIMEDIA PRESENTATION
Use the Internet or library resources to research an early complex village, such as Catal Huyuk. Jericho is another example of a complex village. Create a multimedia presentation that includes

- information and visuals of the layout of the village and its buildings and structures
- images of artifacts and other evidence of culture
- a map showing the village's location
- text for each slide
- documentation of your sources (6.1.2)

Research Links ClassZone.com

Reading Charts Use the chart below to answer the questions. (6.1.3)

The Domestication of Animals		
Animal	**Location**	**Use**
llama	South America	transport, meat
turkey	North America	meat
guinea pig	South America	meat
horse	Asia (southwestern steppes)	transport
dog	Asia (possibly China)	guarding, herding, hunting
camel	Asia (central and Near East)	transport
cat	Africa	killing mice and rats
sheep	Europe, Asia, Africa	meat, wool
goat	Asia	milk, meat
pig	Europe, Asia	meat
cattle	Europe, Asia, Africa	milk, meat
chicken	Asia (southeastern)	meat, eggs

1. How were turkeys, guinea pigs, and pigs used?

A. protection
B. meat
C. transport
D. clothes

2. Which animals were domesticated in South America?

A. turkey, pig
B. horse, goat
C. llama, guinea pig
D. camel, cattle

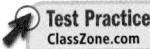
Test Practice ClassZone.com

Additional Test Practice, pp. S1–S33

The Earliest Human Societies • 73

Critical Thinking

Big Ideas: Culture

10. Possible answers: Special skills allowed people to develop new products; trade expanded; social classes developed; government developed.

11. hoes, digging sticks, and sickles

12. Possible answer: People originally lived the nomadic life of hunters and gatherers. Eventually, people learned to farm and raise animals, and this led to a more settled life in villages. Villages became more complex, with specialized labor, social classes, and governments.

Standards-Based Assessment

1. The correct answer is B. Turkeys, guinea pigs, and pigs were all used for meat. These animals were not used for protection, transport, or to make clothes.

2. The correct answer is C. Llamas and guinea pigs were both domesticated in South America. The animals in answers A, B, and D were domesticated but not in South America.

Research Links

Visit **ClassZone.com** for links to Web sites that can be used in the virtual museum exhibit.

Test Practice

Visit **ClassZone.com** to access strategies and tutorials for taking standardized tests.

Formal Assessment
- Chapter Tests, Forms A, B, and C, pp. 24–35

Test Generator
- Chapter Tests, Forms A, B, and C (English and Spanish)

ALTERNATIVE ASSESSMENT RUBRICS

3. Starting with a Story Rubric

	Clarity of Storyboard	**Content of Caption**
4	detailed, clear	detailed, thorough
3	clear	detailed
2	somewhat unclear	not very detailed
1	very unclear	no details

4. Technology Rubric

	Presence of Required Elements	**Level of Organization**
4	includes all	clear
3	includes most	reasonably clear
2	includes some	unclear
1	includes few or none	no organization

Objectives

- Identify the elements of a narrative.
- Research information for use in a narrative about early humans.
- Publish a class magazine.

❶ Focus & Motivate

Preview Explain that students will use facts about early humans to write a fictional story. These facts should come from Unit 1 of the textbook and from students' own research.

❷ Teach

Talk About It

- What facts or ideas from Chapters 1 and 2 might make a good narrative? *(Possible answers: who created cave paintings and why, what archaeologists do and how they do it, what Lucy's life was like, what life in Catal Huyuk was like)*

- Which people from Chapters 1 and 2 might have had interesting stories to tell? *(Possible answers: people who built Stonehenge, artists who created Lascaux cave paintings or other prehistoric art, people who made the first stone tools, the hunter of the Alps, residents of Catal Huyuk)*

- What conflicts would be interesting to write about? *(Possible answers: hunting for food, surviving extreme weather conditions)*

- **Critical Thinking: Forming and Supporting Opinions** Early humans faced many changes. Which changes would be most interesting to read about in a narrative? Why? *(Possible answers: ice age, because weather made it difficult to survive; creating the first tools, because those eventually led to today's technology; domesticating animals, because what we eat and wear today is still affected by the animals we raise)*

Writing About History

Narratives:
A Story About Early Humans

CALIFORNIA STANDARDS
Writing 2.1 Write fictional or autobiographical narratives.

Purpose: To write a narrative for a class magazine about early humans
Audience: Your class

In this unit, you read stories about teenagers who discovered cave paintings, anthropologists who found Lucy's skeleton, and the ice man's fate. Another name for a story is a **narrative**.

Some narratives are based mostly on imagination. Historians, though, write narratives about events that really happened. Their stories are based on facts. But without the ability to interpret information, a historian could not turn the factual evidence from artifacts into a story of the past.

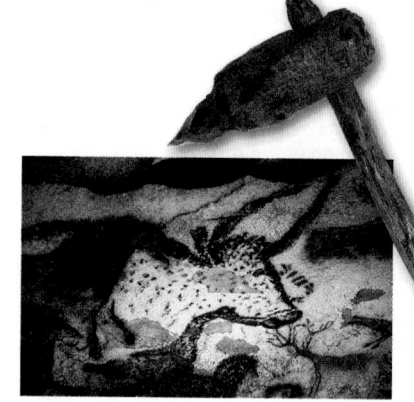

▲ Lascaux Cave painting and prehistoric tool

Organization & Focus

Your assignment is to write a narrative about early humans. A narrative has three basic parts. The **beginning** sets the scene and starts the action. The **body** presents a conflict. The **resolution** settles the conflict and ends the story. The first step in writing a narrative is to focus on a topic.

Choosing a Topic Here are some ways to help you think of topics about early humans to write about.

- Note facts or ideas from Chapters 1 and 2 that might make a good narrative.
- Review the images in these chapters. What story might exist behind each one?
- Talk to a classmate. Share ideas that might work as good stories.

Identifying Purpose and Audience For this writing assignment, your purpose and audience are provided above. In general, to plan a narrative, consider the following two questions:

- Why are you writing this story? Thinking about what interests you about this topic will help you decide on your purpose.
- Who will read this story? Your writing will change based on the ages, education levels, and interests of your audience.

DIFFERENTIATING INSTRUCTION

English Learners

Review Narrative Terms
Students may be unfamiliar with terms related to writing a narrative. Explain that setting means where and when the story takes place. Characters are the people (or even animals) in the story. Point of view means beliefs and opinions. The main conflict is the problem in the story—without a conflict, a story is not very interesting. Resolved means finding a solution for the conflict.

Inclusion

Brainstorm Ideas
You may wish to pair students and have them research and write together. Have them look through Unit 1 and brainstorm ideas. Encourage students to use the Research Links for Unit 1, available on **ClassZone.com**. Then use the chart on page 75 to help them focus.

Finding Details Organize information about your topic in a chart like the one below. List words and phrases that will make the narrative vivid and engaging.

Narrative Elements	Main Point	Vivid Details
What is the setting?		
Who are the characters?		
What is the point of view of the person telling the story?		
What is the main conflict?		
How is the conflict resolved?		

Outlining and Drafting Create an outline for your story using the details from your chart. Then write the first draft. Transition words and phrases, such as *later, next,* and the *following day,* can tell the order of events. Include dialogue if you wish.

Research & Technology

You can find information to use in your narrative in a library or on the Internet. Use notecards to record facts and ideas that will help you decide what to write. Try to make your story as real as possible.

Technology Tip Before you go online, have a search strategy. Identify specific questions and keywords. Ask a librarian to recommend search engines and directories.

Evaluation & Revision

Work on your narrative until you are ready to share it. Here are some ways to check your draft and improve it.

- Read it aloud and ask for feedback.
- Write a title.
- Check all details.

When you are done, create a neat, clean copy.

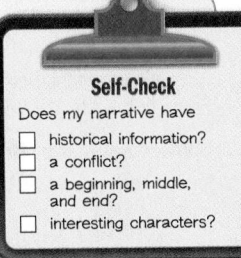

Self-Check
Does my narrative have
- [ ] historical information?
- [ ] a conflict?
- [ ] a beginning, middle, and end?
- [ ] interesting characters?

Publish & Present

To create the magazine, divide up these tasks.
- Design front and back covers and create illustrations.
- Organize the stories and create a table of contents.
- Think of a title for the magazine.
- Share the magazine with other social studies classes.

75

ANSWERS

Narrative Rubric

	Structure of Narrative	Use of Research	Errors in Mechanics
4	sophisticated, with interesting characters and setting, a believable conflict, and effective transitions	extensive and precise with several sources	few or none
3	detailed and organized, with characters, setting, conflict, and transitions	two or three sources	some
2	sometimes confusing; characters, setting, or conflict lack focus	one source	many
1	weak and disorganized; lacks characters, setting, or conflict	no sources	many major

Begin the Unit

Quick Look

Chapter 3 describes the development of human civilization in Mesopotamia, including the civilization of Sumer.

Chapter 4 explores the development of empires in the ancient world and the ways in which government grew to meet the challenges of ruling vast territories.

Interact with History ▶

Purpose

To help students comprehend the dramatic achievements of the first civilizations by picturing themselves in a historical situation—being taken prisoner into Babylon

Visual Learning

Ask a student volunteer to read the text and questions aloud. Point out that the text and three question on these pages help guide students to an answer of the main question on page 76. Discuss the three questions before discussing the main question.

Interact ANSWERS

- What does your first sight of the city tell you about Babylon? *(It is a large city, and its people have great technical skills in building. The people value military strength.)*

- What skills must the Babylonians have to build such a structure? *(Possible answers: They must have architectural skills; they must have advanced construction skills.)*

- What purpose do the soldiers on the wall serve? *(They help protect Babylon from an attack.)*

- What qualities do bulls and dragons have in common? Why might the Babylonians admire them? *(Possible answers: Bulls and dragons are powerful and fierce. Perhaps the Babylonians admire them because they suggest strength.)*

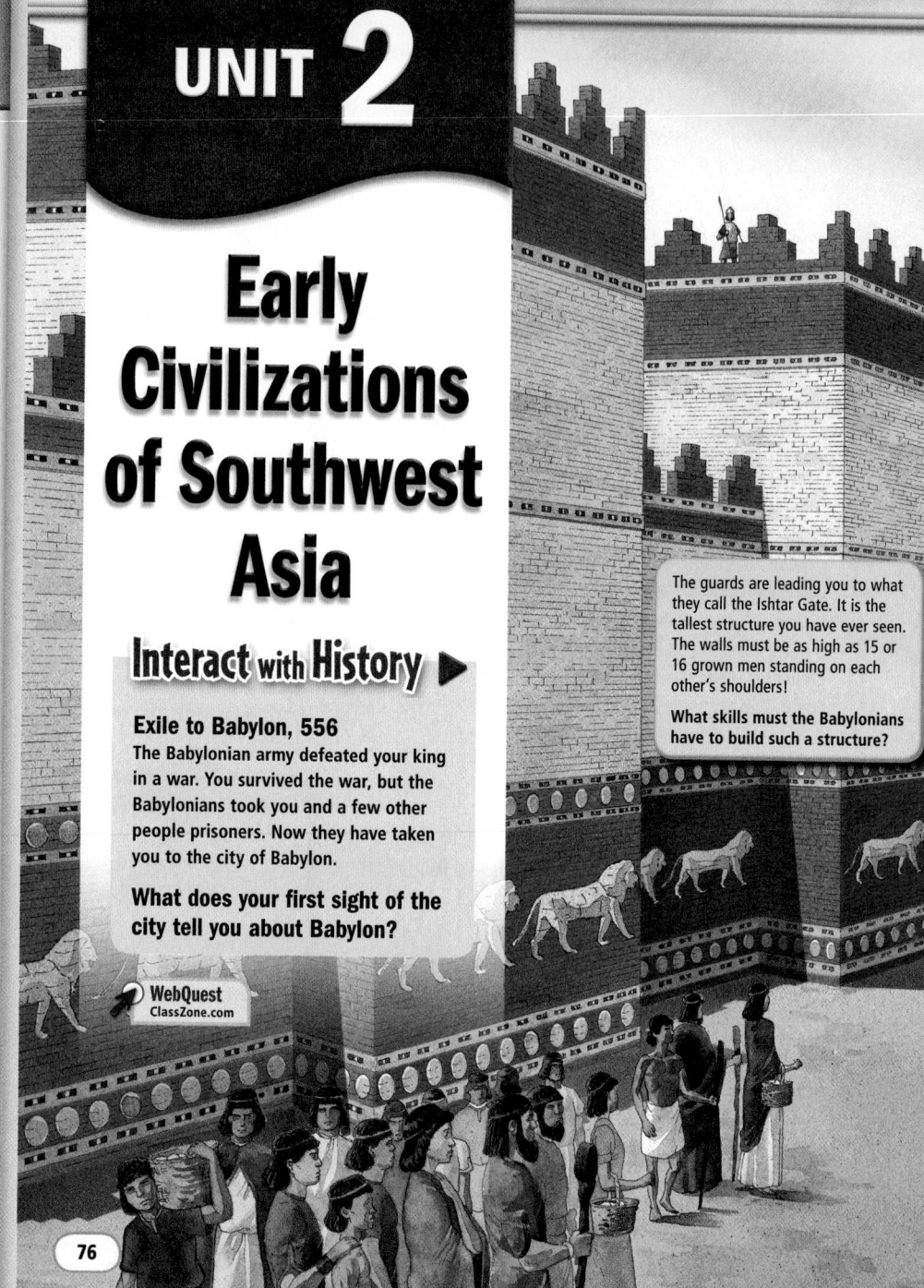

UNIT **2**

Early Civilizations of Southwest Asia

Interact with History ▶

Exile to Babylon, 556
The Babylonian army defeated your king in a war. You survived the war, but the Babylonians took you and a few other people prisoners. Now they have taken you to the city of Babylon.

What does your first sight of the city tell you about Babylon?

WebQuest ClassZone.com

The guards are leading you to what they call the Ishtar Gate. It is the tallest structure you have ever seen. The walls must be as high as 15 or 16 grown men standing on each other's shoulders!

What skills must the Babylonians have to build such a structure?

76

TECHNOLOGY

Web Quest: Hammurabi's Code

Visit **ClassZone.com** to lead your students through a WebQuest on Hammurabi's Code and how it affected life for ordinary Babylonians. Each student will choose to play the role of a type of Babylonian citizen. The student will then examine how the code of law might affect him or her.

When to Use This project works well as an introduction to Chapter 4 or as an end-of-chapter activity.

Class Time Two class periods

Materials Needed At least one computer with access to the World Wide Web and a printer

Customizing for Your Classroom

- If computer time is limited, have small groups rotate through stations, finding information from encyclopedias, library books, or their textbook as well as the Web sites.

- Encourage Spanish speakers to use the textbook's Spanish glossary.

- Pair students who may have difficulty reading with stronger readers to ensure they understand the language of Hammurabi's Code.

On top of the gate and the surrounding walls stand armed men. They hold spears and bows and arrows. You didn't realize that the army that defeated your king was only a part of the full strength of Babylon.

What purpose do the soldiers on the wall serve?

The bricks of the gate are the most amazing color—a blue that is as dark as the evening sky. Pictures of dragons and bulls decorate the walls.

What qualities do bulls and dragons have in common? Why might the Babylonians admire them?

Chapter 3
Ancient Mesopotamia

Chapter 4
Early Empires

77

Correcting Misconceptions

In some religious traditions, Babylon symbolizes a place of luxury and corruption. This could be partly due to some passages in the Bible. Ask students if they are familiar with this image. Explain that Babylon was also a great city of learning and government.

More About . . .

The Wonders of Babylon

At its height, Babylon was reputed to be home to some of the most amazing sights of the ancient world. One such sight was the great Tower of Babel, which was a religious symbol that may have been dedicated to a Babylonian god. Another wonder was the so-called Hanging Gardens of Babylon. Descriptions of the gardens suggest they were a series of terraces built one on top of the other, in which beautiful plants grew. Water was pumped to the top of the gardens by a special system, which may have been powered by slaves.

WHY STUDY EARLY CIVILIZATIONS OF SOUTHWEST ASIA?

- The civilizations of Southwest Asia were the world's first great civilizations.

- Many of the advances that make civilization possible, such as written language and complex government, were first developed in these places.

- The development of social classes continues to happen in societies today.

- The geographic factors that helped give rise to these great civilizations also help explain the rise of later great civilizations.

- The land of Mesopotamia, where these civilizations emerged, remains a critical area in world affairs today.

CHAPTER 3 PLANNING GUIDE: Ancient Mesopotamia

Chapter Overview	Copymasters		Assessment
Mesopotamia was the site of great achievement in early human history, including the development of the world's first civilization.	**In-Depth Resources: Unit 2** • Family Newsletter (English and Spanish), pp. 1–2 • Visual Summary, p. 6 • Vocabulary Study Guide, p. 8 **Character Education** **Reading Study Guide,** p. 29	**Bringing Social Studies Alive,** Chapter 3 **Document-Based Questions: Strategy and Practice** **Reading Toolkit,** L8–L10 **Modified Lesson Plans for English Learners,** pp. 19–24	**Chapter Review,** pp. 106–107 **Formal Assessment** • Chapter Tests, Forms A, B, and C, pp. 43–57 **Test Generator** **Integrated Assessment Book** **Online Test Practice**
LESSON 1 **Geography of Mesopotamia** pp. 82–87 **OBJECTIVE** Analyze how the geography of Mesopotamia influenced life in the region.	**In-Depth Resources: Unit 2** • Reading Skill: Summarizing, p. 3 • Vocabulary Cards, p. 9 • Skillbuilder Practice: Categorizing, p. 7 • Reteaching Activity, p. 15	**Interdisciplinary Projects** • Science, p. 14 **Reading Study Guide,** p. 23	**Lesson Review,** p. 86 **Formal Assessment** • Lesson Quiz, p. 40 **California Daily Standards Practice Transparencies,** TT8
LESSON 2 **The First Civilization** pp. 88–97 **OBJECTIVE** Learn about the development of the first civilization in Sumer.	**In-Depth Resources: Unit 2** • Reading Skill: Making Generalizations, p. 4 • Vocabulary Cards, p. 9 • Geography Practice: Oldest Cities of the World, p. 11 • Literature: from "A Praise Poem of the Shulgi," p. 14 • Reteaching Activity, p. 16	**Interdisciplinary Projects** • Language Arts, p. 15 **Reading Study Guide,** p. 25	**Lesson Review,** p. 95 **Formal Assessment** • Lesson Quiz, p. 41 **California Daily Standards Practice Transparencies,** TT9
LESSON 3 **Life in Sumer** pp. 98–105 **OBJECTIVE** Study Sumerian society and the innovations that developed there.	**In-Depth Resources: Unit 2** • Reading Skill: Categorizing, p. 5 • Vocabulary Cards, p. 9 • Primary Source: Sumerian Proverbs, p. 13 • Reteaching Activity, p. 17	**History Makers** • Leonard Woolley, p. 5 **Interdisciplinary Projects** • Math, p. 13; Civics, p. 16 **Reading Study Guide,** p. 27	**Lesson Review,** p. 103 **Formal Assessment** • Lesson Quiz, p. 42 **California Daily Standards Practice Transparencies,** TT10

Integrated Technology

 eEdition Plus Online

EasyPlanner Plus Online

eTest Plus Online

 Audio CDs
- Reading Study Guide
- Reading Study Guide in Spanish
- The World's Music

 CD-ROMs
- Power Presentations
- eEdition
- EasyPlanner
- Test Generator

 Ancient Civilizations Video Series
- Ancient Mesopotamia

---

 eEdition CD-ROM

 Map Transparencies
- MT5 Climates of Southwest Asia

 Humanities Transparencies
- HT5 Stone Vessel

 Critical Thinking Transparencies
- CT10 Summarizing

 ClassZone.com

---

 eEdition CD-ROM

 Map Transparencies
- MT6 Ancient City of Ur

 Humanities Transparencies
- HT6 Bull with a Human Head

 Critical Thinking Transparencies
- CT11 Making Generalizations

 ClassZone.com

---

 eEdition CD-ROM

 Critical Thinking Transparencies
- CT12 Categorizing
- CT13 Chapter 3 Visual Summary

 ClassZone.com

Overview of California Resources

	Lesson 1	Lesson 2	Lesson 3
California Reading Toolkit	L8	L9	L10
California Modified Lesson Plans for English Learners	p. 19	p. 21	p. 23
California Daily Standards Practice Transparencies	TT8	TT9	TT10
California Standards Enrichment Workbook	pp. 21–24	pp. 23–26, 37–38	pp. 23–26, 37–38
California Standards Planner and Lesson Plans	L15	L17	L19
California Online Test Practice	ClassZone.com	ClassZone.com	ClassZone.com
California Test Generator CD-ROM			
California EasyPlanner CD-ROM			
California eEdition CD-ROM			

Chart Key

P E Pupil Edition	CD-ROM	Internet
Copymaster	Audio	Overhead Transparency
	Video	

PREVIEWING RESOURCES FOR DIFFERENTIATED INSTRUCTION

English Learners

In-Depth Resources in Spanish
- Reading Skill and Strategy **A**
- Skillbuilder Practice
- Geography Practice **C**
- Vocabulary Study Guide **B**

In-Depth Resources: Unit 2
- Family Newsletter (English and Spanish)

Reading Study Guide (Spanish)

Reading Study Guide Audio CD
(Spanish)

Test Generator
Chapter Test (Spanish)

Plus

Modified Lesson Plans for English Learners

Multi-Language Glossary of Social Studies Terms

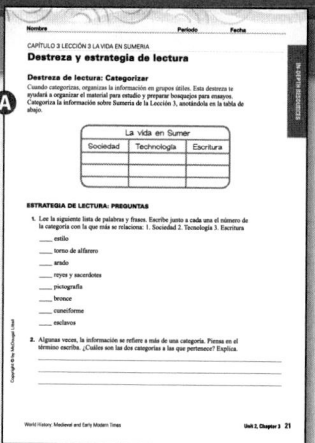
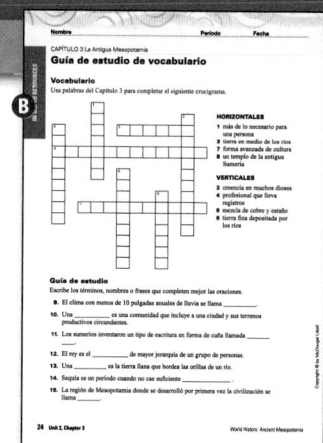

Struggling Readers

In-Depth Resources: Unit 2
- Vocabulary Study Guide
- Skillbuilder Practice **B**
- Geography Practice
- Reteaching Activities
- Family Newsletter **C**

Reading Study Guide A

Reading Study Guide Audio CD

Reading Toolkit

Formal Assessment
Chapter Test, Form A

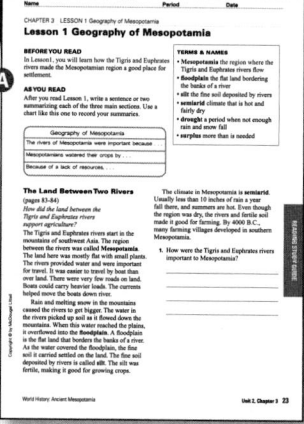
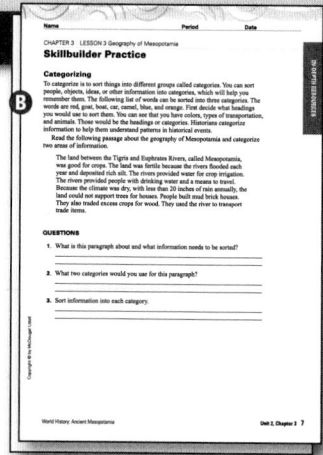

Inclusion

EasyPlanner CD-ROM
- Reading Skill and Strategy
- Vocabulary Study Guide **A**
- Geography Practice **B**
- Reteaching Activities **C**

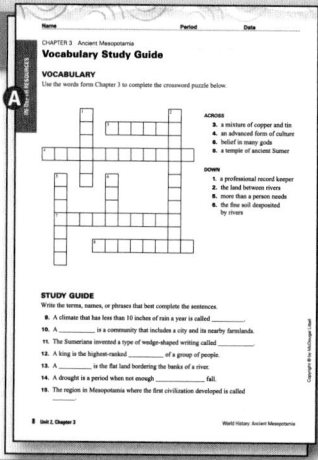
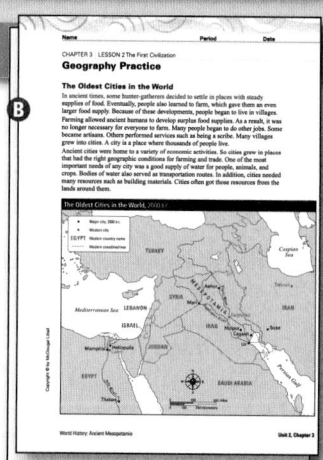

Gifted and Talented Students

In-Depth Resources: Unit 2
- Primary Source **A**
- Literature

History Makers B

Interdisciplinary Projects C

Formal Assessment
Chapter Test, Form C

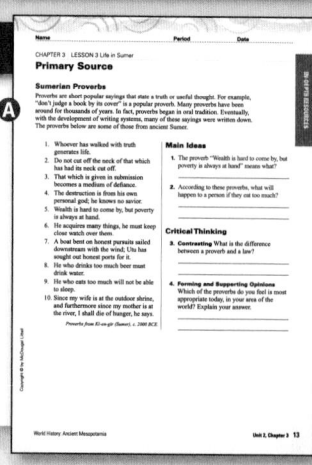

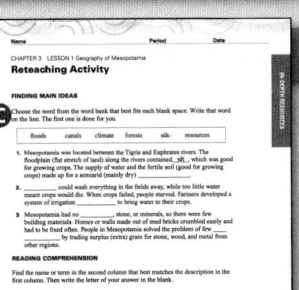

Activities in the Teacher's Edition for English Learners

- Identify How Writing is Organized, p. 84
- Make a Generalization, p. 91
- Interpret a Map, p. 96
- Categorize Information, p. 102

Activities in the Teacher's Edition for Struggling Readers

- Read Aloud, p. 85
- Write Paragraph Summaries, p. 90
- Write a Job Description, p. 94
- Record the Sequence, p. 101
- Create a Venn Diagram, p. 104

Activities in the Teacher's Edition for Inclusion Students

- Role-Play: Be a Trader, p. 85
- Chart Information, p. 91
- Create a Diagram, p. 94
- Interpret a Map, p. 96
- Restate Proverbs, p. 102

Activities in the Teacher's Edition for Gifted and Talented Students

- Build an Irrigation Model, p. 84
- Create a Poster of Sumerian Civilization, p. 90
- Create a Pictograph System, p. 101
- Create a Board Game, p. 104

Integrated Technology

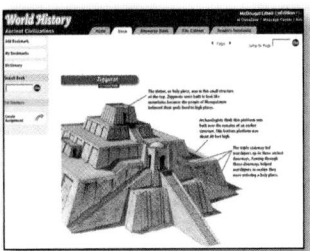

eEdition CD-ROM
- Interactive Visuals
- Interactive Maps
- Starting with a Story

ClassZone.com
- WebQuests
- Research Links
- Internet Activities
- Homework Helper
- Chapter Quiz
- Current Events
- Test Practice

Power Presentations CD-ROM
- Lecture Notes
- Media Gallery
- Chapter Review Game

Critical Thinking Transparencies
- CT10 Summarizing
- CT11 Making Generalizations
- CT12 Categorizing
- CT13 Chapter 3 Visual Summary

California Daily Standards Practice Transparencies, TT8–TT10

Map Transparencies
- MT5 Climates of Southwest Asia
- MT6 Ancient City of Ur

Humanities Transparencies
- HT5 Stone Vessel
- HT6 Bull with a Human Head

Test Generator CD-ROM

EasyPlanner CD-ROM

Ancient Civilizations Video Series
Ancient Mesopotamia

Begin the Chapter

Objective

Describe the development of the first human civilizations and the factors that helped give rise to them.

Quick Look

Lesson 1 describes the geographic features of Mesopotamia, where the first civilizations would emerge.

Lesson 2 describes the first civilization and its growth.

Lesson 3 explores the life and culture of the first civilization at Sumer.

Before You Read:
Previewing Key Concepts

Previewing key concepts helps students prepare for what they will be reading and helps them identify critical information.

Have students follow these steps:

- Read the Before You Read instructions and follow the steps.

- Repeat this process for each lesson as you read, using the main ideas listed on the first page of each lesson.

- As you read the lesson, look for answers to your questions, and jot down information as it comes up.

- After you have finished the lesson, make sure you have answered each question fully. Review the lesson if you need more information.

- At the end of the chapter, think about what you have learned about ancient Mesopotamia.

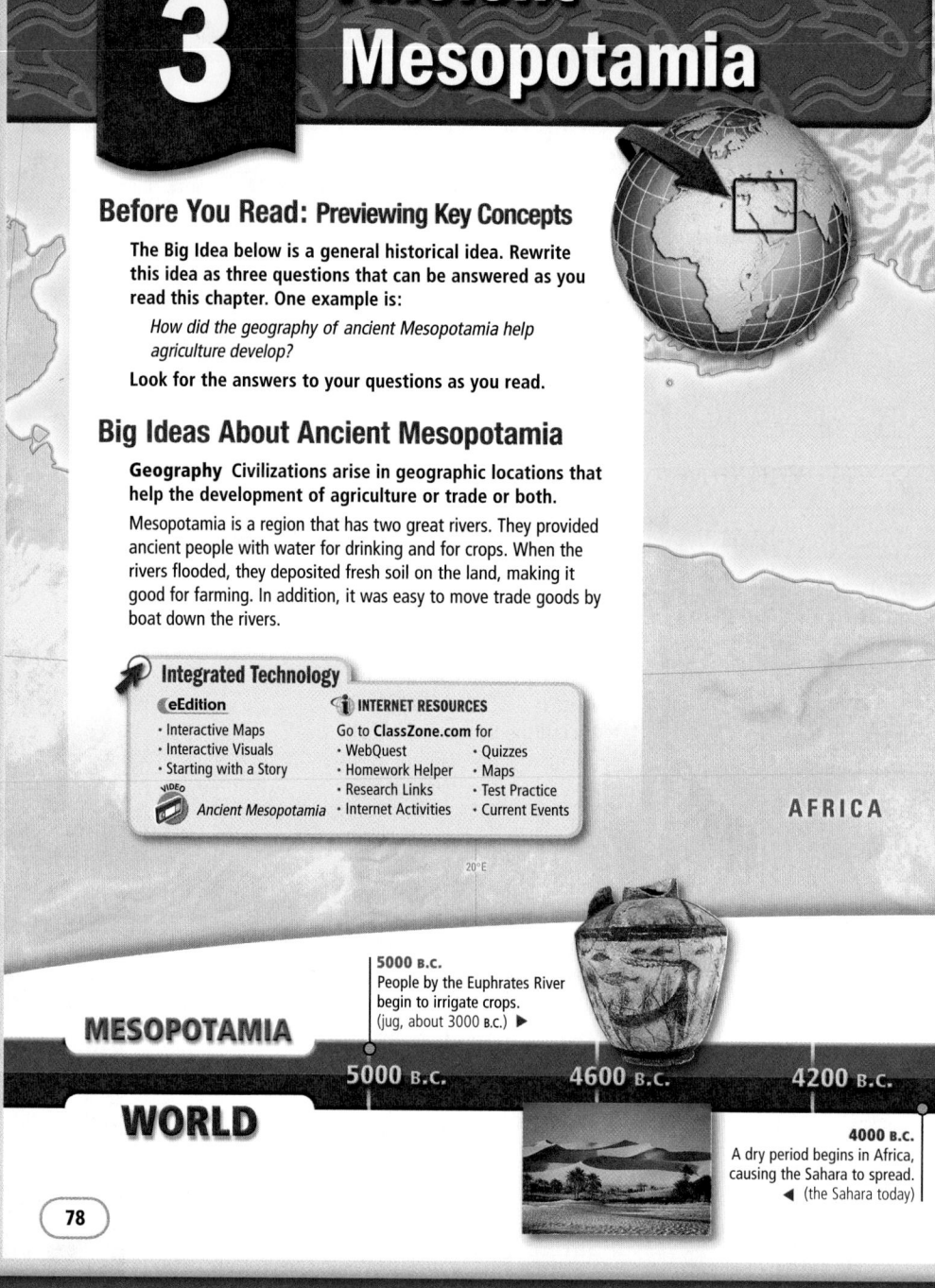

Chapter 3 Ancient Mesopotamia

Before You Read: Previewing Key Concepts

The Big Idea below is a general historical idea. Rewrite this idea as three questions that can be answered as you read this chapter. One example is:

How did the geography of ancient Mesopotamia help agriculture develop?

Look for the answers to your questions as you read.

Big Ideas About Ancient Mesopotamia

Geography Civilizations arise in geographic locations that help the development of agriculture or trade or both.

Mesopotamia is a region that has two great rivers. They provided ancient people with water for drinking and for crops. When the rivers flooded, they deposited fresh soil on the land, making it good for farming. In addition, it was easy to move trade goods by boat down the rivers.

Integrated Technology

eEdition
- Interactive Maps
- Interactive Visuals
- Starting with a Story

VIDEO *Ancient Mesopotamia*

INTERNET RESOURCES
Go to **ClassZone.com** for
- WebQuest
- Homework Helper
- Research Links
- Internet Activities
- Quizzes
- Maps
- Test Practice
- Current Events

AFRICA

20°E

5000 B.C.
People by the Euphrates River begin to irrigate crops. (jug, about 3000 B.C.) ▶

MESOPOTAMIA

5000 B.C.   4600 B.C.   4200 B.C.

WORLD

4000 B.C.
A dry period begins in Africa, causing the Sahara to spread.
◀ (the Sahara today)

78

TIME LINE DISCUSSION

Use the time line to help students establish a time frame for the events and developments that led to the emergence of the earliest civilizations *(sometime around 3300 B.C.).*

- According to the time line, about how long after the introduction of irrigation along the Euphrates River did farming villages begin to grow into cities? *(about 1,500 years)*

- According to the time line, which came first: the development of cities or of a system of writing? *(the development of cities)*

- How long ago did writing develop in Mesopotamia? *(about 5,000 years ago)*

- How long after the development of cities in Mesopotamia did cities begin to emerge in the Indus River Valley? *(about 1,000 years)*

Mesopotamia, 2400 B.C.
INTERACTIVE

Caspian Sea

ASIA

ZAGROS MOUNTAINS

MESOPOTAMIA

Tigris River

Euphrates River

Karkheh River

Aras River

Syrian Desert

Mediterranean Sea

Jordan River

Kish

SUMER
• Umma
Nippur •
Lagash •
Eridu • • Ur

Persian Gulf

Red Sea

ARABIAN PENINSULA

| 0 | 75 | 150 miles |
| 0 | 75 | 150 kilometers |

Fertile soil deposited by rivers
Sumerian cultural area
Modern coastline

Timeline:

3500 B.C.
Farming villages grow into cities.

3000 B.C.
The first system of writing is in use.
◄ (tablet, about 2100 B.C.)

2400 B.C.
King Urukagina of Lagash reforms government.

3400 B.C.   3000 B.C.   2600 B.C.   2200 B.C.

3100 B.C.
King Narmer unifies Egypt.

2600–2500 B.C.
People in the Indus Valley build cities.
◄ (city ruins today)

79

RECOMMENDED RESOURCES

Books for the Teacher
Roaf, Michael. *The Cultural Atlas of Mesopotamia and the Ancient Near East.* New York: Facts on File, 1990. Study of the history, geography, and archaeology of this region.

Roux, Georges. *Ancient Iraq.* London: Penguin Books, 1992. History of the Mesopotamian civilizations of ancient times.

Videos
Mesopotamia. 52 minutes. Richmond: Time-Life Video, 1995. Follows archaeologists searching biblical sights in the fertile crescent.

Internet
To access these sites, visit the Research Links for this chapter at **ClassZone.com**.

The British Museum. This site includes a rich collection of information on the geography and culture of ancient Mesopotamian civilizations.

Providence College's CivWeb. Includes descriptions and links to many sources of information on Mesopotamian culture.

Introduce the Big Ideas
Read aloud the text about the Big Ideas. Have students think about how the geography of their region has affected development. For example, do students live in coastal areas, where trade has been important? Do they live in farming areas, where agriculture has spurred development? Here are some other Big Ideas that you may want to emphasize in this chapter.

Culture
Ways of living changed as people came together to live in Mesopotamian cities, leading to the growth of rich cultures.

Government
In Mesopotamian civilizations, the need to develop codes of behavior and the need for protection led to the development of government.

Science and Technology
New inventions and discoveries helped make possible larger and more complex cities and civilizations.

Talk About It
Interpreting Maps
Ask students to examine the map and its key. What geographic features are present in the area where all the cities are shown? *(rivers and fertile soil)* What natural barriers appear to limit the extent of the Sumerian cultural area? *(the Syrian Desert, the Zagros Mountains, and the Persian Gulf)*

INTERACTIVE

An interactive version of this map is available on the eEdition and Power Presentations CD-ROMs.

Find Out More
What countries and cultures exist in this part of the world today? Have students use an encyclopedia, maps in this book, and other sources to find out about settlement in this region of the modern world.

Watch the Video
Ancient Mesopotamia helps students discover how ancient peoples lived and worked. This 23 minute video is part of the Ancient Civilizations for Children video series.

Objective

Describe some of the challenges associated with the transition from a hunting-and-gathering system to an agricultural system.

Introducing the Story

Importance of Farming

The ability to farm helped humans produce large amounts of food, which in turn enabled people to settle in large numbers in a single place—a village. However, as settlements grew, they became more vulnerable to any sort of disruption in the food supply. Large numbers of people depended on farmers' crops for their survival, and drought, floods, or other environmental conditions could wreak havoc on these crops.

Vocabulary Preview

penetrate to enter or push into

evaporate to turn liquid into vapor

Reading the Story Aloud

1. **The teacher as reader:** Read a section of the passage, modeling for students the difference between evenly paced reading and unevenly paced reading.

2. **The students as readers:** Have students read a section of the passage to a partner, pausing before or after specific words or sentences to emphasize ideas.

Starting with a Story

Students can also follow along as they listen to the story on the eEdition or Power Presentations CD-ROMs.

Starting with a Story

THE Long Dry Spell

CALIFORNIA STANDARDS
Reading 3.3
Analyze the influence of setting on the problem and its resolution.

Background: The first people in Southwest Asia (sometimes referred to as the Middle East) were hunters and gatherers. In some places, they found animals and plants that people began to raise themselves. Some plants that people learned to grow were wild grains. So as people learned how to plant crops for themselves, they began to settle in villages.

This change happened over time more than 8,000 years ago. The new way of life was not always easy. Imagine you are there as your village fights for its life.

Ancient people learned to grow wheat for food. ▶

80

ADDITIONAL RESOURCES

Books for the Student

Oakes, Lorna and Dr. John Haywood. *Find Out About Mesopotamia: What Life Was Like in Ancient Sumer, Babylon and Assyria.* London: Southwater Publishing, 2004. Explores the cultures of the ancient civilizations of Mesopotamia.

Pilbeam, Mavis. *Mesopotamia and the Fertile Crescent.* Austin: Steck-Vaughn, 1999. Traces the development of the earliest civilizations from prehistoric times.

Videos

Ancient Mesopotamia. 23 minutes. Wynnewood: Schlessinger Media, 1998. Dramatization of archaeological explorations into ancient civilizations of Mesopotamia.

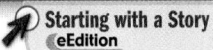

Y ou are a farmer in Southwest Asia. The oldest members of your family decided several years ago to settle in a new village near a river. They knew the river had something special about it that would make this place suitable for farming.

Every year the river floods and puts a fresh layer of rich, dark mud on the fields. This mud provides moisture to the soil and somehow seems to help plants grow. You depend on the flood to be able to farm.

This year the flood never happened because there wasn't enough rain. With no moisture, the soil was hard when you were ready to plant. Your sharpened digging stick barely penetrated the soil enough for you to put the seeds in the ground.

Now the weather is hot and dry, and the tiny plants are struggling to survive. Every day the scorching sun beats down on them. Their leaves wilt. Large cracks are appearing in the ground, and crops are dying.

The brutal heat makes it difficult to work. Yet every day you must walk to the river with animal-skin bags to get water for the plants. You repeat the trip hour after hour, until your legs feel like they won't support you any longer. Your back aches from carrying water and from bending over your crops. The plants need every drop of moisture they can get. But the heat of the sun seems to evaporate the water as soon as it hits the ground.

At times like this, farming seems like fighting a losing battle. If your crops die, your family won't have enough food. Trudging back and forth to the river, you pray to the gods for help. Sick with worry, you wonder how to avoid this situation in the future.

What can you invent to make farming easier?

Reading & Writing

1. **READING: Setting** Setting is the place and time of a story. How did setting influence the problem in this story?

2. **WRITING: Explanation** Write a description of your invention. Explain how it works step by step. Conclude by summarizing how the invention will change farming.

CALIFORNIA STANDARDS Writing 2.2
Write expository compositions.

(81)

STARTING WITH A STORY

Talk About It

Ask students the following questions to begin the discussion:

- What feature of the environment makes the sight of this village attractive to the farming family? *(It is next to a river that floods the fields every year, providing the fields with fertile soil.)*

- What are the effects of the lack of adequate rainfall in the region of the river? *(It keeps the river from flooding; it makes the ground hard and difficult to work; it affects the crops that are currently growing.)*

- How is the village coping with the lack of water? *(Its inhabitants are carrying water from the river to the fields by hand.)*

- Why is it so important to get water into the fields? *(Without water, the plants will die, and the people of the village will not have enough to eat.)*

What can you invent to make farming easier?

Students may mention an invention that somehow gets water to the fields with less labor. This invention would help farmers worry less about the lack of rainfall, allowing them to grow needed crops in spite of poor weather.

Making Personal Connections

Connect the discussion to today by discussing the kinds of issues that threaten our security. Students might mention the threat of environmental harm, economic hardship, illness, or war.

ACTIVITIES ANSWERS

1. READING Possible answer: The place has a hot climate and lack of rain. These conditions are killing the crops. During the time of the story, people did not have the technology to irrigate their fields or plows to break up the soil.

2. WRITING

2. Writing Rubric

	Invention Idea	Detail of Instructions	Content of Summary
4	creative, helpful	complete, easy to follow	clearly explains impact of invention
3	helpful	complete	explains impact of invention reasonably well
2	moderately helpful	somewhat complete	impact of invention unclear
1	not helpful	very difficult to follow	no impact explained

❶ Plan & Prepare

Objectives

- Describe the geographic features of Mesopotamia and the ways in which they contributed to the spread of agriculture.
- Explain how early farmers managed to control water supplies in the region.
- Summarize ways in which ancient people in Mesopotamia managed in a land with scarce resources.
- **Language Objective:** Examine how text organization makes new information easier to understand.

Quick Look

Lesson 1 describes the geographic features and conditions that prevailed in Mesopotamia.

❷ Focus & Motivate

Preview Tell students that this lesson explores the environment in which the first farmers of Mesopotamia lived. Ask students to think about ways that their environment affects their lives—for example, what clothes they wear, where they build their houses, and so on.

Introduce the Main Ideas The three main ideas relate to the Big Idea that "Civilizations developed in places that supported agriculture or trade or both." Help students look for this Big Idea as you go through the lesson.

Reading Skill: Summarizing Remind students that summarizing involves repeating only the main points and details.

SAMPLE ANSWERS FOR DIAGRAM

Geography of Mesopotamia
The rivers of Mesopotamia were important because they provided water for farmers and a means of travel.
Mesopotamians watered their crops by building canals to carry water to their fields.
Because of a lack of resources, they traded with people from distant lands.

Lesson 1

▶ MAIN IDEAS

1 **Geography** The land between the Tigris and Euphrates rivers was a good region for agriculture.

2 **Geography** The environment of Mesopotamia presented several challenges to the people who lived there.

3 **Geography** Mesopotamians changed their environment to improve life.

▶ TAKING NOTES

Reading Skill: Summarizing

To summarize is to restate a passage in fewer words. After you read Lesson 1, write a sentence or two summarizing each of the three main sections. Use a chart like this one to record your summaries.

Geography of Mesopotamia
The rivers of Mesopotamia were important because . . .
Mesopotamians watered their crops by . . .
Because of a lack of resources, . . .

 Skillbuilder Handbook, page R3

▲ **Ram** This figurine shows a ram caught in a thicket. It is made of gold, shell, and a blue stone called lapis.

CALIFORNIA STANDARDS

6.2.1 Locate and describe the major river systems and discuss the physical settings that supported permanent settlement and early civilizations.

6.2.2 Trace the development of agricultural techniques that permitted the production of economic surplus and the emergence of cities as centers of culture and power.

HI 2 Students understand and distinguish cause, effect, sequence, and correlation in historical events, including the long- and short-term causal relations.

HOW TO TEACH THE CALIFORNIA STANDARDS

Standard	Content	Student Question or Activity	Instruction
6.2.1	**Page 84** Describes the physical environment of the Tigris and Euphrates river valley	**Page 86** Students describe how the Tigris and Euphrates rivers supported early settlement.	Have volunteers locate the Tigris and Euphrates rivers on a world map. Discuss reasons why early people selected this area for permanent settlement.
6.2.2	**Page 86** Explains how agricultural surplus led to trade	**Page 86** Students explain how irrigation was connected to trade.	Discuss which posed a greater threat to the Mesopotamians: flood or drought. Ask students to support their opinions with facts from the lesson.
HI 2	**Page 85** Summarizes how the lack of resources affected the Mesopotamians	**Page 86** Students tell how the lack of natural resources affected the Mesopotamians.	Ask students if building mud walls would be effective in keeping out thieves and invading peoples. Have students offer alternative solutions to this problem.

Geography of Mesopotamia

TERMS & NAMES
Mesopotamia
floodplain
silt
semiarid
drought
surplus

Build on What You Know Think of a time when you have seen pictures of a flood on television or in newspapers. Floods cause destruction by washing away objects in their path. Do you think a flood can also have good consequences?

The Land Between Two Rivers

① ESSENTIAL QUESTION How did the land between the Tigris and Euphrates rivers support agriculture?

The Tigris (TY•grihs) and Euphrates (yoo•FRAY•teez) rivers are in Southwest Asia. They start in the mountains of what are now Turkey and Kurdistan. From there they flow through what is now Iraq southeast to the Persian Gulf. (See the map on pages 78–79.)

Mesopotamia The region where these two rivers flow is called **Mesopotamia** (MEHS•uh•puh•TAY•mee•uh). The name means "land between the rivers." This land was mostly flat with small, scrubby plants.

The rivers provided water and means of travel. In ancient times, it was easier to travel by boat than over land. Boats can carry heavy loads. River currents helped move boats that were traveling down river. Also, few roads existed.

The rivers flooded each year, depositing fertile soil on the land. The rivers also provided water for crops.

Connect to Today

Euphrates River
Even today, people of Mesopotamia farm the land next to the Euphrates River. The flat land by a river is a floodplain. ▼

83

Terms & Names

Mesopotamia the region between the Tigris and Euphrates Rivers

floodplain the flat land bordering a river

silt the fine soil deposited by floodwaters

semiarid having little rainfall and warm temperatures

drought period of little rainfall

surplus an amount of a good, such as food, in excess of what is needed

❸ Teach

The Land Between Two Rivers

🖊 6.2.1, 6.2.2

Talk About It

- **Critical Thinking: Making Decisions**
  How did the climate of Mesopotamia likely affect early farmers' decisions about where to settle and build farming villages? *(The dry climate would require that farm fields be within a short distance of the riverbanks.)*

California Resources

California Reading Toolkit, L8
California Modified Lesson Plans for English Learners, p. 19
California Daily Standards Practice Transparencies, TT8
California Standards Enrichment Workbook, pp. 21–22, 23–24
California Online Test Practice
California Test Generator CD-ROM
California Standards Planner and Lesson Plans, L15
California EasyPlanner CD-ROM
California eEdition CD-ROM

LESSON 1 PROGRAM RESOURCES

ON LEVEL

In-Depth Resources: Unit 2
- Family Newsletter, pp. 1–2 (English and Spanish)
- Reading Skill: Summarizing, p. 3
- Skillbuilder Practice: Categorizing, p. 7

Formal Assessment
- Lesson Quiz, p. 40

ENGLISH LEARNERS

In-Depth Resources in Spanish
- Reading Skill: Summarizing, p. 19
- Skillbuilder Practice: Categorizing, p. 23

Modified Lesson Plans for English Learners, p. 19

Reading Study Guide (Spanish), p. 23

Reading Study Guide Audio CD (Spanish)

STRUGGLING READERS

In-Depth Resources: Unit 2
- Reading Skill: Summarizing, p. 3
- Reteaching Activity, p. 15

Reading Toolkit, L8

Reading Study Guide, p. 23

Reading Study Guide Audio CD

GIFTED AND TALENTED STUDENTS

Humanities Transparencies
- HT5 Stone Vessel

Interdisciplinary Projects
- Science, p. 14

INCLUSION

EasyPlanner CD-ROM
- Reading Skill: Summarizing
- Vocabulary Study Guide
- Reteaching Activity

TECHNOLOGY

eEdition CD-ROM
- Starting with a Story

Power Presentations CD-ROM

Map Transparencies
- MT5 Climates of Southwest Asia

Humanities Transparencies
- HT5 Stone Vessel

Critical Thinking Transparencies
- CT10 Summarizing

Test Generator CD-ROM

ClassZone.com

In-Depth Resources: Unit 2
• Reading Skill: Summarizing, p. 3
• Skillbuilder Practice:Categorizing, p. 7

Vocabulary Strategy

The Prefix *Semi*
Point out that the prefix *semi-* can also mean partially or somewhat. Ask students to use a dictionary to find other words that have this prefix and to note how the different parts of the word are put together. For example, the word *semiformal* means somewhat formal.

Teach

Controlling Water by Irrigation

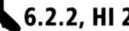 **6.2.2, HI 2**

Talk About It

• What were some of the problems related to floods in Mesopotamia? *(It was not easy to predict when a flood would come or how severe it would be.)*

• **Critical Thinking: Understanding Cause and Effect** In what ways did the people of Mesopotamia respond to the challenges of their environment? *(They built irrigation systems to provide steady water supplies to their fields, and they built dams to control flooding.)*

History from Visuals

Ancient Irrigation
Tell students to review the diagram on this page and to read the labels that go with it. Make sure that they see how the system enabled farmers to allow a controlled amount of water from the river to enter their fields.

• Why do you think the canals became smaller as they reached individual fields? *(The main canals were designed to provide water to a number of fields, so each field only needed a small share of the water.)*

GEOGRAPHY SKILLBUILDER ANSWER
Controlling the amount of water prevented fields from being flooded.

 Map Transparencies
• MT5 Climates of Southwest Asia

Fertile Soil Almost every year, rain and melting snow in the mountains caused the rivers to swell. As the water flowed down the mountains, it picked up soil. When the rivers reached the plains, water overflowed onto the **floodplain**, the flat land bordering the banks. As the water spread over the floodplain, the soil it carried settled on the land. The fine soil deposited by rivers is called **silt**. The silt was fertile, which means it was good for growing crops.

A Semiarid Climate Usually, less than 10 inches of rain fell in southern Mesopotamia a year. Summers were hot. This type of climate is called **semiarid**. Although the region was dry, ancient people could still grow crops because of the rivers and the fertile soil. Farming villages were widespread across southern Mesopotamia by 4000 B.C.

REVIEW What made Mesopotamia a good region for farming?
the rivers and the fertile soil

Controlling Water by Irrigation

2 ESSENTIAL QUESTION How did the climate affect farmers?

Being a farmer is difficult. Crops need the right amount of water to thrive. The floods and the semiarid climate in Mesopotamia meant that farmers often had either too much water or too little.

Vocabulary Strategy

The **prefix** *semi-* means "half." The word *arid* means "dry." A *semiarid* region has some rain, but remains fairly dry.

The yearly flood was unpredictable, making it hard to know when to plant. Sometimes, the flood washed everything away. At other times, the flood did not come, and drought occurred.

Geography

Ancient Irrigation
The model below shows how an ancient irrigation system worked.

1 Gates controlled how much water flowed from the river.

2 Main canals led from the river. They sloped gently downward to keep the water flowing.

3 Medium-sized branch canals led away from the main canals.

4 Small feeder canals led water directly to the fields.

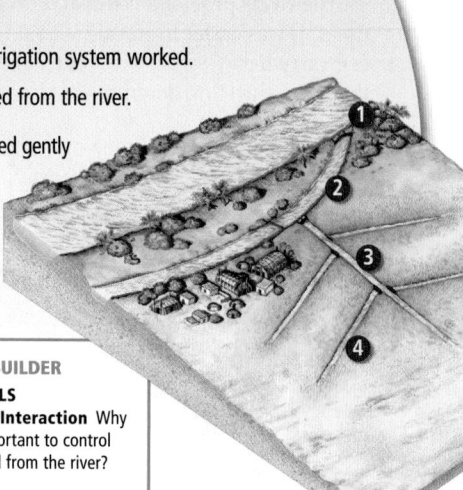

GEOGRAPHY SKILLBUILDER
INTERPRETING VISUALS
Human-Environment Interaction Why do you think it was important to control how much water flowed from the river?

84 • Chapter 3

DIFFERENTIATING INSTRUCTION

Gifted and Talented Students

Build an Irrigation Model
Have students use clay or other similar materials to build a working model of an irrigation system. Models should include main and feeder canals, as well as gates to control the flow of water. Students can use the Internet, their textbook, or other resources to find possible designs for their model.

English Learners

Identify How Writing is Organized
Explain to students that authors organize their writing in many ways: titles text, illustrations, labels, captions, and sidebars. Scan the text and point out examples of these organizational devices in the lesson. Have students describe the purpose of each device.

Floods and Droughts The yearly flood was unpredictable. No one knew when the flood would occur. It might come in April or as late as June. Farmers could not predict when to plant. Also, the flood's size depended on how much snow melted in the mountains in spring and how much rain fell. If there was too much, the flood might be violent and wash everything away. If there was too little rain and melting snow, the flood would not come.

A **drought** is a period when not enough rain and snow fall. In a semiarid region, drought is a constant danger. During a drought, the river level would drop, making it hard to water crops. If crops failed, people starved.

Irrigation By about 6000 B.C., farmers built canals to carry water from the rivers to their fields. Such a system is called irrigation. Often, the silt in the water clogged the canals. Workers had to clean out the silt to keep the water flowing. They also built dams to hold back excess water during floods.

REVIEW How did Mesopotamians water their crops during droughts?
They used irrigation canals to bring water to crops.

Finding Resources

③ **ESSENTIAL QUESTION** How did Mesopotamians cope with a lack of resources?

Since the beginning of time, humans have had to solve problems in the environment. For example, Mesopotamia had no forests to provide wood. The region also lacked stone and minerals, such as metals.

Mud Houses and Walls Because of that lack of resources, Mesopotamians had few building materials. Since they could not build with wood or stone, they used mud for bricks and plaster. However, mud buildings crumbled easily and had to be repaired often.

Also, Mesopotamia was easy to invade because it had few mountains or other natural barriers. As a result, people from other regions often came to steal from the Mesopotamians or conquer them. The ancient Mesopotamians wanted to protect themselves, but they had no trees or stone to build barriers. So people built mud walls around their villages.

Connect to Today
▲ **Building of Mud and Reeds** This style of building has been used in the region for at least 5,000 years and is still used today.

Ancient Mesopotamia • 85

(margin text) hey used mud to build houses and defensive walls. They traded surplus grain for tone, wood, and metals rom other egions.

Teach

Finding Resources

🖊 **6.2.1, 6.2.2**

Talk About It

- How did the people of Mesopotamia cope with the lack of wood, stone, and metal in the region? *(They used mud and they traded for materials that they needed.)*

- What factor made Mesopotamia subject to attack from outside invaders? *(a lack of natural barriers, such as mountain ranges)*

- What made it possible for Mesopotamians to trade for goods they needed? *(agricultural surpluses, such as grain)*

- **Critical Thinking: Summarizing** How did the environment of Mesopotamia help contribute to the need to organize people? *(Possible answer: The lack of resources forced people to expend a lot of labor on tasks such as digging irrigation canals and building structures out of mud, which in turn required organization.)*

More About . . .

Mesopotamian Buildings
Mesopotamians often used reeds to build their structures, and, as the picture on this page shows, this building style is sometimes used today. They also built many structures out of mud bricks. Unlike the stone used in the buildings of many other ancient civilizations, these mud bricks have generally not survived to modern times. As a result, the ancient civilizations of Mesopotamia have presented modern scholars with few intact ruins for study.

DIFFERENTIATING INSTRUCTION

Inclusion

Role-Play: Be a Trader
Divide students into groups of two. Have each pair review the section on Finding Resources. Then, have them act out an imaginary scene in which a Mesopotamian trader seeks to obtain resources from a distant source.

Struggling Readers

Read Aloud
Have students form pairs. Ask students to take turns reading the paragraphs of the Finding Resources section aloud to each other. Encourage them to help each other pronounce and understand troublesome words or sentences and ask questions if they need help.

④ Assess & Reteach

Assess Have students work in pairs on the questions and note the location of the answers.

 Formal Assessment
- Lesson Quiz, p. 40

Reteach On a blank sheet of paper, have each student write down each heading and subheading in the lesson in the form of a question. Tell students to exchange their questions with another student. Then, have them review the content of the lesson to determine the answers to the questions.

 In-Depth Resources: Unit 2
- Vocabulary Cards, p. 9
- Reteaching Activity, p. 15

 Homework Helper

Visit **Classzone.com** for a lesson review, a flip-card activity, and links to related Web sites.

 Humanities Transparencies
- HT5 Stone Vessel

Finding Resources Mesopotamians obtained some stone, wood, and metal outside their own land. They were able to trade for these things because they grew a surplus of grain. **Surplus** means more than they needed for themselves.

Jobs such as digging canals, building walls, and trading had to be done over and over. Community leaders began to organize groups of people to do the work at the right time. Lesson 2 explains more about the organization of society.

REVIEW Why was trade important in Mesopotamia?

> Mesopotamians had to trade surplus grain for things they didn't have in their own land, such as wood, metal, and stone.

Lesson Summary
- The Tigris and Euphrates rivers made the soil of Mesopotamia good for growing crops.
- The people of Mesopotamia developed an irrigation system to bring water to crops.
- Mesopotamia had few resources. People traded surplus crops to get what they needed.

Why It Matters Now . . .
The Mesopotamians had to overcome a lack of resources. Today people still work to solve shortages of water, food, and resources.

1 Lesson Review

Homework Helper
ClassZone.com

Terms & Names
1. Explain the importance of

Mesopotamia	silt	drought
floodplain	semiarid	surplus

Using Your Notes

Summarizing Use your completed chart to answer the following question:
2. How did the Mesopotamians change the environment to deal with geographic challenges? (HI 1)

Geography of Mesopotamia
The rivers of Mesopotamia were important because . . .
Mesopotamians watered their crops by . . .
Because of a lack of resources, . . .

Main Ideas
3. What did the Tigris and Euphrates rivers provide for ancient Mesopotamians? (6.2.1)
4. How did the lack of natural resources affect Mesopotamians? (HI 2)
5. How did Mesopotamian farmers obtain the right amount of water for their crops? (6.2.2)

Critical Thinking
6. **Understanding Causes** How was irrigation connected to trade? (6.2.2)
7. **Drawing Conclusions** How did Mesopotamians create a successful society? (HI 2)

Activity **Writing Job Descriptions** Create a job description for a worker in Mesopotamia. Some possible jobs include irrigation system planner, canal digger, wall builder, trader, and project scheduler. Form a small group, and share your job descriptions. (Writing 2.2)

---

1 Lesson Review Answers

Terms & Names
1. • Mesopotamia, p. 83
   • floodplain, p. 84
   • silt, p. 84
   • semiarid, p. 84
   • drought, p. 85
   • surplus, p. 86

Using Your Notes
See page 48 for an example of a complete chart.
2. Possible answers: They dealt with drought by building irrigation canals; they dealt with floods by building dams; they dealt with a lack of barriers by building walls to protect their communities.

Main Ideas
3. water, a means of transportation, and fertile soil
4. Without wood and stone, they had to use mud for building.
5. They dug canals and ditches to irrigate their fields year-round. They built dams and gates to protect against excess water.

Critical Thinking
6. Irrigation allowed farmers to grow surplus grain, which could be traded for resources from other places.
7. They organized people to solve problems and learned how to alter the environment to meet their needs.

Activity Rubric

	Quality of Description	Number of Errors
4	imaginative, detailed, accurate	no more than one spelling or punctuation errors
3	detailed, accurate	two or three errors
2	few details, some inaccuracies	four or five errors
1	no details, inaccurate	more than five errors

Make a Diagram

Goal: To explore the geographic relationship between resources and settlement in river valley civilizations

Materials & Supplies
- posterboard
- colored markers or pencils
- ruler
- books on earth science or encyclopedias

Prepare

1 Reread the paragraph "Fertile Soil" on page 84. Also, research the processes by which rivers pick up soil, carry it to other places, and deposit it on floodplains.

2 Learn the terms *erosion* and *deposition*.

Do the Activity

1 Create a diagram showing a river flowing from mountains through a floodplain to a gulf. (Use the diagram at right as a model.) Draw an arrow to show which way the river is flowing.

2 Label the following areas: mountains, river, floodplain, gulf.

3 Color the fertile region green. (Use the map on page 79 as a model.)

4 Add captions to explain how rivers pick up soil and how they deposit it on the floodplain.

Follow-Up

Where do you think ancient farmers built villages? Explain.

Extension

Writing a Comparison Research in books or ask a science teacher which U.S. river systems deposit soil on floodplains. Write a paragraph comparing those river systems to the ones in Mesopotamia.

CALIFORNIA STANDARDS
6.2.1 Locate and describe the major river systems and discuss the physical settings that supported permanent settlement and early civilizations.

87

ACTIVITY: MAKE A DIAGRAM

Objectives

- Describe the ways in which rivers impact their surrounding environment.
- Create a diagram using information collected from secondary sources.

Suggestions for Completing the Activity

- Invite students to learn more about rivers, flooding, and erosion through library books and the Internet.
- Mention to students that encyclopedias might be a good source of information about erosion and deposition.
- Remind students to follow each step of the activity, including placing labels and descriptions on the diagram.

ACTIVITY ANSWERS

Follow-Up Answer

Possible answer: Ancient farmers would have built villages at the lower part of the river where it flooded plains. They would want to take advantage of the water and fertile soil.

Extension Rubric

	Quality of Comparison	Explanation of Concepts	Number of Errors
4	includes at least two comparisons and contrasts	completely accurate	no more than one spelling or punctuation error
3	includes at least one comparison and one contrast	mostly accurate	two or three errors
2	includes only a comparison or a contrast	somewhat accurate	four or five errors
1	no comparison or contrast	not accurate	more than five errors

❶ Plan & Prepare

Objectives

- Describe the characteristics that define a civilization.
- Trace the factors that led to the development of the first civilization.
- Describe the first civilization at Sumer.
- **Language Objective:** Make generalizations based on lesson information and personal experiences.

Quick Look

Lesson 2 explores the changes in human life that marked the emergence of the first civilization at Sumer.

❷ Focus & Motivate

Preview Inform students that this lesson will examine what characteristics mark a civilization. Ask students to think as they read this lesson about how these characteristics are present in their own civilization.

Introduce the Main Ideas The three main ideas relate to the Big Idea that "Civilizations developed in places that supported agriculture or trade or both." Help students look for this Big Idea as you go through the lesson.

Reading Skill: Making Generalizations Tell students that making generalizations is the skill of making broad judgments based on a set of facts or information.

SAMPLE ANSWERS FOR CHART

Civilization in Sumer	
Advanced cities	Babylon, Ur, Uruk, Hit
Specialized workers	priest, artisan
Complex institutions	the temple, government
Record keeping	writing
Advanced technology	bronze

Lesson 2

▶ **MAIN IDEAS**

❶ **Culture** Food surpluses, new technology, and advanced social organization led to a complex way of life. It is called civilization.

❷ **Government** A new type of government developed in Sumer that included a city and its surrounding lands.

❸ **Government** Religion dominated life in Sumer, but in time, powerful men who were not priests became the political rulers.

▶ **TAKING NOTES**

Reading Skill: Making Generalizations
As you read Lesson 2, use your own words to record information about Sumer on a chart like this. You will be asked to make a generalization, or broad judgment, later.

Civilization in Sumer	
Advanced cities	
Specialized workers	
Complex institutions	
Record keeping	
Advanced technology	

 Skillbuilder Handbook, page R8

▲ **Votive Statues** Sumerian artists made these statues to worship the gods when people were busy doing other things. Notice how big their eyes are from gazing at the gods.

CALIFORNIA STANDARDS

6.2.2 Trace the development of agricultural techniques that permitted the production of economic surplus and the emergence of cities as centers of culture and power.

6.2.3 Understand the relationship between religion and the social and political order in Mesopotamia and Egypt.

6.2.9 Trace the evolution of language and its written forms.

HI 2 Students understand and distinguish cause, effect, sequence, and correlation in historical events, including the long- and short-term causal relations.

HOW TO TEACH THE CALIFORNIA STANDARDS

Standard	Content	Student Question or Activity	Instruction
6.2.2	**Pages 90–91** Lists traits of civilization	**Page 95** Students tell why food surpluses are necessary for civilization to develop.	Discuss the basic traits of civilization. Ask students which characteristic they believe is most important in an advanced society.
6.2.3	**Page 94** Describes how Sumerian priests became political leaders in Mesopotamia	**Page 95** Students explain why a priest's job was so important in Sumer.	Explain that religious leaders were also the political leaders in Sumer. Have students debate the role of religion in government.
HI 2	**Pages 94–95** Explains the relationship between warfare and the establishment of kings as political leaders in Sumer	**Page 95** Students describe how warfare changed the Sumerian government.	Point out that with economic success societies develop more power. Tell students to look in the lesson for ways that Mesopotamia became more powerful.

The First Civilization

Build on What You Know Cities today have a wide range of cultural options. These include sports, entertainment, museums, and restaurants. They also offer people the chance to gain a good education or a promising job. As you are about to read, even the earliest cities were places of opportunity and culture.

The Rise of Civilization

① ESSENTIAL QUESTION How did civilization develop in the region of Sumer?

The rise of agriculture enabled people to settle in villages. They didn't have to search for food. As more people decided to live in communities, villages grew larger. In time, they became cities. City leaders had to start organizing workers to solve problems, such as building and cleaning irrigation canals. Over time, society and culture grew more complex. These changes led to an advanced form of culture called **civilization**. Most historians think the first civilization rose about 3300 B.C. in **Sumer**, which was a region in southern Mesopotamia.

The rise of agriculture enabled people to settle in villages. Eventually, the villages grew larger and became cities. Over time, the society and culture in cities grew more complex. These changes led to an advanced form of culture known as civilization.

Ruins of Ur The ancient Sumerian city of Ur once stood on the banks of the Euphrates. The river has shifted over time. Now it is ten miles away. ▼

89

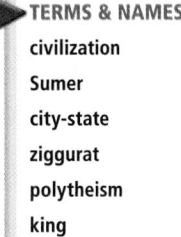

Terms & Names

civilization an advanced form of culture

Sumer an ancient region of southern Mesopotamia

city-state a political unit that includes a city and its nearby farmlands

ziggurat an ancient Sumerian or Babylonian temple that rose in a series of steplike levels

polytheism a belief in many gods or goddesses

king the leader of a group of people

❸ Teach

The Rise of Civilization

6.2.2

Talk About It

- **Critical Thinking: Finding Main Ideas** Why are civilizations considered "advanced" and "complex"? *(They involve a great variety of people, occupations, and economic statuses.)*

California Resources

California Reading Toolkit, L9
California Modified Lesson Plans for English Learners, p. 21
California Daily Standards Practice Transparencies, TT9
California Standards Enrichment Workbook, pp. 23–24, 25–26, 37–38
California Online Test Practice
California Test Generator CD-ROM
California Standards Planner and Lesson Plans, L17
California EasyPlanner CD-ROM
California eEdition CD-ROM

LESSON 2 PROGRAM RESOURCES

ON LEVEL
In-Depth Resources: Unit 2
- Reading Skill: Making Generalizations, p. 4
- Vocabulary Study Guide, p. 8
- Geography Practice: Oldest Cities in the World, p. 11

Formal Assessment
- Lesson Quiz, p. 41

ENGLISH LEARNERS
In-Depth Resources in Spanish
- Reading Skill, p. 20
- Vocabulary Study Guide, p. 24
- Geography Practice: Oldest Cities in the World, p. 25

Modified Lesson Plans for English Learners, p. 21
Reading Study Guide (Spanish), p. 25
Reading Study Guide Audio CD (Spanish)

STRUGGLING READERS
In-Depth Resources: Unit 2
- Reading Skill: Making Generalizations, p. 4
- Vocabulary Study Guide, p. 8
- Reteaching Activity, p. 16

Reading Toolkit, L9
Reading Study Guide, p. 25

Reading Study Guide Audio CD

GIFTED AND TALENTED STUDENTS
In-Depth Resources: Unit 2
- Literature: A Praise Poem of the Shulgi, p. 14

Interdisciplinary Projects
- Language Arts, p. 15

INCLUSION
EasyPlanner CD-ROM
- Reading Skill: Making Generalizations
- Vocabulary Study Guide
- Reteaching Activity

TECHNOLOGY
eEdition CD-ROM
Power Presentations CD-ROM
Map Transparencies
- MT6 City of Ur

Humanities Transparencies
- HT6 Bull with a Human Head

Critical Thinking Transparencies
- CT11 Making Generalizations

Test Generator CD-ROM
ClassZone.com

In-Depth Resources: Unit 2
• Reading Skill: Making Generalizations, p. 4
• Geography Practice: Oldest Cities of the World, p. 11

More About . . .

Sumerian Artists
In the 1920s, an archaeological study in the Sumerian city of Ur unearthed an amazing collection of Sumerian works of art, which rivaled the findings of the tomb of Tutankhamen in Egypt. Included were a large number of beautiful objects, including musical instruments, jewelry, and more. Sumerian artists crafted their fine work from gold, semiprecious stones, and other materials obtained by trade from distant lands. These items reveal that artistic skill had developed to a very high level in Ur.

History from Visuals

Interpreting Tables
Make sure students are reading the table correctly. Point out that the left column identifies the category and the right column gives examples.

• What examples of advanced technology are included in the table? *(irrigation, bronze tools)*

Traits of Civilization Five traits characterize civilization: advanced cities, specialized workers, complex institutions, record keeping, and advanced technology.

1. **Advanced Cities** Civilization is closely linked to life in cities. At first, cities became important because farmers needed a place to store and trade their surplus grain. As cities grew, they began to offer other advantages. For example, the cities of Sumer had large temples where people prayed. Cities also offered many different types of work.

2. **Specialized Workers** In general, a society needs food surpluses before civilization can develop. Having a food surplus allows people to do other types of work besides farming. Workers can specialize, which means to do a job that requires special skills. For example, Sumerian workers built houses, made jewelry, sewed clothes, or created pottery. When people specialize, the quality of their work improves because they can develop their skill.

Because cities are crowded, people must learn to live together. They also have to cooperate on projects, such as building irrigation canals. As a result, some people took on

Civilization in Sumer

Basic Traits of Civilization	Examples from Sumer	
Advanced cities	Kish, Nippur, Ur	
Specialized workers	priest, king, artisan	
Complex institutions	the temple, the army, schools	
Record keeping	writing	
Advanced technology	irrigation, bronze tools	

Kings City-states in ancient Sumer were ruled by kings. King Gudea ruled the city-state Lagash. ▶

DIFFERENTIATING INSTRUCTION

Gifted and Talented Students

Create a Poster of Sumerian Civilization
Have students use library or Internet resources to find additional information and illustrations with which to make a poster about Sumerian civilization. The posters should provide illustrated examples showing that Sumer was indeed a civilization.

Struggling Readers

Write Paragraph Summaries
Divide the class into groups of five. Within each group, assign each student one of the five traits of a civilization. Have each group member study his or her paragraph and write a one-sentence summary of it. Then, have each student present his or her summary to the rest of the group.

the job of organizing society. In early Sumerian cities, priests did that job. They ran society and acted as judges.

3. **Complex Institutions** In time, religion and government became institutions. An institution is a group of people who have a specific purpose. Often it exists to help society meet its needs. For example, schools are institutions that exist to educate children. An army is an institution that exists to protect a society. Sometimes society uses an army to conquer others.

4. **Record Keeping** Societies must keep track of many things. For example, the rulers may want to measure the food supplies stored in the city. Keeping records usually involves writing, but not always. In Mesopotamia, people started by using wooden counting sticks. Later, they invented the world's first system of writing. (You will learn about this in Lesson 3.)

5. **Advanced Technology** Societies advance as people learn better ways to do things. For example, the people of Sumer learned to use canals to irrigate crops. They also created new tools and used new materials. For instance, the Sumerians began to make tools of bronze (a mixture of copper and tin). Bronze tools replaced tools made of copper, which is a softer metal.

REVIEW Why was Sumer a good example of civilization?
It had large cities with specialized workers, complex institutions, and a system of record keeping. It also used advanced technology.

Sumerian City-States

② **ESSENTIAL QUESTION** What new type of community developed in Sumer?

Sumerian cities offered many advantages to people who lived in the surrounding lands. Cities were centers of trade, learning, and religion. Most people still lived in the countryside. Even so, over time the cities began to rule the surrounding lands and villages.

A community that included a city and its nearby farmlands was called a **city-state**. The nearby land might include several villages. Between 10,000 and 100,000 people might have lived in a city. Each city-state ruled itself.

Sumer developed a type of community called the city-state, which is a city and its nearby farmlands.

Helmet and Sword This gold helmet and bronze sword are examples of advanced technology. They also show the skill of the specialized workers who made them.

More About . . .

Bronze Tools
The arrival of the technology for making bronze is a significant development in the history of a particular culture. It is common for historians to refer to a particular culture's Bronze Age as a way of characterizing its level of development. Different cultures around the world followed a similar progression from the use of copper to the use of bronze and, finally, to the use of iron. The time line of this progression, however, differs from culture to culture. The people of Mesopotamia were among the first in the world to develop the technology for making bronze.

Teach

Sumerian City-States

6.2.3

Talk About It

- What was a city-state? *(It was a self-governing state that consisted of a city and the lands in the immediate area.)*

- Where were most of the Sumerian city-states located, and why? *(They were located near the mouths of the Tigris and Euphrates rivers because the soil was especially fertile in that region.)*

- **Critical Thinking: Making Inferences** What can you infer about the role of religion in Sumer from the fact that the ziggurat was the center of city life? *(Possible answer: City life was strongly influenced and shaped by religious concerns.)*

DIFFERENTIATING INSTRUCTION

English Learners

Make a Generalization
Explain to students that a generalization is a broad judgment that is supported by facts. A generalization includes signal words such as *all*, *most*, and *never*. Tell students that they will need to listen for facts as the lesson is read out loud, restate several of these facts, and use the restated facts and a signal word to make a generalization.

Inclusion

Chart Information
Have small groups work on the board to add information to the chart that the class started on page 88. Have students who have difficulty extracting information from text act as the scribes for each group by writing information on the board that other group members dictate. All group members can copy the information from the board onto their own generalization charts.

More About . . .

Sumerian City-States

Though related by language and culture, the city-states of Sumer were often in conflict with one another over access to scarce resources. War among the city-states was common, as was war with forces outside of Sumer. Over time, various city-states would conquer others, and the rule of monarchs would expand or contract. This regular warfare was a major influence on the development of new technology, as each city-state anxiously sought to gain a military advantage over its rivals.

History from Visuals

Analyzing Infographics

- In what sense did the ziggurat resemble a mountain? *(Possible answers: It went progressively higher from its outer edges to its center. It was wider at the base and pointed at the top.)*

- What feature of the ziggurat helped remind people that entering the ziggurat meant entering a holy place? *(the arched doorways)*

- What occupied the top of the ziggurat? *(a shrine)*

Map Transparencies
- MT6 City of Ur

The City-States of Sumer By 3000 B.C., Sumer had at least 12 city-states. Some of the more famous ones were Kish, Nippur, and Ur. As the map on page 94 shows, most city-states were located near the mouths of the Tigris and Euphrates rivers. The land was especially fertile there. As a result, farmers grew more food. Food surpluses supported a larger population.

Ur was the hometown of Abraham, who is an important person in three religions: Judaism, Christianity, and Islam. You will read about Abraham in Chapter 10.

Life in the City The cities of Sumer grew gradually. Because of this, they did not look the way many U.S. cities look today. Instead of straight streets that cross at right angles, Sumerian cities had narrow, winding streets. As you learned in Lesson 1, protective walls surrounded the city. Gates in the wall allowed people to come and go.

People built their houses of mud walls that were several feet thick. Such thick walls helped to keep out heat. Narrow tunnels ran through the walls, carrying fresh air from the outside into the house. People first made the doorways by placing a horizontal beam over two vertical posts. Then they built the mud walls around the doorways.

A house consisted of a series of rooms arranged around a courtyard. The builders covered the courtyard with a loose roof of palm leaves over wooden planks. This roof helped protect people from the hot sun. The cooking area was usually located out in the courtyard so the smoke could escape through gaps in the roof.

The Ziggurat: City Center If you were to visit a Sumerian city, one building would stand out from all the rest. The largest and most important structure in a Sumerian city was the temple. It was called a **ziggurat** (ZIHG•uh•RAT). Ziggurats were first built about 2200 B.C.

The ziggurat was not just a temple; it was the center of city life. The ziggurat functioned as a sort of city hall. This was because the priests ran the irrigation systems. People came to the ziggurat to pay the priests for their services with grain and other items. As a result, the priests controlled the storage of surplus grain. The priests ended up controlling much of the wealth of the city-state.

REVIEW What was life like in Sumerian cities?

People lived in houses built of thick mud walls around central courtyards. The ziggurat was the center of city life and functioned as a city hall.

INTERDISCIPLINARY ACTIVITIES

Art

Create a Sumerian City Street Scene

Have students use what they have read about the appearance and activities of a Sumerican city-state to create a picture of typical activities at a ziggurat. Encourage students to use the illustration of the ziggurat on page 93 and the photograph of the votive statues on page 88 to help them visualize what they want to depict in their own drawing.

Math

Calculate the Population of Sumer

Have students use the estimates of the population of the different city-states given in the text and the numbers of different Sumerian city-states to estimate the population of Sumer. *(City populations ranged from 10,000 to 100,000, and there were at least 12 city-states. This means the population of Sumer may have ranged between 120,000 and 1,200,000.)*

In early Sumer, priests were the leaders. As the city-states became wealthier, they came under attack. Powerful men who could protect the city-states became kings.

Changes in Leadership

③ ESSENTIAL QUESTION How did the leadership of Sumer change?

As you just read, priests played an important political role in Sumer. People also went to them to ask the gods for help. The priests advised the people on how to act to please the gods.

Sumerian Religion The Sumerians believed in many gods and goddesses. A belief in many gods and goddesses is called **polytheism**. Sumerians believed that four main gods created the world and ruled over it. These were the gods of sky, wind, foothills (hills that are near mountains), and fresh water. Each city-state worshiped its own god. In addition, Sumerians had thousands of lesser gods. The Sumerians believed their gods looked and acted like people.

Vocabulary Strategy

The **prefix** poly- means "many," and the **root word** theism means "belief in a god."

Ziggurat
INTERACTIVE

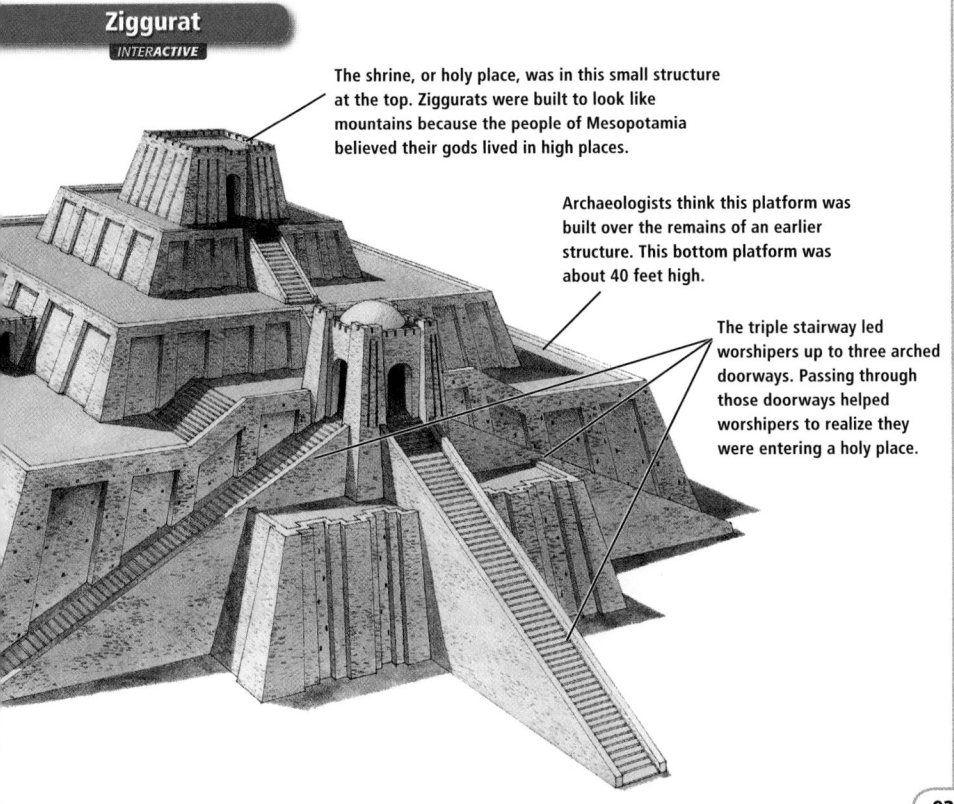

The shrine, or holy place, was in this small structure at the top. Ziggurats were built to look like mountains because the people of Mesopotamia believed their gods lived in high places.

Archaeologists think this platform was built over the remains of an earlier structure. This bottom platform was about 40 feet high.

The triple stairway led worshipers up to three arched doorways. Passing through those doorways helped worshipers to realize they were entering a holy place.

93

Teach

Changes in Leadership

🖊 **6.2.3, H12**

Talk About It

- Why were priests considered leaders in Sumer? *(The priests were thought to have influence with the gods and therefore over all aspects of Sumerian life.)*

- What did Sumerians see as their responsibilities to the gods? *(They felt they were required to work for the gods and to pray and make offerings to them.)*

- What development in Sumer led to the emergence of kings as new types of leaders? *(warfare among city-states and with outsiders)*

- **Critical Thinking: Finding Main Ideas** Explain why the job of being king in Sumer could be considered an example of specialization. *(Possible answer: As the problems and challenges of city life became more complicated, Sumerians began to seek more specialized types of leadership.)*

 Humanities Transparencies
- HT6 Bull with a Human Head

INTERDISCIPLINARY ACTIVITIES

Language Arts

Describe a Ziggurat
Have students assume the role of a reporter visiting a Sumerian city from afar. Instruct them to write a colorful description of a ziggurat that explains what it looks like and what role it plays in the life of the city.

Language Arts

Write a Poem About Leadership
Tell students to write a 4–5 stanza poem. This poem should tell about the character traits and deeds that, in the student's opinion, a great leader might exhibit or do.

History from Visuals

Interpreting Maps

Instruct students to review this map to see the locations of the Sumerian city-states. Explain that both the Tigris and Euphrates rivers flow down into the Persian Gulf.

- Ask students how this may have influenced the location of the Sumerian city-states. *(Possible answer: Flooding was probably more likely to occur further down the river, making the land there more suitable for farming.)*

GEOGRAPHY SKILLBUILDER ANSWER

Most cities were located very near the Tigris or Euphrates rivers and the Persian Gulf. These locations gave the cities access to water and transportation.

More About . . .

Sumerian Kings

There were many Sumerian kings, but perhaps the most famous is Gilgamesh. He was the king of Uruk who lived about 2700 B.C. Gilgamesh is the main subject of one of the oldest written stories in history—*The Epic of Gilgamesh.* This is a collection of stories and myths about the king, who was worshiped as a god following his death.

In-Depth Resources: Unit 2
- Literature: A Praise Poem of the Shulgi, p. 14

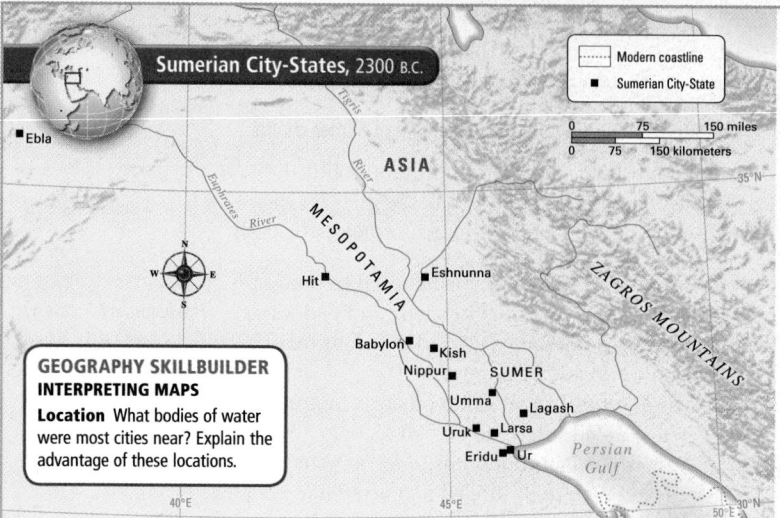

Sumerian City-States, 2300 B.C.

..... Modern coastline
■ Sumerian City-State

0   75   150 miles
0   75   150 kilometers

Ebla
ASIA
Euphrates River
Tigris River
MESOPOTAMIA
ZAGROS MOUNTAINS
Hit
Eshnunna
Babylon
Kish
Nippur
SUMER
Umma
Lagash
Uruk
Larsa
Eridu
Ur
Persian Gulf

GEOGRAPHY SKILLBUILDER
INTERPRETING MAPS
Location What bodies of water were most cities near? Explain the advantage of these locations.

Priests Become Leaders Life in Sumer had many dangers, such as floods, droughts, and invasions. The Sumerians believed the gods could prevent these troubles. To protect their cities, people tried to please the gods. Each god had many priests. The priests worked to satisfy the gods and claimed to have influence with them. Because of that claim, people accepted the priests as leaders.

Service to the Gods Sumerians thought of the gods as rich landowners who created humans to work for them. Priests, ordinary people, and even rulers said prayers and made offerings to the gods. Everyone took part in rituals and followed religious rules. Many of those rituals took place at the ziggurat.

Sumerians believed that the souls of dead people went to the land of no return. It was a gloomy place that was also called the underworld. Some scholars think the hardships of Sumerian life caused Sumerians to expect continued unhappiness after death.

New Leaders in Sumer Around 3000 B.C., as city-states became richer, other groups of people began to attack them to take their wealth. Some attackers came from other regions. Others came from rival city-states. In such dangerous times, the people of the city-state often asked a powerful man to rule them and protect the city.

At first, such leaders led the city-states only during wars. Eventually, they took control of the cities full-time. These new leaders took over some of the priests' jobs. They maintained the canals, managed the surplus grain, and acted as judges.

DIFFERENTIATING INSTRUCTION

Struggling Readers

Write a Job Description
Have students write a job description for a Sumerian priest. Students should use the description of the various jobs of the priest given in the text as the basis of their description.

Inclusion

Create a Diagram
Have students create a diagram that shows the progression in Sumerian society from leadership by priests to leadership by kings. The diagram should show what the roles of the priests were, how and why they changed, and how kings emerged as the leaders of Sumerian life.

In time, this new type of ruler became a **king**, who is the highest-ranked leader of a group of people. The area a king ruled was called a kingdom. Sumer became a kingdom under one king by 2375 B.C.

The priests still remained important because their job was to keep the gods happy and keep evil away. The people believed that the gods let the kings rule.

▲ **Ring** A Sumerian artisan created this ring about 3000 B.C.

REVIEW How did kings take over as rulers of Sumer?
Powerful men protected the cities from attack and eventually became the full-time rulers.

Lesson Summary

- Sumer had a complex society and culture. Historians consider it the first civilization.
- Sumerian city-states were a form of government that included cities and the land around them.
- Priests were the first leaders in Sumer, but kings became leaders when the need for defense grew.

Why It Matters Now . . .

Cities first became important in Sumer. People today still move to cities to find jobs, education, and culture.

---

❹ Assess & Reteach

Assess Divide students into small groups and have them answer the questions. Then ask groups to take turns presenting answers to the class. Discuss whether any groups answered questions differently.

 Formal Assessment
- Lesson Quiz, p. 41

Reteach Have students read the lesson summary. For each item, have them find information or examples from the lesson that support that item.

 In-Depth Resources: Unit 2
- Vocabulary Cards, p. 9
- Reteaching Activity, p. 16

🖰 Homework Helper

Visit **Classzone.com** for a lesson review, a flip-card activity, and links to related Web sites.

---

2 Lesson Review

🖰 **Homework Helper**
ClassZone.com

Terms & Names

1. Explain the importance of

civilization	city-state	polytheism
Sumer	ziggurat	king

Using Your Notes

Making Generalizations Use your completed chart to answer the following question:

2. What is the relationship between specialized workers and complex institutions? State your answer as a generalization. (HI 3)

Civilization in Sumer	
Advanced cities	
Specialized workers	
Complex institutions	
Record keeping	
Advanced technology	

Main Ideas

3. Why are food surpluses necessary for civilization to develop? (6.2.2)

4. In what way did the ziggurat function like a city hall? (6.2.2)

5. What did people in Sumer think their gods were like? (6.2.3)

Critical Thinking

6. **Making Inferences** Why was a priest's job so important in Sumer? (6.2.3)

7. **Understanding Cause and Effect** How did warfare change the government in Sumer? (HI 2)

Activity

Making a Poster Create a poster listing the five traits of civilization and giving examples from a modern society, such as the United States. (HI 3)

Ancient Mesopotamia • 95

---

2 Lesson Review Answers

Terms & Names

1. • civilization, p. 89
   • Sumer, p. 89
   • city-state, p. 91
   • ziggurat, p. 92
   • polytheism, p. 93
   • king, p. 95

Using Your Notes

See page 88 for an example of a completed chart.

2. Possible answer: Some specialized workers, such as priests, work in complex institutions. Some institutions, such as schools, train workers in specialized skills.

Main Ideas

3. Without food surpluses, everyone has to work at providing food. With food surpluses, some people are free to do other jobs. This makes specialized workers and complex institutions possible.

4. In the ziggurat, the priests ran the irrigation systems and accepted payment for their work. They also stored much of the city-state's wealth in the ziggurat.

5. Sumerians thought of the gods as rich landowners who created humans to work for them. They also believed that the gods could prevent troubles.

Critical Thinking

6. Possible answer: The priests were leaders in society because they had influence with the gods. The priests also managed the irrigation systems and collected payment for doing so.

7. Possible answer: Powerful men who ruled during wars became the full-time leaders and took over many of the priests' jobs.

Ancient Mesopotamia • 95

Objectives

- Demonstrate skill at interpreting a thematic map.
- Explain the relationship among the various regions where writing developed and draw conclusions about the spread of writing.
- **Language Objective:** Identify elements that are necessary to read and understand the information on a map.

❶ Focus & Motivate

Preview Remind students that in Chapter 1, they learned about the major role maps play in the study of Earth and its history. Ask students why being able to interpret maps properly is such an important skill. *(It makes it possible for a student to "unlock" the information that is given in a map.)*

❷ Teach

Talk About It

- What information does the map on page 97 contain? *(information on where and when written language developed in the ancient world)*
- What does the key of this map allow you to see? *(the extent of written language in various 500-year periods between 3000 B.C. and 1500 B.C.)*
- What is a common feature of most of the places where writing developed? *(a river)*
- **Critical Thinking: Comparing and Contrasting** What does the map show that the time line does not? *(The map shows the location of the places where writing developed and other features of their geography; the time line only names the places.)*

Skillbuilder   Extend Lesson 2

Reading a Map

Goal: To use a map to draw conclusions about the evolution of written language

CALIFORNIA STANDARDS
6.2.9 Trace the evolution of language and its written forms.
CST 3 Students use a variety of maps and documents to identify physical and cultural features of neighborhoods, cities, states, and countries and to explain the historical migration of people, expansion and disintegration of empires, and the growth of economic systems.

Learn the Skill

Maps are representations of features on Earth's surface. Some maps show political features such as borders. Other maps show physical features such as mountains. A third type of map is the thematic map, which shows specific types of information such as where certain languages are spoken.

S See the Skillbuilder Handbook, page R9.

Practice the Skill

❶ Read the title of the map at the right. It will tell you what information the map shows. This thematic map shows where the first writing systems developed.

❷ Read the map key. It is usually in a box. It will tell you what the various symbols and colors on the map mean. Notice that on this map, color is used to show the time period a written language developed. A photograph of one of the writing systems accompanies the map.

❸ Notice the relationship among the various regions shown on the map. See what conclusions you can draw. For example, this map shows that Sumer and Egypt were the first regions where people used writing systems. The next regions to have writing systems were located next to Sumer and Egypt. From this, you can draw the conclusion that writing spread from Sumer and Egypt to their neighbors.

❹ Sometimes, you can use maps as a source of information for written documents or visual presentations. The time line below presents the information on the map in a different way.

Example:

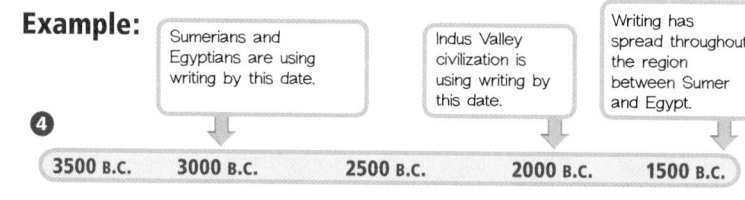

❹

| 3500 B.C. | 3000 B.C. | 2500 B.C. | 2000 B.C. | 1500 B.C. |

Sumerians and Egyptians are using writing by this date.

Indus Valley civilization is using writing by this date.

Writing has spread throughout the region between Sumer and Egypt.

DIFFERENTIATING INSTRUCTION

English Learners

Interpret a Map

Explain that reading a map requires learning specialized vocabulary: titles, labels, inset, captions, symbols, illustration, photos and colors. Guide students as they locate and explain the information each map element provides for the reader.

Inclusion

Summarize a Map

Pair students with vision impairments with other students. Instruct teams to turn to the map that appears on page 97. Working together, have them interpret, describe, and summarize the information contained in the map. Summaries should refer to the map title and the key and other information on the map.

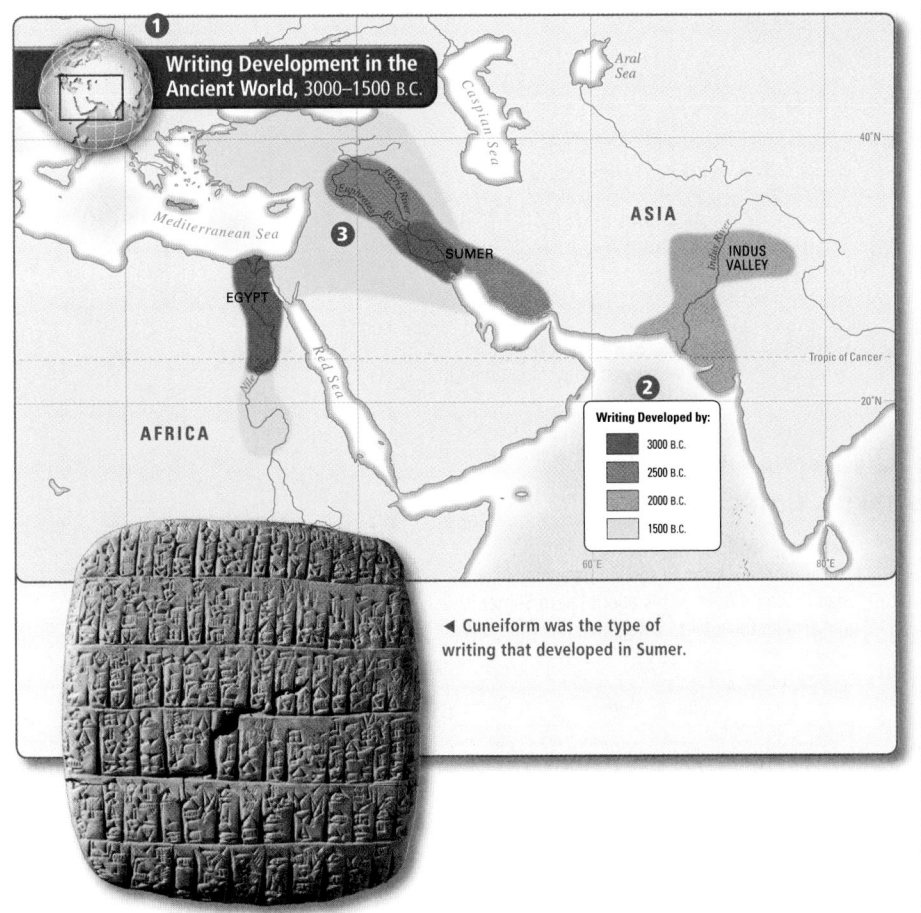

Writing Development in the Ancient World, 3000–1500 B.C.

Aral Sea

Caspian Sea

ASIA

SUMER

INDUS VALLEY

40°N

EGYPT

Mediterranean Sea

AFRICA

Red Sea

Nile

Tropic of Cancer

20°N

Writing Developed by:

■	3000 B.C.
■	2500 B.C.
■	2000 B.C.
■	1500 B.C.

60°E   80°E

◀ Cuneiform was the type of writing that developed in Sumer.

Apply the Skill

Look at the map on pages 78–79. It is a thematic map showing the region where the Tigris and Euphrates rivers deposited fertile soil and the region where Sumerian culture was found. Write a brief description of the relationship between these two regions.

APPLY THE SKILL

Rubric

	Description of Relationship	Number of Errors
4	clear, accurate, well supported	no more than one spelling or punctuation error
3	accurate and well supported	two or three errors
2	somewhat accurate	Four or five errors
1	not accurate	more than five errors

❶ Plan & Prepare

Objectives

- Describe the key features of Sumerian society.
- Describe the major technological advance of the Sumerian people.
- Explain the Sumerian role in the development of written language.
- **Language Objective:** Classify details by category to make nonfiction text more comprehensible and meaningful.

Quick Look

Lesson 3 focuses on the complex nature of Sumerian society and the many important advances that came from it.

❷ Focus & Motivate

Preview Tell students that this lesson will look at the major accomplishments of Sumerian society. Ask students to consider how their lives today depend on some of the Sumerian inventions. *(Possible answer: They might mention how various forms of transportation, such as the car, depend on the wheel. They also might mention that the plow is used to provide some of their food.)*

Introduce the Main Ideas The three main ideas relate to the Big Idea that "Civilizations developed in places that supported agriculture or trade or both." Help students look for this Big Idea as you go through the lesson.

Reading Skill: Categorizing Tell students that categorizing involves putting pieces of information into general groups. The chart shown on this page has already identified some categories for this lesson.

SAMPLE ANSWERS FOR CHART

Life in Sumer		
Society	Technology	Writing
unequal classes	plow and wheel	pictograph
slaves	bronze	cuneiform
women belonged to all classes	mathematics	

Lesson 3

▶ **MAIN IDEAS**

① **Culture** Sumerian society was divided into several classes, with kings at the top and slaves at the bottom.

② **Science and Technology** Sumerians invented tools and developed special knowledge to improve their lives.

③ **Culture** Sumerians created a written language called cuneiform that was based on picture writing.

▶ **TAKING NOTES**

Reading Skill: Categorizing
To categorize means to sort information. As you read Lesson 3, take notes about life in Sumer. Use a chart like this one to categorize the information you gather.

Life in Sumer		
Society	Technology	Writing

S **Skillbuilder Handbook, page R6**

▲ **Woman with Pottery**
The woman shown in this figurine holds a pot that was probably made on a potter's wheel—a Sumerian invention.

CALIFORNIA STANDARDS

6.2.2 Trace the development of agricultural techniques that permitted the production of economic surplus and the emergence of cities as centers of culture and power.

6.2.3 Understand the relationship between religion and the social and political order in Mesopotamia and Egypt.

6.2.9 Trace the evolution of language and its written forms.

Framework In studying each ancient society, students should examine the role of women and the presence or absence of slavery.

HOW TO TEACH THE CALIFORNIA STANDARDS

Standard	Content	Student Question or Activity	Instruction
6.2.2	**Page 100** Traces the development of agricultural technology, including the plow and wheel	**Page 103** Students explain why the plow was an important tool for farmers.	Compare land and water transportation after the invention of the wheel. Ask students which was more efficient for transporting goods in Sumer.
6.2.3	**Page 99** Outlines the members of the social classes in Sumerian society	**Page 103** Students explain how religion affected who was in the upper class.	Discuss how social classes develop. Ask students to think about who decides which people belong in which class.
6.2.9	**Pages 101–102** Traces the evolution of writing from pictographs to cuneiform	**Page 103** Students describe how writing evolved in Sumer.	Have several volunteers create pictographs to represent world history on the board. Decide as a class which pictograph best represents history, and have students redraw the pictograph onto their history notebooks.

Life in Sumer

TERMS & NAMES

bronze

pictograph

stylus

cuneiform

scribe

Build on What You Know Think about society today. Consider the differences between the people who have money and power and the people who don't have much of either one. Similar differences existed in ancient Sumer.

Sumerian Society

①ESSENTIAL QUESTION What were the social classes that made up Sumerian society?

As Sumerian society grew more complex, it divided into several social groups, or classes. Many societies are divided into unequal classes. Class systems often define who usually has power and who usually does the less desirable jobs.

Social Classes The king and the priests were at the top of the upper classes of Sumer. The Sumerians believed their kings and priests had a link to the gods, so they had great influence over people. The upper class also included landowners, government officials, and rich merchants.

The in-between classes included all free people. Most people in Sumer were in this group, including many farmers and artisans. Slaves made up the lowest class.

The upper class included kings, priests, landowners, officials, and merchants. The in-between class included all free people not in the upper class. Slaves made up the lowest class.

◄ **The Standard of Ur**
A standard is a flag or symbol carried on a pole. This decorated panel shows many people in Sumerian society, including farmers. The panel is about 8.5 inches by 19.5 inches.

Terms & Names

bronze a metal made of copper and tin

pictograph a picture or drawing that represents a word or an idea

stylus a sharpened reed used to press markings into clay tablets

cuneiform a type of writing made up of wedge-shaped markings

scribe a person who specializes in writing and serves as a record keeper

❸ Teach

Sumerian Society

6.2.3

Talk About It

• What is the effect of a class system on a society? *(It affects who has power and who does less-desirable jobs.)*

• **Critical Thinking: Making Inferences** Which class in Sumerians society made it possible to get the least desirable jobs done? *(Possible answer: The class of enslaved people.)*

California Resources

California Reading Toolkit, L10

California Modified Lesson Plans for English Learners, p. 23

California Daily Standards Practice Transparencies, TT10

California Standards Enrichment Workbook, pp. 23–24, 25–26, 37–38

California Online Test Practice

California Test Generator CD-ROM

California Standards Planner and Lesson Plans, L19

California EasyPlanner CD-ROM

California eEdition CD-ROM

LESSON 3 PROGRAM RESOURCES

ON LEVEL

In-Depth Resources: Unit 2
• Reading Skill: Categorizing, p. 5
• Vocabulary Cards, p. 9

Formal Assessment
• Lesson Quiz, p. 42

ENGLISH LEARNERS

In-Depth Resources in Spanish
• Reading Skill: Categorizing, p. 21

Modified Lesson Plans for English Learners, p. 23

Reading Study Guide (Spanish), p. 27

Reading Study Guide Audio CD (Spanish)

STRUGGLING READERS

In-Depth Resources: Unit 2
• Reading Skill: Categorizing, p. 5
• Vocabulary Cards, p. 9
• Reteaching Activity, p. 17

Reading Toolkit, L10

Reading Study Guide, p. 27

Reading Study Guide Audio CD

GIFTED AND TALENTED STUDENTS

In-Depth Resources: Unit 2
• Primary Source: Sumerian Proverbs, p. 13

History Makers
• Leonard Woolley, p. 5

Interdisciplinary Projects
• Math, p. 13
• Civics, p. 16

INCLUSION

EasyPlanner CD-ROM
• Reading Skill: Categorizing
• Reteaching Activity

TECHNOLOGY

eEdition CD-ROM

Power Presentations CD-ROM

Critical Thinking Transparencies
• CT12 Categorizing
• CT13 Chapter 3 Visual Summary

Test Generator CD-ROM

ClassZone.com

In-Depth Resources: Unit 2
• Reading Skill: Categorizing, p. 5

Teach

Sumerian Science and Technology

6.2.2

Talk About It

- What are two examples of significant inventions with which the Sumerians are credited? *(the plow and the wheel)*

- What are two ways that the Sumerians used wheels? *(They used wheels to help transport goods and as a potter's wheel to make pottery.)*

- How have Sumerian developments in mathematics affected the world? *(These developments have influenced the ways we measure time as well as degrees in a circle.)*

- **Critical Thinking: Identifying Issues and Problems** How might knowledge of geometric shapes help in construction? *(Knowing how to make objects that have certain shapes and angles enables the building of orderly, solid structures.)*

More About . . .

The Invention of the Wheel
Some scholars believe that the Sumerians may have first developed the wheel in the form of a potter's wheel. It was after this that somebody in Sumer recognized the potential of the wheel as a way to move objects on the ground. The invention was quickly put to work, and human society began to use machines to reduce labor.

Slaves Some past societies have used slaves as a source of cheap labor. Most slaves in Sumer were taken as prisoners during war. In other cases, if Sumerian parents died or were very poor, their children might become slaves who worked in the temple. At times, a free person might borrow more money than he or she could repay. Such persons became slaves until they worked off the debt.

Slaves had some rights. They could conduct business and borrow money. Slaves could also buy their freedom.

Role of Women All of the social classes included women, so their social positions varied widely. In general, women in early Sumer had more rights than they did in later Mesopotamia.

Some upper-class women became priestesses, which was a role of honor. Free women could own land, and they could work as merchants and artisans, such as weavers. Still, the main role for most women was raising their children.

> **REVIEW** Why were kings and priests in the highest class?
> They were believed to have a link to the gods, which gave them great influence over people.

Sumerian Science and Technology

 ESSENTIAL QUESTION What tools did the Sumerians invent?
the plow, the wheel, the potter's wheel
Sumerians were good at solving problems. They invented tools and developed special knowledge to improve their lives. They were first to invent some of the things we use daily.

Early Inventions Historians believe that Sumerians may have invented the plow (about 6000 B.C.) and the wheel (about 3500 B.C.). These inventions helped Sumerians a great deal in their daily lives.

The plow was the first important tool invented to help farmers. The first plows were often simple digging sticks with handles. They could be pulled or pushed, first by people, then by animals. Plows broke up hard soil, which made planting easier. Also, water could sink more deeply into plowed soil. As a result, the roots of plants received more water.

The Sumerians used the wheel in many ways, such as on wagons to transport goods. Wheeled wagons helped farmers take their crops to market more easily and quickly. However, transporting goods on the river was still more efficient.

Wheel Early wheels were usually made from wood with tires made of leather. ▼

INTERDISCIPLINARY ACTIVITIES

Language Arts

Write a Press Release
Have students write a press release announcing the invention of the wheel. Students can use library or Internet resources to learn about key features of a press release. Then, have them announce the wheel's invention, including information about the many benefits of the wheel.

Science

Create a Table
Have students work individually to create a table of major Sumerian science and technology developments. The table should consist of two columns. The major developments discussed in the text can be listed in the left column. The significance of the invention can be recorded in the right column. Students should illustrate their table.

One special kind of wheel was the potter's wheel. Before the invention of the potter's wheel, people made pottery by shaping coils of clay by hand. With the potter's wheel, Sumerians could make more pottery faster. Pots were important storage containers for surplus food.

Sumerians were among the first people to use **bronze**, a mixture of copper and tin. Bronze was stronger than copper so tools lasted longer and stayed sharper. Bronze tools became another item that Sumerians could trade.

Mathematics The Sumerians developed arithmetic to keep records of crops and trade goods. Their number system was based on the number 60. So today, we have 60 seconds in a minute and 60 minutes in an hour. Circles contain 360 degrees. Eventually, the measurement of time helped with the creation of calendars.

Sumerians used a triangle and a measuring rope to set land boundaries. They understood geometric shapes such as rectangles, triangles, and squares. They used those shapes to make bricks, build ramps, and dig canals.

REVIEW How did new tools make life better for the Sumerians? The plow made planting easier. The wheel helped people transport things faster. The potter's wheel made pottery making faster. Bronze tools lasted longer and stayed sharper.

Creation of Written Language

3 ESSENTIAL QUESTION How did the Sumerians invent writing?

Sumerians invented writing by 3000 B.C. to meet the needs of business. As trade expanded, merchants needed records of exchanges. They also wanted to label goods.

Picture Writing At first, Sumerians used clay tokens that had an image of a product, such as a cow, to keep track of goods. They sealed the tokens in clay containers to make sure that no one tampered with them. The Sumerians marked the outside of the containers so people would know what was inside them.

The marks outside the container would be a symbol of the product. Such symbols are known as **pictographs**, which means "picture writing." In time, Sumerians stopped using tokens. They just drew the pictographs on clay tablets.

Side annotation: They began by using symbols called pictographs to keep track of trade goods. In time, these symbols began to stand for ideas as well as objects. Later, they began to use symbols made of wedges and lines instead of pictures. This system of writing is called cuneiform.

▲ **Nail Head** This bronze figurine of a god decorates a nail. It shows both the technical and artistic skills of the ancient Sumerians.

Visual Vocabulary

pictograph

Ancient Mesopotamia • 101

Teach

Creation of Written Language

6.2.9, REP 4

Talk About It

- In what way did business spur the development of writing? *(As business expanded, people needed a way to keep records.)*

- What did the first writing look like? *(It was made up of pictures or symbols that represented specific objects.)*

- Why was the use of symbols to represent sounds a significant change in the development of language? *(It made possible the writing of more words.)*

- **Critical Thinking: Identifying Issues and Problems** What kind of an effect do you think the development of writing had on Sumerian culture? *(Possible answers: Writing helped link Sumerians with their past by making it possible to keep accurate records and pass on stories and information. Writing helped create a new specialized job—the scribe—and required new learning.)*

Visual Vocabulary

Direct students' attention to the picture of the pictograph on this page. Point out each figure and its picture-like quality. Remind students of the meaning of the term *pictograph*.

DIFFERENTIATING INSTRUCTION

Struggling Readers

Record the Sequence
Have student pairs review the section on the development of writing. Pairs should identify three events in its development. Then, on a blank sheet of paper, students should write the numerals one, two, and three. Next to these numerals have them write the developments in order of occurrence, including one sentence about each development.

Gifted and Talented Students

Create a Pictograph System
Tell students to create pictographs for each of the subjects they study at school, as well as pictographs for different types of assignments—reading, reports, worksheets, and so on. Have students use their pictograph system to create a record of their week at school.

Interpreting Primary Sources

Sumerian Proverbs

- What were two ways mentioned in which cuneiform was used? *(Cuneiform was used for keeping records and writing proverbs.)*

- Why are proverbs sometimes difficult to understand? *(They are unique to the culture from which they came.)*

DOCUMENT–BASED QUESTION ANSWER

Possible answers: Based on the proverbs, the Sumerians felt that the truth was very important. They felt that possessions were a burden because they had to be protected.

More About . . .

Cuneiform

Cuneiform writing was inscribed on clay tablets, which, if important enough to be saved for future reading, could be dried. Cuneiform writing evolved and changed over the centuries and became extremely complex. It included marks that stood for specific things, ideas, and letters. Sometimes the same mark served more than one purpose.

 In-Depth Resources: Unit 2
- Primary Source: Sumerian Proverbs, p. 13

Background: Cuneiform was used to write many kinds of records. These were often written on small clay tablets like the one shown. Cuneiform was also used for literature, such as proverbs. A proverb is a short saying containing wisdom or advice. Proverbs are found in many cultures.

It is not always easy to understand the meaning of ancient proverbs because every culture is different. What do you think these proverbs mean?

from *Sumerian Proverbs*

Translated by Edmund I. Gordon

Whoever has walked with truth generates life.

Tell a lie and then tell the truth; it will be considered a lie!

He acquires many things; he must keep close watch over them.

Possessions are sparrows in flight which can find no place to alight.

DOCUMENT–BASED QUESTION

Judging from these proverbs, how did the Sumerians feel about truth? How did they feel about possessions?

Cuneiform At first, pictographs showed actual objects. Later, they also stood for ideas. In time, the Sumerians began to use pictographs to stand for sounds too. By combining sounds, they could write more words.

The Sumerians used a sharpened reed called a **stylus** to press markings into a clay tablet. Because of its shape, the stylus made marks that were wedge shaped. Over time, the Sumerians stopped using pictures and began to use symbols made entirely of these wedge shapes. This wedge-shaped writing is called **cuneiform** (KYOO•nee•uh•FAWRM).

The writing system was very complex. The Sumerian language contained about 600 different symbols. Learning all those symbols took years. As a result, few people were able to read and write. The people who specialized in writing were called **scribes**. They were professional record keepers. Other people in Sumerian society respected them highly.

Written History At first, Sumerians used records mostly for business dealings. Later, people started writing about wars, floods, and the reigns of their kings. These records are Sumer's written history.

DIFFERENTIATING INSTRUCTION

English Learners

Categorize Information

Tell students that details from the text can be organized into 3 categories: societies, technology, and writings. Have students revisit the text to generate examples for each of these categories. Have students use a similar sentence pattern when sharing their findings in class. Example: (*The plow and the wheel*) belong to the same category because they are all examples of (*technology.*)

Inclusion

Restate Proverbs

Pair students and have each pair choose three proverbs from the Primary Source material on page 102. For each proverb, the pair should restate the proverb in their own words. Students who have difficulty with motor skills may find it helpful to use a computer to write their restatements. Others may be more comfortable with a verbal restatement. Then gather all pairs and have them discuss the meanings of the proverbs.

Other cultures in Mesopotamia and elsewhere adopted the cuneiform writing system from the Sumerians. Archaeologists have found thousands of cuneiform tablets in Southwest Asia. One king owned a library of more than 24,000 clay tablet records and histories from all over the region of Mesopotamia.

They were the most highly educated people in the society and performed an important function.

 REVIEW Why were scribes highly respected in Sumer?

Lesson Summary

- Sumerian society had several classes. Kings and priests were at the top of society. Slaves were at the bottom.
- Inventions, such as the wheel and the plow, and mathematical knowledge improved Sumerian life.
- The Sumerians created a system of writing to record business transactions and histories.

Why It Matters Now . . .

The Sumerians developed the first system of writing. Writing makes it easier for people to pass on knowledge from generation to generation.

▲ **Scribe** This sculpture of a scribe was made later in Mesopotamian history. Notice that he is holding a stylus.

---

❹ Assess & Reteach

Assess Have students work through the assessment in pairs, except for the activity.

📝 **Formal Assessment**
- Lesson Quiz, p. 42

Reteach Have students create an outline for the lesson, using the major headings and subheadings of the lesson.

📝 **In-Depth Resources: Unit 2**
- Vocabulary Cards, p. 9
- Reteaching Activity, p. 17

➤ **Homework Helper**

Visit **Classzone.com** for a lesson review, a flip-card activity, and links to related Web sites.

---

3 Lesson Review

Homework Helper
ClassZone.com

Terms & Names

1. Explain the importance of
   bronze   stylus   scribe
   pictograph   cuneiform

Using Your Notes

Categorizing Use your completed chart to answer the following question:

2. Which invention or technology do you think was most important? Explain why. (6.2.2)

Life in Sumer		
Society	Technology	Writing

Main Ideas

3. How did religion affect who was in the upper class? (6.2.3)

4. Why was the plow such an important tool for farmers? (6.2.2)

5. How did writing evolve in Sumer? (6.2.9)

Critical Thinking

6. **Making Inferences** Why was the invention of cuneiform an important development? (6.2.9)

7. **Drawing Conclusions** Why do historians identify the beginning of history with the beginning of writing? (6.2.9)

Activity **Internet Activity** Choose one of the Sumerian inventions and use the Internet to research it. Then give a presentation on its importance. Include visuals with captions in your presentation. (6.2.2, 6.2.9)
INTERNET KEYWORDS: *plow, wheel, cuneiform*

Ancient Mesopotamia • 103

---

3 Lesson Review Answers

Terms & Names

1. • bronze, p. 101
   • pictograph, p. 101
   • stylus, p. 102
   • cuneiform, p. 102
   • scribe, p. 102

Using Your Notes

See page 98 for an example of a complete chart.

2. Possible answers: the wheel because it helps to transport things and people; writing because of its crucial role in recording knowledge

Main Ideas

3. Sumerians believed that the king and priests had links to the gods and, as a result, had great influence over people. Because of this, kings and priests formed the upper class.

4. It made farming easier and increased crop yields.

5. Writing began with pictographs that stood for objects, ideas, and sounds. Over time, pictographs evolved into symbols that used wedges and lines.

Critical Thinking

6. Possible answers: Cuneiform was the first writing system. It allowed people to record food supplies, business deals, historical events, and literature.

7. Possible answers: Writing gave people a way to record events and tell the stories of their lives.

Activity Rubric

	Detail of Explanation	Use of Media	Quality of Presentation
4	clear, detailed	two or more media used well and imaginatively	neat, attractive
3	reasonably well detailed	two media used well	neat
2	few details	one media used correctly	a bit sloppy
1	vague, no details	poor usage of one	sloppy

Ancient Mesopotamia • 103

Objectives

- Describe some of the major inventions of ancient Mesopotamia.
- Explore how ancient inventions still influence the world today.
- Synthesize information from visuals and text and use that information in discussion and writing.
- **Language Objective:** Classify details by category to make nonfiction text more comprehensible and meaningful.

❶ Focus & Motivate

Preview Briefly discuss how the challenges people face today are different from those that faced the people of Mesopotamia—and how they might be the same. Tell students that these two pages explore how people today benefit from the ancient Mesopotamians' efforts to solve problems and meet challenges.

❷ Teach

Talk About It

- What are two inventions of the Mesopotamians that help farmers today? *(Mesopotamians developed the plow and the wheel, both of which are relied upon by farmers today.)*

- What "problem" do you think the Mesopotamians who invented the board game were trying to address? *(Possible answer: boredom, how to pass time, or a way to learn how to think strategically/logically)*

- **Critical Thinking: Comparing and Contrasting** In what ways have people today improved on Mesopotamian inventions? In what ways are people today still using Mesopotamian inventions as they were created thousands of years ago? *(Possible answers: People today have improved the plow in various ways. However, board games and wheels are still similar today to the way they were thousands of years ago.)*

Research Links
ClassZone.com

Extend Lesson 3

Mesopotamian Inventions

Purpose: To learn about the ancient Mesopotamian inventions of the plow, board games, and the potter's wheel

The ancient Mesopotamians are a good example of people who solved problems—and changed history by doing so. They invented technology that helped to grow crops and to create pottery more efficiently. Ever since, people all over the world have used those inventions. But don't think that ancient Mesopotamians were so serious that they worked all the time. They also invented some ways to have fun!

CALIFORNIA STANDARDS
6.2.2 Trace the development of agricultural techniques that permitted the production of economic surplus and the emergence of cities as centers of culture and power.

Plow

▶ **Past** The sun can bake the soil as hard as a brick. Seeds thrown on top of such hard ground usually don't sprout. Because of this, early farmers had to find a way to loosen the soil. They invented the plow, which has a blade that cuts into soil and turns it over. The plow helped farmers to grow surplus crops.

▼ **Present** Today's plows are bigger and use metal blades to turn over the soil. Now tractors instead of animals pull plows. Even there, we owe a debt to the ancient Mesopotamians. We wouldn't have tractors without the wheel—and they invented that too.

plow

104 • Chapter 3

DIFFERENTIATING INSTRUCTION

Struggling Readers

Complete a Venn Diagram

Have students compare and contrast how the three Mesopotamian inventions shown here were used in the past and are used today with a Venn diagram.

Gifted and Talented Students

Create a Board Game

Have students write the rules and design the playing board and pieces of a new board game. Students can use ideas from the Mesopotamian board game shown here to create their game.

Board Games

▼ **Past** This game comes from a tomb at Ur. Scholars think the goal was to move your pieces from one end to the other while an opponent blocked the narrow bridge.

▶ **Present** Checkers is a board game that many people still enjoy. The object is to capture all of your opponent's pieces.

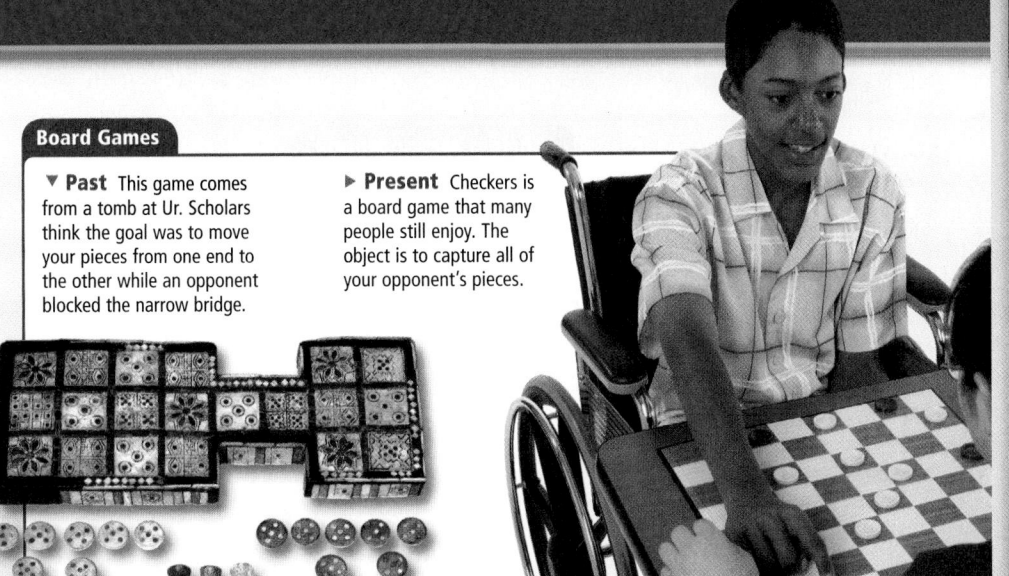

Research Links
Visit **ClassZone.com** for editor-approved, age-appropriate research links related to this topic.

More About . . .

The "Royal Game of Ur"
Archaeologists working in Ur in the 1920s and 1930s discovered a number of game boards in the tombs of Sumerian royalty. The game boards were hollow, and inside were a number of playing pieces and odd-shaped dice. There were no rules found for the game, though experts have created rules for what they believe the game might have been like. Players today can even obtain electronic versions of this game for play on the Internet.

Pottery

▶ **Past** It is possible to create pottery entirely by hand, but the potter's wheel provides several advantages. Artisans can make pots with more even, streamlined shapes. And the process is much faster, so artisans could produce more pots than before.

▼ **Present** If you go to any craft fair, you can still find pottery that artisans make on a simple potter's wheel. Many people create pottery as a way to express their artistic side.

Activities

1. **TALK ABOUT IT** Which of these inventions has had the greatest effect on your life? Explain.

2. **WRITE ABOUT IT** Create instructions for the ancient board game shown here. Write them out, using a numbered, step-by-step format. (Writing 1.3)

Ancient Mesopotamia • 105

ACTIVITIES ANSWERS

1. **TALK ABOUT IT** Possible answer: The plow, which has helped make possible our high standard of living by helping produce large amounts of food.

2. **WRITE ABOUT IT**

2. Writing Rubric

	Clarity of Instructions	Utilization of Pieces	Level of Creativity
4	clear, complete	rules use all pieces and features of the game board	rules produce a fun, exciting game
3	complete	rules use most of the pieces and features of the game board	rules produce a fun game
2	unclear	rules use some of the pieces and features of the game board	rules produce a somewhat interesting game
1	incomplete	rules use few of the pieces or features of the game board	rules produce an uninteresting game

Terms & Names

1. Possible answer: Flooding rivers deposited silt on the floodplain.
2. Possible answer: The first civilization arose in Sumer.
3. Possible answer: The Sumerians practiced polytheism at the ziggurat.
4. Possible answer: Pictographs developed into cuneiform.

Main Ideas

Geography of Mesopotamia (pages 82–87)

5. The flooding enriched the soil. But too much flooding could damage crops. Also, flooding was unpredictable. As a result, farmers had a difficult time predicting when to plant.
6. Without irrigation, successful farming was impossible in the semiarid climate.

The First Civilization (pages 88–97)

7. Advances in agriculture led to food surpluses. Having a food surplus allowed some people to focus on work other than farming. As a result, people began to specialize in doing jobs that spurred the development of cities.
8. The temple was the center of a Sumerian city. It controlled religion and the economy

Life in Sumer (pages 98–105)

9. Women could serve as priestesses. Some slaves worked in the temples.
10. It consisted of wedge-shaped characters on clay tablets. The characters stood for things, ideas, and sounds.

▶ **VISUAL SUMMARY**   **Ancient Mesopotamia**

Geography (6.2.1)
- Rivers made agriculture possible.
- Challenges included floods, drought, and lack of resources.

Culture (6.2.9)
- Sumerians developed the first writing system.
- Sumerian society was divided into classes.

Belief Systems (6.2.3)
- Sumerians worshiped many gods.
- The temple was called a ziggurat.

Government (6.2.3)
- City-states were the form of government throughout Sumer.
- First, priests ruled in Sumer. Later, powerful men became kings.

Science & Technology (6.2.2)
- Irrigation helped provide a steady source of water for crops.
- Sumerians invented the wheel and the plow.

▶ **TERMS & NAMES**

Explain why the words in each set below are linked with each other.

1. **floodplain** and **silt**
2. **Sumer** and **civilization**
3. **ziggurat** and **polytheism**
4. **pictograph** and **cuneiform**

▶ **MAIN IDEAS**

Geography of Mesopotamia (pages 82–87)
5. How did the flooding of the Tigris and Euphrates rivers both help and hurt farmers? (6.2.1)
6. Why was irrigation so important to agriculture in Mesopotamia? (6.2.2)

The First Civilization (pages 88–97)
7. How did advances in agriculture contribute to the rise of cities? (6.2.2)
8. What role did the temple play in Sumerian society? (6.2.3)

Life in Sumer (pages 98–105)
9. What roles did women and slaves have in Sumerian religion? (6.2.3)
10. What are the characteristics of Sumerian cuneiform writing? (6.2.9)

ALTERNATIVE ASSESSMENT RUBRICS

1. Writing Rubric

	Level of Persuasiveness	Number of Errors
4	very persuasive	zero or one grammatical or spelling errors
3	persuasive	two or three such errors
2	somewhat persuasive	four or five such errors
1	not persuasive	more than five such errors

2. Science Rubric

	Accuracy of Content	Effectiveness of Style
4	contains all required elements	neat, organized, attractive
3	contains most required elements	neat and organized
2	contains some required elements	somewhat organized
1	contains few or no required elements	not organized

CRITICAL THINKING Big Ideas: Geography

11. UNDERSTANDING CAUSES How did the geography of Mesopotamia help civilization develop there? (6.2.1)

12. EXPLAINING HISTORICAL PATTERNS Judging from the history of Sumer, what geographic conditions would help other ancient civilizations to develop? (HI 3)

13. UNDERSTANDING EFFECTS How did inventions and special knowledge support agriculture in Sumer? (6.2.2)

ALTERNATIVE ASSESSMENT

1. WRITING ACTIVITY Review the section "Changes in Leadership" on pages 93–95. Decide whether you think kings or priests made better leaders in ancient Sumer. Then write a persuasive paragraph trying to convince readers to adopt your position. (6.2.3)

2. INTERDISCIPLINARY ACTIVITY— SCIENCE Use books or the Internet to research bronze. Make a poster that explains how bronze is made, what it was used for, and how it helped the economy of Sumer. Use photocopies or draw examples of bronze objects. (HI 6)

3. STARTING WITH A STORY Review the invention that you thought of to help the farmer. How did your ideas compare with what you learned in the chapter? Draw pictures for a wall mural that would illustrate the development of agriculture techniques in Mesopotamia. (6.2.2)

Technology Activity

4. PLANNING A MULTIMEDIA PRESENTATION Use the Internet or the library to research scribes in Sumer. Work with a partner to plan a multimedia presentation. (6.2.9)

- Who could become a scribe?
- How were scribes educated?
- What kinds of work did they do?

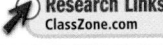
Research Links ClassZone.com

Reading a Chart Use the chart below to answer the questions. (6.2.9)

Early Development of Writing		
word	pictograph	cuneiform
bird		
cow		
fish		
mountain		
water		

1. What do all of the words on the chart have in common?

A. They name a person's actions.
B. They name abstract ideas.
C. They name human emotions.
D. They name things from nature.

2. Which of the following statements is true of the way cuneiform looked?

A. It was made of realistic pictures of objects.
B. It was similar to our alphabet.
C. It was made of wedges and lines.
D. It used symbols that were larger than pictographs.

Test Practice ClassZone.com

Additional Test Practice, pp. S1–S33

Critical Thinking

Big Ideas: Geography

11. Possible answer: The rivers enriched the soil and provided fresh water that could support large communities. The rivers also were transportation routes that promoted the growth of trade.

12. Possible answer: Other ancient civilizations probably developed near rivers that provided water and means of transport. The rivers may have flooded, depositing fertile soil on the land.

13. Possible answer: The wheel and the plow made farming easier and increased crop yields. Sumerians used math to keep track of their crops and animals, survey fields, and plan their irrigation systems.

Standards-Based Assessment

1. The correct answer is letter D. All these items are from the natural world. Answers A through C do not describe the words on the chart.

2. The correct answer is letter C. Cuneiform was made up of wedges and lines. Cuneiform is not made of realistic pictures of objects, nor is it similar to our alphabet. Cuneiform did not use symbols larger than pictographs.

 Research Links

Visit **ClassZone.com** for links to Web sites that can be used in the multimedia presentation.

 Test Practice

Visit **ClassZone.com** to access strategies and tutorials for taking standardized tests.

📝 **Formal Assessment**
- Chapter Tests, Forms A, B, and C, pp. 43–57

💿 **Test Generator**
- Chapter Tests, Forms A, B, and C (English and Spanish)

ALTERNATIVE ASSESSMENT RUBRICS

3. Starting with a Story Rubric

	Quality of Illustration	Level of Illustration
4	detailed, accurate	very creative
3	accurate	creative
2	somewhat accurate	somewhat creative
1	not accurate	not creative

4. Technology Rubric

	Clarity of Answers	Effectiveness of Presentation
4	clear	neat, attractive
3	adequate	neat
2	vague or incomplete	a bit sloppy
1	incorrect or missing	sloppy

CHAPTER 4 PLANNING GUIDE: Early Empires

Chapter Overview

The first empires, which began in the Fertile Crescent of Mesopotamia, brought about important developments in the growth of civilization.

Copymasters

 In-Depth Resources: Unit 2
- Family Newsletter (English and Spanish), pp. 19–20
- Visual Summary, p. 24
- Vocabulary Study Guide, p. 26

 Character Education

 Reading Study Guide, p. 37

 Bringing Social Studies Alive, Chapter 4

 Document-Based Questions: Strategy and Practice

 Reading Toolkit, L11–L13

 Modified Lesson Plans for English Learners, pp. 25–30

Assessment

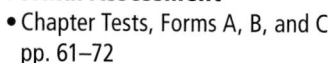 **Chapter Review,** pp. 136–137

Formal Assessment
- Chapter Tests, Forms A, B, and C, pp. 61–72

Test Generator

Integrated Assessment Book

Online Test Practice

LESSON 1

Mesopotamian Empires
pp. 112–117

OBJECTIVE Study the key individuals and developments of civilization's first empires.

 In-Depth Resources: Unit 2
- Reading Skill: Summarizing, p. 21
- Vocabulary Cards, p. 27
- Primary Source: from the Code of Hammurabi, p. 31
- Skillbuilder Practice: Making Decisions, p. 25
- Reteaching Activity, p. 33

 Interdisciplinary Projects
- Math, p. 19

 Reading Study Guide, p. 31

Lesson Review, p. 116

Formal Assessment
- Lesson Quiz, p. 58

California Daily Standards Practice Transparencies, TT11

LESSON 2

Assyria Rules the Fertile Crescent
pp. 118–127

OBJECTIVE Analyze the rise and fall of the Assyrian and Chaldean Empires.

 In-Depth Resources: Unit 2
- Reading Skill: Understanding Cause and Effect, p. 22
- Vocabulary Cards, p. 27
- Reteaching Activity, p. 34

 Interdisciplinary Projects
- Language Arts, p. 21; Art, p. 22

 Reading Study Guide, p. 33

Lesson Review, p. 123

Formal Assessment
- Lesson Quiz, p. 59

California Daily Standards Practice Transparencies, TT12

LESSON 3

Persia Controls Southwest Asia
pp. 128–135

OBJECTIVE Explore the rise of the Persian Empire.

 In-Depth Resources: Unit 2
- Reading Skill: Identifying Issues and Problems, p. 23
- Vocabulary Cards, p. 27
- Literature: Autobiography, by Darius, p. 32
- Geography Practice: The Royal Road, p. 29
- Reteaching Activity, p. 35

 History Makers
- Cyrus, p. 7

 Interdisciplinary Projects
- Science, p. 20

Reading Study Guide, p. 35

Lesson Review, p. 133

Formal Assessment
- Lesson Quiz, p. 60

California Daily Standards Practice Transparencies, TT13

Integrated Technology

 eEdition Plus Online

EasyPlanner Plus Online

eTest Plus Online

 Audio CDs
- Reading Study Guide
- Reading Study Guide in Spanish
- The World's Music

 CD-ROMs
- Power Presentations
- eEdition
- EasyPlanner
- Test Generator

 **Ancient Civilizations Video Series**
- Ancient Mesopotamia

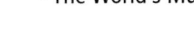 **eEdition CD-ROM**

 Map Transparencies
- MT7 The Babylonian Empire

 Critical Thinking Transparencies
- CT14 Summarizing

 ClassZone.com

---

 eEdition CD-ROM

 Humanities Transparencies
- HT7 Cylinder Seals from Assyria

 Critical Thinking Transparencies
- CT15 Understanding Cause and Effect

 ClassZone.com

---

 eEdition CD-ROM

 Map Transparencies
- MT8 Expansion of the Persian Empire

 Humanities Transparencies
- HT8 Stairway from Persepolis

 Critical Thinking Transparencies
- CT16 Identifying Issues and Problems
- CT17 Chapter 4 Visual Summary

 ClassZone.com

Overview of California Resources

	Lesson 1	Lesson 2	Lesson 3
California Reading Toolkit	L11	L12	L13
California Modified Lesson Plans for English Learners	p. 25	p. 27	p. 29
California Daily Standards Practice Transparencies	TT11	TT12	TT13
California Standards Enrichment Workbook	pp. 21–22, 27–28	pp. 45–46	pp. 45–46, 57–58
California Standards Planner and Lesson Plans	L21	L23	L25
California Online Test Practice	ClassZone.com	ClassZone.com	ClassZone.com
California Test Generator CD-ROM			
California EasyPlanner CD-ROM			
California eEdition CD-ROM			

Chart Key

PE	Pupil Edition		CD-ROM		Internet
	Copymaster		Audio		Overhead Transparency
			Video		

PREVIEWING RESOURCES FOR DIFFERENTIATED INSTRUCTION

English Learners

In-Depth Resources in Spanish
- Reading Skill and Strategy
- Skillbuilder Practice **B**
- Geography Practice
- Vocabulary Study Guide

In-Depth Resources: Unit 2
- Family Newsletter (English and Spanish) **C**

Reading Study Guide (Spanish) **A**

Reading Study Guide Audio CD
(Spanish)

Test Generator
Chapter Test (Spanish)

Plus

Modified Lesson Plans for English Learners

Multi-Language Glossary of Social Studies Terms

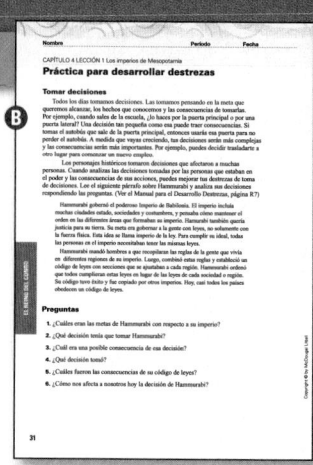

Struggling Readers

In-Depth Resources: Unit 2
- Vocabulary Study Guide **B**
- Skillbuilder Practice **C**
- Geography Practice
- Reteaching Activities **A**
- Family Newsletter

Reading Study Guide

Reading Study Guide Audio CD

Reading Toolkit

Formal Assessment
Chapter Test, Form A

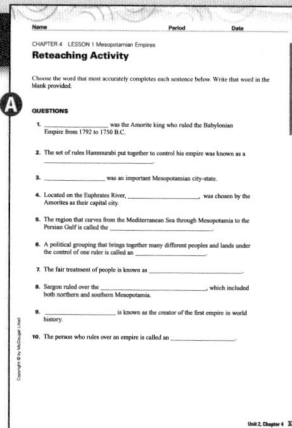

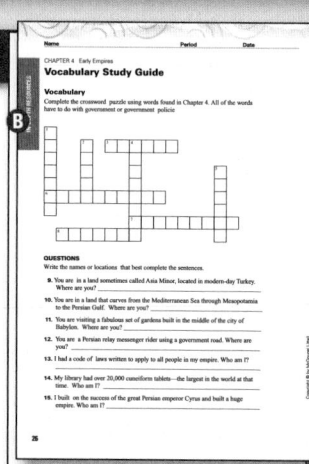

Inclusion

EasyPlanner CD-ROM
- Reading Skill and Strategy **B**
- Vocabulary Study Guide **A**
- Geography Practice
- Reteaching Activities **C**

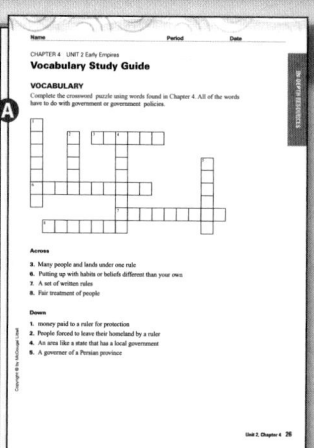

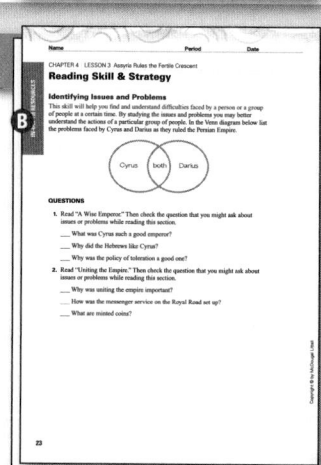

Gifted and Talented Students

In-Depth Resources: Unit 2
- Primary Source
- Literature **A**

History Makers **B**

Interdisciplinary Projects **C**

Formal Assessment
Chapter Test, Form C

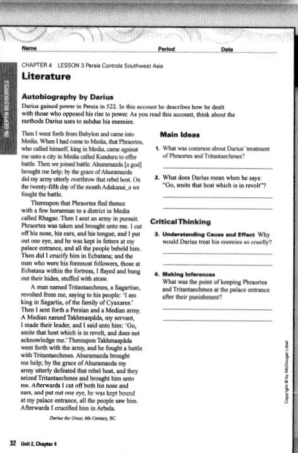

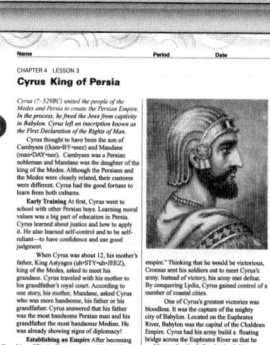

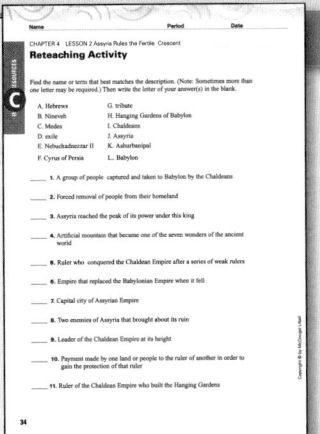

Activities in the Teacher's Edition for English Learners

- Framing Historical Questions, p. 114
- Comparing and Contrasting, p. 120
- Preview Dialogue, p. 125
- Finding Main Ideas, p. 132
- Comparing and Contrasting, p. 134

Activities in the Teacher's Edition for Struggling Readers

- Discuss Key Vocabulary Words, p. 115
- Create a Sequence, p. 121
- Write Headline Summaries, p. 131
- Role-Play Darius's Court, p. 134

Activities in the Teacher's Edition for Inclusion Students

- Use Sticky Notes, p. 114
- Prepare Enlarged Photocopies, p. 120
- Role-Play the Ruler, p. 132

Activities in the Teacher's Edition for Gifted and Talented Students

- Hold a Debate, p. 115
- Report on Mesopotamian Antiquities, p. 121
- Compare Landscapes, p. 125
- Write a Biographical Sketch, p. 131

Integrated Technology

eEdition CD-ROM

- Interactive Visuals
- Interactive Maps
- Starting with a Story

ClassZone.com

- WebQuests
- Research Links
- Internet Activities
- Homework Helper
- Chapter Quiz
- Current Events
- Test Practice

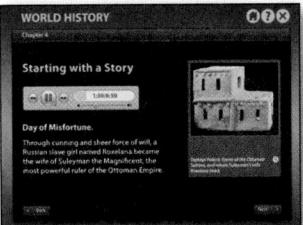

Power Presentations CD-ROM

- Lecture Notes
- Media Gallery
- Chapter Review Game

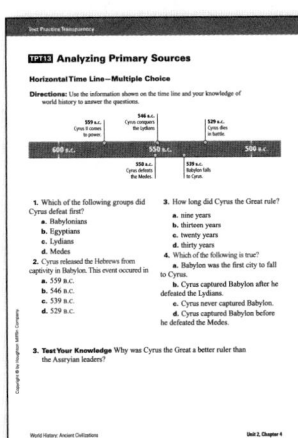

Critical Thinking Transparencies

- CT14 Summarizing
- CT15 Understanding Cause and Effect
- CT16 Identifying Issues and Problems
- CT17 Chapter 4 Visual Summary

California Daily Standards Practice Transparencies, TT11–TT13

Map Transparencies

- MT7 The Babylonian Empire
- MT8 Expansion of the Persian Empire

Humanities Transparencies

- HT7 Cylinder Seals from Assyria
- HT8 Stairway from Persepolis

Test Generator CD-ROM

EasyPlanner CD-ROM

Ancient Civilizations Video Series

- Ancient Mesopotamia

Early Empires • 107D

Begin the Chapter

Objective

Describe the location and extent of the first empires and the key points in their development.

Quick Look

Lesson 1 explores the key individuals and developments of the first Mesopotamian Empires.

Lesson 2 describes the rise and fall of the Assyrian Empire.

Lesson 3 summarizes the key events and individuals of the Persian Empire.

Before You Read: Knowledge Rating

Remind students that knowledge rating is a strategy that helps students prepare to read and set a purpose for what they will be learning. Students identify their level of knowledge about certain key terms—and at the same time are alerted to words and concepts to which they need to pay special attention. Tell students that to use knowledge rating effectively, they should follow these steps:

• Read the list of terms that you should look for as you read the chapter. Write the words on a sheet of paper.

• Consider each term and use the rating scale to note your level of knowledge about the word.

• As you read, note the definition of each term, and write it down on your sheet. Pay special attention to those terms that you rated 1 and 2.

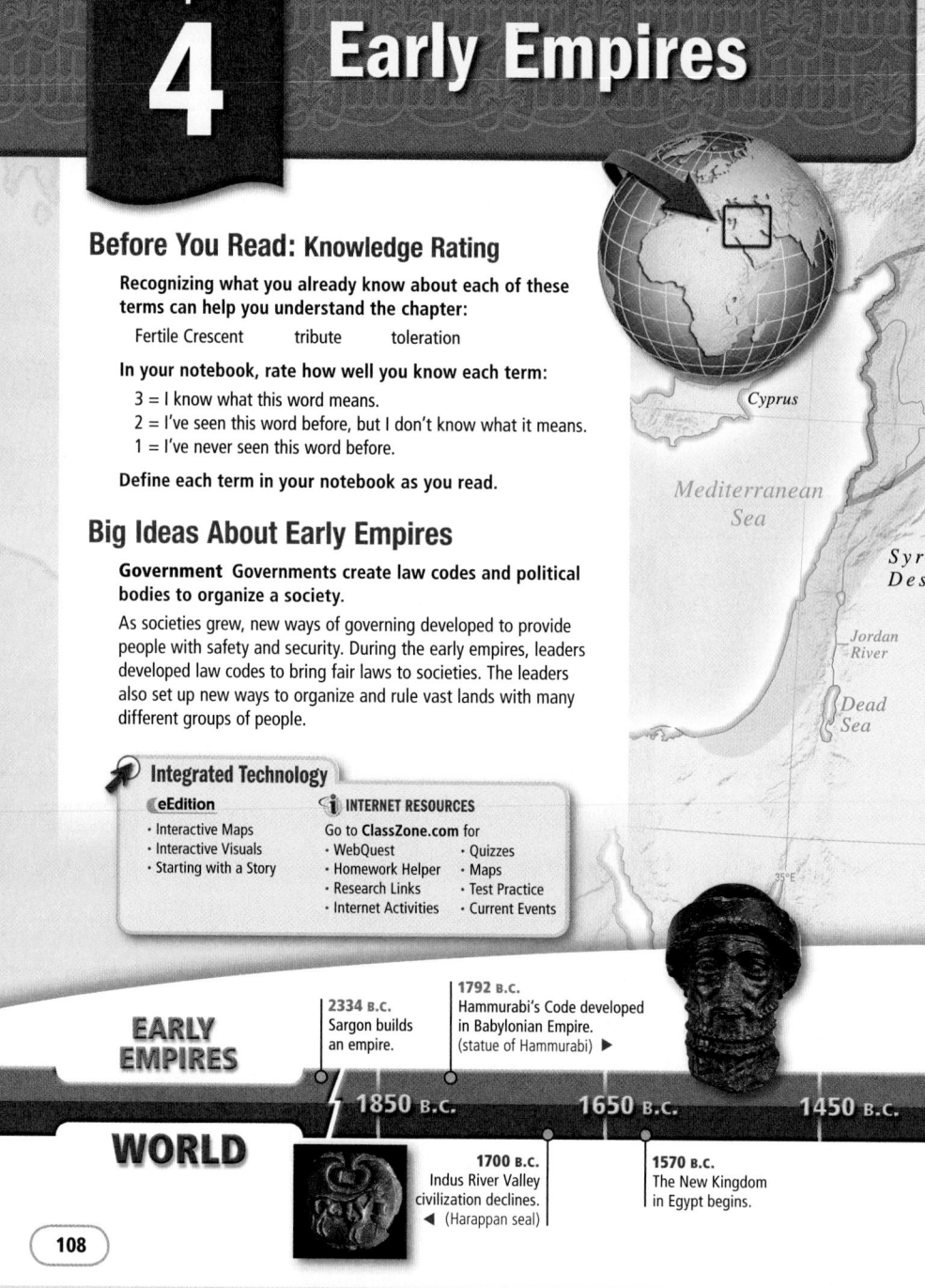

Chapter 4 — Early Empires

Before You Read: Knowledge Rating

Recognizing what you already know about each of these terms can help you understand the chapter:

Fertile Crescent   tribute   toleration

In your notebook, rate how well you know each term:

3 = I know what this word means.
2 = I've seen this word before, but I don't know what it means.
1 = I've never seen this word before.

Define each term in your notebook as you read.

Big Ideas About Early Empires

Government Governments create law codes and political bodies to organize a society.

As societies grew, new ways of governing developed to provide people with safety and security. During the early empires, leaders developed law codes to bring fair laws to societies. The leaders also set up new ways to organize and rule vast lands with many different groups of people.

Integrated Technology

eEdition
• Interactive Maps
• Interactive Visuals
• Starting with a Story

INTERNET RESOURCES
Go to **ClassZone.com** for
• WebQuest   • Quizzes
• Homework Helper • Maps
• Research Links   • Test Practice
• Internet Activities • Current Events

EARLY EMPIRES

2334 B.C. Sargon builds an empire.

1792 B.C. Hammurabi's Code developed in Babylonian Empire. (statue of Hammurabi) ▶

1850 B.C.   1650 B.C.   1450 B.C.

WORLD

1700 B.C. Indus River Valley civilization declines. ◀ (Harappan seal)

1570 B.C. The New Kingdom in Egypt begins.

108

Cyprus

Mediterranean Sea

Syria Deser

Jordan River

Dead Sea

35°E

TIME LINE DISCUSSION

Use the time line to help students develop an understanding of the events and individuals associated with the rise of early empires.

• According to the time line, who is the first to build an empire? *(Sargon, in 2334 B.C.)*

• How many years passed between the establishment of Sargon's empire and the development of Hammurabi's Code? *(542 years)*

• According to the time line, which empire appeared first—the Assyrian or the Persian empire? *(the Assyrian Empire)*

• According to the time line, which two empires developed nearest to each other in time? *(the Assyrian and Persian empires)*

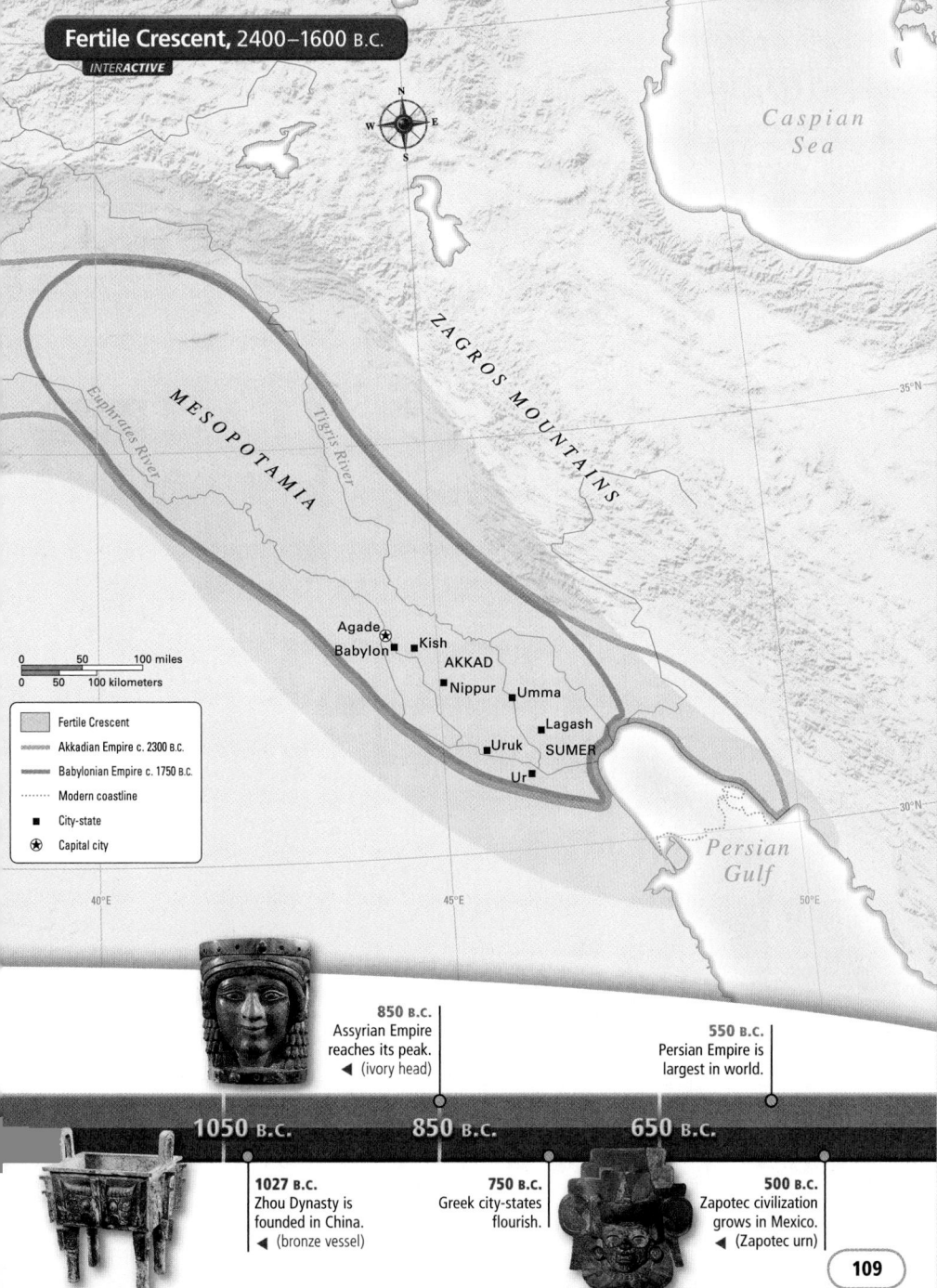

Fertile Crescent, 2400–1600 B.C.
INTERACTIVE

Caspian Sea

ZAGROS MOUNTAINS

MESOPOTAMIA

Euphrates River

Tigris River

Agade ✪
Babylon ■ ■ Kish
AKKAD
■ Nippur
■ Umma
■ Lagash
■ Uruk SUMER
Ur ■

Persian Gulf

35°N

30°N

40°E   45°E   50°E

0   50   100 miles
0   50   100 kilometers

▢ Fertile Crescent
╌╌ Akkadian Empire c. 2300 B.C.
╌╌ Babylonian Empire c. 1750 B.C.
····· Modern coastline
■ City-state
✪ Capital city

850 B.C.
Assyrian Empire
reaches its peak.
◄ (ivory head)

550 B.C.
Persian Empire is
largest in world.

1050 B.C.   **850 B.C.**   **650 B.C.**

1027 B.C.
Zhou Dynasty is
founded in China.
◄ (bronze vessel)

750 B.C.
Greek city-states
flourish.

500 B.C.
Zapotec civilization
grows in Mexico.
◄ (Zapotec urn)

109

RECOMMENDED RESOURCES

Books for the Teacher
Boardman, John; I. E. S.
Edwards, E. Sollberger, and
N. G. L. Hammond, eds. *The
Cambridge Ancient History.
Volume 3. Part 2. The
Assyrian and Babylonian
Empires and Other States
of the Near East.* Cambridge:
Cambridge UP, 1992. Thorough
history of the empires of
Mesopotamia.

Briant, Pierre. *From Cyrus to
Alexander: A History of the
Persian Empire.* Warsaw, IN:
Eisenbraun, 2002. Overview

of the history of the Persian
Empire.

Harper, Robert Francis. *The
Code of Hammurabi, King
of Babylon.* TN: University
Press of the Pacific, 2002.
A translation of the code
along with supporting
documentation.

Videos
Mesopotamia. 20 Minutes.
Wheeling, Il: Film Ideas, Inc.
Discussion of the ancient
civilizations and empires of
Mesopotamia.

Internet
To access these sites, visit the
Research Links for this chapter
at **ClassZone.com.**

The British Museum. Provides
an extensive online exhibit on
the civilizations and empires of
Mesopotamia.

Fordham University. Its
Ancient History Sourcebook
includes large amounts of
information on the empires of
Mesopotamia and Persia.

Introduce the Big Ideas
Have students think about their own lives and
how they depend on laws to keep them safe.
What might happen if there were no laws for
guiding traffic? What if there were no laws
protecting people from those who wish to
harm them? Help students understand that as
communities grew larger and more complex, the
need for systems of law and order grew.

Here are some other Big Ideas that you may
want to emphasize in this chapter:

Culture
The spread of civilization and the building of
empires meant that information, ideas, and
ways of living also spread and were adapted into
different cultures.

Science and Technology
New inventions and techniques enabled the
development of great military power in some
empires.

Geography
Empires spread, which helped promote the
spread of ideas and beliefs.

Talk About It
Interpreting Maps
Ask students to look at the map on this page
and read the key. What did the Akkadian and
Babylonian Empires have in common? *(They were
located in the Fertile Crescent, and made up in
large part by Mesopotamia.)* What geographic
features appear to characterize the Fertile
Crescent? *(Possible answer: The land is relatively
flat and has many rivers.)*

INTERACTIVE

An interactive version of this map is available on
the eEdition and Power Presentations CD-ROMs.

Find Out More
Use a world map to determine what countries
exist on the land that now lies at the northwest
end of the Persian Gulf, which was underwater in
ancient times? *(parts of Iraq, Iran, and Kuwait)*

Watch the Video
Ancient Mesopotamia explores the land that was
home to some of the world's first civilizations.
This 23-minute video is part of the Ancient
Civilizations for Children™ series.

Objective

Describe the need for, and impact of, codes of law in the development of civilizations.

Introducing the Story

Day of Misfortune

This story uses an account of a typical sort of dispute, between a homeowner and a builder, to illustrate the need for legal systems to settle disagreements. Ask students to think about how such common disputes might have led to the development of legal codes.

Vocabulary Preview

shekel a unit of money used in the ancient world

shifty sneaky

Reading the Story Aloud

1. **The teacher as reader:** Read the story aloud with expression, so that students hear the drama and understand the emotional impact of the events.

2. **The students as readers:** Have student readers direct their voices to the furthest points of the room so that they can be heard by everyone in the class.

Starting with a Story

Students can also follow along as they listen to the story on the eEdition or Power Presentations CD-ROMs.

Starting with a Story

Day of Misfortune

Background: To build unity in his empire, Hammurabi, the ruler of Babylon, created a set of laws that applied to all people in the empire. The laws covered acts that affected the community, such as business conduct and crime. Imagine that you live in a brand-new house in the Babylonian Empire. Unfortunately, the roof of the house has caved in. Now, you and your father are talking to the builder about who is responsible for the damage.

Model of a typical Mesopotamian house ▶

CALIFORNIA STANDARDS
Reading 3.6
Identify and analyze features of themes conveyed through characters, actions, and images.

110

ADDITIONAL RESOURCES

Books for the Student
Nardo, Don. *The Assyrian Empire (World History)*. San Diego: Lucent Books, 1998. History of the people and leaders of the Assyrian Empire.

Zeinert, Karen. *The Persian Empire (Cultures of the Past)*. Tarrytown: Benchmark Books, 1997. Recounting of the rise and fall of the Persian Empire.

Schomp, Virginia. *Ancient Mesopotamia: The Sumerians, Babylonians, and Assyrians (People of the Ancient World)*. New York: Franklin Watts, 2004. Overview of the history of the Fertile Crescent.

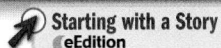
Starting with a Story
eEdition

My father pointed to the house and said to the builder, "You can see the damage." I stood with them in front of our ruined house. The roof of our new house had a huge hole in it. The roof supports had fallen through the second floor and into the first floor.

My father turned to me. "Stay here, son," he said. He took the builder inside with him. They looked up at the sky from the first floor.

I could tell that my father was getting angry. The builder seemed not to care. "You made mistakes when you built my house," my father told him, his voice rising. "I paid you the right number of shekels, so you have to rebuild at your expense." "No," the builder snapped. His face looked mean. I watched his shifty eyes as he snarled, "There's nothing that says I have to do it."

"Oh, yes there is!" cried my father. "The code of laws by King Hammurabi says a builder has to make repairs at his own expense if a house falls down. Not only that, the law says you have to pay for everything that was damaged in the house."

My father kept talking to the builder. "You are lucky no one was home at the time. If the collapse had killed me, by law you would have been put to death." For the first time, the builder looked a bit worried.

"If my son, here, had been killed, your son would have had to die." My father seemed to be getting somewhere now. The builder looked more worried.

The builder started to back away from us. Then he started running. "Stop! Come back here!" my father shouted at him. I turned to my father. "Isn't he going to obey the code of law? What do we do next?"

Why are laws necessary?

Reading & Writing

1. **READING: Theme** A theme is the subject or idea that a story is about. Look at the illustration and think about the question at the end of the story. Talk with a partner to decide what the theme of this story is. As you read other stories in this book, watch to see if this theme recurs.

2. **WRITING: Persuasion** Imagine that you are the father in this story. Write a persuasive speech listing your complaints about the builder of your house. Then present your speech to your classmates.

CALIFORNIA STANDARDS **Writing 2.5**
Write persuasive compositions.

111

Talk About It

Ask students the following questions to begin the discussion:

- Why is the father angry? *(He believes that the builder of the house is responsible for the collapse and that the builder seems unwilling to accept that responsibility.)*

- In what way does the builder respond to the accusation of the father? *(He says that there is no way to make him fix the problems.)*

- Why does the builder become nervous? *(He realizes that he may be punished under the law.)*

- What do you think is going to happen next in the story? *(Possible answer: The father will contact local leaders to see how to have the law used against the builder.)*

Why are laws necessary?

Laws allow for the fair settlement of disputes; laws help prevent disputes by encouraging people to treat each other fairly.

Making Personal Connections

Connect the discussion to today by asking students to think about ways in which they depend on laws to protect them. Students should recognize that laws generally help them feel safer and more secure.

READING & WRITING ACTIVITIES

1. **READING** Possible answer: Laws are important and it is important to obey them.

2. **WRITING**

2. Writing Rubric

	Level of Persuasiveness	Use of Mechanics	Style of Presentation
4	very persuasive	no spelling or punctuation errors	lively, interesting
3	persuasive	one or two spelling or punctuation errors	lively
2	somewhat persuasive	three or four spelling or punctuation errors	somewhat lively
1	not persuasive	more than four spelling or punctuation	not lively, uninteresting

❶ Plan & Prepare

Objectives

- Trace the development of the first empires in Mesopotamia.
- Describe the significance of Hammurabi's Code of Law.
- **Language Objective:** Demonstrate understanding of text information by creating and responding to questions.

Quick Look

Lesson 1 traces the development of human civilization's first empires, including the contributions of Hammurabi, an early emperor.

❷ Focus & Motivate

Preview Tell students that this lesson will explore the development of the first empires in human history. Ask students to think about ways in which their country is similar to, and different from, these first empires.

Introduce the Main Ideas The three main ideas relate to the Big Idea that "Governments create law codes and political bodies to organize a society." Help students look for this Big Idea as you go through the lesson.

Reading Skill: Summarizing Remind students that summarizing involves repeating only the main points and details.

SAMPLE ANSWERS FOR CHART

Topic	Statement
Geography	Flat lands with fewer barriers are easier to conquer.
A strong king	A strong king can bring together different lands and people.
A law code	A law code can unite people under one government because they feel they are being treated fairly.

Lesson 1

▲ **Bust of Sargon** Sargon of Akkad created the world's first empire 4,500 years ago.

▶ MAIN IDEAS

1 **Geography** Powerful city-states expanded to control much of Mesopotamia.

2 **Government** Babylon built a large empire in the Fertile Crescent.

3 **Government** Hammurabi created one of the first codes of law.

▶ TAKING NOTES

Reading Skill: Summarizing

Summarizing means restating the main idea and important details about a subject. As you read Lesson 1, make a summary statement about each of the topics listed. Record them on a list of your own.

Topic	Statement
Geography	
A strong king	
A law code	

 Skillbuilder Handbook, page R3

HOW TO TEACH THE CALIFORNIA STANDARDS

Standard	Content	Student Question or Activity	Instruction
6.2.1	Page 114 Describes the physical geography of the Fertile Crescent	Page 116 Students tell which empires controlled the Fertile Crescent.	Instruct students to trace the outline of the Fertile Crescent on copies of a world map.
6.2.4	Page 115 Outlines the definition and purpose of Hammurabi's Code	Page 116 Students explain why Hammurabi's Code was an important landmark in the growth of civilization.	Explain that Hammurabi's Code is sometimes referred to as the "eye-for-an-eye" code. Have students discuss reasons why this is or is not an apt description.
HI 1	Page 115 Explains the central problem of control in society and Hammurabi's solution to that problem	Page 116 Students identify the purpose of Hammurabi's Code.	Ask students to share ways that their lives might be different if Hammurabi's Code were enforced in the United States today.

Mesopotamian Empires

TERMS & NAMES

empire

emperor

Fertile Crescent

Hammurabi

code of law

justice

Build on What You Know How big is the state where you live? What kinds of activities take place in the capital of your state? Most of the Mesopotamian city-states were smaller than the state you live in. The city-states were centers of culture and power.

The First Empire Builders

1 ESSENTIAL QUESTION Who controlled Mesopotamia? Sargon

From about 3000 to 2000 B.C., ambitious kings of the city-states of Sumer fought over land. The land was flat and easy to invade. More land would give more wealth and power to the king. However, no single king was able to control all of the city-states in Mesopotamia.

Sargon Builds an Empire About 2350 B.C., a powerful leader named Sargon took control of both northern and southern Mesopotamia. Sargon of Akkad is known as the creator of the first empire in world history. An **empire** brings together many different peoples and lands under the control of one ruler. The person who rules is called an **emperor**.

Sumerian Ruins
Doorways are visible in these ruins of the once important Sumerian city of Uruk. ▼

113

Terms & Names

empire a collection of many peoples and lands under the control of one ruler

emperor the ruler of an empire

Fertile Crescent a region that stretches from the Mediterranean Sea to the Persian Gulf

Hammurabi the ruler of the Babylonian Empire from 1792 to 1750 B.C.

code of law a set of written rules

justice fair treatment of people

❸ Teach

The First Empire Builders
(6.2.2, HI 1)

Talk About It

• **Critical Thinking: Finding Main Ideas** How did the formation of empires encourage trade? *(it was safer and easier to move goods)*

California Resources

California Reading Toolkit, L11
California Modified Lesson Plans for English Learners, p. 25
California Daily Standards Practice Transparencies, TT11
California Standards Enrichment Workbook, pp. 21–22, 27–28
California Online Test Practice
California Test Generator CD-ROM
California Standards Planner and Lesson Plans, L21
California EasyPlanner CD-ROM
California eEdition CD-ROM

LESSON 1 PROGRAM RESOURCES

ON LEVEL
In-Depth Resources: Unit 2
• Family Newsletter (English and Spanish), pp. 19–20
• Reading Skill: Summarizing, p. 21
• Vocabulary Study Guide, p. 26
• Vocabulary Cards, p. 27
• Skillbuilder Practice, Making Decisions, p. 25

Formal Assessment
• Lesson Quiz, p. 58

ENGLISH LEARNERS
In-Depth Resources in Spanish
• Reading Skill: Summarizing, p. 27
• Skillbuilder Practice, p. 31

Modified Lesson Plans for English Learners, p. 25
Reading Study Guide (Spanish), p. 31
Reading Study Guide Audio CD (Spanish)

STRUGGLING READERS
In-Depth Resources: Unit 2
• Reading Skill: Summarizing, p. 21
• Vocabulary Study Guide, p. 26
• Vocabulary Cards, p. 27
• Reteaching Activity, p. 33
Reading Toolkit, L11
Reading Study Guide, p. 31

Reading Study Guide Audio CD

GIFTED AND TALENTED STUDENTS
In-Depth Resources,: Unit 2
• Primary Source: from the Code of Hammurabi, p. 31

Interdisciplinary Projects
• Math, p. 19
• Language Arts, p. 21

INCLUSION
EasyPlanner CD-ROM
• Reading Skill: Summarizing
• Vocabulary Study Guide
• Reteaching Activity

TECHNOLOGY
eEdition CD-ROM
• Starting with a Story
Power Presentations CD-ROM
Map Transparencies
• MT7 The Babylonian Empire

Critical Thinking Transparencies
• CT14 Summarizing

Test Generator CD-ROM

ClassZone.com

In-Depth Resources: Unit 2
• Reading Skill: Summarizing, p. 21

More About . . .

Sargon of Akkad
Sargon was a real person, but much of what we know of him today is actually legend. According to this legend, Sargon was abandoned as an infant and set adrift in a basket on the Euphrates River. He was rescued and, with the help of the goddess Ishtar, rose to build his great empire. After rising to power, he built the city after which his empire is named.

Teach

The Babylonian Empire

HI 1

Talk About It

• What eventually happened to the Akkadian empire? *(It fell apart due to attacks from outside and fighting among the city-states within the empire.)*

• Why did Hammurabi need other people to help him control the lands and keep order? *(Possible answer: The Babylonian Empire extended across too large an area for him to control on his own.)*

• **Critical Thinking: Making Generalizations** How would you characterize the leadership of Hammurabi? *(Possible answer: Hammurabi was well organized and he was involved in many aspects of Babylonian life.)*

 Map Transparencies
• MT7 The Babylonian Empire

The Akkadian Empire Sargon's empire was called the Akkadian Empire. Eventually, Sargon ruled over lands that stretched in a curve from the Mediterranean Sea through Mesopotamia to the Persian Gulf. This region is called the **Fertile Crescent** (see map on page 109). Unlike the dry region around it, the Fertile Crescent had rich soil and water that made the area good for farming.

Sargon's conquests helped to spread Akkadian ideas and ways of life. One of the most important ideas shared in the empire was the Akkadian system of writing.

The creation of an empire is a pattern that repeats in history. Empires are important because they change the way people live. They may bring peace to the peoples there. They encourage trade, which makes more goods available. Empires often include people from several cultures. The ideas, technology, and customs of the different peoples may be shared by all.

REVIEW How do empires change the lives of people who live in them?
Their lands may be more peaceful and goods more plentiful, and ideas and customs are shared with others.

The Babylonian Empire

2 **ESSENTIAL QUESTION** Which empires ruled the Fertile Crescent?
the Akkadian and Babylonian empires
The empire of Akkad lasted for about 200 years. It fell apart because of attacks by outside peoples. Fighting also took place among city-states within the empire.

Babylonians Expand About 2000 B.C., people known as the Amorites began to invade and take control of the city-states of Sumer. They chose the city of Babylon, which was located on the Euphrates River, for their capital.

From 1792 to 1750 B.C., a powerful Amorite king named **Hammurabi** (HAM•uh•RAH•bee) ruled the Babylonian Empire. Hammurabi expanded control over many city-states. Soon, his empire stretched across Mesopotamia and other parts of the Fertile Crescent.

Hammurabi used governors to help him control the lands. He sent out people to collect tax money and appointed judges to help keep order. Hammurabi also watched over agriculture, irrigation, trade, and the construction of buildings.

REVIEW How did Hammurabi control his huge empire?
Hammurabi used governors to help him control the lands, sent out people to collect tax money, and appointed judges to help keep order.

▲ **Statue of Hammurabi**
This statue from about 1760 B.C. shows Hammurabi praying.

DIFFERENTIATING INSTRUCTION

English Learners

Frame Historical Questions
Model how to identify important details from the text to formulate, ask, and respond to questions. Use any of the following question forms: Who? What? When? Where? Why? Have students work with a partner to practice formulating, asking and responding to questions about the lesson.

Inclusion

Use Sticky Notes
As students read the lesson, have them use sticky notes to mark words, sentences, or paragraphs that they have difficulty understanding. When they're done reading, have students work in small groups and help each other clarify information in the lesson. As questions are answered, students can remove the sticky notes until none remain.

Hammurabi's Law Code

❸ ESSENTIAL QUESTION Why did Hammurabi create a law code?
to control people in the empire

Hammurabi ruled a vast empire of many peoples with different ideas, ways of life, and sets of laws. He needed a set of rules that all his people could obey.

A Code of Laws Hammurabi believed a **code of law** would help to control the empire. A code of law is a set of written rules for people to obey. He sent out people to collect the existing rules. After studying these rules, Hammurabi put together a single code of law. The code, written in cuneiform, was displayed on huge pillars near a temple.

Justice for All The code's goal was to bring **justice**, fair treatment of people, to the people. In addition to identifying acts of wrongdoing, the code gave rights to people living in the land. Even women and children had rights, which was not the case in many ancient cultures. Punishments were different for each social class. (See Primary Source below.)

Primary Source

Background: Hammurabi's Code is sometimes called the "eye for an eye" code. It included 282 laws covering business, property, and conduct toward other people. The laws help us understand what was important to the people in Hammurabi's empire.

This scene is from the upper section of a pillar with the law code of Hammurabi. The laws were written on the lower section so that people could see them. ▶

from *Code of Hammurabi*
Translated by L. W. King

195. If a son strike his father, his hands shall be hewn [cut off].
196. If a man put out the eye of another man, his eye shall be put out.
197. If a man break another man's bone, his bone shall be broken.
202. If any one strike the body of a man higher in rank than he, he shall receive sixty blows with an ox-whip in public.
204. If a freed man strike the body of another freed man, he shall pay ten shekels in money.
205. If the slave of a freed man strike the body of a freed man, his ear shall be cut off.

DOCUMENT–BASED QUESTION
What do the laws tell you about justice at the time?

DIFFERENTIATING INSTRUCTION

Gifted and Talented Students

Hold a Debate
Divide students into two teams to hold a debate. The first team should support the position "Laws are necessary for the protection of individuals and society." The second team should support an opposing position "Laws are not necessary for the protection of individuals and society." Give each team time to discuss its position and to develop its arguments. Each team should also choose 1–3 people to present its arguments.

Struggling Readers

Discuss Key Vocabulary Words
Have students form small groups to talk about some of the complex words on pages 115 and 116. Allow students to work together to explore the words *justice* and *legacy*. Have student groups write two sentences that demonstrate their understanding of these terms.

Teach

Hammurabi's Law Code

 6.2.4

Talk About It

- From what was Hammurabi's code of law created? *(the existing rules of the different peoples in his empire)*
- Why would Hammurabi care about the rights of women and children? *(to protect them)*
- Why would Hammurabi want to replace the use of personal revenge to solve problems? *(Possible answer: Personal revenge was an unfair and often brutal way to solve problems.)*
- **Critical Thinking: Summarizing** Write a sentence summarizing Hammurabi's legacy. *(Possible answer: He established the notion that society should be ruled by laws and that the laws should apply to all people, not just a few.)*

📝 **In-Depth Resources: Unit 2**
- Skillbuilder Practice: Making Decisions, p. 25
- Primary Source: from the Code of Hammurabi, p. 31

Interpreting Primary Sources

Code of Hammurabi
- Why do you think Hammurabi's Code is referred to as the "eye-for-an-eye" code? *(Some of the laws follow the pattern of an eye for an eye—that is, the idea of punishment for a crime resembling the nature of the crime itself.)*
- What do these specific laws tell you about the issues that concerned people during Hammurabi's reign? *(Possible answer: People were probably concerned about personal safety and well being.)*

DOCUMENT–BASED QUESTION ANSWER

People were considered unequal in Babylonian society. Punishments were harsher for people of lower rank, especially slaves.

❹ Assess & Reteach

Assess Divide students into small groups and have them answer the questions. Then ask groups to take turns presenting answers to the class. Discuss whether any groups answered questions differently.

 Formal Assessment
• Lesson Quiz, p. 58

Reteach Have each student use the lesson title and its headings and subheadings to create an outline of the content of this lesson. Beneath each subheading, list details that support the ideas listed.

 In-Depth Resources: Unit 2
• Vocabulary Cards, p. 27
• Reteaching Activity, p. 33

 Homework Helper

Visit **Classzone.com** for a lesson review, a flip-card activity, and links to related Web sites.

Hammurabi's Legacy The code established the idea that the government should provide protection and justice for the people. Hammurabi wanted to replace the belief in personal revenge as a way of solving problems. Hammurabi's Code set out the belief that society should be run by the rule of law. That means the law should be applied to all people, not just a few. By placing the laws on pillars where they could be seen, it also suggests everyone has a right to know the laws and the punishments for breaking them.

REVIEW What was the purpose of Hammurabi's Code?

to make the government responsible for protection and justice and to create a rule of law in society

Lesson Summary
• Sargon of Akkad built an empire of many different peoples under one ruler and one government.
• Hammurabi expanded the Babylonian Empire and brought its peoples together by wise government.
• Hammurabi created a single code of law that set up well-defined rules of treatment for all.

Why It Matters Now . . .
Hammurabi's Code established the idea that rule of law is an important part of society. Rule of law that guarantees fair treatment is practiced in most countries today.

1 Lesson Review

Homework Helper
ClassZone.com

Terms & Names
1. Explain the importance of

empire	Fertile Crescent	code of law
emperor	Hammurabi	justice

Using Your Notes
Summarizing Use your completed chart to answer the following question:
2. How does a strong king become an emperor? (HI 1)

Topic	Statement
Geography	
A strong king	
A law code	

Main Ideas
3. Which empires gained control of the Fertile Crescent? (6.2.1)
4. Why did Hammurabi think his empire needed a single code of law? (6.2.4)
5. What basic ideas about the law did Hammurabi's Code set up? (6.2.4)

Critical Thinking
6. **Making Inferences** How did the geography of Mesopotamia affect the history of the region? (HI 1)
7. **Drawing Conclusions** Why is the development of Hammurabi's Code an important landmark in the growth of civilization? (6.2.4)

Activity

Creating a Code of Law Develop a code of law for use in your classroom. Include penalties for failing to meet the rules. Have classmates compare your list with theirs. (6.2.4)

116 • Chapter 4

---

1 Lesson Review Answers

Terms & Names
1. • empire, p. 113
 • emperor, p. 113
 • Fertile Crescent, p. 114
 • Hammurabi, p. 114
 • code of law, p. 115
 • justice, p. 115

Using Your Notes
See page 112 for an example of a completed chart.
2. To become an emperor, a king must conquer lands outside his own and control them with a single government.

Main Ideas
3. the Akkadian Empire and the Babylonian Empire
4. He ruled many lands with many different peoples, and he wanted to gain control of the lands by making his subjects feel they were being treated fairly.
5. The code set up the idea that the government was responsible for what happens in society and that society should be run by rule of law.

Critical Thinking
6. Possible answer: The land was very flat. This feature of geography made the city-states easy to invade by conquerors like Sargon.
7. Rule of law allows a civilization to regulate its citizens in a fair manner and eliminates belief in personal revenge.

Activity Rubric

	Development of Law Code	Penalties
4	logical, consistent, fair	clearly stated, appropriate
3	fair	reasonable
2	some unfair	harsh or unclear
1	unfair or too few rules	missing or confusing

Build a Monument

Goal: To evaluate the reign of Hammurabi and to create a monument detailing his accomplishments

Prepare

1. Research the reign of Hammurabi. Make a list of his accomplishments.

2. Reread the information on Hammurabi on pages 114–116 in this chapter.

3. Research existing monuments to U.S. presidents or other world leaders.

Do the Activity

1. Look at your list of Hammurabi's achievements. Decide which are the most impressive and should be listed on the monument.

2. Brainstorm how you might show the achievements of Hammurabi visually.

3. Sketch a suitable monument for Hammurabi.

4. Transfer your drawing to construction paper. Cut it out and tape it together.

Follow-Up

1. Which of Hammurabi's accomplishments did you select? Why?

2. Why do people erect monuments to leaders?

Extension

Design Contest Have a design contest with others in your class to select the most appropriate design for Hammurabi's monument.

CALIFORNIA STANDARDS
6.2.4 Know the significance of Hammurabi's Code.

Materials & Supplies

- gray or tan construction paper
- markers
- scissors asnd tape
- ruler

Optional: books on Babylonia, Hammurabi, and U.S. presidential monuments

117

ACTIVITY: BUILD A MONUMENT

Objectives

- Describe key accomplishments of the reign of Hammurabi and create a model of a monument to him based on monuments that exist today.

- **Language Objective:** Write a descriptive paragraph on the accomplishments of Hammurabi.

Suggestions for Completing the Activity

- Encourage students to find more information about Hammurabi and about monuments using library books and the Internet.

- Suggest students consider monuments found in Washington, D.C., as a starting point. Examples include the Washington Monument, Jefferson Memorial, and Lincoln Memorial.

- Discuss with students how monuments celebrate the achievements of people visually.

- Remind students to follow each step of the activity.

ACTIVITY ANSWERS

Follow-Up Answers

1. Students may select different accomplishments, but many will name his code of laws.
2. Possible answers: to honor them, to celebrate their achievements, to help later generations remember them

Extension Rubric

	Design of Monument	Effort on Model
4	worthy of a great leader	carefully done
3	good	adequate
2	average	needs work
1	unimpressive	poorly done

❶ Plan & Prepare

Objectives

- Describe the rise and fall of the Assyrian Empire in the Fertile Crescent.
- Describe Assyrian innovations in building and ruling an empire.
- Trace the rise and fall of the Assyrian Empire's successor—the Chaldean Empire.
- **Language Objective:** Compare and contrast details of selected people, characters, events, and ideas.

Quick Look

Lesson 2 explores the rise and fall of two additional empires of the Fertile Crescent—the Assyrian Empire and the Chaldean Empire.

❷ Focus & Motivate

Preview Tell students that this lesson will continue its exploration into the growth of large empires in the Fertile Crescent. Ask students to compare these new empires with those that came before.

Introduce the Main Ideas The three main ideas relate to the big idea that "Governments create law codes and political bodies to organize a society." Help students look for this Big Idea as you go through the lesson.

Reading Skill: Understanding Cause and Effect Tell students that every cause has an effect, and that effects can themselves be causes of other effects.

SAMPLE ANSWERS FOR CHART

Causes	Effects
Assyrian military machine	built a huge empire
Cruelty to captured peoples	made enemies who, in turn, united against them
Huge empires	developed new methods of government

Lesson 2

▶ MAIN IDEAS

❶ Science and Technology Assyria built a military machine that was greatly feared by others in the region.

❷ Government Assyria used several different methods to control its empire.

❸ Government The Chaldeans replaced the Assyrians as the main power in Mesopotamia and other parts of the Fertile Crescent.

▶ TAKING NOTES

Reading Skill:
Understanding Cause and Effect

Finding causes and effects will help you understand the events in Lesson 2. Look for the effect of each cause listed in the chart. Fill in the effects on a chart of your own.

Causes	Effects
Assyrian military machine	
Cruelty to captured peoples	
Huge empires	

Ⓢ Skillbuilder Handbook, page R26

▲ **Jeweled Pendant** This ornament for a necklace is made from gold and precious stones. It shows a sacred palm tree.

CALIFORNIA STANDARDS

6.2 Students analyze the geographic, political, economic, religious, and social structures of the early civilizations of Mesopotamia, Egypt, and Kush.

6.3.4 Discuss the locations of the settlements and movements of Hebrew peoples, including the Exodus and their movement to and from Egypt, and outline the significance of the Exodus to the Jewish and other people.

HI 2 Students understand and distinguish cause, effect, sequence, and correlation in historical events, including long- and short-term causal relations.

HOW TO TEACH THE CALIFORNIA STANDARDS

Standard	Content	Student Question or Activity	Instruction
6.2	**Pages 120–122** Describe the political and social structure of two Mesopotamian civilizations	**Page 123** Students compare various aspects of the Assyrian and Chaldean empires.	Explain that history often repeats itself. As they read the lesson, have students look for ways that the Chaldeans followed in the footsteps of the Assyrians.
6.3.4	**Page 122** Addresses an important episode in the history of the Hebrew people	**Page 123** Students explain what happened to the Hebrews when they rebelled against the Chaldeans.	After reading, ask students to write a paragraph describing how they would have felt if they had been a Hebrew, and they had just learned that their sacred temple in Jerusalem had been destroyed because of the rebellion.
HI 2	**Page 120** Describes the steps Assyria took to govern its conquered lands	**Page 123** Students list the causes for Assyria's improvements in government.	Ask students to debate which method of rule would earn more obedience from its subjects: cruel and harsh or tolerant and fair. Have students debate both sides of the issue.

Assyria Rules the Fertile Crescent

TERMS & NAMES

exile

tribute

Hanging Gardens of Babylon

Terms & Names

exile forced removal from one's homeland

tribute money paid to a conquering ruler for protection

Hanging Gardens of Babylon magnificent structure of gardens built in Babylon by Nebuchadnezzar

Build on What You Know In the last lesson, you learned that early empires in Mesopotamia conquered land that stretched into the Fertile Crescent. These empires needed strong armies and wise leaders to hold them together. When the Babylonian Empire fell, another took its place—Assyria.

A Mighty Military Machine

1 ESSENTIAL QUESTION How was Assyria able to build an empire?
They used a powerful military.
Assyria was located in northern Mesopotamia, an area of rolling hills. To protect their lands, the rulers built a powerful army and set out to control the neighboring lands. The Assyrian army proved they were second to none.

A Powerful Army The Assyrians fought fiercely on foot, on horseback, and with chariots. Assyrian soldiers used the latest inventions for war. They carried iron swords and iron-tipped spears. Few of their enemies had iron weapons. The Assyrians attacked city walls with battering rams. They used ladders to scale the walls of cities. They even dug tunnels under city walls to get soldiers inside.

Once inside the city, they slaughtered the inhabitants. One Assyrian king boasted that he had destroyed 89 cities, 820 villages, and had burned the city of Babylon. As a result, the Assyrians were greatly feared by other peoples.

Stone Carving Assyrian warriors attack the walls and burn a neighboring city. ▼

119

❸ Teach

A Mighty Military Machine

◣ **6.2, HI 2**

Talk About It

- **Critical Thinking: Understanding Cause and Effect** How do you think others felt about Assyrians as a result of their harsh treatment of conquered people? (*Possible answers: They were feared; people wanted to see them conquered.*)]

California Resources

California Reading Toolkit, L12
California Modified Lesson Plans for English Learners, p. 27
California Daily Standards Practice Transparencies, TT12
California Standards Enrichment Workbook, pp. 45–46
California Online Test Practice
California Test Generator CD-ROM
California Standards Planner and Lesson Plans, L23
California EasyPlanner CD-ROM
California eEdition CD-ROM

LESSON 2 PROGRAM RESOURCES

ON LEVEL

In-Depth Resources: Unit 2
- Reading Skill: Understanding Cause and Effect, p. 22
- Vocabulary Cards, p. 27

Formal Assessment
- Lesson Quiz, p. 59

ENGLISH LEARNERS

In-Depth Resources in Spanish
- Reading Skill: Understanding Cause and Effect, p. 28

Modified Lesson Plans for English Learners, p. 27

Reading Study Guide (Spanish), p. 33

Reading Study Guide Audio CD (Spanish)

STRUGGLING READERS

In-Depth Resources: Unit 2
- Reading Skill: Understanding Cause and Effect, p. 22
- Vocabulary Cards, p. 27
- Reteaching Activity, p. 34

Reading Toolkit, L12

Reading Study Guide, p. 33

Reading Study Guide Audio CD

GIFTED AND TALENTED STUDENTS

Interdisciplinary Projects
- Art, p. 22

INCLUSION

EasyPlanner CD-ROM
- Reading Skill: Understanding Cause and Effect
- Vocabulary Study Guide
- Reteaching Activity

TECHNOLOGY

eEdition CD-ROM

Power Presentations CD-ROM

Humanities Transparencies
- HT7 Cylinder Seals from Assyria

Critical Thinking Transparencies
- CT15 Understanding Cause and Effect

Test Generator CD-ROM

ClassZone.com

In-Depth Resources: Unit 2
* Reading Skill: Understanding Cause and Effect, p. 22

Teach

Assyria Builds a Huge Empire

6.2, HI 1

Talk About It

* Why did the Assyrian Empire need special systems of organization? *(The empire was huge in size, making efficient organization a critical issue.)*

* **Critical Thinking: Compare and Contrast** Compare the intended purpose of the Assyrian method of ruling with the actual effects of this method. *(Possible answer: The Assyrians hoped to rule by power and fear, but in fact their methods inspired resentment and caused their subjects to unite against them.)*

Humanities Transparencies
* HT7 Cylinder Seals from Assyria

History from Visuals

Interpreting Maps
Have students identify the Tigris and Euphrates rivers, so they can see how the extent of the Assyrian Empire compares to the territory of earlier Mesopotamian empires.

* What was the most distant land that the Assyrians conquered? *(Egypt)*

* What geographic features formed the western and northern boundaries of the Assyrian Empire? *(Zagras and Taurus mountains)*

Extension Ask students if they think the empire would have expanded south. *(Possible answer: No, the Arabian peninsula is covered by desert.)*

GEOGRAPHY SKILLBUILDER ANSWER

The Nile, the Euphrates, and the Tigris

Harsh Treatment of Captured People The Assyrians were cruel to the peoples they defeated. Enemies who surrendered were allowed to choose a leader. But those who refused to submit to Assyrian control were taken captive. The Assyrians killed or made slaves of captives. They speared enemy leaders and burned their cities. They sent captured peoples into **exile**. This means that they forced people to move from their homelands to other lands, often far away.

> **REVIEW** Why were the Assyrians feared by their enemies?
> The Assyrians were ferocious fighters and cruel to the people they captured.

Assyria Builds a Huge Empire

2 ESSENTIAL QUESTION How did Assyria control its empire?

Between 850 and 650 B.C., the Assyrians conquered many lands. They added Syria, Babylonia, Egypt, and Palestine to the empire. Assyria reached its peak of power under the rule of Ashurbanipal (AH•shur•BAH•nuh•PAHL) from 668 to 627 B.C. Under his leadership, the Assyrians controlled almost all of the Fertile Crescent.

A Huge Empire The Assyrian Empire grew so large that it needed to be very well organized. The Assyrians governed the conquered lands by choosing a governor or native king from that land to rule under their direction. The Assyrians provided the army that protected all of the lands.

Each ruler in a conquered land had to send **tribute** to the Assyrian emperor. This meant that the ruler had to pay for the protection given by the Assyrian army. Tribute brought money and goods into the empire's treasury. If any ruler failed to pay tribute, the army destroyed cities in that land. People of the land were forced into exile.

Assyrians chose a local governor or king to rule under their direction and provided an army to protect the land.

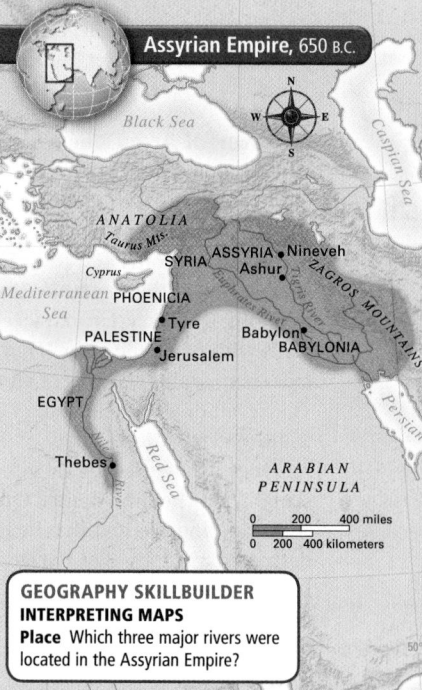

Assyrian Empire, 650 B.C.

Black Sea
ANATOLIA
Taurus Mts.
Cyprus
SYRIA   ASSYRIA • Nineveh
Ashur
Mediterranean PHOENICIA
Sea   • Tyre
PALESTINE   Babylon•
• Jerusalem   BABYLONIA
EGYPT
Thebes•   ARABIAN
Red Sea   PENINSULA
Caspian Sea
ZAGROS MOUNTAINS
Persian Gulf

0   200   400 miles
0   200   400 kilometers

GEOGRAPHY SKILLBUILDER
INTERPRETING MAPS
Place Which three major rivers were located in the Assyrian Empire?

DIFFERENTIATING INSTRUCTION

English Learners

Compare and Contrast
Tell students often the word *both* is used to compare two things that are similar. When they find two things are different the word *but* is used to contrast two things. Using details about the Assyrian Empire and the Babylonian Empire model a comparing and a contrasting statement. Have students make their own comparing and contrasting statements using *but* or *both*.

Inclusion

Prepare Enlarged Photocopies
For students who are visually impaired, prepare enlarged photocopies of the lesson and have students follow along with the text while listening to the lesson on the audio CD.

History Makers

Ashurbanipal (c. 668–627 B.C.)

Ashurbanipal, an Assyrian king, sent people to find and bring back copies of writings from throughout the empire. His collection contained over 20,000 cuneiform tablets. The collection included dictionaries, myths, and stories. He kept writings on special subjects such as science, geography, medicine, and religion. He even had some reports by spies.

Ashurbanipal set up a huge library in the capital at Nineveh (shown at the left). The library organized the collected texts by subject, like books in a modern library. However, Nineveh's enemies leveled the library. When archaeologists dug up the library's ruins, they found tablets. The tablets became the main source of information about ancient Mesopotamia.

◀ This is an artist's idea of what the library in Nineveh looked like.

The Assyrians made many enemies by their cruel actions. The leaders worried that exiled peoples might try to gather a force strong enough to defeat the Assyrians. They were right. The Assyrians had to put down many revolts.

Assyria Crumbles In 609 B.C., the Assyrian Empire fell. Two of its enemies, the Medes (meedz) and the Chaldeans (kal•DEE•uhnz), joined forces to defeat the Assyrians. These forces completely destroyed the city of Nineveh by burning it to the ground. For centuries afterward, only mounds of earth marked the location of the once great capital.

REVIEW Why did the Assyrians receive tribute?
The Assyrian army protected all the lands in the empire.

A New Babylonian Empire

3 **ESSENTIAL QUESTION** Who replaced the Assyrian Empire? Chaldeans, or New Babylonians

In time, Assyria's neighbors, the Chaldeans, ruled much of the former Assyrian empire. The city of Babylon became the capital of the Chaldeans' new empire. Remember that Babylon was the capital of the first Babylonian empire. Sometimes the Chaldeans are called the New Babylonians.

Early Empires • 121

History Makers

Ashurbanipal

The Assyrian Empire was one of great military might, and its emperors achieved power by being great warriors. However, Ashurbanipal was different in the ranks of Assyrian rulers, in that he was also a scholar. It was not a requirement that Assyrian kings know how to read and write, and Ashurbanipal's skill in this area was unusual. Linked to this skill was great curiosity. His great collection of texts is a major source of present-day knowledge of Assyria.

Teach

A New Babylonian Empire

◥ **6.2, 6.3.4, HI 1**

Talk About It

- Which people took power from the Assyrians? *(the Chaldeans)*

- What city did the Chaldeans choose as their capital? *(Babylon)*

- Why would Nebuchadnezzar rebuild the city in the way he did? *(to reflect the glory of his reign)*

- **Critical Thinking: Understanding Cause and Effect** In what way do you think religious conflict enabled the defeat of the Chaldeans? *(Possible answers: A Chaldean leader tried to replace a popular god. This made people upset and less willing to support their leader militarily. This left the empire vulnerable to attack.)*

DIFFERENTIATING INSTRUCTION

Gifted and Talented Students

Report on Mesopotamian Antiquities
Tell students that many Mesopotamian artifacts and records, such as those of Ashurbanipal's library, were, until recently, under the control of officials of Saddam Hussein's Iraqi regime. Have students use library and Internet sources to write a brief report on the effects of the Iraqi war and the ousting of Hussein on these ancient treasures.

Struggling Readers

Create a Sequence
Have students work in small groups to read through this section and create a sequence chart about the rise and fall of different empires. Have the group create a series of four boxes on a sheet of paper. Then, starting at the beginning of the lesson, write down the names of the ruling empires in the order they occur.

More About . . .

Nebuchadnezzar

Like Ashurbanipal, Nebuchadnezzar was an emperor who, though skilled in war, was known for something other than military might. Nebuchadnezzar's legacy is his vast building program. His long reign of more than 40 years features many great building projects in Babylon and beyond. In addition to the accomplishments mentioned in the text, he built a bridge over, and a tunnel under, the Euphrates River. He also built a wall between the Euphrates and the Tigris to help protect the city from attack from the north. Much of what is known of the great king comes from the Old Testament of the Bible.

More About . . .

The Ishtar Gate

German archaeologists excavated the ruins of the Ishtar Gate in the early 1900s. Through painstaking effort, experts were able to piece together the broken bricks and rebuild a portion of the spectacular structure. The part shown here is from the processional wall. It can be seen at the Pergamon Museum in Berlin, Germany. There is also a reproduction of the Ishtar Gate in modern-day Babylon, Iraq.

Chaldeans Take Assyrian Lands The Chaldean Empire reached its peak between 605 and 562 B.C. The Chaldeans were led by Nebuchadnezzar II (NEHB•uh•kuhd•NEHZ•uhr) who drove the Egyptians out of Syria and captured trading cities on the Mediterranean coast.

Like the Assyrians, the Chaldeans faced revolts by captured people. The Hebrews, a group of people living in lands near the Mediterranean Sea coast, rebelled in 598 B.C. Nebuchadnezzar seized Jerusalem, which was the capital city of the Hebrews. The Hebrews' sacred temple there was destroyed. The Chaldeans held thousands of Hebrews captive in Babylon for about 50 years.

Height of Wealth and Power Nebuchadnezzar rebuilt the city of Babylon and constructed the huge, colorful Ishtar Gate. Processions into the city went through this gate. An enormous ziggurat called the Tower of Babel loomed 300 feet above the city. Chaldean astronomers used the tower to study the skies. It is said that to please his wife, Nebuchadnezzar built an artificial mountain covered with trees and plants. It was called the **Hanging Gardens of Babylon**. The gardens were built in such a way that they appeared to float above the ground. They became one of the Seven Wonders of the World. (See the Reader's Theater, pages 124–127.)

Processional Way A portion of the walls leading to Ishtar Gate in Babylon features lions that were symbols of the goddess Ishtar. ▼

INTERDISCIPLINARY ACTIVITIES

Language Arts

Write Interview Questions
Ask students to pretend that they are given the opportunity to interview Nebuchadnezzar about his empire and his accomplishments. Have students write five interview questions for the great king. Then have students write pretend answers from Nebuchadnezzar.

Art

Design a Wall
The Ishtar Gate included the symbols that represented important Babylonian gods. Have students work together to design their own wall and gate for your school. The wall and gate should feature symbols that are meaningful to the students and staff. Have students draw a picture of their wall, along with an explanation of the meaning of each symbol they include.

The Empire Fades Weak rulers followed Nebuchadnezzar II. In addition to the weak rulers, internal conflicts about religion upset and divided the Chaldeans. This made it easy for Cyrus of Persia to conquer the land. You will learn more about Cyrus in the next lesson.

REVIEW What were some features of the Chaldean capital of Babylon? the famous Ishtar gate, a huge ziggurat, and the Hanging Gardens

▲ **Detail from the Ishtar Gate** This is one of the mythical dragons found on the Ishtar Gate. The dragons were believed to dwell in ancient Babylon.

Lesson Summary

- The Assyrian military used new kinds of weapons and ways of fighting. The military was very cruel to captured peoples.
- The Assyrians' highly organized government controlled the conquered lands.
- The Chaldeans conquered Assyrian lands. Their empire reached its peak under Nebuchadnezzar II.

Why It Matters Now . . .

The Assyrian Empire showed that to control large areas of land with many people, an empire must have a highly organized government and a strong military.

2 Lesson Review

Homework Helper ClassZone.com

Terms & Names

1. Explain the importance of

    exile   tribute   Hanging Gardens of Babylon

Using Your Notes

Understanding Cause and Effect Use your completed chart to answer the following question:

2. What caused Assyria to improve its methods of government? (HI 2)

Causes	Effects
Assyrian military machine	
Cruelty to captured peoples	
Huge empires	

Main Ideas

3. What tactics did the Assyrians use to defeat their enemies? (6.2)

4. How did the Assyrians maintain control of their lands? (6.2)

5. What happened to the Hebrews when they rebelled against the Chaldeans? (6.3.4)

Critical Thinking

6. **Making Inferences** What can happen when a country follows a policy of cruelty toward captured peoples, as Assyria did? (6.2)

7. **Comparing** In what ways were the Assyrians and the Chaldeans alike? (6.2)

Activity   **Internet Activity** Use the Internet to research the wonders of Babylon under Nebuchadnezzar II. Create a guide for tourists. (6.2)
INTERNET KEYWORDS: *Babylon, Nebuchadnezzar*

Early Empires • **123**

---

4 Assess & Reteach

Assess Have students work on their own to answer the questions and then meet in groups to discuss their answers.

 Formal Assessment
- Lesson Quiz, p. 59

Reteach Have students read the three items in the Lesson Summary. Then, have them work individually to find information from the lesson to write an additional sentence that completes or adds to each summary item.

 In-Depth Resources: Unit 2
- Vocabulary Cards, p. 27
- Reteaching Activity, p. 34

Homework Helper

Visit **Classzone.com** for a lesson review, a flip-card activity, and links to related Web sites.

---

2 Lesson Review Answers

Terms & Names

1. • exile, p. 120
   • tribute, p. 120
   • Hanging Gardens of Babylon, p. 122

Using Your Notes

See page 118 for an example of a completed chart.

2. Assyria had to improve methods of government because of the size of its empire. Many captured lands and peoples required better organization for control.

Main Ideas

3. The Assyrians used the latest inventions, such as weapons made with iron. They used chariots, battering rams, and cavalry as well as foot soldiers. The Assyrians also were very cruel to captured peoples.

4. The Assyrians chose the person who ruled in each conquered land. They forced payments of tribute in return for protection by the Assyrian army.

5. They were taken into captivity, moved to Babylon, and their temple at Jerusalem was destroyed.

Critical Thinking

6. Possible answer: A country can make many enemies. Peoples sent into exile can join forces to overthrow their conqueror.

7. Possible answers: Both faced revolts by captured peoples; both destroyed cities and placed captured people in exile.

Activity Rubric

	Level of Information	Guide Design
4	extensive, thorough	colorful, exciting layout
3	good detail	appealing with some illustrations
2	some detail	adequate
1	little or no detail	poorly done; few or no illustrations

Early Empires • **123**

Objectives

- Explore aspects of the building of the Hanging Gardens of Babylon
- **Language Objective:** Compare and contrast details of selected people, characters, events, and ideas.

❶ Focus & Motivate

Connect to the Big Idea

Science and Technology As civilizations grew and expanded, they faced new challenges. They met these challenges in part by developing new inventions.

Connect to Prior Knowledge

Have students recall what they learned in Lesson 2 about Nebuchadnezzar and his reign as emperor. *(Nebuchadnezzar was well known for building magnificent structures, such as the Ishtar Gate.)*

THE HANGING GARDENS OF BABYLON

Background: The year is 580 B.C. The place: Babylon, an ancient city in what is now Iraq. The ruler, Nebuchadnezzar II, is currently the most powerful king in the region. To strengthen his power, he has married Amytis, a princess from a land called Media, which was located in present-day Iran.

CAST OF CHARACTERS

Amytis: (uh•MIH•tuhs) queen and wife of Nebuchadnezzar II

Merodach: (mih•ROH•DAK) the royal architect

Sammu: slave to the royal family

Essam: the royal engineer

Nebuchadnezzar II: (NEHB•uh•kuhd•NEHZ•uhr) King of the Chaldeans

Narrator

CALIFORNIA STANDARDS
6.2 Students analyze the geographic, political, economic, religious, and social structures of the early civilizations of Mesopotamia, Egypt, and Kush.

ADDITIONAL RESOURCES

Books for the Student

Cox, Reg and Neil Morris. *The Seven Wonders of the Ancient World.* Parsippany: Silver Burdett Press, 1996. Examines the great architectural achievements of the past, including the Hanging Gardens of Babylon.

Curlee, Lynn. *The Seven Wonders of the Ancient World.* New York: Atheneum, 2002. Text and illustrations explore the Seven Wonders of the World, which include the Hanging Gardens of Babylon.

Videos

The Seven Wonders of the World, Volume 2: Wonders of the East. 95 minutes. Los Angeles: Family Home Entertainment, 1999. Video tour of the ancient wonders of the world.

DVDs

The Seven Wonders of the Ancient World. 60 minutes. London: Atlantic Productions, 2002. Exploration of the seven wonders of the world.

Amytis: Sammu, did you bring my palm oil? My face is as dry as the desert wind in this dreadful land!

Sammu: Right here, my queen.

Narrator: Amytis has been very unhappy since King Nebuchadnezzar brought her from Media. She is a Median princess, and the king married her to help keep peace between the two lands. But Amytis is so miserable. If she insists on returning to Media, her father will not be pleased. Look, here come the king and the queen.

Amytis: You said that I would live in a paradise as your wife. But I think I left paradise when I left Media.

Nebuchadnezzar: But my queen, Babylon is one of the largest and most beautiful cities in the world. Look at the great city walls, the Tower of Babel, the paved boulevards.

Amytis: In the Median mountains where I lived, the breezes were comfortable. The trees provided cool shade and sweet fruit. It's so hot and dusty here. It's nothing like my beautiful Media!

Narrator: Nebuchadnezzar knew that he must please Amytis to keep peace with her father in Media. He hurries to speak with her.

Nebuchadnezzar: My sweet, what if I give you what you desire? Cool gardens, green trees, flowers, and clear water right here in Babylon. Will you stay?

Amytis: Of course. But how can you do that?

Nebuchadnezzar: (*boasting*) I am the most powerful king the world has known. I will find a way. Sammu, fetch my royal architect and engineer.

Sammu: Yes, my king.

Nebuchadnezzar: Merodach, I charge you to create a spectacular mountain garden, right here on the palace grounds. It must have trees and flowers and clear running water. Essam, you will take the plans and figure out how to make this work. Do you both understand?

Merodach and Essam: Yes, my king. It will be done.

Narrator: Months later the king, the royal architect, and the royal engineer go over the architect's plans.

(continued)

---

❷ Teach

Talk About It

- Assign students the roles in the play and have them practice the play before reading it aloud to the class.

- Encourage students to read and perform the play in a dramatic fashion.

- As an option, you may want to assign other students roles in production. These can include directing the performance, videotaping it, creating sets and costumes, and so on.

- Why did Nebuchadnezzar decide to propose the building of the gardens? *(to help satisfy his homesick wife)*

- **Critical Thinking: Making Inferences** What can you infer from the fact that Nebuchadnezzar is so anxious to preserve peace with Amytis's father? *(Possible answer: Amytis's father might pose a threat to Nebuchadnezzar and his empire.)*

More About . . .

Media
Media was an ancient country in West Asia that generally occupied the lands of present-day southern Azerbaijan and western Iran. The Medes ruled over Persia during Sargon's reign between 722 and 705 B.C. and captured Nineveh, the capital of Assyria, in 612 B.C. Media eventually became part of the Parthian kingdom in the second century B.C.

DIFFERENTIATING INSTRUCTION

English Learners

Preview Dialogue
Have students work in small groups to read over the dialogue to the play prior to the in-class reading. Have students identify any difficult words or phrases and use dictionaries to look them up. Students should share questions with the rest of the class.

Gifted and Talented Students

Compare Landscapes
To help build background for the play, have students use library or Internet resources to do more research on Babylon and Media. Students should create a chart that compares and contrasts the two lands on such measures as landforms, rainfall, and vegetation.

Teach

Talk About It

- How does Merodach propose to help make the garden remind Amytis of home? *(by bringing in plants native to her homeland and creating an artificial mountain)*

- How does Essam propose to overcome the lack of water in the region? *(by using a new invention called a chain pump to carry water to the top of the mountain)*

- Who will operate the chain pump? *(slaves)*

- **Critical Thinking: Comparing and Contrasting** Contrast Nebuchadnezzar's concern for his wife with his attitude toward other people. *(Possible answer: Nebuchadnezzar is willing to go to enormous expense to satisfy his wife because her father is a powerful ally, but he has no regard for the fate of slaves who will operate the garden pump.)*

Merodach: We can build a huge tower with terraces that will be filled with dirt. We will import trees that grow in our queen's Median homeland: date palms, cypress, fig, and pomegranate. Perfumed flowers too. And we can clear spaces for shaded canopies to protect our fair queen from the midday sun. Of course, we will need something to keep evil spirits away from her precious soul. I propose guarding the stairway with giant statues of winged lions that have copies of your majesty's head. The gods themselves could not offer better protection.

Nebuchadnezzar: Her own green mountain, in the midst of this desert! Amytis would love that. Remember just one thing: it rarely rains here. We can irrigate our flat farmlands from the rivers, but how will we move water uphill to keep an entire forest alive?

Essam: (*smiling*) I've designed what I call a chain pump. My system uses a large wheel at the bottom of the "mountain," and one at the top. They are connected by a chain, from which hang many buckets for water. As slaves turn the

◀ **Hanging Gardens** This is an artist's idea of what the Hanging Gardens looked like.

INTERDISCIPLINARY ACTIVITIES

Science

Diagram the Chain Pump
Have students create a diagram of the chain pump as described in this selection. The illustration should include all the parts mentioned in the text. Remind students to label the parts.

Language Arts

Write a New Scene
Have students write a new scene for this play that investigates the experiences and feelings of the slaves who operate the chain pump. The scene might explore their feelings about their plight and their reaction to the hanging garden itself.

bottom wheel, the chain dips buckets into an irrigation pool and carries them upward. At the top, the buckets dump into an upper pool with channels to carry water to every plant in the monument.

Nebuchadnezzar: Well done, both of you! Let's get started immediately.

Merodach: Your worship, these hanging gardens will probably be the most expensive building project ever. And the chain pump will need to be operated by shifts of men all day and night. It will require much gold and many slaves.

Nebuchadnezzar: Not a problem. Since I captured Jerusalem, we have a fresh supply of both gold and slaves.

Narrator: Nebuchadnezzar built his Hanging Gardens of Babylon, and they were called one of the Seven Wonders of the World. Nebuchadnezzar presented the gardens to Amytis.

Nebuchadnezzar: Amytis, my sweet, here are your new gardens. Now, perhaps, you will not want to go home to Media.

Amytis: Oh, my king! They are the most wonderful gardens ever!

Narrator: Amytis loves her human-made mountain, and spends almost all of her time

there. This has made life easier for the king. Nebuchadnezzar and Amytis enjoy relaxing in the gardens.

Amytis: Sammu, we need more pomegranates and dates in this basket. Go pick us some, then come back and fan me.

Sammu: Yes, my queen. Right away.

Amytis: My king, I think we should invite the Egyptian pharaoh for a royal visit. I want all the world to see and admire my beautiful gardens. They will be a vision of beauty for all eternity!

Narrator: Amytis was partially right. There was nothing like the Hanging Gardens of Babylon anywhere. But somewhere along the line they were destroyed, along with the Chaldean civilization. The only way you can see them now, my friends, is with your imagination.

Activities

1. **TALK ABOUT IT** What do you think might have happened to the Hanging Gardens?

2. **WRITE ABOUT IT** Write a new scene in which Amytis has a party for the Egyptian royal family to show off her Hanging Gardens of Babylon. What might guests see and do at such an elegant event? (Writing 2.4)

Teach

Talk About It

- Besides making his wife happy, why might Nebuchadnezzar want to build the gardens? *(to show how powerful he was)*

- Why does Amytis want to invite the Egyptian pharaoh for a visit? *(Amytis wants to make the pharaoh's wife jealous and spread the word of her garden.)*

- What was the fate of the Hanging Gardens of Babylon? *(They were destroyed at some point in history.)*

- **Critical Thinking: Making Inferences** What can you conclude about the power of Nebuchadnezzar based on this story? *(He was powerful and rich enough to build great monuments in the empire.)*

More About . . .

The Seven Wonders of the World
In addition to the Hanging Gardens of Babylon, there are six other wonders of the ancient world. The Pyramids of Giza, in present-day Egypt, are the only surviving wonder. They were built long before the Hanging Gardens. All of the other wonders were built after the Hanging Gardens. They include the Statue of Zeus and the Colossus of Rhodes, both in present-day Greece; the Temple of Artemis and the Mausoleum of Halicarnassus, both in present-day Turkey; and the Pharos of Alexandria, in present-day Egypt.

ACTIVITIES ANSWERS

1. **TALK ABOUT IT** Possible answers: They were destroyed by enemies; they died because they became too expensive to maintain.

2. **WRITE ABOUT IT**

2. Writing Rubric

	Description of Event	Expression in Dialogue	Use of Standard English
4	clear and concise	entertaining	consistent and correct
3	adequate	interesting	consistent
2	some details	ordinary	inconsistent
1	few details	boring	incorrect

❶ Plan & Prepare

Objectives

- Describe the rise of the Persian Empire in Asia.
- Analyze the accomplishments of Cyrus and Darius, two notable Persian leaders.
- **Language Objective:** Preview the text and retain information using SQ3R strategy.

Quick Look

Lesson 3 traces the emergence of the powerful Persian Empire under Cyrus and Darius.

❷ Focus & Motivate

Preview Tell students that this lesson will look beyond the Fertile Crescent and to the rise of a great new empire in the region—the Persian Empire. Remind students of the pattern of rises and falls among early empires.

Introduce the Main Ideas The three main ideas relate to the Big Idea "Governments create law codes and political bodies to organize a society." Help students look for this Big Idea as you go through the lesson.

Reading Skill: Identifying Issues and Problems Tell students that identifying the issues and problems facing a leader or society provides context for understanding why a leader may take certain actions.

SAMPLE ANSWERS FOR DIAGRAM

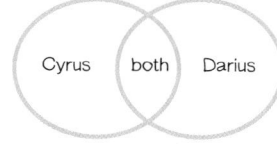

Cyrus uniting different lands under empire

both ruling over large area, diverse peoples

Darius ruling empire that was huge in size

Lesson 3

▶ **MAIN IDEAS**

❶ **Geography** Persia's location between Mesopotamia and India was a bridge between eastern and western Asia.

❷ **Government** Cyrus used a policy of toleration to control the Persian Empire.

❸ **Government** To better govern, Persia divided its lands into smaller units.

▶ **TAKING NOTES**

Reading Skill: Identifying Issues and Problems
A study of problems faced by rulers in Lesson 3 can help you understand the growth of governments. Use a Venn diagram to identify the issues and problems faced by Cyrus and Darius.

Cyrus — both — Darius

Ⓢ **Skillbuilder Handbook, page R28**

▲ **Drinking Vessel** A winged lion decorates a gold drinking vessel. Winged lions symbolizing speed and power were associated with Persia.

CALIFORNIA STANDARDS

6.3.4 Discuss the locations of the settlements and movements of Hebrew peoples, including the Exodus and their movement to and from Egypt, and outline the significance of the Exodus to the Jewish and other people.

6.4.5 Outline the founding, expansion, and political organization of the Persian Empire.

HI 3 Students explain the sources of historical continuity and how the combination of ideas and events explains the emergence of new patterns.

CST 3 Students use a variety of maps and documents to identify physical and cultural features of neighborhoods, cities, states, and countries and to explain the historical migration of people, expansion and disintegration of empires, and the growth of economic systems.

128 • Chapter 4

HOW TO TEACH THE CALIFORNIA STANDARDS

Standard	Content	Student Question or Activity	Instruction
6.3.4	Page 131 Describes the settlement of the Hebrews under Cyrus's rule	Page 133 Students describe how Cyrus treated the Hebrews.	Before reading, explain that Cyrus led swift, deadly attacks in the Mesopotamian region. Have students predict how he treated the conquered Hebrews.
6.4.5	Pages 130–132 Outlines the founding and expansion of the Persian Empire	Page 133 Students illustrate common problems Cyrus and Darius faced during their reigns.	Explain that the Persian Empire expanded to include a geographic area larger than the United States. Discuss the difficulties of governing an area so large.
HI 3	Page 131 Describes the rule of Cyrus the Great	Page 133 Students explain the impact of Cyrus's policy of toleration.	After reading, discuss how the patterns of rule changed in Mesopotamia both before and after Cyrus's rule.
CST 3	Page 130 Illustrates the Persian Empire and the route of the Royal Road	Page 130 Students list which cities were connected by the Royal Road.	Provide students with a map of the Persian Empire in 500 B.C. Have students label major Persian cities and trace the route of the Royal Road.

Persia Controls Southwest Asia

TERMS & NAMES

Anatolia

toleration

province

satrap

Royal Road

Build on What You Know In Lessons 1 and 2, you learned about empires that were built in the lands of the Fertile Crescent. To the east of these empires was the land of the Medes, which was called Media. These lands bridged east and west Asia.

A Land Between East and West

① ESSENTIAL QUESTION What was the land of the Persians like?

mountainous with fertile valleys and some high plateaus

The Medes controlled lands that included the Persians. Modern-day Iran lies on Persian land. It is marked by geographic differences.

Mountains, Deserts, and a Plateau The area Persia would control was isolated from the rest of the Fertile Crescent. Mountain ranges cut off the land from the sea and from the rest of the continent. These ranges are the Zagros, the Caucasus (KAW•kuh•sus), and the Hindu Kush. (See the map on page 130.) Most people lived at the edge of a high plateau in the middle of the region or in mountain valleys. Iron, copper, and semiprecious gems could be found in the land.

Iranian Valley
Fertile valleys still exist between the mountain ranges in the lands once known as Persia. ▼

129

Terms & Names

Anatolia land within modern-day Turkey

toleration acceptance of habits, beliefs, and practices of others

province a political division of a country

satrap a Persian governor

Royal Road a road in Persia used for government purposes

❸ Teach

Between East and West

6.4.5, 6.3.4

Talk About It

- **Critical Thinking: Explaining Geographic Patterns** How did Persia's location affect its development? *(It was often invaded but was also a trade center.)*

California Resources

California Reading Toolkit, L13

California Modified Lesson Plans for English Learners, p. 29

California Daily Standards Practice Transparencies, TT13

California Standards Enrichment Workbook, pp. 45–46, 57–58

California Online Test Practice

California Test Generator CD-ROM

California Standards Planner and Lesson Plans, L25

California EasyPlanner CD-ROM

California eEdition CD-ROM

LESSON 3 PROGRAM RESOURCES

ON LEVEL

In-Depth Resources: Unit 2
- Reading Skill: Identifying Issues and Problems, p. 23
- Vocabulary Cards, p. 27
- Geography Practice: The Royal Road, p. 29

Formal Assessment
- Lesson Quiz, p. 60

ENGLISH LEARNERS

In-Depth Resources in Spanish
- Reading Skill: Identifying Issues and Problems, p. 29
- Geography Practice, p. 33

Modified Lesson Plans for English Learners, p. 29

Reading Study Guide (Spanish), p. 35

Reading Study Guide Audio CD (Spanish)

STRUGGLING READERS

In-Depth Resources: Unit 2
- Reading Skill: Identifying Issues and Problems, p. 23
- Vocabulary Cards, p. 27
- Reteaching Activity, p. 35

Reading Toolkit, L13

Reading Study Guide, p. 35

Reading Study Guide Audio CD

GIFTED AND TALENTED STUDENTS

In-Depth Resources: Unit 2
- Literature: Autobiography by King Darius, p. 32

History Makers
- Cyrus, p. 7

Interdisciplinary Projects
- Science, p. 20

INCLUSION

EasyPlanner CD-ROM
- Reading Skill: Identifying Issues and Problems
- Vocabulary Study Guide
- Reteaching Activity

TECHNOLOGY

eEdition CD-ROM

Power Presentations CD-ROM

Map Transparencies
- MT8 Expansion of the Persian Empire

Humanities Transparencies
- HT8 Stairway from Persepolis

Critical Thinking Transparencies
- CT16 Identifying Issues and Problems
- CT17 Chapter 4 Visual Summary

Test Generator CD-ROM

ClassZone.com

In-Depth Resources: Unit 2
- Reading Skill: Identifying Issues and Problems, p. 23
- Geography Practice: The Royal Road, p. 29

History from Visuals

Interpreting Maps

Have students observe the extent of the Persian Empire compared to the extent of the empires of the Fertile Crescent.

- Based on what you have read about the empires of the Fertile Crescent, what do you think were some of the issues and challenges facing the Persian Empire? *(Possible answer: managing the many different peoples living under the empire)*

Extension Have students look at a modern world map to see some of the present-day countries that have land that was once occupied by the Persians. What present-day country is Sardis a part of? *(Turkey)*

GEOGRAPHY SKILLBUILDER ANSWER

Susa, Nineveh, and Sardis

INTERACTIVE

An interactive version of this map is available on the eEdition and Power Presentations CD-ROMs.

Teach

Cyrus Founds the Persian Empire

6.3.4, 6.4.5, HI 3

Talk About It

- What was the vision that inspired Cyrus? *(to unite all the lands around Persia into one large empire)*

- How did Cyrus differ in his approach to conquered peoples compared with Ashurbanipal and Nebuchadnezzar? *(He treated them with respect and tolerance.)*

- **Critical Thinking: Understanding Cause and Effect** Why do you think Cyrus decided to treat conquered people the way he did? *(Possible answers: He believed it was easier to govern people who were not always in revolt; he believed it was the right way to treat others.)*

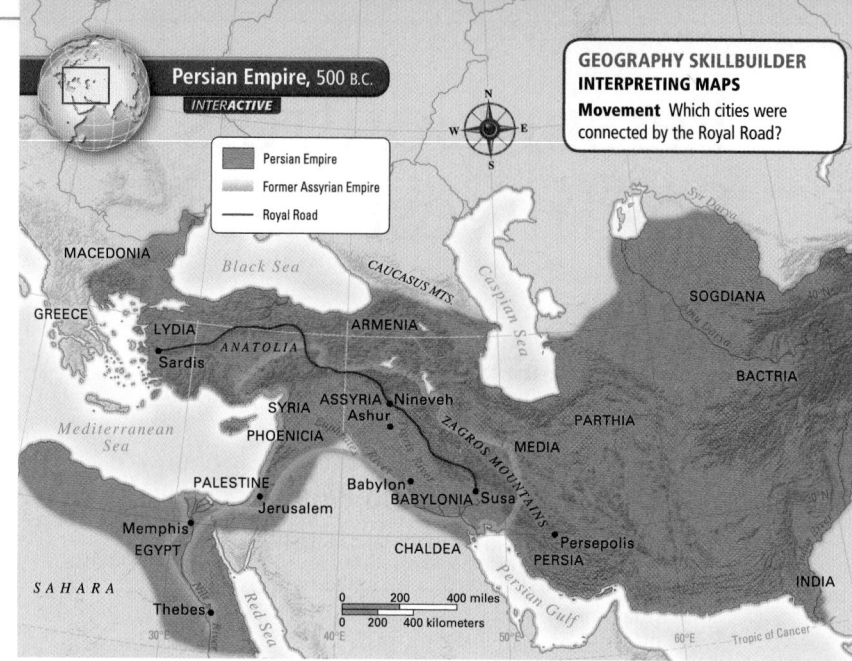

Persian Empire, 500 B.C.
INTERACTIVE

- Persian Empire
- Former Assyrian Empire
- Royal Road

GEOGRAPHY SKILLBUILDER
INTERPRETING MAPS
Movement Which cities were connected by the Royal Road?

MACEDONIA · Black Sea · CAUCASUS MTS · Caspian Sea · SOGDIANA · GREECE · LYDIA · Sardis · ANATOLIA · ARMENIA · BACTRIA · SYRIA · ASSYRIA · Nineveh · ZAGROS MOUNTAINS · PARTHIA · Mediterranean Sea · Ashur · MEDIA · PHOENICIA · PALESTINE · Babylon · BABYLONIA · Susa · Memphis · Jerusalem · Persepolis · EGYPT · CHALDEA · PERSIA · SAHARA · Persian Gulf · INDIA · Thebes · Red Sea

0   200   400 miles
0   200   400 kilometers

Persians Occupy the Land Nomadic invaders often swept in and occupied the lands of the Medes. The nomads came from the plains of Central Asia. They were related to other nomadic people who would later move into Europe and into India. The result of these invasions was much mixing of nomads' customs with other societies that lived there. About 1000 B.C., Persians entered the region. They created many tiny kingdoms that thrived through trade in horses and minerals with eastern and western Asia. These kingdoms grew in power and began to threaten the Medes' control of the land.

REVIEW How did the presence of nomadic tribes affect Persia?
The result was to mix customs and ways of life.

Cyrus Founds the Persian Empire

He used respect and toleration to rule.

2 ESSENTIAL QUESTION What was the rule of Cyrus like?

The Medes ruled Persia until a brilliant, powerful Persian king named Cyrus (SY•ruhs) took control. He was known as Cyrus the Great. Cyrus had a vision of conquering the lands around Persia and uniting these lands as one large empire. Then he set out to accomplish his goal.

INTERDISCIPLINARY ACTIVITIES

Language Arts

Address the Conquered People
Have students assume the role of Cyrus. Have each student prepare and deliver a speech to a group of people he has conquered. Student speeches should reflect Cyrus's military skill and also his beliefs in the treatment of conquered peoples.

Music

Write Song Lyrics
Cyrus was celebrated by the Jewish people as the man who allowed them to return to their homelands and rebuild their sacred temple in Jerusalem. Working in small groups, have students select a familiar song and rewrite the lyrics to create a song that honors Cyrus. Have volunteers perform their songs for the class.

Comparisons Across Cultures

Treatment of Captured Peoples

Ashurbanipal and the Assyrians	Cyrus, Darius, and the Persians
Used policies of cruelty	Used policies of toleration
Tortured leaders	Allowed leaders to remain in power
Burned cities	Did not destroy homes
Sent people into exile	Allowed people to keep their own gods and culture
Collected tribute	Collected tribute

▲ This is an artist's idea of the surrender of a conquered leader to Assyrian king Sennacherib.

Fearless Military Leader Cyrus led swift, deadly attacks in the region. First, Cyrus conquered **Anatolia**, also called Asia Minor. It lies within modern-day Turkey. Then, between 550 and 539 B.C., Cyrus conquered the Fertile Crescent lands that had once been controlled by the Assyrians and the Chaldeans. His empire was immense.

A Wise Emperor Cyrus needed ways to control lands filled with many different peoples. Unlike the Assyrians who ruled through cruelty, Cyrus set up a policy of **toleration**. This meant allowing people to keep their customs and beliefs. Cyrus allowed the conquered peoples to continue to worship their own gods, speak their own languages, and practice their own ways of life. However, they did have to pay tribute.

Cyrus's policies of respect and toleration made friends instead of enemies. For example, the Hebrew people (see Lesson 2) who had been captured by the Chaldeans greatly liked Cyrus because he freed them. He also allowed them to rebuild their temple and the city of Jerusalem. Cyrus's policy of toleration made governing the empire much easier. There were fewer revolts, and the people lived in peace.

REVIEW Why can Cyrus be considered a wise emperor?

His policies of toleration treated people with respect. His policies reduced unrest and brought peace.

Early Empires • 131

Teach

Darius Expands the Empire

6.4.5

Talk About It

- Why was Darius I forced to deal with rebellions in the Persian Empire? *(The successors of Cyrus did not faithfully follow his policies.)*

- What did Darius focus on after putting down the rebellions? *(He expanded the Persian Empire.)*

- What steps did Darius take to manage the vast empire he had created? *(He divided it into provinces and named satraps to govern them.)*

- **Critical Thinking: Summarizing** What steps did Darius take to unite the empire? *(Possible answers: He built a road that allowed for communication and trade; he adopted a monetary system that made it easier to conduct trade in the empire.)*

 In-Depth Resources: Unit 2
- Literature: Autobiography by King Darius, p. 32

 Map Transparencies
- MT8 Expansion of the Persian Empire

 Humanities Transparencies
- HT8 Stairway from Persepolis

More About . . .

Darius
Like Cyrus, who ruled before him, Darius is sometimes remembered as Darius the Great. It was Darius who expanded the Persian Empire to its greatest extent, as seen on the map on page 130. Also, like Cyrus, Darius demonstrated great religious tolerance. By embracing the gods of the many diverse peoples of his empire, he was able to win much loyalty.

Darius Expands the Empire

 ESSENTIAL QUESTION How did Darius control his empire?

He divided the land into smaller units and appointed governors and spies.

Cyrus built a stable empire of many peoples by his policy of toleration. After he died, a weak, less-tolerant ruler faced rebellions in the empire. Then a strong leader named Darius (duh•RY•uhs) came to power.

Darius Extends Persian Control The new emperor, Darius I, spent his first years as emperor dealing with rebellious peoples. After he put down the revolts, he moved to conquer lands as far east as India. The Persian Empire grew to 2,800 miles from east to west. (The distance from New York City to Los Angeles is about 2,500 miles.)

Political Organization The empire was so large that Darius added new policies to those set up by Cyrus. Darius divided the empire into 20 **provinces**. Each province, which was an area of land similar to a state, had a local government.

Darius set up governors called **satraps** (SAY•traps) to carry out his orders in the provinces and to collect taxes. He appointed a military commander for each satrap. He also sent out spies called "king's eyes and ears" to be sure his satraps followed orders. These policies allowed him to have greater control over all of the lands.

Uniting the Empire The policy of provinces ruled by satraps was only one way to unite the empire. Darius started the use of a **Royal Road**, or road for government purposes. The Royal Road was 1,775 miles long. The eastern end of the road was in Susa, and the western end was in Sardis on the Anatolian Peninsula. Royal messages were sent by a relay of messengers.

About every 15 miles there was a relay station where the messengers could get a fresh horse. Royal messages could move from one end of the road to the other in about seven days. Military troops and mail also moved along it from all parts of the empire to the capital. The road also promoted trade and business throughout the empire.

Connect to Today

Ruins at Persepolis
Winged and bearded bull-like figures guard the Gate of All Nations at the Persian royal palace. ▼

DIFFERENTIATING INSTRUCTION

English Learners

Find Main Ideas
Survey the headings and subheadings in this section. Model turning a heading and a subheading into questions. Guide students as they make formulate three questions for the section. Tell students they must listen for the answers to these questions as you read the text aloud. Have students ask and respond to the questions to see if they have been answered.

Inclusion

Role-Play the Ruler
Have students write or dictate statements from the perspective of either Darius or Cyrus describing his accomplishments as ruler of Persia. Have volunteers take turns presenting their statements to the class and have the class guess which ruler the student is describing.

Darius set up a law code based on Hammurabi's model. From the Lydians, a conquered people, Darius took the idea of *minted coins*. The coins were good throughout the empire. They promoted business and made it easy to pay taxes.

Enemies of Persia Darius planned a march against Egyptian rebels in 486 B.C., but he died that year. His son Xerxes (ZURK•seez) had to deal with Egypt. You will read about Egypt in the next chapter. Xerxes would also have to deal with the Greeks. You will read about them in Chapter 11.

REVIEW Why did Darius divide the empire into provinces?
Darius had more control over the areas and was able to reduce conflict.

Visual Vocabulary

Minted coins is a term for coins that are issued by the government and are official money.

Lesson Summary
- Tiny Persian kingdoms thrived due to trade.
- Cyrus the Great ruled the Persian Empire with a policy of toleration.
- Darius formed provinces and appointed satraps to improve government.

Why It Matters Now . . .
The Persians showed that lands ruled with policies of toleration could be stable and peaceful.

3 Lesson Review

 Homework Helper
ClassZone.com

Terms & Names
1. Explain the importance of

Anatolia	province	Royal Road
toleration	satrap	

Taking Notes
Identifying Issues and Problems Use your completed Venn diagram to answer the following question:

2. What common problems did Cyrus and Darius face during their reigns? (6.4.5)

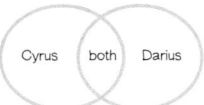
Cyrus — both — Darius

Main Ideas
3. How did people in early Persian kingdoms earn their living? (6.4.5)
4. How did Cyrus treat the Hebrew people in the lands he captured? (6.3.4)
5. In what ways did the Royal Road and minted coins help Darius unite the empire? (6.4.5)

Critical Thinking
6. **Making Inferences** How did Cyrus's policy of toleration change the way empires were ruled? (HI 3)
7. **Comparing and Contrasting** How did the policies of Cyrus and Darius contrast with those of the Assyrians? (6.4.5)

Activity

Making a Map Take out the world map you created in Chapter 2. Add to the map by outlining the expansion of the Persian Empire under Darius. (CST 3)

Early Empires • 133

Vocabulary Strategy

Visual Vocabulary
Direct students' attention to the illustrations of coins. Help students recognize that these coins were made by a central authority—a mint—and were essentially identical to each other. This meant that all coins would mean the same thing—represent the same value—in different parts of the empire.

❹ Assess & Reteach

Assess Have students work in pairs on the questions and note the locations of the answers.

 Formal Assessment
- Lesson Quiz, p. 60

Reteach Have students review the headings in the section. Then, have them state the main idea for each.

In-Depth Resources: Unit 2
- Vocabulary Cards, p. 27
- Reteaching Activity, p. 35

Homework Helper
Visit **Classzone.com** for a lesson review, a flip-card activity, and links to related Web sites.

---

3 Lesson Review Answers

Terms & Names
1. • Anatolia p. 131
   • toleration, p. 131
   • province, p. 132
   • satrap, p. 132
   • Royal Road, p. 132

Using Your Notes
See page 128 for an example of a completed diagram.
2. Cyrus and Darius had huge empires and added lands by conquest. These lands were filled with conquered peoples who had different customs and religions. Cyrus and Darius faced the need to bring these people together in order to have a stable empire. Cyrus and Darius made changes in government to help solve the problem.

Main Ideas
3. by trading horses and minerals with traders from eastern and western Asia
4. Cyrus allowed the Hebrews to return to their homelands and to repair their temple in Jerusalem.
5. The Royal Road helped Darius communicate with distant parts of the empire. The Royal Road and minted coins promoted trade and business.

Critical Thinking
6. The policies reduced tensions among the conquered people. The people were less likely to revolt if they were happy. A peaceful land is much easier to rule.
7. The Assyrians were cruel to the captured peoples. They were faced with many revolts. Persian policies of toleration made governing much easier.

Activity Rubric

	Accuracy of Map
4	no errors
3	few errors
2	several errors
1	mostly inaccurate

Early Empires • 133

Objectives

- Explore daily life in the court of Darius, the Persian Emperor.
- Analyze and interpret information from an infographic.
- **Language Objective:** Create a statement comparing and contrasting details about the court of Darius.

❶ Focus & Motivate

Preview Explain that Darius was the leader of what was then the most powerful empire in the world. This Daily Life feature explores how Darius communicated his power to the world around him.

❷ Teach

Talk About It

- What appears to be the largest and most grand-looking part of the Court of Darius? *(the audience hall)*

- How did the audience hall compare to the place where conquered people waited to pay their tribute? *(Possible answer: The audience hall was an impressive indoor area while the area where people waited to pay tribute looked like an open courtyard.)*

- Why do you think Darius's court needed such a large treasure room? *(Darius collected a great deal of tribute from conquered peoples.)*

- **Critical Thinking: Making Inferences** What did the Court of Darius "say" about the Persian Emperor? *(It reflected the idea that he was a wealthy and powerful leader of a great empire.)*

 Humanities Transparencies
- HT8 Stairway at Persepolis

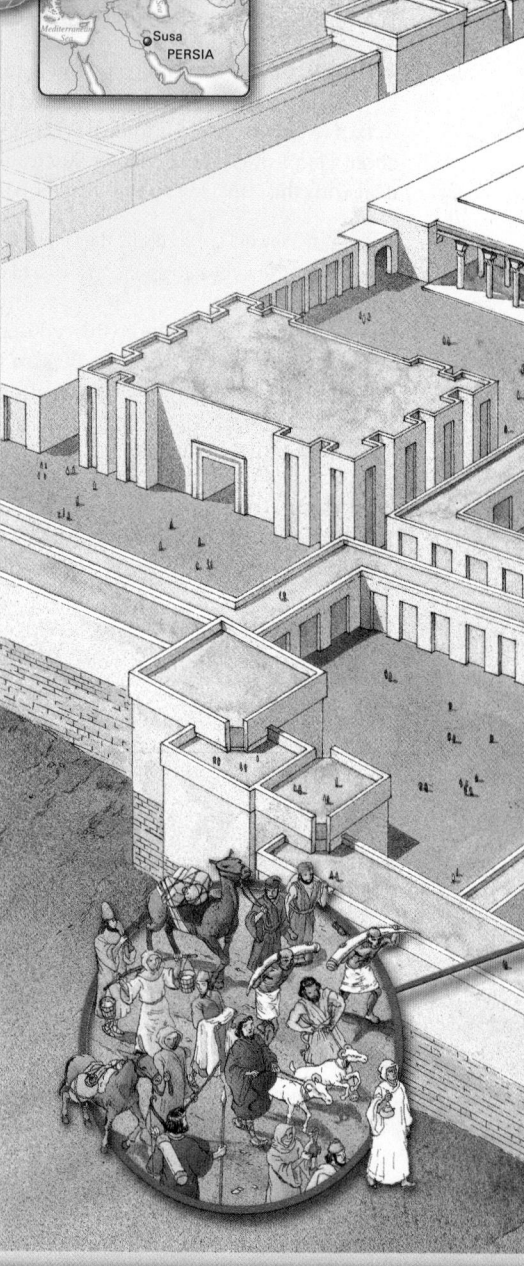

Daily Life
Extend Lesson 3

Research Links
ClassZone.com

The Court of Darius

Purpose: To learn about life at the court of the Persian emperor Darius

Darius's palace was designed to impress all who came there. It was set on the base of a hill on a platform 50 feet above the plain. Its enormous size proclaimed the power of the emperor. The palace at Persepolis was one of three palaces used by the Persian emperors. Darius held court here in the wintertime.

Ⓐ Entrance Gate The palace had two entrance gates where representatives of conquered peoples waited to present tribute to the emperor. They brought animals such as bulls and horses. Other tribute included gold, ivory, cloth, grain, and precious gems.

Ⓑ Treasure Room The treasure room held large quantities of gold and silver. Some of it was made into serving plates and drinking vessels. Precious stones such as lapis lazuli, carnelian, and turquoise decorated some of these pieces. Other stones were used in fine jewelry.

Ⓒ Ladies' Court Upper-class women were not expected to do any work. Many servants attended to the ladies of the court. The women generally stayed in the ladies' court unless commanded to appear before the emperor.

Ⓓ Audience Hall Darius met with officials of his empire and received ambassadors from other countries in this hall. The hall had 36 columns inside and 36 columns outside to support the roof. The walls featured brightly colored tiles showing such things as human-headed lions and ranks of royal guards.

CALIFORNIA STANDARDS
6.4.5 Outline the founding, expansion, and political organization of the Persian Empire.

134 • Chapter 4

DIFFERENTIATING INSTRUCTION

English Learners

Compare and Contrast
Guide students in a discussion about how the details in the captions are illustrated in the scenes. Formulate and model a comparing and contrasting statement using some of the details. Encourage students to use both and but as they share their own comparing and contrasting statements with their classmates.

Struggling Readers

Role-Play Darius's Court
Group students in teams of three. Have them each assume the role of one of the three groups of people mentioned in this feature. Then, have them offer a brief three- or four-sentence dramatic presentation to the class about their day at court. Ask the class to try to guess what group each student represents.

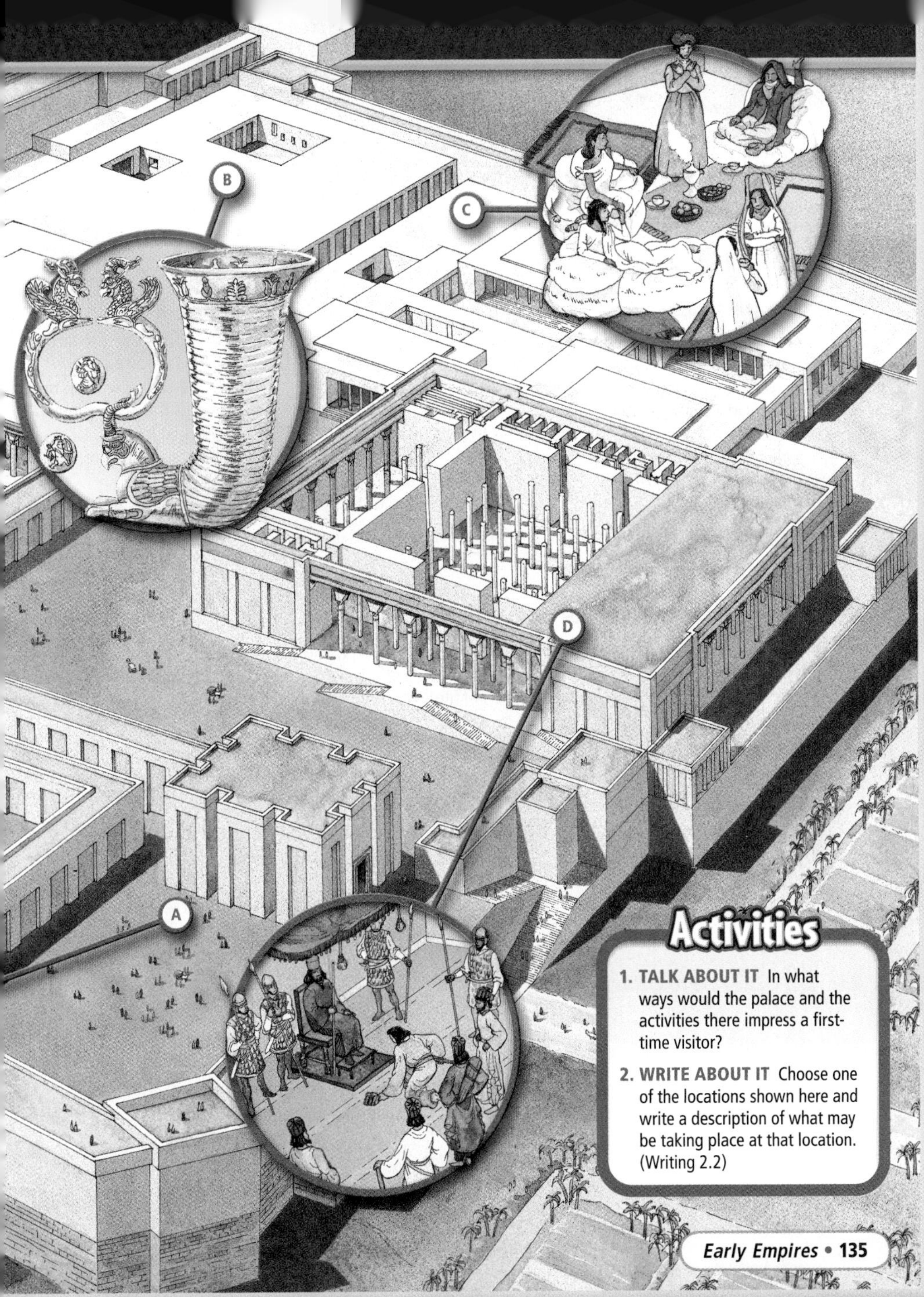

Research Links

Visit **ClassZone.com** for age-appropriate
Web sites related to this topic.

More About . . .

Persepolis

Persepolis means "city of the Persians." Darius established the city and its magnificent palace buildings, though it may have taken 100 years to complete in all its glory. In 331 B.C., Persepolis was destroyed by invading Greek armies. It was written that it took 25,000 pack animals to carry off the enormous treasures in its storehouses. The city lay in ruins until the 1930s, when archaeologists began the careful excavation of the site.

Activities

1. **TALK ABOUT IT** In what ways would the palace and the activities there impress a first-time visitor?

2. **WRITE ABOUT IT** Choose one of the locations shown here and write a description of what may be taking place at that location. (Writing 2.2)

Early Empires • 135

ACTIVITIES ANSWERS

1. **TALK ABOUT IT** Possible answers: its raised situation; its enormous size; the conquered peoples waiting to present tribute to the emperor; the riches of the treasure room; the number of servants

2. **WRITE ABOUT IT**

2. Writing Rubric

	Language Style	Details in Description	Errors in Mechanics
4	vivid	rich and full	few or none
3	descriptive	clear, some detail	some
2	somewhat descriptive	adequate	many
1	vague	too few	major

Terms & Names

1. The Fertile Crescent lies south of Anatolia, includes Mesopotamia, and extends from the Mediterranean Sea to the Persian Gulf. These lands were parts of early empires.

2. Hammurabi set up one of the earliest codes of law in world history. His code of law became a model for later rulers. The code set up the rule of justice for all.

3. To govern his vast empire, Darius established many provinces, under the rule of satraps, and he used the Royal Road to link distant parts of his empire.

Main Ideas

Mesopotamian Empires (pages 112–117)

4. The Fertile Crescent includes the lands of Mesopotamia and stretches in an arc from the Mediterranean Sea to the Persian Gulf.

5. They may bring peace, encourage trade, and ideas and technologies.

6. Hammurabi's Code helped different groups of people feel that they were being treated fairly. Individuals and groups knew their rights under the law. The code helped Hammurabi govern his many peoples.

Assyria Rules the Fertile Crescent (pages 118–127)

7. The Assyrians were able to conquer many lands because their army was very fierce and used new ways of fighting.

8. The Assyrians were cruel to peoples with different religious beliefs and ways of life.

9. Tribute was paid for the protection of the army of the conquering country.

Persia Controls Southwest Asia (pages 128–135)

10. Cyrus used toleration to keep the people happy so that they would not rebel.

11. Darius expanded his government because he conquered many more lands. The Persian Empire reached as far as western India. Darius had to find ways to control so many different peoples, some at a great distance from the capital city.

12. It allowed the movement of troops, mail, and goods throughout the empire. It also helped unite the empire.

▶ **VISUAL SUMMARY**

Early Empires

Government (6.2)
- First empire is created.
- Code of law developed.
- Empire divided into smaller units for easier rule.
- Policies of toleration are used to control captured people.

Culture (6.2)
- System of writing helps record keeping.
- Library is built by Ashurbanipal.
- Hanging Gardens are built by Nebuchadnezzar.
- Tower of Babel rises above the city of Babylon.

Economics (6.2)
- Tribute used to support the empire.
- Minted coins help business and the government.
- Royal Road links the Persian Empire.

▶ **TERMS & NAMES**

Explain why the words in each set below are linked with each other.

1. **empire, Fertile Crescent,** and **Anatolia**

2. **Hammurabi, code of law,** and **justice**

3. **province, satrap,** and **Royal Road**

▶ **MAIN IDEAS**

Mesopotamian Empires (pages 112–117)

4. Which lands are a part of the region known as the Fertile Crescent? (6.2.1)

5. How do empires change the lives of the people who live in them? (HI 1)

6. Why was Hammurabi's Code a step toward better government? (6.2.4)

Assyria Rules the Fertile Crescent (pages 118–127)

7. Why were the Assyrians able to build such a large empire? (6.2)

8. How did Assyrians treat peoples with different religious beliefs and ways of life? (6.2)

9. Why did conquered people have to pay tribute? (6.2)

Persia Controls Southwest Asia (pages 128–135)

10. What policies did Cyrus use to keep his empire under control? (6.4.5)

11. Why did Darius expand his government? (6.4.5)

12. Why was the Persian Royal Road important? (6.4.5)

ALTERNATIVE ASSESSMENT RUBRICS

1. Writing Rubric

	Similarities and Differences	Purpose and Conclusion
4	many examples	clear and logical
3	some examples	clear
2	few examples	unclear
1	no examples	missing

2. Science Rubric

	Clarity of Captions	Visual Appeal
4	clear and concise	strongly appealing
3	clear	above average
2	vague	average
1	missing	messy

CRITICAL THINKING

Big Ideas: Government

13. **MAKING INFERENCES** How does a uniform code of law improve a leader's ability to rule effectively? (6.2.4)

14. **EXPLAINING HISTORICAL PATTERNS** What pattern of governmental leadership can be seen in the reigns of Hammurabi, Cyrus, and Darius? (6.4.5)

15. **COMPARING** How successful were the policies of Assyria compared with those of Persia? (6.4.5)

ALTERNATIVE ASSESSMENT

1. **WRITING ACTIVITY** Select two rulers from this chapter to compare and contrast. Write an expository paragraph about them. (Writing 2.2)

2. **INTERDISCIPLINARY ACTIVITY—SCIENCE AND TECHNOLOGY** Use printed sources or the Internet to research ancient warfare equipment such as that the Assyrians invented. Create a poster to illustrate your findings. (6.2)

3. **STARTING WITH A STORY**

Review the story titled "Day of Misfortune." Work with a few classmates to rewrite the story as a scene in a play. Include an ending that tells what happened to the builder. Perform your scene. (6.2.4)

Technology Activity

4. **MAKING A MULTIMEDIA PRESENTATION** Use the Internet or printed sources to find illustrations of Mesopotamian or Persian objects found by archaeologists. Work with a small group to make a multimedia presentation. (6.2)
   • What objects were found?
   • What activities do they represent?

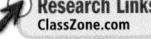
Research Links
ClassZone.com

Reading Tables Use the table below to answer the questions. (6.2)

Size and Population of Ancient Empires			
Empire	**Empire Size in Square Miles**	**Major City**	**City Size (Approximate Population)**
Akkadia	2,509,664	Agade	35,000
Sumer	386,102	Ur	65,000
Babylonia	640,930	Babylon	60,000
Assyria	3,602,333	Nineveh	120,000

Source: *Institute for Research on World Systems*

1. **Which of the following statements about empire land size is correct?**
   A. Assyria's land size is much smaller than Babylonia's land size.
   B. Assyria's land size is much larger than Sumer's land size.
   C. Sumer's land size and Babylonia's land size are about the same.
   D. All of the empires are about the same size.

2. **Based on the population size of the major cities, which statement is correct?**
   A. Agade and Nineveh were the largest cities.
   B. Babylon and Nineveh were similar in size.
   C. Babylon and Ur were similar in size.
   D. Nineveh was ten times larger than any other city.

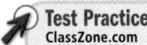
Test Practice
ClassZone.com

Additional Test Practice, pp. S1–S33

Critical Thinking

Big Ideas: Government

13. A uniform code of law makes the law the same for all groups regardless of their own cultural traditions. The expectations are the same for all, making ruling a less difficult task.

14. Possible answer: All three were powerful rulers who established larger empires. They also established policies to enable better control of their empires.

15. Possible answer: Both Assyria and Persia had huge empires. Assyria faced much opposition from the conquered peoples because of its cruelty. Persia was more successful with policies of toleration.

Standards-Based Assessment

1. B is the correct answer; Assyria's land size is much larger than Sumer's land size.

2. C is the correct answer; Babylon and Ur were similar in size.

Research Links
Visit **ClassZone.com** for links to Web sites that can be used in the multimedia presentation

Test Practice
Visit **ClassZone.com** to access strategies and tutorials for taking standardized tests.

Formal Assessment
   • Chapter Tests, Forms A, B, and C, pp. 61–72

Test Generator
   • Chapter Tests, Forms A, B, and C (English and Spanish)

ALTERNATIVE ASSESSMENT RUBRICS

3. Starting with a Story Rubric

	Expression of Dialogue	Plausibility of Conclusions	Stage Directions
4	vibrant	plausible, logical ending	clear and complete
3	interesting	plausible ending	complete
2	adequate	unlikely ending	incomplete
1	poor	vague	missing

4. Technology Rubric

	Clarity of Explanation	Quality of Illustrations	Accuracy of Captions
4	clear and instructive	clear and detailed	clear and concise
3	clear	some detail	accurate
2	unfocused	poor examples	adequate
1	unclear or missing	poor example	unclear or missing

Objectives

- Identify parts of an expository composition.
- Research information for an expository composition about the origin or impact of empires.
- Prepare and share a final copy of the composition.

❶ Focus & Motivate

Preview Ask students where they would find examples of expository writing other than in a textbook. *(Possible answers: instruction manuals, newspapers, cookbooks)* Have them volunteer occasions when they have used expository writing in the past.

❷ Teach

Talk About It

- What key words signal cause-and-effect relationships? *(Possible answers: because, as a result of, consequently, before)*

- Which ideas from pages 113–114 might be included in a composition that explains the effects of an empire? *(Possible answers: strong and powerful kings take over the lands of weaker rulers; empires encourage trade; include people from several cultures; ideas and customs such as writing are shared by everyone)*

- What should readers know after reading the introduction to this composition? *(Readers should know what the writer is intending to prove about either the causes or effects of empires.)*

- **Critical Thinking: Evaluating Information** If the body of the composition is organized in order of importance from least to most, which effect might be discussed last? Why? *(Possible answer: Empires change the way people live.)*

Writing About History

Expository Writing: Explanations
The Origins and Impacts of Empires

Writing Model
ClassZone.com

CALIFORNIA STANDARDS
Writing 2.2 Write expository compositions.

Purpose: To write an expository composition about empires

Audience: Your learning partner

In this unit, you read many explanations. For example, you read how the land in Mesopotamia became fertile because of flooding and how fertile land made crops grow. These explanations are examples of **expository writing,** or writing that informs. Historians use expository writing to explain past events and their impact on human life.

◀ Sargon

Organization & Focus

Your assignment is to write a 500- to 700-word expository composition about the origins or impacts of empires. An expository composition has three main parts. The **introduction** gets the reader interested and states a clear thesis, or main idea. The **body** provides supporting details in the form of facts and examples. The **conclusion** summarizes the information and restates the thesis.

Historical expositions often have chronological sequence or cause and effect as their organizational pattern. In this essay, cause-and-effect organization will best help you to explain the origins or impacts of empires.

Choosing a Topic Reread pages 113–114. With a learning partner, identify paragraphs that deal with the causes of the rise of empires and those that deal with empires' effects. Finally, you and your partner should divide the topic, so that one will write about the origins and the other about the impacts.

Identifying Purpose and Audience When your purpose is to explain, you need to use facts and examples to support your main idea. Through discussion, try to get an idea of what kinds of facts and examples will help your learning partner understand your thesis.

DIFFERENTIATING INSTRUCTION

Gifted and Talented Students

Extend the Assignment
Have students write a composition that explains both the causes and effects of empires. Encourage them to develop relationships among their ideas.

Struggling Readers

Chart Causes and Effects
Together with students, use the text to identify the causes and effects of empires. Have students record these ideas on a cause-and-effect chart before completing the rest of the assignment.

Research & Technology

Finding Details Review Chapters 3 and 4. Look for information to support your thesis, and record it in a chart like the one below. Review your notes and create categories for them. Possible categories include the themes of this program: Geography, Culture, Economics, Government, Belief Systems, and Science & Technology. Use your category names as key words to search for more information.

 **Technology Tip** To do additional research on the Internet, you might visit an online database, or collection of well-organized information. Your librarian might be able to suggest a database with information on your topic.

Thesis:	
Supporting Facts	Supporting Examples

Outlining and Drafting When you have the facts and examples you need, decide on the best order for them. One possibility is order of importance, with the most important information saved for last. Another is a category-by-category order with the categories arranged for logical flow. Outline your composition, and then compose the first draft.

Evaluation & Revision

When revising, pay attention to the order of your ideas and the flow of paragraphs. Use the Self-Check to see if your explanation accomplishes its purpose. When you are satisfied that it does, prepare a final copy. Use your word processor to check spelling.

Self-Check
Does my explanation have
- [ ] a clear introduction, with the main idea, or thesis, stated?
- [ ] supporting examples and facts logically arranged?
- [ ] a conclusion that restates the main idea?

Publish & Present

Exchange compositions with your partner, and read his or her work. Then discuss what you learned from reading your partner's composition and from writing your own.

139

More About . . .

Thesis Statements
The thesis statement is one key to a good essay. It states the point that the writer wishes to make about the topic of the paper and is usually placed near the end of the first paragraph.

Before writing a thesis statement, students should read through their research. As they read, students should ask themselves what they want to prove about their topic. The answer to this question is their thesis.

ANSWERS

Expository Writing Rubric

	Structure of Composition	Content of Composition	Errors in Mechanics
4	effective introduction with strong thesis statement, developed body paragraph(s), and sound conclusion	shows thorough understanding of topic; excellent use of facts	few or none
3	solid introduction, body, and conclusion	shows good understanding of topics; good use of facts	some
2	undeveloped but distinct introduction, body, and conclusion	shows some understanding of topic; some use of facts	many
1	weak and disorganized	shows little or no understanding; few facts	many major

Begin the Unit

Quick Look

Chapter 5 describes the development of ancient Egyptian civilization and the reigns of important pharaohs.

Chapter 6 examines societies and civilizations in other parts of Africa during the same time period.

Interact with History ▶

Purpose

To help students connect with ancient Africans by imagining themselves in a historical situation—building a pyramid in ancient Egypt

Visual Learning

Invite a volunteer to read aloud the text and questions, and tell students to put themselves in the situation described. Explain that the text and three questions on the illustration give clues to the answer to the main question. Discuss these questions before discussing the main one.

Interact ANSWERS

- What problems might you face in building a pyramid? *(lack of workers, lack of skilled workers, dangers from moving such huge blocks)*

- What different types of workers would you need to build the pyramid? *(laborers, supervisors/overseers, architects, engineers, stonecutters, artists)*

- What are some of the dangers involved in this process? *(Workers could be crushed to death if the blocks slipped. Workers could be injured or killed working so hard in the hot sun.)*

- What are the advantages of finishing the blocks at the quarry? at the pyramid? *(Quarry—Finished blocks would be lighter, and there would be less mess to clean up at the site. Pyramid—Finished blocks would not be damaged in transit.)*

UNIT 3

Ancient Africa

Interact with History ▶

Building the Great Pyramid, about 2550 B.C.
You are an overseer working to build the tomb of the pharaoh, or ruler. Many laborers and skilled craftspeople will be needed to complete the pyramid in time.

What problems might you face in building a pyramid?

WebQuest
ClassZone.com

Thousands of workers were needed to build the pyramid. Many were farmers who worked during the season when the Nile was flooded.

What different types of workers would you need to build the pyramid?

140

TECHNOLOGY

WebQuest: Ancient Egypt

Visit **ClassZone.com** to lead your students through a WebQuest on ancient Egypt. Students will create an architect's report to a pharaoh, explaining the design of a particular pyramid.

When to Use This project works well as an introduction to the chapter or as an end-of-chapter activity.

Class Time Two class periods

Materials Needed At least one computer with access to the World Wide Web and a printer.

Customizing for Your Classroom

- If computer time is limited, have small groups rotate through stations, finding information from encyclopedias, magazines, or the textbook as well as Web sites.

- Encourage Spanish speakers to use the textbook's Spanish Glossary. Point out terms such as *pirámide* (pyramid) and *faraón* (pharaoh) that are similar in both languages.

Each stone block weighed about 2.5 tons—which is about as heavy as a small pickup truck. The ancient Egyptians had not started using the wheel yet. So they had to drag the blocks on sleds up wooden ramps.

What are some of the dangers involved in this process?

Artisans had to finish rough stone blocks to be the perfect size and shape. This created a huge pile of stone chips. Archaeologists are not sure if the finishing was done at the quarry or at the pyramid site.

What are the advantages of finishing the blocks at the quarry? at the pyramid?

141

Correcting Misconceptions

Ask students to describe how movies depict ancient Egypt. When students have finished this unit, ask them to write down two ways in which the movies were inaccurate.

More About . . .

When and Where Pyramids Were Built

The pharaohs of the Old and Middle Kingdoms ordered the pyramids to be built. About 80 have been discovered so far. Many are located near Memphis probably because it was the capital city of Egypt during much of this period.

WHY STUDY WORLD HISTORY?

- The monuments the ancient Egyptians created still impress people with their size and beauty.

- Geography influences people's lives today, just as the Nile influenced ancient Egyptians' lives long ago.

- People use writing to communicate with each other and to keep records, as the ancient Egyptians and Aksumites did.

- Societies currently use trade to make themselves richer, as Hatshepsut did during the New Kingdom.

- Many people are curious as to whether there is life after death.

- Today many people believe in religions based on a single god, as the pharaoh Akhenaton and King Ezana did.

- Empires often increase and decrease in power, as ancient Egypt and Kush did.

- Societies still influence each other, as Egyptian religion, language, and customs influenced the Kushites.

- Desertification continues to be a problem in the Sahel and in many other parts of the world.

CHAPTER 5 PLANNING GUIDE: Ancient Egypt

Chapter Overview

The development of agriculture along the Nile River permitted the growth of other occupations and of ancient Egyptian civilization.

Copymasters

In-Depth Resources: Unit 3
- Family Newsletter (English and Spanish), pp. 1–2
- Visual Summary, p. 7
- Vocabulary Study Guide, p. 9

Character Education

Reading Study Guide, p. 47

Bringing Social Studies Alive, Chapter 5

Document-Based Questions: Strategy and Practice

Reading Toolkit, L14–L17

Modified Lesson Plans for English Learners, pp. 31–38

Assessment

Chapter Review, pp. 182–183

Formal Assessment
- Chapter Tests, Forms A, B, and C, pp. 81–95

Test Generator

Integrated Assessment Book

Online Test Practice

LESSON 1
Gift of the Nile
pp. 146–153

OBJECTIVE Explain how ancient Egyptians used the fertile land along the Nile and other natural resources.

In-Depth Resources: Unit 3
- Reading Skill: Understanding Cause and Effect, p. 3
- Vocabulary Cards, p. 11
- Skillbuilder Practice: Drawing Conclusions from Sources, p. 8
- Reteaching Activity, p. 17

Interdisciplinary Projects
- Science, p. 26

Reading Study Guide, p. 39

Lesson Review, p. 151

Formal Assessment
- Lesson Quiz, p. 77

California Daily Standards Practice Transparencies, TT14

LESSON 2
Life in Ancient Egypt
pp. 154–163

OBJECTIVE Describe Egyptian social roles, technological advances, and religious beliefs.

In-Depth Resources: Unit 3
- Reading Skill: Categorizing, p. 4
- Vocabulary Cards, p. 11
- Primary Source: Herodotus' Account of Life in Egypt, p. 15
- Reteaching Activity, p. 18

Interdisciplinary Projects
- Math, p. 25; Language Arts, p. 27

Reading Study Guide, p. 41

Lesson Review, p. 161

Formal Assessment
- Lesson Quiz, p. 78

California Daily Standards Practice Transparencies, TT15

LESSON 3
The Pyramid Builders
pp. 164–171

OBJECTIVE Tell how and why Egyptians built pyramids during the Old Kingdom and the Middle Kingdom.

In-Depth Resources: Unit 3
- Reading Skill: Summarizing, p. 5
- Vocabulary Cards, p. 11
- Geography Practice: Types of Pyramids, p. 13

- Literature: Boufra's Tale, p. 16
- Reteaching Activity, p. 19

Reading Study Guide, p. 43

Lesson Review, p. 170

Formal Assessment
- Lesson Quiz, p. 79

California Daily Standards Practice Transparencies, TT16

LESSON 4
The New Kingdom
pp. 172–181

OBJECTIVE Identify important changes that happened during the reigns of Hatshepsut, Akhenaten, and Ramses II.

In-Depth Resources: Unit 3
- Reading Skill: Explaining Chronological Order and Sequence, p. 6
- Vocabulary Cards, p. 11
- Reteaching Activity, p. 20

Interdisciplinary Projects
- Health, p. 28

History Makers
- Hatshepsut, p. 9

Reading Study Guide, p. 45

Lesson Review, p. 177

Formal Assessment
- Lesson Quiz, p. 80

California Daily Standards Practice Transparencies, TT17

Integrated Technology

 eEdition Plus Online

EasyPlanner Plus Online

eTest Plus Online

 Audio CDs
- Reading Study Guide
- Reading Study Guide in Spanish
- The World's Music

 CD-ROMs
- Power Presentations
- eEdition
- EasyPlanner
- Test Generator

 Ancient Civilizations Video Series
- Ancient Egypt

---

 eEdition CD-ROM

 Map Transparencies
- MT9 Natural Resources in Ancient Egypt

 Critical Thinking Transparencies
- CT18 Understanding Cause and Effect

 ClassZone.com

---

 eEdition CD-ROM

 Humanities Transparencies
- HT9 Hieroglyphs

 Critical Thinking Transparencies
- CT19 Categorizing

 ClassZone.com

---

 eEdition CD-ROM

 Critical Thinking Transparencies
- CT20 Summarizing

 ClassZone.com

---

 eEdition CD-ROM

 Map Transparencies
- MT10 The New Kingdom of Egypt, 1550–1070 B.C.

 Humanities Transparencies
- HT10 Royal Family in Adoration Before the Aton

 Critical Thinking Transparencies
- CT21 Explaining Chronological Order and Sequence
- CT22 Chapter 5 Visual Summary

 ClassZone.com

Overview of California Resources

	Lesson 1	Lesson 2	Lesson 3	Lesson 4
California Reading Toolkit	L14	L15	L16	L17
California Modified Lesson Plans for English Learners	p. 31	p. 33	p. 35	p. 37
California Daily Standards Practice Transparencies	TT14	TT15	TT16	TT17
California Standards Enrichment Workbook	pp. 21–24, 31–32	pp. 23–26, 29–30, 37–38	pp. 25–26, 29–30	pp. 25–26, 33–34
California Standards Planner and Lesson Plans	L27	L29	L31	L33
California Online Test Practice	ClassZone.com	ClassZone.com	ClassZone.com	ClassZone.com
California Test Generator CD-ROM				
California EasyPlanner CD-ROM				
California eEdition CD-ROM				

Chart Key

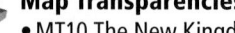 **PE** Pupil Edition	 **CD-ROM**	**Internet**
Copymaster	**Audio**	**Overhead Transparency**
	Video	

PREVIEWING RESOURCES FOR DIFFERENTIATED INSTRUCTION

English Learners

In-Depth Resources in Spanish
- Reading Skill and Strategy Ⓐ
- Vocabulary Study Guide Ⓑ
- Skillbuilder Practice
- Geography Practice Ⓒ

In-Depth Resources: Unit 3
- Family Newsletter (English and Spanish)

Reading Study Guide (Spanish)

Reading Study Guide Audio CD
(Spanish)

Test Generator
Chapter Test (Spanish)

Plus

Modified Lesson Plans for English Learners

Multi-Language Glossary of Social Studies Terms

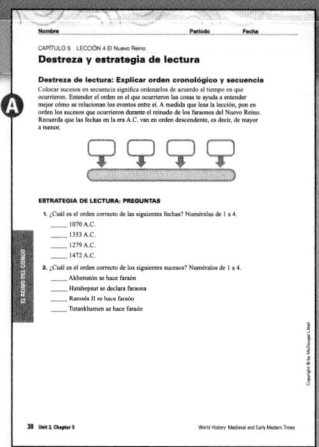
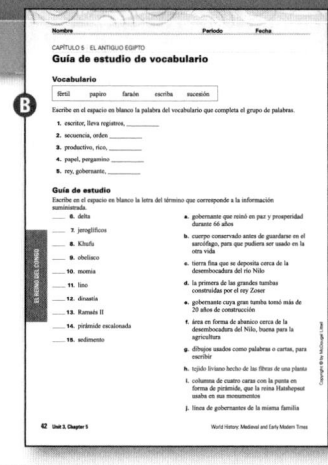

Struggling Readers

In-Depth Resources: Unit 3
- Vocabulary Study Guide
- Skillbuilder Practice Ⓑ
- Geography Practice
- Reteaching Activities
- Family Newsletter Ⓒ

Reading Study Guide Ⓐ

Reading Study Guide Audio CD

Reading Toolkit

Formal Assessment
Chapter Test, Form A

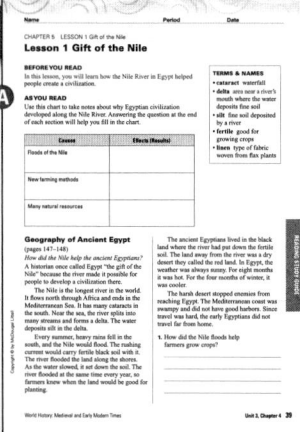
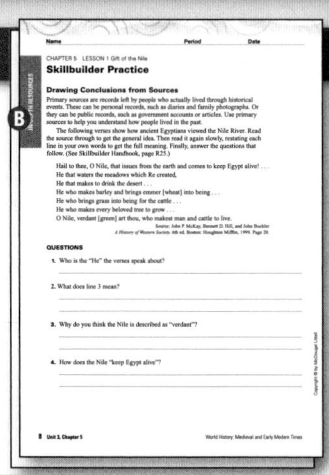

Inclusion

EasyPlanner CD-ROM
- Reading Skill and Strategy Ⓒ
- Vocabulary Study Guide
- Geography Practice Ⓐ
- Reteaching Activities Ⓑ

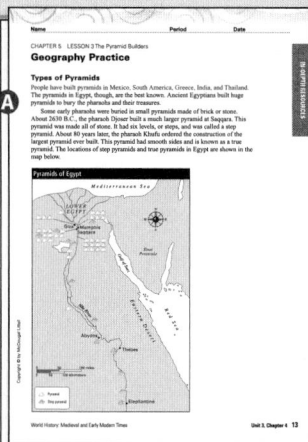
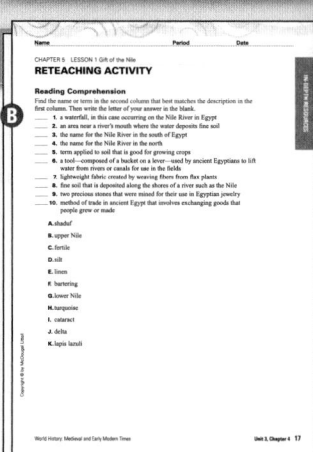

Gifted and Talented Students

In-Depth Resources: Unit 3
- Primary Source Ⓐ
- Literature

History Makers Ⓑ

Interdisciplinary Projects Ⓒ

Formal Assessment
Chapter Test, Form C

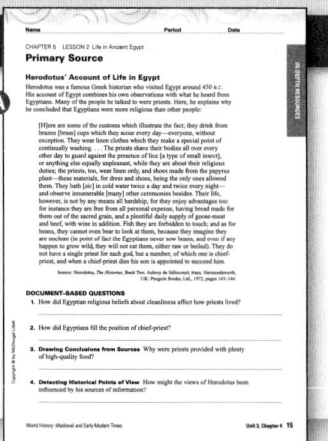

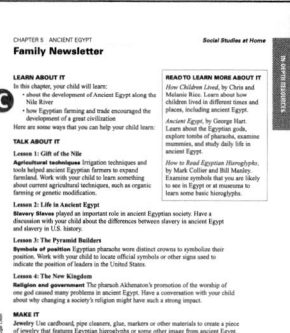

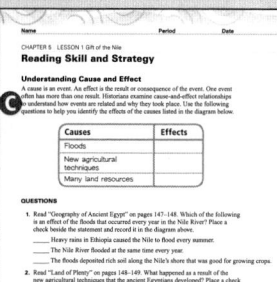

Activities in the Teacher's Edition for English Learners

- Create Visual Vocabulary Items, p. 148
- Understand Vocabulary, p. 152
- Identify Related Words, p. 156
- Decode Compound Words, p. 159
- Make Word Squares, p. 166
- Compare and Contrast Rulers, p. 175
- Read a Play, p. 179
- Make a Cartoon Strip, p. 180

Activities in the Teacher's Edition for Struggling Readers

- Focus on Vocabulary, p. 148
- Role-Play: Be a Trader, p. 152
- Create Job Descriptions, p. 157
- Identify Main Ideas, p. 159
- Be a Reporter, p. 167
- Examine Photographs, p. 169
- Use the Review Question, p. 174
- Draw a Map, p. 180

Activities in the Teacher's Edition for Inclusion Students

- Take Audio Notes, p. 149
- Enlarge Images, p. 156
- Divide and Conquer, p. 162
- Use the Graphic Organizer, p. 167
- Practice Remembering, p. 174

Activities in the Teacher's Edition for Gifted and Talented Students

- Create a Diorama, p. 149
- Draw a U.S. Social Pyramid, p. 157
- Create Your Own Calendar, p. 162
- Create a Poster on King Tut's Treasures, p. 169
- List Research Questions, p. 175
- Design Props, p. 179

Integrated Technology

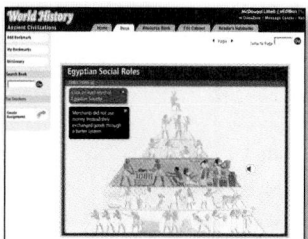

eEdition CD-ROM

- Interactive Visuals
- Interactive Maps
- Starting with a Story

ClassZone.com

- WebQuests
- Research Links
- Internet Activities
- Homework Helper
- Chapter Quiz
- Current Events
- Test Practice

Power Presentations CD-ROM

- Lecture Notes
- Media Gallery
- Chapter Review Game

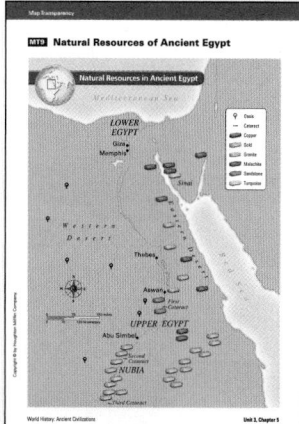

Critical Thinking Transparencies

- CT18 Understanding Cause and Effect
- CT19 Categorizing
- CT20 Summarizing
- CT21 Explaining Chronological Order and Sequence
- CT22 Chapter 5 Visual Summary

California Daily Standards Practice Transparencies, TT14–TT17

Map Transparencies

- MT9 Natural Resources in Ancient Egypt
- MT10 The New Kingdom of Egypt, 1550–1070 B.C.

Humanities Transparencies

- HT9 Hieroglyphs
- HT10 Royal Family in Adoration Before the Aton

Test Generator CD-ROM

EasyPlanner CD-ROM

Ancient Civilizations Video Series
Ancient Egypt

Begin the Chapter

Objective

Analyze the geographic, political, economic, religious, and social structures of early Egypt.

Quick Look

Lesson 1 explains how the Nile River affected ancient Egypt.

Lesson 2 describes the jobs, technology, and beliefs found there.

Lesson 3 explores government and culture during the Old and Middle kingdoms.

Lesson 4 focuses on important pharaohs of the New Kingdom.

Before You Read: K-W-L

To use K-W-L, the reader stops to think about what he or she already knows about a topic. Then the reader focuses on what he or she wants to know about it. Both steps help set a purpose for reading, which improves the student's motivation and ability to focus.

Explain to students that to use K-W-L effectively, they should follow these steps:

- Think about what you already know about ancient Egypt. Have you seen movies or television shows about it? Maybe you have read magazine articles or books about the pyramids, Cleopatra, or King Tut.

- Think about what you want to learn about ancient Egypt. The pictures on this page and on the previous two pages may give you some ideas.

- At the end of the chapter, think about what you have learned about ancient Egypt. You may have more questions now than those you listed at the beginning of the chapter.

Chapter 5 — Ancient Egypt

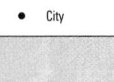

Before You Read: K-W-L

Considering what you have already learned about ancient Egypt will help prepare you to read this chapter. Record the answers to the following questions in your notebook:

- What do you already know about Egypt?
- Study the map and time line on these pages. What do they tell you about Egypt's land and its people?
- What do you want to **learn** about Egypt?

Big Ideas About Ancient Egypt

Geography Civilizations developed in places that supported agriculture or trade or both.

Ancient Egypt developed along the Nile River. Rich farmland along the Nile provided plenty of food for the Egyptians. The river also became a trading highway. Farming and trade encouraged the development of a great civilization in Egypt.

Integrated Technology

eEdition
- Interactive Maps
- Interactive Visuals
- Starting with a Story

VIDEO Ancient Egypt

INTERNET RESOURCES
Go to **ClassZone.com** for
- WebQuest
- Homework Helper
- Research Links
- Internet Activities
- Quizzes
- Maps
- Test Practice
- Current Events

Desert
Fertile area
— Cataract
• City

AFRICA

0   75   150 miles
0   75   150 kilometers

20°E

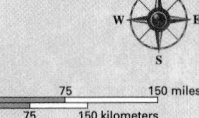

EGYPT

3100 B.C.
Upper and Lower Egypt are united.

3000 B.C.

2550 B.C.
Work on Khufu's Great Pyramid begins in Giza. (Great Pyramid is at far right.) ▶

2500 B.C.

WORLD

2500 B.C.
Harappan culture rises in the Indus Valley. ◀ (Harappan elephant seal)

142

TIME LINE DISCUSSION

Use the time line to help students establish a mental time frame for the civilization of ancient Egypt (from about 3100 to about 1200 b.c.) and to preview information that will be covered in the chapter.

- About how many years of Egyptian history does this chapter cover? *(about 2,000 years)*
- What event marks the beginning of this period of Egyptian history? *(the union of Upper and Lower Egypt)*

- Which two events occurred during the 2500s, and where did they take place? *(Khufu's pyramid begins in Giza; Harappan culture rises in the Indus Valley.)*
- Which event occurs earlier—the issue of Hammurabi's Code or Hatshepsut's rise to power? *(Hammurabi)*

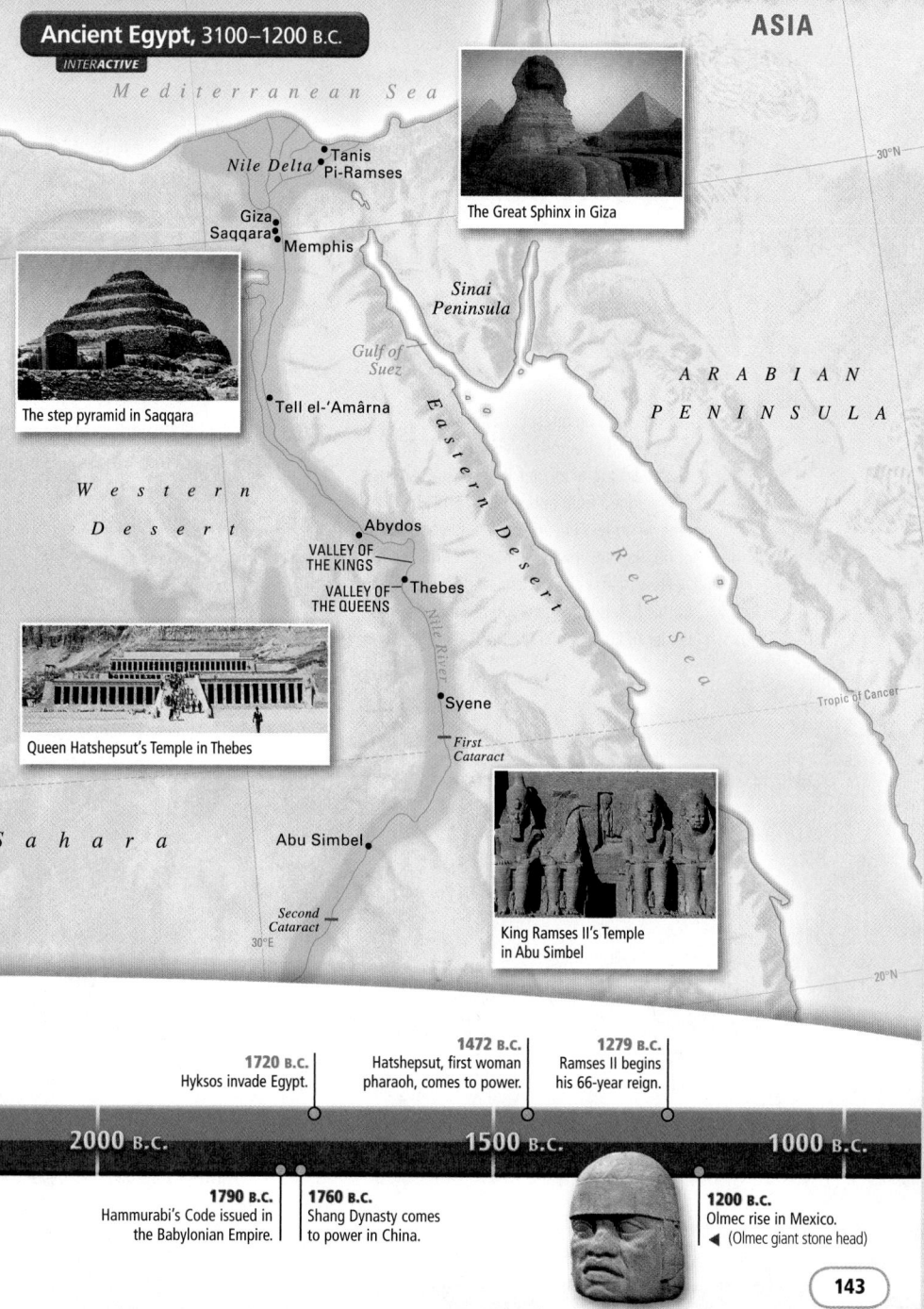

Ancient Egypt, 3100–1200 B.C.
INTERACTIVE

Mediterranean Sea

ASIA

Nile Delta
- Tanis
- Pi-Ramses

The Great Sphinx in Giza

- Giza
- Saqqara
- Memphis

Sinai Peninsula

Gulf of Suez

The step pyramid in Saqqara

- Tell el-'Amârna

ARABIAN PENINSULA

Eastern Desert

Western Desert

- Abydos
- VALLEY OF THE KINGS
- VALLEY OF THE QUEENS
- Thebes

Red Sea

Queen Hatshepsut's Temple in Thebes

- Syene

Sahara

- Abu Simbel

First Cataract

Tropic of Cancer

King Ramses II's Temple in Abu Simbel

Second Cataract
30°E

30°N

20°N

1472 B.C.
Hatshepsut, first woman pharaoh, comes to power.

1279 B.C.
Ramses II begins his 66-year reign.

1720 B.C.
Hyksos invade Egypt.

2000 B.C.   1500 B.C.   1000 B.C.

1790 B.C.
Hammurabi's Code issued in the Babylonian Empire.

1760 B.C.
Shang Dynasty comes to power in China.

1200 B.C.
Olmec rise in Mexico.
◄ (Olmec giant stone head)

143

CHAPTER 5

Introduce the Big Ideas

Read aloud the text about Big Ideas. Ask students to think about how geography affects their daily lives. For example, rivers, lakes, or mountains might make travel difficult.

Here are some other Big Ideas that you may want to emphasize in this chapter:

Belief Systems
Belief systems and religions may shape governments and societies.

Science and Technology
New inventions and techniques change the way humans live their daily lives.

Talk About It

Interpreting Maps
Ask students to read the map key and examine the map. Where was the fertile land in Egypt located? *(along the Nile River)* Why do you think most of the cities also developed along the Nile? *(The river provided the means to ship food and other goods to religious and trade centers.)*

INTERACTIVE

An interactive version of this map is available on the eEdition and Power Presentations CD-ROMs.

Find Out More

In what part of the country do most Egyptians live today? How do they make a living? Have students look in an encyclopedia or yearbook to find out if the Nile continues to be important to Egypt's economy today.

Watch the Video

In *Ancient Egypt*, archaeologist Arizona Smith and a young detective-in-training explore King Tut's tomb and learn about the Rosetta Stone. This video is part of the Ancient Civilizations Video Series.

RECOMMENDED RESOURCES

Books for the Teacher
Montet, Pierre. *Everyday Life in Egypt in the Days of Ramesses the Great.* Philadelphia: University of Pennsylvania Press, 1980. Discusses the society, religion, and everyday life of people of all classes.

Sauneron, Serge. *The Search for God in Ancient Egypt.* Ithaca: Cornell University Press, 2001. Examines how ancient Egyptian priests viewed their deities.

Videos
Egypt: Quest for Immortality. 50 minutes. Time-Life Video and Television, 1995. Explores the riches of the pharaohs' tombs.

Pharaoh's Obelisk. 60 minutes. A NOVA Production. WGBH Video, 2004.

Internet
To access these sites, visit the Research Links for this chapter at **ClassZone.com**.

The Ancient Egyptian Culture Exhibit. EMuseum at Minnesota State University, Mankato. Includes detailed maps as well as photographs of artifacts. Challenging reading level.

The British Museum: Ancient Egypt. Includes games and animations.

Objective

Describe the impact that strong leaders have on a society.

Introducing the Story

Ramses II

Ramses II had at least 6 wives and possibly more than 100 children. He outlived a number of his older sons, who would have been his heirs. His 13th son followed him to the throne.

Ramses is famous for his extensive building program. Besides his own tomb in the Valley of the Kings, he also had a huge mausoleum built for his children and many temples. He covered Egypt with more monuments and buildings than any other pharaoh.

Vocabulary Preview

empire group of lands or nations united under one ruler

golden age period of peace and prosperity

casket box for dead body

Reading the Story Aloud

1. **The teacher as reader:** Read the story aloud with expression so that students hear the drama and understand the emotional impact of the events.

2. **The students as readers:** Give student readers a few minutes to read the story to themselves before reading it aloud to the rest of the class.

Starting with a Story

Students can also follow along as they listen to the story on the eEdition or Power Presentations CD-ROMs.

Starting with a Story

THE DEATH OF RAMSES II

CALIFORNIA STANDARDS
Reading 1.1 Read aloud narrative and expository text fluently and accurately and with appropriate pacing, intonation, and expression.

Background: Egypt was one of the longest-lasting world empires. For almost 3,000 years, kings called pharaohs ruled the land. One of the most dazzling of all was Ramses II (RAM•SEEZ), who reigned from about 1279 to 1213 B.C. At a time when few Egyptians lived beyond the age of 40, Ramses II was in charge for 66 years!

Now he has finally died, and Egypt prepares for his funeral. Imagine you are there as the leader of Egypt's golden age is laid to rest.

Statue of Ramses II ▶

144

ADDITIONAL RESOURCES

Books for the Student

Kallen, Stuart. *Pyramids.* San Diego: Lucent Books, 2002. Explores the questions that still puzzle archaeologists about the building of the pyramids.

Moscovitch, Arlene. *Egypt: The Culture.* New York: Crabtree Publishing, 2000. Provides information about everyday life, beliefs, and archaeological treasures of ancient Egypt.

Videos

Ancient Egypt. Five 15-minute episodes. Case Television Production for Channel Four. Public Media Education, 1995. VHS. Designed for grades 4 through 9.

Egypt: Quest for Eternity. 60 minutes. Produced by National Geographic Society and WQED/Pittsburgh, 1993. Distributed by Columbia Tristar Home Video. DVD or VHS.

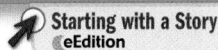
Starting with a Story
eEdition

You are a professional mourner, a person whose job is to cry at funerals. In the past, you've helped to bury some important people—but never a pharaoh! Your white mourning robe is spotless. You spent hours preparing the wreath of flowers to crown your head.

No one remembers any other pharaoh. Ramses II ruled Egypt when your grandparents were children. Some people thought he would live forever. Now he's dead and headed for his tomb in the Valley of the Kings. The ceremony began at his temple at Abu Simbel. At that temple, four 66-foot statues of Ramses II guard the entrance. Inside the secret chambers, priests preserved the pharaoh's body for burial.

Next, a royal barge carried Ramses' casket on the Nile River. Inside is the pharaoh's mummy, wrapped in orange linen and wearing a gold mask. Hundreds of important Egyptians are waiting at the tomb.

It's time to begin the procession. You line up with other mourners behind a group of slaves carrying Ramses' most important possessions. There is his sword! Could it be the one he carried into battle when he fought Egypt's enemy, the Hittites? Who will stop the Hittites now?

Tearing your hair and beating your chest, you wail your song of sorrow: "Great lord of our empire! Provider of lasting peace! Builder of temples that reach for the sun! Don't leave us! Without you, we are fatherless children!"

Sometimes you fake your cries at funerals, but today you mean every word. Trembling with fear, you wonder what will happen now.

What do you hope the new pharaoh will be like?

Reading & Writing

1. **READING: Reading Aloud** What parts of this story benefit most from being read with appropriate intonation and expression?

2. **WRITING: Narration** Suppose you are waiting to hear Ramses' son, the new pharaoh, speak for the first time. Write a brief scene in which you discuss your hopes and fears for Egypt with others in the crowd.

CALIFORNIA STANDARDS Writing 2.1
Write narratives.

(145)

Talk About It

Ask students the following questions to begin the discussion:

- From whose point of view is the story told? *(a professional mourner's)*

- Why is the mourner troubled by the funeral she is attending? *(because it is the funeral of a pharaoh who has ruled during her entire life, and she is worried that the next pharaoh may not be as capable and successful a ruler)*

- What are some present-day funeral customs? *(dark clothing, flowers, music)*

- How do today's customs compare with those of ancient Egypt? *(Similarities—People attend funerals and often show grief. Differences—People usually wear dark colors, not white; no professional mourners.)*

What do you hope the new pharaoh will be like?

Students may say that they want an intelligent pharaoh who will provide for his people. Some students may answer that they want a fierce warrior who will protect them; others may want a leader who preserves peace and encourages trade.

Making Personal Connections

Connect the discussion to today by discussing what people want in a president, a governor, or other elected official. Students may say that many of the same qualities are desired but that elected officials do not serve for life as pharaohs did.

READING & WRITING ACTIVITIES

1. READING Possible answers: the narrator's descriptions of Ramses' possessions; the narrator's song of sorrow

2. WRITING

2. Writing Rubric

	Quality of Dialogue	Specific Hopes and Fears	Number of Errors
4	detailed and lively	many	few or none
3	detailed	several	some
2	adequate	some	many
1	unclear	few or none	many major

❶ Plan & Prepare

Objectives

- Explain how the flooding of the Nile River benefited the ancient Egyptians.
- Describe how Egyptians used the fertile land along the Nile.
- Identify other natural resources that Egyptians used.
- **Language Objective:** Understand and use geographic terms such as *fertile*, *delta*, and *silt*.

Quick Look

Lesson 1 focuses on the Nile and other influences on the Egyptian economy.

❷ Focus & Motivate

Preview Explain that this lesson focuses on environment. Ask students to identify ways their environment affects their lives. For example, weather influences the clothes they wear.

Introduce the Main Ideas The three main ideas relate to the Big Idea that "Civilizations developed in places that supported agriculture or trade or both." Help students look for this Big Idea as you go through this lesson.

Reading Skill: Understanding Cause and Effect Remind students that a single cause can have more than one effect.

SAMPLE ANSWERS FOR CHART

Causes	Effects
Floods	deposited rich soil that was good for growing crops
New agricultural techniques	expanded farmland
Many land resources	mined copper and iron for tools and weapons; used gold and precious stones for jewelry; fished and hunted wildlife; traded surplus goods

---

Lesson 1

▶ **MAIN IDEAS**

❶ **Geography** The Nile River helped Egypt develop a civilization.

❷ **Economics** The fertile land provided everything Egyptians needed.

❸ **Economics** The Nile and other resources influenced Egypt's economy.

▶ **TAKING NOTES**

Reading Skill:
Understanding Cause and Effect

Following causes and effects will help you understand the main ideas in this lesson. In Lesson 1, look for the effects of each event listed in the chart. Record them on a chart of your own.

Causes	Effects
Floods	
New agricultural techniques	
Many land resources	

S Skillbuilder Handbook, page R26

▲ **Lotus Pendants** This necklace once belonged to an Egyptian king. The pendants at the bottom are lotus buds. The lotus, a water lily that grows in the Nile River, is a symbol of Egypt.

CALIFORNIA STANDARDS

6.2.1 Locate and describe the major river systems and discuss the physical settings that supported permanent settlement and early civilizations.

6.2.2 Trace the development of agricultural techniques that permitted the production of economic surplus and the emergence of cities as centers of culture and power.

6.2.6 Describe the role of Egyptian trade in the eastern Mediterranean and Nile valley.

HOW TO TEACH THE CALIFORNIA STANDARDS

Standard	Content	Student Question or Activity	Instruction
6.2.1	**Page 147** Describes the physical geography of the Nile River system	**Page 151** Students tell why Egypt developed along the Nile River.	Tell students that the Nile is the longest river in the world and spans more than 4,000 miles. Have students trace the path of the Nile on a world map.
6.2.2	**Page 149** Summarizes the agricultural techniques used by the Egyptians	**Page 151** Students explain how geography affected Egypt's economy.	Besides agriculture, have students brainstorm economic activities that helped the Egyptian economy prosper. Record students' responses on the board.
6.2.6	**Page 151** Explains the role of Egyptian transportation and trade in the Nile Valley	**Page 151** Students describe how trade along the Nile came about.	Using a world map, have students list the countries through which the Nile River flows today.

Gift of the Nile

TERMS & NAMES
cataract
delta
silt
fertile
linen

CHAPTER 5 • LESSON 1

Build on What You Know Have you ever received a gift that was very important to you? How did it affect your life? The Nile River was so important to Egypt that 2,500 years ago, an ancient Greek historian called Egypt "the gift of the Nile."

Geography of Ancient Egypt

1 **ESSENTIAL QUESTION** Why was the Nile River important? *provided water for drinking and for crops*

The Greek historian knew what he was talking about. The Nile River fed Egyptian civilization for hundreds of years.

The Longest River The Nile is 4,160 miles long—the world's longest river. It begins near the equator in Africa and flows north to the Mediterranean Sea. In the south it churns with cataracts. A **cataract** (KAT•uh•RAKT) is a waterfall. Near the sea the Nile branches into a delta. A **delta** is an area near a river's mouth where the water deposits fine soil called **silt**. In the delta, the Nile divides into many streams.

The river is called the upper Nile in the south and the lower Nile in the north. For centuries, heavy rains in Ethiopia caused the Nile to flood every summer. The floods deposited rich soil along the Nile's shores. This soil was **fertile**, which means it was good for growing crops. Unlike the Tigris and Euphrates, the Nile River flooded at the same time every year, so farmers could predict when to plant their crops.

The Nile Valley
Fertile land in Egypt stretches along the Nile and then gives way to desert. As a result, Egypt was a narrow country. ▼

147

Terms & Names

cataract a waterfall

delta the area near a river's mouth where the water deposits fine soil

silt fine soil deposited by a river

fertile good for growing crops

linen a type of fabric woven from flax plants

❸ Teach

Geography of Ancient Egypt
6.2.1

Talk About It

- **Critical Thinking: Drawing Conclusions**
  Why was it a benefit that the Nile flooded at the same time each year? *(People could be prepared and plan their lives around it.)*

California Resources

California Reading Toolkit, L14
California Modified Lesson Plans for English Learners, p. 31
California Daily Standards Practice Transparencies, TT14
California Standards Enrichment Workbook, pp. 21–24, 31–32
California Online Test Practice
California Test Generator CD-ROM
California Standards Planner and Lesson Plans, L27
California EasyPlanner CD-ROM
California eEdition CD-ROM

LESSON 1 PROGRAM RESOURCES

ON LEVEL
In-Depth Resources: Unit 3
- Family Newsletter (English and Spanish), pp. 1–2
- Reading Skill: Understanding Cause and Effect, p. 3
- Skillbuilder Practice: Drawing Conclusions from Sources, p. 8
- Vocabulary Study Guide, p. 9
- Vocabulary Cards, p. 11

Formal Assessment
- Lesson Quiz, p. 77

ENGLISH LEARNERS
In-Depth Resources in Spanish
- Reading Skill: Understanding Cause

and Effect, p. 35
- Skillbuilder Practice: Drawing Conclusions from Sources, p. 41
- Vocabulary Study Guide, p. 42

Modified Lesson Plans for English Learners, p. 31

Reading Study Guide (Spanish), p. 39

Reading Study Guide Audio CD (Spanish)

STRUGGLING READERS
In-Depth Resources: Unit 3
- Reading Skill: Understanding Cause and Effect, p. 3
- Vocabulary Study Guide, p. 9

- Vocabulary Cards, p. 11
- Reteaching Activity, p. 17

Reading Toolkit, L14

Reading Study Guide, p. 39

Reading Study Guide Audio CD

GIFTED AND TALENTED STUDENTS
Interdisciplinary Projects
- Science, p. 26

INCLUSION
EasyPlanner CD-ROM
- Reading Skill: Understanding Cause and Effect
- Vocabulary Study Guide
- Reteaching Activity

TECHNOLOGY
eEdition CD-ROM
- Starting with a Story

Power Presentations CD-ROM

Map Transparencies
- MT9 Natural Resources in Ancient Egypt

Critical Thinking Transparencies
- CT18 Understanding Cause and Effect

Test Generator CD-ROM

ClassZone.com

In-Depth Resources: Unit 3
- Reading Skill: Understanding Cause and Effect, p. 3
- Skillbuilder Practice: Drawing Conclusions from Sources, p. 8

Teach

Land of Plenty
📞 **6.2.1, 6.2.2**

Talk About It

- How did the Egyptians expand their farmland? *(irrigation canals carried river water to dry areas)*

- What kinds of crops did Egyptians grow? *(wheat, vegetables, fruits, flax)*

- How did Egyptians use the wheat that they grew? *(They ground the wheat into flour to make bread.)*

- **Critical Thinking: Making Inferences** What did the Egyptians first have to produce from the flax before they could weave it into linen fabric? *(thread)*

History from Visuals

Interpreting Maps
Ask students to locate the Nile delta on the map and then compare it with the satellite image. Point out that a river is continually building up its delta as it deposits silt.

- What part of the Nile delta does the brown area in the satellite image show? *(new delta land being built up)*

GEOGRAPHY SKILLBUILDER ANSWER
The direction of the wind and currents aided transportation. Going south, Egyptians could raise a sail and let the winds blow them. Returning north, they could drift with the current.

Red Land, Black Land The ancient Egyptians lived in narrow bands of land on each side of the Nile. They called this region the black land because of the fertile soil that the floods deposited. The red land was the barren desert beyond the fertile region.

Weather in Egypt was almost always the same. Eight months of the year were sunny and hot. The four months of winter were sunny but cooler. Most of the region received only an inch of rain a year. The parts of Egypt not near the Nile were a desert.

Isolation The harsh desert acted as a barrier to keep out enemies. The Mediterranean coast was swampy and lacked good harbors. For these reasons, early Egyptians stayed close to home.

REVIEW What did the floods of the Nile River provide for farmers?
rich black soil

Land of Plenty

② **ESSENTIAL QUESTION** How did Egyptians use the land around the Nile?
for food, flaz, and building materials
Each year, Egyptian farmers watched for white birds called ibises (EYE•bihs•uhz), which flew up from the south. When the birds

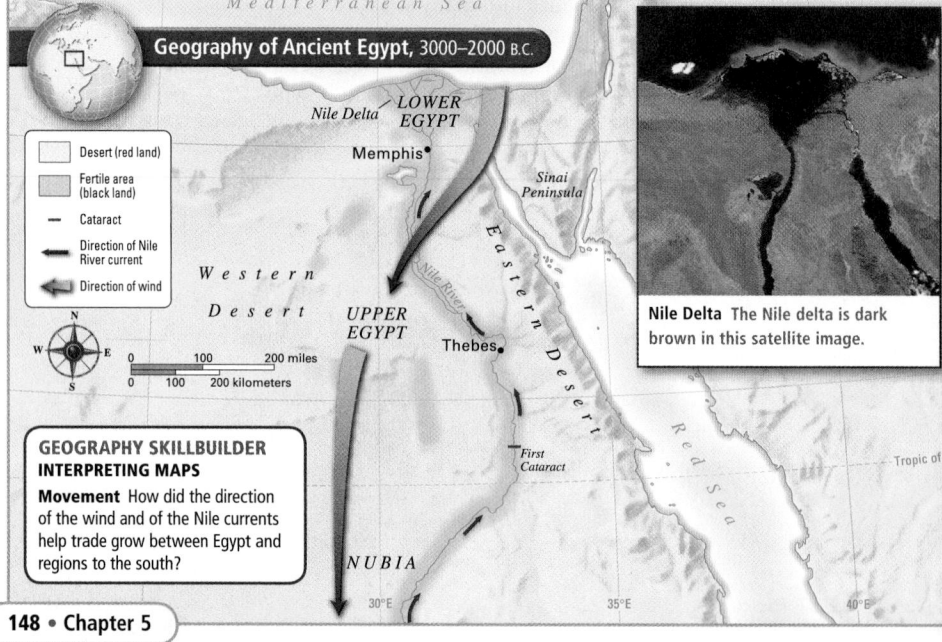

Geography of Ancient Egypt, 3000–2000 B.C.

Mediterranean Sea

Nile Delta — LOWER EGYPT
Memphis•

☐ Desert (red land)
▓ Fertile area (black land)
— Cataract
⬅ Direction of Nile River current
⬅ Direction of wind

Western Desert

UPPER EGYPT
Thebes•

Sinai Peninsula

Eastern Desert

Nile River

First Cataract

Red Sea

NUBIA

0   100   200 miles
0   100   200 kilometers

30°E   35°E   40°E

Tropic of C

Nile Delta The Nile delta is dark brown in this satellite image.

GEOGRAPHY SKILLBUILDER INTERPRETING MAPS
Movement How did the direction of the wind and of the Nile currents help trade grow between Egypt and regions to the south?

DIFFERENTIATING INSTRUCTION

English Learners

Create Visual Vocabulary Items
Have pairs draw pictures that show the meanings of the terms *fertile*, *delta*, and *silt*. Then have pairs write or say a definition of each term in their own words. Make sure students understand how the terms relate to ancient Egypt. For example, the silt was rich and fertile soil, so the Egyptians could grow food on it.

For more support, see *Modified Lesson Plans for English Learners*, pp. 31–32.

Struggling Readers

Focus on Vocabulary
Ask students to read through the lesson one section at a time and jot down any words they are unfamiliar with, such as the words *barren* and *barrier* on this page. Explain what the words mean. Then have small groups read through the section aloud with you, asking each student to read one paragraph.

arrived, the annual flood waters would soon follow. After the waters drained away, farmers could plant seeds in the fertile soil.

Agricultural Techniques By about 2400 B.C., farmers used technology to expand their farmland. Working together, they dug irrigation canals that carried river water to dry areas. Then they used a tool called a shaduf (shah•DOOF) to spread the water across the fields. These innovative, or new, techniques gave them more farmland.

Egyptian Crops Ancient Egyptians grew a large variety of foods. They were the first to grind wheat into flour and to mix the flour with yeast and water to make dough rise into bread. They grew vegetables such as lettuce, radishes, asparagus, and cucumbers. Fruits included dates, figs, grapes, and watermelons.

Egyptians also grew the materials for their clothes. They were the first to weave fibers from flax plants into a fabric called **linen**. Lightweight linen cloth was perfect for hot Egyptian days. Men wore linen wraps around their waists. Women wore loose, sleeveless dresses. Egyptians also wove marsh grasses into sandals.

Egyptian Houses Egyptians built houses using bricks made of mud from the Nile mixed with chopped straw. They placed narrow windows high in the walls to reduce bright sunlight. Egyptians often painted walls white to reflect the blazing heat. They wove sticks and palm trees to make roofs. Inside, woven reed mats covered the dirt floor. Most Egyptians slept on mats covered with linen sheets. Wealthy citizens enjoyed bed frames and cushions.

Egyptian nobles had fancier homes with tree-lined courtyards for shade. Some had a pool filled with lotus blossoms and fish. Poorer Egyptians simply went to the roof to cool off after sunset. They often cooked, ate, and even slept outside.

REVIEW What agricultural techniques did ancient Egyptians use?
Egyptians watched for ibises to know when to plant seeds, dug irrigation canals, and used a tool called a shaduf to spread water.

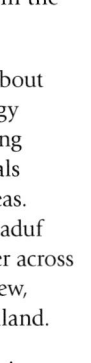

Connect to Today

▲ **Shaduf** A shaduf is a bucket on a lever. It was used to lift water from the Nile or canals. Some Egyptians still use shadufs today.

Vocabulary Strategy

The word *linen* has **multiple meanings**. Sheets and tablecloths are often called linens because they used to only be made from linen cloth.

Ancient Egypt • **149**

More About . . .

Irrigation Systems
The Egyptians captured river water during floods in artificial basins, or reservoirs, and then channeled it to fields and gardens during the growing season through a network of canals or ditches. These ditches could be opened and closed as needed.

Vocabulary Strategy

Multiple-Meaning Words
Tell students that the intended meaning of a multiple-meaning word can often be determined from the way the word is used in a sentence. Offer these two sentences as examples:

- *My mother's suit is made of* **linen.**
- *Change the bed* **linens** *before the guests arrive.*

Ask students to generate other examples.

More About . . .

Sacred Ibises
The ancient Egyptians watched for ibises to signal when the Nile would flood. The ibis was sacred to the god Thoth, who was frequently represented with the body of a human and the head of an ibis.

Ibises fed on amphibians and small aquatic animals that lived in the river. They also ate grasshoppers, locusts, and other insects that harmed crops.

DIFFERENTIATING INSTRUCTION

Inclusion

Take Audio Notes
Have students who are visually impaired take notes by making an audio or video recording with a classmate. Remind them to use the word *because* to explain causes and effects in the lesson. For example, farmers dug canals to bring in water because they needed more farmland.

Gifted and Talented Students

Create a Diorama
Group students and have them design a diorama of an Egyptian settlement with farm fields along the Nile, irrigation canals through the fields, and houses along the edges of the fields. Students can make a table-sized illustration of the river, fields, and outlying desert and then place model houses on the illustration to form a diorama.

Teach

Geography Shapes Egyptian Life

 6.2.1, 6.2.6

Talk About It

- What did Egyptians make from the minerals and stones they mined? *(tools, weapons, and jewelry)*
- What tools did Egyptians use for fishing and hunting? *(rafts, nets, harpoons, hammers, spears, boomerangs)*
- **Critical Thinking: Making Inferences** What items might an Egyptian farmer exchange by bartering? *(The farmer might exchange fruits, vegetables, or grains for copper or iron tools and weapons, turquoise jewelry, or fish and wild game.)*

Map Transparencies
- MT9 Natural Resources in Ancient Egypt

History from Visuals

Interpreting Visuals

- What kind of weapon does the hunter appear to be using? *(some kind of throwing stick)*
- On what is the hunter standing? *(a raft)*
- Who is on the raft with him? *(a woman, a child, and a bird)*

Geography Shapes Egyptian Life

farming, mining, fishing, hunting, transportation, trade

③ ESSENTIAL QUESTION What economic activities developed in Egypt?

Egypt's economy depended on farming. However, the natural resources of the area allowed other economic activities to develop too.

Mining The Egyptians wanted valuable metals that were not found in the black land. For example, they wanted copper to make tools and weapons. Egyptians looked for copper as early as 6000 B.C. Later they learned that iron was stronger, and they sought it as well. Ancient Egyptians also desired gold for its bright beauty. The Egyptian word for gold was *nub*. Nubia was the Egyptian name for the area of the upper Nile that had the richest gold mines in Africa.

Mining minerals was difficult. Veins (long streaks) of copper, iron, and bronze were hidden inside desert mountains in the hot Sinai Peninsula, east of Egypt. Even during the cool season, chipping minerals out of the rock was miserable work.

Egyptians mined precious stones too. They were probably the first people in the world to mine turquoise (TUR•KWOYZ). The Egyptians also mined lapis lazuli (LAP•ihs LAZ•uh•lee). These beautiful blue stones were used in jewelry.

Fishing and Hunting The Nile had fish and other wildlife that Egyptians wanted. To go on the river, Egyptians made lightweight rafts by binding together reeds. They used everything from nets to harpoons to catch fish. One ancient painting even shows a man ready to hit a catfish with a wooden hammer.

More adventurous hunters speared hippopotamuses and crocodiles along the Nile. Egyptians also captured quail with nets. They used boomerangs to knock down flying ducks and geese. (A boomerang is a curved stick that returns to the person who threw it.)

▲ **Hunter** This wall painting from a tomb shows a man hunting marsh birds.

INTERDISCIPLINARY ACTIVITIES

Art

Imitate Egyptian Art
Have students create a drawing that imitates Egyptian art and that combines pictures and calligraphy, just as the wall painting shown on this page combines pictures and hieroglyphs. Suggest that students portray themselves in an everyday activity and then use calligraphy to identify the people in the drawing and explain what is happening.

Math

Create a Barter System
Divide the class into small groups and have each group prepare a barter exchange list, in which they identify at least ten items for trading and tell what each is worth. For example, one notebook might be worth ten pencils. After the groups finish, have them share their lists with the class.

Transportation and Trade Eventually, Egyptians equipped their reed boats with sails and oars. The Nile then became a highway. The river's current was slow, so boaters used paddles to go faster when they traveled north with the current. Going south, they raised a sail and let the winds that blew in that direction push them.

The Nile provided so well for Egyptians that sometimes they had surpluses, or more goods than they needed. They began to trade with each other. Ancient Egypt had no money, so people exchanged goods that they grew or made. This method of trade is called bartering.

REVIEW How did geography affect Egypt's economy?
Egyptians mined copper, iron, gold, lapis lazuli, and turquoise; they hunted and fished along the Nile; they traded up and down the Nile.

Lesson Summary
- The Nile River created a fertile land in a desert.
- The Egyptians used technology to expand their farms and grow many crops.
- Ancient Egyptians also mined, fished, hunted, and traded.

Why It Matters Now . . .
Ancient Egyptians invented many things we use today, such as yeast bread, turquoise jewelry, and linen clothes.

Turquoise Jewelry
This bracelet has turquoise and other precious stones. ▼

1 Lesson Review

 Homework Helper
ClassZone.com

Terms & Names
1. Explain the importance of

| cataract | silt | linen |
| delta | fertile | |

Using Your Notes
Understanding Cause and Effect Use your completed chart to answer the following question:
2. How did new agricultural techniques make the Egyptians more prosperous? (6.2.2)

Causes	Effects
Floods	
New agricultural techniques	
Many land resources	

Main Ideas
3. Why did Egypt develop along the Nile? (6.2.1)
4. How did irrigation canals expand farmland in Egypt? (6.2.2)
5. How did trade along the Nile come about? (6.2.6)

Critical Thinking
6. **Making Inferences** How did climate affect the daily lives of Egyptians? (6.2.1)
7. **Drawing Conclusions** Analyze the gifts of the Nile in terms of innovation and cultural endurance. (6.2.1)

Activity
Making a Sketch Create a sketch showing the different types of economic activities that took place in ancient Egypt. (6.2.2)

Ancient Egypt • **151**

④ Assess & Reteach

Assess Have pairs take turns answering the questions. Ask volunteers to share their completed charts for item 2.

 Formal Assessment
- Lesson Quiz, p. 77

Reteach Divide the class into three groups. Assign each group one of the subsections in this lesson—"Geography of Ancient Egypt," "Land of Plenty," or "Geography Shapes Egyptian Life." Each group should work together to list three or four important ideas in its subsection. Have groups share responses with the class. Make sure that each group takes notes on the subsections that the other groups covered.

 In-Depth Resources: Unit 3
- Vocabulary Cards, p. 11
- Reteaching Activity, p. 17

Homework Helper
Visit **ClassZone.com** for a lesson review, a flip-card activity, and links to related Web sites.

1 Lesson Review Answers

Terms & Names
1. • cataract, p. 147
   • delta, p. 147
   • silt, p. 147
   • fertile, p. 147
   • linen, p. 149

Using Your Notes
See page 146 for an example of a completed chart.
2. By making more land and water available for crops, the Egyptians had more to trade with other groups.

Main Ideas
3. The Nile provided fertile soil, water, transportation, and food.

4. Canals carried water to land that did not have enough, expanding land for farming.
5. People had more goods than they needed. They built boats and sailed up and down the Nile to trade with each other.

Critical Thinking
6. Deserts stopped Egyptians from traveling too far. They also kept invaders out. Regular floods meant that farmers knew when to plant crops.
7. Fertile soil and warm weather meant that Egyptians could farm and hunt. With more goods than they needed, they had time to create art and jewelry. They also learned how to mine, build ships, and barter.

Activity Rubric

	Number of Activities	Quality of Illustrations
4	many	clear and detailed
3	several	clear, with some detail
2	some	vague
1	few or none	sloppy or inaccurate

Ancient Egypt • **151**

Objectives

- Understand and describe the role of Egyptian trade in the eastern Mediterranean and Nile valley.
- Analyze and interpret information from an infographic.

❶ Focus & Motivate

Preview Explain that the Daily Life feature will give students more information about how Egyptians traveled and traded.

❷ Teach

Talk About It

- What items are these traders bringing with them? *(goats, sheep, fruit, barley, wheat)*
- Why did the traders lower the sail when traveling north? *(The winds usually blew south. The current carried boats north.)*
- **Critical Thinking: Drawing Conclusions** What dangers might Egyptian traders have faced? *(Possible answers: bad weather, robbers, crocodile attacks)*

Daily Life
Extend Lesson 1

Research Links
ClassZone.com

Life on the Nile River

Purpose: To learn about the life of Egyptian traders on the Nile River

If you were an Egyptian trader, you would sail the Nile River in a boat that looks much like the one shown here. Traders carried their goods in reed boats that they sailed up and down the Nile. As shown below, the simple boat held everything the traders needed for their trip on the river.

Ⓐ Hull In the hull below the boat's deck, you store barrels of fruit and sacks of barley and wheat.

Ⓑ Sails You raise your linen sail to catch the wind when you travel south on the Nile against the current. You lower the sail when you travel with the current north on the Nile.

Ⓒ Oars The boat has a basket and oar at either end. Once the boat sets sail, you or another trader will stand in the basket and use the oar to steer.

Ⓓ On Deck There is much activity on the boat's deck, as you store more goods and tie up the sheep and goats you plan to barter.

Ⓔ River Animals A pair of ibises and some hippos feed as you load your boat. But you keep your eye on the crocodiles—the most dangerous animals on the Nile.

CALIFORNIA STANDARDS
6.2.6 Describe the role of Egyptian trade in the eastern Mediterranean and Nile valley.

DIFFERENTIATING INSTRUCTION

English Learners

Understand Vocabulary
This feature includes terms that are probably unfamiliar to English learners. Explain that barley and wheat are grains that are often used in bread or to feed animals.

Have a volunteer point out where the hull and oars are on the ship. If necessary, draw a hull and oars on the board to be sure students understand the terms.

Struggling Readers

Role-Play: Be a Trader
Divide the class into small groups. Have each group choose a person to play the role of a trader in ancient Egypt. The other students in the group will be the trader's customers.

Groups should use what they have learned to create and answer questions such as, "What do you have to trade?" and "How did you get here?" Invite volunteers to act out their questions and answers for the class.

Research Links

Visit **ClassZone.com** for age-appropriate Web sites related to this topic.

More About . . .

When Crocodiles Attack

Crocodiles are smaller than they used to be. Modern crocodiles are rarely over 20 feet long, but by studying fossils, scientists have learned that Nile crocodiles were nearly 30 feet long.

Crocodiles are fast-moving and highly intelligent reptiles. They have been known to attack humans, but they usually eat fish and birds. A crocodile floats in the water, resembling a drifting log, and then uses its powerful tail to smack its prey into the river.

Activities

1. **TALK ABOUT IT** What were some of the advantages of being an Egyptian trader? What were some of the disadvantages?

2. **WRITE ABOUT IT** Imagine you are an Egyptian trader and write a diary entry about a day spent sailing the Nile. You could write about the goods you're planning to trade or about the animals you see during your trip. (Writing 2.2)

Ancient Egypt • **153**

ACTIVITIES ANSWERS

1. **TALK ABOUT IT** Possible answers: Advantages—access to rare goods from other places, ability to travel. Disadvantages—no money, so have to barter; danger from storms, thieves, and crocodiles

2. **WRITE ABOUT IT**

2. Writing Rubric

	Level of Knowledge	Style of Language	Number of Errors
4	detailed	vivid	few or none
3	adequate	descriptive	some
2	some	somewhat descriptive	many
1	little or none	vague	many

❶ Plan & Prepare

Objectives

- Identify jobs and social roles of ancient Egyptians.
- Describe Egyptian advances in calendars, geometry, medicine, and writing.
- Explain Egyptian religious beliefs.
- **Language Objective:** Understand and use terms related to writing, such as *scribe*, *hieroglyph*, and *papyrus*.

Quick Look

Lesson 2 focuses on the structure of Egyptian society and how science, technology, and religion influenced it.

❷ Focus & Motivate

Preview Suggest that students compare modern jobs with the kinds the ancient Egyptians held.

Introduce the Main Ideas The three main ideas relate to the Big Idea "Belief systems and religions may shape governments and societies." Help students look for this Big Idea as you go through this lesson.

Reading Skill: Categorizing Tell students that a category names the subject of a group of ideas. Point out that the boldfaced headings in a lesson categorize the information in that lesson.

SAMPLE ANSWERS FOR DIAGRAM

Egyptian Culture

- **Religion** believed in happy afterlife, believed in many gods, created mummies
- **Work and family** specialized jobs, complex social order, fairly equal rights for women, school for some boys
- **Learning** developed world's first 365-day calendar, developed geometry, performed surgery, developed writing system

---

Lesson 2

▶ MAIN IDEAS

① **Economics** Egyptians developed a complex society with many different jobs and social roles.

② **Science and Technology** Egyptians made advances in calendars, geometry, medicine, and other areas.

③ **Belief Systems** Egyptians believed in many gods and a happy life after death.

▶ TAKING NOTES

Reading Skill: Categorizing Sorting information into groups helps you understand patterns in history. In Lesson 2, look for three categories of Egyptian culture and details about them. Record the information on a web diagram.

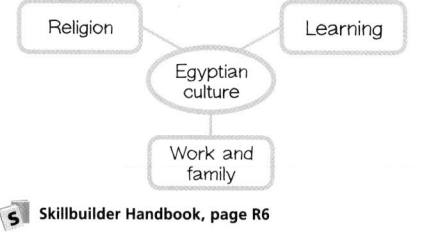

Religion — Egyptian culture — Learning

Work and family

🅢 Skillbuilder Handbook, page R6

▲ **Cat Mummy** Some Egyptians made their dead pets into mummies and gave them a formal burial. Cats were especially honored in Egypt.

CALIFORNIA STANDARDS

6.2.2 Trace the development of agricultural techniques that permitted the production of economic surplus and the emergence of cities as centers of culture and power.

6.2.3 Understand the relationship between religion and the social and political order in Mesopotamia and Egypt.

6.2.5 Discuss the main features of Egyptian art and architecture.

6.2.9 Trace the evolution of language and its written forms.

HI 2 Students understand and distinguish cause, effect, sequence, and correlation in historical events, including the long- and short-term causal relations.

HOW TO TEACH THE CALIFORNIA STANDARDS

Standard	Content	Student Question or Activity	Instruction
6.2.2	**Page 155** Describes the effects of economic surplus	**Page 161** Students tell why some Egyptians became artisans.	Discuss how the Egyptian civilization would have been different without agricultural surplus.
6.2.3	**Page 156** Illustrates social, political, and religious roles in Egyptian society	**Page 157** Students describe the levels of Egyptian society.	Ask students which Egyptian social roles were affiliated with religion? (*pharaoh, priests and nobles*)
6.2.5	**Page 158** Connects geometry to Egyptian architecture	**Page 158** Students summarize some advances in Egyptian learning.	Explain that mummification was an art form for the Egyptians. Discuss reasons why so much effort was put into this process.
6.2.9	**Pages 158–159** Traces the evolution of writing in Egypt	**Page 161** Students explain how hieroglyphs were used.	Discuss how long it would take to learn how to write using hieroglyphs.
HI 2	**Page 158** Explains how Egyptians applied practical knowledge of various subjects	**Page 161** Students tell why Egyptian advances in learning were important.	After reading the lesson, create a class chart listing practical ways that Egyptians applied their knowledge of astronomy, geometry, and medicine.

Life in Ancient Egypt

TERMS & NAMES

scribe

hieroglyph

papyrus

afterlife

embalm

mummy

Build on What You Know As you have seen, Egypt prospered along the Nile. This prosperity made life easier and provided greater opportunities for many Egyptians.

Work and Family Life

1 ESSENTIAL QUESTION How did work and social roles affect people in ancient Egypt? *work roles expanded, social roles limited Egyptians*

When farmers produce food surpluses, the society's economy begins to expand. Cities emerge as centers of culture and power, and people learn to do jobs that do not involve agriculture. For example, some ancient Egyptians learned to be **scribes**, people whose job was to write and keep records.

Specialized Jobs As Egyptian civilization grew more complex, people took on jobs other than that of a farmer or scribe. Some skilled artisans erected stone or brick houses and temples. Other artisans made pottery, incense, mats, furniture, linen clothing, sandals, or jewelry.

A few Egyptians traveled to the upper Nile to trade with other Africans. These traders took Egyptian products such as scrolls, linen, gold, and jewelry. They brought back exotic woods, animal skins, and live beasts.

Luxor, Egypt Skilled artisans helped to build this temple and the shafts with pointed tops, which are called obelisks. ▼

155

Terms & Names

scribe a person whose job was to write and keep records

hieroglyph a picture that stands for a word or letter

papyrus a paperlike material made from a reed of the same name

afterlife life that takes place in another world after death

embalm to preserve a body after death

mummy a body that has been dried so it won't decay

❸ Teach

Work and Family Life

✎ **6.2.2, 6.2.3, HI 2**

Talk About It

- **Critical Thinking: Making Inferences**
  What job would the child of a farmer in ancient Egypt most likely learn? *(farming, because most children learned their parents' jobs)*

California Resources

California Reading Toolkit, L15

California Modified Lesson Plans for English Learners, p. 33

California Daily Standards Practice Transparencies, TT15

California Standards Enrichment Workbook, pp. 23–26, 29–30, 37–38

California Online Test Practice

California Test Generator CD-ROM

California Standards Planner and Lesson Plans, L29

California EasyPlanner CD-ROM

California eEdition CD-ROM

LESSON 2 PROGRAM RESOURCES

ON LEVEL

In-Depth Resources: Unit 3
- Reading Skill: Categorizing, p. 4
- Vocabulary Cards, p. 11

Formal Assessment
- Lesson Quiz, p. 78

ENGLISH LEARNERS

In-Depth Resources in Spanish
- Reading Skill: Categorizing, p. 36

Modified Lesson Plans for English Learners, p. 33

Reading Study Guide (Spanish), p. 41

Reading Study Guide Audio CD (Spanish)

STRUGGLING READERS

In-Depth Resources: Unit 3
- Reading Skill: Categorizing, p. 4
- Vocabulary Cards, p. 11
- Reteaching Activity, p. 18

Reading Toolkit, L15

Reading Study Guide, p. 41

Reading Study Guide Audio CD

GIFTED AND TALENTED STUDENTS

In-Depth Resources: Unit 3
- Primary Source: Herodotus' Account of Life in Egypt, p. 15

Interdisciplinary Projects
- Math, p. 25
- Language Arts, p. 27

INCLUSION

EasyPlanner CD-ROM
- Reading Skill: Categorizing
- Reteaching Activity

TECHNOLOGY

eEdition CD-ROM

Power Presentations CD-ROM

Humanities Transparencies
- HT9 Hieroglyphs

Critical Thinking Transparencies
- CT19 Categorizing

Test Generator CD-ROM

ClassZone.com

In-Depth Resources: Unit 3
• Reading Skill: Categorizing, p. 4

More About . . .

Egyptian Artisans
Egyptian artisans were highly respected within their communities. Most worked in workshops, where they gained training and experience. Some workshops were devoted to making objects just for temples or just for the pharaoh.

History from Visuals

Interpreting Visuals

• What group is at the base of the pyramid, and therefore is also the largest? *(laborers and slaves)*

• What group is the next largest? *(farmers)*

• How does the shape of the pyramid relate to the levels in Egyptian society? *(As you go up the pyramid, its decreasing size corresponds to the decreasing population in each level.)*

SKILLBUILDER ANSWER
People are seen performing different types of work, from bottom to top: construction, serving meals; producing food; making crafts and selling goods; keeping records; performing religious ceremonies. The hardest physical labor is done by people in the bottom level, who must drag and carry loads.

INTERACTIVE
An interactive version of this infographic is available on the eEdition and Power Presentations CD-ROMs.

More About . . .

The Egyptian Military
The Egyptian army was made up primarily of draftees who were selected from all parts of the country. The governor of each territory chose a certain number of men to serve in the pharaoh's army. In wartime, they were supplemented by mercenaries and troops from allied countries.

The army had divisions of archers, infantry, and, after 1900 B.C., charioteers. Their weapons included clubs, spears, axes, throwing sticks, and shields as well as bows and arrows.

Rulers and Priests As Egypt grew, so did its need to organize. Egyptians created a government that divided the empire into 42 provinces. Many officials worked to keep the provinces running smoothly. Egypt also created an army to defend itself.

One of the highest jobs in Egypt was to be a priest. Priests followed formal rituals and took care of the temples. Before entering a temple, a priest bathed and put on special linen garments and white sandals. Priests cleaned the sacred statues in temples, changed their clothes, and even fed them meals.

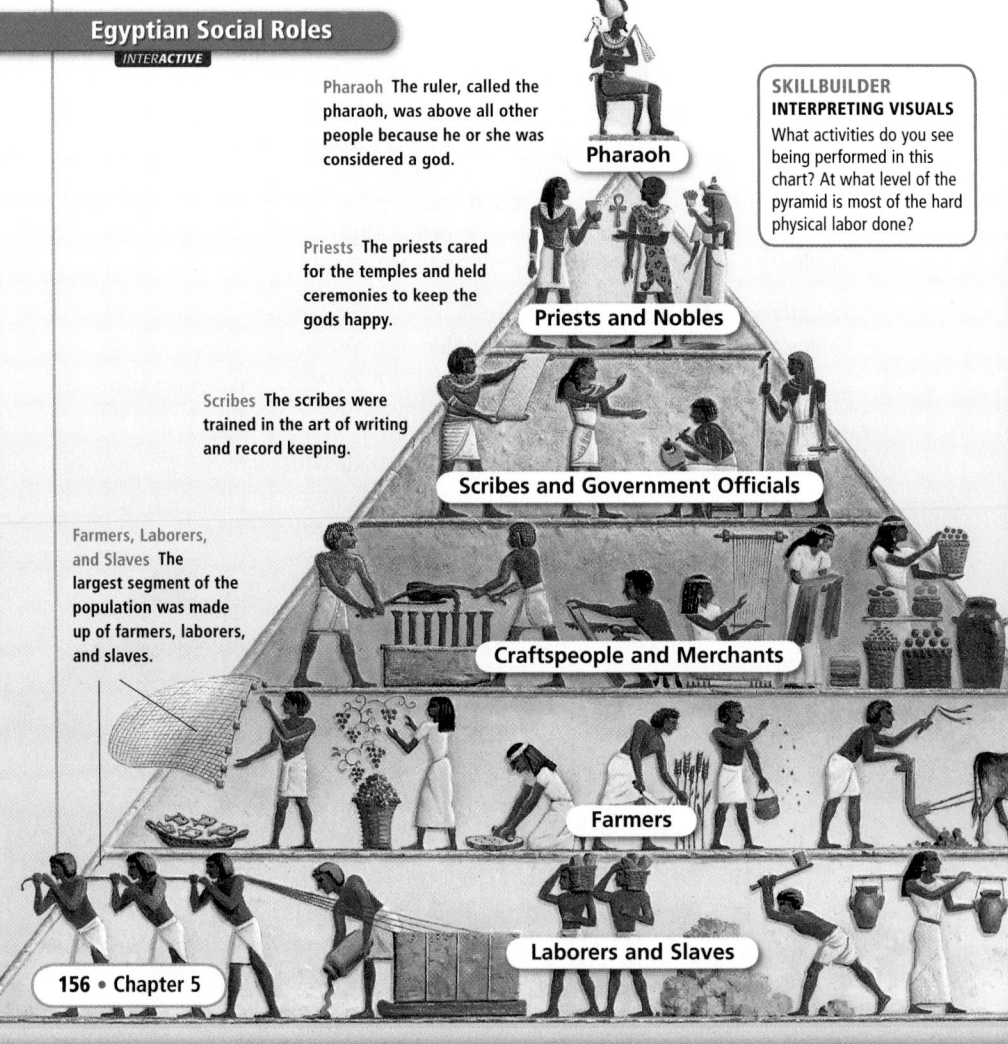

Egyptian Social Roles
INTERACTIVE

Pharaoh The ruler, called the pharaoh, was above all other people because he or she was considered a god.

Pharaoh

Priests The priests cared for the temples and held ceremonies to keep the gods happy.

Priests and Nobles

Scribes The scribes were trained in the art of writing and record keeping.

Scribes and Government Officials

Farmers, Laborers, and Slaves The largest segment of the population was made up of farmers, laborers, and slaves.

Craftspeople and Merchants

Farmers

Laborers and Slaves

156 • Chapter 5

SKILLBUILDER
INTERPRETING VISUALS
What activities do you see being performed in this chart? At what level of the pyramid is most of the hard physical labor done?

DIFFERENTIATING INSTRUCTION

English Learners

Identify Related Words
Tell students that the word *scribe* comes from a Latin word that means "to write." Ask students if they know words in other languages with that meaning. *(Possible answers: Escribir is Spanish and écrire is French; both mean "to write.")* Ask what English word is similar to *papyrus. (paper)* Have pairs create sentences that use *scribe* and *papyrus.*

For more support, see *Modified Lesson Plans for English Learners,* pp. 33–34.

Inclusion

Enlarge Images
Students who have visual impairments may benefit from the enlarged version of the "Egyptian Social Roles" feature, available on the eEdition and Power Presentations CD-ROMs.

Together, the priests and the ruler held ceremonies to please the gods. Egyptians believed that if the gods were angry, the Nile would not flood. As a result, crops would not grow, and people would die. So the ruler and the priests tried hard to keep the gods happy and to maintain the social and political order.

Slaves Slaves were at the bottom of society. In Egypt, people became slaves if they owed a debt, committed a crime, or were captured in war. In general, Egyptian slaves were treated well and were usually freed after a period of time. One exception was the slaves who had to work in the mines. Many died from the exhausting labor.

Life for Women Egypt was one of the best places in the ancient world to be a woman. Unlike other ancient African cultures, in Egyptian society men and women had fairly equal rights. For example, they could both own and manage their own property.

The main job of most women was to care for their children and home, but some did other jobs too. Some women wove cloth. Others worked with their husbands in fields or workshops. Some women, such as Queen Tiy, even rose to important positions in the government.

Childhood Children in Egypt played with toys such as dolls, animal figures, board games, and marbles. Their parents made the toys from wood or clay. Boys and girls also played rough physical games with balls made of leather or reeds.

Boys and some girls from wealthy families went to schools run by scribes or priests. Most other children learned their parents' jobs. Almost all Egyptians married when they were in their early teens.

> **REVIEW** What were the levels of Egyptian society?
> pharaoh, priests, scribes, merchants and craftspeople, farmers and laborers and slaves

Expanding Knowledge

2 **ESSENTIAL QUESTION** How did learning advance in ancient Egypt?

new ideas and techniques in astronomy, geometry, medicine, and writing

As in many ancient societies, much of the knowledge of Egypt came about as priests studied the world to find ways to please the gods. Other advances came about because of practical discoveries.

Ancient Egypt • 157

 In-Depth Resources: Unit 3
• Primary Source: Herodotus' Account of Life in Egypt, p. 15

Teach

Expanding Knowledge
6.2.5, 6.2.9, HI 2
Talk About It

• How did the Egyptians develop the idea for a 365-day calendar? *(They observed that the star Sirius always returned to the same position in the sky every 365 days.)*

• On what material did the Egyptians write? *(papyrus)*

• **Critical Thinking: Comparing and Contrasting** How do the letters of the English alphabet differ from hieroglyphs? *(All English letters stand for sounds, not words or ideas. English letters do not look like physical objects.)*

DIFFERENTIATING INSTRUCTION

Struggling Readers

Create Job Descriptions
Have small groups use the text to write job descriptions for people at each level of Egyptian society. Discuss the type of information they should include, such as the skills needed for each job and the materials workers would use. Ask students to record the information on a chart and then to present it orally.

Gifted and Talented Students

Draw a U.S. Social Pyramid
Direct small groups to draw and label a pyramid that shows the social levels in U.S. society. Allow time for groups to share and compare their pyramids. Then discuss how students' pyramids compare with Egyptian society.

More About . . .

Uses of Egyptian Astronomy

The Egyptians used measurements from the stars to align pyramids and temples with Earth's four cardinal directions. The priest-astronomers were amazingly accurate in marking the foundations of buildings. For example, the four sides of the Great Pyramid at Giza (discussed on page 167) are aligned to face north, east, south, and west with less than a half degree of error.

More About . . .

Egyptian Math

The Egyptians used only the operations of addition and subtraction, not multiplication and division. To multiply and divide, they used tables of duplication. For example, to find the product of 7 times 5, they would refer to a table that doubled the multiplier.

```
 1 x 5 =   5
 2 x 5 =  10
 4 x 5 =  20
 8 x 5 =  40
16 x 5 =  80
32 x 5 = 160
```

Since 1 + 2 + 4 equals 7, they would add 5 + 10 + 20 to get 35 as the answer. (1 x 5 = 5 plus 2 x 5 = 10 plus 4 x 5 = 20) To divide, they would reverse this process.

Astronomy Egyptian priests studied the sky as part of their religion. About 5,000 years ago, they noticed that a star now called Sirius (SIHR•ee•uhs) appeared shortly before the Nile began to flood. The star returned to the same position in 365 days. Based on that, Egyptians developed the world's first practical calendar.

Geometry The Egyptians developed some of the first geometry. Each year the Nile's floods washed away land boundaries. To restore property lines, surveyors measured the land by using ropes that were knotted at regular intervals.

Geometric shapes such as squares and triangles were sacred to Egyptians. Architects used them in the design of royal temples and monuments.

Medicine Egyptian doctors often prepared dead bodies for burial, so they knew the parts of the body. That knowledge helped them perform some of the world's first surgery. Some doctors specialized in using medicines made of herbs.

Egyptian medicine was far from perfect. Doctors believed that the heart controlled thought and the brain circulated blood, which is the opposite of what is known now. Some Egyptian treatments would raise eyebrows today. One "cure" for an upset stomach was to eat a hog's tooth crushed inside sugar cakes!

Hieroglyphs Beginning about 3000 B.C., Egyptians developed a writing system using hieroglyphs. **Hieroglyphs** (HY•uhr•uh•GLIHFS) are pictures that stand for different words or sounds. Early Egyptians created a hieroglyphic system with about 700 characters. Over time the system grew to include more than 6,000 symbols.

The Egyptians also developed a paper-like material called **papyrus** (puh•PY•ruhs) from a reed of the same name. Egyptians cut the stems into strips, pressed them, and dried them into sheets that could be rolled into scrolls. Papyrus scrolls were light and easy to carry. With them, Egyptians created some of the first books.

REVIEW What advances in learning did the Egyptians make? They created a 365-day calendar, developed accurate surveying methods, learned to use herbs for medicine, developed a writing system, and learned to make papyrus.

▲ **Scribe** A person who wanted to be a scribe had to study many years to learn all of the hieroglyphs.

INTERDISCIPLINARY ACTIVITIES

Math

Calculate Like Egyptians

Tell students about the ancient Egyptians' use of duplication tables described in "More About Egyptian Math" on this page. Write the duplication table on the board, and have students use it to find the answers to the following multiplication problems:

13 x 5 (40 + 20 + 5 = 65)

27 x 5 (80 + 40 + 10 + 5 = 135)

31 x 5 (80 + 40 + 20 + 10 + 5 = 155)

Science

Explain the Return of Sirius

Ask students to write a paragraph or draw a diagram to explain the return of Sirius to the same position every 365 days. They may need to use reference books or the Internet for more information. Students should learn that the stars do not move, but their position in the night sky changes because of Earth's orbit around the sun, which takes about 365 days.

Primary Source

Hieroglyphs

The ancient Egyptians used hieroglyphs in many ways, as shown in this carving of Senusret I, a ruler from the 1900s B.C.

- They could be simple picture writing. For example, a wavy line might mean "water."

- Some pictures stood for ideas. A circle often meant Re, the sun god.

- Finally, some signs also came to represent sounds. For example, the signs below represent the name of Cleopatra, a foreign queen who would later rule Egypt.

KL E O P A T-R A-T

DOCUMENT–BASED QUESTION
What do you think is the purpose of the hieroglyphs on this carving?

These symbols represent the name of ruler Senusret I.

These pictures stand for the idea "given life."

These symbols represent the name of the Egyptian god Amon.

Beliefs and Religion

3 **ESSENTIAL QUESTION** What religious beliefs did Egyptians hold?

many gods, a happy life after death

We know from their writing and their art that, in general, the Egyptians had a positive view of life. The black land provided most of the Egyptians' needs. As a result, they did not have to struggle to make a living.

Life After Death Their positive outlook shaped their religion and led them to believe that the gods favored them. Egyptians believed that their prosperity could continue with a happy afterlife. An **afterlife** is a life believed to follow death. Not every ancient culture shared Egyptians' beliefs. For example, the Sumerians thought that the afterlife was miserable.

Vocabulary Strategy

Afterlife is a **compound word.** You can divide it into the words *after* and *life.* An afterlife is a life believed to follow death.

DIFFERENTIATING INSTRUCTION

English Learners

Decode Compound Words
List on the board some other compound words used in this lesson.

workshops	everyday
paperlike	today
jackal-headed	

Help students identify the two words in each compound word and then determine the meaning of the compound.

Struggling Readers

Identify Main Ideas
Tell students that the main idea of a paragraph is often stated in the first or second sentence. Sometimes, however, the main idea is implied and can be stated by summarizing the paragraph.

To give students practice in identifying main ideas, have them list the main idea of each paragraph under the heading "Beliefs and Religion."

Interpreting Primary Sources

Hieroglyphs

- Can you identify three ways that hieroglyphs were used? *(as pictures for words, as symbols for ideas, and as signs for sounds)*

- Why might it be difficult to interpret hieroglyphs? *(The symbols could represent different things.)*

Note that some English words have more than one meaning also.

DOCUMENT–BASED QUESTION **ANSWER**
so that the Egyptian people would think of Senusreti as a god and accept his rule

 Humanities Transparencies
- HT9 Hieroglyphs

Teach

Beliefs and Religion

6.2.3, 6.2.5, HI 2

Talk About It

- How did the Egyptian belief about the afterlife differ from the Sumerians' belief? *(The Egyptians thought the afterlife was happy, and the Sumerians thought it was miserable.)*

- Why did Egyptians make mummies? *(Egyptians believed they would need their bodies in the afterlife, so they embalmed bodies after death.)*

- **Critical Thinking: Summarizing** What did Egyptians do to achieve a happy afterlife? *(They were embalmed if they could afford it, and they lived a good life in order to be judged worthy by the gods.)*

Vocabulary Strategy

Compound Words
Point out that some compound words are hyphenated, such as *one-sided, long-lived,* and *empty-handed.* Ask students to generate examples of non-hyphenated compound words. *(Possible answers: classroom, bookmark)* Have students identify the words that make up each compound word and tell its meaning.

Interpreting Visuals
Tell students that the god Anubis is depicted with the head of a jackal and appears at the center of the scale in the painting. The god Toth, depicted as a baboon in this painting, recorded the results of the judgment. Ask students to identify what animals are combined in the goddess Amemet, who is kneeling before Toth. *(the head of a crocodile, the forebody of a lion, and the hind-quarters of a hippopotamus)*

Point out the characteristic features of Egyptian art in this papyrus painting, such as the combination of pictures with hieroglyphic writing, the stylized (as opposed to realistic) depiction of the characters, and the flatness (or lack of perspective or depth).

More About . . .

The Afterlife and Mummification
The ancient Egyptians based their belief in the afterlife on their observations of nature: the sun and moon appeared and disappeared; plants died and new plants grew from seeds.

Originally, Egyptians believed that only the pharaohs could attain the afterlife. Over time, however, the belief arose that everyone had the opportunity. Mummification helped a person attain immortality, but it was not considered an absolute requirement.

▲ **Judgment of the Dead** Egyptians believed that bad deeds made a heart heavy. They thought that the god Anubis weighed each dead person's heart, as shown in this Egyptian art. If it was lighter than a feather, the reward was a happy afterlife. If the heart was heavier than a feather, Anubis fed it to a monster.

Many Gods As you have learned in Chapter 3, polytheism is a belief in many gods. The Egyptians worshiped gods that were related to the afterlife and to parts of nature—such as the sun, the river, and plant life. Some of the most important Egyptian gods included

- Re (ray)—the sun god (later called Amon-Re)
- Osiris (oh•SY•rihs)—a god who judged Egyptians after death
- Isis (EYE•sihs)—a fertility goddess who was Osiris' wife
- Anubis (uh•NOO•bihs)—a god of the dead

Making Mummies Egyptians thought they would need their bodies in the afterlife, so they embalmed dead people. **Embalm** means to preserve a body after death. First, embalmers removed all organs except the heart. Next, they filled the body with a mixture of salt and herbs to create a mummy. A **mummy** is a body that has been dried so it won't decay. When dry, the mummy was wrapped in hundreds of yards of linen strips. The whole process of embalming and wrapping took about 70 days. Embalming was expensive, and not everyone could afford it.

INTERDISCIPLINARY ACTIVITIES

Science

Compare Embalming Techniques
Encourage interested students to research present-day embalming techniques and find out how long the bodies remain preserved. Have students give an oral report to the class, comparing these techniques and how long they last with those of the ancient Egyptians.

Science

Investigate the Effect of Environment on Preservation
Ask students to hypothesize why many artifacts from ancient Egypt are so well-preserved. Suggest that students test environmental influences on preservation. For example, students could make two scrolls and bury one in a container of dry sand and another in a container of wet mud. After a week, they could compare the conditions of the scrolls.

The mummy was placed in a coffin inside a tomb. The tomb also held everyday objects, furniture, and food. Scenes from the person's life were painted on the walls. The Egyptians expected these pictures to become real so that the dead person could use them in the afterlife.

REVIEW What did the Egyptians think happened after death?
They believed they would be judged and then lead
Lesson Summary a life in another world.

- The Egyptians developed a calendar, early geometry, medical knowledge, and hieroglyphic writing.
- Ancient Egypt had a complex society with specialized jobs. Women and slaves lived better there than in many other ancient lands.
- The Egyptians believed in many gods related to nature. They also believed in a happy afterlife.

Why It Matters Now . . .
The ancient Egyptians were the first people known to develop a formal religion based on a belief in the afterlife. Such a belief is part of most religions today.

Anubis Egyptians believed the jackal-headed god Anubis weighed their hearts after death. ▼

2 Lesson Review

 Homework Helper
ClassZone.com

Terms & Names

1. Explain the importance of

| scribe | papyrus | embalm |
| hieroglyph | afterlife | mummy |

Using Your Notes

Categorizing Use your completed web diagram to answer the following question:

2. What jobs did Egyptians hold? (6.2.3)

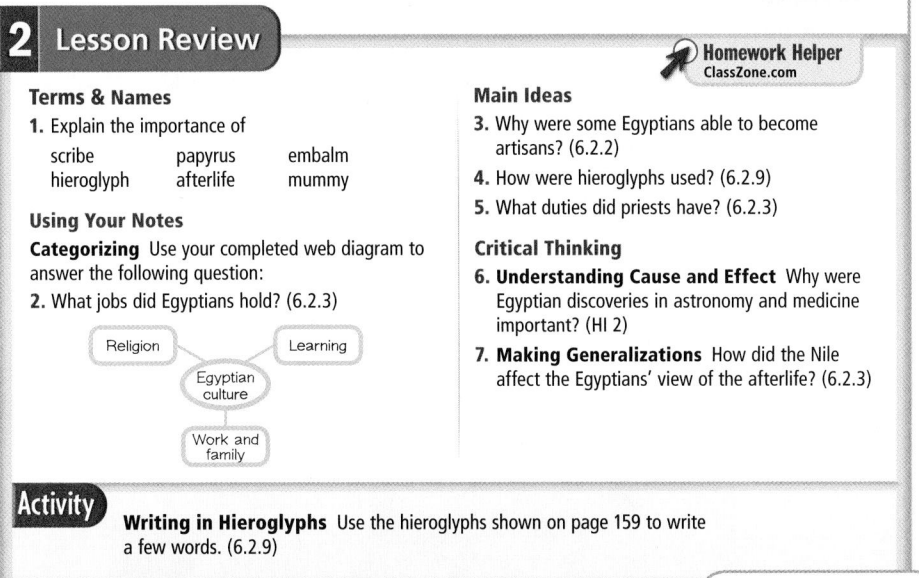

Main Ideas

3. Why were some Egyptians able to become artisans? (6.2.2)
4. How were hieroglyphs used? (6.2.9)
5. What duties did priests have? (6.2.3)

Critical Thinking

6. **Understanding Cause and Effect** Why were Egyptian discoveries in astronomy and medicine important? (HI 2)
7. **Making Generalizations** How did the Nile affect the Egyptians' view of the afterlife? (6.2.3)

Activity

Writing in Hieroglyphs Use the hieroglyphs shown on page 159 to write a few words. (6.2.9)

Ancient Egypt • 161

❹ Assess & Reteach

Assess Have pairs of students use the lesson review questions to quiz each other, taking turns answering the questions.

 Formal Assessment
- Lesson Quiz, p. 78

Reteach Have students use signals to indicate their familiarity with the vocabulary terms in this section. Write the terms on the board. As you point to each term and say it aloud, have students hold up zero fingers if they don't understand the term; one finger if they have a vague idea of what it means; two fingers if they are fairly sure of the word's meaning; and three fingers if they know the word and can use it in a sentence.

You may wish to have students close their eyes or rest their heads on their desks as they signal so they avoid seeing others' responses.

 In-Depth Resources: Unit 3
- Vocabulary Cards, p. 11
- Reteaching Activity, p. 18

🔍 Homework Helper

Visit **ClassZone.com** for a lesson review, a flip-card activity, and links to related Web sites.

2 Lesson Review Answers

Terms & Names

1. • scribe, p. 155
   • hieroglyph, p. 158
   • papyrus, p. 158
   • afterlife, p. 159
   • embalm, p. 160
   • mummy, p. 160

Using Your Notes

See page 154 for an example of a completed diagram.
2. laborer, farmer, scribe, artisan, trader, merchant, government official, priest, pharaoh

Main Ideas

3. Food surpluses meant that not everyone had to be a farmer.
4. They were used to keep records, and they were written on tomb walls to describe people there.
5. Priests followed formal rituals, took care of the temple, cleaned sacred statues, changed the clothing on statues, and fed the statues meals.

Critical Thinking

6. Advances in astronomy led to the world's first practical calendar. Advances in medicine led to some of the world's first surgery.
7. The Nile provided most of what the Egyptians needed, so they generally had a positive outlook on life. This positive outlook led to a positive view of the afterlife.

Activity Rubric

	Number of Symbols	Ease of Decoding
4	many	fluent
3	several	easy
2	some	with some effort
1	few	with great effort

Ancient Egypt • 161

Objectives

- Describe the main features of Egyptian art and architecture.
- Explain how the knowledge and advancements of ancient Egyptians affect people today.
- Synthesize information from visuals and text and use that information in discussion and writing.

❶ Focus & Motivate

Preview Briefly discuss how students' lives are different from those of the ancient Egyptians. Explain that these two pages concentrate on similarities between life in ancient Egypt and life today.

❷ Teach

Talk About It

- How is the ancient Egyptian calendar similar to the modern Western calendar? *(Both have 365 days.)*
- Would you want to be operated on with the ancient surgical instruments shown here? Why or why not? *(Most students will say that the ancient instruments look dangerous.)*
- How does the pyramid at the Louvre differ from the Egyptian pyramids? *(appears to be made of glass and metal, not stone; lit from within)*
- **Critical Thinking: Making Inferences** How would students' lives be different if, like the ancient Egyptians, we had no names for units of time shorter than one hour? *(Possible answers: Clocks would have only one hand; all school periods would be at least an hour long.)*

Connect to Today
Extend Lesson 2

Research Links
ClassZone.com

The Legacy of Egypt

Purpose: To learn about the impact that Egyptian knowledge and learning have on people today

You may feel little connection with the ancient Egyptians as you learn about their civilization. Yet our civilization owes a great deal to the Egyptians. They left behind a rich heritage in science and mathematics that we continue to build on today.

CALIFORNIA STANDARDS
6.2.5 Discuss the main features of Egyptian art and architecture.

Calendars

▶ **Past** Around 4000 B.C., the Egyptians developed a 365-day calendar based on the star Sirius. This fragment from a tomb painting shows the Egyptian concept of time. The red circles represent the months of the year. The large circles, which are divided into 24 hours, symbolize religious holidays.

▶ **Present** The Egyptian calendar is the basis for the modern Western calendar. Still, the calendar in the handheld computer shown here can do things that ancient Egyptians never dreamed of—including measuring minutes and seconds. Egyptians did not have names for units of time smaller than an hour.

162 • Chapter 5

DIFFERENTIATING INSTRUCTION

Gifted and Talented Students

Create Your Own Calendar
Have small groups brainstorm and map out a new kind of calendar. For example, each month might have four weeks of ten days each. Encourage students to think about whether their new calendar would be consistent with the seasons as the years pass.

Inclusion

Divide and Conquer
Students who have difficulty reading may benefit from the Divide and Conquer technique. Pair students and have each pair read one of the three subsections in this feature. Then combine the pairs and have a group discussion in which each pair summarizes what they read and takes notes on what the other pairs read.

Medical Knowledge

▼ **Past** Egyptian doctors treated physical injuries, such as wounds and broken bones, much like doctors today. They examined the patient, conducted tests, and made their diagnosis. Egyptians were also the first to use surgical instruments, such as those shown here.

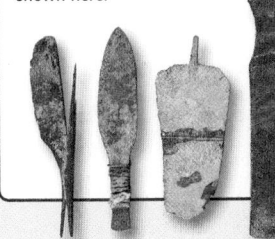

▶ **Present** Egyptian medicine provided the foundation for modern medicine. Our instruments have become more sophisticated, such as those used for laser surgery. But doctors today still use the three categories that Egyptians used to describe a patient's condition: favorable, uncertain, and unfavorable.

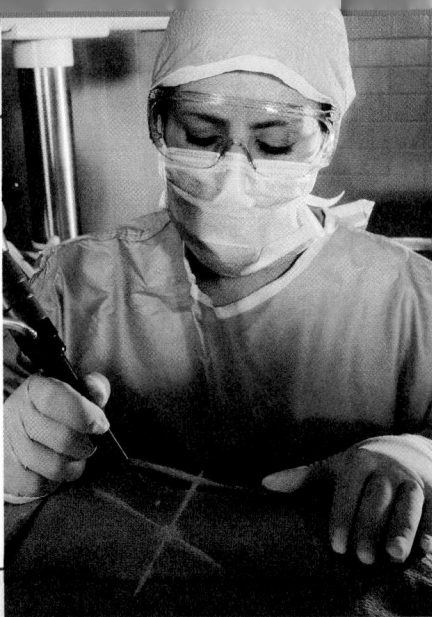

Architecture

▶ **Past** Egyptians measured fields using such geometric shapes as triangles. Architects also used this shape when they built their great stone pyramids. You will learn more about Egyptian pyramids in the next lesson.

▼ **Present** The magnificent pyramids of ancient Egypt have left their mark on Western architecture. The glass pyramid at the Louvre Museum in Paris is just one example of Egyptian influence.

Activities

1. **TALK ABOUT IT** What do these advances in knowledge and learning tell you about ancient Egyptian civilization?

2. **WRITE ABOUT IT** What will our civilization be remembered for? Write a paragraph telling what you think our legacy will be. (Writing 2.2)

Ancient Egypt • 163

Research Links
Visit **ClassZone.com** for age-appropriate Web sites related to this topic.

More About . . .

Egyptian Surgery
Egyptian doctors had a thorough understanding of anatomy. Ancient Egyptian writings described the exact location of the heart within the body. Egyptian doctors knew that the heart could have problems such as what we now call arrhythmia (irregular heartbeat). They used splints, bandages, and sutures in treating the wounded.

However, Egyptians did not know about germs. Instead, they thought that evil gods or magic caused some ailments.

More About . . .

Egyptian Medicine
The Egyptians' extensive medical knowledge impressed people from other ancient cultures. In the *Odyssey,* Homer wrote, "In Egypt, the men are more skilled in medicine than any of human kind." Ancient sources indicate that rulers of other lands asked pharaohs to send doctors to them.

ACTIVITIES ANSWERS

1. TALK ABOUT IT Possible answers: Egyptians were skilled in math; religion was important to them; they built large-scale projects, including the pyramids; they worked hard at treating the sick.

2. WRITE ABOUT IT

2. Writing Rubric

	Response to Question	Degree of Organization	Number of Errors
4	thoughtful and detailed	has introduction and conclusion	few or none
3	adequate	fairly good	some
2	vague or illogical	somewhat disorganized	many
1	off-topic or confusing	little or none	many major

❶ Plan & Prepare

Objectives

- Explain how government and religion were linked in ancient Egypt.
- Describe how the Great Pyramid of Giza was built and what it contained.
- Identify the differences between the Middle Kingdom and the Old Kingdom.
- **Language Objective:** Understand and use terms related to rulers, such as *dynasty*, *succession*, and *pharaoh*.

Quick Look

Lesson 3 focuses on the rule of the pharaohs and the building of pyramids during the Old Kingdom and on the decline of central power during the Middle Kingdom.

❷ Focus & Motivate

Preview Ask students why U.S. presidents don't use tax money to build huge monuments to themselves as the Egyptians did. *(Spending of tax money has to be approved by Congress.)*

Introduce the Main Ideas The three main ideas relate to the Big Idea "Belief systems and religions may shape governments and societies." Help students look for this Big Idea as you go through the lesson.

Reading Skill: Summarizing Have students use the graphic organizer to summarize ideas as they read.

Main ideas/ details:	Main ideas/ details:	Main ideas/ details:
built pyramids to honor pharaohs, to bury pharaohs inside	Great Pyramid built by Pharaoh Khufu, largest pyramid ever built, took 20 years and about 20,000 laborers	inside tomb several passageways to confuse robbers, filled with treasures, wall paintings showing pharaohs

Summary about Pyramids

Lesson 3

▶ MAIN IDEAS

① **Government** Egypt united under a central government that ruled for centuries.

② **Culture** Pharaoh Khufu built a huge monument to proclaim his glory.

③ **Government** Egypt entered a period of change as centralized rule weakened.

▶ TAKING NOTES

Reading Skill: Summarizing To summarize means to condense information into fewer words. Jot down the main ideas and important details in Lesson 3 in a diagram like the one below. Then use them to help you write a summary of the lesson.

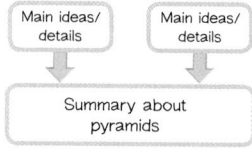

Main ideas/ details	Main ideas/ details

Summary about pyramids

S **Skillbuilder Handbook, page R3**

▲ **Ankh** The ankh (ahnk) was a symbol of life for ancient Egyptians. Tomb art often shows pharaohs and gods holding ankhs.

HOW TO TEACH THE CALIFORNIA STANDARDS

Standard	Content	Student Question or Activity	Instruction
6.2.3	**Page 166** Explains the relationship between government and religion in Egypt	**Page 166** Students tell how religion and government were linked in ancient Egypt.	Remind students that Egyptians considered the pharaohs to be godlike. Have students give details from the text to support this statement.
6.2.5	**Pages 166–169** Describes the architecture and art of the Egyptian pyramids	**Page 170** Students describe some of the main features of Egyptian art.	Find out what students already know about Egyptian pyramids, art, and mummies. Discuss from what sources students learned this information.
CST 1	**Pages 169–170** Summarizes major changes in the history of ancient Egypt	**Page 170** Students explain how Egypt experienced change during the Middle Kingdom.	Have students write a paragraph from the perspective of a robber who is lost in the passages of one of the pyramids. Encourage students to discuss their motivation for stealing and different emotions they might be feeling.

The Pyramid Builders

TERMS & NAMES
dynasty
succession
pharaoh
pyramid
step pyramid
Khufu

Build on What You Know You have read about the upper and lower Nile. There were also two kingdoms called Upper Egypt and Lower Egypt. They united into a strong empire.

The Old Kingdom

① ESSENTIAL QUESTION What kind of government ruled Egypt after it was united? a strong central government

Legend says a king named Narmer united Upper and Lower Egypt. Some historians think Narmer actually represents several kings who gradually joined the two lands. After Egypt was united, its ruler wore the Double Crown. It combined the red Crown of Lower Egypt with the white Crown of Upper Egypt. (See page 166.)

The First Dynasty The first dynasty of the Egyptian empire began about 2925 B.C. A **dynasty** (DY•nuh•stee) is a line of rulers from the same family. When a king died, one of his children usually took his place as ruler. The order in which members of a royal family inherit a throne is called the **succession**. More than 30 dynasties ruled ancient Egypt.

Historians divide ancient Egyptian dynasties into the Old Kingdom, the Middle Kingdom, and the New Kingdom. The Old Kingdom started about 2575 B.C., when the Egyptian empire was gaining strength.

Pyramids These structures, called pyramids, were built as monuments over the tombs of rulers. ▼

Terms & Names

dynasty line of rulers from the same family

succession the order in which members of a royal family inherit a throne

pharaoh the title of king in ancient Egypt

pyramid structure with triangular sides that meet at a point

step pyramid a pyramid with sides that rise in a series of steps

Khufu pharaoh who built the Great Pyramid

❸ Teach

The Old Kingdom

⬏ **6.2.3, CST 1**

Talk About It

- **Critical Thinking: Making Inferences** Did the ancient Egyptians believe that the gods made mistakes? *(No, they blamed the pharaoh for angering the gods if there were hard times.)*

California Resources

California Reading Toolkit, L16
California Modified Lesson Plans for English Learners, p. 35
California Daily Standards Practice Transparencies, TT16
California Standards Enrichment Workbook, pp. 25–26, 29–30
California Online Test Practice
California Test Generator CD-ROM
California Standards Planner and Lesson Plans, L31
California EasyPlanner CD-ROM
California eEdition CD-ROM

LESSON 3 PROGRAM RESOURCES

ON LEVEL

In-Depth Resources: Unit 3
- Reading Skill: Summarizing, p. 5
- Vocabulary Cards, p. 11
- Geography Practice: Types of Pyramids, p. 13

Formal Assessment
- Lesson Quiz, p. 79

ENGLISH LEARNERS

In-Depth Resources in Spanish
- Reading Skill: Summarizing, p. 37
- Geography Practice: Types of Pyramids, p. 43

Modified Lesson Plans for English Learners, p. 35

Reading Study Guide (Spanish), p. 43
Reading Study Guide Audio CD (Spanish)

STRUGGLING READERS

In-Depth Resources: Unit 3
- Reading Skill: Summarizing, p. 5
- Vocabulary Cards, p. 11
- Reteaching Activity, p. 19

Reading Toolkit, L16
Reading Study Guide, p. 43
Reading Study Guide Audio CD

GIFTED AND TALENTED STUDENTS

In-Depth Resources: Unit 3
- Literature: Baufra's Tale, p. 16

INCLUSION

EasyPlanner CD-ROM
- Reading Skill: Summarizing
- Reteaching Activity

TECHNOLOGY

eEdition CD-ROM
Power Presentations CD-ROM
Critical Thinking Transparencies
- CT20 Summarizing

Test Generator CD-ROM
ClassZone.com

In-Depth Resources: Unit 3
- Reading Skill: Summarizing, p. 5
- Geography Practice: Types of Pyramids, p. 13

More About . . .

The Rule of Pharaohs
As both the political and religious leader of the Egyptians, the pharaoh had two titles: "Lord of the Two Lands" and "High Priest of Every Temple." The title "Lord of the Two Lands" referred to the pharaoh as ruler of Upper Egypt and Lower Egypt. As political ruler, he owned the land, determined the laws, taxed the people, and defended the country. As religious leader, he constructed temples and conducted rituals.

Teach

Khufu's Great Pyramid

6.2.5

Talk About It

- Why did pharaohs build pyramids? *(They were permanent monuments to the pharaoh and the palace of the pharaoh in the afterlife.)*

- Why was building the Great Pyramid hard work? *(Miners had to cut the stone with copper tools. The stone slabs had to be moved and dragged by hand.)*

- What was found inside the pyramids? *(wall paintings, sculptures, food, furniture, and other items needed for the afterlife)*

- **Critical Thinking: Identifying Issues and Problems** How might the Egyptians have prevented robbers from breaking into the pharaohs' tombs and stealing the treasures? *(Possible answers: posting guards, setting traps)*

| Crown of Upper Egypt | Crown of Lower Egypt | Double Crown of Upper and Lower Egypt |

Pharaohs Rule The king of Egypt became known as the **pharaoh** (FAIR•oh). The word *pharaoh* meant "great house," and it was originally used to describe the king's palace. Later it became the title of the king himself. The pharaoh ruled from the capital city of Memphis.

The ancient Egyptians thought the pharaoh was a child of the gods and a god himself. Egyptians believed that if the pharaoh and his subjects honored the gods, their lives would be happy. If Egypt suffered hard times for a long period, the people blamed the pharaoh for angering the gods. In such a case, a rival might drive him from power and start a new dynasty.

Because the pharaoh was thought to be a god, government and religion were not separate in ancient Egypt. Priests had much power in the government. Many high officials were priests.

REVIEW How were religion and government linked in ancient Egypt?
People viewed the pharaoh as a god, and many priests were high officials.

Khufu's Great Pyramid

2 **ESSENTIAL QUESTION** How did Pharaoh Khufu proclaim his glory? built a huge monument

The first rulers of Egypt were often buried in an underground tomb topped by mud brick. Soon, kings wanted more permanent monuments. They replaced the mud brick with a small pyramid of brick or stone. A **pyramid** (PIHR•uh•mihd) is a structure shaped like a triangle, with four sides that meet at a point.

DIFFERENTIATING INSTRUCTION

English Learners

Make Word Squares
To help students learn the terms and names, have them make word squares. Use the example to demonstrate. Have students work with partners to make word squares for each of the vocabulary words.

After students complete the word squares, model the correct pronunciation of each word and have students repeat it.

For more support, see *Modified Lesson Plans for English Learners*, pp. 35–36.

Word Square

Word	Symbol or picture
dynasty *Translation (Spanish)* dinastía	
Meaning	**Sentence**
line of rulers from the same family	In a dynasty, the son of a ruler usually becomes the next ruler.

About 2630 B.C., King Djoser (ZHOH•suhr) built a much larger pyramid over his tomb. It is called a **step pyramid** because its sides rise in a series of giant steps. It is the oldest-known large stone structure in the world.

The Great Pyramid About 80 years later, a pharaoh named **Khufu** (KOO•FOO) decided he wanted a monument that would show the world how great he was. He ordered the construction of the largest pyramid ever built. Along its base, each side was about 760 feet long. The core was built from 2.3 million blocks of stone.

Building the Great Pyramid was hard work. Miners cut the huge blocks of stone using copper saws and chisels. These tools were much softer than the iron tools developed later. Other teams of workers pulled the stone slabs up long, sloping ramps to their place on the pyramid. Near the top of the pyramid, the ramps ended. Workers dragged each heavy block hundreds of feet and then set it in place.

Farmers did the heavy labor of hauling stone during the season when the Nile flooded their fields. Skilled stonecutters and overseers worked year-round. The Great Pyramid took nearly 20 years to build. An estimated 20,000 Egyptians worked on it. A city called Giza (GEE•zuh) was built for the pyramid workers and the people who fed, clothed, and housed them.

Visual Vocabulary

pyramid

step pyramid

History Makers

Khufu (ruled during the 2500s B.C.)

Khufu was one child who followed his father's example. His father, Snefru (SNEHF•ROO), was a warrior king who brought prosperity to Egypt. Snefru celebrated his deeds by building the first true pyramid as his burial monument.

Khufu liked the pyramid's design, but he decided that bigger was even better. His Great Pyramid was the tallest structure on Earth for over 4,300 years. Can you imagine the spectacular riches a ruler like that must have included in his tomb? We can only imagine because grave robbers emptied the chambers inside the pyramid long ago. The only object left from Khufu's funeral is a ship discovered in 1954. This 125-foot ship was meant to transport Khufu's soul through the afterlife along the path of the sun god.

Ancient Egypt • **167**

More About . . .

Preventing Tomb Robbery

The ancient Egyptians tried various methods to foil potential tomb robbers. They blocked passageways with granite plugs, built false doorways, designed hidden rooms, and sealed the tombs. In some cases, they also inscribed a curse on the tomb entrance. One such curse read, "As for anybody who shall enter this tomb in his impurity: I shall wring his neck as a bird's." The legend of the "mummy's curse" comes from such inscriptions.

History from Visuals

Interpreting Visuals

Explain that the entrance to the pyramid is at the end of the escape passage. The air shafts may have been built for religious reasons because they point to certain stars.

- How many chambers were built inside the Great Pyramid? *(three)*

- How is the king's chamber different from the queen's? *(The king's chamber is much larger.)*

INTERACTIVE

An interactive version of this infographic is available on the eEdition and Power Presentations CD-ROMs.

Grave Robbers Eventually, Egyptians stopped building pyramids. One reason is that the pyramids drew attention to the tombs inside them. Grave robbers broke into the tombs to steal the treasure buried with the pharaohs. Sometimes they also stole the mummies.

Egyptians believed that if a tomb was robbed, the person buried there could not have a happy afterlife. During the New Kingdom, pharaohs began building more secret tombs in an area called the Valley of the Kings. The burial chambers were hidden in mountains near the Nile. This way, the pharaohs hoped to protect their bodies and treasures from robbers.

Inside the Tombs Both the pyramids and later tombs had several passageways leading to different rooms. This was to confuse grave robbers about which passage to take. Sometimes relatives, such as the queen, were buried in the extra rooms.

Tombs were supposed to be the palaces of pharaohs in the afterlife. Mourners filled the tomb with objects ranging from food to furniture that the mummified pharaoh would need. Some tombs contained small statues that were supposed to be servants for the dead person.

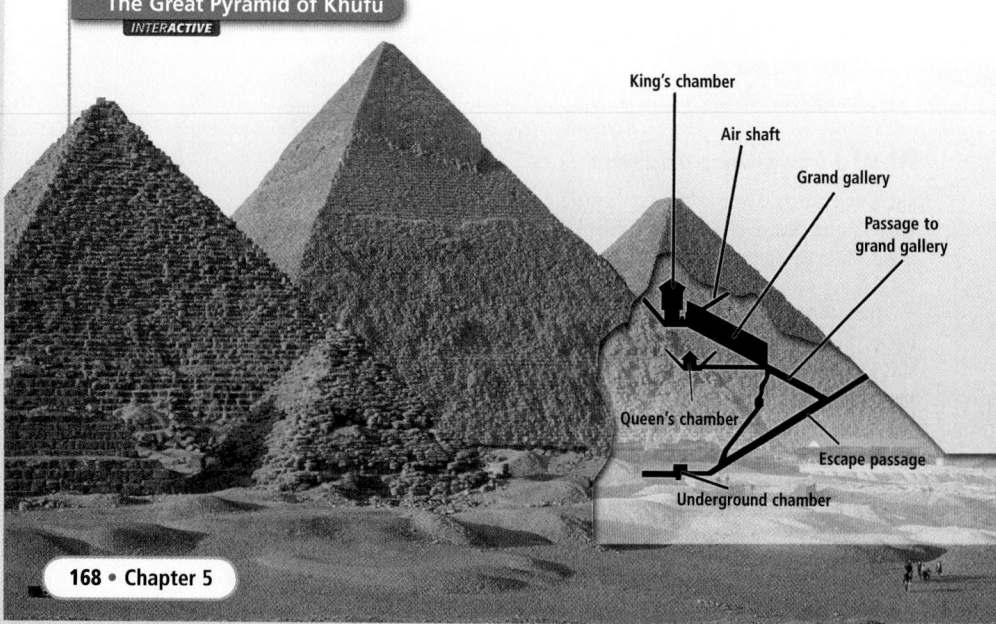

The Great Pyramid of Khufu
INTERACTIVE

King's chamber
Air shaft
Grand gallery
Passage to grand gallery
Queen's chamber
Escape passage
Underground chamber

INTERDISCIPLINARY ACTIVITIES

Science

Diagram a Pyramid Complex
The pyramid of Khufu, like other pyramids, was part of a larger complex. Have students research the parts of Khufu's pyramid complex on the Internet or in the library and make a labeled diagram of it.

Art

Identify Features of Egyptian Art
Have students use the Internet or library books to locate a wall painting from an Egyptian royal tomb. Ask students to share the painting with the class, explain what the painting depicts, and identify features that are typical of Egyptian art.

Egyptian artists decorated royal tombs with wall paintings and sculptures carved into the walls. Art was meant to glorify both the gods and the dead person. A sculpture of a dead pharaoh had "perfect" features, no matter how he really looked. Artists also followed strict rules about how to portray humans. Paintings showed a person's head, arms, and legs from the side. They showed the front of the body from the neck down to the waist.

Wall paintings showed pharaohs enjoying themselves so they could have a happy afterlife. One favorite scene was of the pharaoh fishing in a papyrus marsh. Warlike kings were often portrayed in battle. Scenes might also show people providing for the needs of the dead person. Such activities included growing and preparing food, caring for animals, and building boats.

As hard as the pharaohs tried to hide themselves, robbers stole the treasures from almost every tomb. Only a secret tomb built for a New Kingdom pharaoh was ever found with much of its treasure untouched. The dazzling riches found in this tomb show how much wealth the pharaohs spent preparing for the afterlife.

REVIEW Why did Khufu decide to build such a large pyramid?
He wanted to show the world how great he was.

Middle Kingdom

3 **ESSENTIAL QUESTION** What happened to Egypt when centralized rule weakened? Kings became less powerful, and outsiders invaded Egypt.

By about 2130 B.C., Egyptian kings began to lose their power to local rulers of the provinces. For about 500 more years, the kings held Egypt together, but with a much weaker central government. This period of Egyptian history is called the Middle Kingdom.

Old and Middle Kingdoms
2575–1630 B.C.

Mediterranean Sea

LOWER EGYPT
Nile Delta
Giza
Saqqara • Memphis
30°N
Western Desert
• Herakleopolis
UPPER EGYPT
Eastern Desert
Red Sea

0   150   300 miles
0   150   300 kilometers

• Thebes
25°N

First Cataract

Old Kingdom (2575 B.C.–2130 B.C.)
Additional area of Middle Kingdom (1980 B.C.–1630 B.C.)

Second Cataract
NUBIA
30°E   35°E   20°N

GEOGRAPHY SKILLBUILDER
INTERPRETING MAPS
Location On what body of water were most Egyptian cities located?

Ancient Egypt • 169

DIFFERENTIATING INSTRUCTION

Gifted and Talented Students

Create a Poster on King Tut's Treasures
Have students conduct Internet research to find out about King Tut. Ask students to create a poster that answers the following questions:

• Who was King Tutankhamen?

• Where was his tomb?

• When was the tomb discovered and by whom?

• What kinds of treasures were found in his tomb?

Struggling Readers

Examine Photographs
To reinforce the text's description of the inside of royal tombs, show students numerous photographs from books or the Internet. Encourage students to identify common features and subjects of Egyptian art. Point out the "perfect" features of a pharaoh and the way the human body is portrayed: showing the head and legs from the side and the torso from the front.

History from Visuals

Interpreting Maps
Have students examine the map and key.

• How did the Middle Kingdom differ from the Old Kingdom? *(The Middle Kingdom spread out farther to the east, west, and south, and it covered a later period.)*

• To what region in the south did the Middle Kingdom extend? *(Nubia)*

Extension Have students compare this map with a present-day map of eastern Africa. Ask what present-day country is located where Nubia was. *(Sudan)*

GEOGRAPHY SKILLBUILDER ANSWER
the Nile River

Teach

Middle Kingdom
CST 1

Talk About It

• How did the power of the pharaoh during the Middle Kingdom differ from that of the Old Kingdom? *(The kings lost power to the governors of the provinces.)*

• How were the Hyksos able to conquer Egypt? *(with better weapons and horse-drawn chariots)*

• **Critical Thinking: Making Inferences** What weakness of the Middle Kingdom, besides poorer weapons and lack of horse-drawn chariots, might have helped the Hyksos conquer Egypt? *(a weak central government)*

More About . . .

Tutankhamen's Tomb
The untouched treasure was found in the tomb of Tutankhamen, who is sometimes called King Tut. The tomb of this seemingly unimportant pharaoh who reigned for only about ten years is particularly famous for the magnificent gold objects it contained.

Inside a stone sarcophagus, Tutankhamen's mummy lay within three coffins. The inner coffin was made of solid gold, and the two outer ones were wood covered with gold. Four shrines of gold hammered over wood were also found in the burial chamber, and the body was covered with jewelry. The king's funeral mask was made of gold as well.

Ancient Egypt • 169

❹ Assess & Reteach

Assess Group students, and have the students in each group number off. Ask a question from the Lesson Review, and allow group members to agree on an answer. Then call out a number for a person from each group to give the group's answer.

 Formal Assessment
  • Lesson Quiz, p. 79

Reteach Divide the class into small groups. Have each group work together to complete the Reteaching Activity for Lesson 3. Share and discuss answers. If students are still uncertain about key terms in the lesson, have them quiz each other using Vocabulary Cards.

 In-Depth Resources: Unit 3
  • Vocabulary Cards, p. 11
  • Reteaching Activity, p. 19

 Homework Helper

Visit **ClassZone.com** for a lesson review, a flip-card activity, and links to related Web sites.

Invasions Rulers during the Middle Kingdom also faced challenges from outside Egypt. A nomadic people called the Hyksos (HIHK•sohs) invaded Egypt from the northeast. Their army conquered by using better weapons and horse-drawn chariots, which were new to Egyptians. After about 100 years, the Egyptians drove out the Hyksos and began the New Kingdom. You will study this period in Lesson 4.

REVIEW How was the Middle Kingdom different from the Old Kingdom?
The central government was weaker during the Middle Kingdom.

Lesson Summary

  • For thousands of years, Egypt remained a unified country ruled by a series of dynasties.
  • The Egyptians built pyramids to honor pharaohs. Tombs inside the pyramids held treasures to be used in the afterlife.
  • The Middle Kingdom was a time when the central government lost power to the provinces.

Why It Matters Now . . .

Ancient Egypt still fascinates people. Books and movies portray the mystery of mummies and tombs. People wear jewelry and use household objects modeled on Egyptian artifacts.

3 Lesson Review

Homework Helper
ClassZone.com

Terms & Names

1. Explain the importance of

dynasty	pharaoh	step pyramid
succession	pyramid	Khufu

Using Your Notes

Summarizing Use your completed diagram to answer the following question:

2. What was the purpose of the pyramids? (6.2.5)

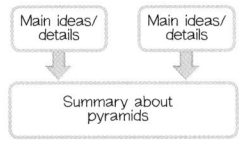

Main Ideas

3. Why were religion and government not separate in ancient Egypt? (6.2.3)

4. What were some of the main features of Egyptian art? (6.2.5)

5. What group was able to conquer Egypt during the Middle Kingdom? (CST 1)

Critical Thinking

6. **Evaluating Information** Why did Egypt experience a period of change during the Middle Kingdom? (CST 1)

7. **Making Decisions** Did pyramids accomplish their purpose? Consider what they did for a pharaoh while he lived and after he died. (6.2.3)

Activity

Writing a Narrative Look at the illustration on pages 140–141 and reread "The Great Pyramid" on page 167. Write a narrative story about one of the workers. (Writing 2.1)

---

3 Lesson Review Answers

Terms & Names

1. • dynasty, p. 165
   • succession, p. 165
   • pharaoh, p. 166
   • pyramid, p. 166
   • step pyramid, p. 167
   • Khufu, p. 167

Using Your Notes

See page 164 for an example of a completed organizer.

2. The pyramids were thought to be the palaces of the pharaohs in the afterlife; they housed the mummy of the pharaoh; they were monuments to the greatness of a pharaoh.

Main Ideas

3. The pharaoh was a god-king.
4. Possible answers: detailed, showed scenes from everyday life, showed gods and goddesses, often included writing
5. the Hyksos

Critical Thinking

6. Rulers of the provinces became more powerful, which made the pharaoh less powerful.
7. Yes—They showed the pharaohs' power and authority; they were memorials for the pharaohs. No—They used money and labor that could have been used to better peoples' lives and improve trade.

Activity Rubric

	Use of Details	Understanding of Concepts	Errors in Mechanics
4	vivid	thorough	few or none
3	descriptive	good	some
2	somewhat descriptive	some	many
1	vague	little or none	many major

Make A Pyramid

Goal: To understand the art and architecture of ancient Egypt by creating a pyramid and decorating its walls

Materials & Supplies
- yellow or tan construction paper
- ruler and protractor
- scissors and tape
- markers

Optional: Book on Egyptian tombs

Prepare

1. Research Egyptian pyramids and art. Study the images in this chapter and in books about Egypt.

2. Reread the information on pyramids on pages 166–169.

Do the Activity

1. Draw and cut out a six-inch square. Then draw and cut out four six-inch equilateral triangles (triangles whose sides are of equal length).

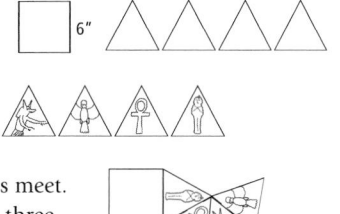

2. Decorate one side of each triangle with the type of art you think would be found inside a tomb.

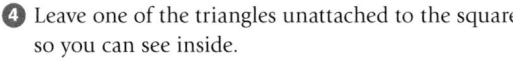

3. Tape the four triangles together so that their top points meet. Then tape the bottom sides of three of the triangles to three sides of the square base. Make sure the art goes on the inside.

4. Leave one of the triangles unattached to the square so you can see inside.

Follow-Up

1. How is an understanding of geometry related to building a pyramid?

2. How do the images that you put inside the pyramid relate to Egyptian beliefs?

Extension

Making a Presentation Show your pyramid to the class. Explain why you created your art and how it expresses Egyptian beliefs about life after death.

CALIFORNIA STANDARDS
6.2.5 Discuss the main features of Egyptian art and architecture.

ACTIVITY: MAKE A PYRAMID

Objective

Draw conclusions about Egyptian beliefs from primary sources and apply the information by making a model.

Suggestions for Completing the Activity

- Tell students that the triangles should have 60-degree angles.

- To ensure that students make squares and triangles of the correct size, you might make templates from posterboard and have them use the templates to trace the shapes.

- Remind students that their artwork should be related to Egyptian beliefs about the afterlife.

ACTIVITY ANSWERS

Follow-Up Answers

1. The lengths of the sides of the square and the triangles must be the same in order to fit together to form a pyramid.

2. Possible answers: based on Egyptian hieroglyphs, gods and goddesses, art, daily life, or social structure

Extension Rubric

	Explanation of Concepts	Style of Speaking	Number of Errors
4	thorough	very clear	few or none
3	adequate	fairly clear	some
2	vague	vague	many
1	poor	unclear	many major

❶ Plan & Prepare

Objectives

- Identify the main achievements of Queen Hatshepsut.
- Explain how Akhenaton tried to change Egyptian religion and art.
- Describe the achievements of Ramses II.
- **Language Objective:** Use terms of comparison and contrast to describe two important rulers, Hatshepsut and Ramses II.

Quick Look

Lesson 4 focuses on the reigns of Hatshepsut, Akhenaton, and Ramses II.

❷ Focus & Motivate

Preview Explain that this lesson focuses on important rulers of the New Kingdom. Ask students what they think is the most important achievement of the current U.S. president.

Introduce the Main Ideas The New Kingdom brings together the Big Ideas about Belief Systems and Geography.

Reading Skill: Explaining Chronological Order and Sequence Draw a time line on the board extending from 2000 B.C. to A.D. 2000 to demonstrate how the order of the numbers changes.

SAMPLE ANSWERS FOR TIME LINE

1472 B.C. Hatshepsut declares herself ruler of Egypt. She expands trade.

1353 B.C. Akhenaton replaces the old gods with one god, Aton.

1333 B.C. Tutankhamen becomes pharaoh. He worships the old gods.

1279 B.C. Ramses II becomes pharaoh. He brings peace, stability, and prosperity.

1213 B.C. Ramses II dies and the central government starts to weaken.

1070 B.C. Foreign powers begin to rule Egypt.

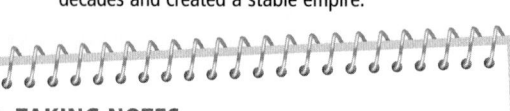

Lesson 4

▶ **MAIN IDEAS**

❶ **Economics** Queen Hatshepsut ruled as pharaoh and expanded trade during the New Kingdom.

❷ **Belief Systems** Akhenaton tried to change Egyptian religion by replacing the old gods with one god called Aton.

❸ **Government** Ramses II ruled Egypt for decades and created a stable empire.

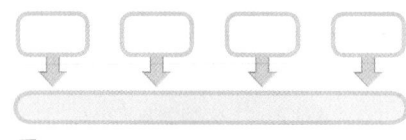

▶ **TAKING NOTES**

Reading Skill:
Explaining Chronological Order and Sequence

Placing events in sequence means putting them in order based on the time they happened. As you read Lesson 4, note things that happened in the reigns of the pharaohs discussed. Create a time line like the one below to put events in order.

S **Skillbuilder Handbook, page R15**

▲ **King Tut** British archaeologist Howard Carter found the tomb of New Kingdom pharaoh Tutankhamen in 1922. The mummy was protected by this gold mask.

CALIFORNIA STANDARDS

6.2.3 Understand the relationship between religion and the social and political order in Mesopotamia and Egypt.

6.2.7 Understand the significance of Queen Hatshepsut and Ramses the Great.

CST 2 Students construct various time lines of key events, people, and periods of the historical era they are studying.

HOW TO TEACH THE CALIFORNIA STANDARDS

Standard	Content	Student Question or Activity	Instruction
6.2.3	**Page 175** Explains the connection between political power and religion in ancient Egypt	**Page 177** Students tell how Akhenaton tried to change the way Egyptians worshiped.	Have students share whether or not they would have supported Akhenaton's changes if they had lived in ancient Egypt.
6.2.7	**Pages 173–174, 175–176** Summarizes the accomplishments of Hapshepsut and Ramses the Great	**Page 177** Students explain the importance of Hatshepsut and Ramses II.	Discuss reasons why King Tut is more famous than other Egyptian rulers even though he ruled for such a short time.
CST 2	**Pages 173–176** Provides key dates and details about ancient Egyptian history	**Page 172** Students construct a time line of key events and people from ancient Egyptian history	Before reading, write the names of rulers featured in Lesson 4 on cards and challenge students to put them in the correct sequence.

The New Kingdom

TERMS & NAMES

Hatshepsut

obelisk

Ramses II

Build on What You Know You read a little about the dazzling reign of Ramses II in Starting with a Story. He was a powerful pharaoh of the New Kingdom.

A Woman Pharaoh

1 ESSENTIAL QUESTION What was the significance of Queen Hatshepsut's rule? expanded trade, built monuments

The New Kingdom included some of Egypt's most powerful rulers. These pharaohs set up a new capital city of Thebes, 450 miles south of the old capital at Memphis. They strengthened Egypt by expanding the empire.

Taking Power Queen **Hatshepsut** (hat•SHEHP•SOOT) was the first woman to rule as pharaoh. She was the wife of a pharaoh who died soon after he took power. Hatshepsut then ruled with her stepson, Thutmose III (thoot•MOH•suh). In 1472 B.C., she declared herself the only ruler. She wore a false beard reserved for pharaohs alone.

Trade Grows Unlike other New Kingdom pharaohs, Hatshepsut did not only expand Egypt by waging war. She also wanted to make Egypt richer through trade. Her biggest trading expedition crossed the eastern desert to the Red Sea. Large ships sailed south to an African land called Punt (poont). Traders brought back rare herbs, spices, scented woods, live monkeys, and potted trees for making incense.

Hatshepsut's Temple
Queen Hatshepsut had this temple constructed to honor herself. It was cut into a mountain. ▼

Ancient Egypt • 173

Terms & Names

Hatshepsut an Egyptian queen who declared herself pharaoh in 1472 B.C. and expanded trade

obelisk a four-sided shaft with a pyramid-shaped top

Ramses II the pharaoh who ruled Egypt from 1279 to 1213 B.C. and created a stable empire

3 Teach

A Woman Pharaoh
6.2.7, CST 2

Talk About It

- **Critical Thinking: Making Inferences**
  How did Thutmose III feel about Hatshepsut? How do you know? *(He resented her. He tried to destroy all records of her reign.)*

California Resources

California Reading Toolkit, L17
California Modified Lesson Plans for English Learners, p. 37
California Daily Standards Practice Transparencies, TT17
California Standards Enrichment Workbook, pp. 25–26, 33–34
California Online Test Practice
California Test Generator CD-ROM
California Standards Planner and Lesson Plans, L33
California EasyPlanner CD-ROM
California eEdition CD-ROM

LESSON 4 PROGRAM RESOURCES

ON LEVEL
In-Depth Resources: Unit 3
- Reading Skill: Explaining Chronological Order and Sequence, p. 6
- Vocabulary Cards, p. 11

Formal Assessment
- Lesson Quiz, p. 80

ENGLISH LEARNERS
In-Depth Resources in Spanish
- Reading Skill: Explaining Chronological Order and Sequence, p. 38

Modified Lesson Plans for English Learners, p. 37

Reading Study Guide (Spanish), p. 45

Reading Study Guide Audio CD (Spanish)

STRUGGLING READERS
In-Depth Resources: Unit 3
- Reading Skill: Explaining Chronological Order and Sequence, p. 6
- Vocabulary Cards, p. 11
- Reteaching Activity, p. 20

Reading Toolkit, L17

Reading Study Guide, p. 45

Reading Study Guide Audio CD

GIFTED AND TALENTED STUDENTS
History Makers
- Hatshepsut, p. 9

Interdisciplinary Projects
- Health, p. 28

INCLUSION
EasyPlanner CD-ROM
- Reading Skill: Explaining Chronological Order and Sequence
- Reteaching Activity

TECHNOLOGY
eEdition CD-ROM

Power Presentations CD-ROM

Map Transparencies
- MT10 The New Kingdom of Egypt, 1550–1070 B.C.

Humanities Transparencies
- HT10 The Royal Family in Adoration Before the Aton

Critical Thinking Transparencies
- CT21 Explaining Chronological Order and Sequence
- CT22 Chapter 5 Visual Summary

Test Generator CD-ROM

ClassZone.com

In-Depth Resources: Unit 3
• Reading Skill: Explaining Chronological Order and Sequence, p. 6

Teach

A Reforming Pharaoh

 6.2.3

Talk About It

• Why did the priests become angry with Akhenaton? *(When he closed the temples of all gods but Aton, the priests lost power and feared that the gods would be angry.)*

• Why was Akhenaton's new religion short-lived? *(Tutankhamen restored the worship of the old gods after Akhenaton's death.)*

• **Critical Thinking: Understanding Cause and Effect** What were two effects of Akhenaton's decision to replace the old gods with one god? *(The priests became angry, and he had to move to a new capital city to avoid conflict with them.)*

History from Visuals

Interpreting Maps
Have students examine the trade routes on the map and use the legend to identify items that Egypt obtained from other lands.

• What is the most distant land to which Egyptians sailed? *(India)* What did they obtain there? *(grain)*

• With what cities or lands along the Mediterranean Sea did Egypt trade? *(Cyprus, Hittite Empire, Crete, Mycenae, Troy)*

• What did Egypt obtain from Mycenae? *(silver)* from Cyprus? *(copper)*

Extension Have students compare this map with a physical map of the region. Identify why the trade routes do not extend west across northern Africa. *(It is desert.)*

GEOGRAPHY SKILLBUILDER ANSWER
Gold was taken overland as far as the Nile. It could then be transported by boat.

INTERACTIVE

An interactive version of this infographic is available on the eEdition and Power Presentations CD-ROMs.

Hatshepsut's Monuments Like other pharaohs, Hatshepsut was eager to proclaim her glory. One type of monument she erected was the obelisk (AHB•uh•lihsk). An **obelisk** is a four-sided shaft with a pyramid-shaped top. (See page 155.) Hatshepsut had tall obelisks carved from blocks of red granite. On them, artisans used hieroglyphs to record her great deeds.

Mysterious End After ruling 15 years, Hatshepsut disappeared. She may have died peacefully, or Thutmose III may have killed her. After her death, Thutmose became pharaoh and tried to destroy all records of Hatshepsut's reign. We know about her because archaeologists restored her damaged temple and tomb.

REVIEW How did Hatshepsut try to make Egypt richer? by expanding trade

A Reforming Pharaoh

2 ESSENTIAL QUESTION How did Akhenaton try to change Egyptian religion?
replaced old gods with one god
As you read earlier, the Egyptians believed that angry gods caused suffering. In spite of this, one pharaoh dared to defy the gods.

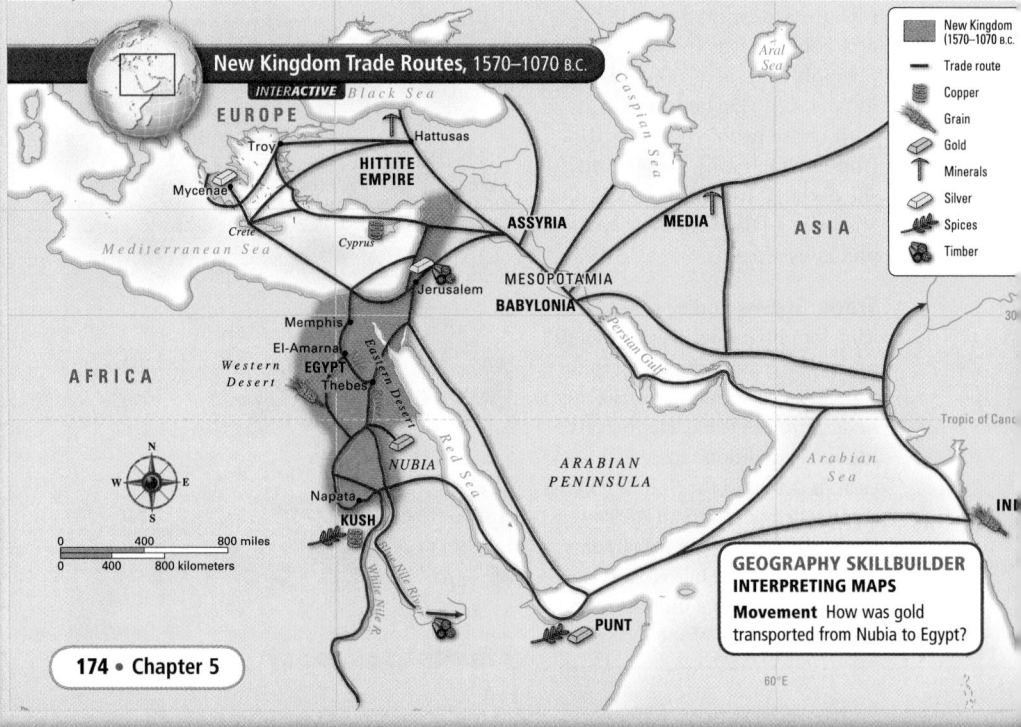

New Kingdom (1570–1070 B.C.)
— Trade route
Copper
Grain
Gold
Minerals
Silver
Spices
Timber

New Kingdom Trade Routes, 1570–1070 B.C.
INTERACTIVE

GEOGRAPHY SKILLBUILDER
INTERPRETING MAPS
Movement How was gold transported from Nubia to Egypt?

174 • Chapter 5

DIFFERENTIATING INSTRUCTION

Inclusion

Practice Remembering
Point out the title "A Woman Pharaoh" and have students read the text under it. Ask them to close their books and tell you everything they remember. Write answers on the board, leaving space under each.

When students run out of ideas, ask them to open their books and verify their answers. Have students copy the corrected information into their notebooks.

Struggling Readers

Use the Review Question
Have students follow along silently as you read aloud the review question on this page. Tell them to look for the answer to that question as they quietly read the text to themselves. Discuss the answer and find the places on the map that are mentioned in the text.

A New Belief When Akhenaton (AH•kuh•NAHT•n) became pharaoh in 1353 B.C., he lifted a sun god called Aton to the highest status. He then closed the temples of other gods. In this way, he promoted the worship of one god for the first time in Egyptian history.

Priests who served the other gods suddenly lost power. They became furious. They also feared that the pharaoh's actions had angered the old gods. To avoid conflict with those priests, Akhenaton moved about 200 miles away from them to a new capital city called Akhetaton (AH•kuh•TAHT•n).

Realistic Art Akhenaton's new ways of thinking affected art. As Lesson 3 explained, Egyptian artwork usually tried to show perfect beauty. Under Akhenaton, that changed. For the first time, a pharaoh was shown realistically. For example, carvings of Akhenaton show his large stomach.

Reform Ends Akhenaton's new religion did not last long. Three years after his death, a young relative named Tutankhamen (TOOT•ahng•KAH•muhn) became pharaoh in 1333 B.C. This boy relied on advisers to help him rule Egypt. They convinced Tutankhamen to reject the new religion and worship the old gods.

▲ **Nefertiti** Historians consider this bust to be a realistic image of Akhenaton's wife, Nefertiti (NEHF•uhr•TEE•tee).

REVIEW What reforms did Akhenaton make?
replaced worship of old gods with that of the sun god, Aton, had artists create realistic works

A Powerful Pharaoh

 ESSENTIAL QUESTION How did Ramses II expand Egypt? conquest, a peace treaty

In 1279 B.C., 44 years after Tutankhamen died, **Ramses II** (RAM•SEEZ) took the throne. His 66-year reign was among the longest in history. He expanded the Egyptian empire.

Empire Builder Unlike Hatshepsut, Ramses II—also called Ramses the Great—wanted to make Egypt powerful through war. Under Ramses' rule, Egypt extended its territory south into the African kingdom of Nubia. The empire also stretched to the eastern rim of the Mediterranean Sea. There it bordered the empire of a people called the Hittites.

Ancient Egypt • 175

DIFFERENTIATING INSTRUCTION

English Learners

Compare and Contrast Rulers
Have small groups reread the material on Hatshepsut and Ramses II. Each group should create a chart that compares and contrasts the two. For more support, see *Modified Lesson Plans for English Learners*, pp. 37–38.

Hatshepsut	Ramses II
female	male
traded with other countries	fought with other countries
ruled a shorter time	ruled a longer time

Gifted and Talented Students

List Research Questions
Have students list questions that occur to them as they read this lesson. Ask students to share their questions and form a group list. Then assign the questions to various students and have them do Internet or library research to try to find the answers. For example, students may want to compare Hatshepsut with Nefertiti or learn more about Egyptian art.

Art Under Akhenaton
Akhetaton was a city of at least 20,000 people and the site of an artistic renaissance. Akhenaton's palaces were covered with art; even the floors of one palace were painted with scenes from nature.

The sun god called Aton was considered the source of all life. Birds, fish, plants, and fruit were all considered worthy subjects. Humans were shown in everyday scenes. For example, the pharaoh and Nefertiti were depicted playing with their children.

Humanities Transparencies
• HT10 The Royal Family in Adoration Before the Aton

More About . . .

Nefertiti
Akhenaton's wife Nefertiti is perhaps better known today than the pharaoh himself is. Famous for her great beauty, Nefertiti was the chief royal wife. (Like other pharaohs, Akhenaton had more than one wife.)

Nefertiti also held the position of priestess. Scholars believe that she actively participated in the religious changes her husband promoted.

Teach

A Powerful Pharaoh
 6.2.7, CST 2

Talk About It

• How long did Ramses II rule Egypt? (*66 years*)

• How did Ramses II expand Egypt's empire? (*by adding territory through war*)

• **Critical Thinking: Evaluating Information** Of the three New Kingdom pharaohs in this lesson, which do you think had the greatest effect on Egypt? Why? (*Possible answers: Hatshepsut, for improving trade; Akhenaton, for starting a new religion and supporting a new kind of art; Ramses II, for extending Egypt's territory and providing stability*)

Map Transparencies
• MT10 The New Kingdom of Egypt, 1550–1070 B.C.

Ancient Egypt • 175

▲ **Abu Simbel** Four giant statues of Ramses guarded his temple at Abu Simbel, which was near the Nile. Each statue was as tall as a six-story building.

Military Leader The Egyptians and Hittites had long been enemies. Soon after he became pharaoh, Ramses led an army into battle against the Hittites. Nobody really won the battle, but Ramses claimed victory. His real success came after the battle. The treaty he negotiated with the Hittites was the first known peace treaty in world history.

Ramses' Reign Ramses was bold in honoring himself. He built a city called the House of Ramses. Four 66-foot statues of himself guarded his temple. The statues' ears were three feet long! Unlike Akhenaton, Ramses did not want his statues to show how he really looked. He wanted to appear godlike.

Ramses II reigned until 1213 B.C., when he was more than 90 years old. Having one ruler for 66 years made the Egyptian government *stable*. His reign was also a time of peace. After the treaty with the Hittites, no enemy threatened Egypt while Ramses ruled.

Life was calm and happy in other ways too. The Nile flooding was even more reliable than usual during Ramses' reign. Egyptian crops were more plentiful than ever.

Vocabulary Strategy

Stable is a **multiple-meaning** word. Here it means "not likely to change."

Egypt's Decline Egypt was never quite the same after Ramses died. Gradually, the central government weakened. After about 1070 B.C., a series of foreign powers ruled Egypt.

INTERDISCIPLINARY ACTIVITIES

Language Arts

Compare Pharaohs and Presidents
Have students write a paragraph comparing U.S. presidents and Egyptian pharaohs. Suggest that they include information such as length of term in office, method of succession, and powers.

Art

Design a Monument
Suggest that students design a monument that a modern pharaoh might build to honor his or her life and accomplishments.

- What would make a ruler today worthy of being remembered?
- What would make a more memorable image: a portrait, a building, words carved into stone, or something else?

One of those rulers was Alexander the Great, the king of Macedonia who conquered Egypt. (You will read about Alexander in Chapter 12.) After his death, Macedonians continued to rule Egypt. The last Macedonian ruler was the famous queen Cleopatra. Eventually the powerful Roman Empire would conquer Egypt.

REVIEW What were Ramses II's accomplishments?

Lesson Summary

- Hatshepsut was the first woman to rule as pharaoh. She expanded Egypt's trade with other lands.
- Akhenaton tried to change Egypt's religion to a belief in one god, but his religion did not last after his death.
- Ramses II built an extensive empire and ruled for 66 years. His reign was a time of peace and prosperity.

▲ **Cleopatra** After Rome conquered Egypt, Cleopatra killed herself. She feared she would be taken to Rome as a prisoner.

Why It Matters Now . . .

The ancient Egyptians rejected Akhenaton's idea of one supreme god, but that idea later became widespread. Today many people believe in religions based on a single god.

Ramses extended Egypt's territory, negotiated a peace treaty, and built a monument to himself. He lived a long life, and Egypt remained at peace.

---

4 Lesson Review

 Homework Helper
ClassZone.com

Terms & Names

1. Explain the importance of

    Hatshepsut   obelisk   Ramses II

Using Your Notes

Explaining Sequence Use your completed time line to answer the following question:

2. Which pharaoh reigned the longest? (CST 2)

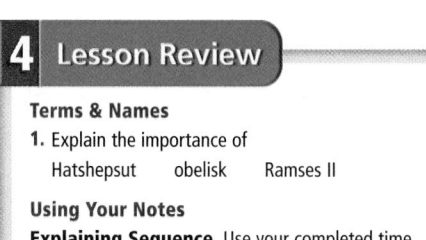

Main Ideas

3. What was unusual about the reign of Hatshepsut? (6.2.7)

4. How did Akhenaton try to change the way the Egyptians worshiped? (6.2.3)

5. Why was the government of Egypt stable under Ramses II? (6.2.7)

Critical Thinking

6. Forming and Supporting Opinions Why do you think Thutmose tried to erase all records of Hatshepsut's reign? (6.2.7)

7. Comparing and Contrasting In what ways were the reigns of Akhenaton and Ramses II different? (6.2.7)

Activity **Internet Activity** Use the Internet to research one of the pharaohs in this lesson. Then make a sketch for the pharaoh's Web page. (6.2.7)
INTERNET KEYWORD: *pharaoh's name*

Ancient Egypt • 177

---

❹ Assess & Reteach

Assess Organize students in groups of four. Have each group work together to answer questions 3, 4, and 5 in the Lesson Review. Discuss answers as a class.

 Formal Assessment
- Lesson Quiz, p. 80

Reteach On the board, write the names of the three pharaohs covered in this lesson: Hatshepsut, Akhenaton, and Ramses II. Call on volunteers to identify the main ideas about each one, and write their responses on the board.

In-Depth Resources: Unit 3
- Vocabulary Cards, p. 11
- Reteaching Activity, p. 20

Homework Helper
Visit **ClassZone.com** for a lesson review, a flip-card activity, and links to related Web sites.

---

4 Lesson Review Answers

Terms & Names

1. • Hatshepsut, p. 173
    • obelisk, p. 174
    • Ramses II, p. 175

Using Your Notes

See page 172 for an example of a completed organizer.

2. Ramses II

Main Ideas

3. Hatshepsut was a woman.

4. He replaced all gods with one god.

5. The ruler remained the same for over 60 years.

Critical Thinking

6. He was jealous of her fame; he was angry that she had ruled in his stead; he was angry that a woman had been pharaoh.

7. Akhenaton worshiped one god, which angered the priests. Ramses II worshiped the old gods.

Activity Rubric

	Number of Details	Use of Information	Links to Sources
4	many	extensive	several
3	several	some	some
2	some	little	few
1	few	none	none

Ancient Egypt • 177

Objective

Build understanding of the significance of Queen Hatshepsut's expedition to Punt.

❶ Focus & Motivate

Connect to the Big Idea

Geography Civilizations developed in places that supported agriculture or trade or both. In the case of Egypt, both agriculture and trade were important. The Nile River supported agriculture. Egypt's location along three waterways—the Nile River, the Mediterranean Sea, and the Red Sea—supported trade.

Connect to Prior Knowledge

Have students tell what they learned in Lesson 4 about Hatshepsut's expedition to Punt. *(Her biggest trading expedition crossed the eastern desert to the Red Sea. Large ships sailed south to an African land called Punt. Traders brought back rare herbs, spices, scented woods, live monkeys, and potted trees.)*

More About . . .

The Land of Punt

Punt was located near present-day Sudan. The land produced myrrh, frankincense, and other fragrant products that the Egyptians valued for use in religious ceremonies and in cosmetics.

Hatshepsut sent five ships with 30 rowers to sail down the Red Sea to the land of Punt. Scholars have learned details about the trip and the items obtained from inscriptions and murals on the walls of Hatshepsut's temple near Luxor in the Valley of the Kings.

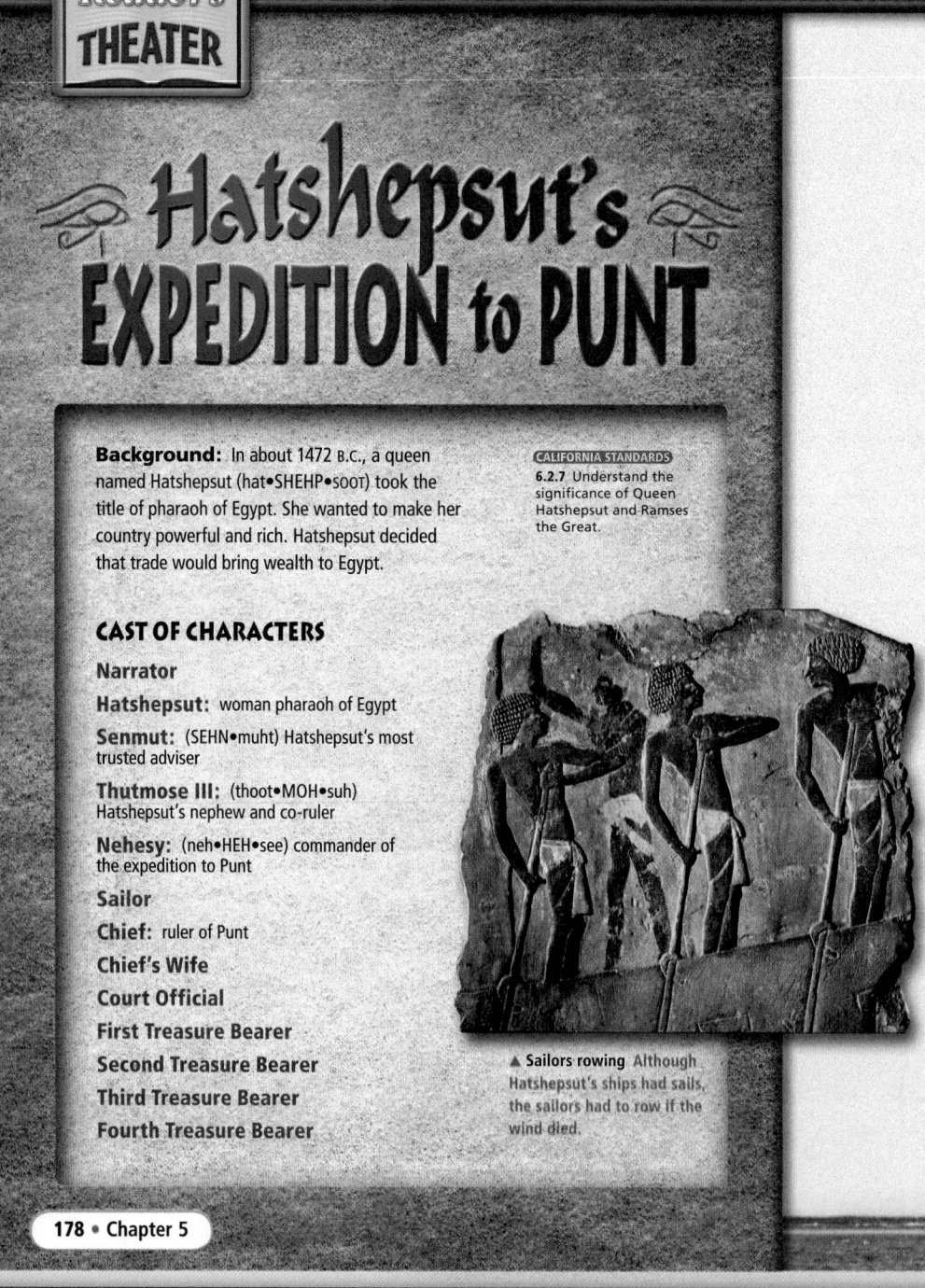

Reader's THEATER Extend Lesson 4

Hatshepsut's EXPEDITION to PUNT

Background: In about 1472 B.C., a queen named Hatshepsut (hat•SHEHP•soot) took the title of pharaoh of Egypt. She wanted to make her country powerful and rich. Hatshepsut decided that trade would bring wealth to Egypt.

CALIFORNIA STANDARDS
6.2.7 Understand the significance of Queen Hatshepsut and Ramses the Great.

CAST OF CHARACTERS

Narrator

Hatshepsut: woman pharaoh of Egypt

Senmut: (SEHN•muht) Hatshepsut's most trusted adviser

Thutmose III: (thoot•MOH•suh) Hatshepsut's nephew and co-ruler

Nehesy: (neh•HEH•see) commander of the expedition to Punt

Sailor

Chief: ruler of Punt

Chief's Wife

Court Official

First Treasure Bearer

Second Treasure Bearer

Third Treasure Bearer

Fourth Treasure Bearer

▲ **Sailors rowing** Although Hatshepsut's ships had sails, the sailors had to row if the wind died.

178 • Chapter 5

ADDITIONAL RESOURCES

Books for the Student
Andronik, Catherine M. *Hatshepsut, His Majesty, Herself.* New York: Atheneum, 2001. Well-written, readable account with personal details.

Brierley, Anthony. *Explorers of the Ancient World.* New York: Peter Bedrick Books, 1995. Covers the expedition to Punt. Struggling readers may find the maps and reading level helpful.

Greenblatt, Miriam. *Hatshepsut and Ancient Egypt.* New York: Benchmark Books, 2000.

Videos
Great Egyptians. 25 minutes. New York: Discovery Channel Films, 2001. Segments on Hatshepsut, Tutankhamen, and Cleopatra can be presented alone.

CD-ROMs
Ancient Egypt. Silver Spring: Discovery Channel School, 2002. Allows students to explore ancient Egyptian history and life at their own pace.

Narrator: When King Thutmose II died, his son Thutmose III became pharaoh. Because the boy was so young, his stepmother, Queen Hatshepsut, ruled in his place. Within a few years, the queen proclaimed herself to be pharaoh. Hatshepsut also had big plans for Egypt. She discussed her plans with Senmut.

Hatshepsut: I want to make Egypt great again. I want to repair the old temples and build new ones.

Senmut: Great Pharaoh, such a plan will please the gods. But where will Egypt gain the fine building materials to carry out such projects?

Hatshepsut: The god Amon-Re (AH•muhn•RAY) has told me to trade with the land of Punt, which is rich in valuable goods. We will send a trading expedition there.

Thutmose III: (*angry whisper*) This is terrible news. If Hatshepsut succeeds in her plan, she will earn great glory. I will never get rid of her and be able to rule by myself.

Narrator: After hearing of Hatshepsut's plan for the expedition to Punt, Senmut sent for Nehesy. He was a skilled sea captain.

Nehesy: You sent for me, your highness?

Hatshepsut: Our ancient writings tell of a rich land called Punt. To reach it, you must sail the length of the Red Sea and then down the coast of the lands to the south. Do you think you can find this place?

Nehesy: Oh, yes. I'm sure I can find this land.

▲ **Hatshepsut** The royalty of Egypt wore colorful jewelry, as shown on this figure of Hatshepsut.

Hatshepsut: Good. I want you to take a fleet and sail to Punt. Take my trusted adviser Senmut with you. He will trade with the people of Punt and bring back materials to make our temples great again.

Narrator: Nehesy did as the pharaoh commanded. He gathered together five great ships. Each was about 80 feet long and had a single giant sail.

Senmut: Are you sure you can make this voyage, Nehesy? Our people are used to sailing on the Nile, not on the wide seas.

(continued)

Ancient Egypt • 179

Talk About It

- Assign each of the roles in the play to students, and have them practice the play before reading it aloud to the class.
- Emphasize that students should perform a dramatic reading, which means using gestures and changes in inflection to convey meaning.
- Assign other students the roles of helping to direct the reading or videotaping the final performance.
- Why did Hatshepsut send the expedition to Punt? (*The people there had valuable goods that were rare or unavailable in Egypt.*)
- **Critical Thinking: Making Inferences** What do you think will happen when the expedition reaches Punt? (*Possible answers: The people there will be surprised or afraid; the Egyptians will trade goods with them.*)

More About . . .

Hatshepsut's Construction Projects
As pharaoh, Hatshepsut carried out a major building program. She rebuilt the sections of the temple at Karnak erected by her father, Thutmose I, adding obelisks and a tower. She also built a temple cut into rock at Beni-Hasan.

DIFFERENTIATING INSTRUCTION

English Learners

Read a Play
Make sure students understand how a play is read. Point out the pronunciation guides and demonstrate how to put the emphasis on the right syllable. Direct students' attention to the stage direction for Thutmose III's first speech.

Gifted and Talented Students

Design Props
Have students read the play and come up with ideas for a few simple props for the different characters. Students can work with partners or in small groups to make the props.

Teach

Talk About It

- Why were the ruler and his wife surprised to see the Egyptians? *(Egypt was far away; the people of Punt did not realize that the Egyptians even knew about their land.)*
- What trade items did the Egyptians bring? *(weapons, jewelry, food)*
- **Critical Thinking: Drawing Conclusions** Why do you think the Egyptians brought these types of trade items? *(Possible answers: easy to transport; Egyptians were proud of their skill at metalworking; Egyptian jewelry and food would probably seem exotic to the people of Punt)*

More About . . .

Egyptian Trade
Egyptian merchant ships had carried goods up and down the Nile as far as Aswan for centuries, but around 2300 B.C., waterways were built around the cataracts that allowed vessels to continue south. The Mediterranean trade routes took Egyptian ships to Syria, Crete, and Cyprus.

The Egyptians traded their plentiful grain for olive oil and wine. Under Thutmose III, their ships were also used to transport conquering armies.

More About . . .

Nile Boats
Shipping was an important industry in ancient times. Nile boats were made from wooden planks and curved up at the stern and bow. They were steered by large oars, and the single sail was taken down when traveling against the wind.

The crews might have as many as 20 men, mostly rowers. The ships that sailed the Mediterranean and Red seas were similar but larger.

Nehesy: When the wind is behind the sail, it will push us forward. When the wind dies or blows the wrong way, my 30 oarsmen will row the ship.

Senmut: That sounds like a good plan, but are you sure we will be safe?

Nehesy: We are perfectly safe. I have given orders that we must always stay within sight of the coast, so we cannot get lost.

Senmut: All right, Nehesy. I believe the voyage is in good hands under your leadership.

Narrator: After many months, the fleet came to a land with huge trees. The Egyptians could see a village with round huts that had cone-shaped thatch roofs.

Sailor: Look over there! I think that's the land of Punt! We made it!

Narrator: The ruler of the country and his wife came to meet the ships and learned they were from Egypt.

Chief: How did you come here? We thought this land was unknown to Egypt.

Chief's Wife: Did you come down the roads of the heavens? You must have followed the sun's path.

Senmut: We sailed down the Red Sea and then along the coast of this land. O Great Chief, I bring you greetings from Pharaoh Hatshepsut. I have brought many gifts to honor you. I also have trade goods to exchange for the goods of your country.

Chief: Come to my house. My servants will prepare a meal for us, and you and I can bargain.

Narrator: Senmut showed the Chief of Punt the trade items he had brought.

Senmut: My people are good metal workers. I have brought you bronze daggers and axes, and also beautiful necklaces. We also brought wheat bread, dried fruits, and honeycakes.

Narrator: The chief and Senmut agreed to a trade. Then the Egyptians loaded their ships and returned home. When they reached the coast of Egypt, they traveled over land to the capital at Thebes.

Trade goods The Egyptians took bronze knives and jewelry to Punt. They traded them for wood, ivory, fragrant-smelling incense, leopard skins, and live monkeys.

DIFFERENTIATING INSTRUCTION

English Learners

Make a Cartoon Strip
Group students and have them work together to sketch a cartoon strip that portrays the action in the play. Students can simplify the script to include dialogue in the cartoon strip.

Struggling Readers

Draw a Map
Ask students to draw a map of the route that Hatshepsut's expedition took to reach Punt. (See page 174.) Students' maps might include symbols for the items traded.

Court Official: O Great Hatshepsut, your expedition to Punt has returned. Senmut has arrived with a caravan of goods from the ships.

Hatshepsut: Show him in.

Senmut: Your highness, the chief of Punt greeted us with friendliness, and our trade mission was successful. We have gained many great treasures for Egypt. I will have them brought before you.

First Treasure Bearer: Great Pharaoh, I bring you chests of gold.

Hatshepsut: Good. I will use this to adorn my obelisks and other monuments.

Second Treasure Bearer: Highness, I bring logs of dark ebony wood and great tusks of ivory. Our artisans can use these materials to make beautiful things.

Third Treasure Bearer: Mighty Pharaoh, I bring baboons and monkeys for your amusement. And leopards for their exotic spotted skins.

Fourth Treasure Bearer: Your highness, I bring great quantities of incense.

Hatshepsut: This will please the priests, who burn incense in the temples.

Senmut: Great Pharaoh, we have saved the best treasure for last. The Chief of Punt sold us 31 myrrh trees, which his people carefully planted in tubs for the journey. I will plant the trees in the

courtyard of your great temple. With the sap of these trees, our priests can make their own incense.

Hatshepsut: Senmut, you have done well. And Nehesy, I am pleased with you too.

Nehesy: Thank you, your highness.

Thutmose III: (*angry whisper*) I was certain this trade mission would fail. But it has succeeded more than Hatshepsut dared to hope. She is right that the priests will be happy. Now they will love Hatshepsut and support her rule. I must wait for a better time to seize the throne.

Narrator: Years later, Thutmose III did become the sole pharaoh of Egypt. No one knows what happened to Hatshepsut. Maybe Thutmose killed her or maybe she died of old age. We do know that Thutmose tried to erase her name from history. He failed, and the record of Hatshepsut's deeds still amazes the world.

Activities

1. **TALK ABOUT IT** What qualities of a good ruler did Hatshepsut have?

2. **WRITE ABOUT IT** Write a new scene in which Senmut and the chief bargain over the exchange of goods. Show how each person tried to get the most he could from the exchange. (Writing 2.1)

Ancient Egypt • 181

Teach

Talk About It

- How did the Egyptians get back to Hatshepsut? *(They sailed back from Punt, then traveled overland with the goods to get to the capital city.)*

- What was the reaction of Thutmose III to the success of the trading party? Why? *(He was angry because he knew that the expedition's success would make it harder for him to take power away from Hatshepsut.)*

- **Critical Thinking: Evaluating Information** How does the value that the Egyptians placed on the different trade items show the importance of religion in their lives? *(They valued the myrrh trees the most because the priests could use them to make their own incense for religious ceremonies.)*

More About . . .

Incense
Incense was used by ancient peoples in religious ceremonies and it is still used today. The Egyptians used it daily in the rituals performed for the sun god Re and in funeral rites. The aromatic resins used to make incense were also used in perfumes, medicines, cosmetics, and embalming. Other fragrant parts of plants—such as flowers, seeds, and bark—were used to make incense as well.

ACTIVITIES ANSWERS

1. **TALK ABOUT IT** Possible answers: She was courageous, reasonable, intelligent, practical, peaceful, and religious.

2. **WRITE ABOUT IT**

2. Writing Rubric

	Accuracy of Scene	Realism of Dialogue	Number of Errors
4	very detailed	very realistic	few or none
3	somewhat detailed	somewhat realistic	some
2	general	stilted	many
1	unclear	unrealistic	many major

Terms & Names

1. Delta and silt are terms related to rivers.

2. A scribe was trained to write hieroglyphs.

3. A pharaoh ruled, and those in his family who followed him made up a dynasty.

4. Hatshepsut and Ramses II were two of the most powerful New Kingdom pharaohs.

Main Ideas

Gift of the Nile
(pages 146–153)

5. Boats could easily travel up and down the river, making trade with the interior of Africa and trade on the Mediterranean Sea possible.

6. The Egyptians expanded their farmland by building canals to bring water from the Nile to desert areas.

Life in Ancient Egypt
(pages 154–163)

7. The symbols can stand for an actual object, a letter, or an idea.

8. They embalmed bodies to preserve them for the afterlife.

The Pyramid Builders
(pages 164–171)

9. The Egyptians believed the pharaoh was a god.

10. The tomb of the pharaoh, food, furniture, and other items to be used in the afterlife were all found inside pyramids. Also found were passageways to confuse robbers and sometimes chambers for other members of the pharaoh's family.

The New Kingdom
(pages 172–181)

11. Hatshepsut made Egypt richer through trade, and she built tall obelisks as monuments.

12. Ramses II ruled for a very long time, making the empire stable.

▶ **VISUAL SUMMARY**

Ancient Egypt

Geography (6.2.1)
- Nile provided silt and water, transportation.
- Desert acted as a natural barrier.

Economy (6.2.6)
- Traded with parts of Africa, Arabia, and Mediterranean countries
- A prosperous land with many specialized jobs

Belief Systems (6.2.3)
- Many gods; pharaoh was one
- Believed in a happy afterlife

Science & Technology (6.2.9)
- Developed calendar, astronomy, medicine
- Developed written language—hieroglyphs

Government (6.2.3)
- Upper and Lower Egypt united as one country
- Pharaohs and dynasties kept control; priests served as officials

▶ **TERMS & NAMES**

Explain why the words in each set below are linked with each other.

1. **delta** and **silt**
2. **scribe** and **hieroglyph**
3. **dynasty** and **pharaoh**
4. **Hatshepsut** and **Ramses II**

▶ **MAIN IDEAS**

Gift of the Nile (pages 146–153)

5. Why was the Nile so valuable for trade and transportation? (6.2.6)

6. How did Egyptian farmers use the Nile to expand their farmland? (6.2.2)

Life in Ancient Egypt (pages 154–163)

7. What are the characteristics of the hieroglyphic system? (6.2.9)

8. Why did the Egyptians embalm bodies? (6.2.3)

The Pyramid Builders (pages 164–171)

9. Why did the Egyptians have such great respect for the pharaohs? (6.2.3)

10. What items were found inside pyramids? (6.2.5)

The New Kingdom (pages 172–181)

11. What were the important accomplishments of Queen Hatshepsut? (6.2.7)

12. Why was the reign of Ramses II so successful? (6.2.7)

ALTERNATIVE ASSESSMENT RUBRICS

1. Writing Rubric

	Accuracy of Description	Number of Errors
4	thoughtful and detailed	few or none
3	detailed	some
2	shows some knowledge	many
1	unclear	many major

2. Science Rubric

	Clarity of Explanation	Accuracy of Illustration
4	clear	attractive and age-appropriate
3	adequate	neat
2	vague or incomplete	somewhat neat
1	incorrect or missing	sloppy

CRITICAL THINKING Big Ideas: Geography

13. DRAWING CONCLUSIONS How did the geography of Egypt help civilization develop there? (6.2.1)

14. UNDERSTANDING CAUSE AND EFFECT How did the geography of ancient Egypt affect the building of pyramids and other structures? (6.2.5)

15. EXPLAINING HISTORICAL PATTERNS Why do you think successful agriculture encourages the development of civilizations? (6.2.2)

ALTERNATIVE ASSESSMENT

1. WRITING ACTIVITY Write a descriptive paragraph about an artifact in the chapter. Identify the object and the page on which it is found. (Writing 2.2)

2. INTERDISCIPLINARY ACTIVITY—SCIENCE Research to learn about the Egyptian calendar. Make a poster explaining the calendar. (HI 2)

3. STARTING WITH A STORY Review the narrative you wrote about the new pharaoh. Draw a picture that illustrates the scene. (6.2.7)

Technology Activity

4. CREATING A MULTIMEDIA PRESENTATION Use the Internet or the library to research and compare Egyptian pyramids with those of Meso-America. Work with a partner to make a multimedia presentation. (6.2.5)

- Include maps that show where pyramids are located in Egypt and Meso-America.
- Show slides of pyramids from Egypt and Meso-America.
- Supply text for each slide.
- Provide documentation of your sources.

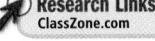
Research Links
ClassZone.com

Reading Charts Use the chart below to answer the questions. (6.2.5)

Pyramids Around the World

PYRAMID	LOCATION & APPROX. DATE	HEIGHT (meters)	NOTES
Djoser step pyramid	Saqqara, Egypt 2630 B.C.	60	First step pyramid
Bent pyramid	Dahshur, Egypt 2600 B.C.	105	First attempt at a true pyramid
Khufu's Great Pyramid	Giza, Egypt 2550 B.C.	147	True pyramid
Pyramid of the Sun	Teotihuacán, Mexico 100 B.C.	65	Step pyramid
Temple of the Giant Jaguar	Tikal, Guatemala A.D. 700	45	Step pyramid

Sources: *Encyclopedia Britannica; World Book*

1. Which of the following pyramids is not in Egypt?
- A. Djoser step pyramid
- B. Bent pyramid
- C. Khufu's Great Pyramid
- D. Temple of the Giant Jaguar

2. Which of the following is tallest?
- A. Djoser step pyramid
- B. Bent pyramid
- C. Pyramid of the Sun
- D. Temple of the Giant Jaguar

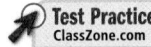
Test Practice
ClassZone.com

Additional Test Practice, pp. S1–S33

Critical Thinking

Big Ideas: Geography

13. The Nile River provided soil, water, food, and transportation for the Egyptian people. Deserts kept invaders out so that the civilization could develop with little interference.

14. The geography affected the materials used and the design, location, and architecture of the structures.

15. It allows people to concentrate on other jobs, develop other interests, and improve their lives.

Standards-Based Assessment

1. The correct answer is D, Temple of the Giant Jaguar. It is in Guatemala.

2. The correct answer is B, the Bent pyramid. The three other options are shorter than 105 meters.

 Research Links

Visit **ClassZone.com** for links to Web sites that can be used in the multimedia presentation.

 Test Practice

Visit **ClassZone.com** to access strategies and tutorials for taking standardized tests.

Formal Assessment
- Chapter Tests, Forms A, B, and C, pp. 81–95

 Test Generator
- Chapter Tests, Forms A, B, and C (English and Spanish)

ALTERNATIVE ASSESSMENT RUBRICS

3. Starting with a Story Rubric

	Accuracy of Illustration	Effectiveness of Style
4	effective	attractive
3	good	neat
2	shows some knowledge	somewhat neat
1	shows little or no knowledge	sloppy

4. Technology Rubric

	Use of Maps and Slides	Use of Text
4	extensive	accurate text for each slide
3	good	some text for most slides
2	acceptable	several errors
1	incorrect or missing	many major errors

Chapter Overview	Copymasters		Assessment

Geography, trade, and migration were important factors in the development of African civilizations.

In-Depth Resources: Unit 3
- Family Newsletter (English and Spanish), pp. 21–22
- Visual Summary, p. 26
- Vocabulary Study Guide, p. 28

Character Education

Reading Study Guide, p. 55

Bringing Social Studies Alive, Chapter 6

Document-Based Questions: Strategy and Practice

Reading Toolkit, L18–L20

Modified Lesson Plans for English Learners, pp. 39–44

Chapter Review, pp. 208–209

Formal Assessment
- Chapter Tests, Forms A, B, and C, pp. 99–110

Test Generator

Integrated Assessment Book

Online Test Practice

LESSON 1

Nubia and the Land of Kush

pp. 188–195

OBJECTIVE Study the rise of the civilizations of Nubia and Kush.

In-Depth Resources: Unit 3
- Reading Skill: Explaining Sequence, p. 23
- Vocabulary Cards, p. 29
- Geography Practice: The Nubian Kingdoms of Kush, p. 31
- Skillbuilder Practice: Interpreting Charts, p. 27
- Reteaching Activity, p. 35

Interdisciplinary Projects
- Science, p. 32

Reading Study Guide, p. 49

Lesson Review, p. 193

Formal Assessment
- Lesson Quiz, p. 96

California Daily Standards Practice Transparencies, TT18

LESSON 2

The Kingdom of Aksum

pp. 196–201

OBJECTIVE Analyze the rise and fall of the kingdom of Aksum.

In-Depth Resources: Unit 3
- Reading Skill: Finding Main Ideas, p. 24
- Vocabulary Cards, p. 29
- Primary Source: Crowning the King, by Stuart C. Munro-Hay, p. 33
- Reteaching Activity, p. 36

History Makers
- Ezana, p. 11

Interdisciplinary Projects
- Math, p. 31

Reading Study Guide, p. 51

Lesson Review, p. 200

Formal Assessment
- Lesson Quiz, p. 97

California Daily Standards Practice Transparencies, TT19

LESSON 3

West, Central, and Southern Africa

pp. 202–207

OBJECTIVE Learn about civilizations in west, central, and southern Africa.

In-Depth Resources: Unit 3
- Reading Skill: Explaining Geographic Patterns, p. 25
- Vocabulary Cards, p. 29
- Literature: African Griots, by Nikiprowetzky, p. 34
- Reteaching Activity, p. 37

Interdisciplinary Projects
- Language Arts, p. 33; Art, p. 34

Reading Study Guide, p. 53

Lesson Review, p. 207

Formal Assessment
- Lesson Quiz, p. 98

California Daily Standards Practice Transparencies, TT20

eEdition Plus Online

EasyPlanner Plus Online

eTest Plus Online

 Audio CDs
- Reading Study Guide
- Reading Study
  Guide in Spanish
- The World's Music

 CD-ROMs
- Power Presentations
- eEdition
- EasyPlanner
- Test Generator

 eEdition CD-ROM

 **Map Transparencies**
- MT11 Northeastern Africa: Physical

 Humanities Transparencies
- HT11 Shoulder Necklace from Meroë

 **Critical Thinking Transparencies**
- CT23 Explaining Sequence

 ClassZone.com

 eEdition CD-ROM

 Critical Thinking Transparencies
- CT24 Finding Main Ideas

 ClassZone.com

 eEdition CD-ROM

 Map Transparencies
- MT12 The Nok Culture

 Humanities Transparencies
- HT12 Nok Sculpture

 Critical Thinking Transparencies
- CT25 Explaining Geographic Patterns
- CT26 Chapter 6 Visual Summary

 ClassZone.com

Overview of California Resources

	Lesson 1	Lesson 2	Lesson 3
California Reading Toolkit	L18	L19	L20
California Modified Lesson Plans for English Learners	p. 39	p. 41	p. 43
California Daily Standards Practice Transparencies	TT18	TT19	TT20
California Standards Enrichment Workbook	pp. 21–22, 35–36	pp. 35–36	pp. 17–18
California Standards Planner and Lesson Plans	L35	L37	L39
California Online Test Practice	ClassZone.com	ClassZone.com	ClassZone.com
California Test Generator CD-ROM			
California EasyPlanner CD-ROM			
California eEdition CD-ROM			

Chart Key

PE Pupil Edition   CD-ROM   Internet

Copymaster   Audio   Overhead Transparency

Video

In-Depth Resources in Spanish

- Reading Skill and Strategy
- Skillbuilder Practice **B**
- Geography Practice
- Vocabulary Study Guide

In-Depth Resources: Unit 3

- Family Newsletter (English and Spanish) **C**

Reading Study Guide (Spanish) **A**

Reading Study Guide Audio CD
(Spanish)

Test Generator
Chapter Test (Spanish)

Plus

Modified Lesson Plans for English Learners

Multi-Language Glossary of Social Studies Terms

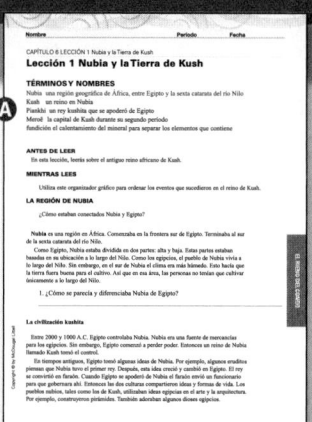

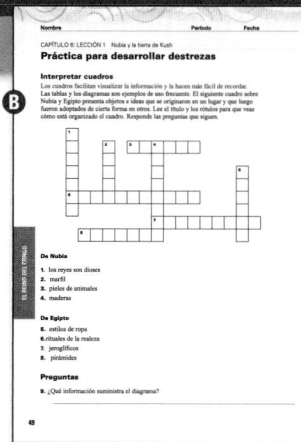

In-Depth Resources: Unit 3

- Vocabulary Study Guide **B**
- Skillbuilder Practice **C**
- Geography Practice
- Reteaching Activities **A**
- Family Newsletter

Reading Study Guide

Reading Study Guide Audio CD

Reading Toolkit

Formal Assessment
Chapter Test, Form A

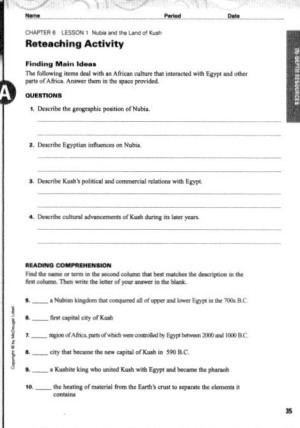

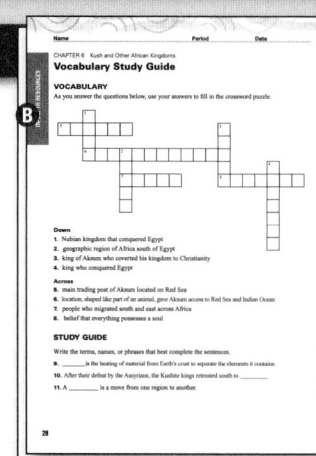

EasyPlanner CD-ROM

- Reading Skill and Strategy **A**
- Vocabulary Study Guide **B**
- Geography Practice
- Reteaching Activities **C**

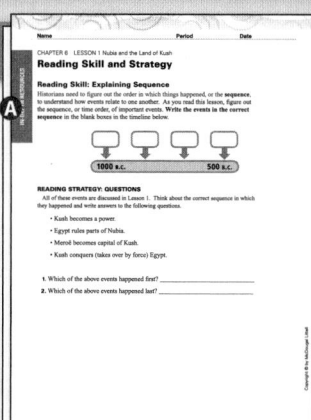

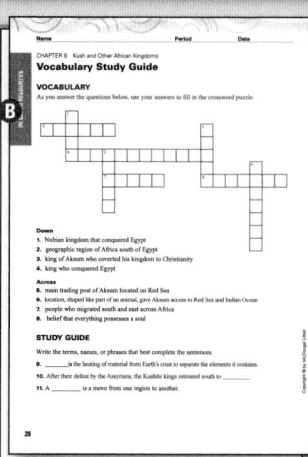

In-Depth Resources: Unit 3

- Primary Source
- Literature **A**

History Makers **B**

Interdisciplinary Projects **C**

Formal Assessment
Chapter Test, Form C

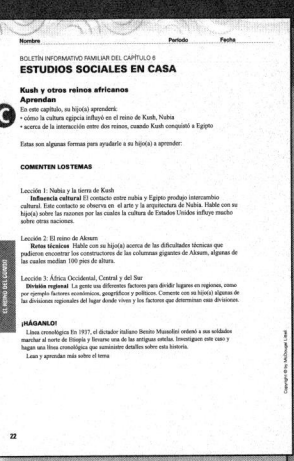

Activities in the Teacher's Edition for English Learners

- Make a Time Line, p. 192
- Word Webs, p. 198
- Use Context Clues, p. 204

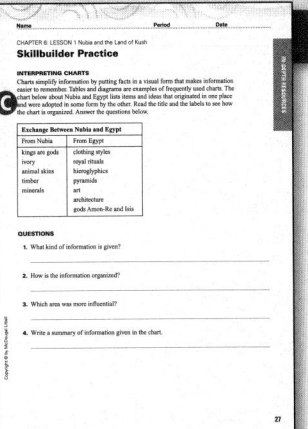

Activities in the Teacher's Edition for Struggling Readers

- Make a Time Line, p. 190
- Review Key Terms, p. 194
- Shrink the Paragraphs, p. 199
- Place the Lesson on a Map, p. 205

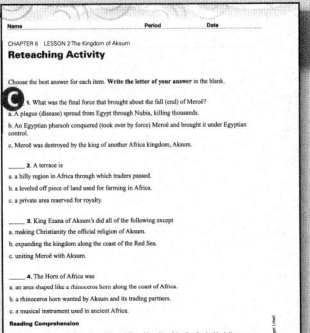

Activities in the Teacher's Edition for Inclusion Students

- Paired Reading, p. 192
- Use Flash Cards, p. 198
- Find Causes and Effects, p. 204

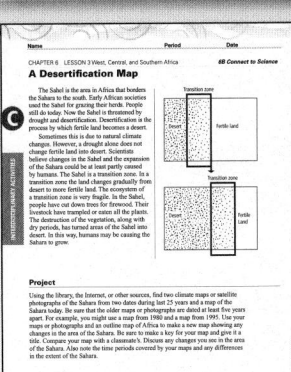

Activities in the Teacher's Edition for Gifted and Talented Students

- Make an Expanded Time Line, p. 190
- Create a "Kush Catalog," p. 194
- Write a Biographical Sketch, p. 199
- Report on the Iron Age, p. 205

Integrated Technology

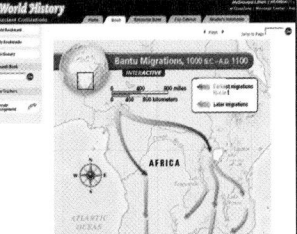

eEdition CD-ROM

- Interactive Visuals
- Interactive Maps
- Starting with a Story

ClassZone.com

- WebQuests
- Research Links
- Internet Activities
- Homework Helper
- Chapter Quiz
- Current Events
- Test Practice

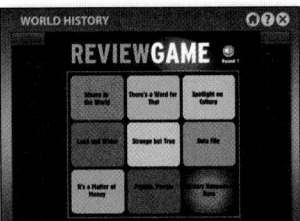

Power Presentations CD-ROM

- Lecture Notes
- Media Gallery
- Chapter Review Game

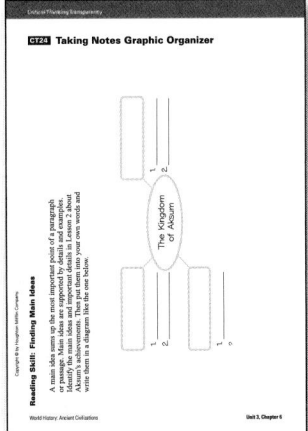

Critical Thinking Transparencies

- CT23 Explaining Sequence
- CT24 Finding Main Ideas
- CT25 Explaining Geographic Patterns
- CT26 Chapter 6 Visual Summary

California Daily Standards Practice Transparencies, TT18–TT20

Map Transparencies
- MT11 Northeastern Africa: Physical
- MT12 The Nok Culture

Humanities Transparencies
- HT11 Shoulder Necklace from Meroë
- HT12 Nok Sculpture

Test Generator CD-ROM

EasyPlanner CD-ROM

Begin the Chapter

Objective

Analyze the major civilizations that developed on the African continent and how geography influenced the development of these civilizations and cultures.

Quick Look

Lesson 1 traces the development of the civilizations of Nubia, including the kingdom of Kush.

Lesson 2 describes the rise and fall of Aksum on the Horn of Africa.

Lesson 3 summarizes the development of human civilization in west, central, and southern Africa.

Before You Read: Knowledge Rating

Remind students that knowledge rating is a strategy that helps them set a purpose for what they will be reading. Students identify their level of knowledge about words and concepts that will be in upcoming lessons. In the process, they identify information for which they will need to be especially alert. Tell students that to use knowledge rating effectively, they should follow these steps:

- Read carefully the list of terms and words for which you should be on the lookout as you read the chapter. Write the words on a sheet of paper.

- Consider each term, and use the rating scale to note your level of knowledge about the word.

- As you come upon the terms in the chapter, note the definition of the term, and write it down on your sheet of paper. Pay special attention to those terms that you rated with a 1 and 2.

---

6 Kush and Other African Kingdoms

Before You Read: Knowledge Rating

Recognizing what you already know about each of these terms can help you understand the chapter:

Kush	Meroë	Aksum
Ezana	griot	Bantu

In your notebook, rate how well you know each term:

3 = I know what this word means.

2 = I've seen this word, but I don't know what it means.

1 = I've never seen this word before.

Define each term in your notebook as you read.

Big Ideas About the Kush Civilization

Culture Ways of living change as humans interact with each other.

Kush civilization was influenced by Egyptian culture. Kush was under the rule of Egypt for hundreds of years. Kush adopted Egyptian customs, religion, hieroglyphs, and architecture. Later, Kush conquered Egypt. The two cultures influenced each other.

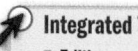

Integrated Technology

eEdition
- Interactive Maps
- Interactive Visuals
- Starting with a Story

(i) INTERNET RESOURCES
Go to **ClassZone.com** for
- WebQuest
- Homework Helper
- Research Links
- Internet Activities
- Quizzes
- Maps
- Test Practice
- Current Events

AFRICA

751 B.C.
Piankhi, a Kushite king, conquers Memphis in Egypt.

500 B.C.
Nok people make iron tools.
(Nok head) ▶

800 B.C.   650 B.C.   500 B.C.

WORLD

461 B.C.
Age of Pericles begins in Greece.
◀ (marble bust of Pericles)

184

TIME LINE DISCUSSION

Use the time line to help students develop an understanding of the time frame for the development of early civilizations in different parts of Africa.

- Which occurred first: The Kush conquest of Memphis or the Age of Pericles in Greece? *(the conquest of Memphis)*

- According to the time line, by what year had iron-making technology developed in Africa? *(500 B.C.)*

- How long after the Pax Romana began were the Bantu migrations underway? *(about 127 years)*

- Which occurred first—the Bantu migrations or the reign of King Ezana? *(The Bantu migrations were underway about 225 years before King Ezana ruled Askum.)*

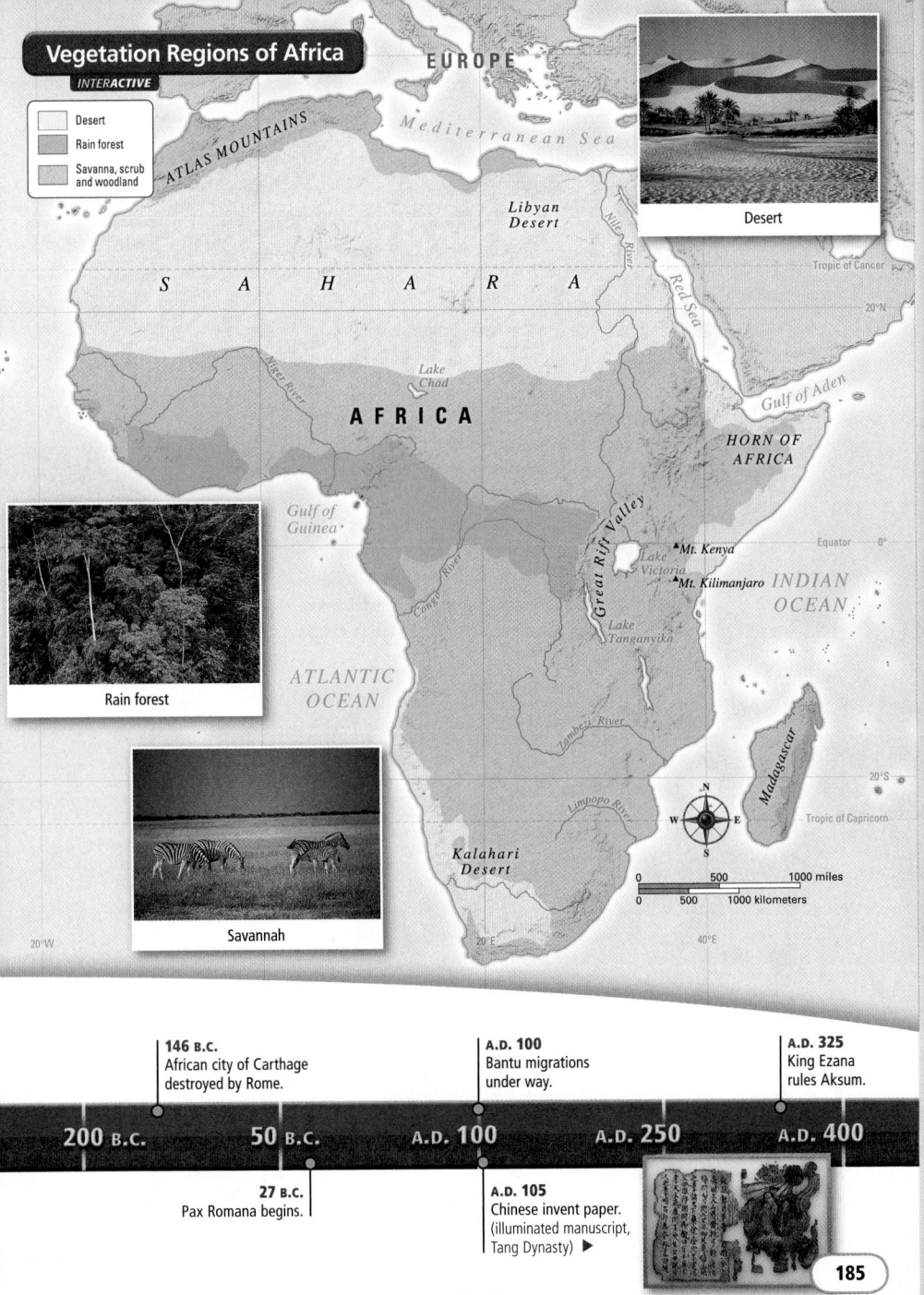

Vegetation Regions of Africa
INTERACTIVE

Key:
- Desert
- Rain forest
- Savanna, scrub and woodland

EUROPE

Mediterranean Sea

ATLAS MOUNTAINS

S A H A R A

Libyan Desert

Niger River

Lake Chad

AFRICA

20°N

Tropic of Cancer

Red Sea

Gulf of Aden

HORN OF AFRICA

Gulf of Guinea

Great Rift Valley

Congo River

▲Mt. Kenya

Lake Victoria

▲Mt. Kilimanjaro

Equator 0°

INDIAN OCEAN

Lake Tanganyika

ATLANTIC OCEAN

Zambezi River

Madagascar

20°S

Limpopo River

Tropic of Capricorn

Kalahari Desert

N / S / E / W compass

0   500   1000 miles
0   500   1000 kilometers

20°W   20°E   40°E

Desert

Rain forest

Savannah

Timeline:

146 B.C. African city of Carthage destroyed by Rome.

A.D. 100 Bantu migrations under way.

A.D. 325 King Ezana rules Aksum.

200 B.C.   50 B.C.   A.D. 100   A.D. 250   A.D. 400

27 B.C. Pax Romana begins.

A.D. 105 Chinese invent paper. (illuminated manuscript, Tang Dynasty) ▶

185

RECOMMENDED RESOURCES

Books for the Teacher
Burstein, Stanley, ed. *Ancient African Civilizations: Kush and Axum.* Princeton: Wiener, 1998. Historical overview of these ancient African civilizations.

Klieman, Kairn A. *"The Pygmies Were Our Compass": Bantu and Batwa in the History of West Central Africa, Early Times to c. 1900 C.E.* Portsmouth: Heinemann, 2003. Traces the history of the Bantu peoples of West Africa.

Monges, Miraim Ma'at-Ka-Re. *Kush, the Jewel of Nubia: Reconnecting the Root System of African Civilization.* Trenton: Africa World, 1997. Explores the impact of Kush on African civilization.

Welsby, Derek A. *The Kingdom of Kush: The Napatan and Meroitic Empires.* Princeton: Wiener, 1998. History of the empires of Kush.

Internet
To access these sites, visit the Research Links for this chapter at **ClassZone.com.**

The Nubia Salvage Project. Provides information on the history of Nubia and examples of archaeological findings.

African History Sourcebook. Includes large amounts of information on ancient Africa.

Introduce the Big Ideas
Read aloud the text about the Big Ideas. Have students think about how culture in the United States is affected by its neighbors in Mexico and Canada. How has United States culture affected our neighbors?

Here are some other Big Ideas that you may want to emphasize in this chapter:

Economics
The desire to trade in African goods brought visitors to Africa and helped enrich kingdoms there.

Geography
The movement of people, goods, and ideas helped shape the history of different regions of Africa.

Science and Technology
African civilizations adopted new technologies and distinctive techniques for building.

Talk About It

Interpreting Maps
Have students look at the map and read the key. What climate exists in the eastern part of Africa from the Horn of Africa northward? *(a desert environment)* How do you think that fact will affect the location of major civilizations in these areas? *(Possible answer: The lack of water will require major settlements to be located along rivers or near the coast.)*

INTERACTIVE

An interactive version of this map is available on the eEdition and Power Presentations CD-ROMs.

Find Out More
Where are the population centers of Africa today? Have students use library or Internet sources to find out. Ask students if the patterns of the past—the location of cities near water supplies—continues to apply today.

Objective

Describe the impact of the cultural mixing that affected Africa, Asia, and Europe.

Introducing the Story

Christianity in Aksum

This story dramatizes the impact of Christianity on the kingdom of Aksum. Christianity helped the African kingdom solidify its economic links with the Roman Empire. It also provided a cultural link, as this story explores.

Vocabulary Preview

conversion the adopting of a new religion

pilgrimage a journey to a holy place

Ten Commandments the basic laws of the Jewish faith

Constantinople the capital of the eastern Roman Empire

Reading the Story Aloud

1. **The teacher as reader:** Read a portion of the story to model how to read it with expression.

2. **The students as readers:** Have students practice reading the passage in pairs, offering each other feedback.

Starting with a Story

Students can also follow along as they listen to the story on the eEdition or on the Power Presentations CD-ROMs.

Starting with a Story

An African's Pilgrimage

CALIFORNIA STANDARDS
Reading 2.3 Connect and clarify main ideas by identifying their relationships to other sources and related topics.

Background: In the third century A.D., a Babylonian prophet wrote that there were four great kingdoms on Earth. These were the kingdoms of China, Persia, Rome, and the African kingdom of Aksum. Rome and Aksum made Christianity their official religion. In 324, Constantine became the Roman Empire's first Christian ruler. Around the same time, King Ezana became the first Christian ruler of Aksum. As you read the following story, think about what it would be like to live in Africa's Christian kingdom.

Church in Aksum, Ethiopia ▶

186

ADDITIONAL RESOURCES

Books for the Student

Jenkins, Earnestine, *A Glorious Past: Ancient Egypt, Ethiopia, and Nubia.* New York: Chelsea House, 1995. Overview of the history of the ancient civilizations of Africa.

Mann, Kenny. *Egypt, Kusk, Aksum: Northeast Africa.* Parsippany: Dillon, 1997. Historical review of the traditions of ancient African kingdoms.

Russman, Edna R. *Nubian Kingdoms.* New York: Watts, 1998. Survey of the history of the Nubian kingdoms.

Service, Pamela F. *The Ancient African Kingdom of Kush.* New York: Cavendish, 1998. Exploration of the history and culture of this great kingdom.

There was a young boy in Aksum. His father was an important official in the court of King Ezana. The father was a devoted servant of the king, and he adopted Christianity after the king made it Aksum's official religion. After his conversion, the father worked hard to raise his son as a Christian. He spent many hours helping him to read the Bible, and the boy grew to love the sacred book's stories and lessons. Even so, it was not until his father took him on a pilgrimage to the Christian holy places that he became truly dedicated to the new faith.

The boy still recalled with great pleasure the day they sailed from the port city of Adulis. King Ezana and Bishop Frumentius had provided resources and guides to take them to Jerusalem. With such preparation, they departed with few cares. On the way to the holy city, the guides ordered stops at many sites familiar from the Bible. One of the most meaningful was Sinai, the mountain where God gave Moses the Ten Commandments. The boy would never forget standing on Sinai's sacred summit and gazing over the surrounding scene. On the way to Jerusalem, they also stopped in Bethlehem, the birthplace of Jesus.

Jerusalem, however, was the spiritual peak of the journey. The boy walked with pilgrims from all over the Christian world as they visited the most important sites. The boy took careful notes because he was expected to report to the king about what he had seen. He met another boy his age and the boy's father, who had traveled to Jerusalem from Constantinople. The young Aksumite traveler was able to speak some Greek and make himself understood to the travelers from Constantinople. He acquired a rich supply of experiences and information to report to his king.

What experiences might the boy take back to Aksum from his pilgrimage?

Reading & Writing

1. **READING: Main Ideas** The main idea sums up the most important point of a paragraph or selection. With a partner, list one or two main ideas from the above passage.

2. **WRITING: Comparison and Contrast** Write a two-paragraph essay in which you compare what the boy's ideas about Jerusalem might have been before his trip with what he might have learned on the journey.

CALIFORNIA STANDARDS Writing 2.2
Write expository compositions.

187

Talk About It

Ask students the following questions to begin the discussion:

- Why did the father adopt Christianity? (*The king, whom he served, made it the official religion of the kingdom.*)
- What event helped the boy achieve dedication to his new faith? (*He went on a pilgrimage to the holy places of his new religion.*)
- What did the boy and his father do on the way to Jerusalem? (*They stopped at different holy sites along the way.*)
- Whom did the boy meet in Jerusalem? (*a pilgrim from Constantinople*)

What experiences might the boy take back to Aksum from his pilgrimage?

Possible answers: He will be able to write about seeing many different sights on his way to Jerusalem and in Jerusalem itself. He will also be able to report about meeting a fellow pilgrim from Constantinople.

Making Personal Connections

Connect the discussion to today by asking students to think about a time they have been exposed to another culture. How did the sights and scenes make them feel? (*Possible answers: amazed, awed, excited*)

READING & WRITING ACTIVITIES

1. **READING** Possible answers: (1) The boy's pilgrimage to the holy lands of Christianity helped strengthen his faith. (2) Jerusalem, with its pilgrims from all over the world, was the spiritual highlight of the journey.

2. **WRITING**

2. Writing Rubric

	Level of Comparison	Number of Errors
4	thorough and believable	zero or one spelling or punctuation errors
3	believable	two or three spelling or punctuation errors
2	somewhat believable	four or five spelling or punctuation errors
1	not believable	more than five spelling or punctuation errors

❶ Plan & Prepare

Objectives

- Describe the geographic features of Nubia.
- Summarize the development of the land of Kush.
- Describe notable features of the Kush civilization.
- **Language Objective:** Use signal words to describe the sequence of events in the lesson.

Quick Look

Lesson 1 explores Kush—the great civilization that arose in the African region of Nubia.

❷ Focus & Motivate

Preview Tell students that this lesson will explore the rise of another great civilization of the Nile River Valley, which was heavily influenced by Egypt. Ask students to think about how different states in the same region of the United States share certain cultural features.

Introduce the Main Ideas The three main ideas relate to the Big Idea that "Ways of living change as humans interact with each other." Help students look for this Big Idea as you go through the lesson.

Reading Skill: Explaining Sequence Tell students that understanding the sequence of events can help you recognize how events are related to one another.

SAMPLE ANSWERS FOR TIME LINE

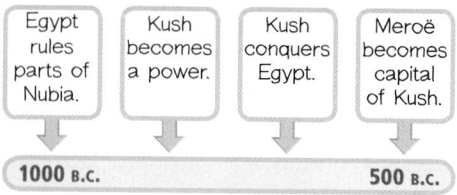

| Egypt rules parts of Nubia. | Kush becomes a power. | Kush conquers Egypt. | Meroë becomes capital of Kush. |

1000 B.C.   **500 B.C.**

Lesson 1

▸ **MAIN IDEAS**

① **Geography** The region of Nubia had connections with Egypt.

② **Government** A powerful king of Kush conquered Egypt and ruled as pharaoh.

③ **Economics** Meroë was an important economic center linking Egypt and the interior of Africa.

▸ **TAKING NOTES**

Reading Skill: Explaining Sequence

To sequence events means to put them in order based on the time they happened. As you read Lesson 1, make a note of things that happened in the Kushite kingdoms. Create a time line like the one below to put events in order.

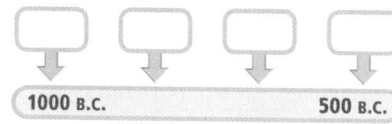

1000 B.C.   **500 B.C.**

S **Skillbuilder Handbook, page R15**

▲ **Nubian Pottery** This Nubian pottery vessel decorated with giraffes is an example of the goods traded in Kush.

CALIFORNIA STANDARDS

6.2.1 Locate and describe the major river systems and discuss the physical settings that supported permanent settlement and early civilizations.

6.2.8 Identify the location of the Kush civilization and describe its political, commercial, and cultural relations with Egypt.

CST 3 Students use a variety of maps and documents to identify physical and cultural features of neighborhoods, cities, states, and countries and to explain the historical migration of people, expansion and disintegration of empires, and the growth of economic systems.

HOW TO TEACH THE CALIFORNIA STANDARDS

Standard	Content	Student Question or Activity	Instruction
6.2.1	**Page 189** Describes the region of Nubia and the geographic factors that supported settlement.	**Page 193** In question 3, students explain how the Nile was important to the relationship between Egypt and Kush.	Explain that water sources were important in the relationship between Egypt and Kush because the Nile supported permanent settlements and aided in trade.
6.2.8	**Pages 190–192** Analyzes the political, commercial, and cultural ties between the Kush civilization and Egypt	**Page 193** In the Making a Map activity, students place Kush and its two capitals on a map.	Discuss how the location of Meroë was ideal for producing iron and that it had access to gold. Its position allowed it to become a major trading center. Encourage students to reread The Kushite Capital of Meroë to find details to put in their letters.
CST 3	**Page 190** The map shows Kush and surrounding area. It identifies physical and cultural landmarks.	**Page 190** Students determine bodies of water important to Kush by interpreting the map using the map key and map labels.	Have a volunteer locate the Mediterranean, the Red Sea, and the Nile River on the map on page 190. Discuss why these bodies of water would have been important to Kush because the trade of goods that were scarce elsewhere brought wealth to the kingdom.

Nubia and the Land of Kush

TERMS & NAMES
Nubia
Kush
Piankhi
Meroë
smelting

Build on What You Know Have you ever traveled on a river or visited a river town? The Egyptians lived downstream on the lower, or northern, end of the Nile River. Now you will learn about another culture that developed to the south that interacted with Egypt and other parts of Africa.

The Region of Nubia

1 ESSENTIAL QUESTION In what ways were Nubia and Egypt connected?   by the Nile River

Nubia (NOO•bee•uh) is the name for a geographic region of Africa. (See the map at the top of the next page.) Nubia extended from the southern boundary of Egypt southward to include present-day Sudan. Its southern boundary was south of the Nile River's sixth cataract.

Upper and Lower Nubia Like Egypt, Nubia was divided into upper (southern, upstream) and lower (northern, downstream) areas. Like the Egyptians, the people of Nubia lived along the Nile. However, in southern Nubia, unlike in Egypt, a climate that provided greater moisture meant farming was not limited to the Nile valley.

REVIEW What geographic feature connected Egypt and Nubia?
the Nile River

Connect to Today

▼ **The Upper Nile** The Nile River begins in Burundi and then travels north through Uganda, Sudan (shown below), and Egypt before it empties into the Mediterranean Sea.

189

Terms & Names

Nubia a region of Africa that covers parts of Egypt and Sudan

Kush a powerful ancient kingdom of Nubia

Piankhi a Kushite king who conquered Egypt

Meroë the capital of Kush starting about 590 B.C. and a center of trade

smelting the process of heating mineral-bearing material to separate the elements

❸ Teach

The Region of Nubia

6.2.1, 6.2.8

Talk About It

- **Critical Thinking: Compare and Contrast** How was Nubia similar to and different from Egypt? *(People in both places lived along the Nile, and both regions had an upper and lower area. Unlike Egypt, Nubia's climate favored farming beyond the Nile Valley.)*

California Resources

California Reading Toolkit, L18
California Modified Lesson Plans for English Learners, p. 39
California Daily Standards Practice Transparencies, TT18
California Standards Enrichment Workbook, pp. 21–22, 35–36
California Online Test Practice
California Test Generator CD-ROM
California Standards Planner and Lesson Plans, L35
California eEdition CD-ROM

LESSON 1 PROGRAM RESOURCES

ON LEVEL

In-Depth Resources: Unit 3
- Family Newsletter (English and Spanish), pp. 21–22
- Reading Skill: Explaining Sequence, p. 23
- Vocabulary Study Guide, p. 28
- Vocabulary Cards, p. 29
- Skillbuilder Practice, p. 27
- Geography Practice, p. 31

Formal Assessment
- Lesson Quiz, p. 96

ENGLISH LEARNERS

In-Depth Resources in Spanish
- Reading Skill, p. 45

- Vocabulary Study Guide, p. 50
- Skillbuilder Practice, p. 49
- Geography Practice, p. 51

Modified Lesson Plans for English Learners, p. 39

Reading Study Guide (Spanish), p. 49

Reading Study Guide Audio CD (Spanish)

STRUGGLING READERS

In-Depth Resources: Unit 3
- Reading Skill, p. 23
- Vocabulary Study Guide, p. 28
- Vocabulary Cards, p. 29
- Reteaching Activity, p. 35

Reading Toolkit, p. L18
Reading Study Guide, p. 49
Reading Study Guide Audio CD

GIFTED AND TALENTED STUDENTS

Interdisciplinary Projects
- Science, p. 32

INCLUSION

EasyPlanner CD-ROM
- Reading Skill: Explaining Sequence
- Vocabulary Study Guide
- Reteaching Activity

TECHNOLOGY

eEdition CD-ROM
- Starting with a Story

Power Presentations CD-ROM

Map Transparencies
- MT11 Northeastern Africa: Physical

Critical Thinking Transparencies
- CT23 Explaining Sequence

Humanities Transparencies
- HT11 Shoulder Necklace from Meroë

Test Generator CD-ROM

ClassZone.com

Teach

The Kuṣh Civilization

 6.2.8, CST 3

Talk About It

- What were the effects of Egyptian rule of Nubia on Nubian culture? *(Nubian culture was influenced by Egyptian culture.)*

- What significant event happened in the 700s B.C. between Nubia and Egypt? *(The Nubian kingdom of Kush conquered Egypt.)*

- What geographic factor helped Napata emerge as an important center in Kush? *(It was located at the head of a road used to transport goods along a stretch of the Nile that was not navigable.)*

- **Critical Thinking: Making Generalizations** In what way did technology influence the decline of Kush under Taharqa? *(Possible answer: The technology of their weapons was not advanced enough to resist the Assyrians.)*

 In-Depth Resources: Unit 3
- Reading Skill: Explaining Sequence, p. 23
- Skillbuilder Practice, p. 27

Human Transparencies
- MT11 Northeastern Africa: Physical

History from Visuals

Interpreting Maps
Help students recognize the boundaries of the Egyptian Empire at its height and the Kingdom of Kush.

- Which part of the Egyptian empire did the kingdom of Kush eventually conquer? *(Possible answer: the part along the Nile River)*

GEOGRAPHY SKILLBUILDER ANSWER

the Nile River, the Mediterranean Sea, and the Red Sea

The Kush Civilization

2 ESSENTIAL QUESTION What were some of the achievements of Piankhi?

united Egypt and Kush; established dynasty on throne of Egypt

Egypt controlled parts of Nubia between 2000 and 1000 B.C. During these centuries, Nubia was a source of goods for Egypt. But as Egypt declined, a Nubian kingdom called **Kush** became a power in the region.

Cultural Relations Between Egypt and Kush In ancient times, Nubia had a strong influence on Egypt. For example, some scholars believe Nubia's monarchy was the earliest in human history. Later, this monarchy was developed in the person of the Egyptian pharaoh.

Then, when Egypt ruled Nubia, the Egyptian pharaoh appointed an official to govern the region. Contact with Egypt resulted in cultural exchanges. Egypt influenced the art and architecture of the Nubian region, including the emerging kingdom of Kush. Nubians also worshiped some of the gods sacred to Egyptians.

Young Kushite nobles went to Egypt where they learned the Egyptian language. They also adopted the customs and clothing styles of the Egyptians. They brought back royal rituals and a hieroglyphic writing system to Kush. Egyptian pyramids were also adapted by builders in Kush.

Kush Rises to Power In the 700s B.C., the Nubian kingdom of Kush conquered all of upper and lower Egypt. In 751 B.C., **Piankhi** (PYANG•kee)—a Kushite king—attacked the Egyptian city of Memphis. By about 36 years later, Piankhi had gained control of Egypt.

From this point on, two periods make up the history of Kush. Each period is based on the location of the capital and king's tomb. The city of Napata was the capital during this first period. Meroë (MEHR•oh•EE) was the capital during the second.

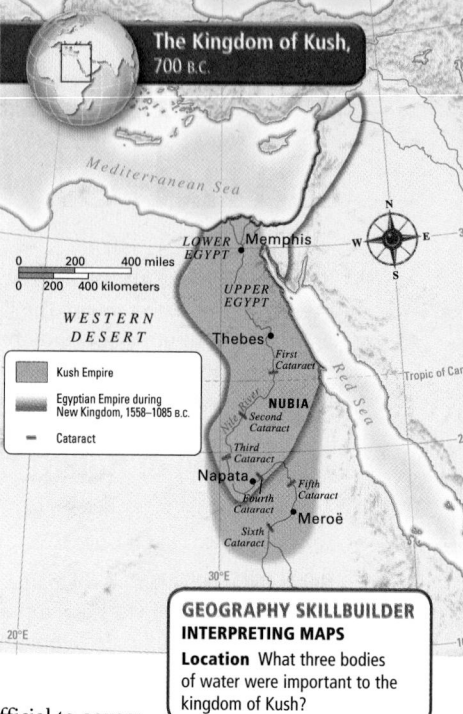

The Kingdom of Kush, 700 B.C.

Mediterranean Sea

LOWER EGYPT • Memphis

UPPER EGYPT

WESTERN DESERT

Thebes • First Cataract

Tropic of Can

0 200 400 miles
0 200 400 kilometers

Kush Empire

Egyptian Empire during New Kingdom, 1558–1085 B.C.

— Cataract

NUBIA
Second Cataract

Third Cataract

Napata • Fifth Cataract

Fourth Cataract • Meroë

Sixth Cataract

Red Sea

30°E

20°E

GEOGRAPHY SKILLBUILDER
INTERPRETING MAPS
Location What three bodies of water were important to the kingdom of Kush?

Vocabulary Strategy

Use context clues to figure out the meaning of *sacred*. The rest of the sentence tells you that the word sometimes means "worthy of religious respect or reverence."

DIFFERENTIATING INSTRUCTION

Struggling Readers

Make a Time Line
To help students understand the sequence of events in the emergence of Kush, have them work in teams of two to create a time line of the section "The Kush Civilization." Ask teams to work slowly through the text, taking notes about each development mentioned. Then have them use their notes to make their time line.

Gifted and Talented Students

Make an Expanded Time Line
Have students use information from this section and previous chapters to make a time line of key events during the time period of the rise of the kingdom of Kush. Students may also use library and Internet resources. They should include information about groups such as the Assyrians, Babylonians, and the Persians in their time lines.

Political and Commercial Relations with Egypt Piankhi united Egypt and Kush. Nubia established its own dynasty, or line of royal rulers, on the throne of Egypt. Piankhi was declared Egypt's pharaoh. His reign marked the beginning of Egypt's 25th Dynasty. Although he was the pharaoh, Piankhi did not live in Egypt. Instead, he chose to live in Napata, the capital of Kush.

Napata was located at the head of a road used to move goods around the Nile River's cataracts. Traders used the road when boats loaded with goods were unable to navigate the rough water on certain sections of the river. Nubia was rich in goods that were scarce in Egypt: ivory, animal skins, timber, and minerals. This led to a lively trade along the Nile. Napata was the center for the spread of Egyptian goods and culture to Kush's other trading partners in Africa and beyond.

The Decline of Kush Taharqa (tuh•HAHR•kuh) was a later Kushite ruler of Egypt. Taharqa spent much of his reign fighting the Assyrians, who had invaded and conquered Egypt in 671 B.C.

The Assyrians carried iron weapons that were more powerful than the bronze weapons of the Kushites. A large part of the Assyrian army was made up of foot soldiers, who were armed with bows and arrows.

History Makers

Piankhi (ruled during the 700s B.C.)

Piankhi was a Kushite king who knew when to fight and when to make peace. When a Libyan chief threatened Upper Egypt, Piankhi decided to fight. He defeated the Libyans' land army and their river fleet as well. At the time, Egypt had many weak princes who ruled small areas. They welcomed Piankhi's protection. The Egyptian priests also were eager to have Piankhi come to their defense.

Around 750 B.C., Piankhi united Egypt and became the pharaoh. This marked the beginning of the 25th Dynasty. Having accomplished what he set out to do, Piankhi went home to Napata. There he had a stone slab built that celebrated his deeds. The slab lasted longer than his dynasty, which ended after about 100 years.

▲ **Monument** This black granite monument, which is six feet high, was discovered in Napata. The image of Piankhi is at the center, upper right.

Kush and Other African Kingdoms • 191

Vocabulary Strategy

Using Context Clues
Help students use context clues to figure out the meaning of challenging words. Explain that context is the sentence in which the word appears. The clues are found in the way the word is used and the overall meaning of the sentence. Have students see if they can figure out the meaning of the word *navigate* on this page using context clues.

History Makers

Piankhi
In addition to his accomplishments in life, Piankhi is also noted for his death and burial. His grave is in a complex of pyramids located at el-Kurru. This is one of many pyramid complexes that have been found in Nubia. Nubian use of pyramids for royal burials is somewhat curious because the last of the great Egyptian royal pyramids had been built hundreds of years earlier. The Nubian pyramids, including Piankhi's, are much smaller than the great Egyptian pyramids. Piankhi's was about 26 feet wide at its base and rose at a sharper angle than the traditional Egyptian pyramids.

INTERDISCIPLINARY ACTIVITIES

Science

Compare Iron And Bronze
Have students use library and Internet resources to research and report on the differences between iron and bronze. Students should create a poster that explains the differences between these metals and how they may have affected battles in ancient civilizations.

Language Arts

Create a Monument
Have students write the text for a marker or monument that celebrates some of their own achievements. The monument should present the students' accomplishments in list form. Students may also write down predictions of what they hope to achieve in their lives.

Teach

The Kushite Capital of Meroë

 6.2.8

Talk About It

- Why did the Kushite kings choose Meroë as the site of their new capital? *(It was located on the Nile and on important trade routes.)*

- What kinds of goods did the Kushites trade at Meroë? *(products made from iron, ivory, and gold)*

- **Critical Thinking: Finding Main Ideas** Briefly describe the culture that developed in the Kingdom of Kush. *(Possible answer: The culture was a mixture of Nubian and Egyptian elements, including religion that featured Egyptian and Nubian gods, written language that started with Egyptian-like hieroglyphics, and burial practices that resembled those of Egypt.)*

Human Transparencies
- HT11 Shoulder Necklace from Meroë

More About . . .

Meroë
Meroë's iron industry played a significant part in its economic rise to success. In addition to local supplies of ore, Meroë had access to ample supplies of wood and water, both necessary in the smelting process. The iron produced at Meroë was used in trade and to make tools that enabled more successful agriculture. Eventually, however, the iron industry was hurt by destruction of the forests. This environmental damage played a part in the city's decline after several hundred years of stability.

Horses and Chariots Some Assyrians drove chariots. The Assyrian army also was the first army to have a cavalry—men on horseback.

The Kushite armies under Taharqa were no match for the Assyrians, who took control of Egypt and parts of Kush. After their defeat, the Kushite kings retreated south.

REVIEW How did Piankhi become the Egyptian pharaoh?
He attacked Memphis and eventually gained control of most of Egypt.

The Kushite Capital of Meroë

3 ESSENTIAL QUESTION Why was the Kushite city of Meroë an important economic center?

location on Nile and along trade routes; access to gold and iron

The Kushite kings eventually chose a new capital, **Meroë**, in about 590 B.C. Meroë was located on the Nile and on trade routes leading from the Red Sea to the interior of Africa. It had access to gold and iron.

An Economy of Ironworking and Trade The defeat of Kush by the Assyrians taught the Kushites that they needed iron weapons. The people of Kush learned to smelt iron. **Smelting** is the heating of material from Earth's crust to separate the elements it contains. The Kushites mined rock containing iron ore. Then they heated the rock in small earthen furnaces. The heat caused the iron to separate from other minerals.

Meroë was an ideal location for producing iron. The city was close to iron ore deposits. The Kushites set up smelting furnaces to process the deposits. Meroë traded its iron in central and east Africa, and in Arabia.

Ivory, gold, and products made from them were traded at Meroë. These items were in demand in many other parts of the world. Trade was especially active with Egypt, which was under Greek rule beginning in the fourth century B.C.

A Rich Culture Develops Some of the gods worshiped by the Kushites in Napata and Meroë were similar to those of Egypt. This similarity was especially true of the sun god Amon-Re and Isis, goddess of the moon. Other gods were Nubian in origin.

▲ **Sphinx** This granite sphinx of King Taharqa comes from the Amon Temple at Kawa and dates from about 690 to 664 B.C.

DIFFERENTIATING INSTRUCTION

English Learners

Make a Time Line
Use information from the text to construct a time line of Nubia and the Land of the Kush. Include information about the Kush kingdom, the Kushite Piankhi, Meroë and the practice of smelting of iron ore. Model how to use signal words *(first, next, then)*, dates, and key phrases to sequence events shown on the time line.

Inclusion

Paired Reading
Have students work in pairs to read each section of the text. Partners should alternate reading passages aloud and retelling what they have read in their own words. As students read and retell, they should note questions they have. Discuss these questions as a class.

In Nubia, women played an important role. Amanirenas and Amanishakheto were important Nubian queens. Queen Amanitore and her husband ruled beginning around 12 B.C.

The people of Kush developed a written language. They appear to have at first used hieroglyphics similar to those used by the Egyptians. Later, their language changed to an alphabet of 23 symbols. The language has not yet been translated.

Royal tombs in Kush were built of stone. They were pyramid-shaped with steep sides. These tombs included a chapel attached to the side. Kushite kings were often mummified to preserve their bodies. These traditions continued in Nubia even after they had died out in Egypt.

REVIEW In what ways was Meroë economically important?
Its location on the Nile was ideal for trade with Egypt. Ironworking at Meroë

Lesson Summary was a source of many trade items.
- Nubia and Egypt interacted with each other.
- The Kushite king Piankhi conquered Egypt.
- The Kushite capital of Meroë was a trade center.

Why It Matters Now . . .
By studying the history of Nubia, we learn of the important role played by Africans in ancient history.

▲ **Armlet** This armlet dates from Meroë in the late first century B.C. It is made of gold with fused-glass inlays. On the hinge is the figure of a goddess.

1 Lesson Review

 Homework Helper
ClassZone.com

Terms & Names
1. Explain the importance of

Nubia	Piankhi	smelting
Kush	Meroë	

Using Your Notes
Explaining Sequence Use your completed time line to answer the following question:
2. What event marked the end of the Kushite kingdom based in Napata? (6.2.8)

1000 B.C.   500 B.C.

Main Ideas
3. How was the Nile important to the relationship between Nubia and Egypt? (6.2.1)
4. What was the most significant achievement of Piankhi's rule? (6.2.8)
5. Why did the people of Meroë learn to smelt iron? (6.2.8)

Critical Thinking
6. **Comparing** How did Piankhi's reign differ from that of Taharqa in the control of Egypt? (6.2.8)
7. **Drawing Conclusions** What factors made the Kushites move their capital to Meroë? (CST 3)

Activity **Making a Map** Pull out the world outline map you began in the activity for Chapter 2, Lesson 1. Place the Nubian kingdom of Kush on the map, along with its two capitals of Napata and Meroë. (CST 3)

Kush and Other African Kingdoms • 193

1 Lesson Review Answers

Terms & Names
1. • Nubia, p. 189
   • Kush, p. 190
   • Piankhi, p. 190
   • Meroë, p. 192
   • smelting, p. 192

Using Your Notes
See page 188 for an example of a completed time line.
2. the Assyrian invasion of Egypt and Kush

Main Ideas
3. The Nile served as a major waterway between them. It increased trade between the two areas.
4. He united Egypt and Kush.
5. They learned through their defeat by the Assyrians that iron weapons were important to their safety.

Critical Thinking
6. Possible answer: Piankhi gained control of Egypt, increasing the power of Kush, while Taharqa lost control of Egypt when Kush was defeated by the Assyrians.
7. Possible answer: Meroë offered a good location from which to establish trade and increase the kingdom's wealth. It had access to iron ore, trade routes, and other riches.

❹ Assess & Reteach

Assess Have students work on their own to answer questions, then meet in groups to discuss their answers.

 Formal Assessment
• Lesson Quiz, p. 96

Reteach Have students convert each section heading and subheading into a question and write these questions on a sheet of paper. Next, have students exchange their questions with each other. Finally, have them review the lesson to find answers to each question.

 In-Depth Resources: Unit 3
• Vocabulary Cards, p. 29
• Reteaching Activity, p. 35

Homework Helper
Visit **ClassZone.com** for a lesson review, a flip-card activity, and links to related Web sites.

Activity Rubric

	Accuracy of Map	**Effectiveness of Presentation**
4	accurate	attractive and neat
3	mostly accurate	neat
2	somewhat accurate	somewhat neat
1	inaccurate	sloppy

Kush and Other African Kingdoms • 193

Objectives

- Use a map to identify physical and human characteristics of Kush.
- Identify the relationship between the kingdom of Kush's mineral wealth, access to trade routes, and economic prosperity.

❶ Focus & Motivate

Tell students that being able to collect information from maps about geographic patterns is a key social studies skill. It is a skill they will use throughout their academic careers and their lives.

❷ Teach

Talk About It

- To what geographic feature are the trade routes on this map connected? *(rivers and the Red Sea)*

- Which trade route on this map would likely have served as the route by which goods came into Kush from distant lands, such as India and Arabia? *(probably the route between the Red Sea and the Meroë area)*

- What feature on the Nile River appears to be associated with the location of trade routes? *(Many routes intersect with the river just below the cataracts.)*

- **Critical Thinking: Making Inferences** What does the location of trade routes in Kush relative to rivers and seas suggest about the nature of trade in Kush? *(River and sea transportation were very important.)*

Skillbuilder   Extend Lesson 1

Explaining Geographic Patterns

CALIFORNIA STANDARDS

6.2.8 Identify the location of the Kush civilization and describe its political, commercial, and cultural relations with Egypt.

CST 3 Students use a variety of maps and documents to identify physical and cultural features of neighborhoods, cities, states, and countries and to explain the historical migration of people, expansion and disintegration of empires, and the growth of economic systems.

Goal: To identify the importance of minerals and trade to the economic system of the Kush Empire

Learn the Skill

Recognizing geographic patterns involves seeing the overall shape, organization, or trend of specific geographic characteristics. Look at the chart at the bottom of this page for examples of geographic patterns. Trade routes make up one type of geographic pattern. You read about the Kush Empire and trade in Lesson 1. Trade routes went in and out of Kush in every direction, by land and by sea.

S See the Skillbuilder Handbook, page R16.

Practice the Skill

❶ Look at the title of the map at right to get an idea of the geographic pattern—trade routes and minerals—that it shows.

❷ Identify significant mineral deposits, such as gold and iron, on this map by using the symbols in the legend.

❸ Look at the map to see in what areas trade routes developed. Which part of the continent, if any, was largely untouched by Kush trade routes?

❹ Check the map to see how the location of resources contributed to the development of trade routes.

❺ There are many different examples of geographic patterns. Some of these are given below.

Examples:

❺

GEOGRAPHIC PATTERNS			
Weather Cycles	Economic Changes	Languages	Trade Routes
Monsoon winds in India follow a predictable pattern: winter—from northeast; summer—from southwest.	Oil has transformed the economies of some North African countries.	Bantu languages spread across Africa as a result of Bantu migrations.	Triangular trade developed between Africa, America, and Europe; Silk Roads crossed Asia.

DIFFERENTIATING INSTRUCTION

Struggling Readers

Review Key Terms
Have students work in pairs to review the meaning of key terms and places included on the map. Students should identify terms such as *cataract, Upper Nubia, Lower Nubia, Kush, Meroë, Napata,* and *Thebes.* They can then use their glossary and index to review the meaning and significance of the terms.

Gifted and Talented Students

Create a "Kush Catalog"
Have students use library or Internet resources to research the many types of goods traded into and out of Kush during its period of greatest prosperity. Have students create an illustrated catalog of the kinds of items a "shopper" in Kush might hope to buy.

Trade Map

The Kush Empire was a center of trade. As the mineral wealth of the Nile valley flowed out of Kush to Egypt (among other places), luxury goods from India and Arabia flowed in. Trade routes developed both over land and by sea to carry goods in and out of Kush.

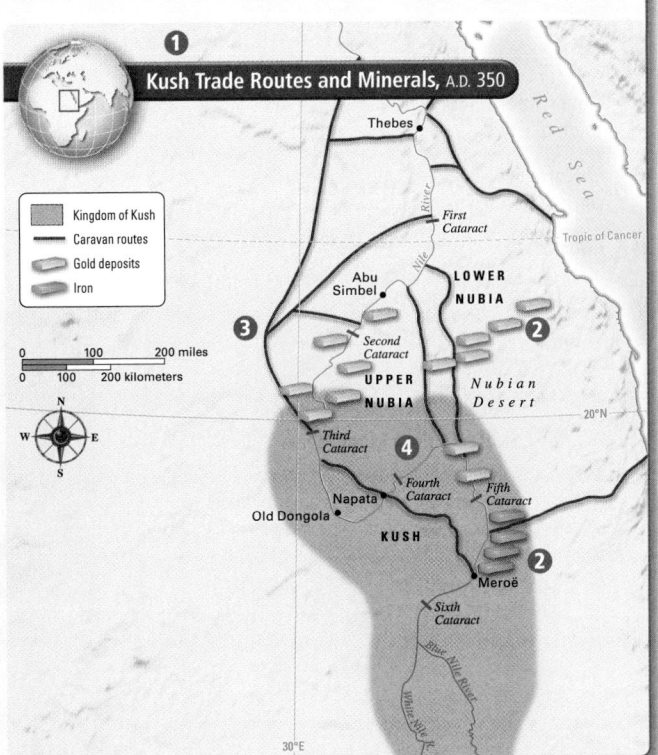

Kush Trade Routes and Minerals, A.D. 350

Kingdom of Kush
Caravan routes
Gold deposits
Iron

0   100   200 miles
0   100   200 kilometers

Thebes
Red Sea
First Cataract
Tropic of Cancer
Abu Simbel
LOWER NUBIA
Second Cataract
UPPER NUBIA
Nubian Desert
20°N
Third Cataract
Fourth Cataract
Fifth Cataract
Napata
Old Dongola
KUSH
Meroë
Sixth Cataract
Blue Nile River
White Nile R.
30°E

Apply the Skill

Look at the maps on the distribution of hunters and gatherers in Chapter 2, Lesson 1, page 52. Make notes on the geographic patterns that you see developing across the time span of the three maps on that page.

More About . . .

Trade in the Kingdom of Kush
One possible factor in the success of Kush as a trading empire was the camel. This animal helped make trade possible with areas in the African interior that had been cut off from civilization along the Nile by vast areas of desert. The camel was brought to the Nile Valley from Asia—perhaps with the Assyrians. The use of the animals spread, and they helped revolutionize the nature of trade on the continent.

Kush and Other African Kingdoms • **195**

APPLY THE SKILL

SAMPLE ANSWER FOR GRAPHIC ORGANIZER

Geographic Pattern		
Distribution of Hunter-Gatherers		
Hunter-gatherers used to be distributed across most of the world.	They became more scattered as time went on.	Today, they are widely scattered and found in only a few parts of the world.

❶ Plan & Prepare

Objectives

- Summarize the development of the kingdom of Aksum.
- Describe notable features of the Aksum civilization.
- Describe how the Aksum civilization reflected a wide range of cultural influences.
- **Language Objective:** Create concept cluster of words and terms from the lesson that are related to the kingdom of Aksum.

Quick Look

Lesson 2 traces the rise of the kingdom of Aksum, which replaced Kush and developed a rich and varied culture.

❷ Focus & Motivate

Preview Tell students that this lesson describes the rise of another great civilization in Africa—and of the influences that produced its rich culture. Ask students to think about how the United States today is enriched by the influences of many different cultures.

Introduce the Main Ideas The three main ideas relate to the Big Idea that "Ways of living change as humans interact with each other." Help students look for this Big Idea as you go through the lesson.

Reading Skill: Finding Main Ideas Tell students that the main ideas are often the first ideas mentioned in a paragraph.

SAMPLE ANSWERS FOR DIAGRAM

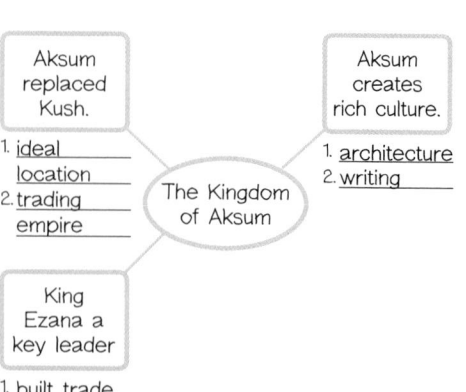

Lesson 2

▶ MAIN IDEAS

1 **Government** A new power, Aksum, rises south of Egypt.

2 **Culture** Ezana expands Aksum's influence and converts to Christianity.

3 **Culture** Aksum's cultural and technical achievements were long lasting.

▶ TAKING NOTES

Reading Skill: Finding Main Ideas

A main idea sums up the most important point of a paragraph or passage. Main ideas are supported by details and examples. Identify the main ideas and important details in Lesson 2 about Aksum's achievements. Then put them into your own words and write them in a diagram like the one below.

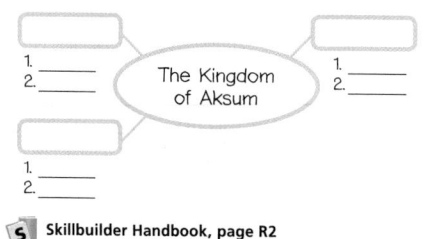

S Skillbuilder Handbook, page R2

▲ **Pillar** This towering stone pillar was built around A.D. 400 to celebrate Aksum's achievements.

CALIFORNIA STANDARDS

6.2.8 Identify the location of the Kush civilization and describe its political, commercial, and cultural relations with Egypt.

HI 1 Students explain the central issues and problems from the past, placing people and events in a matrix of time and place.

CST 3 Students use a variety of maps and documents to identify physical and cultural features of neighborhoods, cities, states, and countries and to explain the historical migration of people, expansion and disintegration of empires, and the growth of economic systems.

HOW TO TEACH THE CALIFORNIA STANDARDS

Standard	Content	Student Question or Activity	Instruction
6.2.8	**Pages 197–198** Discusses how the Kingdom of Kush fell after a king of Aksum destroyed Meroë.	**Page 198** Students consider how Aksum absorbed the territory belonging to Kush and gained access to its trading network.	Have students identify the location of Kush. Discuss why the king of Aksum may have destroyed Meroë. Encourage students to consider that the location of Kush was ideal for trade and the king of Aksum may have wanted to gain access to the trading network established by Kush.
HI 1	**Page 200** States how Aksum farmers adopted the land for farming.	**Page 200** Students explain how the adoption of Christianity as the official religion of Aksum affected the culture.	Ask students to explain the effect of writing on history. Encourage them to think about how useful writing is in daily life. Brainstorm how people might communicate without writing. Have students consider how the language of Aksum has affected the languages used in Ethiopia and Eritrea today.
CST 3	**Page 198** The map shows the Aksum kingdom and trade routes in the region.	**Page 198** Students trace trade routes originating from Aksum to determine access to other countries and continents.	Ask students how the physical features (such as rivers, seas, mountains, deserts, savannah) that traders encountered on a particular trade route from Aksum may have affected economic growth or trade.

The Kingdom of Aksum

TERMS & NAMES

Aksum

Horn of Africa

Adulis

Ezana

terrace

Build on What You Know In Lesson 1 you learned about the kingdom of Kush. South of Kush, a new African kingdom arose as a leading center of political and economic power.

The Rise of Aksum

Aksum had an ideal location with access to the Red Sea, Mediterranean Sea, and Nile River for exchanging goods from the Indian Ocean trade, Persia, and Africa.

1 ESSENTIAL QUESTION Why did trade become important to Aksum?

The kingdom of Kush fell when Meroë was destroyed by a king of **Aksum** (AHK•SOOM). Kush was conquered by Aksum. Aksum was located in modern-day Ethiopia and Eritrea.

Perfect Trade Location Aksum arose in the **Horn of Africa**, an area shaped like a rhinoceros horn. (See map below.) This location gave Aksum access to trade to the Red Sea, Mediterranean Sea, Indian Ocean, and the Nile valley.

Arab traders built colonies and trading posts there. They found the location ideal for exchanging goods from the Indian Ocean trade, Persia, and Africa. Aksum was a meeting place for African, Arabian, and other peoples.

A legend traces the founding of the Ethiopian dynasty of Aksum to Menelik, son of King Solomon of Israel and the Queen of Sheba.

Ethiopia This photograph shows present-day Ethiopia (highlighted on map), where the ancient kingdom of Aksum was located. ▼

197

Terms & Names

Aksum a kingdom that rose to power in the fourth century A.D. in modern-day Ethiopia and Eritrea

Horn of Africa the horn-shaped area in eastern Africa in which Aksum was located

Adulis the main trading port of Aksum

Ezana a powerful king of Aksum who helped the kingdom achieve greatness

terrace a leveled-off area of land

❸ Teach

The Rise of Aksum

6.2.8, HI 1, CST 3

Talk About It

- **Critical Thinking: Finding Main Ideas** Why is it accurate to refer to Aksum as a 'hub' of trade? (*Like spokes from the hub of a wheel, trade routes went in all directions from Aksum.*)

California Resources

California Reading Toolkit, L19
California Modified Lesson Plans for English Learners, p. 41
California Daily Standards Practice Transparencies, TT19
California Standards Enrichment Workbook, pp. 35–36
California Online Test Practice
California Test Generator CD-ROM
California Standards Planner and Lesson Plans, L37
California eEdition CD-ROM

LESSON 2 PROGRAM RESOURCES

ON LEVEL

In-Depth Resources: Unit 3
- Reading Skill: Finding Main Ideas, p. 24
- Vocabulary Study Guide, p. 28
- Vocabulary Cards, p. 29

Formal Assessment
- Lesson Quiz, p. 97

ENGLISH LEARNERS

In-Depth Resources in Spanish
- Reading Skill: Finding Main Ideas, p. 46
- Vocabulary Study Guide, p. 50

Modified Lesson Plans for English Learners, p. 41

Reading Study Guide (Spanish), p. 51

Reading Study Guide Audio CD (Spanish)

STRUGGLING READERS

In-Depth Resources: Unit 3
- Reading Skill: Finding Main Ideas, p. 24
- Vocabulary Study Guide, p. 28
- Vocabulary Cards, p. 29
- Reteaching Activity, p. 36

Reading Toolkit, p. L19

Reading Study Guide, p. 51

Reading Study Guide Audio CD

GIFTED AND TALENTED STUDENTS

In-Depth Resources: Unit 3
- Primary Source: Crowning the King, p. 33

Interdisciplinary Projects
- Math, p. 31

History Makers
- Ezana, p. 11

INCLUSION

EasyPlanner CD-ROM
- Reading Skill: Finding Main Ideas
- Vocabulary Study Guide
- Reteaching Activity

TECHNOLOGY

eEdition CD-ROM

Power Presentations CD-ROM

Critical Thinking Transparencies
- CT24 Finding Main Ideas

Test Generator CD-ROM

ClassZone.com

In-Depth Resources: Unit 3
• Reading Skill: Finding Main Ideas, p. 24

Teach

King Ezana Expands Aksum

CST 3

Talk About It

• What was the sequence of events by which Ezana helped make Aksum a great power? *(He took control of a trading colony on the Arabian Peninsula, then he conquered Kush and destroyed Meroë.)*

• What religion did Ezana adopt for Aksum? *(Christianity)*

• **Critical Thinking: Making Generalizations** What does the spread of Christianity in Aksum suggest about the cultural influences on the African Kingdom? *(Possible answer: The kingdom was influenced by faraway cultures.)*

History from Visuals

Interpreting Maps

Have students spend a few moments examining the map on this page, paying special attention to the many trade routes connected to the kingdom of Aksum.

• Briefly describe the advantages Aksum had in its ability to control international trade. *(Possible answer: It had access to the sea and easy access to population centers in Africa, Europe, and Asia.)*

GEOGRAPHY SKILLBUILDER ANSWER

African interior, Egypt, Mediterranean countries on the Indian Ocean

---

An International Trading Hub Like Kush, Aksum became a trading hub, or center, from which trade spread out in many directions. Traders came from Egypt, other parts of Africa, Arabia, the eastern Mediterranean, Persia, and India.

Adulis (ah•DOO•lihs), a city on the Red Sea, was the main trading port of Aksum. There traders exchanged salt, ivory, cloth, brass, iron, gold, glass, olive oil, and wine. Animal traders purchased animals such as giraffes and elephants.

REVIEW What made Aksum's location ideal for trade?
It allowed access to the Indian Ocean, the Red Sea, the Mediterranean Sea, and to the African interior.

King Ezana Expands Aksum

2 ESSENTIAL QUESTION What was the effect of King Ezana on religion?

At the beginning, Aksum was small. Then, in the A.D. 300s, a bold king added territory and built a powerful nation.

He converted himself and his kingdom to Christianity.

A Trading Nation Ezana (AY•zah•nah) was a strong king who rose to power in Aksum in A.D. 325. First he took control of a trading colony on the coast of the Arabian peninsula. Then, in 350, he conquered Kush and burned Meroë to the ground.

Around this time, the empire of Aksum expanded inland and along the coast of the Red Sea. As a result, the kingdom controlled a large trading network.

Ezana had become king as an infant. While he was being educated, Ezana's mother ruled on his behalf. One of Ezana's teachers taught him about Christianity. When Ezana began to rule he converted to Christianity. He also made Christianity the official religion of Aksum. The Christian church in Aksum was linked to Alexandria, in Egypt, rather than to Rome.

REVIEW How did Ezana influence the culture of Aksum?
He made Christianity the official religion.

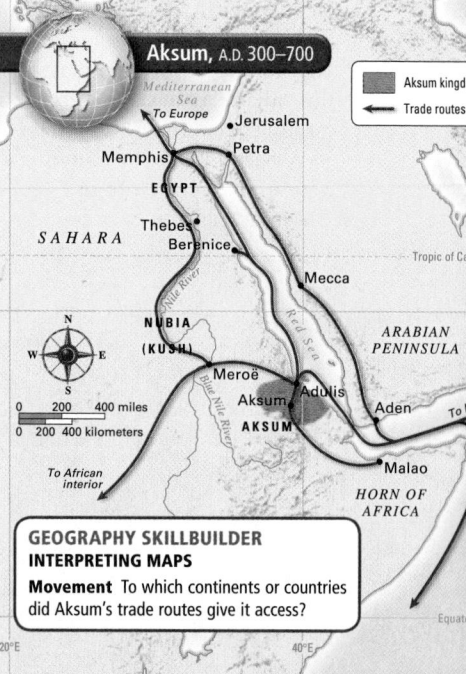

Aksum, A.D. 300–700

GEOGRAPHY SKILLBUILDER
INTERPRETING MAPS
Movement To which continents or countries did Aksum's trade routes give it access?

DIFFERENTIATING INSTRUCTION

Inclusion

Use Flash Cards
Have students make three large cards and label them A through C. To test students' understanding of the text, ask them simple questions about important concepts with three response choices. Questions may also be written on large cards. Students should hold up the card with the letter signifying the correct response.

English Learners

Use Word Webs
Demonstrate how to locate words from the lesson that are related to *Kingdom of Aksum*. Say, *Aksum relates to Kingdom of Aksum and can be written in the word web. The king of Aksum destroyed the kingdom of Meroë.* Have students work with a partner to complete their own word webs. To conclude, have students take turns explaining how each word relates to *the Kingdom of Aksum.*

Primary Source

Background: African rulers in Egypt, Kush, and Aksum had accounts of their military campaigns carved onto stone pillars and thrones.

They followed a standard format. First they described the reasons for going to war. Then they described the war itself. Next they noted the campaign's results. Finally, they gave thanks to the gods or God for victory. The passage quoted on the right was carved onto a throne for King Ezana to celebrate his victory.

from *Aksum: An African Civilization of Late Antiquity*
By Stuart Munro-Hay

And I set up a throne here in Shado [in Aksum] by the might of the Lord of Heaven who has helped me and given me supremacy. May the Lord of Heaven reinforce my reign. And, as he has now defeated my enemies for me, may he continue to do so wherever I go. As he has now conquered for me, and has submitted my enemies to me, I wish to reign in justice and equity, without doing any injustice to my peoples.

 Aksum Crown This is an early crown from the Christian kingdom of Aksum.

> **DOCUMENT–BASED QUESTION**
> Whom is King Ezana thanking? What are his goals for ruling?

Aksum's Achievements

③ ESSENTIAL QUESTION What were some of Aksum's achievements?

architecture (pillars), written language, terraced farming

A unique culture rose in Aksum. Just as the people of Kush blended Nubian and Egyptian influences, so Aksum saw a coming together of cultural influences from the Horn of Africa and southern Arabia.

Architecture Among the most impressive of these achievements were the pillars of Aksum, which builders placed around the country. Some were 60 to more than 100 feet tall. Writing carved on the pillars celebrated great victories or achievements. Builders in Egypt and Kush had used pillars in a similar fashion.

Builders constructed Aksum's tall pillars without mortar. They were carved from single stone slabs. Features included false doors and windows. Builders and architects also built large temples. Later, richly decorated Christian churches replaced the temples.

Kush and Other African Kingdoms • 199

Interpreting Primary Sources

- What were the main purposes of the inscriptions typically made on Aksum pillars or thrones? *(They described the reasons for wars, explained the fighting, told the outcome, then thanked God or the gods for the victory.)*

- What is the purpose of the throne inscription of King Ezana shown here? *(It celebrates the winning of a war.)*

DOCUMENT–BASED QUESTION ANSWER
Ezana is thanking God. Ezana's goals are to rule with justice and equity.

📓 **In-Depth Resources: Unit 3**
- Primary Source: Crowning the King, p. 33

Teach

Aksum's Achievements
🔖 **6.2.8**

Talk About It

- What were the most impressive structures erected in Aksum, and why were they built? *(stone pillars, which were built to celebrate great victories or achievements)*

- In what ways did Aksum farmers adapt to the rugged environment of the region? *(They terraced land and built elaborate irrigation systems.)*

- **Critical Thinking: Finding Main Ideas** In what way did the language of Aksum reflect the multicultural nature of the kingdom? *(The language was brought to Aksum by Arabian traders.)*

DIFFERENTIATING INSTRUCTION

Gifted and Talented Students

Write a Biographical Sketch
Have students use library and Internet sources to learn more about the life of King Ezana and his conversion to Christianity. The report should explain how the king's conversion reflected the multicultural nature of life in Aksum during that time.

Struggling Readers

Shrink the Paragraphs
Have students work in teams of three to five to "shrink" the paragraphs in the two sections on pages 198–200. Each student should take responsibility for one paragraph, which he or she will read and "shrink" down to one summary sentence. When all the students are finished, they should string together their shrunken paragraphs to form a shrunken summary of these pages.

❹ Assess & Reteach

Assess Have students work in pairs on the questions, taking turns answering them.

 Formal Assessment
• Lesson Quiz, p. 97

Reteach Ask students to read the items in the Lesson Summary out loud. Then, for each item, have students review the lesson for information with which to write an additional, follow-up sentence on the topic.

 In-Depth Resources: Unit 3
• Vocabulary Cards, p. 29
• Reteaching Activity, p. 36

 Homework Helper

Visit **ClassZone.com** for a lesson review, a flip-card activity, and links to related Web sites.

A Written Language Aksum had a written language called Ge'ez (gee•EHZ). Arabian migrants brought the language to Aksum. Ge'ez became the basis for three languages that are used in Ethiopia and Eritrea today—Amharic, Tigrinya, and Tigre. Ge'ez is still used in the Ethiopian Church.

Terraced Farming The landscape of Aksum was rugged and hilly. To adapt the land for farming, farmers built terraces. A **terrace** is a leveled-off area of land. Being flat, terraces hold moisture better than hilly land does. Terraced farming increased the amount of land that could be cultivated. Aksum's farmers also built canals, dams, and holding ponds to bring mountain water to the fields.

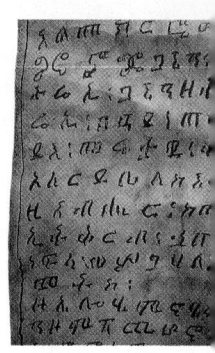

▲ **Scroll** Text written in the Ge'ez language

REVIEW How did Aksum farmers increase productivity?
They built terraces and irrigation systems.

Lesson Summary
• Aksum became a powerful trading center.
• King Ezana expanded Aksum's empire.
• Aksum's unique culture had long-lasting effects.

Why It Matters Now . . .
Many Ethiopians today are Christians, the religion of King Ezana.

---

2 Lesson Review

 **Homework Helper** ClassZone.com

Terms & Names

1. Explain the importance of

Aksum	Adulis	terrace
Horn of Africa	Ezana	

Using Your Notes

Finding Main Ideas Use your completed diagram to answer the following question:

2. What were some of Aksum's major achievements? (CST 3)

[diagram: The Kingdom of Aksum]
1. ___ 2. ___
1. ___ 2. ___
1. ___ 2. ___

Main Ideas

3. What factors led to the rise of Aksum? (6.2.8)
4. How did Ezana expand Aksum's power? (CST 3)
5. What kinds of structures were built in Aksum, and what purpose did they serve? (CST 3)

Critical Thinking

6. **Drawing Conclusions** What did the pillars of Aksum reveal about the culture? (CST 3)
7. **Making Inferences** In what ways did the adoption of Christianity as the official religion affect the culture of Aksum? (HI 1)

Activity

Designing a Coin Write a short motto for King Ezana. The motto should say something memorable about him or his reign. Draw a coin showing the motto and sketch Ezana. (HI 1)

200 • Chapter 6

---

2 Lesson Review Answers

Terms & Names
1. • Aksum, p. 197
   • Horn of Africa, p. 197
   • Adulis, p. 198
   • Ezama, p. 198
   • terrace, p. 200

Using Your Notes
See page 196 for an example of a completed diagram.
2. building a great trading network; spectacular architecture; written language; agricultural innovations

Main Ideas
3. The power of Kush declined; Aksum's location made it a trading center.
4. He added territory and built Aksum into a trading nation.
5. Great pillars celebrated achievements and victories; temples and churches were part of worship.

Critical Thinking
6. Possible answer: Their inscriptions tell of Aksum's history.
7. Possible answer: Many people became Christians. Churches replaced Aksum's temples.

Activity Rubric

	Content of Motto	**Style of Coin**
4	clever and focuses on significant feature	attractive and interesting
3	focuses on significant feature	interesting
2	focuses on less significant feature	fairly interesting
1	irrelevant to Ezana's reign	uninteresting

Design a Pillar

Goal: To understand the architecture of Kush and Aksum, and the purpose it served, by creating a pillar and decorating its sides

Prepare

1 Look at the example of a pillar from Aksum on page 196 and read the caption.

2 Reread the information on the monument of Piankhi in Kush (page 191) and the pillars of Aksum (page 199) in this chapter.

Do the Activity

1 Draw a pillar to fill up a poster board.

2 Design drawings to celebrate the achievements of one of the following: your school, your neighborhood, your city, your state, or your country.

3 Color your drawings with crayons or magic markers.

4 Cut out the pillar from the poster board so that it is free-standing.

5 Give a title to the pillar you have designed.

Follow-Up

1 Why might a pillar be an effective way to celebrate achievement?

2 How do the images you used on your pillar celebrate achievement?

Extension

Making a Presentation Display your pillar in the classroom. Explain what your pillar is meant to celebrate and how it expresses the beliefs of your community.

Materials & Supplies
- poster board
- pens, pencils, or markers
- scissors

CALIFORNIA STANDARDS
6.2.8 Identify the location of the Kush civilization and describe its political, commercial, and cultural relations with Egypt.

ACTIVITY: DESIGN A PILLAR

Objective

Explore a key feature of Aksum culture by designing a monument.

Suggestions for Completing the Activity

- Make sure students look at and read about the Aksum pillar and about the monument of Piankhi so they understand the nature and purpose of these monuments.
- Before they draw and write inscriptions on their pillars, have students plan what they want their pillar to show and say.
- Be sure students give a title to their pillar.
- Encourage neatness and care in drawing, inscribing, and coloring the pillar.

201

ACTIVITY ANSWERS

Follow-Up Answers

1. Pillars are monuments that command attention and are easily recognized and distinctive.
2. Students should be able to explain how the markings on their pillars communicate the desired message.

Extension Rubric

	Content of Drawings	Design of Pillar	Style of Presentation
4	creative and thoughtful selections that demonstrate achievements	attractive design and well organized	clearly and thoroughly explains concepts
3	thoughtful selections that demonstrate achievement	well organized	thoroughly explains concepts
2	selections that vaguely celebrate achievements	not very well organized	adequately explains concepts
1	irrelevant selections	no apparent organization	does not explain concepts

❶ Plan & Prepare

Objectives

- Describe early life in west, central, and southern Africa.
- Describe the key features of the Nok culture.
- Summarize the history of the Bantu migrations.
- **Language Objective:** Use structural and context clues to define words to gain a deeper understanding of the information they read.

Quick Look

Lesson 3 explores developments among the early peoples of west, central, and southern Africa, including the Nok culture and the Bantu migrations.

❷ Focus & Motivate

Preview Tell students that this lesson covers what was taking place in other parts of Africa at the time when Egypt, Kush, and Aksum were achieving greatness. Ask students to think about how regions and cultures differ in different sections of their own continent.

Introduce the Main Ideas The three main ideas relate to the Big Idea that "Ways of living change as humans interact with each other." This lesson discusses how the people of west, central, and southern Africa lived and changed through interactions with each other. Help students look for this Big Idea as you go through the lesson.

Reading Skill: Explaining Geographic Patterns Tell students to remember the five themes of geography—location, place, region, movement, and human-environment interaction—when looking for geographic patterns.

SAMPLE ANSWERS FOR DIAGRAM

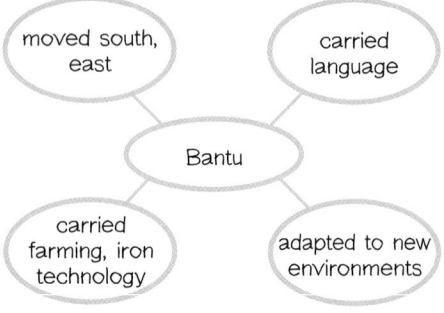

moved south, east

carried language

Bantu

carried farming, iron technology

adapted to new environments

▶ **MAIN IDEAS**

❶ **Geography** The people of west, central, and southern Africa adapted to life in a variety of environments.

❷ **Economics** The Nok people were the first ironworkers of West Africa.

❸ **Geography** Migration by the Bantu people from West Africa populated central and southern Africa.

▶ **TAKING NOTES**

Reading Skill:
Explaining Geographic Patterns
Recognizing geographic patterns means seeing the overall shape or trend of geographic characteristics. In Lesson 3, look for details about the nomadic migrations of the Bantu people of Africa. Record the information on a web diagram.

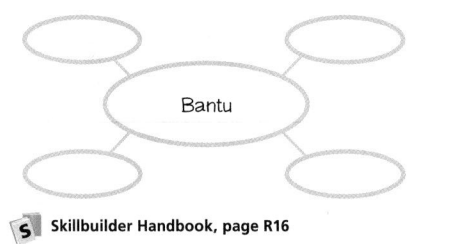

Bantu

Ⓢ **Skillbuilder Handbook, page R16**

▲ **Sculpture** This Nok terra cotta (ceramic clay) sculpture depicts a seated dignitary, a person of high status.

CALIFORNIA STANDARDS

6.1.2 Identify the locations of human communities that populated the major regions of the world and describe how humans adapted to a variety of environments.

CST 1 Students explain how major events are related to one another in time.

HI 1 Students explain the central issues and problems from the past, placing people and events in a matrix of time and place.

HOW TO TEACH THE CALIFORNIA STANDARDS

Standard	Content	Student Question or Activity	Instruction
6.1.2	**Pages 205–207** Explains where the Nok and Bantu lived.	**Page 207** Students create a chart to explain causes and effects of the Bantu migrations.	Discuss what students know about the locations of human communities. Ask students to name some reasons people choose to live in an area and why they might migrate.
CST 1	**Pages 206** Describes the different stages of migration of the Bantu-speaking peoples.	**Page 207** Students explain why the migration of Bantu-speaking peoples was so slow.	Explain that one reason people moved or migrated to other areas is that farmers used slash-and-burn farming that exhausted the soil after a few years, so they moved to find better land.
HI 1	**Pages 203–204** Explains how people coped with problems of climate change.	**Page 207** Students explain why the Bantus overwhelmed the people into whose territory they migrated.	Point out that although the Bantu changed many things about their way of life as they migrated, they held onto their ironmaking skills and their language. Discuss why these things were so important.

West, Central, and Southern Africa

TERMS & NAMES
- animism
- griot
- Nok
- Bantu
- migration

Terms & Names

animism a belief that all things have a soul

griot an official storyteller in early African societies who helped convey history

Nok an early culture of west Africa

Bantu an early culture of west Africa that eventually migrated to other places

migration moving from one region to another

Build on What You Know You have been learning about some of the people living in eastern Africa. You will now learn about the people of west, central, and southern Africa.

Early Life in Africa

1 ESSENTIAL QUESTION What were some of the environments that the people of west, central, and southern Africa had to adapt to?

savannahs and rain forest

As the Sahara dried up, about 4000 B.C., people moved south into West Africa around the Niger River, just as they had moved eastward into the Nile valley. West, central, and southern Africa included savannahs (flat, grassy, mostly treeless plains) and rain forests.

Regions of Africa: West, Central, and Southern Africa

WEST

CENTRAL

SOUTHERN

A Variety of Environments

The rain forests in west and central Africa did not support much farming. People's lives there were very different from the settled lives of farmers in the Nile valley. Savannahs cover more than 40 percent of the African continent. They are mostly covered with grasses. Dry seasons alternate with rainy. These savannahs became the places where most people lived in small groups made up of a number of families.

Kush and Other African Kingdoms • 203

❸ Teach

Early Life in Africa

6.1.2, CST 1, HI 1

Talk About It

- **Critical Thinking: Making Inferences** How did the lack of a written language help shape the culture of early people in west and central Africa? *(Possible answer: It produced an oral culture, in which history was passed on in stories told by griots.)*

California Resources

California Reading Toolkit, L20
California Modified Lesson Plans for English Learners, p. 43
California Daily Standards Practice Transparencies, p. TT20
California Standards Enrichment Workbook, pp. 17–18
California Online Test Practice
California Test Generator CD-ROM
California Standards Planner and Lesson Plans, L39
California eEdition CD-ROM

LESSON 3 PROGRAM RESOURCES

ON LEVEL

In-Depth Resources: Unit 3
- Reading Skill: Explaining Geographic Patterns, p. 25
- Vocabulary Study Guide, p. 28
- Vocabulary Cards, p. 29

Formal Assessment
- Lesson Quiz, p. 98

ENGLISH LEARNERS

In-Depth Resources in Spanish
- Reading Skill: Explaining Geographic Patterns, p. 47
- Vocabulary Study Guide, p. 50

Modified Lesson Plans for English Learners, p. 43
Reading Study Guide (Spanish), p. 53
Reading Study Guide Audio CD (Spanish)

STRUGGLING READERS

In-Depth Resources: Unit 3
- Reading Skill: Explaining Geographic Patterns, p. 25
- Vocabulary Study Guide, p. 28
- Vocabulary Cards, p. 29
- Reteaching Activity, p. 37

Reading Toolkit, p. L20

Reading Study Guide, p. 53
Reading Study Guide Audio CD

GIFTED AND TALENTED STUDENTS

In-Depth Resources: Unit 3
- Literature: African Griots, p, 34

Interdisciplinary Projects
- Language Arts, p. 33
- Art, p. 34

INCLUSION

EasyPlanner CD-ROM
- Reading Skill: Explaining Geographic Patterns
- Vocabulary Study Guide

- Reteaching Activity

TECHNOLOGY

eEdition CD-ROM

Power Presentations CD-ROM

Map Transparencies
- MT12 The Nok Culture

Critical Thinking Transparencies
- CT25 Explaining Geographic Patterns

Humanities Transparencies
- HT12 Nok Sculpture

Test Generator CD-ROM

ClassZone.com

Kush and Other African Kingdoms • 203

In-Depth Resources: Unit 3
- Reading Skill: Explaining Geographic Patterns, p. 25

History from Visuals

Interpreting Infographics
Direct students' attention to the infographic on this page about desertification. Make sure they understand the meaning of the term *desertification*, which is the creation of desert from land that was formerly not desert. Have them read the introductory passage and then the numbered sections. Make sure they recognize that the steps represent a sequence.

- According to the introductory segment, what are two causes of desertification? *(natural climate change and human activity)*

- Which step in this diagram explains how the desertification process begins? *(step 2)*

GEOGRAPHY SKILLBUILDER ANSWER

Possible answer: Desertification would make it difficult or impossible for people to make a living from the land and would likely force them to move.

More About . . .

The Sahara
Prior to 3000 B.C., the Sahara was believed to have been a much wetter place than it is today. Since then, however, it has gradually become the world's largest desert, covering nearly all of North Africa. In this vast expanse, there is little water outside of the occasional oasis. In spite of this, at least two million people live in the Sahara today. Under its surface lie supplies of oil and other minerals. There is also water underground, and irrigation has made settlement possible in some areas.

Geography

Desertification

The Sahara has been expanding for thousands of years. This expansion of dry, desertlike conditions into fertile areas is called desertification.

Normally, desertification results from nature's long-term climate cycles. However, as the illustrations show, human activity has sped up the process.

1 Even areas lush with plant life were subject to desertification.

2 In ancient times, climate change expanded the Sahara. Today farming, overgrazing, and wood burning have expanded the desert.

3 Due to overuse of the land for farming, grazing, and burning wood for fuel, dry grasses died and were replaced by shrubs.

4 Because there was less plant life covering the soil, rain evaporated quickly. The wind then carried away the fertile topsoil, leaving barren wasteland.

GEOGRAPHY SKILLBUILDER
INTERPRETING VISUALS
Human-Environment Interaction
What impact would desertification be likely to have on people in the areas affected?

Herding and Farming South of the Sahara, the savannahs were filled with herds of animals. Mainly because of climate change and also desertification, shown above, the soil was thin and not ideal for farming. As a result, many people were herders. These people kept cattle, goats, and sheep.

Others practiced slash-and-burn farming. This was a very early farming technique. People cleared the land by cutting down and burning trees and the undergrowth. After a few years, the thin soil became exhausted. Then the people moved on to new areas. Experts believe such farming began in Africa sometime around 6000 B.C.

Belief Systems and Language Like other ancient peoples, most Africans believed in more than one god, though they usually believed in one creator god greater than the others. They also thought that there were spirits present in animals, plants,

DIFFERENTIATING INSTRUCTION

Inclusion

Find Causes and Effects
To help students who may have difficulty reading, hand out copies of a cause-effect chart or graphic organizer. Assign pairs of students different short segments of the text. Have students pick out the causes and effects and list them on their charts. Then have students contribute their findings to a class chart on the board, following the order of the text. Suggest that students copy the information from the board into their notes.

English Learners

Use Context Clues
Direct students to the section on *savannahs* on pages 203–204. Write the word on the board. Guide students as they note descriptions and details that define *savannahs* in the context of the lesson. Have students note details to describe: the rainforest, herds that were raised, the grassy plains, and crops that were farmed. To conclude, Ask, How did most people support themselves? Why?

or natural forces. This belief that everything possesses a soul is called **animism**.

These early societies did not have a written language. They preserved their history by telling stories. In some places, storytellers known as **griots** (gree•OHZ) kept the history alive. Their stories were lively retellings of past events.

> **REVIEW** How did people live on the plains of Africa?
> herding and slash-and-burn farming

The Nok Culture

2 **ESSENTIAL QUESTION** What role did ironworking play in Nok culture?

important role; used to make tools and weapons

Many early peoples in West Africa made objects out of materials that decayed, such as plant fiber. Few artifacts survived. However, archaeologists have found evidence of one culture that made objects that have survived.

Sculpture This Nok sculpture shows a half-human, half-bird creature. ▼

Ironworkers Between the Benue and Niger rivers—a distance of about 300 miles—scientists have found small clay statues. In addition, they discovered waste products from ironmaking, charcoal, and iron-smelting furnaces. Archaeologists were surprised to find that iron had been produced in this area before 500 B.C. They had thought, based on previous evidence, that ironmaking occurred only in the eastern part of Africa.

One early West African people who produced iron were called the **Nok**. They lived in an area that today is southeastern Nigeria. It appears that the Nok did not follow the pattern of some early ironmakers in other parts of the world, who first produced copper and then bronze. Instead, the Nok seem to have moved right into ironmaking. They were among the first western African people to make iron.

Using Iron To produce iron, the Nok mined iron ore. Then they smelted the iron. Ironsmiths worked the iron into tools and weapons. Some of the tools and weapons made their way into trade routes across West Africa.

> **REVIEW** What was the pattern of some early ironworkers, and how did the Nok differ?
> Others first produced copper and bronze. Nok went straight to ironmaking, skipping copper and bronze.

Kush and Other African Kingdoms • 205

In-Depth Resources: Unit 3
• Literature: African Griots, p. 34

Teach

The Nok Culture

🔲 **6.1.2, CST 1, HI 1**

Talk About It

• What is one reason that experts know about the Nok culture today? *(They made goods and used materials that have survived, allowing experts to learn about them.)*

• **Critical Thinking: Explaining Historical Patterns** Based on what you have read about other civilizations, what effect do you think iron had on the Nok culture? *(Possible answers: It helped them to be more efficient and productive; it helped them be more powerful in battle; it aided in trade.)*

Map Transparencies
• MT12 The Nok Culture

Humanities Transparencies
• HT12 Nok Sculpture

DIFFERENTIATING INSTRUCTION

Gifted and Talented Students

Report on the Iron Age
Have students use library and Internet resources to report on the development of iron-making technology in early peoples. Students should create brief reports that include specific information about iron in Africa and illustrations of iron tools and weapons from early times.

Struggling Readers

Place the Lesson on a Map
Help students find the different places mentioned in this section on a map. Students may use maps from the front of this book or from library or Internet sources.

Teach

The Bantu Migrations

6.1.2, CST 1, HI 1

Talk About It

- Who were the Bantu people and where were they from originally? *(They were a group of different peoples that spoke Bantu languages. They came originally from the area around where the Nok lived.)*

- What did Bantu farmers do when they encountered new types of environments in their migrations? *(They adapted their methods to those environments.)*

- What skill set the Bantu apart from the people they encountered as they migrated throughout Africa? *(iron making)*

- **Critical Thinking: Summarizing** What effect did the Bantu have as they encountered different peoples and cultures? *(Possible answer: They adapted and adopted parts of those cultures, establishing a new culture in different areas as they moved.)*

History from Visuals

Interpreting Maps
Have students spend a few moments looking at the map on this page. Make sure they read the title and the key.

- According to this map, in which directions did the Bantu migrate first? *(They migrated south and east.)*

GEOGRAPHY SKILLBUILDER ANSWER
Possible answer: The Sahara lay to the north.

The Bantu Migrations

③ ESSENTIAL QUESTION Where did the Bantu peoples first live, and where did they move to?

West Africa; moved south and east throughout Africa

The **Bantu** people lived in the same area as the Nok. The Bantu spread across Africa in what was one of the greatest movements in history. They slowly moved south and east along a frontier, opening up new lands to farming and herding. The Bantu brought farming and iron to Africa south of an imaginary line from Nigeria in the west to Kenya in the east.

Bantu Speakers Some African peoples spoke similar languages based on a parent language that historians called Bantu. The word *Bantu* itself means "the people." The Bantu-speaking peoples were not one group. They were many groups who had similar cultures. They were farmers, herders, and eventually ironworkers.

Migration Begins About 3,000 years ago the Bantu speakers began moving out of their lands near the Benue and Niger rivers in West Africa. They migrated south and east. A **migration** is a move from one region to another.

The migration of the Bantu was a slow process that took thousands of years. Some groups eventually settled in the rain forest along the Congo River. Some Bantu lived in small villages and farmed along the riverbanks. Later, Bantu-speaking groups moved south beyond the forest to the grasslands of southern Africa. There they began raising animals such as cattle and growing grain crops. Bantu farmers adapted the way they farmed to their new environments.

Bantu speakers kept their ability to make iron. Ironmaking set them apart from others living in areas to which the Bantu migrated. Their iron tools helped them in their main task of farming.

Bantu Migrations, 1000 B.C.–A.D. 1100
INTER**ACTIVE**

| 0 | 400 | 800 miles |
| 0 | 400 | 800 kilometers |

→ Earliest migration to A.D. 1
→ Later migrations

AFRICA

GEOGRAPHY SKILLBUILDER
INTERPRETING MAPS
Movement Compare this map with the one on page 185. Why didn't the Bantu speakers migrate north?

INTERDISCIPLINARY ACTIVITIES

Language Arts

Report on the Bantu Languages
Have students use library and Internet resources to learn more about Bantu languages today. Students should use their findings to create an informative poster about the language family, showing, for example, where Bantu languages are spoken, giving examples of Bantu languages, and so on.

Language Arts

Write about the Bantu Migration
Have students write a newspaper feature article about the Bantu migration. They should assume the perspective of a reporter living in the lands into which Bantu people are moving. They should report on what is happening and what the Bantu people are like. Students can use their text and library and Internet resources for information.

Effects of Migration The Bantu speakers moved to areas where other people already lived. The Bantu adopted cattle herding from peoples near present-day Lake Victoria. They displaced hunting-gathering peoples. Bantu speakers exchanged ideas and customs with people in the areas they entered, and intermarried with them. They shared their knowledge of ironmaking and agriculture. As the Bantu speakers migrated, their languages spread.

Mask This mask was created by a Kuba craftsperson. The Kuba were a Bantu-speaking people. ▼

REVIEW To which areas of Africa did the Bantu speakers migrate?
to central and southern Africa

Lesson Summary
- Early societies living on the savannah south of the Sahara practiced herding and farming.
- The Nok made iron tools for use and for trade.
- Migration of Bantu speakers spread the Bantu language and culture.

Why It Matters Now . . .
Despite the great variety of languages and cultures in Bantu-speaking Africa, there are also connections based on a common heritage.

---

3 Lesson Review

Homework Helper
ClassZone.com

Terms & Names
1. Explain the importance of

animism	Nok	migration
griot	Bantu	

Using Your Notes
Explaining Geographic Patterns Use your completed web diagram to answer the following question:

2. In what two ways did most of the peoples of West Africa support themselves and their families? (6.1.2)

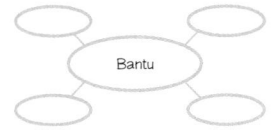

Main Ideas
3. Why did people living on the plains of central Africa practice herding? (6.1.2)
4. Why were archaeologists surprised to discover that the Nok produced iron? (6.1.2)
5. Why was the migration of Bantu speakers so slow? (CST 1)

Critical Thinking
6. **Understanding Causes** Why did the Bantus overwhelm the people into whose territory they migrated? (HI 1)
7. **Comparing** Compare the importance of ironmaking in the Nok and Bantu cultures. (6.1.2)

Activity **Internet Activity** Use the Internet to research the Bantu migrations. Then create a chart showing the causes and effects of the migrations. (6.1.2)
INTERNET KEYWORD: *Bantu migrations*

Kush and Other African Kingdoms • 207

 Assess & Reteach

Assess Have students work on their own to answer the questions, then meet in groups to discuss their answers.

 Formal Assessment
- Lesson Quiz, p. 98

Reteach Have students make an outline of this lesson. Suggest they use the major headings as the main entries (for example: "A. Early Life in Africa.") Then they can fill in details beneath the main entries with information from each section.

 In-Depth Resources: Unit 3
- Vocabulary Cards, p. 29
- Reteaching Activity, p. 37

Homework Helper

Visit **ClassZone.com** for a lesson review, a flip-card activity, and links to related Web sites.

---

3 Lesson Review Answers

Terms & Names
1. • animism, p. 205
   • griot, p. 205
   • Nok, p. 205
   • Bantu, p. 206
   • migration, p. 206

Using Your Notes
See page 202 for an example of a completed diagram.
2. herding and slash-and-burn farming

Main Ideas
3. The soil was too thin to support agriculture.
4. Previous evidence suggested that iron making had occurred only in the eastern part of Africa.
5. Groups of Bantu speakers would migrate to a new place and live there for awhile before moving on.

Critical Thinking
6. The iron tools of the Bantu were superior to those of the people living in the regions to which they migrated.
7. Possible answer: Both the Nok and the Bantu used iron weapons; the Nok used some of the iron tools they made to trade and the Bantu used them to farm.

Activity Rubric

	Content of Chart	Number of Errors
4	clear and accurate causes and effects	zero or one spelling or punctuation errors
3	accurate causes and effects	two or three spelling or punctuation errors
2	causes and effects unclear or somewhat inaccurate	four or five spelling or punctuation errors
1	no causes and effects given	more than five spelling or punctuation errors

Kush and Other African Kingdoms • 207

Terms & Names

1. Piankhi was a powerful king who ruled the kingdom of Kush.

2. Adulis was the main trading port of Aksum.

3. Bantu speakers spread over Africa in a great migration.

Main Ideas

Nubia and the Land of Kush
(pages 188–195)

4. The Nile River served as a natural highway linking the two places.

5. Deposits of iron ore in the area led to the production of iron, which in turn led to the production of iron tools and weapons for local use and trade.

The Kingdom of Aksum
(pages 196–201)

6. He made Christianity the official religion of Aksum.

7. It is used in the Ethiopian Church and provided the basis for three modern-day African languages.

West, Central, and Southern Africa
(pages 202–207)

8. smelting and ironworking

9. The Bantu speakers shared their knowledge of iron production and farming. Bantu languages spread to other people in the area.

▶ **VISUAL SUMMARY**

Kush and Other African Kingdoms

Geography (6.1.2)
- Nubia and Egypt interacted over the centuries.
- The people of Africa lived in different environments.
- Bantu speakers traveled from West Africa to central and southern Africa.

Government (6.2.8)
- The Kush kingdoms conquered Egypt and ruled Egypt and Nubia.
- The kingdom of Aksum absorbed Kush in the region of Nubia.

Economics (6.2.8)
- The Kushite kingdom of Meroë was an economic center linking Egypt and the interior of Africa.
- The Nok people were accomplished ironworkers.

Culture (6.2.8)
- The kingdom of Aksum converted to Christianity.
- Aksum's achievements in architecture, language, and farming were long-lasting.

▶ **TERMS & NAMES**

Explain why the words in each set below are linked with each other.

1. **Piankhi** and **Kush**
2. **Aksum** and **Adulis**
3. **Bantu** and **migration**

▶ **MAIN IDEAS**

Nubia and the Land of Kush (pages 188–195)

4. How did geography help to increase trade between Nubia and Egypt? (6.2.1)

5. In what way did iron contribute to the economic and commercial development of Meroë? (6.2.8)

The Kingdom of Aksum (pages 196–201)

6. What official act of King Ezana led to lasting cultural change? (HI 1)

7. What is the cultural legacy of Geʿez? (CST 3)

West, Central, and Southern Africa (pages 202–207)

8. What processes did the Nok use to produce trade goods? to produce tools? (HI 1)

9. How did the migration of the Bantu speakers affect culture in the areas of central and southern Africa? (HI 1)

ALTERNATIVE ASSESSMENT RUBRICS

1. Writing Rubric

	Content of Report	Style of Presentation
4	creative and accurate details	lively and creative
3	accurate details	creative
2	few and/or inaccurate details	fairly creative
1	no details	creative

2. Geography Rubric

	Accuracy of Map	Creativity of Design
4	accurate	attractive and creative
3	mostly accurate	attractive
2	somewhat accurate	not very attractive
1	inaccurate	sloppy and unattractive

CRITICAL THINKING Big Ideas: Culture

10. **UNDERSTANDING CAUSE AND EFFECT** How did contact with Egypt affect Nubian culture? (6.2.8)

11. **DRAWING CONCLUSIONS** What impact might Meroë's importance as a trade center have had on the interaction of cultures? (6.2.8)

12. **COMPARING AND CONTRASTING** What two cultural influences did Aksum blend? (6.2.8)

ALTERNATIVE ASSESSMENT

1. **WRITING ACTIVITY** You have read about the Bantu migrations in Lesson 3. Write a report about what the migrations might have been like. Read your report to the class. (Writing 2.1)

2. **INTERDISCIPLINARY ACTIVITY— GEOGRAPHY** Work with a partner or a small group. Brainstorm places on or near the Nile that you have learned about in Chapter 6. Draw a map showing each place on your list. Draw symbols or add labels to indicate why each place was important. (CST 3)

3. **STARTING WITH A STORY**

    Review the essay you wrote in which you compared your ideas about Jerusalem before and after your trip. Write a 60-second TV news story about your journey. (Writing 2.1)

Technology Activity

4. **CREATING A NEWSLETTER**
Use the Internet and library to research desertification. Create a newsletter about the topic.
   • Present information on desertification's rate of growth.
   • Show how it has affected Africa.
   • Show what is being done about desertification. (Writing 1.4)

Research Links
ClassZone.com

Reading Charts Use the chart below to answer the questions. (6.2.8)

Interaction of Egypt and Kush	
Language	Kushites brought back hieroglyphic writing to Kush from Egypt.
Religion	Kushites worshiped many Egyptian gods, but had some distinct gods of their own.
Architecture	Kushites built pyramids similar to those of Egypt, but with steeper sides. They also sometimes built temples onto the sides of pyramids.
Art	Kushites produced wall paintings, pottery, jewelry, and sculpture.
Burial practices	Kings were buried in splendid stone-faced pyramids.
Government	The ruler was treated as a god.

1. **What objects were important in both architecture and burial practices?**
   A. sculptures
   B. pyramids
   C. jewelry
   D. hieroglyphics

2. **How would you describe the relationship between Egypt and Kush?**
   A. They influenced each other greatly.
   B. They did not have much influence on each other.
   C. They were enemies.
   D. They had no relationship at all.

 **Test Practice**
ClassZone.com

Additional Test Practice, pp. S1–S33

Kush and Other African Kingdoms • 209

Critical Thinking

Big Ideas: Culture

10. The Nubian culture borrowed from the Egyptian culture. Egyptian styles influenced Nubian art and architecture. People in Nubia began worshiping some of the Egyptian gods.

11. As trade flowed in and out of Meroë, the cultures of Egypt, Kush, other parts of Africa, and Arabia interacted with that of the city.

12. influences from the Horn of Africa and southern Arabia

Standards-Based Assessment

1. The correct answer is B. Pyramids appear in both the "Architecture" and the "Burial Practices" section of the chart.

2. The correct answer is A. The chart includes many examples of how Egypt influenced Kush.

 Research Links

Visit **ClassZone.com** for links to Web sites that can be used in the newsletter.

 Test Practice

Visit **ClassZone.com** to access strategies and tutorials for taking standardized tests.

 Formal Assessment
   • Chapter Tests, Forms A, B, and C, pp. 99–110

 Test Generator
   • Chapter Tests, Forms A, B, and C (English and Spanish)

ALTERNATIVE ASSESSMENT RUBRICS

3. Starting with a Story Rubric

	Content of Essay	Number of Errors
4	thoughtful and detailed	zero or one spelling or punctuation errors
3	detailed	two or three spelling or punctuation errors
2	few details	four or five spelling or punctuation errors
1	no details	five or more spelling or punctuation errors

4. Technology Rubric

	Required Elements	Effectiveness of Style
4	thoroughly covers all required elements	attractive and creative
3	covers most required elements	neat
2	covers some required elements	somewhat neat
1	covers few or no required elements	sloppy

Objectives

- Identify steps for writing a research report.
- Take notes from appropriate sources on a chosen topic.
- Complete a research report with a bibliography.

❶ Focus & Motivate

Preview Ask students what facts about their daily lives might be important to people in the future. Explain that they will be using the text and other sources to learn more about the way the Egyptians or other ancient peoples lived.

❷ Teach

Talk About It

- Which aspects of daily life from Chapters 5 and 6 would be interesting to research? *(Possible answers: Egyptians weaving linen from crops; the people of Kush smelting iron)*

- Who would be a good reader for a report on the kinds of meals enjoyed by ancient Egyptians? *(Possible answers: cafeteria manager, parents, classmates)*

- What is a primary source that might be used for this report? *(Possible answers: a translation of a letter or diary entry; a translation of a document recording facts about a particular aspect of life in Egypt or Kush; a poem or story written by someone during this time period)*

- **Critical Thinking: Explaining Chronological Order and Sequence** Why should a researcher look over each source before taking notes? *(Possible answers: to determine whether it contains enough helpful information; to decide how to organize notes taken from it)*

Writing About History

Research Reports:
Daily Life in Ancient Times

Writing Model
ClassZone.com

CALIFORNIA STANDARDS
Writing 2.3 Write research reports.

Purpose: To write a research report on an aspect of daily life in ancient times

Audience: Someone involved in a similar aspect of your daily life

You read many details in this unit that showed what life in ancient Egypt was like: a hog's tooth crushed in a sweet cake, priests feeding meals to statues, children playing with animal toys. How do historians know these things? They do research. By studying primary and secondary sources, they piece together an understanding of daily life. You can learn more about daily life in ancient times by writing a research report yourself. A **research report** is a composition that pulls together information from several primary sources or secondary sources or both.

▲ Egyptian mural of a hunter

Organization & Focus

Your assignment is to write a 500- to 700-word research report about an aspect of daily life in ancient Egypt or Kush. Possible topics include education, meals, clothing, religion, or sports and games. In addition to an introduction, body, and conclusion, research reports also have a **bibliography**—a list of the sources used in preparing the report.

Choosing a Topic Review Chapters 5 and 6 looking for information on daily life. Think about which aspect of ancient daily life seems most connected to your daily life today. For example, if you are an athlete, you might be especially interested in sports in ancient times. Focus on your subject so that you can cover it thoroughly in your report.

Identifying Purpose and Audience Your purpose is to make ancient history seem meaningful and alive to a reader. Choose a reader who shares your interest in your topic. For example, if you are writing about sports, you might choose your soccer coach for your audience.

DIFFERENTIATING INSTRUCTION

Gifted and Talented Students

Create a Daily Life Feature
Have students develop a feature similar to the Daily Life features in the text. They should incorporate the information they researched for their report. Ask students to use a combination of both text and visuals on large poster-size paper to present their ideas to the class.

Inclusion

Help Students Do Research
Group students who have similar topics. Arrange with the school librarian for groups to do research in the library at different times. It might be helpful to provide the librarian with a list of topics in advance. During their library visit, students should obtain an encyclopedia article and a print-out from a Web site on their topic. Have students begin the note-taking process with these sources. Encourage them to add more if possible.

Finding Details Look for vivid details about your topic, such as the objects people used, the ways they behaved, and any laws, rules, or rituals they had. Take notes on a graphic organizer like the one below.

Aspect of Daily Life		
Objects	Behaviors	Laws, Rules, or Rituals

Research & Technology

Plan on using at least four different sources for your research report.

- a primary source
- a Web site
- an encyclopedia article
- a book

As you research, take notes on note cards. On each card, record the source—the title, author, publisher, date, page number, or Web address. You will need this information for your bibliography.

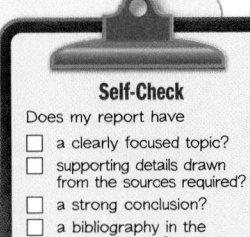

Technology Tip Fortunately for students of ancient civilization, translations of some documents, as well as photographs of some artifacts, are online. Start your Internet research by visiting ClassZone.com, which has links to sites about life in the ancient world.

Outlining and Drafting Group your note cards into categories and arrange the categories in a logical order. Use your categories and notes to outline your report. Follow the outline as you write your draft.

Evaluation & Revision

Share your first draft with test readers to see what still needs work. You may need to do any of the following:

- Add more information or stronger examples.
- Take something out that doesn't belong.
- Move something to a better, more logical location.

When you are satisfied with your report, prepare your bibliography. Use your language arts textbook or school handbook to find the correct format for each source.

Self-Check

Does my report have

- [ ] a clearly focused topic?
- [ ] supporting details drawn from the sources required?
- [ ] a strong conclusion?
- [ ] a bibliography in the proper format?

Publish & Present

Make a neat final copy of your report. Give it to your reader and explain why you chose him or her. Invite comments on your report.

211

More About . . .

Note Cards

Share the following ideas about note cards with students:

- Create a bibliography card for each source. Include all information about the source on this card. Number each card. Each note then taken from this source should have the card number on the top right-hand corner. This number eliminates the need to copy all of the publication information on each card.
- Write only one fact per card.
- Use only the front of the card.

ANSWERS

Research Report Rubric

	Depth of Research	Content of Research	Errors in Mechanics
4	extensive; taken from several varied sources	insightful and interesting; excellent use of transitions	few or none
3	good number of facts; use of appropriate sources	shows good understanding of topic; some use of transitions	some
2	some facts; use of a couple of sources	shows some understanding of topic; little use of transitions	many
1	few facts or limited sources	shows little or no understanding; lacks unity and coherence	many major

Begin the Unit

Quick Look

Chapter 7 examines the development of the first civilizations in the land now called India.

Chapter 8 explores the rich civilization of ancient China.

Chapter 9 traces the emergence and accomplishments of the civilizations in the Americas during ancient times.

Interact with History ▶

Purpose

To help students visualize a key cultural and religious center and gain insight into life in ancient India.

Visual Learning

Ask a student volunteer to read the text and questions aloud. Point out that the text and three question on these pages guide students to answer the main question on this page. Discuss the three questions before discussing the main one.

Interact ANSWERS

- Why do people build holy places? *(Possible answers: to remember key religious leaders; to provide gathering places for the faithful; to provide inspiring religious symbols for the faithful)*

- How might Buddhists feel about a structure that housed part of the Buddha's bodily remains? *(Possible answer: They might revere that structure just as they revere the Buddha.)*

- What lessons might these carved scenes be designed to teach? *(Possible answer: They might teach about how to live a holy life and to rule in a just way.)*

- Why would thinking about life and death help a person to worship? *(Possible answer: Questions about life and death are questions that many religions try to answer.)*

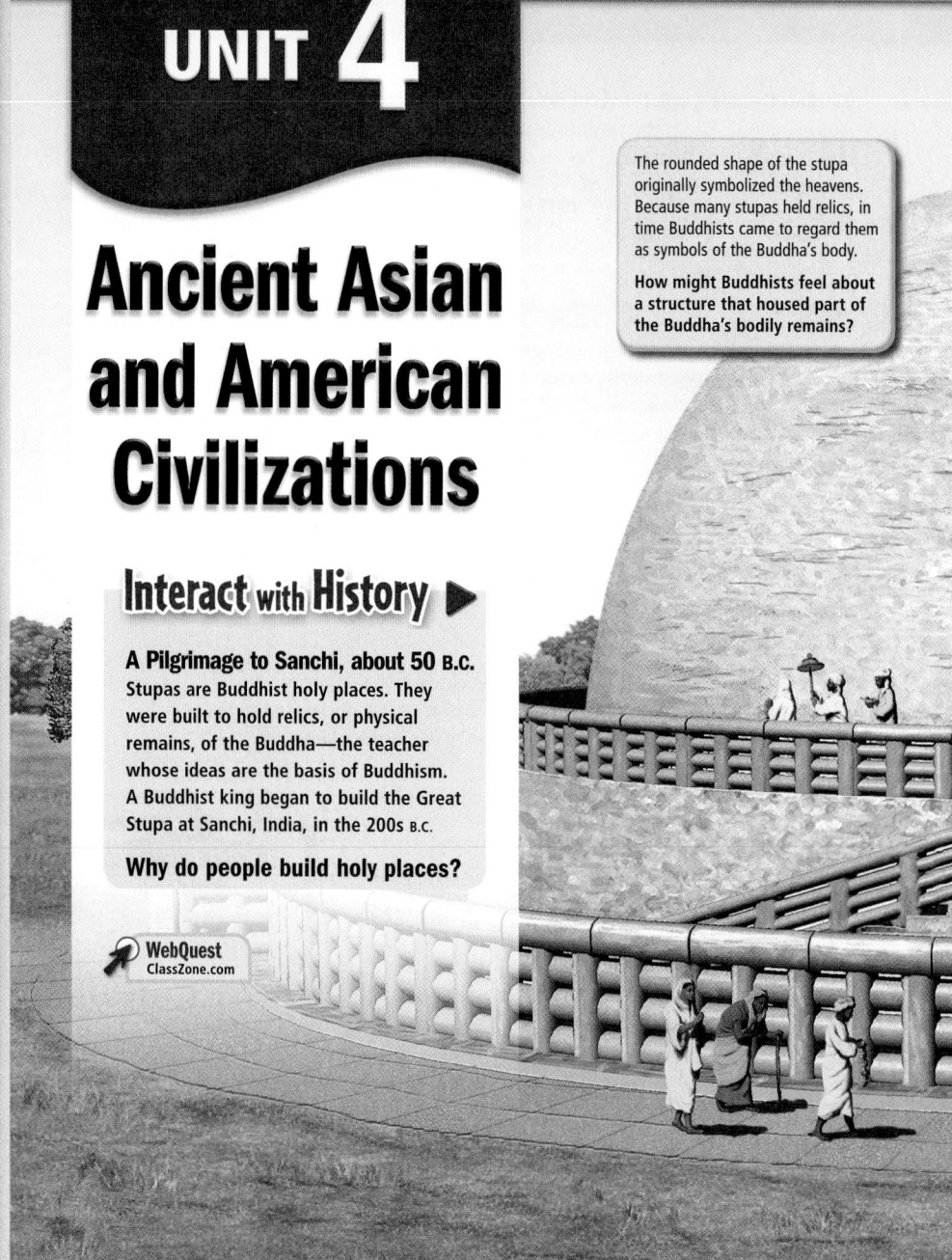

UNIT **4**

Ancient Asian and American Civilizations

The rounded shape of the stupa originally symbolized the heavens. Because many stupas held relics, in time Buddhists came to regard them as symbols of the Buddha's body.

How might Buddhists feel about a structure that housed part of the Buddha's bodily remains?

Interact with History ▶

A Pilgrimage to Sanchi, about 50 B.C. Stupas are Buddhist holy places. They were built to hold relics, or physical remains, of the Buddha—the teacher whose ideas are the basis of Buddhism. A Buddhist king began to build the Great Stupa at Sanchi, India, in the 200s B.C.

Why do people build holy places?

WebQuest ClassZone.com

212

TECHNOLOGY

WebQuest: Exploring Buddhism

Visit **ClassZone.com** to lead your students through a WebQuest on ancient Buddhism and the culture related to it. Students will assume the roles of archaeologists exploring the ruins of ancient Buddhist sites. Students will examine various artifacts that will help them formulate ideas about the culture of ancient Buddhists.

When to Use This project works well as an activity linked to Chapter 7, particularly following Lesson 3.

Class Time 2 class periods

Materials Needed At least one computer with access to the World Wide Web, and a printer.

Customizing for Your Classroom

- If computer time is limited, have small groups rotate through stations, finding information from encyclopedias, library books, or their textbook as well as the Web sites.

- Encourage Spanish speakers to use the textbook's Spanish glossary.

- Pair students who may have difficulty reading with stronger readers to ensure they are able to accurately understand and interpret the information on Buddhist artifacts.

This is the Southern Gateway. Some of the carvings show scenes of the Buddha's birth. Others show events from the life of Asoka, the king who started building this monument. He ruled India according to Buddhist law.

What lessons might these carved scenes be designed to teach?

Worshipers brought offerings of flowers, lamps, and other gifts. Some lay flat on the ground in worship. Others walked around the stupa several times, thinking about the Buddha. To ancient Indians, the circular path stood for the daily path of the sun and the cycle of life and death.

Why would thinking about life and death help a person to worship?

213

Correcting Misconceptions

Ask students what they know about Buddhism and how they picture the Buddha. When students have finished the unit, ask them to discuss what they knew and whether it was correct.

More About . . .

Sanchi

The Great Stupa at Sanchi is perhaps the most important stupa in India, the birthplace of Buddhism. However, the site has no historical significance in the life of the Buddha. It was probably started by Asoka, who built many stupas in his lifetime. Over the centuries, it was expanded and acquired importance as a leading Buddhist site in the world. With the decline of Buddhism in India, the stupa itself fell into decay, until it was restored in the 1800s.

WHY STUDY ANCIENT ASIAN AND AMERICAN CIVILIZATIONS?

- Many of the religious traditions practiced in the world today had their beginnings in the ancient civilizations of Asia.

- The same geographic patterns that help explain the rise of great river-valley civilizations in other parts of the world can be seen in the evolution of civilizations in Asia and the Americas.

- The cultural and scientific accomplishments of the ancient civilizations of India, China, and the Americas continue to enrich our world today.

- Chinese philosophies are still followed by many today.

- Many descendants of early civilizations, such as the Maya, still follow the ancient customs and live in the same regions.

CHAPTER 7 PLANNING GUIDE: Ancient India

Chapter Overview

Invasions, belief systems, and political, economic, and social structures helped shape Indian history.

Copymasters

In-Depth Resources: Unit 4
- Family Newsletter (English and Spanish), pp. 1–2
- Visual Summary, p. 7
- Vocabulary Study Guide, p. 9

Character Education

Reading Study Guide, p. 65

Bringing Social Studies Alive, Chapter 7

Document-Based Questions: Strategy and Practice

Reading Toolkit, L21–L24

Modified Lesson Plans for English Learners, pp. 45–52

Assessment

Chapter Review, pp. 246–247

Formal Assessment
- Chapter Tests, Forms A, B, and C, pp. 119–133

Test Generator

Integrated Assessment Book

Online Test Practice

LESSON 1
Geography and Indian Life
pp. 218–225

OBJECTIVE Analyze how India's geography affected the development of early Indian cities.

In-Depth Resources: Unit 4
- Reading Skill: Making Generalizations, p. 3
- Vocabulary Cards, p. 11
- Geography Practice: Physical Features of India, p. 13
- Reteaching Activity, p. 17

Interdisciplinary Projects
- Science, p. 38

Reading Study Guide, p. 57

Lesson Review, p. 224

Formal Assessment
- Lesson Quiz, p. 115

California Daily Standards Practice Transparencies, TT21

LESSON 2
The Origins of Hinduism
pp. 226–231

OBJECTIVE Explain how the Aryan invasions led to the emergence of Hinduism and the caste system.

In-Depth Resources: Unit 4
- Reading Skill: Summarizing, p. 4
- Vocabulary Cards, p. 11
- Skillbuilder Practice: Explaining Chronological Order and Sequence, p. 8

- Literature: Bhagavad Gita, p. 16
- Reteaching Activity, p. 18

Interdisciplinary Projects
- Language Arts, p. 39

Reading Study Guide, p. 59

Lesson Review, p. 231

Formal Assessment
- Lesson Quiz, p. 116

California Daily Standards Practice Transparencies, TT22

LESSON 3
Buddhism and India's Golden Age
pp. 232–239

OBJECTIVE Trace the rise of Buddhism and the growth of the Maurya and Gupta Empires.

In-Depth Resources: Unit 4
- Reading Skill: Comparing and Contrasting, p. 5
- Vocabulary Cards, p. 11
- Primary Source: Teachings, by the Buddha, p. 15
- Reteaching Activity, p. 19

History Makers
- Asoka, p. 13

Interdisciplinary Projects
- Art, p. 40

Reading Study Guide, p. 61

Lesson Review, p. 239

Formal Assessment
- Lesson Quiz, p. 117

California Daily Standards Practice Transparencies, TT23

LESSON 4
The Legacy of India
pp. 240–245

OBJECTIVE Understand the impact of ancient India on the world today.

In-Depth Resources: Unit 4
- Reading Skill: Categorizing, p. 6
- Vocabulary Cards, p. 11
- Reteaching Activity, p. 20

Interdisciplinary Projects
- Math, p. 37

Reading Study Guide, p. 63

Lesson Review, p. 243

Formal Assessment
- Lesson Quiz, p. 118

California Daily Standards Practice Transparencies, TT24

Integrated Technology

 eEdition Plus Online

EasyPlanner Plus Online

eTest Plus Online

 Audio CDs
- Reading Study Guide
- Reading Study
  Guide in Spanish
- The World's Music

 CD-ROMs
- Power Presentations
- eEdition
- EasyPlanner
- Test Generator

---

 eEdition CD-ROM

 Map Transparencies
- MT13 Harappan Civilization, 2500 B.C.

Critical Thinking Transparencies
- CT27 Making Generalizations

 ClassZone.com

---

 eEdition CD-ROM

 Humanities Transparencies
- HT13 Krishna on an Elephant

Critical Thinking Transparencies
- CT28 Summarizing

 ClassZone.com

---

 eEdition CD-ROM

 Map Transparencies
- MT14 Indian Ocean Trade, A.D. 400

Humanities Transparencies
- HT14 Head of a Buddha

Critical Thinking Transparencies
- CT29 Comparing and Contrasting

 ClassZone.com

---

 eEdition CD-ROM

 Critical Thinking Transparencies
- CT30 Categorizing
- CT31 Chapter 7 Visual Summary

 ClassZone.com

Overview of California Resources

	Lesson 1	Lesson 2	Lesson 3	Lesson 4
California Reading Toolkit	L21	L22	L23	L24
California Modified Lesson Plans for English Learners	p. 45	p. 47	p. 49	p. 51
California Daily Standards Practice Transparencies	TT21	TT22	TT23	TT24
California Standards Enrichment Workbook	pp. 65–66	pp. 67–72, 77–78	pp. 73–78	pp. 77–78
California Standards Planner and Lesson Plans	L41	L43	L45	L47
California Online Test Practice	ClassZone.com	ClassZone.com	ClassZone.com	ClassZone.com
California Test Generator CD-ROM				
California EasyPlanner CD-ROM				
California eEdition CD-ROM				

Chart Key

P E Pupil Edition	CD-ROM	Internet
Copymaster	Audio	Overhead Transparency
	Video	

PREVIEWING RESOURCES FOR DIFFERENTIATED INSTRUCTION

English Learners

In-Depth Resources in Spanish
- Reading Skill and Strategy Ⓐ
- Skillbuilder Practice
- Geography Practice Ⓒ
- Vocabulary Study Guide Ⓑ

In-Depth Resources: Unit 4
- Family Newsletter (English and Spanish)

Reading Study Guide (Spanish)

Reading Study Guide Audio CD (Spanish)

Test Generator
Chapter Test (Spanish)

Plus

Modified Lesson Plans for English Learners

Multi-Language Glossary of Social Studies Terms

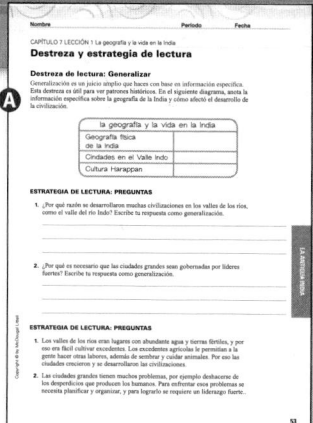
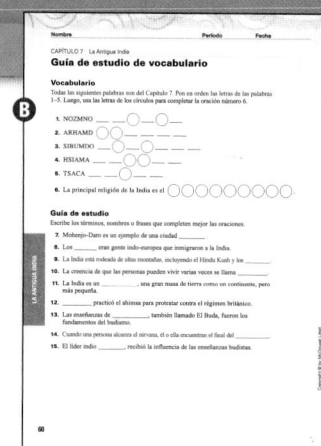

Struggling Readers

In-Depth Resources: Unit 4
- Vocabulary Study Guide
- Skillbuilder Practice Ⓑ
- Geography Practice
- Reteaching Activities
- Family Newsletter Ⓒ

Reading Study Guide Ⓐ

Reading Study Guide Audio CD

Reading Toolkit

Formal Assessment
Chapter Test, Form A

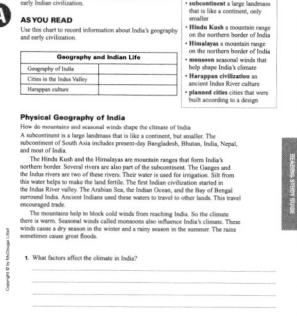
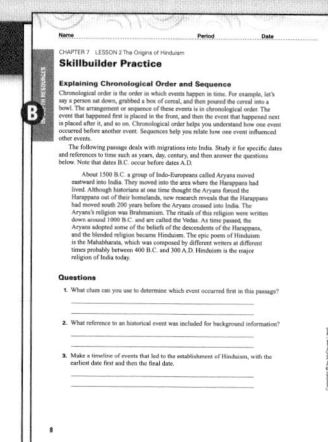

Inclusion

EasyPlanner CD-ROM
- Reading Skill and Strategy Ⓑ
- Vocabulary Study Guide Ⓒ
- Geography Practice
- Reteaching Activities Ⓐ

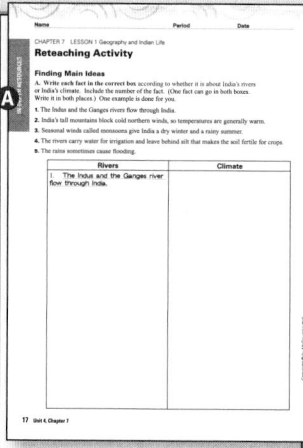
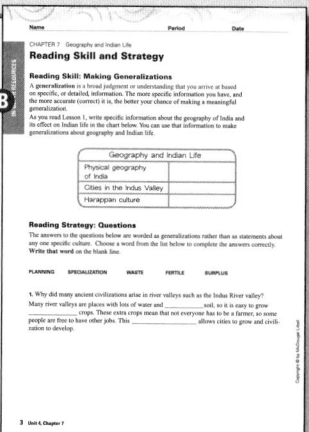

Gifted and Talented Students

In-Depth Resources: Unit 4
- Primary Sources Ⓐ
- Literature

History Makers Ⓑ

Interdisciplinary Projects Ⓒ

Formal Assessment
Chapter Test, Form C

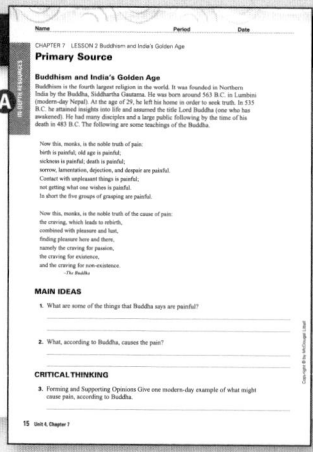

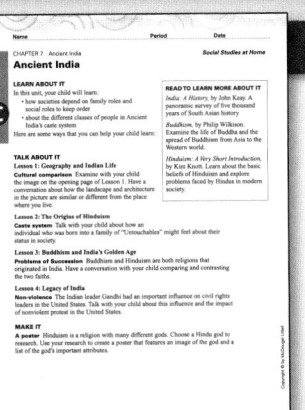

Activities in the Teacher's Edition for English Learners

- Describe Occupations, p. 220
- Study a Chart, p. 228
- Create a Mural, p. 234
- Categorize Information, p. 242
- Create and Answer Questions, p. 244

Activities in the Teacher's Edition for Struggling Readers

- Outline Information, p. 222
- Make a Web Diagram, p. 230
- Create a Time Line, p. 237
- Make a T-Chart, p. 244

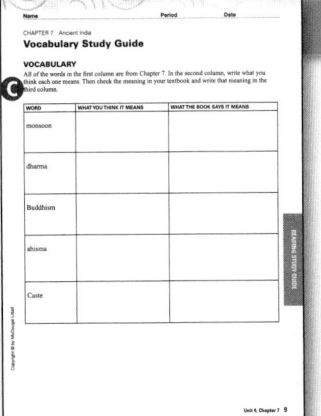

Activities in the Teacher's Edition for Inclusion Students

- Use Interactive Map, p. 220
- Ask Questions, p. 228
- Answer Questions, p. 234
- Use the Graphic Organizer, p. 242

Activities in the Teacher's Edition for Gifted and Talented Students

- Compare and Contrast Civilizations, p. 222
- Create a Poster, p. 230
- Write a Biographical Sketch, p. 237

Integrated Technology

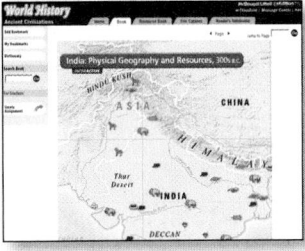

eEdition CD-ROM
- Interactive Visuals
- Interactive Maps
- Starting with a Story

ClassZone.com
- WebQuests
- Research Links
- Internet Activities
- Homework Helper
- Chapter Quiz
- Current Events
- Test Practice

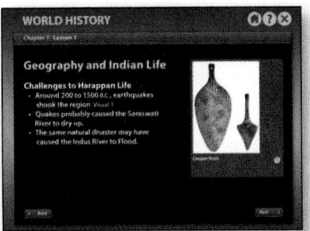

Power Presentations CD-ROM
- Lecture Notes
- Media Gallery
- Chapter Review Game

Critical Thinking Transparencies
- CT27 Making Generalizations
- CT28 Summarizing
- CT29 Comparing and Contrasting
- CT30 Categorizing
- CT31 Chapter 7 Visual Summary

California Daily Standards Practice Transparencies, TT21–TT24

Map Transparencies
- MT13 Harappan Civilization, 2500 B.C.
- MT14 Indian Ocean Trade, A.D. 400

Humanities Transparencies
- HT13 Krishna on an Elephant
- HT14 Head of a Buddha

Test Generator CD-ROM

EasyPlanner CD-ROM

Begin the Chapter

Objective

Analyze the geographic, political, economic, religious, and social structures of ancient Indian civilizations.

Quick Look

Lesson 1 explores the basic geography of the Indian subcontinent and how it affected the development of ancient cities.

Lesson 2 traces the impact of the Aryan migrations, including the development of the caste system and the Hindu religion.

Lesson 3 analyzes the development of Buddhism and its effect on India, including the reemergence of Hinduism and the Guptas.

Lesson 4 describes the legacy of the ancient Indian civilizations.

Before You Read: Knowledge Rating

Learning key terms and vocabulary is central to understanding reading material. Knowledge rating is a strategy that helps students identify words and terms they should be alert for in their upcoming reading. It provides students an opportunity to learn words and concepts ahead of time.

Have students follow these steps:

• Read the "Before You Read" instructions and follow the steps.

• Use a dictionary to look up the meanings of words that you rated 2 and 1. With this information, write sentences using each of the words correctly.

• When you come to these words in your reading, review what you learned about their meaning.

Chapter 7 Ancient India

Before You Read: Knowledge Rating

Recognizing what you already know about each of these terms can help you understand the chapter.

In your notebook, rate how well you know each term.

3 = I know what this word means.

2 = I've seen this word, but I don't know what it means.

1 = I've never seen this word before.

Define each term as you read.

Big Ideas About Ancient India

Culture Many societies rely on family roles and social roles to keep order.

Indians saw themselves as belonging to one of four social classes called castes. These broad classes were divided into many smaller groups based on jobs. In time, a fifth group of people called the untouchables came to be considered the lowest group in society.

Integrated Technology

eEdition
• Interactive Maps
• Interactive Visuals
• Starting with a Story

INTERNET RESOURCES
Go to **ClassZone.com** for
• WebQuest
• Homework Helper
• Research Links
• Internet Activities
• Quizzes
• Maps
• Test Practice
• Current Events

ARABIAN PENINSULA

INDIA

2500 B.C.
Well-planned cities are thriving by the Indus River.
◄ (necklace, 3000 to 2000 B.C.)

1500 B.C.
Aryans begin to migrate into India.

2500 B.C.   2000 B.C.   1500 B.C.

WORLD

1472 B.C.
Queen Hatshepsut begins to rule Egypt.
◄ (statue of Hatshepsut, late 1400s B.C.)

214

TIME LINE DISCUSSION

Use the time line to help students develop a mental time frame for the civilizations of ancient India and to preview information that will be covered in the chapter.

• About how many years of Indian history are covered in this chapter? *(about 2,000 years)*

• About how long after the full establishment of cities on the Indus River did the Aryans begin to arrive in India? *(about 1,000 years)*

• Which event on this time line might Queen Hatshepsut have heard about in Egypt? *(the arrival of Aryans in India)*

• Which came first: the life and death of the Buddha or the reign of King Asoka? *(the life and death of the Buddha)*

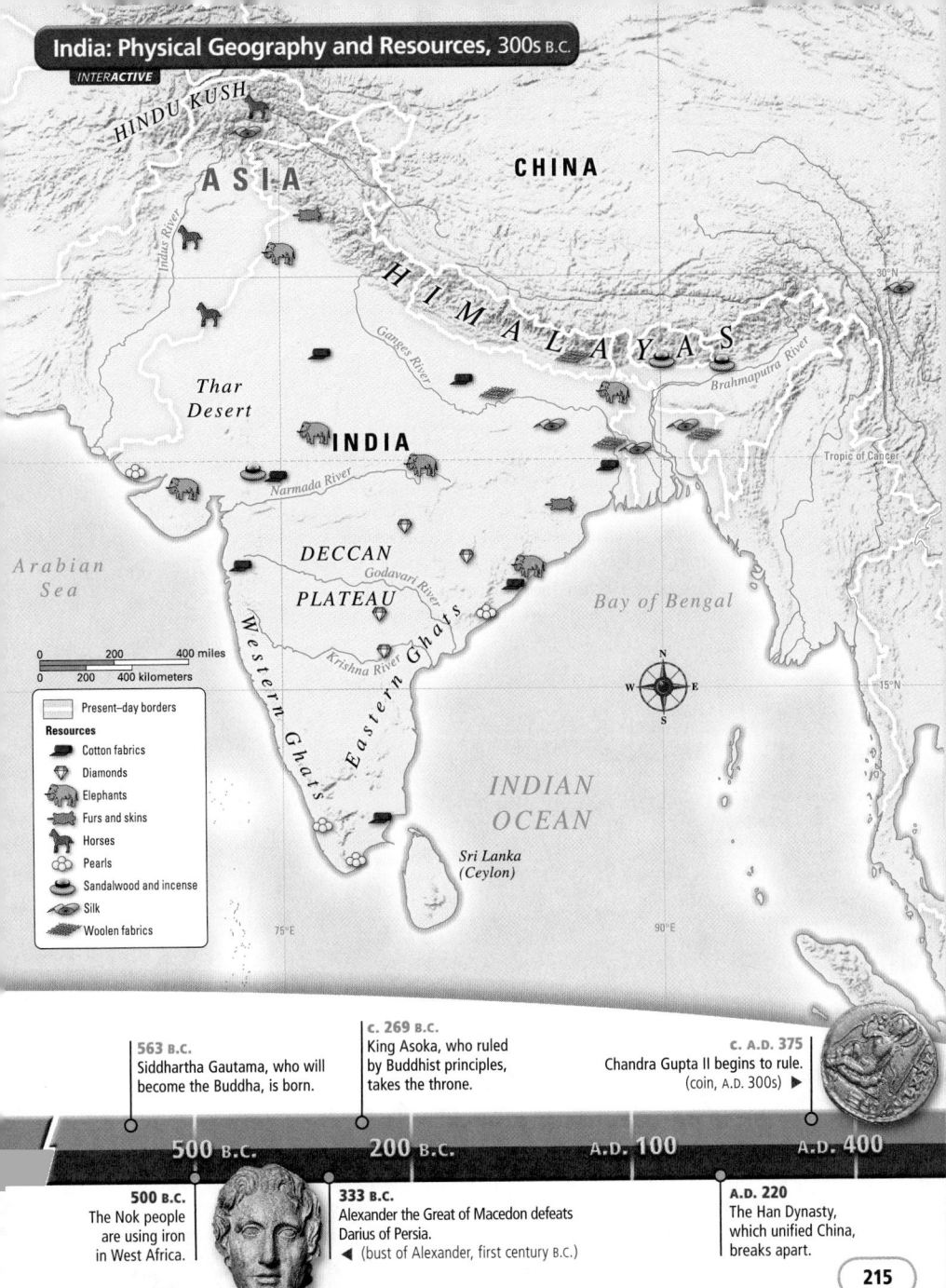

India: Physical Geography and Resources, 300s B.C.

INTER*ACTIVE*

ASIA

HINDU KUSH

CHINA

H I M A L A Y A S

Indus River

Ganges River

Brahmaputra River

30°N

Thar Desert

INDIA

Narmada River

Tropic of Cancer

Arabian Sea

DECCAN PLATEAU

Godavari River

Krishna River

Western Ghats

Eastern Ghats

Bay of Bengal

15°N

N W E S

INDIAN OCEAN

| 0 | 200 | 400 miles |
| 0 | 200 | 400 kilometers |

Present-day borders

Resources
- Cotton fabrics
- Diamonds
- Elephants
- Furs and skins
- Horses
- Pearls
- Sandalwood and incense
- Silk
- Woolen fabrics

Sri Lanka (Ceylon)

75°E   90°E

563 B.C.
Siddhartha Gautama, who will become the Buddha, is born.

c. 269 B.C.
King Asoka, who ruled by Buddhist principles, takes the throne.

c. A.D. 375
Chandra Gupta II begins to rule.
(coin, A.D. 300s) ►

500 B.C.   200 B.C.   A.D. 100   A.D. 400

500 B.C.
The Nok people are using iron in West Africa.

333 B.C.
Alexander the Great of Macedon defeats Darius of Persia.
◄ (bust of Alexander, first century B.C.)

A.D. 220
The Han Dynasty, which unified China, breaks apart.

215

CHAPTER 7

Introduce the Big Ideas

Read aloud the text about the Big Ideas. Have students think about social roles and rules in their current society. Do classes exist in this country today? If so, can people move between them?

Here are other Big Ideas that you might emphasize in this chapter:

Geography
As in Mesopotamia and ancient Egypt, the geography of rivers and the surrounding land played a central role in the development of Indian civilization.

Belief Systems
The different religions that originated in India strongly influenced world culture and history.

Science and Technology
Indian civilizations made contributions in mathematics that continue to affect our world today.

Talk About It

Interpreting Maps
Ask students to look at the map and read the legend. Ask, What is one kind of crop that the people of ancient India raised? *(cotton)* In what ways did people in India depend on animals? *(Possible answers: They traded elephants and horses, collected pearls from oysters, wove fabrics from sheep's wool, and trapped for furs and skins.)*

INTER*ACTIVE*

An interactive version of this map is available on the eEdition and on the Power Presentations CD-ROMs.

Find Out More

India today is the world's second most populous country. What part of India has the largest population today? Ask, What products does this area produce? Use library or Internet sources to learn more about how the economy of India today compares to that of ancient India.

The World's Music
Introduce your students to Indian music by playing track 16 of *The World's Music* audio CD. "Rag Bhairavi" is an example of Indian classical music. *Raga* refers to a repertoire of music which may be sung or played on string or wind instruments.

RECOMMENDED RESOURCES

Books for the Teacher
Cunningham, Alexander. *Ancient Geography of India.* New Delhi: Munshiram Manoharal, 2002. A classic geographic study of ancient India.

Editors of Time-Life Books. *Land of Mystery.* Alexandria: Time-Life Books, 1994. Illustrated journey into the ancient land of India.

Videos
Origins of India's Hindu Civilization. 22 minutes. Huntsville: Educational Video Network, 1994. Overview of the history of the Indian subcontinent and its people.

Lost Treasures of the Ancient World 3: Ancient India 50 minutes. West Long Branch: Kultur Video, 2000. Video profile of the history and architecture of ancient India.

Internet
To access these sites, visit the Research Links for this chapter at **ClassZone.com**.

The British Museum. This online resource provides a range of information on the geographic, religious, and cultural past of India.

Washington State University. This Web site has an extensive collection of information on ancient Indian history.

Ancient India • 215

Objective

Analyze one theory about a significant geographic event in ancient India.

Introducing the Story

The Saraswati River

As with early civilizations in Egypt and Mesopotamia, rivers played a central role in giving rise to ancient Indian civilizations. The fate of the Saraswati River and the people who depended upon it for a living is therefore a compelling story about the challenges of ancient life. For many years, the Saraswati River existed only in myth. Recently, however, scientists have traced its historic path and begun to unlock the secrets of its decline.

Vocabulary Preview

precious rare, valuable

cautiously with great care

dockyard a place where boats are moored

Reading the Story Aloud

1. **The teacher as reader:** Model how to read a section of the passage fluently, reading at a smooth, even pace, with good expression.

2. **The students as readers:** As students read, have them pause briefly for punctuation and read the words within the punctuation marks smoothly.

Starting with a Story

Students can also follow along as they listen to the story on the eEdition or on the Power Presentations CD-ROMs.

Saraswati EARTHQUAKE

Background: Some researchers have developed the theory that sometime around 2000 to 1500 B.C., a major river in India called the Saraswati (suh•RUHS•wuh•tee) dried up. An earthquake may have changed the course of smaller rivers that fed the Saraswati. One river may have turned west to flow into the Indus River. The extra water caused disastrous floods. People who lived on the banks of the Saraswati faced the opposite problem. Their river disappeared. Imagine you live in a city that had been built along the Saraswati.

The Saraswati River ▶

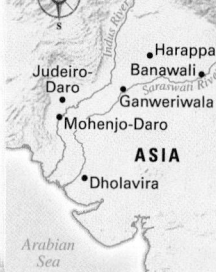

CALIFORNIA STANDARDS
Reading 3.3 Analyze the influence of setting on the problem and its resolution.

216

ADDITIONAL RESOURCES

Books for the Student

Barr, Marilynn G. *India: Exploring Ancient Civilizations.* Carthage, Ill.: Teaching and Learning Company, 2003. Overview of the ancient civilizations of ancient India.

Bowden, Rob. *Settlements of the Indus River.* Chicago: Heinemann, 2004. Exploration of the river-valley civilizations of India's Indus River.

Nelson, Julie. *India.* Austin: Raintree Steck-Vaughn, 2002. Discussion of the key features of India's great ancient civilizations.

Neurath, Marie. *They Lived Like this in Ancient India.* New York: Franklin Watts, 2001. Study of the daily life of people in ancient Indian civilizations.

Starting with a Story
eEdition

You are a trader. For years, you have made a good living sailing a boat down the Saraswati River to the Arabian Sea and then to Mesopotamia. There you sold Indian goods: precious woods, gold, deep red beads, milky white pearls, ivory combs, and fine-spun cotton. In exchange, you bought silver, tin, wool fabric, and grain.

One day, everything suddenly changes. Returning from a trip, you dock your boat in the dockyard built next to the river and go home. Early the next morning, you awake from a sound sleep to feel the house shaking. Dishes clatter, and screams rise from the street. When the shaking finally stops, you cautiously step outside to find out what happened.

The scene outside is shocking. The top floor of the two-story house next door has toppled over, exposing the stairway. Littering the street are piles of mud bricks from the upper stories of other buildings.

Back inside the house, you pick up the broken pieces of painted plates. As you clean up the mess, you have no idea that an even worse disaster is about to strike.

Several hours later, you go outside to check on your neighbors. Walking past the river, you notice that the water level has dropped. All day, it falls until finally nothing is left but a few puddles in the low places of the riverbed. One by one, the boats in the dockyard settle in the mud.

Surely, you tell yourself, the river will return. But the days pass, and nothing changes. Finally, you face the awful fact that the Saraswati has probably dried up forever. You and your neighbors must decide what to do.

Should you rebuild your city or move?

Reading & Writing

1. **READING: Setting** The setting is the time and place of a story. How does the setting contribute to the problem the trader faces?

2. **WRITING: Persuasion** Imagine that you joined a group of your neighbors discussing whether to stay or leave. When they asked for your opinion, you said you wanted to think about it. Now write a letter explaining your opinion and reasons for it. Discuss the costs and benefits of staying versus the costs and benefits of leaving. (HI 6)
   CALIFORNIA STANDARDS Writing 2.5
   Write persuasive compositions.

(217)

Talk About It

Ask students the following questions to begin the discussion:

- In what way did the river provide a livelihood for the main character? *(He used the river as a means of transportation and for the conduct of trade.)*

- What is the "worse disaster" that follows the earthquake? *(The river dries up.)*

- What are some other ways the loss of the Saraswati might affect people living in this area? *(Possible answers: The soil will be less fertile and there will be inadequate water.)*

Should you rebuild your city or move?

Possible answer: It may be necessary to move, because the loss of the river will make it hard to raise food and to trade goods.

Making Personal Connections

Ask how people respond to natural disasters and what resources are available to help. Students may say that disasters bring about relief efforts that help people to overcome the immediate effects of the disaster. Today, governments often assist people in the long term.

READING & WRITING ACTIVITIES

1. **TALK ABOUT IT** Possible answer: The story takes place at a time when an earthquake happens; it takes place long ago when there was no scientific understanding of such events; it takes place in a city that is dependant on a river but whose river has disappeared, jeopardizing life there.

2. **WRITE ABOUT IT**

2. Writing Rubric

	Opinion Stated	Discussion of Reasons	Style of Letter
4	very persuasive	costs and benefits of both choices	lively and interesting
3	persuasive	costs and benefits of one choice	interesting
2	somewhat persuasive	costs <u>or</u> benefits, not both	mainly factual in style
1	not persuasive	neither costs nor benefits	disorganized

❶ Plan & Prepare

Objectives

- Describe the physical features, including the river systems that characterized ancient India.
- Describe the development of early Indian cities.
- Analyze Harappan civilization.
- **Language Objective:** Describe the people of ancient India by using structural and context clues to gain a deeper understanding.

Quick Look

Lesson 1 traces the emergence of great civilizations in ancient India, including the cities of the Indus Valley and the Harappan culture.

❷ Focus & Motivate

Preview Tell students that they will be exploring India, another region where ancient civilizations developed. Have them recall what they have learned about the conditions and circumstances that gave rise to other civilizations.

Introduce the Main Ideas The three main ideas relate to the Big Idea "Societies rely on family roles and social roles to keep order." Help students identify social roles taken by members of the Harappan civilization and discuss how these roles helped to keep order in Harappan society.

Reading Skill: Making Generalizations Tell students that making generalizations involves taking lots of information and organizing it into a brief, general statement.

SAMPLE ANSWERS FOR CHART

Geography and Indian Life	
Physical geography of India	mountainous north, rivers
Cities in the Indus Valley	large, planned, advanced
Harappan culture	widespread, prosperous

Lesson 1

▶ **MAIN IDEAS**

❶ **Geography** In India, mountains and seasonal winds shape the climate and affect agriculture.

❷ **Government** The earliest Indian civilization built well-organized cities near the Indus River.

❸ **Culture** Harappan civilization produced writing, a prosperous way of life, and a widely shared culture.

▶ **TAKING NOTES**

Reading Skill: Making Generalizations

A generalization is a broad judgment based on information. As you read Lesson 1, record information on a chart like the one below. Later, you will be asked to make a generalization.

Geography and Indian Life	
Physical geography of India	
Cities in the Indus Valley	
Harappan culture	

Ⓢ **Skillbuilder Handbook, page R8**

▲ **Priest-King** Scholars believe this seven-inch-tall sculpture is of a priest or king from the ancient city of Mohenjo-Daro.

218 • Chapter 7

HOW TO TEACH THE CALIFORNIA STANDARDS

Standard	Content	Student Question or Activity	Instruction
6.5.1	**Page 220** Describes how the Indus and other rivers gave rise to Indian civilization	**Page 221** Students explain how India's rivers and climate affect agriculture.	Ask students what they know about river systems in earlier civilizations. Discuss the importance of water sources in ancient Egypt and Mesopotamia as well as in India.
CST 3	**Pages 220–221** Describe how climate affected life in India	**Page 220** Students learn how monsoons bring dry winters and wet summers to India.	Discuss with students how everyday life in their community is affected by periods of heavy precipitation as well as by dry spells.
REP 1	**Pages 222–223** Analyzes the cultural features of Harappan civilization	**Page 224** Students think of additional questions that they want answered about Harappan culture.	Ask students to think of a variety of resources that can help them answer any questions that they have.

Geography and Indian Life

TERMS & NAMES
subcontinent
Hindu Kush
Himalayas
monsoon
Harappan civilization
planned city

The mountains help block cold north winds, causing the climate to be warmer. Winds blow from the southwest in summer, bringing rain from the ocean. Winds blowing from the northeast in winter are dry because they lose their moisture passing over the mountains. Because of this, winter is a dry season.

Build on What You Know Have you ever visited a part of the United States with a different climate? Some regions of the country receive much more rainfall than other regions do. As you are about to learn, India has two distinct seasons: a rainy season and a dry season.

Physical Geography of India

❶ ESSENTIAL QUESTION How do mountains and seasonal winds shape the climate of India?

India is a **subcontinent**, which is a large landmass that is like a continent, only smaller. The subcontinent includes present-day Bangladesh, Bhutan, India, Nepal, and most of Pakistan. It is often referred to as South Asia. Geographers think the kite-shaped Indian subcontinent used to be a separate land. It inched north until it hit Asia. The collision pushed up mountains where the two lands met.

Ganges River The Ganges is one of the major rivers of India. Most Indians consider it holy. As the photograph shows, the banks of the Ganges today are heavily populated. ▼

219

Terms & Names

subcontinent a large landmass similar to, but smaller than, a continent

Hindu Kush mountain range north of India

Himalayas mountain range in north India

monsoon a seasonal wind

Harappan civilization an ancient culture that emerged in the Indus River Valley

planned city city built by a design

❸ Teach

Physical Geography of India

6.5.1, CST 3

Talk About It

• **Critical Thinking: Comparing and Contrasting** How are conditions in India similar to those in Sumer? *(Both had rivers that helped establish civilizations.)*

LESSON 1 PROGRAM RESOURCES

In-Depth Resources: Unit 4
• Reading Skill: Making Generalizations, p. 3

Vocabulary Strategy

Synonyms
Remind students that a synonym is word that has the same or similar meaning as another word. Have students test their understanding by coming up with pairs of synonyms using words from this lesson. (For example, they could use *agriculture* and *farming*.)

History from Visuals

Interpreting Maps
Have students read over the text and examine the graphic on this page. Make sure they understand that the two boxes describe the two different monsoons that occur in India. Ask a student volunteer to explain how the symbols on the map help describe the text. *(They show the directions of the different seasonal monsoons.)*

• Where does the summer monsoon get the moisture it later drops as rain? *(It gets moisture from the ocean.)*

GEOGRAPHY SKILLBUILDER ANSWER

The summer monsoon causes the rainy season.

Mountains and Waterways Those high mountains tower over the northern borders of India. They form several mountain ranges, including the **Hindu Kush** (HIHN•doo kush) and the **Himalayas** (HIHM•uh•LAY•uhs).

In addition to tall mountains, the subcontinent has several great rivers. These include the Ganges (GAN•JEEZ) and the Indus. Like other rivers you have studied, these two rivers carry water for irrigation. The silt they deposit makes the land fertile. The Indus River valley was the home of the first Indian civilization. In ancient times, another river called the Saraswati (suh•RUHS•wuh•tee) ran parallel to the Indus. The Saraswati area was also home to great cities. However, it dried up, perhaps because of an earthquake. (See Starting with a Story on pages 216–217.)

The Arabian Sea, Indian Ocean, and Bay of Bengal surround India. Ancient Indians sailed these waters to other ancient lands, such as Mesopotamia. This travel helped encourage trade.

Climate The tall mountains help block cold north winds from reaching much of India. As a result, temperatures are generally warm there. In addition, seasonal winds called **monsoons** shape India's climate. Because of the monsoon, India has a dry season in the winter and a rainy season

Vocabulary Strategy
The word *monsoon* is also sometimes used as a **synonym** for the summer rainy season.

Geography
Monsoons

A monsoon is a seasonal wind. India and Pakistan have two main monsoons: a summer monsoon and a winter monsoon.

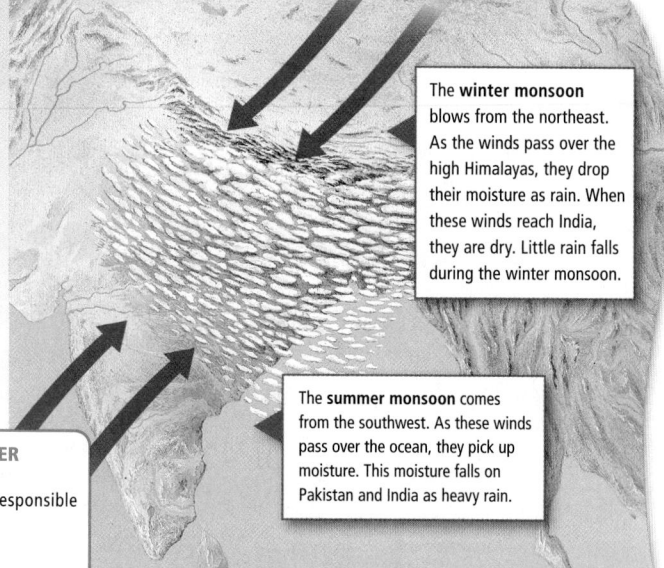

The **winter monsoon** blows from the northeast. As the winds pass over the high Himalayas, they drop their moisture as rain. When these winds reach India, they are dry. Little rain falls during the winter monsoon.

The **summer monsoon** comes from the southwest. As these winds pass over the ocean, they pick up moisture. This moisture falls on Pakistan and India as heavy rain.

GEOGRAPHY SKILLBUILDER
INTERPRETING VISUALS
Region Which monsoon is responsible for causing a rainy season?

220 • Chapter 7

DIFFERENTIATING INSTRUCTION

Inclusion

Use the Interactive Map
Students who have visual impairments or who have difficulty reading may benefit from referring to the interactive map on page 215 as you read aloud the section "Physical Geography of India." Make sure students can point out on the map each feature that is described in the text. The map is available on the eEdition and on the Power Presentations CD-ROMs.

English Learners

Describe Occupations
Have students listen for terms that describe people's occupations as you read the lesson aloud. Have students use structural and context clues to describe occupations that are found throughout the lesson. Some of these occupations include farmers, geographers, the ancient Indians, historians, archaeologists, architects, priests, and kings. Chart students' responses and post.

in the summer. The summer monsoon provides rain for India's crops. But these rains can also cause severe floods.

REVIEW How do India's rivers and climate affect agriculture?
The rivers flood and deposit fertile soil, which helps crops grow; the monsoons create a wet season and a dry season and the wet season provides rain for crops.

Cities in the Indus Valley

2 **ESSENTIAL QUESTION** Why was the earliest Indian civilization located near the Indus River?
The river helped with agriculture and trade, so early people built cities near it.
Huge earth mounds dot the Indus Valley. Near them, people found burnt bricks and tiny stone seals covered with a mysterious writing. These finds caused further exploration of the mounds. Archaeologists uncovered the ruins of an ancient civilization.

▲ **Indus Valley Seal**
This seal clearly shows an elephant, but scholars don't know why. No one has figured out how to read the pictographs above the animal.

Early Inhabitants History in the Indus River valley followed the same pattern as in Sumer and Egypt. As in other regions, civilization along the Indus River began with agriculture. The earliest farmers raised wheat and barley. By 3000 B.C., they were growing cotton and making it into fabric—the first people in Asia to do so. They domesticated cattle, sheep, goats, and chickens. They also learned how to make copper and bronze tools, which were more effective than stone tools.

People in the villages traded with one another. Over time, the Indus Valley people began to trade with people from farther away. The wealth they gained from trade helped them to develop a more complex culture.

Great Cities By 2500 B.C., some villages had grown to be great cities. The Indus and Saraswati valleys contained hundreds of cities. At least 35,000 people may have lived in the largest and best-known cities, Mohenjo-Daro (moh•HEHN•joh•DAHR•oh) and Harappa (huh•RAP•uh). Harappa gave its name to the entire Indus River culture. Today that ancient culture is called **Harappan civilization**.

This civilization featured **planned cities**, which were cities that were built according to a design. Architects surrounded these cities with heavy brick protective walls. City streets crossed each other in a neat grid with square corners. Along the streets were homes, shops, and factories. The cities also had large public buildings that may have been used for religious or government functions.

Ancient India • 221

Teach

Cities in the Indus Valley

6.5.1

Talk About It

- What development marked the start of civilization along the Indus River? *(the development of agriculture)*

- Which crop did the people of the Indus Valley grow before anyone else in Asia? *(cotton)*

- What were some distinctive features of Indus Valley cities? *(Possible answers: their large size; the fact that they were planned; the complexity of systems such as sewers)*

- **Critical Thinking: Making Inferences** Explain how the complexity of the Indus Valley cities suggests strong leadership. *(Possible answer: Organizing the people and resources needed to plan and carry out these systems requires a great deal of power and authority.)*

More About . . .

Mohenjo-Daro
Much of what we know about the cities of the Indus Valley comes from excavations at Mohenjo-Daro. Mohenjo-Daro was about one mile square and carefully planned. Streets were built to ensure drainage, which helped provide a more sanitary environment. Buildings were constructed out of hard bricks, which were baked. These bricks have survived fairly well over the centuries.

INTERDISCIPLINARY ACTIVITES

Art

Create a City Design
The cities of the Indus Valley are known for being carefully planned. Divide students into small groups and have each group create a poster showing its own plan for a well-designed city. The plan should show the locations of streets, neighborhood areas, public areas, and fortifications. Students should include labels to explain their design.

Language Arts

Present a Speech
Have small groups of students suppose that they will be asking a museum for funds to excavate the earth mounds of the Indus Valley. Students should prepare a speech in which they describe the site and explain what they expect to find.

Teach

Harappan Culture

6.5.1, REP 1

Talk About It

- What prevents people today from reading the written records of Harappan civilization? *(No one has learned how to read the Harappan written language.)*

- What evidence exists of religious practice in Harappan civilization? *(structures that may have been used in religious rituals; figurines that may have religious meaning)*

- What do scientists believe may have led to the decline of the Harappan civilization? *(natural disasters, such as floods and earthquakes)*

- **Critical Thinking: Finding Main Ideas** What examples support the idea that Harappan civilization was spread over a wide area? *(Possible answers: People across a wide area used a standard set of weights and measures and kept similar types of statues and toys. Cities followed the same design.)*

Dealing with Problems People in large cities always have to deal with the problem of removing human waste. Harappan cities were very advanced in that area. Almost every house contained a bathroom and a toilet. Underground sewers carried away the waste.

People need to use much planning and organization to build such complex cities. Because of that, historians believe the ancient Harappans must have had powerful leaders. We do not know if priests or kings or a combination of both ruled the Harappans, but their government must have been strong.

REVIEW How was Harappan civilization similar to other ancient civilizations?
arose on a river, began with agriculture, probably had a strong government

Harappan Culture

3 ESSENTIAL QUESTION What were the cultural features of Harappan civilization?

A mysterious form of writing covered the stone seals that people found in the ruined cities. Some of those seals may have indicated types of trade goods.

Some scholars think that the 500 pictographs, or picture signs, of Harappan writing may stand for words, sounds, or both. But they don't really know. No one has figured out how to read the writing of Harappan civilization. Until someone learns to read it, the only way we can learn about the civilization is by studying artifacts.

They used a writing system that has not been deciphered. They had planned cities. They used standard weights and measures, shared artistic styles, and led a prosperous lifestyle.

DIFFERENTIATING INSTRUCTION

Gifted and Talented Students

Compare and Contrast Civilizations
Have students create a poster that compares and contrasts the civilizations of Harappa and either Sumer or Egypt. The posters should use words and images to identify ways in which the cultures were similar and ways in which they differed.

Struggling Readers

Outline Information
Pair struggling readers with more accomplished readers, and have them work together to outline the section entitled "Harappan Culture." Pairs should identify the three major headings, then list two or three details that support each heading. Have student pairs present their outlines to the class.

Harappan Religion Archaeologists have not identified the site of any temples for specific gods. But they have found evidence of religion. Mohenjo-Daro had a huge public bath that may have been used for religious rituals. (Many religions have rituals linked to cleansing. For example, Christian baptism stands for the act of washing away sin.) Archaeologists have found figures of animals, such as bulls, that Indians still regard as holy. They also found clay figurines that may be goddesses or simply dolls.

A Widespread and Prosperous Culture People across a wide region shared Harappan culture. Harappan cities spread across an area that was about 500,000 square miles in size. That region was nearly twice as big as Texas is today. Even so, these cities shared a common design. Those shared designs show how widely the culture had spread.

Harappan people used standard weights and measures. Across the region, they made similar bronze statues and clay toys. These artifacts show that the Harappans could afford to have more than just basic necessities. This was because they gained wealth from agriculture and trade. Archaeologists have found seals from the Indus Valley as far away as Mesopotamia. Indians traded timber, ivory, and beads. Mesopotamians sold the Indians silver, tin, and woolen cloth.

Mohenjo-Daro The ruins of the ancient city show how carefully planned it was. The streets were at right angles, and the walls were well built. The smaller photograph is the Great Bath, which was probably a public bathhouse. ▼

▲ **Pot** This pot was found in the cemetery in the city of Harappa.

More About . . .

Harappan Seals
Much of what we know about Harappan language is taken from a large number of seals—small square clay objects inscribed with pictures and what is believed to be the Harappan script. These objects have been found in Mohenjo-Daro and other Harappan ruins, and also in the faraway lands of Mesopotamia. Scholars debate the meaning of the script, but many agree that the distribution and the art on the seals reveal that the Harappans traded widely.

 Map Transparencies
• MT13 Harappan Civilization 2500 B.C.

INTERDISCIPLINARY ACTIVITIES

Language Arts

Create a Script
The Harappan script, which is found on seals and other artifacts, has long puzzled scholars. Invite students to create a set of five different seals, featuring objects familiar to their daily lives and inscribed with a script of their own design. The script should use symbols to represent different letters and sounds. Have students exchange their seals and see if they can crack each other's code.

Language Arts

Write a Story
Scholars are uncertain as to what happened to the Harappan culture and why it declined. Have students read the story on page 217 about the drying up of the Saraswati River. Invite them to write a similar story to describe the possible effects of severe flooding along the Indus River.

❹ Assess & Reteach

Assess Have students work on their own to answer questions and then meet in groups to discuss their answers.

 Formal Assessment
• Lesson Quiz, p. 115

Reteach Have students convert each section heading and subheading into a question and write these questions on a sheet of paper. Next, have students exchange their questions with each other. Finally, have them review the lesson to find an answer to each question.

 In-Depth Resources: Unit 4
• Vocabulary Cards, p. 11
• Reteaching Activity, p. 17

 Homework Helper

Visit **ClassZone.com** for a lesson review, a flip-card activity, and links to related Web sites.

Challenges to Harappan Life Around 2000 to 1500 B.C., earthquakes shook the region. These quakes probably caused the Saraswati River to dry up. The same natural disaster may have caused the Indus River to flood. The problems forced people to leave their cities. Harappan civilization went into decline. As you will read in Lesson 2, another group of people soon took the place of Harappan civilization.

REVIEW How is the Harappan writing similar to hieroglyphs?
It uses pictures for words, sounds, or both.

Lesson Summary
• The rivers of India and the seasonal monsoons helped make agriculture possible.
• Agricultural wealth led to the rise of a complex civilization in the Indus Valley.
• The prosperous Harappan culture lasted for about 800 years.

Why It Matters Now . . .
Ancient Indians developed products that are still important today. They were the first people to domesticate chickens and the first Asians to produce cotton cloth.

▲ **Copper Tools**
Farmers used these tools for tasks such as weeding and leveling soil.

1 Lesson Review

Homework Helper
ClassZone.com

Terms & Names
1. Explain the importance of

| subcontinent | Himalayas | Harappan civilization |
| Hindu Kush | monsoon | planned city |

Using Your Notes
Making Generalizations Use your completed chart to answer the following question:
2. What are advantages and disadvantages of having monsoons? (6.5.1)

Geography and Indian Life	
Physical geography of India	
Cities in the Indus Valley	
Harappan culture	

Main Ideas
3. What evidence showed archaeologists that an ancient civilization had existed in the Indus Valley? (6.5.1)
4. What economic activities allowed Harappan civilization to begin along the Indus and Saraswati rivers? (6.5.1, CST 3)
5. What evidence suggested that Harappan civilization was prosperous? (6.5.1)

Critical Thinking
6. **Framing Historical Questions** What questions do you still have about Harappan culture? (REP 1)
7. **Understanding Cause and Effect** What are two positive and two negative effects of India's great rivers? (6.5.1)

Activity
Doing a Dig Find a toy, tool, or object in your house or classroom. Study it and describe it as if you were an archaeologist. List five things that it tells you about its owner. (REP 4)

---

1 Lesson Review Answers

Terms & Names
1. • subcontinent p. 219
• Hindu Kush, p. 220
• Himalayas, p. 220
• monsoon, p. 220
• Harappan civilization, p. 221
• planned cities, p. 221

Using Your Notes
See page 218 for an example of a completed chart.
2. Possible answer: Monsoons provide rain to water crops, but they can also cause destructive floods.

Main Ideas
3. seals carved with writing, the ruins of great cities, artifacts of art objects and trade goods
4. agriculture, then trade
5. Possible answers: large, planned cities, artifacts, trade goods from faraway places

Critical Thinking
6. Possible answers: What language did they speak? What was their religion?
7. Possible answers: Positive: enrich the soil for agriculture, provide waterways, provide drinking water. Negative: may flood, change course, or disappear, jeopardizing the life and livelihood of the people who depend on them

Activity Rubric

	Level of Description	Presence of Required Elements
4	creative, insightful	identifies five things the object suggests; uses correct spelling
3	insightful	identifies only four things the object suggests; uses mostly correct spelling
2	somewhat insightful	identifies only three things the object suggests; uses some correct spelling
1	not insightful	identifies fewer than three things the object suggests; uses very little correct spelling

Make a Climate Graph

Goal: To learn about the physical setting that supported the Harappan civilization by creating a bar graph showing average monthly rainfall

Materials & Supplies
- graph paper
- colored markers, pencils, or pens
- ruler

Prepare

❶ Look at examples of bar graphs in your textbooks. Notice how such graphs are constructed. Learn the meaning of the terms *vertical axis* and *horizontal axis*.

❷ Study the chart at right of average monthly rainfall in Islamabad, Pakistan—a city located near the site of ancient Harappa.

Do the Activity

❶ On a piece of graph paper, draw the horizontal axis and the vertical axis. On the vertical axis, mark 11 one-inch measurements up the side and label them.

❷ Below the horizontal axis, write the names of all 12 months. You may abbreviate the names. Space them evenly.

❸ For each month, draw a bar whose height indicates the average amount of rainfall.

Follow-Up

As you learned in Lesson 1, the summer monsoon blows over the Indian Ocean and the Arabian Sea and brings rain to the Indian subcontinent. Look at your graph. In what months does the summer monsoon occur? Would ancient farmers have wanted to plant before or after the summer monsoon? Explain.

Extension

Creating a Line Graph Use almanacs or the Internet to research the average monthly temperatures in Islamabad. Create a line graph to convey this information.

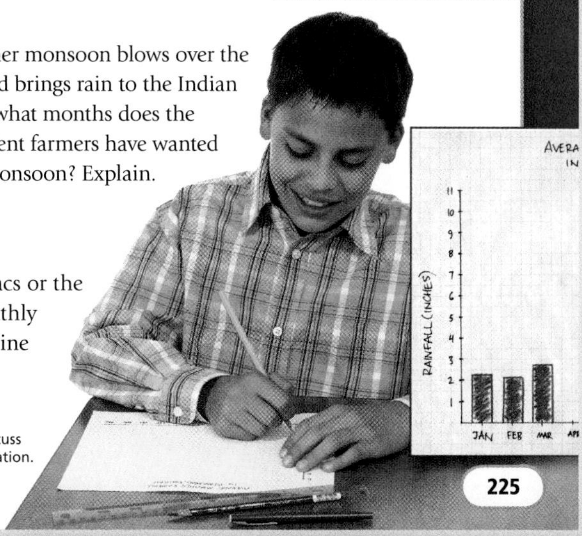

CALIFORNIA STANDARDS
6.5.1 Locate and describe the major river system and discuss the physical setting that supported the rise of this civilization.

Average Monthly Rainfall in Islamabad, Pakistan

Month	Rainfall (inches)
Jan.	2.3
Feb.	2.1
Mar.	2.7
Apr.	2.1
May	1.6
June	1.2
July	10.1
Aug.	9.9
Sep.	3.8
Oct.	1.0
Nov.	0.7
Dec.	1.6

Source: www.worldclimate.com

225

ACTIVITY: CLIMATE GRAPH

Objectives
- Describe an aspect of the physical geography of ancient India.
- Create a graph using statistical information.

Suggestions for Completing the Activity
- Help students find examples of bar graphs from other books. Math books are good sources for bar graphs.
- Explain that the horizontal axis is the line that runs along the bottom of the graph, and that the vertical axis is the line that runs up and down.
- Make sure students are reading the table of information on rainfall in Islamabad.
- Help students follow the steps under Do the Activity properly.

ACTIVITY ANSWERS

Follow-Up Answers
The summer monsoon occurs in July and August. Farmers would plant before the summer monsoon so the rain would water the crops.

Extension Rubric

	Accuracy of Data	Style of Graph
4	accurate, complete information	properly constructed and labeled
3	mostly accurate information	one or two errors in construction and labeling of the graph
2	somewhat accurate information	three or four errors in construction and labeling of the graph
1	inaccurate information	five or more errors in construction and labeling of the graph

① Plan & Prepare

Objectives

- Describe the significance of the Aryan migrations into India.
- Analyze the social structure of the caste system.
- Summarize the features of Brahmanism and Hinduism.
- **Language Objective:** Interpret the information from a chart that supports the text and makes the content more comprehensible.

Quick Look

Lesson 2 explores the effects of the Aryan migrations, which transformed ancient India and led to the development of Hinduism.

② Focus & Motivate

Preview Tell students that this lesson tells of the civilization that followed the Harappan civilization in India and of the organization of the new Aryan society. Remind students of the transition from one civilization to the next in places such as Mesopotamia and Nubia.

Introduce the Main Ideas The three main ideas relate to the Big Idea "Many societies rely on family roles and social roles to keep order." Help students look for this Big Idea in the lesson.

Reading Skill: Summarizing Tell students that summarizing involves creating a brief statement that captures only the central points of a longer passage.

SAMPLE ANSWERS FOR CHART

The Origins of Hinduism
The Aryans migrated *into India from the west.*
Aryan culture changed India by *creating a complex, blended culture.*
The main characteristics of Hinduism are *belief in reincarnation and in the existence of many paths to God.*

Lesson 2

▶ **MAIN IDEAS**

① **Culture** A group of nomadic people moved into India and took over what was left of Harappan civilization.

② **Government** Under Aryan rule, Indian society developed a distinct system of social classes that still affects India today.

③ **Belief Systems** Over time, the belief of the Aryans developed into the religion of Hinduism.

▶ **TAKING NOTES**

Reading Skill: Summarizing

To summarize is to restate a passage in fewer words. After you read Lesson 2, write a paragraph summarizing each of the three main sections. Use a chart like the one below to record your summaries.

The Origins of Hinduism
The Aryans migrated . . .
Aryan culture changed India by . . .
The main characteristics of Hinduism are . . .

 Skillbuilder Handbook, page R3

▲ **Shiva** One of the most important gods of Hinduism is Shiva, the destroyer. This statue shows him dancing on the demon of ignorance.

CALIFORNIA STANDARDS

6.5.2 Discuss the significance of the Aryan invasions.

6.5.3 Explain the major beliefs and practices of Brahmanism in India and how they evolved into early Hinduism.

6.5.4 Outline the social structure of the caste system.

6.5.7 Discuss important aesthetic and intellectual traditions (e.g., Sanskrit literature, including the *Bhagavad Gita;* medicine; metallurgy; and mathematics, including Hindu-Arabic numerals and the zero).

HOW TO TEACH THE CALIFORNIA STANDARDS

Standard	Content	Student Question or Activity	Instruction
6.5.2	**Page 228** Analyzes how the Aryan invasion led to a blending of Indian culture	**Page 231** Students explain the differences between the Aryan and Harappan cultures.	Discuss with students how the United States is a blend of many cultures. Ask students to give examples of the diversity of U.S. culture.
6.5.3	**Page 229** Explains the early Aryan beliefs, known as Brahmanism, which evolved into Hinduism	**Page 231** Students use a chart to help answer how Hinduism grew out of Brahmanism.	Ask students what other civilizations underwent changes in belief systems. Remind them that Christianity came to Aksum after Aksum had absorbed Kush.
6.5.4	**Page 228** Analyzes how Aryan life was organized	**Page 229** Students describe the features of the caste system.	Spark discussion by mentioning that the United States has an informal class system.
6.5.7	**Page 230** Presents an excerpt from the poem *Bhagavad Gita.*	**Page 231** Students identify the values of a warrior culture based on the poem.	Have students compare and contrast the values of a warrior in ancient India to those of a soldier today.

The Origins of Hinduism

TERMS & NAMES
- Aryan
- caste
- Brahmanism
- Hinduism
- reincarnation
- karma

Build on What You Know In Chapter 5, you learned how Egypt battled the Hittites. The Hittites belonged to a group of peoples who all spoke dialects of a language called Indo-European. Scholars believe that the Indo-Europeans may have originally come from Central Asia.

Aryans Move Into India

1 ESSENTIAL QUESTION Who were the Aryans?

Most Indo-Europeans were nomads. They lived in family groups or clans and herded cattle, sheep, and goats. They also were warriors who rode horse-driven chariots. They fought with long bows and arrows and with bronze axes.

The Indo-European Migrations Around 2000 B.C., something drove the Indo-Europeans from their homeland. Historians do not know if a drought, a plague, or an invasion made them leave. Different groups moved to different regions. The Hittites went to Southwest Asia. Many other Indo-Europeans settled in parts of Europe.

They were an Indo-European people who spoke Sanskrit, herded animals, and lived in simple houses. They moved into India beginning about 1500 B.C.

Hindu Kush This mountain range runs along the northwest border of the Indian subcontinent. The Aryan people crossed these mountains to enter India. ▼

HINDU KUSH

HIMALAYAS

227

Terms & Names

Aryans Indo-European people that moved into India about 1500 B.C.

caste a social class based on jobs

Brahmanism early Aryan religion

Hinduism the major religion of India

reincarnation the belief that each person has many lives

karma the belief that the deeds of a person affect what he or she will be in the next life

❸ Teach

Aryans Move Into India
6.5.2

Talk About It

- **Critical Thinking: Summarize** How has thinking about the Aryan invasion changed? *(Historians used to think the Aryans conquered the Harappans. Now, they believe Harappan cities were in ruins before the Aryans arrived.)*

California Resources

California Reading Toolkit, L22
California Modified Lesson Plans for English Learners, p. 47
California Daily Standards Practice Transparencies, TT22
California Standards Enrichment Workbook, pp. 67–72, pp. 77–78
California Online Test Practice
California Test Generator CD-ROM
California Standards Planner and Lesson Plans, L43
California EasyPlanner CD-ROM
California eEdition CD-ROM

LESSON 2 PROGRAM RESOURCES

ON LEVEL

In-Depth Resources: Unit 4
- Reading Skill: Summarizing, p. 4
- Skillbuilder Practice: Explaining Chronological Order and Sequence, p. 8
- Vocabulary Study Guide, p. 9

Formal Assessment
- Lesson Quiz, p. 116

ENGLISH LEARNERS

In-Depth Resources in Spanish
- Reading Skill: Summarizing, p. 54
- Skillbuilder Practice: Explaining Chronological Order and Sequence, p. 59

- Vocabulary Study Guide, p. 9

Modified Lesson Plans for English Learners, p. 47

Reading Study Guide (Spanish), p. 59

Reading Study Guide Audio CD (Spanish)

STRUGGLING READERS

In-Depth Resources: Unit 4
- Reading Skill: Summarizing, p. 4
- Vocabulary Study Guide, p. 9
- Reteaching Activity, p. 18

Reading Toolkit, p. L22

Reading Study Guide, p. 59

Reading Study Guide Audio CD

GIFTED AND TALENTED STUDENTS

In-Depth Resources: Unit 4
- Literature: Bhagavad Gita, p. 16

Interdisciplinary Projects
- Language Arts, p. 39

INCLUSION

EasyPlanner CD-ROM
- Reading Skill: Summarizing
- Vocabulary Study Guide
- Reteaching Activity

TECHNOLOGY

eEdition CD-ROM

Power Presentations CD-ROM

Humanities Transparencies
- HT13 Krishna on an Elephant

Critical Thinking Transparencies
- CT28 Summarizing

Test Generator CD-ROM

ClassZone.com

In-Depth Resources: Unit 4
- Reading Skill: Summarizing, p. 4
- Skillbuilder Practice: Explaining Chronological Order and Sequence, p. 8

History from Visuals

Interpreting Maps

Direct students to read the map title and the contents of the map. Make sure they understand that the map shows the process by which the subcontinent was populated by Aryan peoples.

- How long did it take for the Aryans to spread out across the continent? *(about 1,250 years)*

GEOGRAPHY SKILLBUILDER ANSWER

the Himalayas

INTERACTIVE

An interactive version of this map is available on the eEdition and the Power Presentations CD-ROMs.

Teach

Changes to Indian Life
6.5.4

Talk About It

- What happened when the Aryans encountered the Dravidians? *(Their cultures blended, as each culture shared with the other.)*

- What were the key features of the caste system? *(People were identified with a particular caste depending on their job. There were four broad categories of castes, and eventually a fifth group that was below all the others emerged.)*

- Who were the Brahmans? *(They were priests in the early Aryan religion.)*

- **Critical Thinking: Summarizing** How did Brahmanism change over time? *(Possible answer: People began to question how the world came into being and started to believe that one spirit governed the universe.)*

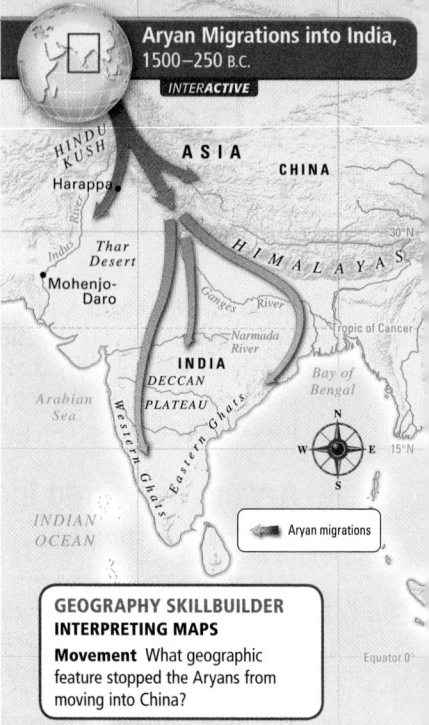

Aryan Migrations into India, 1500–250 B.C.
INTERACTIVE

GEOGRAPHY SKILLBUILDER
INTERPRETING MAPS
Movement What geographic feature stopped the Aryans from moving into China?

The Aryan Invasions In about 1500 B.C., a group of Indo-Europeans called the **Aryans** (AIR•ee•uhnz) traveled east into India. In contrast to the city-dwelling Harappans, the Aryans were herders. They lived in simple houses. They spoke an Indo-European language called Sanskrit.

Did Aryan warriors in chariots conquer the walled cities and force the Harappans to flee south? For years, history books told that story. But new research suggests a different tale. Two hundred years before the Aryans arrived, the largest Harappan cities lay in ruins. As Lesson 1 explained, this destruction may have been the result of earthquakes and floods.

They were a group of Indo-Europeans who moved into India after the Harappan civilization fell. They probably came from Central Asia.

REVIEW Who were the Aryans, and where did they come from?

Changes to Indian Life

 ESSENTIAL QUESTION How was Aryan society organized?

The Aryans entered India gradually. They practiced a mysterious religion that appealed to many Dravidians—the people living in India when they arrived. As a result, Aryan religion and language spread. In turn, the Dravidians taught the Aryans about city life. Because of these interactions, India developed a complex, blended culture.

The Caste System Aryan society was organized into classes: warriors, priests, and commoners. As Indian society grew more complex, these classes developed into what was later called the caste system. A **caste** is a social class whose members are identified by their job. Because there are thousands of different jobs, thousands of groups exist. Broadly, those groups are organized into four categories. (See the chart on the next page.)

After many centuries, a fifth group came into being that was considered below all other groups. This fifth group is called the untouchables. They had to do the jobs no one else wanted.

The Aryans developed the caste system, which organized society into groups based on occupation. These were organized into four broad categories. Much later, a fifth category called the untouchables developed, which was below all other groups.

DIFFERENTIATING INSTRUCTION

Inclusion

Ask Questions
As students to read this lesson and have them ask themselves a question about what they have read at the end of every paragraph. Then have them write down the answer. Go over students' answers, letting them know whether they are focusing on the key point or on supporting details.

English Learners

Study a Chart
Explain that studying details in the chart *The Indian Caste System* will help students gain a deeper understanding of the lesson. Guide students as they describe some of the details in the chart and caption. Ask students what they would like and NOT like about having the same occupation as their father. Have students share their answers aloud with the class.

The Caste System

Indian society divides itself into a complex structure of social classes based partially on jobs. This class structure is called the caste system.

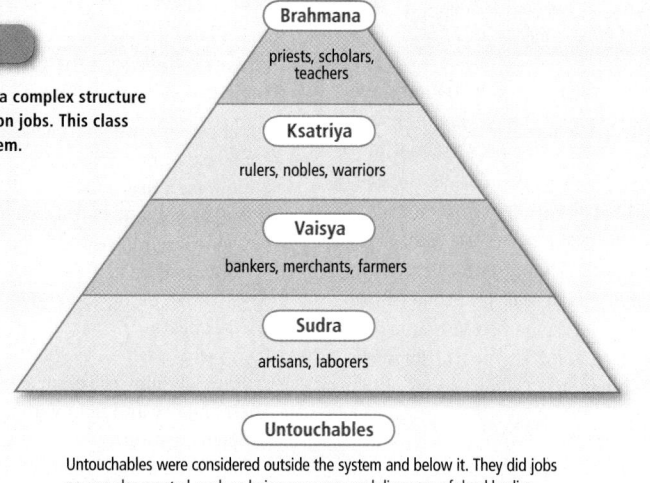

Brahmana
priests, scholars, teachers

Ksatriya
rulers, nobles, warriors

Vaisya
bankers, merchants, farmers

Sudra
artisans, laborers

Untouchables

Untouchables were considered outside the system and below it. They did jobs no one else wanted, such as being sweepers and disposers of dead bodies.

▲ **Sweeper** This sweeper did not choose his job. In traditional India, jobs were passed down from father to son.

Aryan Beliefs and Brahmanism The early religion of the Aryans is now called **Brahmanism**, after the name of the Aryan priests, or Brahmans. The Aryans worshiped many nature gods. The Brahmans made sacrifices to those gods by offering animals to a sacred fire. Over time, the ceremonies became more and more complex. Some lasted for days—or even months. The rituals of the Aryan religion and many hymns to their gods are found in ancient Sanskrit texts called the Vedas.

As time passed, Indians began to question how the world came into being. These questions led to changes in Brahmanism. One change was a belief that one spirit governed the universe.

Later, Indians wrote about their ancient history in such works as the *Mahabharata* (MAH•huh•BAH•ruh•tuh)—an epic poem that retells many legends. The *Bhagavad Gita* (BAH•guh•vahd GEE•tuh) is part of the *Mahabharata*. (See the Primary Source on page 230.)

REVIEW What is the caste system?

Hinduism: The Religion of India

③ **ESSENTIAL QUESTION** How did the religion of Hinduism develop?

The *Bhagavad Gita* is the most important text of Hinduism. **Hinduism** is the modern name for the major religion of India, which grew out of early Brahmanism.

Ancient India • 229

History from Visuals

Interpreting Visuals
Have students read over the text and the diagram on this page. Ask them to read the caption that accompanies the picture.

- What is the significance of the fact that the diagram is shaped like a pyramid? *(It suggests that certain castes were ranked more highly than others were.)*

- What is the significance of the fact that the untouchables are a category that is separate from the rest of the pyramid? *(It suggests that they were held in very low esteem.)*

Teach

Hinduism: The Religion of India

 6.5.3, 6.5.7

Talk About It

- What is the *Bhagavad Gita*? *(It is a central piece of Hindu writing.)*

- What are some of the key features of Hinduism? *(Hindus believe in reincarnation and karma. Though they believe in many gods, they see these as part of one supreme God or life force. They believe that there are many different paths to God.)*

- **Critical Thinking: Finding Main Ideas** What did Hinduism gain from Brahmanism? *(Possible answer: Both religions recognize many gods. Eventually, Brahmanism came to believe that one god governed the universe, a belief shared by Hinduism.)*

📝 **In-Depth Resources: Unit 4**
- Literature: Bhagavad Gita, p. 16

INTERDISCIPLINARY ACTIVITIES

Language Arts

Describe the Caste System
Have students assume the role of a foreign correspondent visiting India from one of the other civilizations they have studied in this book. Ask students to write an article about the caste system of India, describing its features and comparing it to the social system in their own lands. Remind students to describe each caste in a respectful way.

Math

Find Percentages
Have students use library or Internet resources to find the total number of people living in India today. Then have students look up the numbers of Indian speakers of languages such as Hindi, Bengali, Gujarati, and Marathi. Ask students to calculate percentages and to display their findings in a pie graph.

Interpreting Primary Sources

from the *Bhagavad Gita*

Instruct students to read the summary section on the left, to establish the background for the reading. Then, have students read the passage itself.

- What is the basic message that Krishna presents to Arjuna? *(It is important to do your duty.)*
- What does Krishna suggest are the consequences of not fulfilling one's duty? *(The consequences are incurring a sin.)*
- In what way does this passage convey the Hindu idea of fulfilling one's duty? *(It suggests that doing one's duty leads to happiness and not doing it leads to sin.)*

DOCUMENT–BASED QUESTION ANSWER

Winning or losing will each lead to a reward, and fighting is the only way to do his duty and thus avoid sin.

Vocabulary Strategy

The Prefix *re-*

Tell students that learning to recognize prefixes and roots can help them break down and understand many unfamiliar words. Ask students to find another example of a word with the prefix *re-* on this page. *(reborn)* Invite students to search for other words that begin with prefixes. *(Some common prefixes include* de- *and* un-.*)* Have students use a dictionary to try to trace the meanings of these words by breaking down the meanings of the prefixes and the roots.

Humanities Transparencies
- HT13 Krishna on an Elephant

Background: The *Bhagavad Gita* tells the story of a warrior, Prince Arjuna. A great war is about to begin. When he looks at the enemy army, Arjuna sees many friends and relatives. He does not want to fight.

With Arjuna is his chariot driver, Krishna. In reality, Krishna (shown at right) is the god Vishnu in human form. In this excerpt, Krishna tells Arjuna that he must do his duty.

DOCUMENT–BASED QUESTION
What arguments does Krishna use to convince Arjuna that the outcome of the battle is not important?

from the *Bhagavad Gita*
Translated by Ranchor Prime

Do not hesitate in your sacred duty as a warrior.
For a soldier nothing is more sacred than the
    fight for a just cause. . . .
If you do not take up this just fight,
    you will fail in your duty and your
    honor will be lost. . . .
If you die in battle you will
    enter heaven.
If you win
    you will enjoy the earth.
Therefore rise and fight with
    determination.
Fight for the sake of fighting.
Look equally on happiness
    and distress, gain and
    loss, victory and defeat.
In this way you will not incur sin.

Many Gods Hindus worship many gods. Although they believe in many gods, Hindus also recognize one supreme God or life force. Hindus consider the other gods to be parts of the one universal God. The three most important of the other gods are Brahma, the creator; Vishnu, the protector; and Shiva, the destroyer. (Shiva destroys the world so that it can be created anew.) Shiva's wife, Kali, also has many worshipers.

Many Lives Hindus believe in **reincarnation**, which means that each person has many lives. What a person does in each life determines what he or she will be in the next life, according to a doctrine called **karma**. Good deeds allow a person to be reborn as a higher being. Evil deeds cause a person to be reborn as a lower being, such as an insect. (Hindus believe that animals, like humans, have the supreme life force in them. For that reason, many Hindus are vegetarians. They will not eat animals.)

Reincarnation creates a repeating cycle of birth, life, death, and rebirth. The cycle ends only when a person achieves a mystical union with God. To achieve that, a person must come to realize that his or her soul and God's soul are one.

Vocabulary Strategy

The word *reincarnation* uses the **prefix** *re-*, which means "again," and the **root** *carn*, which means "flesh." Therefore, reincarnation means that the soul takes on another body.

DIFFERENTIATING INSTRUCTION

Gifted and Talented Students

Create a Poster
Have students find a passage they like from the *Bhagavad Gita* and use it to create a poster modeled on the Primary Source feature on page 230. Students should write a paragraph that explains the background of the passage. Suggest that students illustrate the poster with a photocopy of authentic Indian art. Alternatively, they may make a drawing based on a piece of Indian art.

Struggling Readers

Make a Web Diagram
Have students work in pairs to create a web diagram of the section "Hinduism: The Religion of India." Starting with a blank sheet of paper, they should draw a circle in the center with the word *Hinduism* in it. Then, have pairs read through each paragraph together and add an item to the web diagram summarizing the content of that paragraph. Have students share their diagrams with the class.

Many Paths to God Hindus believe they connect with God by following their own individual path. Part of that path concerns one's job, which is linked to the caste system. Devout Hindus must faithfully carry out their assigned duties in life.

Hindus have a choice of spiritual practices to grow closer to God. Two of these are also popular in Western countries. Meditation is the practice of making the mind calm. Yoga is a complex practice that includes exercise, breathing techniques, and diet.

REVIEW How can Hindus believe in one God and many different gods at the same time? They think that the other gods are part of the one supreme God.

Lesson Summary

- After Harappan civilization declined, Aryan people brought their culture to India.
- Aryan society developed a class structure that was based on jobs and is called the caste system.
- Hindus worship many gods. They believe in reincarnation and karma.

Why It Matters Now . . .

Hinduism ranks third among world religions in the number of followers (after Christianity and Islam).

2 Lesson Review

 Homework Helper
ClassZone.com

Terms & Names

1. Explain the importance of

Aryan	Brahmanism	reincarnation
caste	Hinduism	karma

Using Your Notes

Summarizing Use your completed chart to answer the following question:

2. How did Hinduism grow out of the beliefs of Brahmanism? (6.5.3)

The Origins of Hinduism
The Aryans migrated . . .
Aryan culture changed India by . . .
The main characteristics of Hinduism are . . .

Main Ideas

3. How did the Aryan culture differ from Harappan culture? (6.5.2)

4. What was the social structure of the Aryan caste system? (6.5.4)

5. How does karma relate to reincarnation? (6.5.3)

Critical Thinking

6. **Recognizing Changing Interpretations** What changed the long-held theory that Aryan invaders drove out the Harappan people? (HI 5)

7. **Drawing Conclusions from Sources** What values of a warrior culture does the passage from the *Bhagavad Gita* express? (6.5.7)

Activity **Internet Activity** Use the Internet to learn about Hindu customs concerning one of these topics: the Ganges River, cows, funerals, diet. Present your findings to the class in an oral presentation. (6.5.3)
INTERNET KEYWORDS: *Hinduism, Ganges*

❹ Assess & Reteach

Assess Divide students into small groups and have them answer the questions. Then ask groups to take turns presenting answers to the class. Discuss whether any groups answered the questions differently.

Formal Assessment
- Lesson Quiz, p. 116

Reteach Ask students to read the items in the Lesson Summary out loud. Then, for each item, have students review the lesson for information which they will use to write an additional, follow-up sentence on the topic.

In-Depth Resources: Unit 4
- Vocabulary Cards, p. 11
- Reteaching Activity, p. 18

 Homework Helper

Visit **ClassZone.com** for a lesson review, a flip-card activity, and links to related Web sites.

---

2 Lesson Review Answers

Terms & Names

1. • Aryan, p. 228
   • caste, p. 228
   • Brahmanism, p. 229
   • Hinduism, p. 229
   • reincarnation, p. 230
   • karma, p. 230

Using Your Notes

See page 226 for an example of a completed chart.

2. From Brahmanism, Hinduism gained several gods, sacred writings, and a belief that one spirit ruled the universe.

Main Ideas

3. The Aryans were herders and warriors; they spoke a different language; they did not build planned cities.

4. It was structured according to inherited social class and job.

5. Hindus believe in reincarnation, which means that each person has many lives. According to the doctrine of karma, what a person does in each life determines what he or she will be in the next life.

Critical Thinking

6. evidence that the Harappan culture had declined long before the Aryans came to India

7. Possible answers: bravery, honor, duty, ignoring emotions, not caring whether you win or lose

Activity Rubric

	Quality of Information	Style of Presentation
4	accurately explains all aspects of Hindu custom	very well organized, uses images or visual aids
3	explains most aspects of Hindu custom	well organized, uses some images or visual aids
2	explains some aspects of Hindu custom	fairly well organized; uses few images or visual aids
1	explains few aspects of Hindu custom	disorganized; uses no images or visual aids

❶ Plan & Prepare

Objectives

- Describe the life and teachings of the Buddha and the spread of Buddhism.
- Describe the growth of the Maurya Empire and the achievements of Asoka.
- Analyze the golden age of the Guptas, including developments in art and science.
- **Language Objective:** Create a mural to compare and contrast the Maurya Empire and the Gupta Empire.

Quick Look

Lesson 3 traces the development of Buddhism in India, along with the flowering of culture that occurred during the time of the Mauryas and the Guptas.

❷ Focus & Motivate

Preview Explain that this lesson traces the further development of religion, culture, and political power in ancient India. Have students recall how the development of major empires influenced religion, culture, and politics in other regions they have studied.

Introduce the Main Ideas The three main ideas further develop the Big Idea "Many societies rely on family roles and social roles to keep order." Help students look for ideas about rulers and social roles as you go through this lesson.

Reading Skill: Comparing and Contrasting Tell students that the skill of comparing and contrasting enables a reader to detect patterns in historical information, which helps increase understanding of content.

SAMPLE ANSWERS FOR DIAGRAM

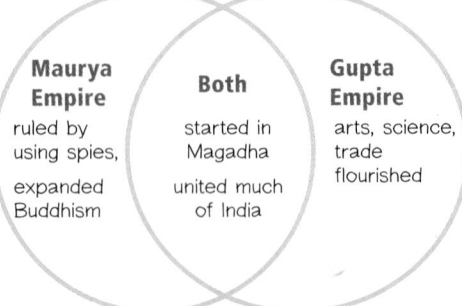

Maurya Empire ruled by using spies, expanded Buddhism

Both started in Magadha united much of India

Gupta Empire arts, science, trade flourished

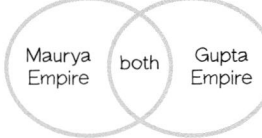

Lesson **3**

▶ **MAIN IDEAS**

❶ **Belief Systems** A teacher called the Buddha developed a new religion that focused on helping people to escape suffering.

❷ **Government** The Maurya rulers united northern India into the first great Indian empire.

❸ **Culture** About 500 years after Asoka's death, a new ruler united northern India and began a golden age of culture.

▶ **TAKING NOTES**

Reading Skill: Comparing and Contrasting

To compare and contrast is to look for similarities and differences. As you read Lesson 3, compare and contrast the Maurya and Gupta empires. Record your notes on a Venn diagram like the one below.

Maurya Empire — both — Gupta Empire

Ⓢ Skillbuilder Handbook, page R4

▲ **Lion** The king Asoka adopted many Buddhist principles. He had his laws and policies carved on pillars in public places. The capitals, or tops, of the pillars were decorated with sculpture.

CALIFORNIA STANDARDS

6.5.5 Know the life and moral teachings of the Buddha and how Buddhism spread in India, Ceylon, and Central Asia.

6.5.6 Describe the growth of the Maurya empire and the political and moral achievements of the emperor Asoka.

6.5.7 Discuss important aesthetic and intellectual traditions (e.g., Sanskrit literature, including the *Bhagavad Gita*; medicine, metallurgy; and mathematics, including Hindu-Arabic numerals and the zero).

Framework While Buddhism did not survive on Indian soil, Jainism, which introduced the idea of *ahimsa*, or nonviolence, has continued to play a role in modern India, especially through Gandhi's idea of nonviolent civil disobedience.

232 • Chapter 7

HOW TO TEACH THE CALIFORNIA STANDARDS

Standard	Content	Student Question or Activity	Instruction
6.5.5	**Pages 233–235** Describe Buddhism and how it spread	**Page 235** Students explain how a Buddhist could achieve an end to suffering.	Discuss with students how Buddhism differs from Hinduism.
6.5.6	**Pages 235–236** Analyze the rise of the Maurya Empire and its ruler Asoka	**Page 235** Students explain how the Maurya rulers turned northern India into an important empire.	Ask students to think about how earlier empires had come into being. As a class, compare and contrast these empires with the Maurya Empire.
6.5.7	**Page 238** Explains advances in Indian mathematics, medicine, and metallurgy	**Page 239** Students identify how these key achievements created a golden age.	Ask students for examples of the damage that rust can cause. Help them see why gupta metallurgy was significant.
Framework	**Page 233** Explains the idea of *ahimsa*.	**Page 239** Students identify Buddhist influences on Asoka.	Ask students to think of leaders who have preached nonviolence. (*Gandhi, Martin Luther King Jr.*) Explain that the idea of nonviolence comes from Jainism.

Buddhism and India's Golden Age

Build on What You Know As you know, Hinduism is the modern name for the major religion that is practiced in India. Other religions also had their beginnings in India. One of these is the religion of Jainism. Jains teach *ahimsa* (uh•HIHM•SAH), which means "nonviolence." Jains practice *ahimsa* very strictly. They believe that every living thing has a soul and should not be hurt. Some Jains even wear masks to avoid accidentally breathing in small insects.

The Rise of Buddhism

① **ESSENTIAL QUESTION** What are the main teachings of the religion of Buddhism? The main teachings are the Four Noble Truths, the Eightfold Path, nirvana, ahimsa, and rejection of the caste system.

Another religion called Buddhism also began in India. **Buddhism** is based on the teachings of **Siddhartha Gautama** (sihd•DAHR•tuh GAW•tuh•muh). He was a prince who gave up his wealth and position to try to understand the meaning of life. Later, when he began to teach what he had learned, he was called the Buddha, or enlightened one.

◀ **Resting Buddha** This carving of a sleeping Buddha is in the Ajanta Caves in India.

Terms & Names

ahimsa nonviolence

Buddhism a religion that is based on the teachings of the Buddha

Siddhartha Gautama the man who became known as the Buddha

nirvana the Buddhist concept of a state of being where suffering ends

dharma the teachings of the Buddha

Asoka the greatest Maurya king

❸ Teach

The Rise of Buddhism

6.5.5

Talk About It

• **Critical Thinking: Comparing** What are beliefs and practices common to Buddhism and Hinduism? *(reincarnation, meditation)*

California Resources

California Reading Toolkit, L23
California Modified Lesson Plans for English Learners, p. 49
California Daily Standards Practice Transparencies, TT23
California Standards Enrichment Workbook, pp. 73–78
California Online Test Practice
California Test Generator CD-ROM
California Standards Planner and Lesson Plans, L45
California EasyPlanner CD-ROM
California eEdition CD-ROM

233

LESSON 3 PROGRAM RESOURCES

ON LEVEL

In-Depth Resources: Unit 4
• Reading Skill: Comparing and Contrasting, p. 5
• Vocabulary Cards, p. 11

Formal Assessment
• Lesson Quiz, p. 117

ENGLISH LEARNERS

In-Depth Resources in Spanish
• Reading Skill: Comparing and Contrasting, p. 55

Modified Lesson Plans for English Learners, p. 49

Reading Study Guide (Spanish), p. 61

Reading Study Guide Audio CD (Spanish)

STRUGGLING READERS

In-Depth Resources: Unit 4
• Reading Skill: Comparing and Contrasting, p. 5
• Vocabulary Cards, p. 11
• Reteaching Activity, p. 19

Reading Toolkit, p. L23

Reading Study Guide, p. 61

Reading Study Guide Audio CD

GIFTED AND TALENTED STUDENTS

In-Depth Resources: Unit 4
• Primary Source: Teachings by Buddha, p. 15

History Makers
• Asoka, p. 13

Interdisciplinary Projects
• Art, p. 40

INCLUSION

EasyPlanner CD-ROM
• Reading Skill: Comparing and Contrasting
• Vocabulary Study Guide

• Reteaching Activity

TECHNOLOGY

eEdition CD-ROM

Power Presentations CD-ROM

Humanities Transparencies
• HT14 Head of Buddha

Map Transparencies
• MT14 Indian Ocean Trade A.D. 400

Critical Thinking Transparencies
• CT29 Comparing and Contrasting

Test Generator CD-ROM

ClassZone.com

In-Depth Resources: Unit 4
- Reading Skill: Comparing and Contrasting, p. 5
- Primary Source: Teachings of Buddha, p. 15

History Makers

Siddhartha Gautama

According to some stories about his life, Siddhartha Gautama was born into the Shakaya clan as a member of the caste known as Ksatriya. During the first three decades of his life, he married, had a child, and lived an extraordinarily privileged and sheltered life. He left all of this behind when he became aware of the reality of suffering.

After rejecting his worldly home in order to seek the truth, Siddhartha practiced extreme self-denial of food and comfort. This nearly cost him his life. However, he discovered the wisdom of the "middle way" between self-denial and the worldly life of his youth. This enabled him to eventually achieve enlightenment and become the Buddha.

The Buddha continued to teach others about the path to enlightenment for the next 45 years. He died at the age of 80.

Vocabulary Strategy

Word Study

Tell students that words such as *nirvana* and *karma* have particular meanings relative to Hinduism and Buddhism, but that they also have a general meaning in the wider culture. Students might hear *nirvana* to mean any state of blissfulness or great happiness. *Karma* is sometimes used to refer loosely to the concept of destiny or fate.

Humanities Transparencies
- HT14 Head of Buddha

History Makers

Siddhartha Gautama (c. 563 to 483 B.C.)

According to Buddhist teaching, as Siddhartha Gautama sat meditating, an evil spirit tempted him to stop seeking truth. First the spirit sent beautiful women, but Siddhartha ignored them. Then flaming rocks began to rain down on him. But as they drew close to Siddhartha, they became flower petals. Finally, the evil spirit asked what right Siddhartha had to look for truth. Siddhartha touched the ground, and a voice thundered, "I bear you witness"—which means to testify in one's favor.

That night Siddhartha's meditation grew even deeper, and he received his great insights. He had become the Buddha. The evil spirit decided to tempt him one last time. "No one will understand your deep truths," the spirit taunted.

The Buddha simply answered, "Some will understand."

The Buddha's Life and Teachings Siddhartha was born a Hindu prince. A priest had predicted that he would become a wandering holy man. To prevent this, Siddhartha's father gave his son every luxury and sheltered him. Siddhartha did not see old age, illness, death, or poverty until he was 29. When he finally did see such troubles, they upset him. He fled his home to search for peace in a world of suffering.

For six years, Siddhartha starved himself, but this sacrifice did not help him find the answers he sought. Then he sat under a fig tree and meditated until he found understanding. This gave him insights into reality, which he called the Four Noble Truths.

1. People suffer because their minds are not at ease.
2. That condition comes from wanting what one doesn't have or from wanting life to be different.
3. People can stop suffering by not wanting.
4. People can stop wanting by following the Eightfold Path.

The Eightfold Path involved having the right opinions, desires, speech, actions, job, effort, concentration, and meditation. This path, the Buddha taught, could lead to **nirvana** (neer•VAH•nuh), or the end of suffering. Reaching nirvana broke the cycle of reincarnation that Buddhists, as well as Hindus, believed in.

DIFFERENTIATING INSTRUCTION

Inclusion

Answer Questions

Create a set of questions to go along with one or more of the headings in the lesson. Divide students into pairs, giving each pair a set of blank cards. Have them answer each question on the cards as they finish reading the corresponding text. Tell them to save the cards to review the material before they are tested on it.

English Learners

Create a Mural

Have students work with a partner to create a mural that depicts life in the Maurya Empire and life in the Gupta Empire. Advise students to revisit the text, as needed. Have them use labels and captions to help describe details in their illustrations. Then have students use their murals to explain the similarities and differences to their classmates. Post murals in classroom.

The Buddha believed in the practice of *ahimsa*. But he didn't worship Hindu gods and goddesses. He also rejected the idea that people in the upper castes were holier than others.

Buddhism Changes After the Buddha died, his followers gathered his teachings to pass on to others. These collected teachings are called the **dharma** (DAHR•muh), which means the true nature of things. Dharma is often shown symbolically as a wheel.

Monks and nuns—men and women who live in religious communities—helped develop the formal religion of Buddhism. Other Buddhists became wandering holy men and tried to live as the Buddha had.

Over time, Buddhism split into many branches. Some branches stressed the importance of being a monk and studying the Buddha's life. Others stressed meditation. Some Buddhists taught that ordinary people could become Buddhas. Such holy people could work to save others through acts of mercy and love. Most Buddhists worshiped the Buddha as a divine being.

REVIEW How could a Buddhist achieve an end to suffering?
by following the Eightfold Path and reaching nirvana

The Maurya Empire

2 **ESSENTIAL QUESTION** How did the Maurya rulers unite northern India into the first great Indian empire? They conquered much territory in northern India.

One reason Buddhism became so influential is that a famous Indian king ruled by its teachings. As you will read, he was the third king of the Maurya dynasty, which united India.

A United India For centuries, separate Aryan kingdoms battled each other. Around 550 B.C., Magadha (MAH•guh•duh), a northeastern kingdom, began to gain strength. About 321 B.C., Chandragupta Maurya (CHUHN•druh•GUP•tuh MOWR•yuh) became king of Magadha. He conquered much territory. His Maurya Empire soon covered much of the subcontinent.

Chandragupta controlled his empire by using spies to learn what people did and an army of soldiers to keep order. Many officials ran the government. To pay these people, Chandragupta taxed land and crops heavily. Surprisingly, legend says that he became a nonviolent Jainist monk at the end of his life.

Connect to Today

▲ **Indian Flag** In the center of the flag of modern India is a Buddhist symbol—the wheel of dharma.

Ancient India • **235**

More About . . .

Buddhism After the Buddha
Following the death of the Buddha, Buddhism remained a relatively small religion confined mainly to India. It was not until the reign of Asoka that Buddhism spread.

Two main schools of Buddhism emerged over time and took root in different parts of the world. The more conservative Theravada became the dominant form of Buddhism in Southeast Asia. This branch stressed the difficult discipline of a monastic life. Another branch, called Mahayana Buddhism, which has a more popular appeal, spread to China, Korea, and Japan.

Teach

The Maurya Empire
✎ 6.5.6

Talk About It

- What change did Chandragupta Maurya bring to India? *(He united much of the subcontinent under a single empire.)*

- What were the most notable features of Asoka's rule? *(He sought to rule India by peaceful means. He was influenced by Buddhism and promoted the spread of that religion.)*

- **Critical Thinking: Understanding Cause and Effect** How did the rise of Buddhism in India affect Hinduism? *(Possible answers: At first, it lessened the practice of Hinduism. However, Hinduism eventually adapted, taking steps to reach out to the people. Eventually, Hinduism regained its place as the major religion of India.)*

INTERDISCIPLINARY ACTIVITIES

Art

Compare Images
Ask students to find images of the Buddha from many Asian cultures, such as Indian, Chinese, Thai, and Japanese, and have them create a poster that compares the images. Have students present their posters to the class, explaining their comparisons. Then display the posters in the classroom.

Language Arts

Retell a Story
Have students use the library or the Internet to find another story about the Buddha's life. Invite students to retell the story to the class.

King Asoka's Edicts

Much of what scholars know about King Asoka comes from a series of policies, or edicts, that he issued during his reign. These were carved into rocks and stone pillars scattered in more than 30 locations across India. These edicts appear in different languages in different parts of what was the Maurya empire.

The Asoka inscriptions tell details of his life and reflect his desire to see Buddhist principles followed in his empire—both on the level of individual behavior and in terms of government policy. Indeed, the empire under Asoka stopped its practice of attacking neighbors and sought more peaceful relations. Better treatment and protection for animals was urged. One edict, for example, details how he planned to eliminate the consumption of meat from his court.

Hindu Gods

Vishnu and Shiva are two gods in what is sometimes referred to as the Hindu trinity. The third major god is Brahma. In this conception, Shiva is the "destroyer"—that is, the destroyer of evil things. Brahma is the creator, and Vishnu is the preserver.

The Hindu gods have many different names in Hindu practice and they take many different forms. For example, Vishnu is linked to two avatars (incarnations), Krishna and Rama. These are human representations of the immortal being. Shiva has many different attributes and is known by hundreds of names.

Asoka, the Buddhist King The greatest Maurya king was Chandragupta's grandson **Asoka** (uh•SOH•kuh), who began to rule in 269 B.C. Early in Asoka's reign, he fought a bloody war and conquered a neighboring kingdom. Afterwards, Asoka decided to rule by Buddhist teachings. He gave up constant warfare. He tried to rule peacefully by law instead.

Asoka had his policies carved on rocks and pillars. Rocks that survive from his reign advise people to be truthful and kind. Others urge people not to kill living things.

Asoka sent out missionaries to spread Buddhism. At the same time, he let people of other religions worship freely. Asoka's officials planted trees, dug wells, set up hospitals, and built rest houses along main roads. These improvements allowed people to travel in more comfort than before. Better travel conditions helped traders and officials.

Changes to Hinduism The popularity of Buddhism meant that fewer people were worshiping Hindu gods. Early Hinduism had a set of complex sacrifices that only priests could perform. They conducted the rites in Sanskrit, which few people spoke anymore. This caused people to feel distant from the gods. Many people turned to Buddhism instead. Rulers who had come under the influence of Buddhism encouraged this shift.

Hindu thought began to change. Starting in the A.D. 600s, poets began to write hymns of praise to the gods Vishnu and Shiva. These poems were written in languages that common people spoke, instead of in Sanskrit. The poems expressed intense love and joy.

The poems became popular across India. As a result, many Indians felt a renewed love for their Hindu gods. This renewal of interest in Hinduism occurred at the same time as a decline in Buddhism. Some Hindu leaders had been actively opposing Buddhism. Eventually, Buddhism lost most of its followers in India. By that time, however, it had spread to many other countries in Asia.

Possible answers: set an example of compassionate and tolerant behavior, tried to govern fairly, sent missionaries to spread Buddhism, improved roads, founded hospitals

REVIEW What were some of Asoka's accomplishments?

Vishnu The god Vishnu remains one of the most popular gods in India. This Indian miniature dates from the 1700s. ▼

INTERDISCIPLINARY ACTIVITIES

Art

Create an Asoka-Style Pillar
Have students use library or Internet sources to read about Asoka's pillars. Then have them work individually to create a drawing of their own pillars. Students should also write an inscription for their pillar that conveys some basic message about how people should behave.

Science

Make a Fact Sheet
Point out that Indian artisans had very advanced methods of metallurgy. One iron pillar that they erected in Delhi has resisted rust since it was erected in about A.D. 400. Have students investigate what causes rust and ask them to create a fact sheet explaining the process. Suggest that students also include a list of tips for preventing rust.

The Golden Age of the Guptas

③ ESSENTIAL QUESTION Who were the Guptas, and when did they rule India? The Guptas were a family that became the second group of rulers to unify India. They began to rule in A.D. 320.

The Maurya Empire collapsed shortly after Asoka died because of poor rule and invasions. Five centuries of conflict followed until the Gupta (GUP•tuh) family took control.

The Gupta Empire Like the Mauryas, the Guptas began as leaders in Magadha. Chandra Gupta I became king in A.D. 320. (He was not related to Chandragupta Maurya.) Right away, he married a king's daughter and gained new lands. Later, his son enlarged the empire by fighting wars. But Chandra Gupta's grandson, Chandra Gupta II, was the greatest ruler of the family. During his reign (A.D. 375 to 415), India had a golden age—a time of great accomplishment.

> **GEOGRAPHY SKILLBUILDER**
> **INTERPRETING MAPS**
> **Region** Which empire was larger? Describe the differences in the regions the two empires controlled.

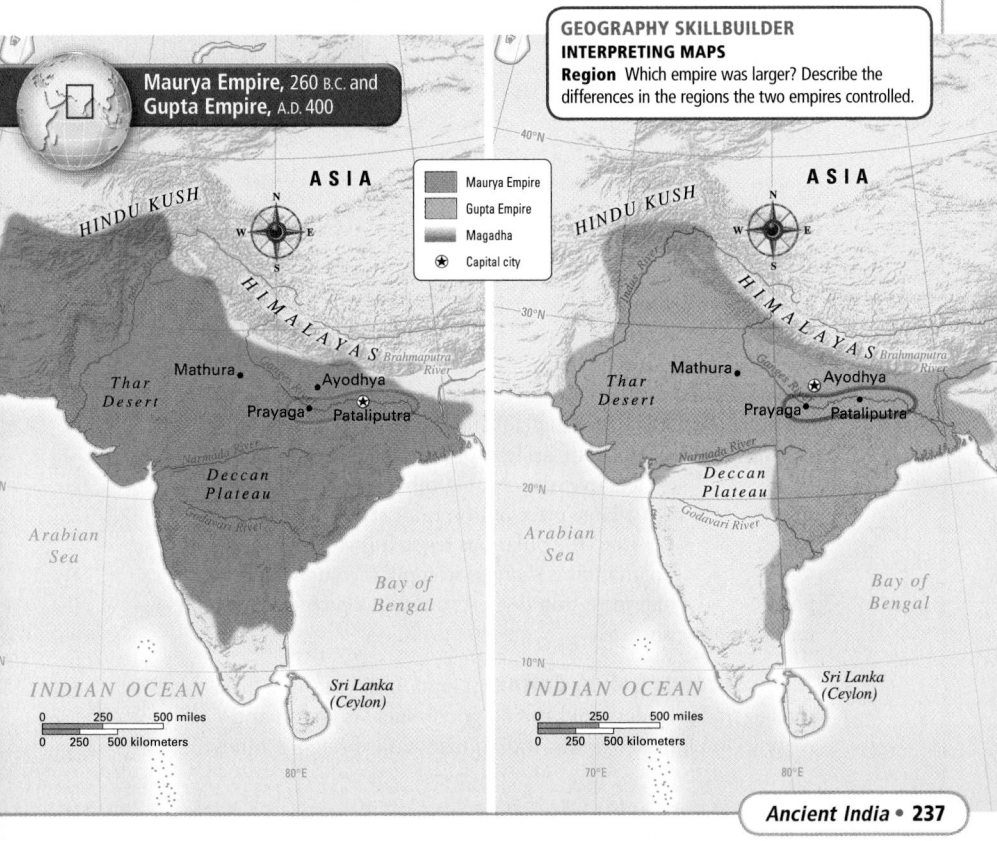

Maurya Empire, 260 B.C. and **Gupta Empire**, A.D. 400

- Maurya Empire
- Gupta Empire
- Magadha
- ⊛ Capital city

Ancient India • 237

DIFFERENTIATING INSTRUCTION

Gifted and Talented Students

Write a Biographical Sketch
Have students use library or Internet resources to learn more about one of the great Indian leaders, Chandra Gupta I or his grandson Chandra Gupta II. Students should collect information about key events in his life, details about his style of rule, and highlights of major achievements from his reign. Students should organize their findings in a brief biographical sketch.

Struggling Readers

Create a Time Line
Have students work individually to create a time line of the events and developments in this lesson. Tell them to use a blank sheet of paper to draw their time line. They should mark the time line with years in even increments from 600 B.C. to A.D. 500. Then work through the lesson, adding events to the time line in the appropriate spots. When students are finished, have them compare their time lines and discuss any inconsistencies.

Teach

The Golden Age of the Guptas

🖊 **6.5.7**

Talk About It

- What led to the collapse of the Maurya Empire? *(poor leadership, invasions)*

- What developments marked India's golden age under Chandra Gupta II? *(a flourishing of arts, literature, math, and science)*

- What developments from the golden age of the Guptas influence our lives today? *(During this period of time, Indians developed the decimal system and the system of numerals we use today. They also determined the value of pi.)*

- **Critical Thinking: Framing Historical Questions** What are some questions a historian might ask about Gupta India that help reveal why it was such a fertile time for Indian art and science? *(Possible answers: What role did India's leadership play in the flowering of Indian culture? How did the size of the empire affect the culture? Were there specific events or individuals who were responsible for key advances?)*

History from Visuals

Interpreting Maps
Instruct students to compare the two maps on this page. Be sure they recognize how the different shadings represent the two Indian empires of Gupta and Maurya.

- What two geographic features limited the northern extent of both empires? *(the Himalayas and the Hindu Kush)*

GEOGRAPHY SKILLBUILDER ANSWER

The Maurya Empire was larger; it controlled the Deccan Plateau and more of the territory west of the Indus River.

More About . . .

The History of Zero

Historically, the use of numbers and mathematics evolved around very basic and concrete problems—counting up farm animals or baskets of crops, for instance. There was no need to have a symbol to represent the absence of something. Human beings were able to solve all sorts of math problems for centuries without a symbol for zero.

Even in cultures that had a place value system, the written record indicates that mathematicians just left a blank space to represent the spot where we would put a zero. However, this approach caused problems when trying to represent a number such as "506." If a blank space is used instead of a zero, "506" would be represented as "5_6." People could easily think that "5_6" meant "56" or "5 and 6" instead of "506." The Indians are credited with developing the use of zero as a position holder in numbers, which avoided the confusion caused by using a blank space. They are also credited with developing the mathematical concept of zero.

Map Transparencies
• MT14 Indian Ocean Trade A.D. 400

Art and Literature Under Chandra Gupta II, Indian arts flourished. Architects erected gracefully designed temples. Artists painted murals and sculpted statues, many of which had religious subjects.

Kalidasa (KAH•lee•DAH•suh) wrote brilliant Sanskrit plays and poems. His most famous play is about a young woman named Sakuntala (SAH•koon•TAH•lah). The king falls in love with her and promises to marry her. Later he forgets her because of a curse laid on him. The couple are reunited in heaven. Today Kalidasa is considered one of the greatest writers India ever had.

Mathematics, Science, and Metallurgy Indian scholars invented the numeral system we use today. They developed the decimal system and the symbol for zero. (The Maya of Central America also came up with the idea of zero independently.)

One mathematician figured out the length of a year. He also estimated the value of pi. Pi is the number that is used to calculate the length of a circle's boundary.

Doctors added new techniques to the ancient practice of Ayurvedic (EYE•yuhr•VAY•dihk) medicine. It is one of the oldest systems of medicine in the world. It promotes health by using diet, exercise, and other methods to maintain energy in the body.

Indian artisans developed advanced methods of metallurgy (metal working). In Delhi, an iron pillar erected about A.D. 400 towers almost 23 feet over the city. No other people were able to manufacture such a large piece of iron until at least 1,000 years later. Unlike most iron, the pillar has resisted rust for 16 centuries. One possible explanation is that the iron pillar contains more phosphorous than most iron does. As a result, a protective coating formed on the surface.

Trade Spreads Indian Culture Gupta India profited from foreign trade. Traders sold Indian goods such as cotton and ivory to foreign merchants. Indian merchants bought Chinese

▲ **Vishnu Temple** During the Gupta period, Hindu temples began to be built with pyramid-shaped roofs. This architectural style remained very influential. (See the photograph of Angkor Wat on page 241.)

INTERDISCIPLINARY ACTIVITIES

Math

Create a Pi Demonstration
Tell students that pi represents a number that is useful in certain kinds of mathematical exercises. Have students use library or Internet resources to learn about pi, what it is and how it works. Then have them create a brief fact sheet that explains pi.

Language Arts

Celebrate the Golden Age of India
Have student use library and Internet resources to learn more about the golden age of the Guptas in India. Then have them work in teams of two or three to write and perform a song that celebrates the glory of this time. The song should mention some of the great achievements of Indian artists and scientists of this era.

goods such as silk. They resold these goods to traders who were traveling west.

Both traders and missionaries spread Indian culture and beliefs. Hinduism spread to parts of Southeast Asia. Buddhism gradually spread to Central Asia, Sri Lanka (formerly called Ceylon), China, and Southeast Asia.

REVIEW Why was the period of Gupta rule a golden age for India? because there were many advances in art, mathematics, science, and technology

Lesson Summary
- A new religion called Buddhism taught people to escape suffering by following a path of right living.
- Influenced by Buddhism, King Asoka tried to rule with peace, law, and good works.
- Under Gupta rule, India had a golden age. The arts, science, metallurgy, and trade prospered.

Why It Matters Now . . .
The spread of Hinduism and Buddhism shaped Asian cultures. Many Asian people still practice those religions today.

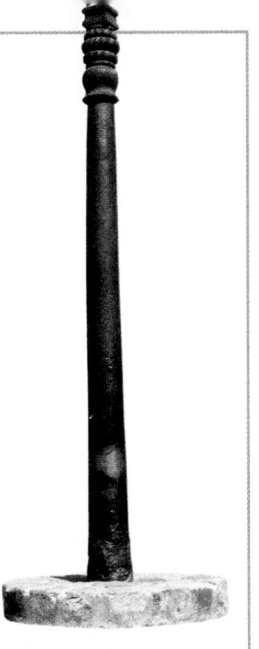

▲ **Iron Pillar** This pillar from the Gupta period stands more than 20 feet high and weighs about 1,300 pounds.

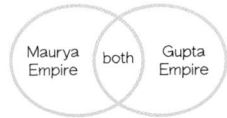 **Lesson Review**

 Homework Helper
ClassZone.com

Terms & Names
1. Explain the importance of

ahimsa	Siddhartha Gautama	dharma
Buddhism	nirvana	Asoka

Using Your Notes
Comparing and Contrasting Use your completed Venn diagram to answer the following question:

2. How were the Maurya and Gupta empires of India alike? (6.5.6)

Maurya Empire — both — Gupta Empire

Main Ideas
3. The Buddha's Eightfold Path stressed right behavior in eight areas. What were they? (6.5.5)

4. How did Buddhism influence Asoka as a ruler? (6.5.6)

5. What were the important achievements in Indian literature? (6.5.7)

Critical Thinking
6. **Comparing** Was Hinduism or Buddhism more similar to ancient Egyptian religion? Why? (6.5.5)

7. **Assessing Credibility of Primary Sources** If historians found an engraved rock pillar from Asoka's time, would that be a primary source or a secondary source? Explain. (REP 4)

Activity

Writing Rules With a group of your friends, agree on three or four basic rules for social conduct. Print your rules on a poster and display it in the classroom. (6.5.6)

Ancient India • 239

---

3 Lesson Review Answers

Terms & Names
1. • *ahimsa*, p. 233
   • Buddhism, p. 233
   • Siddhartha Gautama, p. 233
   • nirvana, p. 234
   • dharma, p. 235
   • Asoka, p. 236

Using Your Notes
See page 232 for an example of a completed diagram.
2. Both began in Maghada; both united northern India; in both, the grandson of the founder was the greatest ruler.

Main Ideas
3. opinions, desires, speech, actions, job, effort, concentration, and meditation

4. Possible answers: He decided to rule peacefully by law and gave up constant warfare; he sent out missionaries to spread Buddhism; he tolerated other religions; he posted laws in public places; he improved conditions for travelers.

5. the *Bhagavad Gita*; the poems and plays of Kalidasa

Critical Thinking
6. Possible answer: Hinduism was most like religion in Ancient Egypt, because both had a belief in many different gods.

7. It would be a primary source because it was produced at the time by someone who took part in the historical events.

---

④ Assess & Reteach

Assess Have students work on their own to answer the questions, then meet in small groups to discuss their answers.

 Formal Assessment
- Lesson Quiz, p. 117

Reteach Pair up students. Within each pair, have students take turns "teaching" the content of each section to the other student. Student teachers should highlight key information in each section and ask review questions of their "student."

 In-Depth Resources: Unit 4
- Vocabulary Cards, p. 11
- Reteaching Activity, p. 19

Homework Helper

Visit **ClassZone.com** for a lesson review, a flip-card activity, and links to related Web sites.

Activity Rubric

	Content of Rules	Style of Presentation
4	appropriate, thoughtful	well organized, neat
3	appropriate	well organized
2	somewhat appropriate	fairly well organized
1	not appropriate	disorganized

Ancient India • 239

❶ Plan & Prepare

Objectives

- Summarize the religious legacy, including Hinduism and Buddhism, left to the world by ancient India.
- Describe the artistic legacy of the ancient Indians.
- Describe the contributions of the ancient Indians to the field of mathematics.
- **Language Objective:** Categorize information to better understand the legacy of India.

Quick Look

Lesson 4 describes the rich legacy left by the ancient Indians in such areas as religion, art, and mathematics.

❷ Focus & Motivate

Preview Explain that this lesson summarizes some of the major contributions that the great civilizations of ancient India made to world thought and culture. Ask students to think about how the ideas and inventions of the ancient Indians continue to enrich the world today.

Introduce the Main Ideas The three main ideas relate to the Big Idea "Ways of living change as humans interact with each other." Help students look for this Big Idea as you go through the lesson.

Reading Skill: Categorizing Tell students that categorizing is a skill for organizing information. Sorting information into categories can help students see relationships and patterns in information.

SAMPLE ANSWERS FOR ORGANIZER

Legacy of India		
Religion	Arts	Mathematics
Hinduism	*Bhagavad Gita*	Hindu-Arabic numerals
Buddhism	architecture	decimal system

Lesson 4

▶ **MAIN IDEAS**

❶ **Belief Systems** Hinduism and Buddhism are practiced in countries besides India and have also influenced people of other faiths.

❷ **Culture** The artistic styles of ancient India influenced other cultures and continue to be used today.

❸ **Culture** The decimal system, numerals, and the concept of the zero transformed the ability to do mathematical calculations.

▶ **TAKING NOTES**

Reading Skill: Categorizing To categorize means to sort information. As you read Lesson 4, take notes about the legacy of India. Use a chart like this one to categorize your information.

Legacy of India		
Religion	Arts	Mathematics

 **Skillbuilder Handbook, page R6**

▲ **Mohandas Gandhi** In the early 20th century, Britain ruled India as a colony. Gandhi was one of the men who led the fight against foreign rule, but he practiced *ahimsa* while doing so. He took part only in nonviolent protests.

CALIFORNIA STANDARDS

6.5.7 Discuss important aesthetic and intellectual traditions (e.g., Sanskrit literature, including the *Bhagavad Gita*; medicine; metallurgy; and mathematics, including Hindu-Arabic numerals and the zero).

Framework While Buddhism did not survive on Indian soil, Jainism, which introduced the idea of *ahimsa*, or nonviolence, has continued to play a role in modern India, especially through Gandhi's idea of nonviolent civil disobedience.

CST 1 Students explain how major events are related to one another in time.

HOW TO TEACH THE CALIFORNIA STANDARDS

Standard	Content	Student Question or Activity	Instruction
6.5.7	**Pages 242–243** Explains how Indian arts and mathematics have influenced modern society.	**Page 243** Students explain which of India's legacies has impacted their lives the most.	Discuss with students how mathematics and art touch their lives every day. Mention that students use Arabic numerals both in and out of school, and that they can see art and architecture nearly everywhere.
Framework	**Page 242** Analyzes how Hindu and Buddhist beliefs continue to influence people in India and around the world.	**Page 243** Students identify which Hindu and Buddhist belief inspired modern-day leaders to practice nonviolence.	Ask students whether they have heard a leader stress the importance of choosing peace over violence. Discuss with students why nonviolent protests might be more effective than protests where fighting occurs.
CST 1	**Page 242** Tells how Arab traders brought Indian numerals to the West.	**Page 243** Students explain why Indian numerals became known as Arabic numerals.	Ask students if they have heard of any other number systems. (*Possible answer: Roman numerals*) Explain that the Roman numeral system does not have a number for zero.

The Legacy of India

Build on What You Know In ancient times, trade spread Indian religion and art to other parts of Asia. Indian culture continues to influence our modern world today.

India's Religious Legacy

1 ESSENTIAL QUESTION How did the religions of India affect other cultures?

Yoga is as old as the *Bhagavad Gita* and as new as the yoga classes taught in health clubs. Its popularity shows that the ancient religious traditions of India are still very much alive.

Hinduism and Buddhism Today Four out of five people living in India today are Hindus. Hindus also live in Nepal, Sri Lanka, Malaysia, and many other countries. Also, about 1 million people in the United States practice Hinduism.

Buddhism did not remain strong in India. Not even 1 percent of Indians today are Buddhists. But the religion is popular in Asia, Western Europe, and the United States.

Both Hinduism and Buddhism spread to other lands. Also, many people of other faiths practice meditation and yoga.

Angkor Wat The Hindu temples at Angkor Wat in Cambodia show how Hinduism and Indian artistic styles spread to Southeast Asia. ▼

241

Terms & Names

Mohandas Gandhi a leader who used nonviolence to oppose the British rule of India

Hindu-Arabic numerals the numerals 1–9, which originated in India

❸ Teach

India's Religious Legacy

6.5.7, CST 1

Talk About It

- What does the popularity of yoga today suggest about the impact of Indian culture? *(Ancient Indian traditions are still influential.)*

- **Critical Thinking: Understanding Cause and Effect** How has *ahimsa* affected the United States in the last century? *(Ahimsa influenced Martin Luther King Jr., who used nonviolent protests to gain rights for African Americans in the 1950s and 1960s.)*

California Resources

California Reading Toolkit, L24
California Modified Lesson Plans for English Learners, p. 51
California Daily Standards Practice Transparencies, TT24
California Standards Enrichment Workbook, pp. 77–78
California Online Test Practice
California Test Generator CD-ROM
California Standards Planner and Lesson Plans, L47
California EasyPlanner CD-ROM
California eEdition CD-ROM

LESSON 4 PROGRAM RESOURCES

ON LEVEL

In-Depth Resources: Unit 4
- Reading Skill: Categorizing, p. 6

Formal Assessment
- Lesson Quiz, p. 118

ENGLISH LEARNERS

In-Depth Resources in Spanish
- Reading Skill: Categorizing, p. 56

Modified Lesson Plans for English Learners, p. 51

Reading Study Guide (Spanish), p. 63

Reading Study Guide Audio CD (Spanish)

STRUGGLING READERS

In-Depth Resources: Unit 4
- Reading Skill: Categorizing, p. 6
- Reteaching Activity, p. 20

Reading Toolkit, p. L24

Reading Study Guide, p. 63

Reading Study Guide Audio CD

GIFTED AND TALENTED STUDENTS

Interdisciplinary Projects
- Math, p. 37

INCLUSION

EasyPlanner CD-ROM
- Reading Skill: Categorizing
- Vocabulary Study Guide
- Reteaching Activity

TECHNOLOGY

eEdition CD-ROM

Power Presentations CD-ROM

Critical Thinking Transparencies
- CT30 Categorizing

Test Generator CD-ROM

ClassZone.com

Teach

India's Artistic Legacy

6.5.7, CST 1

Talk About It

- What are two pieces of Indian literature that continue to influence the world today? *(the* Mahabharata *and the* Bhagavad Gita*)*

- What is one example given of how Indian influences can be seen in buildings elsewhere in the world? *(the temple at Angkor Wat)*

- **Critical Thinking: Explaining Historical Patterns** Why do you think Indian artistic contributions had influence beyond India and continue to influence the world today? *(Possible answer: They were used to express Indian religious belief; those religions spread to other cultures, taking the artistic styles along with them.)*

The Legacy of Indian Mathematics

6.5.7, Framework

Talk About It

- What Indian invention do you use in math class every day? *(the numerals 1–9, 0)*

- **Critical Thinking: Summarizing** How would you summarize the Indian contribution to modern-day mathematics? *(Possible answer: The Indian system of numerals and decimals is the basis for much of the mathematics practiced today.)*

Hindu and Buddhist Influences In the mid-1900s, Indian leader **Mohandas Gandhi** (MOH•huhn•DAHS GAHN•dee) used *ahimsa* (nonviolence) in his fight against British rule. His life inspired U.S. civil rights leader Martin Luther King Jr. In the 1950s and 1960s, King led nonviolent protests to gain rights for African Americans.

Today Hindu and Buddhist influences continue. For example, millions of people from other religions meditate and practice yoga.

> **REVIEW** Which of India's original religions remains most popular in India? Hinduism

▲ **Dance of the** *Ramayana* Indian culture has strongly influenced Southeast Asia. This dancer in Thailand is performing a piece from an Indian epic called the *Ramayana*.

India's Artistic Legacy

2 ESSENTIAL QUESTION How have the Indian arts influenced other cultures?

People in other cultures read Indian epics and act in dramas based on them. Indian artistic and architectural styles have influenced other cultures, such as those in Southeast Asia.

The arts of India have strongly influenced the world. For example, in many Southeast Asian nations, people perform plays based on the ancient Sanskrit epic the *Mahabharata*. The *Bhagavad Gita* has been translated into many languages and is read around the world.

Indian art and architecture have shaped other cultures. For example, ancient Indian artists developed visual symbols to show the Buddha's holiness. These symbols include features such as a topknot of hair. Artists have used such symbols to portray the Buddha ever since. In northwestern Cambodia, ancient builders erected a large Hindu temple called Angkor Wat. Indian influences are seen in the design of those temples.

> **REVIEW** What types of Indian art have influenced other societies? literature, dance, sculpture, architecture

The Legacy of Indian Mathematics

3 ESSENTIAL QUESTION How does the mathematical knowledge of ancient India affect our lives today? We use Hindu-Arabic numerals, the decimal system, and the concept of zero, all of which were developed in India.

The numerals we use originated in India. People in India have been using the numerals for 1 to 9 for more than 2,000 years. Arab traders brought these numerals to the West. As a result, we call them Arabic numerals, or **Hindu-Arabic numerals**.

DIFFERENTIATING INSTRUCTION

Inclusion

Use the Graphic Organizer
Reproduce the Categorizing graphic organizer on page 240. Have pairs of students read the lesson and work together to add information to the organizer. Invite each pair to review and discuss their organizer.

English Learners

Categorize Information
Explain to students that they will group the things they read about into three categories: *Religion, Arts,* and *Mathematics.* Ask students to skim the text to locate details about religion. Chart student responses. Guide students as they identify other details from the text for the other categories. Chart their responses. Read the details you wrote on the chart that were shared by students.

The number system first developed in India and used today is called the decimal system. The name comes from the Latin word *decem,* which means "ten." In a number such as 5,555, each numeral is worth ten times as much as the numeral to its right. The place of a numeral—the ones place, the tens place, the hundreds place, and so on—tells how much that numeral is worth.

The decimal system would not work without a symbol for zero. It would be impossible to write a number like 504 without some way to show that the tens place was empty. In India, the use of the zero goes back about 1,400 years.

REVIEW How does the zero make the decimal system possible? It provides a way to show when a place is empty.

Lesson Summary
- Hinduism and Buddhism are major world religions.
- Indian literature and art shaped other cultures.
- Without the zero, the way we do mathematical calculations would be impossible.

Why It Matters Now . . .
Every day you use at least ten things that were invented in India. You can count on it!

4 Lesson Review

Homework Helper
ClassZone.com

Terms & Names
1. Explain the importance of
Mohandas Gandhi   Hindu-Arabic numerals

Using Your Notes
Categorizing Use your completed chart to answer the following question:
2. Which of India's legacies has made the biggest impact on your life? Explain. (6.5.7)

Legacy of India		
Religion	Arts	Mathematics

Main Ideas
3. What ancient Hindu and Buddhist practice inspired both Mohandas Gandhi and Martin Luther King Jr.? (Framework)
4. Which ancient Indian arts influenced Southeast Asian culture? (6.5.7)
5. What number system did Indian mathematicians invent? (6.5.7)

Critical Thinking
6. **Making Generalizations** What are three main ways Indian religion, art, music, literature, and dance reached the rest of the world? (HI 2)
7. **Explaining Sequence** How did Indian numerals come to be called Arabic numerals? (CST 1)

Activity

Making a Travel Poster Research one of the Indian legacies you learned about. Advertise it on a travel poster about "Old and New India." (6.5.7)

Ancient India • 243

④ Assess & Reteach

Assess Place students in groups of equal size, and have the students in each group number off. Ask a question from the Lesson Review, and allow group members to agree on an answer. Then call out a number for a person from each group to give the group's answer.

 Formal Assessment
- Lesson Quiz, p. 118

Reteach Divide the class into three groups. Assign each group one of the subsections in this lesson—"India's Religious Legacy," "India's Artistic Legacy," or "The Legacy of Indian Mathematics." Each group should work together to list two or three of the most important ideas in its section. Have groups share their responses with the class. Make sure that each group takes notes on the information shared by the other groups.

 In-Depth Resources: Unit 4
- Vocabulary Cards, p. 11
- Reteaching Activity, p. 20

Homework Helper

Visit **ClassZone.com** for a lesson review, a flip-card activity, and links to related Web sites.

4 Lesson Review Answers

Terms & Names
1. • Mohandas Gandhi, p. 242
 • Hindu-Arabic numerals, p. 242

Using Your Notes
See page 240 for an example of a completed organizer.
2. Possible answers: numerals and zero, because students use them every day

Main Ideas
3. *ahimsa,* or nonviolence
4. literature, dance, art, and architecture
5. the decimal system

Critical Thinking
6. Possible answers: trade, missionaries, books, pictures, Indian leaders, teachers
7. Arab traders learned the numerals in India and introduced them to Europeans, who named the numerals for the people who introduced them.

Activity Rubric

	Content of Poster	Style of Poster
4	thorough; multiple examples of legacy	well organized, neat
3	several examples of legacy	well organized
2	few examples of legacy	not well organized
1	no examples of legacy	disorganized

Ancient India • 243

Objectives

- Describe some health practices of ancient India.
- Explain how those practices affect people today.
- Synthesize information from visuals and text, and use that information in discussion and writing.
- **Language Objective:** Preview the text, formulate purpose-setting questions, and answer questions.

❶ Focus & Motivate

Preview Have students discuss how they think their lives might be different from the lives of people who lived in ancient India. Tell them that these pages will explore how their lives today may in fact be touched by some of the practices developed in ancient India.

❷ Teach

Talk About It

- Ask students if they or anyone they know has ever practiced yoga or meditation. Have students discuss how familiar they are with the concept of yoga and its practice. Invite volunteers to demonstrate or name poses or practices they associate with yoga.

- Have students review the illustrations of the herbs and other substances pictured at the top of page 245. How comfortable would they be using medicines like these as part of treatment for a disease? What is their familiarity with herbal treatments and other alternatives to Western medicine?

- Explain to students that vegetarianism is practiced by many people in this country. Ask students what some of the reasons are that people practice this sort of diet. *(Possible answers: respect for animals, a belief that vegetarianism is healthier)*

- **Critical Thinking: Making Inferences** How have ancient Indian practices survived and affected the modern world? *(Possible answers: Some traces of ancient Indian practices are a common part of our lives today, though their original forms and purposes have changed significantly.)*

Research Links
ClassZone.com

Indian Health Practices

Purpose: To learn about ancient Indian medicine

Magazines often feature articles that give health tips. It's a popular subject. In recent years, such articles have focused on diet and exercise. Today a person who eats vegetarian food, practices yoga, and uses scented oils to produce a calm atmosphere is considered modern. But these are not new ideas about how to live a healthy life. Each of them dates back to ancient India.

CALIFORNIA STANDARDS
6.5.7 Discuss important aesthetic and intellectual traditions (e.g. Sanskrit literature, including the *Bhagavad Gita*; medicine; metallurgy; and mathematics, including Hindu-Arabic numerals and the zero.)

Yoga

▶ **Past** This 3,500-year-old seal from Mohenjo-Daro shows a man meditating in a yoga pose. The word *yoga* means "joining" or "union." The purpose of yoga is to help humans unite with the supreme force of the universe. Yoga includes many practices, including exercise, breathing techniques, meditation, and service to others.

▶ **Present** The form of yoga that most Americans know is an exercise routine that consists of practicing certain poses. Each pose is designed to promote balance and to help energy flow through the body in certain ways. In recent decades, this form of yoga has become one of the most popular types of exercise in the United States.

244 • Chapter 7

DIFFERENTIATING INSTRUCTION

Struggling Readers

Make a T-Chart
Have students take the information on this page and organize it in a T-chart. Have them draw a vertical line on a sheet of paper to create two columns. At the top of one column, have them write *Past,* and at the top of the other, have them write *Today*. Students should then look for details in each segment to include in their T-chart, and list the information in the appropriate column.

English Learners

Create and Answer Questions
Have students predict what they think they will learn based on the title, headings, subheadings, and pictures. Then have them formulate *Who? What? When? Where?* and *Why?* questions about the subjects covered. Tell students they must listen for the answers to these questions as you help them read the text. To conclude, have students ask and respond to the questions.

Ayurvedic Medicine

▼ **Past** This ancient system of medicine teaches that each person is made of five elements—space, air, fire, water, and earth—but the combinations differ. As a result, everyone is unique and must have unique remedies. An Ayurvedic physician tries to bring the five elements into a better balance. Remedies include cleansing treatments, special diets, herbs and spices like those below, and oils with healing fragrances.

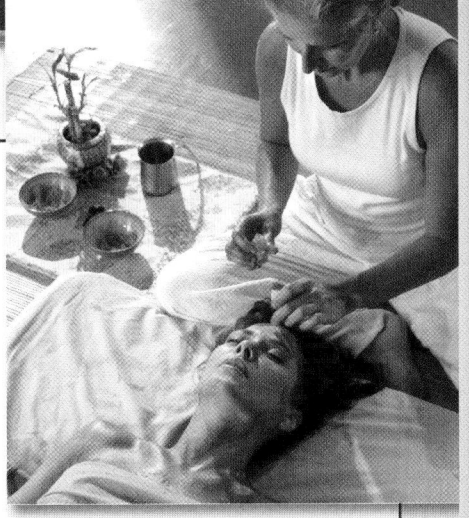

▲ **Present** Today some people use Ayurvedic treatments in addition to Western medicine. For example, this woman is having her forehead massaged with healing oil.

Vegetarianism

▼ **Past** Since ancient times, Hindus have believed that some animals—such as the cow—are sacred. More generally, they believe that animals also share in the universal life force. Because they respect this life force, devout Hindus do not eat meat.

▶ **Present** Indian cooking features a wide variety of vegetarian dishes. Common foods are rice and *dals* (a type of lentils). Some foods are highly spiced. This meal is being served on banana leaves.

More About . . .

Yoga

The popular image of yoga as a form of physical exercise or discipline reflects one part of this complex and multifaceted art. Yoga's richness and complexity is partly a function of its long history. The first written appearance of the word *yoga* is in the Vedic texts of the Brahmans. Over time, through the development of the Hindu religion, the meaning and practice of yoga changed, stressing at various times a spiritual focus and at other times a physical focus. These different traditions have helped produce the wide variety of yoga practices seen today.

More About . . .

Indian Cooking

For many people in this country, Indian food is synonymous with the word *curry*. In fact, curry is a catch-all term for a wide variety of sauces and cooking styles used in India and throughout Asia. Though one can purchase something called "curry powder" in the supermarket, curry is not a single spice but a blend of many different spices. In addition, it represents only one conception of what curry should be and how it should taste.

In India, the dishes we call curries range from mild to very spicy. They feature such herbs as cardamom, cumin, coriander, and turmeric. Many other herbs may be added to this base, depending on the dish.

Activities

1. **TALK ABOUT IT** Why do you think yoga has become so popular in the United States?
2. **WRITE ABOUT IT** Use books or the Internet to find out how to eat enough protein on a vegetarian diet. Write a brief explanation of how to do this. (Writing 2.2)

Ancient India • 245

ACTIVITIES ANSWERS

1. **TALK ABOUT IT** Possible answers: It offers a wide range of benefits, from the physical to the spiritual. It can be practiced in a variety of ways, which allows many people to take part.

2. **WRITE ABOUT IT**

2. Writing Rubric

	Content of Explanation	Number of Errors
4	thorough; complete information about protein in a vegetarian diet	accurate spelling, grammar, and punctuation
3	nearly complete information about protein in a vegetarian diet	fairly accurate spelling, grammar, and punctuation
2	some information about protein in a vegetarian diet	somewhat accurate spelling, grammar, and punctuation
1	little or no information about protein in a vegetarian diet	little accurate spelling, grammar, and punctuation

Terms & Names

1. Both terms refer to mountain ranges that form a natural barrier for the Indian subcontinent.

2. The religion of *Brahmanism* and the class system of *caste* were both part of Aryan culture.

3. Every *Buddhist* hopes to achieve *nirvana*, which means the end of suffering.

4. *Mohandas Gandhi* preached *ahimsa*, a practice of non-violence common to Hinduism and Buddhism.

Main Ideas

Geography and Indian Life
(pages 218–225)

5. They bring warm moist air from the southwest, carrying rain for the fields.

6. near the Indus River

The Origins of Hinduism
(pages 226–231)

7. Aryan culture blended with Dravidian culture to create a complex Indian culture.

8. Hindus believe that the many different gods are part of one supreme God.

Buddhism and India's Golden Age
(pages 232–239)

9. The Four Noble Truths are: 1. People suffer because their minds are uneasy; 2. That condition comes from wanting what one doesn't have or wanting life to be different; 3. People can stop suffering by not wanting; 4. People can stop wanting by following the Eightfold Path.

10. Artists, scientists, and mathematicians made great advances and created lasting works.

The Legacy of India
(pp. 240–245)

11. The practice of *ahimsa* and the example of Gandhi influenced Martin Luther King Jr.

12. It made modern mathematics possible.

VISUAL SUMMARY

Ancient India

Geography (6.5.1)
- The first Indian civilization arose near the Indus and Saraswati rivers.
- Monsoons, or seasonal winds, affect India's climate.

Government (6.5.6)
- Chandragupta Maurya ruled harshly. He used spies, his army, and many officials.
- Asoka tried to rule peacefully, influenced by Buddhism.

Belief Systems (6.5.3, 6.5.5)
- Hinduism is a religion that worships God in many forms and believes in reincarnation.
- Buddhism teaches people to follow a middle way according to the Eightfold Path.

Culture (6.5.7)
- Indian artistic styles spread to other regions of Asia.
- Indians invented the zero, Hindu-Arabic numerals, and the decimal system. They were skilled metal workers.

TERMS & NAMES

Explain why the words in each set below are linked with each other.

1. **Himalayas** and **Hindu Kush**
2. **caste** and **Brahmanism**
3. **Buddhism** and **nirvana**
4. **Mohandas Gandhi** and *ahimsa*

MAIN IDEAS

Geography and Indian Life (pages 218–225)
5. Why do Indian farmers depend on the summer monsoons? (6.5.1)
6. By what body of water were Harappa and Mohenjo-Daro, two of ancient India's large cities, located? (6.5.1)

The Origins of Hinduism (pages 226–231)
7. What cultural impact did the Aryan migrations have on India? (6.5.2)
8. How does Hinduism differ from many religions that worship many gods? (6.5.3)

Buddhism and India's Golden Age (pages 232–239)
9. What are the Four Noble Truths? (6.5.5)
10. Why was the reign of Chandra Gupta II considered India's golden age? (6.5.7)

The Legacy of India (pages 240–245)
11. How did a Hindu belief influence the U.S. civil rights movement? (6.5.7)
12. What makes the Indian idea of the zero so important? (6.5.7)

CRITICAL THINKING Big Ideas: Culture

13. **UNDERSTANDING EFFECT** How did the caste system maintain social order? (6.5.4)
14. **ANALYZING ECONOMIC AND POLITICAL ISSUES** In what way was the caste system related to economic status? (6.5.4)
15. **MAKING INFERENCES** How do you think the Buddha felt about the caste system? Why? (6.5.5)

ALTERNATIVE ASSESSMENT RUBRICS

1. Writing Rubric

	Content of Paragraph	Number of Errors
4	many persuasive reasons, accurate refutation of opposing point of view	few or none
3	some reasons, some refutation	some
2	few reasons, little refutation	many
1	little or no reasons, little or no refutation	many major

2. Math Rubric

	Content of Poster	Number of Errors
4	accurate content, many examples of decimal places	few or none
3	mostly accurate content, several examples	some
2	somewhat inaccurate content, few examples	many
1	many inaccuracies	many and major

ALTERNATIVE ASSESSMENT

1. WRITING ACTIVITY Mohandas Gandhi opposed the caste system and worked to end its influence in India. Write a persuasive paragraph to try to convince the Indian government to fight against the traditional caste system. (Writing 2.5)

2. INTERDISCIPLINARY ACTIVITY— MATH Research the places in the decimal system. Learn the name for as many high numbers as you can: million, billion, trillion, and so on. Make a poster showing the names for these numbers and how they are written: For example, 1 million is written 1,000,000. (6.5.7)

3. STARTING WITH A STORY Review the essay you wrote about the Saraswati River disaster. Draw an editorial cartoon to persuade others to follow your suggestion. (6.5.1)

Technology Activity

4. DESIGNING A WEB PAGE
Use the Internet and the library to find out more about Buddhism in the United States. Then design a Web page using pictures, maps, or graphs to convey the information. (6.5.5)
- Which immigrant groups in the United States practice Buddhism?
- In what states or regions are the most Buddhists to be found?
- What is Zen Buddhism?
- What other forms of Buddhism are practiced in the United States?

Research Links ClassZone.com

Reading a Map
Use the map below to answer the questions. (6.5.5)

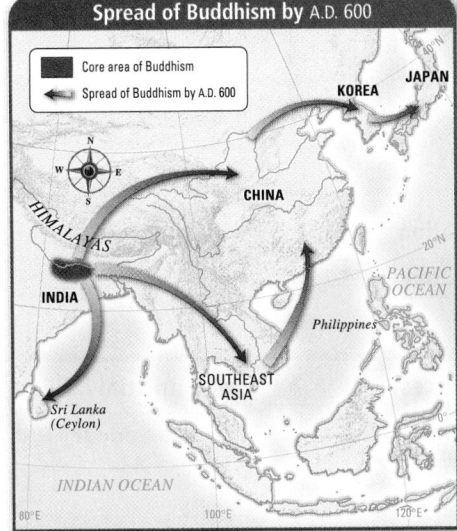
Spread of Buddhism by A.D. 600

- Core area of Buddhism
- Spread of Buddhism by A.D. 600

KOREA, JAPAN, CHINA, HIMALAYAS, INDIA, PACIFIC OCEAN, Philippines, SOUTHEAST ASIA, Sri Lanka (Ceylon), INDIAN OCEAN

1. Where did Buddhism originate?
- A. southern India
- B. northern China
- C. northwestern Korea
- D. northeastern India

2. What is the farthest place from India that Buddhism had spread by A.D. 600?
- A. China
- B. Japan
- C. Korea
- D. Sri Lanka

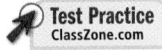
Test Practice ClassZone.com

Additional Test Practice, pp. S1–S33

Critical Thinking

Big Ideas: Culture

13. Possible answer: Each caste knew its place in society and what was expected of it.

14. Possible answer: The four broad castes were based on social class, and generally the higher social classes had more wealth. The castes were also subdivided into smaller groups according to job, which is an economic category.

15. Possible answer: The Buddha came from a wealthy, higher caste family, but money and status did not bring him happiness. After he achieved enlightenment, he taught people to live in moderation and to learn not to desire too much. Therefore, he probably opposed the caste system because it ranked people based on what they did for a living.

Standards–Based Assessment

1. The correct answer is D. The map locates the core area of Buddhism there.

2. The correct answer is B. The area touched by arrows that is the furthest from India is Japan.

Research Links
Visit **ClassZone.com** for links to Web sites that can be used in the newsletter.

Test Practice
Visit **ClassZone.com** to access strategies and tutorials for taking standardized tests.

📝 **Formal Assessment**
- Chapter Tests, Forms A, B, and C, pp. 119–133

💿 **Test Generator**
- Chapter Tests, Forms A, B, and C (English and Spanish)

ALTERNATIVE ASSESSMENT RUBRICS

3. Starting with a Story Rubric

	Content of Cartoon	Effectiveness of Style
4	very persuasive; neatly drawn	well drawn, clear
3	persuasive; adequately drawn	mostly clear
2	somewhat persuasive, messily drawn	somewhat clear
1	not persuasive; sloppily drawn	unclear

4. Technology Rubric

	Elements of Web page	Style of Presentation
4	covers all four questions	attractive, creative
3	covers three questions	creative
2	covers two questions	somewhat creative
1	covers less than two questions	dull

CHAPTER 8 PLANNING GUIDE: Ancient China

Chapter Overview	Copymasters		Assessment

Chapter Overview

Ancient China was influenced by geography, unique philosophies, and powerful dynasties.

Copymasters

In-Depth Resources: Unit 4
- Family Newsletter (English and Spanish), pp. 22–23
- Visual Summary, p. 28
- Vocabulary Study Guide, p. 30

Character Education

Reading Study Guide, p. 75

Bringing Social Studies Alive, Chapter 8

Document-Based Questions: Strategy and Practice

Reading Toolkit, L25–L28

Modified Lesson Plans for English Learners, pp. 53–60

Assessment

Chapter Review, pp. 282–283

Formal Assessment
- Chapter Tests, Forms A, B, and C, pp. 138–149

Test Generator

Integrated Assessment Book

Online Test Practice

LESSON 1

Geography Shapes Life in Ancient China

pp. 252–257

OBJECTIVE Trace the effects of China's geography on the development of civilization.

In-Depth Resources: Unit 4
- Reading Skill: Explaining Geographic Patterns, p. 24
- Vocabulary Cards, p. 31
- Reteaching Activity, p. 37

Reading Study Guide, p. 67

Interdisciplinary Projects
- Math, p. 43

Lesson Review, p. 257

Formal Assessment
- Lesson Quiz, p. 134

California Daily Standards Practice Transparencies, TT25

LESSON 2

China's Ancient Philosophies

pp. 258–265

OBJECTIVE Examine how distinctive philosophies shaped ancient Chinese civilization.

In-Depth Resources: Unit 4
- Reading Skill: Comparing, p. 25
- Vocabulary Cards, p. 31
- Skillbuilder Practice: Cost Benefit Analysis, p. 29
- Literature: Dao DeJing, by Laozi, p. 36

- Primary Source: Teachings, by Confucius, p. 35
- Reteaching Activity, p. 38

Interdisciplinary Projects
- Language Arts, p. 45

Reading Study Guide, p. 69

Lesson Review, p. 263

Formal Assessment
- Lesson Quiz, p. 135

California Daily Standards Practice Transparencies, TT26

LESSON 3

The Qin and the Han

pp. 266–275

OBJECTIVE Explore the development of Qin and Han China.

In-Depth Resources: Unit 4
- Reading Skill: Comparing and Contrasting, p. 26
- Vocabulary Cards, p. 31
- Geography Practice: The Great Wall, p. 33
- Reteaching Activity, p. 39

History Makers
- Wudi, p. 15

Interdisciplinary Projects
- Physical Education, p. 46

Reading Study Guide, p. 71

Lesson Review, p. 271

Formal Assessment
- Lesson Quiz, p. 136

California Daily Standards Practice Transparencies, TT27

LESSON 4

The Legacy of Ancient China

pp. 276–281

OBJECTIVE Study the cultural legacy of ancient China.

In-Depth Resources: Unit 4
- Reading Skill: Categorizing, p. 27
- Vocabulary Cards, p. 31
- Reteaching Activity, p. 40

Interdisciplinary Projects
- Science, p. 44

Reading Study Guide, p. 73

Lesson Review, p. 280

Formal Assessment
- Lesson Quiz, p. 137

California Daily Standards Practice Transparencies, TT28

Integrated Technology

 eEdition Plus Online

EasyPlanner Plus Online

eTest Plus Online

 Audio CDs
- Reading Study Guide
- Reading Study Guide in Spanish
- The World's Music

 CD-ROMs
- Power Presentations
- eEdition
- EasyPlanner
- Test Generator

 Ancient Civilizations Video Series
- Ancient China

---

 eEdition CD-ROM

 Map Transparencies
- MT15 Agricultural Regions of China

 Humanities Transparencies
- HT15 Shang Bronze Elephant

 Critical Thinking Transparencies
- CT32 Explaining Geographic Patterns

 ClassZone.com

---

 eEdition CD-ROM

 Critical Thinking Transparencies
- CT33 Comparing and Contrasting

 ClassZone.com

---

 eEdition CD-ROM

 Humanities Transparencies
- HT16 Women Ironing Silk

 Critical Thinking Transparencies
- CT34 Comparing and Contrasting

 ClassZone.com

---

 eEdition CD-ROM

 Map Transparencies
- MT16 World Known to the Romans and the Chinese, A.D. 100

 Critical Thinking Transparencies
- CT35 Categorizing
- CT36 Chapter 8 Visual Summary

 ClassZone.com

Overview of California Resources

	Lesson 1	Lesson 2	Lesson 3	Lesson 4
California Reading Toolkit	L25	L26	L27	L28
California Modified Lesson Plans for English Learners	p. 53	p. 55	p. 57	p. 59
California Daily Standards Practice Transparencies	TT25	TT26	TT27	TT28
California Standards Enrichment Workbook	pp. 79–82	pp. 83–86	pp. 87–90	pp. 83–84, 91–94
California Standards Planner and Lesson Plans	L49	L51	L53	L55
California Online Test Practice	ClassZone.com	ClassZone.com	ClassZone.com	ClassZone.com
California Test Generator CD-ROM				
California EasyPlanner CD-ROM				
California eEdition CD-ROM				

Chart Key

 **PE** Pupil Edition

 Copymaster

CD-ROM

Audio

Video

Internet

Overhead Transparency

PREVIEWING RESOURCES FOR DIFFERENTIATED INSTRUCTION

English Learners

In-Depth Resources in Spanish
- Reading Skill and Strategy
- Skillbuilder Practice **B**
- Geography Practice
- Vocabulary Study Guide

In-Depth Resources: Unit 4
- Family Newsletter (English and Spanish) **C**

Reading Study Guide (Spanish) **A**

Reading Study Guide Audio CD
(Spanish)

Test Generator
Chapter Test (Spanish)

Plus

Modified Lesson Plans for English Learners

Multi-Language Glossary of Social Studies Terms

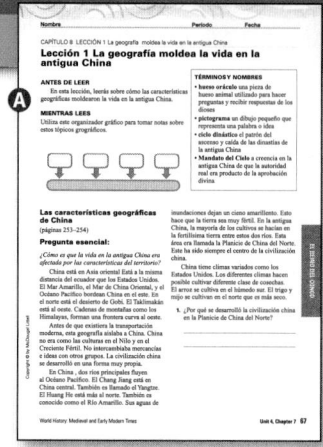

Struggling Readers

In-Depth Resources: Unit 4
- Vocabulary Study Guide **B**
- Skillbuilder Practice **C**
- Geography Practice
- Reteaching Activities **A**
- Family Newsletter

Reading Study Guide

Reading Study Guide Audio CD

Reading Toolkit

Formal Assessment
Chapter Test, Form A

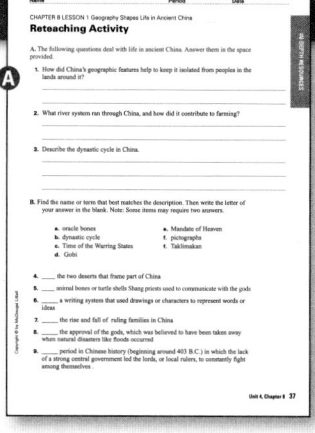
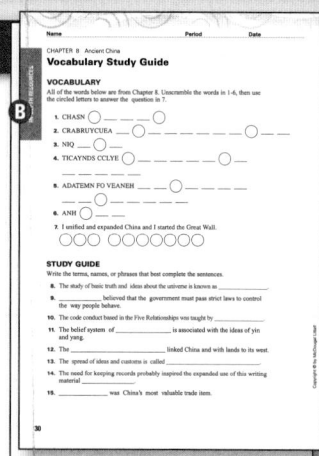

Inclusion

EasyPlanner CD-ROM
- Reading Skill and Strategy **B**
- Vocabulary Study Guide **C**
- Geography Practice
- Reteaching Activities **A**

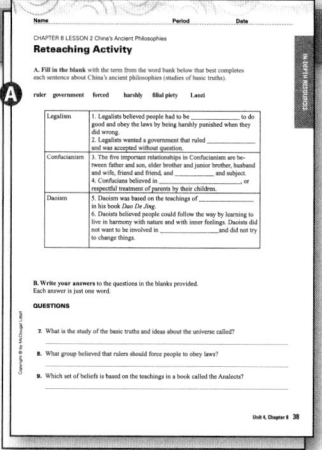
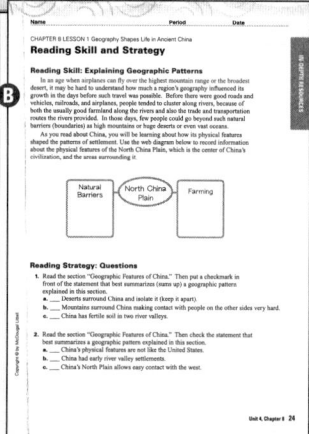

Gifted and Talented Students

In-Depth Resources: Unit 4
- Primary Source
- Literature **A**

History Makers **B**

Interdisciplinary Projects **C**

Formal Assessment
Chapter Test, Form C

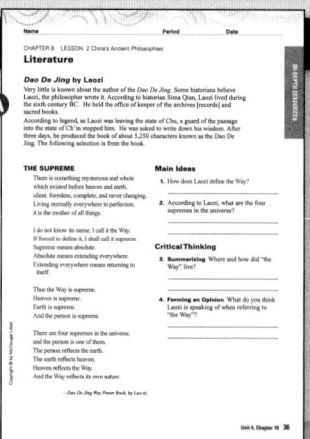

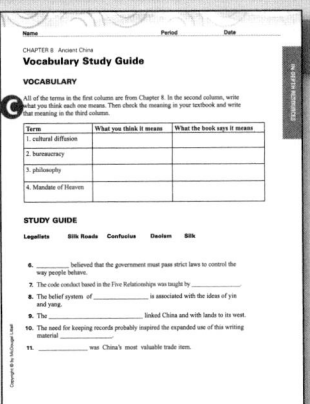

Activities in the Teacher's Edition for English Learners

- Make a Human Map of China, p. 256
- Categorize Key Terms, p. 261
- Define Multiple-Meaning Words, p. 269
- Review Vocabulary, p. 273
- Formulate Questions, p. 278

Activities in the Teacher's Edition for Struggling Readers

- Diagram the Content, p. 255
- Divide and Conquer, p. 262
- Break Down the Paragraphs, p. 264
- Focus on Vocabulary, p. 270
- Diagram the Pits, p. 274
- Illustrate the Content, p. 279

Activities in the Teacher's Edition for Inclusion Students

- Enlarge Images, p. 256
- Take Audio Notes, p. 261
- Stage a Debate, p. 264
- Practice Remembering, p. 269
- List Inventions and Discoveries, p. 278

Activities in the Teacher's Edition for Gifted and Talented Students

- Profile a Shang or Zhou Ruler, p. 255
- Diagram Confucian and Daoist Ideas, p. 262
- Propose "Men of Han" Illustrations, p. 270
- Report on Shi Huangdi's Military, p. 273
- Create a Qin Art Gallery, p. 274
- Catalog Chinese Inventions, p. 279

Integrated Technology

eEdition CD-ROM

- Interactive Visuals
- Interactive Maps
- Starting with a Story

ClassZone.com

- WebQuests
- Research Links
- Internet Activities
- Homework Helper
- Chapter Quiz
- Current Events
- Test Practice

Power Presentations CD-ROM

- Lecture Notes
- Media Gallery
- Chapter Review Game

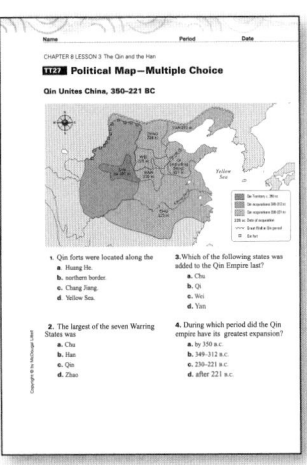

Critical Thinking Transparencies

- CT32 Explaining Geographic Patterns
- CT33 Comparing and Contrasting
- CT34 Comparing and Contrasting
- CT35 Categorizing
- CT36 Chapter 8 Visual Summary

California Daily Standards Practice Transparencies, TT25–TT28

Map Transparencies

- MT15 Agricultural Regions of China
- MT16 World Known to the Romans and the Chinese, A.D. 100

Humanities Transparencies

- HT15 Shang Bronze Elephant
- HT16 Women Ironing Silk

Test Generator CD-ROM

EasyPlanner CD-ROM

Ancient Civilizations Video Series

- Ancient China

Begin the Chapter

Objective

Analyze the geographic, political, economic, religious, and social structures of ancient Chinese civilization.

Quick Look

Lesson 1 explores the basic geography of China and how that geography affected the development of ancient civilization there.

Lesson 2 traces the development of the distinctive philosophies that influenced ancient China.

Lesson 3 analyzes the emergence of the Qin and Han Dynasties in ancient China.

Lesson 4 describes the rich cultural legacy of ancient China.

Before You Read: Predicting

Predicting is a means of setting a purpose for reading. It involves taking prior knowledge about geography and history and using it to identify possible points of discussion in the upcoming reading. This can help students focus on what they will learn.

Have students follow these steps:

- Read the "Before You Read" instructions and follow the steps.

- As students formulate their three questions, suggest they think about other religions or belief systems they have read about in other chapters.

- Encourage students to check for answers as they read the chapter.

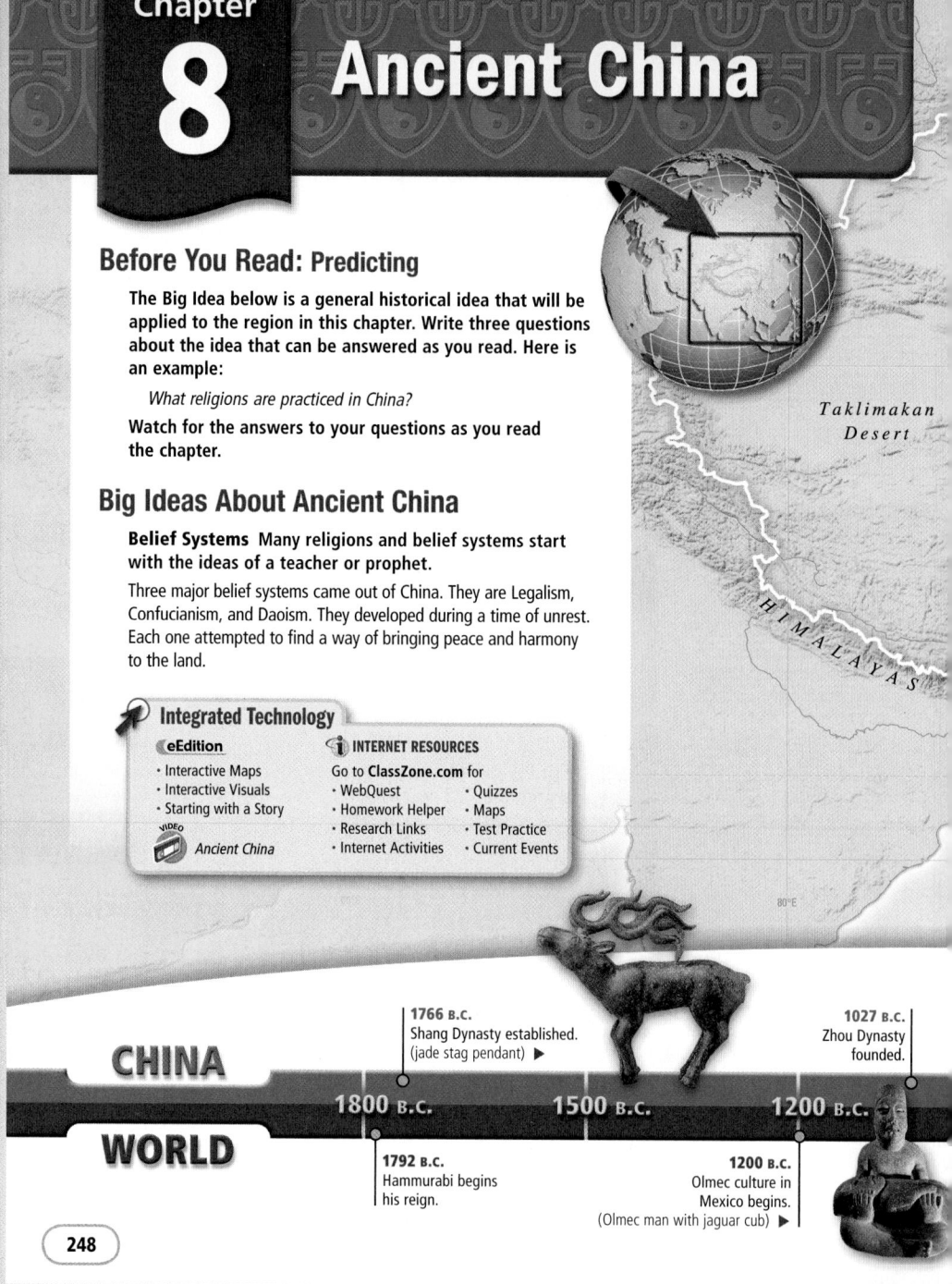

Chapter 8 Ancient China

Before You Read: Predicting

The Big Idea below is a general historical idea that will be applied to the region in this chapter. Write three questions about the idea that can be answered as you read. Here is an example:

What religions are practiced in China?

Watch for the answers to your questions as you read the chapter.

Big Ideas About Ancient China

Belief Systems Many religions and belief systems start with the ideas of a teacher or prophet.

Three major belief systems came out of China. They are Legalism, Confucianism, and Daoism. They developed during a time of unrest. Each one attempted to find a way of bringing peace and harmony to the land.

Integrated Technology

eEdition
- Interactive Maps
- Interactive Visuals
- Starting with a Story

VIDEO *Ancient China*

INTERNET RESOURCES
Go to **ClassZone.com** for
- WebQuest
- Homework Helper
- Research Links
- Internet Activities
- Quizzes
- Maps
- Test Practice
- Current Events

Taklimakan Desert

HIMALAYAS

CHINA

1766 B.C.
Shang Dynasty established.
(jade stag pendant) ▶

1027 B.C.
Zhou Dynasty founded.

1800 B.C.   1500 B.C.   1200 B.C.

WORLD

1792 B.C.
Hammurabi begins his reign.

1200 B.C.
Olmec culture in Mexico begins.
(Olmec man with jaguar cub) ▶

248

TIME LINE DISCUSSION

Use the time line to help students develop a mental time frame for the civilization of ancient China and to preview information that will be covered in the chapter.

- What was the first dynasty to emerge in ancient China? *(the Shang Dynasty)*

- Based on this time line, what general statement can you make about how long a dynasty lasted? *(Dynasties lasted several hundred years.)*

- During which dynasty did Confucius live? *(the Zhou Dynasty)*

- Name one emperor who ruled in China after the establishment of the Roman Empire. *(Liu Bang)*

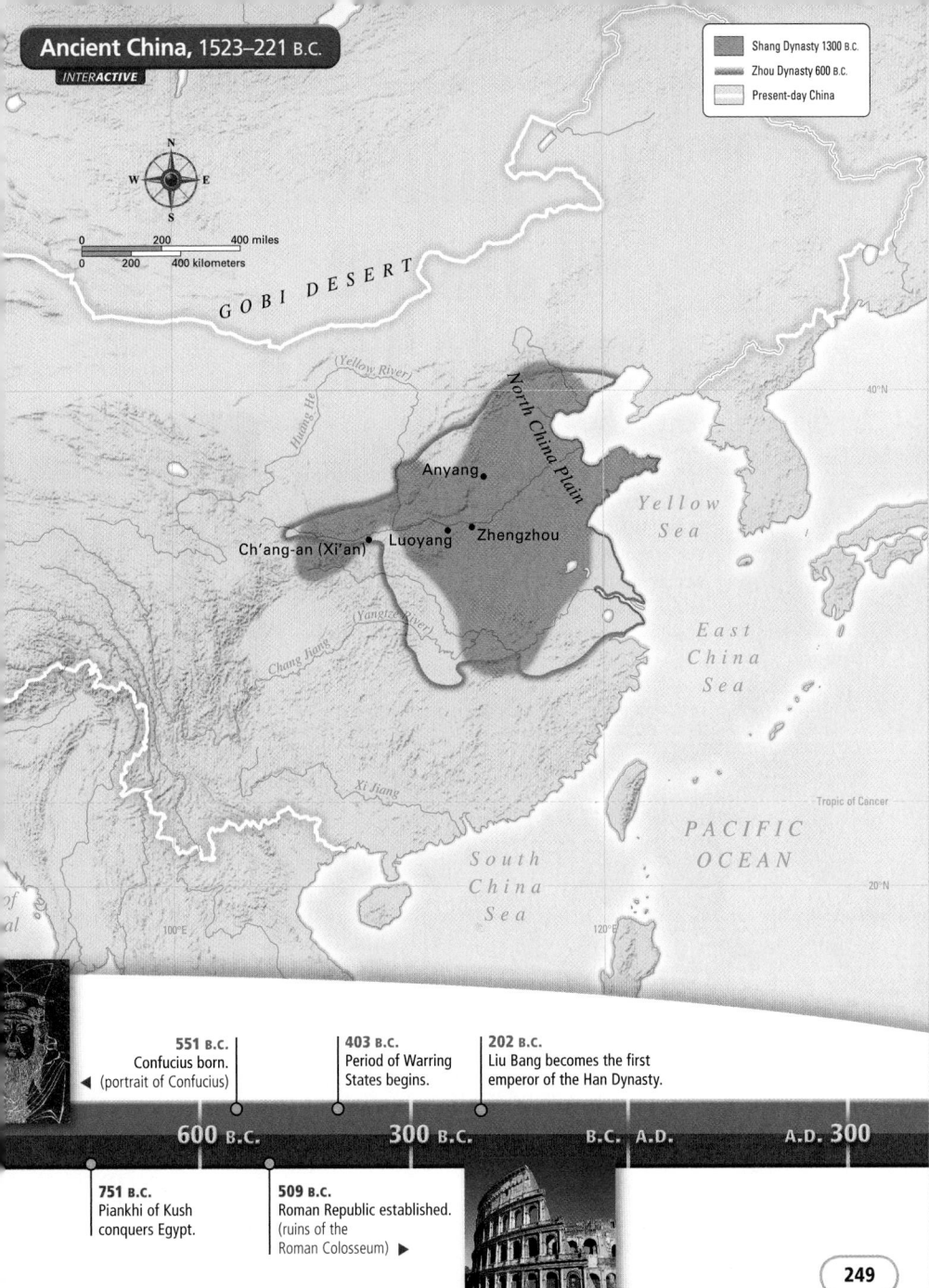

Ancient China, 1523–221 B.C.

INTERACTIVE

Shang Dynasty 1300 B.C.
Zhou Dynasty 600 B.C.
Present-day China

N W E S

0   200   400 miles
0   200   400 kilometers

GOBI DESERT

(Yellow River)

Huang He

North China Plain

Anyang

Ch'ang-an (Xi'an) • Luoyang • Zhengzhou

Yellow Sea

East China Sea

Chang Jiang

(Yangtze River)

Xi Jiang

South China Sea

PACIFIC OCEAN

Tropic of Cancer

40°N

20°N

100°E   120°E

551 B.C.
Confucius born.
◄ (portrait of Confucius)

403 B.C.
Period of Warring
States begins.

202 B.C.
Liu Bang becomes the first
emperor of the Han Dynasty.

600 B.C.   **300 B.C.**   **B.C. A.D.**   **A.D. 300**

751 B.C.
Piankhi of Kush
conquers Egypt.

509 B.C.
Roman Republic established.
(ruins of the
Roman Colosseum) ►

249

RECOMMENDED RESOURCES

Books for the Teacher
Debaine-Francfort, Corinne.
***Discoveries: Search for
Ancient China.*** New York:
Harry N. Abrams, 1999.
Archaeological record of
ancient China.

Loewe, Michael, and Edward L.
Shaughnessy. ***The Cambridge
History of Ancient China:
From the Origins of
Civilization to 221*** B.C.
Cambridge: Cambridge UP,
1999. Part of a multi volume
history of China.

Videos
Chinese. 45 minutes.
Wheeling: Film Ideas, Inc.,
2004. Video exploration of
ancient Chinese civilization.

DVDs
The Silk Road. Three DVDs
totaling 600 minutes. New
York: Central Park Media, 2000.
Film tour of the ancient and
historic places of China and the
Silk Road.

Internet
To access these sites, visit the
Research Links for this chapter
at **ClassZone.com**

**Washington State
University.** This site has
an extensive collection of
information on ancient Chinese
history.

The University of Evansville.
"Exploring Ancient World
Cultures" page includes a
number of essays and resources
on ancient China.

Introduce the Big Ideas

Read aloud the text about the Big Ideas. Have
students think about how, during difficult times,
belief systems may change to meet the needs of
those experiencing hardship.

Here are some other Big Ideas that you may
want to emphasize in this chapter.

Geography

The geography of rivers and the surrounding
land played a central role in the development of
Chinese civilizations.

Talk About It

Interpreting Maps

Ask students to look at the map and read the
legend. How do the ancient Chinese empires
compare to the modern nation of China?
(They were much smaller than modern China.)
What barriers separate China from the other
civilizations that existed around the same time as
the Chinese dynasties? *(Gobi Desert, Taklimakan
Desert, Himalayas)*

INTERACTIVE

An interactive version of this map is available
on the eEdition and on the Power Presentations
CD-ROMs.

Find Out More

China is the most populous country in the
world. Use library or Internet resources to learn
more about the population density of China
today. Where are the major population centers
of modern-day China? Where are today's
population centers found within the boundaries
of ancient Chinese empires located?

Watch the Video

Ancient China presents a fascinating look at
archaeological sites and artifacts such as the
Great Wall, the Emperor Qin's tomb, and bronze
vessels found in the ancient city of Anyang.
This 23-minute video is part of the *Ancient
Civilizations for Children* video series.

The World's Music

Introduce your students to authentic Chinese
music by playing track 18 of *The World's Music*
audio CD. "A Single Bamboo Can Easily Bend" is
an example of folk music from Hunan province in
central China.

Objective

Describe the influence of a major figure in ancient Chinese history.

Introducing the Story

Confucius

Confucius is both a legendary and a historical figure of ancient China. His philosophy has inspired people for hundreds of years. He taught many lessons on the relationships between people. Confucius placed a special responsibility upon rulers to behave properly and set a good example for their people to follow.

Vocabulary Preview

minister a government official

righteous acting in an upright manner

Reading the Story Aloud

1. **The teacher as reader:** Read the story aloud with expression, so that students hear the drama and understand the emotional impact of the events.

2. **The students as readers:** Give student readers a few minutes ahead of time to read the story to themselves before they read it aloud to the rest of the class.

Starting with a Story

Students can also follow along as they listen to the story on the eEdition or on the Power Presentations CD-ROMs.

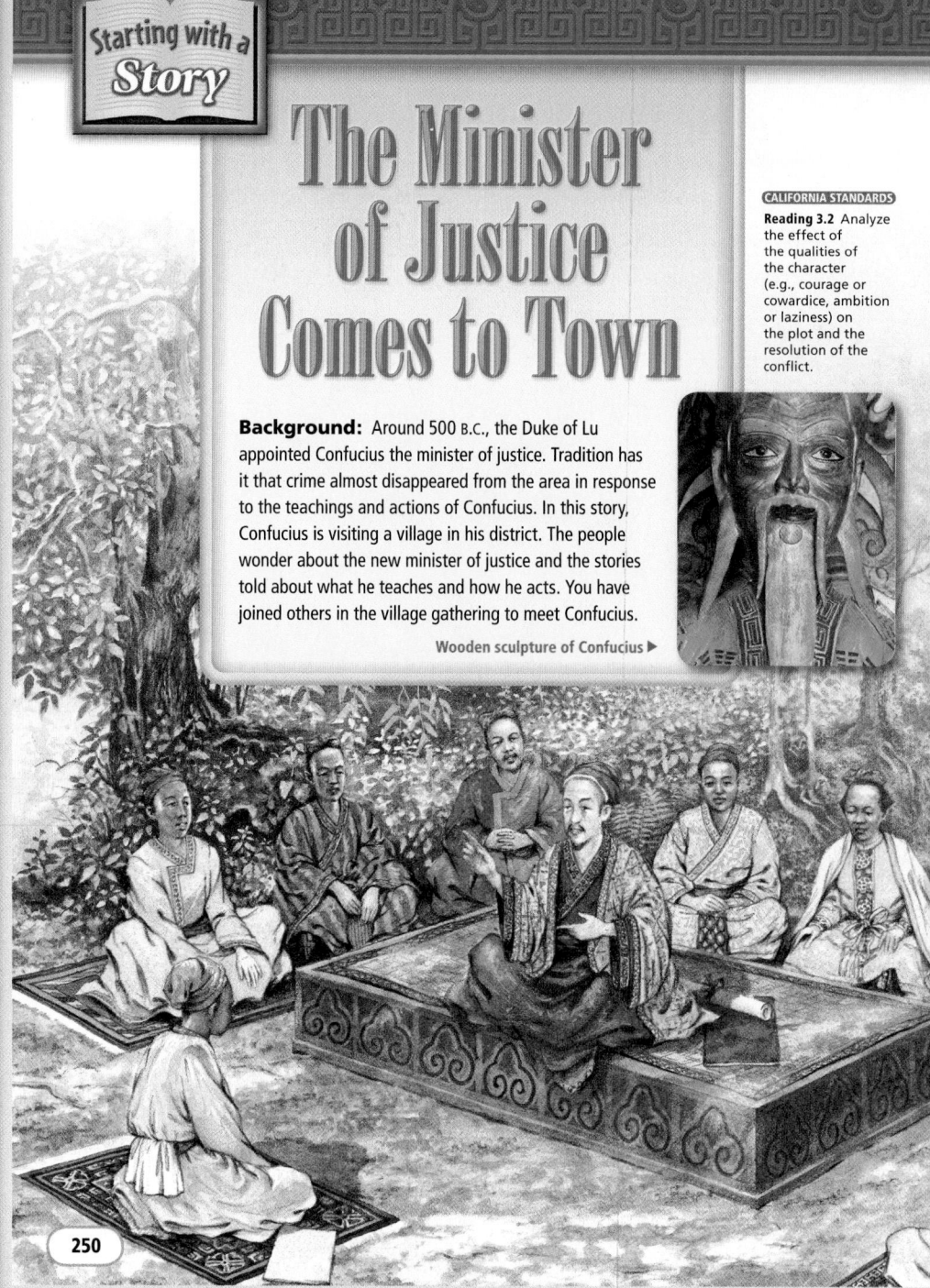

Starting with a Story

The Minister of Justice Comes to Town

Background: Around 500 B.C., the Duke of Lu appointed Confucius the minister of justice. Tradition has it that crime almost disappeared from the area in response to the teachings and actions of Confucius. In this story, Confucius is visiting a village in his district. The people wonder about the new minister of justice and the stories told about what he teaches and how he acts. You have joined others in the village gathering to meet Confucius.

Wooden sculpture of Confucius ▶

250

ADDITIONAL RESOURCES

Books for the Student

Art, Suzanne Strauss. *The Story of Ancient China.* Lincoln: Pemblewick Press, 2001. A lively survey of ancient Chinese history.

Shuter, Jane. *The Ancient Chinese.* Des Plaines: Heinemann Interactive Library, 1998. Overview of different features of ancient Chinese civilization.

Videos

Ancient China. 23 minutes. Wynnewood: Schlessinger Media, 1998. Archaeological journey explores the wonders of ancient China.

Confucius. 50 minutes. New York: A & E Home Video, 1999. Study of the life and wisdom of the great Chinese philosopher.

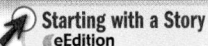

We saw his oxcart coming in the distance. It was Confucius, the great teacher. We waited, excited at his presence. He was our minister of justice. We had heard stories about how crime and violence had disappeared from villages where he was the main official. We thought this sounded too good to be true.

"I am happy that you came," he said, to greet us all. Then he began to speak. "We need to change our ways of living so that we can all live in peace with each other. I have studied how to make this happen." Then he said that peace required us to learn how to treat each other kindly.

He said that we must behave properly with our family members, our neighbors, and the rulers. He went on, "In our families we must show respect for our parents and our ancestors. We must be righteous, or do what is right rather than what brings us profit. Each of us must know our place. Each has a duty to another."

I asked if that meant the government officials, too. They were always cheating the people and acting as if they were gods. Confucius quickly responded. "That includes the highest rulers," he said. "They must set examples of goodness for us. In turn, we must obey them as their subjects."

"Teacher," I asked, "is that all? Will that make crime and violence go away?" He replied, "It may seem too simple, but it will work. However," he cautioned, "all must agree to respect and honor each other."

He rose to leave. I, for one, was willing to try out his ideas. Did anyone else feel the way I did?

What impact do you think Confucius' ideas will have on the village?

Reading & Writing

1. **READING: Character and Plot** What character trait does Confucius suggest is important in creating a peaceful society? How do you think Confucius' ideas will be accepted in the village?

2. **WRITING: Persuasion** Write a letter to the village members explaining why Confucius' ideas will lead to a more peaceful village.

CALIFORNIA STANDARDS Writing 2.5
Write persuasive compositions.

251

STARTING WITH A STORY

Talk About It

Ask students the following questions to begin the discussion:

- Why was the narrator in the story excited by the approach of Confucius? *(Confucius was a great teacher who was known for achieving remarkable results in reducing crime.)*
- What did Confucius suggest was the key to reducing crime and violence? *(People must behave properly in all their different relations with people.)*
- Why was the narrator especially concerned about government officials? *(They had a history of being corrupt.)*

What impact do you think Confucius' ideas will have on the village?

Possible answer: It will help improve life in the community because Confucius has great authority and the people's respect, people will be willing to try his ideas.

Making Personal Connections

Connect the discussion to today by asking about how people treat one another in our society. Do people show respect for others, including rulers and neighbors? Do people think others are acting in ways that are worthy of respect? Students may say that it would be easier to treat people with respect if they were treated the same way in return.

READING & WRITING ACTIVITIES

1. **READING** Respect is important. Some people will like his ideas and want to have the village run on his ideas. Others will say that the only way to have a peaceful society is to have harsh rules.

2. **WRITING** The letter should
   - show an understanding of the principles of Confucius
   - clearly state why Confucius' ideas will work
   - give reasons why other methods have failed

2. Writing Rubric

	Understanding of Confucian Principles	Stating of Position	Depth of Supporting Statements
4	clear	clear and concise	many clearly stated
3	mostly clear	adequate	some
2	some understanding	unclear	some but not clear
1	little understanding	missing	none

Ancient China • **251**

❶ Plan & Prepare

Objectives

- Analyze the physical features, including the river systems, mountain ranges, and deserts, that characterized ancient China.
- Describe the development of the earliest Chinese civilization, the Shang Dynasty.
- Describe the Zhou Dynasty, which followed the Shang Dynasty.
- **Language Objective:** Use structural and context clues to define words and gain a deeper understanding of the information.

Quick Look

Lesson 1 explores the emergence of great civilizations in ancient China, where the oldest continuous civilization in the world was born.

❷ Focus & Motivate

Preview Tell students that the development of Chinese civilization follows a pattern similar to the development of other ancient civilizations, but it also has many distinctive features. Have students recall the map on page 249 and remind them how far away China is from the other early civilizations they have read about.

Introduce the Main Ideas The three main ideas relate to the Big Idea "Civilizations developed in places that supported agriculture or trade or both." Help students look for this Big Idea as you go through the lesson.

Reading Skill: Explaining Geographic Patterns Tell students that explaining geographic patterns can help make connections between content they are reading now and content they have studied earlier. It can help them make sense of what they are learning.

POSSIBLE ANSWERS FOR ORGANIZER

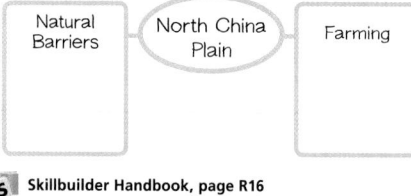

```
Natural          North China          Farming
Barriers           Plain
                                     rivers aided
cut off by                           agriculture
natural
barriers
```

Lesson 1

▶ MAIN IDEAS

❶ Geography Natural barriers isolate China's fertile river valleys from other parts of Asia.

❷ Government The Shang Dynasty ruled China's earliest civilization, which arose near the Huang He.

❸ Government Claiming approval from the gods, the Zhou conquered the Shang and took over China.

▶ TAKING NOTES

Reading Skill: Explaining Geographic Patterns

Facts about geography can help you understand settlement patterns in history. As you read, take notes on the natural barriers and the farming area of China. Record the information on a Web diagram placing the North China Plain in the center circle.

```
Natural          North China          Farming
Barriers           Plain
```

S **Skillbuilder Handbook, page R16**

▲ **Shang Bronze Drinking Vessel** The Shang were famous for their excellent bronzework.

CALIFORNIA STANDARDS

6.6 Students analyze the geographic, political, economic, religious and social structures of the early civilizations of China.

6.6.1 Locate and describe the origins of Chinese civilization in the Huang-He Valley during the Shang Dynasty.

6.6.2 Explain the geographic features of China that made governance and the spread of ideas and goods difficult and served to isolate the country from the rest of the world.

HOW TO TEACH THE CALIFORNIA STANDARDS

Standard	Content	Student Question or Activity	Instruction
6.6	**Pages 253–255** Describes the geography of China and the early political, religious, and social structures of the early Chinese dynasties	**Page 254** Students explain why ancient Chinese civilization grew up on the North China Plain.	Discuss what students have learned about the development of other early civilizations. Explain that China, though it shares many features with other civilizations, developed in its own unique way.
6.6.1	**Pages 253–254** Describes the rivers that played a central role in the development of Chinese civilization.	**Page 257** Students explain why Shang settlements began on the Huang He.	Have students explain how the role the rivers in China played was similar to that of the Tigris, Euphrates, Nile, and Indus rivers. (*All supported agriculture.*)
6.6.2	**Page 253** Describes physical barriers that helped isolate ancient China from the rest of the world.	**Page 257** Students explain how the geographic barriers affected the Shang and Zhou dynasties.	Tell students that China was well isolated from the influence of other civilizations. Ask a volunteer use a textbook or classroom map to point out the various barriers that helped cut off China from the rest of the world.

Geography Shapes Life in Ancient China

TERMS & NAMES

oracle bone

pictograph

dynastic cycle

Mandate of Heaven

Build on What You Know What makes the area you live in a good place for people to live? Think about how the geographic features of your area have affected life there.

Geographic Features of China

1 ESSENTIAL QUESTION What effect did the physical features of China have on its early development?

provided fertile soil for good farming, isolated China from other civilizations

The river valley pattern you studied in Mesopotamia, Egypt, and the Indus Valley was repeated in China. Its civilization developed because two rivers brought water and silt that made farming possible. Cities grew along the banks of the river.

Isolated by Barriers Located on the eastern side of Asia, China lies about the same distance north of the equator as the United States. China's lands are bordered on the east by the Yellow Sea, East China Sea, and the Pacific Ocean. Deserts edge the northern and western lands. To the north is the Gobi Desert and to the west lies the Taklimakan Desert. The Pamir, Tian Shan, and Himalaya mountain ranges form a tight curve on the western border.

Unlike the regions of the Nile and Fertile Crescent, where civilizations interacted with each other, China was geographically isolated. The huge mountain chains, vast deserts, and large expanses of water made the spread of ideas and goods to China difficult. As a result, Chinese civilization developed along very distinct lines.

Gobi Desert One of the largest deserts in the world, the Gobi covers more land than Texas and California combined. ▼

MONGOLIA
GOBI DESERT
NORTH KOREA
SOUTH KOREA
CHINA

253

Terms & Names

oracle bone a bone or shell used in Shang Dynasty religious rituals

pictograph a picture or drawing that represents a word or an idea

dynastic cycle the pattern of the rise and fall of dynasties

Mandate of Heaven ancient Chinese belief that a ruler had the gods' approval

❸ Teach

Geographic Features of China

6.6.1, 6.6.2

Talk About It

- **Critical Thinking: Comparing and Contrasting** In what way was China similar geographically to lands where other ancient civilizations emerged? *(Great rivers produced conditions for successful agriculture.)*

California Resources

California Reading Toolkit, L25
California Modified Lesson Plans for English Learners, p. 53
California Daily Standards Practice Transparencies, TT25
California Standards Enrichment Workbook, pp. 79–82
California Online Test Practice
California Test Generator CD-ROM
California Standards Planner and Lesson Plans, L49
California EasyPlanner CD-ROM
California eEdition CD-ROM

LESSON 1 PROGRAM RESOURCES

ON LEVEL

In-Depth Resources: Unit 4
- Family Newsletter (English and Spanish) pp. 22–23
- Reading Skill: Explaining Geographic Patterns, p. 24
- Vocabulary Study Guide, p. 30
- Vocabulary Cards, p. 31

Formal Assessment
- Lesson Quiz, p. 134

ENGLISH LEARNERS

In-Depth Resources in Spanish
- Reading Skill: Explaining Geographic Patterns, p. 63
- Vocabulary Study Guide, p. 70

Modified Lesson Plans for English Learners, p. 53

Reading Study Guide (Spanish), p. 67

Reading Study Guide Audio CD (Spanish)

STRUGGLING READERS

In-Depth Resources: Unit 4
- Reading Skill: Explaining Geographic Patterns, p. 24
- Vocabulary Study Guide, p. 30
- Vocabulary Cards, p. 31
- Reteaching Activity, p. 37

Reading Toolkit, p. L25

Reading Study Guide, p. 67

Reading Study Guide Audio CD

GIFTED AND TALENTED STUDENTS

Map Transparencies
- MT15 Agricultural Regions of China

Interdisciplinary Projects
- Math, p. 43

INCLUSION

EasyPlanner CD-ROM
- Reading Skill: Explaining Geographic Patterns
- Vocabulary Study Guide
- Reteaching Activity

TECHNOLOGY

eEdition CD-ROM

Power Presentations CD-ROM

Map Transparencies
- MT15 Agricultural Regions of China

Critical Thinking Transparencies
- CT 32 Explaining Geographic Patterns

Humanities Transparencies
- HT15 Shang Bronze Elephant

Test Generator CD-ROM

ClassZone.com

In-Depth Resources: Unit 4
• Reading Skill: Explaining Geographic Patterns, p. 24

More About . . .

The Yellow River

As the text notes, the Yellow River bears a yellow-colored silt that gives it its name. This silt also contributes to another name for the Huang He—China's Sorrow. This name comes from the frequent floods that have occurred along its banks. To help control these floods, the Chinese historically built levees. But the enormous sediment load of the Yellow River has raised the river bed, requiring ever higher levees. Breaches of the levees have been common throughout Chinese history, often with devastating results.

Teach

The Shang Dynasty

 6.6

Talk About It

• Along which river did Chinese civilization first emerge? *(along the Huang He)*

• Who were the Shang kings? *(They were members of the Shang family, who took control of portions of the North China Plain around 1766 B.C.)*

• What was the purpose of oracle bones? *(They were used as a way to ask questions of the gods and get answers.)*

• **Critical Thinking: Understanding Cause and Effect** Explain how the development of a writing system would help unify the large and varied land of China. *(It provided a way for people in many different places to communicate—even if they did not speak the same language.)*

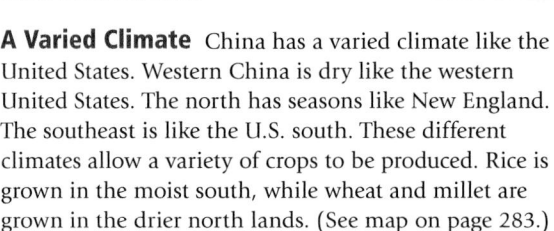

Two River Systems Two major rivers flow toward the Pacific Ocean. The Chang Jiang (chahng jyahng), or the Yangtze, is found in central China. The Huang He (hwahng huh) to the north is also known as the Yellow River. Their floodwaters deposit yellowish silt that makes fertile soil. In ancient times, most Chinese farming was done in the very rich land between these rivers. This land, called the North China Plain, has always been the center of Chinese civilization.

A Varied Climate China has a varied climate like the United States. Western China is dry like the western United States. The north has seasons like New England. The southeast is like the U.S. south. These different climates allow a variety of crops to be produced. Rice is grown in the moist south, while wheat and millet are grown in the drier north lands. (See map on page 283.)

▲ **Chang Jiang (Yangtze River)** This river is the longest river in Asia. It has been and still is a major trade route throughout China. Like the Huang He, it, too, carries yellow silt.

REVIEW Why was the North China Plain the center of Chinese civilization? Most of China's fertile land for farming lies on the North China Plain.

The Shang Dynasty

2 ESSENTIAL QUESTION How did the Chinese language develop?
developed from scratches on oracle bones to pictographs
Around 2000 B.C., farming settlements along the Huang He began to grow into cities. An early civilization began there, and Chinese culture today evolved from that ancient beginning. Therefore, we can say that China is the oldest continuous civilization in the world.

Shang Kings About 1766 B.C., Shang family kings began to control some cities. They set up a dynasty, or rule by generations of one family. The kings were responsible for religious activities. They claimed to rule with the gods' permission. Shang kings controlled the central portion of the North China Plain; their relatives ruled distant areas. The Shang used chariots to defend themselves against the nomads who lived to the north and west. They made war with nomadic people like the Zhou (joh).

INTERDISCIPLINARY ACTIVITIES

Science

Explore the Huang He

Have students research the Huang He and its history and the steps the Chinese have taken to deal with flooding along the great river. Students should use their findings to create a poster that diagrams Chinese levees and the challenge presented by the large sediment load in the river.

Language Arts

Write a Song to the Huang He

Tell students that Huang He is known not only for sustaining Chinese civilization—but also as China's Sorrow. Have students research the history of this river. Then have them write a song that expresses the conflicting emotions the river and its history have produced among the Chinese people.

Shang Families In Shang culture, respect for one's parents and ancestors was very important. Family was closely tied to religion. The Chinese believed that the spirits of their ancestors could bring good fortune to the family. Families paid respect to the father's ancestors by making animal sacrifices in their honor. Men ruled within the family.

Developing Language The Shang kings claimed to be able to influence the gods to help people. Shang kings received messages from the gods through **oracle bones**. These were animal bones or turtle shells on which Shang royal priests scratched questions to the gods. Next, they touched the bones with heated rods to make them crack. The royal priests interpreted the cracks and scratched the answers on the bones. These scratch marks were an early form of a writing system.

Like other ancient peoples, the Shang developed their system of writing with **pictographs**. This system of writing used simple drawings, or characters, for words or ideas. As you can see in the chart to the right, the pictographs are very similar to the modern Chinese characters. Compared to the English alphabet of 26 letters, the Chinese system of writing used a huge number of symbols. To be barely able to read and write, a person had to know at least 1,500 characters. An educated person had to know at least 10,000 characters.

One unique thing about the Chinese syste m of writing is that you can read Chinese without being able to speak it. (A person who speaks a language other than English can still understand 2 + 2 = 4.) The writing system helped unify a large and varied land.

REVIEW How did the Shang develop writing?
Answer The Shang used pictographs to stand for words or ideas.

The Zhou Dynasty

3 **ESSENTIAL QUESTION** How were the Zhou able to conquer Shang lands? Answer They claimed the Mandate of Heaven.

The Zhou people moved down from the northwest. They clashed with the Shang on many occasions. Around 1027 B.C., the Zhou ruler Wu Wang led a force that defeated the Shang.

Visual Vocabulary
Oracle Bone

This oracle bone made of a shoulder blade has inscriptions scratched on it.

Chinese Writing

Ancient	Modern
field	
田	田
water	
巛	水
ox	
半	牛

DIFFERENTIATING INSTRUCTION

Gifted and Talented Students

Profile a Shang or Zhou Ruler
Have students use library or Internet resources to learn about the life and reign of a Shang or Zhou ruler. Students should use their findings to create a timeline of the ruler's life and a brief biographical sketch. Have students share their profiles with the class.

Struggling Readers

Diagram the Content
Have students work alone to create a web diagram of the section "The Shang Dynasty." Students should take a sheet of paper, draw a circle in the center, and write *Shang Dynasty* inside the circle. Then they should draw three circles around this central circle, one for each of the subsections on pages 254–255. In each circle, have students write details from the text. Students should compare their diagrams with others in the class.

History from Visuals

Interpreting Diagrams
Have students review the diagram of Chinese writing. Be sure they recognize that the figures on the left side represent ancient figures, and the figures on the right represent modern-day examples.

• How have Chinese figures changed over the centuries? *(Possible answer: The symbols have not changed much. They have become a little more stylized, or artistic.)*

Visual Vocabulary

Oracle
An oracle can be a place, or shrine. It can also be a person or object. Ask students why people might want to consult an oracle. *(Possible answer: because they want to understand the world, they want to know what will happen)*

Teach

The Zhou Dynasty

6.6

Talk About It

• What event led to the end of the Shang Dynasty and the start of the Zhou Dynasty? *(The Zhou defeated the Shang around 1027 B.C.)*

• What was the Mandate of Heaven? *(It was the belief that rulers had the approval of the gods—and could lose it.)*

• How did the ancient Chinese believe gods signaled their displeasure with a ruler? *(by bringing suffering or misfortune to the people, through natural disasters, uprisings, or invasions)*

• **Critical Thinking: Understanding Cause and Effect** How did the Zhou system of government help contribute to the Time of the Warring States? *(Possible answer: The lack of a central government empowered local rulers, or lords, who fought among themselves.)*

History from Visuals

Interpreting Diagrams

Direct students' attention to the diagram on this page. Explain to students that this diagram shows a cycle—a series of events that happen in the same way over and over throughout history. Ask students what this cycle represents. *(the cycle by which dynasties rose to power then fell from power)* Ask students to point out what device in this diagram indicates where the cycle begins. *(The number one indicates that the cycle starts with that label.)*

• By what technique does the diagram suggest that the cycle, once completed, continued on in the same pattern? *(There is an arrow from the last label, number six, leading back to the first label, number one.)*

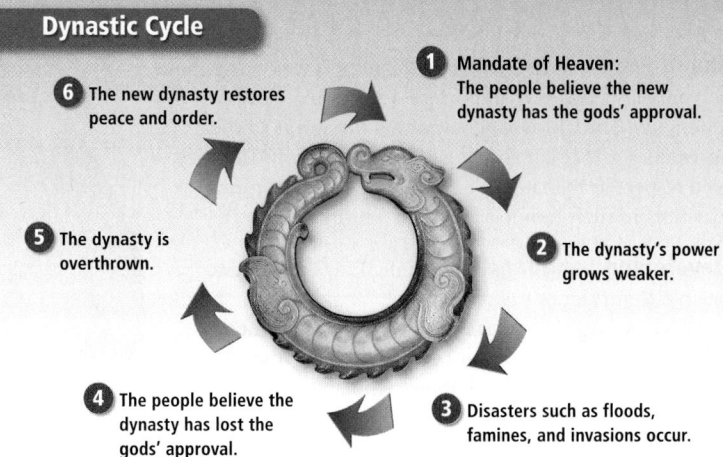

Dynastic Cycle

6 The new dynasty restores peace and order.

1 **Mandate of Heaven:** The people believe the new dynasty has the gods' approval.

5 The dynasty is overthrown.

2 The dynasty's power grows weaker.

4 The people believe the dynasty has lost the gods' approval.

3 Disasters such as floods, famines, and invasions occur.

The Zhou and the Dynastic Cycle The Zhou kings established a new dynasty in China. Chinese dynasties rose and fell in a pattern. Historians call the pattern of the rise and fall of dynasties in China the **dynastic cycle**. Look at the diagram above to see the pattern.

Like the ancient Egyptians, the Zhou kings thought that trouble would come if rulers lost heaven's favor. Eventually, the idea that a good ruler had approval from the gods became a part of Chinese culture. When a ruler was bad or foolish, the people believed the approval of the gods would be taken away. This idea was called the **Mandate of Heaven**. The Chinese people believed that troubles such as peasant uprisings, invasions, floods, or earthquakes meant that the Mandate of Heaven had been taken away. Then it was time for new leaders.

The Zhou adopted many Shang ways. This started a pattern of Chinese culture that developed until the present day.

Zhou Government Like the Shang, the Zhou did not have a strong central government. Kings put people with family ties or other trusted people in charge of regions. Those local rulers, or lords, owed loyalty and military service to the king. In return, the king promised to help protect their lands. As their towns became cities, the lords grew stronger. More groups came under their rule. The lords became less dependent on the king. They began to fight among themselves and with other peoples. The lands they added to their control expanded Chinese territory.

DIFFERENTIATING INSTRUCTION

English Learners

Make a Human Map of China
Write "China is isolated by barriers" on the board. Have one student stand in the middle of the room holding a sign reading "China." Have other students arrange themselves around the student holding signs to represent the Yellow Sea, the East China Sea, the Pacific Ocean, the Gobi Desert, the Taklimakan Desert, the Pamir Mountains, the Tian Shan Mountains, and the Himalayas. Have students note details from the text, to share with classmates, that describe the geographical feature they are representing. To conclude, ask students what the passage on the board means.

Inclusion

Enlarge Images
For students who have visual impairments, draw an enlarged version of the "Dynastic Cycle" on the board, and read aloud the steps of the cycle as you label the chart. Suggest that students think of a wheel. If the number one is written at the top of the wheel and the wheel is set in motion, the position of the number will change, but it will eventually come around to the top again.

The Time of the Warring States Invasion of Chinese lands was a constant theme in Chinese history. After 800 B.C., nomads from the north and west invaded China. In 771 B.C., invaders destroyed the capital city of Hao and killed the king. The king's family escaped to Luoyang and set up a new capital. Because the kings were weak, the lords fought constantly. This led to a period called the Time of the Warring States, which began around 403 B.C.

REVIEW How did the idea of the Mandate of Heaven help the Zhou take over the Shang? The Zhou convinced the Shang that their rulers had lost the approval of the gods.

Lesson Summary

- River valleys supported the rise of Chinese civilization, while some geographic features helped to isolate China from outside contact.
- The Shang developed a dynasty and a culture that included a system of writing.
- The Zhou claimed to rule using the idea of the Mandate of Heaven.

Why It Matters Now . . .

The culture developed by the Shang and the Zhou still influences Chinese ways of life today.

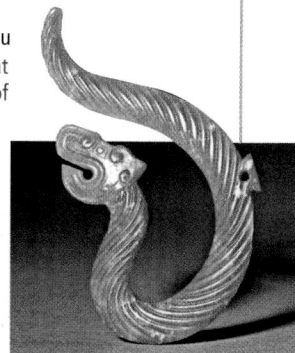
▲ **Jade Dragon Pendant** The dragon is a symbol of power and excellence.

1 Lesson Review

Homework Helper ClassZone.com

Terms & Names

1. Explain the importance of
   oracle bone   dynastic cycle
   pictograph   Mandate of Heaven

Using Your Notes

Explaining Geographic Patterns Use your completed graphic to answer the following question:

2. How did geographic barriers affect Shang and Zhou relations with outside peoples? (6.6.2)

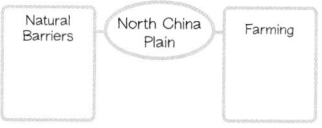

Natural Barriers — North China Plain — Farming

Main Ideas

3. Why did Shang settlements begin along the Huang He? (6.6.1)

4. How did the Shang develop a Chinese language? (6.6)

5. How would the Chinese people know that a ruler had lost the Mandate of Heaven? (6.6)

Critical Thinking

6. **Understanding Cause and Effect** How did the belief in the Mandate of Heaven help the change in government from the Shang to the Zhou? (6.6)

7. **Comparing** In what ways was the settling of the Huang He Valley similar to settlements in other world regions? (6.6.1)

Activity

Creating Elements of Language Develop pictographs and use them in a sentence about your classroom. Have classmates try to determine what you wrote. (6.6)

Ancient China • 257

❹ Assess & Reteach

Assess Have pairs of students use the lesson review questions to quiz each other, taking turns to answer the questions.

 Formal Assessment
- Lesson Quiz, p. 134

Reteach Divide the class into small groups. Have each group work together to complete the Reteaching Activity for Lesson 1. Share and discuss answers. If students are still uncertain about key terms in the lesson, have them quiz each other using Vocabulary Cards.

 In-Depth Resources: Unit 4
- Vocabulary Cards, p. 31
- Reteaching Activity, p. 37

 **Homework Helper**

Visit **ClassZone.com** for a lesson review, a flip-card activity, and links to related Web sites.

---

1 Lesson Review Answers

Terms & Names

1. • oracle bone, p. 255
   • pictograph, p. 255
   • dynastic cycle, p. 256
   • Mandate of Heaven, p. 256

Using Your Notes

See page 252 for an example of a completed organizer.

2. Natural barriers of seas, mountains, and deserts made travel difficult, which isolated the Chinese from trade routes and influence from the west.

Main Ideas

3. The river left behind silt that made the land especially fertile.

4. The Shang developed an early system of writing by using pictographs for words or ideas. The Chinese language today has roots in the Shang system.

5. Natural disasters, rebellions, or invasions signaled the loss of favor of the gods.

Critical Thinking

6. Possible answers: The fighting between the Zhou and the Shang may have been taken as a sign that the Shang had lost the Mandate of Heaven.

7. Like other early civilizations, settlements first appeared along rivers where fertile soil made farming possible. Cities grew from farming villages.

Activity Rubric

	Number of Pictographs	Reflection of Idea	Clarity of Message
4	more than ten	clear	clear message
3	eight or nine	mostly clear	most of message clear
2	six or seven	somewhat vague	some symbols deciphered
1	less than five	vague	undecipherable

❶ Plan & Prepare

Objectives

- Analyze the philosophy of Legalism—what it was and why it came about.
- Describe key details about the life of Confucius and his teachings.
- Describe key details in the life of Laozi and the philosophy of Daoism.
- **Language Objective:** Categorize information to better understand China's belief systems.

Quick Look

Lesson 2 explores the rich philosophical tradition of ancient China, including the philosophies of Legalism, Confucianism, and Daoism.

❷ Focus & Motivate

Preview Explain that this lesson focuses on Chinese philosophy. Ask students if they have ever heard of Confucius and what they know about his life.

Introduce the Main Ideas The three main ideas relate to the Big Idea "Belief systems may shape governments and societies." Tell students to look for ways that belief systems influenced Chinese society.

Reading Skill: Comparing Comparing is a way to recognize patterns in different events or ideas. Recognizing patterns can help you see the relationships between events and ideas.

SAMPLE ANSWERS FOR CHART

Legalism	Confucianism	Daoism
humans wicked	respect in all relationships	all things guided by a universal force
strict laws needed	established clear roles	sought harmony with nature

---

Lesson 2

▶ MAIN IDEAS

❶ Belief Systems Legalists believed that the government must control people through strict laws.

❷ Belief Systems Confucius taught that order would return to China if society was organized around five relationships.

❸ Belief Systems The followers of Daoism taught that people could find virtue by living in harmony with nature.

▶ TAKING NOTES

Reading Skill: Comparing

Comparing can help you see the similarities and differences among sets of things. In this lesson, look for details about the three Chinese philosophies. Identify points that all three philosophies consider important in a chart similar to the one below.

Legalism	Confucianism	Daoism

 **Skillbuilder Handbook, page R4**

▲ **Symbol: The Way** This Chinese symbol is called Dao. It means "the Way" or "the path." It is made up of two characters. The red one means "go forward," and the green one means "head." Taken together, they mean "the way to understanding."

CALIFORNIA STANDARDS

6.6.3 Know about the life of Confucius and the fundamental teachings of Confucianism and Daoism.

6.6.4 Identify the political and cultural problems prevalent in the time of Confucius and how he sought to solve them.

6.6 Students analyze the geographic, political, economic, religious, and social structures of the early civilizations of China.

HOW TO TEACH THE CALIFORNIA STANDARDS

Standard	Content	Student Question or Activity	Instruction
6.6.3	**Pages 260–262** Describes the life and teachings of Confucius **Pages 262–263** Describes the fundamental teachings of Daoism	**Page 262** Students read feature on career of Confucius. **Page 263** Students explain how a Daoist might respond to Confucius' teachings.	Point out the key features of Confucian thought and of Daoist thought, and make sure students see the differences. Encourage students to use resources to learn more about these two ideas.
6.6.4	**Pages 260–262** Describes the political and social environment in which Confucius lived and his attempts to solve problems	**Page 260** Students identify actions that Confucius thought would bring order to China.	Remind students about the events taking place in China when Confucius was alive, including warfare between different groups in China.
6.6	**Pages 259–263** Summarizes the major religious and political thought of early Chinese civilization	**Page 263** Students explain how Legalists thought government should keep peace among people.	Have students review what they learned in Lesson 1 about the social problems facing China during the Shang and Zhou dynasties.

China's Ancient Philosophies

TERMS & NAMES

philosophy
Legalism
Confucianism
filial piety
Daoism

Build on What You Know In the last lesson, you learned about the Time of the Warring States in China. During this time, Chinese society experienced much disorder. Warlords and kings fought with each other to gain control of lands. Scholars wondered what it would take to bring peace to the land. They developed three ways of thinking: Legalism, Confucianism, and Daoism. Each was a **philosophy**, or a study of basic truths and ideas about the universe.

Legalism

1 ESSENTIAL QUESTION How did Legalism suggest that society be controlled? strict laws and force

One philosophy was **Legalism**, or a belief that rulers should use the legal system to force people to obey laws. Those who followed this belief system saw disorder in society. These people decided that a strong government was the answer to China's problems.

Strict Laws and Harsh Punishments Legalists believed that human nature is wicked and that people do good only if they are forced to do it. Legalists believed that the government must pass strict laws to control the way people behaved. They believed that harsh punishments were needed to make people afraid to do wrong.

School of Confucius
Confucius, second figure from the left, meets with his students. ▼

259

Terms & Names

philosophy study of basic truths and ideas

Legalism a philosophy stressing the strict use of laws to control behavior

Confucianism a philosophy taught by Confucius that stresses proper relationships

filial piety the Confucian idea of respect for one's parents and ancestors

Daoism an ancient Chinese philosophy based on the teachings of Laozi

❸ Teach

Legalism

6.6

Talk About It

- **Critical Thinking: Making Inferences**
  Why didn't Legalists want people reading books that presented different philosophies?
  (Possible answer: They did not want people to question the authority of the state.)

California Resources

California Reading Toolkit, L26
California Modified Lesson Plans for English Learners, p. 55
California Daily Standards Practice Transparencies, TT26
California Standards Enrichment Workbook, pp. 83–86
California Online Test Practice
California Test Generator CD-ROM
California Standards Planner and Lesson Plans, L51
California EasyPlanner CD-ROM
California eEdition CD-ROM

LESSON 2 PROGRAM RESOURCES

ON LEVEL

In-Depth Resources: Unit 4
- Reading Skill: Comparing, p. 25
- Vocabulary Cards, p. 31
- Skillbuilder Practice, p. 29

Formal Assessment
- Lesson Quiz, p. 135

ENGLISH LEARNERS

In-Depth Resources in Spanish
- Reading Skill: Comparing, p. 64
- Skillbuilder Practice, p. 69

Modified Lesson Plans for English Learners, p. 55

Reading Study Guide (Spanish), p. 69
Reading Study Guide Audio CD (Spanish)

STRUGGLING READERS

In-Depth Resources: Unit 4
- Reading Skill: Comparing, p. 25
- Vocabulary Cards, p. 31
- Reteaching Activity, p. 38

Reading Toolkit, p. L26
Reading Study Guide, p. 69
Reading Study Guide Audio CD

GIFTED AND TALENTED STUDENTS

In-Depth Resources: Unit 4
- Primary Source: *Teachings*, by Confucius, p. 35
- Literature: *Dao De Jing*, by Laozi, p. 36

Interdisciplinary Projects
- Language Arts, p. 45

INCLUSION

EasyPlanner CD-ROM
- Reading Skill: Comparing
- Reteaching Activity

TECHNOLOGY

eEdition CD-ROM
Power Presentations CD-ROM
Critical Thinking Transparencies
- CT 33 Comparing and Contrasting

Test Generator CD-ROM
ClassZone.com

In-Depth Resources: Unit 4
• Reading Skill: Comparing, p. 25

More About . . .

The Legalists
Legalists actually ruled China for a short period at the beginning of the Qin Dynasty. (The next section covers this dynasty.) During this time, many scholars were killed and books on all subjects, except for practical subjects such as agriculture and medicine, were destroyed. This included many books about Confucian thought. Of course, Confucianism survived this trial and continues to influence the world today.

Teach

Confucianism

6.6.3, 6.6.4

Talk About It

- What did Confucius see as the key to peace and harmony? *(respect between all people)*

- To Confucius, what was the role of government? *(Government's role was to set a good example for people in terms of behavior.)*

- Into what broad categories did the key relationships identified by Confucius fall? *(relationships in the family and relationships in society)*

- **Critical Thinking: Comparing and Contrasting** In what ways were Confucianism and Legalism similar to each other, and in what ways were they different? *(Possible answer: They were similar in that they tried to suggest proper roles and relationships between people and their rulers. They were different in that they had different views concerning what ordinary humans were capable of. Legalists saw people as evil, and Confucianism felt people were worthy of respect.)*

An Increase in Government Control Shang Yang, a supporter of Legalism, wanted to force people to report lawbreakers. In fact, he thought people who did not report lawbreakers should be cut in two. Legalists taught that rulers should reward people who do their duty.

Legalists did not want people to complain about the government or question what it did. They favored arresting people who questioned the government or taught different ideas. They also taught that rulers should burn books that contained different philosophies or ideas.

REVIEW Why did Legalists want a strong government?
Legalists believed that people needed to be strictly controlled to provide an orderly society.

Confucianism

 ESSENTIAL QUESTION What actions did Confucius believe would bring order to China? proper conduct as outlined in the five relationships

Confucius lived from 551 to 479 B.C., in a time of much conflict and unrest in China. He developed ideas to end conflict and have peace in all relationships. According to Confucius, respect for others was absolutely necessary for peace and harmony. Government leaders should set a good example so that people would see what was correct. Confucius' students collected his ideas and recorded them in a book called the *Analects*. The book tells of Confucius' teachings, which together form a belief system known as **Confucianism**.

The Five Relationships Confucius taught a code of proper conduct for people. In Confucianism there were five basic relationships. Each type of relationship had its own duties and its own code of proper conduct. Here are the five relationships.

- father and son
- elder brother and junior brother
- husband and wife
- friend and friend
- ruler and subject

Notice that the relationships fall into two basic categories: proper conduct in the family and proper conduct in society.

Connect to Today

Ceremony Children in Taiwan take part in a ceremony honoring Confucius.▼

INTERDISCIPLINARY ACTIVITIES

Language Arts

Write an Explanation
Have students work individually to write a short explanation in which they summarize in their own words the beliefs of Legalist philosophers. They should include what was expected of ordinary citizens and how citizens were expected to behave.

Language Arts

Have a Discussion
Pair students and have them discuss the Legalist philosophy and the Confucian philosophy. One student should explain the important points of the Legalist philosophy, and the other should explain the important points of the Confucian philosophy. Then have the entire class summarize the beliefs of each philosophy.

Primary Source

Background: Confucius taught filial piety, or respect for one's parents and ancestors. In this selection, he discusses filial piety with his students. He focuses on propriety, or concern about what is proper or correct in society.

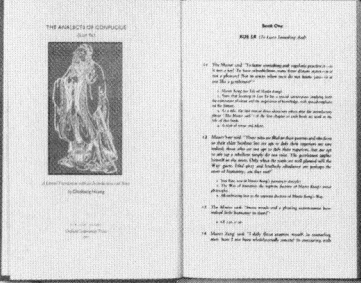

from the *Analects*

By Confucius
Translated by James Legge

"The filial piety of now-a-days means the support of one's parents. But dogs and horses likewise are able to do something in the way of support; — without reverence, what is there to distinguish the one support given from the other?" . . .

Mang I asked what filial piety was. The Master said, "It is not being disobedient." . . .

Fan Chih said, "What did you mean?" The Master replied, "That parents, when alive, should be served according to propriety; that, when dead, they should be buried according to propriety; and that they should be sacrificed to according to propriety."

DOCUMENT–BASED QUESTION
What can you infer from Confucius' teachings about the place of the family in society?

Proper Conduct Confucius believed good conduct and respect began at home. Husbands had to be good to their wives. Wives had to obey every decision of their husbands. Brothers had to be kind to brothers, but a younger brother always had to follow the wishes of his older brother. One of Confucius' most important teachings was about **filial piety**, or treating parents with respect. The Primary Source above is about filial piety.

Confucius was also concerned with people's behavior in society. Authority should be respected. The ruler's responsibility was to live correctly and treat his subjects with respect. If a ruler led in a right, moral way, a subject's duty was to obey. If these behaviors were followed, there would be peace in the society.

The Impact of Confucianism Confucianism set out clear family and social roles. By following these roles, the Chinese people found ways to avoid conflict and live peacefully. Many rulers tried to live up to Confucius' model for a good ruler. By encouraging education, Confucius laid the groundwork for fair and skilled government officials.

Confucius thought rulers should set an example of good morals and conduct.

REVIEW How did Confucius think rulers should behave?

Interpreting Primary Sources

from the *Analects*

- How does Confucius illustrate his point that merely supporting parents is not enough? *(He points out that dogs and horses are able to help support a parent.)*
- What does Confucius say is necessary to distinguish filial piety from the kind of support dogs and horses provide? *(People must show reverence, or deep respect, for parents.)*
- How does Confucius suggest that a person can show filial piety? *(by treating a parent with propriety—in the proper way—at all times)*

DOCUMENT–BASED QUESTION ANSWER

Possible answer: The family is an important place for carrying out proper behavior and social norms.

More About . . .

Filial Piety
In Confucian thought, filial piety is more than a way to ensure good relations in the home. It is a cornerstone of the social structure. The relations between parent and child in the home that Confucius described is the model for all structures in society. Indeed, of all the five relationships, the one between parent and child was considered the most important.

DIFFERENTIATING INSTRUCTION

English Learners

Categorize Key Terms
Explain that the leaders of Chinese society developed three logical ways of thinking that helped them solve problems and make decisions: Legalism, Confucianism, and Daoism. As a class, students should group the things they read about into these three categories. Guide students in identifying key terms, such as *Legalist*, and locating details to help them determine into which category each term fits.

Inclusion

Take Audio Notes
Have students who are visually impaired take notes by making an audiotape or digital recording with a classmate. Suggest that students pause after each section to summarize or make comparisons between the different philosophies.

History Makers

Confucius

Confucius survived a difficult childhood of poverty to become one of the single most influential human beings in history. He was intensely interested in promoting harmonious relationships in his troubled land. Toward this goal, he sought a career in government. However, that career faltered when he lost the favor of the rulers of the time. Following his dismissal, he continued to teach his ideas, earning wide fame and devotion among his many students. His teachings were passed down through the generations and eventually recorded in the *Analects.* Through these writings, people around the world continue to study his ideas about the perfection of human beings and society.

Teach

Daoism

📍 6.6.3

Talk About It

- What is the Dao? *(It is "the way"—a force that guides all existence.)*

- According to Daoists, what is the unique situation facing human beings? *(Humans do not live in harmony with the Dao and must therefore learn to live in harmony with nature and with their inner feelings.)*

- What do the concepts of yin and yang represent in Daoist thought? *(Yin and Yang are two natural forces that interact in an ever-shifting way. Understanding the relationship between yin and yang is necessary to understanding one's place in the world.)*

- **Critical Thinking: Comparing and Contrasting** How did Daoism differ from Confucian thought? *(Possible answer: Daoism stressed that each person had to find their individual way, while Confucius taught that people had certain clearly defined roles.)*

History Makers

Confucius (551–479 B.C.)

The name Confucius is a translation of the Chinese title *Kongfuzi.* It means "Master Kong."

Confucius began his career at the age of 19 as supervisor of a noble family's herds. He then spent years in study and acting as a tutor to children of rich families. He wanted to be a government official so that he could try out his ideas of ways to change society. One of the ideas he taught may sound familiar to you. He said, "What you do not want done to yourself, do not do to others."

Finally, at the age of 51, Confucius was appointed the minister of justice in his home state of Lu. Legend says he was so successful that his town was free of crime and a model of correct behavior. Unfortunately, Confucius had to leave his post and felt he was a failure.

Daoism

3 **ESSENTIAL QUESTION** What did the Daoists believe about society?
individuals had to live in harmony with nature and inner feelings

The third philosophy is said to have begun with Laozi (low•dzuh). No one knows if he really existed, but some say he lived in the 500s B.C. The name Laozi means "Old Master." The book of his teachings is the *Dao De Jing* (*The Book of the Way of Virtue*). The teachings of Laozi are called **Daoism** (DOW•IHZ•uhm). They contrast sharply with Legalism and Confucianism.

The Way Daoists believed that a universal force called the Dao, or the Way, guides all things. All creatures, except humans, live in harmony with this force. To relate to nature and each other, each human being had to find an individual way, or Dao. The individual had to learn to live in harmony with nature and with inner feelings.

Following the Way Daoists did not argue about good and bad, and they did not try to change things. They accepted things as they were. They did not want to be involved with the government.

Daoists tried to understand nature and live in harmony with its rhythms. This included the idea of yin and yang, or two things that interact with each other. The yin (black) stands for all that is cold, dark, and mysterious. The yang (white) represents all

---

DIFFERENTIATING INSTRUCTION

Gifted and Talented Students

Diagram Confucian and Daoist Ideas

Have students use library or Internet resources to learn more about Confucianism and Daoism. Using what they learn, have them create a detailed Venn diagram in which they compare and contrast these two thought systems. Students should share their diagrams with the class.

Struggling Readers

Divide and Conquer

Have partners work together to read through and focus on one segment of the section "Daoism." When students have finished working through their sections, have volunteers from the class offer their own summaries of each segment's meaning. Discuss differences or questions about varying interpretations of the text together.

that is warm, bright, and light. The forces complement each other. The forces are always changing and evolving. Understanding yin and yang helped a person understand how he or she fits into the world.

In the next lesson you will learn how the three philosophies influenced the way in which the rulers of China controlled their lands.

REVIEW Why did Daoism teach that each human had to find an individual way to follow in life?   Because there were no rules for correct conduct, each person had to live in harmony with the forces of nature.

▲ **Yin and Yang Symbol** The outer circle represents "everything". The inner shapes represent the interaction of the forces—Yin and Yang.

Lesson Summary
- Legalists believed humans are wicked and need strict laws with harsh punishments.
- Confucius taught a code of proper conduct, including respect, that humans could learn.
- Daoists held the view that each human must find an individual moral path to follow.

Why It Matters Now . . .
The teachings of Confucianism and Daoism remain influential in China and the world today.

---

2 Lesson Review

 Homework Helper ClassZone.com

Terms & Names
1. Explain the importance of

| philosophy | Confucianism | Daoism |
| Legalism | filial piety | |

Using Your Notes
Comparing Use your completed graphic to answer the following question:
2. Which of the Chinese philosophies stressed the importance of family? (6.6.3)

Legalism	Confucianism	Daoism

Main Ideas
3. How did Legalists believe governments should keep peace among people? (6.6)
4. What was the purpose of Confucius' five relationships? (6.6.4)
5. What did Daoists believe about nature? (6.6.3)

Critical Thinking
6. **Comparing and Contrasting** How did the Legalists' views of human nature contrast with those of the Confucians? (6.6.3)
7. **Making Inferences** How might a Daoist respond to Confucius' teachings? (6.6.3)

Activity **Creating Classroom Rules** Choose one of the three Chinese philosophies and create a set of classroom rules that reflect the basic ideas of that philosophy. Share your rules with others, and decide which rules you would like for your classroom. (6.6.3)

Ancient China • 263

---

❹ Assess & Reteach

Assess Have pairs of students take turns answering the questions. Ask volunteers to share their completed charts for item 2.

 Formal Assessment
- Lesson Quiz, p. 135

Reteach Have students work individually. Tell them to read over the bulleted items in the Lesson Summary. For each item, have them review the appropriate section of the text and write an additional sentence or two to expand on and further explain that idea. Have students share their additional summary sentences with the class.

In-Depth Resources: Unit 4
- Vocabulary Cards, p. 31
- Reteaching Activity, p. 38

Homework Helper
Visit **ClassZone.com** for a lesson review, a flip-card activity, and links to related Web sites.

---

2 Lesson Review Answers

Terms & Names
1. • philosophy, p. 259
   • Legalism, p. 259
   • Confucianism, p. 260
   • filial piety, p. 261
   • Daoism, p. 262

Using Your Notes
See page 258 for an example of a completed chart.
2. Confucianism

Main Ideas
3. by passing strict laws with harsh punishments and by promoting unquestioned authority for government
4. The five relationships promoted a peaceful society.
5. Nature is governed by a universal force and humans should try to live in harmony with it.

Critical Thinking
6. Possible answer: The Legalists held the view that people were selfish and wicked. Confucius held that human beings were capable of and worthy of respect.
7. Possible answer: A Daoist might argue that an individual's own path to understanding did not require adherence to rules about relationships.

Activity Rubric

	Reflection of Philosophy	**Application in the Classroom**	**Number of Errors**
4	clear	good application	none
3	most of its points	mostly applies	few
2	some of its points	applies somewhat	several
1	unclear	does not apply	many

Objectives

- Analyze text that uses the compare-and-contrast organizational pattern.
- Describe the philosophies of Confucius and Laozi.
- **Language Objective:** Use a Venn diagram to formulate statements to compare and contrast two Chinese philosophies.

❶ Focus & Motivate

Preview Remind students that comparing and contrasting is a key skill that can help them understand the forces that helped shape history. Ask students if they can think of words that a writer might use to signal similarities between events or ideas. *(Possible answers: like, similarly, as in).* Ask what kinds of words might signal differences. *(Possible answers: unlike, in contrast, however)* Finally, ask students what kind of graphic organizer is useful for comparing and contrasting two different things. *(a Venn diagram)*

❷ Teach

Talk About It

- Based on the introduction to the Secondary Source, what do Confucius and Laozi both focus on in their philosophies? *(how people should live to achieve a perfect society)*

- What word in the second paragraph suggests that Confucius and Laozi were not the same in their beliefs? *(the word* however*)*

- What word in the third paragraph indicates that the passage is about to point out the way in which Laozi's ideas differed from those of Confucius? *(the word* unlike*)*

- **Critical Thinking: Making Inferences** Which philosopher would most likely make the following statement: "Fulfilling one's duties in society is the way to harmony and order." *(Students should identify this idea as most like Confucius.)*

Comparing and Contrasting

Goal: To analyze a passage to compare and contrast two Chinese philosophies

CALIFORNIA STANDARDS
Reading 2.2 Analyze text that uses the compare-and-contrast organizational pattern.
6.6.3 Know about the life of Confucius and the fundamental teachings of Confucianism and Daoism.

Learn the Skill

Comparing means looking at the similarities and differences between two or more things. **Contrasting** means examining only the differences between them. Historians compare and contrast events, personalities, beliefs, and situations in order to understand them.

Ⓢ See the Skillbuilder Handbook, page R4.

Practice the Skill

❶ Look for two views about a subject that may be compared and contrasted. The sample passage at the right compares two ways of achieving a perfect society.

❷ To find similarities in the views, look for clue words suggesting that two things are alike. Clue words include *both, like, as,* and *similarly.*

❸ To find differences, look for clue words that show how two things are different. Clue words include *by contrast, however, except, yet,* and *unlike.*

❹ Make a Venn diagram like the one below to help you identify similarities and differences between two things. In the overlapping area, list characteristics shared by both subjects. In the separate ovals, list characteristics not shared by the other. The chart below compares and contrasts two Chinese philosophers, Confucius and Laozi.

Example:

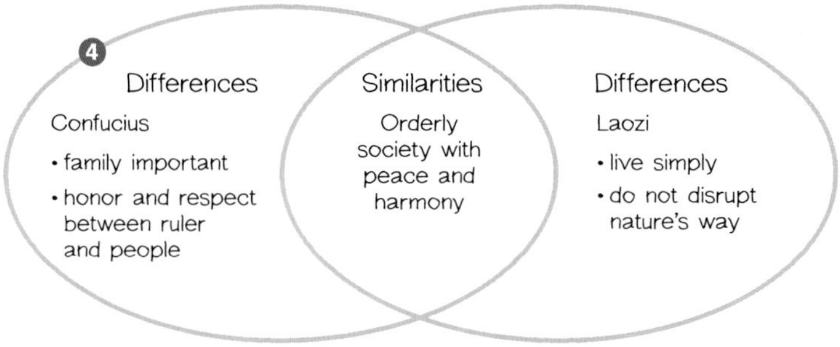

❹ Differences
Confucius
- family important
- honor and respect between ruler and people

Similarities
Orderly society with peace and harmony

Differences
Laozi
- live simply
- do not disrupt nature's way

DIFFERENTIATING INSTRUCTION

Inclusion

Have a Discussion
Pair students and have them discuss the beliefs of Laozi and Confucius. One student should explain the beliefs of Laozi, and the other should explain the beliefs of Confucius. In conclusion, they should decide how the two thinkers' beliefs were similar and how they were different.

Struggling Readers

Break Down the Paragraphs
Pair students and have them work together through the passage on page 265. Instruct them to focus on the second and third paragraphs one at a time. For each paragraph, have them read the passage aloud and list all the key points in the passage about the philosopher's ideas. When they have finished their lists, have the students compare them to see how the lists are similar and different.

Secondary Source

In this selection, the ideas of two Chinese philosophers, Confucius and Laozi, are discussed. The paragraphs focus on how Confucius and Laozi thought people should live to achieve a perfect society.

Two Chinese Philosophies

In China, two philosophers, Confucius and Laozi, looked for ❶ a way to create a perfect society. ❷ Both philosophers wanted people to live in peace and to have an orderly society.

❸ However, the ideas of Confucius are quite different from those of Laozi. Confucius believed family was very important. He said that family members should respect each other. In the community and country, rulers should have respect for the people and the people should respect the ruler. If they do these things, the society will be stable and happy.

Laozi did not agree with the teachings of Confucius. ❸ Unlike Confucius, he believed organizations and human-made systems were not the way to live in harmony. ❸ Instead, Laozi taught that nature provides the best examples of living in harmony. He told his followers to observe the ways of nature and they would know how to live. He stressed living simply and not disrupting the ways of nature. If people did this, he said, there would be peace and harmony in the world.

▲ **Confucius** Confucius wanted to restore order and harmony to China by having all people show respect for one another.

▲ **Laozi** Laozi believed that the natural order of things was important. If people followed nature, they would have a good life.

Apply the Skill

Go back to Chapter 7, Lessons 2 and 3. (See pages 234–242.) Read the information on Hinduism and Buddhism. Make a Venn diagram like the one at the left to help you take notes on the two religions.

SAMPLE ANSWER FOR GRAPHIC ORGANIZER

Differences	Similarities	Differences
Hinduism	belief in reincarnation	Buddhism
• worshiped many gods		• follows Eightfold Path
• main gods Vishnu, Shiva, Brahma		• goal is achieving nirvana
• read *Bhagavad Gita*		• teachings: dharma

More About . . .

Laozi

As the text mentions on page 262, the individual known as Laozi is perhaps a legend. He was said to be a contemporary of Confucius, and the two disagreed sharply over matters of philosophy. Eventually, Laozi became associated with a religious form of Daoism. In this role, Laozi became the object of worship and sacrifice. Some came to consider him the embodiment of the *dao*, and he was called upon to assist leaders in times of difficulty.

❶ Plan & Prepare

Objectives

- Summarize how China became unified under the Qin Dynasty.
- Explore the political contributions of the Han Dynasty.
- Describe daily life in Han China.
- **Language Objective:** Use sentence context to choose the correct dictionary definition for multiple meaning words.

Quick Look

Lesson 3 continues the Section 1 discussion about the development of the ancient Chinese Empire during the Qin and Han dynasties.

❷ Focus & Motivate

Preview Explain that this lesson traces the history of two ancient Chinese dynasties—the Qin and the Han. Ask students to think about how important leadership is in this country. What makes a leader effective or ineffective in the modern world?

Introduce the Main Ideas The three main ideas relate to the Big Idea "Governments create law codes and political bodies to organize a society." Help students look for this Big Idea as you go through the lesson.

Reading Skill: Comparing and Contrasting Comparing and contrasting is a skill that helps you evaluate information about different individuals or events.

SAMPLE ANSWERS FOR VENN DIAGRAM

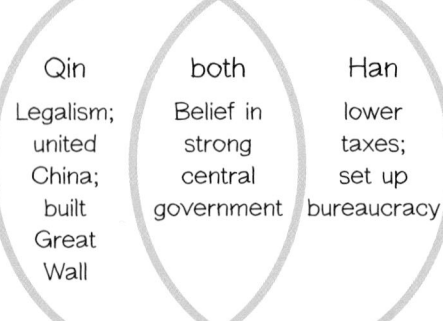

Qin: Legalism; united China; built Great Wall

both: Belief in strong central government

Han: lower taxes; set up bureaucracy

Lesson 3

▶ MAIN IDEAS

1 **Government** Shi Huangdi conquered the warring states, unified China, and built a strong government.

2 **Government** The Han Dynasty took over China and established a strong empire that lasted 400 years.

3 **Culture** Life in Han China set a pattern that is still seen today.

▶ TAKING NOTES

Reading Skill: Comparing and Contrasting

Comparing and contrasting means looking for similarities and differences that can help you understand developments in history. As you read, look for clue words such as *like* or *similarly* that indicate two things are alike in some ways. Compare and contrast the rule of the Qin and Han dynasties. Record your information on a Venn diagram.

Qin — both — Han

S **Skillbuilder Handbook, page R4**

▲ **Jade Funeral Suit** This jade funeral suit is made up of 2,498 jade pieces sewn together with gold thread. The Chinese believed jade would preserve dead bodies for the afterlife.

CALIFORNIA STANDARDS

6.6.5 List the policies and achievements of the emperor Shi Huangdi in unifying northern China under the Qin Dynasty.

6.6.6 Detail the political contributions of the Han Dynasty to the development of the imperial bureaucratic state and the expansion of the empire.

6.6 Students analyze the geographic, political, economic, religious, and social structures of the early civilizations of China.

HOW TO TEACH THE CALIFORNIA STANDARDS

Standard	Content	Student Question or Activity	Instruction
6.6.5	**Pages 267–268** Describes the rule of Shi Huangdi, including Legalist policies, and lists important accomplishments, such as the unification of China and building of the Great Wall	**Page 267** Students explain how the Qin Dynasty unified China.	Tell students to recall what they learned about Legalism and the purpose behind the killing of those who held different philosophies.
6.6.6	**Pages 269–270** Describes the political organization of the Han Dynasty, including the establishment of the Chinese bureaucracy and the expansion of China under Wudi.	**Page 270** Students analyze the hiring of workers for the Han Bureaucracy.	Ask students to consider the advantages of hiring government workers based on their skills and merits.
6.6	**Pages 267–271** Summarizes the political and social developments of Qin and Han China.	**Page 271** Students explain why modern Chinese citizens identify with Han China.	Suggest that students use library or Internet sources to learn more about life in Han China.

The Qin and the Han

TERMS & NAMES
Qin
Shi Huangdi
Han Dynasty
bureaucracy

Build on What You Know At the end of the Zhou period, several states were still at war. As you recall, the Chinese believed in the Mandate of Heaven. According to that belief, wars and other troubles were signs that the ruling dynasty had lost heaven's favor. A new ruler was needed.

The Qin Unified China

1 ESSENTIAL QUESTION How did the Qin Dynasty unify China?

The new ruler of China came from the state of **Qin** (chihn). (Some scholars think the name of China may come from this word.) The new emperor took the name **Shi Huangdi** (shee•hwahng•dee). He would unify and expand China.

A Legalistic Ruler In 221 B.C., Qin ruler Shi Huangdi began ending internal battles between warring states. He then conquered rival states and drove out nomadic invaders. China grew larger than it had been under the Zhou.

Shi Huangdi believed in the Legalist way of running the country. He tried to wipe out Confucian teachings. He had 460 critics and Confucianists killed. He also ordered the burning of books that contained ideas he disliked.

strengthened imperial power, built highways and irrigation projects, standardized weights, measure, coins, and writing

Terra Cotta Army Thousands of clay soldiers were buried at the tomb of Shi Huangdi. ▼

267

Terms & Names

Qin a state of ancient China

Shi Huangdi first emperor of the Qin Dynasty

Han Dynasty a dynasty begun in 202 B.C., which reunified China

bureaucracy the network of appointed officials that assist in providing government

❸ Teach

The Qin Unified China

✎ **6.6.5**

Talk About It

- **Critical Thinking: Finding Main Ideas**
In what way did Shi Huangdi's building of the Great Wall represent his overall approach to government? *(Possible answer: He united many distinct, smaller sections of wall to make one great wall. Likewise, he unified China.)*

California Resources

California Reading Toolkit, L27
California Modified Lesson Plans for English Learners, p. 57
California Daily Standards Practice Transparencies, TT27
California Standards Enrichment Workbook, pp. 87–90
California Online Test Practice
California Test Generator CD-ROM
California Standards Planner and Lesson Plans, L53
California EasyPlanner CD-ROM
California eEdition CD-ROM

LESSON 3 PROGRAM RESOURCES

ON LEVEL

In-Depth Resources: Unit 4
- Reading Skill: Comparing and Contrasting, p. 26
- Vocabulary Cards, p. 31
- Geography Practice, p. 33

Formal Assessment
- Lesson Quiz, p. 136

ENGLISH LEARNERS

In-Depth Resources in Spanish
- Reading Skill: Comparing and Contrasting, p. 65
- Geography Practice, p. 71

Modified Lesson Plans for English Learners, p. 57
Reading Study Guide (Spanish), p. 71
Reading Study Guide Audio CD (Spanish)

STRUGGLING READERS

In-Depth Resources: Unit 4
- Reading Skill: Comparing and Contrasting, p. 26
- Vocabulary Cards, p. 31
- Reteaching Activity, p. 39

Reading Toolkit, p. L27

Reading Study Guide, p. 71

Reading Study Guide Audio CD

GIFTED AND TALENTED STUDENTS

History Makers
- Wudi, p. 15

Interdisciplinary Projects
- Physical Education, p. 46

INCLUSION

EasyPlanner CD-ROM
- Reading Skill: Comparing and Contrasting
- Reteaching Activity

TECHNOLOGY

eEdition CD-ROM

Power Presentations CD-ROM

Humanities Transparencies
- HT16 Women Ironing Silk

Critical Thinking Transparencies
- CT 34 Comparing and Contrasting

Test Generator CD-ROM

ClassZone.com

In-Depth Resources: Unit 4
• Reading Skill: Comparing and Contrasting, p. 26

More About . . .

The Great Wall of China

The Great Wall of China is a structure that truly lives up to its name. Over 4,160 miles (6,700 km) long (3000 km), with all its branches the wall extends over 4,500 miles (7,300 km). The wall stretches into what even today is a lonely, isolated land. The effort of moving supplies and people to build and serve in these remote areas has been considerable.

Created in the Qin Dynasty, the wall has been updated and improved many times. The wall people can see today is mainly the product of the efforts of the Ming Dynasty, which began in the 1300s. Since that work was completed, parts of the wall have been raided by local residents for building materials.

Uniting China Shi Huangdi wanted a strong central government. To gain personal control of the government, he set out to weaken the noble families. He took land away from defeated nobles. Shi Huangdi also forced the nobles to live at the capital so he could watch them. These actions weakened the power of noble families and strengthened the emperor's power.

Shi Huangdi set out to unite the lands under his control. To link the lands together, he built highways and irrigation projects. He forced peasants to work on these projects and set high taxes to pay for them. He also set government standards for weights, measures, coins, and writing. These steps made it easier to trade and do business everywhere in China.

The Great Wall Shi Huangdi planned to build a long wall along China's northern borders to keep out invaders. He forced hundreds of thousands of peasants and criminals to build it. Many workers died from hard labor. The deaths caused great resentment among the people.

The first Great Wall linked smaller walls that had been built during the Time of the Warring States. The earliest walls were built of earth. Later stone and brick were used. The Great Wall has been rebuilt and extended many times.

The Qin Dynasty Ends Shi Huangdi died in 210 B.C. He was buried in an elaborate tomb. Near his tomb, an army of terra cotta (baked clay) soldiers was buried. Archaeologists discovered the soldiers in 1974. (See Literature Connections, pages 272–276.)

The Great Wall
Thousands of people visit a portion of the Great Wall during a holiday. ▼

REVIEW Why did Shi Huangdi kill so many Confucianists?
Shi Huangdi believed in the Legalist way of running government. He did not want Confucian ideas to be used.

INTERDISCIPLINARY ACTIVITIES

Math

Calculate How Long It Would Take to Walk the Wall

Ask students to complete the following math problem:

The Great Wall of China is about 4,160 miles long. If a soldier was able to walk 30 miles a day, how long would it take him or her to walk from one end of the wall to the other? *(It would take more than 138 days—4,160 divided by 30.)*

Language Arts

Write a News Article

Have students use the Internet or other reference sources to find out more about Shi Huangdi's success in unifying China. Then have them write a news article that chronicles his role in Chinese history. Invite them to read their articles to the class.

Han China, 206 B.C.–A.D. 220
INTERACTIVE

Han Empire
Great Wall
Silk Roads

GOBI DESERT

Kashgar
Dunhuang
ASIA
Lanzhou
Ch'ang-an (Xi'an)
Luoyang
Nanjing

KOREA
Sea of Japan
JAPAN
Yellow Sea
East China Sea
PACIFIC OCEAN

HIMALAYAS

INDIA
Bay of Bengal
South China Sea

GEOGRAPHY SKILLBUILDER
INTERPRETING MAPS
Place Which physical feature does the Great Wall border?

The Han Dynasty

② **ESSENTIAL QUESTION** How did the Han rule China? They used a bureaucracy.

Shi Huangdi's son was a less effective ruler than his father. People rebelled during his rule. A civil war broke out during the last years of his reign. Eventually, a military general named Liu Bang (lee•oo bahng) defeated the Qin forces. He ended the civil war and reunified China. In 202 B.C., he started the **Han Dynasty**. The Han Dynasty lasted until about 220 A.D., during the same time period as the Roman Empire.

Han Government Liu Bang kept the Qin policies of strong central government, but he lowered taxes. He made punishments less harsh. In Han China, peasant men owed the government a month of labor per year on the emperor's public projects. He put peasants to work building roads, canals, and irrigation projects.

The Han rulers set up a **bureaucracy**. In this way of governing, officials chosen by the ruler ran offices, or bureaus. The officials helped enforce the emperor's rule. The Han rulers put family members and trusted people in local government positions. They set up a system of tests to find the most educated and ethical people for the imperial bureaucratic state. To do this they tested individuals on their knowledge of Confucianism.

Ancient China • 269

History from Visuals

Interpreting Maps
Ask students to review the map of Han China, including the key that explains the meaning of the map's shading and symbols. Point out to students that for most of its length, the Great Wall of China runs along the border of the Han Empire.

GEOGRAPHY SKILLBUILDER ANSWER

the Gobi Desert

INTERACTIVE

An interactive version of this map is available on the eEdition and Power Presentations CD-ROMs.

Teach

The Han Dynasty

🖊 6.6.6

Talk About It

- Why did civil war erupt in China under the son of Shi Huangdi? *(He was not an effective ruler and people rebelled against him.)*

- What system did Han rulers use to build the most effective bureaucracy? *(They tested people in their knowledge of Confucianism to find the most skilled and qualified people.)*

- According to the text, what was the main contribution of Wudi to the Chinese Empire? *(He expanded the empire through conquest.)*

- **Critical Thinking: Identifying Issues and Problems** The text refers to a variety of problems in the Han Empire, but states that "Somehow they managed to stay in power until A.D. 220." Why was it unusual for a dynasty to survive such troubles? *(Possible answer: The Chinese belief in the Mandate of Heaven dictated that troubles such as those that the Han faced meant it was time for a new dynasty.)*

DIFFERENTIATING INSTRUCTION

English Learners

Define Multiple-Meaning Words
Write the following sentences on the board and ask students to read each one aloud: "At the end of the Zhou *period*, several states were still at war." "Remember to put a *period* at the end of a sentence." Model for students how to identify the correct definition of the word *period* by using a dictionary and sentence context. Have students work with a partner and choose correct definitions of other multiple-meaning words found in the lesson (drove, noble, ruler) by using a dictionary and sentence context.

Inclusion

Practice Remembering
Point out the title "Han Government" and have students read the text under it. Ask them to close their books and tell you everything they remember. Write their responses on the board, leaving space under each. When students run out of ideas, ask them to open their books and verify their answers. Have students copy the corrected information into their notebooks.

Ancient China • 269

Vocabulary Strategy

Using Context Clues
Have students use context clues to try to determine the meaning of the term *martial* in the second paragraph on this page. Help students see that the phrase *because he used war* helps explain the meaning of *martial*—of or having to do with war. Ask students to offer their ideas on the meaning of the common term *court martial* (a court for the armed forces) and *martial law* (rule by the military).

Teach

Life in Han China

6.6, 6.6.6

Talk About It

- In what kind of environment did most Chinese live and work during the Han Dynasty? *(on farms)*

- How might one distinguish between a wealthy farmer and a poor farmer in Han China? *(A wealthy farmer would have an animal to pull the plow, whereas a poor farmer would likely pull the plow by himself or herself.)*

- Briefly describe Han cities. *(Possible answers: They were centers of trade, government, and education. They were crowded and had entertainment. They may also have had street gangs.)*

- **Critical Thinking: Making Inferences** Why do you think many people in China today identify themselves with Han China? *(Possible answer: It was a time when China was successful and prosperous.)*

Empress Rules When Liu Bang died in 195 B.C., his widow, the Empress Lü, ruled for their young son. Lü outlived her son and continued to place infants on the throne. This allowed her to retain power because the infants were too young to rule. When she died in 180 B.C. all her relatives were executed.

Expanding the Empire From 141 to 87 B.C., a descendant of Liu Bang named Wudi (woo•dee) ruled the Han Empire. He was called the Martial Emperor because he used war to expand China. Wudi made many military conquests. He brought southern Chinese provinces, northern Vietnam, and northern Korea under his control. He chased nomadic invaders out of northern China. By the end of his rule, China had grown significantly, in fact nearly as large as it is today.

The Han faced rebellions, peasant revolts, floods, famine, and economic disasters. Somehow they managed to stay in power until A.D. 220.

REVIEW How did the Han rulers find people for government jobs?
The Han rulers set up a system of tests. They tested for knowledge of Confucianism.

Life in Han China

Many lived in small rural villages and worked as farmers. Others lived in cities and worked in business or government.

3 ESSENTIAL QUESTION What was life in Han China like?

Many Chinese today call themselves the people of the Han. They identify strongly with their ancient past. The Han were industrious people whose civilization prospered.

Daily Life in Han China A large part of the Han society lived and worked on farms. Farmers lived in villages near the lands they worked. Most lived in one- or two-story mud houses. Barns, pigsties, and storage buildings were also located there. Rich farmers probably had an ox or two to pull a plow. Poor farmers had to pull the plows themselves. Both rich and poor had a few simple tools to make farming a bit easier.

Chinese farmers wore simple clothing and sandals, much like clothing today. For the cooler months, their clothing was stuffed like a quilt. Farmers in the north raised wheat or millet. Those in the south raised rice. Families kept vegetable gardens for additional food. Fish and meat were available, but expensive. As a result, most people ate small portions of meat and fish.

Women of Han
These ladies of the Chinese court have elaborate dresses and hair styles. ▼

DIFFERENTIATING INSTRUCTION

Gifted and Talented Students

Propose "Men of Han" Illustrations
Point out the pictures of the "Women of Han" on this page. Have students do research in the library or on the Internet to find pictures or descriptions with which to make "Men of Han" illustrations. Students can collect drawings or written descriptions of the clothing and styles worn by men during the Han Dynasty.

Struggling Readers

Focus on Vocabulary
Have students read through the section "Life in Han China" and jot down any words or phrases that are difficult for them to understand. *(Possible examples include the words industrious, prosperous, pigsties, and millet.)* Have students use dictionaries to try to find the meanings of these terms. Tell them they can ask you about those they cannot figure out. After you have explained all the challenging terms, have students reread the section.

City Living Not everyone lived in the country. Han China had cities as well. The cities were centers of trade, education, and government. Merchants, craftspeople, and government officials lived there. In some ways, the cities were not too different from today's cities. They were crowded and had lots of entertainment, including musicians, jugglers, and acrobats. According to some writers, the cities also had street gangs.

REVIEW How were the lives of farmers different from those of city dwellers? Farmers lived in small houses near their fields and possibly in a small village. City dwellers lived in more populated areas.

Flying Horse This bronze statue of a horse is considered one of the finest pieces of Han art. ▼

Lesson Summary

- In 221 B.C., the Qin ruler Shi Huangdi unified China and ruled by harsh Legalist principles.
- The Han Dynasty ruled over a large and successful land.
- The Han Chinese way of life is reflected in Chinese life today.

Why It Matters Now . . .
Strong government remains important in Chinese life today.

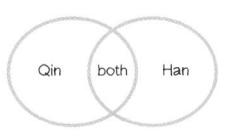

3 Lesson Review

Homework Helper
ClassZone.com

Terms & Names

1. Explain the importance of
   Qin
   Shi Huangdi
   Han Dynasty
   bureaucracy

Using Your Notes

Comparing and Contrasting Use your completed graphic to answer the following question:

2. In what ways were the Qin and Han dynasties similar? (6.6.5, 6.6.6)

Qin — both — Han

Main Ideas

3. What ruling style did Shi Huangdi choose, and how did it affect his rule? (6.6.5)
4. Why was the ruler Wudi important in the achievements of the Han Dynasty? (6.6.6)
5. How is the Chinese way of life today similar to that of Han China? (6.6)

Critical Thinking

6. **Making Inferences** Why were Shi Huangdi's efforts to unify China important? (6.6.5)
7. **Comparing** How were Shi Huangdi's methods of uniting his lands similar to those of Persian rulers? (6.6.5)

Activity **Making a Map** Take out the world map that you started in Chapter 2. Add the borders of Han China to the map and then draw the Great Wall of China. Choose an appropriate symbol for the wall. (6.6)

Ancient China • **271**

---

④ Assess & Reteach

Assess Have pairs of students use the lesson review questions to quiz each other, taking turns answering the questions.

 Formal Assessment
• Lesson Quiz, p. 136

Reteach Have students use numbers to indicate their familiarity with the vocabulary terms in this section. Have the students tear a piece of paper into quarters. Write one of the numbers 0–3 on each quarter. Write the terms on the board. As you point to each term and say it aloud, have students hold up zero if they do not understand the term; one if they have a vague idea what it means; two if they are fairly sure of the word's meaning; and three if they know the word and can use it in a sentence.

📝 **In-Depth Resources: Unit 4**
• Vocabulary Cards, p. 31
• Reteaching Activity, p. 39

🔎 **Homework Helper**

Visit **ClassZone.com** for a lesson review, a flip-card activity, and links to related Web sites.

---

3 Lesson Review Answers

Terms & Names

1. • Qin, p. 267
   • Shi Huangdi, p. 267
   • Han Dynasty, p. 269
   • bureaucracy, p. 269

USING YOUR NOTES
See page 266 for an example of a completed diagram.

2. Both sought to build a strong central government. Both dynasties greatly expanded Chinese territory. Both depended on the work of peasants (though Qin conditions were harsher).

MAIN IDEAS

3. Shi Huangdi was a Legalist. He ruled harshly and tried to wipe out Confucian ideas.
4. Wudi expanded China, brought parts of Vietnam and Korea under Chinese control, and chased nomadic invaders out of northern China.
5. Many Chinese still live in rural areas, raising grains; others live in cities, which are centers of trade, education, and government.

Critical Thinking

6. During the Time of the Warring States, warlords dominated small areas and there was little unity. By changing the way trade and government were done, Shi Huangdi created a China that operated in a similar fashion everywhere.
7. Possible answer: He sought to create a unified land by such measures as building highways and issuing standardized coins.

Activity Rubric

	Location of Borders and Wall	Clarity of Legend or Key	Quality of Map
4	accurate	clear	outstanding
3	mostly accurate	mostly clear	good
2	somewhat inaccurate	misleading	average
1	inaccurate	missing	poor

Ancient China • **271**

Objectives

- Describe the features of Shi Huangdi's buried terra cotta army.
- Analyze literature as a means of learning about history.
- **Language Objective:** Create a concept cluster of words and terms from the lesson that are related to the selection.

❶ Focus & Motivate

Connect to the Big Idea

Belief Systems Belief systems and religions may shape government and societies. In ancient China, belief about what happens after death apparently led emperor Shi Huangdi to have a grand terra cotta army built to guard his tomb. This extraordinary army provides many details about life in the days of ancient China.

Connect to Prior Knowledge

Have students review what they learned in the Lesson 3 about Shi Huangdi. *(He was a Legalist who united China and ordered the construction of the Great Wall of China. He used force to control his people and killed those who held views he considered to be dangerous.)*

More About . . .

Shi Huangdi
Shi Huangdi was uncomfortable with the idea of death and interested in the subject of immortality. This helps explain his decision to have this terra cotta army created to protect his tomb. While much work has been done on the excavation of the soldiers who guard him, Shi Huangdi's body has not been found.

Extend Lesson 3

Literature CONNECTIONS

from THE EMPEROR'S SILENT ARMY

BY JANE O'CONNOR

Background: In 1974, three Chinese farmers digging a well hit a hard object. As they continued to dig, the clay head of a man dressed like an ancient soldier emerged from the ground. The farmers had stumbled across a clay army of about 7,500 soldiers complete with weapons and horse-drawn chariots. The army was buried at the site of the tomb of one of China's greatest emperors, Qin Shinhuang (shee•hwahng•dee). (He is also known as Shi Huangdi.)

CALIFORNIA STANDARDS
Reading 2.0 Students read and understand grade-level-appropriate material. They describe and connect the essential ideas, arguments, and perspectives of the text by using their knowledge of text structure, organization, and purpose.

272 • Chapter 8

ADDITIONAL RESOURCES

Books for the Student
Patent, Dorothy Hinshaw. *The Incredible Story of China's Buried Warriors.* New York: Benchmark Books, 1999. Description of the buried army at Shi Huangdi's tomb.

Peers, Chris J., and Michael Perry. *Imperial Chinese Armies: 200 B.C.–589 A.D.* Oxford: Osprey Publishing, 1995. Discussion of the clothing, equipment, and tactics used by ancient Chinese soldiers.

Lindesay, William, and Guo Baofu. *The Terracotta Army of the First Emperor of China.* Hong Kong: Odyssey Publications, 1999. Pictorial account of the archaeological findings at Shi Huangdi's tomb.

Pancella, Peggy. *Qin Shi Huangdi.* Chicago: Heinemann Library, 2004. Biography of the first Qin emperor.

Videos

Tomb of the Terra Cotta Warriors. 50 minutes. New York: A&E Home Video, 1998. Video exploration of the excavations of the tomb of the terra cotta warriors.

BURIED SOLDIERS

Qin Shinhuang became emperor because of his stunning victories on the battlefield. His army was said to be a million strong. In every respect except for number, the terracotta army is a faithful replica of the real one.

So far terracotta troops have been found in three separate pits, all close to one another. A fourth pit was discovered, but it was empty. The entire army faces east. The Qin kingdom, the emperor's homeland, was in the northwest. The other kingdoms that had been conquered and had become part of his empire lay to the east. So Qin Shihuang feared that any enemy uprising would come from that direction.

The first pit is by far the biggest, more than two football fields long, with approximately six thousand soldiers and horses. About one thousand have already been excavated and restored. None of the soldiers in the army wears a helmet or carries a shield, proof of the Qin soldiers' fearlessness. But the archers stationed in the front lines don't wear any armor either. They needed to be able to move freely in order to fire their arrows with accuracy. And so these frontline sharpshooters, who were the first targets of an approaching enemy, also had the least protection.

Following the vanguard[1] are eleven long columns of foot soldiers and lower-ranking officers, the main body of the army, who once carried spears, battle-axes, and halberds[2]. The soldiers are prepared for an attack from any direction; those in the extreme right and extreme left columns face out, not forward, so that they can block enemy charges from either side. Last of all comes the rear guard, three rows of soldiers with their backs to the rest of the army, ready to stop an attack from behind.

Stationed at various points among the foot soldiers are about fifty charioteers who drove wooden chariots. Each charioteer has a team of four horses and is dressed in full-length armor. In some carts, a general rides beside the charioteer, ready to beat a drum to signal a charge or ring a bell to call for a retreat. . . .

Terra Cotta Army Site

CHINA

□   Tomb of the Terra Cotta Army

    Qin Empire, 221 B.C.–202 B.C.

    Present-day China

---

1. **vanguard:** troops moving at the head of an army.
2. **halberd:** a long-handled weapon used as both spear and a battle-ax.

Ancient China • 273

...IATING INSTRUCTION

...rners

...ulary

...fficult words in the literature
...fined, students may find a
...miliar terms.

...to review the text to locate
...s they do not know. Have
...hese terms on one side of
...n work with them to find
...ch students can write on
...e of the note card. They can
...review meanings or to quiz

Gifted and Talented Students

Report on Shi Huangdi's Military

Shi Huangdi was famed for having a large and powerful military. Have students use library or Internet sources to report on the exploits of this force during the emperor's lifetime. Suggest that students present their findings in the form of a time line of key events. Students can also illustrate their time line with pictures they find or create themselves.

❷ Teach

Talk About It

- What is the significance of the direction in which the terra cotta army is facing? *(The army is facing the direction from which the emperor may have feared future attack.)*

- What does the clothing and equipment of the figures tell about their courage? *(They had little protection—for example, no helmets— which suggests they entered battle with no fear.)*

- How do the soldiers protect against attacks from the side and the back? *(Some of the soldiers face the side and some face to the rear.)*

- **Critical Thinking: Drawing Conclusions from Sources** The passage mentions that one of the pits in which the soldiers have been found was empty. What are some possible explanations for this? *(Possible answer: There were not enough terra cotta soldiers to fill this pit at the time of the emperor's death.)*

Teach

Talk About It

- What information supports the statement that the second pit is a backup force to the main pit? *(It has fewer soldiers. It includes soldiers of all different ranks, plus many horses.)*

- What information supports the statement that the third pit may be army headquarters? *(The soldiers in the third pit are not arranged in formation.)*

- **Critical Thinking: Framing Historical Questions** What questions might you ask that would help you understand what the intended purpose of that fourth pit was? *(Possible answers: What was the customary formation of fighting forces in Shi Huangdi's day? Where is the fourth pit located relative to the other pits?)*

More About . . .

The Terra Cotta Figures

The terra cotta figures in the pits were originally painted with different colors—about 13 have been identified. However, this paint has deteriorated over the centuries. Archaeologists have found that soon after being exposed to the air, the paint disappears. They have been working on methods to protect the paint so that soldiers still in the ground—and there are many—can have their paint preserved.

Pit 2 is far smaller than Pit 1. With an estimated 900 warriors of all different ranks, Pit 2 serves as a powerful back-up force to help the larger army in Pit 1. There are also almost 500 chariot horses and more than 100 cavalry horses.

The terracotta horses are Mongolian[3] ponies, not very big, but muscular and full of power. With their flaring nostrils, bared teeth, and bulging eyes, the chariot horses all look as if they are straining to gallop across a battlefield. The mane of each chariot horse is trimmed short and its tail is braided. That is so it won't get caught in the harness. . . .

Pit 3, by far the smallest, contains fewer than seventy warriors and only one team of horses. Archeologists think that Pit 3 represents army headquarters. That's because the soldiers are not arranged in an attack formation. . . .

Altogether, the three pits of warriors and horses make up an unstoppable army. . . .

REVIEW Which army groups are represented in each pit?

Pit 1: archers, foot soldiers, charioteers; Pit 2: backup forces; Pit 3: army headquarters

3. **Mongolian:** coming from the area of Mongolia.

▼ **Pit 2 Soldiers** These are a backup force for the soldiers in Pit 1.

Top View Diagram of Terra Cotta Army Pits

Filled with army
Empty

Pit 4
Pit 3
Pit 2
Pit 1

N W E S

0   50 meters

DIFFERENTIATING INSTRUCTION

Struggling Readers

Diagram the Pits

To help students get a better picture of the description in this passage, have them work in teams to create diagrams of the different pits. Using the illustrations in the text and additional research, have students create a separate diagram for each room. Students should draw a rough outline of each pit and include notes and illustrations that help explain and describe the contents of each room.

Gifted and Talented Students

Create a Qin Art Gallery

The terra cotta figures in Shi Huangdi's tomb are more than just a rich history. They are also spectacular examples of ancient Chinese art. Have students conduct research to learn more about Chinese art of the time. Have them collect their findings in a gallery of representative artworks. Each page of this gallery should include an image of art from around the Qin era along with a written description of the piece.

About two thousand soldiers have been unearthed, yet, amazingly, so far no two are the same. The army includes men of all different ages, from different parts of China, with different temperaments. A young soldier looks both excited and nervous; an older officer, perhaps a veteran of many wars, appears tired, resigned.[4] Some soldiers seem lost in thought, possibly dreaming of their return home; others look proud and confident. Although from a distance the figures appear almost identical, like giant-size toy soldiers, each is a distinct work of art. . . .

The uniforms of the terracotta figures are exact copies in clay of what real soldiers of the day wore. The soldier's uniform tells his rank in the army. The lowest-ranking soldiers are bareheaded and wear heavy knee-length tunics[5] but no armor. Often their legs are wrapped in cloth shin guards for protection.

The generals' uniforms are the most elegant. Their caps sometimes sport a pheasant feather; their fancy shoes curl up at the toes; and their fine armor is made from small iron fish scales. Tassels on their armor are also a mark of their high rank.

▲ **Mongolian Ponies**
More than 600 horses were found in the tombs. Some were cavalry horses, and others pulled war chariots.

REVIEW How would you describe the uniforms of the soldiers? *The generals' uniforms are more elegant; they have fine armor. The lowest-ranking soldiers have little protection and no armor*

4. **resigned:** giving in passively to sorrow or misfortune.
5. **tunic:** a loose-fitting knee-length garment.

Reading & Writing

1. **READING: Essential Ideas** What information about the emperor's army can you gain from the text, pictures, and diagrams in the story?

2. **WRITING: Response to Literature** Write a speech asking for donations to continue the archaeological work at the site of the tomb. Deliver the speech to your classmates.

CALIFORNIA STANDARDS Writing 2.4
Write responses to literature.

Teach

Talk About It

- According to this source, how many soldiers have been uncovered? *(about 2,000)*

- What is surprising about the appearance of these figures? *(Each figure is unique.)*

- What details help distinguish the different ranks of the soldiers in the pit? *(Their uniforms differ, with the lowest ranking soldiers wearing simple tunics and the generals wearing elaborate clothes.)*

- **Critical Thinking: Making Inferences** Why do you think the soldiers were created with such care, ensuring that each was unique? What does this suggest about the purpose of the terra cotta army? *(Possible answers: The figures had a purpose that went beyond decoration. The figures were meant to be lifelike and suggest that perhaps Shi Huangdi believed in an afterlife.)*

More About . . .

Differences Between the Figures
Experts have noted that the differences between individual figures vary not just from person to person, but from room to room. The expressions and faces of the horses also vary. In addition, the figures vary by rank. The lowest ranking soldiers vary in size, from around five feet, eight inches tall to over six feet. Officers are generally taller.

ACTIVITIES ANSWERS

1. **READING** the number of warriors, the organization of the army, weapons used, clothing of the warriors

2. **WRITING**

2. Writing Rubric

	Information on Site	Account of Discovery	Details about Statues	Requests for Funds
4	complete	interesting and engaging	many rich details	strong and appealing
3	adequate	fairly complete	many details	adequate
2	some	adequate	several	weak
1	little	weak	few/none	missing

❶ Plan & Prepare

Objectives

- Explore the contributions and impact of the Silk Roads on Chinese culture and history.
- Trace the influence of ideas such as Confucianism and Daoism in Chinese history.
- Describe the many contributions of the ancient Chinese to our world.
- **Language Objective:** Formulate, ask, and respond to questions to demonstrate understanding.

Quick Look

Lesson 4 explores the cultural influences that have helped shape China and the ways in which Chinese culture has influenced the world.

❷ Focus & Motivate

Preview Explain that this lesson traces the cultural legacy of ancient China. Ask students if they can identify any major inventions for which the ancient Chinese are credited.

Introduce the Main Ideas The three main ideas relate to the Big Idea "Ways of living change as humans interact with each other." Help students look for this Big Idea as you go through the lesson.

Reading Skill: Categorizing Being able to organize information by putting it into appropriate categories can help students understand what they read.

SAMPLE ANSWERS FOR ORGANIZER

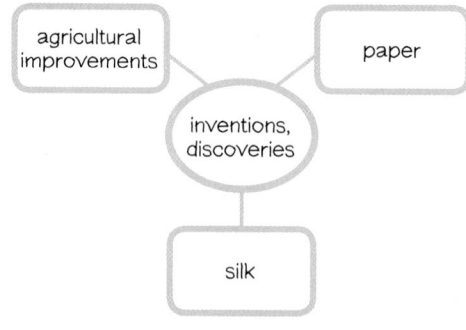

▶ **MAIN IDEAS**

❶ **Geography** The Silk Roads brought cultural and economic changes to China.

❷ **Belief Systems** Chinese philosophies such as Confucianism and Daoism had a lasting influence on East Asia.

❸ **Science and Technology** During Han times, China made many advances in technology, agriculture, and trade.

▶ **TAKING NOTES**

Reading Skill: Categorizing

Sorting information into groups helps you understand important developments in history. Look for categories of ancient China's legacy and details about them. Record the information on a web diagram.

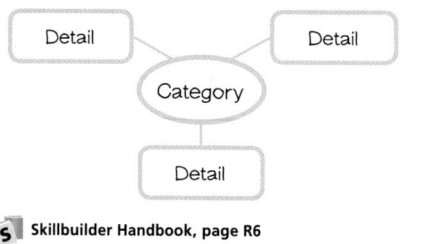

S **Skillbuilder Handbook, page R6**

▲ **Embroidered Silk Tapestry**
This Chinese tapestry shows the Buddha preaching at a site called Vulture Peak.

CALIFORNIA STANDARDS

6.6. Students analyze the geographic, political, economic, religious, and social structures of the early civilizations of China.

6.6.3 Know about the life of Confucius and the fundamental teachings of Confucianism and Daoism.

6.6.7 Cite the significance of the trans-Eurasian "Silk Roads" in the period of the Han Dynasty and Roman Empire and their locations.

6.6.8 Describe the diffusion of Buddhism northward to China during the Han Dynasty.

HOW TO TEACH THE CALIFORNIA STANDARDS

Standard	Content	Student Question or Activity	Instruction
6.6	**Pages 279–280** Presents major Chinese inventions and innovations.	**Page 279** Students explain why most early Chinese inventions were related to farming.	Suggest that students use the Internet or library resources to read more about Chinese innovations in different fields.
6.6.3	**Pages 278** Summarizes the lasting legacy of Confucian and Daoist thought in China	**Page 278** Students tell how Chinese philosophies still impact the world today.	Suggest that students use the library or Internet resources to read about modern-day students of Daoist and Confucian thought.
6.6.7	**Pages 277–278** Describes the nature of the Silk Roads in ancient China	**Page 278** Students analyze the importance of the Silk Roads.	Tell students that the Silk Roads had a big impact on Europe as well. Ask students what they know about Marco Polo.
6.6.8	**Pages 278** Describes the role of the Silk Roads in the spread of Buddhism	**Page 280** Students explain how the Silk Roads helped spread Buddhism.	Tell students that Buddhism took root in China and continues to be an important religious tradition there today.

The Legacy of Ancient China

TERMS & NAMES

Silk Roads

trans-Eurasian

cultural diffusion

Terms & Names

Silk Roads the overland trade routes linking China to the West.

trans-Eurasian involving the continents of Europe and Asia

cultural diffusion the spread of ethnic ideas and customs to other areas of the world

Build on What You Know Trade formed a part of Chinese life. Despite the geographic barriers that separated China from the lands to the west, trade caused Chinese contacts with other lands to increase.

The Silk Roads

❶ ESSENTIAL QUESTION What kinds of goods moved along the Silk Roads? Silk, paper, pottery from China and metals, precious stones, and horses from the west moved along the roads between the east and the west.

During the time of the Han Dynasty, only the Chinese knew how to make silk. It was much desired as a luxury fabric by both the Chinese and people outside of China. Chinese silk was important in opening trading routes to the west.

A Trans-Eurasian Link Overland trade routes were called **Silk Roads** because traders carried silk and other goods on caravan trails. The trails stretched westward from China through central Asia to Mesopotamia and Europe. (See map on pages 278–279.) Because these trails stretched across two continents, Europe and Asia, they were called **trans-Eurasian**. China was part of a huge global trade network.

By 100 B.C., the Silk Roads were well established. Goods leaving China included silk, paper, and pottery. Exchange goods coming from the west included sesame seeds and oil, metals, and precious stones. One trade item the Chinese especially valued was Central Asian horses.

Cultural Diffusion Trade goods were not the only things that moved on the Silk Roads. Ideas and cultural customs moved on the Silk Roads, too. This spread of ideas and customs is called **cultural diffusion**. For example, such things as Central Asian military methods, Buddhism, and western cultural styles reached China. In turn, Chinese art, silks, and pottery influenced the cultures to the west.

Connect to Today

Silk A modern-day seller of silk sells his goods at the ancient Silk Road market at Kashgar in China. ▼

277

❸ Teach

The Silk Roads

↖ **6.6.7, 6.6.8**

Talk About It

- **Critical Thinking: Summarizing** Explain how the trade along the Silk Roads led to the introduction of Buddhism in China. *(Possible answer: Trade linked China to places such as India; Buddhist priests traveled to China, bringing information about the Buddhist religion.)*

In-Depth Resources: Unit 4
• Reading Skill: Categorizing, p. 27

Teach

Influential Ideas and Beliefs

 6.6.3

Talk About It

• What became of Daoism over the centuries in China? *(It became a religion.)*

• **Critical Thinking: Comparing and Contrasting** How are the legacies of Confucianism and Daoism similar and different? *(Both remain influential today. Daoism is a religion that remained widespread only in China, while Confucian thought spread beyond China.)*

History from Visuals

Interpreting Maps
Have students look over the map that spreads across pages 278–279. To ensure that students recognize what part of the globe is highlighted in this map, direct their attention to the small locator map on page 278. Make sure they see that this map stretches all the way from the Mediterranean Sea to China, and that it passes through or near the lands of Mesopotamia, Persia, and India.

• How do you think the presence of the Silk Roads affected life in the cities located along their paths? *(Possible answer: These places probably included people of many cultures and were active trading centers.)*

GEOGRAPHY SKILLBUILDER ANSWER
The Silk Roads split to avoid the Taklimakan Desert.

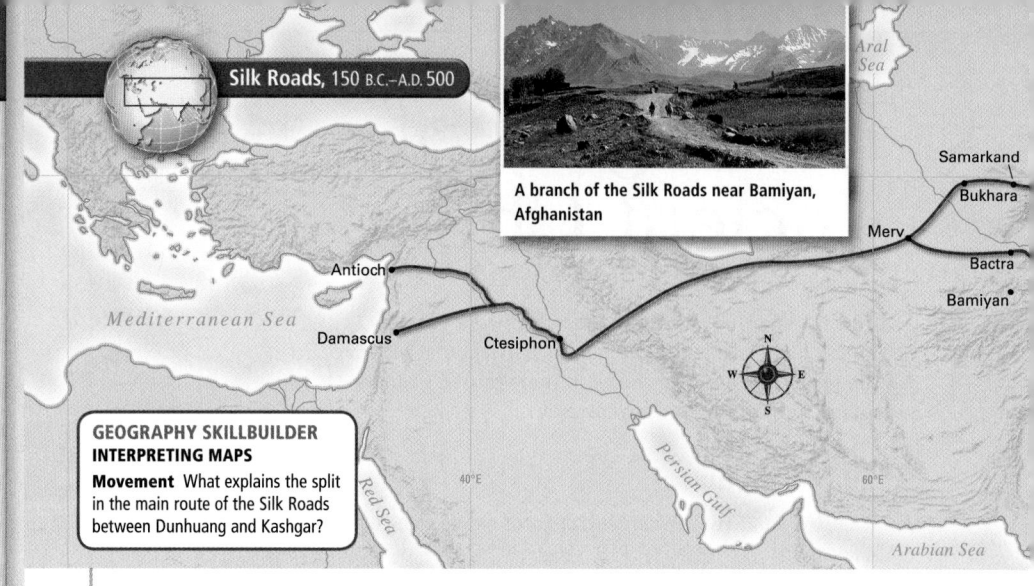

Silk Roads, 150 B.C.–A.D. 500

A branch of the Silk Roads near Bamiyan, Afghanistan

Samarkand
Bukhara
Merv
Bactra
Bamiyan
Antioch
Mediterranean Sea
Damascus
Ctesiphon
Red Sea
40°E
Persian Gulf
60°E
Aral Sea
Arabian Sea

GEOGRAPHY SKILLBUILDER
INTERPRETING MAPS
Movement What explains the split in the main route of the Silk Roads between Dunhuang and Kashgar?

The Spread of Buddhism In Chapter 7, you learned about the beginnings of Buddhism in India. During the Han Dynasty, Buddhist missionaries entered China along the Silk Roads. Buddhism spread to Japan and Korea from China. Chinese Buddhists modified Buddhism to make it fit better with their own traditions.

REVIEW Why were the Silk Roads important to Chinese civilization?
They linked China to lands to the west, facilitated trade, and brought cultural diffusion.

Influential Ideas and Beliefs

2 ESSENTIAL QUESTION How important were Confucianism and Daoism?
They were very important. They set a tone that continues into the present.

Confucianism The standards set by Confucianism remained significant in Chinese government and education. Today, the legacy of Confucius' ideas about social duty are still important in Chinese villages. Confucianism also became a very influential philosophy in Japan, Korea, and Vietnam.

Daoism Daoism had a lasting influence in China. By the sixth century it was a religion with priests, rituals, and volumes of collected writings. Unlike Confucianism, however, Daoism remained primarily a Chinese belief system.

REVIEW Where is Confucianism practiced today?
Confucianism is practiced in China, Korea, Japan, and Vietnam.

DIFFERENTIATING INSTRUCTION

English Learners

Formulate Questions
Model how to use the question words *who*, *what*, *when*, *where*, *why*, and *how* to turn a heading or subheading into a question. For example: Why are they called the Silk Roads? Guide students as they use important details from the text to formulate a response. Have students work with a partner to practice formulating, asking, and responding to questions about the lesson.

Inclusion

List Inventions and Discoveries
Have pairs of students list all of the different inventions and discoveries that they read about. Have each pair compare its list with the list of another pair to see if they got all the items.

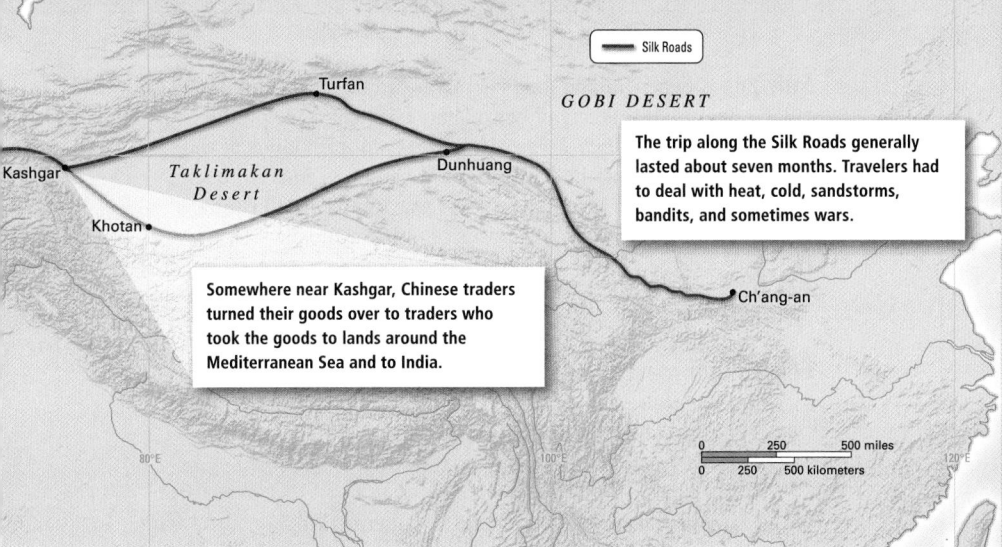

Silk Roads

Turfan

GOBI DESERT

Kashgar

Taklimakan Desert

Dunhuang

Khotan

Ch'ang-an

The trip along the Silk Roads generally lasted about seven months. Travelers had to deal with heat, cold, sandstorms, bandits, and sometimes wars.

Somewhere near Kashgar, Chinese traders turned their goods over to traders who took the goods to lands around the Mediterranean Sea and to India.

Chinese Inventions and Discoveries

③ **ESSENTIAL QUESTION** In which aspects of Chinese life did the Han make great advances?

China had a large and growing population to feed. Because agriculture was so important in China, most of the really important inventions during this period came about in agriculture.

Agricultural Improvements Chinese inventions made life easier for farmers and made more grain available for trade. For example, a better plow and farm tools helped increase crop production. The invention of a collar harness allowed horses to pull heavy loads. The wheelbarrow made it easier for farmers to move heavy loads by hand. Watermills used river power to grind grain. In a land of mostly farmers, these inventions were valuable.

Paper In A.D. 105, paper was invented in China. Before that time, books were made of costly silk. The inexpensive paper was made from a mixture of old rags, mulberry tree bark, and fibers from the hemp plant. Inexpensive paper made books available in a country that valued learning. Paper was important for a bureaucratic government that kept many records.

agricultural improvements, invention of paper, and production of silk

Ancient China • 279

Teach

Chinese Inventions and Discoveries

6.6

Talk About It

- What two inventions helped make it easier to move heavy loads? *(the collar harness and the wheelbarrow)*

- What were two benefits of the many Chinese inventions for agriculture? *(They made more grain available for trade and they made life easier for farmers.)*

- Why was paper such an important invention to the Chinese? *(It provided a low-cost alternative to silk. It made written materials more widely available. It helped the Chinese bureaucracy keep records.*

- **Critical Thinking: Forming and Supporting Opinions** Of the Chinese inventions and innovations mentioned, which do you think had the greatest impact on Chinese culture? Explain. *(Possible answer: silk, because it was very valuable and was able to lure traders from far away, who brought new products and new ideas to China)*

DIFFERENTIATING INSTRUCTION

Gifted and Talented Students

Catalog Chinese Inventions
Have students work in teams to create an illustrated catalog of Chinese inventions or innovations. Students can find information in the library or on the Internet. Each item in the catalog should be illustrated and include a brief description of its importance.

Struggling Readers

Illustrate the Content
Pair a strong reader with a struggling reader, and ask the stronger reader to read the section "Chinese Inventions and Discoveries" to the struggling reader. Tell the struggling reader to make brief notes and then illustrate the content of the section. The student should draw simple pictures of the inventions and innovations mentioned, along with brief descriptions of them.

④ Assess & Reteach

Assess Have students work on their own to answer the questions, then meet in groups to discuss their answers.

 Formal Assessment
• Lesson Quiz, p. 137

Reteach Divide the class into three groups. Assign each group one of the subsections in this lesson—"The Silk Roads," "Influential Ideas and Beliefs," or "Chinese Inventions and Discoveries." Each group should work together to list the three or four most important ideas in its subsection. Have groups share responses with the class. Make sure that each group takes notes on the subsections that the other groups covered.

 In-Depth Resources: Unit 4
• Vocabulary Cards, p. 31
• Reteaching Activity, p. 40

 Homework Helper

Visit **ClassZone.com** for a lesson review, a flip-card activity, and links to related Web sites.

Silk Silk is beautiful and long lasting. It can be dyed brilliant colors. Because it was rare, it became an excellent trade product. Silk allowed the Chinese to get silver and gold from lands to the west of China. At one time, one pound of silk was equal to one pound of gold. Getting gold and silver was important to China because it did not have rich deposits of either mineral.

REVIEW Why was it necessary to make improvements in farming methods in ancient China? China had very little land that could be farmed and many people who needed food from crops.

Lesson Summary
• Trading routes called the Silk Roads brought goods and ideas to and from China.
• Confucianism and Daoism had a lasting influence in China.
• Chinese inventions in agriculture, paper making, and other discoveries improved daily life.

Why It Matters Now . . .
Ancient cultural patterns continue to influence life in China and elsewhere.

4 Lesson Review

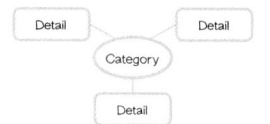

Terms & Names
1. Explain the importance of
   Silk Roads   trans-Eurasian   cultural diffusion

Using Your Notes
Categorizing Use your completed graphic to answer the following question:
2. What ideas or goods did China give the ancient world? (6.6)

```
   Detail          Detail
        \          /
         Category
            |
         Detail
```

Main Ideas
3. What economic changes did the Silk Roads bring to China? (6.6.7)
4. How did the Silk Roads aid in the spread of Buddhism? (6.6.8)
5. Why were most of the early Chinese inventions related to agriculture? (6.6)

Critical Thinking
6. **Understanding Cause and Effect** Why were the Silk Roads important to ancient China? (6.6.7)
7. **Making Inferences** Why might Confucianism continue to influence life in Chinese villages? (6.6.3)

Activity **Internet Activity** Use the Internet to research how silk is made. Create a diagram showing the process. Be sure to clearly label all the steps. (6.6)
INTERNET KEYWORD: *Silk making*

---

4 Lesson Review Answers

Terms & Names
1. • Silk Roads, p. 277
   • trans-Eurasian, p. 277
   • cultural diffusion, p. 277

Using Your Notes
See page 276 for an example of a completed organizer.
2. Among the Chinese contributions were silk, paper, agricultural improvements, and Confucian and Daoist philosophies.

Main Ideas
3. The trade routes brought new goods and metals to China and allowed the Chinese to trade silk and other products with the West.
4. Buddhist missionaries used the roads to travel into China and spread Buddhism.
5. China's large population needed efficient and effective agriculture, especially because it had a small growing area.

Critical Thinking
6. The Silk Roads established trading contact and cultural diffusion between China and the west. It allowed them to sell silk and to get goods and gold and silver in return.
7. Possible answer: Confucianism established patterns of social order and duty that continue to be important to Chinese villagers today.

Activity Rubric

	Accuracy of Labeling	Listing of Steps	Clarity of Diagram
4	all correct	all correct	clear
3	1–2 errors	most correct	mostly clear
2	several errors	one or two missing	parts unclear
1	none correct	missing	unclear

Keep a Silk Roads Journal

Goal: To analyze the nature of goods, landscape, and means of transportation on the Silk Roads by writing journal entries about a trader's experience on the road

Materials & Supplies
- books on the Silk Roads
- writing paper and pen

Prepare

1. Research the products, landscape, and means of transportation found on the Silk Roads.

2. Reread the information and look at the map of the Silk Roads on pages 278–279 in this chapter.

Do the Activity

1. Imagine you are a Chinese trader about to start a trip on the Silk Roads. Decide what items you will trade.

2. Determine a route you would take starting at Chang'an and ending at Kashgar.

3. Decide what type of animals you will use.

4. Write three diary entries about your experience on the Silk Roads. Be sure to include information about the land you are traveling through and other traders you meet.

Follow-Up

1. How did climate and physical geography help you plan your trip?

2. What things must you think about when planning a long trip on the Silk Roads?

Extension

Making a Wall Map Work with a group to create a large map of the Silk Roads. Tape your map to the wall and have other students add products traded on the Silk Roads.

CALIFORNIA STANDARDS
6.6.7 Cite the significance of the trans-Eurasian "Silk Roads" in the period of the Han Dynasty and Roman Empire and their locations.

281

Objectives

- Analyze the functions and features of the Silk Roads.
- Analyze impressions and record them in a journal.

Suggestions for Completing the Activity

- Before students begin their research into the Silk Roads, preview the kinds of information they will be asked to include in their journals. Have students be on the lookout for useful information as they do their research.

- Make sure students include all the required elements for this activity—details about animals used, route, and observations about climate and physical geography.

- Remind students that they are only traveling on one stretch of the Silk Roads and that the details and information they select should be appropriate to it.

ACTIVITY ANSWERS

Follow-Up Answers

1. Students should recognize that climate and geography would affect such factors as clothing choices, time of year for the journey, and type of animals used.

2. Possible answer: where you are traveling, when you are traveling, what you must carry, what lands you will be traveling through

Extension Rubric

	Content of Map	Style of Map
4	accurate, detailed	neatly done, correct spelling
3	accurate	neat, spelling mostly correct
2	somewhat accurate	acceptable, some labels misspelled or missing
1	not accurate	sloppy, labels missing

Terms & Names

1. The *Qin* ruler followed the principles of *Legalism*.

2. *Han Dynasty* rulers set up a *bureaucracy* and a system of examinations to fill many government posts.

3. According to *Confucianism*, the relationship between parent and child should demonstrate *filial piety*.

4. The *Silk Roads* helped promote *cultural diffusion* by making possible the spread of ideas and products between China and areas to the west.

Main Ideas

Geography Shapes Life in Ancient China (pages 252–257)

5. It helped promote agriculture by depositing yellowish silt that made the soil fertile.

6. Marks made by priests on animal bones or shells as part of a religious ritual became the basis for a Chinese system of writing.

China's Ancient Philosophies (pages 258–265)

7. Legalists believed in strict rules and total obedience to the government, while the Daoists believed in few rules and instead stressed finding one's own, individual path.

8. the relationships of ruler and subject; husband and wife; father and son; elder brother and junior brother; and friend and friend

The Qin and the Han (pages 266–275)

9. high taxes and the demand for labor from peasants

10. Han rulers established a bureaucracy in which many posts were filled on the basis of results of exams.

The Legacy of Ancient China (pages 276–281)

11. Central Asian military methods, Buddhism, and western cultural styles reached China along the Silk Roads.

12. Farmers could grow crops more efficiently to feed a large population in a country with very little farmable land.

▶ **VISUAL SUMMARY** 〔 **Ancient China** 〕

Science & Technology (6.6)
- Chinese master the art of bronzeworking.
- A language system develops.
- Advances in agricultural technology produce more food.
- Paper is invented.
- Silk is produced.

Geography (6.6.2, 6.6.7, 6.6.8)
- Early farmers settle in the river valleys of the Huang He and Chang Jiang.
- Physical landforms make contact with other parts of the world difficult.
- Goods, ideas, Buddhism, and cultural practices moved along the Silk Roads.

Government (6.6, 6.6.5, 6.6.6)
- Shang establish first dynasty.
- Mandate of Heaven establishes authority.
- Shi Huangdi and Qin unify China.
- Builders begin the Great Wall.
- Han Dynasty rules for 400 years.

Belief Systems (6.6.3, 6.6.4)
- Legalism calls for strict control of the people.
- Confucius teaches that the five relationships will bring harmony.
- Daoism promotes learning the way of nature to find harmony.

▶ **TERMS & NAMES**

Explain why the words in each set below are linked with each other.

1. **Qin** and **Legalism**
2. **Han Dynasty** and **bureaucracy**
3. **filial piety** and **Confucianism**
4. **Silk Roads** and **cultural diffusion**

▶ **MAIN IDEAS**

Geography Shapes Life in Ancient China (pages 252–257)
5. What made the Huang He so valuable to ancient Chinese civilization? (6.6.1)
6. How did Chinese writing develop? (6.6)

China's Ancient Philosophies (pages 258–265)
7. How did the Legalists and Daoists differ in their views of society? (6.6.3)
8. What five basic human relationships did Confucius teach? (6.6.4)

The Qin and the Han (pages 266–275)
9. Which policies of Qin ruler Shi Huangdi caused the greatest resentment among the people? (6.6.5)
10. What advances in government did the Han make? (6.6.6)

The Legacy of Ancient China (pages 276–281)
11. What are some ideas that reached ancient China because of the Silk Roads? (6.6.7)
12. Why were agricultural improvements important in ancient China? (6.6)

ALTERNATIVE ASSESSMENT RUBRICS

1. Writing Rubric

	Clarity of Description	Discussion of Views	Number of Errors
4	vivid	heartfelt	no errors
3	clear	adequate	few errors
2	needs details	needs more discussion	several errors
1	not clear	poor or missing	many errors

2. Science Rubric

	Description of the Process	Use of Illustrations	Clarity of Explanation
4	correct	engaging	clear and concise
3	mostly correct	attractive	clear
2	mostly incorrect	adequate	somewhat unclear
1	missing	poor or missing	unclear or missing

Critical Thinking

CRITICAL THINKING
Big Ideas: Belief Systems

13. DRAWING CONCLUSIONS How did the teachings of Confucius support the ancient Chinese family structure? (6.6.3)

14. UNDERSTANDING CAUSE AND EFFECT How did Confucianism contribute to the development of the Chinese bureaucracy? (6.6.4)

15. FORMING AND SUPPORTING OPINIONS Which of the three belief systems discussed in this chapter do you think would be the most effective in ruling a land? Explain. (6.6.3)

ALTERNATIVE ASSESSMENT

1. WRITING ACTIVITY Write a diary entry as a person working on the Great Wall. Include a description of your work and also your views about having to do the work. (Writing 2.1)

2. INTERDISCIPLINARY ACTIVITY—SCIENCE Research the paper-making process. Make a poster illustrating the process and tell how it changed Chinese lives. (6.6)

3. STARTING WITH A STORY

Review your letter on the impact of Confucian teachings on society. Write a paragraph supporting the view that strict laws, not simply respect, are needed to control society. (Writing 2.5)

Technology Activity

4. CREATING A MULTIMEDIA PRESENTATION
Use the library or the Internet to research the Qin tomb of Shi Huangdi and a tomb of an Egyptian ruler. Create a multimedia presentation on the tombs. (6.6.5)
Include
- location of tombs
- similarities and differences

Research Links
ClassZone.com

Reading a Map The map below shows climates that are found in China and compares them to locations in North America. Answer the questions about the map. (6.6)

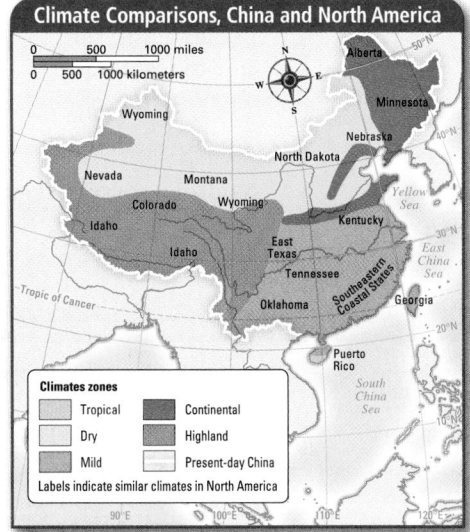

Climate Comparisons, China and North America

Climates zones
Tropical	Continental
Dry	Highland
Mild	Present-day China

Labels indicate similar climates in North America

1. The western lands of China are similar to which state of the United States?
A. Minnesota
B. Idaho
C. Kentucky
D. Oklahoma

2. Which area of China has a climate similar to Nebraska?
A. West Central
B. East Central
C. Northeast
D. Far North

Test Practice
ClassZone.com

Additional Test Practice, pp. S1–S33

Ancient China • 283

Critical Thinking

Big Ideas: Belief Systems

13. Possible answer: Three of the five key relationships identified by Confucius had to do with family relationships. Confucius saw the family as a key component of society.

14. Possible answer: In the Han Dynasty, the Chinese imperial government gave tests about Confucianism to bring fair and honest people into government positions.

15. Students should demonstrate knowledge of each philosophy and defend its strengths and weaknesses in fostering government.

Standards-Based Assessment

1. The correct answer is Idaho. Idaho is the only state in the set that is marked on western lands.

2. The correct answer is C. The labels on the map show that "Nebraska" is similar to the northeast part of China.

Research Links
Visit ClassZone.com for links to Web sites that can be used in the newsletter.

Test Practice
Visit ClassZone.com to access strategies and tutorials for taking standardized tests.

Formal Assessment
- Chapter Test, Forms A, B, and C, pp. 138–149

Test Generator
- Chapter Tests, Forms A, B, and C (English and Spanish)

ALTERNATIVE ASSESSMENT RUBRICS

3. Starting with a Story Rubric

	Statement of Position	Level of Support	Discussion of Counter-arguments
4	clear and concise	outstanding	clearly rebutted
3	clear	solid	mostly rebutted
2	unclear	weak	hardly discussed
1	missing	poor	missing

4. Technology Rubric

	Accuracy of Locations	Comparison of Tombs	Number of Media Used
4	correct	thorough and complete	more than three
3	correct	adequate	two or three
2	incorrect	some comparison	one
1	missing	little comparison	none

CHAPTER 9 PLANNING GUIDE: Ancient America

Chapter Overview

Early civilizations such as the Olmec and Maya emerged in lands south of the present-day United States, leaving behind a rich legacy that is still influential today.

Copymasters

In-Depth Resources: Unit 4
- Family Newsletter (English and Spanish), pp. 41–42
- Visual Summary, p. 47
- Vocabulary Study Guide, p. 49

Character Education

Reading Study Guide, p. 85

Bringing Social Studies Alive, Chapter 9

Document-Based Questions: Strategy and Practice

Reading Toolkit, L29–L32

Modified Lesson Plans for English Learners, pp. 61–68

Assessment

Chapter Review, pp. 314–315

Formal Assessment
- Chapter Tests, Forms A, B, and C, pp. 154–168

Test Generator

Integrated Assessment Book

Online Test Practice

LESSON 1

The Geography of the Americas

pp. 288–293

OBJECTIVE Study the areas of the Americas where the first civilizations developed.

In-Depth Resources: Unit 4
- Reading Skill: Comparing and Contrasting, p. 43
- Vocabulary Cards, p. 51
- Reteaching Activity, p. 57

Interdisciplinary Projects
- Science, p. 50

Reading Study Guide, p. 77

Lesson Review, p. 293

Formal Assessment
- Lesson Quiz, p. 150

California Daily Standards Practice Transparencies, TT29

LESSON 2

Ancient Andean Civilizations

pp. 294–299

OBJECTIVE Analyze the rise of the early civilizations in South America.

In-Depth Resources: Unit 4
- Reading Skill: Drawing Conclusions, p. 44
- Vocabulary Cards, p. 51
- Skillbuilder Practice: Creating a Model, p. 48
- Reteaching Activity, p. 58

Interdisciplinary Projects
- Language Arts, p. 51

Reading Study Guide, p. 79

Lesson Review, p. 299

Formal Assessment
- Lesson Quiz, p. 151

California Daily Standards Practice Transparencies, TT30

LESSON 3

The Olmec of Meso-America

pp. 300–305

OBJECTIVE Trace the development of the Olmec civilization in Meso-America.

In-Depth Resources: Unit 4
- Reading Skill: Categorizing, p. 45
- Vocabulary Cards, p. 51
- Reteaching Activity, p. 59

Reading Study Guide, p. 81

Interdisciplinary Projects
- Physical Education, p. 52

Lesson Review, p. 304

Formal Assessment
- Lesson Quiz, p. 152

California Daily Standards Practice Transparencies, TT31

LESSON 4

The Mayan Civilization

pp. 306–313

OBJECTIVE Learn about the development of the Mayan civilization in Meso-America.

In-Depth Resources: Unit 4
- Reading Skill: Visualizing, p. 46
- Vocabulary Cards, p. 51
- Geography Practice: The Land of the Maya, p. 53
- Literature: Popol Vuh, p. 56
- Primary Source: The Rabbit and the Crab, p. 55
- Reteaching Activity, p. 60

History Makers
- Pacal, p. 17

Interdisciplinary Projects
- Math, p. 49

Reading Study Guide, p. 83

Lesson Review, p. 311

Formal Assessment
- Lesson Quiz, p. 153

California Daily Standards Practice Transparencies, TT32

Integrated Technology

 **eEdition Plus Online**

EasyPlanner Plus Online

eTest Plus Online

 Audio CDs
• Reading Study Guide
• Reading Study
  Guide in Spanish
• The World's Music

 CD-ROMs
• Power Presentations
• eEdition
• EasyPlanner
• Test Generator

 **Ancient Civilizations Video Series**
• Ancient Maya

---

 eEdition CD-ROM

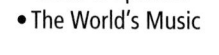 **Map Transparencies**
• MT17 Geographic Regions of South America

 **Critical Thinking Transparencies**
• CT37 Comparing and Contrasting

 **ClassZone.com**

---

 eEdition CD-ROM

 **Humanities Transparencies**
• HT17 Nazca Line Drawing of a Man

 **Critical Thinking Transparencies**
• CT38 Drawing Conclusions

 ClassZone.com

---

 eEdition CD-ROM

 **Critical Thinking Transparencies**
• CT39 Categorizing

 **ClassZone.com**

---

 eEdition CD-ROM

 **Map Transparencies**
• MT18 Archaeological Map of Tikal

 Humanities Transparencies
• HT18 Mayan Ball Game Marker

 **Critical Thinking Transparencies**
• CT40 Summarizing
• CT41 Chapter 9 Visual Summary

 ClassZone.com

Overview of California Resources

	Lesson 1	Lesson 2	Lesson 3	Lesson 4
California Reading Toolkit	L29	L30	L31	L32
California Modified Lesson Plans for English Learners	p. 61	p. 63	p. 65	p. 67
California Daily Standards Practice Transparencies	TT29	TT30	TT31	TT32
California Standards Enrichment Workbook	pp. 113–114	pp. 113–114	pp. 113–114	pp. 113–114
California Standards Planner and Lesson Plans	L57	L59	L61	L63
California Online Test Practice	ClassZone.com	ClassZone.com	ClassZone.com	ClassZone.com
California Test Generator CD-ROM				
California EasyPlanner CD-ROM				
California eEdition CD-ROM				

Chart Key

 Pupil Edition   CD-ROM   Internet

 Copymaster   Audio   Overhead Transparency

 Video

PREVIEWING RESOURCES FOR DIFFERENTIATED INSTRUCTION

English Learners

In-Depth Resources in Spanish
- Reading Skill and Strategy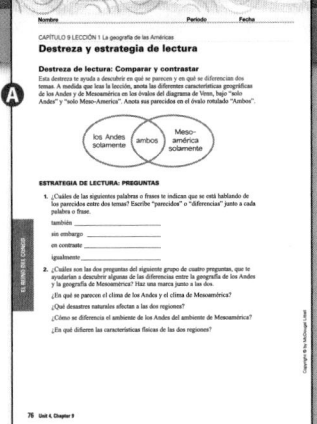
- Skillbuilder Practice
- Geography Practice C
- Vocabulary Study Guide B

In-Depth Resources: Unit 4
- Family Newsletter (English and Spanish)

Reading Study Guide (Spanish)

Reading Study Guide Audio CD
(Spanish)

Test Generator
Chapter Test (Spanish)

Plus

Modified Lesson Plans for English Learners

Multi-Language Glossary of Social Studies Terms

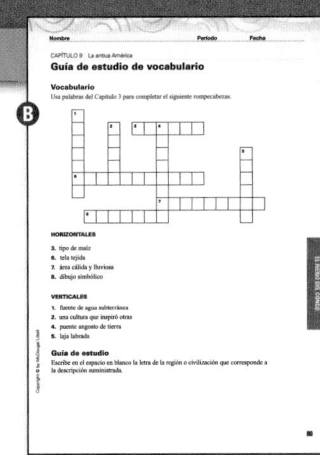

Struggling Readers

In-Depth Resources: Unit 4
- Vocabulary Study Guide
- Skillbuilder Practice B
- Geography Practice
- Reteaching Activities
- Family Newsletter C

Reading Study Guide A

Reading Study Guide Audio CD

Reading Toolkit

Formal Assessment
Chapter Test, Form A

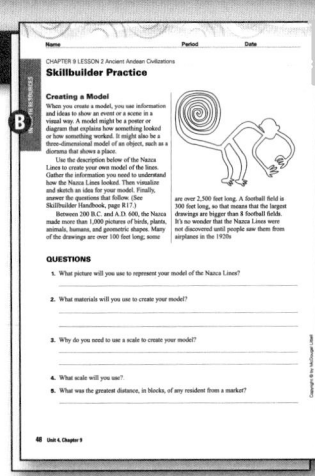

Inclusion

EasyPlanner CD-ROM
- Reading Skill and Strategy A
- Vocabulary Study Guide B
- Geography Practice C
- Reteaching Activities

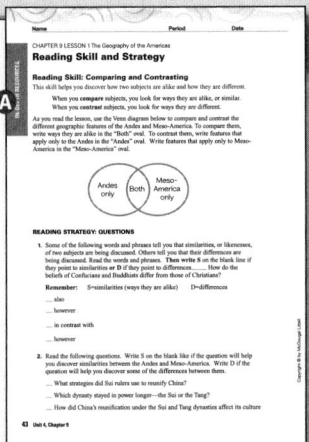

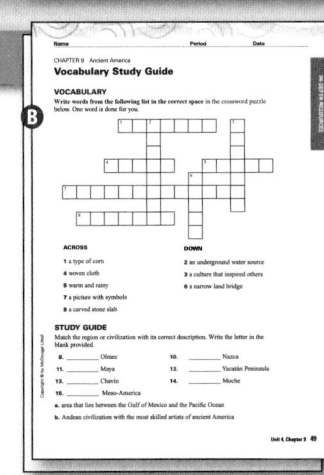

Gifted and Talented Students

In-Depth Resources: Unit 4
- Primary Source A
- Literature

History Makers B

Interdisciplinary Projects C

Formal Assessment
Chapter Test, Form C

Activities in the Teacher's Edition for English Learners

- Locate Key Words, p. 290
- Draw Logical Conclusions, p. 297
- Organize Vocabulary, p. 303
- Create a Mural, p. 310
- Study the Illustration, p. 312

Activities in the Teacher's Edition for Struggling Readers

- Outline the Section, p. 291
- Diagram the Section, p. 298
- Shrink the Paragraphs, p. 302
- Create Vocabulary Cards, p. 309

Activities in the Teacher's Edition for Inclusion Students

- Take Audio Notes, p. 290
- Listen to the Lesson, p. 297
- Create an Olmec Picture Book, p. 303
- Read the Sections Aloud, p. 310
- Play the Mayan Ball Game, p. 312

Activities in the Teacher's Edition for Gifted and Talented Students

- Create an Andes Fact Book, p. 291
- Create a Multimedia Presentation, p. 298
- Write Interview Questions, p. 302
- Report on Mayan Science, p. 309

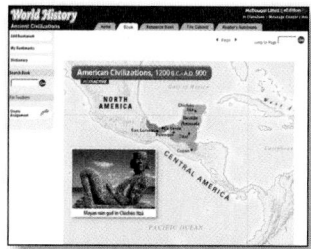

eEdition CD-ROM

- Interactive Visuals
- Interactive Maps
- Starting with a Story

ClassZone.com

- WebQuests
- Research Links
- Internet Activities
- Homework Helper
- Chapter Quiz
- Current Events
- Test Practice

Power Presentations CD-ROM

- Lecture Notes
- Media Gallery
- Chapter Review Game

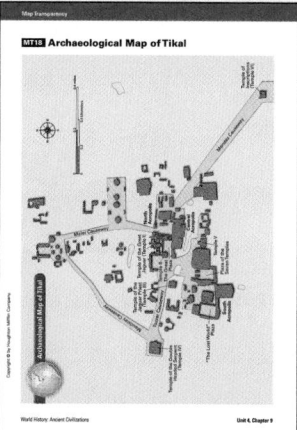

Critical Thinking Transparencies

- CT37 Comparing and Contrasting
- CT38 Drawing Conclusions
- CT39 Categorizing
- CT40 Summarizing
- CT41 Chapter 9 Visual Summary

California Daily Standards Practice Transparencies, TT29–TT32

Map Transparencies

- MT17 Geographic Regions of South America
- MT18 Archaeological Map of Tikal

Humanities Transparencies

- HT17 Nazca Line Drawing of a Man
- HT18 Mayan Ball Game Marker

Test Generator CD-ROM

EasyPlanner CD-ROM

Ancient Civilizations Video Series

- Ancient Maya

Begin the Chapter

Objective

Analyze the geographic, political, economic, religious, and social structures of the early civilizations of South America and Meso-America.

Quick Look

Lesson 1 examines the basic geography of the Americas, focusing on the areas that gave rise to the first civilizations.

Lesson 2 traces the development of the first civilizations of the Andes Mountains in South America.

Lesson 3 describes the history of the Olmec, the first great civilization of Meso-America.

Lesson 4 explores the Meso-American civilization of the Maya.

Before You Read: Anticipation Guide

The anticipation guide involves the strategy of allowing students to apply prior knowledge and preview subjects that will be discussed in the reading ahead. By completing the anticipation guide, students will become more aware of and interested in their reading. Have students do the following:

- Follow the steps in the "Before You Read" section.
- Remind students to record the statements and their opinions in a place where they can easily find them.
- Encourage students to look for, as they read the chapter, evidence that proves or disproves the statements .

Chapter 9 — Ancient America

Before You Read: Anticipation Guide

Copy the statements below in your notebook. Write *agree* or *disagree* next to each one. After you have read the lesson, look over the statements again and see if you have changed your opinion.

- The geography of the Andes Mountains helped civilizations develop there.
- Some ancient American civilizations built pyramids.
- The Maya did not create a very advanced civilization.

Big Ideas About Ancient America

Science and Technology New inventions and techniques change the way humans live their daily lives.

Ancient American cultures arose in difficult environments. These cultures adapted to their challenging conditions by developing new farming techniques and irrigation systems. The techniques allowed them to grow food and build thriving civilizations.

■	Olmec, 1200–400 B.C.
□	Chavín, 900–200 B.C.
■	Nazca, 200 B.C.–A.D. 600
■	Moche, A.D. 100–700
■	Maya, A.D. 250–900

120° W

Integrated Technology

eEdition
- Interactive Maps
- Interactive Visuals
- Starting with a Story

Ancient Maya

INTERNET RESOURCES
Go to **ClassZone.com** for
- WebQuest
- Homework Helper
- Research Links
- Internet Activities
- Quizzes
- Maps
- Test Practice
- Current Events

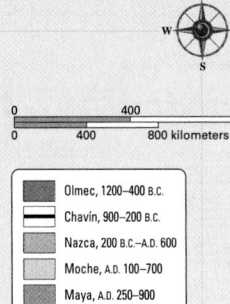

AMERICAS

1200 B.C.
Olmec build the Americas' first known civilization in southeastern Mexico. *(sculpture of Olmec wrestler)* ►

900 B.C.
Chavín culture arises in Peru and influences other cultures in South America.

1200 B.C.   900 B.C.

WORLD

1200 B.C.
Attacked by invaders, Egyptian Empire begins to decline. *(Egyptian sphinx and pyramid)* ►

284

TIME LINE DISCUSSION

Use the time line to help students develop a time frame for the discussion of civilizations in the Americas and to preview information that will be covered in the chapter.

- According to the time line, what was the first South American civilization to emerge? *(the Chavín culture)*
- About how many years passed between the emergence of the Chavín culture and the rise of the Nazca culture in Peru? *(700 years)*

- Which occurred first—the height of the Roman Empire or the Classic Period of the Mayan civilization? *(the height of the Roman Empire)*
- Which civilization in the Americas was rising during the decline of the Egyptian Empire? *(the Olmec civilization)*

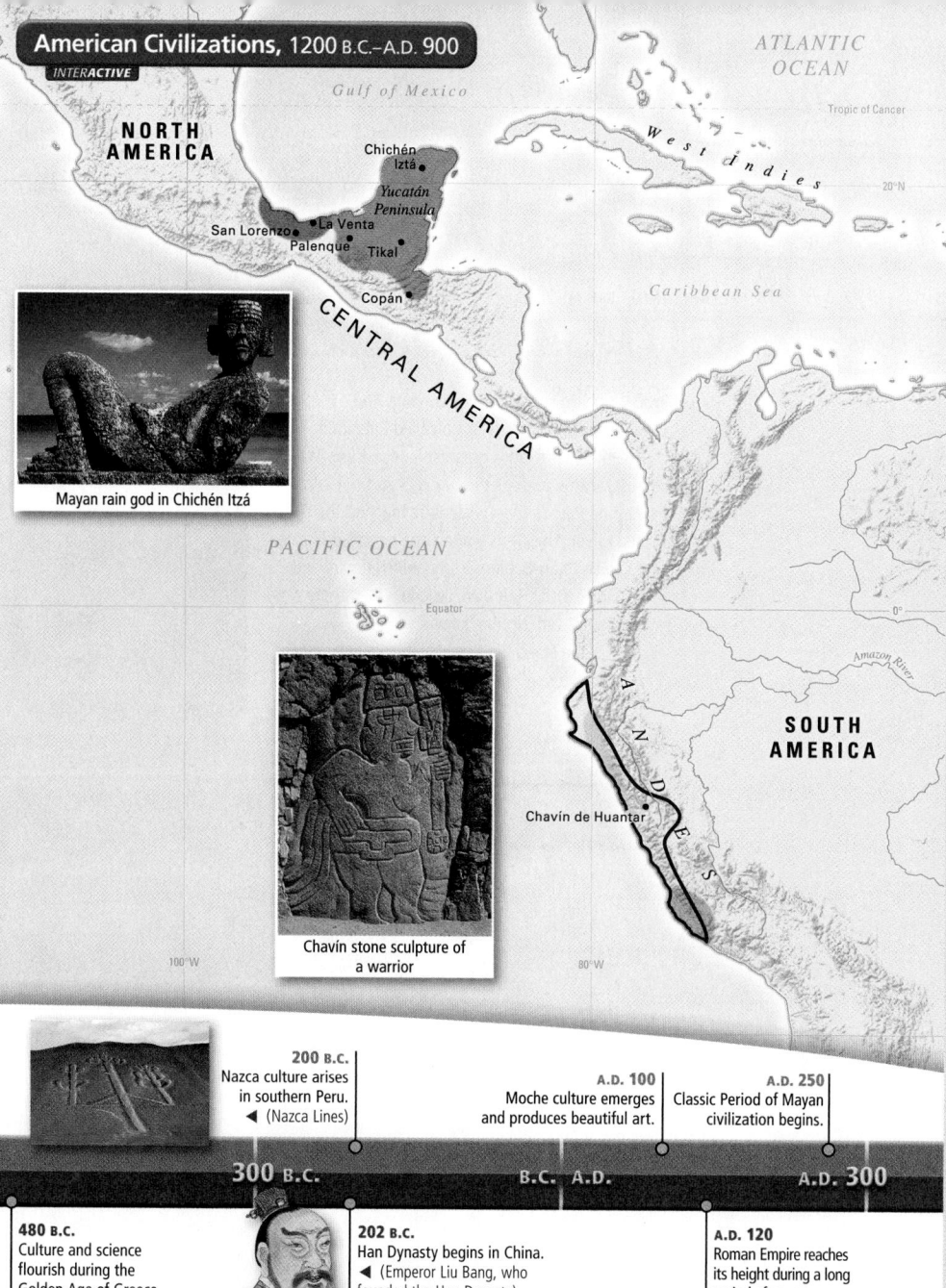

American Civilizations, 1200 B.C.–A.D. 900
INTERACTIVE

NORTH AMERICA

Gulf of Mexico

ATLANTIC OCEAN

Tropic of Cancer

Chichén Itzá
Yucatán Peninsula
San Lorenzo
La Venta
Palenque
Tikal
Copán

West Indies

20°N

Caribbean Sea

CENTRAL AMERICA

Mayan rain god in Chichén Itzá

PACIFIC OCEAN

Equator

Chavín stone sculpture of a warrior

ANDES

Chavín de Huantar

SOUTH AMERICA

Amazon River

0°

100°W

80°W

200 B.C.
Nazca culture arises in southern Peru.
◄ (Nazca Lines)

A.D. 100
Moche culture emerges and produces beautiful art.

A.D. 250
Classic Period of Mayan civilization begins.

300 B.C.

B.C. A.D.

A.D. 300

480 B.C.
Culture and science flourish during the Golden Age of Greece.

202 B.C.
Han Dynasty begins in China.
◄ (Emperor Liu Bang, who founded the Han Dynasty)

A.D. 120
Roman Empire reaches its height during a long period of peace.

285

RECOMMENDED RESOURCES

Books for the Teacher
Benson, Elizabeth P., and Beatriz de la Fuente, eds. *Olmec Art of Ancient Mexico.* Washington: National Gallery of Art, 1996. Guide to the National Gallery exhibition in 1996.

Burger, Richard L. *Chavín and the Origins of Andean Civilization.* New York: Thames, 1995. Includes a history of the Chavín culture of South America.

Videos
Lost Kingdoms of the Maya. 60 minutes. Washington: National Geographic Video, 1993. Film tour of the Central American and Mexican forests that were once home to the ancient Mayan civilization. VHS.

Internet
To access these sites, visit the Research Links for Chapter 9 at **ClassZone.com**.

The online **EMuseum at Minnesota State University, Mankato** features many resources relating to South American cultures.

The **Washington State University Web site** contains extensive information about ancient civilizations in the Americas.

Introduce the Big Ideas

Read aloud the text about the Big Ideas. Discuss the role that new technologies play in students' lives. In what ways do recent technologies help them survive or thrive in their environment? How has technology changed their world in the past few years?

Here are some other Big Ideas that you may want to emphasize in this chapter.

Geography
Civilizations developed in places that supported agriculture or trade or both.

Culture
Modern culture draws on the legacy of many past civilizations.

Talk About It

Interpreting Maps
Instruct students to examine the map and read the legend. Ask students how the locations of these civilizations compare with the locations of those they have read about in earlier chapters. *(Unlike civilizations covered in previous chapters, the American civilizations do not seem to have grown up around major river systems.)*

INTERACTIVE

An interactive version of this map is available on the eEdition and Power Presentations CD-ROMs.

Find Out More

Have students use library or Internet sources to learn more about the people currently living on the lands where ancient civilizations developed long ago. Ask, What is life like today for people living on Mexico's Yucatán Peninsula or in the Andes Mountains of South America?

Watch the Video

Investigate the culture and lasting contributions of the Maya with *Ancient Maya.* This 23-minute video is part of the Ancient Civilizations for Children Series.

Objective

Describe details about the Mayan culture.

Introducing the Story

Archaeological Finds at Palenque

Many of the details in this story come from the rich archaeological record of Palenque. This great city was located in what is now Mexico. Among the ruins were found a number of impressive structures, some of which are featured in the story. Also discovered at the site of Palenque was the tomb of King Pacal II. A stone sarcophagus contained the ancient king's remains as well as many impressive jade pieces, including the death mask referred to in the story and pictured on page 286.

Vocabulary Preview

attendant someone who waits on others

jaguar a large cat native to Central and South America

Reading the Story Aloud

1. **The teacher as reader:** Read the story aloud with expression so that students can hear the drama and better understand the emotional impact of the events.

2. **The students as readers:** Give students a few minutes to preview the story and become familiar with the vocabulary before they read it aloud.

Starting with a Story

Students can also follow along as they listen to the story on the eEdition or Power Presentations CD-ROMs.

Starting with a Story

King Pacal II and His Sons

CALIFORNIA STANDARDS
Reading 2.7 Make reasonable assertions about a text through accurate, supporting citations.

Background: In southern Mexico stand the ruins of an ancient Mayan city-state called Palenque (pah•LEHNG•keh). The city's greatest leader, King Pacal II (pah•KAHL), came to power in A.D. 615 and ruled for 68 years. During Pacal's reign, Palenque reached the height of its power. The city's golden age continued under Pacal's two sons, Chan-Bahlum II (chan•BAH•loom) and Kan-Xul II (kahn•SHOOL). But then, around 800, the city was mysteriously abandoned. No one knows why.

At the time of the story, however, the future looks bright. You are about to see Kan-Xul become king of Palenque.

Pacal's jade death mask ▶

286

ADDITIONAL RESOURCES

Books for the Student

Day, Nancy. *Your Travel Guide to Ancient Maya Civilization.* Minneapolis: Runestone, 2000. This book features a range of information about the Mayan civilization.

Nicholson, Robert. *The Maya.* New York: Chelsea, 1994. The author provides a clear overview of Mayan history and culture.

Videos

Time-Life's Lost Civilizations, part 3. 100 minutes. Alexandria: Time-Life Video and Television, 2002. These installments of a television series cover the Mayan and Incan empires. VHS, DVD.

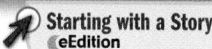
As an attendant in the palace, you have much to do before the ceremony begins. But as you work, placing the gifts and offerings around the throne, you think about Kan-Xul's father.

Pacal the Great made Palenque one of the most powerful Mayan cities in the land. He had beautiful temples built and decorated them with wonderful jade ornaments and stone sculptures. After Pacal died, the city's artists carved statues of the king. They also made necklaces and rings for him to wear on his journey to the underworld. You were one of the few servants to catch a peek of the life-sized jade mask that was placed over the dead king's face. Now you're almost sorry you looked. Whenever you recall the unblinking gaze of its eyes, you shiver.

After Pacal's funeral, slaves carefully lowered a stone block to seal his tomb. The enormous block weighed as much as 70 men. A long speaking tube extended from the tomb. The tube let Pacal's sons talk and pray to their dead father.

Pacal's oldest son, Chan-Bahlum, ruled for 18 years. He continued his father's work. Now that he has died, his brother Kan-Xul will be the king. After you finish the preparations, you stand at the back of the room and watch the ceremony.

Kan-Xul sits on the jaguar throne. He receives the magnificent jade headdress that his father and brother wore before him. His mother stands at his side and watches as Kan-Xul accepts gifts from the noblemen of the city. You happily imagine the many kings who will certainly follow Kan-Xul. Then suddenly, you feel a strange chill. You remember the cold, staring eyes of Pacal's death mask. The eyes seem to behold a darker future. What do they see?

What can happen when a new leader takes power?

Reading & Writing

1. **READING: Supporting Citations** How was Pacal important to his sons and to the people of Palenque? Use citations from the story to support your answer.

2. **WRITING: Description** Imagine that you are a reporter covering the ceremony as Kan-Xul becomes king. Write a short news feature in which you describe what you see.

CALIFORNIA STANDARDS Writing 2.2
Write expository compositions.

287

Talk About It

Ask students the following questions to begin the discussion:

- What is about to take place as the story begins? *(a ceremony in which Kan-Xul will become king)*
- What does the attendant think about as the ceremony approaches? *(He or she thinks about the soon-to-be king's father, who helped make Palenque a great city.)*
- What memory upsets the attendant as he or she thinks about Pacal? *(the vision of his death mask)*
- Why does the memory of the death mask upset the attendant in the story? *(The vision makes the attendant wonder about the future of Palenque.)*

What can happen when a new leader takes power?

Possible answers: Policies can change; the government can be strengthened or weakened; the new leader may not be effective.

Making Personal Connections

Connect the discussion to today by bringing up political elections in the United States. Ask, What methods do we use to transfer power from one leader to the next? What does and does not change when this transition occurs?

READING & WRITING ACTIVITIES

1. READING Pacal passed down a thriving kingdom to his sons; his sons continued to honor Pacal after his death; the people of Palenque believed that the city's golden age would continue.

2. WRITING Students should describe what they see in the illustration. They might also use dialogue to help bring the news feature to life.

2. Writing Rubric

	Description of Ceremony	Errors in Mechanics
4	many interesting, accurate details	few or none
3	several accurate details	some
2	some details	many
1	few or no details	major

❶ Plan & Prepare

Objectives

- Analyze physical features of the Americas, including rivers, mountain ranges, and climate.
- Give details about the geography of the Andes.
- Locate Meso-America and list details about its geographical features.
- **Language Objective** Formulate statements in a Venn diagram to compare and contrast the geographies of the Andes and Meso-America.

Quick Look

Lesson 1 examines the geography of the Americas, focusing on the areas that gave rise to the first civilizations.

❷ Focus & Motivate

Preview Tell students that this lesson will explore the first civilizations that emerged in the Americas. Ask students to think about the variety of geographical features that exist within the United States.

Introduce the Main Ideas The three main ideas relate to the Big Idea "Civilizations developed in places that supported agriculture or trade or both." Help students look for statements related to this Big Idea as they read the lesson.

Reading Skill: Comparing and Contrasting Tell students that comparing and contrasting is a skill that helps readers understand how subjects are alike and how they differ. It also helps them recognize patterns that link different people, places, and ideas.

SAMPLE ANSWERS FOR DIAGRAM

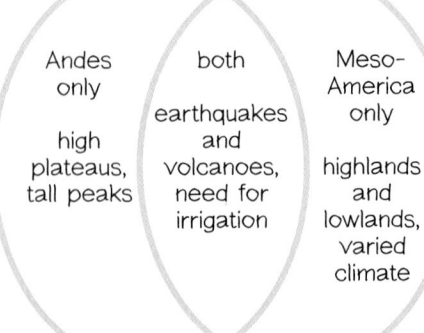

Lesson 1

▶ MAIN IDEAS

❶ Geography The physical geographies of North and South America are very different.

❷ Geography The Andes provide a harsh environment for the people who live there.

❸ Geography Meso-America has a variety of landforms and climates.

▶ TAKING NOTES

Reading Skill: Comparing and Contrasting

When you compare and contrast two subjects, you discover how they are alike and how they are different. As you read Lesson 1, compare and contrast the geography of the Andes with the geography of Meso-America. Use a Venn diagram like the one below to record their similarities and differences.

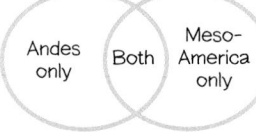

S Skillbuilder Handbook, page R4

▲ **Quetzal Bird** The colorful quetzal (keht•SAHL) bird of Central America was greatly respected by the Maya. They used the bird's feathers to decorate the ceremonial robes of kings and priests.

CALIFORNIA STANDARDS

7.7 Students compare and contrast the geographic, political, economic, religious, and social structures of the Meso-American and Andean civilizations.

7.7.1 Study the locations, landforms, and climates of Mexico, Central America, and South America and their effects on Mayan, Aztec, and Incan economies, trade, and development of urban societies.

CST 3 Students use a variety of maps and documents to identify physical and cultural features of neighborhoods, cities, states, and countries and to explain the historical migration of people, expansion and disintegration of empires, and the growth of economic systems.

HOW TO TEACH THE CALIFORNIA STANDARDS

Standard	Content	Student Question or Activity	Instruction
7.7	**Pages 289–290** Summarizes the general features of the geography of North and South America	**Page 290** Students view a climate map of North and South America and answer a question about the climates of the two continents.	Before students read, ask them to describe similarities and differences in the geography and climate of North and South America. Write students' responses on the board.
7.7.1	**Pages 290–292** Describes the locations, landforms, and climates of Mexico, Central America, and South America	**Page 293** Students explain how climate affects the two main regions in Meso-America.	Have students use the maps on pages 285 and 291 to identify the countries that now exist where the first civilizations of the Andes emerged. Then have students list the present-day countries in Meso-America.
CST 3	**Page 291** Illustrates the Andes Mountain range on a map of South America	**Page 293** Students create a map of Meso-America and the western coast of South America.	Discuss reasons why people might choose to live in mountainous regions. *(to enjoy a cooler climate, to raise animals, to grow new foods)*

The Geography of the Americas

CHAPTER 9 • LESSON 1

TERMS & NAMES

isthmus

tropical

Meso-America

Yucatán Peninsula

slash-and-burn agriculture

Build on What You Know Which do you like best—the mountains, the shore, the desert, the plains? You can find all of these regions in North America. In this lesson, you will compare the geography of North America with that of South America.

Physical Geography of the Americas

1 ESSENTIAL QUESTION What is the physical geography of the Americas like? major mountain ranges and rivers; wide range of climates

Look at the map of North and South America on the following page. You can see that the continents are connected. A narrow land bridge called an **isthmus** links them. However, the geographies and climates of the two continents are very different.

Major Landforms and Rivers Mountains run along the western parts of both continents. North America has a north-south mountain range called the Rocky Mountains. South America has a mountain range called the Andes.

Water flows down these ranges to the continents' great rivers. The major river system of North America is the Mississippi. The Amazon and Paraná (PAR•uh•NAH) rivers are the major systems of South America.

Amazon River
Villagers of the Amazon rain forest paddle a canoe on the river. The Amazon carries more water to the sea than any other river in the world. ▼

289

Terms & Names

isthmus a narrow strip of land

tropical a warm and rainy climate

Meso-America southern Mexico and part of Central America

Yucatán Peninsula land between the Gulf of Mexico and the Caribbean Sea

slash-and-burn agriculture a type of farming in which fields are cleared by burning

❸ Teach

Physical Geography of the Americas

7.7.1

Talk About It

• **Critical Thinking: Explaining Historical Patterns** Where might the first civilizations in the Americas have emerged? *(Possible answer: in areas with water and fertile soil for agriculture)*

California Resources

California Reading Toolkit, L29
California Modified Lesson Plans for English Learners, p. 61
California Daily Standards Practice Transparencies, TT29
California Standards Enrichment Workbook, pp. 113–114
California Online Test Practice
California Test Generator CD-ROM
California Standards Planner and Lesson Plans, L57
California EasyPlanner CD-ROM
California eEdition CD-ROM

LESSON 1 PROGRAM RESOURCES

ON LEVEL

In-Depth Resources: Unit 4
Family Newsletter (English and Spanish), pp. 41–42
Reading Skill: Comparing and Contrasting, p. 43
Vocabulary Study Guide, p. 49
Vocabulary Cards, p. 51

Formal Assessment
Lesson Quiz, p. 150

ENGLISH LEARNERS

In-Depth Resources in Spanish
Reading Skill: Comparing and Contrasting, p. 73
Vocabulary Study Guide, p. 80

Modified Lesson Plans for English Learners, p. 61
Reading Study Guide (Spanish), p. 77
Reading Study Guide Audio CD (Spanish)

STRUGGLING READERS

In-Depth Resources: Unit 4
• Reading Skill: Comparing and Contrasting, p. 43
• Vocabulary Study Guide, p. 49
• Vocabulary Cards, p. 51
• Reteaching Activity, p. 57

Reading Toolkit, p. L29

Reading Study Guide, p. 77
Reading Study Guide Audio CD

GIFTED AND TALENTED STUDENTS

Interdisciplinary Projects
• Science, p. 50

INCLUSION

EasyPlanner CD-ROM
• Reading Skill: Comparing and Contrasting
• Vocabulary Study Guide
• Reteaching Activity

TECHNOLOGY

eEdition CD-ROM
• Starting with a Story

Power Presentations CD-ROM

Map Transparencies
• MT17 Geographic Regions of South America

Critical Thinking Transparencies
• CT37 Comparing and Contrasting

Test Generator CD-ROM

ClassZone.com

Ancient America • **289**

In-Depth Resources: Unit 4
• Reading Skill: Comparing and Contrasting, p. 43

History from Visuals

Interpreting Maps
Direct students' attention to the map on page 290. Explain that the climates of the Americas were a significant factor in the development of early civilizations.

• What type of climate characterizes most of South America and Central America? *(tropical)*

GEOGRAPHY SKILLBUILDER ANSWER
continental, polar

Teach

Geography of the Andes
 7.7, 7.7.1, CST 3

Talk About It

• Where did early civilizations emerge in South America? *(in the Andes Mountains)*

• What factors made agriculture difficult in the Andes? *(The soil could be stony; the climate was harsh, with unpredictable rainfall.)*

• How did farmers in the Andes overcome geographical obstacles? *(They developed irrigation canals and planted crops that were suited to the environment.)*

• **Critical Thinking: Framing Historical Questions** Based on what you have read, what questions do you have about early civilizations in the Andes? *(Possible answers: Why did early people choose to settle in the Andes, where farming was difficult? What kinds of animals lived in the mountains?)*

A Variety of Climates The locations of the two continents has an impact on their seasons. As you can see on the map on this page, North America lies north of the equator. Most of South America lies south of it. As a result, the seasons are reversed. When it is summer in North America, it is winter in South America—and vice versa.

The locations of the continents also affect their climates. Much of North America has a mild or dry climate, with four distinct seasons. Most people live in these climates. Few people live in the northern regions of Canada, where the climate is very cold.

South America also has a wide range of climates. In addition, much of the continent receives a great deal of rainfall. In fact, about half of South America is warm and rainy. These warm and rainy areas are called **tropical** zones. Some areas of North America are also tropical. These areas lie mostly in Central America. The people who built ancient civilizations in this Central American area learned to live and thrive in its tropical climate.

Climates of North and South America

Climate Zones
- Tropical
- Dry
- Mild
- Continental
- Polar
- Highland

PACIFIC OCEAN
ATLANTIC OCEAN
Tropic of Cancer
Equator
Tropic of Capricorn

0   1000   2000 miles
0 1000 2000 kilometers

150°W   120°W   90°W   60°W

GEOGRAPHY SKILLBUILDER
INTERPRETING MAPS
Region What climate zones are found in North America but not in South America?

REVIEW What are some major differences between the geographies and climates of North America and South America? Much of North America lies north of the equator; much of South America lies south. Much of South America is warm and rainy; North America has regions that can be very hot and some that can be very cold.

Geography of the Andes

2 **ESSENTIAL QUESTION** What geographic features are characteristic of the Andes? tall peaks, high plateaus, harsh climates

Ancient civilizations developed on both continents. Some arose high in South America's Andes Mountains. The Andes extend about 5,500 miles from Venezuela in the north to Chile at the southern tip of South America. They consist of very high plateaus surrounded by even higher peaks.

DIFFERENTIATING INSTRUCTION

English Learners

Locate Key Words
Help students locate text that includes comparison words such as *both, each, like, as,* and *similarly* and contrast words such as *but, by contrast, however, except* and *yet.* Direct students to the section "Physical Geography of the Americas." Say to them, "North America and South America are both continents connected by an isthmus. However, the geography and the climate of the two continents are very different." Note these details in a Venn diagram.

Inclusion

Take Audio Notes
Have students who are visually impaired use a tape recorder to take audio notes about the main points of the lesson. Then have pairs listen to the recordings and discuss important ideas from the lesson.

Tall Peaks The peaks of the Andes are the highest in the Americas. Many are over 20,000 feet, or almost four miles high. The highest elevations are covered only by a thin, stony soil. Lower down, the soil is a little richer.

The Andes' location along two colliding plates also makes life there hard. The plate movement causes volcanic activity and earthquakes in the Andes. The climate is severe too. At high altitudes it freezes, and in many places rainfall is unpredictable.

High Plateaus Over a long stretch of the Andes, the mountains split into two ranges. A large group of high plateaus lies between them. This area is filled with hills, valleys, plains, and deserts. A few large rivers water the area. But in the high desert regions, rain almost never falls.

As you might imagine, farming presents a challenge in the Andes. To grow their food, farmers in ancient Andean civilizations developed irrigation canals. These carried water to crops the farmers developed, such as potatoes.

REVIEW What makes the Andes a harsh environment?
poor soil, threat of volcanoes and earthquakes, temperature extremes, unpredictable or no rainfall

Andes Mountains

GUYANA
VENEZUELA   SURINAME
              FRENCH GUIANA
COLOMBIA
ECUADOR
SOUTH
AMERICA
PERU   BRAZIL

BOLIVIA

CHILE   PARAGUAY
Mt. Aconcagua
22,834 ft.
(6,960 m)   URUGUAY
       ARGENTINA

GEOGRAPHY SKILLBUILDER
INTERPRETING MAPS
Human-Environment Interaction
What advantage might the Andes have provided against invaders?

Andes The Andes are the longest mountain range in the world. The top photograph shows a high plateau region. The bottom one shows the more fertile valley region.

Ancient America • 291

History from Visuals

Interpreting Maps
Ask students to review the map on page 291. Point out the mountain range that runs along the west coast of South America. Have students compare this map with the climate map that appears on the opposite page of the spread.

- What climate zones are found along South America's west coast? *(tropical, dry, mild)*
- Do you think the mountains would be the most likely place for the development of an early civilization? *(Possible answer: no, because their environment does not have features ideally suited for agriculture)*

GEOGRAPHY SKILLBUILDER ANSWER
The mountains provided natural protection from enemies.

Map Transparencies
- MT17 Geographic Regions of South America

DIFFERENTIATING INSTRUCTION

Gifted and Talented Students

Create an Andes Fact Book
Have students use library or Internet resources to research the Andes Mountains and create a "fact book" about this region. The book should contain illustrations and information about the physical environment of the Andes—average temperatures, and so on.

Struggling Readers

Outline the Section
Have students work in pairs to outline the content of the section "Geography of the Andes." Each student should assume responsibility for one subsection, identifying its main point and two supporting details. Once a pair have completed their portions, they should combine them and outline the entire section together.

History from Visuals

Interpreting Maps

Direct students' attention to the map on page 292. Ask students to read the title in order to identify the subject of the map. Have students note the shape and outline of Meso-America.

- What Central American countries are in Meso-America? *(parts of Honduras and Nicaragua, along with Guatemala, El Salvador, and Belize)*

GEOGRAPHY SKILLBUILDER ANSWER
the Gulf of Mexico, the Pacific Ocean, and the Caribbean Sea

Teach

Geography of Meso-America

7.7, 7.7.1

Talk About It

- In general, how does the climate of Meso-America compare with the climate of the Andes? *(It is milder.)*

- Briefly describe the two main land regions of Meso-America. *(It has tropical lowlands near the coast and highlands between the Sierra Madre mountains.)*

- How do these two regions differ in terms of climate? *(Lowland areas are wet and tropical, and the highlands are cool and dry.)*

- **Critical Thinking: Understanding Cause and Effect** How did the physical features of Meso-America help shape the development of civilizations there? *(Possible answers: Early civilizations had to find methods of growing crops in the different climates.)*

GEOGRAPHY SKILLBUILDER
INTERPRETING MAPS
Location What three bodies of water surround Meso-America?

Geography of Meso-America

3 ESSENTIAL QUESTION How do the geography and climate of Meso-America contrast with those of the Andes? The climate of Meso-America is milder than the Andes, and the geography is less extreme.
Ancient civilizations arose in North America in a region called **Meso-America**. Meso-America includes southern Mexico and the Central American countries of Guatemala, El Salvador, Belize, and parts of Honduras and Nicaragua. In contrast with the Andes Mountains, Meso-America offers a milder environment.

The Land of Meso-America Meso-America has two main regions: highlands and lowlands. The tropical lowlands hug the coast of the Gulf of Mexico. These areas of dense jungle are also found on the **Yucatán** (YOO•kuh•TAN) **Peninsula**, which lies between the Gulf of Mexico and the Caribbean Sea. The highlands stretch between the mountains of the Sierra Madre mountain system. Like much of the Andes, this region is subject to earthquakes and volcanoes.

Climate Rainfall varies greatly in these two regions. It can rain more than 100 inches a year in the steamy lowlands, providing a good environment for palm, avocado, and cacao trees. As you climb toward the highlands, however, the air becomes cooler and drier. This region receives much less rainfall.

INTERDISCIPLINARY ACTIVITIES

Science

Answer Volcano Trivia

Volcanoes have shaped the landscapes of parts of Meso-America. Have students use library or Internet resources to learn about volcanoes in this region. Have them create a list of trivia questions and answers about how volcanoes work, what active volcanoes exist in Central America and Mexico, and when notable volcanic eruptions have occurred. Have students quiz one another with their trivia questions.

Math

Calculate Averages

Have students review the text, looking for information about how much rain falls in the lowland areas of Meso-America. Have them use this information to calculate how much rain falls on average, each day in this area. *(More than 100 inches of rain falls annually in the lowland areas. Dividing 100 by 365 gives an average daily rainfall of about 0.27 inch.)*

Early Meso-American farmers had to develop advanced agricultural practices to deal with both climates. In the dry highlands, farmers irrigated their fields, which produced corn, beans, and squash. In the lowlands, they practiced **slash-and-burn agriculture**. They cleared a patch of jungle by cutting back and burning it. When the field became less productive, farmers began again with a new piece of land.

 REVIEW How does climate affect the two main regions in Meso-America?

Corn These ears of maize, or corn, are being sold in a Yucatán market. Corn was first developed in Meso-America. ▼

the lowlands receive abundant rainfall; the highlands are drier. Early Meso-American people used advanced agricultural practices to adapt to both climates.

Lesson Summary

- North America and South America have contrasting climates and geographies.
- The Andes Mountains provided a challenging environment for ancient civilizations.
- The climates of Meso-America resulted in the development of different agricultural practices.

Why It Matters Now . . .

Today the potatoes developed in the Andes and the corn developed in Meso-America have become important crops in countries all over the world.

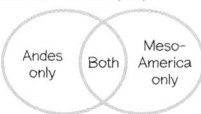 **1 Lesson Review**

 Homework Helper
ClassZone.com

Terms & Names

1. Explain the importance of
   - isthmus
   - tropical
   - Meso-America
   - Yucatán Peninsula
   - slash-and-burn agriculture

Using Your Notes

Comparing and Contrasting Use your completed Venn diagram to answer the following question:

2. How is the geography of the Andes and Meso-America similar? (7.7)

Andes only | Both | Meso-America only

Main Ideas

3. Why are the seasons reversed in North and South America? (7.7.1)
4. Why is farming a challenge in the Andes? (7.7.1)
5. How did farmers grow crops in the rainy lowlands of Meso-America? (7.7.1)

Critical Thinking

6. **Explaining Geographic Patterns** Why did farmers in the Andes and in Meso-America develop advanced agricultural techniques? (7.7)
7. **Making Inferences** What might have happened if ancient peoples in the Americas had not adapted to their environments? (7.7.1)

Activity **Making a Physical Map** Trace a map showing Meso-America and the western coast of South America. Label the major landforms, bodies of water, and regions in both places. Use a legend to identify any symbols or colors on the map. (CST 3)

Ancient America • 293

CHAPTER 9 • LESSON 1

❹ Assess & Reteach

Assess Have students form small groups and then number themselves within their groups. Ask a question from the Lesson Review, and allow the members of each group talk together and agree on an answer. Call out a number, and have the person in each group who was assigned that number share his or her group's answer with the rest of the class.

Formal Assessment
- Lesson Quiz, p. 150

Reteach On the board, write the names of the two regions discussed in this lesson—the Andes and Meso-America. Call on volunteers to identify key details about each region. Record their responses on the board.

In-Depth Resources: Unit 4
- Vocabulary Cards, p. 51
- Reteaching Activity, p. 57

Homework Helper

Visit **ClassZone.com** for a lesson review, a flip-card activity, and links to related Web sites.

---

1 Lesson Review Answers

Terms & Names

1.
   - isthmus, p. 289
   - tropical, p. 290
   - Meso-America, p. 292
   - Yucatán Peninsula, p. 292
   - slash-and-burn agriculture, p. 293

Using Your Notes

See page 288 for an example of a completed diagram.

2. Both contain rugged areas with difficult climates, making agriculture a challenge.

Main Ideas

3. because North America lies to the north of the equator and most of South America lies to the south
4. The highest elevations are covered only by a thin, stony soil; in some parts of the high plateaus, rain almost never falls.
5. by using slash-and-burn agriculture

Critical Thinking

6. The climates in both places were harsh; people had to develop these techniques in order to survive.
7. Possible answers: Their civilizations would not have developed; the area would have remained in its natural state.

Activity Rubric

	Accuracy of Features	Neatness of Map
4	accurately labeled and positioned locations and features, clear legend	very neat and easy to read
3	mostly accurately labeled and positioned locations and features, reasonable legend	neat
2	some accurate locations and features, unclear legend	somewhat neat
1	inaccurate or missing locations, features, or legend	sloppy

Ancient America • 293

❶ Plan & Prepare

Objectives

- Characterize two of the oldest Andean civilizations, the Chavín and the Nazca.
- Describe key features of another ancient Andean civilization, the Moche.
- **Language Objective:** Analyze facts to draw logical conclusions.

Quick Look

Lesson 2 explores the history and culture of three of the oldest civilizations in the Americas—the Andean civilizations of the Chavín, the Nazca, and the Moche.

❷ Focus & Motivate

Preview Tell students that this lesson will examine key features of three civilizations that developed in the Andes Mountains of South America.

Introduce the Main Ideas The three main ideas relate to the Big Idea "Civilizations developed in places that supported agriculture or trade or both."

Reading Skill: Drawing Conclusions To draw conclusions, students must search for significance and meaning by connecting pieces of information.

SAMPLE ANSWERS FOR DIAGRAM

Detail:
Archaeologists have found Chavín religious items.

Detail:
Little is known about Chavín political or economic life.

Conclusion:
Chavín culture was united mainly by religion.

Lesson 2

▶ **MAIN IDEAS**

❶ **Culture** The art of the Chavín, which featured religious images, influenced other cultures.

❷ **Culture** The Nazca civilization left behind beautiful art and mysterious images.

❸ **Science and Technology** The Moche created a complex system of agriculture that supported important city structures.

▶ **TAKING NOTES**

Reading Skill: Drawing Conclusions

When you draw conclusions, you form opinions about what you have read. Draw conclusions about the three ancient Andean civilizations as you read Lesson 2. Use a diagram like the one below to record your conclusions.

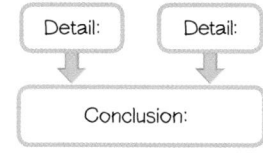

Detail: ——— Detail:

Conclusion:

S Skillbuilder Handbook, page R25

▲ **Chavín Art** This golden ornament of a snarling cat is typical of Chavín religious art. Some archaeologists believe that artwork featuring snarling cats was used in religious rituals of the Chavín.

CALIFORNIA STANDARDS

7.7 Students compare and contrast the geographic, political, economic, religious, and social structures of the Meso-American and Andean civilizations.

CST 3 Students use a variety of maps and documents to identify physical and cultural features of neighborhoods, cities, states, and countries and to explain the historical migration of people, expansion and disintegration of empires, and the growth of economic systems.

HI 5 Students recognize that interpretations of history are subject to change as new information is uncovered.

HOW TO TEACH THE CALIFORNIA STANDARDS

Standard	Content	Student Question or Activity	Instruction
7.7	**Pages 295–299** Describes cultural features of three ancient Andean civilizations	**Page 299** Students compare and contrast features of the Chavín, Nazca, and Moche civilizations.	After students read, have each of them write one sentence explaining which civilization he or she admires most and why. Have volunteers share their opinions with the rest of the class.
CST 3	**Page 296** Illustrates physical features of three South American civilizations	**Page 296** Students use a map to determine which civilization extended farthest along the Andes.	Ask students to locate Peru on a globe and a world map. Tell students that the civilizations they will be reading about in Lesson 2 existed in this region of the world.
HI 5	**Page 295** Explains that our understanding of ancient cultures changes as more discoveries are made	**Page 299** Students tell how recent discoveries have increased our understanding of the Moche culture.	Explain that no explanation of the Nazca Lines is known to be correct. Invite students to briefly research the mythology surrounding the Nazca Lines and to either select an existing theory or create their own theory that explains the meaning of these drawings.

Ancient Andean Civilizations

TERMS & NAMES

Chavín

textile

Nazca

aquifer

Moche

Build on What You Know You have learned about the rugged landscape and harsh climate of the Andes Mountains. Now find out about the people who created civilizations in this tough environment.

The Chavín Civilization

❶ ESSENTIAL QUESTION What was the Chavín civilization?

The ruins of a huge U-shaped temple stand high in the Andes of Peru in a place called Chavín de Huantar (chah•VEEN deh WAHN•tahr). The temple was built by a culture known as the **Chavín**. This culture flourished between about 900 and 200 B.C. Our understanding of the Chavín may increase as more discoveries are made. But for right now, the little we know is based on the ruins of the structures they built.

The Chavín Ruins Archaeologists believe that the Chavín civilization was united mainly by religion. Little is known about their political or economic organization. However, the religious images found at Chavín de Huantar tell us about their culture.

an early, influential Andean civilization

Chavín de Huantar Heads like this one decorated the outer walls of the temple of Chavín de Huantar. The heads may have been designed to frighten away evil spirits. ▼

295

Terms & Names

Chavín an Andean culture that flourished between 900 and 200 B.C.

textile a woven or knitted cloth

Nazca an Andean culture that flourished from 200 B.C. to A.D. 600

aquifer an underground water source

Moche an Andean culture that flourished from A.D. 100 to 700

❸ Teach

The Chavín Civilization

🖎 **7.7, CST 3, HI5**

Talk About It

- **Critical Thinking: Making Inferences**
  What can you infer about the findings at Chavín de Huantar? *(Possible answer: Religion was an important aspect of Chavín culture.)*

California Resources

California Reading Toolkit, L30
California Modified Lesson Plans for English Learners, p. 63
California Daily Standards Practice Transparencies, TT30
California Standards Enrichment Workbook, pp. 113–114
California Online Test Practice
California Test Generator CD-ROM
California Standards Planner and Lesson Plans, L59
California EasyPlanner CD-ROM
California eEdition CD-ROM

LESSON 2 PROGRAM RESOURCES

ON LEVEL

In-Depth Resources: Unit 4
- Reading Skill: Drawing Conclusions, p. 44
- Skillbuilder Practice: Creating a Model, p. 48
- Vocabulary Cards, p. 51

Formal Assessment
- Lesson Quiz, p. 151

ENGLISH LEARNERS

In-Depth Resources in Spanish
- Reading Skill: Drawing Conclusions, p. 74
- Skillbuilder Practice: Creating a Model, p. 79

Modified Lesson Plans for English Learners, p. 63
Reading Study Guide (Spanish), p. 79
Reading Study Guide Audio CD (Spanish)

STRUGGLING READERS

In-Depth Resources: Unit 4
- Reading Skill: Drawing Conclusions, p. 44
- Vocabulary Cards, p. 51
- Reteaching Activity, p. 58

Reading Toolkit, p. L30
Reading Study Guide, p. 79

Reading Study Guide Audio CD

GIFTED AND TALENTED STUDENTS

Interdisciplinary Projects
- Language Arts, p. 51

INCLUSION

EasyPlanner CD-ROM
- Reading Skill: Drawing Conclusions
- Reteaching Activity

TECHNOLOGY

eEdition CD-ROM

Power Presentations CD-ROM

Humanities Transparencies
- HT17 Nazca Line Drawing of a Man

Critical Thinking Transparencies
- CT38 Drawing Conclusions

Test Generator CD-ROM

ClassZone.com

In-Depth Resources: Unit 4
• Reading Skill: Drawing Conclusions, p. 44

History from Visuals

Interpreting Maps

Have students examine the map, paying attention to the title and the map key. Tell students that on the pages to come they will be reading more about the civilizations mentioned in the key.

• Which two civilizations coexisted for several hundred years? *(Nazca and Moche)*

• For which civilization was Cerro Blanco a center? *(the Moche civilization)*

GEOGRAPHY SKILLBUILDER ANSWER

the Chavín

Teach

The Nazca Civilization

 7.7

Talk About It

• Why is the Nazca people's reliance on agriculture surprising? *(The place they lived in receives very little rainfall.)*

• What is distinctive about the Nazca irrigation system? *(It featured underground canals.)*

• What are the Nazca Lines, and what are some of the theories about their meaning? *(They are large drawings made on the ground and visible only from the air. They may have been religious or astronomical in nature, or they may have been related to the flow of surface or underground water.)*

• **Critical Thinking: Finding Main Ideas**
What information might support the theory that the Nazca created the lines as a means of tracing or identifying sources of water? *(Possible answer: the fact that there was so little rainfall in their area.)*

Religion and Art Some archaeologists believe that Chavín de Huantar was a holy city. The culture's ruler-priests may have called on farmers, who made up most of the society, to build the religious center. The farmers probably worked at Chavín de Huantar to fulfill their religious duty. Followers of the Chavín religion probably traveled to the center for special festivals.

The Chavín culture spread across much of northern and central Peru. Archaeologists know this because they have found the Chavín art style in religious images throughout the northern coast of Peru. This style is seen in stone carvings and in beautiful black and red pottery. The Chavín also embroidered images into woven cloth called **textiles**.

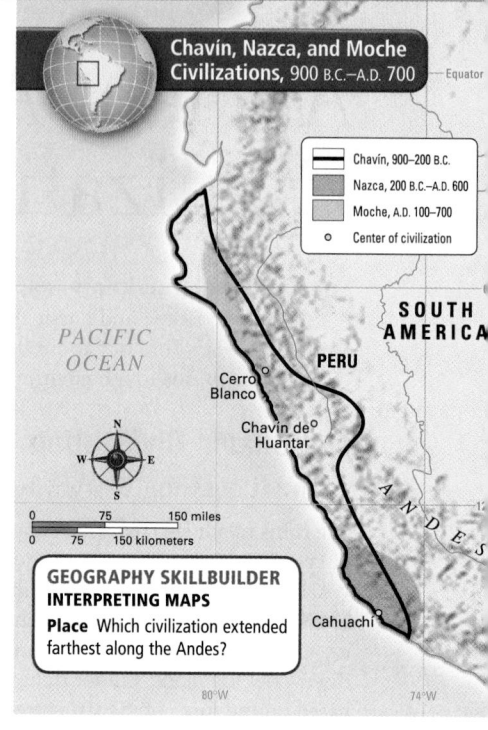

Chavín, Nazca, and Moche Civilizations, 900 B.C.–A.D. 700

Chavín, 900–200 B.C.
Nazca, 200 B.C.–A.D. 600
Moche, A.D. 100–700
○ Center of civilization

PACIFIC OCEAN

SOUTH AMERICA

PERU

Cerro Blanco

Chavín de Huantar

Cahuachi

ANDES

0   75   150 miles
0   75   150 kilometers

GEOGRAPHY SKILLBUILDER
INTERPRETING MAPS
Place Which civilization extended farthest along the Andes?

REVIEW How did the Chavín influence other cultures?
through their religion and religious art

The Nazca Civilization

2 ESSENTIAL QUESTION How did the Nazca adapt to their harsh environment?
They developed irrigation and agricultural techniques.
After the decline of the Chavín, other cultures arose in Peru. One of these was the **Nazca** (NAHZ•kuh) culture, which arose along the southern coast of present-day Peru. The Nazca prospered from around 200 B.C. to A.D. 600.

Irrigation and Agriculture Much about the Nazca remains a mystery. Like the Chavín, little is known about the political and economic structures of the Nazca. One of the things we do know about the Nazca is that they developed an extensive irrigation system. Their economy was based on farming, but the Nazca lived in an area that received less than an inch of rainfall a year. So to water their crops, the Nazca built a network of underground canals.

INTERDISCIPLINARY ACTIVITES

Language Arts

Write a Persuasive Paragraph

Have students do additional research on the Nazca Lines, using library or Internet sources. Then have each student write a paragraph that makes a persuasive argument for one of the theories about the lines. The paragraph should seek to convince readers that the selected theory is the most likely explanation for the creation of the lines.

Art

Design a Line Illustration

Have students look at pictures of the Nazca Lines here and in other sources. Then have them design their own line drawings. Students can select whatever images they would like to draw, as long as the drawings are in the same spirit and style as the Nazca Lines.

Art The Nazca civilization is also known for its beautiful pottery and textiles. Potters crafted bowls and double-spouted pitchers and decorated them with vividly painted people, birds, fish, fruits, and mythical creatures. Textile artists wove the wool of the alpaca, a camel-like animal, into ponchos, shirts, and headbands. They decorated these fine textiles with religious images and animals.

The Nazca Lines Probably the most striking legacy left behind by the Nazca are the Nazca Lines, which are shown below. To this day, no one knows the purpose of the Nazca Lines. Some people believe that the Nazca worshiped mountain or sky gods and created the drawings to please them. Other people believe the lines showed where surface water entered the plain. Still others say that the lines form a giant astronomical calendar and map. The latest theory is that some of them show the routes of **aquifers**, or underground water sources.

> **REVIEW** What is the Nazca culture known for?
> their irrigation system, their beautiful pottery and textiles, the Nazca Lines

Geography

The Nazca Lines

Between 200 B.C. and A.D. 600, the Nazca made more than 1,000 pictures of birds, plants, animals, humans, and geometric shapes on the plains of southeastern Peru. The dry climate and winds in the region preserved the designs.

Most of the drawings are so big that you can't recognize them from the ground. The hummingbird (top) and parrot shown here, for example, are over 100 feet long. Some designs are more than 2,500 feet long. It's no wonder the Nazca Lines remained undiscovered until people saw them from airplanes in the 1920s.

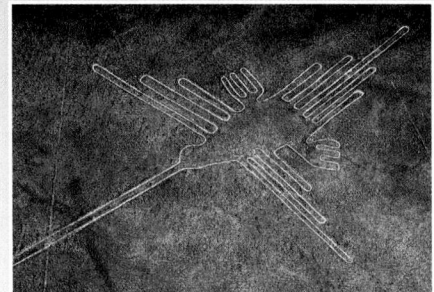

GEOGRAPHY SKILLBUILDER
INTERPRETING VISUALS
Human-Environment Interaction What do the lines suggest about the Nazca?

History from Visuals

Interpreting Visuals
Instruct students to examine the photographs of the two Nazca drawings. Then read aloud the accompanying text.

- What conclusion can you draw from the fact that the line drawings depict many different types of things? *(Possible answer: The Nazca were very artistic.)*

- Why do you think the drawings are so large? *(Possible answers: They were meant to last a long time; they were meant to be seen from a great distance.)*

GEOGRAPHY SKILLBUILDER ANSWER
Possible answer: They were skilled engineers, mathematicians, and artists.

More About . . .

The Nazca Lines
The Nazca Lines appear on a portion of a Peruvian desert plain that is nearly 40 miles long and about 1 mile wide. The lines were created by simply moving the dark stones that litter the plain to the side, revealing the lighter-colored earth underneath.

 In-Depth Resources: Unit 4
- Skillbuilder Practice: Creating a Model, p. 48

 Humanities Transparencies
- HT17 Nazca Line Drawing of a Man

DIFFERENTIATING INSTRUCTION

English Learners

Draw Logical Conclusions
Discuss these facts with students:
- Farming was important to the Nazca.
- The Nazcas received only an inch of rain a year.
- The Nazca supplied water to crops by building underground canals.

Model how to use this information to draw the conclusion: "The Nazca knew how to solve problems." Discuss why this is a logical conclusion. Guide students as they revisit the text to note other facts and to draw a logical conclusion from the facts.

Inclusion

Listen to the Lesson
Have students who are visually impaired use the Reading Study Guide Audio CD to learn more about the Nazca people and other Andean civilizations discussed in this lesson. Students should answer all the questions and exercises in the audio study guide.

Teach

The Moche Civilization

7.7

Talk About It

- From what source did the Moche get water for irrigating their crops? *(rivers in the Andes)*

- Besides agriculture, where did the Moche get their food? *(They hunted and fished, gathered snails and wild plants, and domesticated ducks and llamas.)*

- What evidence supports the statement that the Moche were skilled architects? *(Some of their buildings are still standing.)*

- **Critical Thinking: Comparing and Contrasting** How did the pottery of the Moche, as described in the text, differ from the art of the Chavín and the Nazca? *(Possible answer: Moche pottery depicts scenes of daily life, whereas Chavín and Nazca art features religious images.)*

The Moche Civilization

3 ESSENTIAL QUESTION What does Moche art tell us about their civilization?

While the Nazca rose on the southern coast of Peru, the **Moche** (MOH•chay) culture dominated Peru's hot, dry northern coast between about A.D. 100 and 700. The culture is named for the city of Moche, which may have been the capital of the Moche civilization.

Agriculture Like the Nazca, the Moche used advanced farming techniques to make the most of their environment. The Moche channeled the rivers that flowed from the Andes Mountains into impressive irrigation systems. They used this water to grow corn, beans, squash, avocados, chile peppers, and peanuts. In fact, the Moche enjoyed a wide variety of foods. They hunted and fished, gathered snails and wild plants, and ate domesticated ducks and llamas.

had highly skilled artists; provided details about Moche daily life

▲ **Moche Pottery** Archaeologists believe that this jug pictures an actual person. Some experts consider the Moche the most skilled artists of ancient America.

City Structures In addition to being good engineers, the Moche were also skilled architects. Two large structures still stand in the city of Moche. The Temple of the Sun is a gigantic step pyramid, which you learned about in Chapter 5. The Temple of the Moon is a raised platform topped with big rooms and courtyards.

Some archaeologists believe that the temples may have served as centers of political power for the Moche. They think that nobles ruled over the people. The lower classes, made up of farmers and laborers, probably paid taxes for the repair of the temples and other city structures.

Art Recent discoveries of Moche tombs have increased our understanding of the Moche civilization. Archaeologists have found beautiful jewelry made of gold, silver, and turquoise. Leaders and the wealthy wore this jewelry. They also wore textiles covered with pictures of people, plants, and animals.

DIFFERENTIATING INSTRUCTION

Gifted and Talented Students

Create a Multimedia Presentation

Have students collect information from this lesson and from outside resources, such as library books and the Internet, to make a multimedia presentation about the ancient civilizations of the Andes. The presentation should include illustrations and text descriptions of representative artwork and architecture and other details that tell about the different civilizations.

Struggling Readers

Diagram the Section

Have students work individually to create web diagrams of the section "The Moche Civilization." Each diagram should have the word *Moche* in the center, with several satellite boxes around it. Students should use details from the lesson to fill in these boxes.

In addition, archaeologists have found pottery that tells us about Moche daily life. The pots show doctors with their patients, women weaving cloth, and musicians playing instruments. But we still don't know very much about Moche religious beliefs or why the civilization fell. One day, further archaeological discoveries may answer these questions.

REVIEW How have archaeologists learned about the Moche civilization?
excavating tombs, studying pots and other artwork

Lesson Summary
- Chavín religion spread to a large area along Peru's coast.
- The Nazca developed irrigation systems and etched mysterious lines on the ground.
- The Moche civilization built large cities where artists crafted beautiful jewelry and pottery.

Why It Matters Now . . .
The farming methods used by the ancient Andean civilizations can help people today bring water to their dry fields and develop crops that grow well there.

▲ **Nazca Textile** This colorful poncho was made around A.D. 600. Nazca textiles were sometimes used to show the owner's standing in the society.

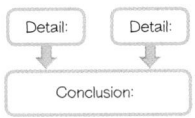
2 Lesson Review

Homework Helper
ClassZone.com

Terms & Names
1. Explain the importance of
   Chavín   Nazca   Moche
   textile   aquifer

Using Your Notes
Drawing Conclusions Use your diagram to answer the following question:
2. What conclusions can you draw about the Chavín culture? (7.7)

> Detail: →
> Detail: →
> Conclusion:

Main Ideas
3. How do archaeologists know that the Chavín influenced other cultures? (7.7)
4. What are the Nazca Lines? (CST 3)
5. How have recent discoveries increased understanding of the Moche? (HI 5)

Critical Thinking
6. **Comparing and Contrasting** Compare and contrast characteristics of the Chavín, Nazca, and Moche civilizations. (7.7)
7. **Identifying Issues and Problems** Why is it difficult to know more about the Chavín, Nazca, and Moche cultures? (HI 5)

Activity
Making a Nazca Line Drawing Sketch a plan for a Nazca Line drawing that would be 100 feet long. Be sure to indicate the scale you use in your drawing. (CST 3)

---

❹ Assess & Reteach

Assess Have pairs of students take turns answering the questions. Ask volunteers to share their completed diagrams for the lesson.

 Formal Assessment
- Lesson Quiz, p. 151

Reteach Have students work individually to review the statements in the Lesson Summary. For each statement, have students go back to the appropriate section of the text and write an additional sentence to expand and further explain the idea. Ask volunteers to share their additional sentences with the rest of the class.

 In-Depth Resources: Unit 4
- Vocabulary Cards, p. 51
- Reteaching Activity, p. 58

 Homework Helper
Visit **ClassZone.com** for a lesson review, a flip-card activity, and links to related Web sites.

---

2 Lesson Review Answers

Terms & Names
1. • Chavín, p. 295
   • textile, p. 296
   • Nazca, p. 296
   • aquifer, p. 297
   • Moche, p. 298

Using Your Notes
See page 294 for an example of a completed diagram.
2. Possible answer: The people were religious and artistic.

Main Ideas
3. They have found Chavín-style religious images throughout the northern coast of Peru.
4. huge drawings of animals, plants, birds, and various shapes etched into the dry plains
5. Pottery has revealed details of the daily life of the Moche.

Critical Thinking
6. Possible answers: All three cultures produced textiles and pottery. Both the Nazca and the Moche used irrigation extensively. Chavín cities were used primarily as religious centers.
7. Possible answers: We have no written sources and must rely on archaeological finds to make inferences about these cultures.

Activity Rubric

	Accuracy of Scale	Quality of Sketch
4	is logical and represents a length of 100 feet	neat, clear, and similar to Nazca style
3	represents a length of 100 feet	neat
2	represents a length other than 100 feet	somewhat messy
1	missing	sloppy or unfinished

❶ Plan & Prepare

Objectives

- Analyze the earliest civilization in the Americas—the Olmec.
- Characterize the Olmec culture and define its legacy.
- **Language Objective:** Classify the lesson vocabulary by category to make the text more comprehensible and meaningful.

Quick Look

Lesson 3 traces the history and contributions of the ancient Olmec civilization.

❷ Focus & Motivate

Preview Tell students that in this lesson they will learn about the Olmec civilization, which arose in what is now Mexico over 3,000 years ago. Tell students that this civilization has challenged many early theories about ancient civilizations in Meso-America.

Introduce the Main Ideas The three main ideas relate to the Big Idea "Civilizations developed in places that supported agriculture or trade or both."

Reading Skill: Categorizing This skill requires students to recognize similarities in pieces of information and then organize information into logical categories.

SAMPLE ANSWERS FOR DIAGRAM

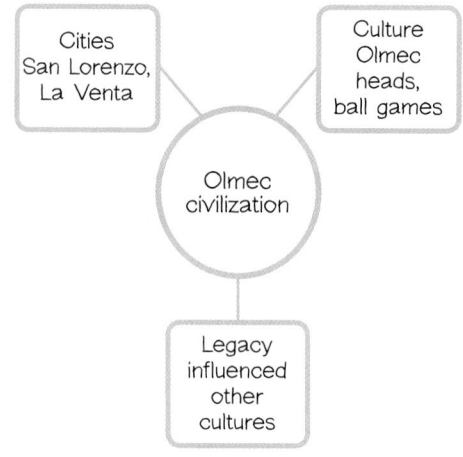

Lesson 3

▶ **MAIN IDEAS**

❶ **Geography** The Olmec lived in a fertile land and developed the first civilization in the Americas.

❷ **Culture** The Olmec had a complex civilization with many great accomplishments in art and learning.

❸ **Culture** Olmec culture spread to other groups of people in Meso-America through trade.

▶ **TAKING NOTES**

Reading Skill: Categorizing

Sorting similar kinds of information into groups helps you understand patterns in history. As you read Lesson 3, look for three categories about Olmec civilization. Record the information you learn about them in a web diagram like the one below.

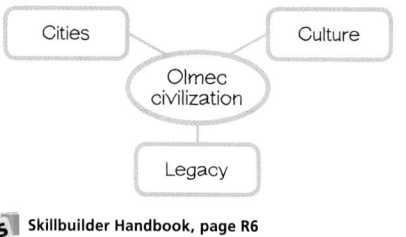

S **Skillbuilder Handbook, page R6**

▲ **Olmec Figure** This Olmec jade figure shows an adult holding a baby. Jade was sacred to the Olmec. They traded throughout much of Meso-America to obtain it.

HOW TO TEACH THE CALIFORNIA STANDARDS

Standard	Content	Student Question or Activity	Instruction
7.7	**Pages 301–303** Describes geographical and cultural features of the Olmec civilization	**Page 304** Students use their web diagrams to identify important parts of Olmec culture.	Have students create an outline of Lesson 3. Students may use the existing structure of the lesson to create headings and subheadings. They should use facts from the reading as supporting details.
HI 2	**Pages 303–304** Describes how Olmec culture influenced later Meso-American civilizations	**Page 304** Students explain the effect of Olmec trade in Meso-America.	Review key features of the Olmec culture, including their buildings, art, and religious beliefs. Have students create a diagram illustrating Olmec influences on the other civilizations treated in Chapter 9.
HI 5	**Pages 301** Explains that discoveries of Olmec ruins challenged earlier theories about ancient people	**Page 304** Students tell why historians changed their minds about how people lived in ancient Meso-America.	Review the time line on pages 284–285. Point out that the Olmec are the earliest known civilization in the Americas.

The Olmec of Meso-America

Build on What You Know You have learned about the ancient Andean civilizations in South America. Now you will read about the Olmec civilization, which arose even earlier in Meso-America. This North American region had better geographical conditions than the Andes.

The Earliest American Civilization

1 ESSENTIAL QUESTION What helped the Olmec develop the first civilization in the Americas? geography, fertile soil

Scholars of Meso-America used to think that in 1200 B.C., people lived only in villages. Then they discovered the remains of a city-based culture in Mexico's lowlands. Archaeologists named Meso-America's first known civilization the **Olmec** (AHL•mehk).

Geography Olmec civilization took root in the jungles along southern Mexico's Gulf coast. Rich soil along the rivers in the region produced generous corn crops for Meso-American farmers, just as the fertile soil around the Nile supported Egyptian farmers. As you have already learned, successful agriculture usually comes before the rise of cities.

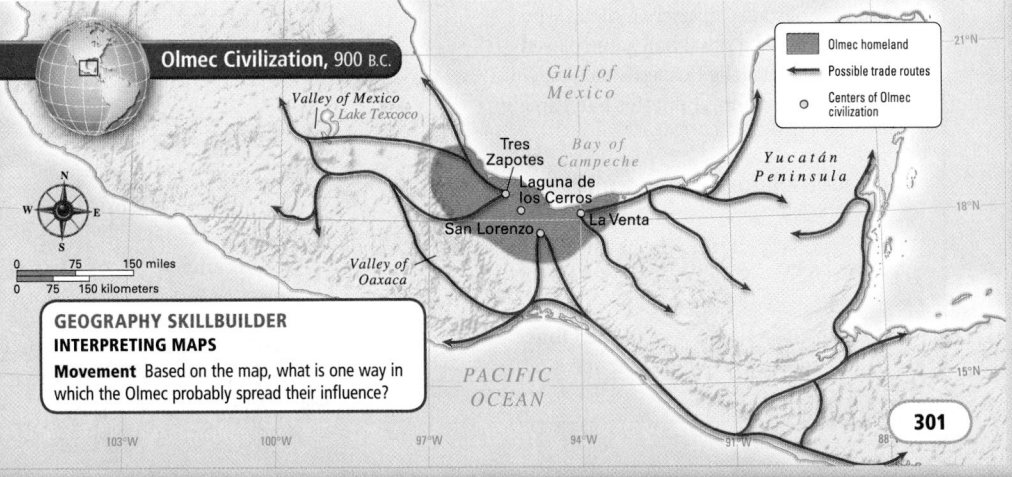

Olmec Civilization, 900 B.C.

Olmec homeland
Possible trade routes
Centers of Olmec civilization

Gulf of Mexico

Valley of Mexico
Lake Texcoco

Tres Zapotes
Bay of Campeche
Laguna de los Cerros
San Lorenzo
La Venta

Yucatán Peninsula

Valley of Oaxaca

PACIFIC OCEAN

0   75   150 miles
0   75   150 kilometers

GEOGRAPHY SKILLBUILDER
INTERPRETING MAPS
Movement Based on the map, what is one way in which the Olmec probably spread their influence?

301

CHAPTER 9 • LESSON 3

Terms & Names

Olmec an ancient civilization that developed in Meso-America over 3,000 years ago

mother culture a culture that influences the customs and ideas of later cultures

3 Teach

The Earliest American Civilization

7.7, HI 5

Talk About It

- **Critical Thinking: Categorizing** In what way was the rise of the Olmec's city-based culture similar to the development pattern of other ancient cities? (*The Olmec had a productive, river-based agricultural system.*)

California Resources

California Reading Toolkit, L31
California Modified Lesson Plans for English Learners, p. 65
California Daily Standards Practice Transparencies, TT31
California Standards Enrichment Workbook, pp. 113–114
California Online Test Practice
California Test Generator CD-ROM
California Standards Planner and Lesson Plans, L61
California EasyPlanner CD-ROM
California eEdition CD-ROM

LESSON 3 PROGRAM RESOURCES

ON LEVEL

In-Depth Resources: Unit 4
- Reading Skill: Categorizing, p. 45
- Vocabulary Cards, p. 51

Formal Assessment
- Lesson Quiz, p. 152

ENGLISH LEARNERS

In-Depth Resources in Spanish
- Reading Skill: Categorizing, p. 75

Modified Lesson Plans for English Learners, p. 65

Reading Study Guide (Spanish), p. 81

Reading Study Guide Audio CD (Spanish)

STRUGGLING READERS

In-Depth Resources: Unit 4
- Reading Skill: Categorizing, p. 45
- Vocabulary Cards, p. 51
- Reteaching Activity, p. 59

Reading Toolkit, p. L31

Reading Study Guide, p. 81

Reading Study Guide Audio CD

GIFTED AND TALENTED STUDENTS

Interdisciplinary Projects
- Physical Education, p. 52

INCLUSION

EasyPlanner CD-ROM
- Reading Skill: Categorizing
- Reteaching Activity

TECHNOLOGY

eEdition CD-ROM

Power Presentations CD-ROM

Critical Thinking Transparencies
- CT39 Categorizing

Test Generator CD-ROM

ClassZone.com

In-Depth Resources: Unit 4
• Reading Skill: Categorizing, p. 45

History from Visuals

Interpreting Maps
Have students review the map and key on page 301.

• Ask students what information they have read that supports the belief that the Olmec traded widely. *(They traded throughout much of Meso-America to obtain jade.)*

GEOGRAPHY SKILLBUILDER ANSWER
trade

Teach

Olmec Culture

 7.7

Talk About It

• Briefly describe what the text refers to as "some of the most amazing finds" at Olmec sites. *(gigantic stone heads that may be statues of rulers, gods, or ancient athletes.)*

• Based on Olmec art, what was the most important god in their culture? *(the jaguar spirit)*

• **Critical Thinking: Making Inferences**
Why do scholars view calendars as evidence of advanced learning? *(Possible answer: Making a calendar requires an ability to calculate, keep records, and observe the movements of stars and planets.)*

More About . . .

Olmec Heads
There are many reasons to be amazed by the colossal Olmec stone heads besides their sheer size. The sculptures were carved from rock that had been transported dozens of miles through difficult terrain. Some experts believe that the Olmec must have transported them along rivers on boats. The sculptures were also created without the aid of metal tools. In spite of this fact, the features are richly detailed and expertly sculpted.

Cities The Olmec built several cities, which served as political centers. One of the cities, now called San Lorenzo, dates back to around 1150 B.C. Archaeologists have found earthen mounds, courtyards, and pyramids in the city. Another Olmec city, now called La Venta, rose around 900 B.C. A 100-foot pyramid discovered there probably once contained the tomb of a great Olmec ruler.

Archaeologists believe that Olmec cities were ruled by powerful dynasties. Administrators, engineers and builders, and artists came below the rulers in the rigid Olmec social structure. Farmers formed the society's largest and lowest class.

REVIEW Why were the Olmec able to build cities?
Their fertile soil and other resources allowed them to build the cities.

Olmec Culture

 ESSENTIAL QUESTION What did the Olmec accomplish in art and learning? built huge stone heads, developed a calendar, may have used picture symbols

San Lorenzo and La Venta have given archaeologists greater insight into Olmec culture. These cities give us a glimpse into Olmec accomplishments in art and learning.

Olmec Art Some of the most amazing finds were huge stone heads. Crafted with simple tools, some heads stand as tall as 9 feet and weigh as much as 20 tons.

Archaeologists do not know who or what the heads represent. They may represent Olmec rulers or gods. Since all of the faces stare out from underneath helmets, they may also represent athletes who played a ritual ball game played during religious festivals. You will learn more about this ball game in Lesson 4.

Religion and Learning Much like the art of the ancient Andean civilizations, Olmec art was often tied to religion. The Olmec worshiped a number of nature gods. But above all, the Olmec worshiped the jaguar spirit.

Olmec Head The stone used for the heads was carried up to 80 miles over mountain ranges, rivers, and swamps. ▼

DIFFERENTIATING INSTRUCTION

Gifted and Talented Students

Write Interview Questions
Have students conduct additional research on the Olmec culture, using library or Internet resources. Then have each student create a list of ten questions he or she would like to ask an Olmec about the Olmec culture. Encourage students to ask questions that would resolve historical debates or answer key questions.

Struggling Readers

Shrink the Paragraphs
Have students work in teams of two. Ask each team to read aloud the section "Olmec Culture." Then assign each team member one of the two subsections. Have students review their subsections and reduce each paragraph to a short summary statement. Have students share their summary statements with their partners, then with the rest of the class.

Primary Source

Jaguar Sculpture

Background: Scholars have not yet been able to decipher Olmec writing. But images of a jaguar, a big cat that still prowls the jungles of Meso-America, appear on many Olmec carvings and other artifacts. The jaguar is an important symbol of Olmec culture. Some historians have even called the Olmec "the people of the jaguar."

The carvings often show an imaginary animal that is part human and part jaguar. Like the three-inch-high sculpture shown here, the creature usually has a snarling mouth and long, curved fangs. The Olmec worshiped the jaguar for its power. They believed that the jaguar could control nature and society.

DOCUMENT–BASED QUESTION
Why do you think the Olmec pictured the jaguar as part human?

Many Olmec sculptures represent this spirit as a half-human, half-jaguar creature. You can learn about these sculptures in the Primary Source feature above.

Advances in learning also reflect religious influence. Some archaeologists believe that the Olmec developed a calendar to keep track of religious ceremonies. They may also have used picture symbols to illustrate the calendar.

REVIEW How was Olmec art tied to religion?
The huge stone heads may have represented gods; the Olmec worshiped the jaguar, which was often represented in carvings and sculpture.

Olmec Legacy

3 ESSENTIAL QUESTION How did the Olmec influence other cultures?
built huge stone heads, developed a calendar, may have used picture symbols

For reasons that are not fully understood, Olmec civilization ended some time after 400 B.C. Invaders, or the Olmec themselves, destroyed most of the monuments in cities such as San Lorenzo and La Venta.

Nevertheless, the Olmec legacy lived on in later Meso-American cultures. A large trading network throughout Meso-America helped spread Olmec influence. As a result, the Olmec are often called Meso-America's **mother culture**.

Vocabulary Strategy
You can use **context clues** to understand the meaning of the term *mother culture*. Words like *legacy*, *spread influence*, and *mother* suggest a culture that supported and inspired others.

Ancient America • 303

Interpreting Primary Sources

Jaguar Sculpture

• Why do some historians refer to the Olmec as "the people of the jaguar"? *(because the jaguar appears so often in Olmec religious art)*

• Why do you think the jaguar figure is often shown with a snarling mouth and long fangs? *(Possible answer: These features demonstrate the ferocity and strength of the jaguar.)*

DOCUMENT–BASED QUESTION ANSWER

Possible answers: to show a close connection between the two; to show humans as being endowed with the strength of a jaguar

Teach

Olmec Legacy

7.7, HI 2

Talk About It

• What happened to the Olmec civilization after 400 B.C.? *(It ended, although experts are not sure why.)*

• What helped to spread Olmec culture throughout the Meso-American region? *(an extensive trading network)*

• **Critical Thinking: Finding Main Ideas** Why do you think the term *mother culture* is used to convey the idea that the Olmec influenced other cultures? *(Possible answer: Mothers are people who have given birth to other people. The Olmec culture was a culture from which other cultures came.)*

DIFFERENTIATING INSTRUCTION

English Learners

Organize Vocabulary
Tell students that vocabulary from the text can be organized into three categories: "cities," "legacy," and "culture." Have students revisit the text to generate examples for each of the three categories. If necessary, have students share their findings with classmates out loud. Note students' work on a chart and have them practice formulating statements. Such as "La Venta belongs in the 'cities' category because it is an Olmec city where the pyramid tomb of a great ruler was found."

Inclusion

Create an Olmec Picture Book
Students who have difficulty reading can create "picture book" versions of this lesson. Pair students and have them use pictures from this lesson or from outside sources to illustrate the main points of the lesson. Students should write brief captions for their illustrations.

④ Assess & Reteach

Assess Organize students into groups of four. Have each group work together to answer questions 3, 4, and 5 in the Lesson Review. Discuss the answers with the class.

 Formal Assessment
• Lesson Quiz, p. 152

Reteach Pair up students and have the pairs take turns teaching the content of the sections to each other. Students should emphasize the key information in each section and ask their "student" review questions.

 In-Depth Resources: Unit 4
• Vocabulary Cards, p. 51
• Reteaching Activity, p. 59

Homework Helper

Visit **ClassZone.com** for a lesson review, a flip-card activity, and links to related Web sites.

Influences Other cultures were particularly influenced by Olmec art styles. These styles—especially the use of the jaguar—can be seen in the pottery and sculpture of later peoples. In addition, the Olmec left behind their ideas for cities, ceremonial centers, and ritual ball games. Their use of picture symbols may also have influenced later writing systems. The Olmec greatly influenced the Mayan civilization, which you will learn about in Lesson 4.

REVIEW Why is Olmec civilization called Meso-America's mother culture?
It was Meso-America's first civilization, and it influenced later cultures in the region.

Lesson Summary
• Successful farming gave rise to a great civilization in Mexico's lowlands.
• The Olmec made great advances in art and learning.
• Trade spread Olmec influence throughout Meso-America.

Why It Matters Now . . .
The Olmec mother culture continues to influence the cultures of Mexico and Central America today.

3 Lesson Review

Homework Helper
ClassZone.com

Terms & Names
1. Explain the importance of
   Olmec   mother culture

Using Your Notes
Categorizing Use your completed web diagram to answer the following question:
2. What were important parts of Olmec culture? (7.7)

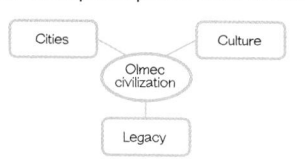

Main Ideas
3. How were classes in the Olmec social structure ordered? (7.7)
4. What does Olmec art tell us about their religious beliefs? (7.7)
5. What was the effect of Olmec trade in Meso-America? (HI 2)

Critical Thinking
6. **Recognizing Changing Interpretations of History** Why did historians change their minds about how people lived in ancient Meso-America? (HI 5)
7. **Comparing and Contrasting** How was the rise of Olmec civilization similar to that of ancient Egypt? (HI 2)

Activity
Writing a Letter Imagine that you are an Olmec artist. Write a letter in which you explain why the jaguar is important to you. (7.7)

304 • Chapter 9

---

3 Lesson Review Answers

Terms & Names
1. • Olmec, p. 301
   • mother culture, p. 303

Using Your Notes
See page 300 for an example of a completed diagram.
2. giant Olmec heads, ball games

Main Ideas
3. rulers first; then administrators, engineers and builders, and artists; farmers last
4. They worshiped the jaguar; they believed the jaguar spirit

controlled nature and society.
5. Olmec influence spread and affected other cultures in the region.

Critical Thinking
6. Possible answers: New findings and information overturned old ideas and assumptions.
7. Possible answers: Both civilizations developed as a result of successful agriculture along the fertile banks of rivers.

Activity Rubric

	Explanation in Letter	**Errors in Mechanics**
4	inventive explanation, incorporates existing theories about both religious and artistic importance	few or none
3	incorporates existing theories about religious or artistic importance	some
2	incorporates theories unrelated to religion or art	many
1	no explanation given	major

Make a Shoebox Time Capsule

Goal: To understand that much of what we know about the Olmec and other ancient American civilizations is based on the artifacts archaeologists have found

Prepare

❶ Get together with a small group of classmates.

❷ Discuss items that represent today's culture in the United States.

Do the Activity

❶ Use the paper and colored pencils to draw two pictures of items that represent U.S. culture.

❷ Cut out each drawing with the scissors.

❸ Label your drawings.

❹ Place all of your group's drawings in a shoebox. Label the box with your group name or number.

Follow-Up

❶ Exchange shoeboxes with another group. What items did this group place in its shoebox?

❷ Pretend you are archaeologists who have discovered the box 1,000 years from now. What insight does each artifact provide about U.S. culture in the 21st century?

Extension

Making Historical Interpretations With your group, take the drawings out of your shoebox. Erase the labels and tear small pieces off the drawings. Then put the drawings back and exchange shoeboxes once again with another group. Try to identify the "ruins" in the shoebox.

Materials & Supplies
- paper
- colored pencils
- scissors
- shoebox

CALIFORNIA STANDARDS
HI 5 Students recognize that interpretations of history are subject to change as new information is uncovered.

Objective

Recognize that our knowledge about a culture changes as archaeologists and historians uncover new information.

Suggestions for Completing the Activity

- Help students brainstorm items that represent the U.S. culture of today.

- Encourage students to think beyond fads, focusing on items or ideas that clearly say "United States."

- Remind students what features are used to characterize other cultures—lasting achievements, daily objects, art, and technology.

305

ACTIVITIES ANSWERS

Follow-Up Answers

1. Items will vary but should be representative of modern U.S. culture.
2. Possible answers: Electronic items were popular in U.S. culture; people liked to listen to music, talk on cell phones, and explore the Internet.

Extension Rubric

	Identification of Objects	Level of Engagement
4	shows understanding of historical interpretation	shows interest and engages actively in the activity
3	shows some understanding of historical interpretation	shows interest and completes the activity
2	shows a basic understanding of historical interpretation	participates in the activity with prompting from classmates or teacher
1	shows little understanding of historical interpretation	demonstrates little or no participation in the activity

❶ Plan & Prepare

Objectives

- Analyze the rise of Mayan civilization, including the location of key Mayan cities.
- Describe daily life among the Maya, including distinctions among social classes and religious practices.
- Summarize the cultural accomplishments of the Maya.
- **Language Objective:** Create a mural showing Mayan life.

Quick Look

Lesson 4 explores the history of the Mayan civilization of Meso-America, including its many artistic and scientific achievements.

❷ Focus & Motivate

Preview Explain that this lesson describes the Mayan civilization of Meso-America. Students will learn about many of the Maya's notable accomplishments.

Introduce the Main Ideas The three main ideas relate to the Big Idea "Modern culture draws on the legacy of many past civilizations." Help students look for statements related to this Big Idea as they read the lesson.

Reading Skill: Summarizing This skill requires students to identify the main point of a passage and restate it in a short summary sentence.

SAMPLE ANSWERS FOR DIAGRAM

```
The Rise of the Maya
        |
    Main idea
The Mayan civilization rose to
great heights between A.D. 250
         and 900.
     /            \
  Detail          Detail
 fabulous       rich culture,
city-states—    including art
 Palenque,       and learning
Copán, Tikal
```

Lesson 4

▶ MAIN IDEAS

❶ Geography Mayan civilization rose in Central America as the Maya adapted to both highlands and lowlands.

❷ Culture Mayan society was divided into classes and shaped by religion.

❸ Culture The Maya produced beautiful art and made important advances in learning.

▶ TAKING NOTES

Reading Skill: Summarizing

When you summarize, you supply only main ideas and important details. Identify the main ideas and important details in each section of Lesson 4. Then put them in your own words and record them in a diagram like the one below.

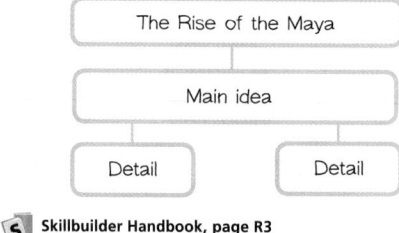

```
The Rise of the Maya
        |
    Main idea
    /        \
 Detail     Detail
```

S Skillbuilder Handbook, page R3

▲ **Mayan Mask** This jade mask, found in a tomb in Tikal, covered the face of a dead Mayan nobleman. The Maya believed that the nobleman would wear the mask during his voyage to the afterlife to protect him from evil spirits.

CALIFORNIA STANDARDS

7.7.1 Study the locations, landforms, and climates of Mexico, Central America, and South America and their effects on Mayan, Aztec, and Incan economies, trade, and development of urban societies.

7.7.2 Study the roles of people in each society, including class structures, family life, warfare, religious beliefs and practices, and slavery.

7.7.3 Explain how and where each empire arose and how the Aztec and Incan empires were defeated by the Spanish.

7.7.4 Describe the artistic and oral traditions and architecture in the three civilizations.

7.7.5 Describe the Meso-American achievements in astronomy and mathematics, including the development of the calendar and the Meso-American knowledge of seasonal changes to the civilizations' agricultural systems.

HOW TO TEACH THE CALIFORNIA STANDARDS

Standard	Content	Student Question or Activity	Instruction
7.7.3	**Page 307** Tells where the Mayan civilization arose	**Page 308** Students tell on which landform most Mayan city-states were located.	Instruct students to visit the library or use the Internet to learn more about the climate of the Yucatán Peninsula.
7.7.2	**Pages 308–309** Describes the roles of Mayan people	**Page 311** Students tell who belonged to the main classes in Mayan society.	Have students compare the social structure of Mayan society with that of a society previously studied.
7.7.1	**Page 307** Describes the effect of geography on Mayan society	**Page 308** Students explain how the Maya developed into a great civilization.	Ask students to predict how Mayan civilization arose. Record students' responses on the board.
7.7.4	**Page 310** Illustrates Mayan architecture	**Page 310** Students compare Mayan and Egyptian architecture.	Have students use blocks to create small models of Mayan and Egyptian pyramids.
7.7.5	**Page 310** Highlights Mayan achievements	**Page 311** Students discuss the Mayan calendar.	Explain that the Aztecs adopted the Mayan calendar with some modifications.

The Mayan Civilization

TERMS & NAMES
Maya
maize
stele
glyph
codex

Build on What You Know You have learned that the Olmec influenced other cultures. Now you'll read about one of them, the Maya, who built a powerful civilization in Meso-America.

The Rise of the Maya

1 ESSENTIAL QUESTION Where did Mayan civilization rise?

from present-day southern Mexico into northern Central America

As the Olmec declined, the **Maya** began to develop a civilization from present-day southern Mexico into northern Central America. This area included the lowlands in the north, the dry forests of the Yucatán Peninsula, and the dense jungles of present-day Mexico and Guatemala. The area also included the highlands in the south. This is a range of cool mountains stretching from southern Mexico to El Salvador.

Early Settlements By about 1500 B.C., people speaking Mayan languages first began settling lowland villages, where they farmed and traded. The first ceremonial centers, where the Maya practiced their religion, appeared in wealthier villages by 500 B.C. Eventually, these villages developed into cities.

Tikal The pyramid shown here is the Temple of the Jaguar. It stands in Tikal, one of the great Mayan cities. ▼

307

❸ Teach

The Rise of the Maya

7.7.1, 7.7.2, 7.7.3

Talk About It

- **Critical Thinking: Making Inferences** Why are the years between A.D. 250 and 900 known as the Classic Period of Mayan civilization? *(During that time, the Maya built magnificent city-states.)*

California Resources

California Reading Toolkit, L32
California Modified Lesson Plans for English Learners, p. 67
California Daily Standards Practice Transparencies, TT32
California Standards Enrichment Workbook, pp. 113–114
California Online Test Practice
California Test Generator CD-ROM
California Standards Planner and Lesson Plans, L63
California EasyPlanner CD-ROM
California eEdition CD-ROM

LESSON 4 PROGRAM RESOURCES

ON LEVEL

In-Depth Resources: Unit 4
- Reading Skill: Summarizing, p. 46
- Vocabulary Cards, p. 51
- Geography Practice: The Land of the Maya, p. 53

Formal Assessment
- Lesson Quiz, p. 153

ENGLISH LEARNERS

In-Depth Resources in Spanish
- Reading Skill: Summarizing, p. 76
- Geography Practice: The Land of the Maya, p. 81

Modified Lesson Plans for English Learners, p. 67

Reading Study Guide (Spanish), p. 83

Reading Study Guide Audio CD (Spanish)

STRUGGLING READERS

In-Depth Resources: Unit 4
- Reading Skill: Summarizing, p. 46
- Vocabulary Cards, p. 51
- Reteaching Activity, p. 60

Reading Toolkit, p. L32

Reading Study Guide, p. 83

Reading Study Guide Audio CD

GIFTED AND TALENTED STUDENTS

In-Depth Resources: Unit 4
- Primary Source: The Rabbit and the Crab, p. 55

History Makers
- Pacal: Mayan King, p. 17

Interdisciplinary Projects
- Math, p. 49
- Literature: Popol Vuh, p. 56

INCLUSION

EasyPlanner CD-ROM
- Reading Skill: Summarizing
- Reteaching Activity

TECHNOLOGY

eEdition CD-ROM

Power Presentations CD-ROM

Humanities Transparencies
- HT18 Mayan Ball Games Marker

Map Transparencies
- MT18 Archaeological Map of Tikal

Critical Thinking Transparencies
- CT40 Summarizing
- CT41 Chapter 9 Visual Summary

Test Generator CD-ROM

ClassZone.com

In-Depth Resources: Unit 4
• Reading Skill: Summarizing, p. 46

History from Visuals

Interpreting Maps

Have students review the map and key, paying special attention to the relief shading. Point out the small locator map to help clarify how the location of the Mayan civilization relates to the locations of other civilizations they have studied.

• Which Mayan city stands out geographically in comparison with the others shown on the map? *(Copán is located in a mountainous region, while the other cities are located in lowland areas.)*

GEOGRAPHY SKILLBUILDER ANSWER

the Yucatán Peninsula

Map Transparencies
• MT18 Archaeological Map of Tikal

Teach

Mayan Life

 7.7.2

Talk About It

• Briefly describe the Mayan social structure that developed over time. *(The king was at the top, followed by the noble class. Below them were merchants and artisans. Farmers and slaves were at the bottom.)*

• Which group made up the largest class in Mayan society? *(Most Maya were farmers, low in the Mayan social structure.)*

• What does the text suggest about how the homes and clothing of Mayan farmers compared with those of Mayan nobles? *(Farmers lived in simpler homes and wore simpler clothing than the nobles.)*

• **Critical Thinking: Finding Main Ideas** Identify two facts in the text that support the statement "Mayan life was shaped by religion." *(Possible answers: The Maya prayed to many gods; they made human sacrifices; their ball games had a religious purpose.)*

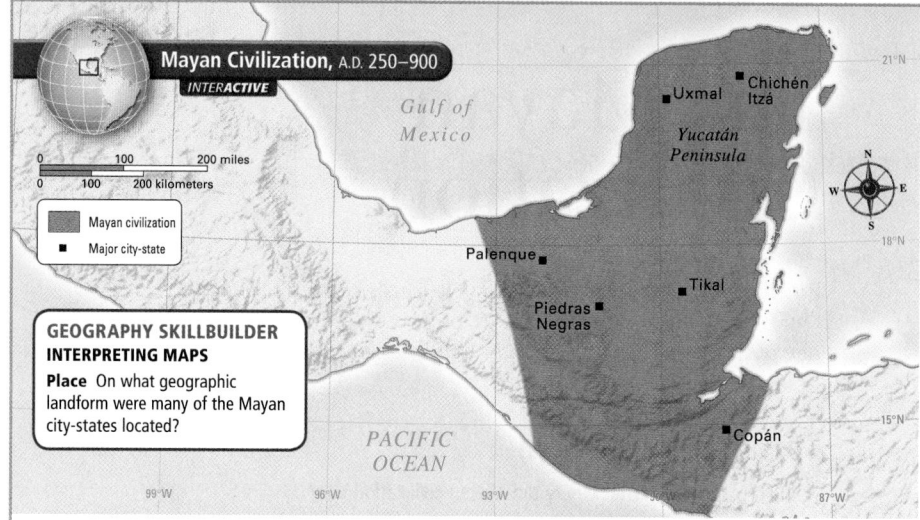

Mayan Civilization, A.D. 250–900
INTERACTIVE

0   100   200 miles
0   100   200 kilometers

▨ Mayan civilization
■ Major city-state

Gulf of Mexico

Uxmal Chichén Itzá
Yucatán Peninsula
Palenque
Piedras Negras Tikal
Copán
PACIFIC OCEAN

GEOGRAPHY SKILLBUILDER
INTERPRETING MAPS
Place On what geographic landform were many of the Mayan city-states located?

Classic Period Recent findings may cause the dates to change, but the period from A.D. 250 to 900 is traditionally known as the Classic Period of Mayan civilization. During this period, the Maya built magnificent city-states with temples, pyramids, and plazas.

Some of the largest city-states included Tikal (tee•KAHL), Copán (koh•PAHN), and Palenque. (You read about Palenque and some of its kings in Starting with a Story on page 286.) Each city-state was independent and was ruled by a king. However, the cities were linked through trade. Cities traded local products, such as salt, textiles, and jade.

REVIEW How did the Maya develop into a great civilization?
They founded small farming villages and built ceremonial centers in the wealthier ones. Eventually, these evolved into cities.

Mayan Life

 ESSENTIAL QUESTION How was Mayan society structured?
king on top, then nobles, merchants and artisans, farmers, and slaves
Thousands of people lived in the city-states. Over time, a clear social structure developed. The Mayan king was at the top of this structure, followed by the noble class, made up of priests and leading warriors. Merchants and artisans came next, followed by farmers and then slaves. Slaves were mostly prisoners captured during wars.

Daily Life Most of the Mayan people lived and worked as farmers. They grew beans, squash, and **maize** (mayz), a type of corn. This corn crop was important to the Maya. In fact, according to Mayan legends, people had been created out of maize.

INTERDISCIPLINARY ACTIVITIES

Art

Diagram the Mayan Social Structure

Have students use information in the lesson and additional resources to create diagrams of the social structure of the Mayan civilization. The diagrams should incorporate illustrations that reveal aspects of daily life among people of the different classes. For example, illustrations may show the types of houses, clothing, or work of people in different classes.

Science

Research Mayan Architecture

Have students use library or Internet resources to learn more about Mayan architecture. Students should share their findings in brief reports that describe the style of the buildings as well as the way they were created without the use of metal tools.

Mayan farmers used a variety of agricultural techniques, including irrigation. To irrigate dry areas, they dug canals that carried water to their fields. They also added rich soil from the canal beds to their fields to lift them above river level. To keep their families dry when the rivers flooded, the farmers built their houses on poles that raised the houses above the ground.

In contrast with the farmers, members of the noble class lived in decorated stone palaces. The Mayan nobles and their children wore beautiful clothes and jade beads.

Religious Beliefs Mayan life was shaped by religion. The Maya prayed to many gods. Their supreme god was the lord of fire. Other gods included the god of the sun, goddess of the moon, and the gods of death, war, corn, and rain.

To gain favor with their gods, the Maya made offerings of animals, plants, and jade. Sometimes they even made human sacrifices. In most large cities, the Maya also played a ritual ball game on a huge court. One of the reasons the Maya played this game is because they believed it would bring life-giving rains. You will learn more about the Mayan ball game in the Daily Life feature on pages 312–313.

Stele This carved stone slab of a Mayan ruler stands in a ceremonial center at Copán. Artistic expression in Copán reached its height during the reign of this ruler. ▼

REVIEW How was Mayan life shaped by religion?
The Maya prayed to many gods; farmers particularly depended on them for good crops and rain.

Mayan Culture

3 **ESSENTIAL QUESTION** What were Mayan achievements in art and learning?
steles, use of zero, calendar, writing system
Mayan art and learning were also linked to religion. Art was produced for religious ceremonies. Religious beliefs led to the development of the calendar and to advances in mathematics and astronomy.

Art Meso-America's tropical climate long ago rotted Mayan art made of wood, bark, feather, and gourds. Only pottery, sculpture, jade work, and **steles** (STEE•leez)—carved stone slabs—have survived. Steles were used to mark special religious dates and celebrate a ruler's reign.

Ancient America • 309

DIFFERENTIATING INSTRUCTION

Gifted and Talented Students

Report on Mayan Science
Have students use library or Internet resources to learn more about the Mayan calendar or the Mayan codices. Students should assemble and present their findings in brief "fact sheets." Each fact sheet should include written information and an illustration.

Struggling Readers

Create Vocabulary Cards
Have students work independently to identify challenging vocabulary terms in this lesson, including the highlighted vocabulary words and any other terms that students don't understand. Then have students write each term on a note card. Provide dictionaries for them to look up the meaning of each word and write it on the back of the card. They may also wish to add illustrations.

More About . . .

Sacrifices in Mayan Civilization
Experts believe that the Maya used both human and animal blood in making sacrifices to their gods. Blood sacrifices were considered necessary in order to nourish the gods. They took several forms. In many cases, a priest or noble would wound himself in order to spill a small amount of blood. In other cases, animals and sometimes humans were killed. Priests removed their hearts in order to appeal to the gods.

 Humanities Transparencies
• HT18 Mayan Ball Game Marker

Teach

Mayan Culture
7.7.4, 7.7.5

Talk About It

• How did religion shape Mayan culture? (*Art was created to serve religious purposes. Religious questions and concerns prompted the development of science and astronomy. The social structure was influenced religious roles.*)

• How did Mayan astronomers and mathematicians demonstrate their advanced knowledge? (*They developed a highly accurate calendar.*)

• How did we learn about the Mayan system of writing? (*by studying glyphs on steles and in books*)

• **Critical Thinking: Understanding Cause and Effect** How might food shortages have affected Mayan cities? (*Possible answer: Cities require a surplus food supply in order to allow specialization of labor. Food shortages may have made it impossible for cities to survive.*)

History from Visuals

Interpreting Visuals

Have students analyze the text and illustrations dealing with the similarities and differences between the Mayan and Egyptian cultures. Point out that the Egyptian civilization and the Mayan civilization developed thousands of miles away from each other at different times and that historians believe neither civilization ever knew the other existed.

- How do you explain the similarities between the Mayan and Egyptian civilizations? *(Possible answers: Both civilizations developed the same kinds of technologies; both cultures had great respect for their dead, so it is not surprising that they built great structures to honor them.)*

SKILLBUILDER ANSWER

The Mayan pyramid has a staircase leading to a temple on top; the Egyptian pyramid is smoother. Both are triangular.

More About . . .

Mayan Calendars

The Maya actually had three different calendar systems. One of these systems kept track of the Mayan religious cycle. This cycle lasted 260 days. They also had a calendar that included 365 days in the year, like our own. In addition, the Maya had a system called the long count, which recorded the number of days that had passed since the (mythical) creation of the Mayan world.

 In-Depth Resources: Unit 4
- Primary Source: The Rabbit and the Crab, p. 55
- Literature: Popol Vuh, p. 56

Comparisons Across Cultures

Mayan and Egyptian Civilizations

The Mayan and the Egyptian civilizations built pyramids and developed writing systems that had striking similarities and differences. Both civilizations used their pyramids as tombs and filled them with treasure. But Mayan pyramids were also used for religious rituals.

Both the Egyptians and the Maya developed writing systems based on picture symbols. However, Mayan symbols—called glyphs—stood for whole words, syllables, or sounds. Egyptian symbols, called hieroglyphs, stood for sounds, ideas, or letters.

Mayan pyramid

Mayan glyphs

Egyptian pyramid

Egyptian hieroglyphs

> **SKILLBUILDER**
> **INTERPRETING VISUALS**
> As you study the Mayan and Egyptian pyramids above, what other similarities and differences do you see?

Achievements in Math and Science In Chapter 7, you learned that ancient Indian mathematicians used a symbol for the zero and positions to show place. The Maya also developed these two important mathematical ideas.

Mayan astronomers and mathematicians applied these ideas to develop a calendar system. The 365-day calendar they created is nearly as accurate as a modern calendar. The calendar helped identify the best times to plant crops and attack enemies. It was also used to keep track of religious holidays.

Writing Only a few writing systems developed in the ancient world. The Maya developed the most advanced writing system in the ancient Americas. Mayan writing on steles and books contains symbolic pictures called **glyphs** (glihfs). Some of these glyphs stood for whole words, syllables, or sounds. The Maya used the glyphs to record important historical events in a bark-paper book called a **codex** (KOH•DEKS). Only four of these books have survived.

DIFFERENTIATING INSTRUCTION

English Learners

Create a Mural

Have students work with partners to create murals showing life in the Mayan social structure. Have students include images of the Mayan king, the noble class, merchants, artisans, farmers, and slaves, showing and explaining how the Mayan people lived and worked. Have students explain their murals to their classmates. Post the murals in the classroom.

Inclusion

Read the Sections Aloud

Pair students and have each pair take turns reading the section titled "Mayan Culture" aloud. Students may alternate paragraphs or subsections. As students read to each other, encourage them to pause at the end of each subsection to summarize what they just read.

Abandoned Cities By 900, the Maya had abandoned their great cities. To this day, no one knows why. Warfare, which broke out in the 700s, may have caused a decline. Overcrowding and overfarming may have led to food shortages. When Spanish conquerors arrived in the 1500s, only small, weak city-states remained. However, Mayan peoples still live in Meso-America. Many of them still speak the Mayan languages, as well as Spanish.

REVIEW How were art and learning linked to religion?

Lesson Summary
- The Maya built magnificent cities.
- A clear class structure developed in the Mayan civilization.
- The Maya created lasting artworks, invented a writing system, and made great advances in astronomy and mathematics.

Why It Matters Now . . .
The influence of Mayan culture is found in the United States as a result of immigration from Meso-America.

Connect to Today

▲ **Maya Today** The modern-day descendants of the ancient Maya follow many traditional practices. For example, these women carry corn much like their ancestors did.

teles marked religious dates; mathematicians and astronomers developed a calendar that helped the Maya keep track of religious holidays.

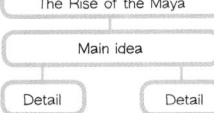 **Lesson Review**

Homework Helper
ClassZone.com

Terms & Names
1. Explain the importance of

Maya	stele	codex
maize	glyph	

Using Your Notes

Summarizing Use your completed diagram to answer the following question:
2. What is the main idea of the section "Mayan Life"? (7.7.2)

> The Rise of the Maya
>
> Main idea
>
> Detail   Detail

Main Ideas
3. What happened during the Classic Period in Mayan civilization? (7.7.3)
4. Who belonged to the main classes in Mayan society? (7.7.2)
5. Why did the Maya develop a calendar? (7.7.5)

Critical Thinking
6. **Understanding Cause and Effect** Why do you think archaeologists were able to find many Mayan steles? (7.7.1)
7. **Comparing and Contrasting** How did the Olmec influence Mayan culture and religion? (7.7.4)

Activity **Internet Activity** Use the Internet to learn more about the Mayan calendar. Create a poster with pictures and captions that shows how the Mayan system worked. (7.7.5)
INTERNET KEYWORD *Mayan calendar*

Ancient America • **311**

CHAPTER 9 • LESSON 4

❹ Assess & Reteach

Assess Have students work individually to answer the questions, then meet in small groups to discuss their answers.

 Formal Assessment
- Lesson Quiz, p. 153

Reteach Have students use hand signals to indicate their familiarity with the vocabulary terms in this lesson. Write the terms on the board. As you point to each term and say it aloud, have students who do not understand the term hold up a closed fist, students who have a vague idea of what it means raise one finger, students who are fairly sure of the word's meaning raise two fingers, and students who know the word and can use it in a sentence raise three fingers.

 In-Depth Resources: Unit 4
- Vocabulary Cards, p. 51
- Reteaching Activity, p. 60

 Homework Helper

Visit **ClassZone.com** for a lesson review, a flip-card activity, and links to related Web sites.

---

❹ Lesson Review Answers

Terms & Names
1. • Maya, p. 307
   • maize, p. 308
   • stele, p. 309
   • glyph, p. 310
   • codex, p. 310

Using Your Notes
See page 306 for an example of a completed diagram.
2. The Maya were divided into distinct classes, all of which were shaped by religion.

Main Ideas
3. The Maya built their great cities and were at the pinnacle of their power.
4. ruler, nobles, merchants, artisans, farmers, slaves
5. to identify the best times to plant crops and attack enemies and to keep track of religious holidays

Critical Thinking
6. because the stone markers were able to survive the region's tropical climate
7. building of pyramids, use of picture symbols, playing of ritual ball game, importance of art to religion

Activity Rubric

	Accuracy of Explanation	Illustrations on Calendar
4	thorough, accurate explanation of how calendar worked	neat, clearly labeled, accurate
3	accurate explanation	labeled, accurate
2	mostly accurate explanation	some labels, mostly accurate
1	inaccurate explanation	missing or inaccurate

Ancient America • **311**

Daily Life
Extend Lesson 4

Research Links
ClassZone.com

Objectives

- Describe the purpose and features of the ball game that was a central part of Mayan culture.
- Explore how activities of daily life reflect a larger culture.
- **Language Objective:** Interpret the aspects of an illustration that support the text and make the content more comprehensible.

❶ Focus & Motivate

Preview Explain that this feature will provide more information about an important Mayan ritual—a game that not only entertained but also hold significant religious meaning.

❷ Teach

Talk About It

- What was the religious importance of the game? *(The people believed that the winners were favored with prosperity from the gods.)*

- What were the consequences of losing the game? *(Possible answers: Fans would be disappointed; the players would be disgraced; the captain of the losing team was often sacrificed to the gods.)*

- **Critical Thinking: Making Inferences** Why do you think the Maya considered it a great honor to play the ball game? *(The honor and future of a city was thought to depend on the outcome of the game. There was great glory for the victors.)*

Playing the Mayan Ball Game

Purpose: To learn about the rules and risks of the Mayan ball game

Ball courts, like this one in Copán, were found in every major Mayan city-state. Most players belonged to the noble class and considered it a great honor to play the Mayan ball game. But the stakes were high. The Maya believed that the gods rewarded the winning team's city with fertile soil and plentiful crops. However, the captain of the losing team was often sacrificed to the gods. Here are some typical features of the Mayan ball game.

Ⓐ Spectators People crowded along the walls above the court to cheer on their team and favorite players.

Ⓑ Temple At the end of the game, the captain of the losing team followed the priest up the staircase to the temple and accepted his fate.

Ⓒ Steles The glyphs on the steles were meant to inspire the home team. They celebrated the city's king and the team's great victories.

Ⓓ Goal It is thought that to win the game, players had to bounce the ball off of carved parrot heads set about 20 to 30 feet off the ground along the court. But this could take hours or even days.

Ⓔ Players Players could not touch the ball with their hands or feet. They could only hit the solid, eight-pound rubber ball with their hips, knees, and elbows. Even though players wore heavy padding, they often got hurt.

CALIFORNIA STANDARDS
7.7.2 Study the roles of people in each society, including class structures, family life, warfare, religious beliefs and practices, and slavery

DIFFERENTIATING INSTRUCTION

Inclusion

Play the Mayan Ball Game
Have students work in teams to create a simulation of the ball game. Review the rules and purpose of the game with each team. Then have students practice passing around a ball without using their hands or feet.

English Learners

Study the Illustration
Tell students that studying the details of the illustration will help them gain a deeper understanding of the text. Have students describe some of the details in the illustration. Discuss how the information in the captions is illustrated in the scene. Say, "Imagine that you may be selected to play the Mayan ball game. What would you like about being part of the team? What would you not like about being on the team?" Have students share out loud with classmates.

Research Links

Visit **ClassZone.com** for age-appropriate Web sites related to the Mayan ball games.

More About . . .

The Mayan Ball Game
The ball used in the Mayan game was usually made of rubber, though other materials were sometimes used. The size and weight of the ball made it a dangerous weapon in and of itself, requiring players to use a variety of pads. The need for padding increased when, in an effort to draw blood, game officials replaced the ball with a stone. Indeed, the game could be quite dangerous and often led to injury. It was also extremely difficult. Scoring a goal was very challenging and often took a very long time.

Activities

1. **TALK ABOUT IT** What does this game tell you about Mayan culture?

2. **WRITE ABOUT IT** Imagine the action as the teams move down the court and put the ball in play. Then write descriptive copy of the action that a television sports announcer might read. (Writing 2.2)

Ancient America • **313**

ACTIVITIES ANSWERS

1. TALK ABOUT IT Possible answer: People believed strongly in and respected the power of their gods; people were strong, willing to make sacrifices for their city.

2. WRITE ABOUT IT

2. Writing Rubric

	Vividness of Description	Errors in Mechanics
4	contains many action verbs and vivid adjectives	few or none
3	contains some action verbs and vivid adjectives	some
2	contains few action verbs and vivid adjectives	many
1	contains no action verbs or vivid adjectives	major

Terms & Names

1. In a *tropical* environment, ancient farmers commonly practiced *slash-and-burn agriculture.*

2. The Nazca made huge pictures on the plains of southeastern Peru. Some people believe these *Nazca Lines* show the routes of *aquifers.*

3. The *Olmec* civilization is considered Meso-America's *mother culture.*

4. The Maya recorded historical events with *glyphs* written in a kind of book called a *codex.*

Main Ideas

The Geography of the Americas
(pages 288–293)

5. People learned how to adapt to and develop agriculture in the challenging environments.

6. The Andes are characterized by high peaks and a dry climate. Much of Meso-America is made up of low-lying regions with a tropical climate.

Ancient Andean Civilizations
(pages 294–299)

7. Artists of both cultures used religious images in their artwork.

8. by studying ruins, tombs, and artwork

The Olmec of Meso-America
(pages 300–305)

9. Archaeologists realized that a city-based culture had developed in Meso-America by 1200 B.C.

10. Olmec art styles, ideas for cities and planned ceremonial centers, the ritual ball game, possibly the use of hieroglyphs

The Mayan Civilization
(pages 306–313)

11. The Mayan civilization developed in an area of lowlands, dry forests, dense jungles, highlands, and mountains that stretched from what is now southern Mexico into northern Central America.

12. pottery, sculpture, jade work, steles, pyramids

▶ **VISUAL SUMMARY**

```
Ancient America
```

Geography (7.1)
- The Andes provided a harsh environment for the Chavín, Nazca, and Moche civilizations.
- The Olmec and Maya lived in fertile land in Meso-America.

Culture (7.7.4)
- Trade helped spread Olmec culture throughout Meso-America.
- Ancient Americans left behind beautiful carvings, pottery, and textiles.
- The Maya built pyramids and temples in their great city-states.

Science and Technology (7.7.5)
- The Moche created irrigation systems.
- The Maya developed a calendar and the concept of zero.

▶ **TERMS & NAMES**

Explain why the words in each set below are linked with each other.

1. **tropical** and **slash-and-burn agriculture**
2. **Nazca** and **aquifer**
3. **Olmec** and **mother culture**
4. **glyph** and **codex**

▶ **MAIN IDEAS**

The Geography of the Americas (pages 288–293)

5. How did civilizations in the Americas arise in difficult environments? (7.7.1)
6. Name some geographical differences between the Andes and Meso-America. (7.7)

Ancient Andean Civilizations (pages 294–299)

7. How were art and religion linked in the Chavín and Nazca cultures? (7.7)
8. How have archaeologists learned about the Chavín, Nazca, and Moche? (HI 5)

The Olmec of Meso-America (pages 300–305)

9. What was the importance of discovering ruins in San Lorenzo and La Venta? (HI 5)
10. What aspects of the Olmec civilization influenced other cultures? (HI 2)

The Mayan Civilization (pages 306–313)

11. Describe the geography of the area where Mayan civilization rose. (7.7.3)
12. What artistic and architectural traditions did the Maya develop? (7.7.4)

▶ **CRITICAL THINKING**

BIG IDEAS: Science and Technology

13. **MAKING INFERENCES** What innovations of the early Andean cultures probably helped later civilizations survive? (7.7)
14. **UNDERSTANDING CAUSE AND EFFECT** How did religious practices in ancient America lead to developments in science? (7.7.2)
15. **EVALUATING INFORMATION** How did the development of the concept of zero help the Maya calculate numbers? (7.7.5)

ALTERNATIVE ASSESSMENT RUBRICS

1. Writing Rubric

	Details in Letter	Style of Writing
4	includes many accurate details	lively, engaging
3	includes some accurate details	somewhat lively and engaging
2	includes few accurate details	not very lively or engaging
1	includes no accurate details	stiff, uninteresting

2. Mathematics Rubric

	Demonstration of Number System	Accuracy of Calculations
4	demonstrates full understanding	no errors
3	demonstrates some understanding	few errors
2	demonstrates little understanding	multiple errors
1	demonstrates no understanding	no calculations

ALTERNATIVE ASSESSMENT

1. **WRITING ACTIVITY** Imagine that you have just flown over and discovered the Nazca Lines. Write a letter to a friend describing them and telling what you think they were used for. (CST 3)

2. **INTERDISCIPLINARY ACTIVITY—MATHEMATICS** Learn about the symbols the Maya used in their number system. Then use the symbols to write a few simple addition problems. (7.7.5)

3. **STARTING WITH A STORY**

   Review the news feature you wrote about the ceremony in Palenque. Use the feature to write a brief scene about what happened after the ceremony. Create dialogue and interesting characters to make the scene come alive. (Writing 2.1)

Technology Activity

4. **WRITING A VIDEO SCRIPT**
   Use the Internet or the library to find out about the hardships archaeologists and explorers suffered to uncover information about the Maya. Then work with a group of classmates to write a video script for a documentary about the explorers. (7.7.1)
   • Include interviews with the archaeologists and explorers.
   • Write a dramatic scene describing their struggles.
   • Use maps and pictures to help illustrate the geography of Meso-America.

Research Links
ClassZone.com

Interpreting Visuals Use this Mayan clay figure of a warrior to answer these questions. (7.7.2)

1. **What class in Mayan society did warriors belong to?**
   A. nobles
   B. merchants
   C. farmers
   D. slaves

2. **Which of the following indicates this warrior's class?**
   A. his modest appearance
   B. his frightened expression
   C. his humble pose
   D. his clothing and jewelry

Test Practice
ClassZone.com

Additional Test Practice, pp. S1–S33

Critical Thinking

Big Ideas: Science and Technology

13. Possible answers: farming and irrigation techniques

14. Possible answer: A desire to keep track of religious holidays led astronomers and mathematicians to develop calendars.

15. Possible answer: The use of zero makes numbers easier to calculate.

Standards-Based Assessment

1. The correct answer is A. Warriors were grouped with nobles in the Mayan social structure. Answers B, C, and D are incorrect because they are lower classes than nobles and warriors.

2. The correct answer is D. The figure's clothing identifies him as a warrior. Answers A, B, and C are incorrect because they do not accurately describe the characteristics of the figure.

 Research Links

Visit **ClassZone.com** for Web sites that can be resources for the multimedia presentation.

 Test Practice

Visit **ClassZone.com** to access strategies and tutorials for taking standardized tests.

 Formal Assessment
   • Chapter Tests, Forms A, B, and C, pp. 154–164

 Test Generator
   • Chapter Tests, Forms A, B, and C, (English and Spanish)

ALTERNATIVE ASSESSMENT RUBRICS

3. Starting with a Story Rubric

	Events in Scene	Style of Writing
4	realistic and compelling continuation of the story	includes realistic dialogue and interesting characters
3	realistic continuation of the story	includes some dialogue and interesting characters
2	unrealistic continuation of the story	includes weak dialogue and characters
1	unrelated to the story	missing dialogue and/or characters

4. Technology Rubric

	Content of Script	Quality of Presentation
4	accurate, thorough, compelling; includes all required elements	well organized, informative
3	accurate, includes all required elements	organized, good information
2	partially accurate, omits one or two required elements	some organization, some facts
1	inaccurate, omits several or all required elements	little organization, few details

❶ Focus & Motivate

Preview Explain to students that they are going to be comparing and contrasting one aspect of two cultures in this assignment. Discuss how making comparisons and contrasts helps them to make decisions. Ask students for examples of comparing and contrasting from their own lives. *(For example, they compare and contrast food items in the lunch line before they make their choice.)*

❷ Teach

Talk About It

- What topics appear to offer a good basis for comparison between ancient China or India and the Americas? *(Possible answers: geography, religion and belief systems, art)*

- Why is it important to narrow the focus of a comparison-and-contrast essay? *(A narrow focus allows more in-depth analysis of the differences and similarities.)*

- What is the function of the conclusion in a comparison-and-contrast composition? *(The conclusion summarizes the differences and similarities and explains why they are significant.)*

- **Critical Thinking: Forming and Supporting Opinions** Would it be surprising to find many similarities between two cultures thousands of miles apart? Explain. *(Possible answers: It would be surprising because the two cultures were too far apart to have shared ideas, they had different climates or physical features with which to contend, and had different influences on their development. It would not be surprising because humans have the same basic needs no matter where or when they live.)*

Writing About History

🔍 **Writing Model**
ClassZone.com

CALIFORNIA STANDARDS
Writing 2.3 Write expository compositions: comparison and contrast.

Expository Writing: Comparison and Contrast
Two Ancient Civilizations

Purpose: To write a composition comparing and contrasting life in ancient India or China to life in the Americas

Audience: Your classmates

You just read about three ancient civilizations that developed over 3,000 years. How can you get a good understanding of the main ideas from such a long span of history? One way is to organize the information by similarities and differences. When you write an essay about similarities and differences, you are writing a type of expository composition called **comparison and contrast**.

▲ Hindu temple and pyramid in Tikal

Organization & Focus

Your assignment is to write a 500- to 700-word expository essay that compares and contrasts ancient Asian and American civilizations. Focus on just one aspect of life so that you can cover it thoroughly.

Choosing a Topic Study the Visual Summaries on pages 246, 282, and 314, and look for topics to compare and contrast. For example, the visual summaries of the three chapters group information by the themes of this book: Geography, Culture, Economics, Government, Belief Systems, and Science & Technology. By using one of the themes, you can compare and contrast an aspect of life in two cultures.

Identifying Purpose and Audience Your communication purpose in this assignment is to compare and contrast, and your audience is your classmates. However, there is another useful purpose for writing this essay. It will help you to review and draw meaning from the unit.

Finding Details Reread all the information in this unit about your topic. Take notes about important details. After you finish your notes, look for details that are similar and those that are different across the two cultures.

Outlining and Drafting You might organize and present your ideas in one of three possible ways, as the chart above right shows.

DIFFERENTIATING INSTRUCTION

Struggling Readers

Use Outlines
After students have taken notes, discuss the methods they can use to organize their ideas. Then have students work on their outlines in class. Circulate to answer questions. Collect the outlines and revise them to help students complete their papers more easily.

Ways to Organize Comparison and Contrast Details		
Point by Point	**Whole by Whole**	**Similarities & Differences**
Presents one aspect at a time, showing both comparisons (similarities) and contrasts (differences)	Presents each subject as a whole, pointing out comparisons and contrasts during the presentation of the second subject	Presents the similarities together and the differences together
Example:	**Example:**	**Example:**
1) Goods traded in China; goods traded in the Americas (how they were alike and different)	1) Trade in China (the goods traded and the effect of trade on the rest of the culture)	1) Trade in China and the Americas were alike in these ways.
2) Effect of trade on Chinese culture; effect of trade on ancient American cultures (how they were alike and different)	2) Trade in ancient America (the goods traded and the effect of trade on the rest of the culture, with references back to the first section using phrases such as "Unlike Chinese trade" or "As in China")	2) Trade in China and the Americas were different in these ways.

Decide which order works best for your topic and create an outline for your essay. Follow your outline as you draft your essay. Be sure to use transitions that highlight the comparisons, such as *like, also, as well,* and the contrasts, such as *in contrast, on the other hand, unlike.*

Research & Technology

As you draft your essay, you may need additional information. One good source would be an encyclopedia, either online or in print. Articles in the same encyclopedia often cover the same general topics for each civilization. That will help you to compare and contrast.

Technology Tip Make the settings in your word processor for margins, tabs, and spacing match the form your school requires. These settings are usually found in the Format menu.

Evaluation & Revision

When you have finished your first draft, put it aside for a day. Then read it as if you had never read it before, to see what might still need work. In particular, check the organization of ideas within and between paragraphs. Make revisions until you are satisfied.

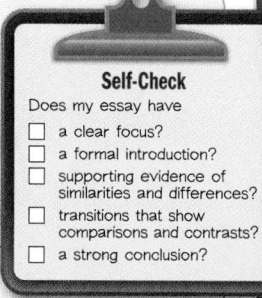
Self-Check
Does my essay have
☐ a clear focus?
☐ a formal introduction?
☐ supporting evidence of similarities and differences?
☐ transitions that show comparisons and contrasts?
☐ a strong conclusion?

Publish & Present

Make a neat final copy of your essay that conforms to your school's guidelines. Share it with your classmates and take turns reading and commenting on each other's work.

317

More About . . .

Taking Notes
To take notes from the textbook or another source, students might use a combination of methods, including quoting, paraphrasing, and summarizing.

- **Direct quotations** should be copied infrequently and only when the original language is so powerful that meaning will be lost if it is paraphrased or summarized. The name of the person being quoted or the source information should be kept with the quotation on the note card.

- **Paraphrases** restate ideas in a new way. Students should read the original text and think about the information. They should then explain each idea in their own words.

- **Summaries** capture what is most important from a passage. A summary identifies the main ideas of the text in the summarizer's own words.

ANSWERS

Comparison-and-Contrast Composition Rubric

	Structure of Composition	Content of Composition	Errors in Mechanics
4	effectively organized; excellent use of transitions	detailed, precise, and interesting	few or none
3	consistent organization; good use of transitions	many good details	some
2	fairly logical organization; a few transitions	some good details	many
1	muddled organization; no transitions	few details	many major

Begin the Unit

Quick Look

Chapter 10 describes the origins and history of the Jews, including their interaction with the Romans in Judea.

Chapter 11 explores the geography, beliefs and customs, and government of ancient Greece, as well as the Persian Wars.

Chapter 12 discusses the history and legacy of classical Greek ideas, the Peloponnesian War, and the importance of Alexander the Great.

Interact with History ▶

Purpose

To help students comprehend the importance of religious life by picturing themselves in a historical situation—visiting the Temple in Jerusalem about 950 B.C.

Visual Learning

Ask a student volunteer to read the text aloud while the class examines the illustration. Have students answer the three illustration questions before discussing the main one.

Interact ANSWERS

- How might religion influence the laws of a society? *(Possible answers: Laws might be based on religious beliefs; religious rules and principles might provide the foundation for a society's laws.)*

- What seems to be the mood of your fellow worshipers? *(Possible answers: happy; cheerful; festive)*

- What problems might you face in traveling to Jerusalem? *(Possible answers: sand; heat; robbers; the cost of three journeys)*

- What gifts might you bring to the temple? *(Possible answers: animals; crops; money)*

UNIT 5

The Roots of Western Ideas

Interact with History ▶

Visiting the Temple of Solomon, about 950 B.C.
You are a visitor from a small village in the countryside to the Temple built by King Solomon in the capital city of Jerusalem. The Temple is the center of religious life. Each year, there are a number of festivals that you attend in Jerusalem.

How might religion influence the laws of a society?

WebQuest ClassZone.com

The music of harps and cymbals fills the air as worshipers enter the Temple courtyards.

What seems to be the mood of your fellow worshipers?

Three times a year you are required to travel to Jerusalem to worship at the great Temple.

What problems might you face in traveling to Jerusalem?

318

TECHNOLOGY

WebQuest: Solomon's Temple

Visit **ClassZone.com** to lead your students through a WebQuest on preparing for a pilgrimage to the Temple. Students will form small groups to research and write dialogues and to draw pictures showing what daily-life activities herders and farmers engaged in, how they would have prepared for the trip to Jerusalem, and how they might have felt in anticipation of a visit to King Solomon's Temple. At the end of the project, students should be able to answer why people went to Jerusalem, why Solomon was so influential, and what daily life was like for the people in this place and time.

When to Use This project can be an introductory or end-of-chapter activity.

Class Time Two to three class periods

Materials Needed At least one computer with access to the World Wide Web and a printer.

Customizing for Your Classroom

- If computer time is limited, have small groups rotate through stations, finding information in encyclopedias, library books, or their textbook as well as the Web sites.

- Encourage Spanish speakers to use the textbook's Spanish glossary.

- Pair students who may have difficulty reading with stronger readers to ensure they understand the quest.

The smoke of gifts burned on a sacrificial fire floats through the air.

What gifts might you bring to the Temple?

319

Correcting Misconceptions

Today, the phrase "animal sacrifice" brings to mind primitive and bloody images. This is due to movie images and generalizations about pagan worship. Ask students what they think of when they hear "animal sacrifice." Explain that the customs of the time led many to offer animals as gifts and that this was a great sacrifice because the animals represented their livelihood.

More About . . .

Solomon's Temple
The Temple is the only ancient Hebrew building known. The Bible describes it as having entrance pylons, courts, and a *naos* (the chamber that housed the Ark of the Covenant). The Temple was destroyed several times. Accounts say that it was made of stone, timber, and metal. Nothing remains of this original structure.

WHY STUDY THE ROOTS OF WESTERN IDEAS?

- These civilizations developed many of the ideas upon which modern civilizations are based.

- Jewish monotheism influenced other world religions, particularly Christianity and Islam.

- Jewish laws, rituals, and writings from this period still influence how Jews practice their religion.

- The Greek alphabet influenced the development of all Western alphabets, including the English alphabet.

- Greece was the birthplace of democracy, setting a model for future generations.

- The blending of cultures under Alexander the Great is an example of how many different cultures can coexist under a single government.

- Greek art, philosophy, literature, and science continue to influence today's world.

CHAPTER 10 PLANNING GUIDE: The Hebrew Kingdoms

Chapter Overview

The Jews introduced new beliefs that influenced Western civilization, and these same beliefs helped them through times of conflict.

Copymasters

 In-Depth Resources: Unit 5
- Family Newsletter (English and Spanish), pp. 1–2
- Visual Summary, p. 6
- Vocabulary Study Guide, p. 8

 Character Education

 Reading Study Guide, p. 93

 Bringing Social Studies Alive, Chapter 10

 Document-Based Questions: Strategy and Practice

 Reading Toolkit, L33–L35

 Modified Lesson Plans for English Learners, pp. 69–74

Assessment

 Chapter Review, pp. 348–349

 Formal Assessment
- Chapter Tests, Forms A, B, and C, pp. 176–187

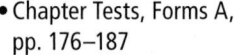 **Test Generator**

 Integrated Assessment Book

 Online Test Practice

LESSON 1
The Origins of the Hebrews
pp. 324–333

OBJECTIVE Trace the development of the Hebrew Kingdom.

 In-Depth Resources: Unit 5
- Reading Skill: Understanding Cause and Effect, p. 3
- Vocabulary Cards, p. 9
- Geography Practice: The Twelve Tribes of Israel, p. 11
- Literature: The Shema, p. 14
- Reteaching Activity, p. 15

 Interdisciplinary Projects
- Science, p. 56; Language Arts, p. 57

 Reading Study Guide, p. 87

 Lesson Review, p. 329

 Formal Assessment
- Lesson Quiz, p. 173

 California Daily Standards Practice Transparencies, TT33

LESSON 2
Kingdoms and Captivity
pp. 334–341

OBJECTIVE Examine the conflicts the Israelites faced as they built a nation.

 In-Depth Resources: Unit 5
- Reading Skill: Explaining Chronological Order and Sequence, p. 4
- Vocabulary Cards, p. 9
- Primary Source: David and Solomon, p. 13
- Reteaching Activity, p. 16

 History Makers
- Moses, p. 19

 Interdisciplinary Projects
- Math, p. 55; Health, p. 58

 Reading Study Guide, p. 89

 Lesson Review, p. 339

 Formal Assessment
- Lesson Quiz, p. 174

 California Daily Standards Practice Transparencies, TT34

LESSON 3
Rome and Judea
pp. 342–347

OBJECTIVE Analyze why the Jews held onto their beliefs even as they left their homeland.

 In-Depth Resources: Unit 5
- Reading Skill: Comparing and Contrasting, p. 5
- Vocabulary Cards, p. 9
- Skillbuilder Practice: Distinguish Fact from Opinion, p. 7
- Reteaching Activity, p. 17

 Reading Study Guide, p. 91

 Lesson Review, p. 346

 Formal Assessment
- Lesson Quiz, p. 175

 California Daily Standards Practice Transparencies, TT35

Integrated Technology

 eEdition Plus Online

EasyPlanner Plus Online

eTest Plus Online

 Audio CDs
- Reading Study Guide
- Reading Study Guide in Spanish
- The World's Music

 CD-ROMs
- Power Presentations
- eEdition
- EasyPlanner
- Test Generator

 **eEdition CD-ROM**

 **Humanities Transparencies**
- HT19 Abraham Giving Thanks

Critical Thinking Transparencies
- CT42 Understanding Cause and Effect

ClassZone.com

 **eEdition CD-ROM**

Map Transparencies
- MT19 Kingdom of David and Solomon, c. 965

Humanities Transparencies
- HT20 David Dancing Before the Ark

Critical Thinking Transparencies
- CT43 Explaining Chronological Order and Sequence

ClassZone.com

eEdition CD-ROM

Map Transparencies
- MT20 Roman Judea, A.D. 70

Critical Thinking Transparencies
- CT44 Comparing and Contrasting
- CT45 Chapter 10 Visual Summary

ClassZone.com

Overview of California Resources

	Lesson 1	Lesson 2	Lesson 3
California Reading Toolkit	L33	L34	L35
California Modified Lesson Plans for English Learners	p. 69	p. 71	p. 73
California Daily Standards Practice Transparencies	TT33	TT34	TT35
California Standards Enrichment Workbook	pp. 39–46	pp. 41–46	pp. 41–46, 103–104
California Standards Planner and Lesson Plans	L65	L67	L69
California Online Test Practice	ClassZone.com	ClassZone.com	ClassZone.com
California Test Generator CD-ROM			
California EasyPlanner CD-ROM			
California eEdition CD-ROM			

Chart Key

 PE Pupil Edition

Copymaster

 CD-ROM

 Audio

Video

 Internet

Overhead Transparency

PREVIEWING RESOURCES FOR DIFFERENTIATED INSTRUCTION

English Learners

In-Depth Resources in Spanish
- Reading Skill and Strategy
- Skillbuilder Practice **B**
- Geography Practice
- Vocabulary Study Guide

In-Depth Resources: Unit 5
- Family Newsletter (English and Spanish) **C**

Reading Study Guide (Spanish) **A**

Reading Study Guide Audio CD
(Spanish)

Test Generator
Chapter Test (Spanish)

Plus

Modified Lesson Plans for English Learners

Multi-Language Glossary of Social Studies Terms

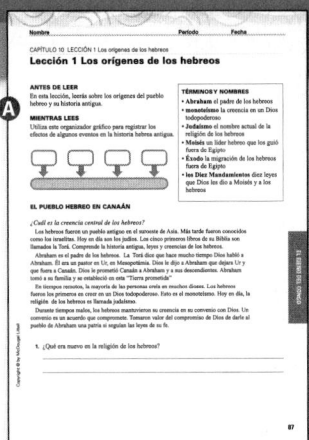

Struggling Readers

In-Depth Resources: Unit 5
- Vocabulary Study Guide **B**
- Skillbuilder Practice **C**
- Geography Practice
- Reteaching Activities **A**
- Family Newsletter

Reading Study Guide

Reading Study Guide Audio CD

Reading Toolkit

Formal Assessment
Chapter Test, Form A

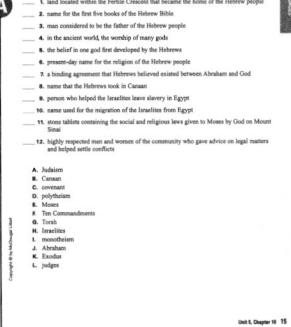
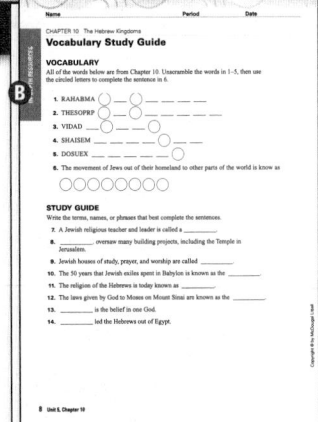

Inclusion

EasyPlanner CD-ROM
- Reading Skill and Strategy **C**
- Vocabulary Study Guide **A**
- Geography Practice
- Reteaching Activities **B**

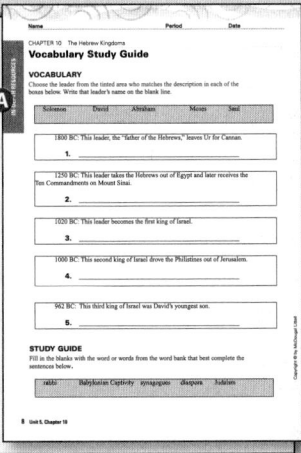
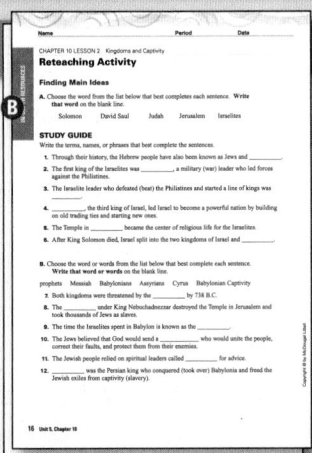

Gifted and Talented Students

In-Depth Resources: Unit 5
- Primary Source
- Literature **A**

History Makers **B**

Interdisciplinary Projects **C**

Formal Assessment
Chapter Test, Form C

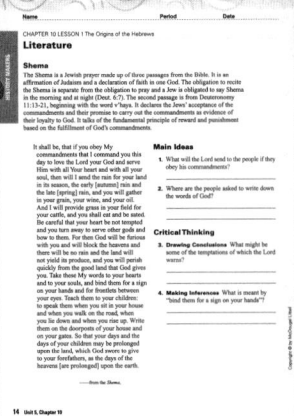

Integrated Technology

eEdition CD-ROM

- Interactive Visuals
- Interactive Maps
- Starting with a Story

ClassZone.com

- WebQuests
- Research Links
- Internet Activities
- Homework Helper
- Chapter Quiz
- Current Events
- Test Practice

Power Presentations CD-ROM

- Lecture Notes
- Media Gallery
- Chapter Review Game

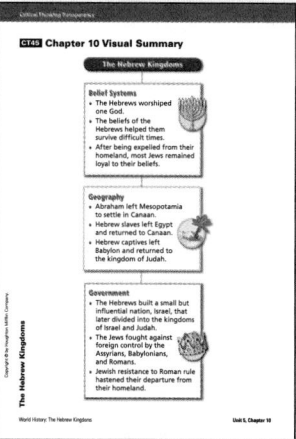

Critical Thinking Transparencies

- CT42 Understanding Cause and Effect
- CT43 Explaining Chronological Order and Sequence
- CT44 Comparing and Contrasting
- CT45 Chapter 10 Visual Summary

California Daily Standards Practice Transparencies, TT33–TT35

Map Transparencies

- MT19 Kingdom of David and Solomon, c. 965
- MT20 Roman Judea, A.D. 70

Humanities Transparencies

- HT19 Abraham Giving Thanks
- HT20 David Dancing Before the Ark

Test Generator CD-ROM

EasyPlanner CD-ROM

Activities in the Teacher's Edition for English Learners

- Create a Word Chart, p. 327
- Explore Descriptive Language, p. 331
- Profile Strong Leaders, p. 337
- Use Signal Words, p. 340
- Create a Mural, p. 344

Activities in the Teacher's Edition for Struggling Readers

- Read Aloud, p. 327
- Write a Headline, p. 332
- Write a Summary Paragraph, p. 336
- Illustrate Text, p. 345

Activities in the Teacher's Edition for Inclusion Students

- Self-Question, p. 328
- Create an Infographic, p. 332
- Preview Text, p. 337
- Read Aloud, p. 340
- Use an Interactive Map, p. 344

Activities in the Teacher's Edition for Gifted and Talented Students

- Research Topics of Interest, p. 328
- Create a Three-Dimensional Map, p. 331
- Create a Poster of Hebrew Kings, p. 336
- Create an FAQ, p. 345

Begin the Chapter

Objective

Describe the development of the Hebrew kingdoms and the difficulties faced by the Jews in maintaining their unity.

Quick Look

Lesson 1 describes the origins of the Hebrews, their beliefs, their time in Egypt, and their return to the Promised Land.

Lesson 2 explains how the Israelites built a nation in difficult times and what internal conflicts they faced.

Lesson 3 explores the Roman occupation of Judea and the way the Jewish people managed to maintain their beliefs.

Before You Read: Predicting

Predicting helps students prepare for what they will be reading and helps them identify critical information. Have students follow these steps:

- Read the chapter and lesson titles.
- Write three questions you think will be answered in the chapter. (Possible questions: What were the origins of the Hebrew people? How did the Hebrew people become captives? What were Rome and Judea?)
- As you read the lesson, look for answers to your questions and jot down information as it comes up.
- After you have finished the lesson, make sure you have answered each question fully. Review the lesson if you need more information.
- At the end of the chapter, think about what you have learned about the Hebrew kingdoms.

Chapter 10 The Hebrew Kingdoms

Before You Read: Predicting

Scan the title of the chapter and the lesson titles. Write three questions you think might be answered in the chapter. One example is

What were the origins of the Hebrew people?

As you find the answers to your questions as you read, write them in your notebook.

Big Ideas About the Hebrew Kingdoms

Belief Systems Belief systems and religions may shape government and societies.

Although the ancient Hebrews were a small group of people, their impact on world history has been great. The Hebrews have contributed to civilizations across Europe, Asia, and the Americas. The beliefs of the Hebrew people have been important in the development of religion and law in Western civilization.

Integrated Technology

eEdition
- Interactive Maps
- Interactive Visuals
- Starting with a Story

INTERNET RESOURCES
Go to **ClassZone.com** for
- WebQuest
- Homework Helper
- Research Links
- Internet Activities
- Quizzes
- Maps
- Test Practice
- Current Events

AFRICA

Assyrian Empire, 650 B.C.
Babylonian Empire, 600 B.C.

SOUTHWEST ASIA

1800 B.C.
Abraham and his family leave Ur on their way to Canaan. (Russian icon showing Abraham and Sara) ▶

c. 1250 B.C.
Moses leads Hebrews out of Egypt.

1800 B.C.   1500 B.C.   1200 B.C.

WORLD

1200 B.C.
Olmec civilization emerges in southeast Mexico. (Olmec jade head) ▶

320

TIME LINE DISCUSSION

Use the time line to help students establish a time frame for the events that led to the establishment of the Hebrew kingdoms.

- How long a period does the time line cover? *(about 2,100 years)*
- According to the time line, which came first—Moses, leading the Hebrews out of Egypt or the destruction of Solomon's Temple? *(Moses, leading the Hebrews out of Egypt)*

- How many years after Abraham left Ur did the Romans destroy Herod's temple? *(about 1,870 years)*
- At the time Moses led the Hebrews out of Egypt, what was happening on the North American continent? *(The Olmec civilization was emerging in southeast Mexico.)*

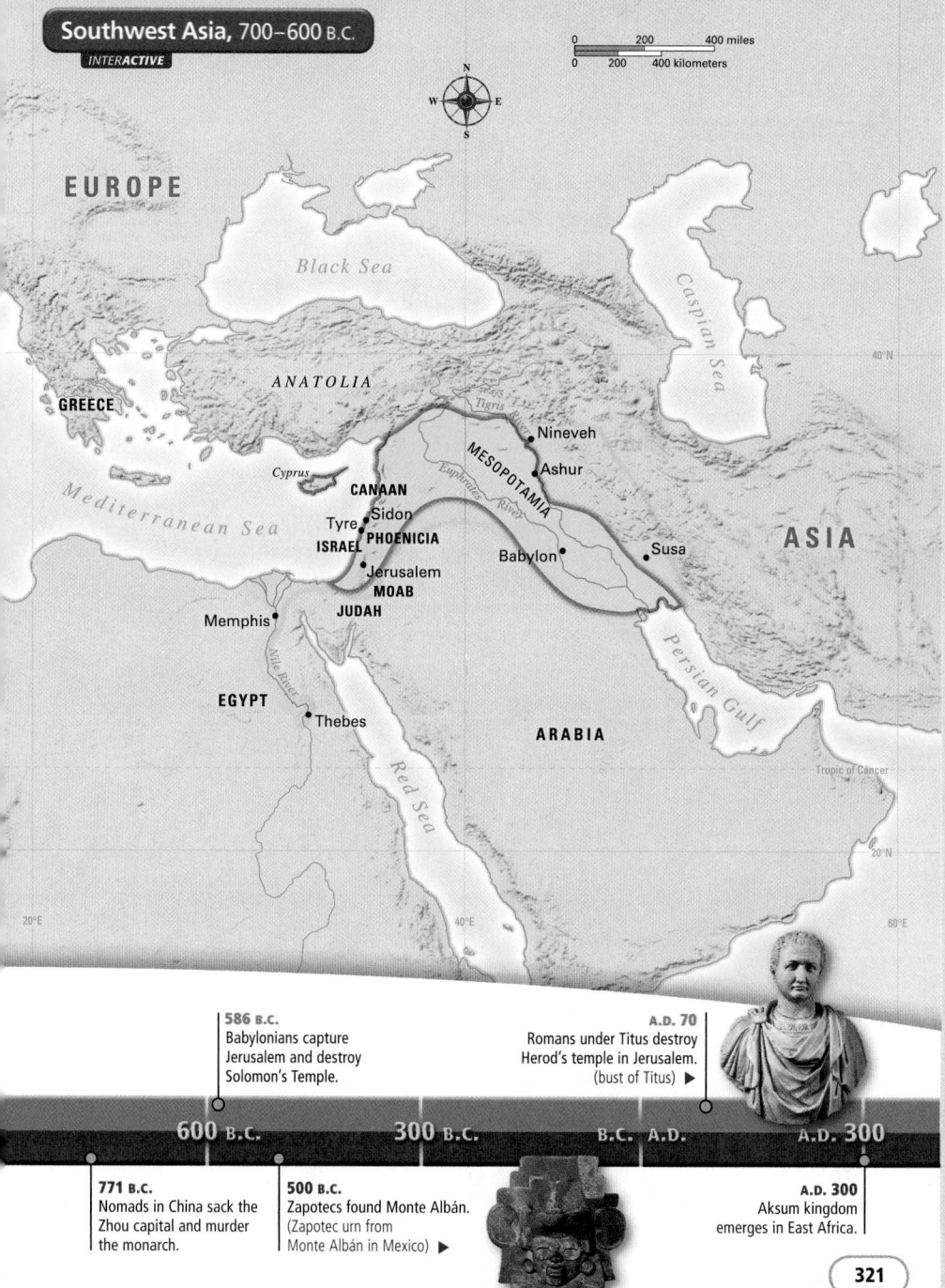

Southwest Asia, 700–600 B.C.
INTER*ACTIVE*

0 200 400 miles
0 200 400 kilometers

EUROPE

Black Sea

Caspian Sea

ANATOLIA

GREECE

40°N

Cyprus

Tigris River

MESOPOTAMIA

Nineveh

Ashur

CANAAN

Mediterranean Sea

Euphrates River

Tyre Sidon
PHOENICIA
ISRAEL

ASIA

Babylon

Susa

Jerusalem
MOAB
JUDAH

Memphis

Nile River

EGYPT

Thebes

Red Sea

Persian Gulf

ARABIA

Tropic of Cancer

20°N

20°E

40°E

60°E

586 B.C.
Babylonians capture
Jerusalem and destroy
Solomon's Temple.

A.D. 70
Romans under Titus destroy
Herod's temple in Jerusalem.
(bust of Titus) ▶

600 B.C.   **300 B.C.**   **B.C. A.D.**   **A.D. 300**

771 B.C.
Nomads in China sack the
Zhou capital and murder
the monarch.

500 B.C.
Zapotecs found Monte Albán.
(Zapotec urn from
Monte Albán in Mexico) ▶

A.D. 300
Aksum kingdom
emerges in East Africa.

321

RECOMMENDED RESOURCES

Books for the Teacher
Payne, David F. *Kingdoms of
the Lord: A History of the
Hebrew Kingdoms from Saul
to the Fall of Jerusalem.*
Grand Rapids: Eerdmans, 1981.

Windeatt, Mary Fabyan. *King
David and His Songs: A
Story of the Psalms.*
Rockford: TAN, 1994.

Videos
Masada. 427 minutes.
Universal City: MCA Home
Video, 1997. 4 videocassettes.

Internet
To access these sites, visit the
Research Links for this chapter
at **ClassZone.com**.

**Heritage: Civilization and
the Jews** This interactive
PBS Web site includes maps,
historical documents, and audio
and video clips.

Moses and the Exodus
Learn more about Moses'
leading the Jews out of Egypt,
with interactive maps, photos,
quizzes, and other features.

CHAPTER 10

Introduce the Big Ideas
Read aloud the text about the Big Ideas. Have
students think about religious ideas that have
affected law and society in the United States.
Ask, for example, What punishable crimes are
directly referred to in the Ten Commandments?
What religious ideas affect the rules and
regulations in your school?

Here are some other Big Ideas that you may
want to emphasize in this chapter.

Culture
The idea of monotheism led to the development
of a new kind of society, in conflict with
polytheistic societies.

Government
The Jews wander for long periods, seeking to
establish their own nation based upon Jewish
law.

Talk About It
Interpreting Maps
Ask students to examine the map and its key.
Ask what earlier civilization was located in the
Assyrian Empire? *(Babylon)* When did the area
change from Assyrian to Babylonian control?
(about 600 B.C.) Where was Canaan located? *(on
the eastern shore of the Mediterranean Sea)*

INTER*ACTIVE*

An interactive version of this map is available on
the eEdition and Power Presentations CD-ROMs.

Find Out More
Have students use an encyclopedia, maps in
this book, and other sources to find out what
countries and cultures exist in this part of
the world today, and have them summarize
information about current conflicts in the region.

The Hebrew Kingdoms • **321**

Objective

Explore how people learn to understand each other and adopt new beliefs.

Introducing the Story

Courageous David

The most well-known story about Ruth's great-grandson, David, describes his defeat of Goliath. According to the Bible, he showed great courage as a boy by using a sling to fight and kill Goliath, a nine-foot-tall Philistine giant. Because of his courage, David became a commander in the army of Saul.

David went on to rule Israel from about 1010 to 962 B.C. David was known as a soldier, writer, and musician and as the father of Solomon.

Vocabulary Preview

famine a severe, widespread food shortage

Reading the Story Aloud

1. **The teacher as reader:** Focus on the characters by creating a Venn diagram on the board and writing *Naomi* and *Ruth* in the two circles. Read a section of the passage and ask students what information to write in each woman's circle. To conclude, ask students to summarize what the women have in common in the overlapping part of the circles.

2. **The students as readers:** Have a student read a section of the passage aloud, and select other students to act out the passage for the class.

 **Starting with a Story**

Students can also follow along as they listen to the story on the eEdition or Power Presentations CD-ROM.

Starting with a Story

Ruth and Naomi

CALIFORNIA STANDARDS
Reading 3.3 Analyze the influence of setting on the problem and its resolution.

Background: The Hebrews settled throughout parts of what are now Israel and Lebanon. Their laws, religious customs, and beliefs were different from those of other peoples in that region. However, Hebrews and other groups sometimes learned to understand each other.

One example of this understanding is the Bible story of Ruth and Naomi. Naomi, with her husband and sons, had left Israel and moved to Moab, a land east of the Dead Sea in present-day Jordan. Naomi's sons married women from Moab, including Ruth. Ruth, who was not a Hebrew, was an ancestor of King David of Israel.

322

ADDITIONAL RESOURCES

Books for the Student

Mann, Kenny. *The Ancient Hebrews.* New York: Benchmark, 1999. Examines the history, culture, religion, daily life, and legends of the Jewish people.

Videos

Israel: Land of Strife, Land of Promise. 30 minutes. Madison: Knowledge Unlimited, 1997. Chronicles the history of Israel, from biblical times through its declaration as an independent Jewish state to its continuing challenges today. VHS.

The Exodus Revealed: Search for the Red Sea Crossing. 82 minutes. Chicago: Questar, 2001. Traces the archaeological evidence for the crossing of the Red Sea. VHS, DVD.

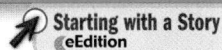
STARTING WITH A STORY

N aomi, her husband, and their sons had come to live in Moab many years ago. They fled a famine in their native land. Once settled in Moab, one of the sons married Ruth, a woman of Moab. In this way, they all became one family.

Now Ruth's husband, father-in-law, and brother-in-law have all died. Ruth's mother-in-law, Naomi, tells her that she is going back to Israel. Ruth tells Naomi that she will go with her. Naomi is touched by Ruth's loyalty but thinks she should reconsider.

Naomi urges Ruth to stay in Moab, where Ruth will find a new husband among her own people. Ruth knows that the Hebrews have a different faith. They do not make statues of gods. They worship only one God.

Ruth thinks about the love and friendship she has for Naomi. She thinks about her dead husband, Naomi's son. Ruth thinks about which group of people, both of whom she loves, she will choose to live with. Then Ruth says to Naomi, "Wherever you go, I will go. Wherever you lodge, I will lodge. Your people shall be my people and your God my God."

When Naomi returns to Israel, Ruth goes with her out of loyalty to Naomi and her family. Later, Ruth marries a Hebrew and declares that she will worship his God. One of their descendants is David, the second king of Israel. David, one of the greatest figures in the history of the Hebrews, represents the coming together of different peoples and traditions.

How might Ruth's decision affect her understanding of other people and cultures?

Reading & Writing

1. **READING: Setting** The setting of the story is the time and place of the action. The time may be past, present, or future. The place may be real or imaginary. With a partner, discuss the time and place of the story of Ruth and Naomi.

2. **WRITING: Exposition** Imagine that you are Ruth. Write a letter to your great-grandson, King David of Israel. Explain to him what your homeland in Moab was like, why you chose to leave, and how your life changed when you moved to a new land.

CALIFORNIA STANDARDS Writing 2.2
Write expository compositions.

323

Talk About It

Ask students the following questions to begin the discussion:

- What made Naomi and her husband leave Israel to go to Moab? *(There was a famine in Israel. They went in search of more food.)*
- Why does Naomi want to return to Israel? *(Her husband and two sons have died. She wants to return home.)*
- Why does Naomi think Ruth should stay in Moab? *(She should live with her own people. She will have to change her religion if she goes to Israel.)*
- Why does Ruth go with Naomi? *(She loves Naomi and is her friend. Ruth's husband is dead, but she is loyal to Naomi.)*

How might Ruth's decision affect her understanding of other people and cultures?

By choosing to leave her native land and follow her mother-in-law, Ruth has decided to embrace another culture and people; this will probably make her more tolerant and understanding of others.

Making Personal Connections

Connect the discussion to today by encouraging students to draw conclusions about how a person decides to make a big change in his or her life. *(by listing pros and cons, talking with other family members, and considering what is right and wrong)*

READING & WRITING ACTIVITIES

1. **READING** Possible answer: The story is set long ago, in the countries of Moab and Israel.
2. **WRITING** Students might read their letters aloud in class.

2. Writing Rubric

	Quality of Exposition	Content of Letter
4	inventive, complete, easy to follow	covers three topics clearly
3	good, complete	covers topics reasonably well
2	fair, somewhat complete	covers topics unclearly
1	unclear, difficult to follow	topics missing or unexplained

❶ Plan & Prepare

Objectives

- Explain the origins and significance of central beliefs of the Hebrews.
- Describe the locations of the settlements of the Hebrew people and Moses' role in Hebrew freedom.
- Summarize what happened when the Hebrews returned to Canaan.
- **Language Objective:** Use structural analysis to determine the meanings of words with prefixes.

Quick Look

Lesson 1 describes Abraham's journey, Hebrew beliefs, the Egyptian captivity, the Exodus, and the return to the Promised Land.

❷ Focus & Motivate

Preview Tell students that this lesson explores the Hebrew search for the Promised Land and the problems they encountered. Ask students what they already know about Abraham, Moses, and the Ten Commandments. *(Possible answers: Abraham was father of the Jews; Moses led the Hebrews out of Egypt; the Ten Commandments are rules for behavior)*

Introduce the Main Ideas The three main ideas relate to the Big Idea that belief systems and religions may shape governments and societies. Help students look for this Big Idea as they read the lesson.

Reading Skill: Understanding Cause and Effect Remind students that a cause is a reason why something else happens and an effect is what happens.

SAMPLE ANSWERS FOR CHART

Causes	Effects
Abraham leaves Ur.	Abraham settles with his family in Canaan.
Moses leads people out of Egypt	Israelites wander in the desert for 40 years.
Moses climbs Mount Sinai.	Moses is given the Ten Commandments.

Lesson 1

▶ **MAIN IDEAS**

❶ Belief Systems The Hebrews believed in one God and tried to follow his commandments.

❷ Geography Enslaved Hebrews returned from Egypt to Canaan to reclaim land.

❸ Government Hebrew leaders called judges attempted to rule according to their understanding of God's laws.

▶ **TAKING NOTES**

Reading Skill: Understanding Cause and Effect
A cause makes something happen. An effect is a result of a cause. Following causes and effects will help you understand the main ideas in this lesson. In Lesson 1, look for the effects of each event or cause listed in the chart. Record them on a chart like the one below.

Causes	Effects
Abraham leaves Ur.	
Moses leads people out of Egypt.	
Moses climbs Mount Sinai.	

 Skillbuilder Handbook, page R26

▲ **Torah Case** The Tik, or Torah case, shown above was made in Iraq in the early 20th century.

CALIFORNIA STANDARDS

6.3.1 Describe the origins and significance of Judaism as the first monotheistic religion based on the concept of one God who sets down moral laws for humanity.

6.3.2 Identify the sources of the ethical teachings and central beliefs of Judaism (the Hebrew Bible, the Commentaries): belief in God,

observance of law, practice of the concepts of righteousness and justice, and importance of study; and describe how the ideas of the Hebrew traditions are reflected in the moral and ethical traditions of Western civilization.

6.3.3 Explain the significance of Abraham, Moses, Naomi, Ruth,

David, and Yohanan ben Zaccai in the development of the Jewish religion.

6.3.4 Discuss the locations of the settlements and movements of Hebrew peoples, including the Exodus and their movement to and from Egypt, and outline the significance of the Exodus to the Jewish and other people.

HOW TO TEACH THE CALIFORNIA STANDARDS

Standard	Content	Student Question or Activity	Instruction
6.3.1	**Page 326** Discusses the central beliefs of Judaism	**Page 326** Students describe how Judaism differed from other religions.	Discuss the differences between monotheism and polytheism.
6.3.2	**Page 327** Explains how Ten Commandments were received	**Page 327** Students identify the types of behavior addressed in the Ten Commandments.	Ask students how modern civilization reflects ideas in the Ten Commandments.
6.3.3	**Page 327** Describes the role of Moses	**Page 329** Students describe the part Moses played in the Exodus from Egypt.	Have students make an outline that details the importance of Moses.
6.3.4	**Page 328** Describes the return of the Israelites to Canaan	**Page 329** Students identify some effects of the return of the Israelites to Canaan.	Have students make a chart of the Israelite journeys discussed in this lesson.

The Origins of the Hebrews

TERMS & NAMES

Abraham

monotheism

Judaism

Moses

Exodus

Ten Commandments

Build on What You Know You have probably noticed that plants grow better in green, well-watered places. And you have learned how early cities developed in the Fertile Crescent. Within this region is an area that, partly because of its fertility, became the home of the Hebrews.

The Hebrew People in Canaan

❶ ESSENTIAL QUESTION What is the central belief of the Hebrews?   belief in one God

The first five books of the Hebrew Bible are called the Torah (TAWR•uh). The Hebrews believed that these holy books, or scriptures, were given to them by God. The Torah gives the early history, laws, and beliefs of the Hebrews. It consists of Genesis, Exodus, Leviticus, Numbers, and Deuteronomy. Later, there were Commentaries, or interpretations, written about the Torah.

From Ur to Canaan A shepherd named **Abraham** was the father of the Hebrews. Abraham lived in Ur, a city in Mesopotamia, about 1800 B.C. According to the Torah, God told Abraham to leave Ur and go to Canaan (KAY•nuhn). Abraham believed that if he went to Canaan, the land would belong to his descendants because it was promised to them by God. Because of this, the Hebrews thought of Canaan as the Promised Land. With his family, Abraham settled in Canaan. (See map below.)

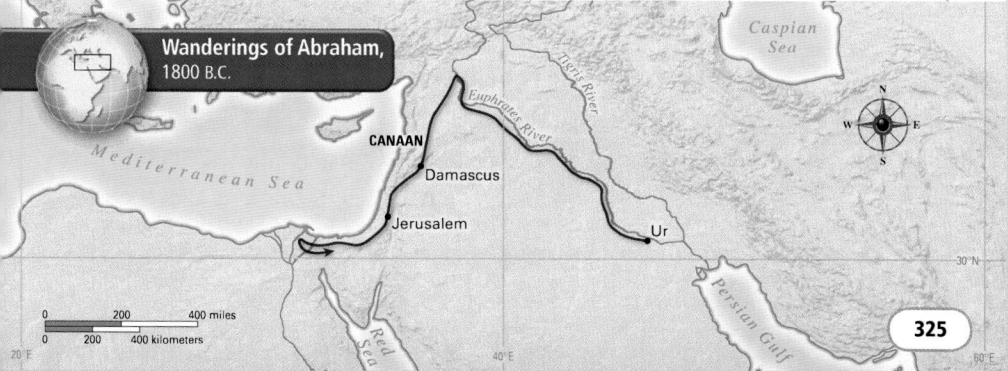

Wanderings of Abraham, 1800 B.C.

Caspian Sea

CANAAN
Damascus
Jerusalem
Ur

Mediterranean Sea

Euphrates River

Tigris River

Red Sea

Persian Gulf

0   200   400 miles
0   200   400 kilometers

325

Terms & Names

Abraham the father of the Hebrews

monotheism a belief in one God

Judaism the Hebrew religion

Moses a leader who helped the Israelites escape from Egypt and received the Ten Commandments

Exodus the migration of the Israelites from Egypt

Ten Commandments stone tablets containing religious rules for the Israelites

❸ Teach

The Hebrew People in Canaan

◤ **6.3.1, 6.3.2, 6.3.4**

Talk About It

- **Critical Thinking: Cause and Effect:** How did Abraham create the foundation of Judaism? *(Abraham's belief that God had spoken to him established the idea of the chosen people.)*

California Resources

California Reading Toolkit, L33
California Modified Lesson Plans for English Learners, p. 69
California Daily Standards Practice Transparencies, TT33
California Standards Enrichment Workbook, pp. 39–46
California Online Test Practice
California Test Generator CD-ROM
California Standards Planner and Lesson Plans, L65
California EasyPlanner CD-ROM
California eEdition CD-ROM

LESSON 1 PROGRAM RESOURCES

ON LEVEL

In-Depth Resources: Unit 5
- Family Newsletter (English and Spanish), pp. 1–2
- Reading Skill: Understanding Cause and Effect, p. 3
- Vocabulary Study Guide, p. 8
- Vocabulary Cards, p. 9
- Geography Practice: The Twelve Tribes of Israel, p. 11

Formal Assessment
- Lesson Quiz, p. 173

ENGLISH LEARNERS

In-Depth Resources in Spanish
- Reading Skill: Understanding Cause and Effect, p. 83

- Geography Practice, p. 89

Modified Lesson Plans for English Learners, p. 69

Reading Study Guide (Spanish), p. 87

Reading Study Guide Audio CD (Spanish)

STRUGGLING READERS

In-Depth Resources: Unit 5
- Reading Skill: Understanding Cause and Effect, p. 3
- Vocabulary Study Guide, p. 8
- Vocabulary Cards, p. 9
- Reteaching Activity, p. 15

Reading Toolkit, L33

Reading Study Guide, p. 87

Reading Study Guide Audio CD

GIFTED AND TALENTED STUDENTS

In-Depth Resources: Unit 5
- Literature: The Shema, p. 14

Interdisciplinary Projects
- Science, p. 56
- Language Arts, p. 57

INCLUSION

EasyPlanner CD-ROM
- Reading Skill: Understanding Cause and Effect
- Vocabulary Study Guide
- Reteaching Activity

TECHNOLOGY

eEdition CD-ROM
- Starting with a Story

Power Presentations CD-ROM

Humanities Transparencies
- HT19 Abraham Giving Thanks

Critical Thinking Transparencies
- CT42 Understanding Cause and Effect

Test Generator CD-ROM

ClassZone.com

In-Depth Resources: Unit 5
- Reading Skill: Understanding Cause and Effect, p. 3
- Geography Practice: The Twelve Tribes of Israel, p. 11
- Literature: The Shema, p. 14

Teach

Canaan to Egypt and Back

6.3.2, 6.3.3, 6.3.4

Talk About It

- How did the Hebrews become known as Israelites? *(They took the name from Abraham's grandson Jacob, who had been given the name Israel. Jacob's sons and grandsons founded the 12 tribes of the Israelites.)*

- What events caused Moses to lead the Israelites out of Egypt? What happened as a result? *(Egypt's pharaoh enslaved the Israelites and forced them to work. They wandered as nomads in the Sinai desert for 40 years.)*

- According to the Bible, where did Moses receive the Ten Commandments? *(at the top of Mount Sinai)*

- **Critical Thinking: Understanding Cause and Effect** How did the Israelites' receiving the Ten Commandments affect the Hebrew religion? *(Possible answer: The Ten Commandments became the basis of their laws and strengthened their belief that God had a covenant with them.)*

Humanities Transparencies
- HT19 Abraham Giving Thanks

▲ **Abraham and Family** This painting shows Abraham and his family during their journey to Canaan.

Judaism and Monotheism Throughout the ancient world, people were polytheists (*poly* means "many"). This means that they worshiped many gods. The Hebrews believed that God spoke to Abraham and gave him important teachings. Abraham taught the belief in one all-powerful God who established moral laws for humanity. This belief is called **monotheism** (*mono* means "one"). **Judaism** today is descended from the religion of the ancient Hebrews. The name comes from the tribe of Judah, one of the 12 tribes descended from Abraham.

According to the Torah, during troubled times the Hebrews held to their belief that they were God's chosen people. They believed that a covenant (KUHV•uh•nuhnt), or a binding agreement, existed between God and Abraham and his descendants. They took courage from God's pledge to give a homeland to Abraham's descendants if they followed the laws of their faith and practiced righteousness and justice.

REVIEW How was Judaism different from other religions?
Most people worshiped many gods; the Hebrews worshiped one God.

Canaan to Egypt and Back

 ESSENTIAL QUESTION Why did the Hebrews go to Egypt? to flee famine in Canaan

Over time, the Hebrews in Canaan took a new name—the Israelites. Their name came from Abraham's grandson Jacob. According to the Torah, he was given the name *Israel*. Jacob had 12 sons. Ten of these sons and two grandsons were the fathers of the 12 tribes.

INTERDISCIPLINARY ACTIVITIES

Language Arts

Analyze a Commandment
To help students understand the historical influence of the Ten Commandments, have them research federal and state laws that are similar to the commandment against stealing.

Language Arts

Profile Abraham
Have students use library resources and the Internet to research and report on the life of Abraham. Tell students to include information about other religions (such as Islam) in which Abraham plays is honored. Invite volunteers to give oral reports on their research.

Moses Leads the Israelites The Torah tells of a terrible famine in Canaan. The starving Israelites went to Egypt, where Jacob's son Joseph served as top adviser to Egypt's pharaoh.

In time, a new pharaoh came to power. He enslaved the Israelites and forced them to work on his building projects. The Torah tells how **Moses** helped the Israelites leave Egypt. The migration of the Israelites from Egypt is known as the **Exodus**.

The Ten Commandments After leaving Egypt, the Israelites wandered in the Sinai desert for 40 years, living as nomads. According to the Torah, Moses climbed to the top of Mount Sinai, where God spoke to him. When Moses came down the mountain, he carried two stone tablets that contained the **Ten Commandments**. These commandments became the basis for the laws of the Israelites. The commandments later became an important part of the moral and ethical traditions of Western civilization.

Vocabulary Strategy

The word *exodus* comes from the Greek word *exodos*. It combines the **root** *hodos*, which means "way" or "journey," with the **prefix** *ex-*, which means "out."

Primary Source

Background: According to the Torah, the Ten Commandments are the ten laws given by God to Moses on Mount Sinai. These orders serve as the basis for the moral laws of the Hebrews.

▲ Moses with tablets of Ten Commandments

The Ten Commandments*

1. I am the Lord thy God. . . . Thou shalt have no other gods before me.
2. Thou shalt not make unto thee any graven image. . . .
3. Thou shalt not take the name of the Lord thy God in vain. . . .
4. Remember the Sabbath day to keep it holy.
5. Honor thy father and thy mother. . . .
6. Thou shalt not kill.
7. Thou shalt not commit adultery.
8. Thou shalt not steal.
9. Thou shalt not bear false witness against thy neighbor.
10. Thou shalt not covet . . . any thing that is thy neighbor's.

Exodus 20:2–17

* Jews and some Christians word the commandments in ways slightly different from this version.

DOCUMENT–BASED QUESTIONS
1. What are the first four commandments concerned with?
2. What do the last six commandments have in common that makes them different from the first four?

The Hebrew Kingdoms • **327**

Teach

Return to the Promised Land

6.3.4

Talk About It

- How long did it take for the Israelites to reclaim Canaan? *(200 years)*

- Who were the judges, and what was their role in Israelite life? *(They were highly respected men and women who gave advice and led the people. The first ones were military leaders, but later judges gave legal advice and settled arguments. They played a key role in keeping the tribes united.)*

- What did Deborah do to help the Israelites? *(She inspired a small force of fighters to defeat a much larger Canaanite force.)*

- **Critical Thinking: Understanding Cause and Effect** How did the judges help to keep the Israelites united? *(They kept the tribes focused on their traditional religion.)*

More About . . .

Hebrew Women
Hebrew tradition tells of many strong women besides Deborah. Esther became the queen of a king of Persia. She outwitted the chief minister, Haman, by getting the king to cancel Haman's order to kill all the Jews. The Jewish festival of Purim celebrates this event.

An Agreement Confirmed The Israelites believed that the giving of the commandments reaffirmed their covenant with God. They thought that God would protect them. The people, in turn, would obey his laws. They believed that God through his commandments had set down moral laws for all humanity.

REVIEW How did the Israelites escape from slavery in Egypt?
Moses led the Israelites out of Egypt.

Return to the Promised Land

❸ **ESSENTIAL QUESTION** What role did the judges play in the life of the ancient Israelites? Judges were military leaders; gave advice on legal matters; helped settle conflicts; helped to keep 12 tribes united.

By the time the Israelites returned to Canaan, many years had passed. The other groups who lived there were subject to powerful rulers who lived in walled cities. Moses picked Joshua to lead the people into Canaan.

The 12 Tribes of Israel All of the Israelites entering Canaan were descendants of Jacob. They were organized into 12 tribes. Each tribe was named after one of Jacob's sons or grandsons. The men of these tribes became Joshua's troops. They formed a fighting force united by their goal of reclaiming the land from the city states. The first city to fall to the Israelites was Jericho. The movement to reclaim Canaan continued for 200 years.

Once the fighting ended, the Israelite soldiers became farmers and herders. The 12 tribes divided the land among themselves. Some received land in the mountains. Others settled on the plains. Tribes that lived near each other formed close ties, because they shared beliefs, problems, and enemies.

Judges Lead the Israelites
During the 200 years of war, no single powerful leader led the Israelites. Instead, they sought advice from many different

Judges This engraving portrays the judge Deborah. ▼

DIFFERENTIATING INSTRUCTION

Inclusion

Self-Question
As students read about the Hebrews, have them pause at the end of every paragraph to ask themselves a question about what they have read. Tell them to write down their answer. Go over students' answers and let them know whether they are focusing on the key points or on supporting details.

Gifted and Talented Students

Research Topics of Interest
Have students list questions that occur to them as they read this lesson. Ask them their questions and make a list of them. Then assign the questions to specific students and have them do Internet or library research to find the answers. For example, students may want to learn more about the fall of Jericho or about the 12 tribes.

leaders called judges. These were highly respected men and women of the community.

The first judges acted as military leaders. Later judges gave advice on legal matters and helped settle conflicts. Judges such as Gideon, Samson, and Samuel gained fame throughout Canaan for their strength and wisdom. Deborah was one of the most famous judges. She inspired a small force of fighters to victory against a large Canaanite force near Mount Tabor.

The judges played a key role in keeping the 12 tribes united. When the Israelites lacked a strong judge as a leader, some tribes turned away from traditional religion. They made offerings to false gods. The judges spoke out against these practices.

REVIEW Who were some of the important judges of Israel? Gideon, Samson, Samuel, Deborah

Lesson Summary
- Abraham led the Hebrews to Canaan.
- Moses gave the Hebrews the Ten Commandments.
- The judges led the Israelites in Canaan.

Why It Matters Now . . .
Judaism was the first monotheistic religion and influenced other world religions, particularly Christianity and Islam.

---

1 Lesson Review

Homework Helper
ClassZone.com

Terms & Names

1. Explain the importance of

Abraham	Judaism	Exodus
monotheism	Moses	Ten Commandments

Using Your Notes

Understanding Cause and Effect Use your completed chart to answer the following question:

2. What was one effect of each of the following causes shown in the chart? (6.3.3)

Causes	Effects
Abraham leaves Ur.	
Moses leads people out of Egypt.	
Moses climbs Mount Sinai.	

Main Ideas

3. What religious beliefs made the Hebrews different from other ancient peoples? (6.3.1, 6.3.2)
4. What part did Moses play in the Exodus from Egypt? (6.3.3, 6.3.4)
5. Why did the return of the Hebrews to Canaan cause conflicts with other peoples living there? (6.3.4)

Critical Thinking

6. **Summarizing** What covenant between God and the Hebrews did the Hebrews believe the Ten Commandments reaffirmed? (6.3.2)
7. **Drawing Conclusions** How did the Hebrew belief in a Promised Land affect their actions in Egypt and Canaan? (6.3.4)

Activity

Making a Map Trace the map that shows the route of Abraham and his family out of Ur on page 325. Add to the map the geographic challenges they faced. (CST 3)

The Hebrew Kingdoms • **329**

---

❹ Assess & Reteach

Assess Have students work in pairs. First, one student should answer a question orally, with the other writing down the answer. Then they should switch roles and continue taking turns until all the questions are answered.

 Formal Assessment
- Lesson Quiz, p. 173

Reteach Have each student write down each heading and subheading in the lesson in the form of a question on an index card. Form teams and have one team give a heading question to the other team. The second team has to find the correct subheading cards to win a point. If the second team can also answer the questions, they receive another point. Finally, have the second team give a question to the first team. Review answers to all questions.

In-Depth Resources: Unit 5
- Vocabulary Cards, p. 9
- Reteaching Activity, p. 15

Homework Helper

Visit **ClassZone.com** for a lesson review, a flip-card activity, and links to related Web sites.

---

1 Lesson Review Answers

Terms & Names

1. • Abraham, p. 325
   • monotheism, p. 326
   • Judaism, p. 326
   • Moses, p. 327
   • Exodus, p. 327
   • Ten Commandments, p. 327

Using Your Notes

See page 324 for an example of a completed chart.

2. Abraham settles with his family in Canaan. Israelites wander in the desert for 40 years. Moses is given the Ten Commandments.

Main Ideas

3. The Hebrews believed in monotheism.
4. Moses led the Hebrews out of Egypt.
5. During the time the Hebrews were gone, other groups had settled in Canaan.

Critical Thinking

6. God would protect the Israelites in return for their obedience to his laws.
7. The belief in a Promised Land gave the Hebrews hope during their slavery in Egypt and inspired them to fight hard to reclaim their land in Canaan.

Activity Rubric

	Quality of Map	Number of Errors
4	well drawn, clearly labeled, detailed, accurate	no more than one factual error
3	fairly well drawn, detailed, accurate	two or three
2	poorly drawn, few details, some inaccuracies	four or five
1	poorly drawn, no details, inaccurate	more than five

The Hebrew Kingdoms • **329**

Objectives

- Build understanding of the qualities that Moses demonstrated leading the Israelites out of Egyptian captivity.
- **Language Objective:** Review descriptive words and phrases to help make the text comprehensible and meaningful.

❶ Focus & Motivate

Connect to the Big Idea

Belief Systems The Israelites wandered for long periods, seeking to establish their own nation based on Hebrew law.

Connect to Prior Knowledge

Have students tell what they learned in Lesson 1 about the Israelites' Exodus. *(The word* exodus *means "a way out." Moses led people on a migration from Egypt, and they wandered for 40 years in the Sinai desert.)*

More About . . .

The Pharaoh and Moses

According to the Bible, Moses was raised by the pharaoh's daughter as her own son. As he grew, he felt compassion for the enslaved Israelites. Once he found out that he was an Israelite, he tried to convince the pharaoh to free them. The pharaoh refused.

Ten plagues came to the people of Egypt. The first nine were plagues of blood, frogs, lice, wild beasts, animal disease, skin disease, hail, locusts, and darkness. After the tenth plague, the death of first born sons, the pharaoh said the Jews could leave. Because the Israelites left in a hurry, they couldn't wait for their bread to rise, so they baked it flat. That is why this bread, matzo, is eaten by Jews today.

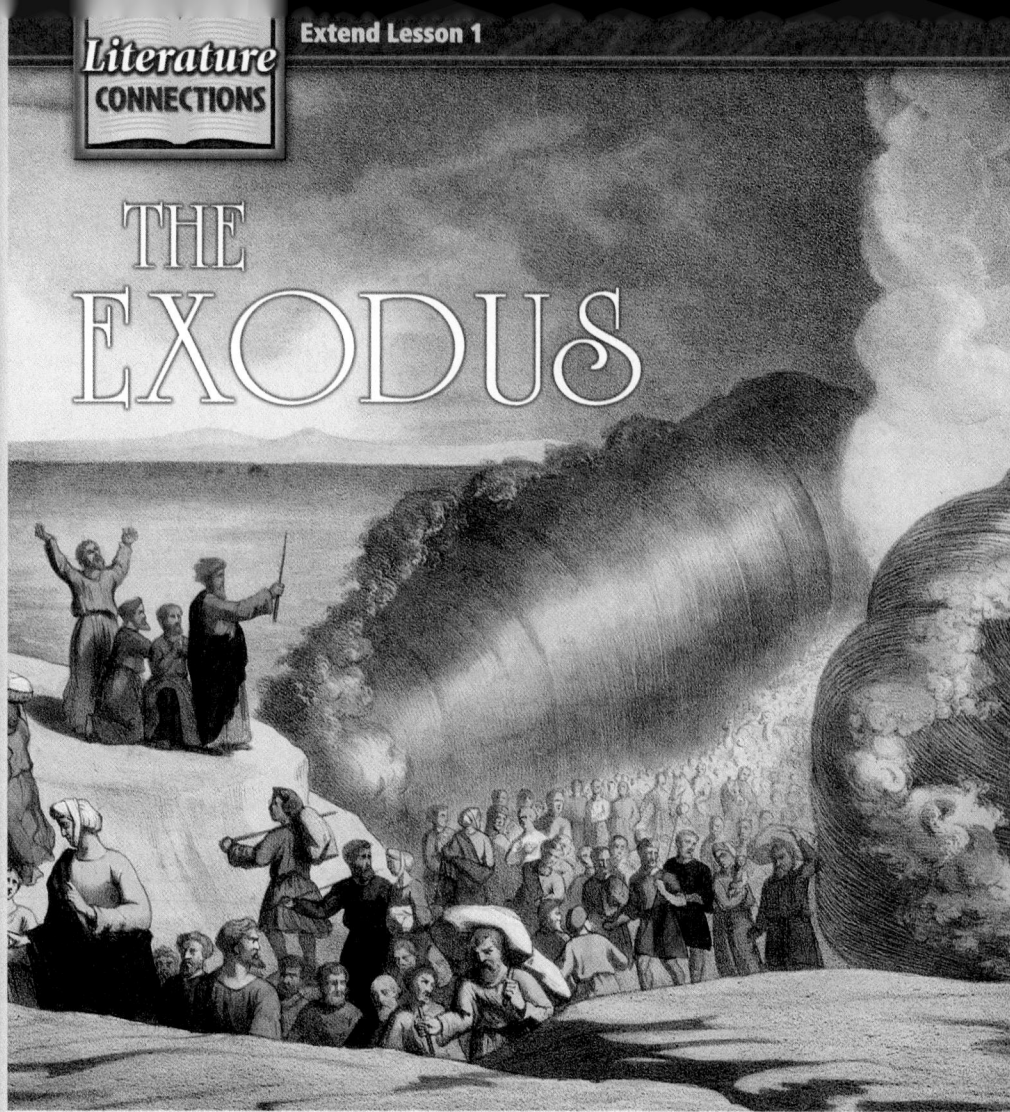

THE EXODUS

Background: According to the Torah, God commanded Moses to lead the Hebrews out of slavery in Egypt. Moses went to the pharaoh and pleaded with him to let the Hebrew people go. After God sent a series of plagues, the pharaoh agreed. Then he changed his mind and led his troops to stop the Hebrews. The Exodus became an inspirational story to other people attempting to flee slavery, such as African Americans in the South before the Civil War. This version of the Exodus is taken from *The Children's Bible: The Old and New Testaments.*

CALIFORNIA STANDARDS
Reading 3.2 Analyze the effect of the qualities of the character (e.g., courage or cowardice, ambition or laziness) on the plot and resolution of the conflict.

330 • Chapter 10

ADDITIONAL RESOURCES

Books for the Student

Auld, Mary. *Exodus from Egypt.* New York: Watts, 2000. A retelling of the story of Moses and the plagues sent by God to convince the pharaoh to let the Israelites leave Egypt.

Taylor, Leighton. *The Red Sea.* Woodbridge: Blackbirch, 1999. Examines the physical features, sea life, and people of the Red Sea.

Videos

Egypt: Beyond the Pyramids. 200 minutes. New York: New Video, 2001. Information about Ramses the Great. VHS, DVD.

Lost Tribes of Israel. 60 minutes. South Burlington: WGBH Boston Video, 2000. Present-day search for the remnants of the lost 10 of the original 12 Hebrew tribes. VHS.

Continuing their journey from Succoth, the Israelites camped at Etham, at the edge of the wilderness. And the Lord went before them by day in a pillar of cloud to show them the way, and by night in a pillar of fire to give them light, so that they could travel by day and night. He did not take away from the people the pillar of cloud by day nor the pillar of fire by night.

It was told to the king of Egypt that the people had fled, and the hearts of Pharaoh and his servants were moved against the people, and they said: "Why have we done this, and let Israel free from serving us?"

Then Pharaoh made ready his chariots and took his people with him. He took six hundred chosen chariots, of all the chariots of Egypt, and put captains over all of them.

The Lord hardened the heart of Pharaoh, king of Egypt, and Pharaoh pursued the children of Israel, for the children of Israel had gone out proudly.

The Egyptians came after them, all the horses and chariots of Pharaoh, his horsemen and his army, and overtook them camping beside the sea, near Pihahiroth, before Baalzephon.

When Pharaoh came near, the children of Israel looked up, and, seeing the Egyptians marching after them, they were very frightened. Then the children of Israel cried out to the Lord, and they said to Moses:

"Were there no graves in Egypt? Have you brought us away to die in the wilderness? Why have you treated us in this way, in bringing us out of Egypt? Did we not tell you in Egypt, 'Let us alone, so that we may serve the Egyptians?' For it would have been better for us to serve the Egyptians than to die in the wilderness."

The Hebrew Exodus, c. 1250 B.C.

Mediterranean Sea · Tyre · CANAAN · Jerusalem · Jordan River · Dead Sea · Ramses · Succoth · Etham · EGYPT · Memphis · Nile River · 30°N · Sinai Peninsula · Ezion-geber · Gulf of Suez · Mt. Sinai · 34°E · Red Sea

0   50   100 miles
0   50   100 kilometers

← Route of Hebrews out of Egypt
● City
▲ Mountain peak

▲ **Moses** This painting, titled *The Parting of the Red Sea*, shows Moses leading the Hebrews in their flight from Egypt.

REVIEW Why were the Israelites upset?

The Hebrew Kingdoms • 331

❷ Teach

Talk About It

- As students read, ask them to note the main idea of each paragraph.
- Have students retell what they have read in their own words.
- Have students use the map to decide where the Israelites started their journey and where they may have stopped along their route to Canaan. Ask students to list these places, numbering them in the order the Israelites reached them.
- Why were the Israelites upset? *(They felt that enough of them had died in Egypt and that Moses was leading them to death. They thought Egyptian slavery was better than death in the wilderness.)*
- **Critical Thinking: Making Predictions** What do you think will happen when the pharaoh and his army catch up with the Israelites? *(Possible answers: They will make them slaves again; Moses and the Israelites will escape; the Israelites will kill the pharaoh's men; the Egyptians will kill the Israelites.)*

More About . . .

The Red Sea
Why is it named the Red Sea? No one knows for sure. There are various theories. Some people think it is because of the the pink and red coral found in it. Others think it refers to the reddish-brown algae that sometimes float on the surface. Many believe it is a misspelling of the name Sea of Reeds, since there are many reddish reeds in this sea. Still others think it refers to the red color of the mountains on the shore.

DIFFERENTIATING INSTRUCTION

English Learners

Explore Descriptive Language
Explain that the author has included many descriptions that can help us understand what the Exodus was like for the Israelites. The Lord's appearance is described as a pillar of cloud by day and a pillar of fire at night. Make sure that students understand that a pillar is a tall structure, whether made of clouds or fire; it could be easily seen and used as a guide to get to Canaan. Locate other descriptive words or phrases and help students understand their meanings in the context of the selection.

Gifted and Talented Students

Create a Three-Dimensional Map
Have groups of students create three-dimensional maps on which they show the path of the Israelites from Egypt to Canaan. Make sure they show terrain, cities, and bodies of water on their maps.

Have groups divide their work by assigning each member a task: doing research, getting materials, making the map, and making a presentation.

Teach

Talk About It

- Why did the Israelites become frightened? *(The Egyptians pursued them with horses and chariots.)*

- What did Moses tell the people to calm their fears? *(The Lord would save them, he would show his power, and they would never see the Egyptians again.)*

- **Critical Thinking: Drawing Conclusions** Why do you think the Israelites continued to follow Moses? *(There seemed to be no escape from the Egyptians, and the faith of Moses was powerful and reassuring.)*

More About . . .

Illuminated Manuscripts
Illuminations are handmade paintings and drawings that illustrate manuscript books. Many people are familiar with the designs used in Celtic books as examples of illuminations.

Illuminations were added to scrolls and codices from the time of ancient Egypts. There are several types of illuminations, including:

- decorated titles and initials in a text
- drawings of flowers, leaves, and other objects
- miniature paintings in margins
- border designs

Designs can be as simple as letters outlined in red ink or as complicated as an entire scene painted in miniature to complement the text. A painting such the one of as Moses and the Red Sea might have taken up more than one page of a manuscript.

In the history of art, illuminated manuscripts preserve a historical record of the changes in artistic styles throughout the centuries.

"Do not be afraid," said Moses to the people. "Stand still and watch the power of the Lord to save you, as he will show you today, for the Egyptians whom you have seen today you shall never see again. The Lord will fight for you if you will be calm."

And God said to Moses: "Why do you cry to me? Tell the children of Israel to go forward. But you must lift up your rod and stretch out your hand over the sea, and divide it. And the children of Israel shall go on dry land through the middle of the sea.

"And you shall see that I will harden the hearts of the Egyptians, and they shall follow you. Then I will show my power over Pharaoh and over all his armies, his chariots and his horsemen. And the Egyptians shall know that I am the Lord, when I have shown my power."

Then the angel of God which went before the camp of Israel moved and went behind them. The pillar of cloud moved from in front of them and rose up behind them. It came between the camp of Israel and the camp of the Egyptians, but it gave light by night to Israel, so that the Egyptians did not come near Israel all that night.

Then Moses stretched out his hand over the sea, and the Lord caused the sea to go back by making a strong east wind blow all that night. It made the sea dry land, and the waters were divided.

The children of Israel walked into the middle of the sea upon the dry ground, and the waters were a wall on their right hand and on their left.

REVIEW What happened when Moses stretched his hand over the sea? The waters of the sea divided so that the Hebrews could pass through.

Exodus This depiction of Moses and the passage of the Red Sea is from a French illuminated manuscript, about 1250 A.D. ▶

DIFFERENTIATING INSTRUCTION

Inclusion

Create an Infographic
Pair up proficient readers with students who have difficulty reading. Have the pairs read the story together. Then ask them to create infographics that present the important points of the story by means of illustrations and captions. Invite students to take turns presenting different portions of their infographics.

Struggling Readers

Write a Headline
Have student pairs review the story and the pictures on pages 330–333 and write newspaper-style headlines that summarize the content. Here are two examples: PILLARS OF CLOUD AND FIRE LEAD JEWS! PHARAOH'S ARMY CLOSING IN FAST!

The Egyptians pursued them and went into the middle of the sea after them, all Pharaoh's horses, his chariots and his horsemen.

When morning came, the Lord looked down on the army of the Egyptians through the pillar of fire and the cloud, and troubled the forces of the Egyptians. He made the wheels fall off their chariots and made them drive heavily, so that the Egyptians said, "Let us flee from the children of Israel, for the Lord fights for them against the Egyptians."

Then God said to Moses: "Stretch out your hand over the sea, so that the waters may come together again and cover the Egyptians, their chariots and their horsemen."

Moses stretched out his hand over the sea, and the sea returned to its bed when the morning appeared. The Egyptians fled before it, but the Lord overthrew the Egyptians in the middle of the sea. The waters returned and covered the chariots and the horsemen, and all the forces of Pharaoh that had followed him into the sea. Not one of them survived.

But the children of Israel had walked on dry land in the middle of the sea, and the waters had formed a wall for them on their right hand and on their left. Thus the Lord saved Israel that day from the hands of the Egyptians, and the Israelites saw the Egyptians dead upon the sea shore.

When Israel saw the great work the Lord did against the Egyptians, the people stood in awe of the Lord, and believed in him and his servant Moses.

▲ **Chariot** A pharaoh in his chariot hunts desert animals.

REVIEW Whom did the Israelites credit for the destruction of their enemies?
the Lord, or God

Reading & Writing

1. **READING: Character** With a partner, discuss the character of Moses as it is revealed in his actions. Then make a list of words that describe his character.

2. **WRITING: Narration** Write a dialogue between two soldiers in Pharaoh's army. Have them discuss their mission in pursuing the Hebrews.

CALIFORNIA STANDARDS Writing 2.1
Write narratives.

The Hebrew Kingdoms • 333

Teach

Talk About It

- Why didn't the Egyptian army capture the Israelites? *(They followed, but the Lord made the wheels fall off their chariots.)*

- How were the Egyptians destroyed? *(The waters closed over them as they retreated.)*

- **Critical Thinking: Analyzing Information** How does the story of the Red Sea show the importance of religious belief to the Israelites? *(Moses told them the Lord would protect them, and the Israelites followed Moses even though they were afraid. The Israelites saw how the Lord protected them and were inspired by Moses' faith.)*

More About . . .

The Parting of the Red Sea
Some scientists have attempted to establish a scientific basis for the parting of the Red Sea. Recently, Russian scientists explained that there is a reef in the Red Sea that was closer to the surface during the time of Moses. If the wind had blowing at 67 miles per hour all night, the reef would have been exposed long enough for the Israelites to cross before the water rose up again.

Many theologians believe that such investigations are not important. They say it is difficult to prove facts from the Bible. Faith is more important, they say, because the stories told are meant to teach important lessons.

ACTIVITIES ANSWERS

1. **READING** Possible answers: faithful; determined; strong; charismatic; obedient; courageous

2. **WRITING** Students might mention pros and cons of the mission. Volunteers might read their dialogues in class, with other students taking one of the two roles.

2. Writing Rubric

	Quality of Dialogue	Description of Mission
4	detailed and lively	clear and accurate
3	detailed	clear, mostly accurate
2	adequate	vague, some errors
1	unclear	vague, many errors

❶ Plan & Prepare

Objectives

- Identify important Israelite leaders and discuss how they helped build a nation.
- Explain why the Israelites split into two kingdoms and describe the outcome of this division.
- Describe the beliefs that sustained the Israelites during the Babylonian Captivity.
- **Language Objective:** List words and phrases to identify the leaders in the kingdom of Israel.

Quick Look

Lesson 2 describes important Israelite leaders, the building and splitting of their nation, and the Babylonian Captivity.

❷ Focus & Motivate

Preview Tell students that this lesson will examine how a strong leader is needed to unify a nation. As they read, ask students to think of examples of how strong or weak leaders can make or break a nation.

Introduce the Main Ideas The three main ideas relate to the Big Idea about belief systems. As students read the lesson, help them look ways in which the beliefs of the Israelites influenced their leaders and government.

Reading Skill: Explaining Chronological Order and Sequence Tell students that putting events in order can help them remember the events better and see how one event leads to another.

SAMPLE ANSWERS FOR TIME LINE

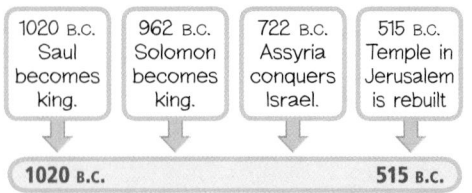

| 1020 B.C. Saul becomes king. | 962 B.C. Solomon becomes king. | 722 B.C. Assyria conquers Israel. | 515 B.C. Temple in Jerusalem is rebuilt |

1020 B.C.   515 B.C.

Lesson 2

▶ MAIN IDEAS

❶ **Government** The Israelites built a small nation.

❷ **Government** Conflict divided the Israelites and made them vulnerable to outside invaders.

❸ **Belief Systems** The exiled Israelites returned to their homeland with beliefs that carried them through difficult times.

▶ TAKING NOTES

Reading Skill:
Explaining Chronological Order and Sequence

To put events in sequence means to put them in order based on the time they happened. As you read Lesson 2, make a note of things that happened in the kingdoms of Israel and Judah. Use a time line like this one to put events in order.

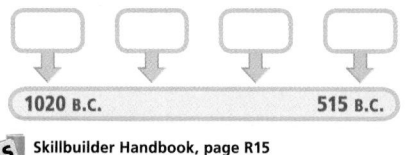

1020 B.C.   515 B.C.

Ⓢ Skillbuilder Handbook, page R15

▲ **Mezuzah** Traditionally, some Jews keep a scroll of an important scripture passage in a mezuzah (a container often attached to a doorpost) like the one shown here.

CALIFORNIA STANDARDS

6.3.2 Identify the sources of the ethical teachings and central beliefs of Judaism (the Hebrew Bible, the Commentaries): belief in God, observance of law, practice of the concepts of righteousness and justice, and importance of study; and describe how the ideas of the Hebrew traditions are reflected in the moral and ethical traditions of Western civilization.

6.3.3 Explain the significance of Abraham, Moses, Naomi, Ruth, David, and Yohanan ben Zaccai in the development of the Jewish religion.

6.3.4 Discuss the locations of the settlements and movements of Hebrew peoples, including the Exodus and their movement to and from Egypt, and outline the significance of the Exodus to the Jewish and other people.

HOW TO TEACH THE CALIFORNIA STANDARDS

Standard	Content	Student Question or Activity	Instruction
6.3.2	**Page 338** Discusses the Jews' central beliefs in the Messiah and prophets	**Page 339** Students describe the role of the prophets in Jewish life in the ancient world.	Have students define what the idea of a Messiah meant to the Israelites and talk about the role of prophets.
6.3.3	**Page 336** Explains who the first Israelite kings were	**Page 339** Students describe Solomon's achievements as king of Israel. **Page 340** Students organize events in the rise and fall of the Hebrew kingdoms.	Read the History Makers feature, asking students what they know about David. Then, discuss the importance of Saul and Solomon.
6.3.4	**Page 338** Describes the Babylonian Captivity	**Page 339** Students explain how the Jews kept their identity in Babylon.	Discuss what the rebuilding of the Temple in Jerusalem meant to the exiles who had returned to Judah.

Kingdoms and Captivity

TERMS & NAMES

David

Solomon

Babylonian Captivity

Messiah

prophets

Build on What You Know You have learned that the Israelites came back to Canaan from Egypt. When they returned, they fought to regain control of the land and clashed with their neighbors.

The Kingdom of Israel

1 **ESSENTIAL QUESTION** Who were some of the early kings of Israel? Saul, David, Solomon

The Israelites' belief in one God and their religious practices set them apart from others in the region. They traded with other groups in Canaan but did not adopt their culture or beliefs. However, sometimes individuals from different groups did mix. One such example is the story of Ruth and Naomi, which you read at the beginning of the chapter.

Saul and David About 1029 B.C., the Israelites faced the Philistines, another people in the area. The Philistines invaded and conquered Israelite territory.

The Israelites agreed to unite under one king in order to fight the Philistines, although many feared a king with too much power. A judge named Samuel shared these concerns, but helped select the first kings of the 12 tribes.

Connect to Today

Judah and Philistia A flock of sheep grazes in hills once part of the kingdom of Judah. ▼

Mediterranean Sea — *Sea of Galilee* — **ISRAEL** — *Jordan River* — **PHILISTIA** — **JUDAH** — *Dead Sea*

335

Terms & Names

David the second king of Israel

Solomon a son of David and king of Israel

Babylonian Captivity a 50-year period when the Israelites were enslaved in Babylon

Messiah "anointed one" looked for by the Jews

prophets spiritual leaders of the Jews

❸ Teach

The Kingdom of Israel

6.3.3

Talk About It

- **Critical Thinking: Explaining Chronological Order and Sequence** Why was Solomon able to accomplish more than Saul or David? *(Possible answer: Saul and David had to fight and defeat the Philistines. Solomon enjoyed peace and was able to foster trade and build the Temple.)*

California Resources

California Reading Toolkit, L34

California Modified Lesson Plans for English Learners, p. 71

California Daily Standards Practice Transparencies, TT34

California Standards Enrichment Workbook, pp. 41–46

California Online Test Practice

California Test Generator CD-ROM

California Standards Planner and Lesson Plans, L67

California EasyPlanner CD-ROM

California eEdition CD-ROM

LESSON 2 PROGRAM RESOURCES

ON LEVEL

In-Depth Resources: Unit 5
- Reading Skill: Explaining Chronological Order and Sequence, p. 4
- Vocabulary Study Guide, p. 8
- Vocabulary Cards, p. 9

Formal Assessment
- Lesson Quiz, p. 174

ENGLISH LEARNERS

In-Depth Resources in Spanish
- Reading Skill: Explaining Chronological Order and Sequence, p. 84
- Vocabulary Study Guide, p. 88

Modified Lesson Plans for English Learners, p. 71

Reading Study Guide (Spanish), p. 89

Reading Study Guide Audio CD (Spanish)

STRUGGLING READERS

In-Depth Resources: Unit 5
- Reading Skill: Explaining Chronological Order and Sequence, p. 4
- Vocabulary Study Guide, p. 8
- Vocabulary Cards, p. 9
- Reteaching Activity, p. 16

Reading Toolkit, L34

Reading Study Guide, p. 89

Reading Study Guide Audio CD

GIFTED AND TALENTED STUDENTS

History Makers
- Moses, p. 19

In-Depth Resources: Unit 5
- Primary Source: David and Solomon, p. 13

Interdisciplinary Projects
- Math, p. 55
- Health, p. 58

INCLUSION

EasyPlanner CD-ROM
- Reading Skill: Explaining Chronological Order and Sequence
- Reteaching Activity

TECHNOLOGY

eEdition CD-ROM

Power Presentations CD-ROM

Humanities Transparencies
- HT20 David Dancing Before the Ark

Map Transparencies
- MT19 Kingdom of David and Solomon, c. 965

Critical Thinking Transparencies
- CT43 Explaining Chronological Order and Sequence

Test Generator CD-ROM

ClassZone.com

In-Depth Resources: Unit 5
• Reading Skill: Explaining Chronological Order and Sequence, p. 4

More About . . .

Philistines

The Philistines fought the Israelites for centuries. They controlled supplies of iron, and their cities were strong and organized.

In the Bible story of Samson and Delilah, Samson was an Israelite judge, and Delilah betrayed him to the Philistines by cutting his hair to make him weak.

In modern times, to be called a philistine is not a compliment. In 17th-century England, the primary meaning of *philistine* was "enemy." At the same time in Germany, it took on the meaning of "a person without culture and taste." Today, *philistine* is used to refer to an uneducated and materialistic person.

History Makers

David

The word *psalm* means "a sacred song, or hymn." Seventy-three psalms are thought to have been written by David. The most famous is Psalm 23, which starts "The Lord is my shepherd; I shall not want. . . ." The symbol of David's musicianship is the harp.

The Bernini sculpture focuses on David's slaying of Goliath. David stands over his armor, exposed and ready to do battle. The sculpture shows David in motion, sling pulled back, ready to turn and throw a stone at Goliath.

Humanities Transparencies
• HT20 David Dancing Before the Ark

David (ruled during the 900s B.C.)

◄ Sculpture of David by Bernini

David organized a central government and made Jerusalem the capital of Israel. He expanded the borders of Israel and helped its economy grow by encouraging trade with Phoenicia, a neighbor on the Mediterranean coast.

According to the Bible, David slew the Philistine giant Goliath. David, who was Israel's second king, was also a fine poet and musician. He is said to have written the beautiful prayers and songs found in the Bible's Book of Psalms. By the time David died, Israel had become an independent and united kingdom mostly at peace with its neighbors.

A New Leader The Israelites chose Saul, a respected military leader, as their first king in 1020 B.C. Under Saul, the Israelites fought the Philistines. These battles forced the Philistines to loosen their control over the Israelites. After Saul's death, the Israelites looked for a new leader.

According to the Bible, Samuel chose a young man named **David** as the next king. The choice was a wise one. In about 1000 B.C., David and the Israelites drove out the Philistines. David won control of Jerusalem.

Solomon David established a line of kings. He chose his son **Solomon** to succeed him. Solomon became the third king of Israel in about 962 B.C. Solomon, too, was a strong leader.

During Solomon's rule, Israel became a powerful nation. Solomon built on the trade ties between Phoenicia and Israel established by David. Solomon also formed new trade alliances.

Solomon oversaw many building projects. His most famous was the Temple in Jerusalem. (See pages 318–319.) The Temple became the center of religious life for the Israelites. People came there from all parts of the kingdom to say prayers and leave offerings. Many also came to ask the wise king to settle their disputes.

REVIEW Why did the Israelites decide to choose a king?
to lead them against the Philistines

DIFFERENTIATING INSTRUCTION

Gifted and Talented Students

Create a Poster of Hebrew Kings

Have students use library or Internet resources to find information and illustrations with which to make posters about Israelite kings. The posters should include names, dates of reigns, and illustrations showing the kings' major accomplishments.

Struggling Readers

Write a Summary Paragraph

Divide the class into groups of five. In each group, assign each student one of the following people or groups: Saul, David, Solomon, Solomon's son, the Assyrians, the Babylonians. Have each student study the assigned person or group and write a one-paragraph summary of his or her findings. Then have each student present his or her summary to the rest of the group.

The Kingdom Divides

2 ESSENTIAL QUESTION What was the outcome of the conflict among the Israelites? *the two kingdoms of Israel and Judah*

Faced by a threat of attack, Israelite tribes formed the kingdom of Israel. When the threat ended, they quarreled and fought.

Israel and Judah King Solomon died in 922 B.C. When Solomon's son became king, the northern tribes refused to pledge their loyalty until he agreed to lighten their taxes and end forced labor on building projects. When he refused, the tribes rebelled. Only the tribes of Judah and Benjamin remained loyal.

Israel split into two separate kingdoms. The northern part continued to be called Israel. The two tribes in the southern area, which included Jerusalem, called their new nation Judah. The words *Judaism* and *Jews* come from the name Judah.

Two separate kingdoms existed for about two centuries. Throughout this period, Jerusalem remained an important center of worship.

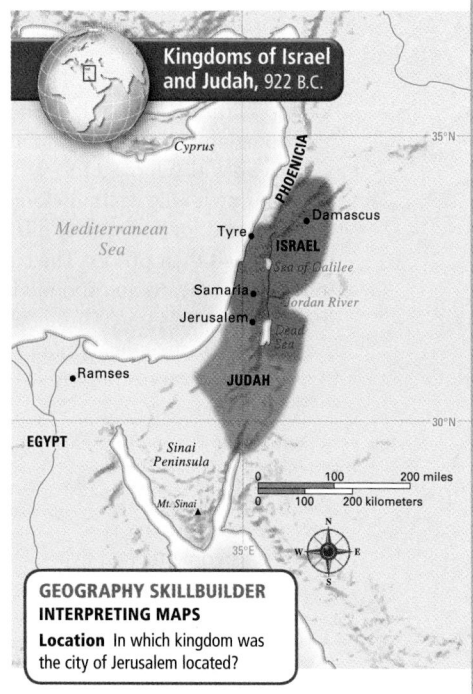

GEOGRAPHY SKILLBUILDER
INTERPRETING MAPS
Location In which kingdom was the city of Jerusalem located?

Assyrians and Babylonians Take the Land By 738 B.C., both kingdoms faced new threats to their independence from the Assyrians. The Assyrians forced Israel and Judah to pay tribute. In 722 B.C., Assyria invaded Israel and conquered it. The kingdom of Israel ended. Around 612 B.C., the Assyrian Empire fell to the Babylonians. (You read about this in Chapter 4.)

For many years, King Nebuchadnezzar ruled Babylonia. In 586 B.C., Nebuchadnezzar captured Jerusalem. When Judah's leaders resisted his rule, the Babylonians destroyed the Temple in Jerusalem. They took thousands of Jews to Babylon as slaves.

REVIEW What conflicts caused Israel to split into two kingdoms?
The northern tribes refused to pledge loyalty to Solomon's son until he lightened their taxes and ended their forced labor. When he refused, northern tribes rebelled.

The Hebrew Kingdoms • 337

DIFFERENTIATING INSTRUCTION

English Learners

Profile Strong Leaders
Explain that Samuel helped the Israelites select their first kings to fight the Philistines. The Israelites chose Saul as their first king in 1020 B.C. Guide students as they skim the text to locate information about other Israelite leaders. Use a chart to model how to note the name, the date, and a brief summary of the career of each leader. Have students work in pairs and share their findings with the rest of the class.

Inclusion

Preview Text
Read aloud the Essential Question for the section "The Kingdom Divides" and model for students how to use the subheadings on the page to predict the answer to the question. *(Possible answer: Because the Israelites were divided, the Assyrians and Babylonians were able to conquer them.)* After students read the text, revisit the Essential Question and confirm the answer. Encourage students to use this strategy as they read each section of the text.

 In-Depth Resources: Unit 5
• Primary Source: King Solomon, p. 13

Teach

The Kingdom Divides

6.3.4

Talk About It

• What problem did the northern tribes have with Solomon's son when he became king? *(He refused to lighten their taxes and free them from forced labor on building projects.)*

• How did the terms *Judaism* and *Jews* originate? *(When the kingdom split in two, the southern kingdom was called Judah after the tribe of Judah. The terms come from the name of this kingdom.)*

• What new dangers threatened the independence of both kingdoms? *(invasions by Assyria and Babylonia)*

• **Critical Thinking: Making Inferences** Why did the division into two kingdoms leave the Israelites open to attack? *(Possible answers: They were not unified because they were fighting; they didn't pay attention to outside threats; they had divided armies.)*

History from Visuals

Interpreting Maps
Have students examine the map and its title.

• Which kingdom had a coastline on the Mediterranean Sea—Israel or Judah? *(Israel)*

• In which kingdom were most cities located? *(Israel)*

Extension Have students compare this map with a present-day map showing the country of Israel. Ask, how does the area of the modern nation compare with the area of Israel in 922 B.C.? *(Present-day Israel includes most of both kingdoms.)*

GEOGRAPHY SKILLBUILDER ANSWER
Judah

 Map Transparencies
• MT19 Solomon's Israel, 962 B.C.

The Hebrew Kingdoms • 337

Teach

Jewish Exiles Return to Judah

⌐ 6.3.2, 6.3.4

Talk About It

- How long were the Israelites captives in Babylon? *(about 50 years)*

- What was the function of the prophets? *(They interpreted God's word, warned people about breaking God's code, criticized rulers who didn't live according to God's laws, and comforted people in times of trouble.)*

- How did the Babylonian Captivity end? *(The Persians conquered Babylonia, and Cyrus freed the Jews and allowed them to return to Judah.)*

- **Critical Thinking: Drawing Conclusions** What strengths did the Jews have that allowed them to survive another captivity? *(Possible answers: They maintained their identity, and that united them; they suffered together and helped each other; they were persistent and willing to rebuild what had been destroyed; they had hope of a Messiah.)*

History from Visuals

Interpreting Visuals
Ask students what an engraving is, and have them study the engraving of Cyrus the Great.

- What is the difference in dress between Cyrus and the Jews in the crowd? *(Cyrus is wearing rich clothing, and the people are dressed in common clothing.)*

- What articles might Cyrus be giving away? *(tikkim, mezuzahs, candles, spices)*

Jewish Exiles Return to Judah

❸ ESSENTIAL QUESTION What hope sustained the Jews in exile?
hope to return to Judah and rebuild the Temple in Jerusalem

The exiles from Judah spent about 50 years in Babylon. This time is known as the **Babylonian Captivity**. During this period, the Israelites became known as the Jews.

Beliefs During the Babylonian Captivity During their years in Babylon, the Jews struggled to keep their identity. They continued to observe religious laws, celebrate holidays, and worship as they had in Judah. They hoped someday to return to their homeland in Judah and rebuild the Temple in Jerusalem.

The exiles also looked forward to a time when they would have their own king again. Before the exile, Hebrew leaders were anointed, or had special oils poured on their heads, when they assumed their offices. The Hebrew word **Messiah** (mih•SY•uh) means an "anointed one" charged with some task or leadership. Throughout the centuries of foreign rule, the people kept hoping for their own king. This was sometimes expressed as a hope for an anointed king, an heir to the throne of David, a Messiah.

During times of trouble, both in Judah and in exile, the Jewish people turned to spiritual leaders called **prophets** for advice. These were men and women thought to have a special ability to interpret God's word. They warned the people when they strayed from the Jewish code of conduct. They criticized rulers who were not living according to God's laws. The prophets also comforted the people in times of trouble.

The Temple Is Rebuilt In 539 B.C., the Persians conquered Babylonia. As you learned in Chapter 4, Lesson 3, the Persian

Cyrus the Great This engraving shows Cyrus giving objects from the destroyed Temple to the Jews. ▼

INTERDISCIPLINARY ACTIVITIES

Art

Create a Banner
Have students review what they have read about the Hebrews' desire to return to Judah. Then have them design banners or flags bearing important symbols of this desire. Encourage students to be imaginative and use colors and appropriate symbols on their banners or flags.

Math

Calculate the Journey from Babylon
Have students use the map on page 331 to calculate approximate distance between Jerusalem and Babylon. *(about 600 miles)*

king Cyrus set up a policy of religious toleration in his empire. In 538 B.C., Cyrus freed the Jewish exiles from captivity and allowed them to return to their homeland in Judah.

Soon after the exiles returned to Judah, they began rebuilding the Temple in Jerusalem. The beautiful Temple Solomon had built lay in ruins. Grass grew between the crumbling walls. Workers completed the new Temple in 515 B.C.

REVIEW How did the exiles maintain their identity in Babylon?
by observing their religious laws, celebrating holidays, and worshiping as they had in Judah

Lesson Summary

- Saul, David, and Solomon were the first kings of Israel.
- After the death of Solomon, the kingdom of Israel split into two smaller kingdoms—Israel and Judah.
- The Babylonian conquest destroyed the Temple and forced the people of Judah into exile in Babylon.

Why It Matters Now . . .

During the years in captivity, the exiles maintained the religious beliefs and practices that are part of Jewish life today.

▲ **Ivory Pomegranate** This ivory fruit is believed to be the only remaining relic from Solomon's Temple. Almost two inches high, the object may have decorated an altar.

 **Lesson Review**

Homework Helper ClassZone.com

Terms & Names

1. Explain the importance of

| David | Babylonian Captivity | prophets |
| Solomon | Messiah | |

Using Your Notes

Explaining Chronological Order and Sequence

Use your completed time line to answer the following question:

2. Which empire destroyed the kingdom of Israel, and which empire took the Jews into captivity? (6.3.4)

1020 B.C.   515 B.C.

Main Ideas

3. What were Solomon's achievements as king of Israel? (6.3.2, 6.3.3)
4. What was the role of prophets in Jewish life in the ancient world? (6.3.2)
5. What event ended the Babylonian Captivity? (6.3.4)

Critical Thinking

6. **Drawing Conclusions** How did fighting among the tribes of Israel make it easier for their enemies to conquer them? (6.3.4)
7. **Making Inferences** Why do you think Jewish exiles wanted to rebuild the Temple as soon as they returned to their homeland? (6.3.2)

Activity

Writing a Narrative Look at the illustration on pages 318–319 and reread "Solomon" on page 336. Write a narrative story about one of the visitors or travelers to the Temple. (Writing 2.1)

The Hebrew Kingdoms • 339

More About . . .

Cyrus the Great

Cyrus was king of Persia from about 576 to 520 B.C. The Jews admired Cyrus because he freed them and helped them to obtain power in Canaan.

The name *Cyrus* means "like the sun" in Persian. He conquered other peoples to protect his land, but he respected the cultures and religions of the conquered peoples. A clay barrel discovered in Babylon in 1879 had a declaration that Cyrus wrote inscribed on it. Some historians feel that this was the first declaration of human rights.

❹ Assess & Reteach

Assess Divide students into small groups and have them answer the questions. Then ask groups to take turns presenting answers to the rest of the class. Discuss whether any groups answered questions differently.

 Formal Assessment
- Lesson Quiz, p. 174

Reteach Have students read the Lesson Summary. For each item, have them find information or examples in the lesson that support the statements.

 In-Depth Resources: Unit 5
- Vocabulary Cards, p. 9
- Reteaching Activity, p. 16

 Homework Helper

Visit **ClassZone.com** for a lesson review, a flip-card activity, and links to related Web sites.

---

2 Lesson Review Answers

Terms & Names

1. • David, p. 336
   • Solomon, p. 336
   • Babylonian Captivity, p. 338
   • Messiah, p. 338
   • prophets, p. 338

Using Your Notes

See page 334 for an example of a completed time line.

2. The Assyrians destroyed the kingdom of Israel, and the Babylonians took the Jews into captivity.

Main Ideas

3. He expanded trade alliances, built the Temple and other buildings in Jerusalem, and increased the power and influence of Israel.
4. They gave advice, warned rulers and people when they acted unjustly or failed to observe the law, and comforted the people in times of trouble.
5. the conquest of Babylonia by the Persians

Critical Thinking

6. Possible answer: When they were united, their military force was stronger, and they were better able to resist their enemies.
7. Possible answer: so that they would have a hopeful symbol of their freedom and return to self-rule and so that they could go back to worshiping with priests, as they had in the past

Activity Rubric

	Number of Details	Understanding of Concepts
4	vivid	thorough
3	descriptive	good
2	somewhat descriptive	some
1	vague	little or none

Objectives

- Use a time line to organize dates in Hebrew history.
- Use a time line to structure events in Hebrew history.
- **Language Objective:** List words and phrases to identify the leaders in the kingdom of Israel.

❶ Focus & Motivate

Preview Tell students that keeping track of the order of historical events will help them remember material better. Challenge students to suggest words and phrases that link two events together. (*Possible answers: next, after, before, then, at that time*)

❷ Teach

Talk About It

- How many years does the time line span? (*505 years*)
- How long did Saul reign? (*58 years*)
- For about how many years did the two Hebrew kingdoms exist separately? (*200 years*)
- After Assyria conquered Israel, how much time passed before the rebuilding of the Temple? (*207 years*)
- About how long was the Babylonian Captivity? (*48 years*)
- **Critical Thinking: Making Inferences** Compare the amount of time the Jews had a kingdom with the amount of time they were captive and without territory. How does this explain why the idea of the Messiah was such a powerful motivator for the Jews? (*Possible answers: The Jews had a kingdom for about 434 years. Then they were captive and without territory for about 48 years. After their long struggles, the idea of a Messiah appealed to them because they wanted to have their own kingdom again.*)

Skillbuilder   Extend Lesson 2

Constructing Time Lines

Goal: To construct a time line in order to understand events in the history of the Hebrews

CALIFORNIA STANDARDS
CST 2 Students construct various time lines of key events, people, and periods of the historical era they are studying.

Learn the Skill

Making a time line is a good way to understand material that includes a lot of dates. Events are placed on a time line in the order that they happened. When events are in the proper order, you can see the relationships among them.

[S] See the Skillbuilder Handbook, page R14.

Practice the Skill

❶ Look for clue words about time as you read the passage at right. These are words such as *first, next, then, before, after, finally,* and *by that time.* Some of these are identified for you in the passage.

❷ Use specific dates provided in the text.

❸ Look for phrases that link two events together to help you find an exact date. For example, to figure out the date of Solomon's death, subtract 40 (the number of years he ruled) from 962, the year his reign began. Remember that B.C. dates decrease as they move forward in time.

❹ Use a time line like the one below to help you put the events in a passage in the right order. Look for the earliest date to know how to mark the beginning of the time line and latest to mark the end of the time line. This time line is based on the passage you just read.

Example:

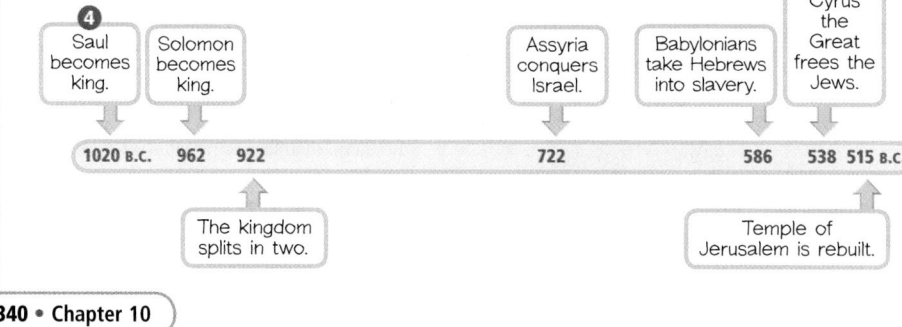

DIFFERENTIATING INSTRUCTION

English Learners

Use Signal Words
Model how to use signal words (*first, next, then, last, later*), specific dates, and key phrases to describe the sequence of events shown on the time line. Say, *Saul becomes king in 1020 B.C. Then, in 962, Solomon becomes king of the Hebrews.* Have students take turns using signal words to describe other events shown on the time line. Make sure students know to use the present tense when reading a time line.

Inclusion

Read Aloud
Read the secondary source aloud with students, stopping at each number to have students look at the example time line on page 340. Point out how the clue words, dates, and phrases are reflected on the time line. Tell students that when they create their own time line for the "Apply the Skill," activity they can stop during reading to jot down each date and event. Then they can put the dates in chronological order. Remind students to look for phrases that link events.

Mosaics

Mosaics are pictures or designs made by attaching small colored stones or tiles to surfaces. Mosaic designs can be made on ceilings, walls, floors, and furniture. They can be found in churches and art galleries.

Modern mosaics frequently appear on floors in houses, on tabletops, and on decorative items, such as trivets.

To make a mosaic, one needs small pieces of stone or ceramic, some grout, and a surface. Put the grout mixture on the surface, arrange the pieces, and let it dry.

Secondary Source

In the following passage, the author describes the history of the Hebrew kingdoms. Notice that the passage covers a long period of time. Use the numbered strategies listed under Practice the Skill to help you follow the order of events.

The Rise and Fall of the Hebrew Kingdoms

The ❶ first king of Israel was Saul. He became king in ❷ 1020 B.C. His successor, King David, expanded the kingdom. He established a dynasty that lasted for about 400 years.

The kingdom of Israel reached its peak during the reign of David's son Solomon. He took the throne in ❷ 962 B.C. and reigned for ❸ 40 years. His greatest achievement was the construction of a great Temple in Jerusalem. ❶ After Solomon's death, the kingdom split in two. The northern kingdom was called Israel, and the southern kingdom was called Judah.

The kingdom was not as strong ❶ after the split. In ❷ 722 B.C., Assyria took over Israel but not Judah. ❶ Then in ❷ 586 B.C., the Babylonians conquered Judah. Thousands of Jews were taken to Babylon as slaves.

The Jews remained slaves in Babylon until ❷ 538 B.C. ❶ At that time, Cyrus the Great of Persia conquered the Babylonians. He freed the Jews and allowed them to return to Palestine. ❶ After their return, the Jews rebuilt the Temple of Jerusalem. It was completed in ❷ 515 B.C.

▲ **Mosaic** King David and King Solomon are shown in this detail from a Byzantine mosaic of the 11th century.

Apply the Skill

Turn to Chapter 13, Lesson 3. Read the sections "Julius Caesar" and "Emperors Rule Rome." Make a time line like the one at left to show the order of events.

APPLY THE SKILL

SAMPLE ANSWERS FOR THE TIME LINE

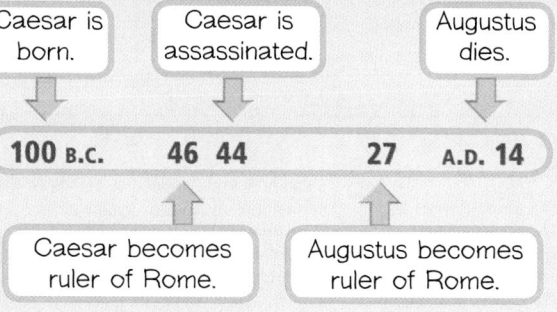

| Caesar is born. | Caesar is assassinated. | Augustus dies. |

| **100** B.C. | **46** **44** | **27** A.D. **14** |

| Caesar becomes ruler of Rome. | Augustus becomes ruler of Rome. |

❶ Plan & Prepare

Objectives

- Describe how the Jews regained control of Jerusalem.
- Explain the consequences of resistance to Roman control.
- Summarize how the Jews kept their faith alive after the Diaspora.
- **Language Objective:** Create a mural to compare and contrast the ways in which the Syrians and the Romans treated their Jewish subjects.

Quick Look

Lesson 3 describes the Jews' struggle for freedom from the Syrians and the Romans and explores how the Jews held on to their faith.

❷ Focus & Motivate

Preview Tell students that this lesson looks at the final stages of Jewish resistance to foreign rule.

Introduce the Main Ideas The three main ideas relate to the Big Idea "Belief systems and religions may shape government and societies." Help students look for this Big Idea as they read the lesson.

Reading Skill: Comparing and Contrasting Tell students that comparing and contrasting helps them understand how things are alike and different. A Venn diagram graphically illustrates this by showing similarities in the overlapping region and differences in the outer regions.

SAMPLE ANSWERS FOR DIAGRAM

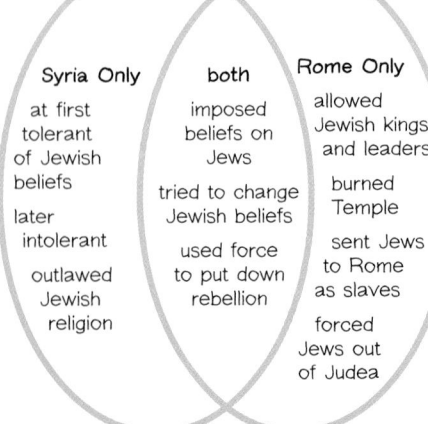

Syria Only
- at first tolerant of Jewish beliefs
- later intolerant
- outlawed Jewish religion

both
- imposed beliefs on Jews
- tried to change Jewish beliefs
- used force to put down rebellion

Rome Only
- allowed Jewish kings and leaders
- burned Temple
- sent Jews to Rome as slaves
- forced Jews out of Judea

Lesson 3

▶ **MAIN IDEAS**

❶ **Government** Jews fought against foreign control and regained self-rule.

❷ **Government** Jewish resistance to Roman control resulted in Jews being driven out of their homeland.

❸ **Belief Systems** Living outside their homeland, many Jews remained loyal to their beliefs.

▶ **TAKING NOTES**

Reading Skill: Comparing and Contrasting
Comparing and contrasting means finding ways in which two things are alike and different. In Lesson 3, look for ways in which the Syrians and Romans were alike and different in their treatment of Jewish rebellions and insert them in a Venn diagram like the one below.

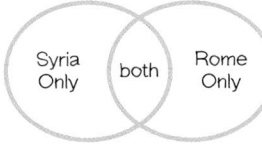

Syria Only | both | Rome Only

S **Skillbuilder Handbook, page R4**

▲ **Menorah** This 18th-century brass menorah comes from eastern Europe. Most menorahs have seven branches. The nine-branched version is used in celebration of Hanukkah.

CALIFORNIA STANDARDS

6.3.2 Identify the sources of the ethical teachings and central beliefs of Judaism (the Hebrew Bible, the Commentaries): belief in God, observance of law, practice of the concepts of righteousness and justice, and importance of study; and describe how the ideas of the Hebrew traditions are reflected in the moral and ethical traditions of Western civilization.

6.3.3 Explain the significance of Abraham, Moses, Naomi, Ruth, David, and Yohanan ben Zaccai in the development of the Jewish religion.

6.3.5 Discuss how Judaism survived and developed despite the continuing dispersion of much of the Jewish population from Jerusalem and the rest of Israel after the destruction of the second Temple in A.D. 70.

6.7.5 Trace the migration of Jews around the Mediterranean region and the effects of their conflict with the Romans, including the Romans' restrictions on their right to live in Jerusalem.

HOW TO TEACH THE CALIFORNIA STANDARDS

Standard	Content	Student Question or Activity	Instruction
6.3.2	**Pages 345–346** Traces how Jews have adhered to their religious beliefs wherever they have settled	**Page 346** Students explain how study kept the faith of the Jews alive.	Create a compare-and-contrast chart. Write "Adopt New Beliefs" and "Refuse to Adopt New Beliefs" above two columns. Have students brainstorm pros and cons.
6.3.3	**Page 344** Explains how Yohanan ben Zaccai received permission for a Jewish scholar's school	**Page 346** Students use the Internet to research Yohanan ben Zaccai	Ask students to discuss why schools might be important in a society and to tell how their school may help keep the traditions of Western society alive.
6.3.5	**Pages 345–346** Explores how Jews kept their faith after the Diaspora	**Page 346** Students explain why the Diaspora changed the way Jews practiced their religion	Review the vocabulary words *rabbi* and *synagogue*. Ask students to explain how rabbis and synagogues reinforced Jewish unity.
HI 1	**Pages 343–346** Describes problems Jews faced as they fought foreign control	**Page 346** Students identify the goal of the revolt led by Judah Maccabeus.	Have students create a time line of Jewish struggles from 198 B.C. to A.D. 70.

Rome and Judea

Build on What You Know The Jews returned to Judah from their long exile in Babylon. As they prepared for self-rule, they recalled how freedom had often been followed by foreign invasion.

Ruled by Foreigners

1 **ESSENTIAL QUESTION** What was the relationship of Judah to Syria?
Judah was controlled by Syria.
The land of Judah lay in the path of conquering armies that marched across the eastern shores of the Mediterranean. Over the years, many different groups, including the Syrians, Greeks, and Romans, controlled the country.

Syria Controls Judah In 198 B.C., the Syrians seized control of Judah. Syrian rulers admired Greek culture. They introduced Greek ideas and beliefs to the Jewish people. Some Jews adopted aspects of Greek culture, and some began to worship Greek gods. Many of the people did not. They continued to observe, or follow, Jewish religious beliefs and practices. Judah's first Syrian rulers allowed the Jews to practice their religion.

In 175 B.C., a new Syrian ruler ordered Jewish priests to make offerings to Greek gods. When the Jews refused, he outlawed their religion and placed statues of Greek gods in the Temple in Jerusalem. The Syrian ruler made it a crime to observe Jewish laws or study the Torah. Some Jews fled to the hills, where they prepared to fight back.

Ancient Ruins The ruins of this ancient Jewish house of worship are located in Capernaum in Israel. ▼

343

Terms & Names

Diaspora the scattering of Jews out of Judea

rabbi a Jewish religious leader and teacher

synagogue a Jewish place of worship

❸ Teach

Ruled by Foreigners

6.3.2, HI 1

Talk About It

- **Critical Thinking: Drawing Conclusions**
  Why was it predictable that the Jews would not adopt new beliefs? *(Possible answer: Their history showed that they had always fought to maintain their laws, they had endured exile, and they had always created ways to keep their faith.)*

California Resources

California Reading Toolkit, L35
California Modified Lesson Plans for English Learners, p. 73
California Daily Standards Practice Transparencies, TT35
California Standards Enrichment Workbook, pp. 41–46, 103–104
California Online Test Practice
California Test Generator CD-ROM
California Standards Planner and Lesson Plans, L69
California EasyPlanner CD-ROM
California eEdition CD-ROM

LESSON 3 PROGRAM RESOURCES

In-Depth Resources: Unit 5
- Reading Skill: Comparing and Contrasting, p. 5
- Skillbuilder Practice: Distinguishing Fact from Opinion, p. 7

Teach

Roman Control

 6.3.3

Talk About It

- How did the Romans control Judea? *(They appointed Jewish kings and religious leaders.)*

- Who were the Zealots? *(Jewish freedom fighters who led an uprising against Roman troops and were defeated by the Roman general Vespasian.)*

- **Critical Thinking: Solving Problems**
  How did Yohanan ben Zaccai help to keep Jewish traditions alive under Roman rule? *(He got permission from Vespasian to set aside a place for Jewish scholars to study.)*

- What name is given to the movement of the Jews to other parts of the world, both before and after the conflict with Rome? *(Diaspora)*

Map Transparencies
- MT20 Roman Judea, 63 B.C. to A.D. 70

Rebels Fight Syria A Jewish priest along with his five sons led the fight to drive out the Syrians. One of his sons, Judah Maccabeus, led the revolt.

Judah Maccabeus had a difficult task. His tiny fighting force, called the Maccabees, faced the much larger, better-equipped Syrian army. But the Maccabees' knowledge of the countryside gave them an advantage. In battle after battle, the rebels defeated the Syrian forces. By 164 B.C., the Maccabees had regained control of Jerusalem.

REVIEW Why did the Jews rebel against their Syrian rulers?
Syrian rulers ordered Jewish priests to make offerings to Greek gods, outlawed Jewish religion, placed statues of Greek gods in the Temple in Jerusalem, and outlawed study of the Torah.

Roman Control

2 ESSENTIAL QUESTION What was the result of Jewish resistance to Roman rule? destruction of Jerusalem and the Temple and a further scattering of the Jews

The independence of the Jews did not last. After less than a century of self-rule, another foreign power took control.

Rome Conquers Judea In 63 B.C., the Romans conquered Judah, which the Romans called Judea. Roman rulers kept strict control over Judea. The Jews were allowed to have Jewish kings and religious leaders, but these kings and leaders were appointed by Rome.

Resistance to Roman Rule The people of Judea disagreed about how to deal with the Romans. Some wanted to cooperate. Others favored fighting to free Judea.

In A.D. 66, a group of Jews known as the Zealots led a rebellion in Judea against Roman authority in the province. Roman leaders responded by sending General Vespasian to crush the uprising.

Some Jews feared the Romans would destroy the Temple. A teacher named Yohanan ben Zaccai hurried to Vespasian's camp. He asked the general to set aside a place for Jewish scholars to study. The school that ben Zaccai set up kept alive the traditions of the Jews.

Masada Zealots held out against the Romans in the fortress of Masada, which overlooks the Dead Sea in Israel. ▼

DIFFERENTIATING INSTRUCTION

English Learners

Create a Mural
Have students work with partners to create murals that depict Jewish life under Syrian rule and Jewish life under Roman rule. Advise students to revisit the text as needed and to use labels and captions to describe details in their illustrations. Have students use their murals to explain the similarities and differences to their classmates. Post the murals in the classroom.

Inclusion

Use an Interactive Map
Students who have visual impairments may benefit from the enlarged, interactive version of the map available on the Power Presentations and eEdition CD-ROMs.

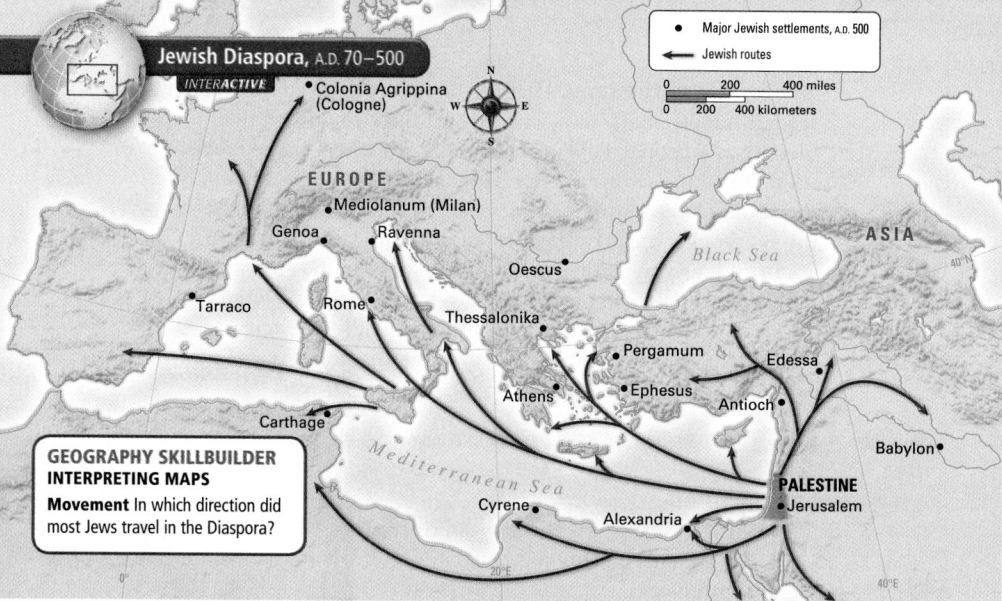

Jewish Diaspora, A.D. 70–500
INTERACTIVE

Colonia Agrippina (Cologne)

EUROPE

Mediolanum (Milan)
Genoa
Ravenna
Tarraco
Rome
Oescus
Thessalonika
Athens
Pergamum
Ephesus
Edessa
Antioch
Babylon
Carthage
Cyrene
Alexandria

PALESTINE
Jerusalem

Black Sea
ASIA
Mediterranean Sea

• Major Jewish settlements, A.D. 500
← Jewish routes

0   200   400 miles
0 200 400 kilometers

GEOGRAPHY SKILLBUILDER
INTERPRETING MAPS
Movement In which direction did most Jews travel in the Diaspora?

Vespasian put his son Titus in charge of the Roman troops in Judea. In A.D. 70, Titus put down the rebellion, burning the second Temple and taking Jerusalem. Some Zealots fought on at Masada, a fortress overlooking the Dead Sea, but it was taken.

The Diaspora The destruction by the Romans of the second Temple and of Jerusalem in A.D. 70 hastened the movement of the Jews out of Judea. This movement of the Jews to other parts of the world, which had begun peacefully centuries earlier, is known as the **Diaspora** (dy•AS•puhr•uh), a Greek word meaning "scattered." The Romans sent many Jews to Rome as slaves. Some Jews remained in Jerusalem.

REVIEW What was the lasting effect of Jewish resistance to Roman rule? *the destruction of Jerusalem and the Temple; an increase in the movement of Jews out of Judea*

Judaism—An Ongoing Faith

3 ESSENTIAL QUESTION What happened to Jewish beliefs when the Jews were in exile? *They were maintained through study and careful observance of beliefs and laws in practice.*

Although the Jews were scattered throughout the Roman Empire, many stayed faithful to their religious beliefs. Despite their scattering, they continued to try to practice the biblical concepts of righteousness and justice.

The Hebrew Kingdoms • 345

Teach

Judaism—An Ongoing Faith

6.3.2, 6.3.5

Talk About It

- What did Jews do to maintain their identity as a people after the destruction of the Temple in A.D. 70? *(Spiritual leaders and teachers, called rabbis, read the Torah and Commentaries in synagogues, Jewish places of worship.)*

- How did Jews make sure their traditions would be passed on to their children? *(They created schools where children studied the Torah and learned the prayers of their faith.)*

- **Critical Thinking: Drawing Conclusions** Are the laws, rituals, and writings from this period still an important part of how Jews practice their religion? *(Possible answers: Yes, Jews still study the Torah, use the same religious objects, commemorate the events of this time, worship in synagogues, and have rabbis and Hebrew schools; no, there are different groups of Jews, not all of which follow the same rituals and some of which are more orthodox than others.)*

History from Visuals

Interpreting Maps
Ask students to read the map title and the map key.

- What major Jewish settlement was farthest from from Jerusalem? *(Colonia Agrippina)*

- How many major Jewish settlements are shown on the map? *(18)*

GEOGRAPHY SKILLBUILDER **ANSWER**
Most Jews traveled west and north.

INTERACTIVE
An interactive version of this map is available on the eEdition and Power Presentations CD-ROMs.

DIFFERENTIATING INSTRUCTION

Struggling Readers

Illustrate Text
Have small groups review the section "Judaism—An Ongoing Faith." Ask groups to identify three important ways the Jews maintained their identity in exile. Then, on a blank sheet of paper, each group should write the numerals 1, 2, and 3. Next to these numerals, have them write the ways in order of occurrence. Finally, have each group illustrate their three ways and make a presentation to the class.

Gifted and Talented Students

Create an FAQ
Have student pairs each take one event in Hebrew history (for example, Abraham's journey to Canaan, Egyptian captivity, Babylonian captivity, Exodus, building of first Temple) and research interesting details about the event. Have each pair write three questions and answers about the event. Then have all the pairs collect their questions and answers in a binder entitled "Frequently Asked Questions About Jewish History." Students can take turns using the FAQ to quiz one another.

❹ Assess & Reteach

Assess Have students work through the assessment in pairs, except for the activity.

 Formal Assessment
• Lesson Quiz, p. 175

Reteach On the board, create a chart for the lesson, with the headings "Syria," "Rome," "Diaspora," and "Final Exile." With the class, discuss information that should be included under each heading and write it on the chart. Have students copy the chart in their notebooks.

 In-Depth Resources: Unit 5
• Vocabulary Cards, p. 9
• Reteaching Activity, p. 17

 **Homework Helper**

Visit **ClassZone.com** for a lesson review, a flip-card activity, and links to related Web sites.

Teachers and the Law After the Romans destroyed the second Temple, many Jews worried that they would lose their identity as a people. Religious leaders and teachers called **rabbis** tried to make sure this did not happen. Wherever Jews settled, they built places for prayer and worship called **synagogues**. At the synagogue, the people gathered to hear the rabbis read the Torah and interpretations, or Commentaries, on the Torah.

The Jews also held onto their faith by carefully following the laws and observing the customs of their religion. They created schools where Jewish children studied the Torah and learned the prayers of their faith.

through rabbis, synagogues, study of the Torah, following Jewish laws and customs

REVIEW How did Jews keep their culture alive?

Lesson Summary
• The Jews overthrew their Syrian rulers.
• The Romans harshly put down a Jewish revolt.
• The Jews held onto their faith.

Why It Matters Now . . .
The laws, rituals, and writings from this period are an important part of how Jews practice their religion today.

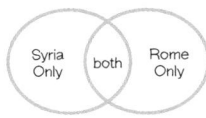
▲ **Torah** A rabbi and teenager read from the Torah.

3 Lesson Review

 **Homework Helper**
ClassZone.com

Terms & Names

1. Explain the importance of
   Diaspora   rabbi   synagogue

Using Your Notes

Comparing and Contrasting Use your completed Venn diagram to answer the following question:

2. How were the Syrians and Romans alike and different in the way they dealt with Jewish rebellion? (6.3.5)

Syria Only   both   Rome Only

Main Ideas

3. What was the goal of the revolt led by Judah Maccabeus and his brothers against the Syrians? (6.7.5)

4. How did the Romans punish the Jews of Judea for resisting Roman rule? (6.3.5)

5. What are three ways Jews kept their faith strong after the Diaspora? (6.3.5)

Critical Thinking

6. **Making Inferences** How did study keep the faith of the Jews alive? (6.3.2)

7. **Drawing Conclusions** Why did the Diaspora change the way that the Jews practiced their religion? (6.3.5)

Activity **Internet Activity** Use the Internet to research one of the people in this lesson, such as Judah Maccabeus or Yohanan ben Zaccai. Then make a sketch for the leader's Web page. (6.3.3)
INTERNET KEYWORDS Judah Maccabeus, Yohanan ben Zaccai

---

3 Lesson Review Answers

Terms & Names

1. • Diaspora, p. 345
   • rabbi, p. 346
   • synagogue, p. 346

Using Your Notes

See page 342 for an example of a completed diagram.

2. Possible answers: At first Syria was tolerant of Jewish beliefs but later it became intolerant and outlawed the Jewish religion. Rome appointed Jewish kings and leaders but burned the Temple and forced Jews out of Judea, sending many to Rome as slaves. Both countries imposed their beliefs on Jews, tried to change Jewish beliefs, and used force to put down Jewish rebellions.

Main Ideas

3. They wanted to drive the Syrians from Judah.
4. They destroyed the Temple and forced many to leave Judea.
5. They studied the Torah, listened to and studied with rabbis, and built and worshiped in synagogues.

Critical Thinking

6. Rabbis and other teachers taught the Torah and the Commentaries, or interpretations of the Torah. Schools were created to teach and pass on Jewish laws and traditions.

7. After the destruction of the second Temple and their exile from Jerusalem, the Jews did not have a central place of worship or priests to lead the services and ceremonies.

Activity Rubric

	Content of Representation	Quality of Sketch
4	good details present	demonstrates grade-level artistic skill, neatly drawn
3	most details present	drawn reasonably neatly
2	some details missing	drawn somewhat sloppily
1	no details	sloppy

Design a Fortress

Goal: To understand the history of the Hebrew kingdoms by designing a fortress such as the one at Masada

Materials & Supplies
- blank drawing paper
- pen, marker or colored pencils

Optional: book on forts and castles

Prepare

1. Research fortresses, including Masada.
2. You will need blank paper and a marker, a pen, or colored pencils.

Do the Activity

1. Draw a blueprint for a fortress from overhead, showing the location of all of the important features of the fort.
2. Draw the fortress from a different angle. For example, you might draw it as it would appear to those outside of it.
3. Call out various elements of your drawing and illustrate them in greater detail. For example, you might draw a close-up of watchtowers or a drawbridge.
4. Label the elements in your drawing, such as moats, drawbridges, walls, and so forth.

Follow-Up

1. How does a fortress represent self-defense rather than aggression?
2. What supplies might you need inside a fortress to withstand a long siege?

Extension

Making a Presentation Each person should show his or her drawing to the rest of the class and explain why a fortress might be important for survival. Drawings might be displayed on a wall in the classroom.

CALIFORNIA STANDARDS
6.3.5 Discuss how Judaism survived and developed despite the continuing dispersion of much of the Jewish population from Jerusalem and the rest of Israel after the destruction of the second Temple in A.D. 70.

347

ACTIVITY: DESIGN A FORTRESS

Objectives

- Understand the types of materials used for and the appearance of fortresses in the Hebrew kingdoms.
- Create a fortress, using information collected from secondary sources.

Suggestions for Completing the Activity

- Invite students to use library resources and the Internet to learn more about fortresses like Masada and ways in which the natural environment was used for defense.
- Tell students that encyclopedias might be a good source of information about the construction of fortresses.
- Remind students to follow each step of the activity, including the blueprint, the sketch from a different angle, the close-up sketches, and the labels.

ACTIVITY ANSWERS

Follow-Up Answers

1. A fortress is a place for people to seek refuge from attackers; by definition, it is a place to defend against an assault.
2. food, water, weapons

Extension Rubric

	Content of Drawing	Explanation of Concepts	Appearance of Drawing
4	very detailed	thorough	attractive and neat
3	many details	adequate	neat
2	few details	vague	somewhat neat
1	no details	unclear	sloppy

Terms & Names

1. Abraham traveled to Canaan, where he could practice monotheism.

2. Moses led the Israelites out of Egypt, and this journey is called the Exodus.

3. David and Solomon were both great Hebrew kings.

4. A rabbi is a spiritual leader and teacher who performs his duties in a synagogue, or Jewish house of worship.

Main Ideas

The Origins of the Hebrews
(pages 324–333)

5. The Hebrews believed in one God and believed they had a covenant with him.

6. Moses received the Ten Commandments, the basis of Hebrew law.

7. The judges acted as military leaders, gave advice on legal matters, and settled disputes.

Kingdoms and Captivity
(pages 334–341)

8. Solomon's projects helped establish a powerful nation, with Jerusalem as the center of religious life. However, his levying of taxes and forced labor to build these projects caused the kingdom to split into two.

9. The kingdom of Israel ended.

10. They struggled to maintain their identity and hoped for a Messiah to deliver them. They also relied on prophets, who gave advice, enforced the laws, and comforted the people.

Rome and Judea
(pages 342–347)

11. The Jews gained temporary independence but lost it to the Romans in less than a century.

12. The Zealots led the fight against the Romans.

13. The Romans conquered Jerusalem and destroyed the second Temple.

Chapter **10** Review

▶ VISUAL SUMMARY

> **The Hebrew Kingdoms**

Belief Systems (6.3.2)
- The Hebrews worshiped one God.
- The beliefs of the Hebrews helped them survive difficult times.
- After being expelled from their homeland, most Jews remained loyal to their beliefs.

Geography (6.3.4)
- Abraham left Mesopotamia to settle in Canaan.
- Hebrew slaves left Egypt and returned to Canaan.
- Hebrew captives left Babylon and returned to the kingdom of Judah.

Government (6.3.5)
- The Hebrews built a small but influential nation, Israel, that later divided into the kingdoms of Israel and Judah.
- The Jews fought against foreign control by the Assyrians, Babylonians, and Romans.
- Jewish resistance to Roman rule hastened their departure from their homeland.

▶ TERMS & NAMES

Explain why the words in each set below are linked with each other.

1. **Abraham** and **monotheism**
2. **Moses** and **Exodus**
3. **David** and **Solomon**
4. **rabbi** and **synagogue**

▶ MAIN IDEAS

The Origins of the Hebrews (pages 324–333)

5. What made the religion of the Hebrews different from the religions of other groups in the ancient world? (6.3.1, 6.3.2)

6. Why might the Hebrew leader Moses be known as "The Lawgiver"? (6.3.3)

7. What are three ways the judges helped the Hebrews? (6.3.2)

Kingdoms and Captivity (pages 334–341)

8. How did Solomon's building projects help and hurt Israel? (HI 1)

9. What happened to the Israelites after Israel was conquered by the Assyrians? (6.3.4)

10. How did the Babylonian conquest change the way the people of Judah lived? (6.3.4)

Rome and Judea (pages 342–347)

11. How did the Maccabee victory affect the government of Judah? (HI 1)

12. Which group of Jews led the fight to resist Roman rule? (6.3.5)

13. How did the Romans punish the people of Judea for rebelling? (6.3.5)

▶ CRITICAL THINKING
Big Ideas: Belief Systems

14. **MAKING INFERENCES** How did the Ten Commandments reflect Jewish beliefs? (6.3.2)

15. **DRAWING CONCLUSIONS** What important Jewish belief was passed on to other religions? (6.3.2)

16. **UNDERSTANDING CONTINUITY AND CHANGE** What beliefs and practices helped Jews pass on their religion? (6.3.2)

ALTERNATIVE ASSESSMENT RUBRICS

1. Writing Rubric

	Level of Persuasiveness	Number of Errors
4	very persuasive, mentions all qualities and details	zero or one grammatical or spelling error
3	persuasive	two or three errors
2	somewhat persuasive	four or five errors
1	not persuasive, no details	more than five errors

2. Science Rubric

	Poster Elements	Effectiveness of Design
4	demonstrates thorough research	neat, organized, attractive
3	demonstrates mostly complete research	neat and organized
2	demonstrates some research	somewhat organized
1	demonstrates little research	not organized

ALTERNATIVE ASSESSMENT

1. **WRITING ACTIVITY** Choose one of the kings discussed in this chapter. Write a persuasive paragraph telling whether you think the person was a good king. Be sure to use information from the chapter to support your opinion. (Writing 2.5)

2. **INTERDISCIPLINARY ACTIVITY—SCIENCE** According to tradition, the Hebrews wandered 40 years in the Sinai desert before entering Canaan. Use books or the Internet to research the climate, plants and animals, and the soil of the desert. Choose a plant or animal that lives in the desert. Make a poster showing how that animal or plant has adapted to life in the desert. (6.3.4)

3. **STARTING WITH A STORY** Review the letter you wrote to your great-grandson. Draw a picture of some aspect of life in Moab or Israel to include with your letter. (6.3.3)

Technology Activity

4. **MAKING A MULTIMEDIA PRESENTATION** Use the Internet or the library to find out more about Judah and the Maccabees. Working in a group, create a multimedia presentation. (HI 1)

- Who were the Maccabees?
- How were the Maccabees able to defeat a larger, better-equipped enemy?
- How do Jews today commemorate the Maccabee victory?

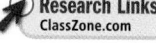
Research Links ClassZone.com

Interpreting Primary Sources The Ark of the Covenant was important to the Hebrews. It was said to contain the original tablets with the Ten Commandments given by God to Moses on Mount Sinai. Use the following description of the Ark from the Torah to answer the questions. (6.3.2)

Primary Source

Bezalel [a craftsman] made the ark of acacia wood—two and a half cubits long [about 50 inches], a cubit and a half wide, and a cubit and a half high. He overlaid it with pure gold, both inside and out, and made a gold molding around it. He cast four gold rings for it and fastened them to its four feet, with two rings on one side and two rings on the other. Then he made poles of acacia wood and overlaid them with gold. And he inserted the poles into the rings on the sides of the ark to carry it. He made the . . . cover of pure gold—two and a half cubits long and a cubit and a half wide. Then he made two cherubim [angels] out of hammered gold at the ends of the cover.

Exodus 37:1–7

1. What precious metal is used in building the Ark?
   A. silver
   B. gold
   C. platinum
   D. copper

2. Why might the Hebrews have used precious metal?
   A. long lasting
   B. tarnish resistant
   C. rust proof
   D. worthy of God

Test Practice ClassZone.com

Additional Test Practice, pp. S1–S33

The Hebrew Kingdoms • 349

Critical Thinking

Big Ideas: Belief Systems

14. The Ten Commandments outlined a belief in one God and laid the foundation of how the Jews ought to worship and live in accordance with God's laws.

15. The idea of belief in one God—monotheism—was passed on to other religions.

16. Jewish beliefs were passed on by establishing synagogues where rabbis taught the Torah and schools where children were taught religious practices and prayers.

Standards-Based Assessment

1. The correct answer is B.

2. The correct answer is D. The Jews used a metal that was precious and therefore worthy of God.

Research Links
Visit **ClassZone.com** for links to Web sites that can be used in the multimedia presentation.

Test Practice
Visit **ClassZone.com** to access strategies and tutorials for taking standardized tests.

Formal Assessment
- Chapter Tests, Forms A, B, and C, pp. 176–187

Test Generator
- Chapter Tests, Forms A, B, and C (English and Spanish)

ALTERNATIVE ASSESSMENT RUBRICS

3. Starting with a Story Rubric

	Quality of Illustration	Level of Creativity
4	detailed, accurate	very creative
3	accurate	creative
2	somewhat accurate	somewhat creative
1	not accurate	not creative

4. Technology Rubric

	Organization of Text	Variety of Graphics
4	well organized, includes all three information points	has variety in links, maps, and graphics; easy to follow
3	adequately organized, includes at least two information points	has variety in links, maps, and graphics; fairly clear
2	vague, includes one point	has little variety in links, maps, and graphics; hard to follow
1	incorrect or missing	has little or no variety in links, maps, and graphics; sloppy design

Many factors, including geography, culture, beliefs, and trade, helped develop ancient Greek civilization.

 In-Depth Resources: Unit 5
- Family Newsletter (English and Spanish), pp. 18–19
- Visual Summary, p. 24
- Vocabulary Study Guide, p. 26

 Character Education

Reading Study Guide, p. 103

 Bringing Social Studies Alive, Chapter 11

 Document-Based Questions: Strategy and Practice

 Reading Toolkit, L36–L39

 Modified Lesson Plans for English Learners, pp. 75–82

 Chapter Review, pp. 386–387

Formal Assessment
- Chapter Tests, Forms A, B, and C, pp. 192–206

Test Generator

Integrated Assessment Book

Online Test Practice

LESSON 1

The Geography of Ancient Greece

pp. 354–359

OBJECTIVE Analyze the geography of Greece and the early days of Greek civilization.

 In-Depth Resources: Unit 5
- Reading Skill: Understanding Effect, p. 20
- Vocabulary Cards, p. 27
- Geography Practice: Mycenaean Civilization, about 1300 B.C., p. 29
- Skillbuilder Practice: Evaluating Information, p. 25
- Reteaching Activity, p. 33

 **Interdisciplinary Projects**
- Science, p. 62

 Reading Study Guide, p. 95

 Lesson Review, p. 359

 Formal Assessment
- Lesson Quiz, p. 188

 California Daily Standards Practice Transparencies, TT36

LESSON 2

Beliefs and Customs

pp. 360–369

OBJECTIVE Explore Greek gods and myths, and early Greek literature.

 In-Depth Resources: Unit 5
- Reading Skill: Making Generalizations, p. 21
- Vocabulary Cards, p. 27
- Literature: *The Odyssey*, by Homer, p. 32
- Reteaching Activity, p. 34

 History Makers
- Homer, p. 21

 **Interdisciplinary Projects**
- Language Arts, p. 63; Physical Education, p. 64

Reading Study Guide, p. 97

 Lesson Review, p. 365

 Formal Assessment
- Lesson Quiz, p. 189

California Daily Standards Practice Transparencies, TT37

LESSON 3

The City-State and Democracy

pp. 370–377

OBJECTIVE Study the history of Greek government.

 In-Depth Resources: Unit 5
- Reading Skill: Categorizing, p. 22
- Vocabulary Cards, p. 27
- Primary Source: Poem, by Solon, p. 31
- Reteaching Activity, p. 35

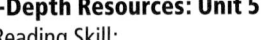 **Reading Study Guide,** p. 99

 Lesson Review, p. 376

Formal Assessment
- Lesson Quiz, p. 190

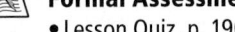 **California Daily Standards Practice Transparencies,** TT38

LESSON 4

Sparta and Athens

pp. 378–385

OBJECTIVE Compare and contrast the city-states of Athens and Sparta, including how they were affected by the Persian Wars.

 In-Depth Resources: Unit 5
- Reading Skill: Comparing and Contrasting, p. 23
- Vocabulary Cards, p. 27
- Reteaching Activity, p. 36

 Interdisciplinary Projects
- Math, p. 61

 Reading Study Guide, p. 101

 Lesson Review, p. 383

 Formal Assessment
- Lesson Quiz, p. 191

 California Daily Standards Practice Transparencies, TT39

eEdition Plus Online

EasyPlanner Plus Online

eTest Plus Online

 **Audio CDs**
- Reading Study Guide
- Reading Study Guide in Spanish
- The World's Music

 CD-ROMs
- Power Presentations
- eEdition
- EasyPlanner
- Test Generator

 Ancient Civilizations Video Series
- Ancient Greece

---

 eEdition CD-ROM

 Map Transparencies
- MT21 Greece Today

 Critical Thinking Transparencies
- CT46 Understanding Effect

 ClassZone.com

---

 eEdition CD-ROM

 Humanities Transparencies
- HT21 Head of Zeus

 Map Transparencies
- MT22 Ancient Olympia

 Critical Thinking Transparencies
- CT47 Making Generalizations

 ClassZone.com

---

 eEdition CD-ROM

 Critical Thinking Transparencies
- CT48 Categorizing

 ClassZone.com

---

 eEdition CD-ROM

 Humanities Transparencies
- HT22 Woman at an Altar

 Critical Thinking Transparencies
- CT49 Comparing and Contrasting
- CT50 Chapter 11 Visual Summary

 ClassZone.com

Overview of California Resources

	Lesson 1	Lesson 2	Lesson 3	Lesson 4
California Reading Toolkit	L36	L37	L38	L39
California Modified Lesson Plans for English Learners	p. 75	p. 77	p. 79	p. 81
California Daily Standards Practice Transparencies	TT36	TT37	TT38	TT39
California Standards Enrichment Workbook	pp. 49–50	pp. 55–56	pp. 49–54	pp. 53–54, 59–60
California Standards Planner and Lesson Plans	L71	L73	L75	L77
California Online Test Practice	ClassZone.com	ClassZone.com	ClassZone.com	ClassZone.com
California Test Generator CD-ROM				
California EasyPlanner CD-ROM				
California eEdition CD-ROM				

Chart Key

PE Pupil Edition	CD-ROM	Internet
Copymaster	Audio	Overhead Transparency
	Video	

English Learners

In-Depth Resources in Spanish
- Reading Skill and Strategy Ⓐ
- Skillbuilder Practice
- Geography Practice Ⓒ
- Vocabulary Study Guide Ⓑ

In-Depth Resources: Unit 5
- Family Newsletter (English and Spanish)

Reading Study Guide (Spanish)

Reading Study Guide Audio CD
(Spanish)

Test Generator
Chapter Test (Spanish)

Plus

Modified Lesson Plans for English Learners

Multi-Language Glossary of Social Studies Terms

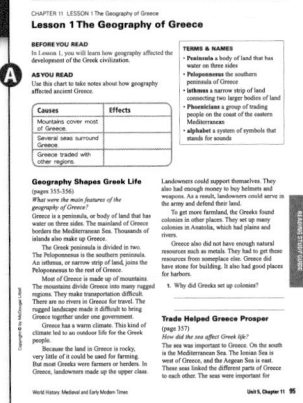
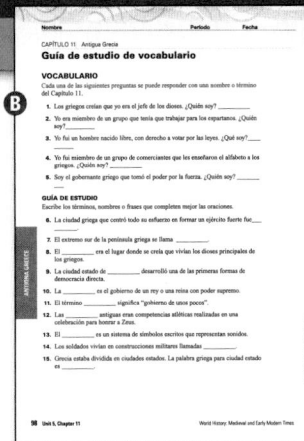

Struggling Readers

In-Depth Resources: Unit 5
- Vocabulary Study Guide
- Skillbuilder Practice Ⓑ
- Geography Practice
- Reteaching Activities
- Family Newsletter Ⓒ

Reading Study Guide Ⓐ

Reading Study Guide Audio CD

Reading Toolkit

Formal Assessment
Chapter Test, Form A

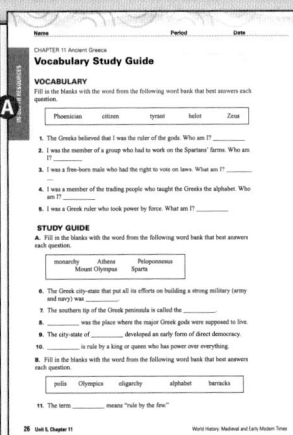
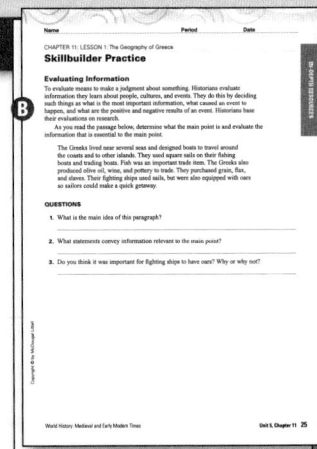

Inclusion

EasyPlanner CD-ROM
- Reading Skill and Strategy
- Vocabulary Study Guide Ⓐ
- Geography Practice Ⓑ
- Reteaching Activities Ⓒ

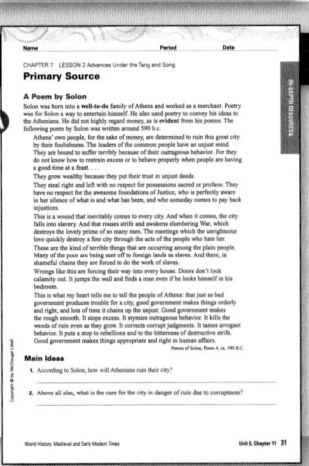
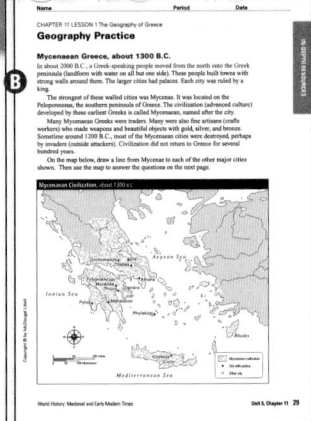

Gifted and Talented Students

In-Depth Resources: Unit 5
- Primary Source Ⓐ
- Literature

History Makers Ⓑ

Interdisciplinary Projects Ⓒ

Formal Assessment
Chapter Test, Form C

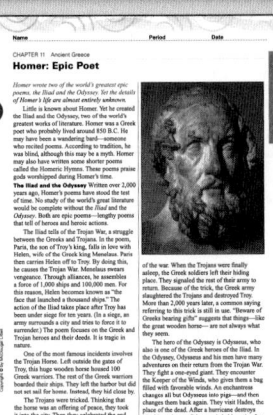

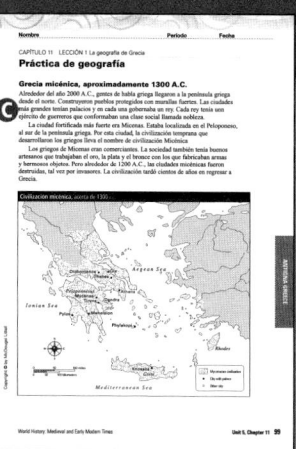

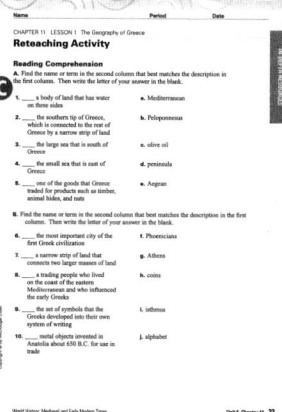

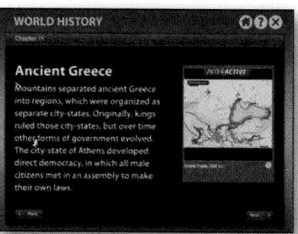

Begin the Chapter

Objective

Explain how the geography, trade, beliefs, and culture of ancient Greece influenced the development of its government.

Quick Look

Lesson 1 describes how the mountains of Greece led to sea travel and trade, which brought new learning to the Greeks.

Lesson 2 explains the relationship between Greek mythology and religion, how Greeks honored their gods, and important early Greek literature.

Lesson 3 traces the development of Greek government from monarchy, aristocracy, and oligarchy to a limited democracy.

Lesson 4 compares and contrasts Athenian government and society with Spartan government and society and describes the roles of Athens and Sparta in the Persian Wars.

Before You Read: Predicting

Predicting helps students prepare to read by asking them to think about what they already know about the chapter ideas. Have students follow these steps:

- Read the chapter and lesson titles.
- Write three questions you think will be answered in the chapter.
- As you read the lesson, look for answers to your questions, and jot down information as it comes up.
- After you have finished the lesson, make sure you have answered each question fully. Review the lesson if you need more information.
- At the end of the chapter, think about what you have learned about ancient Greece.

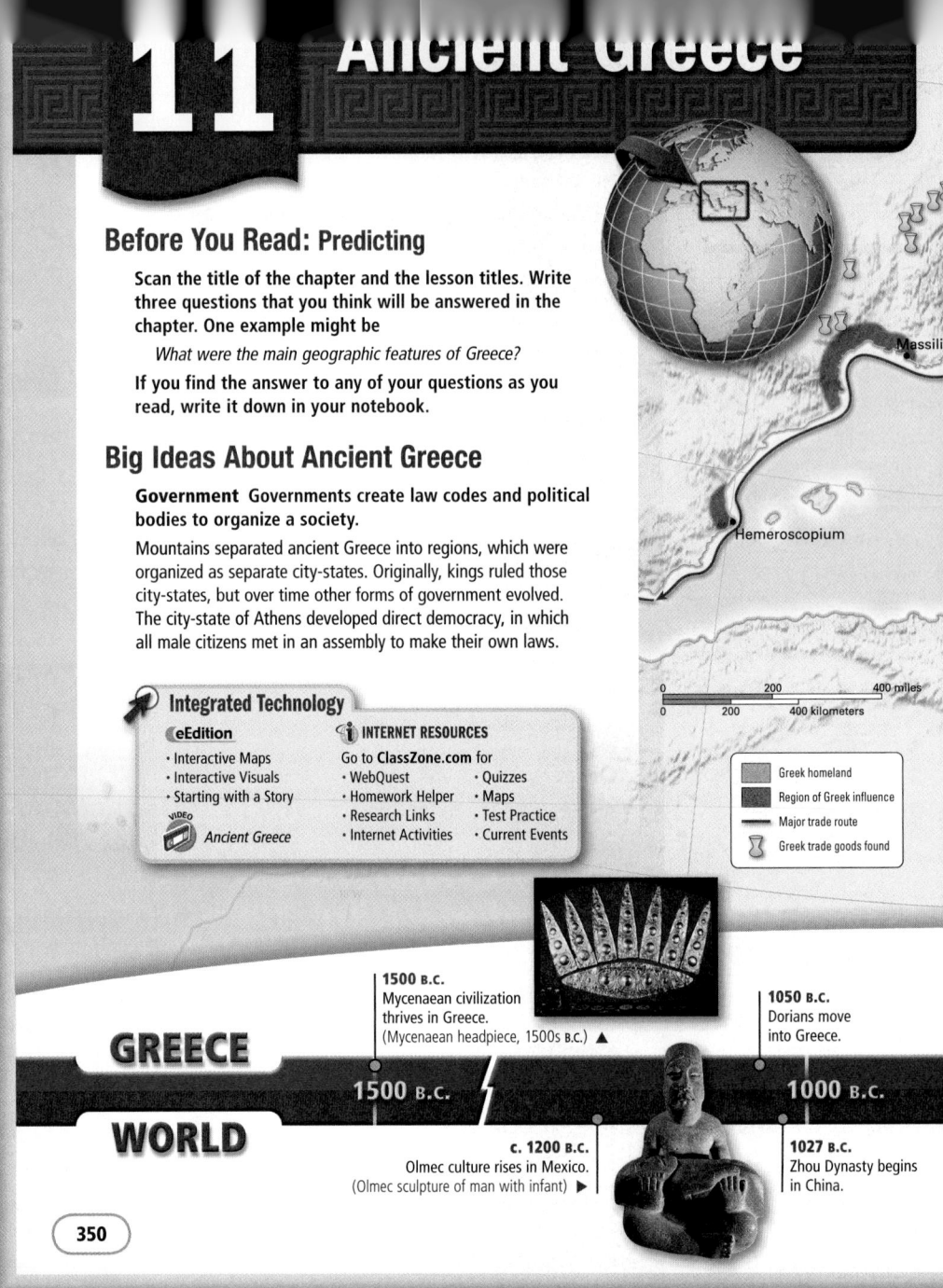

11 Ancient Greece

Before You Read: Predicting

Scan the title of the chapter and the lesson titles. Write three questions that you think will be answered in the chapter. One example might be

What were the main geographic features of Greece?

If you find the answer to any of your questions as you read, write it down in your notebook.

Big Ideas About Ancient Greece

Government Governments create law codes and political bodies to organize a society.

Mountains separated ancient Greece into regions, which were organized as separate city-states. Originally, kings ruled those city-states, but over time other forms of government evolved. The city-state of Athens developed direct democracy, in which all male citizens met in an assembly to make their own laws.

Integrated Technology

eEdition
- Interactive Maps
- Interactive Visuals
- Starting with a Story

Ancient Greece

INTERNET RESOURCES
Go to **ClassZone.com** for
- WebQuest
- Homework Helper
- Research Links
- Internet Activities
- Quizzes
- Maps
- Test Practice
- Current Events

Massilia

Hemeroscopium

0 — 200 — 400 miles
0 — 200 — 400 kilometers

- Greek homeland
- Region of Greek influence
- Major trade route
- Greek trade goods found

GREECE

1500 B.C.
Mycenaean civilization thrives in Greece. (Mycenaean headpiece, 1500s B.C.) ▲

1050 B.C.
Dorians move into Greece.

1500 B.C. — 1000 B.C.

WORLD

c. 1200 B.C.
Olmec culture rises in Mexico. (Olmec sculpture of man with infant) ▶

1027 B.C.
Zhou Dynasty begins in China.

350

TIME LINE DISCUSSION

Remind students to read the time line from left to right. Ask them what parts of the world are mentioned in the bottom half of the time line. Have a volunteer point them out on a world map.

- How long a period does the time line cover? *(about 1,100 years)*
- What is the earliest event listed on the time line? *(Mycenaean civilization thrives in Greece)*

- According to the time line, which came first: Olmec culture rises in Mexico or the Greeks use an alphabet? *(Olmec culture rises in Mexico)*
- What two events took place within about 73 years of each other? When did they take place? *(Buddha is born in about 563 B.C. and Athenians win the Battle of Marathon in 490 B.C.)*

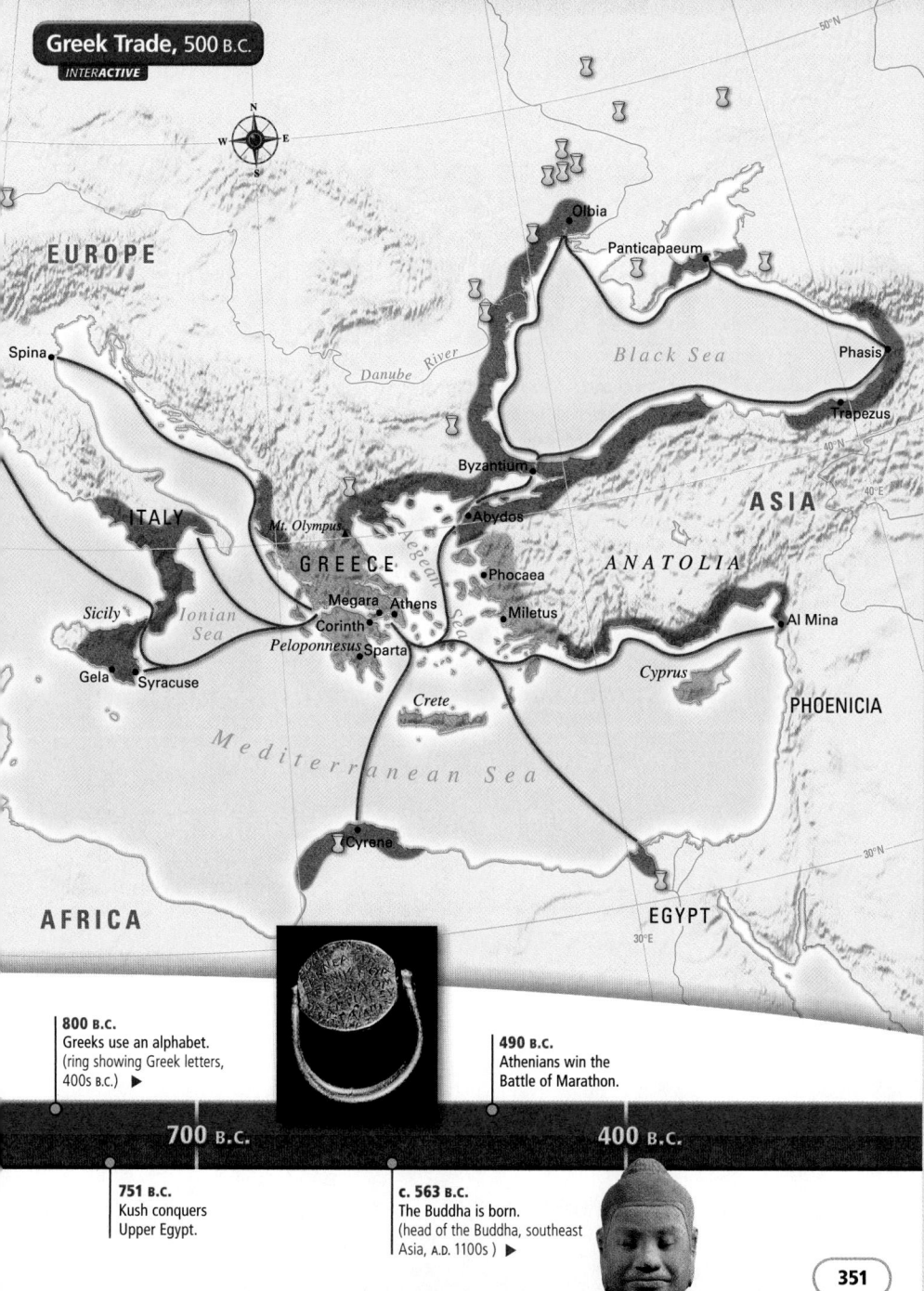

Greek Trade, 500 B.C.
INTERACTIVE

EUROPE

Spina

Olbia

Panticapaeum

Danube River

Black Sea

Phasis

Trapezus

Byzantium

ITALY

Mt. Olympus

Abydos

GREECE

ASIA

Phocaea

ANATOLIA

Sicily

Ionian Sea

Megara Athens

Corinth

Miletus

Peloponnesus Sparta

Al Mina

Gela Syracuse

Crete

Cyprus

PHOENICIA

Mediterranean Sea

Cyrene

AFRICA

EGYPT

800 B.C.
Greeks use an alphabet.
(ring showing Greek letters,
400s B.C.) ▶

490 B.C.
Athenians win the
Battle of Marathon.

700 B.C.

400 B.C.

751 B.C.
Kush conquers
Upper Egypt.

c. 563 B.C.
The Buddha is born.
(head of the Buddha, southeast
Asia, A.D. 1100s) ▶

351

RECOMMENDED RESOURCES

Books for the Teacher
Pomeroy, Sarah. *Ancient Greece: A Political, Social, and Cultural History.* New York: Oxford University Press, 1999. Traces Greek civilization to 146 B.C.

Sacks, David. *Encyclopedia of the Ancient Greek World.* New York: Facts on File, 1995. Examines Greek culture and civilization in a logical, readable format.

Videos
The Real Olympics. 120 minutes. Alexandria: PBS Home Video, 2004. Explores the original games and events. VHS, DVD.

The Spartans. 180 minutes. Alexandria: PBS Home Video, 2003. Traces the rise and fall of ancient Sparta and its influence on later Western culture. Includes key battles and individuals. VHS, DVD.

Internet
To access these sites, visit the Research Links for this chapter at **ClassZone.com**.

PBS.org has various projects: Daily Athenian: Greek Newspaper Project; Interview a Famous Greek; and Two Faces of Greece: Athens and Sparta.

The Museum at UPenn. This museum has a useful Web site about the ancient Greek world.

Introduce the Big Ideas
Read aloud the text about the Big Ideas. Have students think about what laws and political bodies exist in their school in order to organize and run it smoothly.

Here are some other Big Ideas that you can emphasize in this chapter:

Geography
The mountains of Greece affected its agriculture, and the seas allowed the Greeks to develop a vast trade network.

Belief Systems
The Greeks told myths to support their beliefs about values and the world.

Talk About It
Interpreting Maps
Review the symbol key with students. Have students take one symbol, find it on the map, and make a summary sentence describing it. *(Possible answer: Major trade routes—Most Greek trade routes traveled west, south, and east.)* Then ask: What was the farthest trade city from Athens that is shown on the map? *(Hemeroscopium)*

INTERACTIVE

An interactive version of this map is available on the eEdition and Power Presentations CD-ROMs.

Find Out More
Have students use the Internet to find out what goods the Greeks traded in 500 B.C.

Watch the Video
Ancient Greece invites students to explore the history and culture of ancient Greece. This 23-minute video is part of the Ancient Civilizations for Children Video Series.

The World's Music
Introduce your students to Greek music by playing track 8 of *The World's Music* audio CD. "You Birds of the Valley" is an example of folk music from Roumeli, a region in central Greece.

Objective

Analyze how personal differences sometimes need to be ignored in order to work for a greater good.

Introducing the Story

Darius and the Persians

The Persian Empire under Darius consisted of western Asia and Egypt. The Greeks established a few city-states on the coast of Anatolia in western Asia. These city-states resisted Darius's rule. They were conquered by Darius in 494 B.C.

Athens had helped these city-states, so Darius wanted to punish Athens and add more territory to his empire. Darius tried twice to conquer Athens. At the time this story takes place, Darius and his army are camped on the Marathon plain, twenty miles from Athens.

Vocabulary Preview

city-state a form of government with an independent city and its surrounding territory

rival a competitor, an opponent

plead to beg

Reading the Story Aloud

1. **The teacher as reader:** Track similarities and differences between Athens and Sparta on a chart on the board. Read a paragraph of the passage. Then ask students what information to write under *Athens* or *Sparta.* To conclude, ask them to summarize reasons why Sparta should or should not join with Athens against Persia.

2. **The students as readers:** Select three groups of students to be Athenians, Spartans, and Persians. As a student reads a paragraph of the passage, have the appropriate group pantomime the actions.

 **Starting with a Story**

Students can also follow along as they listen to the story on the eEdition or Power Presentations CD-ROMs.

THE PERSIAN INVASION

CALIFORNIA STANDARDS
Reading 2.2 Analyze text that uses the compare-and-contrast organizational pattern.

Background: Ancient Greece was not a unified country. It was made up of independent city-states (states made of a city and its surrounding lands). Two of the leading city-states were Athens and Sparta. In 490 B.C., the mighty Persian Empire dominated Southwest Asia. The Persian king Darius decided to conquer Greece.

Darius and his army have just landed near Athens. Imagine that you are hearing the news in your home state of Sparta. Athens is 150 miles away. You wonder whether this fight has anything to do with you.

Sculpture of a Spartan warrior, possibly a king ▶

352

ADDITIONAL RESOURCES

Books for the Student

Honan, Linda. ***Spend the Day in Ancient Greece.*** Hoboken: Wiley, 1998. Describes a typical day in the life of an ancient Greek family.

MacDonald, Fiona. ***Curious Kids Guide: Ancient Greece.*** New York: Kingfisher, 2002. Answers questions about ancient Greece such as why the Olympics were started.

Videos

Athens and Ancient Greece. 60 minutes. Chicago: Questar, Inc., 1994. Computer graphics re-create the vivid colors used on Greek buildings and discusses myths versus historical fact about ancient Greece. VHS.

The Greeks: Crucible of Civilization. 150 minutes. Alexandria: PBS Video. Atlantic Productions Ltd., 2000. Discusses Greek history through the eyes and words of famous Greeks. VHS, DVD.

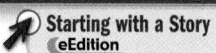
Yｏｕ are a soldier in Sparta. All of the free men in Sparta are soldiers. Your father and grandfather were soldiers. All of the men in your family for more than 150 years have been soldiers.

Sparta's army is its great strength and the source of its pride. From the time you were a boy, you trained to be a soldier. You learned to be tough. You and your friends played at war, preparing for the real thing.

Athens is Sparta's main rival. Its way of life is different. Men there spend most of their time talking about politics. Boys in Athens study debate, music, and poetry. You wonder what kind of people would waste their time on such things.

An Athenian messenger has just arrived to tell the Spartan rulers that the Persian army has landed near Athens. He ran for two days to bring the news. He pleads with the rulers, "The enemy's force is enormous. There are 600 ships and more than 15,000 soldiers, many of them with horses. We have only about 10,000 soldiers. Athens desperately needs the help of your powerful army. Will you not join us in this fight?"

You've heard about the Persian Empire. Their rulers have been conquering their neighbors for more than 100 years. Their lands stretch from the Mediterranean Sea to the border of India. Persians now rule over Egypt.

Such a powerful empire might eliminate your rival for you. Then Sparta would be the greatest city-state in Greece. Why should Spartans die for men who would rather be politicians than warriors? Then a horrible thought occurs to you. What if the Persians don't stop with Athens? What if they decide to come after Sparta next?

Do you help your rival against a greater enemy?

Reading & Writing

1. **READING: Compare and Contrast** How were Athens and Sparta similar and different? Compare and contrast them.

2. **WRITING: Persuasion** Suppose that the rulers of Sparta have asked your advice. Think about the reasons for and against helping Athens. Then write a letter to the ruler explaining what you think Sparta should do.

CALIFORNIA STANDARDS Writing 2.5
Write persuasive compositions.

353

Talk About It

Ask students the following questions to begin the discussion:

- What was Sparta's greatest strength? *(its army)*

- What was education like for an Athenian boy? *(Boys learned about debating, music, and poetry.)*

- Why does Athens need Sparta's help? *(The Persians' huge army has just landed near Athens.)*

- What reasons does Sparta have for NOT helping the Athenians? *(Athens is their rival; Sparta could become the most powerful city-state with Athens' demise.)*

Do you help your rival against a greater enemy?

Students may say that you should help because the enemy could come after you next. Other students may say that you have good enough soldiers to defeat any army.

Making Personal Connections

Connect the discussion to today by encouraging students to think of recent examples of people who sacrificed personal concerns for the greater good. *(Students may give examples of athletes, social reformers, and soldiers.)*

READING & WRITING ACTIVITIES

1. **READING** Possible answers: Similar: They were both independent Greek city-states; they were both in danger of being attacked by the Persians. Different: Athens placed importance on politics, education, and the arts; Sparta placed importance on military strength.

2. **WRITING** Students' letters should explain why Sparta should or should not help Athens.

2. Writing Rubric

	Organization of Exposition	Clarity of Content
4	well organized; letter parts creatively presented	states pros and cons clearly
3	organized; letter parts well presented	states pros and cons reasonably well
2	unorganized; letter parts missing	states pros and cons unclearly
1	incomplete, unclear	missing pros and cons, unexplained

❶ Plan & Prepare

Objectives

- Describe the effect of mountains on Greek life.
- Explain how the sea unified Greece and brought new ideas.
- Summarize the beginnings of Greek culture.
- **Language Objective:** Create a concept cluster using terms from the lesson that relate to the geography of Greece.

Quick Look

Lesson 1 describes geography and trade in ancient Greece and the beginnings and early development of Greek civilization.

❷ Focus & Motivate

Preview Tell students that this lesson explains how the geography of Greece affected life there. Ask students to describe the geography of their area and speculate about how it influences life there. *(Possible answers: farmland—food production; coastline—shipping)*

Introduce the Main Ideas The three main ideas relate to the Big Idea "The mountains of Greece affected its agriculture, and the seas allowed the Greeks to develop a vast trade network." Help students look for this Big Idea in the lesson.

Reading Skill: Understanding Effects Remind students that a single cause can have more than one effect.

SAMPLE ANSWERS FOR CHART

Causes	Effects
Mountains cover most of Greece.	transportation difficult; hard to unify area
Several seas surround Greece.	unified cities; fish; new ideas from others
Greece traded with other regions.	introduced alphabet, coins, and products

---

Lesson 1

▶ MAIN IDEAS

❶ Geography Rugged mountains divided Greece into many regions.

❷ Geography The sea linked the regions of Greece to each other and to foreign regions. Sea trade became common.

❸ Culture Trade helped the early Greeks develop a sophisticated culture.

▶ TAKING NOTES

Reading Skill: Understanding Effects

An effect is an event or action that is the result of a cause. Copy a chart like the one below on your own paper. As you read Lesson 1, look for the effects of the causes that are listed.

Causes	Effects
Mountains cover most of Greece.	
Several seas surround Greece.	
Greece traded with other regions.	

⬛ⓢ **Skillbuilder Handbook, page R26**

▲ **Pottery Plate** The sea was very important to the ancient Greeks. For one thing, it provided them with a variety of seafood, as shown on this plate.

CALIFORNIA STANDARDS

6.4.1 Discuss the connections between geography and the development of city-states in the region of the Aegean Sea, including patterns of trade and commerce among Greek city-states and within the wider Mediterranean region.

CST 3 Students use a variety of maps and documents to identify physical and cultural features of neighborhoods, cities, states, and countries and to explain the historical migration of people, expansion and disintegration of empires, and the growth of economic systems.

HI 2 Students understand and distinguish cause, effect, sequence, and correlation in historical events, including the long- and short-term causal relations.

HOW TO TEACH THE CALIFORNIA STANDARDS

Standard	Content	Student Question or Activity	Instruction
6.4.1	**Page 357** Describes the development of cities by the sea, the growth of shipbuilding, and Greek trade goods	**Page 357** Students explain how the sea helped Greek economy.	Have students look at the map in the Chapter Opener on pages 350–351. Ask them to describe all the peoples with which the Greeks could have traded.
CST 3	**Page 356** Explains the various land uses in Greece	**Page 356** Students use a map to figure out whether more land was used for growing grains and olives or for grazing animals.	Mention to students that much of Greece's land was not conducive for farming.
HI 2	**Page 358** Describes how Greek culture was revived through contact with the Phoenicians	**Page 359** Students explain how trade with other peoples helped Greek culture flourish again.	Discuss how writing is used in business and how money makes trade easier.

The Geography of Greece

TERMS & NAMES
peninsula
Peloponnesus
isthmus
Phoenician
alphabet

Terms & Names

peninsula land with water on three sides

Peloponnesus the peninsula that forms the southern part of Greece

isthmus a narrow strip of land

Phoenicians a people of Southwest Asia who began to trade around 1100 B.C.

alphabet a system of symbols

Build on What You Know Has construction or an accident ever blocked the road your family wanted to take? How did you get around the problem? Mountains prevented the ancient Greeks from traveling over land. This lesson will explain their other methods of travel.

Geography Shapes Ancient Greek Life

1 ESSENTIAL QUESTION What were the main features of the geography of Greece?

The mainland of Greece sticks out into the Mediterranean Sea. It is a **peninsula**, a body of land that has water on three sides. Greece also includes thousands of islands.

A gulf of water almost divides the Greek peninsula in two. The southern tip forms a second peninsula called the **Peloponnesus** (PEHL•uh•puh•NEE•suhs). A narrow strip of land called an **isthmus** (IHS•muhs) links the Peloponnesus to the rest of Greece. (See the map on page 351.)

Landscape and Climate
Mountains cover 70 to 80 percent of Greece. The mountains divided it into many regions. The uneven landscape made transportation over land difficult. Greece had no large rivers on which people could travel. The rugged landscape made it hard to unite Greece under a single government.

Greece has mild, rainy winters and hot, dry summers. In much of Greece, temperatures range from about 50°F in winter to 80°F in summer. The warm climate encouraged outdoor life. For example, outdoor athletic competitions such as races were an important part of Greek culture.

Greece is a peninsula with a long coastline. A gulf of water almost divides it in two, creating a second peninsula. Mountains cover 70 to 80 percent of Greece. There are no major rivers.

Coastline of Greece
Because of its long coastline, Greece has many ports. This port, Piraeus, is near the capital and ancient city of Athens. ▼

355

❸ Teach

Geography Shapes Ancient Greek Life
6.4.1

Talk About It

• **Critical Thinking: Drawing Conclusions** How did Greece's geography contribute to its need for trade? *(Greeks needed metals and products they could not grow.)*

California Resources

California Reading Toolkit, L36
California Modified Lesson Plans for English Learners, p. 75
California Daily Standards Practice Transparencies, TT36
California Standards Enrichment Workbook, pp. 49–50
California Online Test Practice
California Test Generator CD-ROM
California Standards Planner and Lesson Plans, L71
California EasyPlanner CD-ROM
California eEdition CD-ROM

LESSON 1 PROGRAM RESOURCES

ON LEVEL
In-Depth Resources: Unit 5
• Family Newsletter (English and Spanish), pp. 18–19
• Reading Skill: Understanding Effect, p. 20
• Skillbuilder Practice: Evaluating Information, p. 25
• Geography Practice: Mycenaean Civilization, p. 29

Formal Assessment
• Lesson Quiz, p. 188

ENGLISH LEARNERS
In-Depth Resources in Spanish
• Reading Skill, p. 91
• Skillbuilder Practice, p. 97
• Geography Practice, p. 99

Modified Lesson Plans for English Learners, p. 75

Reading Study Guide (Spanish), p. 95

Reading Study Guide Audio CD (Spanish)

STRUGGLING READERS
In-Depth Resources: Unit 5
• Reading Skill, p. 20

• Reteaching Activity, p. 33
Reading Toolkit, L36
Reading Study Guide, p. 95
Reading Study Guide Audio CD

GIFTED AND TALENTED STUDENTS
Interdisciplinary Projects
• Science, p. 62

INCLUSION
EasyPlanner CD-ROM
• Reading Skill: Understanding Cause and Effect
• Reteaching Activity

TECHNOLOGY
eEdition CD-ROM
• Starting with a Story

Power Presentations CD-ROM

Map Transparencies
• MT21 Greece Today

Critical Thinking Transparencies
• CT46 Understanding Effect

Test Generator CD-ROM

ClassZone.com

In-Depth Resources: Unit 5
- Reading Skill: Understanding Cause and Effect, p. 20
- Skillbuilder Practice: Evaluating Information, p. 25

History from Visuals

Interpreting Maps

Tell students to locate a peninsula, an isthmus, and the Peloponnesus on the map. Have them look at the symbol key and rank the land use in descending order with the top being "most land use" and the bottom being "least land use." Read the text aloud.

- Using the text and land use key, what color do you think indicates where mountains are located? *(orange, because animals grazed on rocky, infertile land, which could indicate mountains)*

GEOGRAPHY SKILLBUILDER ANSWER
grazing animals

More About . . .

Olives

In ancient times, olive oil was used to light lamps, to make food, and in ceremonies to bless people and Greek kings. It is made by pressing olives and separating the oil from the fruit. In recent years it has grown to be one of the most used oils because it is very healthy. It is easily digested and has no cholesterol. Many believe it can protect against heart disease.

In the first Olympic games, athletes were given an olive wreath because it was sacred to the ancient Greeks. Greek legend says that Poseidon, god of the sea, and Athena, goddess of wisdom, took part in a contest. Athena made an olive tree grow on the Acropolis. Poseidon caused rushing water to flow from the Acropolis. Athena became the protector of Athens and the Parthenon was erected as her temple. Greeks still consider the olive tree a gift from the gods.

 Map Transparencies
- MT21 Greece Today

Geography

Land Use in Greece

Mountains cover 70 to 80 percent of Greece. As a result, only about 20 to 30 percent of Greek land was good for farming. Even so, the ancient Greeks found ways to make the best use of the land that they had.

- They grew grain on the few open plains. Olive trees grew on the edges of those plains.
- The Greeks planted grapevines on the lower slopes of hills.
- Sheep and goats grazed on land that was too rocky or too infertile to grow crops.

> **GEOGRAPHY SKILLBUILDER**
> **INTERPRETING MAPS**
> **Region** Was more land used for growing grains and olives or for grazing animals?

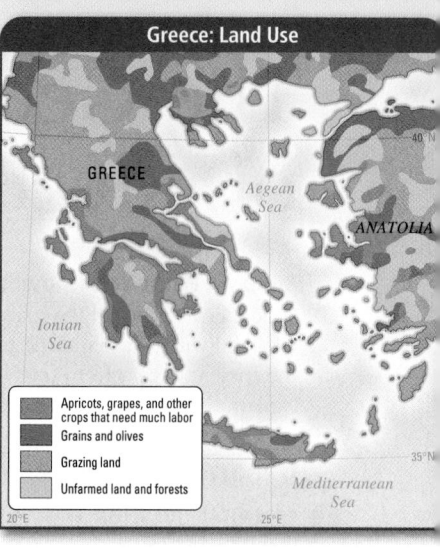

Greece: Land Use

GREECE
Aegean Sea
ANATOLIA
Ionian Sea
Mediterranean Sea

- Apricots, grapes, and other crops that need much labor
- Grains and olives
- Grazing land
- Unfarmed land and forests

Agriculture Greek land was rocky, so only about 20 to 30 percent of it was good for farming. Even so, more than half of all Greeks were farmers or herders. Most farmland was located in the valleys between mountains.

In Greek society, landowners were part of the upper class. In general, only men owned property. A person who owned land could support himself. He had enough wealth to pay for equipment such as helmets, shields, and swords. This allowed him to serve in the army and defend his homeland. As a result, people respected landowners, who had a higher place in society than merchants or poor people.

In order to get more farmland, the Greeks founded colonies in other regions. The western end of Anatolia had broad plains and rivers. The Greeks founded many colonies there.

Resources The lack of farmland was not the only problem. Greece also lacked natural resources such as precious metals. The Greeks had to find those resources somewhere else.

One resource that Greece did have was stone for building. Greece also had plenty of good sites for harbors.

REVIEW How did the mountains affect life in Greece?
They made travel difficult and hindered unification of the country; they limited the amount of land that was suitable for farming.

DIFFERENTIATING INSTRUCTION

English Learners

Create a Geography Word Web

Demonstrate how to locate words from the lesson that relate to the geography of ancient Greece. Explain that these terms or phrases may include location, place, region, and movement. For example, tell students that the word *sea* belongs in the geography word web because ancient Greeks used seas as water highways or roads for travel and trade. Have students work with a partner to create a word web. Then ask students to take turns explaining how their words relate to the geography of ancient Greece.

Struggling Readers

Focus on Vocabulary

Ask students to read through the lesson one section at a time and jot down any words they are unfamiliar with, such as the words *infertile* and *merchants* on this page. Explain what the word means. Then have small groups read through the section aloud with you. Ask each student to read one paragraph.

Trade Helps Greece Prosper

② **ESSENTIAL QUESTION** How did the sea affect Greek life?

Most places in Greece are less than 100 miles from the sea. Because overland travel was difficult, the Greeks used the seas as highways that linked the regions of Greece and also helped encourage trade. The sea also provided fish for the Greek diet.

Just as rivers influenced other ancient cultures, the sea influenced Greece. Greece has a long coastline, and most places in Greece are less than 100 miles from the coast. In fact, many cities were built directly on harbors.

Highways of Water Several seas played a major role in the life of ancient Greece. The largest was the Mediterranean Sea to the south. The Ionian and Aegean seas were branches of the Mediterranean. The Ionian Sea is west of Greece. The Aegean Sea is east of Greece.

These "highways of water" linked most parts of Greece to each other. The Greeks used the seas as transportation routes.

A Seafaring People The Greeks became skilled sailors and shipbuilders. They built rowing ships for fighting and sailing ships for trading. Some warships had two or three levels of oars on each side. Most sailing ships had a single mast and square sail.

The Ionian and Aegean seas are not very large. Small ships could sail around them by staying near the coast or by sailing from island to island. Once the Greeks learned these routes, they could sail to other regions.

The sea was a source of fish, an important part of the Greek diet. The Greeks traded fresh fish from the sea to local ports along the coast. The Greeks also dried some kinds of fish so that they could be transported over great distances.

Trade and Commerce Greece did not produce much grain, but some regions produced surplus olive oil, wine, wool, and fine pottery. Greek city-states bought and sold surplus goods from each other. In addition, Greeks traded these items to other regions around the Black Sea and the Mediterranean Sea, including Egypt and Italy.

The main products that the Greeks bought were grain, timber for building, animal hides, and slaves. The Greeks also traded for nuts, figs, cheese, and flax, which was used to make linen.

REVIEW How did the sea help the Greek economy?
The Greeks used the seas as trade routes to get materials they needed from other places. They also caught fish, which became a trade item.

▲ **Greek Ship** In recent times, people built this ship to show how ancient Greek fishing ships looked.

Ancient Greece • 357

Teach

Trade Helps Greece Prosper

✎ **6.4.1**

Talk About It

- How do we know that the sea was very important to Greek life? *(Greece has a long coastline; most places are less than 100 miles from the coast; many cities were built directly on harbors.)*

- The Greeks became skilled sailors and shipbuilders. How did this affect their way of life? *(They could use the sea for both war and trade.)*

- **Critical Thinking: Drawing Conclusions** How did the sea help the Greek economy? *(It connected one part of the country to the other; it gave them fish to eat and encouraged trade. Trade brought new ideas to the Greeks that helped develop their economy and culture.)*

History from Visuals

Interpreting Visuals
Have students reread the text about the description of Greek ships. Then have them point out the various details on the Greek ship in the illustration.

- Why do you think the Greeks would use rowing ships for fighting and sailing ships for trading? *(Rowing helps to give control and maneuverability to a ship and allows warriors to attack without interference; Sailing moves a ship at a faster speed to travel long distances to trade and does not tire the rowers.)*

INTERDISCIPLINARY ACTIVITIES

Art

Illustrate a Greek ship
Have students look for information and pictures on the Internet about the design and materials used to make Greek ships. Then have them make a design plan showing how to construct a Greek ship. Make sure they include the materials to use and explain whether the ship would be used for sailing or fighting.

Language Arts

Role-Play Greek Traders
Tell students that they are going to be involved in a play in which they are a group of Greek sailors who are preparing to travel to a distant land. Tell students that they are making the trip in order to trade goods with a region such as Egypt or Italy. Invite them to present their plays to the class.

Teach

The Earliest Greeks

CST 3, HI 2

Talk About It

- Where and when did the first Greek civilization develop? *(on the Peloponnesus around 2000 B.C.)*

- How would you describe life in Mycenaean Greece? *(A king ruled each city; many people were traders; the culture had writing, gold jewelry, bronze weapons, and fine pottery.)*

- **Critical Thinking: Making Inferences** How did trading with the Phoenicians help stimulate the development of Greek culture? *(From the Phoenicians, the Greeks learned writing, the alphabet, and how to use coins. The Greeks used these skills to develop literature, gain new ways of governing, and build a strong economy through trade.)*

Comparisons Across Cultures

Analyzing Charts

Ask students to look at the characters from the Phoenician, Greek, and modern alphabet.

- What two Phoenician and Greek characters look most like their modern counterparts? *(Possible answers: O, H, and E)*

- What modern letters are missing from the Phoenician and Greek alphabets? *(G, J, V, W, and Z)*

More About . . .

Mycenaean Occupations

A clay tablet discovered by archaeologists from the Mycenaean civilization had a list of over 100 occupations. The list included shipwrights, bakers, dry cleaners, woodcutters, messengers, saddlers, shepherds, doctors, potters, foresters, carpenters, and weavers.

The Earliest Greeks

3 ESSENTIAL QUESTION How did trade influence Greek culture?
Trade exposed the Greeks to other cultures, from whom they adopted the alphabet and the use of coins.

The Greek culture of sailing and trading developed over thousands of years. The earliest Greeks had moved onto the Greek peninsula about 2000 B.C.

Mycenaean Civilization The first Greek civilization was built on the Peloponnesus. It was named after its most important city, Mycenae (my•SEE•nee). A king ruled each city of Mycenaean Greece. The Mycenaeans were traders. Their culture featured writing, gold jewelry, bronze weapons, and fine pottery. Their civilization collapsed about 1200 B.C., perhaps because of invaders.

After the fall of the Mycenaeans, Greek culture declined. People no longer kept written records. Without such records, historians know little about the period from 1200 to 750 B.C.

New Advances in Greek Culture In time, Greek culture made advances again. One reason for this is that the Greeks learned from other people, such as the **Phoenicians** (fih•NISHSH•uhnz). They were another important trading people, who lived on the coast of the eastern Mediterranean. By trading with other people, the Phoenicians spread their system of writing. It used 22 symbols to stand for sounds. Such a system of symbols is called an **alphabet**.

Comparisons Across Cultures

Alphabets

Writing systems change over time. The Greeks borrowed the Phoenician alphabet of 22 letters but wrote the symbols differently. Also, the Greeks added two letters. Since the time of ancient Greece, their alphabet has evolved into the one used in the United States today.

▲ American Sign Language is a language for the deaf that uses gestures to convey meaning. It includes an alphabet.

Culture	Characters from Alphabet																								
Phoenician	𐤀	𐤁	𐤂	𐤃	𐤄	𐤅		𐤆	𐤇	𐤈	𐤉		𐤊	𐤋	𐤌	𐤍	𐤎	𐤏	𐤐		𐤑	𐤒	𐤓	𐤔	𐤕
Greek	A	B	Γ	Δ	E		Z	H	Θ	I		K	Λ	M	N	Ξ	O	Π		P	Σ	T	Y		X	Ψ
Modern	A	B	C	D	E	F	G	H		I	J	K	L	M	N	O	P		Q	R	S	T	U	V	W	X	Y	Z

DIFFERENTIATING INSTRUCTION

Inclusion

Write and Administer Greek Quizzes

Have students work in pairs. Have each pair write 5 questions about ancient Greece. (For example, students might ask, "Greeks learned the alphabet from what culture?") Students should also write an answer key for their questions. When pairs have finished, have them exchange their quizzes with each other. Have the pairs take turns quizzing each other and correcting the quizzes.

Gifted and Talented Students

Make a Review Game

Have students create a review game using index cards. Have them make sets of cards to play a matching review game. One card should contain an idea, term, or name related to this lesson. The matching card should contain a short explanation, definition, or description. Students lay the cards face down and take turns turning over one card and then another to match it. If the cards match, set them aside. If not, turn them back over and go to the next player.

The Greeks picked up the Phoenician alphabet between 900 and 800 B.C. They changed some letters to suit their language. The Greek alphabet later evolved into our own alphabet of 26 letters.

The Greeks also learned about coins from trading with other peoples. Coins were invented about 650 B.C. in Anatolia. Most parts of Greece were making their own coins by 500 B.C.

Eventually, the Greeks also developed new forms of literature and government. You will learn more about these developments in Lessons 2 and 3.

Greek Coins This coin is from the city of Athens, Greece. One side shows the goddess Athena, for whom Athens was named. The other side shows an owl, which was a symbol of Athena's wisdom. ▼

REVIEW What did the Greeks learn from trading with other peoples?
the use of coins, the use of the alphabet

Lesson Summary

- The mountainous geography of Greece limited agriculture and political unity.
- The Greeks depended on the sea to connect with each other and with the wider world.
- Trade brought an alphabet and coins to Greece.

Why It Matters Now . . .
The Greek alphabet influenced the development of all Western alphabets, including the English alphabet.

---

1 Lesson Review

Homework Helper
ClassZone.com

Terms & Names

1. Explain the importance of
   peninsula   Peloponnesus   isthmus
   Phoenician   alphabet

Using Your Notes

Understanding Effects Use your completed chart to answer the following question:

2. What effects did the geography of Greece have on settlement patterns? (CST 3)

Causes	Effects
Mountains cover most of Greece.	
Several seas surround Greece.	
Greece traded with other regions.	

Main Ideas

3. How did the geography of the Greek peninsula affect the political organization of the region? (6.4.1)
4. How did the seas affect Greek trade patterns? (6.4.1)
5. How did trade with other peoples contribute to Greek civilization? (6.4.1)

Critical Thinking

6. **Analyzing Causes** Why did the Greeks develop trade with other regions? (HI 2)
7. **Contrasting** What were two major differences between the civilizations of Greece and Mesopotamia? (6.4.1)

Activity **Making a Map** Take out the world map you started in Chapter 2. Using the map on page 351 as a model, add the Greek homeland to your map. You should also add the cities of Athens and Sparta. (CST 3)

---

❹ Assess & Reteach

Assess Have pairs take turns answering questions. Ask volunteers to share their completed charts.

📓 **Formal Assessment**
- Lesson Quiz, p. 188

Reteach Divide the class into three groups. Assign each group one of the three sections of this lesson. Each group should list the main ideas in its section and share responses with the class.

📓 **In-Depth Resources: Unit 5**
- Vocabulary Cards, p. 27
- Reteaching Activity, p. 33

🔎 **Homework Helper**
Visit **ClassZone.com** for a lesson review, a flip-card activity, and links to related Web sites.

---

1 Lesson Review Answers

Terms & Names

1. • peninsula, p. 355
   • Peloponnesus, p. 355
   • isthmus, p. 355
   • Phoenician, p. 358
   • alphabet, p. 358

Using Your Notes

See page 354 for an example of a completed chart.

2. Cities were located by the sea; the mountainous geography also encouraged the Greeks to found colonies overseas.

Main Ideas

3. The rugged landscape divided Greece into many regions, so it was difficult for Greece to be united under one government.
4. The seas allowed Greek regions to trade with one another and with the wider Mediterranean world.
5. The Phoenician alphabet influenced the Greek system of writing, and the Greeks started using coins in their trade.

Critical Thinking

6. Possible answer: The ancient Greeks had a limited amount of certain resources, such as grain and precious metals. However, they had a surplus of other resources, such as olive oil and wool. To gain needed resources, the ancient Greeks began to trade their surplus resources for needed resources.
7. Possible answers: Greek civilization did not produce grain surpluses. Sea trade was more common in Greece.

Activity Rubric

	Quality of Map Addition	**Number of Errors**
4	very well-drawn, clearly labeled, detailed, accurate	none or one
3	well-drawn, detailed, accurate	two or three
2	fairly well-drawn, few details, some inaccuracies	four or five
1	no details, inaccurate	more than five

❶ Plan & Prepare

Objectives

- Describe how Greeks viewed interactions with gods.
- Explain how the Greeks honored their gods.
- Discuss what constitutes Greek epic poems and fables.
- **Language Objective:** Identify elements of a myth—characters, setting, conflict, explanation, journey, and symbols—to help make the text more comprehensible.

Quick Look

Lesson 2 explores Greek gods and myths, the ways Greeks honored their gods, and early Greek literature.

❷ Focus & Motivate

Preview Draw a K-W-L chart on the board. Brainstorm what students already know, do not yet know, and would like to know about Greek religion. Fill in the chart as they read the lesson.

Introduce the Main Ideas The three main ideas relate to the Big Idea "The Greeks told myths to support their beliefs about values and the world." Help students look for this Big Idea in the lesson.

Reading Skill: Making Generalizations Explain that making broad judgments helps connect one idea to another to summarize learning.

SAMPLE ANSWERS FOR CHART

Greek Religious Beliefs	Greek Literature
Gods were worshiped by Greeks.	Greeks wrote myths that described gods.
Gods were involved in people's lives.	Greeks wrote many stories about interaction between gods and people.
Gods held much power.	Stories such as the *Odyssey* told about gods working with and against humans.

Lesson 2

▶ **MAIN IDEAS**

❶ **Belief Systems** Like other ancient peoples, the Greeks believed their gods controlled the human and natural worlds.

❷ **Belief Systems** The Greeks honored their gods by worshiping them and by holding festivals and games in their honor.

❸ **Culture** Early Greek literature included stories that taught lessons, and long poems that told of adventures.

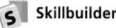

▶ **TAKING NOTES**

Reading Skill: Making Generalizations

As you read Lesson 2, look for information that will help you make a generalization, or broad judgment, about the relationship between Greek beliefs and literature. Record the information on a chart like the one below.

Greek Religious Beliefs	Greek Literature

S **Skillbuilder Handbook, page R8**

▲ **Greek Vase** This vase shows a scene from a Greek myth. The hero Heracles (also called Hercules) rescued Alcestis from the underworld after she offered to die in place of her husband, the king of Thessaly.

CALIFORNIA STANDARDS

6.4.4 Explain the significance of Greek mythology to the everyday life of the people in the region and how Greek literature continues to permeate our literature and language today, drawing from Greek mythology and epics, such as Homer's *Iliad* and *Odyssey*, and from *Aesop's Fables*.

REP 3 Students distinguish relevant from irrelevant information, essential from incidental information, and verifiable from unverifiable information in historical narratives and stories.

REP 4 Students assess the credibility of primary and secondary sources and draw sound conclusions from them.

HOW TO TEACH THE CALIFORNIA STANDARDS

Standard	Content	Student Question or Activity	Instruction
6.4.4	**Page 362** Explains how myths functioned in people's lives	**Page 362** Students explain the connection between Greek myths and religion.	Discuss with students how an explanation of the creation of the world might have helped ancient peoples feel more secure about life.
REP 3	**Page 361** Compares Egyptian and Greek religions	**Page 365** Students analyze ways in which Egyptian and Greek religions were similar and different.	Review the concepts of Egyptian religion with students and compare them to those of Greece on a chart.
REP 4	**Page 362** Relates the story of Prometheus	**Page 365** Students identify the lesson the Greeks might have learned from the story of Prometheus.	Discuss how stories can teach us how to live—whether the story actually happened or not.

Beliefs and Customs

TERMS & NAMES

Zeus

Mount Olympus

myth

Olympics

epic poem

fable

Build on What You Know Like other ancient peoples, the Greeks were polytheistic—they worshiped many gods. But you won't find gods with animal heads in Greece as you did in Egypt. Greek gods looked like humans, yet were more powerful and more beautiful than any human could be.

Greek Gods and Myths

The Greeks believed in **1** many gods. These gods had divine and human qualities. They were very powerful and had a wide range of human emotions. The Greeks believed their 12 main gods lived on Mount Olympus.

ESSENTIAL QUESTION What was Greek religion like?

To the Greeks, the gods were not distant beings. They became involved in people's lives, and the Greeks loved to tell stories about them. These vivid tales showed that the gods were sometimes cruel and selfish.

The Gods of Greece The Greek gods had both divine and human qualities. For example, they were very powerful and could shape human events. Yet they had a wide range of human emotions, including love, anger, and jealousy. The gods and goddesses of Greece constantly competed with one another.

Zeus (ZOOS) was the ruler of the gods. The Greeks believed that he and 11 other major gods and goddesses lived on **Mount Olympus** (uh•LIHM•puhs), the highest mountain in Greece. (See the box on pages 362–363.) The Greeks also worshiped many less-important gods.

Each city had a special god or goddess to protect it. For example, Athena (one of the 12 who lived on Olympus) was the protector of Athens. She was the goddess of wisdom, a warrior, and the patron of crafts such as weaving.

Mount Olympus
The ancient Greeks believed that their most important gods lived on this mountain. As a result, this group is frequently called the Olympian gods. ▼

361

Terms & Names

Zeus ruler of the Greek gods

Mount Olympus the highest mountain in Greece; gods were believed to have lived there

myth a story that people tell to explain beliefs about their world

Olympics games held every four years

epic poem a long poem about ancient heroes

fable a short story that usually involves animals and teaches a moral.

❸ Teach

Greek Gods and Myths

6.4.4

Talk About It

- **Critical Thinking: Making Generalizations** How were Greek myths and religion connected? *(Myths told of the world's creation and actions of gods.)*

California Resources

California Reading Toolkit, L37
California Modified Lesson Plans for English Learners, p. 77
California Daily Standards Practice Transparencies, TT37
California Standards Enrichment Workbook, pp. 55–56
California Online Test Practice
California Test Generator CD-ROM
California Standards Planner and Lesson Plans, L73
California EasyPlanner CD-ROM
California eEdition CD-ROM

LESSON 2 PROGRAM RESOURCES

ON LEVEL

In-Depth Resources: Unit 5
- Reading Skill: Making Generalizations, p. 21
- Vocabulary Study Guide, p. 26

Formal Assessment
- Lesson Quiz, p. 189

ENGLISH LEARNERS

In-Depth Resources in Spanish
- Reading Skill: Making Generalizations, p. 92
- Vocabulary Study Guide, p. 98

Modified Lesson Plans for English Learners, p. 77

Reading Study Guide (Spanish), p. 97
Reading Study Guide Audio CD (Spanish)

STRUGGLING READERS

In-Depth Resources: Unit 5
- Reading Skill: Making Generalizations, p. 21
- Vocabulary Study Guide, p. 26
- Reteaching Activity, p. 34

Reading Toolkit, L37
Reading Study Guide, p. 97
Reading Study Guide Audio CD

GIFTED AND TALENTED STUDENTS

History Makers
- Homer, p. 21

In-Depth Resources: Unit 5
- Literature: The Odyssey, p. 32

Interdisciplinary Projects
- Language Arts, p. 63
- Physical Education, p. 64

INCLUSION

EasyPlanner CD-ROM
- Reading Skill
- Vocabulary Study Guide
- Reteaching Activity

TECHNOLOGY

eEdition CD-ROM

Power Presentations CD-ROM

Map Transparencies
- MT22 Ancient Olympia

Humanities Transparencies
- HT21 Head of Zeus

Critical Thinking Transparencies
- CT47 Making Generalizations

Test Generator CD-ROM

ClassZone.com

In-Depth Resources: Unit 5
• Reading Skill: Making Generalizations, p. 21

Teach

Honoring the Gods

6.4.4

Talk About It

• How did the Greeks honor their gods? *(They created statues and built temples, held festivals, and made sacrifices.)*

• What were the first Olympic games like, and why were they created? *(They took place in a stadium in the city of Olympia and were held every four years. They honored Zeus. Only men competed, and the first games included only a foot race.)*

• What festival allowed Greek girls to honor the goddesses? What was it like? *(It was a festival held at the same time as the Olympics, and it honored Hera, the wife of Zeus. The festival featured a foot race in three age categories.)*

• **Critical Thinking: Drawing Conclusions** How do you know that Greek gods and goddesses were important in daily Greek life? *(Possible answers: Greeks spent time and money building temples and sculptures; certain days of each month were dedicated to a god or goddess; they created the Olympics to honor the gods.)*

History from Visuals

Interpreting Visuals
Ask students to look at the sculpture of Zeus on this page.

• How would you describe the physical characteristics of Zeus? *(Possible answers: athletic body; strong, lean muscles; determined, confident look on his face)*

• What does the position of the arm of Zeus say about him? *(Possible answer: He is ready to go to battle.)*

Humanities Transparencies
• HT21 Head of Zeus

Greek Mythology **Myths** are stories that people tell to explain beliefs about their world. Myths often begin as oral stories. Later they might be written down.

The Greeks created myths to explain the creation of the world and of human beings. Many myths described the gods and goddesses and how they related to one another and to humans. For example, the myth of Prometheus (pruh•MEE•thee•uhs) tells how he stole fire from the gods and gave it to humans. Zeus punished him for this by chaining him to a rock. Every day, an eagle ate his liver—which grew back every night. Today, Prometheus is seen as a hero who defied unjust authority.

Other myths portrayed Greek heroes and heroines. The Reader's Theater on pages 366–369 is based on the myth of a young woman named Atalanta, who was a skilled hunter and runner.

REVIEW How were Greek myths and religion connected?
Many Greek myths told stories of the gods and goddesses.

Honoring the Gods

2 **ESSENTIAL QUESTION** How did the Greeks honor their gods?

Like other ancient peoples, the Greeks believed it was important to honor the gods. An angry god could cause trouble. The Greeks created statues of the gods and built temples as places for the gods to live. They also held special events to honor the gods.

Holy Festivals Certain days of each month were holy to different gods and goddesses or to aspects of nature. For example, each month began with the new moon, and the festival of Noumenia was held. People celebrated holy days with sacrifices and public ceremonies.

The most important festivals honored the 12 Olympian gods. For example, there was a great festival to honor Athena. A new robe was woven for her statue in the main temple. The festival also included a procession, races and other athletic games, and poetry recitals.

They created statues of the gods and built temples for them. They celebrated holy days, held festivals, and took part in athletic games to honor the gods.

Greek Gods and Goddesses

Zeus was the father of many other gods. Some of his children were Aphrodite, Apollo, Athena, and Hermes. ▼

DIFFERENTIATING INSTRUCTION

English Learners

Identify Elements of a Myth
Tell students that myths are tales that explain people's beliefs about their world. Guide students as they discuss the elements of the myth about the god, Zeus. Use a graphic to chart student responses. Have students work with a partner to complete a graphic with details about other mythical gods. Share their findings with classmates.

Struggling Readers

Make a Chart
Have students create a two-column chart in which they list the following concepts in the left column: Greek gods, Zeus, Mount Olympus, myths, holy festivals, Olympics, epic poems, and fables. As they read the lesson, have students write information about each concept in the right column. Then ask them to summarize the chart information by writing a generalization about each entry.

The Olympics In Greece, games were always part of religious festivals. The largest and most elaborate of these were the Olympics. The **Olympics** were games held every four years as part of a major festival that honored Zeus. They took place in a stadium built in the city of Olympia. Only men competed in these contests.

The oldest records of winners at the Olympics date to 776 B.C. But the games might have been going on for centuries before that. The first Olympics included only a foot race. Over time, longer races and other events were added. Events included wrestling, the long jump, the javelin throw, and the discus throw. These games tested skills that were valuable to soldiers.

Unmarried girls competed in a festival to honor the goddess Hera. Hera was Zeus' wife, and her festival was held at the same time as the Olympics. This festival featured a foot race in three different age categories.

REVIEW Why did the Greeks hold the Olympics?
to honor the god Zeus with athletic contests in hopes of gaining his favor

Connect to Today

▲ **Olympics for All** In modern times, a wider variety of athletes has the chance to compete in the Olympic games than ever before.

◄ Demeter was a fertility goddess who was especially linked with growing grain.

▲ Athena was the goddess of wisdom and also a warrior. Athena had no mother. She sprang from the forehead of Zeus.

Apollo was the god of archery, healing, music, poetry, and prophecy. Later, he was honored as the god of the sun. Zeus and Apollo were the most widely worshiped gods. ▶

Other Greek Gods and Goddesses	
Ares	god of war
Aphrodite	goddess of love
Artemis	goddess of the hunt
Hephaestus	god of fire
Hera	wife of Zeus; protector of marriage
Hermes	messenger of the gods
Hestia	goddess of home life
Poseidon	god of the seas and earthquakes

Ancient Greece • 363

More About . . .

The Olympics
The ancient Olympic games started in about 776 B.C. Greek athletes came from many different parts of the region. A particularly fierce rivalry existed between Athens and Sparta.

According to tradition, the foot race, called a stadion, was the only event until about 724 B.C. when other events were added. Archaeologists have restored the original stadium that contained an oval track about 600 yards long, stands for spectators, and changing rooms for athletes.

The Olympic marathon was not a part of the games until the Athens Olympics of 1896. It celebrates a man named Pheidippides, a runner who warned the Spartans about the invasion of Persia at Marathon in 490 B.C. The Olympic torch was not used until the games of 1928. Later it was used in the Olympic torch relay.

History from Visuals

Interpreting Visuals
* Name two gods and two goddesses who do not appear in the chart. *(Apollo, Zeus, Athena, and Demeter)*
* If you added Hecate to the chart, what description would you give her? *(Possible answer: Hecate was goddess of the night and the moon.)*

 Map Transparencies
* MT22 Ancient Olympia

DIFFERENTIATING INSTRUCTION

Inclusion

Listen to the Lesson
Have students who are visually impaired use the Reading Study Guide Audio CD to learn more about the beliefs and customs of ancient Greece that are discussed in this lesson. Students should answer all the questions and exercises in the audio study.

Gifted and Talented Students

Research Myths
Have students select a Greek myth or fable from the lesson to read and research. Each group should decide what the myth or fable reflects about Greek beliefs. Have the students share their research with the class and discuss the Greek beliefs that these myths or fables illustrate.

Teach

Early Greek Literature

\ **6.4.4, REP 3, REP 4**

Talk About It

- What are two famous Greek epic poems, and what events do they convey? *(The* Iliad *is the story of the Trojan War and the Greek warrior, Achilles. The* Odyssey *describes the ten-year journey of the Greek hero, Odysseus, returning from the Trojan War.)*

- **Critical Thinking: Making Inferences**
  How did stories about heroes and heroines influence civilization? *(Possible answers: They gave people someone to look up to; they helped create a culture's history; they helped a culture recognize its values.)*

More About . . .

The Trojan War
The actual Trojan War probably happened between Mycenae and Troy around 1200 B.C. This war may have been caused by a dispute over the control of trade in the Dardanelles. Over time, this conflict was transformed into an epic poem of gods and goddesses, love and betrayal and revenge and honor. This story still entertains readers some 2,800 years after it was created by Homer.

More About . . .

Words and Greek Myths
Many words used today come from Greek mythology. The word *atlas* is from the story of Atlas who had to hold the world on his shoulders. A handsome man is called an *Adonis* after the myth of Adonis. An odyssey, a long, adventurous journey, comes from Homer's tale about Odysseus's long journey home. The word *narcissist* comes from the tale of Narcissus who couldn't stop looking at himself in a pool of water.

 In-Depth Resources: Unit 5
- Literature: The Odyssey, p. 32

Early Greek Literature

② **ESSENTIAL QUESTION** What literature did the early Greeks produce?
They wrote epic poems, such as the Iliad and Odyssey. Aesop wrote down fables that taught a moral, such as "The Hare and the Tortoise."

In addition to stories about gods, the Greeks told stories about their ancient heroes. Much of what we know about the early Greeks comes from stories passed down through generations and from long poems that told stories. These long poems are called **epic poems**. According to tradition, a blind man named Homer composed the most famous epics.

Epics of Homer Homer's epic the *Iliad* is about the Trojan War, which started because a Trojan stole a Greek king's wife. In the *Iliad*, the Greeks surrounded the city of Troy for more than nine years, trying to capture it. The *Iliad* is famous for its portrayal of heroes. For example, no one could defeat the Greek warrior Achilles (uh•KIHL•eez). When he was a baby, his mother dipped him in a river that would make him live forever. But an arrow wounded Achilles in his one weak spot—the heel his mother held as she lowered him in the water—so he died.

For centuries, people thought Homer's story was fiction. Around 1870, archaeologists discovered the ruins of ancient Troy. A real war did take place there, but it did not happen exactly as the *Iliad* portrays it.

Homer's other major epic was the *Odyssey*. It describes the adventures of the Greek hero Odysseus (oh•DIHS•YOOS) after the Trojan War. The Greek gods decided that Odysseus' trip home should take ten years. During that time, he and his men encountered many dangers. The gods sometimes helped Odysseus and sometimes worked against him.

These ancient stories still influence speech and art today. For instance, we use the phrase *Achilles' heel* to refer to a person's weakest area.

Aesop's Fables A **fable** is a short story, usually involving animals, that teaches a moral lesson. A storyteller named Aesop (EE•suhp) is credited with writing down many ancient Greek fables.

Achilles The ancient Greek epics still influence our culture. For example, in 2004, the movie *Troy* retold the story of the Trojan War. Here the warrior Achilles does battle. ▼

INTERDISCIPLINARY ACTIVITIES

Science

Learn About the Moon
The moon and its phases were important to ancient beliefs. Have students do research about the scientific phases of the moon and ancient beliefs about it. Then have students create a poster that gives a scientific explanation about the phases of the moon. The poster should explain any ancient beliefs associated with the moon's phases.

Physical Education

Compete in the Olympics
If possible, create a "Classroom Olympics" with the physical education teacher. Have students volunteer to be competitors that represent Athens or Sparta. Also, have other students work at setting up the race and playing the roles of spectators. Encourage the use of flyers for the event, announcers at the event, and prizes.

One of Aesop's best-known fables is "The Hare and the Tortoise." In it, a hare (rabbit) makes fun of a tortoise (turtle) for being slow. The tortoise challenges the hare to a race. The hare is so sure he will win that he lies down for a nap. The tortoise never stops but goes at a slow, steady pace to the finish line. The hare wakes up too late for his speed to save him. We still use this story today to encourage people to work steadily at a task that seems impossible to accomplish.

Cyclops On Odysseus' long voyage, a one-eyed monster called a Cyclops made him and his men prisoners. The Cyclops ate several of the men before Odysseus defeated him. ▼

REVIEW Why are Homer's epics important?

They tell stories about early Greeks and are part of Greek mythology because they tell us about gods and heroes.

Lesson Summary

- The ancient Greeks created stories about their gods, who were important to their daily lives.
- The ancient Greeks honored their gods through festivals that included rituals and athletic games.
- Early Greeks wrote fables and epic poems.

Why It Matters Now . . .

Greek mythology, epics, and fables continue to influence our literature, language, and movies.

---

2 Lesson Review

 **Homework Helper**
ClassZone.com

Terms & Names

1. Explain the importance of

Zeus	myth	epic poem
Mount Olympus	Olympics	fable

Using Your Notes

Making Generalizations Use your completed chart to answer the following question:

2. How were Greek religious beliefs and Greek literature linked? Write your answer as a generalization. (6.4.4)

Greek Religious Beliefs	Greek Literature

Main Ideas

3. Why was mythology important to the lives of ancient Greeks? (6.4.4)

4. What role did religious festivals play in Greek life? (6.4.4)

5. How are the *Iliad* and the *Odyssey* connected? (6.4.4)

Critical Thinking

6. Drawing Conclusions from Sources What lesson might the Greeks have learned from the myth of Prometheus? (REP 4)

7. Comparing and Contrasting In what key ways were the religions of Egypt and Greece similar and different? (REP 3)

Activity

Writing a Fable Consider a moral lesson that is important to you. Working with a group, create a story that uses animals to teach that lesson. (6.4.4)

---

❹ Assess & Reteach

Assess Have pairs of students use the lesson review questions to quiz each other, taking turns answering the questions.

📝 **Formal Assessment**
- Lesson Quiz, p. 189

Reteach Divide the class into three groups. Assign each group one of the three sections in this lesson. Each group should list the main ideas in its subsection and share responses with the class.

📝 **In-Depth Resources: Unit 5**
- Vocabulary Cards, p. 27
- Reteaching Activity, p. 34

 Homework Helper

Visit **ClassZone.com** for a lesson review, a flip-card activity, and links to related Web sites.

---

2 Lesson Review Answers

Terms & Names

1. • Zeus, p. 361
- Mount Olympus, p. 361
- myth, p. 362
- Olympics, p. 363
- epic poem, p. 364
- fable, p. 364

Using Your Notes

See page 360 for an example of a completed chart.

2. Possible answer: Greek literature included many stories about the gods and about the beginnings of things; these reflected Greek beliefs.

Main Ideas

3. Possible answer: It explained Greek beliefs about the world. It also described gods and goddesses and how they related to each other and to humans.

4. Greeks used festivals to honor their gods on a regular basis.

5. The *Iliad* tells the story of the Trojan War, including how Odysseus helped the Greeks win. The *Odyssey* tells the story of Odysseus's adventures on his journey home after the war.

Critical Thinking

6. It was important not to anger the gods because the gods might punish them.

7. Possible answer: Religion was very important in both cultures. Both believed in many gods and honored them with statues, temples, and rituals. In Egypt, some gods were animals or had animal heads. In Greece, the gods looked and acted like humans.

Activity Rubric

	Content of Fable	**Style of Fable**
4	includes details about animal characters and a moral	done well
3	includes animal characters and a moral	neat
2	missing characters or a moral	acceptable
1	includes no elements of a fable	messy

Objectives

- Illustrates how Atalanta survived and triumphed in life.
- **Language Objective:** Identify elements of a myth—characters, setting, conflict, explanation, journey, and symbols—to help make the text more comprehensible.

❶ Focus & Motivate

Connect to the Big Idea

Beliefs The Greeks told myths to support their beliefs about values and the world.

Connect to Prior Knowledge

Have students tell what they learned about myths in Lesson 2. *(Myths explained the creation of the world, the actions of Greek heroes and heroines, and life lessons.)* Have students read the background for "Atalanta's Last Race" and predict what lesson will be learned from the story. *(Possible answers: Atalanta's athletic skills will win the approval of her father; Atalanta will defeat men in foot races; Atalanta will use her athletic skills to get revenge on her father for leaving her.)*

More About . . .

Women and the Olympics
You already know that women competed separately in races in honor of Hera. Women were not allowed to compete in the first Olympics and only unmarried women could watch them. Married women could be put to death if they attended.

Callipateira, a widow, broke the rule by coming disguised as a man. She was discovered, but since her son, brothers, and father had been Olympic winners, they let her live.

Olympic rules did allow one married woman, the priestess of Demeter, to attend and have a seat of honor.

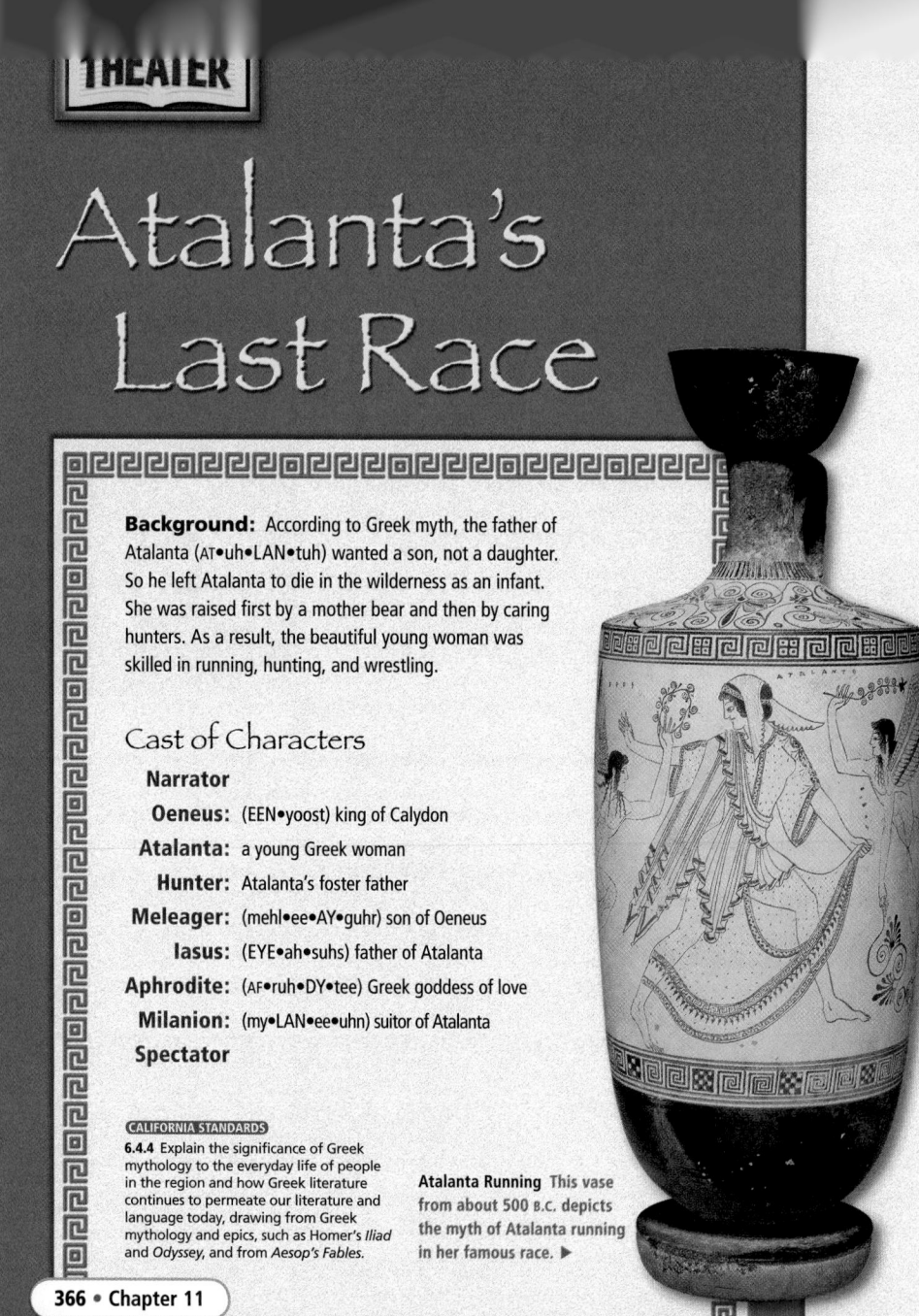

Atalanta's Last Race

Background: According to Greek myth, the father of Atalanta (AT•uh•LAN•tuh) wanted a son, not a daughter. So he left Atalanta to die in the wilderness as an infant. She was raised first by a mother bear and then by caring hunters. As a result, the beautiful young woman was skilled in running, hunting, and wrestling.

Cast of Characters

Narrator

Oeneus: (EEN•yoost) king of Calydon

Atalanta: a young Greek woman

Hunter: Atalanta's foster father

Meleager: (mehl•ee•AY•guhr) son of Oeneus

Iasus: (EYE•ah•suhs) father of Atalanta

Aphrodite: (AF•ruh•DY•tee) Greek goddess of love

Milanion: (my•LAN•ee•uhn) suitor of Atalanta

Spectator

CALIFORNIA STANDARDS
6.4.4 Explain the significance of Greek mythology to the everyday life of people in the region and how Greek literature continues to permeate our literature and language today, drawing from Greek mythology and epics, such as Homer's *Iliad* and *Odyssey*, and from *Aesop's Fables*.

Atalanta Running This vase from about 500 B.C. depicts the myth of Atalanta running in her famous race. ▶

366 • Chapter 11

ADDITIONAL RESOURCES

Books for the Student

Bailey, Linda. ***Adventures in Ancient Greece.*** Tonawanda: Kids Can Press, 2002. Illustrations of ancient Olympic games.

Caselli, Giovanni. ***In Search of Troy: One Man's Quest for Homer's Fabled City.*** New York: Peter Bedrick Books, 1999. Explores Heinrich Schliemann's archaeological search for Troy.

Middleton, Haydn. ***Ancient Greek Women.*** Chicago: Heinemann Library, 2003. Details life of Greek women.

Tames, Richard. ***Ancient Greek Children.*** Chicago: Heinemann Library, 2003. Describes clothes, toys and games, sports, family life, and education.

Woff, Richard. ***The Ancient Greek Olympics.*** New York: Oxford University Press, 1999. Describes the history, tradition, and competitive events

connected with the ancient Olympic games.

Videos

The First Olympics: Blood, Honor, and Glory. 137 minutes. South Burlington: A&E Home Video, 2004. Describes ancient Olympic events as brutal contests including boxing, wrestling, and chariot racing. VHS, DVD.

The Gods of Olympus. 23 minutes. Wynnewood: Schlessinger Media, 2004. Overview of Greek gods. VHS.

Narrator: The goddess Artemis (AHR•tuh•mihs) is angry at King Oeneus because he forgot to make sacrifices to her. So she has sent a wild boar to destroy his country of Calydon (KAL•ih•DAHN). The king has asked the best hunters in Greece for help. When they arrive, Atalanta is with them. She stands before the king, looking lovely in her simple woolen robe. A quiver of arrows hangs over her left shoulder. Her right hand clasps her bow.

Oeneus: Who are you, young woman? I have need of skilled hunters, not foolish girls.

Atalanta: Your majesty, I think you will find that I am as skilled as any man here. I have spent my life in the woods.

Hunter: I can speak for her, my lord. Atalanta has lived among us since she was a small girl. She once killed two centaurs[1] single-handedly. In our land, she is known as "the pride of the woods."

Oeneus: Very well, let us see what she can do. We need all the help we can get.

Narrator: The king's son Meleager falls in love with Atalanta instantly. Although some of the men dislike the idea of hunting with a woman, Meleager insists that she go with them.

Meleager: Come, Atalanta, you can hunt by my side. If you are as skilled as the hunters say, I will be glad of your presence. In fact, I should like you always near me.

_____

1. **centaur** (SEHN•TAWRZ): a creature with the head, arms, and chest of a man, and the body and legs of a horse.

Atalanta: I am happy to be your friend, Meleager, and I look forward to the hunt. But I only care for men as fellow hunters. I don't plan to ever get married.

Narrator: When the hunters surround the boar, it attacks and kills two men. Atalanta stays calm, and it is her arrow that first strikes the animal. Meleager then moves in for the kill.

(continued)

Artemis The goddess Artemis, sister of Apollo, was another female in Greek mythology who was a skilled hunter. ▶

Ancient Greece • **367**

DIFFERENTIATING INSTRUCTION

English Learners

Identify Mythical Elements
Remind students that determining the elements of a myth will help them organize important details and can help them understand and remember what they read. Guide students as they locate and discuss elements for the myth, "Atalanta's Last Race." Use a graphic to chart students' responses. To conclude, ask students to explain if they think Atalanta would have still agreed to marry Milanion if she had won the race.

Gifted and Talented Students

Design Props
Have students read the play and create a few props for the different characters. Students can work with partners or in small groups to make the props. Have students explain why the props were chosen for each character.

❷ Teach

Talk About It

• Assign each of the roles to students, and have them practice the play before reading it aloud to the class.

• Emphasize that students should perform a dramatic reading, which means using gestures and changes in inflection to convey meaning.

• Assign other students the roles of helping to direct the reading or videotaping the performance.

• Why did King Oeneus send out hunters? *(The goddess Artemis was angry at the king and sent a wild boar to destroy his country. The hunters had to kill the boar.)*

• How did the king feel about having a female hunter join them? *(Possible answer: He was not convinced that she could help them.)*

• **Critical Thinking: Making Predictions** What do you think will happen when Meleager tries to kill the boar? *(Possible answers: He will kill the boar and thank Atalanta for her help; the boar will attack and wound him, and Atalanta will save him.)*

More About . . .

Wild Boars
The domestic pig is a descendant of the boar. Wild boars do still exist; they are strong animals with hairy bodies and will use their tusks as weapons. They move mostly at night and will eat nearly anything. Herds of boars can destroy a whole crop field in one night. Wolves and tigers are the boar's natural enemies.

Boars are a prominent symbol on Greek vases and one of the animals pictured on ancient Greek coins. The boar was one of the symbols of the goddess Hecate.

Teach

Talk About It

- What happened to Meleager after he killed the boar? *(He gave the boar hide to Atalanta and died after fighting with his uncles.)*

- When did Atalanta meet her father, Iasus? *(after she won a wrestling match)*

- Why did Aphrodite think that Atalanta needed to be taught a lesson? *(Atalanta believed she was too good for love. Being the goddess of love, Aphrodite was bothered by Atalanta's attitude.)*

- **Critical Thinking: Drawing Conclusions** Why do you think that Aphrodite felt it was not normal for Atalanta to reject love? *(Possible answers: She thought that as a woman, Atalanta should want to marry a man and settle down. She thought that it was not natural for a woman to keep defeating men in foot races.)*

More About . . .

Aphrodite

Aphrodite was born from the foam of the sea and was so beautiful that any man who saw her fell in love. She appears in a story in which Paris has to decide the most beautiful of three goddesses—Hera, Athena, and Aphrodite. He chooses Aphrodite because she promised him Helen of Troy, the most beautiful woman in the world. The love affair between Helen and Paris leads to the Trojan War.

Meleager: Although it is my knife that has killed this beast, I insist that the honor go to Atalanta. She shall have the boar skin as a trophy.

Narrator: Meleager's uncles quarrel with him because he honored Atalanta. This quarrel leads to his death. But Atalanta's fame is just beginning. After defeating a great hero in a wrestling match, she meets her father, Iasus.

Iasus: Congratulations, daughter. I am very proud of you and would like to welcome you back to my home. I see that you will be almost like a son to me. But I understand that many young men want to marry you.

Atalanta: Don't worry, Father, I will never marry a man unless he can beat me in a foot race. (*Aside*) And I know there is no man alive who can do that.

Narrator: Atalanta enjoys defeating all the young men who come to race with her. No matter how fast they are, she is faster. She cares nothing for their promises of love. Her actions do not go unnoticed by Aphrodite, the goddess of love on Mount Olympus.

Aphrodite: It has come to my attention that there is a wild, young maiden who thinks she is too good for love. I may need to teach her a lesson.

Narrator: As it happens, a young man named Milanion wants very much to marry Atalanta. He is smart enough to know he cannot rely on his speed to beat her. He calls upon Aphrodite.

Milanion: Aphrodite, will you help me to marry Atalanta?

◀ **Running Girl** In Sparta, girls were trained in athletics because it taught them to be strong. Also, every four years at a festival in Hera's honor, unmarried girls competed in races.

368 • Chapter 11

DIFFERENTIATING INSTRUCTION

Inclusion

Record a Message

For students who have difficulty with writing skills, have them record a message describing what it would have been like to attend Atalanta's last race. Instruct them to include an opening sentence, at least three supporting details, and a summary sentence. Encourage them to create an outline with brief notes before making their recordings.

Struggling Readers

Design a Storyboard

Have students draw a storyboard in which they illustrate the main events of Atalanta's last race. Then have them write a caption to accompany each illustration. You may want to divide the work among groups by assigning each group one section.

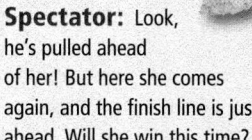

Aphrodite: I will gladly help tame this young woman who refuses to honor me. Here are three magical golden apples. Their beauty is so dazzling that anyone who sees them will feel she must have them. Use them wisely and you will succeed.

Milanion: Thank you, goddess, for your wise and generous assistance.

Narrator: The day arrives when Milanion and Atalanta are to race. Atalanta looks so confident of her skill that Milanion almost despairs of being able to succeed in his plan.

Milanion: I must not lose courage. Aphrodite is on my side.

Narrator: The race begins. Milanion is swift, but Atalanta is pulling ahead. He rolls his first golden apple right in front of her.

Atalanta: Oh my! What is this? I've never seen anything so lovely. I'll just reach down and scoop it up.

Milanion: She barely lost her stride! I've caught up with her, but now she is racing ahead again. I've got to slow her down even more.

Narrator: This time, Milanion throws his apple to Atalanta's side. She has to move to the right to pick it up.

Spectator: Look, he's pulled ahead of her! But here she comes again, and the finish line is just ahead. Will she win this time?

Milanion: This is my last chance. I must distract her long enough for me to reach the goal ahead of her. Here goes.

Narrator: The third golden apple rolls right in front of Atalanta and onto the side of the racecourse. She sees it glinting in the green grass and follows it.

Atalanta: I must have that gorgeous glowing ball. But wait, what's this? Milanion is sprinting past me. He has won!

Milanion: (*panting for breath*) Atalanta, do not be angry with me. I only acted out of my great love for you. I will be extremely honored to be your husband.

Atalanta: I admire your skill and your wit. And I see that Aphrodite is your friend. I will honor my promise and be your wife.

Activities

1. **TALK ABOUT IT** Why might Atalanta prefer not to marry?

2. **WRITE ABOUT IT** Imagine that you are a spectator watching the race between Atalanta and Milanion. Write a paragraph describing the details of the race—the sights, the sounds, and other important impressions. (6.4.4)

Ancient Greece • 369

Teach

Talk About It

- How did Milanion attempt to slow Atalanta down in their race? (*He threw the three golden apples from Aphrodite in front of Atalanta to distract her.*)

- Why did Milanion finally win the race? (*Atalanta went to the side of the race course to pick up the third apple.*)

- Why did Atalanta decide to marry Milanion? (*She promised to do so if she lost the race.*)

- **Critical Thinking: Analyzing Information** Why did Milanion need help to win a race with Atalanta? (*Possible answers: She was faster than Milanion; she beat every other man in all races; she was strong and determined; she did not want to get married.*)

More About . . .

Golden Apples
Golden apples often appear in myths when a god or goddess wishes to give a reward to humans. Many ancient cultures used the golden apple as a symbol. Today's modern Golden Apple Awards reflect the ancient idea of golden apples as rewards.

ACTIVITIES ANSWERS

1. **TALK ABOUT IT** Possible answers: She can do what men can do; she does not need support or protection; she is not in love with any man; she was abandoned by her father and might feel that no man deserves her trust.

2. **WRITE ABOUT IT**

2. Writing Rubric

	Description of Race	Number of Errors
4	imaginative, full details describe characters, sights, and sounds	few or none
3	details describe characters, sights, and sounds	several
2	few details, includes basic characters	many
1	no details, inaccurate	many major

❶ Plan & Prepare

Objectives

- Describe Greek political organization.
- Trace the evolution of Greek government from kingdom to democracy.
- Compare limited and unlimited democracy.
- **Language Objective:** Categorize lesson vocabulary to make nonfiction text more comprehensible and meaningful.

Quick Look

Lesson 3 focuses on the history of Greek government, including the city-state.

❷ Focus & Motivate

Preview Ask students to define what makes a democracy. *(In a democracy, the people make the political decisions.)*

Introduce the Main Ideas The three main ideas relate to the Big Idea "Governments create law codes and political bodies to organize a society." Help students look for this Big Idea in the lesson.

Reading Skill: Categorizing Tell students that categorizing involves putting pieces of information into categories.

SAMPLE ANSWERS FOR CHART

Types of Government		
Monarchy	Oligarchy	Democracy
right to rule given to king by gods	small group of citizens rule; right to rule by wealth or land ownership	all citizens take part; right to decisions not based on wealth/social class
king's son inherited the throne	run government for own reasons	decisions made by vote; majority wins

---

Lesson 3

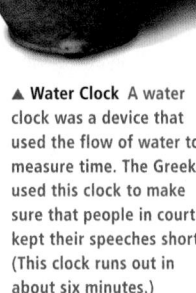

▶ MAIN IDEAS

① **Government** Instead of being a unified country, Greece was organized into separate city-states.

② **Government** Different political systems evolved in the various city-states. Some governments changed because of conflicts between rich and poor.

③ **Government** The city-state of Athens developed democracy, which is rule by the people.

▶ TAKING NOTES

Reading Skill: Categorizing

To categorize means to sort information. As you read Lesson 3, use your own words to take notes about types of government on a chart like this one.

Types of Government		
Monarchy	Oligarchy	Democracy

S **Skillbuilder Handbook, page R6**

▲ **Water Clock** A water clock was a device that used the flow of water to measure time. The Greeks used this clock to make sure that people in court kept their speeches short. (This clock runs out in about six minutes.)

CALIFORNIA STANDARDS

6.4.1 Discuss the connections between geography and the development of city-states in the region of the Aegean Sea, including patterns of trade and commerce among Greek city-states and within the wider Mediterranean region.

6.4.2 Trace the transition from tyranny and oligarchy to early democratic forms of government and back to dictatorship in ancient Greece, including the significance of the invention of the idea of citizenship (e.g., from *Pericles' Funeral Oration*).

6.4.3 State the key differences between Athenian, or direct, democracy and representative democracy.

HI 2 Students understand and distinguish cause, effect, sequence, and correlation in historical events, including the long- and short-term causal relations.

HOW TO TEACH THE CALIFORNIA STANDARDS

Standard	Content	Student Question or Activity	Instruction
6.4.1	**Pages 371–372** Describes the geography of Greece and city settlement patterns	**Page 371** Students explain how Greece was organized politically.	Have students use knowledge from the previous lesson to discuss how Greek geography resulted in city-states developing independently.
6.4.2	**Pages 372–375** Traces the various stages of Greek government	**Pages 372–375** Students identify the different political systems that evolved in Greece.	Have students create an event line that plots the evolving of Greek government.
6.4.3	**Page 375** Explains differences between direct and indirect democracy	**Page 376** Students analyze what made democracy in Athens a limited democracy.	Have a class discussion comparing the characteristics of Athens' form of democracy with democracy in the United States.
HI 2	**Pages 373–375** Analyzes how rebellion brought about change in Greek government	**Page 376** Students explain the role of tyrants in the development of Greek democracy.	Discuss how tyrants who take power illegally can lead to people wanting a voice in the government.

The City-State and Democracy

TERMS & NAMES
polis
aristocracy
oligarchy
tyrant
citizen
democracy

Terms & Names

polis the Greek word for city-state

aristocracy rule by the upper classes

oligarchy rule by the few

tyrant a ruler who takes power illegally

citizen a person who is loyal to and protected by a government

democracy a government in which citizens make political decisions

Build on What You Know As you read in Lesson 1, the Mycenaean civilization fell about 1200 B.C. After a decline, Greek culture gradually started to advance again. This led to the rise of Greek civilization. Like ancient Sumer, Greece was a region of people who shared a common language and common beliefs. In spite of that cultural unity, Greece was divided politically.

The Rise of City-States

① ESSENTIAL QUESTION How was Greece organized politically?
It was organized into separate city-states, which were cities and their surrounding lands.
In Lesson 1, you learned how geography divided Greece into small regions. Because of this, the basic form of government was the city-state. A city-state is a state made of a city and its surrounding lands. The colonies founded by Greeks around the Mediterranean were also city-states.

Greek City-States City-states became common in Greece about 700 B.C. In Greek, the word for city-state was **polis**. Most city-states were small. Geographic features, such as mountains, limited their size. Athens and Sparta were the largest Greek city-states. Their lands included the plains that surrounded the center city.

Most Greek cities had fewer than 20,000 residents. Because a city-state was fairly small, the people who lived there formed a close community.

Agora Most Greek cities, such as Athens shown here, had an agora—an open marketplace that also had temples and other public buildings. Men often met there to talk politics. ▶

371

❸ Teach

The Rise of City-States
6.4.1

Talk About It

- **Critical Thinking: Making Inferences**
Why do you think acropolises stopped being used mainly for military purposes? (*Possible answers: The population of city-states expanded beyond the protective walls of their acropolises; city-states began to rely on strong armies to protect them instead of acropolises.*)

In-Depth Resources: Unit 5
• Reading Skill: Categorizing, p. 22

More About . . .

The Acropolis
The Acropolis in Athens started as a
fortification and developed into a temple
dedicated to Athena. A stone temple in her
honor was built around 600 B.C. When the
Persians invaded, they destroyed the temple.
Pericles urged the rebuilding of the Acropolis
in the last half of the 5th century B.C. A new
temple to Athena, the Parthenon, was built.
Today the ruin of the Parthenon is world
famous.

Teach

Forms of Government

 6.4.2

Talk About It

• What group of people had little power
in all forms of government and how did
they contribute to change in government?
*(Poor people had no voice in monarchies,
aristocracies, or oligarchies. At times their
anger made them rebel. People who wanted to
take power often gained the support of these
rebels. As a result, the poor many times backed
tyrants who took power illegally.)*

• **Critical Thinking: Identifying Issues
and Problems** How did poor people's
resentment and rebellion lead to democratic
government? *(Possible answer: Solon made
reforms that helped prevent revolts by the
poor. Some of these reforms laid the basis for
a democratic government.)*

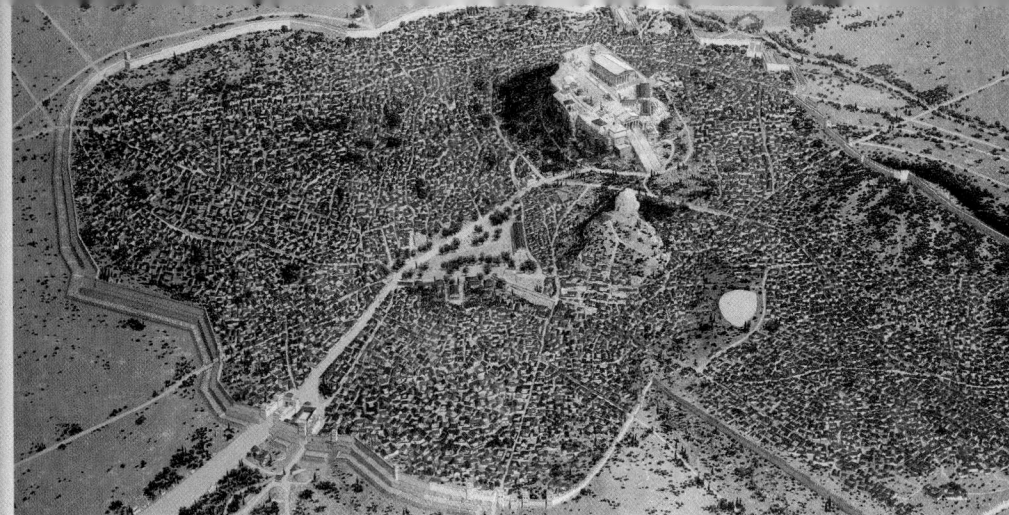

▲ **Athens from the Air**
A modern artist painted
this watercolor showing
Athens and its surrounding
lands. Notice how the
Acropolis is much higher
than everything else.

Layout of the City The center of city life was the
agora. The agora was an open space where people came
for business and public gatherings. Male citizens met
there to discuss politics. Festivals and athletic contests
were held there. Statues, temples, and other public
buildings were found in and around the agora. (See
Daily Life on pages 384–385.)

Many cities had a fortified hilltop called an acropolis. The
word means "highest city." At first, people used the acropolis
mainly for military purposes; high places are easier to defend.
Later the Greeks built temples and palaces on the flat tops of
these hills. Ordinary houses were built along the hill's base.

REVIEW What was the role of the agora in a Greek city?
It was the center of city life where people gathered for all kinds of public activities, such as
business gatherings, political discussions, and festivals.

Forms of Government

② ESSENTIAL QUESTION What different political systems evolved in the
city-states of Greece? Monarchy, oligarchy, and rule by a tyrant were different political systems
used in Greece.
Each city-state of Greece was independent. The people of each
one figured out what kind of government worked best for them.
As a result, different city-states used different political systems.
Some city-states kept the same system of government for
centuries. Others slowly changed from one system to another.

INTERDISCIPLINARY ACTIVITIES

Language Arts

Deliver a Persuasive Speech
Have students write and present a speech
to ordinary citizens in Greece from the
viewpoint of a Greek tyrant who is working
to help poor people by bringing change to
the country. Their speeches should include
arguments against the oligarchy whom the
tyrant helped overthrow. The arguments
should be supported by facts and examples.
Remind students to choose the most
effective order for their arguments.

Art

Create a Diorama
Have students work in groups to create a
diorama of the Acropolis in ancient Athens.
Have them research the layout on the
Internet before beginning the project. Each
group should write research notes and make
a design plan before creating their diorama.

Monarchs and Aristocrats The earliest form of government in Greece was monarchy (MAHN•uhr•kee). A monarch is a king or queen who has supreme power. Therefore, a monarchy is a government that a king or queen rules. Most Greek city-states started out as monarchies but changed over time.

Aristocracy (AR•ih•STAHK•ruh•see) is another name for the upper class or nobility. In Greece, the aristocracy were people who were descended from high-born ancestors. Some aristocrats believed that their ancestors were mythical heroes.

The Greek city-state of Corinth began as a monarchy. Later, an aristocracy ruled it. In fact, by the 700s B.C., most of the Greek city-states had moved from monarchy to rule by an aristocracy.

Oligarchy Some city-states developed a political system called **oligarchy** (AHL•ih•GAHR•kee). Oligarchy means "rule by the few." It is similar to aristocracy because in both cases, a minority group controls the government.

The main difference between the two is the basis for the ruling class's power. When aristocrats rule, they do so because of their inherited social class. In an oligarchy, people rule because of wealth or land ownership. In some Greek city-states, an oligarchy replaced aristocratic rule. In others, the aristocracy and the oligarchy shared power.

Tyrants Poor people were not part of government in either monarchy, aristocracy, or oligarchy. Often, the poor came to resent being shut out of power. At times, they rebelled.

Sometimes a wealthy person who wanted to seize power made use of that anger. He would ask poor people to support him in becoming a leader. Such leaders were called tyrants. In Greece, a **tyrant** was someone who took power in an illegal way. Today the term *tyrant* means a cruel leader. To the Greeks, a tyrant was simply someone who acted like a king without being of royal birth. Some Greek tyrants worked to help the poor. Some created building programs to provide jobs. Others enacted laws canceling the debts that poor people owed to the wealthy.

Tyrants played an important role in the development of rule by the people. They helped overthrow the oligarchy. They also showed that if common people united behind a leader, they could gain the power to make changes.

Vocabulary Strategy
The term *aristocracy* is from the Greek **root words** *aristos*, which means "best," and *kratos*, which means "power." The term *oligarchy* is from the **root words** *oligos*, which means "few," and *arkhe*, which means "rule."

REVIEW How were oligarchy and aristocracy similar?
They were both political systems in which a few wealthy people had control of the government.

Vocabulary Strategy

Root Words
Have students make a three-column chart with the column headings **Word**, **Root**, and **Meaning** from left to right. Have them list the words from the Vocabulary Strategy and then the words *polis*, *monarchy*, and *democracy* in the **Word** column. Then have students look for the roots and meanings of each word and write them in the chart.

More About . . .

Tyrants
Some tyrants had popular support even though they obtained power illegally. Tyrants usually came to power when the poor were dissatisfied or when there was some kind of crisis. Often, they were extremely popular when they first took power. However, their power was very unstable. Unless they made sweeping reforms, their rule through military force and fear could fall to a new tyrant. The word *tyrant* took on a negative meaning with the growth of democracy.

DIFFERENTIATING INSTRUCTION

English Learners

Classify Vocabulary
Have students work in small groups to explain the difference between a monarchy, aristocracy, oligarchy, and democracy. Tell students to locate key vocabulary from the text that can be classified into these four categories. Show students how to find examples for each category. Help students formulate statements to support their findings. Have them practice reading their statements out loud.

Inclusion

Student Teachers
Have students who have difficulty reading work with a partner. Then have each student take turns reading the sections and asking the review questions that follow. Have the student teachers help their partners find the correct answers in the text.

Teach

Athens Builds a Limited Democracy

 6.4.3, HI 2

Talk About It

- What was one of Greece's major legacies to the world? *(the idea of citizenship)*

- What reforms did Solon make? *(He freed slaves and outlawed slavery for citizens, allowed all citizens to serve in the assembly and elect leaders, and made laws less harsh.)*

- What reforms did Cleisthenes make? *(He took power from nobles, organized citizens based on where they lived rather than on wealth, and allowed any citizen to vote on laws.)*

- What is the difference between a direct and indirect democracy? *(direct—all citizens meet to vote on laws; indirect—people elect representatives to make laws)*

- Which people were excluded from Greece's limited democracy? *(women, slaves, and foreigners)*

- **Critical Thinking: Identifying Issues and Problems** What problems could arise when some people are excluded from taking part in government? *(Possible answers: dissatisfaction, poverty, rebellion)*

History Makers

Solon
Solon was an aristocrat and a poet. When he returned after his ten-year journey, Athens was in the middle of a civil war. Solon tried and failed to get Pisistratus, Athens' first tyrant, removed from office.

In-Depth Resources: Unit 5
- Primary Source: Poem by Solon, p. 31

Athens Builds a Limited Democracy

 ESSENTIAL QUESTION How did limited democracy develop in Athens?
People in the lower classes began to demand more power. The reforms of two leaders, Solon and Cleisthenes, gave people more power and led to an early form of democracy.

By helping tyrants rise to power, people in the lower classes realized they could influence government. As a result, they began to demand even more political power.

Citizenship One of the major legacies of ancient Greece is the idea of citizenship, which the Greeks invented. In today's world, a **citizen** is a person who is loyal to a government and who is entitled to protection by that government. To the Greeks, a citizen was a person with the right to take part in ruling the city-state. A citizen had to be born to parents who were free citizens. In much of ancient Greece, people of both upper and lower classes were citizens, but only upper-class citizens had power.

By demanding political power, the lower-class citizens were asking for a major change to their society. Such a change does not happen quickly. During the 500s B.C., two leaders in Athens made gradual reforms that gave people more power. Those leaders were Solon and Cleisthenes (KLIHS•thuh•NEEZ).

Solon and Cleisthenes In the 500s B.C., trouble stirred in Athens. Many poor farmers owed so much money that they were forced to work their land for someone else or to become slaves. The lower classes were growing angry with the rulers.

History Makers

Solon (c. 630 to 560 B.C.)

Solon was called one of the Seven Wise Men of Greece. Although he was the son of a noble family, he reduced the nobles' power. He is known for his political reforms and his poetry. Poetry was the way he communicated with the citizens.

About 600 B.C., Solon recited a poem to encourage the Athenians in a war. He persuaded them to resume the war and save the honor of Athens.

Solon's reforms did not make all Athenians happy. The nobles wished he had made fewer changes. Poor farmers wished that he had given them more land. Tired of having to justify his reforms, Solon left on a trip for ten years. He traveled to Egypt and Cyprus, among other places. He wrote poems about his journey.

INTERDISCIPLINARY ACTIVITIES

Language Arts

Create a Pamphlet
Have students find out more about citizenship in ancient Greece. Ask them to work individually or in pairs to design a pamphlet that might be sent to people in ancient Greece. This pamphlet should identify the rights that the ancient Greeks have as citizens. Encourage students to include illustrations as well as text.

Language Arts

Write a Press Release
Explain what a press release is and show students examples. Then have students write a press release announcing the reforms of Solon or Cleisthenes that led to giving common people more power. Combine students who wrote about Solon and those who wrote about Cleisthenes into groups to create a final press release to present to the class.

About 594 B.C., the nobles elected Solon to lead Athens. He made reforms that helped prevent a revolt by the poor. First he freed people who had become slaves because of debts. He made a law that no citizen could be enslaved.

Solon also organized citizens into four classes based on wealth, not birth. Rich men had more power—yet this was still a fairer system than the old one that limited power to nobles. Solon allowed all citizens to serve in the assembly and help elect leaders. He also reformed the laws to make them less harsh.

Around 500 B.C., Cleisthenes increased the citizens' power even more. He took power away from the nobles. He organized citizens into groups based on place of residence, not wealth. Any citizen could now vote on laws.

Direct Democracy Athens moved toward an early form of democracy. **Democracy** is a government in which the citizens make political decisions. The Athenian style of democracy is called a direct democracy. In such a system, all the citizens meet to decide on the laws. (Indirect democracy, in which people elect representatives to make laws, is more common today. The United States is an example.)

Jury box and tokens
Juries in Athens voted by putting tokens in this box. The token with the hollow center spoke meant "guilty," and the other meant "not guilty." ▼

PATTERNS in HISTORY Forms of Government

	Monarchy	Oligarchy	Direct Democracy
Who ruled	A king or queen ruled the government.	A small group of citizens ruled the government.	All citizens took part in the government (but not all people were citizens).
Basis for rule	Many kings or queens claimed that the gods gave them the right to rule. The monarch's son usually was the next ruler.	Aristocratic birth, wealth, or land ownership gave this group the right to rule.	Neither wealth nor social status affected the right to make decisions.
Type of rule	The king or queen often had supreme power over everyone else.	The ruling group ran the government for their own purposes.	Decisions were made by voting. The majority won.

Ancient Greece • **375**

History from Visuals

Jury Box and Tokens

- What other manual ways can you think of for votes to be counted? *(Possible answers: papers in a hat, raising hands, saying aloud yes or no)*

- Why do you think methods to anonymously count votes developed? *(Possible answers: People wanted privacy; they did not want others to criticize their vote; a vote should be an individual choice rather than a group choice.)*

Patterns in History

Forms of Government

Reading from left to right, what pattern do you see in how many people were involved in government? *(As forms of government developed, more and more people took part in them.)*

DIFFERENTIATING INSTRUCTION

Struggling Readers

Chart Connections
Give students an enlarged copy of the chart on this page. Have student pairs find the text that applies to each category, write the page and paragraph number under it, and read the information aloud. Ask them to add one note under each category after they read the material aloud.

Gifted and Talented Students

Research the Seven Wise Men of Greece
Have students research the men in addition to Solon who are included in the "Seven Wise Men of Greece." Ask students to include where and when they lived, what they did, and why they were considered wise. Then ask students to make a list of the traits that a wise person might have.

❹ Assess & Reteach

Assess Have students complete the category chart on page 376. Then have them create a category chart to compare limited and unlimited democracy. Discuss their findings as a class.

 Formal Assessment
• Lesson Quiz, p. 190

Reteach Have students work in groups of three to write a review of this lesson. Have each member take one of the three sections, summarize it, and share it with the other group members. Create a class summary with information from all groups.

 In-Depth Resources: Unit 5
• Vocabulary Cards, p. 27
• Reteaching Activity, p. 35

🔑 Homework Helper

Visit **ClassZone.com** for a lesson review, a flip-card activity, and links to related Web sites.

Limited Democracy Athens had a limited democracy. It did not include all of the people who lived in the city-state. Only free adult males were citizens who could take part in the government. Women, slaves, and foreigners could not take part. Noncitizens were not allowed to become citizens.

REVIEW How did reformers change the government of Athens? They enacted laws that gave more power to the citizens and paved the way for democracy.

• The people of Greece lived in independent city-states.
• Greek city-states had various types of government: monarchy, oligarchy, and direct democracy.
• Over time, the male citizens of Athens gained the power to make political decisions.

Why It Matters Now . . .

Athens is often called the birthplace of democracy. Many people in today's world are seeking to replace other forms of government with democracy.

▲ **Ostracism** If Athenians thought someone was a danger to the city-state, they would ostracize, or send that person away for ten years. People voted to ostracize someone by scratching his or her name on a piece of pottery called an ostracon.

---

3 Lesson Review

🔑 **Homework Helper**
ClassZone.com

Terms & Names

1. Explain the importance of

polis　　oligarchy　　citizen
aristocracy　　tyrant　　democracy

Using Your Notes

Categorizing Use your completed chart to answer the following question:

2. In which form of government do the fewest people share power? (6.4.2)

Types of Government		
Monarchy	Oligarchy	Democracy

Main Ideas

3. How did the geography of Greece lead to the rise of city-states? (6.4.1)
4. What was the role of tyrants in the development of democracy in Greece? (6.4.2)
5. What made democracy in Athens a limited democracy? (6.4.3)

Critical Thinking

6. **Understanding Causes** What were the key factors leading to the rise of tyrants? Explain. (HI 2)
7. **Drawing Conclusions** Why was the invention of the idea of citizenship important to the development of democracy? (6.4.2)

Activity　**Making a Poster** Find out how a person qualifies as a citizen in the United States. How can a noncitizen become a citizen? Make a poster comparing citizenship in Athens with citizenship in the United States. (6.4.3)

---

3 Lesson Review Answers

Terms & Names

1. • polis, p. 371
   • aristocracy, p. 373
   • oligarchy, p. 373
   • tyrant, p. 373
   • citizen, p. 374
   • democracy, p. 375

Using Your Notes

See page 370 for an example of a completed chart.

2. monarchy

Main Ideas

3. Mountains and seas divided the country into small, separate regions. As a result, independent city-states became the main form of government.
4. They encouraged the people to unite behind a leader in order to get a share of political power.
5. Many people did not have citizenship.

Critical Thinking

6. Possible answer: The aristocracy and the oligarchy often ignored the needs of the poor. As a result, the poor became angry. A tyrant used this anger by asking the poor to support him in becoming a leader.
7. Possible answer: Citizenship encouraged people to be loyal to a government and to get involved in the political process.

Activity Rubric

	Quality of Poster	Number of Errors
4	very well-drawn, clearly labeled, detailed, accurate	no more than one factual error
3	well-drawn, detailed, accurate	two or three errors
2	fairly well-drawn, few details, some inaccuracies	four or five errors
1	no details, inaccurate	more than five errors

Make Vocabulary Cards

Goal: To learn English words that are based on Greek roots

Prepare

1 The Greek word *polis*, which you learned in this chapter, is the root of many English words, including *politics*.

2 Other terms from the chapter use Greek words as prefixes and roots. For example, democracy comes from word *demos*, which means "the people," and *kratos*, which means "power."

Do the Activity

1 Working with a partner, find other words in the dictionary that are based on the Greek word *polis*. Look up words beginning with the letters *pol* and check their origin. Word origins are given at the beginning or at the end of the definition.

2 Look up the following types of government in the dictionary: monarchy, aristocracy, oligarchy. Note the meaning of each term and the Greek roots of the words.

3 Make a vocabulary card for each word that comes from *polis* and for each of the government terms. Write the English word on the front of the card. On the back, write the word's meaning and origin.

Follow-Up

Take turns quizzing each other until you know the meaning of the words.

Extension

Locating Cities on a Map Use a map of the United States to find cities that end in *polis*, such as Indianapolis. Make a list.

CALIFORNIA STANDARDS
Reading 1.0 Word Analysis, Fluency, and Systematic Vocabulary Development Students use their knowledge of word origins and word relationships, as well as historical and literary context clues, to determine the meaning of specialized vocabulary and to understand the precise meaning of grade-level-appropriate words.

Materials & Supplies
- a dictionary that gives word origins
- pens or pencils
- notecards
- a map of the United States

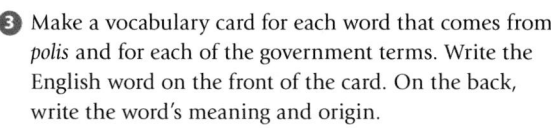

377

ACTIVITY: VOCABULARY CARDS

Objectives

- To learn decoding skills to predict new word meanings.
- Create vocabulary cards based on Greek roots.

Suggestions for Completing the Activity

- Demonstrate how to use the dictionary to find word origins, and explain how to read them.
- Model for students how to read a dictionary entry. Make sure they understand the parts of an entry.
- Make sure you have enough dictionaries that contain word origins to distribute to the class.

ACTIVITY ANSWERS

Follow-Up Answer
Observe students using their vocabulary cards. Assess their ability to work with the cards in an efficient and productive manner.

Extension Rubric

	Listing of Cities	Presentation of List
4	contains many possible examples	neat, clearly written
3	contains some possible examples	mostly neat, clearly written
2	contains few possible examples	somewhat neat, unclear
1	contains one or no examples	sloppy, unclear

❶ Plan & Prepare

Objectives

- Describe Spartan government and its militaristic society.
- Outline Athenian society and its politically active citizens.
- Explain how the Persian Wars led to Greek unification.
- **Language Objective:** Create a mural to compare and contrast life in Sparta and life in Athens.

Quick Look

Lesson 4 focuses on comparing and contrasting Athenian and Spartan society and the effect of the Persian Wars on both.

❷ Focus & Motivate

Preview Tell students that in this lesson they will learn about the beginnings of democracy in Athens and the militaristic society of Sparta. Write "Sparta: Military state" on the board and ask students to list its characteristics.

Introduce the Main Ideas The three main ideas relate to the Big Idea "Governments create law codes and political bodies to organize a society." Help students look for this Big Idea as you go through the lesson.

Reading Skill: Comparing and Contrasting Review comparing and contrasting with students and answer any questions they have.

SAMPLE ANSWERS FOR DIAGRAM

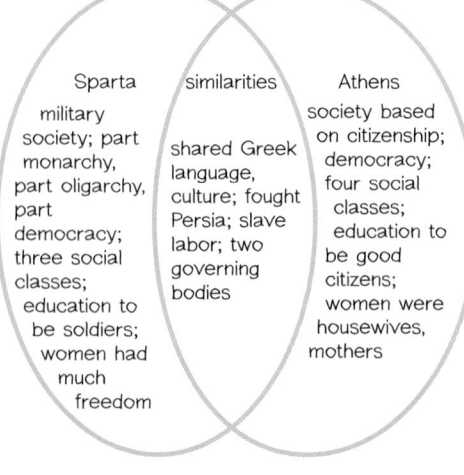

Sparta
military society; part monarchy, part oligarchy, part democracy; three social classes; education to be soldiers; women had much freedom

similarities
shared Greek language, culture; fought Persia; slave labor; two governing bodies

Athens
society based on citizenship; democracy; four social classes; education to be good citizens; women were housewives, mothers

---

Lesson 4

▶ **MAIN IDEAS**

❶ **Government** Sparta built a state in which every part of life was organized around the need to have a strong army.

❷ **Government** Athenian citizens were expected to participate actively in government.

❸ **Government** A Persian invasion endangered Greece, so some city-states united to fight their enemy.

▶ **TAKING NOTES**

Reading Skill: Comparing and Contrasting
Use a Venn diagram to take notes comparing and contrasting life in Sparta and Athens. Think about where you would rather have lived. Underline the details in your notes that influenced your decision.

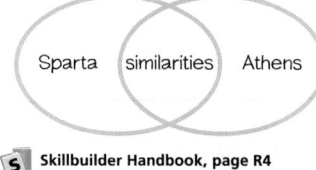

Sparta   similarities   Athens

🄢 **Skillbuilder Handbook, page R4**

▲ **Athena** The goddess Athena was associated closely with the city of Athens. She was wise and was supposed to give good advice in war. Because she is a warrior goddess, she is often shown wearing a helmet.

CALIFORNIA STANDARDS

6.4.3 State the key differences between Athenian, or direct, democracy and representative democracy.

6.4.6 Compare and contrast life in Athens and Sparta, with emphasis on their roles in the Persian and Peloponnesian wars.

HI 2 Students understand and distinguish cause, effect, sequence, and correlation in historical events, including the long- and short-term causal relations.

Framework In studying each ancient society, students should examine the role of women and the presence or absence of slavery.

HOW TO TEACH THE CALIFORNIA STANDARDS

Standard	Content	Student Question or Activity	Instruction
6.4.6	**Pages 379–380** Examines the structure and government of Spartan society **Page 381** Examines the structure and government of Athenian society	**Page 383** Students identify ways in which Sparta and Athens were similar.	Have students complete the Venn diagram on page 378 to compare and contrast life in both city-states.
HI 2	**Page 383** Analyzes why the Persian invasion led to Greek unity	**Page 383** Students explain how the Persian invasion led to Greek unity.	Have students discuss why rivals sometimes need to work together in order to succeed.
Framework	**Pages 379–381** Examines the role of women and slaves in Sparta and Athens	**Page 383** Students contrast the role of women in Sparta and Athens.	Ask students why women might have gained rights during periods of war in the past. (*Possible answers: Family life became less important; because men were fighting, women replaced them in the workplace.*)

Sparta and Athens

TERMS & NAMES

Athens
Sparta
helot
barracks
Marathon

Terms & Names

Athens a city-state of ancient Greece

Sparta a city-state of ancient Greece

helot a slave

barracks military houses

Marathon a plain near Athens

Build on What You Know You've read about **Athens**. Its main rival was **Sparta**, a large city-state in the Peloponnesus. Life there was quite different from life in Athens.

Sparta's Military State

① **ESSENTIAL QUESTION** What did Spartan society emphasize the most?

military strength and building a strong army because it needed to keep the helots in submission

About 715 B.C., Sparta conquered a neighboring area to gain land. This conquest changed Sparta. The Spartans forced the defeated people to become slaves called **helots** (HEHL•uhtz). They worked mostly on farms and had to give the Spartans half their crops. The helots rebelled many times. Although they greatly outnumbered the Spartans and fought hard, the Spartans put down the revolts. Fear of these revolts led Sparta to become a state that focused everything on building a strong army.

Government and Society Sparta had a government that was part monarchy, part oligarchy, and part democracy. Two kings ruled Sparta, and five elected supervisors ran the government. The Council of Elders, made up of 30 older citizens, proposed laws. All Spartan citizens were part of the Assembly. It elected officials and voted on the laws proposed by the Council.

Three social groups made up Spartan society. Citizens lived in the city and spent all their time training to be soldiers. Free noncitizens lived in nearby villages. They had no political rights. The lowest group was the helots. Their labor fed Sparta, making it possible for free Spartans to be full-time soldiers.

Spartan Warrior As this statue shows, Spartans valued military strength. Probably only an officer of a high rank could wear the crested helmet shown here. ▶

379

❸ Teach

Sparta's Military State

6.4.6, Framework

Talk About It

- **Critical Thinking: Drawing Conclusions** In what way were the helots an important class in Sparta? *(Possible answer: They did much of the work, freeing up Spartans to be soldiers.)*

California Resources

California Reading Toolkit, L39
California Modified Lesson Plans for English Learners, p. 81
California Daily Standards Practice Transparencies, TT39
California Standards Enrichment Workbook, pp. 53–54, 59–60
California Online Test Practice
California Test Generator CD-ROM
California Standards Planner and Lesson Plans, L77
California EasyPlanner CD-ROM
California eEdition CD-ROM

LESSON 4 PROGRAM RESOURCES

ON LEVEL

In-Depth Resources: Unit 5
- Reading Skill: Comparing and Contrasting, p. 23

Formal Assessment
- Lesson Quiz, p. 191

ENGLISH LEARNERS

In-Depth Resources in Spanish
- Reading Skill: Comparing and Contrasting, p. 94

Modified Lesson Plans for English Learners, p. 81

Reading Study Guide (Spanish), p. 101

Reading Study Guide Audio CD (Spanish)

STRUGGLING READERS

In-Depth Resources: Unit 5
- Reading Skill: Comparing and Contrasting, p. 23
- Reteaching Activity, p. 36

Reading Toolkit, L39

Reading Study Guide, p. 101

Reading Study Guide Audio CD

GIFTED AND TALENTED STUDENTS

Interdisciplinary Projects
- Math, p. 61

INCLUSION

EasyPlanner CD-ROM
- Reading Skill: Comparing and Contrasting
- Reteaching Activity

TECHNOLOGY

eEdition CD-ROM

Power Presentations CD-ROM

Humanities Transparencies
- HT22 Woman at an Altar

Critical Thinking Transparencies
- CT49 Comparing and Contrasting
- CT50 Chapter 11 Visual Summary

Test Generator CD-ROM

ClassZone.com

In-Depth Resources: Unit 5
• Reading Skill: Comparing and Contrasting, p. 23

Visual Vocabulary

Barracks
Point out to students that the barracks, or military housing, shown here contain beds and little else. The barracks are very spartan, or simple and plain. Tell students that the word *spartan* comes from the word *Sparta.*

Interpreting Primary Sources

from *Parallel Lives*

• What type of modern school is structured like this Spartan school? *(a military boarding school)*

• Looking at the illustration, what might Lycurgus be saying? *(Possible answers: start training early in life; make boys strong, obedient, and willing to take punishment; make them work together so that in battle they work as a unit)*

DOCUMENT–BASED QUESTION ANSWER

They learned to be brave and strong and to obey orders.

Education The goal of Spartan society was to have a strong army. At age seven, boys moved into military houses called **barracks**. Their education stressed discipline, duty, strength, and military skill. (See Primary Source below.) The boys learned to read just enough to get by.

All male citizens entered the army at the age of 20 and served until they were 60. Even after men got married, they had to eat with their fellow soldiers.

Visual Vocabulary

Barracks

Women Spartan society expected its women to be tough, emotionally and physically. Mothers told their sons, "Bring back this shield yourself or be brought back on it." (Spartans carried dead warriors home on their shields.) Education for girls in Sparta focused on making them strong. They had athletic training and learned to defend themselves.

The emphasis on the army made family life less important in Sparta than in other Greek city-states. In Sparta husbands and wives spent much time apart. Women had more freedom. They were allowed to own property. A wife was expected to watch over her husband's property if he was at war.

REVIEW How did Spartan education support the military?
Boys were trained only in things that were important to soldiers. Girls were trained to be strong.

Primary Source

Background: Plutarch (PLOO•TAHRK) was a Greek historian who lived between A.D. 46 and about 120. One of the people he wrote about was Lycurgus (ly•KUR•guhs), the leader of Sparta who created its strong military institutions. This passage describes how boys were trained in Sparta by being placed in companies, or military units.

380

from *Parallel Lives*
By Plutarch
(based on the translation by Aubrey Stewart and George Long)

As soon as the boys were seven years old Lycurgus took them from their parents and enrolled them in companies. Here they lived and ate in common and shared their play and work. One of the noblest and bravest men of the state was appointed superintendent of the boys, and they themselves in each company chose the wisest and bravest as captain. They looked to him for orders, obeyed his commands, and endured his punishments, so that even in childhood they learned to obey.

◀ Lycurgus discusses the meaning of education in this 17th-century painting.

DOCUMENT–BASED QUESTION
What did Spartan boys learn that made them good soldiers?

DIFFERENTIATING INSTRUCTION

English Learners

Create a Mural
Have student pairs create a mural that depicts the similarities and differences of Spartan and Athenian life. Have them use captions to describe the detail in the illustration. Model contrasting statements by using *but, however,* and *except.* Use *both, like,* and *similarly* to make comparing statements. Have students formulate comparing and contrasting statements about Athenian and Spartan life as shown in the murals.

Inclusion

Divide and Conquer
Have students form small groups, and have each group read one of the three subsections of "Sparta's Military State." Then gather the groups together and discuss what each group learned from their reading. Students should use these discussions to help them as they reread "Sparta's Military State."

Athens' Democratic Way of Life

2 ESSENTIAL QUESTION What was the government of Athens like?

As you learned in Lesson 3, over time Athens developed a direct democracy. All of its citizens met to vote on laws. Only free men were citizens.

Athens had two governing bodies. Citizens served in the army and served on juries. Foreigners, women, slaves, and children were not citizens.

Government and Society Athens had two governing bodies. The Council of Four Hundred took care of day-to-day problems. The Assembly voted on policies proposed by the council.

Citizens had to serve in the army whenever they were needed. They also had to serve on juries. Juries usually had several hundred people to hear charges against a person. In Athens, all citizens were equal in the courts. There were no professional lawyers or judges. Citizens argued their case directly before the jury.

Solon's reforms had organized citizens into four classes based on income. Foreigners, women, children, and slaves were not citizens.

Slaves made up one-third of the population. They worked in homes, agriculture, industry, and mines. Some slaves worked alongside their masters. Some even earned wages and were able to buy their freedom.

▲ **Knucklebones Players** These two women are playing knucklebones, an ancient game similar to the child's game of jacks. It is called that because it was originally played with the knucklebones (anklebones) of a sheep.

Education Boys of wealthy families started school at age six or seven. Education prepared them to be good citizens. They studied logic and public speaking to help them debate as adults in the Assembly. They also studied reading, writing, poetry, arithmetic, and music. Athletic activities helped them develop strong bodies.

Women Athenians expected women to be good wives and mothers. These roles were respected because they helped to keep the family and society strong. In addition, some women fulfilled important religious roles as priestesses in temples. In spite of their importance to society, Athenian women had much less freedom than Spartan women.

Women could inherit property only if their fathers had no sons. Girls did not attend school. They learned household duties from their mothers. A few learned to read and write.

REVIEW What were the duties of an Athenian citizen?
He took part in the assembly and served in the military and on juries.

Ancient Greece • 381

Teach

Athens' Democratic Way of Life

6.4.6

Talk About It

- What were the responsibilities of citizens in Athens? *(They served in the army and on juries of several hundred people; they had to argue their own court cases.)*

- How was the education of boys and girls different in Athenian society? *(Boys went to school at age six or seven; they studied logic, public speaking, reading, writing, poetry, arithmetic, music, and athletics. Girls mostly learned to be good wives and mothers and to do household duties.)*

- **Critical Thinking: Comparing and Contrasting** How was the education of Spartan and Athenian boys alike and different? *(Both went to school at about age seven and both were trained to be strong. Spartan boys lived away from families and studied little besides being a soldier. Athenian boys lived at home and studied subjects that would make them skilled debaters and good citizens.)*

More About . . .

Games
We still play many games that people have played throughout history. Athenian boys played a game with a stick and ball similar to field hockey. Pictures show girls and boys throwing balls to each other. Juggling is seen on Greek pottery vases. Marbles were played with clay or marble balls. Versions of backgammon and checkers were played by Greeks and Romans.

 Humanities Transparencies
- HT22 Woman at an Altar

DIFFERENTIATING INSTRUCTION

Struggling Readers

Practice a Pre-Reading Strategy
Have volunteers read aloud the lesson title, section titles, and headings. As each title or heading is read, ask students what they think it means. Then ask them to predict what they will read about in the section. Challenge student to explain how the Essential Questions and the heading that follows each one are related to each other.

Gifted and Talented Students

Play a Game
Have groups research ancient and modern hand games, such as knucklebones and jacks, in more detail. First, ask students to interview parents and grandparents about the games they played as children and report back to the class. Next, research knucklebones and jacks and provide playing pieces and a list of rules for each game. Then teach the games to the class.

Teach

The Persian Wars

6.4.5, HI 2

Talk About It

- Why did the Persians want to go to war with Athens? *(Athens had helped Greek colonies in Anatolia to revolt against Persia. Even though the colonies lost, Persia wanted to punish Athens for interfering.)*

- Without the help of Sparta, how did the outnumbered Greeks win the battle at Marathon? *(They drew the Persians into the center of their army and closed in around them. Greek spears were more effective than Persian arrows at close range.)*

- **Critical Thinking: Drawing Conclusions** Why do you think the Spartans did not arrive earlier to help the Athenians? *(Possible answers: The Spartans debated over whether to help their rival, Athens, or to stay out of the fight. The Spartans realized that if Persia defeated the Athenians, they might try to defeat the Spartans next.)*

History from Visuals

Interpreting Maps

- What map information indicates that Persia was stronger than the Greeks? *(The color purple indicates the extent of the Persian Empire and its allies. It is much larger than the color orange, which indicates the Greek allies.)*

- Where did the Persians win a battle with the Greeks? *(Thermopylae)*

GEOGRAPHY SKILLBUILDER ANSWER

Possible answer: It was safer to be near land than out in the open sea; most of the coast was controlled by Persia, so it would be easy to get supplies.

The Persian Wars

3 ESSENTIAL QUESTION What happened when Persia invaded Greece?

As you know, Persia conquered much of Southwest Asia. A king and a highly organized government ruled the resulting empire.

In the 500s B.C., Persia conquered Anatolia, a region with many Greek colonies. In 499 B.C., some Greeks in Anatolia revolted against Persian rule. Athens, which had a strong navy, sent ships and soldiers to help them. The revolt failed, but Persia decided to punish Athens for interfering. In 490 B.C., the Persians arrived near Athens on the plain of **Marathon**. The Athenians sent a runner to ask Sparta for help, but the Spartans came too late.

The Athenians were greatly outnumbered, so they had to use a clever plan. First they drew the Persians toward the center of the Greek line. Then the Greeks surrounded them and attacked. In close fighting, Greek spears were more effective than Persian arrows. The Persians lost 6,400 men. The Greeks lost only 192.

Legend says that a soldier ran from Marathon about 25 miles to Athens to tell of the victory. When he reached Athens, he collapsed and died. Modern marathons are based on his long run.

During the first invasion, the Greeks defeated the Persians on the plain of Marathon. During the second invasion, the Athenian navy defeated the Persian navy.

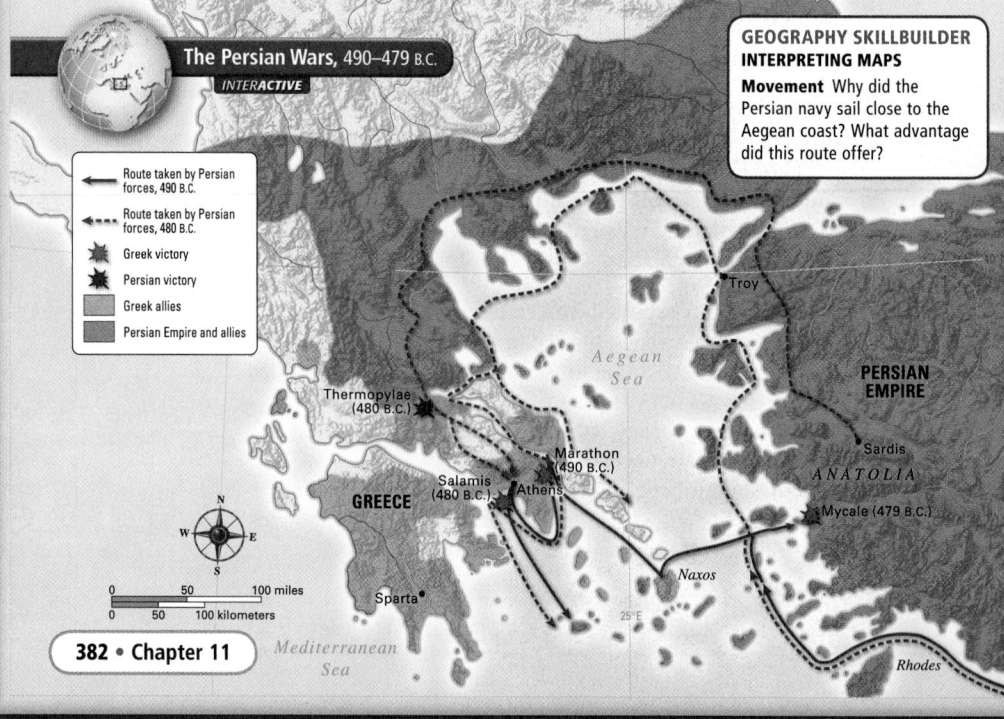

The Persian Wars, 490–479 B.C.
INTERACTIVE

- → Route taken by Persian forces, 490 B.C.
- ⇢ Route taken by Persian forces, 480 B.C.
- ✹ Greek victory
- ✸ Persian victory
- ▢ Greek allies
- ▢ Persian Empire and allies

GEOGRAPHY SKILLBUILDER
INTERPRETING MAPS
Movement Why did the Persian navy sail close to the Aegean coast? What advantage did this route offer?

Troy
Aegean Sea
PERSIAN EMPIRE
Thermopylae (480 B.C.)
Sardis
ANATOLIA
Marathon (490 B.C.)
Salamis (480 B.C.) Athens
Mycale (479 B.C.)
GREECE
Naxos
Sparta
Rhodes
Mediterranean Sea

0   50   100 miles
0   50   100 kilometers

382 • Chapter 11

INTERDISCIPLINARY ACTIVITIES

Math

Create a Mileage Map

Give groups an enlarged copy of the Persian Wars map on this page. Have groups pretend they are the Persian leader in 490 or 480 B.C. Have each group create a mileage map that shows the cities traveled to and the approximate distances between them on the map. Make Troy the starting point. When the maps are complete, have groups compare and contrast the cities traveled to and the distances covered on both maps.

Language Arts

Design a Crossword Puzzle

Tell students to use the terms, names, and other important words in this lesson to make a crossword puzzle. For the clues, have students use the definitions given in the book or write their own. Encourage students to use information from the maps and captions as well as the text.

Greek Victory In 480 B.C., Persia again invaded Greece. In spite of past quarrels with each other, several Greek city-states united against Persia. An army of 300 Spartans guarded the narrow pass at Thermopylae (thuhr•MAHP•uh•lee) to stop a Persian army from reaching Athens. The Spartans held the pass for two days before the Persians killed them all. Their sacrifice gave the Athenians time to prepare for battle.

The Athenians left their city to fight a naval battle against the Persians. The battle took place in a narrow body of water where the large Persian fleet could barely move. Smaller, more mobile Greek ships sunk about 300 Persian ships, and the war ended. You will read more about Greece after the war in Chapter 12.

REVIEW How did the Persian Wars bring the Greek city-states together?
Some city-states realized they needed to put aside their differences and unite in order to defeat a much stronger enemy.

Lesson Summary

- Sparta organized its state around its strong army.
- Athens valued democratic government and culture.
- Some Greek city-states united to defeat the Persians.

Why It Matters Now . . .

Defeating the Persians allowed Greek democracy and culture to continue. This culture greatly influenced later world civilization.

---

4 Lesson Review

 **Homework Helper**
ClassZone.com

Terms & Names
1. Explain the importance of

Athens	helot	Marathon
Sparta	barracks	

Using Your Notes
Comparing and Contrasting Use your completed Venn diagram to answer the following question:
2. What were some ways that Athens and Sparta were alike? (6.4.6)

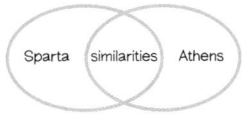

Main Ideas
3. What form of government existed in ancient Sparta? (6.4.6)
4. How were direct democracy and education related in Athens? (6.4.3)
5. What roles did Athens and Sparta play in defeating the Persians? (6.4.6)

Critical Thinking
6. **Understanding Causes** How did the conquest of the helots make it necessary for Sparta to be a military state, and how did the conquest make such a state possible? (HI 2)
7. **Contrasting** How was the role of women different in Athens and Sparta? (6.4.6, Framework)

Activity Internet Activity Use the Internet to learn more about the Persian Wars. Then create one panel for a mural about the wars. Illustrate one battle or another event. (6.4.6)
INTERNET KEYWORDS: *Battle of Marathon, Battle of Salamis, Thermopylae*

Ancient Greece • 383

---

❹ Assess & Reteach

Assess Group students and have each member number off. Ask a question from the lesson review, and allow group members to agree on an answer. Then call out a number and have that person from each group give the group's answer.

 Formal Assessment
- Lesson Quiz, p. 191

Reteach Divide the class into small groups. Have each group work together to complete the Reteaching Activity for Lesson 4. Share and discuss answers. If students are still uncertain about key terms in the lesson, have them quiz each other using Vocabulary Cards.

In-Depth Resources: Unit 5
- Vocabulary Cards, p. 27
- Reteaching Activity, p. 36

Homework Helper

Visit **ClassZone.com** for a lesson review, a flip-card activity, and links to related Web sites.

---

4 Lesson Review Answers

Terms & Names
1. • Athens, p. 379
   • Sparta, p. 379
   • helot, p. 379
   • barracks, p. 380
   • Marathon, p. 382

Using Your Notes
See page 378 for an example of a completed diagram.
2. Possible answers: Both shared in Greek language and culture; both fought against Persia; both used slave labor

Main Ideas
3. Sparta's government combined monarchy, oligarchy, and democracy. Sparta had kings, supervisors, a council, and an Assembly.
4. Athenians educated boys to become active citizens with skills to take part in a democratic government. Women had no political power, so the education of girls was not seen as important.
5. Possible answer: Athens defeated the Persians at Marathon and Salamis. The Spartans fought the Persians at Thermopylae, allowing Athenians time to prepare.

Critical Thinking
6. Possible answer: Sparta became a military state to prevent helot revolts. Helot labor produced the food that fed Spartan society, allowing Spartan citizens to spend all their time in the army.
7. Possible answer: Spartan women could own property, but Athenian women could not. In Athens, women's main roles were to be good wives and mothers. Girls were trained in household duties.

Activity Rubric

	Content of Mural	**Quality of Illustration**
4	displays historical event accurately with many details	very well-drawn
3	displays event well with most details	well-drawn
2	displays event with some details	fairly well-drawn
1	incomplete, few details	poorly drawn

Ancient Greece • 383

Objectives

- Describe the role of the agora in daily Greek life.
- Analyze and interpret information from an infographic.
- **Language Objective:** Interpret information from the illustrations that supports the text and makes the content more comprehensible.

❶ Focus & Motivate

Preview Ask students to describe a typical town or city center near where they live. Discuss what types of merchants and services are located there and what kind of conversation one would expect to find. Tell students that they are going to learn more details about the agora and its place in ancient Greek life.

❷ Teach

Talk About It

- What are some items that Greek merchants are selling? *(cloth, shoes, fish, vegetables, fruit, milk, and eggs)*
- Why were political discussions held in the agora? *(Discussing politics was important to citizens, and the mild weather of Athens made it possible to hold discussions outdoors.)*
- **Critical Thinking: Drawing Conclusions** How does a center such as the agora unify a city? *(Possible answers: Since everyone comes to the same place, people feel connected to neighbors; merchants can help each other out; people can relax together as well as do business.)*

More About . . .

Greek Word Origins
The term *agoraphobia* comes from two Greek roots, *agor* (marketplace) and *phobia* (intense fear). Agoraphobics are people who have an abnormal fear of leaving their homes to go out into the open. Other words with the root *phobia* are *hydrophobia*, *arachnophobia*, and *xenophobia*.

Daily Life

Extend Lesson 4

Life in the Agora

Purpose: To learn about daily life in Athens

Imagine a place that is a shopping mall, city hall, sports arena, and place of worship all in one. The agora of an ancient Greek city was just such a place. An agora was an open space with buildings around it and roads leading into it. People went there to buy and sell goods, to worship at the nearby temples, and to take part in government. This illustration shows the agora of ancient Athens in about 500 B.C.

Ⓐ **Fish Seller** Merchants set up stalls in the open space to sell goods. Because the Greeks lived near the sea, they ate much fish. Fresh fish was sold locally; it would spoil if it was transported very far. (Dried fish could be stored and traded to distant regions.)

Ⓑ **Cloth Seller** Sheep could graze on land that was too poor to farm, so most Greeks wore clothes made from wool. They also wore some linen, made from flax bought in Egypt.

Ⓒ **Political Discussions** Direct democracy required citizens to be very involved in government, so political discussions were popular in Athens. Because the weather was so mild, men often held such discussions outdoors.

Ⓓ **Shoemaker** Craftspeople, such as this shoemaker, often set up shop in the stoa. A stoa was a building made of a roof held up by long rows of columns. Stoas were also used for political meetings and as places for teachers to meet with their students.

Ⓔ **Farmers** Farmers sold their own vegetables, fruit, milk, and eggs at the market. First they had to transport the food to the city. Using an animal to carry the heavy load was the easiest method. Some poor farmers carried goods on their backs.

CALIFORNIA STANDARDS
6.4.6 Compare and contrast life in Athens and Sparta, with emphasis on their roles in the Persian and Peloponnesian Wars.

384 • Chapter 11

DIFFERENTIATING INSTRUCTION

English Learners

Interpret an Illustration
Tell students that studying the details of the illustration will help them gain a deeper understanding of the text. Have students describe some of the details in the illustration. Discuss how the details in the captions are shown in the scenes. Have them identify the jobs depicted in the illustration. Ask students, "What job would you choose?" Have them explain why.

Struggling Readers

Role-Play a Day in the Agora
Divide the class into small groups. Have the students in each group choose a role to play. The roles include a fish seller, cloth seller, farmer, shoemaker, and discusser of politics. Have each group role-play a day in the agora and have other class members be their customers or join in on a political discussion.

Research Links

Visit **ClassZone.com** for age-appropriate Web sites related to this topic.

More About . . .

The Stoa

A stoa protected people from the weather and was a place to talk about issues of the day. Sometimes, it marked the boundaries of the agora. The word *stoic* derives from the word *stoa,* which means *porch.* The Stoics were Greek philosophers who believed in wisdom, restraint, and using reason to live life. Their leader Zeno and his group met on the Stoa Poecile in the Greek marketplace and discussed their philosophy. Combining where they met and what they believed, the word *stoic* has come to mean a person who is unaffected by emotions and exercises restraint and reason.

Activities

1. **TALK ABOUT IT** Do you think the farmers were more likely to sell their goods at the open-air stalls or inside the stoa? Why?

2. **WRITE ABOUT IT** Imagine that you are from a rural village, and you have visited Athens for the first time. Write a description of your visit to the agora. (Writing 2.1)

Ancient Greece • 385

ACTIVITIES ANSWERS

1. **TALK ABOUT IT** Possible answer: Farmers would more likely be in the open-air stalls with the merchants because farmers are selling products. Craftspeople used tools and supplies and were more likely to be in the permanent structure.

2. **WRITE ABOUT IT**

2. Writing Rubric

	Description of Agora	Errors in Mechanics
4	includes stops at several places, vivid detail and language	zero or one
3	includes stops at a few places, good detail and language	two or three
2	includes stops at one or two places, average detail and language	four or five
1	confused detail and language	more than five

REVIEW

Terms & Names

geography
5. isthmus
8. peninsula

culture
1. alphabet
4. fable
6. myth

government
2. aristocracy
3. democracy
7. oligarchy
9. polis
10. tyrant

Main Ideas

The Geography of Ancient Greece
(pages 354–359)

11. Most cities were built on harbors near the coast to take advantage of trade.

12. sailing and shipbuilding

Beliefs and Customs
(pages 360–369)

13. Homer wrote epics that described heroes such as Achilles and Odysseus and showed how Greek gods influenced humans.

14. Both epic poems and fables have been passed down through generations and still influence our culture. Epics are long poems about heroes and gods; fables are short animal stories that teach a lesson.

The City-State and Democracy
(pages 370–377)

15. Solon outlawed citizen slavery and gave non-noble but wealthy citizens some power. Cleisthenes gave all citizens power to vote on laws.

16. Athens had direct democracy in which all the citizens met to make laws. Most democracy today is indirect democracy. Citizens elect representatives to make laws for them.

Sparta and Athens
(pages 378–385)

17. In Sparta, they were unpaid laborers. In Athens, they sometimes earned wages and were able to buy their freedom.

18. Sparta was part monarchy, oligarchy, and democracy, while Athens was a democracy; Sparta focused on military strength, while Athens focused on democracy and cultural pursuits; Spartan women had more freedom than Athenian women.

VISUAL SUMMARY

Ancient Greece

Geography (6.4.1)
- Greece did not have much good farmland.
- Most places in Greece were close to the sea. The Greeks used the seas as highways.

Economics (6.4.1)
- The Greeks built their economy on farming and sea trade.
- They learned to use coins from other trading people.

Culture (6.4.4)
- Early Greek literature included Aesop's fables and the epic poems the *Iliad* and the *Odyssey*.
- The Greeks learned the alphabet from the Phoenicians and adapted it to their language.

Government (6.4.2)
- Different city-states had different forms of government, including monarchy, rule by aristocrats, and oligarchy.
- Athens developed limited, direct democracy.

TERMS & NAMES

Sort the words in the list below into three categories: geography, government, culture. Be prepared to explain your decisions.

1. alphabet
2. aristocracy
3. democracy
4. fable
5. isthmus
6. myth
7. oligarchy
8. peninsula
9. polis
10. tyrant

MAIN IDEAS

The Geography of Greece (pages 354–359)
11. How did the geography of Greece affect the location of cities? (6.4.1)
12. What skills did the Greeks need to master to become successful traders? (6.4.1)

Beliefs and Customs (pages 360–369)
13. In what ways did Homer use mythology? (6.4.4)
14. How were epic poems and fables the same? How were they different? (6.4.4)

The City-State and Democracy (pages 370–377)
15. How did government in Athens evolve into early forms of democracy? (6.4.2)
16. How was Athenian democracy different from democracy in the world today? (6.4.3)

Sparta and Athens (pages 378–385)
17. What roles did slaves play in Sparta and Athens? (6.4.6)
18. How were Athens and Sparta different? (6.4.6)

ALTERNATIVE ASSESSMENT RUBRICS

1. Writing Activity Rubric

	Level of Persuasiveness	Errors in Mechanics
4	very persuasive, gives many details	zero or one
3	persuasive, gives some details	two or three
2	somewhat persuasive, few details	four or five
1	not persuasive, little detail	more than five

2. Literature Rubric

	Elements of Poster	Effectiveness of Design
4	reflects thorough research	neat, organized, attractive
3	mostly complete research	neat and organized
2	some research	somewhat organized
1	little or no research	unorganized, messy

CRITICAL THINKING

Big Ideas: Government

19. ANALYZING POLITICAL ISSUES Why would the rugged geography make it difficult to unify Greece? Explain the potential problems. (6.4.1)

20. EXPLAINING HISTORICAL PATTERNS Considering their cultures, why do you think democracy developed in Athens and not in Sparta? (6.4.6)

21. UNDERSTANDING EFFECTS How did Solon's reforms change Athenian society? (6.4.2)

ALTERNATIVE ASSESSMENT

1. WRITING ACTIVITY Review your notes about Sparta and Athens. Write an essay persuading your readers which city-state was better to live in and why. (6.4.6)

2. INTERDISCIPLINARY ACTIVITY— LITERATURE Read several of Aesop's fables. Choose one besides *"The Hare and the Tortoise."* Make a poster illustrating the fable and its lesson. (6.4.4)

3. STARTING WITH A STORY Review the letter you wrote about helping Athens. Write a report to the Spartan assembly. Describe the results of the Battle of Marathon, and recommend how Sparta and Athens should deal with Persia in the future. (Writing 2.5)

Technology Activity

4. DESIGNING A VIDEO GAME Use the Internet or library to research the *Odyssey*. Work with a partner to design a video game about Odysseus' adventures as he journeyed home. (6.4.4)

- How did he escape from the Cyclops?
- What were Scylla and Charybdis?
- How did he escape from Calypso?

Research Links
ClassZone.com

Reading a Map Use the map and graph below to answer the questions. (6.4.1)

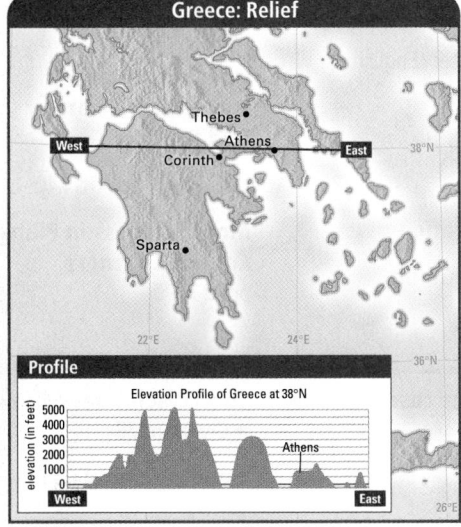

Greece: Relief

Profile

Elevation Profile of Greece at 38°N

1. At what elevation is Athens located?

A. about 400 feet
B. about 650 feet
C. about 950 feet
D. about 1,200 feet

2. Which of the following general statements is supported by the elevation profile?

A. Greece is a country of many lakes.
B. Greece is a country of many plains.
C. Greece is a country of many harbors.
D. Greece is a country of many mountains.

 Test Practice
ClassZone.com

Additional Test Practice, pp. S1–S33

Critical Thinking

Big Ideas: Government

19. Possible answers: The mountainous land made it difficult to travel among regions. It was likely hard for a central government to communicate laws and policies to outer regions, to collect taxes, and to send troops to put down rebellions or to defend borders. In addition, the central government would not always know what was going on in outlying regions.

20. Possible answer: Athens valued individual excellence in learning and the arts. Its citizens were taught public speaking. Democracy, in which individuals must contribute to government, was suited to Athens' culture. Sparta had a strict military society; they valued discipline and obedience, not individual freedom and self-expression.

21. Possible answer: He abolished debt slavery and made the laws less harsh. He divided society into four classes based on income, not birth. More people had a voice in the government.

Standards-Based Assessment

1. The correct answer is C. The elevation of Athens is about 950 feet as is shown by the elevation profile.

2. The correct answer is D. Greece is a country of mountains as is shown by the many high elevations of the elevation profile.

Research Links

Visit **ClassZone.com** for links to Web sites that can be used in the multimedia presentation.

Test Practice

Visit **ClassZone.com** to access strategies and tutorials for taking standardized tests.

Formal Assessment
- Chapter Tests, Forms A, B, and C, pp. 192–206

Test Generator
- Chapter Tests, Forms A, B, and C, (English and Spanish)

ALTERNATIVE ASSESSMENT RUBRICS

3. Starting with a Story Rubric

	Content of Report	Elements of Report
4	well-organized, includes all required elements	very creative
3	organized, includes most elements	creative
2	vague, includes some elements	somewhat creative
1	incorrect or missing content	not creative

4. Technology Rubric

	Level of Research	Quality of Game Ideas
4	extensive	variety in links, maps, and graphics; clear
3	good	clear, some variety
2	adequate	unclear, little variety
1	poor	sloppy, no variety

CHAPTER 12 PLANNING GUIDE: Classical Greece

Chapter Overview

Classical Greece influenced many aspects of the modern world, such as politics, science, and the arts.

Copymasters

In-Depth Resources: Unit 5
- Family Newsletter (English and Spanish), pp. 37–38
- Visual Summary, p. 43
- Vocabulary Study Guide, p. 45

Character Education

Reading Study Guide, p. 113

Bringing Social Studies Alive, Chapter 12

Document-Based Questions: Strategy and Practice

Reading Toolkit, L40–L43

Modified Lesson Plans for English Learners, pp. 83–90

Assessment

Chapter Review, pp. 420–421

Formal Assessment
- Chapter Tests, Forms A, B, and C, pp. 211–222

Test Generator

Integrated Assessment Book

Online Test Practice

LESSON 1
The Golden Age of Greece
pp. 392–397

OBJECTIVE Examine the ways in which Athens flourished under Pericles.

In-Depth Resources: Unit 5
- Reading Skill: Finding Main Ideas, p. 39
- Vocabulary Cards, p. 47
- Geography Practice: The Acropolis, p. 49
- Reteaching Activity, p. 53

Interdisciplinary Projects
- Civics, p. 70

Reading Study Guide, p. 105

Lesson Review, p. 397

Formal Assessment
- Lesson Quiz, p. 207

California Daily Standards Practice Transparencies, TT40

LESSON 2
Peloponnesian War
pp. 398–403

OBJECTIVE Study the conflict between Sparta and Athens and the effects that the Peloponnesian War had on Greek city-states.

In-Depth Resources: Unit 5
- Reading Skill: Comparing and Contrasting, p. 40
- Vocabulary Cards, p. 47
- Primary Source: Funeral Oration, by Pericles, p. 51
- Reteaching Activity, p. 54

Interdisciplinary Projects
- Language Arts, p. 69

Reading Study Guide, p. 107

Lesson Review, p. 402

Formal Assessment
- Lesson Quiz, p. 208

California Daily Standards Practice Transparencies, TT41

LESSON 3
Alexander the Great
pp. 404–409

OBJECTIVE Analyze the changes that occurred due to the conquering of Greece by Alexander the Great.

In-Depth Resources: Unit 5
- Reading Skill: Understanding Cause and Effect, p. 41
- Vocabulary Cards, p. 47
- Skillbuilder Practice: Assessing Credibility of Sources, p. 44
- Reteaching Activity, p. 55

Reading Study Guide, p. 109

Lesson Review, p. 409

Formal Assessment
- Lesson Quiz, p. 209

California Daily Standards Practice Transparencies, TT42

LESSON 4
The Legacy of Greece
pp. 410–419

OBJECTIVE Understand the influence of Greek ideas on the modern world.

In-Depth Resources: Unit 5
- Reading Skill: Finding Main Ideas, p. 42
- Vocabulary Cards, p. 47
- Literature: Oedipus the King, by Sophocles, p. 52
- Reteaching Activity, p. 56

History Makers
- Aristotle, p. 23

Interdisciplinary Projects
- Math, p. 67; Science, p. 68

Reading Study Guide, p. 111

Lesson Review, p. 417

Formal Assessment
- Lesson Quiz, p. 210

California Daily Standards Practice Transparencies, TT43

Integrated Technology

 eEdition Plus Online

EasyPlanner Plus Online

eTest Plus Online

 Audio CDs
- Reading Study Guide
- Reading Study Guide in Spanish
- The World's Music

 CD-ROMs
- Power Presentations
- eEdition
- EasyPlanner
- Test Generator

 Ancient Civilizations Video Series
- Ancient Greece

---

 eEdition CD-ROM

 Map Transparencies
- MT23 Seven Wonders of the World

 Critical Thinking Transparencies
- CT51 Finding Main Ideas

 ClassZone.com

---

 eEdition CD-ROM

 Critical Thinking Transparencies
- CT52 Comparing and Contrasting

 ClassZone.com

---

 eEdition CD-ROM

 Map Transparencies
- MT24 The Successors to Alexander's Empire

 Humanities Transparencies
- HT23 Alexander the Great Preparing to Dive

 Critical Thinking Transparencies
- CT53 Understanding Cause and Effect

 ClassZone.com

---

 eEdition CD-ROM

 Humanities Transparencies
- HT24 Mosaic of Masks

Critical Thinking Transparencies
- CT54 Finding Main Ideas
- CT55 Chapter 12 Visual Summary

 ClassZone.com

Overview of California Resources

	Lesson 1	Lesson 2	Lesson 3	Lesson 4
California Reading Toolkit	L40	L41	L42	L43
California Modified Lesson Plans for English Learners	p. 83	p. 85	p. 87	p. 89
California Daily Standards Practice Transparencies	TT40	TT41	TT42	TT43
California Standards Enrichment Workbook	pp. 51–54	pp. 51–52, 59–60	pp. 51–52, 61–62	pp. 63–64
California Standards Planner and Lesson Plans	L79	L81	L83	L85
California Online Test Practice	ClassZone.com	ClassZone.com	ClassZone.com	ClassZone.com
California Test Generator CD-ROM				
California EasyPlanner CD-ROM				
California eEdition CD-ROM				

Chart Key

PE Pupil Edition   CD-ROM    Internet

📝 Copymaster   🔊 Audio   Overhead Transparency

🎬 Video

PREVIEWING RESOURCES FOR DIFFERENTIATED INSTRUCTION

English Learners

In-Depth Resources in Spanish
- Reading Skill and Strategy
- Skillbuilder Practice **B**
- Geography Practice
- Vocabulary Study Guide

In-Depth Resources: Unit 5
- Family Newsletter (English and Spanish) **C**

Reading Study Guide (Spanish) **A**

Reading Study Guide Audio CD
(Spanish)

Test Generator
Chapter Test (Spanish)

Plus

Modified Lesson Plans for English Learners

Multi-Language Glossary of Social Studies Terms

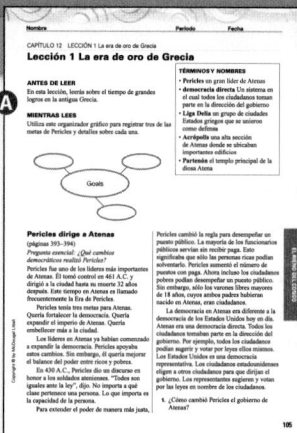
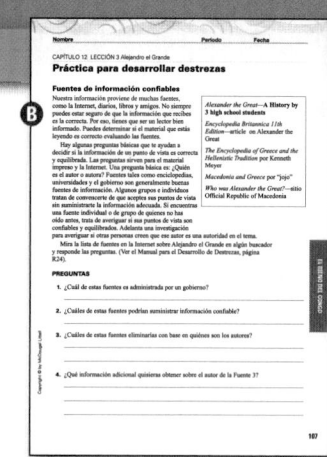

Struggling Readers

In-Depth Resources: Unit 5
- Vocabulary Study Guide **B**
- Skillbuilder Practice **C**
- Geography Practice
- Reteaching Activities **A**
- Family Newsletter

Reading Study Guide

Reading Study Guide Audio CD

Reading Toolkit

Formal Assessment
Chapter Test, Form A

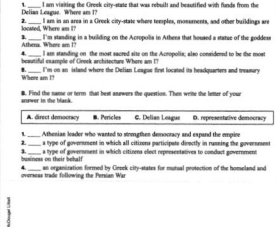
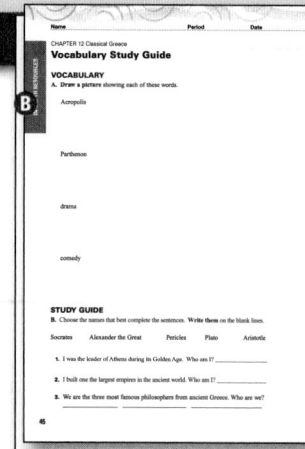

Inclusion

EasyPlanner CD-ROM
- Reading Skill and Strategy **B**
- Vocabulary Study Guide **A**
- Geography Practice
- Reteaching Activities **C**

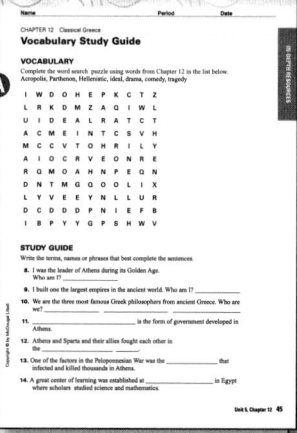
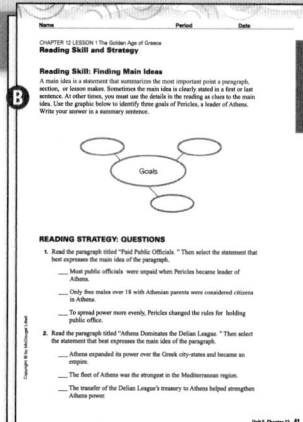

Gifted and Talented Students

In-Depth Resources: Unit 5
- Primary Source
- Literature **A**

History Makers **B**

Interdisciplinary Projects **C**

Formal Assessment
Chapter Test, Form C

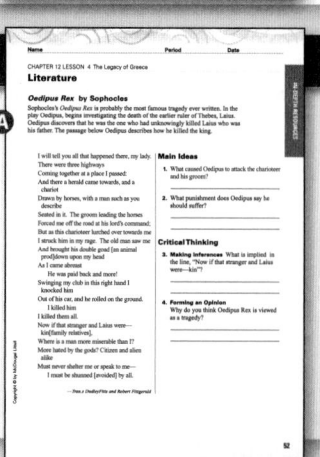

Activities in the Teacher's Edition for English Learners

- Preview the Text, p. 394
- Identify Adjectives, p. 400
- Use Cause-and-Effect Key Words, p. 407
- Compare and Contrast, p. 413
- Study Topic Sentences, p. 415
- Analyze Photographs and Text, p. 418

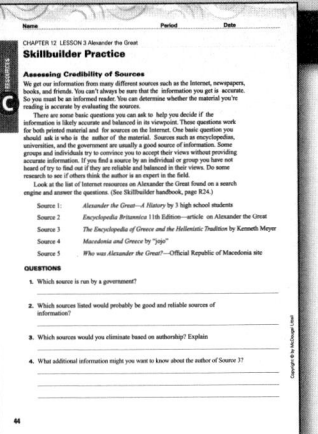

CHAPTER 12 LESSON 3 Alexander the Great
Skillbuilder Practice

Activities in the Teacher's Edition for Struggling Readers

- Focus on Vocabulary, p. 394
- Outline Essential Questions, p. 400
- Record the Sequence, p. 407
- Create Vocabulary Cards, p. 412
- Make Review Charts, p. 415

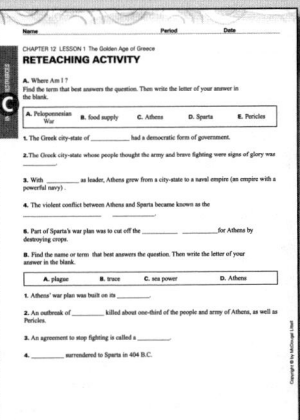

CHAPTER 12 LESSON 1 The Golden Age of Greece
RETEACHING ACTIVITY

Activities in the Teacher's Edition for Inclusion Students

- Conduct an Acropolis Tour Guide, p. 395
- Role-Play a Spartan or Athenian, p. 401
- Design a Catapult, p. 406
- Compose a Tragedy/Comedy Song, p. 412
- Throw a Discus, p. 418

CHAPTER 12 LESSON 1 The Golden Age of Greece   12D Connect to Civics
Advocating a Form of Government

Activities in the Teacher's Edition for Gifted and Talented Students

- Compare Architecture, p. 395
- Analyze a Battle, p. 401
- Create a Map of the Ancient World, p. 406
- Build a Building with Columns, p. 413

Integrated Technology

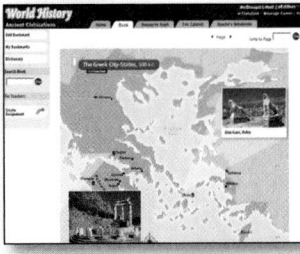

eEdition CD-ROM

- Interactive Visuals
- Interactive Maps
- Starting with a Story

ClassZone.com

- WebQuests
- Research Links
- Internet Activities
- Homework Helper
- Chapter Quiz
- Current Events
- Test Practice

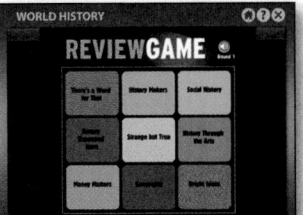

Power Presentations CD-ROM

- Lecture Notes
- Media Gallery
- Chapter Review Game

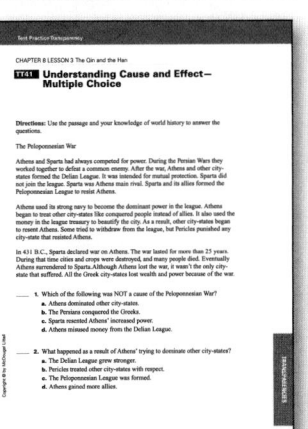

Critical Thinking Transparencies

- CT51 Finding Main Ideas
- CT52 Comparing and Contrasting
- CT53 Understanding Cause and Effect
- CT54 Finding Main Ideas
- CT55 Chapter 12 Visual Summary

California Daily Standards Practice Transparencies, TT40–TT43

Map Transparencies

- MT23 Seven Wonders of the World
- MT24 The Successors to Alexander's Empire

Humanities Transparencies

- HT23 Alexander the Great Preparing to Dive
- HT24 Mosaic of Masks

Test Generator CD-ROM

EasyPlanner CD-ROM

Ancient Civilizations Video Series

- Ancient Greece

Begin the Chapter

Objective

Explain the legacy of classical Greece on the modern world, including ideas about democracy, architecture, philosophy, and science.

Quick Look

Lesson 1 traces the expansion of democracy, the building of wealth, and the beautification of Athens under Pericles.

Lesson 2 analyzes the continuing conflict between Sparta and Athens and the weakening of the city-states following the Peloponnesian War.

Lesson 3 describes how the conquests of Alexander the Great spread Greek culture and influence throughout the known world.

Lesson 4 examines how Greek ideas about architecture, philosophy, and science influenced the development of modern civilizations.

Before You Read: Anticipation Guide

Anticipation statements help students use prior knowledge, encourages them to make personal connections, and gives them clues about what they are about to read. Have students follow these steps.

- Read the three statements.
- Decide whether you agree or disagree. Make an educated guess if you are not sure.
- Say, "When I read the statement, if you agree with it stand up. Be prepared to give reasons why. If you disagree stay seated and be prepared to give reasons why."
- Look for information that supports or contradicts each statement as you read the chapter.
- At the end of the chapter, review the statements and summarize whether you now agree or disagree.

Before You Read: Anticipation Guide

Copy the statements below in your notebook. Write *agree* or *disagree* next to each one. After you read the lesson, check to see if you have changed your mind about each.

- The Golden Age of Greece lasted about a hundred years.
- Alexander the Great's empire was bigger than the Persian empire.
- The Greeks studied philosophy more than science.

Big Ideas About Classical Greece

Geography Migration, trade, warfare, and the action of missionaries spread ideas and beliefs.

Greek ideas about the arts, architecture, sciences, and philosophy spread to parts of Asia through Alexander the Great and his armies. Greek culture blended with the cultures of conquered lands including Egypt, Persia, and India to create a new one. Millions of people who lived in Alexander's empire shared that new culture. The culture continued long after Alexander died.

Tholos Temple, Delphi

Ionian Sea

Integrated Technology

eEdition
- Interactive Maps
- Interactive Visuals
- Starting with a Story

INTERNET RESOURCES
Go to **ClassZone.com** for
- WebQuest
- Homework Helper
- Research Links
- Internet Activities
- Quizzes
- Maps
- Test Practice
- Current Events

0	50 100 miles
0	50 100 kilometers

Area of Greek settlement/Ancient Greece

■ Major city-state

🏛 Major temple or shrine

18°E

GREECE

477 B.C.
The Golden Age of Athens begins. (Parthenon) ▶

431 B.C.
The Peloponnesian War begins.

500 B.C.   475 B.C.   450 B.C.

WORLD

500 B.C.
Nok people of Africa make iron tools.

483 B.C.
Siddhartha Gautama, the Buddha, dies.

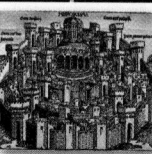

445 B.C.
Jews rebuild the walls of Jerusalem.
◀ (illustration of Jerusalem)

388

TIME LINE DISCUSSION

Explain that a time line is a way to illustrate the sequence of historical events. Ask students what the advantages and disadvantages of a time line are. *(Possible answers: advantages— fast way to see information; easy to study; see cause and effect. disadvantages—not much detail; cannot see information in depth)*

- How long a period does the time line cover? *(about 175 years)*
- How much time passed between the beginning of the Peloponnesian War and the peak of Alexander's empire? *(105 years)*
- List the events in Greek history that you learn about in the time line. *(the beginning date of Golden Age, Peloponnesian War, death of Socrates, and the height of Alexander's empire)*

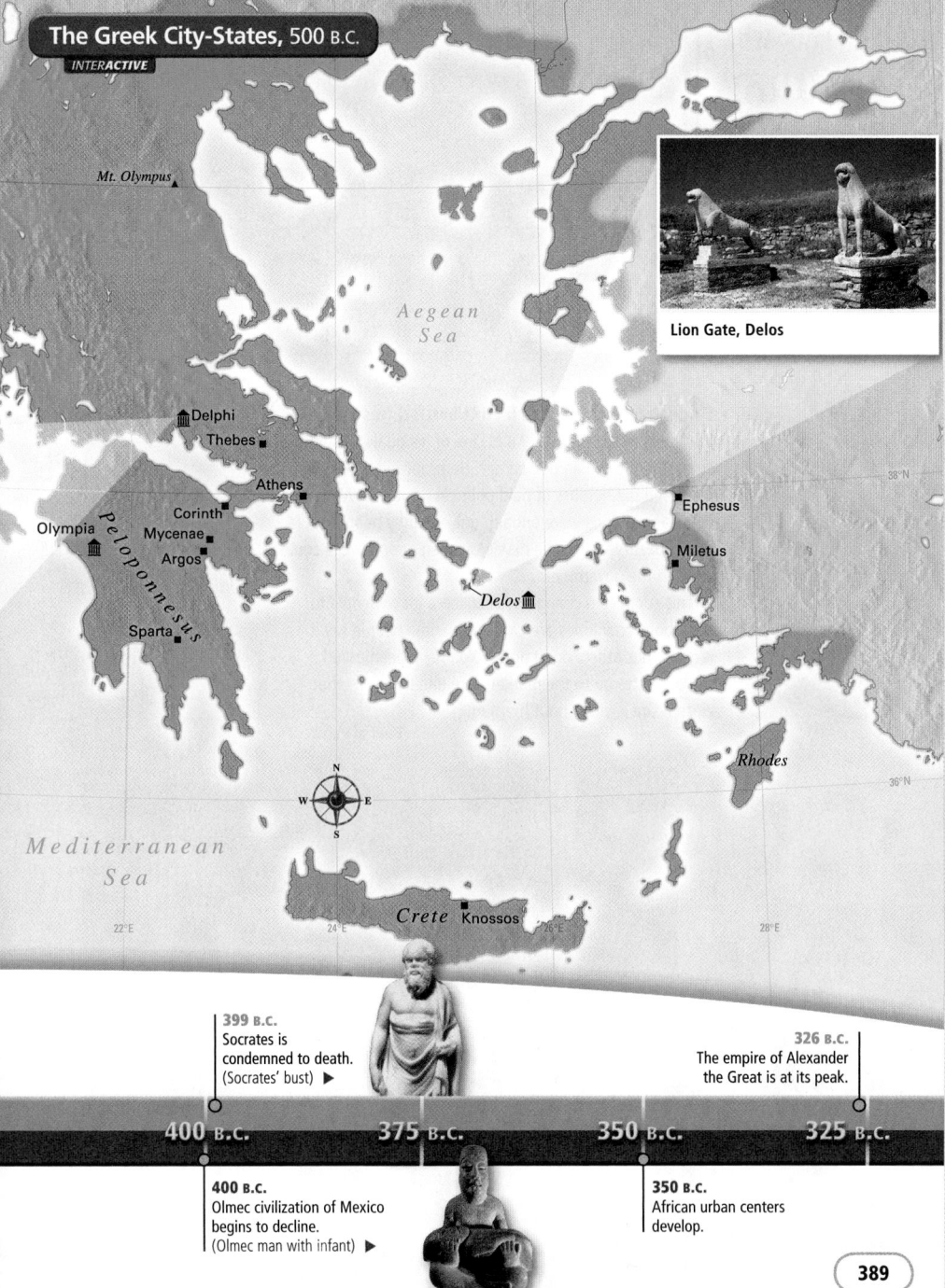

The Greek City-States, 500 B.C.
INTER*ACTIVE*

Mt. Olympus

Aegean Sea

Lion Gate, Delos

Delphi
Thebes
Athens
Corinth
Olympia
Mycenae
Argos
Sparta

Peloponnesus

Ephesus
Miletus

Delos

Rhodes

Mediterranean Sea

Crete   Knossos

N W E S

38°N

36°N

22°E   24°E   26°E   28°E

399 B.C.
Socrates is
condemned to death.
(Socrates' bust) ▶

326 B.C.
The empire of Alexander
the Great is at its peak.

400 B.C.   375 B.C.   350 B.C.   325 B.C.

400 B.C.
Olmec civilization of Mexico
begins to decline.
(Olmec man with infant) ▶

350 B.C.
African urban centers
develop.

389

RECOMMENDED RESOURCES

Books for the Teacher
Aird, Hamish. *Pericles: The Rise and Fall of Athenian Democracy.* New York: Rosen, 2003. Focuses on Pericles' youth, war, the Golden Age, and problems.

Boardman, John. *Oxford Illustrated History of Greece and the Hellenistic World.* Oxford: Oxford UP, 2001. Covers architecture, philosophy, visual arts, military strategy and science from eighth century B.C. through the third century B.C.

Jones, A. H. M. *Athenian Democracy.* Baltimore: Johns Hopkins, 1986. Discusses the politics, government, and social conditions of Greece in an easy and understandable way.

Videos
In the Footsteps of Alexander the Great. 240 minutes. Alexandria, VA: PBS Home Video, 1998. Divided into four parts, tells of Alexander's youth and invasions of Persia, Afghanistan, and India. Follows the 20,000-mile journey of Alexander's conquests.

Internet
To access these sites, visit the Research Links for this chapter at **ClassZone.com**.

PBS Empires. Interactive site exploring fifth-century Athens, virtual Socrates and early philosophers, speaking like a Greek, and occupations.

Introduce the Big Ideas
Read aloud the text about the Big Ideas. Ask students how ideas and beliefs are spread in today's world. *(Possible answers: via the Internet, television, phone, global travel)* Discuss how ideas are constantly spreading in the world and how a global society might accelerate that spread.

Here are some other Big Ideas that you may want to emphasize in this chapter.

Culture
Ways of living change as humans interact with each other.

Science and Technology
New scientific discoveries change human understanding of the world.

Talk About It
Interpreting Maps
Review the symbol key with students. Then ask the following questions: What major temple or shrine was on an island? *(Delos)*

Where is Olympia located? *(on the Peloponnesus north and west of Sparta)*

INTER*ACTIVE*

An interactive version of this map is available on the eEdition and Power Presentations CD–ROMs.

Find Out More

Have students use an encyclopedia, books, or the Internet to learn how Greek ideas spread in the world of Classical Greece.

Watch the Video

If you have not done so, show *Ancient Greece*, the 23-minute video about the history and culture of ancient Greece.

The World's Music

If you have not done so, introduce your students to authentic Greek music by playing track 8 of *The World's Music* audio CD. "You Birds of the Valley" is an example of folk music from Roumeli, a region in central Greece.

Objective

Analyze the qualities that make an effective public official.

Introducing the Story

Point of View

Write the words *Agree* and *Disagree* on the board. Give the class this statement: It is impossible for a poor person to serve in a government. Find out how many agree or disagree and their reasons. Then, introduce the story by saying that Pericles felt that democracy needed all of its citizens to be strong.

Vocabulary Preview

propose to state an idea for consideration

holler to cry, to call, or to shout loudly

Reading the Story Aloud

1. **The teacher as reader:** As you read, stop and ask questions aloud in order to model the comprehension process. For example, after reading the first paragraph, say, "I wonder who wouldn't like poor citizens to get paid." Ask students to listen as you read on, and when your question is answered, to raise their hands.

2. **The students as readers:** Have individual students continue the question process by reading from the third paragraph to the end, stopping to ask their own comprehension questions. Ask listeners to answer the questions when they can.

Starting with a Story

Students can also follow along as they listen to the story on the eEdition or Power Presentations CD-ROMs.

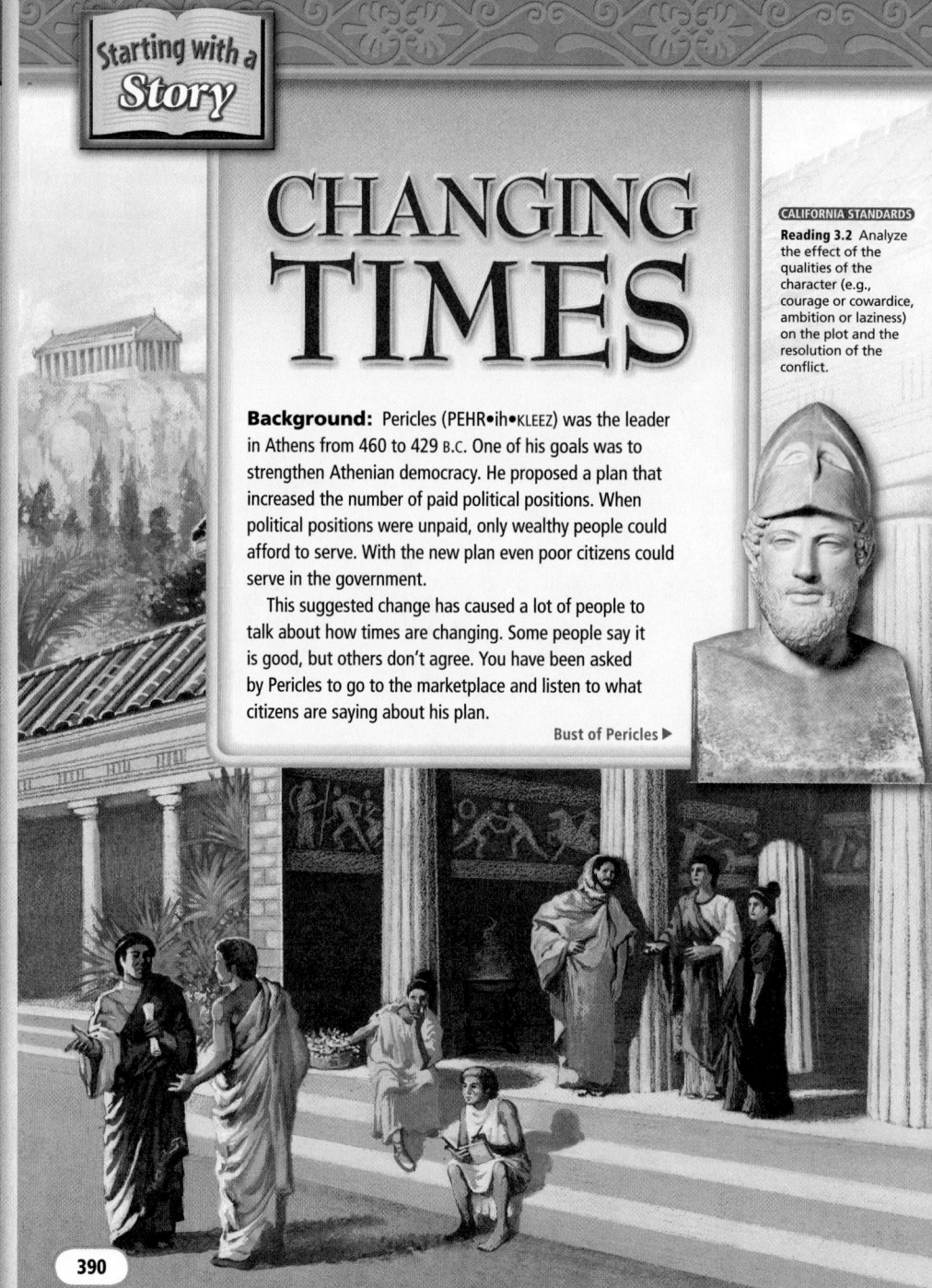

Starting with a Story

CHANGING TIMES

CALIFORNIA STANDARDS
Reading 3.2 Analyze the effect of the qualities of the character (e.g., courage or cowardice, ambition or laziness) on the plot and the resolution of the conflict.

Background: Pericles (PEHR•ih•KLEEZ) was the leader in Athens from 460 to 429 B.C. One of his goals was to strengthen Athenian democracy. He proposed a plan that increased the number of paid political positions. When political positions were unpaid, only wealthy people could afford to serve. With the new plan even poor citizens could serve in the government.

This suggested change has caused a lot of people to talk about how times are changing. Some people say it is good, but others don't agree. You have been asked by Pericles to go to the marketplace and listen to what citizens are saying about his plan.

Bust of Pericles ▶

390

ADDITIONAL RESOURCES

Books for the Student

Burrell, Roy and Peter Connolly. ***Oxford First Ancient History.*** Oxford: Oxford UP, 1997. Lively book about ancient Mediterranean life for middle-school age. Includes cultures already studied as well as Greece and Rome.

Crompton, Samuel Willard. ***Alexander the Great.*** Philadelphia: Chelsea, 2003. Details life and accomplishments of Alexander.

Nardo, Don. ***The Age of Pericles.*** San Diego: Lucent Books, 1996. Outlines life in Greece during the time of Pericles.

Videos

Alexander the Great. 50 minutes. Stratford Upon Avon: Cromwell Productions, 1996. Analyzes the military genius of Alexander. VHS.

Athens: Triumph and Tragedy. 50 minutes. New York: A&E Entertainment. 2000. Investigates the age of Pericles, how buildings were built and used, and how we construct knowledge from ruins. VHS.

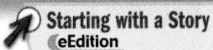
Starting with a Story
eEdition

They were shouting. "Pericles wants more public officials to get paid," one of them hollered above the rest. "Poor citizens will be able to serve the government of Athens. I don't like that!"

The wealthy citizens were talking about the proposed policy change. Pericles was due to arrive at any moment. I was acting as his "eyes and ears" in the market place. Later, I would tell Pericles what I heard being said by the citizens of Athens.

"But I think Pericles is right," another man said. "Any citizen who wants to serve in the government should be able to do so. Pericles says being poor shouldn't prevent a man from serving our city."

"Yes," another man agreed. Several others nodded. "A poor man can serve Athens. A poor man is just as intelligent as a rich man. How can we ask the poor to obey our government if they cannot be public officials?"

"You're right. If a man is poor, it's not his fault!" piped up a fourth citizen. "Blame it on the gods!"

"Rich men are much better educated," a fifth man argued. "That's why only the rich should serve Athens."

Another man answered him. "But Pericles said that no one needs to be ashamed of poverty. The real shame is not trying to escape it."

Just then I heard footsteps. Pericles was coming! I needed to move away from the crowd. Later, he asked me if I had some advice for him based on what I heard. I knew what I would say and hoped he would agree with my advice.

What advice would you give Pericles?

Reading & Writing

1. **READING: Character and Plot** What character trait does Pericles show when supporting the rights of a poor citizen to serve in the government? What other character traits will he need to actually get the plan passed?

2. **WRITING: Persuasion** Think about what you heard. Think about the qualities needed to be a good public official. Then write a position paper outlining points that will help Pericles persuade people that his plan is the correct one.

CALIFORNIA STANDARDS Writing 2.5
Writing persuasive compositions.

391

READING & WRITING ACTIVITIES

1. **READING** Possible answer: Pericles shows respect and concern for the rights of all citizens. He will need to be persuasive and persistent to get the policy enacted.

2. **WRITING**

2. Writing Rubric

	Statement of Position	Points of Support	Deals with Objections
4	clear and concise	many clearly stated	deals with objections
3	clear but not precise	three or more	meets most objections
2	unclear	two or more	deals with a few
1	none/vague	missing/one	missing

Talk About It

Ask students the following question to begin the discussion:

- What did Pericles want? *(to have poor people be able to serve in government)*

- What were the reasons that poor citizens might serve as well as the wealthy? *(They were just as intelligent; poverty is no one's fault.)*

- What did Pericles believe a person should be ashamed of? *(not trying to escape from poverty.)*

- What is Pericles' strongest character trait? *(Possible answers: determination, fairness, wisdom)*

What advice would you give Pericles?

Students may say that Pericles should give the poor a voice not only to keep them from rebelling but also because it is the right thing to do.

Making Personal Connections

Have students draw conclusions about why a democracy needs educated citizens. *(Possible answers: People need to read to vote and learn information; people need to learn how to think to make decisions based on reason.)*

❶ Plan & Prepare

Objectives

- Describe how democracy grew under Pericles.
- Explain how Pericles expanded the wealth and power of Athens.
- Summarize Pericles' beautification program in Athens.
- **Language Objective:** Preview the text to create purpose-setting questions.

Quick Look

Lesson 1 describes how Pericles strengthened democracy, how Athens participated in the Delian League, and how Athens became a beautiful city.

❷ Focus & Motivate

Preview Tell students that this lesson explains how democracy gained strength in Athens. Ask students to list characteristics of a strong democracy and why these characteristics are important. *(Possible answers: All people participate so that there is no rebellion; there is more than one person in charge so that no one becomes a dictator; there are courts so all get a fair hearing.)*

Introduce the Main Ideas The three main ideas relate to the Big Idea "Ways of living change as humans interact with each other." Help students look for this Big Idea in the lesson.

Reading Skill: Finding Main Ideas Explain that main ideas usually are included in a text's headings and subheadings.

SAMPLE ANSWERS FOR DIAGRAM

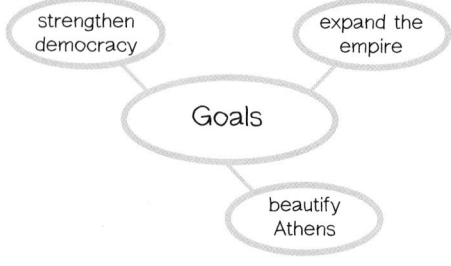

Lesson 1

▶ MAIN IDEAS

❶ Government Democracy expanded under the leadership of Pericles.

❷ Economics Pericles expanded the wealth and power of Athens through the Delian League.

❸ Culture Pericles launched a program to make Athens beautiful.

▶ TAKING NOTES

Reading Skill: Finding Main Ideas

Identifying the main ideas and finding details about those ideas will help you understand the material in the lesson. In Lesson 1, look for three goals set by Pericles, and find details about them. Record the information in a web diagram.

S **Skillbuilder Handbook, page R2**

▲ **Porch of the Caryatids** The porch is part of the Erectheum, a temple that honors several gods and goddesses. The columns are sculptures of maidens (caryatids).

CALIFORNIA STANDARDS

6.4 Students analyze the geographic, political, economic, religious, and social structures of the early civilizations of Ancient Greece.

6.4.2 Trace the transition from tyranny and oligarchy to early democratic forms of government and back to dictatorship in ancient Greece, including the significance of the invention of the idea of citizenship (e.g., from *Pericles' Funeral Oration*).

6.4.3 State the key differences between Athenian, or direct, democracy and representative democracy.

HOW TO TEACH THE CALIFORNIA STANDARDS

Standard	Content	Student Question or Activity	Instruction
6.4	**Page 396** Explains what an acropolis is	**Page 397** Students explain why it was important to beautify the Acropolis in Athens.	Review *agora* and *stoa* as two traditional parts of a Greek City. Then discuss how an *acropolis* is another traditional part of a Greek city layout.
6.4.2	**Page 395** Outlines the steps Athens took to become the strongest power in the Delian League	**Page 395** Students explain how Athens expanded its power.	Have students decide in groups if Athens' use of the treasury showed that they used a democratic process, and explain why or why not.
6.4.3	**Page 395** Charts the similarities and differences between Athenian and United States democratic forms	**Page 397** Students compare the role of citizens in Athens with citizens in the United States.	Have students give an example in their own words of each characteristic of these two forms of democracy.

The Golden Age of Greece

TERMS & NAMES
Pericles
direct democracy
Delian League
Acropolis
Parthenon

CHAPTER 12 • LESSON 1

Terms & Names

Pericles one of Athens' greatest leaders

direct democracy all citizens participate directly in running the government

Delian League an organization of Greek city-states formed for mutual protection after the Persian War

Acropolis the "high city" part of Athens

Parthenon a building in Athens constructed for Athena

Build on What You Know Have you ever had a time when you were really successful in the things you were doing? A period of great achievement is sometimes called a golden age. Ancient civilizations, such as the Han Dynasty in China and the Gupta in India, had golden ages. Greece too had a golden age, during the time of Pericles.

Pericles Leads Athens

① ESSENTIAL QUESTION What democratic changes did Pericles bring?
paid public officials

After the Persian Wars that you read about in Chapter 11, one of Athens' greatest leaders, **Pericles**, emerged. By 460 B.C., Pericles was the strongest leader in Athens. He remained the leader until his death 31 years later. He was so important that this time in Athens is often called the Age of Pericles.

Pericles had three goals for Athens. The first was to strengthen democracy. The second was to expand the empire. The third was to beautify Athens.

Pericles Strengthens Democracy

Remember that, before Pericles, leaders in Athens had begun to expand democracy. Pericles supported those reforms. He wanted, however, to change the balance of power between the rich and the poor.

About 430 B.C., Pericles gave his view of democracy in a speech honoring Athenian soldiers killed in war. "Everyone is equal before the law," he said. What counts in public service "is not membership of a particular class, but the actual ability which the man possesses."

Connect to Today

Ruins of Ancient Athens Parts of ancient Athens sit above the modern city. ▼

393

❸ Teach

Pericles Leads Athens

🔖 **6.4.2, 6.4.3**

Talk About It

- **Critical Thinking: Making Inferences**
  How did Pericles' idea of "everyone is equal before the law" reduce the power of the wealthy? *(Possible answer: Wealthy people would now have to exhibit ability, not just money or power, to be in government.)*

LESSON 1 PROGRAM RESOURCES

ON LEVEL

In-Depth Resources: Unit 5
- Family Newsletter, (English and Spanish), pp. 37–38
- Reading Skill: Finding Main Ideas, p. 39
- Vocabulary Cards, p. 47
- Geography Practice: The Acropolis, p. 49

Formal Assessment
- Lesson Quiz, p. 207

ENGLISH LEARNERS

In-Depth Resources in Spanish
- Reading Skill: Finding Main Ideas, p. 101

- Geography Practice: The Acropolis, p. 109

Modified Lesson Plans for English Learners, p. 83
Reading Study Guide (Spanish), p. 105
Reading Study Guide Audio CD (Spanish)

STRUGGLING READERS

In-Depth Resources: Unit 5
- Reading Skill: Finding Main Ideas, p. 39
- Vocabulary Study Guide, p. 45
- Reteaching Activity, p. 53

Reading Toolkit, L40
Reading Study Guide, p. 105
Reading Study Guide Audio CD

GIFTED AND TALENTED STUDENTS

Interdisciplinary Projects
- Civics, p. 70

INCLUSION

EasyPlanner CD-ROM
- Reading Skill: Finding Main Ideas
- Vocabulary Study Guide
- Reteaching Activity

TECHNOLOGY

eEdition CD-ROM
- Starting with a Story

Power Presentations CD-ROM

Map Transparencies
- MT23 Seven Wonders in the World

Critical Thinking Transparencies
- CT 51 Finding Main Ideas

Test Generator CD-ROM

ClassZone.com

In-Depth Resources: Unit 5
- Reading Skill: Finding Main Ideas, p. 39
- Geography Practice: The Acropolis, p. 49

History Makers

Pericles

Pericles did not rule Athens alone. He and nine other generals ran the military affairs of Athens. What set Pericles apart was his charisma. *Charisma* is a word of Greek origin that means the power or quality of attracting, personal magnetism or charm. It comes from the Greek root *kharis*, which means "favor." Pericles' vision of democracy combined with his charisma made him stand out from other men of his time.

Comparisons Across Cultures

Athenian and U.S. Democracy

Ask students to review the chart on page 395 and summarize the information it presents. *(It shows characteristics of direct and representative democracies and what they have in common.)*

According to the chart, what are the differences in the citizens in each democracy? *(Citizens in Athens were male, 18, and children of citizens. Citizens in the United States are male and female. They are people born in this country as well as immigrants who have become citizens.)*

Have students compare each point and discuss the differences between the two forms of democracy.

Paid Public Officials To spread power more evenly, Pericles changed the rule for holding public office. Most public officials were unpaid before he came to power. This meant that only wealthy people could afford to serve in government in Athens. Pericles increased the number of public officials who were paid. Now even poor citizens could hold a public office if elected or chosen randomly. However, to be a citizen an individual had to be a free male, over 18, and the son of Athenian-born parents.

Direct Democracy The form of democracy practiced in Athens was not the kind practiced in the United States today. The form used in Athens was called **direct democracy**. In a direct democracy all citizens participate in running the government. For example, all citizens in Athens could propose and vote directly on laws. By comparison, the United States has representative democracy, or a republic. U.S. citizens—male and female—elect representatives to take care of government business. These representatives propose and vote on laws. Study the chart on page 395 to find other differences.

REVIEW How is direct democracy different from representative democracy?
In direct democracy all citizens participate in government activities. In a representative democracy selected individuals do this task.

History Makers

Pericles (495–429 B.C.)

Pericles' speaking skills set him apart from other Athenians. He was so skilled that most regarded him as the best speaker of the time. Some people said that when he spoke, his words were like thunder and lightning.

Once, Pericles and another Athenian were involved in a wrestling match. Pericles lost. But his powers of speech were so great that he actually convinced the spectators that he won the match, even though they saw him lose!

His ability to speak so well made it possible for him to persuade Athenian citizens to back his reforms. These reforms brought about major changes in Athenian life. Unfortunately, toward the end of his life, Pericles was involved in several political scandals. As a result, he briefly stepped down from his position of leadership but later was reinstated. He is still thought of as one of the greatest leaders of Greece.

394 • Chapter 12

DIFFERENTIATING INSTRUCTION

English Learners

Preview the Text

Demonstrate how to turn headings and subheadings into *who, what, when, where, why, how* questions. The first heading can become "How did Pericles lead Athens?" Write the question on a chart. Help students skim the text to find a response to the question. Have student pairs work to turn headings into questions and chart them. Then have students scan the text to find responses. For more support, see *Modified Lesson Plans for English Learners*, p. 83.

Struggling Readers

Focus on Vocabulary

Have partners list the subsection headings of the section "Pericles Leads Athens" as main ideas and leave two lines to write details. As students read, have them discuss the section with a partner and agree on the details to be included under each subsection head. Have pairs share their details with another pair and explain the subsection in their own words.

Comparisons Across Cultures

Athenian and U.S. Democracy

Athenian Democracy
Direct Democracy

- Citizenship: male; 18 years old; born of citizen parents
- Assembly of all citizens votes on laws.
- Leader is selected randomly or elected.
- Council of Five Hundred prepares business for the assembly.
- As many as 500 jurors could serve.

Both

- Political power is held by all citizens.
- Government has three branches.
- Law-making branch passes laws.
- Executive branch carries out laws.
- Judicial branch holds trials.

U.S. Democracy
Representative Democracy

- Citizenship: born in United States or completed citizenship process
- Representatives are elected to law-making body.
- Leader is elected.
- Executive branch has elected and appointed officials.
- Juries usually have 12 jurors.

Expanding the Empire

② ESSENTIAL QUESTION How did Athens become more powerful?
Pericles took funds from the Delian League to build a huge navy.
Greek wealth depended on overseas trade. Athens was determined to protect its overseas trade and its homeland. At the end of the Persian War, the Greek city-states formed a league for mutual protection. It was called the **Delian League**.

Delian League Athens helped to organize this league. It was called the Delian League because its headquarters and treasury were located at first on the island of Delos. Pericles used money from the league's treasury to build a strong navy. The naval fleet was made up of at least 300 warships.

Athens Dominates the Delian League The fleet of Athens was the strongest in the Mediterranean region. Because Athens now had a superior navy, it took over leadership of the Delian League. In 454 B.C., the Delian League's treasury was moved to Athens. The transfer of the Delian League's treasury helped to strengthen Athens' power. Athens started treating the other members of the league as if they were conquered people, not allies. Eventually, Athens dominated all of the city-states to such an extent that they became part of an Athenian empire.

REVIEW How did the power of Athens expand?
Pericles used the Delian League's money to build a strong naval fleet for Athens. Then Athens dominated the other city-states.

Classical Greece • **395**

Teach

Expanding the Empire

 6.4

Talk About It

- What was the Delian League? *(an organization of Greek city-states formed to give mutual protection after the Persian War)*

- How did the league help Pericles build a navy? *(He used money from the league's treasury to build a fleet of at least 300 warships.)*

- What was the result of the Delian League's treasury being moved to Athens from Delos? *(Athens became leader of the league and gained more power; it started treating other members of the league like conquered people instead of allies.)*

- **Critical Thinking: Making Inferences** What problems might have resulted from Athens' treatment of league members as conquered people? *(Possible answers: Members would be resentful and rebel, possibly taking control of Athens; they would probably not help Athens to face other enemies.)*

More About . . .

The Delian League
The Delian League was formed by Sparta, Athens, Greek cities in Asia Minor, and other Greek and island city-states to protect each other from Persia. Each city-state had one vote. The Persians were a constant threat, especially to the cities in Asia Minor. The league waged war to regain cities in Asia Minor. This democratic alliance was weakened by Athens becoming a superior force and exercising its authority above the will of other league members.

DIFFERENTIATING INSTRUCTION

Inclusion

Conduct an Acropolis Tour Guide
Give students a layout map of the buildings on the Acropolis and provide one detail about each building. Then have them conduct a pretend tour of the Acropolis, using the details to point out the buildings.

Gifted and Talented Students

Compare Architecture
Have groups research various buildings in the United States that have been influenced by ancient Greek architecture. Have each group select a building, describe its construction, and connect it to Greek architectural styles. Present the buildings to the class.

Teach

Beautifying Athens

 6.4

Talk About It

- Why were the other city-states angry with Pericles? *(He used money meant for mutual protection for his own projects in Athens.)*

- What did Pericles do to beautify Athens? *(He paid artists, architects, and sculptors to create sculptures and buildings out of gold, ivory, and marble. He rebuilt the Acropolis area and constructed the Parthenon, which was dedicated to Athena, the goddess who protected Athens.)*

- **Critical Thinking: Making Inferences** In what way might rebuilding a city after it was in ruins make the city even better? *(Possible answers: Mistakes and problems in previous layouts could be corrected; builders could locate places such as markets, churches, and schools in more central areas.)*

Beautifying Athens

③ ESSENTIAL QUESTION How did Pericles beautify Athens?
rebuilt Acropolis, added sculptures and beautiful buildings

Athens was a city in ruins when the war with Persia ended in 480 B.C. Parts of it were burned, and most of the buildings were destroyed. Pericles saw this destruction as a chance to rebuild, glorify, and beautify Athens.

Rebuilding Athens The Greek city-states paid a tribute to the Delian League organization. The funds were supposed to help build the power of the league. Instead, Pericles used these funds to beautify Athens. He did not ask approval from the members of the league to use the money. This action made other city-states angry.

Pericles spent the money to purchase gold, ivory, and marble to create sculptures and construct beautiful buildings. Pericles also used the money to pay artists, architects, and sculptors for these projects.

The Acropolis One of the areas rebuilt was the **Acropolis** (uh•KRAHP•uh•lihs), or the "high city" part of Athens. An acropolis is an area in a Greek city where important temples, monuments, and buildings are located. The Persians had destroyed the temples and smashed the statues in Athens during the war.

One of the buildings constructed was the **Parthenon** (PAHR•thuh•NAHN). Its purpose was to house a statue of Athena, a goddess. Athenians thought of her as a warrior who protected Athens. Athena was also the goddess of wisdom, arts, and handicrafts.

Acropolis The Parthenon, seen at right, is a temple dedicated to Athena. ▶

INTERDISCIPLINARY ACTIVITIES

Art

Build a Parthenon Model
Have students look for information and pictures on the Internet about the design and materials used to build the Parthenon. Then have them create a plan and construct a model of the Parthenon. Make sure they include a summary of all the parts of the building to point out to the class.

Language Arts

Organize a Debate
Divide students into two teams. Have one team take the role of Pericles and the Athenians defending their right to use the Delian League's money to rebuild Athens. The other team should include various league representatives who argue that they have other needs for the money. Have groups brainstorm and organize their arguments, list them, and then have the debate in class.

The Parthenon is considered the most magnificent building on the Acropolis. It is a masterpiece of architectural design, especially known for its graceful proportions and sense of harmony and order. Another temple on the Acropolis was one dedicated to Athena Nike, the goddess of victory. The most sacred site on the hill is the Erechtheum (ehr•ihic•THEE•uhm). It is considered the most beautiful example of Greek architecture. You can see its porch at the beginning of this lesson. Legend says it marks the site where the god Poseidon and the goddess Athena had a contest to see who would be the patron god of the city. Athena won.

REVIEW How did Pericles finance his program to make Athens beautiful?
Pericles used money from the treasury of the Delian League without its approval.

Lesson Summary

- Pericles strengthened democracy in Athens by paying public officials.
- Pericles expanded the empire by building a strong naval fleet.
- Pericles rebuilt and beautified Athens.

Why It Matters Now . . .

Athenian democracy, art, and architecture set standards that remain influential in the world today.

---

1 Lesson Review

 Homework Helper
ClassZone.com

Terms & Names

1. Explain the importance of

Pericles	Delian League	Parthenon
direct democracy	Acropolis	

Using Your Notes

Finding Main Ideas Use your completed graphic to answer the following question:

2. How did Pericles advance democracy? (6.4.2)

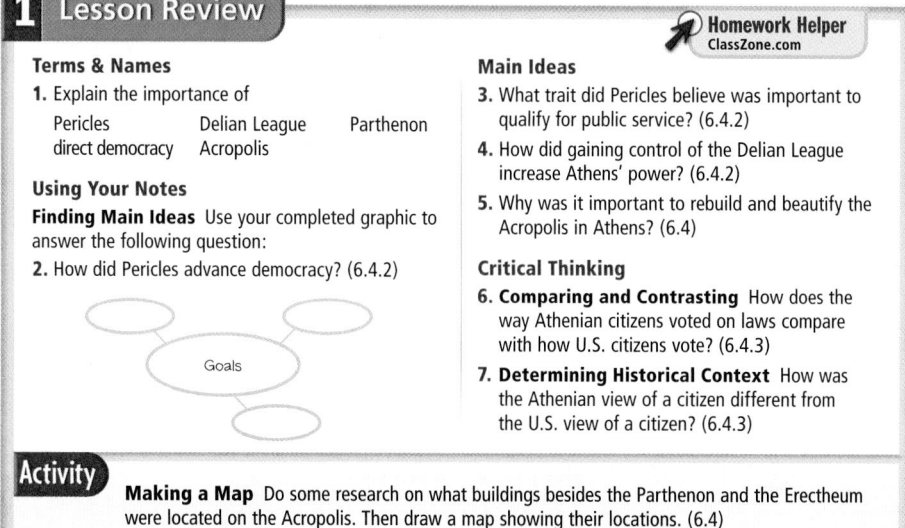

Goals

Main Ideas

3. What trait did Pericles believe was important to qualify for public service? (6.4.2)
4. How did gaining control of the Delian League increase Athens' power? (6.4.2)
5. Why was it important to rebuild and beautify the Acropolis in Athens? (6.4)

Critical Thinking

6. **Comparing and Contrasting** How does the way Athenian citizens voted on laws compare with how U.S. citizens vote? (6.4.3)
7. **Determining Historical Context** How was the Athenian view of a citizen different from the U.S. view of a citizen? (6.4.3)

Activity **Making a Map** Do some research on what buildings besides the Parthenon and the Erectheum were located on the Acropolis. Then draw a map showing their locations. (6.4)

Classical Greece • 397

---

❹ Assess & Reteach

Assess Have students find the answers to the lesson review and write the pages on which they found them. Call out a page number and have student volunteers give an answer from that page.

 Formal Assessment
- Lesson Quiz, p. 207

Reteach Divide the class into three groups. Assign each group one of the sections in this lesson. Each group should call out an answer from the section and the other group members should create the question that the information answers.

 In-Depth Resources: Unit 5
- Vocabulary Cards, p. 47
- Reteaching Activity, p. 53

Homework Helper

Visit **ClassZone.com** for a lesson review, a flip-card activity, and links to related Web sites.

---

1 Lesson Review Answers

1. • Pericles, p. 393
   • direct democracy, p. 394
   • Delian League, p. 395
   • Acropolis, p. 396
   • Parthenon, p. 396

Using Your Notes

See page 392 for an example of a completed diagram.

2. Pericles began a policy of paying people who served in public office.

Main Ideas

3. Pericles believed that ability, rather than social class, was important for public office.
4. Control of the league gave Athens access to its funds, which Athens used to build ships and strengthen its own power.
5. The Acropolis, or "high city," in Athens was the place for temples and important buildings. The Persians had destroyed these structures during the war.

Critical Thinking

6. Male citizens in Athens voted directly on laws. In the United States, citizens elect representatives who vote on laws.
7. The Athenian view of citizenship was much narrower than the U.S. view which includes males, females, and naturalized citizens.

Activity Rubric

	Number of Buildings	Accuracy of Map	Quality of Map
4	four or more	locations are correct	colorful, has all map elements
3	three or more	locations are correct	has all map elements
2	two or three	some locations are incorrect	missing some elements
1	none or one	all are incorrect	poorly done

Classical Greece • 397

❶ Plan & Prepare

Objectives

- Explain the reasons for war between Athens and Sparta.
- Outline the events and describe the results of the Peloponnesian War.
- **Language Objective:** Write descriptions of the war strategies used by Sparta and Athens.

Quick Look

Lesson 2 explores the causes and effects of the Peloponnesian War that led to the weakening of Greek city-states.

❷ Focus & Motivate

Preview Review what students already know about Athens and Sparta by making a three-columned chart on the board with *Athens, Sparta,* and *Questions or Comments* as headings.

Introduce the Main Ideas The three main ideas relate to the Big Idea "New ideas and beliefs can challenge a government's authority, leading to change." Help students look for this Big Idea in the lesson.

Reading Skill: Comparing and Contrasting Tell students to look for words that signal comparison (*like, both also, related*) and contrast (*but, yet, however, different from*) as they read the lesson.

SAMPLE ANSWERS FOR CHART

War Strategy	
Athens	Sparta
Rely on sea power and bring food in by sea	Cut off Athenian food supply
Allow Spartans to destroy countryside	Take control of countryside around Athens

---

Lesson 2

▶ MAIN IDEAS

❶ Government Athens and Sparta and their allies fought a war over Athens' growing power.

❷ Government Athens lost the Peloponnesian War.

❸ Government More than 25 years of war weakened all of the Greek city-states.

▶ TAKING NOTES

Reading Skill: Comparing and Contrasting

Comparing and contrasting the war strategies of Athens and Sparta will help you understand the outcome of the war. In Lesson 2, look for the differences between the war strategies of the two city-states. Record the differences on a chart like the one below.

War Strategy	
Athens	Sparta

 **Skillbuilder Handbook, page R4**

▲ **Spartan Soldier**
Sparta had the most powerful army of all the Greek city-states.

CALIFORNIA STANDARDS

6.4.2 Trace the transition from tyranny and oligarchy to early democratic forms of government and back to dictatorship in ancient Greece, including the significance of the invention of the idea of citizenship (e.g., from *Pericles' Funeral Oration*).

6.4.6 Compare and contrast life in Athens and Sparta, with emphasis on their roles in the Persian and Peloponnesian Wars.

HI 1 Students explain the central issues and problems from the past, placing people and events in a matrix of time and place.

HI 2 Students understand and distinguish cause, effect, sequence, and correlation in historical events, including long- and short-term causal relations.

HOW TO TEACH THE CALIFORNIA STANDARDS

Standard	Content	Student Question or Activity	Instruction
6.4.2	**Page 400** Identifies the importance of democracy and citizenship as described in a passage from *Pericles' Funeral Oration*	**Page 400** Students infer why Pericles paid tribute to Athenian life as well as those who died in the Peloponnesian War.	Ask students if they have ever been to a war memorial in the United States. Discuss the ways in which the memorials honor citizens from a variety of backgrounds.
6.4.6	**Page 400** Explains the reasons for opposition to Athens	**Page 400** Students identify the causes of the war between Athens and Sparta.	Review Pericles' use of Delian League funds. Then review Pericles' action against opposing city-states.
HI 1	**Page 400** Describes what city-states did to oppose Athens	**Page 402** Students analyze the forming of the Peloponnesian League.	Have students compare and contrast the Delian and Peloponnesian leagues.
HI 2	**Page 401** Connects the outbreak of the plague to Athens seeking a truce with Sparta	**Page 401** Students describe the conditions that led to Athens surrendering to Sparta.	Discuss what might happen to an army that had been fighting for 25 years. Ask students which of their conclusions might apply to Athens.

Peloponnesian War

Terms & Names

Peloponnesian War the war between Athens and Sparta that begin in 431 B.C.

plague an easily-spread, deadly disease

truce an agreement to stop fighting

Build on What You Know In Chapter 11, you learned that important differences existed between Athens and Sparta. Tensions had been building between Athens and Sparta for years. Sparta did not like Athens growing more powerful.

The Outbreak of War

❶ ESSENTIAL QUESTION What led Athens and Sparta to fight a war?
fear of Athens' power, Athens' naval empire, Athenian settlers moving into other lands
There were many differences between the city-states of Athens and Sparta. For example, Athens had a democratic form of government. Sparta had a culture that glorified military ideals. Both wanted to be the most powerful city-state in the region. This competition led to clashes between the two city-states and their allies.

Causes of the War There were three main reasons war broke out. First, some city-states feared Athens because of its grab for power and prestige. Second, under the leadership of Pericles, Athens grew from a city-state to a naval empire. Third, some Athenian settlers began to move into the lands of other city-states.

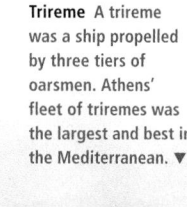

Trireme A trireme was a ship propelled by three tiers of oarsmen. Athens' fleet of triremes was the largest and best in the Mediterranean. ▼

❸ Teach

The Outbreak of War

🔲 6.4.6, HI 2

Talk About It

- **Critical Thinking: Making Inferences**
  Why would other city-states fear Athenian settlers moving into their lands? *(Possible answers: Athenians might eventually conquer the city-states; Athenian power might grow even more and other city-states might not have a voice in their own destiny.)*

California Resources

California Reading Toolkit, L41
California Modified Lesson Plans for English Learners, p. 85
California Daily Standards Practice Transparencies, TT41
California Standards Enrichment Workbook, pp. 51–52, pp. 59–60
California Online Test Practice
California Test Generator CD-ROM
California Standards Planner and Lesson Plans, L81
California EasyPlanner CD-ROM
California eEdition CD-ROM

399

LESSON 2 PROGRAM RESOURCES

ON LEVEL

In-Depth Resources: Unit 5
- Reading Skill: Comparing and Contrasting, p. 40
- Vocabulary Study Guide, p. 45
- Vocabulary Cards, p. 47

Formal Assessment
- Lesson Quiz, p. 208

ENGLISH LEARNERS

In-Depth Resources in Spanish
- Reading Skill: Comparing and Contrasting, p. 102
- Vocabulary Study Guide, p. 108

Modified Lesson Plans for English Learners, p. 85

Reading Study Guide (Spanish), p. 107

Reading Study Guide Audio CD (Spanish)

STRUGGLING READERS

In-Depth Resources: Unit 5
- Reading Skill: Comparing and Contrasting, p. 40
- Vocabulary Study Guide, p. 45
- Vocabulary Cards, p. 47
- Reteaching Activity, p. 54

Reading Toolkit, L41

Reading Study Guide, p. 107

Reading Study Guide Audio CD

GIFTED AND TALENTED STUDENTS

Interdisciplinary Projects
- Language Arts, p. 69

In-Depth Resources: Unit 5
- Primary Source: Pericles' Funeral Oration, p. 51

INCLUSION

EasyPlanner CD-ROM
- Reading Skill: Comparing and Contrasting

- Vocabulary Study Guide
- Reteaching Activity

TECHNOLOGY

eEdition CD-ROM

Power Presentations CD-ROM

Critical Thinking Transparencies
- CT 52 Comparing and Contrasting

Test Generator CD-ROM

ClassZone.com

In-Depth Resources: Unit 5
• Reading Skill: Comparing and Contrasting, p. 40

Teach

The War Rages

🖋 6.4.2, 6.4.6, HI 1

Talk About It

• What advantages did Sparta and Athens each have in the war? *(Sparta had the best army and could not be attacked by sea; Athens had the best navy and could strike Sparta's allies by sea.)*

• When did Athens sign a truce to stop fighting with Sparta? *(421 B.C.)* When did Athens finally surrender? *(404 B.C.)*

• What did Pericles do to counteract Sparta's destruction of the countryside? *(He persuaded people to allow Sparta to destroy the countryside and had people move into the city, supplying them with food by sea.)*

• **Critical Thinking: Making Generalizations** What might happen to armies when they fight over many years? *(Possible answers: They become weaker, smaller, and more open to attack; they miss their families; they stop believing in the war.)*

In-Depth Resources: Unit 5
• Primary Source: Pericles' Funeral Oration, p. 51

Interpreting Primary Sources

Pericles' Funeral Oration

• How does Pericles describe democracy? *(Administration is in hands of the many, not the few.)*

• What does Pericles say about citizens being involved in public service? *(Being excellent and distinguished merits the reward of public service whether a person is poor or not.)*

DOCUMENT–BASED QUESTION ANSWER

Possible answers: He wants to unite people; he needs to help them believe that democracy is worth dying for.

Athens Disliked The other city-states also resented how Athens spent money from the Delian League, intended for the mutual protection of all the city-states. Athens used some of the money to beautify its city. Because of this practice several city-states tried to break free of Athenian power. Pericles' policy was to punish any city-state that resisted Athens.

Sparta headed a league of city-states to stand up to the power of the Delian League. It is called the Peloponnesian League because many of the city-states were located on the Peloponnesus. Finally, in 431 B.C., Sparta declared war on Athens. This conflict was called the **Peloponnesian War**.

> **REVIEW** What were the causes of the war between Athens and Sparta?
> City-states controlled by Athens resented its power.
> Other city-states resented Athens using league funds for itself.

The War Rages

2 ESSENTIAL QUESTION What happened during the Peloponnesian War?
Athens and allies fought Sparta and allies; Spartan side won.
Each side in the war had advantages and disadvantages. Sparta had the better land-based military force, and its location could not be attacked by sea. Athens had the better navy and could strike Sparta's allies by sea. These differences shaped the war strategy of each side.

Primary Source

Pericles' Funeral Oration

Background: Pericles spoke to honor Athenians killed in action during the first year of the Peloponnesian War, which began in 431 B.C. Parts of his speech paid tribute to democracy in Athens as well.

from *The History of the Peloponnesian War*

By Thucydides (Translated by Rex Warner)

It is true that we are called a democracy, for the administration is in the hands of the many and not of the few. But while the law secures equal justice to all alike in their private disputes, the claim of excellence is also recognized; and when a citizen is in any way distinguished, he is preferred to the public service, not as a matter of privilege, but as the reward of merit. Neither is poverty a bar, but a man may benefit his country whatever be the obscurity [insignificance] of his condition.

> **DOCUMENT–BASED QUESTION**
> Why do you think Pericles praises Athenian life in a tribute to the war dead?

400

DIFFERENTIATING INSTRUCTION

English Learners

Identify Adjectives
Explain to students that adjectives describe nouns and that some tell what kind or how many. Tell them that adjectives can be used to compare things. On the board, write "Athens had a democratic government, and Sparta's government was controlled by military power." Help students identify the words that tell what kind or how. Note these details in a graphic.

Struggling Readers

Outline Essential Questions
Have pairs turn the Essential Questions from the lesson into sentence starter statements and write them on a sheet of paper. For example, "What led Athens and Sparta to fight a war?" becomes "Athens and Sparta fought a war because . . ." Then have them reread the subheading, look for the answer, discuss it, and complete the statement. Have pairs compare their sentences with other pairs.

Peloponnesian War, 431–404 B.C.

MACEDONIA

Amphipolis (422 B.C.)

Spartalos (429 B.C.)

Byzantium

Cyzicus (410 B.C.)

Cynossema (411 B.C.)

Ionian Sea

Aegean Sea

PERSIAN EMPIRE

GREECE

Thebes

Corinth

Athens

Notium (407 B.C.)

Ephesus

Miletus

Athens and allies
Sparta and allies
Athenian victory
Spartan victory

Sparta

Sphacteria (425 B.C.)

Mediterranean Sea

GEOGRAPHY SKILLBUILDER
INTERPETING MAPS
Place Around which sea did most of the battles take place?

History from Visuals

Interpreting Maps

- How many victories are shown for Athens? for Sparta? *(Both had three victories.)*
- Which side occupied land near the Persian Empire? *(Athens and its allies)*
- Which side had more territory accessible by sea only? *(Athens)*

GEOGRAPHY SKILLBUILDER ANSWER

Aegean Sea

More About . . .

The Plague

The plague started in Athens in 430 B.C. The symptoms included high fever, inflamed eyes, sore throat, coughing, extreme thirst, vomiting, and red blisters on the skin. Many thousands died. Thucydides, a Greek historian, wrote, "They became infected by nursing one another and died like sheep. . . . Bodies of dying men lay one upon another. . . . The temples. . .were full of corpses of those who had died in them."

Strategies of War Sparta's strategy was to cut off the Athenian food supply by destroying crops. The Spartans did this by taking control of the countryside around Athens.

Athens' strategy was to avoid battles on land and to rely on sea power. Pericles persuaded the Athenians to allow the Spartans to destroy the countryside. He brought people from the areas surrounding Athens inside the city walls. The people would be safe there and Athens would be supplied with food by sea.

Disaster Strikes Athens Because of Pericles' plan to bring people into Athens, the city became badly overcrowded. In the second year of the war, an outbreak of a **plague** took many lives in Athens. The plague was a disease that spread easily and usually caused death. Athens lost as many as one-third of its people and armed forces. Pericles, too, died from the plague.

In 421 B.C., Athens signed a **truce**, or an agreement to stop fighting. Athens finally surrendered to Sparta in 404 B.C.

REVIEW What caused Pericles' strategy to fail?
A plague broke out in the overcrowded city causing the deaths of many Athenians.

Classical Greece • 401

DIFFERENTIATING INSTRUCTION

Inclusion

Role-Play a Spartan or Athenian

Review the characteristics of Athenian and Spartan society with students. Write a list of the characteristics on the board and ask students to choose to be either an Athenian or a Spartan army officer. Explain that they are going to role-play being a general in charge of troops and that they have to convince their soldiers to keep on fighting by reminding them what they are fighting for.

Gifted and Talented Students

Analyze a Battle

Have students select one of the battles shown on the map on page 401 and write an analysis of why they think that Athens or Sparta won the battle. Remind students to think about what they know about the strengths and weaknesses of both city-states and have them draw a conclusion about the outcome. If the outcome is unexpected, ask students to explain why this might be so.

Teach

Consequences of the War

 6.4.6, HI 1

Talk About It

- What two losses did the city-states suffer during the war? *(economic and military power)*
- **Critical Thinking: Identifying Issues and Problems** Why did Philip of Macedonia think that it was possible to take over Greece? *(Possible answers: Years of fighting and the plague weakened Greece enough for Philip to defeat them easily.)*

❹ Assess & Reteach

Assess Divide students into small groups and have them answer all of the Essential and Review questions for the lesson. Ask groups to take turns presenting answers to the class. Discuss whether any groups answered questions differently.

 Formal Assessment
- Lesson Quiz, p. 208

Reteach Have students read the lesson summary. For each item, have them find information or examples from the lesson that support that item.

 In-Depth Resources: Unit 5
- Vocabulary Cards, p. 47
- Reteaching Activity, p. 54

Homework Helper

Visit **ClassZone.com** for a lesson review, a flip-card activity, and links to related Web sites.

Consequences of the War

3 ESSENTIAL QUESTION What was the result of the Peloponnesian War?
All of the Greek city-states were weakened.
The Peloponnesian War lasted for over 27 years. Cities and crops were destroyed, and thousands of Greeks died. All of the Greek city-states suffered losses of economic and military power.

To the north of the Greek city-states, King Philip II of Macedon came to power in 359 B.C. Planning to build an empire, he looked south toward the weakened Greek city-states.

REVIEW What was the long-term effect of the Peloponnesian War?
The city-states lost economic and military power and were vulnerable to attack by Philip of Macedonia.

Lesson Summary

- The wealth, prestige, policies, and power of Athens caused resentment among other city-states.
- A plague that killed many Athenians helped Sparta defeat Athens.
- The Peloponnesian War weakened all of the Greek city-states for 50 years.

Why It Matters Now . . .

The Peloponnesian War shows that countries that wage war may lose power and prestige instead of gaining it.

2 Lesson Review

Homework Helper
ClassZone.com

Terms & Names

1. Explain the importance of
   Peloponnesian War   plague   truce

Using Your Notes

Comparing and Contrasting Use your completed graphic to answer the following question:

2. How was the war strategy of Athens different from that of Sparta? (6.4.6)

War Strategy	
Athens	Sparta

Main Ideas

3. Why did smaller city-states resent Athenian control? (6.4.2)
4. What was the Peloponnesian League and who led it? (HI 1)
5. Why did the Greek city-states lose power after the Peloponnesian War? (6.4.6)

Critical Thinking

6. **Making Generalizations** What can happen to both sides in a war when the fighting goes on for many years? (HI 2)
7. **Making Inferences** What might have helped the Greek city-states to be more cooperative at the end of the Peloponnesian War? (6.4.6)

Activity

Writing a Persuasive Composition Write a persuasive composition in which Pericles tries to convince people to leave their land and move into Athens to be safe from Spartan attacks. (6.4.6)

---

2 Lesson Review Answers

Terms & Names

1. • Peloponnesian War, p. 400
   • plague, p. 401
   • truce, p. 401

Using Your Notes

See page 398 for an example of a completed chart.

2. Pericles had a strong navy. Athens could be supplied with food by sea and the navy could attack Sparta's allies.

Main Ideas

3. They resented Athens using Delian League funds which were designated for mutual protection.
4. It was a group consisting of Sparta and its allies who opposed Athens and its allies. Sparta was the leader.
5. They lost crops, and cities were destroyed.

Critical Thinking

6. Both sides grow weak from the fighting. They may lose land, crops, and/or trade.
7. The Greek city-states had to decide to put their combine interests above their individual interests. They needed a strong power to unite them.

Activity Rubric

	Identifies Dangers	Gives Reasons for Moving	Addresses Concerns
4	two or more clearly stated	several compelling	all
3	two or more	two	most
2	one	one	some
1	none	vague	little

Create a Storyboard

Goal: To analyze the roles of Athens and Sparta in the Peloponnesian War and to create a storyboard portraying the events of that war

Materials & Supplies
- books on the Peloponnesian War
- poster board
- markers

Prepare

1. Research the roles Athens and Sparta played in the Peloponnesian War. Look for important events that occurred during this war.

2. Reread the information in Lesson 2 of this chapter.

Do the Activity

1. Make a list of six to eight events that occurred during the Peloponnesian War. Include events that were not battles.

2. Decide on a visual way to show the events you selected.

3. Divide the poster board into sections based on the number of events you selected.

4. Draw one event scene in each of the sections on the board.

Follow-Up

1. What event that was not a battle had a major influence on the course of the war?

2. Did Sparta actually win the war? Explain.

Extension

Making a Display Create a class storyboard by taking one section from each board made by the members of the class and taping them together. Then, using the storyboard display, explain the events of the war and their impact on Greece.

CALIFORNIA STANDARDS
6.4.6 Compare and contrast life in Athens and Sparta, with emphasis on their roles in the Persian and Peloponnesian Wars.

403

Objective

- To describe the sequence of events and the roles of Sparta and Athens in the Peloponnesian War.

- Create a visual presentation of written information.

Suggestions for Completing the Activity

- As a class, list the events of the war on the board for Sparta and Athens.

- Have students count the number of events and decide on how many sections to use on their poster board.

- Have students decide what elements each event needs to have included in its box.

- Have students bring or draw sample visuals before completing the final board.

ACTIVITY ANSWERS

Follow-Up Answers

1. Possible answers: Sparta and other city-states form the Peloponnesian League; an outbreak of a plague hits Athens; Athens signs a truce with Sparta.

2. Possible answer: Sparta did not really win because they had been greatly weakened by the war, opening up the possibility of invasion by a stronger enemy.

Extension Rubric

	Content of Storyboard	**Presentation of Card**
4	contains all important events	neat, clearly drawn or designed
3	contains most events	mostly neat and drawn or designed
2	missing several events	somewhat neat, not clearly drawn or designed
1	missing most or all events	not neat, not clearly drawn or designed

❶ Plan & Prepare

Objectives

- Describe Philip of Macedonia's conquest of Greece.
- Trace the expansion of Alexander's empire across parts of Europe and Asia.
- Explain the influence of Greek culture in Alexander's empire.
- **Language Objective:** Complete cause-and-effect chains to understand the events in the lesson.

Quick Look

Lesson 3 focuses on the Macedonian conquest of Greece and parts of Europe and Asia by Philip and Alexander of Macedonia.

❷ Focus & Motivate

Preview Ask students to scan the lesson and list any names and places they find. Then ask them what they know about each and what they want to know. Locate the places on a classroom map.

Introduce the Main Ideas The three main ideas relate to the Big Idea "Migration, trade, warfare, and the action of missionaries spread ideas and beliefs." Help students look for this Big Idea in the lesson.

Reading Skill: Understanding Cause and Effect Explain to students that history is often written with a cause-and-effect structure.

SAMPLE ANSWERS FOR CHART

Causes	Effects
Weak governments	Philip able to conquer them
New weapons of warfare	Strengthened Philip II's well-trained professional army
Foreign conquests	Spread of Greek cultures and a new blend of cultural styles known as Hellenistic

---

Lesson 3

▶ MAIN IDEAS

❶ **Government** Philip II of Macedonia conquered Greece.

❷ **Government** Alexander built a huge empire that spread across parts of Europe and Asia.

❸ **Geography** Alexander spread Greek culture and influence throughout his empire.

▶ TAKING NOTES

Reading Skill: Understanding Cause and Effect

Following causes and effects can help you understand patterns in history. In this lesson, look for the effects of conditions listed in the chart. Record them on a chart of your own.

Causes	Effects
Weak governments	
New weapons of warfare	
Foreign conquests	

 Skillbuilder Handbook, page R26

▲ **Philip II, King of Macedonia**
Philip had dreams of defeating both the Greeks and the Persians.

404 • Chapter 12

HOW TO TEACH THE CALIFORNIA STANDARDS

Standard	Content	Student Question or Activity	Instruction
6.4.2	**Page 406** Describes Philip's takeover of Greece and the loss of democracy	**Page 409** Students explain how Philip ended democratic practices.	Have students review "Philip Conquers Greece" on page 406 to find out what happened to democracy in Greece.
6.4.7	**Page 406** Traces the rise of Alexander and his quest to build an empire.	**Page 406** Students explain how Alexander built an empire.	Have students summarize how Philip built a professional army and how Alexander carried on the empire.
HI 2	**Page 406** Describes how the Peloponnesian War led to Greece being conquered by Philip	**Page 406** Students explain why the Greek city-states were open to attack by Philip and his army.	List the effects of the Peloponnesian War on Greek city-states. Then have students describe how the condition left them open to attack.
HI 3	**Page 406** Outlines Alexander's path to creating an empire and the changes he instituted.	**Page 409** Students analyze how Hellenistic culture developed.	Have students review "A Blend of Cultures" and "Alexandria" on pages 408–409 and give examples of each change instituted by Alexander.

Alexander the Great

Build on What You Know While the Greek city-states were busy fighting each other, a new power was rising in the north. The king there was strong. You have learned that a strong ruler can often unite a divided people.

The Kingdom of Macedonia

① **ESSENTIAL QUESTION** Who conquered the Greek city-states? Philip II, King of Macedonia

The new power to the north of Greece was the country of Macedonia (MAS•ih•DOH•nee•uh). Its king, Philip II, was 23 years old, strong and fearless. He had plans to build an empire that included the lands of Greece and of Persia.

A Military Genius As a teenager, Philip had been a hostage in the Greek city of Thebes. There he observed its army and its military tactics. Philip learned of the advantages of a professional army, or an army of full-time soldiers, rather than one made up of citizen-soldiers.

Philip organized a well-trained professional army. He devised new battle formations and tactics. He experimented with the combined use of cavalry and infantry. He supplied his soldiers with new weapons, like the catapult. A **catapult** is a military machine that was used to hurl stones at enemy forces and city walls. His soldiers also used battering rams to smash through closed gates.

Alexander the Great
The detail is from this mosaic. It shows Philip's son, Alexander, in battle. ▼

405

Terms & Names

catapult a military machine that threw stones at enemy forces

Alexander the Great a ruler who built a vast empire east through Central Asia and brought about a cultural blending

Hellenistic a culture that combined Greek, Persian, Egyptian, and Indian styles

Alexandria an important Egyptian city and learning center founded by Alexander the Great

❸ Teach

The Kingdom of Macedonia

⬛ 6.4.7

Talk About It

- **Critical Thinking: Making Inferences** What experiences did Alexander have that would help him rule well? *(Possible answers: He trained in his father's army; he watched his father from childhood.)*

California Resources

California Reading Toolkit, L42
California Modified Lesson Plans for English Learners, p. 87
California Daily Standards Practice Transparencies, TT42
California Standards Enrichment Workbook, pp. 51–52, 61–62
California Online Test Practice
California Test Generator CD-ROM
California Standards Planner and Lesson Plans, L83
California EasyPlanner CD-ROM
California eEdition CD-ROM

LESSON 3 PROGRAM RESOURCES

ON LEVEL

In-Depth Resources: Unit 5
- Reading Skill: Understanding Cause and Effect, p. 41
- Vocabulary Cards, p. 47
- Skillbuilder Practice: Assessing Credibility of Sources, p. 44

Formal Assessment
- Lesson Quiz, p. 209

ENGLISH LEARNERS

In-Depth Resources in Spanish
- Reading Skill: Understanding Cause and Effect, p. 103
- Skillbuilder Practice: Assessing Credibility of Sources, p. 107

Modified Lesson Plans for English Learners, p. 87
Reading Study Guide (Spanish), p. 109
Reading Study Guide Audio CD (Spanish)

STRUGGLING READERS

In-Depth Resources: Unit 5
- Reading Skill: Understanding Cause and Effect, p. 41
- Vocabulary Cards, p. 47
- Reteaching Activity, p. 55

Reading Toolkit, L42

Reading Study Guide, p. 109

Reading Study Guide Audio CD

GIFTED AND TALENTED STUDENTS

Humanities Transparencies
- HT23 Alexander the Great Preparing to Dive

INCLUSION

EasyPlanner CD-ROM
- Reading Skill: Understanding Cause and Effect
- Vocabulary Study Guide
- Reteaching Activity

TECHNOLOGY

eEdition CD-ROM
- Starting with a Story

Power Presentations CD-ROM

Humanities Transparencies
- HT23 Alexander the Great Preparing to Dive

Map Transparencies
- MT24 The Successors to Alexander's Empire

Critical Thinking Transparencies
- CT 53 Understanding Cause and Effect

Test Generator CD-ROM

ClassZone.com

In-Depth Resources: Unit 1
- Reading Skill: Understanding Cause and Effect, p. 41
- Skillbuilder Practice: Assessing Credibility of Sources, p. 44

Teach

Alexander Tries to Conquer the World

6.4.2, 6.4.7

Talk About It

- Why were Greek city-states fearful of rebelling against Alexander? *(He destroyed Thebes using cruel tactics.)*

- In what two places was Alexander successful before crossing Mesopotamia and attacking the Persian Empire directly? *(Anatolia and Egypt)*

- Why was Alexander's empire split after his death? *(Alexander had not unified the empire. No one was strong enough to take control, so the empire was divided among three key generals.)*

- **Critical Thinking: Understanding Cause and Effect** What is one pattern can you see as the cause of a leader's inability to keep building an empire? *(Possible answers: Armies get tired; building an empire takes time and effort; taking control can make subjects rebellious.)*

 Map Transparencies
- MT24 The Successors to Alexander's Empire

More About . . .

Bucephalus

When Alexander was about twelve years old, he tamed Bucephalus, a horse that no one else could tame. Alexander watched the horse for some time and realized that he was afraid of his own shadow. So, Alexander spoke gently to him and turned him toward the sun. Since Bucephalus couldn't see his shadow, Alexander was able to ride him. After seeing this feat, Alexander's father was believed to have said that Alexander would have to find another kingdom, because Macedonia wouldn't be big enough for him.

Philip Conquers Greece After conquering the lands around Macedonia, Philip focused on the Greek city-states. After the Peloponnesian War, the Greeks were too weak and disorganized to unite against Philip. In 338 B.C., Philip completed the conquest of the Greeks. Philip became the ruler of the Greek city-states. His dictatorial rule ended Greek democratic practices. He brought Greek troops into his army and prepared to attack Persia.

Alexander Takes Over However, in 336 B.C., Philip was assassinated at his daughter's wedding. His 20-year-old son Alexander took the throne. Many wondered if such a young man was ready to take control of Macedonia.

REVIEW Why were the Greek city-states open to an attack by Philip?
After the Peloponnesian War, the Greek city-states were weakened and disorganized.

Alexander Tries to Conquer the World

2 **ESSENTIAL QUESTION** How did Alexander build an empire? He gained control of Greece, conquered Persia and took its lands, and took lands in Central Asia and India. Alexander was well-prepared for the job of king. He had been tutored by the finest Greek scholars and trained in the Macedonian army. He continued his father's plan of creating an empire.

Alexander Defeats Persia Before Alexander could attack Persia, the Greek city-state of Thebes rebelled. Alexander destroyed the city. His cruel tactics made other Greek city-states too fearful to rebel. Next, Alexander moved his troops to Anatolia, where he attacked and defeated Persian forces. He used bold tactics, such as using thousands of troops to charge straight at the enemy. In the beginning, Alexander met sharp resistance from the Persians, but he was successful.

Next, instead of going directly to Persia, he turned south and entered Egypt, which the Persians controlled. The Egyptians welcomed Alexander because they hated the Persians. They even chose him to be their pharaoh. Alexander then moved his forces from Egypt across Mesopotamia toward Persia. Finally, he struck Persepolis, the royal capital of the Persians. By 331 B.C., Alexander controlled the Persian Empire.

Alexander Alexander rides his favorite horse Bucephalus. ▼

DIFFERENTIATING INSTRUCTION

Inclusion

Design a Catapult
Give students photographs, information, and questions about the catapult and battering ram. Have student pairs make a tape recording in which one partner asks the questions and the other partner answers them.

Gifted and Talented Students

Create a Poster
Have students research the development of the catapult and the battering ram, and create a poster illustrating them. Have them include the parts of the weapons, when they were developed, by whom, and how they were used. Present the posters to the class and discuss why the weapons would be useful to an army.

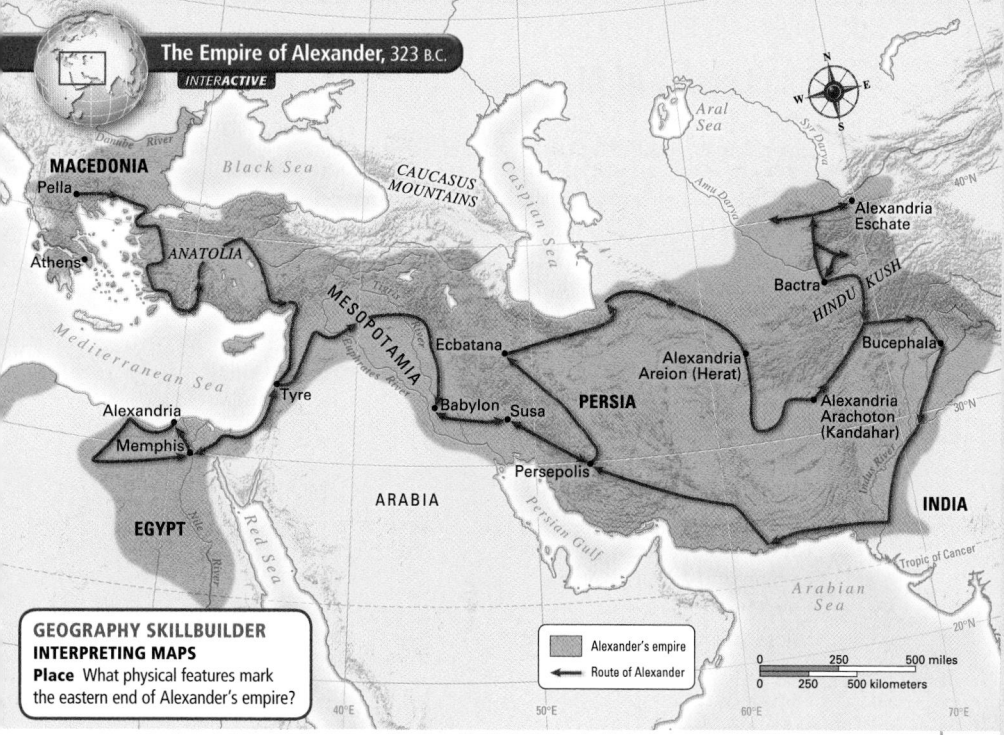

The Empire of Alexander, 323 B.C.
INTERACTIVE

MACEDONIA
Pella

Black Sea

CAUCASUS MOUNTAINS

Aral Sea

Athens

ANATOLIA

Caspian Sea

Alexandria Eschate

Bactra

HINDU KUSH

MESOPOTAMIA

Mediterranean Sea

Ecbatana

Bucephala

Tyre

Alexandria Areion (Herat)

Alexandria

Babylon Susa

PERSIA

Alexandria Arachoton (Kandahar)

Memphis

Persepolis

ARABIA

Persian Gulf

INDIA

EGYPT

Red Sea

Arabian Sea

Tropic of Cancer

GEOGRAPHY SKILLBUILDER
INTERPRETING MAPS
Place What physical features mark the eastern end of Alexander's empire?

[legend]
Alexander's empire
Route of Alexander

0   250   500 miles
0   250   500 kilometers

Alexander's Other Conquests In the next three years, Alexander pushed his armies eastward to conquer parts of Central Asia. In 326 B.C., they reached the Indus River Valley and India. Alexander urged his armies to continue eastward, but they refused to go any further. They had been fighting for 11 years and had marched thousands of miles from home. Alexander was forced to turn back.

In 323 B.C., Alexander and his armies returned to Babylon. While they paused there, Alexander fell ill with a fever and died within days. He was 32 years old. Although he did not live to an old age, he managed to create a great empire. Because of his achievements, he is remembered as **Alexander the Great**.

Alexander did not have time to unify his empire. After he died, military leaders fought among themselves to gain control of the empire. Not one of Alexander's generals was strong enough to take control of the entire empire. Eventually, three key generals divided the empire.

REVIEW How far eastward in Asia did Alexander build his empire?
Alexander and his forces reached the Indus River Valley and India.

Classical Greece • 407

DIFFERENTIATING INSTRUCTION

Teach

The Legacy of Alexander

 HI 2, HI 3

Talk About It

- What is Hellenistic culture? *(It is a blend of Greek, Persian, Egyptian, and Indian styles and customs.)*

- How was learning affected by the spreading of cultures across the empire? *(Scholars could share knowledge, which led to new discoveries in science and medicine.)*

- Why was the lighthouse at Alexandria important? *(It was an important center of learning until the second century A.D.)*

- **Critical Thinking: Identifying Issues and Problems** What problems might occur with the blending of cultures as in Alexander's empire? *(Possible answer: Individual cultures and languages might disappear.)*

Humanities Transparencies
- HT23 Alexander the Great Preparing to Dive

More About . . .

The Lighthouse at Alexandria
One of the three generals to take control of Alexander's empire was Ptolemy Soter. He controlled Egypt and began constructing the lighthouse on the island of Pharos. The lighthouse guided ships using fires at night and reflected sun rays in daylight. It is said that its mirror could reflect over 20 miles away. It was so famous that it appeared on Roman coins. The lighthouse was considered one of Seven Wonders of the Ancient World. The lighthouse was apparently damaged by earthquakes in the 4th and 14th centuries, and collapsed around 1326. The modern French, Spanish, and Italian words for *lighthouse* come from *Pharos*, the name of this famous monument.

The Legacy of Alexander

3 ESSENTIAL QUESTION How did culture change under Alexander's rule?
Greek, Persian, Egyptian, and Indian cultures blended to form Hellenistic culture.
Alexander and his armies carried their culture and customs everywhere they went. As Alexander conquered one land after another, he set up colonies. He also built cities based on Greek culture. He named many of them Alexandria, after himself. The historian Plutarch, who lived a few centuries later, wrote that Alexander actually named 70 cities Alexandria.

A Blend of Cultures Alexander left Greeks behind to rule his lands. Greek became the common language in the lands he controlled. At the same time, Alexander adopted Persian clothing styles and Persian customs. He urged his armies to do the same. Some of the Greek settlers married Persian women and adopted Persian ways. In Egypt, the Greek rulers accepted Egyptian culture and blended it with Greek styles. In India, the same blending occurred.

This blend of Greek, Persian, Egyptian, and Indian styles and customs became known as **Hellenistic** culture. *Hellas* was the Greek name for Greece. This culture influenced the lands of the empire for hundreds of years. Learning was especially affected by the mingling of cultures. The combined knowledge of the Greeks, Egyptians, Arabs, and Indians made new discoveries possible in science and medicine. You will learn more about this in Lesson 4.

Alexandria The most famous of the Hellenistic cities was **Alexandria**, Egypt, which Alexander founded in 332 B.C. The city was an important center of learning until the second century A.D. A library there contained major collections of Greek, Persian, Egyptian, Hebrew, and other texts. Scholars from the Mediterranean area and from Asia came to Alexandria to study.

▲ **Iranian Manuscript** This manuscript depicts Hellenistic art. Aristotle, a Greek thinker, teaches astronomy to Persians. He is dressed in Persian-style clothing.

INTERDISCIPLINARY ACTIVITIES

Science

Create a Map of the Ancient World
Ask students to research the Seven Wonders of the Ancient World. Have students create a map of the world, then label the sites of each wonder and be prepared to tell the class the history of one of them. Assign various students a specific wonder to describe in detail.

Language Arts

Write Journal Entries
Have students create journal entries for Alexander's path to build his empire. Have various students choose one leg of the journey and include the city where they start out, the mileage to the next city, and a description of what they see along the way. Encourage students to research the cities in books or on the Internet to find interesting things to write about.

Also located in Alexandria was the Temple of the Muses. Muses are goddesses who rule the arts and sciences. Many examples of the arts and sciences were stored there. Today we call such a location a museum. Alexandria also had an enormous lighthouse whose light could be seen 35 miles away. It is considered one of the Seven Wonders of the World.

REVIEW How did Hellenistic culture develop?
Alexander and his armies took Greek ways with them wherever they went.

They also adopted the styles of the cultures they conquered in Egypt, Persia, and India.

▲ **Lighthouse at Alexandria**
The image above is an artist's idea of what the lighthouse may have looked like.

Lesson Summary

- Philip II, king of Macedonia, conquered Greece.
- Alexander the Great conquered the Persian Empire and parts of Central Asia.
- Hellenistic culture—a blend of Greek, Persian, Egyptian, and Indian cultures—was created.

Why It Matters Now . . .

The blended culture created by Alexander's empire forms a basis for culture in the countries that exist in those lands today.

3 Lesson Review

 Homework Helper
ClassZone.com

Terms & Names

1. Explain the importance of
   catapult   Hellenistic
   Alexander the Great   Alexandria

Using Your Notes

Understanding Cause and Effect Use your completed graphic to answer the following question:

2. What were the effects of Alexander's conquest of a vast area? (HI 2)

Causes	Effects
Weak governments	
New weapons of warfare	
Foreign conquests	

Main Ideas

3. What happened to Greek democratic practices when Philip of Macedonia conquered Greece? (6.4.2)

4. Why did Alexander's empire include Central Asia but not India? (6.4.7)

5. How did Alexander spread Greek influence in new cities he founded? (HI 3)

Critical Thinking

6. **Understanding Cause and Effect** How did the Peloponnesian War lead to Alexander's success as a conqueror? (HI 2)

7. **Making Inferences** What made Hellenistic culture unique? (6.4.7)

Activity **Calculating the Size of the Empire** Go to the map on page 407. Use the scale to calculate the distance from east to west of Alexander's empire. How does it compare to the distance of the continental United States from east to west? (6.4.7)

Classical Greece • 409

❹ Assess & Reteach

Assess Have pairs complete the chart for question 2. Then summarize the effects with the whole class.

 Formal Assessment
- Lesson Quiz, p. 209

Reteach Divide students into three groups. Assign each group one of the three subheadings in this lesson. Each group is responsible for writing the causes and effects of events that appear in their particular subsection on separate index cards. Have students present their section to the class, with one group member calling out a cause and another member responding with the effect.

 In-Depth Resources: Unit 5
- Vocabulary Cards, p. 47
- Reteaching Activity, p. 55

Homework Helper

Visit **ClassZone.com** for a lesson review, a flip-card activity, and links to related Web sites.

3 Lesson Review Answers

Terms & Names

1. • catapult, p. 405
   • Alexander the Great, p. 407
   • Hellenistic, p. 408
   • Alexandria, p. 408

Using Your Notes

See page 404 for an example of a completed chart.

2. Alexander's conquests resulted in the spread of Greek culture and a new blend of cultural styles called Hellenistic culture.

Main Ideas

3. His dictatorial rule ended Greek democratic practices.

4. Alexander's armies had been away from home for 11 years and refused to go farther.

5. Alexander built his cities on a Greek model and left Greeks behind to rule them.

Critical Thinking

6. Because the Greek city-states were weak, Philip was able to conquer them. His son Alexander then used Greece as a base for further conquests.

7. The culture developed because different groups lived close together and each adopted valuable aspects of the other's culture.

Activity Answer

The approximate distance east to west in Alexander's empire is about 3,250 miles.
The approximate distance east to west in the continental United States is about 3,000 miles.

Classical Greece • 409

❶ Plan & Prepare

Objectives

- Describe how the concepts and styles of Greek architecture and art are still influential today.
- Explain the basis of Western knowledge from Greek study of logic and reason.
- Trace the development of the scientific standards from Hellenistic science.
- **Language Objective:** Design "Then and Now" posters to compare and contrast life in ancient Greece and modern-day United States.

Quick Look

Lesson 4 focuses on the development of Greek art, architecture, philosophy, and science that set standards still in use today.

❷ Focus & Motivate

Preview Write the word *philosophy* on the board and explain that its Greek roots mean "love" + "wisdom" = "love of wisdom." Discuss what a philosopher is and what topics might interest them.

Introduce the Main Ideas The three main ideas relate to the Big Idea "New inventions and techniques change the way humans live their daily lives." Help students look for this Big Idea.

Reading Skill: Finding Main Ideas As students read, tell them to stop and ask, "What did I just read?" and take notes about main ideas that relate to their charts.

SAMPLE ANSWERS FOR CHART

The Arts & Architecture	History & Philosophy	Science & Technology
Greeks invented dramaas an art form.	Greeks practiced direct democracy.	Greeks made important discoveries about planets and stars.
Greeks aimed to capture the ideal in their art.	Greeks wrote down their history.	Math is needed to do astronomy.
Buildings had columns and graceful proportions.	Greeks had two ideas about the universe.	Archimedes explained the law of the lever.

Lesson 4

▶ MAIN IDEAS

❶ **Culture** Greek art and architecture introduced new styles and concepts that set standards for generations of artists around the world.

❷ **Culture** The Greek love of reason and logic influenced the development of Western knowledge.

❸ **Science and Technology** Hellenistic science provided much of the scientific knowledge of the world until the modern age.

▶ TAKING NOTES

Reading Skill: Finding Main Ideas

Looking for the main ideas as you read can help you understand the value of a period in history. As you read this lesson, look for the cultural and scientific contributions made by people of the Greek and Hellenistic cultures. Record these contributions on a list for each of the three headings in Lesson 4.

The Arts & Architecture	History & Philosophy	Science & Technology

 **Skillbuilder Handbook, page R2**

▲ **Hellenistic Sculpture** This sculpture is titled *Winged Victory of Samothrace*. The sculpture features Nike, the goddess of victory.

CALIFORNIA STANDARDS

6.4.8 Describe the enduring contributions of important Greek figures in the arts and sciences (e.g., Hypatia, Socrates, Plato, Aristotle, Euclid, Thucydides).

HI 1 Students explain central issues and problems from the past, placing people and events in a matrix of time and place.

HI 4 Students recognize the role of chance, oversight, and error in history.

HOW TO TEACH THE CALIFORNIA STANDARDS

Standard	Content	Student Question or Activity	Instruction
6.4.8	**Page 415** Outlines the contributions of Socrates, Plato, and Aristotle in philosophy	**Page 414** Students explain how reason and logic in Classical Greece influenced the development of Western knowledge.	Have students research the Socratic method, Platonic ideal, and Aristotelian logic. Discuss each as a class.
HI 1	**Page 414** Explains the pattern of questioning that happens in a culture during a prolonged wars.	**Page 417** Students explain why both Chinese and Greek thinkers searched for basic truths during times of conflict.	Brainstorm with the class about what effects war has on a society. Then ask class to formulate the questions a society might ask itself about these effects.
HI 4	**Page 416** Discusses Ptolemy's astronomical error and the fact that it was believed for 1,400 years.	**Page 417** Students explain what was wrong with Ptolemy's theory on the solar system.	Ask students to pretend they are Ptolemy's peers and review his findings. Give sample questions such as, "What math did you use to make your theory?"

The Legacy of Greece

TERMS & NAMES
drama
tragedy
comedy
ideal
philosophy

CHAPTER 12 • LESSON 4

Build on What You Know You have learned about the great art, literature, and thought of Chinese and Indian civilizations. Greek civilization spread through the actions of Alexander the Great. Later, the Hellenistic culture spread to Mediterranean countries and into Asia.

The Arts and Architecture

①ESSENTIAL QUESTION What new elements did Greek art and architecture introduce? *drama, use of the ideal in sculpture, columns*

The Greeks invented drama as an art form. **Drama** was a written work designed for actors to perform. The Greeks built the first theaters in the western world.

Drama Greek drama was a part of every city's religious festival. Wealthy citizens spent money to sponsor the production of the dramas. Writers submitted plays to the city leader, who chose the ones he thought were the best. Then a play was assigned to a troupe of actors for production. When the plays were performed, contests were held to award prizes to the best writers.

Ancient Theater
The theater at Epidaurus is built into a hillside. ▼

411

Terms & Names

drama a written art form created by the Greeks

tragedy a serious dramatic work invented by the Greeks

comedy a drama that pokes fun at politics, people, and ideas of the day

ideal a style of Greek art focusing on as perfect a form as possible

philosophy the study of basic truths and ideas about the universe

❸ Teach

The Arts and Architecture

6.4.8

Talk About It

- **Critical Thinking: Drawing Conclusions**
  What topics do you think were used in Greek dramas? *(Possible answers: heroes, myths, gods, and goddesses)*

California Resources

California Reading Toolkit, L43
California Modified Lesson Plans for English Learners, p. 89
California Daily Standards Practice Transparencies, TT43
California Standards Enrichment Workbook, pp. 63–64
California Online Test Practice
California Test Generator CD-ROM
California Standards Planner and Lesson Plans, L85
California EasyPlanner CD-ROM
California eEdition CD-ROM

LESSON 4 PROGRAM RESOURCES

ON LEVEL

In-Depth Resources: Unit 5
- Reading Skill: Finding Main Ideas, p. 42
- Vocabulary Cards, p. 47

Formal Assessment
- Lesson Quiz, p. 210

ENGLISH LEARNERS

In-Depth Resources in Spanish
- Reading Skill: Finding Main Ideas, p. 104
- Visual Summary, p. 105

Modified Lesson Plans for English Learners, p. 89

Reading Study Guide (Spanish), p. 111
Reading Study Guide Audio CD (Spanish)

STRUGGLING READERS

In-Depth Resources: Unit 5
- Reading Skill: Finding Main Ideas, p. 42
- Vocabulary Cards, p. 47
- Reteaching Activity, p. 56

Reading Toolkit, L43
Reading Study Guide, p. 111
Reading Study Guide Audio CD

GIFTED AND TALENTED STUDENTS

History Makers
- Aristotle, p. 23

In-Depth Resources: Unit 5
- Literature: Oedipus the King by Sophocles, p. 52

Interdisciplinary Projects
- Math, p. 67
- Science, p. 68

INCLUSION

EasyPlanner CD-ROM
- Reading Skill: Finding Main Ideas
- Vocabulary Study Guide

- Reteaching Activity

TECHNOLOGY

eEdition CD-ROM
Power Presentations CD-ROM
Humanities Transparencies
- HT24 Mosaic of Masks

Critical Thinking Transparencies
- CT54 Finding Main Ideas
- CT55 Chapter 12 Visual Summary

Test Generator CD-ROM
ClassZone.com

In-Depth Resources: Unit 5
- Reading Skill: Finding Main Ideas, p. 42

Humanities Transparencies
- HT24 Mosaic of Masks

More About . . .

Masks

The human face is the part of us that shows who we are. Masks, which hide the face, were worn in Greek drama to hide the actor's identity so that the actor could be transformed into something or someone else. Our modern word *person* comes from *persona*, the Latin word for "mask."

We know about Greek masks from vases that have been found. Masks, however, have been used for centuries. They were used in the Egyptian, Aztec, Mayan, and Incan civilizations for various reasons. They were also used in theaters in China, India, and Japan. Many tribal societies still use masks today. Masks, of course, are also used during Halloween, a time when people can take on a new personality.

More About . . .

Aristophanes

Aristophanes' plays were awarded many prizes. Although his plays are funny and relaxed, Aristophanes himself had little sense of humor and rarely showed emotion. He did not like change and often made jokes about politicians of his day in his plays. Modern audiences may not understand many of these jokes, but his plays are still quite humorous today. Some of his other plays are *Acharnians*, *The Clouds*, *Lysistrata*, and *Peace*.

Actors The actors in plays were men, who also played the parts of women. The actors wore colorful costumes and masks to portray their characters. The stage sets were colorful as well. Dancing was important in Greek festivals and plays. Often the plays included a large chorus that danced, sang, and recited poetry. Drama had two forms: tragedy and comedy.

Tragedy and Comedy The first form, **tragedy**, was a serious drama that presented the downfall of an important character, such as a king. Common themes for tragedy included love, war, and hate. One example is the hero in the play *Oedipus Rex* (EHD•uh•puhs rehks) by Sophocles (SAHF•uh•KLEEZ). In the play, a good, intelligent ruler named Oedipus kills a man. Later, Oedipus finds out that the man he killed was really his own father.

The second form of drama, called **comedy**, was a less serious dramatic work. Comedies often made fun of politics, important people, and ideas of the time. Comedies usually ended happily. Aristophanes (AR•ih•STAHF•uh•neez), who was born in the time of Pericles, was a great writer of comedy. One of his plays, *The Birds*, makes fun of those who would gain power. In the play, a king becomes a bird and founds a city in the sky. The city is called Cloudcuckooland. The hero blocks the gods from interfering with his rule and declares himself the king of the universe.

Sculpture Greek artists aimed to capture the **ideal** in their work. In other words, they tried to portray objects, including humans, in as perfect a form as possible. The artists tried to create a sense of order, beauty, and harmony in every work. Since the Greeks spent much of their time out-of-doors, works of art were located outside and were of a large scale. Many Greek sculptures portrayed the gods. The sculptures were placed in temples. These temples were built to honor the gods.

One of the most famous statues was created to honor the goddess Athena. In 447 B.C., Pericles appointed the sculptor Phidias (FIHD•ee•uhs) to direct the building of the Parthenon as a house for Athena. Phidias created a statue of Athena that was placed inside. He used gold and ivory to make the statue. It stood more than 30 feet tall when it was finished.

▲ **Dramatic Masks**
The mask at the top represented comedy. The lower mask was used in tragedy.

DIFFERENTIATING INSTRUCTION

Inclusion

Compose a Tragedy/Comedy Song
Review the characteristics of tragedy and comedy with students. Discuss examples of tragic and comic stories from contemporary life, using newspapers, television, or radio. Then pair students and ask them to compose a song that conveys comedy and tragedy.

Struggling Readers

Create Vocabulary Cards
Have students create word cards using index cards. Make sure that students use large index cards or create their own large cards from paper. For each vocabulary word in the lesson, tell them to create cards with four sections that include the following: a definition, an example, an illustration or picture, and the word used in a sentence. Use the vocabulary word as the card title.

Architecture Greek architects designed temples, theaters, meeting places, and wealthy citizens' homes. Like the sculptors, the architects worked to create beautiful buildings with graceful proportions. Several distinct elements appeared in architectural works. One element was a column.

Often a series of columns, called a colonnade, was placed around the outside of a building. The space between the top of a column and the roof is called a *pediment*. Sculptures or paintings usually were placed in the pediments. The Parthenon displayed the temple form that was most often used (see page 396). It had a four-sided colonnade around a room built to house the statue of the goddess Athena. Sculptured designs that portrayed scenes in Athena's life were put in the pediments of the Parthenon.

Visual Vocabulary

pediment

REVIEW What was the goal of Greek artists?
Greek artists aimed to show objects in ideal form.

Visual Vocabulary

Pediments in Greek Architecture
Explain that the term *pediment* is from the Latin word *periment*, which was an alteration of pyramid. On a building, the pediment is the triangular piece above the columns that helps support the roof.

History from Visuals

Greek Columns
Have students study the three types of columns shown on this page. Then ask the following questions:

• Which type of column has the most decorative design? *(Corinthian)*

• What is one difference between the Doric and Ionic columns? *(Possible answers: The Doric column has a simpler design; the Ionic column has a thinner column.)*

Greek Columns

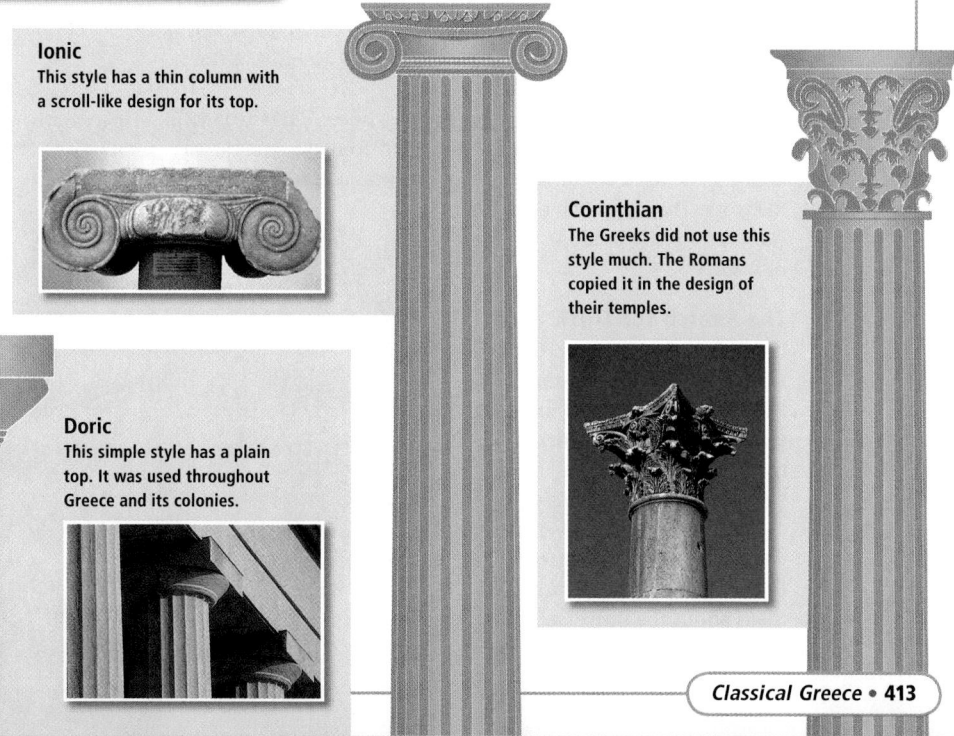

Ionic
This style has a thin column with a scroll-like design for its top.

Corinthian
The Greeks did not use this style much. The Romans copied it in the design of their temples.

Doric
This simple style has a plain top. It was used throughout Greece and its colonies.

Classical Greece • 413

DIFFERENTIATING INSTRUCTION

English Learners

Compare and Contrast
Direct students to the ancient theater photo on page 411. Ask students to note some similarities and differences between this ancient theater and a theater in their community. Note student responses in a chart. Have students create posters illustrating the similarities and differences.

Gifted and Talented Students

Build a Building with Columns
Have students use clay or other similar materials and cardboard to create a simple building with columns. Models should include a floor and roof in addition to the columns. Students can use the Internet, their textbook, or other resources to find possible designs for their model.

Teach

History, Philosophy, and Democracy

6.4.8, HI 1

Talk About It

- What was Plato's ideal government like? *(It was not a democracy; it had a philosopher-king who would be wise, calm, and reasonable.)*

- What was new about the way Greeks wrote history? *(They not only told stories but also examined them to try to determine facts.)*

- Who was Herodotus? *(He was considered the father of history and wrote a history of the Persian Wars called* History.*)*

- What two ideas did Greek philosophers have about the universe? *(It is put together in an orderly way; laws of nature control it.)*

- **Critical Thinking: Detecting Historical Points of View** Socrates once said, "An unexamined life is not worth living." How does this quote reflect his philosophy? *(Possible answer: Life is not good if a person does not question and think about it.)*

More About . . .

Socrates, Plato, and Aristotle
These three philosophers are responsible for some of our ideas about education. The Socratic method is still used to train students in analytical thinking. Plato wrote a series of dialogues that continued Socrates' method. Aristotle's Lyceum, which was an Athenian school, helped form the basis for an adult education movement that began in Massachusetts in the 1800s in which people debated ideas on current topics. These ideas helped shape school curricula and establish libraries and museums.

History, Philosophy, and Democracy

2 ESSENTIAL QUESTION How did the Greek love of reason and logic influence the development of Western thought?
They introduced history based on facts and philosophy based on natural law. Perhaps the greatest legacy the Greeks left for the world was the idea of democracy and ways to run a government.

Democracy Becomes Reality The citizens of some Greek city-states practiced direct democracy. Unfortunately, citizenship was limited to a few people. But, for the first time, citizens had a voice in their government. The government was more open and more fair than any government had been. The Greeks' ideas have been copied in many places over time. Democracy continues to be a goal for many nations where it does not yet exist.

Herodotus and Thucydides The Greeks were among the first civilizations to write down their history. They did not just tell stories about their past. They examined the past to try to determine the facts and significance of a historical event.

Herodotus (hih•RAHD•uh•tuhs) has been called the Father of History. He was interested in learning and recording the stories about events. Herodotus was born in 484 B.C. and traveled widely as a young man. He wrote an account of the Persian Wars called *History*.

Another Greek historian, Thucydides (thoo•SIHD•ih•DEEZ), wrote a history of the Peloponnesian War. To make sure he was accurate, he used documents and eyewitness accounts to create his work. This approach set a standard for the writing of history.

The Search for Truth After the Peloponnesian War, Greek thinkers began to question their values. In this questioning they were like the Chinese thinkers before and during the Time of the Warring States. In the search to find answers, the Greeks developed **philosophy**, or the study of basic truths and ideas about the universe.

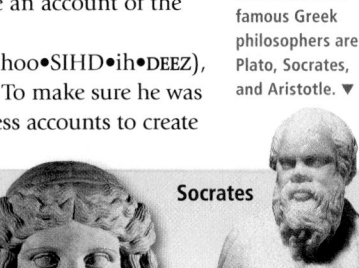

Greek Philosophers
The three most famous Greek philosophers are Plato, Socrates, and Aristotle. ▼

Socrates

Plato

INTERDISCIPLINARY ACTIVITIES

Language Arts

Write a Biographical Sketch
Have students use library and Internet resources to research and write a brief biographical sketch about either Herodotus or Thucydides. Students should explain the importance of their historian's writings as well as how the historian did research for his work.

Language Arts

Research Famous Quotes Booklet
Have three student groups research well-known quotations attributed to Socrates, Plato, or Aristotle. Each group member should be responsible for one quote. The group should then decide what category the quote belongs under, such as government, life, or love, and organize the quotations into categories. Have groups share and discuss their quotations with the rest of the class. Compile all of the quotes into a class booklet.

Greek philosophers had two basic ideas about the universe. First, they assumed that the universe is put together in an orderly way. They believed that laws of nature control the universe. Second, the philosophers assumed that people could understand these laws. The philosophers used these two ideas when they sought the truth.

Socrates Over a period of time, Greece had many famous philosophers. One of them was Socrates (SAHK•ruh•TEEZ), who lived from 470 to 399 B.C. He encouraged his young students to examine their beliefs by asking them a series of questions. This question-and-answer style of teaching is called the Socratic method.

▲ **Death of Socrates**
Socrates' supporters gather with him as he drinks poison.

Young people liked the teaching of Socrates. But his enemies accused him of causing young people to rebel. They brought him to trial. Socrates told the court that he was teaching young people to think about their values and actions. The jury did not agree with his actions and sentenced him to death. Socrates died by drinking a poison called hemlock.

Plato and Aristotle One of Socrates' best students was Plato. He was born about 427 B.C. Plato wrote about an ideal government in a book titled *The Republic*. He did not describe a democracy. Instead, he believed that a philosopher-king should rule. This king would be wise, calm, and reasonable—like a philosopher. Plato started an important school of higher learning called the Academy. It stayed open for about 900 years.

Aristotle (AR•ih•STAHT•uhl) was Plato's brightest student. Aristotle lived from 384 to 322 B.C. He invented a method of debating that followed rules of logic. Later, the rules of logic were applied to studies in science. Aristotle opened his own school in Athens called the Lyceum. In addition to his great philosophical work, Aristotle also spent three years tutoring Alexander the Great.

Aristotle

> **REVIEW** How did Herodotus and Thucydides influence the writing of history today?
> Herodotus tried to record facts in his stories. Thucydides wanted accuracy. He used documents and eyewitness accounts.

Classical Greece • 415

Teach

Science and Technology

6.4.8, HI 4

Talk About It

- What important discoveries about astronomy were made by Hellenistic scholars? *(the circumference of Earth; the relationship of the sun, the moon, and Earth to each other; the estimated size of the sun.)*

- What kinds of discoveries were developed by Hellenistic mathematicians and physicists? *(geometry, the law of the lever, the compound pulley, a water-lifting device, and ideas which led to the invention of pumps and steam engines)*

- What was Hypatia noted for? *(She was the first noted female mathematician, and was also an astronomer. She wrote about works of Ptolemy and Euclid, and was the leader of a philosophical movement based on Plato's ideas.)*

- **Critical Thinking: Identifying Issues and Problems** Why is it important to constantly ask questions and come to new conclusions in science? *(Possible answer: Incorrect ideas, such as Ptolemy's Earth-centered universe, can lead to false knowledge.)*

History from Visuals

Greek Astronomy
Have students study the three diagrams shown at the bottom of this page. Then ask the following questions:

- According to Ptolemy, where was the sun located? *(between Venus and Mars)*

- Which Greek view of astronomy was most accurate? *(the estimate of Earth's circumference)*

- What can you infer from Aristarchus' inaccurate estimate of the sun's size? *(Possible answer: Aristarchus probably thought that the sun was much closer to Earth than it really was.)*

Science and Technology

3 ESSENTIAL QUESTION Why is Hellenistic science so important?
Important discoveries in astronomy, mathematics, and physics come from Hellenistic science. Hellenistic scholars preserved and expanded the scientific and mathematical knowledge of the thinkers of Greece, Egypt, and India.

Astronomy Some important discoveries about the planets and the stars came from scientists studying at Alexandria. For instance, Eratosthenes (EHR•uh•TAHS•thuh•NEEZ) found a way to estimate the circumference, or distance around Earth.

Another scientist at Alexandria, Aristarchus (AR•ih•STAHR•kus), studied the relationship of the sun, moon, and Earth to each other. He also estimated the size of the sun. The scientist Ptolemy (TAHL•uh•mee) studied the universe. Unfortunately for the world of science, Ptolemy placed Earth at the center of the universe. This incorrect view persisted for 1,400 years!

Mathematics and Physics Knowledge of very complicated mathematics is needed to do work in astronomy. Hellenistic mathematicians developed several kinds of math. The mathematician Euclid (YOO•klihd) created a geometry text complete with proofs for his work. The work of Euclid is still the basis for geometry.

Archimedes (AHR•kuh•MEE•deez) explained the law of the lever. As an inventor, he developed the compound pulley. He is also believed to have created a device to lift water. He intended his water-lifting device to be used for the irrigation of fields.

Greek Astronomy

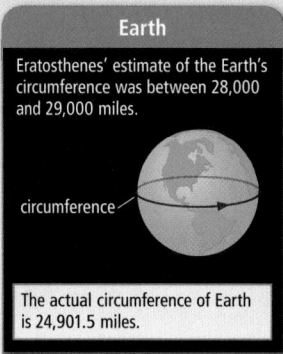

Earth
Eratosthenes' estimate of the Earth's circumference was between 28,000 and 29,000 miles.

circumference

The actual circumference of Earth is 24,901.5 miles.

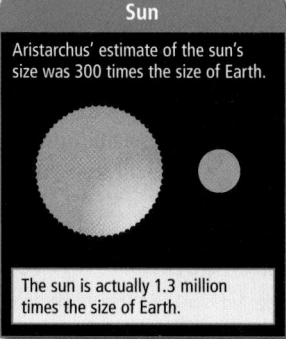

Sun
Aristarchus' estimate of the sun's size was 300 times the size of Earth.

The sun is actually 1.3 million times the size of Earth.

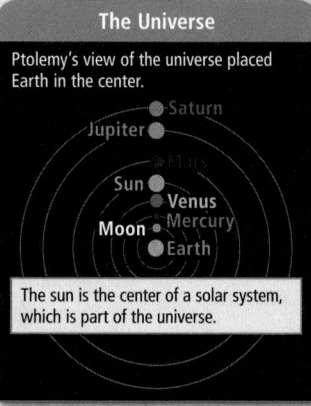

The Universe
Ptolemy's view of the universe placed Earth in the center.

Saturn
Jupiter
Mars
Sun
Venus
Moon
Mercury
Earth

The sun is the center of a solar system, which is part of the universe.

INTERDISCIPLINARY ACTIVITIES

Science

Make Posters
Have students research Ptolemy's and Copernicus' models of the universe and create a poster showing a visual representation of both. Students should include labels and an explanation of how the models are different. Then ask the class to discuss how people might have felt to know that Earth was not the center of the universe.

Math

Research the Life of Euclid
Have students investigate the life of Euclid, including the way in which he developed geometry. Have students include mathematical formulas and explain why they continue to be important in mathematics today.

The ideas of Archimedes were used to build pumps and eventually to create a steam engine.

The first noted female mathematician, Hypatia (hy•PAY•shuh), taught at Alexandria. Hypatia was also an astronomer. She wrote about the works of Ptolemy and about Euclid and geometry as well. She was also the leader of a philosophical movement based on the works of Plato.

REVIEW In what areas of math and science did Greek thinkers work?
Greek thinkers worked in astronomy, geometry, and physics.

Lesson Summary

- Greek and Hellenistic writers, artists, and architects invented new and beautiful styles.
- Greek philosophy and history set standards of logic, reason, and record keeping.
- Hellenistic scientists made important discoveries about the world.

Why It Matters Now . . .

The Greek and Hellenistic cultures set enduring standards in art, philosophy, and science.

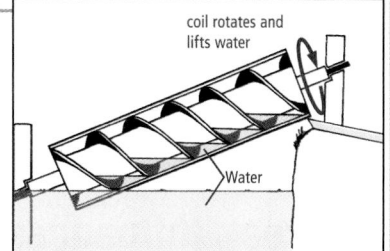
coil rotates and lifts water
Water

▲ **Archimedes' Water-Lifting Device**
The device is a large coil open at both ends. It is placed inside a water tight tube. As the coil turns it brings up water from a lower level.

4 Lesson Review

 Homework Helper
ClassZone.com

Terms & Names

1. Explain the importance of

| drama | comedy | philosophy |
| tragedy | ideal | |

Using Your Notes

Finding Main Ideas Use your completed graphic to answer the following question:

2. What two ideas about the universe did Greek philosophers accept? (6.4.8)

The Arts & Architecture	History & Philosophy	Science & Technology

Main Ideas

3. What qualities did Greek architects strive for in their work? (6.4.8)

4. What teaching style is identified with Socrates, and what was it like? (6.4.8)

5. What important discoveries about Earth, the planets, and the sun came from the scientists of Alexandria? (6.4.8)

Critical Thinking

6. **Determining Historical Context** What was wrong with Ptolemy's theory? (HI 4)

7. **Explaining Historical Patterns** Why did both Chinese and Greek thinkers develop ideas about philosophy during times of war and disorder? (HI 1)

Activity

Internet Activity Use the Internet to research inventions of ancient Greeks. Design a Web page that illustrates and explains those inventions. (6.4.8)
INTERNET KEYWORD: *Greek inventions*

Classical Greece • 417

❹ Assess & Reteach

Assess Have students complete the chart in question 2 of the lesson review.

 Formal Assessment
• Lesson Quiz, p. 210

Reteach Divide students into teams and have them create questions and answers from the main ideas in this lesson on separate pieces of paper. Collect the questions and answers and have teams compete in a contest to see who can come up with the most correct answers. If an answer is given, the team must come up with the question it answers. If a question is asked, the team must give the answer.

 **In-Depth Resources: Unit 5**
• Reteaching Activity, p. 56
• Vocabulary Cards, p. 47

Homework Helper

Visit **ClassZone.com** for a lesson review, a flip-card activity, and links to related Web sites.

4 Lesson Review Answers

Terms & Names

1. • drama, p. 411
   • tragedy, p. 412
   • comedy, p. 412
   • ideal, p. 412
   • philosophy, p. 414

Using Your Notes

See page 410 for an example of a completed chart.

2. Greek philosophers assumed that the universe works in an orderly way according to laws. They believed that people could understand these laws.

Main Ideas

3. Greek architects tried to make beautiful buildings with graceful proportions.

4. Socrates used a question-and-answer teaching method.

5. the circumference of the earth; the size of the sun; placement of planets in the universe

Critical Thinking

6. Ptolemy placed Earth at the center of the universe. This mistake was not corrected for many centuries.

7. Times of war and disorder cause people to question what is important and what might be needed to bring about peace and harmony.

Activity Rubric

	Number of Inventions	Explanation	Illustration
4	three or more	clear and concise	outstanding detail
3	three or more	adequate	clear
2	two	vague	somewhat unclear
1	one	missing	poorly done

Classical Greece • 417

Objectives

- Explain the main features of the Olympics, Greek architecture, and Greek juries.
- Describe the continuing influence of Greece in sports, architecture, and law.
- Analyze and interpret information in order to talk and write about it.
- **Language Objective:** Analyze photographs that enhance the text found in captions to make reading more meaningful and comprehensible.

❶ Focus & Motivate

Preview Invite students to talk about what they know about the Olympics and Greek architecture and how they continue to influence modern life.

❷ Teach

Talk About It

- What are some similarities between the ancient and modern Olympic games? *(Both are held every four years; both are sports events; both stress being in good shape.)*
- What are two differences between the games? *(Only men competed in the past; the modern Olympics is split into summer and winter games.)*
- What idea from nature did the Greeks use to construct their buildings? *(They found a ratio in nature that they believed created perfect proportions.)*
- What are two ways in which Greek and modern juries are alike? *(Jury pools are selected randomly and are paid.)*
- **Critical Thinking: Drawing Conclusions** Why is a jury composed of a group of citizens better than having one person decide a case? *(Possible answers: Having a group decide is more likely to be fair and unbiased, with the case being discussed thoroughly.)*

Greek Influences Today

Purpose: To explore places where Greek influence can be found in today's world

The Greeks have influenced our ideas in many different areas. They strived to achieve the ideal in all areas of life. They paid especially close attention to those aspects of life that were a part of the polis. Today, we can clearly see the Greek influence in sports, architecture, and jury selection.

CALIFORNIA STANDARDS
6.4 Students analyze the geographic, political, economic, religious, and social structures of early civilizations of Ancient Greece.

Olympics

▶ **Past** The Olympics were held in Olympia every four years. Only men could compete. Sports included boxing, wrestling, running, jumping, javelin and discus throwing, and events using horses. This statue of an ancient discus thrower shows the ideal form.

▼ **Present** The modern Olympics are held every four years. There are so many events that the games were split into the Summer Games and the Winter Games. Cathy Freeman (center), gold medal winner in the 400 meter dash in 2000, represented Australia.

418 • Chapter 12

DIFFERENTIATING INSTRUCTION

English Learners

Analyze Photographs and Text
Tell students that analyzing the photographs will help them gain a deeper understanding of the text. Have students discuss what each photograph shows about the Olympics, architecture, and jury selection. Note their observations, then have them read the text. Ask how the text helps them understand the topics. Discuss how the photographs and text work together to explain the topics.

Inclusion

Throw a Discus
Have students find out more about the discus. Then have them create a model of a discus, make a list of the rules for the sport, and demonstrate how to throw a discus for the class.

Architecture

▼ Past Greek architects looked to nature to find the ideal form for building. They found a ratio in nature that they believed created perfect proportions. They used it in their buildings and especially with their columns. The result was a graceful structure like the Temple of Hephaestus.

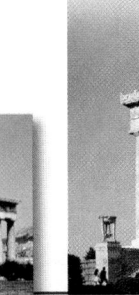

▼ Present Many buildings copy the Greek style. The columns lend a sense of importance and authority to the building. The building below is the Lincoln Memorial in Washington, D.C.

Jury Selection

▶ Past Athens had a pool of about 6,000 qualified jurors. Trials required as many as 500 jurors. Jurors were paid. At right is a jury selection device from ancient Greece. Each juror had a metal plate with his name on it. The plates were randomly placed in the slots. Then rows of the plates were selected for a specific trial.

▼ Present The adult population of citizens of a district make up the jury pool. Jurors are randomly called to serve and are paid a small amount. Juries are made up of 12 persons, although there can be as few as 6. Potential jurors are sent a legal order to serve. The order must be obeyed.

Activities

1. **TALK ABOUT IT** Why do you think jurors are paid?

2. **WRITE ABOUT IT** Use the library or the Internet to research the development of the modern Olympic games. Write a research report describing your findings. (Writing 2.3)

Research Links

Visit **ClassZone.com** for age-appropriate Web sites related to this topic.

More About . . .

The Golden Ratio

The Greeks knew how to calculate *Phi,* or the Golden Ratio. It is an ideal proportion in which the shorter part is to the longer part as the longer part is to the whole. The Greeks knew that people enjoyed looking at rectangles with this ratio even though they could not explain why. The Golden Ratio is seen in several places in the Parthenon, considered the most perfect structure ever made. The Golden Ratio was used by Leonardo Da Vinci in art and sculpture. Curiously, this ratio is reflected in nature and can be found in every spiral form from snail shells to galaxies.

ACTIVITIES ANSWERS

1. **TALK ABOUT IT** Possible answer: Originally jurors were paid so that all citizens could participate in trials, not just the rich who could afford to miss work. The tradition continues into the present day.

2. **WRITE ABOUT IT**

2. Writing Rubric

	Main Ideas	Supports Main Ideas with Facts and Details	Use of Standard English
4	clearly stated, well organized	many rich details	one or no errors
3	adequately stated and organized	some details	two or three errors
2	adequately stated, but poorly organized	few details	some errors
1	poorly stated, poorly organized	little support	many errors

Terms & Names

1. Pericles was responsible for expanding direct democracy in Athens.

2. Resentment of the Delian League was one of the causes of the Peloponnesian War.

3. Alexander the Great's empire became the birthplace of Hellenistic culture.

4. Tragedy and comedy are both forms of drama invented by the Greeks.

Main Ideas

The Golden Age of Greece (pages 392–397)

5. Pericles expanded democracy, created an empire, and beautified the city of Athens. These actions led to a period of high achievement called the Golden Age.

6. Both have citizens exercising political power, and both have three branches of government.

The Peloponnesian War (pages 398–403)

7. The Greek city-states paid a tribute to the Delian League. Pericles used the money to strengthen the power of Athens and beautify its Acropolis.

8. Athens shaped its war strategy around its naval power, and Sparta shaped its around its land-based military.

Alexander the Great (pages 404–409)

9. The war weakened the Greek city-states so that they could not unite under a central power of their own. This enabled Philip to conquer them.

10. Alexander the Great founded many cities based on Greek models. He left Greeks in charge of lands he conquered.

The Legacy of Greece (pages 410–419)

11. Greek sculptors aimed to create ideal images. Greek architects had the same goal of creating structures of beauty and grace.

12. Greek philosophy focused on reason and logic. The Greek thinkers believed that laws ruled the universe and people could understand these laws.

▶ **VISUAL SUMMARY**

Classical Greece

Culture (6.4)
- Developed the basis of western philosophy
- Established rules for the writing of history
- Set out rules of logic

Arts (6.4.8)
- Created drama
- Used the ideal as the basis for the arts
- Set artistic standards for art and architecture

Science & Technology (6.4.8)
- Made important discoveries about Earth and the planets
- Devised new mathematics
- Developed inventions such as compound pulley and water lifting devices

Government (6.4.3)
- Created and used direct democracy
- Expanded citizen participation in government
- Alexander built an enormous empire including land in Asia, Africa, and Europe

▶ **TERMS & NAMES**

Explain why the words in each set below are linked with each other.

1. Pericles and **direct democracy**
2. Delian League and **Peloponnesian War**
3. Alexander the Great and **Hellenistic**
4. tragedy and comedy

▶ **MAIN IDEAS**

The Golden Age of Greece (pages 392–397)

5. How did the three goals of Pericles bring a Golden Age to Greece? (6.4)

6. What aspects of Athenian direct democracy are similar to democracy as practiced by the United States? (6.4.3)

Peloponnesian War (pages 398–403)

7. Why did other city-states in the Delian League resent Athens? (6.4.6)

8. How did Athens and Sparta shape their war strategies? (6.4.6)

Alexander the Great (pages 404–409)

9. How did the Peloponnesian War help Philip II of Macedonia conquer Greece? (6.4.7)

10. How did Alexander the Great introduce Greek ideas to Egypt and Central Asia? (6.4.7)

The Legacy of Greece (pages 410–419)

11. What qualities did Greek sculptors and architects seek to portray? (6.4.8)

12. What are the basic ideas in Greek philosophy? (6.4.8)

▶ **CRITICAL THINKING** Big Ideas: Geography

13. UNDERSTANDING CAUSE AND EFFECT Why didn't the democratic ideas of Greek city-states spread throughout the empire of Alexander the Great? (6.4.7)

14. MAKING INFERENCES How did the conquests of Alexander the Great change the cultures of the conquered lands? (HI 1)

15. UNDERSTANDING CONTINUITY AND CHANGE How did the Greek scientists expand knowledge about the world? (HI 3)

ALTERNATIVE ASSESSMENT RUBRICS

1. Writing Rubric

	Plot	Setting	Points of View
4	engaging	vividly described	two, well written
3	adequate	adequately described	two
2	thin	vaguely described	one, but well written
1	missing	missing	one

2. Science Rubric

	Hypothesis	Steps	Conclusion
4	clear and well stated	many-documented	clearly stated
3	clear	some	adequate
2	somewhat unclear	few	false or poorly stated
1	missing	none	missing

ALTERNATIVE ASSESSMENT

1. WRITING ACTIVITY Review the section about Socrates in Lesson 4. Use books or the Internet to learn more about Socrates' trial. Working with a partner, write a short scene for a play about the trial of Socrates. Be sure to include parts for Socrates, his students, and his enemies. (Writing 2.1)

2. INTERDISCIPLINARY ACTIVITY— SCIENCE Use books or the Internet to research the ideas of Archimedes about levers. Duplicate some of Archimedes' experiments. Prepare a lab report on your activities. (6.4.8)

3. STARTING WITH A STORY

 Review your letter of advice to Pericles about paid public officials. Use the Internet to find what paid public positions exist in your hometown or state. Also find out what qualifications are required for those positions and how the positions are filled. Prepare a report with your findings. (6.4.3)

Technology Activity

4. CREATING A VIDEO SCRIPT Use the Internet or the library to research modern buildings that show the influence of Greek architecture. Create a video script for a presentation on the influence of Greek architecture on modern buildings. (6.4.8)
Include
- the location of the modern buildings
- images of the modern and Greek buildings
- comparisons of modern buildings and Greek buildings

Research Links
ClassZone.com

Using a Time Line The time line below shows changes in Greece from 479 B.C. to 323 B.C. Use it to answer the questions below. (6.4.2)

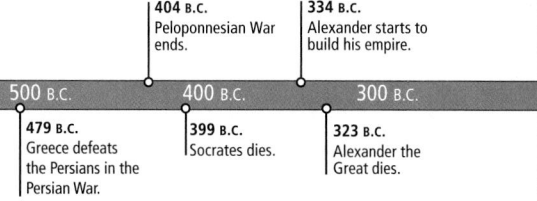

1. Which of the events listed above occurred first?

A. death of Socrates
B. death of Alexander
C. Peloponnesian War
D. Persian War

2. Which of the following statements is correct?

A. Socrates and Alexander lived at the same time.
B. The Peloponnesian War ended before Alexander built an empire
C. The Persian War occurred after the Peloponnesian War.
D. It took Alexander 10 years to build his empire.

 **Test Practice**
ClassZone.com

Additional Test Practice, pp. S1–S33

Classical Greece • 421

Critical Thinking

Big Ideas: Geography

13. When Phillip conquered the city-states, he eliminated democratic practices.

14. All the cultures were affected by cultural diffusion. New ideas and ways of governing became a part of life in the conquered lands. Learning and knowledge changed as well.

15. These scientists made advances in astronomy, mathematics, and physics that expanded knowledge and understanding about the world and the solar system.

Standards-Based Assessment

1. The correct answer is letter D. The other three events occurred later.

2. The correct answer is letter B. Alexander died about ten years after he started to build his empire.

 Research Links

Visit **ClassZone.com** for links to Web sites that can be resources for the multimedia presentation.

 Test Practice

Visit **ClassZone.com** to access strategies and tutorials for taking standardized tests.

 Formal Assessment
- Chapter Tests, Forms A, B, and C, pp. 211–222

 Test Generator
- Chapter Tests, Forms A, B, and C, (English and Spanish)

ALTERNATIVE ASSESSMENT RUBRICS

3. Starting with a Story Rubric

	List of Positions	Qualifications	Information
4	throrough	clearly described	complete
3	adequate	complete	mostly complete
2	missing some	more information needed	missing some
1	few or none	missing	none or little

4. Technology Rubric

	Forms of Media	Location Identified	Explanation
4	more than three	clear and includes a map	clear and concise
3	three	clearly described	complete
2	two	poorly described	vague
1	one or none	missing	missing

Objectives

- Identify important elements of persuasive writing.
- Research information about influential Hebrew or Greek leaders.
- Display a final copy of a persuasive letter and a sketch of a recommended leader.

❶ Focus & Motivate

Preview Explain to students that they will be using what they learned in the preceding three chapters to write a persuasive letter. Discuss with students the purpose of persuasion. Have them identify instances when they have tried to convince someone to agree with them or act a certain way. What kinds of argument and support did they use?

❷ Teach

Talk About It

- Who are possible candidates from Chapters 10, 11, and 12 for the historical society's statue? (*Possible answers: Moses; David; Solomon; Cyrus; Homer; Socrates; Plato; Aristotle; Pericles; Alexander the Great*)

- Why is it important to continue looking for candidates even after a possible choice has been found? (*Possible answers: There might be a stronger choice that has been forgotten or overlooked; knowing all of the possibilities will help in preparing arguments against the other choices.*)

- It could be argued that Aristotle should be chosen for the statue because of the influence his ideas had on later philosophers. What are some examples of Aristotle's achievements that support this argument? (*Possible answers: Aristotle established the Lyceum; his rules of logic were later applied to science; he tutored Alexander the Great.*)

- **Critical Thinking: Making Decisions** What are some ways in which a writer might capture the reader's attention in the opening paragraph of the letter? (*Possible answers: The writer might start the letter with a question or direct quotation; an amusing anecdote might be included in the introduction.*)

Writing About History

Writing Model
ClassZone.com

CALIFORNIA STANDARDS
Writing 2.5 Write persuasive compositions.

Persuasive Writing:
Honoring an Ancient Leader

Purpose: To persuade a historical society to honor the leader of your choice with a statue
Audience: Members of the historical society

You read on page 394 that Pericles convinced people who saw him lose a wrestling match that he had really won. How did he do that? He used persuasion. Writing intended to convince another person to adopt your opinion or position is called **persuasive writing**.

Pericles ▶

Organization & Focus

A historical society has raised money to erect a statue. Its goal is to honor the ancient Hebrew or ancient Greek who had the most-lasting influence on history. Your assignment is to write a 500- to 700-word letter to persuade the society to honor the leader of your choice.

Choosing a Topic Skim Chapters 10, 11, and 12. In your notebook, write the name of each leader you find. Take notes about his or her accomplishments and lasting influence. Even if you find a leader you want to recommend, keep reviewing the chapters. To write a good persuasive letter, you will need to show why your leader is a better choice than other leaders. So you will need details about them too. When you've finished, review your notes and make your choice.

Identifying Purpose and Audience Your purpose is to use facts, examples, and reasons to convince others to adopt your opinion. Your audience is the members of a historical society. Because they are familiar with history, you won't have to provide much background information. You can focus on giving solid and convincing reasons.

Finding Supporting Evidence Gather facts, examples, and reasons to prove that your leader is the best choice. Also, anticipate the leaders others might suggest, and gather evidence against those choices.

DIFFERENTIATING INSTRUCTION

Gifted and Talented Students

Debate Choices
Have students use their research to prepare for a debate. The debate might be between groups of students or between individuals, depending on students' choices of historical figures. Have students in the audience choose the most persuasive group or individual.

Struggling Readers

Complete a Chart
To help students gather information, draw a chart on the board, with several rows and three columns with the following headings: "Person," "Accomplishments," "Lasting Influence." Have them complete the chart as a class.

Outlining and Drafting Make an outline of the three main parts of your persuasive letter. The **introduction** should grab the readers' interest and state your recommendation. The **body** of your letter should offer facts and examples as supporting evidence for your recommendation. The body of your letter should also show why other recommendations—counterarguments—are not as good as yours. The **conclusion** should tie everything together and make a strong appeal.

Research & Technology

Give your readers a strong sense of your leader's personality. One way to do this is to describe actions that demonstrate the leader's best characteristics. You can find additional information about the life of your leader in the library or online. Record helpful information on a chart like the one below.

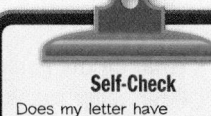
Technology Tip Not all information on the Internet is accurate. Learn to evaluate online sources. For example, museums and encyclopedias are reliable. If you have questions about a source, ask your teacher or librarian.

Characteristics	Actions that Demonstrate Them

Evaluation & Revision

Exchange first drafts with a classmate. Use the following guide to evaluate your partner's letter:

- Is the thesis statement clear?
- How strong are the main arguments and evidence?
- Were counterarguments addressed well?
- Were you convinced by the letter? Why or why not?

Listen carefully to your partner's comments. Rework your letter until you are satisfied that you have addressed your partner's major concerns.

Self-Check
Does my letter have
- [ ] an awareness of my audience and purpose?
- [ ] an introduction that states my recommendation?
- [ ] well-organized and convincing evidence?
- [ ] a strong conclusion with a final appeal?

Publish & Present

Make a neat final copy of your letter. Make a sketch to go along with it to show what the statue might look like. Post your letter and drawing on the bulletin board and read what others have posted there.

423

Logical Fallacies
Propaganda and logical fallacies weaken arguments. Instead of presenting valid points, these techniques or errors—including those described below—rely on appeals to emotion and flawed logic.

- **Begging the question** is answering a question or supporting a claim by simply restating the question or claim in different words. *Everyone must help so that we can work together to solve this problem.*

- **Card stacking** occurs when only one side of an issue is presented. Important evidence that may weaken an argument is ignored.

- **Arguing from ignorance** is stating that something is true because it has not been proved false. *We have never found evidence of life on other planets, so it doesn't exist.*

ANSWERS

Persuasive Letter Rubric

	Structure of Letter	Content of Letter	Errors in Mechanics
4	effectively organized, includes all components of a letter, contains many transitions	shows strong knowledge of individual, extensive development of arguments	few or none
3	good organization, contains some transitions, includes major components of a letter	shows familiarity with individual, development of each argument	some
2	fairly logical organization, contains a few transitions, includes some components of a letter	shows some understanding of individual, some details	many
1	muddled organization, no transitions	few details	many major

Begin the Unit

Quick Look

Chapter 13 examines the effects of geography and social structure on ancient Rome.

Chapter 14 analyzes the origins and early spread of the Christian religion.

Interact with History ▶

Purpose

To understand how the games at the Colosseum reflected the social structure and values of ancient Rome

Visual Learning

Ask a volunteer to read aloud the text while the class examines the illustration. Then discuss the questions on the illustration before answering the main question.

Interact ANSWERS

- What do the games at the Colosseum suggest about the world of ancient Rome? *(Possible answers: The emperor had a great deal of power over the people; the people accepted cruelty and violence.)*

- What effect do you think this show of power had on the Roman people? *(Possible answer: It probably made them fear their emperor's awesome power.)*

- How would you describe the architecture of the Colosseum? *(Possible answers: efficient; ingenious; advanced)*

- What traits do you think were necessary to be a gladiator? *(Possible answer: A gladiator needed to be brave, strong, and a good fighter.)*

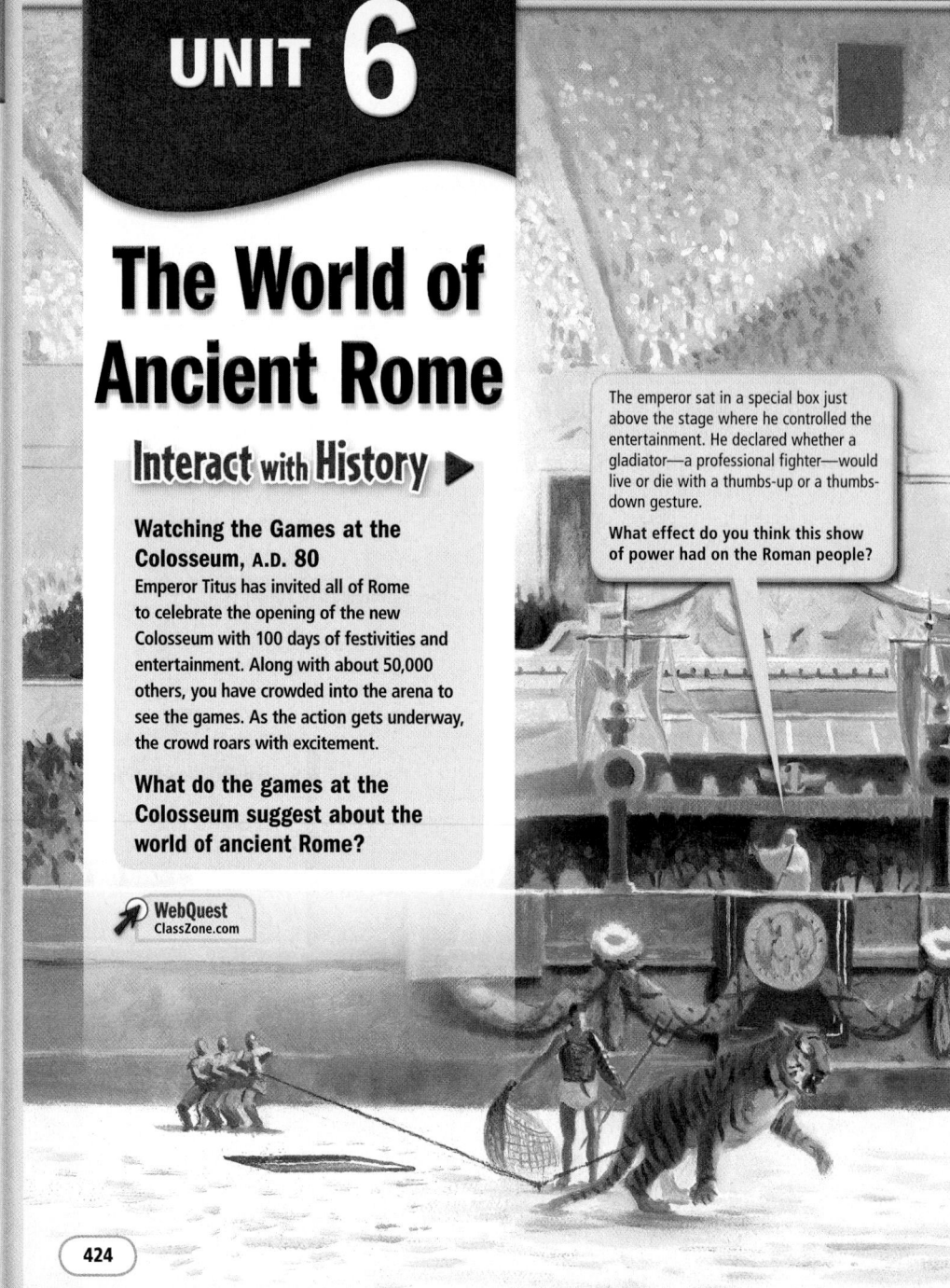

UNIT 6

The World of Ancient Rome

Interact with History ▶

Watching the Games at the Colosseum, A.D. 80
Emperor Titus has invited all of Rome to celebrate the opening of the new Colosseum with 100 days of festivities and entertainment. Along with about 50,000 others, you have crowded into the arena to see the games. As the action gets underway, the crowd roars with excitement.

What do the games at the Colosseum suggest about the world of ancient Rome?

WebQuest
ClassZone.com

The emperor sat in a special box just above the stage where he controlled the entertainment. He declared whether a gladiator—a professional fighter—would live or die with a thumbs-up or a thumbs-down gesture.

What effect do you think this show of power had on the Roman people?

424

TECHNOLOGY

WebQuest: The World of Ancient Rome

Visit **ClassZone.com** to lead your students on a WebQuest through ancient Rome. Students will imagine they have just returned from a day of watching animal and gladiator fights at the Colosseum. Students will draw pictures of the experience and write letters to friends or relatives. They should explain what it was like to be a gladiator, what the Colosseum was like, and what the festivities there reveal about Roman culture and the power of the emperor.

When to Use This project works well as an introduction to the chapter or as an end-of-chapter activity.

Class Time Two class periods

Materials Needed At least one computer with access to the World Wide Web and a printer.

Customizing for Your Classroom

- If computer time is limited, have small groups rotate through stations, finding information in encyclopedias, magazines, the textbook, and the Web sites on **ClassZone.com**.

- Encourage Spanish speakers to use the textbook's Spanish glossary.

- Pair students who may have difficulty reading with stronger readers to ensure they are able to accurately understand and interpret the information on gladiators and the Colosseum.

Spectators could quickly enter and exit the Colosseum through 80 arched entrances. Overhead stretched a cloth awning to protect the public from the sun. Beneath the arena, rope-operated elevators could bring thousands of animals to the surface at once.

How would you describe the architecture of the Colosseum?

The crowd might see lions attacking bulls or hunters killing unusual animals. But most eagerly anticipated were the games that pitted a gladiator against another person or a wild animal. Before they began to fight, the gladiators greeted the emperor: "We who are about to die salute you."

What traits do you think were necessary to be a gladiator?

425

Correcting Misconceptions

Ask students to state two facts about the Roman Empire. When students have finished the unit, ask them to write down whether their facts were accurate or inaccurate.

More About . . .

Gladiators
The shows at the Colosseum and other arenas began with a procession of gladiators, followed by a fake fight with wooden swords. Then a trumpet sounded, and the real gladiators began to fight. There were different classes of gladiators, who used different types of weapons and different methods of fighting. Some fought with short swords and shields, some fought with daggers, and some fought with nets and tridents. Most gladiators were either slaves or criminals. Some served as bodyguards to politically powerful men. A gladiator who survived several fights might be given his freedom.

WHY STUDY THE WORLD OF ANCIENT ROME?

- As a result of Rome's influence, there are still many cultural connections between areas of Europe, Asia, and Africa that border the Mediterranean.

- Some of the most basic values and institutions of the United States, such as civic duty and a separate judicial branch, began in the Roman Republic.

- Rome faced the problems of maintaining peace, law, and order. Modern governments face similar problems.

- Ancient Rome was a mixture of different cultures and beliefs, like many modern societies.

- Ruins of the Roman Forum—the religious, cultural, and political heart of Rome—still stand today.

- Societies still use trade to make themselves richer, as the Romans did during the Pax Romana.

- The Colosseum is a lasting symbol of the power of the Roman Empire. Many stadiums built since have been modeled on the Colosseum.

- One-third of the people in the world today are Christian.

- Millions of people today are members of the Roman Catholic and eastern Orthodox Churches.

CHAPTER 13 PLANNING GUIDE: The Rise of Rome

Chapter Overview

Geography and politics influenced the rise of ancient Rome, which eventually expanded from a republic into a powerful empire.

Copymasters

In-Depth Resources: Unit 6
- Family Newsletter (English and Spanish), pp. 1–2
- Visual Summary, p. 7
- Vocabulary Study Guide, p. 9

Character Education

Reading Study Guide, p. 123

Bringing Social Studies Alive, Chapter 13

Document-Based Questions: Strategy and Practice

Reading Toolkit, L44–L47

Modified Lesson Plans for English Learners, pp. 91–98

Assessment

Chapter Review, pp. 460–461

Formal Assessment
- Chapter Tests, Forms A, B, and C, pp. 231–245

Test Generator

Integrated Assessment Book

Online Test Practice

LESSON 1
The Geography of Ancient Rome
pp. 430–435

OBJECTIVE Analyze the geography of Rome and life in the region during Rome's early days.

In-Depth Resources: Unit 6
- Reading Skill: Categorizing, p. 3
- Vocabulary Cards, p. 11
- Reteaching Activity, p. 17

Interdisciplinary Projects
- Math, p. 73

Reading Study Guide, p. 115

Lesson Review, p. 435

Formal Assessment
- Lesson Quiz, p. 227

California Daily Standards Practice Transparencies, TT44

LESSON 2
The Roman Republic
pp. 436–441

OBJECTIVE Study political and social features of the Roman Republic.

In-Depth Resources: Unit 6
- Reading Skill: Understanding Cause and Effect, p. 4
- Vocabulary Cards, p. 11
- Skillbuilder Practice: Understanding Cause and Effect, p. 8
- Reteaching Activity, p. 18

Interdisciplinary Projects
- Language Arts, p. 75

Reading Study Guide, p. 117

Lesson Review, p. 441

Formal Assessment
- Lesson Quiz, p. 228

California Daily Standards Practice Transparencies, TT45

LESSON 3
Rome Becomes an Empire
pp. 442–451

OBJECTIVE Trace the changes that occurred in Rome after the collapse of the republic.

In-Depth Resources: Unit 6
- Reading Skill: Constructing Time Lines, p. 5
- Vocabulary Cards, p. 11
- Geography Practice: Caesar's Military Campaigns, p. 13
- Primary Source: Cicero's Fears for the Republic, p. 15
- Literature: Caesar, by Plutarch, p. 16

- Reteaching Activity, p. 19

History Makers
- Julius Caesar, p. 25

Interdisciplinary Projects
- Physical Education, p. 76

Reading Study Guide, p. 119

Lesson Review, p. 449

Formal Assessment
- Lesson Quiz, p. 229

California Daily Standards Practice Transparencies, TT46

LESSON 4
The Daily Life of Romans
pp. 452–459

OBJECTIVE Discuss the beliefs, roles, and culture of the people of ancient Rome.

In-Depth Resources: Unit 6
- Reading Skill: Summarizing, p. 6
- Vocabulary Cards, p. 11
- Reteaching Activity, p. 20

Interdisciplinary Projects
- Science, p. 74

Reading Study Guide, p. 121

Lesson Review, p. 458

Formal Assessment
- Lesson Quiz, p. 230

California Daily Standards Practice Transparencies, TT47

Integrated Technology

 eEdition Plus Online

EasyPlanner Plus Online

eTest Plus Online

 Audio CDs
- Reading Study Guide
- Reading Study Guide in Spanish
- The World's Music

 **CD-ROMs**
- Power Presentations
- eEdition
- EasyPlanner
- Test Generator

 Ancient Civilizations Video Series
- Ancient Rome

 **eEdition CD-ROM**

 Critical Thinking Transparencies
- CT56 Categorizing

 ClassZone.com

---

 eEdition CD-ROM

 Map Transparencies
- MT25 Growth of the Roman Empire

 Critical Thinking Transparencies
- CT57 Understanding Cause and Effect

 ClassZone.com

---

 eEdition CD-ROM

 Humanities Transparencies
- HT25 Roman Soldiers

 Map Transparencies
- MT26 Roman Britain

 Critical Thinking Transparencies
- CT58 Constructing Time Lines

 ClassZone.com

---

 eEdition CD-ROM

 Humanities Transparencies
- HT26 Roman Aqueduct

 Critical Thinking Transparencies
- CT59 Summarizing
- CT60 Chapter 13 Visual Summary

 ClassZone.com

Overview of California Resources

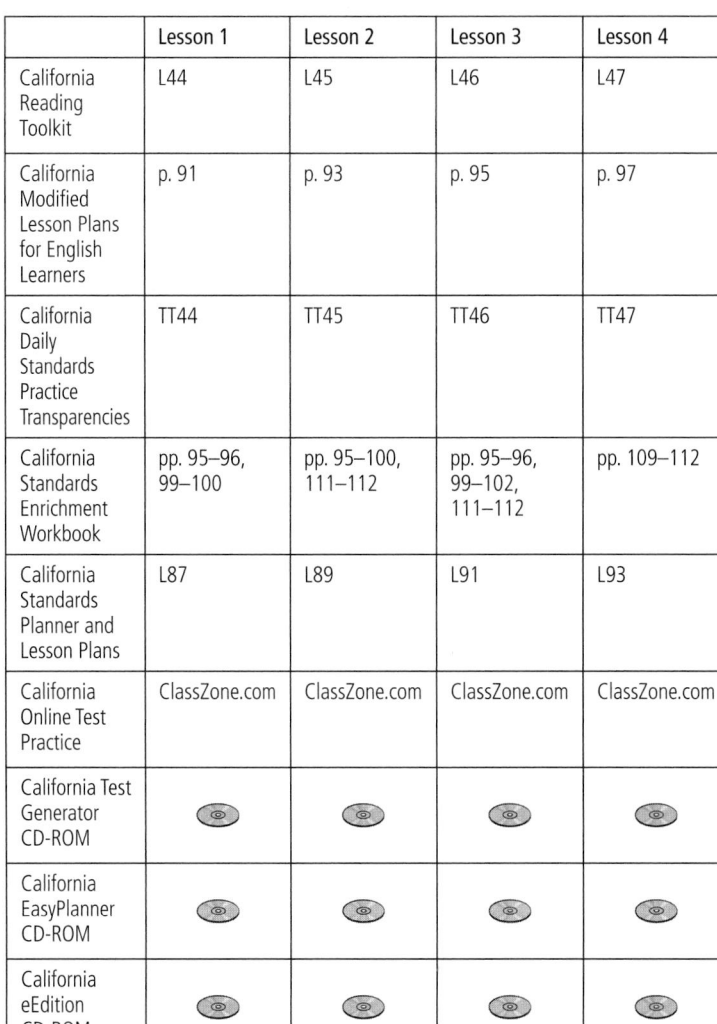

	Lesson 1	Lesson 2	Lesson 3	Lesson 4
California Reading Toolkit	L44	L45	L46	L47
California Modified Lesson Plans for English Learners	p. 91	p. 93	p. 95	p. 97
California Daily Standards Practice Transparencies	TT44	TT45	TT46	TT47
California Standards Enrichment Workbook	pp. 95–96, 99–100	pp. 95–100, 111–112	pp. 95–96, 99–102, 111–112	pp. 109–112
California Standards Planner and Lesson Plans	L87	L89	L91	L93
California Online Test Practice	ClassZone.com	ClassZone.com	ClassZone.com	ClassZone.com
California Test Generator CD-ROM	◎	◎	◎	◎
California EasyPlanner CD-ROM	◎	◎	◎	◎
California eEdition CD-ROM	◎	◎	◎	◎

Chart Key

 P E Pupil Edition

 Copymaster

 CD-ROM

 Audio

 Video

Internet

Overhead Transparency

PREVIEWING RESOURCES FOR DIFFERENTIATED INSTRUCTION

English Learners

In-Depth Resources in Spanish
- Reading Skill and Strategy A
- Skillbuilder Practice
- Geography Practice C
- Vocabulary Study Guide B

In-Depth Resources: Unit 6
- Family Newsletter (English and Spanish)

Reading Study Guide (Spanish)

Reading Study Guide Audio CD
(Spanish)

Test Generator
Chapter Test (Spanish)

Plus

Modified Lesson Plans for English Learners

Multi-Language Glossary of Social Studies Terms

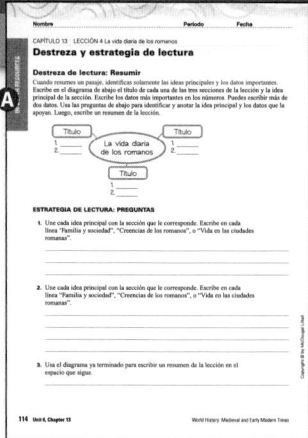
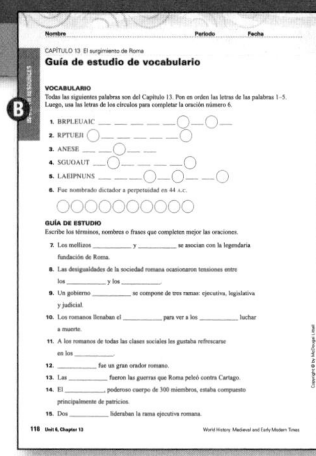

Struggling Readers

In-Depth Resources: Unit 6
- Vocabulary Study Guide
- Skillbuilder Practice B
- Geography Practice
- Reteaching Activities
- Family Newsletter C

Reading Study Guide A

Reading Study Guide Audio CD

Reading Toolkit

Formal Assessment
Chapter Test, Form A

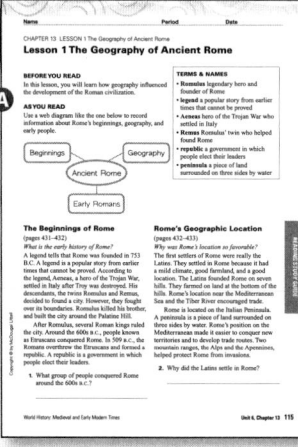
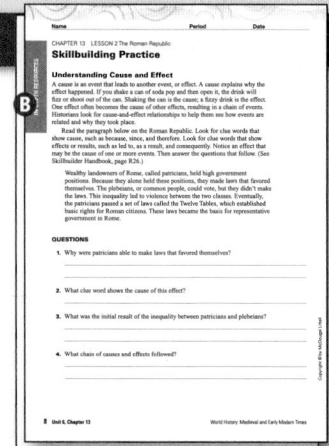

Inclusion

EasyPlanner CD-ROM
- Reading Skill and Strategy A
- Vocabulary Study Guide B
- Geography Practice C
- Reteaching Activities

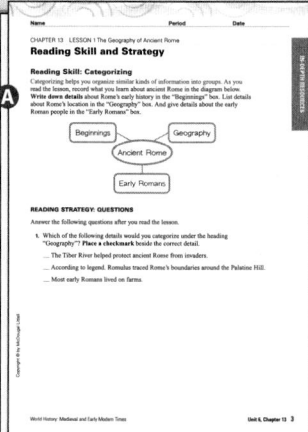
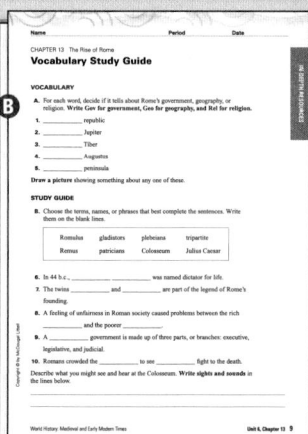

Gifted and Talented Students

In-Depth Resources: Unit 6
- Primary Source A
- Literature

History Makers B

Interdisciplinary Projects C

Formal Assessment
Chapter Test, Form C

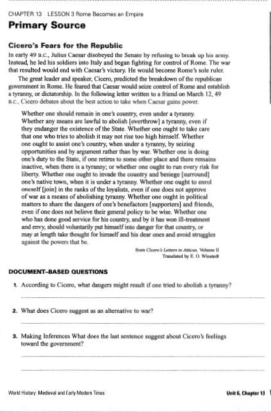
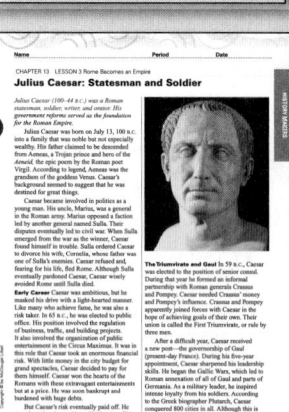

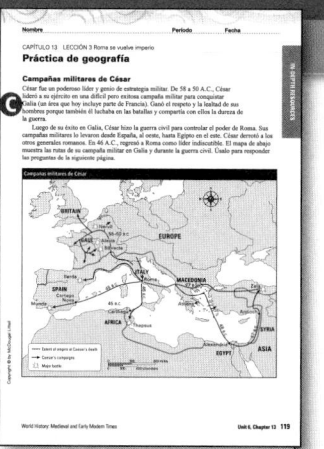

Activities in the Teacher's Edition for English Learners

- Make a Geography Word Web, p. 432
- Make Comparison Statements, p. 438
- Identify Important Figures, p. 447
- Write a Journal Entry, p. 450
- Make Opinion Statements, p. 455

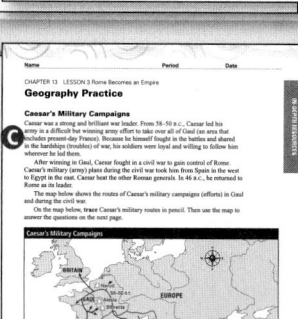

Activities in the Teacher's Edition for Struggling Readers

- Sort Fact from Fiction, p. 432
- Divide and Conquer, p. 434
- Use the Review Questions, p. 439
- Identify Key Players, p. 444
- List Achievements, p. 447
- Summarize, p. 450
- Preread Text, p. 454

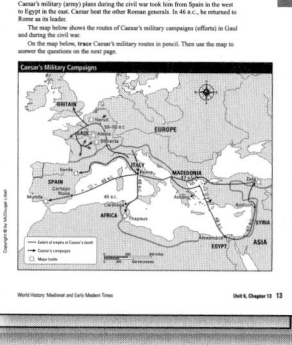

Activities in the Teacher's Edition for Inclusion Students

- Take Audio Notes, p. 438
- Role-Play a Roman Citizen, p. 444
- Remember Details, p. 445
- Practice Remembering, p. 454
- Learn About Public Baths, p. 457

Activities in the Teacher's Edition for Gifted and Talented Students

- Plan a Day's Work on a Roman Farm, p. 434
- Analyze the Pros and Cons of Rome's Government, p. 439
- Report on Cicero's Career, p. 445
- Make a Game, p. 455
- Research Bathing Through History, p. 457

eEdition CD-ROM

- Interactive Visuals
- Interactive Maps
- Starting with a Story

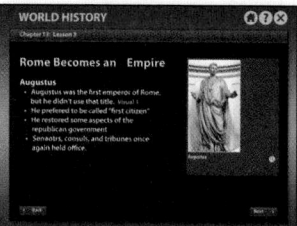

ClassZone.com

- WebQuests
- Research Links
- Internet Activities
- Homework Helper
- Chapter Quiz
- Current Events
- Test Practice

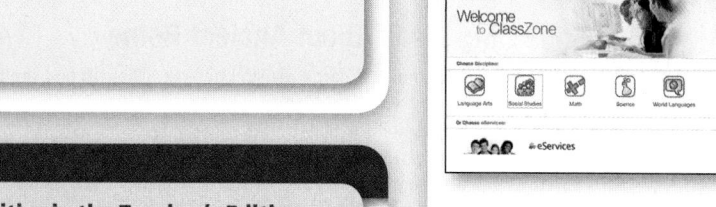

Power Presentations CD-ROM

- Lecture Notes
- Media Gallery
- Chapter Review Game

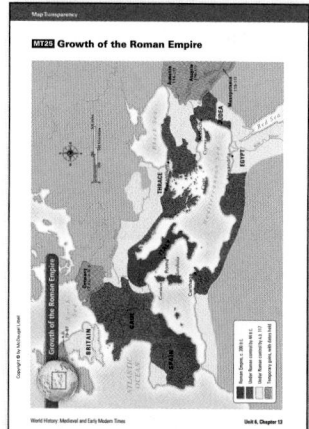

Critical Thinking Transparencies

- CT56 Categorizing
- CT57 Understanding Cause and Effect
- CT58 Constructing Time Lines
- CT59 Summarizing
- CT60 Chapter 13 Visual Summary

California Daily Standards Practice Transparencies, TT44–TT47

Map Transparencies

- MT25 Growth of the Roman Empire
- MT26 Roman Britain

Humanities Transparencies

- HT25 Roman Soldiers
- HT26 Roman Aqueduct

Test Generator CD-ROM

EasyPlanner CD-ROM

Ancient Civilizations Video Series

- Ancient Rome

Begin the Chapter

Objective

Analyze how geography and culture influenced civilization in Rome.

Quick Look

Lesson 1 examines why Rome's geographic location was favorable and what life was like for the early Romans.

Lesson 2 describes early Roman social classes and the division of the government into three parts.

Lesson 3 explores the unrest in the Roman Republic under Julius Caesar and describes the empire founded by Augustus after Caesar was assassinated.

Lesson 4 describes the everyday life of ancient Romans and explores family roles and religious beliefs.

Before You Read: Predicting

Making predictions will help students focus their reading. Before they make their predictions, allow them to page through the chapter. Encourage students to look at the illustrations as well as the lesson titles and subheadings.

Chapter 13 The Rise of Rome

Before You Read: Predicting

Scan the titles of the chapter and the lessons. In your notebook, write three questions you think will be answered in the chapter. One example is

What was life like in ancient Rome?

Fill in the answers to your questions as you find them.

Big Ideas About Ancient Rome

Economics A large division between the rich and the poor often creates problems.

In ancient Rome, anger arose between powerful, wealthy landholders and poor farmers. This anger led to the development of a more representative form of government. Later, conflict between the two classes would lead to civil war.

Integrated Technology

eEdition
· Interactive Maps
· Interactive Visuals
· Starting with a Story
Ancient Rome

INTERNET RESOURCES
Go to **ClassZone.com** for
· WebQuest   · Quizzes
· Homework Helper · Maps
· Research Links   · Test Practice
· Internet Activities · Current Events

ATLANTIC
OCEAN

20°W

ROME

753 B.C.
According to legend, Rome is founded.
◄ (bronze head of wolf)

509 B.C.
Rome becomes a republic.

800 B.C.   600 B.C.

WORLD

750 B.C.
Greek city-states flourish.
(Greek temple in Sicily) ►

426

TIME LINE DISCUSSION

Use the time line to help students preview information that will be covered in the chapter. Point out the civilizations that are covered in the bottom portion of the time line. Have volunteers point out their locations on a world map.

• What time frame does this chapter cover? *(about 750 B.C. to A.D. 117)*

• What structure illustrates the Greek city-states? *(a Greek temple in Sicily)*

• How many years after becoming a republic did Rome defeat Carthage? *(363 years)*

• How many years after its legendary founding did Rome reach its greatest extent? *(870 years)*

The Roman Empire at Its Height, A.D. 117
INTERACTIVE

North Sea

BRITAIN
London

Rhine River

ASIA

Danube River

Carpathian Mts.

EUROPE

GAUL

ALPS

DACIA

Corsica

ITALY

Black Sea

Rome

THRACE
Byzantium

SPAIN

Sardinia

Balearic Islands

GREECE

ANATOLIA

Sicily

Carthage

Crete

Cyprus

Antioch

Euphrates River

Tigris River

Mediterranean Sea

SYRIA

JUDEA

Atlas Mountains

AFRICA

Alexandria

EGYPT

ARABIA

Nile River

Red Sea

0   250   500 miles
0   250   500 kilometers

☐ Roman Republic, 264 B.C.
☐ Areas added at empire's height, A.D. 117

Tropic of Cancer

146 B.C.
Rome defeats Carthage in the Punic Wars.

27 B.C.
Augustus becomes the first emperor of Rome.
◄ (cameo of young Augustus)

A.D. 117
Rome reaches its greatest extent.

200 B.C.   **B.C. A.D.**   **A.D. 200**

321 B.C.
Maurya empire is founded in India.

202 B.C.
Liu Bang reunifies China and starts the Han Dynasty.
(clay horse from the Han Dynasty) ▶

A.D. 30
Jesus is crucified.

A.D. 100
Moche culture arises in South America.

(427)

RECOMMENDED RESOURCES

Books for the Teacher

Boatwright, Mary T., et al. **The Romans: From Village to Empire.** 2nd ed. New York: Oxford UP, 2004. Three historians draw on primary sources to provide a definitive history. Includes illustrations, a time line, and a glossary.

Wells, C. M. **The Roman Empire.** Cambridge: Harvard UP, 1992. Covers Rome from 44 B.C. to A.D. 235. Includes an excellent bibliography.

Videos

Ancient Rome. 49 minutes. Princeton: Films for the Humanities & Sciences, 1999. Three-dimensional re-creations allow students to see Rome as it was before the empire collapsed. VHS, DVD.

The Emperor's Gift: Rome's Colosseum. 26 minutes. Princeton: Films for the Humanities & Sciences, 1996. The engineering, architecture, and civic function of the Colosseum. VHS, DVD.

Roman City. 56 minutes. Allexandria: PBS Video, 1994. Life in the frontier territory of Gaul. VHS.

Internet

To access these sites, visit the Research Links for this chapter at **ClassZone.com**.

PBS.org has various projects: A Roman Empire Information Fair; A Roman Empire Trivia Game; Making Decisions that Affect an Empire; and Religion's Role in the Roman Empire.

Introduce the Big Ideas

Read aloud the text about the Big Ideas. Have students think about divisions between rich and poor in modern society. Talk about how governments create law codes and political bodies to lessen inequalities.

Here are some other Big Ideas that you may want to emphasize in this chapter.

Geography

Civilizations developed in places that supported agriculture or trade or both.

Culture

Many societies rely on family roles and social classes to keep order.

Government

New ideas and beliefs can challenge a government's authority, leading to change.

Economics

Societies trade the surplus goods that they produce to obtain goods they lack.

Talk About It

Interpreting Maps

Ask students to examine the map. Ask, Where is Rome located? _(on the Mediterranean coast, near the center of the "boot" of Italy)_ Have students describe the location of Rome in relation to the rest of the empire in A.D. 117. _(near the center of the empire)_

INTERACTIVE

An interactive version of this map is available on the eEdition and Power Presentations CD-ROMs.

Find Out More

Where are Italy's borders today? What present-day countries occupy the area along the northern coast of Africa that was formerly part of the Roman Empire? _(Morocco, Algeria, Tunisia, Libya, Egypt)_ Have students look in an atlas to find the answers to these questions.

Watch the Video

Ancient Rome invites students to explore the history and culture of ancient Rome. This video is part of the Ancient Civilizations for Children Video series.

Objective

Understand why people come to distrust a leader who has too much power.

Introducing the Story

The Quest for Power in Rome

In ancient Rome, ambitious men vied for political power because it brought wealth and influence. Those who achieved political office were given military commands. By conquering and looting other cities, they enriched themselves and their armies and increased the loyalty of their followers. There was a great deal of rivalry between senators, many of whom would do anything to increase their power.

In 83 B.C., Sulla, a successful general with a loyal army of 120,000 men, expected to be given political power by the Senate. Instead, he was declared an outlaw by the Senate, which was controlled by his enemies. Sulla marched on Rome during the civil war that lasted from 88–82 B.C., when more than 200,000 people were killed. After this, Romans became suspicious and uncomfortable whenever a leader seemed to have too much power.

Vocabulary Preview

senator a citizen who is a member of a council that has legislative power in a government

toga a loose one-piece outer garment

plot a secret plan to accomplish a hostile or illegal deed

Reading the Story Aloud

1. **The teacher as reader:** To dramatize the story, read with animation and expression.

2. **The students as readers:** Have students read through the story on their own to familiarize themselves with it. Then have one student read aloud as other students act out the scenario.

 **Starting with a Story**

Students can follow along as they listen to the story on the eEdition or Power Presentations CD-ROMs.

THE Assassination OF Julius Caesar

CALIFORNIA STANDARDS
Reading 3.3 Analyze the influence of setting on the problem and its resolution.

Background: In 49 B.C., Julius Caesar became the sole ruler of Rome. At first, Caesar was a popular and effective leader. But in time, the Senate, Rome's governing body, resented his power. On March 15, 44 B.C., some of the senators took action.

The Senate held a meeting on that fateful day. The senators entered one by one and, finally, Caesar came into the chamber. And then an incredible scene unfolded.

Bust of Julius Caesar ▶

428

ADDITIONAL RESOURCES

Books for the Student

Adkins, Lesley, and Roy A. Adkins. ***Handbook to Life in Ancient Rome.*** New York: Oxford UP, 1994. Detailed, readable reference written by archaeologists.

McKay, Alexander Gordon. ***Houses, Villas, and Palaces in the Roman World.*** Reprint ed. Baltimore: Johns Hopkins UP, 1998. Describes Roman homes, with illustrations of plans and reconstructions.

Shelton, Jo-Ann. ***As the Romans Did: A Sourcebook in Roman Social History.*** 2nd ed. New York: Oxford UP, 1998. Covers aspects of Roman family life, housing, education, entertainment, and religion.

Videos

The Roman Empire in Northern Europe. 30 minutes. New York: Ambrose Video, 1999. VHS.

CD-ROMs

Romans. Princeton: Films for the Humanities & Sciences, 1997. This CD-ROM is packed with pictures, videos, and animations introducing life in Roman times.

Caesar took his seat in the center of the chamber. According to custom, he was the only one allowed to sit. Before Caesar called the meeting to order, the senators talked in small groups. Then one of the men stepped forward to ask Caesar a question. He even grabbed Caesar's shoulder. Angrily, the ruler waved him away, but the senator seemed determined to gain his attention.

While Caesar argued with his questioner, another senator moved forward. Silently, he drew out a knife and wounded the ruler with his weapon. Caesar cried out in surprise and rose from his chair. He pulled out a knife from the folds of his toga and defended himself. The senator stumbled backward, but the others moved forward. They all drew out their knives. It was a plot!

Caesar made no sound as the senators attacked him. He pulled the hood of his toga over his head and adjusted the garment over his feet. As he fell to the ground, the toga covered his body. When the senators finally stepped back, Caesar was dead.

One of the senators ordered a pair of servants to remove the body. The people of Rome would soon learn that their ruler had been killed. No one—not even the senators—knew what would happen to Rome next.

What might drive people to overthrow their leader?

Reading & Writing

1. **READING: Setting** Setting is when and where a story takes place. How does this story's setting help the senators carry out their plot?

2. **WRITING: Persuasion** The date is March 14, 44 B.C. You are a Roman senator who opposes the plot against Caesar. Write a speech in which you explain and support your position for letting Caesar continue his rule.

CALIFORNIA STANDARDS Writing 2.5
Write persuasive compositions.

429

STARTING WITH A STORY

Talk About It
Ask students the following questions to begin the discussion:

- One senator wanted to ask Caesar a question and even grabbed his shoulder. Why do you think he did that? (*Possible answers: he may have been trying to warn Caesar; he may have been trying to distract Caesar.*)

- Why do you think Caesar adjusted his toga over his head and feet? (*Possible answer: He knew he would be killed and wanted to die with as much dignity as he could manage.*)

- What do you think will happen in Rome next? (*Possible answers: There will be riots in the streets; another dictator will take power.*)

What might drive people to overthrow their leader?

Students may say that people might try to overthrow a leader who has too much power or who abuses power. Leaders who are corrupt or cruel may also be overthrown.

Making Personal Connections
Connect the discussion to today by discussing how leaders are chosen in the United States. Discuss what people can do if they dislike the choices that their leaders make. (*Possible answers: vote people out of office; write petitions; contact legislators; form groups to put pressure on politicians*)

READING & WRITING ACTIVITIES

1. **READING** Possible answer: The senators are gathered for a normal meeting, where they are alone with Caesar and can take him by surprise.

2. **WRITING** Students might point out that another ruler would be just as bad and that the Senate should try to use legal means to limit Caesar's power.

2. Writing Rubric

	Content of Speech	Organization of Speech	Errors in Mechanics
4	shows thorough understanding of the political situation	has introduction, supporting details, and conclusion	few or none
3	shows good understanding	has beginning, middle, and end	some
2	shows basic understanding	includes some irrelevant content	many
1	shows little or no understanding	poorly organized, hard to follow	many major

❶ Plan & Prepare

Objectives

- Understand geographic factors that helped ancient Romans build a civilization.
- Analyze what life was like in early Roman society.
- **Language Objective:** Create a web of words and terms from the lesson that are related to the geography of ancient Rome.

Quick Look

Lesson 1 focuses on the geographic and social factors that contributed to the civilization of ancient Rome.

❷ Focus & Motivate

Preview Explain that this lesson describes the early history of Rome. Explain that Rome grew from a city into a huge empire. Ask students to predict the factors that led to Rome's growth. *(Possible answers: favorable location, hard work, successful farming)*

Introduce the Main Ideas The three main ideas relate to the Big Idea "Civilizations developed in places that supported agriculture or trade or both." Encourage students to look for statements related to this Big Idea as they read the lesson.

Reading Skill: Categorizing Have students pause after reading each section to look for details to add to their web diagrams.

SAMPLE ANSWERS FOR DIAGRAM

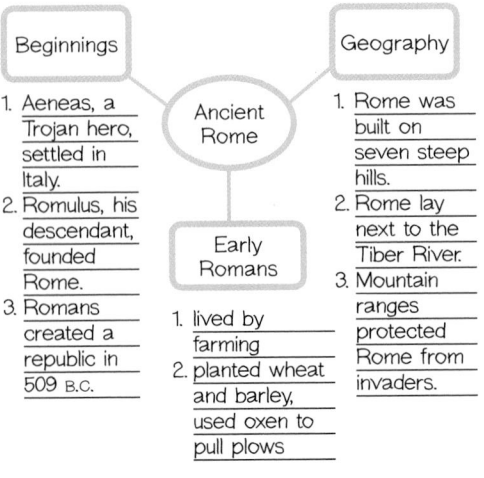

Lesson 1

▶ **MAIN IDEAS**

1. **Culture** Stories about the beginnings of Rome are a mix of legend and historical fact.
2. **Geography** The people who settled Rome chose a geographic location that was good for defense, travel, and trade.
3. **Economics** To survive, Roman farmers relied on discipline and hard work.

▶ **TAKING NOTES**

Reading Skill: Categorizing

Sorting similar kinds of information into groups helps you understand patterns in history. As you read Lesson 1, look for details about the three categories given for ancient Rome. Record the information you learn about them in a web diagram like the one below.

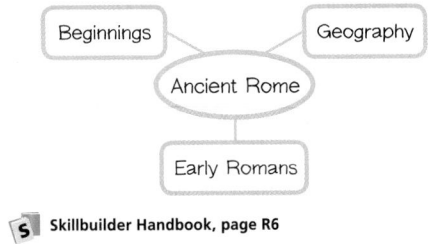

Skillbuilder Handbook, page R6

▲ **Symbol of Rome** This statue of the goddess Roma represents ancient Rome. Romans believed that the goddess protected them and their city.

CALIFORNIA STANDARDS

Framework Students should learn about everyday life in Roman society, including slavery, social conflict, and the rule of Roman law.

6.7.1 Identify the location and describe the rise of the Roman Republic, including the importance of such mythical and historical figures as Aeneas, Romulus and Remus, Cincinnatus, Julius Caesar, and Cicero.

6.7.3 Identify the location of and the political and geographic reasons for the growth of Roman territories and expansion of the empire, including how the empire fostered economic growth through the use of currency and trade routes.

HI 2 Students understand and distinguish cause, effect, sequence, and correlation in historical events, including the long- and short-term causal relations.

HOW TO TEACH THE CALIFORNIA STANDARDS

Standard	Content	Student Question or Activity	Instruction
6.7.1	**Pages 431–432** Describes the importance of mythical and historical figures	**Page 435** Students explain the legend of Rome's founding.	Have students identify the significant mythical and historical figures involved in Rome's founding and growth.
6.7.3	**Pages 432–433** Explains how Rome's location was advantageous to growth and trade	**Page 435** Students explain how hard-working families contributed to economic growth. **Page 460** Students describe the geography of Rome.	Have a volunteer locate Rome on a classroom map. Explain that Rome's location allowed expansion in all directions.
HI 2	**Page 432–433** Explains how Rome's location led to its success in farming and trade	**Page 435** Students compare the role of the Tiber in Rome's development with that of the Nile in Egypt.	Have a volunteer locate the Tiber and the Nile on a classroom map. Explain that the Nile acted as a kind of highway for the ancient Egyptians, letting them travel and trade their goods.

The Geography of Ancient Rome

TERMS & NAMES

Romulus
legend
Aeneas
Remus
republic
peninsula

Build on What You Know You have probably seen movies about ancient Rome, with its Colosseum and gladiators. These films show Rome at its height, but they only tell part of the story. The founding of the civilization owes much to its geography.

The Beginnings of Rome

1 ESSENTIAL QUESTION What is the early history of Rome?

a mix of real history (Rome's beginning with the overthrow of foreign kings) and legend (the founding involving Aeneas, Romulus, and Remus)

The history of ancient Rome begins with the overthrow of foreign kings in 509 B.C. But Romans like to date the history of their city to 753 B.C. That is when a legendary hero called **Romulus** (RAHM•yuh•luhs) is said to have founded Rome.

A **legend** is a popular story from earlier times that cannot be proved. The legend about Rome's founding begins with **Aeneas** (ih•NEE•uhs), a hero of the Trojan War. You learned about the Trojan War in Chapter 11. According to the legend, Aeneas settled in Italy after Troy was destroyed.

Palatine Hill Traces of settlements dating from around 1000 B.C. have been found on the Palatine Hill. ▼

431

Terms & Names

Romulus a legendary hero said to have founded Rome

legend a popular story from early times that cannot be proved

Aeneas a hero of the Trojan War

Remus the twin brother of Romulus

republic a government in which people elect their leaders

peninsula a body of land surrounded on three sides by water

3 Teach

The Beginnings of Rome
6.7.1

Talk About It

- **Critical Thinking: Summarizing** Who were Romulus and Remus? *(legendary founders of Rome)*

California Resources

California Reading Toolkit, L44
California Modified Lesson Plans for English Learners, p. 91
California Daily Standards Practice Transparencies, TT44
California Standards Enrichment Workbook, pp. 95–96, 99–100
California Online Test Practice
California Test Generator CD-ROM
California Standards Planner and Lesson Plans, L87
California EasyPlanner CD-ROM
California eEdition CD-ROM

LESSON 1 PROGRAM RESOURCES

ON LEVEL

In-Depth Resources: Unit 6
- Family Newsletter (English and Spanish), pp. 1–2
- Reading Skill: Categorizing, p. 3
- Vocabulary Study Guide, p. 9
- Vocabulary Cards, p. 11

Formal Assessment
- Lesson Quiz, p. 227

ENGLISH LEARNERS

In-Depth Resources in Spanish
- Reading Skill: Categorizing, p. 111
- Vocabulary Study Guide, p. 118

Modified Lesson Plans for English Learners, p. 91

Reading Study Guide (Spanish), p. 115

Reading Study Guide Audio CD (Spanish)

STRUGGLING READERS

In-Depth Resources: Unit 6
- Reading Skill: Categorizing, p. 3
- Vocabulary Study Guide, p. 9
- Vocabulary Cards, p. 11
- Reteaching Activity, p. 17

Reading Toolkit, L44

Reading Study Guide, p. 115

Reading Study Guide Audio CD

GIFTED AND TALENTED STUDENTS

Interdisciplinary Projects
- Math, p. 73

INCLUSION

EasyPlanner CD-ROM
- Reading Skill: Categorizing
- Vocabulary Study Guide
- Reteaching Activity

TECHNOLOGY

eEdition CD-ROM
- Starting with a Story

Power Presentations CD-ROM

Critical Thinking Transparencies
- CT56 Categorizing

ClassZone.com

In-Depth Resources: Unit 6
• Reading Skill: Categorizing, p. 3

Teach

Rome's Geographic Location

6.7.3, HI 2

Talk About It

• Why did the Latins live so far from their fields? *(The fields were on fertile land at the bottom of hills. The farmers lived at the top of the hills so that they could defend themselves against enemy attacks.)*

• What bodies of water are near Rome? *(the Tiber River and the Mediterranean Sea)*

• **Critical Thinking: Drawing Conclusions** Why was Rome's location near the Mediterranean Sea an advantage? *(Rome was in a good location to engage in sea trade with cities all around the Mediterranean.)*

History from Visuals

Interpreting Maps
Have students locate and name the seven hills of Rome.

• Which hill would you choose to live on if you wanted to feel safe? Why? *(the Palatine Hill, because it is surrounded by other hills)* Explain that the Palatine Hill was the hill on which Rome's original settlement was built.

GEOGRAPHY SKILLBUILDER ANSWER

Servian Wall, Appian Way

INTERACTIVE

An interactive version of this map is available on the eEdition and Power Presentations CD-ROMs.

The Founding of Rome The legend continues with the twins Romulus and **Remus** (REE•muhs), the descendants of Aeneas according to some versions. They were abandoned by their mother but rescued by a wolf. When the twins grew up, they decided to found a city but fought over its location. Romulus killed his brother and traced Rome's boundaries around the Palatine Hill.

After Romulus, a series of Roman kings ruled the city. Sometime in the 600s B.C., however, the Etruscans conquered Rome. The Etruscans were a people from northern Italy. But the Romans wanted self-rule. In 509 B.C., they overthrew the Etruscan king and formed a republic. A **republic** is a government in which people elect their leaders. You will learn about the Roman Republic in Lesson 2.

REVIEW Why are the dates 753 B.C. and 509 B.C. important?
753 B.C. is the legendary founding by Romulus. 509 B.C. marks the beginning of the Roman Republic.

Rome's Geographic Location

2 ESSENTIAL QUESTION Why was Rome's location so favorable?
It had a mild climate, good farmland, and a strategic location. After the overthrow of the Etruscans, Rome grew from a city into a country and then into a vast empire. Its location helped make this growth possible.

Hills and River In reality, people founded Rome, not figures from legend. The first settlers of Rome were the Latins. They came from a region surrounding Rome. They chose the spot for its mild climate, good farmland, and strategic location.

The Latins and later settlers built Rome on seven steep hills. (See map at right.) During the day, settlers farmed the fertile plain at the base of the hills. At night, they returned to their hilltop homes, from which they could defend themselves against an enemy attack.

Seven Hills of Rome, about A.D. 125
INTERACTIVE

Pantheon · Tiber River · Quirinal Hill · Viminal Hill · Servian Wall · Capitoline Hill · Palatine Hill · Esquiline Hill · Roman Forum · Colosseum · Caelian Hill · Circus Maximus · Aventine Hill · Appian Way

GEOGRAPHY SKILLBUILDER
INTERPRETING MAPS
Human-Environment Interaction
What human-made structures helped protect Rome from invasion?

DIFFERENTIATING INSTRUCTION

English Learners

Make a Geography Word Web
Demonstrate how to make a word web of geography terms from the lesson. For example, say, "The word *hills* belongs in the geography word web because ancient Rome was built on seven steep hills." Draw a word web on the board and add *hills* to it. For more support, see *Modified Lesson Plans for English Learners*, p. 91.

Struggling Readers

Sort Fact from Fiction
On the board, write the heading "The Founding of Rome." Under the heading, begin two lists, labeled "Fact" and "Fiction." Then call out details from the legend and from the actual history of the founding of Rome, such as "Romulus and Remus" and "Latins first settled in Rome." Have students decide whether each detail should be listed as fact or fiction.

Geography

The Tiber River

During Rome's earliest times, the Tiber provided a source of water for farming and drinking. Later, the river provided a route for travel and trade. Small ships could sail up the Tiber to Rome and down the Tiber to the Mediterranean. But the river also offered protection from invaders, since Rome was located away from the mouth of the sea.

GEOGRAPHY SKILLBUILDER
INTERPRETING VISUALS
Human-Environment Interaction
What does the photograph suggest about the importance of the Tiber to Romans today?

Rome had other advantages. It was located a short distance from the Mediterranean Sea on several ancient trade routes. It also lay next to the Tiber River. As you learned in the Geography feature above, this river played an important role in Rome's development.

Italian Peninsula Rome's location on the Italian Peninsula also played an important role in its development. The peninsula stretches south from Europe into the Mediterranean Sea. A **peninsula** is a piece of land surrounded on three sides by water. As you can see on the map on page 427, the Italian Peninsula is shaped like a boot. Its heel points toward Greece, while its toe points across the sea to Africa.

Italy's location on the Mediterranean made it relatively easy for Roman ships to reach the other lands around the sea. This position made it easier for Rome to eventually conquer and gain new territories. It also helped the development of trade routes.

The two main mountain ranges of Italy helped protect Rome. The Alps border Italy on the north, and the Apennines (AP•uh•NYNZ) form Italy's spine. But Italy's mountains didn't separate early settlements the way the mountains of Greece did. Italy also had more large plains than Greece. This made farming easier.

REVIEW How did its geography help Rome grow?
Its location on the seven hills and near the Tiber River, as well as its location in Italy, helped the city develop.

The Rise of Rome • 433

INTERDISCIPLINARY ACTIVITIES

Science

Report on Roman Building Materials
Tell students that the Romans used building materials such as volcanic stones, travertine, bricks, and concrete. Explain that the use of concrete helped the Romans create new forms of architecture. Have students research the composition of the concrete that the Romans developed and describe its special properties.

Teach

Lives of Early Romans

6.7.3

Talk About It

- Why were only landowners allowed to join the army at one time? (*Landowners could pay for their own equipment; leaders thought that property owners would fight harder to defend the city.*)

- How did some farmers increase their wealth? (*They bought more land and built larger farms.*)

- **Critical Thinking: Understanding Cause and Effect** How did having more land help farmers increase their wealth even more? (*Possible answer: They could grow more crops and have enough left over to sell or trade for goods.*)

Lives of Early Romans

3 **ESSENTIAL QUESTION** What was life like for the early Romans?
hard, since most were farmers

Like many ancient peoples, the early Romans lived by farming. But even though the land was fertile, life on a Roman farm was not easy.

Working the Land Most early Romans worked small plots of land. They planted grains such as wheat and barley. They also grew beans, vegetables, and fruit. Later they learned to grow olives and grapes. They also raised pigs, sheep, goats, and chickens. They used oxen to pull their plows.

Farmers who owned land also served in the army. In fact, for a time only landowners were allowed to join the army. Roman leaders believed that property owners would fight harder to defend the city. Landowners were also able to pay for their own military equipment.

Over time, some farmers grew richer than others. They bought more land and built larger farms, or estates. A gap developed between small farmers and the owners of the estates. This gap would later produce divisions in Roman politics and government.

Farm Life At first, most Roman farmers lived in simple homes made of mud or timber. They did not have much furniture. In addition, the farmers lived in extended families. This large family group might have included grandparents, aunts and uncles, nieces and nephews, and cousins.

Connect to Today

Italian Farm Grapes, like these shown here, are still a popular crop in Italy. In ancient Rome, only wealthy farmers, who could afford to wait a few years to harvest the first crop, grew grapes. ▼

DIFFERENTIATING INSTRUCTION

Struggling Readers

Divide and Conquer
Students who have difficulty reading may benefit from the "divide and conquer" technique. Pair students and have each partner read one of the two subsections on the lives of early Romans. Then have the partners get together and take turns summarizing what they read.

Gifted and Talented Students

Plan a Day's Work on a Roman Farm
Have small groups plan work schedules for a day in the life of a typical Roman farm family. Remind students that the family might include grandparents, aunts, uncles, and cousins. Point out that everyone had to work from dawn to dusk to produce the food the family would need.

The members of a Roman farm family had to work very hard. They farmed the land with simple tools and fetched water from a well or nearby spring. The small amount of land on most farms had to produce enough food to feed the family. This meant that everyone had to be disciplined about his or her responsibilities.

The qualities of discipline, loyalty, and hard work that these early farmers developed would help Rome succeed. They were the qualities that made Roman armies so successful. When soldiers went to war, they had to obey orders and do their jobs. This attitude would help Rome conquer all of Italy.

REVIEW Why was discipline important to early Romans?
Small farmers needed discipline to survive, and the army also needed discipline to succeed.

Lesson Summary

- Legend and fact shaped Rome's early history.
- Rome's geography encouraged the growth of Roman civilization.
- Roman society benefited from the hard work and discipline of Roman farmers.

Why It Matters Now . . .

There are still many cultural connections among Mediterranean areas of Europe, Asia, and Africa as a result of Rome's influence.

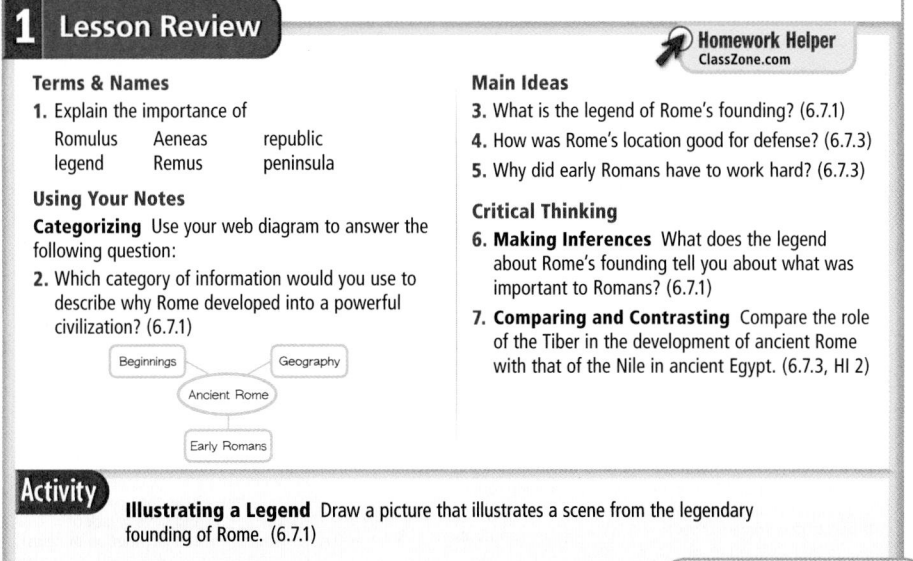

1 Lesson Review

Homework Helper
ClassZone.com

Terms & Names

1. Explain the importance of
   Romulus   Aeneas   republic
   legend   Remus   peninsula

Using Your Notes

Categorizing Use your web diagram to answer the following question:

2. Which category of information would you use to describe why Rome developed into a powerful civilization? (6.7.1)

Beginnings   Geography
Ancient Rome
Early Romans

Main Ideas

3. What is the legend of Rome's founding? (6.7.1)
4. How was Rome's location good for defense? (6.7.3)
5. Why did early Romans have to work hard? (6.7.3)

Critical Thinking

6. **Making Inferences** What does the legend about Rome's founding tell you about what was important to Romans? (6.7.1)
7. **Comparing and Contrasting** Compare the role of the Tiber in the development of ancient Rome with that of the Nile in ancient Egypt. (6.7.3, HI 2)

Activity

Illustrating a Legend Draw a picture that illustrates a scene from the legendary founding of Rome. (6.7.1)

The Rise of Rome • 435

1 Lesson Review Answers

Terms & Names

1. • Romulus, p. 431
   • legend, p. 431
   • Aeneas, p. 431
   • Remus, p. 432
   • republic, p. 432
   • peninsula, p. 433

Using Your Notes

See page 430 for an example of a completed diagram.

2. "Geography" or "Early Romans"

Main Ideas

3. Aeneas, a Trojan War hero, settled in Italy. His descendant Romulus founded Rome.
4. Rome was built on steep hills that could be defended.
5. They were common farmers who had to struggle to feed their families.

Critical Thinking

6. Possible answer: The legend suggests that the Romans wanted to be tied to ancient Greece and to classical heroes.
7. Possible answers: Both provided routes for trade and travel; the Nile was more important to farming than the Tiber.

❹ Assess & Reteach

Assess Have small groups answer one or two of the review questions each. Then have them explain their answers to the the rest of the class.

 Formal Assessment
• Lesson Quiz, p. 227

Reteach Have students complete the Reteaching Activity for Lesson 1 and share and discuss their answers. If students are still uncertain about key terms in the lesson, have them quiz one another, using the Vocabulary Cards.

 In-Depth Resources: Unit 6
• Vocabulary Cards, p. 11
• Reteaching Activity, p. 17

 **Homework Helper**

Visit **ClassZone.com** for a lesson review, a flip-card activity, and links to related Web sites.

Activity Rubric

	Content of Picture	Quality of Illustration
4	clearly depicts the legend	clear and neat
3	depicts some details related to the legend	neat
2	depicts few details related to the legend	somewhat neat
1	shows little or no relation to the legend	sloppy

The Rise of Rome • 435

❶ Plan & Prepare

Objectives

- Examine the effects of self-rule on Roman society.
- Describe how Rome's republican government was organized.
- Analyze the causes and effects of Roman expansion.
- **Language Objective:** Interpret information in a chart to compare the government of the Roman Republic with the government of the present-day United States.

Quick Look

Lesson 2 focuses on Roman expansion and the organization of Roman government and society.

❷ Focus & Motivate

Preview Ask students whether our society today has a class system similar to that of the Romans.

Introduce the Main Ideas The main ideas in this lesson are related to the Big Idea that divisions between rich and poor often create problems.

Reading Skill: Understanding Cause and Effect Remind students to look for words and phrases that signal causes and effects, such as *because, as a result,* and *led to.*

SAMPLE ANSWERS FOR CHART

Causes	Effects
Romans no longer wanted a monarchy.	They founded a republic.
Plebeians were not equal to the patricians.	A constitution was established.
Rome expanded its territories.	Roman conquerors became wealthier and increased the difference between rich and poor.

Lesson 2

▶ MAIN IDEAS

① **Economics** Early Roman society was divided into two unequal classes.

② **Government** The Roman Republic had a government divided into three parts, similar to the U.S. government today.

③ **Government** To gain more land and wealth, Rome began to expand by conquering neighboring peoples.

▶ TAKING NOTES

Reading Skill: Understanding Cause and Effect
Causes explain why an event happens. Effects are the results of the event. As you read Lesson 2, look for the effects of each event listed in the chart below.

Causes	Effects
Romans no longer wanted a monarchy.	
Plebeians were not equal to the patricians.	
Rome expanded its territories.	

 Skillbuilder Handbook, page R26

▲ **Founder** Lucius Junius Brutus helped found the Roman Republic. He led a citizen army that drove the last Etruscan king from Rome.

CALIFORNIA STANDARDS

6.7.1 Identify the location and describe the rise of the Roman Republic, including the importance of such mythical and historical figures as Aeneas, Romulus and Remus, Cincinnatus, Julius Caesar, and Cicero.
6.7.2 Describe the government of the Roman Republic and its significance (e.g., written constitution and tripartite government, checks and balances, civic duty).
6.7.3 Identify the location of and the political and geographic reasons for the growth of Roman territories and expansion of the empire, including how the empire fostered economic growth through the use of currency and trade routes.
7.1.1 Study the early strengths and lasting contributions of Rome (e.g., significance of Roman citizenship; rights under Roman law; Roman art, architecture, engineering, and philosophy; preservation and transmission of Christianity) and its ultimate internal weaknesses (e.g., rise of autonomous military powers within the empire, undermining of citizenship by the growth of corruption and slavery, lack of education, and distribution of news).

HOW TO TEACH THE CALIFORNIA STANDARDS

Standard	Content	Student Question or Activity	Instruction
6.7.1	**Page 438** Explains why Cincinnatus was named dictator	**Page 441** Students identify lands Rome conquered.	Discuss how the locations of conquered nations increased Rome's strength and importance.
6.7.2	**Page 438** Explains Rome's tripartite government	**Page 439** Students identify the three branches of the Roman Republic.	Ask students to discuss how Rome's tripartite government is reflected in the U.S. government.
6.7.3	**Page 440** Describes how Rome expanded as a result of the Punic Wars	**Page 441** Students name lands that Rome conquered.	On a classroom map, point out the locations of conquered lands and note Rome's central location.
7.1.1	**Page 441** Describes the effects of Rome's expansion on farmers	**Page 441** Students discuss the effects of Rome's expansion.	Point out that Rome's expansion increased some people's wealth but also caused an increase in poverty for others.

The Roman Republic

TERMS & NAMES
patrician
plebeian
Senate
consul
Cincinnatus

Build on What You Know You have already learned that Rome overthrew its kings and formed a republic. This change to self-rule would not only affect Rome's government. It would also affect Roman society.

Early Strengths of Roman Society

1 ESSENTIAL QUESTION How was Roman society structured?
It had two classes—patricians and plebeians.
As Rome developed into a complex civilization, two classes arose. Inequalities between them would lead to conflict. This conflict, however, would eventually define Roman citizenship and the rights of citizens under Roman law.

Patricians and Plebeians The upper-class **patricians** (puh•TRIHSH•uhnz) were wealthy landowners who held all of the highest positions in government. The **plebeians** (plih•BEE•uhnz) were mostly common farmers. Like all male Roman citizens, they could vote, but they couldn't hold important government positions.

Resentment over the patricians' power caused tension. Finally, the patricians passed a written constitution, called the Twelve Tables, around 450 B.C. The Twelve Tables established basic rights and duties for Roman citizens.

Roman Forum Ruins of the Roman Forum, the religious, cultural, and political heart of Rome, still stand today. In the early days of the republic, the Senate met in a small building in the Forum. ▼

REVIEW Why did the division of Roman society cause tension?
because the patricians were able to hold positions of power, while the plebeians were not

437

Terms & Names

patrician class of people made up of wealthy landowners and government officials

plebeian class of mostly common farmers

Senate a government body of 300 members that advised Roman leaders

consul one of a pair of leaders of Rome's executive branch of government

Cincinnatus a dictator chosen by the consuls to defend Rome from attack in 458 B.C.

❸ Teach

Early Strengths of Roman Society

6.7.1

Talk About It

- **Critical Thinking: Making Inferences** Would the Twelve Tables prevent further class conflict? (*Possible answer: no, because differences between the two classes still existed.*)

California Resources

California Reading Toolkit, L45
California Modified Lesson Plans for English Learners, p. 93
California Daily Standards Practice Transparencies, TT45
California Standards Enrichment Workbook, pp. 95–100, pp. 111–112
California Online Test Practice
California Test Generator CD-ROM
California Standards Planner and Lesson Plans, L89
California EasyPlanner CD-ROM
California eEdition CD-ROM

LESSON 2 PROGRAM RESOURCES

ON LEVEL

In-Depth Resources: Unit 6
- Reading Skill: Understanding Cause and Effect, p. 4
- Skillbuilder Practice: Understanding Cause and Effect, p. 8
- Vocabulary Cards, p. 11

Formal Assessment
- Lesson Quiz, p. 228

ENGLISH LEARNERS

In-Depth Resources in Spanish
- Reading Skill: Understanding Cause and Effect, p. 112
- Skillbuilder Practice: Understanding Cause and Effect, p. 117

Modified Lesson Plans for English Learners, p. 93

Reading Study Guide (Spanish), p. 117

Reading Study Guide Audio CD (Spanish)

STRUGGLING READERS

In-Depth Resources: Unit 6
- Reading Skill: Understanding Cause and Effect, p. 4
- Vocabulary Cards, p. 11
- Reteaching Activity, p. 18

Reading Toolkit, L45

Reading Study Guide, p. 117

Reading Study Guide Audio CD

GIFTED AND TALENTED STUDENTS

Interdisciplinary Projects
- Language Arts, p. 75

INCLUSION

EasyPlanner CD-ROM
- Reading Skill: Understanding Cause and Effect
- Reteaching Activity

TECHNOLOGY

eEdition CD-ROM

Power Presentations CD-ROM

Map Transparencies
- MT25 Growth of the Roman Empire

Critical Thinking Transparencies
- CT57 Understanding Cause and Effect

ClassZone.com

In-Depth Resources: Unit 6
- Reading Skill: Understanding Cause and Effect, p. 4
- Skillbuilder Practice: Understanding Cause and Effect, p. 8

Teach

Republican Government

6.7.2

Talk About It

- What bodies made up the legislative branch of government in the Roman Republic? Who were the members of each? *(the Senate, whose members were mostly patricians, and the assemblies, whose members were mostly plebeians)*

- What was the job of the consuls? *(to command the army and direct the government for one year)*

- Why might the consuls appoint a dictator? *(so that Rome could have a leader with absolute power in a time of crisis)*

- **Critical Thinking: Drawing Conclusions** Do you think that having two consuls might be better than having one president? *(Possible answers: yes, because it would prevent one person from having too much power; no, because if they disagreed on important issues, conflict might result.)*

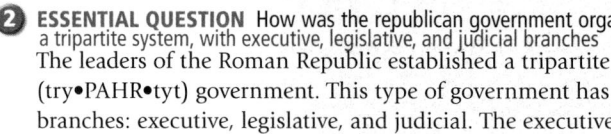

Republican Government

2 **ESSENTIAL QUESTION** How was the republican government organized?
a tripartite system, with executive, legislative, and judicial branches

The leaders of the Roman Republic established a tripartite (try•PAHR•tyt) government. This type of government has three branches: executive, legislative, and judicial. The executive branch enforces a country's laws. The legislative branch makes the laws. And the judicial branch interprets the laws in court.

Legislative and Judicial The legislative branch of Roman government included the Senate and the assemblies. The **Senate** was a powerful body of 300 members that advised Roman leaders. Most senators were patricians. The assemblies were mainly made up of plebeians. Their representatives protected the rights of plebeians.

The judicial branch consisted of eight judges who served for one year. They oversaw the courts and governed the provinces.

Executive Two **consuls** led Rome's executive branch. They commanded the army and directed the government for one year. Each consul had the power to veto, or overrule, the other.

In times of crisis, the consuls could choose a dictator—a leader with absolute power—to rule in their place for a limited time. In 458 B.C., a man named **Cincinnatus** (SIHN•suh•NAT•uhs) was made dictator to defend Rome from attack. According to legend, he defeated the enemy and returned power to the consuls in a single day.

Senators In this 19th-century painting, a speaker addresses his fellow members of the Roman Senate. ▼

438 • Chapter 13

DIFFERENTIATING INSTRUCTION

English Learners

Make Comparison Statements
Direct students to the chart "Comparing Republican Governments." Model how to use information from the chart to formulate comparison statements. Use key words such as *both, each, like, as,* and *similarly.* Say, "Like the government of the Roman Republic, the government of the United States is based on a set of laws." For more support, see *Modified Lesson Plans for English Learners,* p. 93.

Inclusion

Take Audio Notes
Have students who are visually impaired take notes on the lesson by making audiotapes or digital recordings with partners. Remind them to use the word *because* in explaining causes and effects in the lesson.

Executive

Rome

Two consuls, elected for one year: led government and commanded army

United States

A president, elected for four years: heads government and military

Legislative

Rome

Senate of 300 members: advised consuls and set policies

Assemblies: made laws and selected officials

United States

Senate of 100 members: makes laws and advises president

House of Representatives of 435 members: makes laws

Legal Code

Rome

Twelve Tables: basis of Roman law, which established citizens' legal, economic, property, and social rights

United States

U.S. Constitution: basis of U.S. law, which sets forth both individual rights and governmental powers

Judicial

Rome

Eight judges: oversaw courts and governed provinces

United States

Supreme Court of nine justices: interprets the Constitution and federal law

SKILLBUILDER
INTERPRETING VISUALS
What similarities do you see in the governments of the Roman Republic and the United States?

History from Visuals

Interpreting Visuals

- Why do lines connect the "Legislative" and "Judicial" boxes to the "Executive" box? *(to show how the branches of government interact with one another)*

- According to the chart, which branch of the Roman government was most like the corresponding branch of the U.S. government? Describe any differences. *(Possible answer: The legislative branch was most similar because it advised the executive branch and made laws. However, the Roman legislative branch also set policies.)*

SKILLBUILDER ANSWER

tripartite structure, similar powers and duties, system of checks and balances, basis is legal code

Legacy of Roman Law The U.S. government adopted several features of the Roman Republic. You can compare the two systems in the chart above. Like the Roman government, the United States has a tripartite system. The U.S. system of checks and balances makes sure that one branch of the government doesn't have too much power. This system is like the veto, which limited the power of Roman consuls. In addition, like Rome, the United States has a written constitution on which its government is based.

Citizenship is also an important part of a republican government. In the Roman Republic, only free adult males were citizens and could vote. Only these citizens enjoyed the protection of Roman law. They also were expected to perform civic duties. That means that they were expected to serve their nation. Cincinnatus showed civic duty by defeating the enemy and stepping down from power. American citizens show civic duty by voting, taking part in jury duty, and paying taxes.

REVIEW What made up the three branches of the Roman Republic?
executive—consuls and dictators; legislative—Senate and assemblies; judicial—eight judges

The Rise of Rome • 439

DIFFERENTIATING INSTRUCTION

Struggling Readers

Use the Review Questions
Have students follow along silently as you read aloud the review question on this page. Tell students to look for the answer to the question in the text or in the chart on this page. Discuss the answer.

Gifted and Talented Students

Analyze the Pros and Cons of Rome's Government
Have partners discuss the pros and cons of the way Rome's republican government was organized. For example, what was good or bad about having two consuls? Was their term of office too short? Then have each student write three paragraphs giving his or her opinion of the organization of Rome's government. Invite students to suggest ways that the organization might have been improved.

Teach

The Republic Expands

 6.7.3, 7.1.1

Talk About It

- How did Rome treat conquered peoples? *(Rome allowed them to govern themselves, but they had to pay taxes and provide soldiers for the army.)*

- Why did Rome allow conquered peoples so much freedom? *(Possible answers: to gain their loyalty; to make it easier to govern them)*

- **Critical Thinking: Drawing Conclusions** Why were the Romans interested in conquering other peoples? *(Possible answer: to gain wealth and slaves.)*

History from Visuals

Interpreting Maps

Have students examine the map and key.

- Where were Carthage and Rome located? *(on opposite sides of the Mediterranean Sea)*

- How do their locations help to explain the rivalry between Carthage and Rome? *(Each wanted to control trade in the Mediterranean.)*

Extension Have students use an atlas to identify the present-day country containing the site of Carthage. *(Tunisia)*

GEOGRAPHY SKILLBUILDER ANSWER

Possible answer: He wanted to stage a surprise attack.

Map Transparencies
- MT25 Growth of the Roman Empire

The Republic Expands

 ESSENTIAL QUESTION How did Rome expand? wars, including Punic Wars

For hundreds of years after the founding of the republic, Rome expanded its territories. By the 300s B.C., the Romans dominated central Italy. Eventually, they conquered the Etruscans to the north and the Greek city-states to the southeast. By 275 B.C., all of the Italian Peninsula was under Roman control.

In general, Rome did not impose harsh rule on conquered peoples. The republic offered Roman citizenship to most of the conquered peoples and allowed them to govern themselves. In return, they had to pay taxes and provide soldiers for the Roman army.

The Punic Wars Rome needed these soldiers to fight in the *Punic Wars*, which began in 264 B.C. The Punic Wars were a series of three long wars against Carthage, a rich trading city in North Africa.

Rome won each of the Punic Wars but almost lost the second. Hannibal, a general from Carthage, crossed the Alps with a herd of elephants and nearly captured Rome. The Roman general Scipio (SIHP•ee•OH) defeated him in 202 B.C. In 146 B.C., Rome finally captured and destroyed Carthage. By the end of the wars, Roman territory extended from Spain to Greece. (See the map below.)

Vocabulary Strategy

The **specialized vocabulary** term *Punic Wars* refers to the series of wars between Rome and Carthage. Carthage was once a colony of Phoenicia, a group of sea-trading city-states on the Mediterranean. *Punic* comes from the Latin word *Phoenician*.

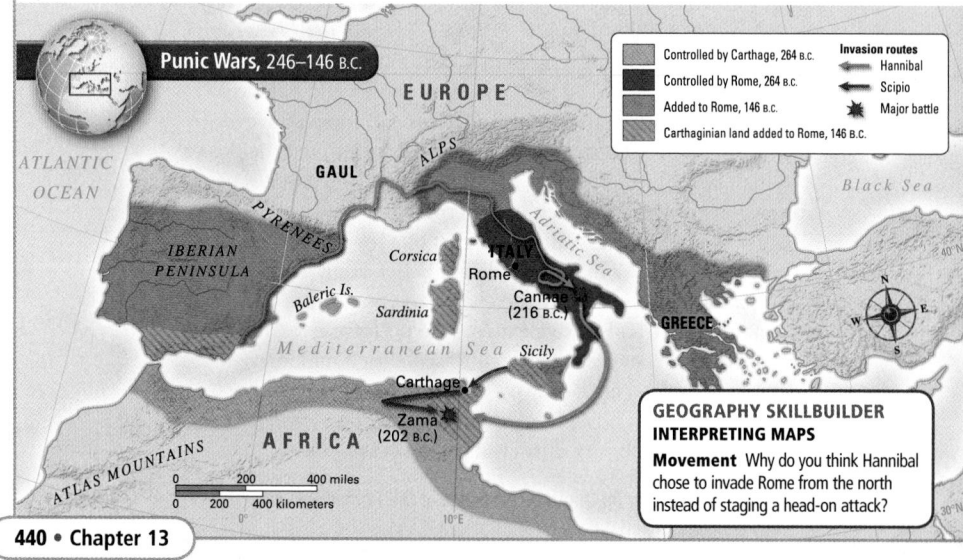

Punic Wars, 246–146 B.C.

| Controlled by Carthage, 264 B.C. |
| Controlled by Rome, 264 B.C. |
| Added to Rome, 146 B.C. |
| Carthaginian land added to Rome, 146 B.C. |

Invasion routes
Hannibal
Scipio
Major battle

**GEOGRAPHY SKILLBUILDER
INTERPRETING MAPS**
Movement Why do you think Hannibal chose to invade Rome from the north instead of staging a head-on attack?

INTERDISCIPLINARY ACTIVITIES

Art

Illustrate Hannibal's March
Have students use the Internet to research Hannibal's march on Rome, which he began in 218 B.C. Ask students to create an illustrated map or time line that shows the crossing of the Alps, the setbacks Hannibal encountered, and the battles he engaged in before being defeated by the Romans.

Language Arts

Write an Acrostic Poem
Have individual students use what they have learned about the Roman Republic to write acrostic poems about it. In an acrostic poem, the first letters of the line spell out a word or phrase when read from top to bottom. For example, an acrostic based on *Roman Republic* would have 13 lines.

Effects of Expansion The Roman conquerors brought back great wealth and many slaves. They bought large estates and farmed them with slave labor. But because many small farmers couldn't compete, they lost their farms. As a result, unemployment and poverty increased. The gap between rich and poor grew wider. This, in turn, produced more anger and tension between the classes.

REVIEW What was the result of Roman expansion?
new lands, great wealth, a wider gap between rich and poor

Lesson Summary
- Early Rome was divided into two classes—patricians and plebeians.
- The Roman Republic was a tripartite system that provided a model for the U.S. government.
- Roman expansion brought new lands and great wealth for Rome.

Why It Matters Now . . .
Some of the most basic values and institutions of the United States, such as civic duty and a separate judicial branch, began in the Roman Republic.

▲ **Laurel Wreath** Roman generals wore a wreath made of laurel leaves after winning a major battle. The Romans adopted this symbol of victory from ancient Greece.

2 Lesson Review

 Homework Helper
ClassZone.com

Terms & Names
1. Explain the importance of

patrician	Senate	Cincinnatus
plebeian	consul	

Using Your Notes
Understanding Cause and Effect Use your completed chart to answer the following question:
2. What happened when Romans no longer wanted a monarchy? (6.7.1)

Causes	Effects
Romans no longer wanted a monarchy.	
Plebeians were not equal to the patricians.	
Rome expanded its territories.	

Main Ideas
3. In what ways were the Roman social classes unequal? (6.7.2)
4. What is the legacy of Roman law? (7.7.1)
5. What lands did Rome conquer? (6.7.1, 6.7.3)

Critical Thinking
6. **Explaining Historical Patterns** Why do you think the Roman Republican government has influenced the governments of other countries? (7.7.1)
7. **Making Inferences** What benefits do you think the Romans gained from their treatment of conquered peoples? (6.7.1)

Activity
Writing a Dialogue Write a brief dialogue between Cincinnatus and the consuls who appointed him dictator. Remember that he served for only one day. (6.7.1)

The Rise of Rome • 441

2 Lesson Review Answers

Terms & Names
1. • patrician, p. 437
   • plebeian, p. 437
   • Senate, p. 438
   • consul, p. 438
   • Cincinnatus, p. 438

Using Your Notes
See page 436 for an example of a completed chart.
2. They founded a republic.

Main Ideas
3. Patricians were wealthy landowners who held the highest positions in the government. Plebeians were mostly common farmers and were barred from holding important government positions.
4. tripartite system, checks and balances, written laws, civic duty
5. Italian Peninsula, Carthage, region from Spain to Greece

Critical Thinking
6. Possible answers: because it is a balanced and fair form of government; because citizens are given a voice
7. Possible answer: The conquered peoples may have been more likely to accept Rome and less likely to rebel.

④ Assess & Reteach

Assess Have students answer the questions in pairs. One student should answer a question orally and the other should write down the answer. Then have students switch roles and continue taking turns until all of the questions are answered.

Formal Assessment
• Lesson Quiz, p. 228

Reteach Divide the class into small groups and have each group outline one section of the lesson. Then have groups share and discuss their outlines.

In-Depth Resources: Unit 6
• Vocabulary Cards, p. 11
• Reteaching Activity, p. 18

Homework Helper
Visit **ClassZone.com** for a lesson review, a flip-card activity, and links to related Web sites.

Activity Rubric

	Understanding of Concepts	Content of Dialogue	Errors in Mechanics
4	thorough	interesting and realistic	few or none
3	good	realistic	some
2	some	rambling or confusing	many
1	little or none	incoherent	many major

❶ Plan & Prepare

Objectives

- Trace the events that led to the overthrow of the Roman Republic.
- Describe the influence of Julius Caesar and Augustus on the transition from republic to empire.
- **Language Objective:** Identify the people who were involved in the rise of the Roman Empire in order to make the text more meaningful and comprehensible.

Quick Look

Lesson 3 focuses on problems created by the expansion of the Roman Republic.

❷ Focus & Motivate

Preview Ask students to predict the changes that expansion brought to Rome's government.

Introduce the Main Ideas The main ideas of this lesson are related to the Big Idea that new ideas and beliefs can challenge a government's authority, leading to change.

Reading Skill: Constructing Time Lines Remind students to leave spaces between events entered on their time lines so that they can insert other events later.

SAMPLE ANSWERS FOR TIME LINE

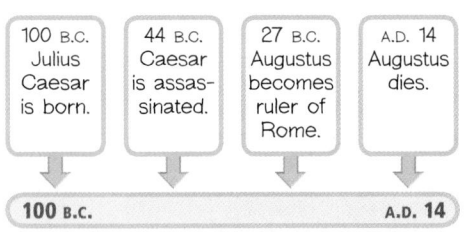

| 100 B.C. Julius Caesar is born. | 44 B.C. Caesar is assassinated. | 27 B.C. Augustus becomes ruler of Rome. | A.D. 14 Augustus dies. |

100 B.C.   A.D. 14

Lesson 3

▶ MAIN IDEAS

❶ Government Angry poor people, power-hungry generals, and ambitious politicians threatened the Roman Republic.

❷ Government Julius Caesar gained absolute control of the republic but did not rule long.

❸ Government After Caesar was assassinated, Augustus founded an empire that enjoyed peace and prosperity for about 200 years.

▶ TAKING NOTES

Reading Skill: Constructing Time Lines
When you place events in order on a time line, you get a sense of the relationships among events. Create a time line like the one shown below to keep track of the dates and events in Lesson 3.

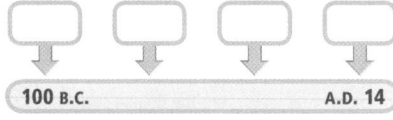

100 B.C.   A.D. 14

Ⓢ Skillbuilder Handbook, page R14

▲ **Imperial Eagle** A Roman soldier carried a bronze or silver image of an eagle raised on a pole, like the one shown in this small figurine, into battle. The eagle represented the strength of the Roman Empire.

CALIFORNIA STANDARDS

6.7.1 Identify the location and describe the rise of the Roman Republic, including the importance of such mythical and historical figures as Aeneas, Romulus and Remus, Cincinnatus, Julius Caesar, and Cicero.

6.7.3 Identify the location of and the political and geographic reasons for the growth of Roman territories and expansion of the empire, including how the empire fostered economic growth through the use of currency and trade routes.

6.7.4 Discuss the influence of Julius Caesar and Augustus in Rome's transition from republic to empire.

7.1.2 Discuss the geographic borders of the empire at its height and the factors that threatened its territorial cohesion.

CST 2 Students construct various time lines of key events, people, and periods of the historical era they are studying.

442 • Chapter 13

HOW TO TEACH THE CALIFORNIA STANDARDS

Standard	Content	Student Question or Activity	Instruction
6.7.1	**Pages 444–445** Describes the rise of Julius Caesar	**Page 449** Students explain how Caesar gained power.	Discuss Caesar's reforms. Explain that many believed he was a tyrant.
6.7.3	**Pages 448–449** Describes how traders used Rome's network of trade routes	**Page 449** Students explain the causes of economic growth during the Pax Romana.	Point out that good trade routes and a common currency made it easier for Romans to engage in trade and accumulate wealth.
6.7.4	**Page 443** Explains the role of Julius Caesar in the fall of the republic	**Page 449** Students summarize the end of the Roman Republic.	Have students compare and contrast the goals and achievements of Julius Caesar and Augustus.
7.1.2	**Page 449** Describes the division between rich and poor	**Page 449** Students explain how expansion threatened the Roman Republic.	Point out that the wealthy were those who benefited most from Rome's expansion.
CST 2	**Page 442** Tells students to construct a time line.	**Page 449** Students use their time line to answer a question.	Have students ask questions based on their time lines.

Rome Becomes an Empire

TERMS & NAMES
civil war
Julius Caesar
Cicero
Augustus
Pax Romana

Build on What You Know In Lesson 2, you learned about the changes expansion brought to Roman society. Expansion would also change the balance of power in Rome's republican government. These changes would lead to the overthrow of the republic.

Conflicts at Home

1 **ESSENTIAL QUESTION** What led to conflict in Rome?

differences between rich and poor in society

As Rome expanded, many wealthy Romans neglected their civic duties. They thought only about gaining even more power and wealth. This increased the differences between rich and poor. As a result, the threat of uprisings grew.

Reform Fails Reformers tried to relieve these problems. They wanted to break up the huge estates and give land to the poor. But the wealthy landowners in the Senate felt threatened. They opposed the reforms and had the reformers killed.

Connect to Today

Colosseum The Colosseum is a lasting symbol of the power of the Roman Empire. Many stadiums built since have been modeled on the Colosseum. ▼

443

Terms & Names

civil war an armed conflict between groups within the same country

Julius Caesar a Roman general who was appointed dictator for life in 44 B.C.

Cicero a Roman consul and great orator

Augustus ruler of Rome from 27 B.C. to A.D. 14

Pax Romana a period of peace and stability that lasted for about 200 years

❸ Teach

Conflicts at Home
6.7.3, 7.1.2

Talk About It

- **Critical Thinking: Summarizing** What were the sources of the conflict that led to civil war between the patricians and the plebeians? *(Possible answer: greed for wealth and land and a desire for power)*

California Resources

California Reading Toolkit, L46

California Modified Lesson Plans for English Learners, p. 95

California Daily Standards Practice Transparencies, TT46

California Standards Enrichment Workbook, pp. 95–96, 99–102, 111–112

California Online Test Practice

California Test Generator CD-ROM

California Standards Planner and Lesson Plans, L91

California EasyPlanner CD-ROM

California eEdition CD-ROM

LESSON 3 PROGRAM RESOURCES

ON LEVEL

In-Depth Resources: Unit 6
- Reading Skill: Constructing Time Lines, p. 5
- Vocabulary Cards, p. 11
- Geography Practice: Caesar's Military Campaigns, p. 13

Formal Assessment
- Lesson Quiz, p. 229

ENGLISH LEARNERS

In-Depth Resources in Spanish
- Reading Skill: Constructing Time Lines, p. 113
- Geography Practice: Caesar's Military Campaigns, p. 119

Modified Lesson Plans for English Learners, p. 95

Reading Study Guide (Spanish), p. 119

Reading Study Guide Audio CD (Spanish)

STRUGGLING READERS

In-Depth Resources: Unit 6
- Reading Skill: Constructing Time Lines, p. 5
- Vocabulary Cards, p. 11
- Reteaching Activity, p. 19

Reading Toolkit, L46

Reading Study Guide, p. 119

Reading Study Guide Audio CD

GIFTED AND TALENTED STUDENTS

In-Depth Resources: Unit 6
- Primary Source: Cicero's Fears for the Republic, p. 15
- Literature: Plutarch's Biography of Caesar, p. 16

History Makers
- Julius Caesar, p. 25

Interdisciplinary Projects
- Physical Education, p. 76

INCLUSION

EasyPlanner CD-ROM

- Reading Skill: Constructing Time Lines
- Reteaching Activity

TECHNOLOGY

eEdition CD-ROM

Power Presentations CD-ROM

Map Transparencies
- MT26 Roman Britain

Humanities Transparencies
- HT25 Roman Soldiers

Critical Thinking Transparencies
- CT58 Constructing Time Lines

ClassZone.com

In-Depth Resources: Unit 6
- Reading Skill: Constructing Time Lines, p. 5
- Geography Practice: Caesar's Military Campaigns, p. 13

Vocabulary Strategy

Word Family

Ask students to use two words in sentences that come from the Latin root *civis*. Two possible examples are:

- It is our civic duty to vote in elections.
- Our society owes a great deal to Roman civilization.

Teach

Julius Caesar

 6.7.1, 6.7.4

Talk About It

- What important skills did Caesar have that helped him achieve great power? *(He was a successful general and a good politician.)*

- Why did the Senate order Caesar to break up his army? *(Possible answer: Many senators distrusted Caesar's great ambition and wanted to prevent him from becoming too powerful.)*

- How did Caesar respond to the Senate's order to disband his army? *(He led his army into Italy and fought for control of Rome.)*

- **Critical Thinking: Forming and Supporting Opinions** Was Caesar a true reformer who wanted to help people, or was he a power-hungry tyrant? Explain your answer. *(Possible answers: He was a true reformer because he helped the poor; he was a tyrant because he defied the Senate.)*

 In-Depth Resources: Unit 6
- Literature: Plutarch's Biography of Caesar, p. 16

Civil War At the same time, generals who had conquered other lands became ambitious for power at home. They hired poor farmers to serve under them as soldiers. Increasingly, these soldiers shifted their loyalty from the republic to their general. The generals' desire for power led to conflict.

Eventually, civil war broke out. A **civil war** is an armed conflict between groups within the same country. On one side were the generals who supported the cause of the plebeians. On the other were generals who were backed by patricians and senators.

A general named Marius fought for the plebeians, while a general named Sulla fought for the patricians. The struggle went on for years. Finally, in 82 B.C., the patricians won. Sulla took power and became a dictator.

REVIEW Who fought in the civil war?
Generals who supported the cause of the plebeians fought against generals backed by patricians.

Julius Caesar

 ESSENTIAL QUESTION Who was Julius Caesar?
a Roman general who became dictator of Rome
After Sulla died, other generals rose to power. One of them was **Julius Caesar**. Caesar was born around 100 B.C. into an old noble family. He was a man of many talents and great ambition. But to achieve real power, he knew he had to win on the battlefield.

Military Leader Caesar first saw military action in Asia Minor—part of present-day Turkey—and Spain. But he proved himself to be a great general in Gaul, the area now known as France.

The Gauls were fierce fighters. But in a brilliant military campaign, Caesar defeated the Gauls and captured the entire region. His conquests won new lands and great wealth for Rome. The victories also won fame and fortune for Caesar.

Vocabulary Strategy

The word *civil* is part of a **word family** that includes the words *civic*, *civilian*, and *civilization*. They all come from the Latin root *civis*, meaning "citizen."

▲ **Caesar** In this 19th-century wood engraving, soldiers bow down to Caesar after he won an important battle in 47 B.C. After the battle, Caesar had the following message sent back to Rome: "I came, I saw, I conquered."

DIFFERENTIATING INSTRUCTION

Inclusion

Role-Play a Roman Citizen
Review the characteristics of plebeians and patricians with students. Write a list of the characteristics on the board and tell each student to choose to be either a plebeian or a patrician. Then have students role-play being members of the groups, trying to convince their generals to keep on fighting by reminding them what they are fighting for.

Struggling Readers

Identify Key Players
Tell students to make a list of the powerful men they have read about in this lesson. Next to each name, have students write down the role the person played in Roman society and one or two reasons why he is well known.

Dictator for Life In addition to his military skills, Caesar was also a good politician. He gained a reputation as a reformer who supported the common people. This, plus his military fame, made him popular with the plebeians.

But Caesar also had enemies. Many powerful Romans, including patrician senators, opposed Caesar. One of his opponents was **Cicero** (SIHS•uh•ROH), a key Roman consul and perhaps the greatest speaker in Roman history. Cicero was a strong supporter of the republic. He distrusted Caesar and the ruler's great desire for power. (You can learn more about the relationship between Cicero and Caesar by reading Cicero's letter in the Primary Source feature below.)

When Caesar returned from Gaul, the Senate ordered him to break up his army. Instead, he led his soldiers into Italy and began fighting for control of Rome. After several years, Caesar emerged victorious. In 46 B.C., he returned to Rome, where he had the support of the people and the army. That same year, the Senate appointed him the sole Roman ruler. In 44 B.C., Caesar was named dictator for life.

Primary Source

Background: Although Cicero opposed Caesar, he could still be polite to Rome's sole ruler. In 45 B.C., Cicero invited Caesar to be a guest in his home. The ruler arrived with 2,000 men. Cicero described the visit in a letter to a friend. In this excerpt from the letter, you can sense that Cicero is not comfortable with Caesar.

from *Cicero's Selected Works*
A Letter by Cicero
Translated by Michael Grant

In other words, we were human beings together. Still, he was not the sort of guest to whom you would say "do please come again on your way back." Once is enough! We talked no serious politics, but a good deal about literary matters. In short, he liked it and enjoyed himself. . . . There you have the story of how I entertained him—or had him billeted [camped] on me; I found it a bother, as I have said, but not disagreeable.

> **DOCUMENT–BASED QUESTION**
> Why do you think Cicero and Caesar avoided talking about politics?

The Rise of Rome • 445

More About . . .

Cicero
Cicero (106–43 B.C.) was born into a wealthy family and was educated in Rome and in Greece. He gained fame as a great orator and was elected consul in 63 B.C. An opponent of Caesar's dictatorship, Cicero retired from public life during Caesar's reign and concentrated on writing philosophy and poetry. He was also a prolific letter writer. More than 800 letters written by Cicero between 67 and 43 B.C. survive. About half of these letters were sent to his friend and publisher Titus Pomponius Atticus. Cicero was murdered during the power struggle that followed Caesar's murder.

Interpreting Primary Sources

from *Cicero's Selected Works*

- What did Cicero mean when he wrote "we were human beings together"? *(Possible answer: They interacted as equals, not as ruler and subject.)*

- What might you conclude about the recipient of Cicero's letter? *(Possible answer: The recipient was a trusted friend who shared Cicero's political views.)*

DOCUMENT–BASED QUESTION ANSWER

because their opposing views would probably have led to an argument

 In-Depth Resources: Unit 6
- Primary Source: Cicero's Fears for the Republic, p. 15

DIFFERENTIATING INSTRUCTION

Inclusion

Remember Details
After students read the information about Cicero, have them close their books and create graphic organizers from memory. Tell students to take turns remembering and writing down details about Cicero's life and beliefs. When they finish, tell them to check their graphic organizers against the book and make any necessary changes.

Gifted and Talented Students

Report on Cicero's Career
Tell students Cicero's fame as a great orator has endured. Have students use the Internet and other research sources to learn about Cicero's career. Remind students that Cicero did not support Caesar's rise to power. Ask, Whom did he support? Why didn't he support Caesar? Have students present their findings to the rest of the class.

Teach

Emperors Rule Rome

6.7.4, CST 2

Talk About It

- What events led to the fall of the Roman Republic? *(the death of Caesar, the civil war that followed, and the rise of Octavian, or Augustus, to power)*

- What positive changes did Augustus bring to Rome? *(Possible answers: He rebuilt Rome, organized government services, created a strong military, and built roads, bridges, and tunnels.)*

- What are three factors that contributed to Rome's expanding economy? *(Roman roads, protection provided by the Roman military, and the use of a common currency)*

- **Critical Thinking: Evaluating Information** Would the Pax Romana have been possible if Rome had remained a republic? *(Possible answers: yes, with the right leadership from the consuls and the senate; no, it required the vision and determination of a strong leader)*

Caesar's Reforms Caesar governed as an absolute ruler, but he started a number of reforms. He expanded the Senate by including supporters from Italy and other regions. He also enforced laws against crime and created jobs for the poor. Despite these reforms, some Romans feared that Caesar would make himself king. Not only would he rule for a lifetime, but his family members would also rule after him. Roman hatred of kings went back to the days of Etruscan rule.

▲ **Silver Coin** This coin was issued after Caesar's assassination. One side of the coin (*top*) shows a profile of one of the assassins. The other side shows a cap of liberty between two daggers. ▼

Assassination and Legacy Concern over Caesar's growing power led to his downfall. As you read in Starting with a Story, Caesar was assassinated in 44 B.C. by a group of senators. The leaders of the conspiracy were eventually killed or committed suicide.

Historians still disagree about Caesar's rule, just as Romans did at the time. Some say he was a reformer who worked to help the people. Others say he was a power-hungry tyrant. In either case, Caesar's rule and his death would bring an end to the republic.

> **REVIEW** Why was Caesar killed?
> Some people felt he was too powerful.

Emperors Rule Rome

3 ESSENTIAL QUESTION What happened to Rome after Caesar's death?
Augustus came to power; republic ended; Rome became an empire.
After Caesar's death, several Roman leaders struggled to gain power. One of these men was Caesar's great-nephew and adopted son, Octavian (ahk•TAY•vee•uhn).

This struggle led to civil war, which lasted for years. The war destroyed what was left of the Roman Republic. Eventually, Octavian defeated his enemies. In 27 B.C., he became the unchallenged ruler of Rome. In time, he took the name **Augustus** (aw•GUHS•tuhs), which means "exalted one," or person of great rank and authority.

Augustus Rebuilds Rome Augustus was the first emperor of Rome, but he didn't use that title. He preferred to be called "first citizen." He restored some aspects of the republican government. Senators, consuls, and tribunes once again held office. But Augustus had power over all of them.

446 • Chapter 13

INTERDISCIPLINARY ACTIVITIES

Language Arts

Debate Caesar's Role in Roman History

Was Caesar a great reformer, or was he a power-hungry tyrant? Did he improve the Roman Republic, or did he destroy it? Encourage students to conduct research into these issues and have groups take sides and debate Caesar's role in Roman history.

Art

Create a Mural

Have students research the temples, theaters, and monuments that were built during Augustus' reign. Ask them to draw a mural that shows what Rome might have looked like under Augustus. In addition to depicting important architecture, students should include scenes that illustrate some of the government and social reforms that Augustus made.

History Makers

Augustus (63 B.C.–A.D. 14)

As a child, Augustus was weak and sickly. He continued to suffer from illnesses throughout his life. Yet he lived a long life and became the powerful ruler of a great empire.

Despite his enormous power, Augustus liked to present himself as an average citizen with simple tastes. He lived in a small house and slept in a bedroom no larger than a cell. He wore plain robes woven by his wife. His favorite foods were those of the common people—bread, cheese, and olives. Augustus also believed in a strict moral code. He sent his own daughter into exile for not living up to this code.

Augustus once said that his highest honor was to be called the father of his country by the Roman people. But after his death, the Romans worshiped Augustus as a god.

History Makers

Augustus

Octavian was only 12 years old when he made his first public speech, a funeral oration for his grandmother Julia, the sister of Julius Caesar. Octavian was 18 when Caesar was murdered. Learning that Caesar had named him as his heir, Octavian went to Rome and managed to win over many of Caesar's troops.

Many of those vying for power in the wake of Caesar's death underestimated the young man's political abilities. Assuming the name Augustus, for example, was a clever and subtle public-relations ploy. The name implied his superiority. At the same time, he gained favor by downplaying his power and stressing his simple values and concern for the poor.

Augustus governed well. He brought the provinces under control and strengthened the empire's defenses. He also began a civil service. A civil service is a group of officials employed by the government. The Roman civil service collected taxes, oversaw the postal system, and managed the grain supply.

Augustus also rebuilt and beautified Rome. He built grand temples, theaters, and monuments. He replaced many old brick buildings with structures in marble. Under Augustus, Rome became a magnificent imperial capital.

The Roman Peace The reign of Augustus began a long period of peace and stability in the Roman Empire. This period is called the **Pax Romana**, or "Roman Peace." The Pax Romana lasted for about 200 years. During this time, the empire grew to its greatest size, about 2 million square miles.

Under Augustus, the Roman army also became the greatest fighting force in the world. Around 300,000 men served in the army. They guarded the empire's frontiers. They also built roads, bridges, and tunnels that helped tie the empire together. In addition, Augustus created a strong Roman navy that patrolled the Mediterranean Sea.

The Rise of Rome • 447

DIFFERENTIATING INSTRUCTION

English Learners

Identify Important Figures

Explain that many people were affected the rise and fall of the Roman Empire. Say, "One group, known as the reformers, wanted to give land to the poor by breaking up wealthy estates. This led to disagreements with landowners who were interested only in getting richer and more powerful." Ask students to identify other people who were involved in the rise and fall of the Roman Empire. For more support, see *Modified Lesson Plans for English Learners*, p. 95.

Struggling Readers

List Achievements

As they read, have pairs of students list the various achievements and improvements of Augustus. Then have two pairs compare lists. Invite students to refer to the text to check information and to add to their lists as needed.

History from Visuals

Interpreting Maps

Have students study the trade routes indicated on the map.

- Across which three continents was trade in the Roman Empire conducted? *(Europe, Africa, and Asia)*

- What product found in Greece was also found in Italy? *(marble)*

GEOGRAPHY SKILLBUILDER ANSWER

grain and textiles

More About . . .

Agriculture

Wealthy Romans bought land in Italy, Gaul, and other areas, such as North Africa, where they planted grapes and olives. The wealthy owners lived in Rome or other cities, while their estates, or villas, were managed by foremen. Small family farms could not compete with the large villas, which had lower labor costs. This deepened the divide between the rich and the poor in Roman society.

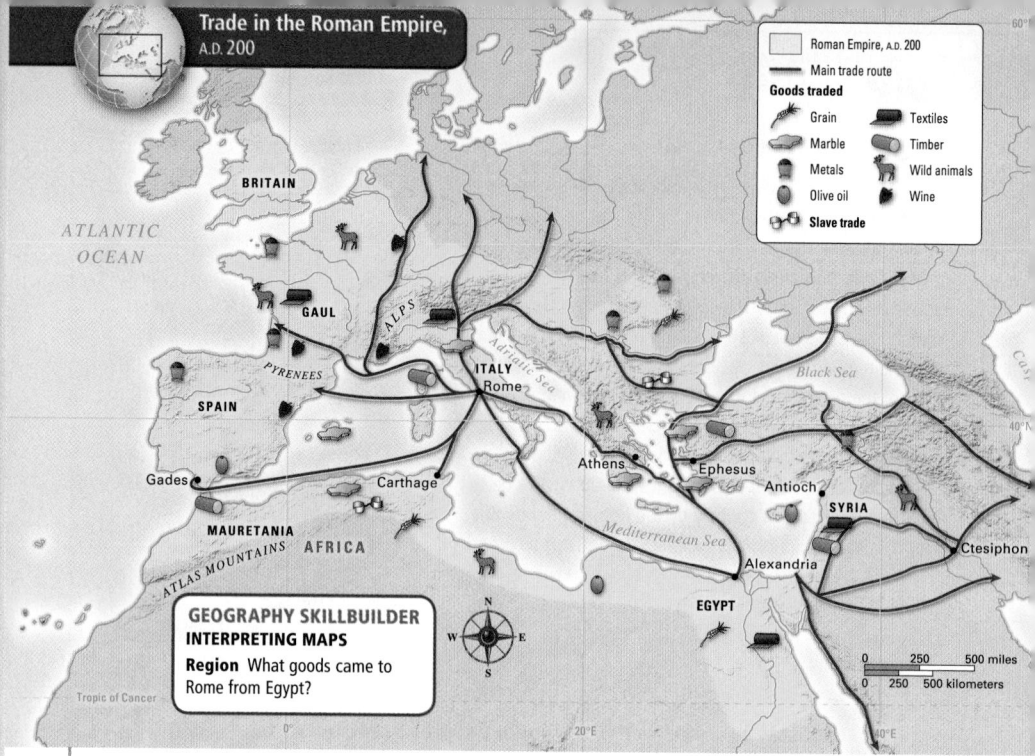

Trade in the Roman Empire, A.D. 200

Roman Empire, A.D. 200
Main trade route
Goods traded
Grain   Textiles
Marble   Timber
Metals   Wild animals
Olive oil   Wine
Slave trade

GEOGRAPHY SKILLBUILDER
INTERPRETING MAPS
Region What goods came to Rome from Egypt?

A Strong Economy The Pax Romana continued long after Augustus died in A.D. 14. Many other emperors ruled after Augustus. Some were good rulers, while others were not. But the government begun under Augustus was so effective that the empire continued to do well.

Agriculture and Trade Agriculture and trade helped the empire prosper. Farming remained the basis of the Roman economy, but industry also grew. The manufacture of pottery, metal goods, and glass increased. So did the production of wine, olive oil, and other food products.

The empire fostered economic growth through the use of trade routes. Traders sailed across the Mediterranean Sea to Spain, Africa, and western Asia. They also traveled by land to Gaul and other parts of Europe. Through trade, Rome acquired valuable goods not available at home. Traders brought back grain, ivory, silk, spices, gold and silver, and even wild animals. Much of this trade relied on the quality of Roman roads. It also relied on the security provided by the Roman military.

INTERDISCIPLINARY ACTIVITIES

Math

Find the Value of a Denarius

Have students use the Internet and other reference sources to find out how much money a moderately successful Roman farmer might have earned in A.D. 14. Ask students to calculate the annual income in terms of present-day dollars. How much could a denarius buy compared with a dollar?

Science

Diagram Olive Oil Production

Have students create a diagram that shows the steps in the production of olive oil for trade. The diagram should answer questions such as the following: What conditions are needed to grow olives? How is oil obtained from the olives? How is it stored and shipped?

Currency The Roman economy was also united by a common currency, or money. In Augustus' time, a silver coin called a denarius (dih•NAHR•ee•uhs) was used throughout the empire. A common form of money made trade between different parts of the empire much easier. Traders could buy and sell without having to change their money into another currency.

Rome's expanding economy largely benefited those who were already wealthy. As a result, the division between rich and poor became deeper. You will learn about this division in Lesson 4.

REVIEW What were the contributions of the first Roman emperor?
Augustus brought peace and stability to the Roman Empire.

Lesson Summary

- The results of Roman expansion produced social conflict and civil war.
- Julius Caesar gained power and became a dictator but was then assassinated.
- The reign of Augustus began a long period of imperial rule and peace in the Roman Empire.

Why It Matters Now . . .

Rome faced the problems of how to maintain peace, law, and order. Modern governments face similar problems.

▲ **Motto** SPQR stands for "the Senate and the people of Rome." This was the motto of the Roman Empire.

3 Lesson Review

 Homework Helper ClassZone.com

Terms & Names

1. Explain the importance of

civil war	Cicero	Pax Romana
Julius Caesar	Augustus	

Using Your Notes

Constructing Time Lines Use your completed time line to answer the following question:

2. How long did Julius Caesar serve as dictator for life? (CST 2)

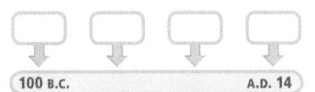

100 B.C.   A.D. 14

Main Ideas

3. How did expansion threaten the Roman Republic? (6.7.3, 7.1.2)
4. How did Caesar gain power? (6.7.1, 6.7.4)
5. How did Roman government change under Augustus? (6.7.4)

Critical Thinking

6. **Summarizing** What events and circumstances brought the Roman Republic to an end? (6.7.3)
7. **Understanding Cause and Effect** What factors encouraged economic growth during the Pax Romana? (6.7.4)

Activity

Making a Map Add Rome to the world map that you have been working on throughout this book. Outline and label the Roman Empire at its height in A.D. 117. (7.1.2)

❹ Assess & Reteach

Assess Have students form groups of four. Have each group work together to answer questions 3, 4, and 5 of the Lesson Review. Discuss the answers with the class.

 Formal Assessment
- Lesson Quiz, p. 229

Reteach Divide students into small groups. Read aloud each subheading in the lesson and ask students to give a main idea or detail related to the subheading. If students are uncertain about key terms in the lesson, have them quiz one another, using the Vocabulary Cards.

 **In-Depth Resources: Unit 6**
- Vocabulary Cards, p. 11
- Reteaching Activity, p. 19

Homework Helper

Visit **ClassZone.com** for a lesson review, a flip-card activity, and links to related Web sites.

3 Lesson Review Answers

Terms & Names

1. • civil war, p. 444
   • Julius Caesar, p. 444
   • Cicero, p. 445
   • Augustus, p. 446
   • Pax Romana, p. 447

Using Your Notes

See page 442 for an example of a completed time line.

2. for just a few months

Main Ideas

3. Wealth from expansion widened the gap between rich and poor, provoking unrest.
4. He became a great general and leader. He used his army to gain power.
5. Augustus became an emperor and the supreme ruler.

Critical Thinking

6. Possible answers: Rome's expansion led to unrest due to the increasing gap between rich and poor. Generals and politicians fought for power. Finally, Julius Caesar took power as dictator.
7. Possible answer: peace and stability, better roads and military security, the development of a vast trade network, and a common currency

Activity Rubric

	Content of Map	Style of Map
4	accurately shows the borders of the Roman Empire	neatly done, correct spelling
3	shows borders, mostly accurate	neatly done, spelling mostly correct
2	borders shown inaccurately	acceptable, some labels misspelled or missing
1	borders missing	sloppy, labels missing

Objectives

- Understand and describe the role of the military in the Roman Empire.
- Analyze and interpret information in an infographic.
- **Language Objective:** Write a journal entry to describe life in a Roman fort.

❶ Focus & Motivate

Preview Discuss what students know about army life today. Explain that on these pages they will learn what life was like for soldiers in the Roman army.

❷ Teach

Talk About It

- Why did soldiers carry shields? *(to protect themselves from enemy arrows and spears)*
- Why might the commander be reading or writing in the wax tablet? *(Possible answer: might be reading the day's schedule or recording the day's events)*
- **Critical Thinking: Drawing Conclusions** What might have motivated Roman citizens and conquered peoples to join the army as common soldiers? *(Possible answers: a desire for continued employment; a hope of rising through the ranks to a position of power; a desire to become a Roman citizen)*

Humanities Transparencies
- HT25 Roman Soldiers

Map Transparencies
- MT26 Roman Britain

Life in a Roman Fort

Purpose: To learn about the daily life of a soldier in a Roman fort

The Romans built permanent forts on the frontiers of the empire. These forts helped Rome both defend and expand its empire. Some of the forts, like the one shown here, were located in Britain. Officers called centurions commanded the forts and the ordinary soldiers. Many Roman citizens joined the army but had to sign on for 25 years of service. Conquered peoples were also invited to join. They became Roman citizens when their service ended.

Each fort housed officers and about 500 soldiers. When they weren't on patrol, the soldiers spent much of their time in and around their barracks. Eighty men and one centurion lived in each barracks.

Ⓐ **Uniform and Equipment** A soldier guarding the fort wore a wool tunic, protective chain mail, an iron helmet, and leather sandals. He carried a spear, a sword, and a shield with his unit's emblem.

Ⓑ **Centurion's Rooms** A commander had several rooms to himself. Like all centurions, he wore a helmet with a crest that helped his soldiers identify him during a battle.

Ⓒ **Mess Rooms** Eight men shared a pair of mess rooms. This is where they slept, cooked, and ate.

Ⓓ **Free Time** The soldiers didn't have much free time, but when they did, they sometimes played games. Board games were popular pastimes.

Ⓔ **Weapons** Soldiers defended the fort by throwing spears or shooting arrows at the enemy. Sometimes they also used this machine, called a ballista. It could throw steel-tipped arrows about 300 to 400 yards.

CALIFORNIA STANDARDS
6.7.3 Identify the location of and the political and geographic reasons for the growth of Roman territories and expansion of the empire, including how the empire fostered economic growth through the use of currency and trade routes.

DIFFERENTIATING INSTRUCTION

English Learners

Write a Journal Entry
Help students complete the writing activity on page 451, in which they describe a typical day at the fort. Say, "Imagine that you are a Roman soldier. What do you like about being a soldier at the fort? What do you dislike about being a soldier at the fort?" Have students share and brainstorm with classmates. For more support, see *Modified Lesson Plans for English Learners,* p. 95.

Struggling Readers

Summarize
Read aloud the description of each inset as students examine it. Then ask students to describe, in their own words, what is happening in the illustration.

Roman Forts

A Roman fort was usually rectangular. There were two main streets, intersecting at right angles to divide the fort into quarters. At the center of the fort, where the two streets met, was the administration center. Soldiers' barracks were usually placed near the perimeter of the fort. Other buildings within the fort included stables and granaries. The fort was usually surrounded by a wall and a ditch.

Activities

1. **TALK ABOUT IT** What words would you use to describe the life of a Roman soldier?

2. **WRITE ABOUT IT** Imagine you are a Roman soldier and write a diary entry describing a typical day. (Writing 2.2)

The Rise of Rome • 451

ACTIVITIES ANSWERS

1. **TALK ABOUT IT** Possible answers: rough, dangerous, busy, boring

2. **WRITE ABOUT IT**

2. Writing Rubric

	Level of Knowledge	Style of Language	Errors in Mechanics
4	shows thorough understanding of life in a Roman fort	vivid	few or none
3	shows good understanding	descriptive	some
2	shows basic understanding	somewhat descriptive	many
1	shows little or no understanding	vague	many major

❶ Plan & Prepare

Objectives

- Understand how Roman families and society were organized.
- Trace the influences of other cultures on Roman religious beliefs.
- Describe what life was like in Roman cities.
- **Language Objective:** Form and support opinions about the advantages and disadvantages of living in Roman cities.

Quick Look

Lesson 4 looks at everyday life in ancient Rome.

❷ Focus & Motivate

Preview Ask students to predict how family roles changed during the Roman Empire. Have them write down their predictions and revisit them at the end of the lesson.

Introduce the Main Ideas The main ideas in this lesson are related to the Big Idea that many societies rely on family roles and social classes to keep order.

Reading Skill: Summarizing Remind students that main ideas are not always stated.

SAMPLE ANSWERS FOR GRAPHIC ORGANIZER

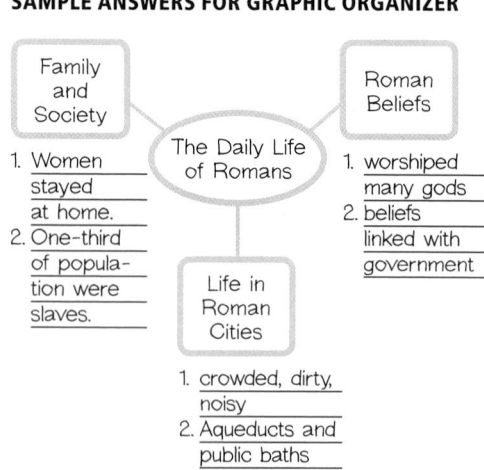

► MAIN IDEAS

❶ **Culture** Roles in Roman family life and society were clearly defined.

❷ **Belief Systems** Roman religious beliefs were influenced by other cultures and linked with government.

❸ **Culture** Although they were overcrowded and dirty, Roman cities were also places of interesting innovations and entertainments.

► TAKING NOTES

Reading Skill: Summarizing

When you summarize, you supply only main ideas and the most important details. Record the main ideas and important details in each section of Lesson 4 in a diagram like the one below.

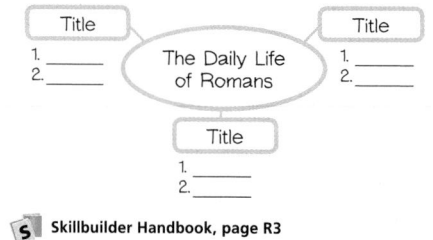

📄 **Skillbuilder Handbook, page R3**

▲ **Household Mosaic** This mosaic was set in front of a house in Pompeii, an ancient Roman city. The words at the bottom of the mosaic tell visitors to "beware of dog."

CALIFORNIA STANDARDS

Framework Students should learn about everyday life in Roman society, including slavery, social conflict, and the rule of Roman law.

6.7 Students analyze the geographic, political, economic, religious, and social structures during the development of Rome.

6.7.8 Discuss the legacies of Roman art and architecture, technology and science, literature, language, and law.

7.1.1 Study the early strengths and lasting contributions of Rome (e.g., significance of Roman citizenship; rights under Roman law; Roman art, architecture, engineering,

and philosophy; preservation and transmission of Christianity) and its ultimate internal weakness (e.g., rise of autonomous military powers within the empire, undermining of citizenship by the growth of corruption and slavery, lack of education, and distribution of news).

HOW TO TEACH THE CALIFORNIA STANDARDS

Standard	Content	Student Question or Activity	Instruction
6.7	**Pages 453–454** Describes the organization of Roman families and society **Page 455** Describes religious influences in Roman public life	**Page 458** Students list who belonged to the main Roman social classes, what the relationship of religion to government was in Rome, and what the city of Rome was like.	Ask students to discuss how family life in Rome was different from family life in the United States today.
6.7.8	**Page 457** Describes how Romans used technology to build aqueducts, bridges, and public baths	**Page 458** Students list architectural innovations that improved Roman city life.	Ask students to imagine what life would be like today if we had no running water and no bridges.
7.1.1	**Page 456** Describes the effects of blending ideas and customs	**Page 458** Students explain how Rome's urban problems affected the development of later cities.	Discuss what later civilizations learned from the problems Rome encountered and from the ways Rome attempted to solve the problems.

The Daily Life of Romans

Terms & Names

aqueduct a channel or pipe that carries water from a spring, stream, or lake into towns

Colosseum a large arena in Rome

gladiator a trained warrior who engaged in combat to the death to entertain the public

Build on What You Know Remember that, in the earliest days of Rome, extended families lived and worked on small farms. Family members knew what was expected of them. During the Roman Empire, family roles became more structured—and so did roles in society.

Family and Society

① ESSENTIAL QUESTION How were the family and society organized?
father was head of family; society consisted of upper, middle, and lower classes

The head of the Roman family was the father. He owned all the property and had control over other members of the household. The father's power was limited, however, by public opinion and custom. Roman society disapproved of a father punishing his family without good cause.

Women Women in a Roman family enjoyed more freedom than women in Greece. Like women in most parts of the world, Roman women were expected to run the household and take care of the children. But they also could inherit property, and they ran the family business when their husbands were away. Still, Roman women had little power outside the home and could not vote.

Emperor's Villa While most Romans lived in poor conditions, the emperors lived in luxury. A large number of slaves took care of this emperor's villa. ▼

453

❸ Teach

Family and Society
6.7

Talk About It

• **Critical Thinking: Forming and Supporting Opinions** What was the most unfair aspect of the Roman class system? Explain your answer. *(Possible answer: slavery, because slaves did all of the hard work and many were treated badly)*

California Resources

California Reading Toolkit, L47
California Modified Lesson Plans for English Learners, p. 97
California Daily Standards Practice Transparencies, TT47
California Standards Enrichment Workbook, pp. 109–112
California Online Test Practice
California Test Generator CD-ROM
California Standards Planner and Lesson Plans, L93
California EasyPlanner CD-ROM
California eEdition CD-ROM

LESSON 4 PROGRAM RESOURCES

ON LEVEL

In-Depth Resources: Unit 6
• Reading Skill: Summarizing, p. 6
• Vocabulary Cards, p. 11

Formal Assessment
• Lesson Quiz, p. 230

ENGLISH LEARNERS

In-Depth Resources in Spanish
• Reading Skill: Summarizing, p. 114

Modified Lesson Plans for English Learners, p. 97

Reading Study Guide (Spanish), p. 121

Reading Study Guide Audio CD (Spanish)

STRUGGLING READERS

In-Depth Resources: Unit 6
• Reading Skill: Summarizing, p. 6
• Vocabulary Cards, p. 11
• Reteaching Activity, p. 20

Reading Toolkit, L47

Reading Study Guide, p. 121

Reading Study Guide Audio CD

GIFTED AND TALENTED STUDENTS

Humanities Transparencies
• HT26 Roman Aqueduct

Interdisciplinary Projects
• Science, p. 74

INCLUSION

EasyPlanner CD-ROM
• Reading Skill: Summarizing
• Reteaching Activity

TECHNOLOGY

eEdition CD-ROM

Power Presentations CD-ROM

Critical Thinking Transparencies
• CT59 Summarizing
• CT60 Chapter 13 Visual Summary

ClassZone.com

In-Depth Resources: Unit 6
• Reading Skill: Summarizing, p. 6

More About . . .

Roman Women

Upper-class girls learned to read and write, but they usually did not receive much further education in the liberal arts. Even so, some aristocratic women became accomplished writers, artists, or musicians.

There is not much information about lower-class women, but archaeological finds indicate that they worked as waitresses, nurses, weavers, midwives, and food sellers. In Roman society, boys were valued more highly than girls. In poor families, infant girls were sometimes abandoned, because when a girl married, her family was expected to pay a dowry, or gift to the husband's family. Many women died in childbirth. The life expectancy for Roman women was 34 years, as opposed to 46 years for men.

Teach

Roman Beliefs

6.7

Talk About It

• What beliefs did the Romans borrow from the Etruscans? *(the belief that gods had human forms and the belief in rituals designed to predict the future)*

• How did Greek religion influence Roman religion? *(The Romans borrowed many of the Greek gods and gave them different names.)*

• **Critical Thinking: Making Inferences** How did the link between religion and government help to shape Roman society? *(Possible answer: It made people respect the emperor more, made them more willing to obey him, and made them less likely to question the emperor's decisions.)*

Children Most parents gave their children some education at home. Boys from wealthy families were often sent to private schools, while daughters stayed at home and learned household skills. Girls usually married by age 14, while boys married later.

Social Classes Over time, Roman social classes changed. The old division between patricians and plebeians evolved into upper and lower classes. Patricians and some wealthy plebeians became part of the upper class. A new middle class also developed. Prosperous business leaders and officials belonged to this middle class. Farmers formed one of the lower classes

Slaves made up the lowest—and largest—class in society. Up to one-third of the population were slaves. Some were prisoners of war. Others became slaves because their parents were slaves. Slaves were found throughout Roman society. They worked in low-level clerical positions. However, slaves also performed all jobs requiring physical labor. They worked in mines, on large estates, and as servants. Many suffered cruel treatment. Slave revolts were common, but none of them succeeded. Thousands of slaves died in these revolts.

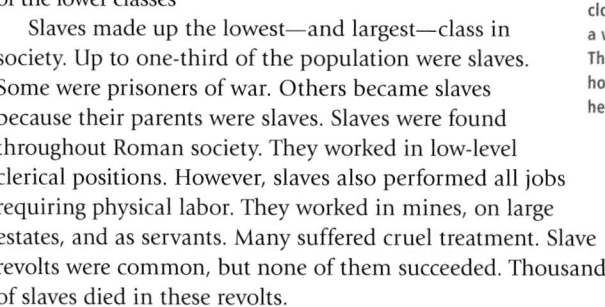

▲ **Upper-Class Woman** The young woman in this wall painting wears the clothes and hairstyle of a wealthy Roman citizen. The book and pen she holds are also signs of her class and education.

REVIEW What were the roles in a typical Roman family?
The father was the head of the family; his wife ran the household; the children received some education, but boys could receive more.

Roman Beliefs

 ESSENTIAL QUESTION What religious beliefs did the Romans hold?
worshiped hundreds of spirits and household gods; borrowed Etruscan rituals and Greek gods
Religious beliefs bound Roman society together. From the earliest times, the Romans worshiped hundreds of spirits. They believed that these spirits lived in everything around them, including rivers, woods, and fields. Roman families also believed that household gods protected them. They set up shrines in their homes to honor these spirits.

DIFFERENTIATING INSTRUCTION

Inclusion

Practice Remembering
Point out the heading "Social Classes" and have students read the text that follows it. Ask them to close their books and and tell you everything they remember. Write answers on the board, leaving space under each.

When students run out of ideas, ask them to open their books and verify their answers. Have students copy the corrected information into their notebooks.

Struggling Readers

Preread Text
Have volunteers read aloud the lesson title, section titles, and other headings. As each is read, ask students what they think it means. Then ask them to predict what they will read about after it. Challenge students to explain how the headings in each section are related to the section's Essential Question.

Religious Influences Later, Roman beliefs were influenced by other cultures. The Etruscans and Greeks particularly affected Roman religion. The Romans adopted the Etruscan idea of gods in human form. They also adopted Etruscan rituals designed to predict the future. The Romans believed these rituals could reveal whether a specific action, such as a battle, would have a good result.

The Romans borrowed many of their gods from the Greeks. For instance, the Roman god Jupiter, father of the gods, had many of the characteristics of the Greek god Zeus. Apollo, the Greek god of music and poetry, became a key Roman god of the same name. The chart below lists some of the gods that Rome borrowed from Greece.

Religion and Public Life As in ancient Egypt, religion and government were linked in Rome. Priests were government officials, and the emperor was the head of the church. Roman gods were also symbols of the state. Romans were expected to honor these gods in public ceremonies.

Over time, even the emperor himself became a god. At first, the Romans only worshiped emperors after death. But eventually they honored living rulers as gods. Loyalty to the emperor became the same as loyalty to the gods.

REVIEW What influences helped form Roman religion?
rituals and ideas from the Etruscans and Greeks

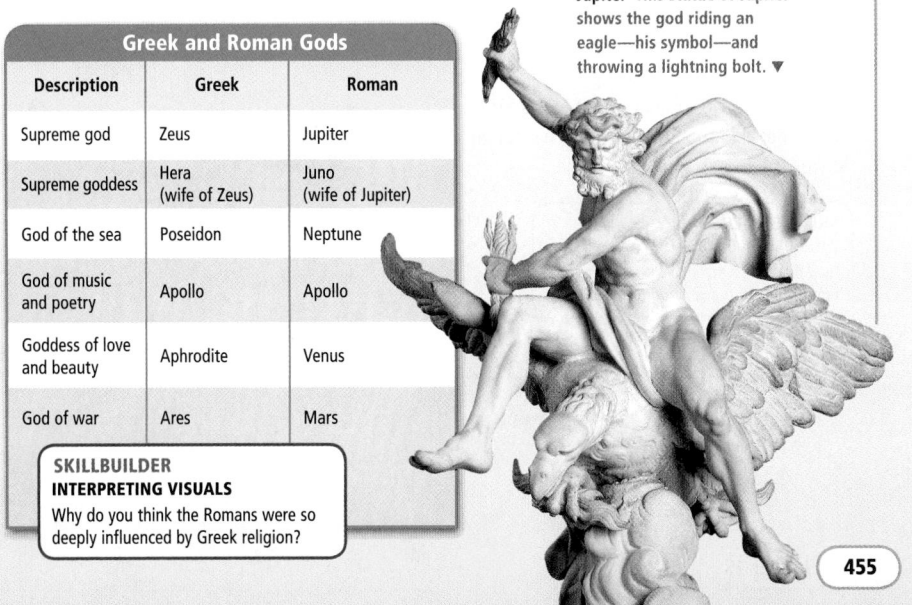

Jupiter This statue of Jupiter shows the god riding an eagle—his symbol—and throwing a lightning bolt. ▼

Greek and Roman Gods

Description	Greek	Roman
Supreme god	Zeus	Jupiter
Supreme goddess	Hera (wife of Zeus)	Juno (wife of Jupiter)
God of the sea	Poseidon	Neptune
God of music and poetry	Apollo	Apollo
Goddess of love and beauty	Aphrodite	Venus
God of war	Ares	Mars

SKILLBUILDER
INTERPRETING VISUALS
Why do you think the Romans were so deeply influenced by Greek religion?

455

Teach

Life in Roman Cities

6.7.8, 7.1.1

Talk About It

- What were the lives of poor Romans and wealthy Romans like? *(Possible answer: Poor Romans lived in cramped, rundown apartments and had little to eat; wealthy Romans lived in luxury in the countryside and ate a wide variety of unusual foods.)*

- **Critical Thinking: Evaluating Information** Which of the Romans' solutions to urban problems do you think was most effective. Why? *(Possible answers: sewers, plumbing, and aqueducts, because they made life easier and helped clean up unsanitary conditions; public baths, because they helped people relax and socialize; chariot races and gladiator fights, because they gave people an outlet for strong emotions and violence)*

History from Visuals

Interpreting Visuals

- What two things did bathers do before they soaked in the hot room? *(First they took a dip in the water in the cold room; then they went to the warm room, where they scraped off dirt by using oil and a metal tool.)*

SKILLBUILDER ANSWER

They placed the cold room farthest from the furnace.

Life in Roman Cities

3 ESSENTIAL QUESTION What was life like in Roman cities? difficult for poor, luxurious for rich

At the height of the Roman Empire, the city of Rome had nearly 1 million people. Other Roman cities, such as Alexandria in Egypt, were also large. However, Rome was the center of the empire. People from all over the empire moved to Rome. This mix of people produced a lively blend of ideas and customs.

The Crowded City The number of people also created some problems. Rome's city center was crowded, dirty, and noisy. Much of the city's population was unemployed and poor. These people lived in large, rundown apartment buildings. They had small rooms with no running water or toilets. They often dropped their trash out the windows, sometimes injuring people walking in the streets below. Fire was also a constant danger. These problems were common in other Roman cities as well.

Poor Romans also had little to eat. Typical foods were bread, olives, and fruit. But the government provided free grain to keep people happy and avoid public unrest.

Architecture of the Roman Public Bath

Archaeologists have discovered that the typical Roman public bath was built on a foundation of pillars. Roman architects constructed a furnace that opened into the area beneath the bath. When slaves burned wood in the furnace, hot air flowed around the pillars. This hot air heated the rooms and water above.

SKILLBUILDER
INTERPRETING VISUALS
How did Roman architects make sure the temperature in the cold room stayed low?

Heat from the furnace was channeled beneath the bath house.

furnace

INTERDISCIPLINARY ACTIVITIES

Science

Be a Health Inspector
Have students research the sanitation problems of cities in the Roman Empire. Ask them to list conditions and practices that were particularly dangerous or unhealthy. Have students investigate diseases prevalent at the time that might have been prevented by enacting and enforcing health codes.

Science

Make an Aqueduct
Ask students to use the Internet and other research sources to find out how the Romans built aqueducts. Have small groups build models of aqueducts.

By contrast, wealthy Romans enjoyed a life of luxury. They lived in large, comfortable homes in the countryside. They spent their time going to the theater and enjoying themselves. They also held fancy dinner parties. These meals featured fine foods like dates, oysters, and ham. They also included unusual dishes like salted jellyfish, roast parrot, and boiled flamingo tongue.

Structures of City Life The Romans came up with a number of practical solutions to some of their urban problems. They built sewer and plumbing systems to improve sanitation. They also built **aqueducts** (AK•wih•DUHKTS) to carry fresh water from springs, streams, and lakes into towns. The water traveled through a system of channels and pipes. Most of these were underground. However, some were supported on high arched bridges. Many of these aqueduct bridges survive and are still used today.

Public baths were another important part of city life. Most towns and even most Roman forts had public bathhouses. Romans of all classes visited the baths to bathe and socialize. You can learn more about the architecture and technology of a typical Roman public bathhouse in the feature below.

cold room

Bathers usually began with a dip in the icy water in the cold room.

warm room

In the comfort of the warm room, bathers used oil and a metal tool to scrape off dirt.

hot room

The steamy hot room was nearest to the furnace. Here, bathers soaked after getting clean.

DIFFERENTIATING INSTRUCTION

Inclusion

Learn About Public Baths
Provide students with photos and information and then have them write questions and answers about Roman public baths. Have each student pair make a tape recording in which one partner asks the questions and the other partner answers them.

Gifted and Talented Students

Research Bathing Through History
Tell students that during the Middle Ages the Roman Catholic Church actually discouraged bathing. Ask students to research and compare bathing practices and bathhouses in different parts of the world throughout history. Have students report their findings to the rest of the class.

Vocabulary Strategy

Root Word
Ask students to fill in the blank in the following sentence with a word that contains the root of *colossus:*

The reformers made a _____ mistake when they threatened the landowners. *(colossal)*

Invite students to suggest synonyms of *colossal. (enormous, huge, gigantic)*

❹ Assess & Reteach

Assess Ask volunteers to answer question 1 of the Lesson Review. Have students write answers to questions 3 through 5. Then have pairs trade papers and check answers. Lead students in a class discussion of questions 2, 6, and 7.

 Formal Assessment
• Lesson Quiz, p. 230

Reteach Divide the class into small groups and have each group identify key terms in a section of the lesson. Have groups exchange key terms and use the terms in main-idea sentences.

 In-Depth Resources: Unit 6
• Vocabulary Cards, p. 11
• Reteaching Activity, p. 20

Homework Helper
Visit **ClassZone.com** for a lesson review, a flip-card activity, and links to related Web sites.

Roman Sports To distract Romans from the problems of city life, the government provided entertainment at large public arenas. One of these was the Circus Maximus (MAK•suh•muhs), a large oval stadium used for chariot races. As you learned on pages 424–425, another famous arena was the **Colosseum**. There, Romans could watch **gladiators**, or trained warriors, fight to the death. The spectacles they watched combined bravery and violence, honor and cruelty.

REVIEW How did the Roman government try to solve some of the problems of city life? provided free grain; built sanitation systems and aqueducts; provided entertainment

Vocabulary Strategy

Colosseum comes from the Latin **root word** *colossus,* meaning "huge statue." The Colosseum was, in fact, named for a huge statue of an emperor that once stood beside the arena.

Lesson Summary
• Family life and social classes were important in ancient Rome.
• Romans worshiped many gods both privately at home and in public ceremonies.
• Roman city life was challenging, but the government tried to ease some of its problems.

Why It Matters Now . . .
Ancient Rome was a mixture of different cultures and beliefs, just like many modern societies.

4 Lesson Review

Homework Helper
ClassZone.com

Terms & Names
1. Explain the importance of
   aqueduct   Colosseum   gladiator

Using Your Notes
Summarizing Use your completed diagram to answer the following question:
2. What architectural innovations improved Roman city life? (6.7.8, 7.1.1)

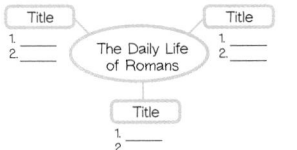

Title
1.
2.

The Daily Life of Romans

Title
1.
2.

Title
1.
2.

Main Ideas
3. Who belonged to the main social classes during the time of the Roman Empire? (6.7)
4. What was the relationship of religion to government in ancient Rome? (6.7)
5. What was the city of Rome like? (6.7)

Critical Thinking
6. **Forming and Supporting Opinions** How would worshiping the emperor while he lived affect the Romans' view of their ruler? (6.7)
7. **Understanding Continuity and Change** How did Rome's urban problems affect the development of cities in later civilizations? (6.7.8, 7.1.1)

Activity **Internet Activity** Use the Internet to find out more about how aqueduct bridges worked. Then draw a diagram that illustrates how these bridges carried water to Roman cities. (6.7.8)
INTERNET KEYWORD *Roman aqueduct*

458 • Chapter 13

---

4 Lesson Review Answers

Terms & Names
1. • aqueduct, p. 457
   • Colosseum, p. 458
   • gladiator, p. 458

Using Your Notes
See page 452 for an example of a completed graphic organizer.
2. sanitation facilities, aqueducts, public baths

Main Ideas
3. Patricians and wealthy plebeians belonged to the upper class; prosperous business leaders and officials belonged to the middle class; farmers and slaves made up two of the lower classes.
4. They were joined. Priests were officials, and the emperor was the religious leader. He was even considered a god.
5. It was large, crowded, dirty, and noisy. It had many problems but was also an interesting place.

Critical Thinking
6. Possible answer: Most Romans would accept what the emperor said without question.
7. The Romans built aqueducts and sanitation systems to address some of their problems. Later civilizations adopted and further developed these innovations.

Activity Rubric

	Content of Diagram	Quality of Illustration	Number of Errors
4	shows thorough understanding	clear, detailed, easy to follow	few or none
3	shows good understanding	neat, detailed, fairly easy to follow	some
2	shows basic understanding	lacking some details	many
1	shows little or no understanding	details incorrect or missing, sloppy	many major

Make a Mosaic

Goal: To create a mosaic, a picture made of small colored tiles, that celebrates the legacy of Roman art

Materials & Supplies
- paper and pencil
- poster board
- paint and paintbrush
- scissors
- glue or paste

Prepare

1. Study the mosaic on page 452.
2. Look at Roman mosaics in books on ancient Rome.

Do the Activity

1. Draw a sketch of your design on a piece of paper. You might draw a simple geometric design or an animal or a flower.
2. Copy the design onto a piece of poster board.
3. Paint several pieces of paper in different colors. After the paint dries, cut the paper into small pieces. These will be your mosaic tiles.
4. Glue your tiles onto the design on your poster board. Use your pencil sketch as a guide. Let your mosaic dry.

Follow-Up

1. Do you think that Roman artists who created mosaics also had to be skilled mathematicians? Explain.
2. What modern mosaics have you seen? How do these compare with the one you made?

Extension

Making Inferences What do the mosaics you have seen in this lesson and in books on ancient Rome suggest about how Romans valued beauty?

CALIFORNIA STANDARDS
6.7.8 Discuss the legacies of Roman art and architecture, technology and science, literature, language, and law.

459

ACTIVITY: MAKE A MOSAIC

Objectives
- Explore the legacy of Roman art.
- Create a mosaic picture.

Suggestions for Completing the Activity

- If students cannot think of designs, suggest that they get ideas from coloring books or from clip art that they can find on the Internet.
- After students draw their designs, they can color the designs to help them determine the colors they will need for their mosaic tiles.

ACTIVITY ANSWERS

Follow-Up Answers
1. Possible answer: yes, because the artists had to carefully plan and measure the figures in their mosaics to get the correct proportions
2. Students will probably say that the modern mosaics they have seen are much more complicated and abstract.

Extension Answer
Students will probably note that Romans greatly valued beauty in their everyday lives.

Activity Rubric

	Design of Mosaic	Presentation
4	well-proportioned	very neat
3	fairly well-proportioned	fairly neat
2	proportions are basically all right	not very neat
1	proportions are wrong	sloppy

Terms & Names

1. Patricians and plebeians were the two main social classes of early Rome.

2. The Senate was a powerful body of Rome's legislative branch. Two consuls led the executive branch.

3. Julius Caesar and Augustus were two great Roman leaders. Caesar was the last ruler of the Roman Republic, and Augustus was the first ruler of the Roman Empire.

4. Gladiators fought in the Colosseum.

Main Ideas

The Geography of Ancient Rome
(pages 430–435)

5. It was in the center of Italy, just inland from the sea, on the Tiber River. It was set on seven steep hills, with plains around it.

6. These behaviors helped Rome build a strong and disciplined army and made citizens disposed to obey their leaders.

The Roman Republic
(pages 436–441)

7. Two consuls commanded the army and directed the government; they could appoint a dictator in time of crisis.

8. The patricians gained more wealth and bought large estates. The plebeians could not compete and lost their farms.

Rome Becomes an Empire
(pages 442–451)

9. expanded the Senate, enforced laws against crime, created jobs, became dictator for life

10. built up a strong army and navy; constructed roads, bridges, and tunnels; expanded trade; developed a single currency

The Daily Life of Romans
(pages 452–459)

11. The rich lived in large homes, ate well, and went to the theater. The poor lived in crowded, dangerous conditions.

12. aqueducts, bathhouses, Colosseum

► **VISUAL SUMMARY**

The Rise of Rome

Geography (6.7.1)
- Hills and the Tiber River helped protect Rome from enemies.
- Rome's location in Italy made it easier to reach and conquer other lands.

Culture (6.7, 6.7.8)
- Roman family life and society were highly structured.
- Romans built aqueducts and sanitation systems to ease the problems of city life.

Government (6.7.2, 7.7.1)
- The Roman Republic had a government divided into three parts.
- Roman government influenced modern republics.

Economics (6.7.3)
- A vigorous trade developed in the Roman Empire.
- A common currency united the empire.

Belief Systems (6.7)
- Romans worshiped many gods.
- Roman religion was linked with government.

► **TERMS & NAMES**

Explain why the words in each set below are linked with each other.

1. **patrician** and **plebeian**
2. **Senate** and **consul**
3. **Julius Caesar** and **Augustus**
4. **gladiator** and **Colosseum**

► **MAIN IDEAS**

The Geography of Ancient Rome (pages 430–435)
5. Describe the geography of Rome. (6.7.3)
6. How did hard work and discipline help Roman civilization grow? (6.7.1)

The Roman Republic (pages 436–441)
7. What powers did the executive branch have in the Roman Republic? (6.7.2, 7.7.1)
8. Why did the gap between patricians and plebeians widen with Rome's expansion? (6.7.1)

Rome Becomes an Empire (pages 442–451)
9. What did Julius Caesar accomplish as ruler of the Roman Republic? (6.7.1, 6.7.4)
10. How did Augustus encourage the expansion of the Roman Empire? (6.7.3, 6.7.4)

The Daily Life of Romans (pages 452–459)
11. How did life differ for the rich and poor in Roman cities? (6.7)
12. What structures in Roman cities have influenced modern structures? (6.7.8)

► **CRITICAL THINKING** Big Ideas: Economics

13. **EXPLAINING HISTORICAL PATTERNS** How did the advantages gained by some early farmers affect Rome's development? (6.7.1)
14. **ANALYZING ECONOMIC AND POLITICAL ISSUES** How did class divisions bring about the end of the Roman Republic? (6.7.2)
15. **IDENTIFYING ISSUES AND PROBLEMS** What steps did the empire take to avoid another civil war between rich and poor? (6.7)

ALTERNATIVE ASSESSMENT RUBRICS

1. Writing Rubric

	Accuracy of Description	Errors in Mechanics
4	thoughtful and detailed	few or none
3	detailed	some
2	shows some knowledge	many
1	unclear	many major

2. Civics Rubric

	Use of Visuals	Understanding of Content
4	extensive and creative	thorough
3	good	adequate
2	acceptable	vague
1	incorrect or missing	poor

ALTERNATIVE ASSESSMENT

1. WRITING ACTIVITY Imagine that you are a plebeian in the Roman Empire. Write a journal entry about a day in your life. Describe where and how you live. Tell what you see and do on an ordinary day. (Writing 2.2)

2. INTERDISCIPLINARY ACTIVITY—CIVICS Create a poster in which you use photographs and drawings to compare the Roman Republic with the U.S. republic. (6.7.2, 7.7.1)

3. STARTING WITH A STORY

 Review the speech you wrote trying to persuade other senators to let Julius Caesar live. Now that you have read the chapter, decide whether you think Caesar's death was good for Rome. Write a paragraph explaining and supporting your opinion. (Writing 2.5)

Technology Activity

4. RECORDING A NEWS REPORT Work with a group of classmates to prepare a radio news report on the opening of the Colosseum. Use information from the chapter as the basis for your report. Do further research on the Internet, if necessary. Tape the news report and play it for your class. (6.7.8)

• Provide background information on the construction and opening of the Colosseum.

• Interview gladiators and ordinary citizens to get their opinions of the arena and its entertainment.

• Discuss what impact you think the Colosseum will have on public entertainment in the future.

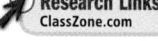
Research Links
ClassZone.com

Interpreting Visuals Use the sculpture below, which shows Roman soldiers fighting from on top of their fort, to answer the questions. (6.7.3, 7.1.2)

1. What advantages do the Roman soldiers appear to have in this battle?

A. They are fighting on the ground.
B. They are fighting with bows and arrows.
C. They are fighting more fiercely.
D. They are fighting from inside their fort.

2. Which sentence best describes the Roman soldiers?

A. They all look frightened.
B. They all are on horseback.
C. They all carry shields and wear helmets.
D. They are not ready for battle.

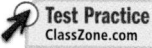
Test Practice
ClassZone.com

Additional Test Practice, pp. S1–S33

Critical Thinking

Big Ideas: Economics

13. Some farmers grew richer than others and bought large estates. In time, they gained power. Their descendants would become the patricians of Roman society, whose power the plebeians would come to resent.

14. Poor plebeians clashed with rich patricians over their desire for more rights and a better life. These struggles brought some changes to the republic. However, the conflict continued, and reformers again demanded change. Eventually this struggle led to civil war and the end of the republic.

15. The government used free grain and entertainment to limit unrest.

Standards-Based Assessment

1. The correct answer is D. A is incorrect because they are not on the ground, B is incorrect because the enemy is fighting with bows and arrows and C is incorrect because the image cannot convey degrees of fierceness.

2. The correct answer is C. The other statements are not supported by the image.

 Research Links

Visit **ClassZone.com** for links to Web sites that can be used in the multimedia presentation.

 Test Practice

Visit **ClassZone.com** to access strategies and tutorials for taking standardized tests.

Formal Assessment
• Chapter Tests, Forms A, B, and C, pp. 231–245

Test Generator
• Chapter Tests, Forms A, B, and C (English and Spanish)

ALTERNATIVE ASSESSMENT RUBRICS

3. Starting with a Story Rubric

	Clarity of Explanation
4	thorough, includes extensive information from the chapter
3	thoughtful, includes some information from the chapter
2	vague, includes little information from the chapter
1	illogical or unclear

4. Technology Rubric

	Report	Presentation
4	well organized, thoroughly researched	clear
3	detailed, shows some research	fairly clear
2	somewhat disorganized, shows little research	vague
1	disorganized, shows little research	unclear

CHAPTER 14 PLANNING GUIDE: The Birth of Christianity

Chapter Overview	Copymasters	Assessment

Chapter Overview

Christianity began within the Jewish religion and eventually spread to Rome, where Catholicism was born.

Copymasters

 In-Depth Resources: Unit 6
- Family Newsletter (English and Spanish), pp. 21–22
- Visual Summary, p. 26
- Vocabulary Study Guide, p. 28

 Character Education

Reading Study Guide, p. 131

 Bringing Social Studies Alive, Chapter 14

 Document-Based Questions: Strategy and Practice

 Reading Toolkit, L48–L50

 Modified Lesson Plans for English Learners, pp. 99–104

Assessment

 Chapter Review, pp. 488–489

 Formal Assessment
- Chapter Tests, Forms A, B, and C, pp. 249–260

 Test Generator

 Integrated Assessment Book

 Online Test Practice

LESSON 1

The Origins of Christianity

pp. 466–475

OBJECTIVE Trace the beginnings of Christianity and the life and death of Jesus.

 In-Depth Resources: Unit 6
- Reading Skill: Explaining Sequence, p. 23
- Vocabulary Cards, p. 29
- Literature: The Gospel of John, p. 34
- Reteaching Activity, p. 35

 History Makers
- Jesus, p. 27

 Interdisciplinary Projects
- Language Arts, p. 81

 Reading Study Guide, p. 125

 Lesson Review, p. 471

Formal Assessment
- Lesson Quiz, p. 246

 California Daily Standards Practice Transparencies, TT48

LESSON 2

The Early Christians

pp. 476–481

OBJECTIVE Analyze the actions of the first Christians and the spread of Christianity.

 In-Depth Resources: Unit 6
- Reading Skill: Comparing and Contrasting, p. 24
- Vocabulary Cards, p. 29
- Skillbuilder Practice: Understanding Continuity and Change, p. 27
- Geography Practice: Paul's Journeys, p. 31
- Primary Source: Letter to the Romans, by Paul, p. 33
- Reteaching Activity, p. 36

 Interdisciplinary Projects
- Science, p. 80

 Reading Study Guide, p. 127

 Lesson Review, p. 481

 Formal Assessment
- Lesson Quiz, p. 247

California Daily Standards Practice Transparencies, TT49

LESSON 3

Rome and Christianity

pp. 482–487

OBJECTIVE Study the reaction of Rome to Christianity and the beginnings of the Roman Catholic Church.

 In-Depth Resources: Unit 6
- Reading Skill: Finding Main Ideas, p. 25
- Vocabulary Cards, p. 29
- Reteaching Activity, p. 37

 Interdisciplinary Projects
- Math, p. 79; Art, p. 82

 Reading Study Guide, p. 129

 Lesson Review, p. 486

 Formal Assessment
- Lesson Quiz, p. 248

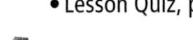 **California Daily Standards Practice Transparencies,** TT50

Integrated Technology

 eEdition Plus Online

EasyPlanner Plus Online

eTest Plus Online

 **Audio CDs**
- Reading Study Guide
- Reading Study Guide in Spanish
- The World's Music

 CD-ROMs
- Power Presentations
- eEdition
- EasyPlanner
- Test Generator

---

 eEdition CD-ROM

 Map Transparencies
- MT27 Jerusalem at the Time of Jesus

 Humanities Transparencies
- HT27 The Sermon on the Mount

 Critical Thinking Transparencies
- CT61 Explaining Sequence

 ClassZone.com

---

 eEdition CD-ROM

 Humanities Transparencies
- HT28 The Conversion of Saul

 Critical Thinking Transparencies
- CT62 Comparing and Contrasting

ClassZone.com

---

 eEdition CD-ROM

 Map Transparencies
- MT28 Christian Communities in the First Century

 Critical Thinking Transparencies
- CT63 Finding Main Ideas
- CT64 Chapter 14 Visual Summary

 ClassZone.com

Overview of California Resources

	Lesson 1	Lesson 2	Lesson 3
California Reading Toolkit	L48	L49	L50
California Modified Lesson Plans for English Learners	p. 99	p. 101	p. 103
California Daily Standards Practice Transparencies	TT48	TT49	TT50
California Standards Enrichment Workbook	pp. 105–106	pp. 105–108	pp. 105–108, 111–112
California Standards Planner and Lesson Plans	L95	L97	L99
California Online Test Practice	ClassZone.com	ClassZone.com	ClassZone.com
California Test Generator CD-ROM	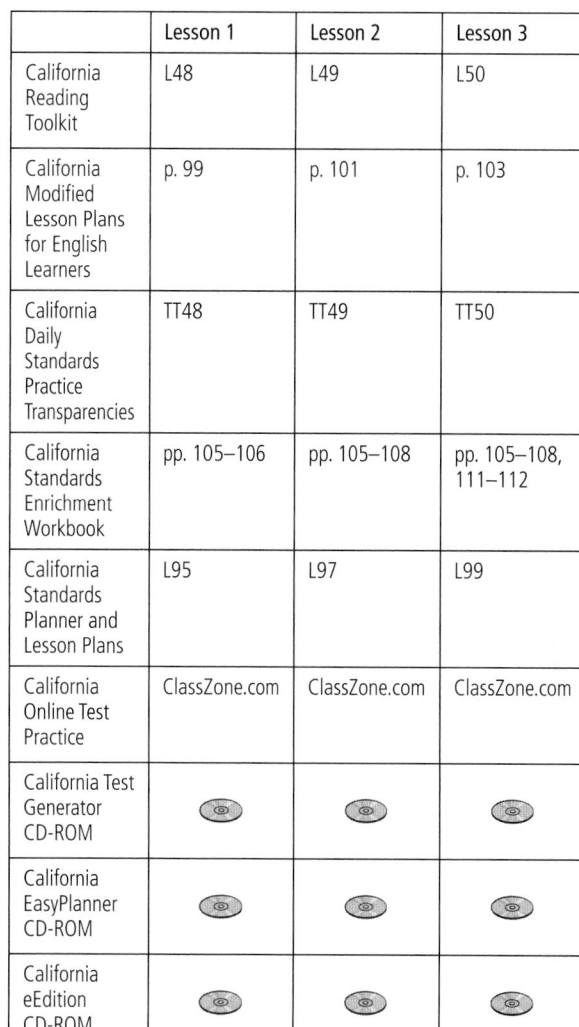		
California EasyPlanner CD-ROM			
California eEdition CD-ROM			

Chart Key

 P E Pupil Edition

 Copymaster

 CD-ROM

 Audio

 Video

 Internet

Overhead Transparency

PREVIEWING RESOURCES FOR DIFFERENTIATED INSTRUCTION

English Learners

In-Depth Resources in Spanish
- Reading Skill and Strategy
- Skillbuilder Practice **B**
- Geography Practice
- Vocabulary Study Guide

In-Depth Resources: Unit 6
- Family Newsletter (English and Spanish) **C**

Reading Study Guide (Spanish) **A**

Reading Study Guide Audio CD (Spanish)

Test Generator
Chapter Test (Spanish)

Plus

Modified Lesson Plans for English Learners

Multi-Language Glossary of Social Studies Terms

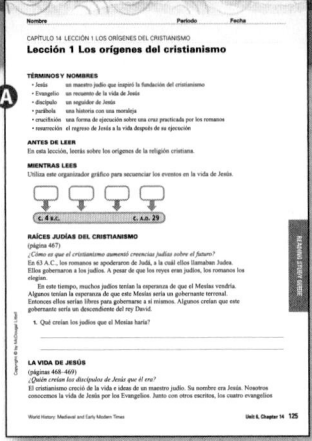

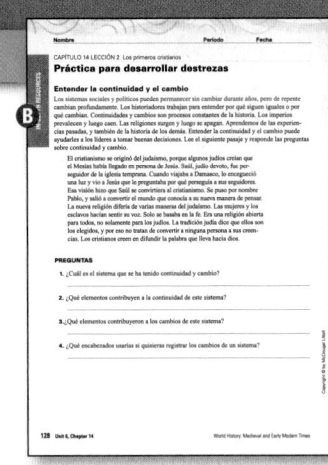

Struggling Readers

In-Depth Resources: Unit 6
- Vocabulary Study Guide **B**
- Skillbuilder Practice **C**
- Geography Practice
- Reteaching Activities **A**
- Family Newsletter

Reading Study Guide

Reading Study Guide Audio CD

Reading Toolkit

Formal Assessment
Chapter Test, Form A

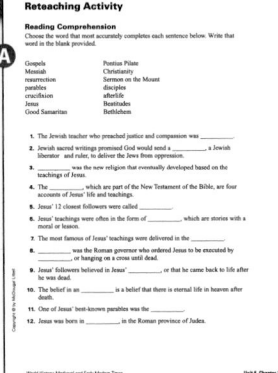

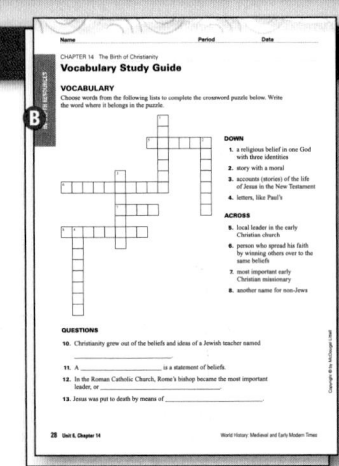

Inclusion

EasyPlanner CD-ROM
- Reading Skill and Strategy **A**
- Vocabulary Study Guide **B**
- Geography Practice
- Reteaching Activities **C**

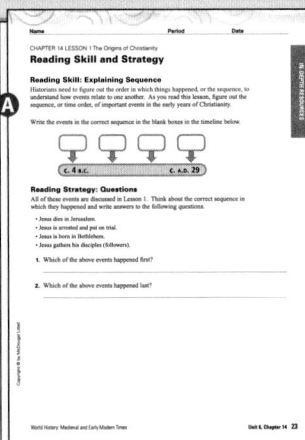

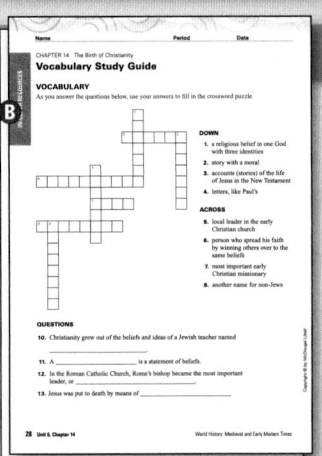

Gifted and Talented Students

In-Depth Resources: Unit 6
- Primary Source
- Literature **A**

History Makers **B**

Interdisciplinary Projects **C**

Formal Assessment
Chapter Test, Form C

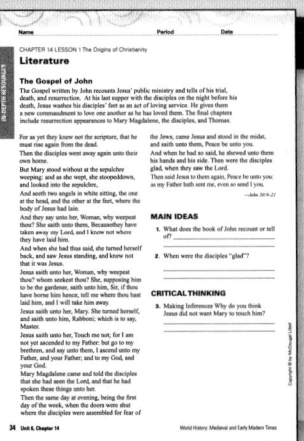

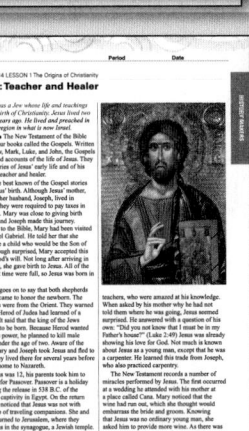

Activities in the Teacher's Edition for English Learners

- Retell a Story, p. 468
- Explain Fact and Opinion, p. 473
- Compare Before and After, p. 478
- Create Word Webs, p. 485

Activities in the Teacher's Edition for Struggling Readers

- Create a Time Line, p. 468
- Act Out the Story, p. 473
- Explore Additional Vocabulary, p. 480
- Compare Constantine and Theodosius, p. 484

Activities in the Teacher's Edition for Inclusion Students

- Listen to the Lesson, p. 470
- Illustrate the Story, p. 474
- Take Audio Notes, p. 480
- Dramatize the Content, p. 484

Activities in the Teacher's Edition for Gifted and Talented Students

- Compile a Roman Fact Sheet, p. 470
- Rewrite the Parable, p. 474
- Report on the Pharisees, p. 478
- Create a Constantinople Poster, p. 485

Integrated Technology

eEdition CD-ROM

- Interactive Visuals
- Interactive Maps
- Starting with a Story

ClassZone.com

- WebQuests
- Research Links
- Internet Activities
- Homework Helper
- Chapter Quiz
- Current Events
- Test Practice

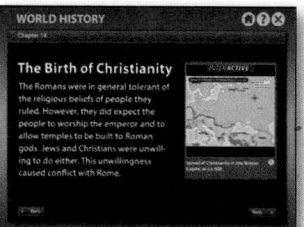

Power Presentations CD-ROM

- Lecture Notes
- Media Gallery
- Chapter Review Game

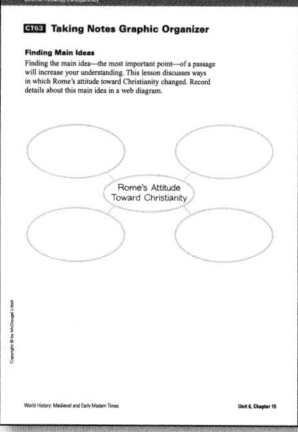

Critical Thinking Transparencies

- CT61 Explaining Sequence
- CT62 Comparing and Contrasting
- CT63 Finding Main Ideas
- CT64 Chapter 14 Visual Summary

California Daily Standards Practice Transparencies, TT48–TT50

Map Transparencies

- MT27 Jerusalem at the Time of Jesus
- MT28 Christian Communities in the First Century

Humanities Transparencies

- HT27 The Sermon on the Mount
- HT28 The Conversion of Saul

Test Generator CD-ROM

EasyPlanner CD-ROM

The Birth of Christianity • **461D**

Begin the Chapter

Objective

Analyze the origins and early spread of the Christian religion.

Quick Look

Lesson 1 explores the foundation of Christianity within the Jewish religion and the life and death of Jesus.

Lesson 2 summarizes the experiences of some of the earliest Christians—Jesus' disciples—as they sought to spread Christianity.

Lesson 3 traces the history of Christianity in Rome, where it finally took root and evolved into the Roman Catholic Church.

Before You Read: Previewing Key Concepts

Previewing key concepts helps students be more aware of the Big Ideas woven throughout the upcoming chapter. This strategy will enable students to set a purpose for their reading and maintain the necessary focus.

Have students follow these steps:

- Follow the directions in the "Before You Read" section.

- Instruct students to keep their questions in a place where they can easily find them again.

- Encourage students to check for answers as they read the chapter.

Chapter 14

The Birth of Christianity

Before You Read: Previewing Key Concepts

The Big Idea below is a general historical idea that will be applied to the Mediterranean region in this chapter. Rewrite this idea as a question that can be answered as you read. Here is an example of a question:

How did Christian beliefs challenge Rome?

Watch for the answer(s) to your question as you read the chapter.

Big Ideas About the Birth of Christianity

Government New ideas and beliefs can challenge a government's authority, leading to change.

The Romans were in general tolerant of the religious beliefs of people they ruled. However, they did expect the people to worship the emperor and to allow temples to be built to Roman gods. Jews and Christians were unwilling to do either. This unwillingness caused conflict with Rome.

Integrated Technology

eEdition
- Interactive Maps
- Interactive Visuals
- Starting with a Story

INTERNET RESOURCES
Go to **ClassZone.com** for
- WebQuest
- Homework Helper
- Research Links
- Internet Activities
- Quizzes
- Maps
- Test Practice
- Current Events

MEDITERRANEAN REGION

26–29 Jesus conducts his public ministry.

70 Romans storm Jerusalem and destroy the Temple complex.

120 Roman Empire reaches its height under Hadrian.

A.D. 25   75   125

WORLD

65 Buddhism takes root in China.

100 Moche culture arises in South America.
(deer-head figure, Peru) ▶

462

TIME LINE DISCUSSION

Use the time line to help students develop a time frame for the spread of Christianity and to preview information that will be covered in the chapter.

- Which event on this time line occurred closest to the public ministry of Jesus? *(Buddhism taking root in China)*

- In what year did the Romans destroy the Temple in Jerusalem *(70)*

- About how many years after the end of Jesus' ministry did Constantine end the persecution of Christians? *(about 284 years)*

- Did the Han Dynasty fall before or after the Roman Empire had reached its greatest height? *(after)*

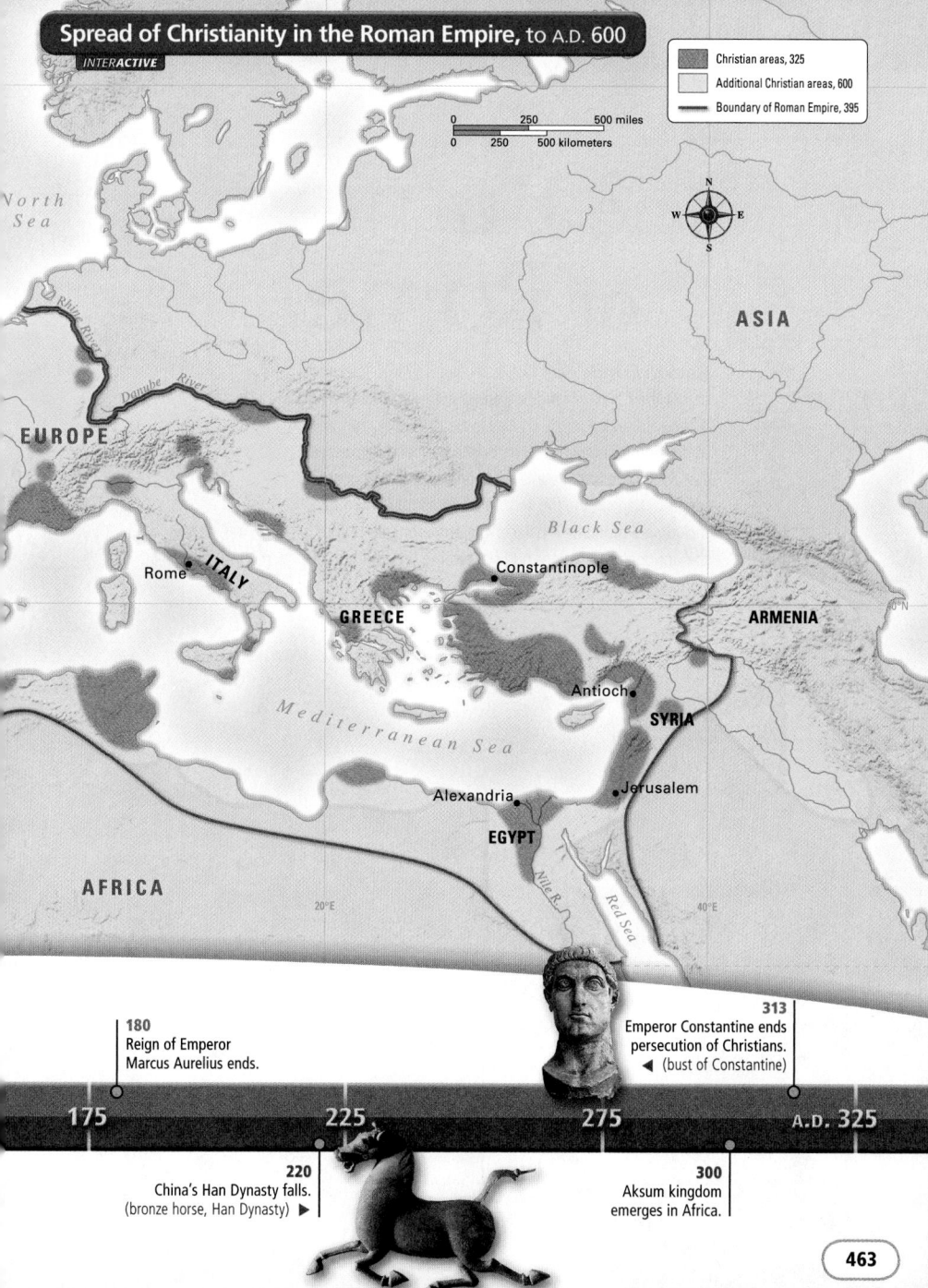

Spread of Christianity in the Roman Empire, to A.D. 600

INTERACTIVE

▨	Christian areas, 325
▢	Additional Christian areas, 600
—	Boundary of Roman Empire, 395

0   250   500 miles
0 250 500 kilometers

North Sea

ASIA

EUROPE

Rhine River

Danube River

Black Sea

Constantinople

Rome ITALY

GREECE

ARMENIA

Mediterranean Sea

Antioch

SYRIA

Alexandria

Jerusalem

EGYPT

AFRICA

20°E

Nile R.

Red Sea

40°E

180
Reign of Emperor
Marcus Aurelius ends.

313
Emperor Constantine ends
persecution of Christians.
◄ (bust of Constantine)

175   225   275   A.D. 325

220
China's Han Dynasty falls.
(bronze horse, Han Dynasty) ▶

300
Aksum kingdom
emerges in Africa.

463

CHAPTER 14

Introduce the Big Ideas

Read aloud the text about the Big Ideas. Direct students to think about government and its influence on people's religious beliefs. What do they think would happen if people's beliefs conflicted with their government leaders? Here are some other Big Ideas that you may want to emphasize in this chapter.

Belief Systems

Christianity grew out of Jewish beliefs and the teachings of Jesus.

Geography

Christianity spread in part because of the tireless efforts of missionaries, such as Paul.

Belief Systems

Christianity eventually became the official religion of the Roman Empire.

Talk About It

Interpreting Maps

Instruct students to look at the map and read the key. Have students briefly describe the state of Christianity in 325. *(It existed in scattered locations throughout the Roman Empire.)* What happened to Christianity from 325 to 600? *(It spread throughout the lands of the old empire and beyond.)*

INTERACTIVE

An interactive version of this map is available on the eEdition and Power Presentations CD-ROMs.

Find Out More

Have students use library or Internet resources to learn what parts of the world Christianity is practiced in today. Is it still the dominant religion in the Mediterranean region? Where else has it taken root?

RECOMMENDED RESOURCES

Books for the Teacher

Ellegård, Alvar. *Jesus: One Hundred Years Before Christ.* Woodstock: Overlook Press, 1999. Story of the life of Jesus and the development of Christianity.

Valée, Gérard. *The Shaping of Christianity: The History and Literature of Its Formative Centuries (100–800).* New York: Paulist Press, 1999. History of the early Christian movement.

Videos

The Rise of Christianity: The First 1,000 Years. 200 minutes. New York: A & E Home Video, 1998. Four-cassette history of the founding and spread of Christianity.

DVDs

Religions of the World. 50 minutes. Wynnewood: Schlessinger Media, 2003. The second disc in this 6-disc set covers the history of Orthodox and Roman Catholic Christianity.

Internet

To access these sites, visit the Research Links for this chapter at **ClassZone.com.**

The **World Civilizations Internet Resources** on the Web site of Washington State University has extensive information on early Christianity.

The **Public Broadcasting System's** site has an online Frontline Series that explores recent scholarship on the life of Jesus and the early Christian Church.

Objective

Read a dramatization of the persecution experienced by early Christians in Rome.

Introducing the Story

The Burning of Rome

Nero is a colorful figure in Roman history. He became emperor as a teenager, allegedly after his mother assassinated his predecessor, her own husband, Claudius. As emperor, he earned a reputation for ambition and selfishness. In addition to rumors that he had started the fire, word spread that Nero had watched the city's inhabitants suffering while playing music. Partly in an effort to quell public anger, he blamed the Christians for setting the blaze—perhaps to fulfill a prophecy that the city would burn. Christians at the time were a small group that Nero regularly and cruelly tormented.

Vocabulary Preview

execution putting a person to death

Reading the Story Aloud

1. **The teacher as reader:** Read the story aloud with expression so students hear the drama and understand the emotional impact of the events.

2. **The students as readers:** Give student readers a few minutes ahead of time to scan the story before reading it aloud to the rest of the class.

Starting with a Story

Students can also follow along as they listen to the story on the eEdition or Power Presentations CD-ROMs.

The Burning of Rome

Background: Fire! In A.D. 64, wind swept flames across the Circus Maximus, Rome's huge racing arena. Afterward, much of the city lay in ruins. A nasty rumor about Rome's emperor, Nero, began to spread almost as fast as the fire had. People whispered that the unpopular emperor had set the fire so that he could rebuild Rome, including a grand new palace. The emperor said that the unpopular Christians had started the fire. But not all Romans blamed the Christians, as you will read.

Roman coin depicting Nero ▶

464

ADDITIONAL RESOURCES

Books for the Student

Morgan, Julian. *Constantine: Ruler of Christian Rome.* New York: Rosen Publishing Group, 2003. Description of the life and rule of the Roman Emperor who helped establish and spread Christianity.

Nardo, Don. *The Rise of Christianity.* San Diego: Lucent Books, 2001. Includes a history of the Christian faith.

Videos

Ancient Rome. 200 minutes. New York: A & E Home Video, 1998. Historical overview of the great empire, including a segment on the rise of Christianity.

The baker is opening his shop near Rome's Christian neighborhood. Every morning, Christians come to buy bread at his bakery. Some Romans hate the Christians because they keep to themselves and refuse to worship the Roman gods. It's true that they don't go to the theater and the races and their men don't join the army. They're also poor, and they wear old clothes. But they're good neighbors and good customers. The Christians the baker knows would never start a fire.

The baker was lucky. His shop still smells smoky, but at least it didn't burn in the fire. As he sets things back in order, he feels sad that his Christian customers suffered so terribly. Because they were unpopular, they were easy for the emperor to blame. To stop people from saying that he set the fire, Nero told everyone it was the fault of the Christians.

The baker has heard that hundreds of Christians who survived the fire died terrible deaths afterward. At Nero's order, many were burned, while others were hanged on crosses or ripped apart by dogs. Nero conducted these executions right in his gardens. The public was invited, but the baker was too disgusted to go.

It's difficult for the baker to understand the Christians' religion. Even so, he doesn't believe any group should suffer such an awful punishment. He wonders whether the Christians who survived will be too afraid to come back to buy his bread.

What do you think will happen to the Christians in Rome?

Reading & Writing

1. **READING: Character** An important person in a story is a main character. Think about the character of Nero in this story. With a partner, discuss the character of the emperor Nero as revealed in his actions. Then make a list of words to describe the emperor.

2. **WRITING: Persuasion** Imagine that you have observed Nero's executions of Christians. You know that they didn't set the fire. You want to persuade others to join a revolt against the cruel emperor. Think about the consequences of a revolt. Then make a poster to persuade others to support your cause.

CALIFORNIA STANDARDS Writing 2.5
Write persuasive compositions.

465

Talk About It

Ask students the following questions to begin the discussion:

- According to the story, why do some Romans dislike the Christians? *(They don't worship Roman gods, and they keep to themselves.)*

- What does the baker think about the Christians? *(He knows they are different, but he doesn't believe they would start a fire.)*

- According to the story, what happened to many Christians following the fire? *(They were held responsible for the fire, and many were killed in terrible ways.)*

- What is the baker's fear for the future, following the punishment of the Christians? *(He worries that they will stay away from his business.)*

What do you think will happen to the Christians in Rome?

Possible answers: They will leave the empire; they will gain support as people realize they were unfairly punished.

Making Personal Connections

Connect the discussion to today by asking what students think about people who are "different" in some way. How do people respond to those who hold different beliefs or follow different practices? Are students suspicious of those who are different? Accepting? Interested?

READING & WRITING ACTIVITIES

1. **READING** Possible answers: cruel, vengeful, vicious
2. **WRITING** Students' posters should acknowledge the danger of revolt but appeal to a sense of justice.

2. Writing Rubric

	Level of Persuasiveness	Impact of Presentation
4	very persuasive; addresses possible consequences and outcomes	visually powerful; communicates message quickly, clearly
3	somewhat persuasive; addresses possible consequences and outcomes	communicates message quickly, clearly
2	not very persuasive; missing either consequences or outcomes	somewhat unclear; lacks immediate impact
1	not persuasive; no consequences or outcomes included	difficult to read; no impact

❶ Plan & Prepare

Objectives

- Describe the Jewish roots of Christianity.
- Summarize the key points in the life and teachings of Jesus.
- Analyze the significance of the death of Jesus.
- **Language Objective:** Work cooperatively in order to participate in a retelling.

Quick Look

Lesson 1 traces the history of the birth of the Christian religion, including the life and death of Jesus.

❷ Focus & Motivate

Preview Tell students that this lesson will explore the origins of Christianity. Ask students to think about how this religion has affected our country and helped shape its past and present.

Introduce the Main Ideas The three main ideas relate to the Big Idea "Many belief systems start with the ideas of a teacher or prophet." Help students look for this big idea as you go through the lesson.

Reading Skill: Explaining Sequence Tell students that sequence is vital in understanding the relationship between events in history and in determining causes and effects.

SAMPLE ANSWERS FOR TIME LINE

Jesus born in Bethlehem	Jesus becomes a traveling teacher	Jesus angers Roman leaders	Jesus is crucified

c. 4 B.C.   c. A.D. 29

▶ MAIN IDEAS

❶ Belief Systems Christianity built upon the Jewish belief in one God and the concept of a Messiah.

❷ Belief Systems The disciples of Jesus came to believe that he was the Messiah.

❸ Belief Systems According to the Gospels, Jesus was executed but rose from the dead. Christians believe that this makes freedom from sin and death possible for everyone.

▶ TAKING NOTES

Reading Skill: Explaining Sequence

To sequence events is to put them in an order based on when they happened. As you read Lesson 1, make notes of things that happened in the life of Jesus. Create a time line like this one to sequence the events.

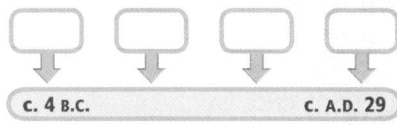

c. 4 B.C.   c. A.D. 29

S Skillbuilder Handbook, page R15

▲ **Cross** The cross is a symbol of Christianity. Some crosses are simple objects made of wood. Some are made of gold and adorned with jewels, like the one shown above.

CALIFORNIA STANDARDS

6.7.6 Note the origins of Christianity in the Jewish Messianic prophecies, the life and teachings of Jesus of Nazareth as described in the New Testament, and the contribution of St. Paul the Apostle to the definition and spread of Christian beliefs (e.g., belief in the Trinity, resurrection, salvation).

CST 3 Students use a variety of maps and documents to identify physical and cultural features of neighborhoods, cities, states, and countries and to explain the historical migration of people, expansion and disintegration of empires, and the growth of economic systems.

HI 1 Students explain the central issues and problems from the past, placing people and events in a matrix of time and place.

HOW TO TEACH THE CALIFORNIA STANDARDS

Standard	Content	Student Question or Activity	Instruction
6.7.6	**Pages 467–471** Describes the life and teachings of Jesus of Nazareth	**Pages 467–471** Students answer several questions about the Jewish tradition and Jesus' life, teachings, and death.	Have students use information in this lesson to create a fact sheet about the historical figure of Jesus. This fact sheet should identify key details of Jesus' life, teachings, and the meaning of his death.
CST 3	**Page 468** Illustrates the geographical region in which Jesus lived and taught	**Page 468** Students examine a map of the region in which Jesus lived and taught.	Have students use library or Internet resources to research the history of Jerusalem and write a brief summary of its religious history and significance.
HI 1	**Pages 467–471** Explains the conflict between Jesus and Jewish and Roman authorities	**Page 471** Students explain how Jewish and Roman leaders viewed Jesus when he came to Jerusalem.	Based on previous chapters, review the history of the Romans and their relationships with the Jews, as well as their relationships with other conquered peoples.

The Origins of Christianity

TERMS & NAMES

Jesus

Gospel

disciple

parable

crucifixion

resurrection

Build on What You Know Religion plays an important role in many people's lives, perhaps your own as well as others'. A new religion called Christianity grew out of Jewish beliefs and the ideas of a Jewish teacher named **Jesus**.

Christianity's Jewish Roots

① **ESSENTIAL QUESTION** How did Christianity build on Jewish beliefs about the future? Some Jewish writings promised a Messiah, an earthly ruler who would deliver the Jews from oppression. In 63 B.C., the Romans conquered the Jewish kingdom of Judah, also called Judea. Although the Jews had their own kings, these Jewish rulers had to be approved by Rome.

During their history, the Jews had frequently been treated badly. Many wanted to be delivered from oppression and from foreign rulers. Some Jewish sacred writings promised a Messiah. Some people believed that this would be an earthly ruler sent by God. However, there were many different Jewish opinions about what to expect from a Messiah. Some believed that this ruler would be descended from King David, the ruler of Israel in the 900s B.C. Some Jews believed the Messiah would free them.

REVIEW What did some Jews believe the Messiah would do? deliver them from oppression

Connect to Today

Bethlehem This photograph shows the Church of the Nativity *(below left)* in Bethlehem, supposedly built upon the site of Jesus' birth. The building to the right is a monastery. ▼

467

Terms & Names

Jesus Jewish teacher whose ideas, life, and death are central to the Christian religion

Gospel written account of Jesus' life

disciple a follower of Jesus during his lifetime

parables stories with a moral

crucifixion a form of execution in which the person is hung from a cross

resurrection coming back to life after death

❸ Teach

Christianity's Jewish Roots

🔖 **6.7.6**

Talk About It

• **Critical Thinking: Making Inferences** What can you infer from this passage about the way the Jews regarded the Romans? *(Possible answer: Jews wanted to be freed from oppression and foreign rule.)*

California Resources

California Reading Toolkit, L48

California Modified Lesson Plans for English Learners, p. 99

California Daily Standards Practice Transparencies, TT48

California Standards Enrichment Workbook, pp. 105–106

California Online Test Practice

California Test Generator CD-ROM

California Standards Planner and Lesson Plans, L95

California EasyPlanner CD-ROM

California eEdition CD-ROM

LESSON 1 PROGRAM RESOURCES

ON LEVEL

In-Depth Resources: Unit 6
• Family Newsletter (English and Spanish), pp. 21–22
• Reading Skill: Explaining Sequence, p. 23
• Vocabulary Cards, p. 29

Formal Assessment
• Lesson Quiz, p. 246

ENGLISH LEARNERS

In-Depth Resources in Spanish
• Reading Skill: Explaining Sequence, p. 121

Modified Lesson Plans for English Learners, p. 99

Reading Study Guide (Spanish), p. 125

Reading Study Guide Audio CD (Spanish)

STRUGGLING READERS

In-Depth Resources: Unit 6
• Reading Skill: Explaining Sequence, p. 23
• Vocabulary Study Guide, p. 28
• Vocabulary Cards, p. 29
• Reteaching Activity, p. 35

Reading Toolkit, L48

Reading Study Guide, p. 125

Reading Study Guide Audio CD

GIFTED AND TALENTED STUDENTS

In-Depth Resources: Unit 6
• Literature: from the Gospel of John, p. 34

Interdisciplinary Projects
• Language Arts, p. 81

History Makers
• Jesus, p. 27

INCLUSION

EasyPlanner CD-ROM
• Reading Skill: Explaining Sequence
• Vocabulary Study Guide
• Reteaching Activity

TECHNOLOGY

eEdition CD-ROM
• Starting with a Story

Power Presentations CD-ROM

Humanities Transparencies
• HT27 The Sermon on the Mount

Map Transparencies
• MT27 Jerusalem

Critical Thinking Transparencies
• CT61 Explaining Sequence

Test Generator CD-ROM

ClassZone.com

The Birth of Christianity • 467

In-Depth Resources: Unit 6
• Reading Skill: Explaining Sequence, p. 23

 Map Transparencies
• MT27 Jerusalem at the Time of Jesus

History from Visuals

Interpreting Maps
Direct students to look over the map, paying special attention to the title, the subtitle, and the key. Be sure students also check the locator map, to ensure that they know where this region is located in the world. Tell students that some of the points on the map refer to places where Jesus delivered important teachings or performed miracles— they will be discussed later in the text. Suggest that students refer back to this map as they read about these events.

> Based on this map, roughly how large was the area in which Jesus lived his life and conducted his teachings? *(Jesus lived and worked in an area that was about 70 miles by 20 miles or 110 kilometers by 30 kilometers.)*

Vocabulary Strategy

Using Context Clues
Remind students that *context* means the sentence or sentences in which the word is used. By understanding the overall meaning of the passage, it can clarify what different words mean.

Teach

The Life of Jesus

🖋 **6.7.6, CST 3**

Talk About It

• What was Jesus' connection to the Jewish faith? *(He was born a Jew and followed many Jewish traditions and teachings.)*

• In what form did Jesus give many of his famous teachings? *(in the form of parables, or stories that offered a moral)*

• **Critical Thinking: Finding Main Ideas**
What were some of Jesus' main teachings? *(Possible answer: justice, compassion, and the coming of God's kingdom)*

The Life of Jesus

Some of his followers claimed he was the Messiah.

 ESSENTIAL QUESTION Who did the disciples of Jesus believe he was?

As a Jew born in the Roman province of Judea, Jesus followed many of the teachings of Judaism. However, he also taught certain ideas and practices that seemed to have put him at odds with some Jewish leaders.

Birth and Early Life We know about Jesus from four accounts called the **Gospels**, written after his death by Matthew, Mark, Luke, and John. The Gospels and other writings make up the New Testament.

According to the Gospels, Jesus was born in Bethlehem and grew up in Nazareth. Christians would later celebrate his birth on the holiday of Christmas. In the Gospel account, Jesus was raised by Mary and by Joseph, a carpenter.

Jesus' Followers As a young adult, Jesus became a traveling teacher. Biblical accounts say he cured the sick and lame and performed other miracles, such as turning water to wine.

Jesus began to gather followers. His closest followers were called **disciples**. Jesus' 12 disciples were Peter, Andrew, James, John, Philip, Bartholomew, Thomas, Matthew, James (son of Alphaeus), Simon, Thaddaeus, and Judas Iscariot.

The Teachings of Jesus Jesus preached justice, compassion, and the coming of God's kingdom. He often delivered these messages in the form of **parables**, or stories with morals. Three of Jesus' best-known parables are those of the Good Samaritan, the Prodigal Son, and the Lost Sheep. (See Literature Connection, pages 472–475.)

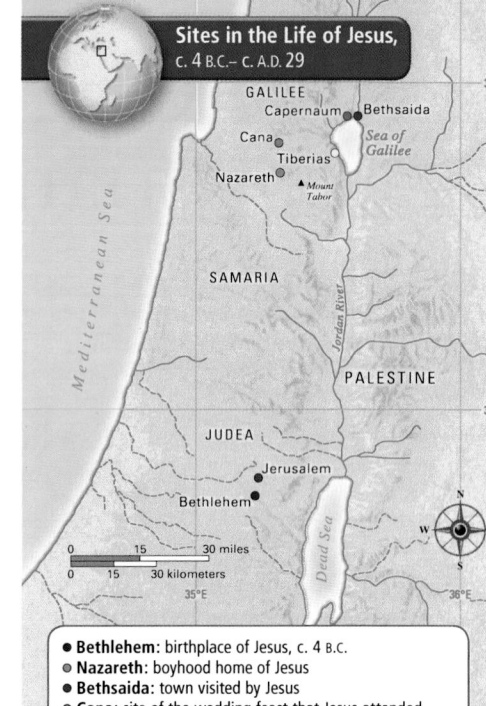

Sites in the Life of Jesus, c. 4 B.C.– c. A.D. 29

• **Bethlehem**: birthplace of Jesus, c. 4 B.C.
• **Nazareth**: boyhood home of Jesus
• **Bethsaida**: town visited by Jesus
• **Cana**: site of the wedding feast that Jesus attended
• **Capernaum**: near site of Sermon on the Mount
○ **Tiberias**: Roman city on Sea of Galilee
• **Jerusalem**: capital where Jesus was executed, c. A.D. 29

Vocabulary Strategy

The meaning of the word *disciple* can be figured out by using **context clues.** The rest of the sentence tells you that disciples are close followers. *Disciple* comes from a Latin word meaning "student" or "pupil."

DIFFERENTIATING INSTRUCTION

English Learners

Summarize Biographical Events
To be sure that students have comprehended the textbook, have them work in pairs to summarize the important events in the life of Jesus, as explained on pages 468–469. The students should use the following format to summarize:
Setting:
People:
Events:

Struggling Readers

Create a Time Line
Using information from the text, have students create a time line of Jesus' life. The time line should include major events and be labeled and illustrated. Have students present their time lines to the class.

Jesus' most famous teachings were given in the Sermon on the Mount. The sermon opens with the Beatitudes (bee•AT•ih•TOODZ), or blessings. In this sermon, Jesus encouraged people not only to obey the law but also to change their hearts. People shouldn't simply refrain from killing; they should also love and pray for their enemies. Jesus encouraged his followers to live simply and humbly.

Despite his teachings, Jesus angered some people who heard him preach. For example, Jesus forgave people who had broken religious laws, but many Jewish leaders thought only God could grant this kind of forgiveness. Jesus also associated with sinners, whom religious leaders treated as outcasts. Most shocking was the claim of some of Jesus' followers that he was the Messiah they had long been waiting for.

REVIEW What form did Jesus' teachings often take? parables

Primary Source

Background: One of Jesus' most famous sermons is called the Sermon on the Mount. In this speech, he made a number of memorable statements that have become known as the Beatitudes. Some of them are at right. Below is the Sermon on the Mount as pictured in a French manuscript of the 1200s.

from *the Beatitudes*

- Blessed are the poor in spirit, for theirs is the kingdom of heaven.
- Blessed are those who mourn, for they shall be comforted.
- Blessed are the meek, for they shall inherit the earth.
- Blessed are those who hunger and thirst for righteousness, for they shall be satisfied.
- Blessed are the merciful, for they shall obtain mercy.
- Blessed are the pure in heart, for they shall see God.
- Blessed are the peacemakers, for they shall be called sons of God.

Matthew 5:3–9

DOCUMENT–BASED QUESTION
What do these sayings of Jesus suggest about his view of the oppressed? Does he seem to identify with the rich and powerful or the poor and weak?

The Birth of Christianity • **469**

INTERDISCIPLINARY ACTIVITIES

Language Arts

Report on the Sermon on the Mount
Have students assume the role of a reporter and write a brief report about Jesus' Sermon on the Mount. The report should answer the questions of *who, what, where, when, why,* and *how.*

Art

Create an Illustrated Map
Have small groups of students use reference books or the Internet to find pictures of the sites shown on the map on page 468. Then have them create a map of the Sites in the Life of Jesus and use the images to illustrate the sites.

Teach

The Death of Jesus

 6.7.6, HI 1

Talk About It

- In what way did Jesus threaten Roman authority? *(He was seen by some as the liberator of the Jews.)*

- Why was Jesus arrested? *(He criticized the way the Jewish Temple was being run.)*

- How was Jesus punished for his crime? *(He was executed by the Romans.)*

- **Critical Thinking: Finding the Main Idea** To his followers, what was the significance of Jesus' resurrection? *(It demonstrated that he was divine and that he died to help bring about God's kingdom on earth.)*

More About . . .

Crucifixion

Execution by crucifixion was a Roman technique that was designed to produce horrible suffering and set a terrible example for observers. The exact methods used during crucifixion are still under debate and probably varied from situation to situation. However, it was common for officials to position victims in such a way as to cause prolonged and terrible pain. The executions were generally public, often occurring along the most crowded roads. Though the Gospels state that Jesus was removed from the cross and buried after death, victims' bodies were sometimes left on the cross.

📝 **In-Depth Resources: Unit 6**
- Literature, from the Gospel of John, p. 34

The Death of Jesus

③ ESSENTIAL QUESTION What belief about Jesus did Christians think made an afterlife possible?

the belief that Jesus had sacrificed himself to bring about God's kingdom

Jesus had made enemies among the Roman rulers as well as among his fellow Jews. The claim that he was the Messiah, or Jewish liberator and ruler, threatened the Romans because it questioned their political power and authority. The claim also shocked many Jewish leaders.

Arrest and Trial According to three of the Gospels, Jesus' followers hailed him as king when he journeyed to Jerusalem to celebrate the Jewish holiday of Passover. In that city's holy Temple, Jesus publicly criticized how the Temple was being run.

These public challenges to Rome and Jewish authorities appointed by Rome sealed his fate. Jewish leaders arrested Jesus and turned him over to the Romans for punishment.

The Story of the Resurrection The Roman governor, Pontius Pilate, ordered Jesus to be executed by **crucifixion**, or hanging on a cross until he suffocated. After Jesus died, a huge stone was placed in front of the tomb where he was buried.

On the third day after his execution, according to the Gospels, some of his followers reported that the stone had moved and the tomb lay empty. Others said they had seen Jesus and had even walked and talked with him.

These accounts of Jesus' **resurrection**, or return to life, proved to many of his followers that he was divine. They came to believe that Jesus had been willing to give up his own life for the sake of God's kingdom. Through his death and resurrection, God was bringing new life into the world. This was a world in which sin would no longer prevail and even death would be defeated. Jesus' followers said anyone who believed this would share in the life of God.

▲ **Tomb** This burial chamber dating from the time of Jesus was sealed with a round stone.

DIFFERENTIATING INSTRUCTION

Gifted and Talented Students

Compile a Roman Fact Sheet
Have students use their texts and outside resources to learn about Roman rule in Jerusalem. Students should present their findings in a fact sheet that describes when the Romans conquered Jerusalem, how they ruled Jerusalem, how the Jews regarded Roman rule, and other details about the occupation.

Inclusion

Listen to the Lesson
Have students who have difficulty seeing work in pairs and listen to the lesson on audio CD. Students should stop the CD frequently to answer questions in the text. They should also take careful notes about their reading. Have students exchange notes at the end of the lesson and offer each other ideas on how to improve them.

According to Christians, Jesus' crucifixion took place on a Friday, and his resurrection on a Sunday. The Christian holidays Good Friday and Easter Sunday, which recall these two events, have been celebrated ever since.

REVIEW What event made Jesus' followers believe their leader was divine?
his resurrection

Lesson Summary

- Some Jews believed a Messiah would give them political power and religious freedom.
- Jesus' teachings stressed compassion, justice, and the coming of God's kingdom.
- Accounts of Jesus' resurrection made some people believe Jesus was divine.

Why It Matters Now . . .

Jesus and his earliest followers were Jewish. Eventually, however, more and more non-Jews converted to Christianity. Today about a third of the people in the world are Christians.

▲ **Relief Sculpture**
The fish is a Christian symbol dating from ancient times. This fourth-century fish with a cross is from a Christian cemetery in Egypt.

---

1 Lesson Review

Homework Helper
ClassZone.com

Terms & Names

1. Explain the importance of

Jesus	disciple	crucifixion
Gospel	parable	resurrection

Using Your Notes

Explaining Sequence Use your completed graphic to answer the following question:

2. What actions of Jesus in Jerusalem preceded his arrest? (6.7.6)

c. 4 B.C.   c. A.D. 29

Main Ideas

3. What great power ruled over Judea in the time of Jesus? (See map on page 463.) (CST 3)

4. How do we know about Jesus' life and about his teachings? (6.7.6)

5. What did accounts of Jesus' resurrection prove to his followers? (6.7.6)

Critical Thinking

6. Determining Historical Context What historical conditions made some Jews in Judea likely to accept Jesus as their Messiah? (6.7.6)

7. Comparing and Contrasting How did Jewish and Roman leaders view Jesus when he came to Jerusalem? (6.7.6, HI 1)

Activity

Writing a Parable Think of an important lesson you would like to teach. Then write a brief story to teach your lesson. Read your parable aloud to your class. (Writing 2.1)

The Birth of Christianity • 471

❹ Assess & Reteach

Assess Group students and have the students in each group number off. Ask a question from the Lesson Review and allow group members to agree on an answer. Then, call out a number and have a person from each group give their group's answer.

 Formal Assessment
- Lesson Quiz, p. 246

Reteach Write the three subheadings in this lesson on the board ("Christianity's Jewish Roots," "The Life of Jesus," and "The Death of Jesus"). Call on volunteers to identify key details about each one. Record students' responses on the board.

 In-Depth Resources: Unit 6
- Vocabulary Cards, p. 29
- Reteaching Activity, p. 35

 **Homework Helper**
Visit **ClassZone.com** for a lesson review, a flip-card activity, and links to related web sites.

---

1 Lesson Review Answers

Terms & Names

1.
- Jesus, p. 467
- Gospel, p. 468
- disciple, p. 468
- parable, p. 468
- crucifixion, p. 470
- resurrection, p. 470

Using Your Notes

See page 466 for an example of a completed chart.

2. He visited the Temple and criticized how it was run. This challenged official authority.

Main Ideas

3. Rome
4. from the Gospels
5. that he was divine

Critical Thinking

6. Possible answers: The Jews were oppressed under Roman rule and looked for a leader who would deliver them.

7. Possible answers: Both groups found Jesus a threat—the Jews because certain ideas of Jesus put him at odds with Jewish leaders; and the Romans because the claim that he was the Messiah threatened their political rule.

Activity Rubric

	Moral in Parable	Storytelling Style
4	illustrates a lesson clearly and creatively	compelling and easy to follow
3	illustrates a lesson clearly	easy to follow some
2	story's link to a lesson is weak	unclear few
1	story does not teach a lesson	incomplete

Objectives

- Analyze specific lessons that are representative of the teachings of Jesus.
- **Language Objective:** Formulate fact and opinion statements to describe characters in the literaature selection.

❶ Focus & Motivate

Connect to the Big Idea

Belief Systems Many religions and belief systems stem from the ideas of a single teacher or prophet. In the case of Christianity, Jesus, a Jewish man living under Roman control, assumed this role. The lessons he taught during his lifetime are central to many of the teachings of Christianity.

Connect to Prior Knowledge

Remind students what they have already read about Jesus and his teachings, in particular the parables through which he presented many of his lessons. (*Parables were stories with morals that demonstrated the basic principles Jesus wanted to teach.*)

More About . . .

Jesus' Parables

There are dozens of parables that appear in the Gospels and some of the same parables appear in more than one Gospel. They range from a few words to several verses, and they often relate to a limited set of themes. One common theme is nature—for example, a famous parable talks about the behavior of seeds planted in different types of soil as a way of illustrating the depth of one's faith. Many other parables relate to people engaged in work or attending weddings or other gatherings.

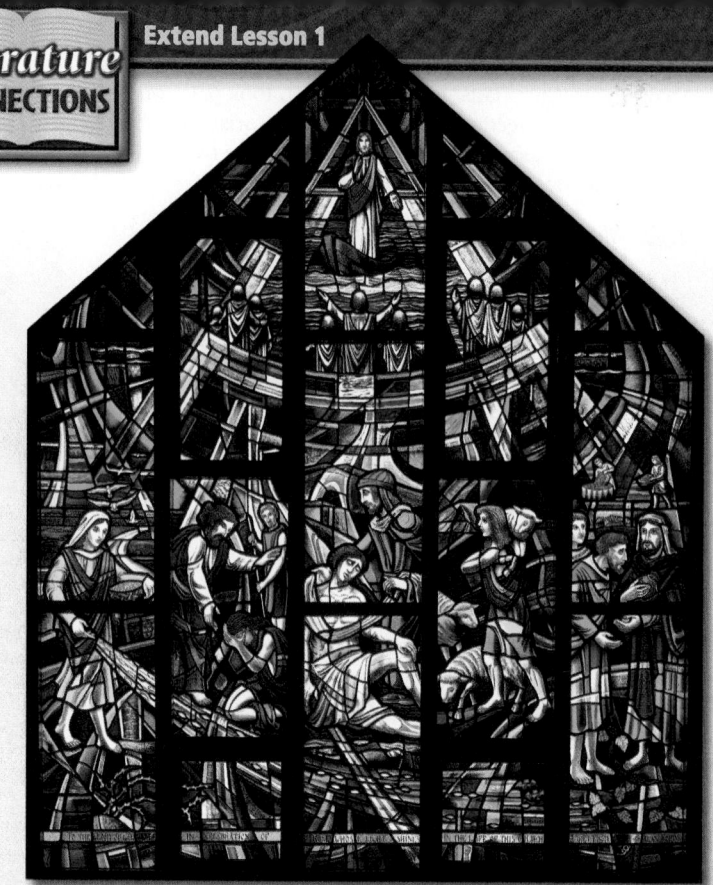

Two Parables of Jesus

Background: Jesus was a teacher. He often taught by telling parables, or stories that teach lessons. His teachings were based upon ideas from the Jewish tradition. Two of his most famous parables are those of the Good Samaritan and the Prodigal Son. The latter deals with God's call for the lost soul to repent. These versions of the parables in the Gospel of Luke are taken from *Everlasting Stories* by Lois Rock. (See page R54 in the Primary Source Handbook for the Parable of the Lost Sheep.)

CALIFORNIA STANDARDS
Reading 3.6 Identify and analyze features of themes conveyed through characters, actions, and images.

472 • Chapter 14

ADDITIONAL RESOURCES

Books for the Student

Dobson, Danae. *Parables for Kids: Eight Contemporary Stories Based on Best-Loved Bible Parables.* Wheaton: Tyndale House, 1999. Contains a retelling of eight parables.

Empson, Lila, and Vicki J. Kuyper. *Jesus Speaks to Teens: Not Your Ordinary Meditations on the Words of Jesus.* Minneapolis, MN: Bethany House Publishers, 2004. Bible readings featuring the words of Jesus, with specific focus on issues facing young people.

Keating, Susan. *Jesus: Religious Leader.* Broomhall: Mason Crest Publishers, 2003. Includes a biography of Jesus.

Videos

Parables: A New Look at Familiar Stories. 60 minutes. Brewster: Paraclete Video Productions, 2000. Video retelling of famous parables from the Bible.

The Good Samaritan

One day as Jesus was sitting with his disciples, a teacher of the Law approached. He smiled a broad smile—the sort of smile that is hard to trust.

"Ah, Teacher," he said to Jesus, bowing a little too low. Jesus raised his eyebrows. "There is one question that has been puzzling me dreadfully, and after hearing so much from everyone about what a wise person you are, I thought I'd ask you. What must I do to receive eternal life?"

"What do the scriptures say?" Jesus answered.

The man replied, "'Love the Lord your God with all your heart, with all your soul, with all your strength, and with all your mind' and 'Love your fellow human beings as you love yourself.'"

"You are right," replied Jesus. "Do this and you will live." And he smiled at the man.

The teacher wasn't going to be dismissed that easily. "Whom should I consider my fellow human beings?" he asked.

Jesus replied, "Once upon a time, there was a man traveling from Jerusalem to Jericho . . . a lonely road, if ever there was one. As he traveled, he was attacked by bandits. They snatched his purse, beat him up, took all he had, and left him for dead."

"I'm entirely with you in condemning the criminal element in society," interrupted the man. Jesus seemed not to notice.

"It just so happened that a priest was going that way," Jesus continued. "He saw the man, but walked by on the other side."

"Isn't it hard to know what to do when you find yourself at the scene of a crime," the teacher commented.

"Next," said Jesus, "came a Levite.[1] He went over to look, then hurried away."

"A real dilemma for a Levite." The man certainly liked to talk. "After all, he couldn't risk touching a dead body if he was on the way to the Temple, because that would have made him unfit to carry out his duties on account of the Law that says . . ."

One of the disciples yawned, and Jesus started to talk again. "A Samaritan was also traveling that way . . ."

"Don't you wish that Samaritans would stay in Samaria with their own strange, regional ways and leave us alone?" added the man.

The Good Samaritan The Samaritan helps the wounded traveler in this detail of a stained glass window. ▼

---

1. **Levite:** a member of the tribe of Levi, chosen to assist the Temple priests.

The Birth of Christianity • 473

❷ Teach

Talk About It

- Invite student volunteers to read the story aloud. Encourage them to read the story dramatically to help improve their understanding of the characters and events.

- Ask student to discuss the characters in the story. Then, ask the following questions:

- The text describes the teacher of the Law as having a "smile that is hard to trust." What does this mean? *(Possible answer: It is a smile that says, "I am your friend," when it is clear that the person is not a friend.)*

- What does the text mean when it says that the teacher of the Law "wasn't going to be dismissed that easily?" *(Possible answer: The teacher wanted to get into a conflict with Jesus or catch him in some sort of controversy.)*

- How does the teacher of the Law respond to the different examples of people who don't help the injured man? *(He seems to understand why the people didn't help the injured man.)*

- **Critical Thinking: Finding the Main Idea** What message do you think Jesus is trying to tell the teacher of the Law with this story? *(Possible answer: He is suggesting that people need to treat other people with kindness, the way they'd want to be treated, and that this is more important than what job people hold or their social status.)*

DIFFERENTIATING INSTRUCTION

Struggling Readers

Creating a Timeline
To help students comprehend the two parables, have the students work in pairs. Each pair should select one parable and create a time line of incidents in the parable. Then each pair should share its time line with the class.

English Learners

Explain Fact and Opinion
An opinion is a statement that tells what a person believes or feels but cannot be proven. A fact is a statement that can be proven. Write the following statement on the board: "I feel the teacher in the story was rude when he interrupted Jesus." Guide students as they explain why the statement is a fact or an opinion.

Teach

Talk About It

- Early in the parable, what does the son ask of the father? *(He asks if he can have his share of his inheritance now rather than later.)*

- What is the father's reaction to his son's request? *(He thinks the son is making a mistake, but he grants the request anyway.)*

- What does the son do with the money he receives for his inheritance? *(He squanders it.)*

- **Critical Thinking: Finding the Main Idea** How do you think the father might feel about his son's request for his inheritance and his decision to leave home? *(Possible answers: He may be sad that his son is anxious to leave. He may be worried that his son is making a mistake. He may be angry that his son is going against his wishes.)*

"And," said Jesus, "he saw the man and felt sorry for him. He tended the man's wounds, lifted him onto his donkey, and took him to an inn. He paid the innkeeper to take care of him, promising to return and pay any extra that might be needed."

Then Jesus asked, "Which of the three treated the man who was robbed as he himself would have liked to have been treated?"

"The one who was kind to him," sulked the man.

"You go and do the same," said Jesus.

> **REVIEW** Who treated the crime victim best? the Samaritan

The Prodigal Son

Jesus told this story:

"There was once a man who had two sons. They worked together on the land and made a good living. As he grew up, the younger son began to dream of what he would do if he had his father's riches, and then he made a plan.

"'Father,' he announced one day, 'when you die, I will inherit some of your wealth. I want to have it now, while I am young.'

"'My dear son, I fear you are making a mistake,' pleaded the father. But it was no use. Sorrowfully, his father divided his property between his two sons.

"Within days, the son sold it and set off for a country far away. There he found much on which to spend his money, with extravagant lodgings and stylish clothes and rich food. Friends gathered around him, eager to come to his parties. He was delighted. But his money soon dwindled away.

"Then, out of nowhere, famine struck the land and the price of everything soared. With nothing left to sell, the young man became desperate.

"He found himself a job . . . but it was of the very worst kind, looking after pigs. He carried a basketful of bean pods to the field they had

The Prodigal Son The father welcomes his returning son in this detail of a stained glass window. ▼

474 • Chapter 14

DIFFERENTIATING INSTRUCTION

Inclusion

Illustrate the Story
Pair students and have them create a comic-strip version of this parable. Each student should identify at least four key scenes in this story, then create drawings to illustrate them. Have partners combine their drawings to tell the whole parable.

Gifted and Talented Students

Rewrite the Parable
Have students rewrite the parable from the point of view of the father. To help them gain more insight into the father's perspective, students may want to use library or Internet resources to read other versions of the parable. Remind students that the behavior of the characters in their revised parables should remain consistent with the original version.

rooted into dust and tipped the food on the ground in front of them. I wish I could eat bean pods, he thought, as he watched them munching. No one gives me anything.

"He began to think of the family farm and the servants who had looked after the flocks. 'They always had more than enough to eat,' he remembered. Then he lifted his head. 'I shall go back to my father,' he said, 'and admit that I have done wrong.'

"So he made the long journey home. But while he was still a long way off, his father saw him. He ran to greet him and kissed him. The son hung his head. 'Father, I have sinned against God and against you. I am no longer fit to be called your son. Treat me as one of your hired workers.'

"His father simply waved his hand. 'Hurry!' he called to the servants. 'Bring a robe for my son, a ring for his finger, and shoes for his feet. Then let us prepare a feast.'

"So it was done. The party began, and the elder son returned from the fields to hear music and dancing. 'What's going on?' he asked a servant.

"'Your brother has come back,' he was told. 'Your father has prepared a feast to celebrate.'

"At that, the elder brother grew so angry he would not even go into the house. His father came out to welcome him in.

"'I have worked for you all these years and yet you have done nothing for me!' the son complained.

"The father replied, 'You are always here with me, and everything I have is yours. But we had to celebrate and be happy—your brother was dead, but now he is alive; he was lost, but now he has been found.'"

REVIEW Why was the older brother angry?

He had obeyed his father and worked hard and yet he had not been rewarded.

Reading & Writing

1. **READING: Theme** In which of these parables does the theme of forgiveness seem important?

2. **WRITING: Narration** Imagine that you are the elder son in the Parable of the Prodigal Son. Write a narrative of your brother's return, in which you explain your point of view.

CALIFORNIA STANDARDS Writing 2.1
Write narratives.

The Birth of Christianity • 475

Teach

Talk About It

- What happens to the son immediately after he squanders all his money? *(He gets a lowly job and realizes that he is even worse off than the servants at his family's home.)*

- What does the son assume he will have to do now that he has squandered all of his money? *(He thinks he will have to work as a servant.)*

- What does the son do when he arrives back at his home? *(He apologizes to his father for his actions.)*

- How does the father respond to his son's return? *(He welcomes him and throws a big party.)*

- How does the son's older brother react to these events? *(He thinks it is unfair that his father gives so much attention to the prodigal son after having given him, the loyal son, so little.)*

- **Critical Thinking: Finding the Main Idea** What do you think the message of this parable is? *(Possible answers: It is never too late to seek forgiveness. Family is more important than money.)*

ACTIVITIES ANSWERS

1. **READING** Most students will probably cite the parable of the Prodigal Son. The father forgives his wayward son his transgressions and urges the older son to be forgiving as well.

2. **WRITING** Volunteers might read their narratives to the class.

2. Writing Rubric

	Conventions of Narrative	Errors in Mechanics
4	includes many interesting details; accurately reflects point of view of older brother	few or none
3	includes some detail; reflects point of view of older brother	some
2	does not reflect point of view of older brother	many
1	is incomplete or unrelated to the parable	major

The Birth of Christianity • 475

❶ Plan & Prepare

Objectives

- Analyze the activities of the disciples and their efforts to spread the Christian faith after the crucifixion.
- Describe the conversion of Saul, an early persecutor of the Christians.
- Summarize Paul's role in spreading Christianity.
- **Language Objective:** Complete a graphic to describe Paul's beliefs before and after his conversion.

Quick Look

Lesson 2 examines the efforts of early Christians in the years following Jesus' crucifixion as they struggled to establish the church.

❷ Focus & Motivate

Preview Tell students that following the crucifixion, the small number of Christians faced much difficulty in spreading their faith. This lesson covers the early years of these people's efforts to carry on Jesus' message.

Introduce the Main Ideas The three main ideas relate to the Big Idea "Migration, trade, warfare, and the action of missionaries spread ideas and beliefs." Help students look for this big idea as you read the lesson.

Reading Skill: Compare and Contrast Comparing and contrasting is a way for students to organize information and make sense of it.

SAMPLE ANSWERS FOR CHART

Saul	Paul
was a Jewish scholar	was a Christian
persecuted Christians	suffered persecution
traveled to stamp out Christianity	traveled to spread Christianity

---

Lesson 2

▶ **MAIN IDEAS**

❶ **Belief Systems** The disciples of Jesus spread his teachings and tried to convince others to believe in him.

❷ **Belief Systems** After having a vision of Jesus, Saul changed from being a persecutor of Christians to a leader of Christians.

❸ **Geography** Paul traveled to many of the great cities of the Roman Empire, seeking to convert people to Christianity.

▶ **TAKING NOTES**

Reading Skill: Comparing and Contrasting

Comparing and contrasting involves finding similarities and differences between two or more things. As you read Lesson 2, compare and contrast Paul's beliefs before and after his conversion, in a chart like the one below.

Saul	Paul

S **Skillbuilder Handbook, page R4**

▲ **Communion Cup** This Russian chalice of gold and precious stones was made in 1598.

CALIFORNIA STANDARDS

6.7.6 Note the origins of Christianity in the Jewish Messianic prophecies, the life and teachings of Jesus of Nazareth as described in the New Testament, and the contribution of St. Paul the Apostle to the definition and spread of Christian beliefs (e.g., belief in the Trinity, resurrection, salvation).

6.7.7 Describe the circumstances that led to the spread of Christianity in Europe and other Roman territories.

HI 2 Students understand and distinguish cause, effect, sequence, and correlation in historical events, including the long- and short-term causal relations.

HOW TO TEACH THE CALIFORNIA STANDARDS

Standard	Content	Student Question or Activity	Instruction
6.7.6	**Pages 479–480** Summarizes Paul's conversion and mission to spread Christian beliefs	**Page 481** Students tell how Paul changed Christianity.	Explain that Paul experienced a complete reversal in his beliefs about Christianity. Have volunteers describe a time in their lives when their beliefs about something changed dramatically.
6.7.7	**Page 480** Describes the circumstances that led to the spread of Christianity throughout Rome and Europe	**Page 481** Students explain why Christianity appealed to women and Gentiles.	Tell students that Paul's Epistles were sent to Christian communities in different parts of the Roman Empire. Have students use library or Internet resources to report on one of these communities.
CST 3	**Pages 478–479** Illustrated time line places key events of the birth of Christianity into historical context	**Pages 478–479** Students use a time line to learn about the events that took place in the early Christian church.	Ask students to find more information about the spread of Christianity in Europe between the times of Paul and Constantine. Have them write entries for the time line on pages 478–479.

The Early Christians

► TERMS & NAMES
Gentile
persecute
Paul
missionary
Epistle

Build on What You Know In Chapter 13 you learned that the Romans worshiped many gods. In contrast, the Jews worshiped one God and tried to obey God's law. The first Christians also obeyed the law of Moses.

Jesus' Disciples

1 **ESSENTIAL QUESTION** What did Jesus' disciples do after his death? They tried to convert other Jews to a belief in Jesus as the Messiah. Jesus' first disciples were Jews. Eventually, they developed beliefs and practices that would cause a break from Judaism.

The Early Church The disciples thought that Jesus had fulfilled Jewish prophecies about the Messiah. The disciples tried to convince other Jews to accept Jesus as the Messiah.

The early church stressed sharing property as well as practicing charity, helping prisoners, and taking common meals. Women and slaves were eager to join, perhaps because the new church taught that all its members were equal. These beliefs helped to set the early church apart from other religions of the time. The disciples hoped to spread Jesus' message and convert others to their beliefs.

Ephesus This view shows the ruins of a street and temple in the Roman city of Ephesus in Anatolia, where early Christians preached. ▼

477

Terms & Names

Gentile term for those who are not Jewish

persecute to harass, such as a religion

Paul an important Christian missionary

missionary a person who spreads his or her faith by converting others to his or her religion.

Epistle one of the letters of Paul to Christian churches that became part of the New Testament

❸ Teach

Jesus' Disciples

↖ **6.7.6**

Talk About It

• **Critical Thinking: Understanding Cause and Effect** How did the question of whether or not Christianity was part of Judaism affect the early Christians? *(Possible answer: It led to some controversy among them, and it gave cause to the Romans to ignore them.)*

California Resources

California Reading Toolkit, L49
California Modified Lesson Plans for English Learners, p. 101
California Daily Standards Practice Transparencies, TT49
California Standards Enrichment Workbook pp. 105–108
California Online Test Practice
California Test Generator CD-ROM
California Standards Planner and Lesson Plans, L97
California EasyPlanner CD-ROM
California eEdition CD-ROM

LESSON 2 PROGRAM RESOURCES

ON LEVEL

In-Depth Resources: Unit 6
• Reading Skill: Comparing and Contrasting, p. 24
• Vocabulary Cards, p. 29
• Skillbuilder Practice: Understanding Continuity and Change, p. 27
• Geography Practice: Paul's Journeys, p. 31

Formal Assessment
• Lesson Quiz, p. 247

ENGLISH LEARNERS

In-Depth Resources in Spanish
• Reading Skill: Comparing and Contrasting, p. 122

Modified Lesson Plans for English Learners, p. 101

Reading Study Guide (Spanish), p. 127

Reading Study Guide Audio CD (Spanish)

STRUGGLING READERS

In-Depth Resources: Unit 6
• Reading Skill: Comparing and Contrasting, p. 24
• Vocabulary Study Guide, p. 28
• Vocabulary Cards, p. 29
• Reteaching Activity, p. 36

Reading Toolkit, L49

Reading Study Guide, p. 127
Reading Study Guide Audio CD

GIFTED AND TALENTED STUDENTS

In-Depth Resources: Unit 6
• Primary Source: A Letter from Paul, p. 33

Interdisciplinary Projects
• Science, p. 80

INCLUSION

EasyPlanner CD-ROM
• Reading Skill: Comparing and Contrasting
• Vocabulary Study Guide

• Reteaching Activity

TECHNOLOGY

eEdition CD-ROM

Power Presentations CD-ROM

Humanities Transparencies
• HT28 The Conversion of Saul

Critical Thinking Transparencies
• CT62 Comparing and Contrasting

ClassZone.com

The Birth of Christianity • 477

In-Depth Resources: Unit 6
- Reading Skill: Comparing and Contrasting, p. 24
- Skillbuilder Practice: Understanding Continuity and Change, p. 27
- Primary Source: A Letter from Paul, p. 33

Humanities Transparencies
- HT28 The Conversion of Saul

Teach

The Conversion of Saul

6.7.6, 6.7.7, CST 3

Talk About It

- What was Saul's original reaction to Christianity? *(He actively opposed Christianity.)*

- What event caused Saul to change his mind about Christianity? *(On the road to Damascus, he had a conversion and began believing that Jesus was the Messiah.)*

- What happened when Paul reached the city of Damascus? *(He became a Christian and went to work converting Gentiles.)*

- **Critical Thinking: Summarizing** How did Paul's cultural background help him in his missionary work? *(Possible answers: He had vast knowledge of Jewish law, which helped him among Jews. He was influenced by Greek culture, and he held Roman citizenship, which allowed him to travel freely in the lands of the Roman Empire.)*

History from Visuals

Interpreting Visuals
Have students review the time line in order to get a clear understanding of the time frame in which the events covered in this chapter occurred.

- How long after the crucifixion of Jesus did Paul begin his teachings? *(about 11 years)*

- How many years passed between Jesus' crucifixion and the persecution of Christians in Rome under Nero? *(about 35 years)*

- How many years separated Nero's persecution of Christians and Constantine's decision to grant them freedom of worship? *(about 249 years)*

Conflict Arises Jews divided the world into Jews and **Gentiles** (JEHN•TYLZ), or non-Jews. The first members of churches were Jews. A debate divided them over whether to convert non-Jews to Christianity. Some thought that Gentiles should observe the Torah, while others thought that this was unnecessary.

At first, Roman leaders ignored the early Christians. Like the Christians themselves, the Romans viewed Christianity as a sect, or division, of Judaism. Jewish leaders disagreed with this view.

REVIEW On what beliefs was the early Christian church based?
giving charity, caring for prisoners, sharing meals, sharing property

The Conversion of Saul

2 ESSENTIAL QUESTION What change did Saul undergo?
He changed from actively persecuting the church to becoming a member and then a leader in the new movement.

One Jewish leader, Saul, actively **persecuted**—that is, oppressed or harassed—the early church. Saul was a Pharisee, a religious scholar who had studied Jewish law. He wrote about how he persecuted the church and tried to destroy it.

The Road to Damascus While pursuing runaway converts on the road to Damascus, Saul to his own astonishment experienced a sudden conversion. According to his own account, Saul felt that God had revealed Jesus as His son to him, and appointed him to proclaim Jesus among the Gentiles. Saul came to believe that Jesus was the Jewish Messiah.

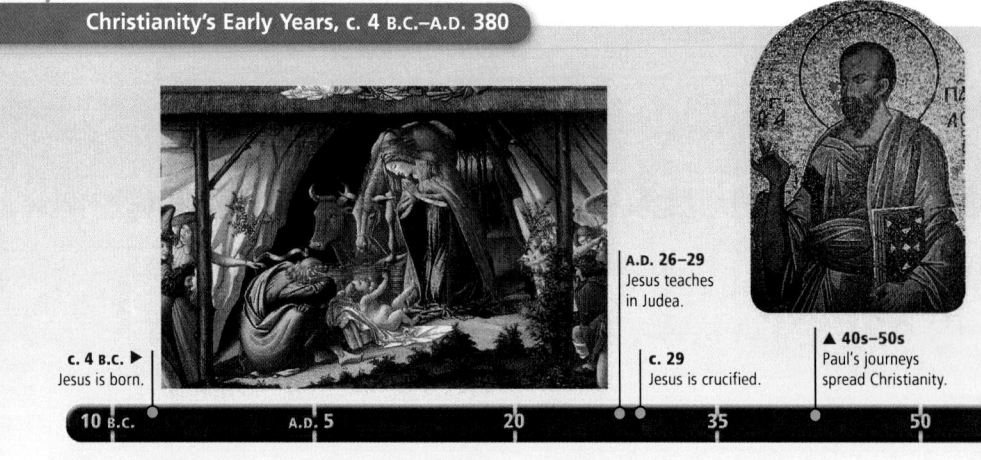

Christianity's Early Years, c. 4 B.C.–A.D. 380

c. 4 B.C. ▶
Jesus is born.

A.D. 26–29
Jesus teaches in Judea.

c. 29
Jesus is crucified.

▲ 40s–50s
Paul's journeys spread Christianity.

10 B.C.   A.D. 5   20   35   50

478 • Chapter 14

DIFFERENTIATING INSTRUCTION

English Learners

Compare Before and After
Have students listen as you read the passage *The Conversion of Saul*. Discuss what Saul was like before his conversion and what Saul was like after his conversion. Note details on the graphic below.

Saul Before the Conversion	Saul After the Conversion

Gifted and Talented Students

Report on the Pharisees
Saul was a Pharisee. Have students use library and Internet resources to learn more about these people, including what role they served in the time of Jesus, how Jesus regarded them, and what part they play in the Gospels. Have students write a brief report to share their findings.

Saul Becomes a Believer When Saul reached Damascus, he didn't persecute the members of the church; he joined them. There he studied his new faith and began to convert Gentiles.

Saul's cultural and political background helped him convert a variety of nonbelievers. As a Pharisee, Saul knew Jewish law. He had been born in Tarsus, a city in Asia Minor heavily influenced by Greek culture. By birth, Saul held Roman citizenship. This allowed him to travel freely through the empire.

When he traveled, Saul used his Roman name, **Paul**. After three years in Damascus, Paul was ready to travel as a **missionary**, or person who spreads his faith by converting others to his religion.

> **REVIEW** What happened to Saul on the road to Damascus?
> He became a Christian.

Paul's Journeys Spread Christianity

3 ESSENTIAL QUESTION Where did Paul travel, and why?
He made four trips throughout parts of the Roman Empire.
During Paul's lifetime, the Roman Empire was experiencing the Pax Romana, or "Roman peace." That made the empire's excellent roads safer for Paul's widespread travels.

The Journeys Nonetheless, Paul's travels weren't easy. He made four missionary journeys. Each one took several years. Paul wrote that he faced "dangers from rivers, dangers from bandits, . . . dangers in the wilderness, dangers at sea."

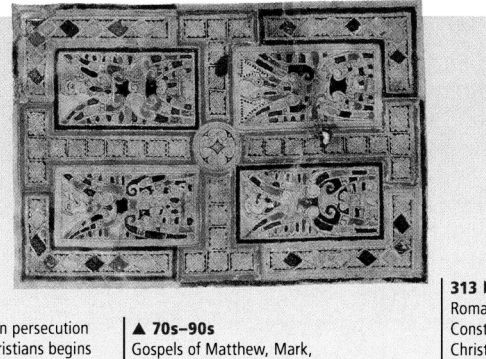

64
Roman persecution of Christians begins under Nero.

▲ 70s–90s
Gospels of Matthew, Mark, Luke, and John are written.

313 ▶
Roman emperor Constantine grants Christians freedom of worship.

380
Emperor Theodosius makes Christianity Rome's official religion.

65   80   95   400

The Birth of Christianity • 479

Teach

Paul's Journeys Spread Christianity

6.7.6, 6.7.7

Talk About It

- What factor helped make Paul's travels easier? *(He was traveling in the midst of the Pax Romana.)*

- How did Paul help set Christianity apart from Judaism? *(He explained that it was not necessary to convert to Judaism before becoming a Christian.)*

- What is the significance of Paul's letters? *(They helped explain Christian belief and inspired Christians to live the proper life, and they eventually became part of the New Testament.)*

- **Critical Thinking: Identifying Issues and Problems** Read the quotation from Paul's letters on page 480. According to this passage, what is the one thing that unites all people? *(believing in Christ)*

INTERDISCIPLINARY ACTIVITIES

Language Arts

Write an Expository Paragraph
Have students show that they have understood the section headed "Paul's Journeys Spread Christianity" by having them write an expository paragraph in which they explain in their own words the historical information about how Paul spread Christianity through the Roman Empire.

Art

Create a Map
Have students work in small groups to do research to find out where Paul journeyed throughout the Roman Empire. Then have them create a map that shows Paul's journeys. Remind them that their maps should include keys and other elements of a map.

More About . . .

Paul's Letters
The letters of Paul form a significant portion of the New Testament. There are over a dozen letters thought to be written by Paul. They generally follow a standard format, beginning with an introduction that identifies Paul as the author and continuing on to cover a variety of topics. In general, there is agreement that these letters were written by Paul. In other cases, scholars believe the letters may have been written by someone other than Paul, perhaps a follower of Paul carrying on his work.

Changes to Christianity

Paul and other Christian missionaries brought about changes that made it possible for Christianity to spread throughout the Roman Empire. For years, Paul and other early Christian leaders struggled over whether Gentiles had to become Jews before becoming Christians. Paul argued that conversion to Judaism was unnecessary. Paul's idea helped separate Christianity from Judaism. It also made the new religion more appealing to Gentiles. As a result, Christianity began to spread throughout the empire.

▲ **Paul** The apostle Paul was the most important early Christian missionary.

The Letters Almost everywhere Paul went, he started new churches. He kept in touch with these churches by writing letters, delivered by other missionaries. Paul's letters explained Christian beliefs and urged converts to live according to God's laws. He preached that salvation was available to all people if they accepted Jesus.

Paul's letters became an important part of the New Testament. They are among the **Epistles** ("letters"). In one famous Epistle, Paul wrote that believing in Christ broke down all barriers between people: "There is neither Jew nor Greek, there is neither slave nor free, there is neither male nor female; for you are all one in Christ Jesus."

Paul's Death Paul had wanted to travel to Rome to speak before the emperor and spread his Christian faith. He did reach Rome, but not in the way he had hoped.

Near the end of his career, Paul returned to Jerusalem. He was taken into custody by the Romans when it was rumored that he had brought Gentiles into the Temple. After staying in prison for two years, Paul demanded to be tried before Caesar in Rome.

Paul left on his final journey in late autumn of A.D. 59. After arriving in Rome in the spring of A.D. 60, Paul remained under house arrest for two years. He wrote several letters from captivity. There his story abruptly ended. Paul probably died in Rome, possibly a victim of the persecution started by Nero.

480 • Chapter 14

DIFFERENTIATING INSTRUCTION

Struggling Readers

Explore Additional Vocabulary
In addition to the names and vocabulary terms highlighted in this lesson, there are a number of important words with which students may be unfamiliar. For example, have students work in teams to look up the definitions of the words *Christ* and *apostle*. Invite volunteers to share their definitions with the class. Encourage students to identify any other unfamiliar words and seek their definitions.

Inclusion

Take Audio Notes
Have students who are visually impaired take notes by making a recording with a classmate. Encourage students to abbreviate the information as if they were taking written notes. Remind them to include key words and ideas that will promote a clear understanding of causes and effects or comparisons and contrasts.

The Legacy of Paul Paul was the most influential of the early apostles, or messengers of Jesus, because of his many journeys and letters. He helped spread the church from Jesus' homeland out to the nations of the world.

REVIEW How did Paul change Christianity?
His conversion of Gentiles helped to spread Christianity.

Lesson Summary

- Jesus' disciples tried to persuade other Jews and debated whether to seek Gentile converts.
- Saul, a persecutor of Christians, became the most important early Christian missionary.
- Paul's conversion of Gentiles established Christianity as a new faith.

Why It Matters Now . . .

More than any other person, Paul contributed to the growth of Christianity as a worldwide religion. All over the world, many churches and cities are named in his honor.

▲ Relief Sculpture
This Roman sailing ship of the first century A.D. was the kind of ship in which Paul would have made many of his journeys.

4 Assess & Reteach

Assess Have students work in pairs to answer the questions and record the page numbers on which they found the answers.

 Formal Assessment
- Lesson Quiz, p. 247

Reteach Have students review the bulleted Lesson Summary items. Then have students work individually to write one or two supporting sentences for each item.

 In-Depth Resources: Unit 6
- Vocabulary Cards, p. 29
- Reteaching Activity, p. 36

Homework Helper

Visit **ClassZone.com** for a lesson review, a flip-card activity, and links to related Web sites.

---

2 Lesson Review

Homework Helper ClassZone.com

Terms & Names

1. Explain the importance of
   Gentile   Paul   Epistle
   persecute   missionary

Using Your Notes

Comparing and Contrasting Use your completed chart to answer the following question:

2. How did Paul's view of Christians change after his conversion? (6.7.6)

Saul	Paul

Main Ideas

3. Why were women and slaves particularly eager to become Christians? (6.7.7)
4. What qualifications did Paul possess that made him an effective missionary? (6.7.6)
5. What decision made Christianity appealing to Gentile converts? (6.7.7)

Critical Thinking

6. **Understanding Cause and Effect** How did the Pax Romana contribute to the spread of Christianity? (HI 2)
7. **Assessing Credibility of Sources** Why are the Epistles useful sources for learning about Paul's experiences? (6.7.6)

Activity Internet Activity Use the Internet to research Paul's journeys and make a thematic map of them. Use illustrations or symbols to show some things that happened to him. (6.7.6)
INTERNET KEYWORD: *Paul's missionary journeys*

The Birth of Christianity • 481

---

2 Lesson Review Answers

Terms & Names

1. • Gentile, p. 478
   • persecute, p. 478
   • Paul, p. 479
   • missionary, p. 479
   • Epistle, p. 480

Using Your Notes

See page 476 for a completed chart.

2. Before his conversion he persecuted Christians. After his conversion, he attempted to teach others about Christian beliefs.

Main Ideas

3. The new church stressed the equality of all.
4. He was a religious and knowledgeable Jew, he knew Greek culture, and he was a Roman citizen.
5. the decision not to require conversion to Judaism first

Critical Thinking

6. Possible answers: The relative safety of the roads allowed Paul to travel extensively through the Roman Empire. Had this important missionary been unable to travel so freely, Christianity might not have spread or become a world religion.
7. Possible answers: The Epistles of Paul were written at the time or close to the time of the events described. Also, they were first-hand accounts written by Paul.

Activity Rubric

	Accuracy of Events & Locations	**Presentation of Map**
4	complete, accurate representation of Paul's experiences	neat, colorfully illustrated, clear
3	accurate representation of Paul's experiences	clear some
2	incomplete or inaccurate representation of Paul's experiences	confusing few
1	significantly incomplete or inaccurate representation of Paul's experiences	unclear

The Birth of Christianity • 481

❶ Plan & Prepare

Objectives

- Analyze the relationship between Rome and the early Christian church.
- Describe the conversion of Constantine and his impact on the Christian church.
- Trace the early development of the Roman Catholic Church.
- **Language Objective:** Create a concept cluster of words and terms from the lesson that are related to Constantine, the Roman emperor.

Quick Look

Lesson 3 describes the role of the Roman Empire in the development of Christianity.

❷ Focus & Motivate

Preview Remind students that in the early days of Christianity, Rome did not welcome the new religion. In this lesson, students will explore the relationship between the Roman Empire and the early Christians.

Introduce the Main Ideas The three main ideas relate to the Big Idea "Belief systems and religions may shape governments and societies." Help students look for this Big Idea as you go through the lesson.

Reading Skill: Finding Main Ideas Tell students that main ideas are often, but not always, presented in the first sentence of a paragraph.

SAMPLE ANSWERS FOR DIAGRAM

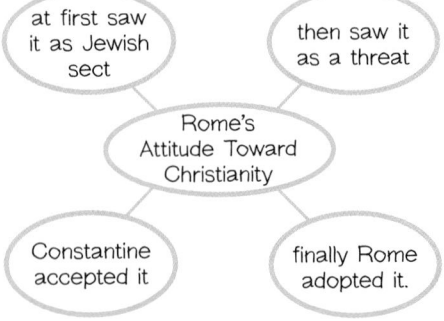

Lesson 3

▶ **MAIN IDEAS**

❶ **Government** Rome became hostile to Jews and Christians because both groups challenged Roman authority.

❷ **Government** The Roman emperor Constantine accepted Christianity and ended persecutions.

❸ **Government** The church developed into a complex institution with many levels of authority.

▶ **TAKING NOTES**

Reading Skill: Finding Main Ideas

Finding the main idea—the most important point—of a passage will increase your understanding. This lesson discusses ways in which Rome's attitude toward Christianity changed. Record details about this main idea in a web diagram.

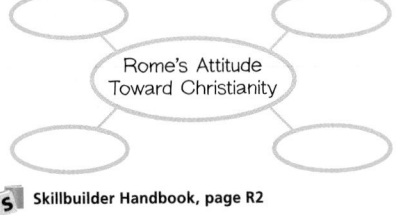

Rome's Attitude Toward Christianity

Skillbuilder Handbook, page R2

▲ **Bronze Statue** The Roman emperor Valentinian holds aloft a Christian cross, showing the conversion of the Roman Empire to Christianity.

CALIFORNIA STANDARDS

6.7.6 Note the origins of Christianity in the Jewish Messianic prophecies, the life and teachings of Jesus of Nazareth as described in the New Testament, and the contribution of St. Paul the Apostle to the definition and spread of Christian beliefs (e.g., belief in the Trinity, resurrection, salvation).

6.7.7 Describe the circumstances that led to the spread of Christianity in Europe and other Roman territories.

7.1.3 Describe the establishment by Constantine of the new capital in Constantinople and the development of the Byzantine Empire, with an emphasis on the consequences of the development of two distinct European civilizations, Eastern Orthodox and Roman Catholic, and their two distinct views on church-state relations.

482 • Chapter 14

HOW TO TEACH THE CALIFORNIA STANDARDS

Standard	Content	Student Question or Activity	Instruction
6.7.6	**Page 486** Defines specific Christian beliefs, including the creed, the Trinity, and holy sacraments	**Page 486** Students explain the importance of the term *Trinity*.	Tell students that the concept of the Trinity was a point of contention among early Christians and that Paul addressed **this issue in his teachings.**
6.7.7	**Pages 484** Traces the history and legalization of Christianity in the Roman Empire	**Pages 485** Students describe the significance of the Edict of Milan.	Have students learn more about Theodosius and record their findings in a brief biographical sketch similar to the "History Makers" feature on page 485.
7.1.3	**Pages 484–485** Summarizes the contributions of Constantine to the development of Christianity in Rome	**Page 484** Students explain the effect Constantine had on the spread of Christianity.	Ask a volunteer to locate Constantinople (now Istanbul), on a world map. Remind students that this city served as capital of the Roman Empire after Rome.

Rome and Christianity

▶ TERMS & NAMES
bishop
pope
catholic
creed
Trinity

Terms & Names

bishop local leader of the Church

pope the bishop of Rome, the most important bishop in the Catholic Church

catholic universal

creed statement of beliefs

Trinity union of three persons—Father, the Son, and the Holy Spirit—in one God

Build on What You Know In Chapter 13, you learned that the Roman religion included elements drawn from the religions of other peoples. An important issue facing the ancient world was how Rome would react to the new religion of Christianity.

Rome's Policy Toward Other Religions

1 ESSENTIAL QUESTION Why was Rome hostile to Christians and Jews?
because they seemed to undermine Roman authority and government
Rome tolerated the alien religious practices of the people it conquered. It exempted Jews from the requirement to worship Roman gods, including the emperor. However, Rome would not let the religions of subject peoples inspire rebellion. When a Jewish revolt began in the Temple in Jerusalem, the Romans destroyed the Temple.

A Christian Threat As more Gentiles joined the Christian movement, the Romans became alarmed. Some Gentiles claimed that they should not have to worship the emperor. The appeal of Christianity to slaves and women also caused alarm. Finally, Christian talk about a Lord who would establish a kingdom seemed to imply an end to the Roman Empire.

Connect to Today
Rome This view shows the Sant'Angelo Bridge over the Tiber River at dusk, with St. Peter's Basilica in the background. ▼

INTERACTIVE

483

❸ Teach

Rome's Policy Toward Other Religions
✎ 6.7.7

Talk About It

- **Critical Thinking: Finding the Main Idea** Why did Roman rulers feel threatened by Christianity? *(Possible answer: It continued to gain members, threatening the Roman leaders' power.)*

California Resources

California Reading Toolkit, L50
California Modified Lesson Plans for English Learners, p. 103
California Daily Standards Practice Transparencies, TT50
California Standards Enrichment Workbook, pp. 105–108, 111–112
California Online Test Practice
California Test Generator CD-ROM
California Standards Planner and Lesson Plans, L99
California EasyPlanner CD-ROM
California eEdition CD-ROM

LESSON 3 PROGRAM RESOURCES

ON LEVEL

In-Depth Resources: Unit 6
- Reading Skill: Finding Main Ideas, p. 25
- Vocabulary Cards, p. 29

Formal Assessment
- Lesson Quiz, p. 248

ENGLISH LEARNERS

In-Depth Resources in Spanish
- Reading Skill: Finding Main Ideas, p. 123

Modified Lesson Plans for English Learners, p. 103

Reading Study Guide (Spanish), p. 129

Reading Study Guide Audio CD (Spanish)

STRUGGLING READERS

In-Depth Resources: Unit 6
- Reading Skill: Finding Main Ideas, p. 25
- Vocabulary Study Guide, p. 28
- Vocabulary Cards, p. 29
- Reteaching Activity, p. 37

Reading Toolkit, L50

Reading Study Guide, p. 129

Reading Study Guide Audio CD

GIFTED AND TALENTED STUDENTS

Interdisciplinary Projects
- Math, p. 79
- Art, p. 82

INCLUSION

EasyPlanner CD-ROM
- Reading Skill: Finding Main Ideas
- Vocabulary Study Guide
- Reteaching Activity

TECHNOLOGY

eEdition CD-ROM

Power Presentations CD-ROM

Map Transparencies
- MT28 Christian Communities in the First Century

Critical Thinking Transparencies
- CT63 Finding Main Ideas
- CT64 Chapter 14 Visual Summary

ClassZone.com

In-Depth Resources: Unit 6
- Reading Skill: Finding Main Ideas, p. 25

 Map Transparencies
- MT28 Christian Communities in the First Century

More About . . .

Persecution of Christians

Students have read about the incidents following the fire in Rome. These were among the most spectacular and horrific incidents. But other emperors, including Diocletian, also won reputations for their terrible treatment of Christians. In addition, there are indications that some Christians actively sought martyrdom at the hands of the Romans. Among some, the idea of suffering for one's faith was an opportunity sought to prove one's devotion.

Teach

The Conversion of Constantine

📞 **6.7.6, 6.7.7, 7.1.3**

Talk About It

- What was Constantine's attitude toward Christianity when he first became emperor? *(He was probably hostile or indifferent, since he permitted the persecution of Christians.)*

- What changed Constantine's mind about the persecution of Christians? *(He believed he had received an answer to a prayer.)*

- What was Constantine's contribution to the spread of Christianity in Rome? *(He legalized Christianity, built Christian churches, and made Christianity part of the Roman culture.)*

- **Critical Thinking: Compare and Contrast** How were Constantine and Theodosius alike and different? *(Possible answers: They were alike in that they both supported Christianity. They were different in that Constantine permitted other religions, while Theodosius required Romans to practice Christianity.)*

The Roman Persecutions Roman doubts about Christianity soon led to active hostility. Nero blamed the Christians for a fire that leveled much of Rome in A.D. 64. Many Christians were tortured and killed because of their religion. Yet the conversions continued. During the Roman persecutions, catacombs—underground cemeteries with secret passages—provided a hiding place for Christians. However, a key event would bring the persecutions to an end.

Christians' refusal to worship the emperor threatened the Romans' political authority. They also feared that growing numbers of Christians would undermine their rule.

REVIEW Why did the Romans feel threatened by Christianity?

The Conversion of Constantine

2 **ESSENTIAL QUESTION** What was Constantine's policy toward Christianity?

At first, he tolerated the persecution of Christians; then he made Christianity legal in the empire; then, at the end of his life, he formally converted to Christianity.

In A.D. 306, Constantine (KAHN•stuhn•TEEN) became the Roman emperor. Like those before him, he had allowed the persecution of Christians. In 312, however, he was waging a battle for leadership of Rome.

The Cross as Sign In the midst of the fighting, Constantine prayed for help. Later he reported seeing a Christian cross in the sky along with these words: "In this sign you will conquer." He ordered his soldiers to put the symbol of the cross on their shields and battle flags. Constantine and his troops were victorious.

The Legalization of Christianity The victorious Constantine immediately ended the persecution of Christians. Then, in the Edict of Milan, he made Christianity one of the empire's legal religions and returned property that had been seized during the persecutions. Constantine also built churches, used Christian symbols on coins, and made Sunday a holy day of rest and worship. But Rome's first Christian emperor delayed his own baptism, or formal conversion, until the end of his life.

▲ **Catacomb** This picture of a catacomb in Rome shows burial niches and a painting of Jesus.

DIFFERENTIATING INSTRUCTION

Inclusion

Research Biographical Information

Have students research Constantine's life. After doing preliminary research, they should select an important incident from his life and share that information with the class in a brief (1- to 2-minute) oral report.

Struggling Readers

Compare Constantine and Theodosius

To help students understand the changes brought about by Constantine and Theodosius, have students work in pairs to create a Venn Diagram. Have them fill in the diagram to show how these two emperors were alike and different in their contributions to the spread of Christianity in the Roman Empire.

Constantine

Constantine was a fierce and successful warrior. He was also a serious student of his new religion. The emperor wrote a special prayer for his troops, and he even traveled with a movable chapel in a tent. Constantine decreed the building of many Christian churches in the Roman Empire.

Constantine established Constantinople (now Istanbul, Turkey) as a new capital. It was a center of Christianity for the next thousand years. He was buried in Constantinople's Church of the Apostles in A.D. 337. Memorials to the 12 apostles surrounded Constantine's tomb. The first Christian emperor considered himself to be Jesus' 13th apostle.

History Makers

Constantine

Constantine was born in the 270s in what is today Serbia. He enjoyed a highly successful career as a soldier before he became emperor. He worshiped Mars, the god of war, and Apollo.

As emperor and a Christian, Constantine sought to bring some unity to a Christian community that had, by that time, broken into a number of different groups with various beliefs. One result was the development of the creed discussed on page 486, which tried to resolve key disputes in Church doctrine.

While Constantine is revered as a leader of the early Christians, he was a powerful ruler who was not above using force.

Christianity Changes Rome In 380, Emperor Theodosius decreed Christianity Rome's official religion. Eleven years later, Theodosius closed down all the pagan temples. "All the peoples we rule," he said, "shall practice that religion that Peter the Apostle transmitted to the Romans."

REVIEW What did the Edict of Milan decree?
that Christianity was a legal religion in the Roman Empire

Beginnings of the Roman Catholic Church

3 ESSENTIAL QUESTION What were some of the beliefs of the early church?
Trinity; that God is present everywhere; the sacraments
The practice of Christianity in Roman cities took on a common structure. Priests and deacons obeyed **bishops**, or local church leaders. Roman Catholic tradition says that Rome's first bishop was the apostle Peter. Much later, Rome's bishop gradually became the most important bishop, or **pope**. This was the beginning of the Roman Catholic Church. *Catholic* means "universal."

The Birth of Christianity • 485

Teach

Beginnings of the Roman Catholic Church

6.7.6, 6.7.7, 7.1.3

Talk About It

- Describe how the practice of Christianity in Roman cities took on a common structure. *(Priests in churches obeyed local leaders, called bishops. The bishop in Rome was the most important bishop and came to be called the pope.)*

- What feature did the creed adopted by early Church leaders include? *(a belief in the Trinity)*

- **Critical Thinking: Summarizing** What do you think was the impact of the development of sacraments and monasteries? *(Possible answer: These developments helped create a culture that was common to all Catholics, thus uniting them.)*

DIFFERENTIATING INSTRUCTION

Gifted and Talented Students

Create a Constantinople Poster
Have students do additional research on the city of Constantinople, which Constantine established as his capital. Students should create a poster that highlights some of the key cultural features of the city, including its art, architecture, and defenses.

English Learners

Create Word Webs
Demonstrate how to locate words from the lesson that are related to Constantine, the Roman Emperor. Victorious relates to Constantine, the Roman Emperor, because he was victorious in the battle for leadership of Rome. Have students work with a partner to complete their own word webs. To conclude, have students take turns to explain how each word relates to Constantine.

④ Assess & Reteach

Assess Have students work on their own to answer the questions, then meet in groups to discuss their answers.

 Formal Assessment
• Lesson Quiz, p. 248

Reteach Have students use signals to indicate their familiarity with the vocabulary terms in this section. Write the terms on the board. As you point to each term and say it aloud, have students hold up a closed fist if they do not understand the term; one finger if they have a vague idea of what it means; two fingers if they are fairly sure of the word's meaning; and three fingers if they know the world and can use it in a sentence.

 In-Depth Resources: Unit 6
• Vocabulary Cards, p. 29
• Reteaching Activity, p. 37

🔍 Homework Helper

Visit **ClassZone.com** for a lesson review, a flip-card activity, and links to related Web sites.

Beliefs and Practices Some early Christian writers, called church fathers, developed a **creed**, or statement of beliefs. This creed featured a belief in the **Trinity**, or union of three divine persons—Father, Son (Jesus), and Holy Spirit—in one God. A church father from North Africa, Augustine, wrote about a God who was present everywhere. The church also developed sacraments—religious rites—such as baptism and communion, based on events in the life of Jesus.

To live the ideal Christian life and to celebrate these sacraments together, Christian men formed communities called monasteries. As the church grew, men entered the higher orders of the church, becoming bishops, priests, and deacons. Christianity changed from a small sect to a powerful, wealthy religion.

REVIEW What is Rome's bishop called? the pope

Lesson Summary
• Rome saw the new religion of Christianity as a threat.
• Constantine embraced Christianity in A.D. 312.
• The Roman Catholic Church traces its roots to the apostle Peter.

Why It Matters Now . . .
One-third of the people in the world today are Christian.

3 Lesson Review

🔍 **Homework Helper** ClassZone.com

Terms & Names
1. Explain the importance of
   bishop   catholic   Trinity
   pope   creed

Using Your Notes
Finding Main Ideas Use your completed diagram to answer the following question:
2. What decision made by Theodosius had a big impact on Roman religion? (6.7.7)

Rome's Attitude Toward Christianity

Main Ideas
3. How did the Romans view Christianity at first? (6.7.7)
4. What effect did the Edict of Milan have? (6.7.7)
5. What three persons are said to make up the Trinity? (6.7.6)

Critical Thinking
6. **Understanding Cause and Effect** What effect did Emperor Constantine have on the spread of Christianity? (7.1.3)
7. **Making Inferences** Why do you think the bishop of Rome became the most important of all the bishops? (6.7.7)

Activity
Making a Time Line Chart the important events in the early history of the church on a time line. Be sure to include the sources for your dates. (CST 2)

---

3 Lesson Review Answers

Terms & Names
1. • bishop, p. 485
   • pope, p. 485
   • catholic, p. 485
   • creed, p. 486
   • Trinity, p. 486

Using Your Notes
See page 482 for an example of a completed diagram.
2. Theodosius made Christianity the official religion of Rome.

Main Ideas
3. as a potential threat
4. It established Christianity as a legal religion in Rome and returned property seized during the persecutions.
5. Father, Son, and Holy Spirit

Critical Thinking
6. Possible answer: Constantine's embrace of the previously unpopular religion helped set the stage for its later acceptance as Rome's state religion.
7. Possible answers: the importance of Rome's first bishop, the Apostle Peter, who was charged by Jesus to be the foundation of the Church; the central role of Rome in embracing and spreading the religion; Christianity's status as the state religion of the Roman Empire, of which Rome was the center

Activity Rubric

	Accuracy of Dates & Sources	Presentation of Time Line
4	thorough, accurate, well-documented	neat, well-organized, labeled
3	accurate, well-documented	neat, labeled
2	some accurate information; not all items documented	messy, somewhat disorganized, incomplete labels
1	inaccurate, incomplete information; missing or poor documentation	sloppy, poor organization, missing labels

Make a World-Religions Pie Graph

Goal: To understand the sizes of the major religions of the world

Prepare

❶ Gather resources, such as world almanacs, encyclopedias, and books from the library.

❷ Make a list of religions you find in these resources.

Do the Activity

❶ Use the resources you've identified to find out the numbers of members of the major religions of the world. Major religions you might research include the following: Christianity, Islam, Judaism, Hinduism, and Buddhism. You might also have categories "Other" (for members of all the many other religions in the world) and "Nonreligious" (for residents of officially atheistic countries, such as China).

❷ Construct a pie graph showing the size of each religion. The bigger the percentage of believers, the bigger the slice of the graph.

❸ Choose a color for each religion or category, and color in each slice of the graph.

Follow-Up

❶ Which religion has the most members?

❷ Which religion has the second greatest number?

❸ What other generalizations can you make on the basis of the graph?

Extension

Making a Presentation Display your completed pie graph in the classroom.

CALIFORNIA STANDARDS
6.7.7 Describe the circumstances that led to the spread of Christianity in Europe and other Roman territories.

Materials & Supplies
- blank sheet of paper
- markers or crayons of different colors
- a ruler to draw lines for sections of the pie graph
- research sources, such as world almanacs or encyclopedias

487

ACTIVITY: MAKE A PIE GRAPH

Objective

Describe the relative size of the populations for various world religions today.

Suggestions for Completing the Activity

- Provide students with up-to-date materials so statistics about various populations are current.

- Help students resolve any conflicts regarding sources, differences in definitions, counting methods, and other possibly confusing issues.

- Review with students the format and purpose of a pie graph. Explain that the whole circle represents the entire world population, and each "slice" represents the population of a given group.

ACTIVITY ANSWERS

Follow-Up Answers
1. Students' graphs may vary but should show Christianity as having the most members.
2. Students' graphs may vary but should show Islam as claiming the second largest number of followers.
3. Students may say that there are many different world religions, and that each has a large number of members.

Extension Rubric

	Accuracy of Data	Presentation of Graph
4	complete, accurate	neat, attractive, easy to read
3	complete, mostly accurate	neat, clear
2	somewhat incomplete or inaccurate	messy, confusing
1	incomplete or inaccurate	sloppy, unclear

Terms & Names

1. The four Gospels tell about the deeds of Jesus and his 12 disciples.

2. Paul was probably the early Christian Church's most important missionary.

3. The pope is the bishop of Rome.

Main Ideas

The Origins of Christianity
(pages 466–475)

4. Possible answers: People should not simply obey the law but should also change their hearts; people should love their enemies; people should live simply; people should not seek to accumulate things.

5. Jesus' birth, crucifixion, and resurrection

The Early Christians
(pages 476–481)

6. Judaism

7. the decision not to require initial conversion to Judaism

Rome and Christianity
(pages 482–487)

8. The Romans destroyed it in response to a Jewish uprising.

9. Possible answers: baptism and communion

VISUAL SUMMARY

The Birth of Christianity

Belief Systems (6.7.6)
- Christianity built upon Jewish beliefs.
- The disciples of Jesus believed that he was the Messiah.
- Christians believe that Jesus rose from the dead and that this made an afterlife possible.
- Jesus' disciples and, later, other apostles like Paul spread the teachings of Jesus.

Geography (6.7.6)
- Paul traveled around the eastern Roman Empire trying to convince Gentiles to believe in Jesus.

Government (6.7.7)
- Jews and Christians challenged the authority of Rome.
- Constantine converted to Christianity and made it one of the official religions of the empire.
- The Christian church developed into a complex institution.

TERMS & NAMES

Explain why the words in each pair below are linked with each other.

1. **Gospel** and **disciple**
2. **Paul** and **missionary**
3. **bishop** and **pope**

MAIN IDEAS

The Origins of Christianity (pages 466–475)

4. What is one important message from the Sermon on the Mount? (6.7.6)

5. What events do the Christian holidays of Christmas, Good Friday, and Easter Sunday commemorate? (6.7.6)

The Early Christians (pages 476–481)

6. What religion did Jesus and his earliest disciples follow? (6.7.6)

7. What early decision helped attract Gentile converts to Christianity and separate it from Judaism? (6.7.6)

Rome and Christianity (pages 482–487)

8. What happened to the Temple in Jerusalem in A.D. 70? (6.7.5)

9. What are two examples of Christian sacraments? (6.7.6)

CRITICAL THINKING

Big Ideas: Government

10. **MAKING INFERENCES** What beliefs did Jesus preach that might have brought him into conflict with Rome? (6.7.6)

11. **DRAWING CONCLUSIONS** Why might Christians have been blamed by the Roman authorities for the fire that destroyed Rome in A.D. 64? (6.7.7)

12. **SUMMARIZING** How did the emperor Constantine help spread Christianity? (7.1.3)

ALTERNATIVE ASSESSMENT RUBRICS

1. Writing Rubric

	Thoroughness of Report	Errors in Mechanics
4	answers all five questions using vivid details	few or none
3	answers all five questions; includes some detail	some
2	answers three or four of the five questions; lacks detail	many
1	answers two or fewer of the five questions; lacks detail	major

2. Geography Rubric

	Evidence of Research	Presentation of Report
4	includes all required elements; thorough, accurate	clearly communicated; well organized; integrates maps appropriately
3	includes required elements, accurate	clearly communicated; organized; integrates maps
2	missing some elements; mostly accurate	somewhat confusing; includes no maps
1	includes incomplete or inaccurate information	unclear, sloppy, includes no maps

ALTERNATIVE ASSESSMENT

1. WRITING ACTIVITY Imagine that you were a reporter present at the Sermon on the Mount or one of the other events described in this chapter. Explain to your readers what you have seen. Describe the people present, the words spoken, and the meaning of the event. Remember the questions of the newspaper reporter as you write up your account: (Writing 2.2)

- Who?
- What?
- Where?
- When?
- How?
- Why?

2. INTERDISCIPLINARY ACTIVITY— GEOGRAPHY Research how many miles Paul traveled on his various journeys. Describe the dangers he faced in various places. What dangers might a modern traveler face on the same routes? Using maps, make a brief oral report about your findings. (6.7.7)

3. STARTING WITH A STORY

 Review the poster you made about replacing Nero. Research what happened to Nero, and write the headline and first paragraph of a news story explaining his overthrow. (Writing 2.2)

Technology Activity

4. CREATING A MULTIMEDIA PRESENTATION
Use the Internet or library to research the sayings of Jesus and other religious leaders. Create a multimedia presentation in which you compare and contrast these sayings. Include
- sayings of Buddha and Confucius
- images of the religious leaders
- a comparison chart
- text for each slide
- documentation of your sources (6.7.6)

Research Links
ClassZone.com

Reading Charts Latin was the language of the western Roman Empire and the Roman Catholic Church. Use the chart below to answer the questions. (6.7.7)

The Influence of Latin		
Latin Word	**Meaning**	**Related Words in English**
pontifex	high priest	pontiff
dominus	lord	domain, dominion
senatus	supreme council of state	senate, senator
provincia	governed territory	province
legio	body of soldiers	legion, legionnaire
Caesar	emperor, prince	kaiser, czar
episcopus	overseer	episcopal, bishop
cardinalis	principal, pivotal	cardinal
sedes	seat	Holy See
catholicus	universal	catholic

1. What two elements in the Roman world do the Latin words in the chart apply to?

A. Temple in Jerusalem and Roman Forum
B. Roman army and roads
C. Roman government and the Roman Catholic Church
D. capitals of Rome and Constantinople

2. What sorts of activities do the Latin words in the chart relate to?

A. sports and athletic competition
B. music and entertainment
C. government and authority
D. business and commerce

 **Test Practice**
ClassZone.com

Additional Test Practice, pp. S1–S33

Critical Thinking

Big Ideas: Government

10. Possible answers: sympathy for the outcast, equality, nonviolence, belief in God

11. Possible answers: Christians had customs and beliefs that differed from other Roman citizens. They refused to worship Roman gods. They were also becoming more numerous, threatening Roman authority.

12. He made Christianity a legal religion, built churches, and established center of Christianity in what is now Turkey.

Standards-Based Assessment

1. The correct answer is C. Answers A, B, and D are incorrect because few of the words in the chart relate to those topics.

2. The correct answer is C. A, B, and D are incorrect because none of the words in the chart relate to sports, music, or business.

 **Research Links**
Visit **ClassZone.com** for links to Web sites that can be used in the newsletter.

 **Test Practice**
Visit **ClassZone.com** to access strategies and tutorials for taking standardized tests.

 Formal Assessment
- Chapter Tests, Forms A, B, and C, pp. 249–260

 Test Generator
- Chapter Tests, Forms A, B, and C (English and Spanish)

ALTERNATIVE ASSESSMENT RUBRICS

3. Starting with a Story Rubric

	Details in Story	Writing Style
4	realistic and compelling; incorporates facts from history	realistic representation of newspaper style; few or no mechanical errors
3	realistic; incorporates facts from history	reasonable representation of newspaper style; some errors
2	unrealistic; includes inaccurate or unrelated facts from history	adequate representation of newspaper style; many errors
1	unrelated to actual events in history	incomplete or includes major errors

4. Technology Rubric

	Comparisons in Report	Organization of Presentation
4	includes all elements; comparisons valid	well written, well organized, interesting
3	includes all required elements	well written
2	missing an element; confusing comparisons	poorly written
1	missing many elements; no comparisons	incomplete, disorganized

CHAPTER 15 PLANNING GUIDE: Rome's Decline and Legacy

Chapter Overview	Copymasters		Assessment
The Roman Empire, which eventually fell and left the Byzantine Empire in its wake, left a rich legacy for the world.	**In-Depth Resources: Unit 6** • Family Newsletter (English and Spanish), pp. 38–39 • Visual Summary, p. 44 • Vocabulary Study Guide, p. 46 **Character Education** **Reading Study Guide,** p. 141	**Bringing Social Studies Alive,** Chapter 15 **Document-Based Questions: Strategy and Practice** **Reading Toolkit,** L51–L54 **Modified Lesson Plans for English Learners,** pp. 105–112	**Chapter Review,** pp. 522–523 **Formal Assessment** • Chapter Tests, Forms A, B, and C, pp. 265–279 **Test Generator** **Integrated Assessment Book** **Online Test Practice**
LESSON 1 **An Empire in Decline** pp. 494–499 **OBJECTIVE** Trace the causes of the decline of the Roman Empire.	**In-Depth Resources: Unit 6** • Reading Skill: Understanding Cause and Effect, p. 40 • Vocabulary Cards, p. 47 • Reteaching Activity, p. 53	**History Makers** • Constantine, p. 29 **Interdisciplinary Projects** • Art, p. 88 **Reading Study Guide,** p. 133	**Lesson Review,** p. 498 **Formal Assessment** • Lesson Quiz, p. 261 **California Daily Standards Practice Transparencies,** TT51
LESSON 2 **The Fall of the Roman Empire** pp. 500–507 **OBJECTIVE** Analyze the fall of Rome.	**In-Depth Resources: Unit 6** • Reading Skill: Explaining Sequence, p. 41 • Vocabulary Cards, p. 47 • Reteaching Activity, p. 54	**Reading Study Guide,** p. 135	**Lesson Review,** p. 505 **Formal Assessment** • Lesson Quiz, p. 262 **California Daily Standards Practice Transparencies,** TT52
LESSON 3 **The Byzantine Empire** pp. 508–513 **OBJECTIVE** Study the features of the Byzantine Empire, which preserved Roman culture after the fall of Rome.	**In-Depth Resources: Unit 6** • Reading Skill: Summarizing, p. 42 • Vocabulary Cards, p. 47 • Skillbuilder Practice: Detecting Historical Points of View, p. 45 • Geography Practice: Constantinople, p. 49	• Primary Source: A Description by Emperor Constantine Porphyrogenitus, p. 51 • Reteaching Activity, p. 55 **Interdisciplinary Projects** • Math, p. 85 **Reading Study Guide,** p. 137	**Lesson Review,** p. 513 **Formal Assessment** • Lesson Quiz, p. 263 **California Daily Standards Practice Transparencies,** TT53
LESSON 4 **The Legacy of Rome** pp. 514–521 **OBJECTIVE** Explore the cultural legacy of the Roman Empire.	**In-Depth Resources: Unit 6** • Reading Skill: Finding Main Ideas, p. 43 • Vocabulary Cards, p. 47 • Literature: The *Aeneid*, by Virgil, p. 52 • Reteaching Activity, p. 56	**Interdisciplinary Projects** • Science, p. 86; Language Arts, p. 87 **Reading Study Guide,** p. 139	**Lesson Review,** p. 519  **Formal Assessment** • Lesson Quiz, p. 264 **California Daily Standards Practice Transparencies,** TT54

Integrated Technology

 eEdition Plus Online

EasyPlanner Plus Online

eTest Plus Online

 Audio CDs
- Reading Study Guide
- Reading Study
  Guide in Spanish
- The World's Music

 CD-ROMs
- Power Presentations
- eEdition
- EasyPlanner
- Test Generator

---

 eEdition CD-ROM

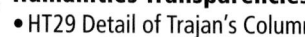 **Humanities Transparencies**
- HT29 Detail of Trajan's Column

 Map Transparencies
- MT29 Roads of the Roman Empire

 Critical Thinking Transparencies
- CT65 Understanding Cause and Effect

 ClassZone.com

---

 eEdition CD-ROM

 Humanities Transparencies
- HT30 Gothic Jewelry

 Map Transparencies
- MT30 Europe, A.D. 500

 **Critical Thinking Transparencies**
- CT66 Explaining Sequence

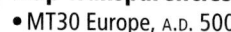 **ClassZone.com**

---

 eEdition CD-ROM

 Critical Thinking Transparencies
- CT67 Summarizing

 ClassZone.com

---

 eEdition CD-ROM

 Critical Thinking Transparencies
- CT68 Finding Main Ideas
- CT69 Chapter 15 Visual Summary

 ClassZone.com

Overview of California Resources

	Lesson 1	Lesson 2	Lesson 3	Lesson 4
California Reading Toolkit	L51	L52	L53	L54
California Modified Lesson Plans for English Learners	p. 105	p. 107	p. 109	p. 111
California Daily Standards Practice Transparencies	TT51	TT52	TT53	TT54
California Standards Enrichment Workbook	pp. 111–112	pp. 111–112	pp. 111–112	pp. 109–112
California Standards Planner and Lesson Plans	L101	L103	L105	L107
California Online Test Practice	ClassZone.com	ClassZone.com	ClassZone.com	ClassZone.com
California Test Generator CD-ROM	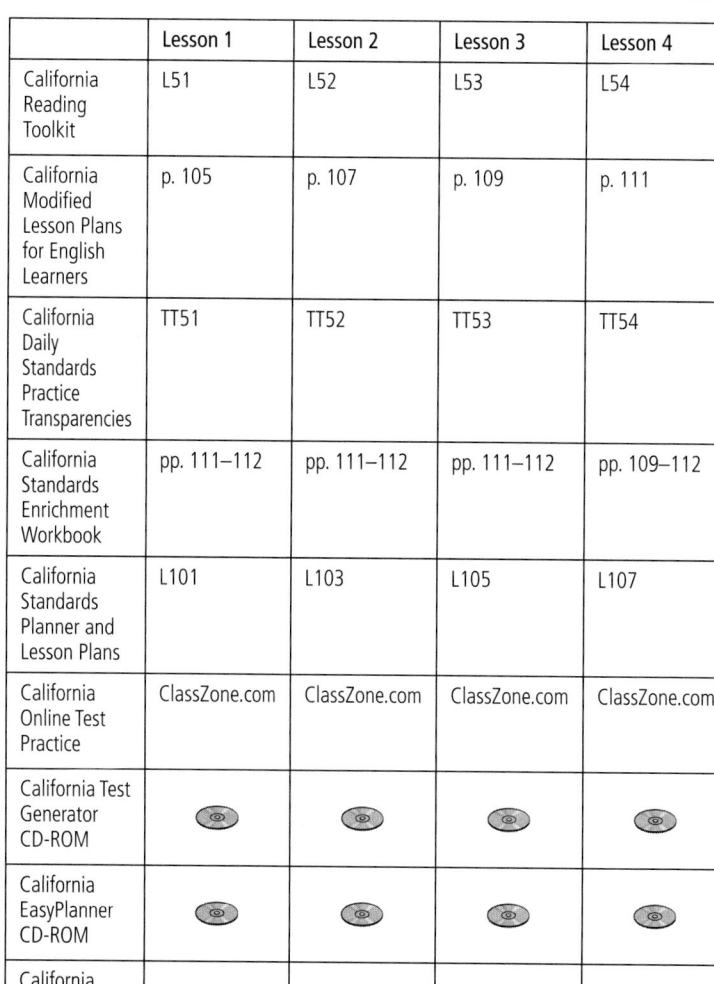			
California EasyPlanner CD-ROM				
California eEdition CD-ROM				

Chart Key

 Pupil Edition   CD-ROM   Internet

 Copymaster   Audio   Overhead Transparency

 Video

English Learners

In-Depth Resources in Spanish
- Reading Skill and Strategy Ⓐ
- Skillbuilder Practice
- Geography Practice Ⓒ
- Vocabulary Study Guide Ⓑ

In-Depth Resources: Unit 6
- Family Newsletter (English and Spanish)

Reading Study Guide (Spanish)

Reading Study Guide Audio CD
(Spanish)

Test Generator
Chapter Test (Spanish)

Plus

Modified Lesson Plans for English Learners

Multi-Language Glossary of Social Studies Terms

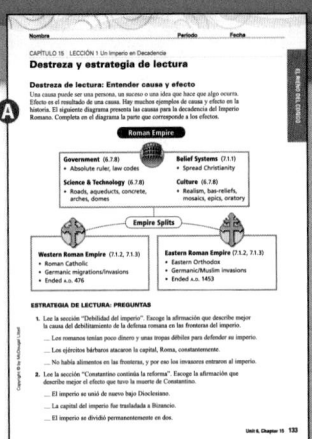
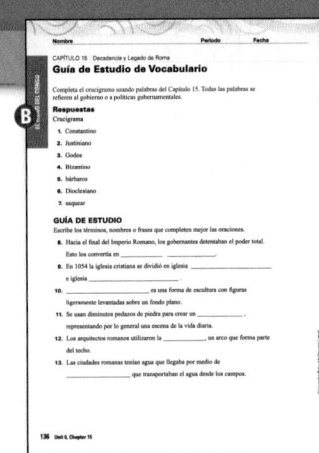

Struggling Readers

In-Depth Resources: Unit 6
- Vocabulary Study Guide
- Skillbuilder Practice Ⓑ
- Geography Practice
- Reteaching Activities
- Family Newsletter Ⓒ

Reading Study Guide Ⓐ

Reading Study Guide Audio CD

Reading Toolkit

Formal Assessment
Chapter Test, Form A

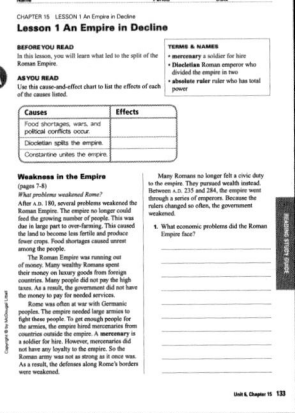
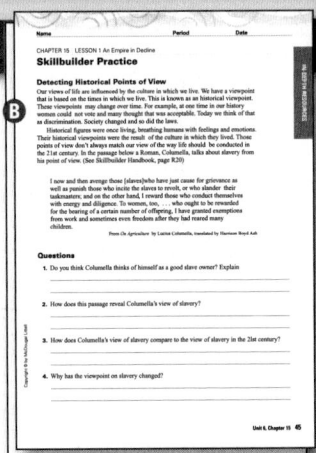

Inclusion

EasyPlanner CD-ROM
- Reading Skill and Strategy Ⓑ
- Vocabulary Study Guide Ⓒ
- Geography Practice
- Reteaching Activities Ⓐ

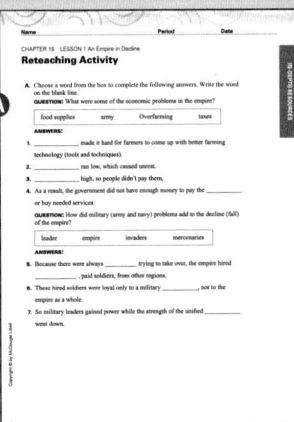

Gifted and Talented Students

In-Depth Resources: Unit 6
- Primary Source Ⓐ
- Literature

History Makers Ⓑ

Interdisciplinary Projects Ⓒ

Formal Assessment
Chapter Test, Form C

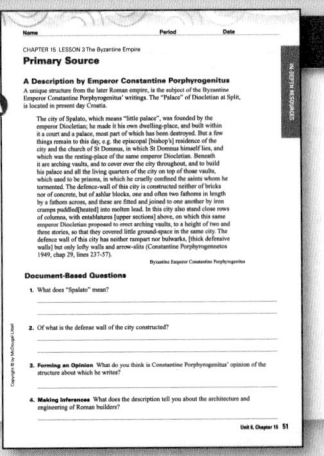

Activities in the Teacher's Edition for English Learners

- Find Solutions, p. 496
- Write Descriptions, p. 502
- Examine Attitudes, p. 506
- Compare and Contrast, p. 511
- Categorize Details, p. 516

Activities in the Teacher's Edition for Struggling Readers

- Diagram the Content, p. 496
- Shrink the Paragraphs, p. 503
- Rewrite the Passage, p. 506
- Create Character Profiles, p. 510
- Read the Sections Aloud, p. 518
- Make Vocabulary Cards, p. 520

Activities in the Teacher's Edition for Inclusion Students

- Listen to the Lesson, p. 497
- Practice Remembering, p. 502
- Take Audio Notes, p. 510
- Read Content Aloud, p. 516
- Divide and Conquer, p. 520

Activities in the Teacher's Edition for Gifted and Talented Students

- Create a History in Maps, p. 497
- Report on the Huns in China, p. 503
- Create Organizational Charts, p. 511
- Explore Roman Roots in U.S. Government, p. 518

Integrated Technology

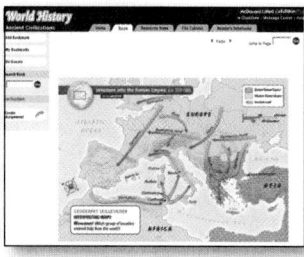

eEdition CD-ROM

- Interactive Visuals
- Interactive Maps
- Starting with a Story

ClassZone.com

- WebQuests
- Research Links
- Internet Activities
- Homework Helper
- Chapter Quiz
- Current Events
- Test Practice

Power Presentations CD-ROM

- Lecture Notes
- Media Gallery
- Chapter Review Game

Critical Thinking Transparencies

- CT65 Understanding Cause and Effect
- CT66 Explaining Sequence
- CT67 Summarizing
- CT68 Finding Main Ideas
- CT69 Chapter 15 Visual Summary

California Daily Standards Practice Transparencies, TT51–TT54

Map Transparencies

- MT29 Roads of the Roman Empire
- MT30 Europe, A.D. 500

Humanities Transparencies

- HT29 Detail of Trajan's Column
- HT30 Gothic Jewelry

Test Generator CD-ROM

EasyPlanner CD-ROM

Rome's Decline and Legacy • 489D

Begin the Chapter

Objective

Analyze the decline of the Roman Empire and the legacy it left for the world.

Quick Look

Lesson 1 describes the weaknesses that gradually emerged in the Roman Empire and their effects on the empire.

Lesson 2 describes the events that led to the actual fall of Rome.

Lesson 3 explores the Byzantine Empire—the remnant of the Roman Empire that continued after its fall.

Lesson 4 summarizes the cultural legacy of the Roman Empire to the rest of the world, in the arts, technology, law and government, and religion.

Before You Read: K-W-L

K-W-L is a strategy for activating prior knowledge and preparing students for what they will be learning. This helps set a purpose for reading and improves students' motivation and ability to focus.

Have students follow these steps:

- Read the "Before You Read" instructions and follow the steps.

- Think about what you already know about the Roman Empire from earlier chapters, from other books, and from movies and television programs you have seen.

- Think about what you'd like to learn about the Roman Empire and its fall.

- At the end of the chapter, think about what you have learned about the Roman Empire's fall and legacy.

Chapter 15
Rome's Decline and Legacy

Before You Read: K-W-L

Considering what you have already learned about Rome will help prepare you to read this chapter. Record the answers to the following questions in your notebook:

- What do you already know about Rome?
- Study the map on these pages. What does it tell you about what has happened in the Roman Empire?
- What do you want to learn about the legacy of Rome?

Big Ideas About Rome's Decline and Legacy

Economics Nomadic peoples often attack settlements to gain the goods that civilizations produce.

Roman armies spent a lot of time fighting people who wanted to enter the empire. Some nomads wanted the protection of the Roman Empire. Others wanted to take over Roman lands. They disrupted trade and took valuable goods.

Integrated Technology

eEdition
- Interactive Maps
- Interactive Visuals
- Starting with a Story

INTERNET RESOURCES
Go to ClassZone.com for
- WebQuest
- Homework Helper
- Research Links
- Internet Activities
- Quizzes
- Maps
- Test Practice
- Current Events

ATLANTIC OCEAN

30°W   20°W

ROME

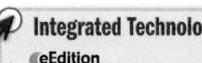

161
Marcus Aurelius begins his reign. (relief of Marcus Aurelius) ▲

285
Diocletian reorganizes the empire.

324
Constantine reunifies the Roman Empire.

476
Western Roman Empire falls.

200   300   400

WORLD

220
Han Dynasty collapses.

325
King Ezana rules African kingdom of Aksum. (pillar from Aksum) ▶

490

TIME LINE DISCUSSION

Use the time line to help students develop a mental time frame for the discussion of the fall of the Roman Empire and to preview information that will be covered in the chapter.

- What do the events of 285 and 324 suggest about the Roman Empire at that time? *(Possible answer: The empire was having trouble with its government and was in fact breaking into different parts.)*

- About how many years passed between Constantine's reunification of the empire and the fall of the Western Roman Empire? *(more than 150 years)*

- How long after the fall of the Western Roman Empire did the Christian Church break into two branches? *(578 years)*

- For how many years did the Byzantine Empire stand after the fall of the Western Roman Empire? *(977 years)*

The Division of the Roman Empire, A.D. 395

INTERACTIVE

North Sea
Baltic Sea
BRITAIN
London
FRANKS
ASIA
VANDALS
GOTHS
EUROPE
GAUL
ALPS
ITALY
Adriatic Sea
Corsica
Rome
MACEDONIA
Black Sea
Constantinople
(Byzantium)
SPAIN
Sardinia
ANATOLIA
Córdoba
Athens
Antioch
Sicily
Crete
SYRIA
Carthage
Cyprus
Mediterranean Sea
PALESTINE
LIBYA
Alexandria
Jerusalem
AFRICA
EGYPT
SAHARA

Eastern Roman Empire
Western Roman Empire
GOTHS Major Germanic peoples

0   300   600 miles
0 300 600 kilometers

527
Justinian comes to power
in the Byzantine Empire.
◄ (mosaic of Justinian)

1054
Christian church splits
into two branches.

1453
Byzantine Empire
falls to the Turks.

600   900   1200   1500

630
Muhammad unifies the people
of the Arabian peninsula.

900s
Mayan civilization
declines.
◄ (Mayan pyramid)

1279
Kublai Khan conquers China.
◄ (painting of Kublai Khan)

491

RECOMMENDED RESOURCES

Books for the Teacher
Burns, Thomas S. *Rome and the Barbarians, 100 B.C.– A.D. 400.* Baltimore: Johns Hopkins UP, 2003. History of the Romans' encounters with "Barbarians."

Kirby, John T., ed. *Roman Republic and Empire, 264 B.C.E.–476 C.E.* Detroit: Gale, 2001. Historical overview of the Roman Republic and the Roman Empire.

Mango, Cyril, ed. *The Oxford History of Byzantium.* Oxford: Oxford UP, 2002. History of the Byzantine Empire.

Videos
Ancient Rome. 200 minutes. New York: A&E Home Video, 1998. Four-cassette history of Rome. VHS.

Barbarians. 200 minutes. New York: A&E Home Video, 2003. Two-disc exploration of the Huns, the Goths, and other groups. DVD.

Internet
To access these sites, visit the Research Links for this chapter at **ClassZone.com**.

WebChron: The Web Chronology Project. North Park University site with an extensive selection of articles and links to sources on the history of the Roman Empire.

Internet Medieval Sourcebook. Contains a wide range of resources on Byzantine history and culture.

Introduce the Big Ideas
Read aloud the text about the Big Ideas. Direct students to think about what they have learned about civilizations, cities, and economic specialization. Ask students to think about why civilizations such as Rome may have been tempting targets for nomadic peoples.

Here are some other Big Ideas that you may want to emphasize in this chapter.

Government
The challenges of ruling the vast Roman Empire, with many people and many different beliefs, undermined Rome's authority and led to change.

Government
In the Byzantine Empire, the disorganized body of Roman law was collected and edited to create a new legal system.

Science and Technology
The Roman skill at building created a legacy of architecture and engineering that is still influential today.

Talk About It

Interpreting Maps
Instruct students to look at the map and read the key. Ask students to offer their opinions about how the division of the empire into two parts may have helped the empire survive. *(Possible answer: The entire empire was very large, and dividing it into halves made it easier to govern those halves.)*

INTERACTIVE

An interactive version of this map is available on the eEdition and Power Presentations CD-ROMs.

Find Out More
Have students use library or Internet resources to compare this map with a map of Europe today. Ask, What is Rome's position in the world today? *(It is the capital of Italy.)* What is the position of Constantinople? *(It is now called Istanbul, and it is the most populous city in Turkey.)*

Objective

Explore a scenario that illustrates the growing conflict between the Germanic groups on the Roman Empire's frontier and the Romans.

Introducing the Story

The Arrival of the Goths

The Goths had long lived on the northern and eastern borders of the Roman Empire. Occasionally, they had fought with the Romans, and they were highly skilled warriors. They were no match, however, for the Huns, a fearsome fighting force from Asia that stormed into the region in the fourth century. The Huns overwhelmed their opponents. After learning of the Huns' conquest of other groups in the region, the Goths decided to seek refuge in the Roman Empire.

Vocabulary Preview

honor glory; fame

Read the Story Aloud

1. **The teacher as reader:** Read the story aloud with expression, so that students hear the drama and understand the emotional impact of the events.

2. **The students as readers:** Give student readers a few minutes to read the story to themselves before they read it aloud to the rest of the class.

Starting with a Story

Students can also follow along as they listen to the story on the eEdition or Power Presentations CD-ROMs.

Starting with a Story

THE ARRIVAL OF THE GOTHS

CALIFORNIA STANDARDS
Reading 2.3 Connect and clarify main ideas by identifying their relationships to other sources and related topics.

Background: The Goths were Germanic peoples who lived north and east of the Western Roman Empire. In A.D. 375, a fierce Asian people called the Huns began to invade the Goths' territory. The Huns killed hundreds of people and burned villages and fields. Fearing for their lives, some Goths fled to the Western Roman Empire. There, they asked the Romans for protection. Imagine that you are an observer as the Goths arrive at the border of the Roman Empire.

Sculpture of a Roman soldier triumphing over a barbarian ▶

492

ADDITIONAL RESOURCES

Books for the Student
Harvey, Bonnie *Attila the Hun.* Philadelphia: Chelsea, 2003. Biographical account of Attila the Hun and description of his effort to conquer the Roman Empire.

Marston, Elsa. *The Byzantine Empire.* New York: Benchmark, 2003. History of the society and culture of the Byzantine Empire, which grew from the falling Roman Empire.

Mellor, Ronald. *The Ancient Roman World.* Oxford: Oxford UP, 2004. Overview of the history, culture, and people of the Roman Empire.

Videos
Roman. 40 minutes. Wheeling: Film Ideas, 2004. Part of the Timelines of Ancient Civilization series, with part 2 focusing on the history of the Roman Empire, starting with the end of the Roman Republic. VHS, DVD.

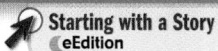
F ear of the Huns caused the western Goths to ask the Romans for protection. The Romans agreed to let the Goths cross the river into their empire. First, however, the Romans said the Goths must give up their weapons. But Goth warriors believed they had no honor without weapons. So they paid the Romans money or did favors for them in order to keep their weapons.

The river crossing was hard. The water was high and flowed swiftly. The floodwaters swept many people to their deaths.

Then the Goths entered a camp guarded by Roman soldiers. The governors of the region were supposed to feed the people. Instead, the Roman soldiers sold the people food—disgusting stuff that no Roman would eat. For example, some meat came from animals that died of disease. In exchange, the Romans took everything of value the Goths had.

Now the Romans are also buying Goth children and making them their slaves. Many Goth parents believe slavery is better than starvation. But they are bitter about making such a cruel choice.

Anger is growing. One Goth says, "We told the Romans that if they helped us, we would accept their religion and fight their enemies. As soon as we have nothing left to offer, they will starve us."

Some people propose going to the governors and explaining the Goths' suffering. "Maybe they will make the soldiers treat us better," one argues.

Others mutter about getting revenge. "We are men of honor. We still have weapons, and we can fight the Romans."

Should the Goths fight back or seek a peaceful solution?

Reading & Writing

1. **READING: Main Ideas** What is the main idea of this story? How do you think it might be related to the main idea of this chapter?

2. **WRITING: Persuasion** Write the outline for a speech in which you try to persuade the Goths whether to fight back or to seek peace. Be sure to give reasons supporting your decision. If possible, deliver your speech to the class.

CALIFORNIA STANDARDS Writing 2.5
Write persuasive compositions.

493

STARTING WITH A STORY

Talk About It

Ask students the following questions to begin the discussion:

- Why did the Goths seek entry into the Roman Empire? *(They were trying to get protection from the Huns.)*

- What can you infer about the Huns from the Goths' fear of them? *(The Huns must have been a powerful people, and the Goths must have believed they could not defeat them.)*

- How did the Romans treat the Goths once they were within Roman borders? *(The Romans took advantage of the Goths and treated them poorly.)*

- What responses to the Romans' treatment of them are the Goths considering? *(They are considering making an appeal to a higher authority or fighting back.)*

Should the Goths fight back or seek a peaceful solution?

Possible answers: The Goths should recognize that they have no hope unless they fight back; the Goths have come this far to avoid fighting, so they should do what they can to avoid battle.

Making Personal Connections

Connect the discussion to today by asking about how this country responds to people who need our help. Does this country welcome people who are suffering at the hands of others? Do we take advantage of people who are struggling or weak? How do you think this country should respond to those who need our help?

READING & WRITING ACTIVITIES

1. **READING** Goths have entered Roman territory, and the Romans are taking advantage of them. This chapter is about the decline and fall of Rome. The Goths' entry into Roman territory will cause problems.

2. **WRITING**

2. Writing Rubric

	Statement of Position	Number of Supporting Statements	Attention to Counterarguments
4	clear and concise	many	all anticipated and answered
3	clear	some	a few anticipated
2	barely adequate	few	not anticipated
1	unclear	none	not anticipated

❶ Plan & Prepare

Objectives

- Summarize the weaknesses that emerged in the Roman Empire following the death of Marcus Aurelius.
- Describe Diocletian's attempt to strengthen the empire by dividing it.
- Analyze Constantine's ongoing efforts at reform in the Roman Empire.
- **Language Objective:** Identify the problems that led to the decline of the Roman Empire.

Quick Look

Lesson 1 explores the events and developments that signaled the decline of the Roman Empire in the centuries after the reign of Marcus Aurelius.

❷ Focus & Motivate

Preview Ask students to recall what they have learned about the histories of other great civilizations—how they rose to greatness and then fell.

Introduce the Main Ideas The three main ideas relate to the Big Idea "Nomadic peoples often attack settlements to gain the goods that civilizations produce." Help students look for statements related to this Big Idea as they read the lesson.

Reading Skill: Understanding Cause and Effect Remind students that a cause is something that takes place—an event or development—that makes something happen. An effect is something that occurs as result of the cause.

SAMPLE ANSWERS FOR CHART

Causes	Effects
Food shortages, wars, and political conflicts occur.	The empire is weakened.
Diocletian splits the empire.	Civil war breaks out over succession.
Constantine unites the empire.	His successors can not rule the whole empire, and it permanently splits.

Lesson 1

▶ **MAIN IDEAS**

❶ **Culture** A series of problems—including food shortages, wars, and political conflicts—weakened the Roman Empire.

❷ **Government** Because the empire was so huge, Diocletian divided it into eastern and western regions to make governing more efficient.

❸ **Government** Emperor Constantine reunited the eastern and western empires and tried to restore the Roman Empire to greatness.

▶ **TAKING NOTES**

Reading Skill: Understanding Cause and Effect
Finding causes and effects will help you understand patterns in history. Look for the effect of each event listed in the chart below. Record them on a chart of your own.

Causes	Effects
Food shortages, wars, and political conflicts occur.	
Diocletian splits the empire.	
Constantine unites the empire.	

 Skillbuilder Handbook, page R26

▲ **Emperor Trajan's Column**
The surface of this 130-foot column is carved with scenes of Trajan's wars against outsiders.

CALIFORNIA STANDARDS

7.1.1 Study the early strengths and lasting contributions of Rome (e.g., significance of Roman citizenship; rights under Roman law; Roman art, architecture, engineering, and philosophy; preservation and transmission of Christianity) and its ultimate internal weaknesses (e.g., rise of autonomous military powers within the empire, undermining of citizenship by the growth of corruption and slavery, lack of education, and distribution of news).

7.1.2 Discuss the geographic borders of the empire at its height and the factors that threatened its territorial cohesion.

7.1.3 Describe the establishment by Constantine of the new capital in Constantinople and the development of the Byzantine Empire, with an emphasis on the consequences of the development of two distinct European civilizations, Eastern Orthodox and Roman Catholic, and their two distinct views on church-state relations.

494 • Chapter 15

HOW TO TEACH THE CALIFORNIA STANDARDS

Standard	Content	Student Question or Activity	Instruction
7.1.1	**Pages 495–496** Traces the major weaknesses of the Roman Empire as it approached its fall	**Pages 494, 496** Students identify problems that weakened the Roman Empire. They also create a chart.	Discuss the effects of each of the major weaknesses of the empire. Help students see how these weaknesses undermined the strength of the empire.
7.1.2	**Pages 496–497** Discusses the size of the empire and the factors that led to its division	**Page 498** Students answer a question about civil war.	Have students do some outside research on the barbarian groups that lived on Rome's frontiers.
7.1.3	**Page 497** Discusses the establishment of Constantinople by Constantine	**Page 498** Students describe the role of Constantine in the strengthening of the Roman Empire.	Review the many contributions of Constantine to the Roman Empire, including his role in promoting Christianity.

An Empire in Decline

Build on What You Know Did you ever have a problem you thought you could solve, then realized you could not find the right solution for it? In this lesson you will learn that the Roman Empire began to develop difficult problems for which there seemed to be no obvious solutions.

Weakness in the Empire

① ESSENTIAL QUESTION What problems weakened Rome?
agricultural, economic, military, and political

After the death of Emperor Marcus Aurelius in A.D. 180, a series of problems began to weaken the empire. These economic and political problems were difficult to solve.

Economic Problems The empire could no longer feed its many people. Some farmland had been destroyed by warfare. But the biggest problem was improving farm production. With many slaves to do the work, plantation owners chose not to develop more-productive farming technology. As a result, the land wore out and harvests did not increase. Food shortages caused unrest.

The empire was running low on money. Taxes were high, so many people did not pay them. Without tax money, the government could not pay the army or buy needed services.

Hadrian's Wall
Hadrian's Wall marked the geographic border of the Roman Empire on the island of Britain. Like the Great Wall of China, this wall was supposed to help keep out invaders. ▼

495

Terms & Names

mercenary a soldier who is hired to fight for a foreign government

Diocletian a Roman emperor who took power in A.D. 284

absolute ruler a ruler who holds complete power in a government

❸ Teach

Weakness in the Empire
🔖 7.1.1

Talk About It

- **Critical Thinking: Summarize** How would you summarize the basic problems facing the Roman Empire in the years after the death of Marcus Aurelius? *(Possible answer: The empire became too large and unmanageable, so that it was hard for it to meet the needs of its people and provide for its own defense.)*

California Resources

California Reading Toolkit, L51
California Modified Lesson Plans for English Learners, p. 105
California Daily Standards Practice Transparencies, TT51
California Standards Enrichment Workbook, pp. 111–112
California Online Test Practice
California Test Generator CD-ROM
California Standards Planner and Lesson Plans, L101
California EasyPlanner CD-ROM
California eEdition CD-ROM

LESSON 1 PROGRAM RESOURCES

ON LEVEL

In-Depth Resources: Unit 6
- Family Newsletter (English and Spanish), pp. 38–39
- Reading Skill: Understanding Cause and Effect, p. 40
- Skillbuilder Practice: Detecting Historical Points of View, p. 45
- Vocabulary Study Guide, p. 46
- Vocabulary Cards, p. 47

Formal Assessment
- Lesson Quiz, p. 261

ENGLISH LEARNERS

In-Depth Resources in Spanish
- Reading Skill, p. 129

- Vocabulary Study Guide, p. 136
- Skillbuilder Practice, p. 135

Modified Lesson Plans for English Learners, p. 105

Reading Study Guide (Spanish), p. 133

Reading Study Guide Audio CD (Spanish)

STRUGGLING READERS

In-Depth Resources: Unit 6
- Reading Skill, p. 40
- Vocabulary Study Guide, p. 46
- Vocabulary Cards, p. 47
- Reteaching Activity, p. 53

Reading Toolkit, L51
Reading Study Guide, p. 133
Reading Study Guide Audio CD

GIFTED AND TALENTED STUDENTS

History Makers
- Constantine, p. 29

Interdisciplinary Projects
- Art, p. 88

INCLUSION

EasyPlanner CD-ROM
- Reading Skills
- Vocabulary Study Guide
- Reteaching Activity

TECHNOLOGY

eEdition CD-ROM
- Starting with a Story

Power Presentations CD-ROM

Humanities Transparencies
- HT29 Detail of Trajan's Column

Map Transparencies
- MT29 Roads of the Roman Empire

Critical Thinking Transparencies
- CT65 Understanding Cause and Effect

Test Generator CD-ROM

ClassZone.com

In-Depth Resources: Unit 6
• Reading Skill: Understanding Cause and Effect, p. 40

More About . . .

Roman Mercenaries

The Roman army made an extensive use of mercenaries. It was common for Roman officials to contract with groups such as the Vandals and the Goths. The Romans provided payment to the groups in return for their commitment of a certain number of soldiers.

Over time, the Romans began to offer groups the opportunity to settle in Roman territory instead of cash payments. It was one such arrangement that students read about in the Starting with a Story feature at the start of this chapter.

Vocabulary Strategy

Multiple Meanings

Tell students that when they encounter a word that they think they know but which does not seem to make sense, they should check the word's meaning in a dictionary. Sometimes the meanings of multiple-meaning words can be quite similar, but sometimes they can be very different. For example, *discipline*, used on this page, can mean two very different things.

Teach

Diocletian Divides the Empire

7.1.2

Talk About It

• Why did the size of the Roman Empire make it hard to govern? *(It was hard to get news from all parts of the empire, so that it was difficult to know when problems arose.)*

• What steps did Diocletian take to make management of the empire easier? *(He made changes in the military and in the economy. He divided the empire.)*

• **Critical Thinking: Identifying Issues and Problems** How might taking absolute power have helped Diocletian rule the Roman Empire? *(Possible answer: It may have made decision making faster or smoother.)*

Military Problems Rome was constantly at war with nomadic peoples in the north and northeast, as well as with the people who lived along its eastern borders. The empire needed larger armies to respond to so many threats, so it hired foreign mercenaries. A **mercenary** is a soldier for hire.

Mercenaries often had no loyalty to the empire. They pledged their allegiance to an individual military leader. Having armies that were loyal to only one man created independent military powers within the empire. In addition, mercenaries were not as disciplined as Roman soldiers. This lack of discipline made the army less effective. The result was a weakened defense along the empire's borders.

Political and Social Problems The sheer physical size of the Roman Empire made it hard to govern. Government officials found it was not easy to obtain news about affairs in some regions of the empire. This made it more difficult to know where problems were developing. Also, many government officials were corrupt, seeking only to enrich themselves. These political problems destroyed a sense of citizenship. Many Romans no longer felt a sense of duty to the empire. Many chose to get rich in business rather than serve in the government.

Other aspects of Roman society also suffered. The cost of education increased, so poor Romans found it harder to become educated. In addition, distributing news across the large empire became more difficult. People grew less informed about civic matters.

REVIEW What problems weakened the Roman Empire? Problems with agriculture, the economy, the military, and the political situation led to a weakened empire.

Diocletian Divides the Empire

2 **ESSENTIAL QUESTION** What steps did Diocletian take to solve the empire's problems? He restored order, introduced economic reforms, and eventually divided the empire.
A rapidly changing series of emperors also weakened the government. During a 49-year period (from A.D. 235 to 284), Rome had 37 emperors. Some of them were military leaders who used their armies to seize control. With emperors changing so often, the Roman people had little sense of orderly rule.

Vocabulary Strategy

The word *mercenary* can have **multiple meanings**. It has come to refer to anyone who, like the Roman mercenaries, does something only to get money.

The Tetrarchs This statue recognizes four emperors who ruled at the same time. ▼

DIFFERENTIATING INSTRUCTION

English Learners

Find Solutions

Ask, What could we do if there were not enough desks for everyone in this classroom? Accept students' logical responses and explain that these are possible solutions. Explain that the Roman Empire had problems that needed solutions. Guide students as they discuss the problems with agriculture, money, the military, and Roman politics. Have students work in small groups to discuss possible solutions. Have them present their solutions to the rest of the class.

Struggling Readers

Diagram the Content

Have students work in pairs to create web diagrams of the first section, "Weakness in the Empire." Have each pair place the title of the section in a circle in the middle of a sheet of paper. Then have them create satellite circles around the center circle, corresponding to the section's subsections. Finally, have them search the text for details to complete the diagram.

Diocletian Restores Order In A.D. 284, the emperor **Diocletian** (DY•uh•KLEE•shunn) took power. He changed the way the army operated by permanently placing troops at the empire's borders. He also introduced economic reforms, including keeping prices low on goods such as bread, to help feed the poor.

During his reign, Diocletian no longer bothered to consult with the Senate. He issued laws on his own. Diocletian was an **absolute ruler**, one who has total power.

Splitting the Empire Diocletian soon realized that he could not effectively govern the huge empire. In A.D. 285, he reorganized it in two, taking the eastern portion for himself. He chose this area for its greater wealth and trade, and its magnificent cities. He appointed Maximian to rule the Western Empire. The two men ruled for 20 years.

In A.D. 306 a civil war broke out over control of the empire. Four military commanders—including Constantine—fought for control of the two halves of the empire.

REVIEW Why did civil war break out in the Roman Empire?
After Diocletian and Maximian stepped down, four military commanders fought for control of the empire.

Constantine Continues Reform

❸ ESSENTIAL QUESTION How did Constantine change the empire?
He reunified it under a single emperor and moved the capital.
In Chapter 14, you learned that Constantine made it lawful to be a Christian. Now you will learn how he became emperor and reunited the Roman Empire.

A Single Emperor Constantine was a western Roman military commander who fought to gain control of Italy during the civil war. In A.D. 312, he entered Rome as the new emperor of the empire's western half. By A.D. 324, he had taken control of the Eastern Empire as well. The empire was reunited and Constantine became the sole emperor.

A New Capital In a bold move, Constantine shifted the empire's capital from Rome to Byzantium. Byzantium was an ancient Greek city located in what is now Turkey. At a crossroads between east and west, the city was well placed for defense and trade. Constantine enlarged and beautified his new capital, which he renamed Constantinople. Today the city is called Istanbul.

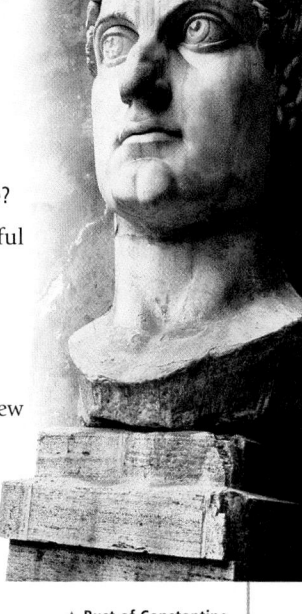

▲ **Bust of Constantine**
Constantine was an important emperor who reunited the Roman Empire.

DIFFERENTIATING INSTRUCTION

Gifted and Talented Students

Create a History in Maps
Have students use library and Internet resources to create map-based histories of the Roman Empire. Students should collect or create a range of maps showing how the empire grew, changed, and ultimately shrank. The maps should clearly indicate what time periods they cover. Have students present their map histories to the rest of the class.

Inclusion

Listen to the Lesson
Pair students who have vision impairments with ones who do not. Have the students who can see well read the lesson aloud. The readers should stop to ask all review questions, and each pair should work together to find the answers.

 Map Transparencies
• MT29 Roads of the Roman Empire

More About . . .

Diocletian
Diocletian took control of the Roman Empire at a very difficult and chaotic time in the empire's history, as described on pages 495–496. Diocletian realized that establishing order was necessary, and he was willing to take harsh measures to achieve that goal. For example, he declared that people working in certain professions would be unable to change their jobs. This was an effort to ensure continuity in certain key professions.

Diocletian also sought to unify the empire by stressing the practice of state religion. This effort led to the persecution of Christians under his rule.

Teach

Constantine Continues Reform
🏹 **7.1.3**

Talk About It

• How did Constantine come to be emperor of the empire's western half? *(He gained power during the civil war that followed the end of the rule of Diocletian and Maximian.)*

• Why did Constantine march on Rome? *(He wanted to gain control of the Western Roman Empire.)*

• What features made Byzantium a good choice for a new capital? *(It was well placed for defense and for trade.)*

• **Critical Thinking: Explaining Historical Patterns** Why do you think Constantine was able to keep the empire united but his successors were not? *(Possible answer: It took a very strong leader to control the whole empire. Constantine had the necessary strength, but others did not.)*

 History Makers
• Constantine, p. 29

❹ Assess & Reteach

Assess Group students, and have the students in each group number off. Ask a question from the Lesson Review, and allow group members to agree on an answer. Then call out a number so that the corresponding student in each group can give the group's answer.

 Formal Assessment
- Lesson Quiz, p. 261

Reteach On the board, write the names of the two main emperors covered in this lesson—Diocletian and Constantine. Call on volunteers to identify the main ideas about each one, and write their responses on the board.

 In-Depth Resources: Unit 6
- Vocabulary Cards, p. 47
- Reteaching Activity, p. 53

🔗 Homework Helper

Visit **ClassZone.com** for a lesson review, a flip-card activity, and links to related Web sites.

Final Division Constantine planned to have each of his three sons rule a portion of the empire after his death. His plan was unwise, for Constantius II, Constantine II, and Constans I created unrest by competing with one another. A period of conflict followed. In 395, the empire was permanently divided into east and west again.

REVIEW How did Constantine strengthen the Roman Empire?
He unified the eastern and western empires.

Lesson Summary
- The Roman Empire declined because of a combination of economic, military, and political reasons.
- Diocletian reorganized the empire to increase efficiency in government.
- Constantine unified the empire and moved its capital to Byzantium, which he renamed Constantinople.

Why It Matters Now . . .
The mistakes made by the Roman emperors remind us that to retain power and control, rulers must successfully deal with many different problems.

1 Lesson Review

🔗 **Homework Helper**
ClassZone.com

Terms & Names
1. Explain the importance of
    mercenary   Diocletian   absolute ruler

Using Your Notes
Understanding Cause and Effect Use your completed chart to answer the following question:
2. How do the causes and effects illustrate the decline of the empire? (7.1.1)

Causes	Effects
Food shortages, wars, and political conflicts occur.	
Diocletian splits the empire.	
Constantine unites the empire.	

Main Ideas
3. Why was the empire in trouble economically? (7.1.1)
4. What reforms did Diocletian introduce to solve the empire's problems? (7.1.2)
5. What did Constantine do to try to restore the empire to greatness? (7.1.3)

Critical Thinking
6. **Understanding Causes** How did constantly changing emperors affect the strength of the Roman Empire? (7.1.1)
7. **Making Inferences** Of the problems listed in this lesson, which one was most difficult for the ordinary Roman? (7.1.1)

Activity
Making a Collage Study the problems faced by the Roman Empire that were explained in this lesson. Then create a collage showing those problems. (7.1.1)

498 • Chapter 15

---

1 Lesson Review Answers

Terms & Names
1. • mercenary, p. 496
   • Diocletian, p. 497
   • absolute ruler p. 497

Using Your Notes
See page 494 for an example of a completed chart.
2. Each effect caused the next set of effects to occur.

Main Ideas
3. The empire could no longer feed its people, and it was not collecting enough taxes to operate successfully.

4. He reorganized the army and the government and introduced economic changes.
5. He unified the empire. He moved the capital to Byzantium.

Critical Thinking
6. Possible answer: People had little sense of orderly rule, and their faith in the power of the emperor was weakened.
7. Possible answers: high taxes; the lack of food

Activity Rubric

	Selection of Words and Images	Quality of Presentation
4	wide variety, clear relationship to Rome's problems	neat, attractive design
3	some variety, some relationship	attractive design
2	several words and images, unclear relationship	somewhat disorderly
1	few words and images, no relationship	sloppy and poorly executed

Hold a Debate

Goal: To debate the historical issue "What was the most serious problem in the late Roman Empire?"

Prepare

❶ Form a small group with three or four other students. Assign roles such as reader, note taker, and presenter.

❷ Reread pages 495–496. Take notes about the problems that the empire faced.

❸ Read the quotations on this page. They offer different opinions about the problems faced by the empire.

Do the Activity

❶ As a team, discuss the problems the quotations describe. Also, discuss other problems explained in this lesson.

❷ Decide which problem was the most serious. Which was hardest for the empire to solve? List your reasons for your choice.

❸ Hold a class debate. One student from each team should give a short speech explaining why the problem the team chose was the most serious. Finally, the class should discuss the various problems and reach a group decision.

Follow-Up

How would you respond to a person who said Rome fell because of barbarian invasions? Explain.

Extension

Doing Additional Research Use books or the Internet to research other problems of the empire. Write a paragraph summarizing what you have learned.

CALIFORNIA STANDARDS
7.1.1

Materials & Supplies
- note cards
- pens or pencils
- books on Roman history

from *The Book of the Ancient Romans* by **Dorothy Mills**

Perhaps the greatest danger of all to Rome . . . was the change in . . . the old Roman ideal of discipline and duty, of self-control and self-restraint. . . . By the second century A.D. there was practically none of it left.

from *The Ancient World: Rome* by **Sean Sheehan and Pat Levy**

So much time was spent [by soldiers and governors] fighting over who would be emperor that little attention was paid to the far reaches of the empire.

from *Ancient Rome* by **Judith Simpson**

By the third century A.D., the army was stretched too far and taxes were raised to cover the Empire's costs. Farmers who could not afford the taxes abandoned their farms, and cities suffered as the economy slumped and their markets declined.

from *History of the World: The Roman Empire* by **Don Nardo**

[After 192] Rome needed several good, strong emperors. . . . Instead, a long series of ambitious, weak, brutal, or inept [lacking skill] rulers occupied the throne.

499

Objective

Debate the problems that faced the Roman Empire.

Suggestions for Completing the Activity

- Make sure students have accurately identified the key problems of the empire.

- Encourage students to use outside sources to learn more about the problems in the empire.

- Make sure teams clearly understand the problems and can defend their selections as the most serious problems facing the empire.

- Suggest that team spokespersons practice their presentations in front of their teams. The teams can suggest improvements to the presentations.

ACTIVITY ANSWERS

Follow-Up Answer
Students may say that there were several problems that contributed to Rome's fall in addition to the barbarian invasions, including food shortages and internal political conflicts.

Extension Rubric

	Content of Paragraph	Errors in Mechanics
4	well researched; thorough, accurate information	no more than one grammatical or spelling error
3	well researched, accurate information	2–3 spelling or grammatical errors
2	some factual errors	4–5 spelling or grammatical errors
1	largely inaccurate	more than 5 spelling or grammatical errors

❶ Plan & Prepare

Objectives

- Describe the status of the two Roman empires following the permanent split in A.D. 395.
- Describe the effects of the ongoing invasions by barbarian groups on the Roman Empire.
- Summarize the events of the fall of Rome.
- **Language Objective:** Identify details that explain life during the fall of the Roman Empire.

Quick Look

Lesson 2 traces the events that led to the final fall of Rome and the end of the Roman Empire.

❷ Focus & Motivate

Preview Have students recall what they have read about changes and challenges facing the Roman Empire in the time of Diocletian and Constantine. Tell students that they will be reading about a new set of problems facing the Roman Empire.

Introduce the Main Ideas The three main ideas relate to the Big Idea "Nomadic peoples often attack settlements to gain the goods that civilizations produce." Help students look for statements related to this Big Idea as they read the lesson.

Reading Skill: Explaining Sequence Tell students that they can properly identify sequence by paying close attention to dates and to signal words such as *then, next,* or *later.*

SAMPLE ANSWERS FOR TIME LINE

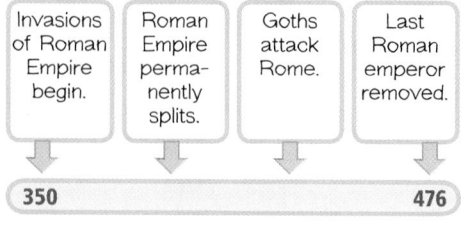

| Invasions of Roman Empire begin. | Roman Empire permanently splits. | Goths attack Rome. | Last Roman emperor removed. |

350 ——————————————— 476

Lesson 2

▶ MAIN IDEAS

❶ **Economics** The Western Roman Empire was much weaker than the more prosperous Eastern Roman Empire.

❷ **Geography** Invading groups of Germanic peoples overran the already weakened Western Empire.

❸ **Government** Invading Germanic peoples raided Rome and overthrew the last Roman emperor, ending the Western Empire.

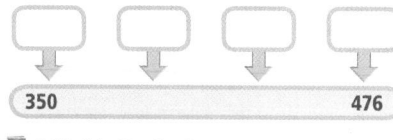

▶ TAKING NOTES

Reading Skill: Explaining Sequence

Knowing the order in which events happen can help you understand the time period you are studying. In this lesson, look for events that bring about the fall of the Roman Empire. Use a time line like the one below to help you identify the sequence of events.

350 ——————————————— 476

Ⓢ Skillbuilder Handbook, page R15

▲ **Gothic Jewelry** The Goths produced finely crafted jewelry from gold and semi-precious gems.

CALIFORNIA STANDARDS

7.1.1 Study the early strengths and lasting contributions of Rome (e.g., significance of Roman citizenship; rights under Roman law; Roman art, architecture, engineering, and philosophy; preservation and transmission of Christianity) and its ultimate internal weaknesses (e.g., rise of autonomous military powers within the empire, undermining of citizenship by the growth of corruption and slavery, lack of education, and distribution of news).

7.1.2 Discuss the geographic borders of the empire at its height and the factors that threatened its territorial cohesion.

CST 1 Students explain how major events are related to one another in time.

HI 5 Students recognize that interpretations of history are subject to change as new information is uncovered.

500 • Chapter 15

HOW TO TEACH THE CALIFORNIA STANDARDS

Standard	Content	Student Question or Activity	Instruction
7.1.1	**Pages 501–504** Describes the weaknesses that remained after the division of the Roman Empire and the effects of attacks by barbarian groups	**Page 502** Students discuss the weakness of the Western Empire. **Page 505** Students discuss the collapse of the Western Empire.	Have students research what Rome was like at the time of the Goths' attack in A.D. 410 and the attack affected the once-great capital.
7.1.2	**Page 501** Describes differences between the western and eastern empires and how these differences help explain the weakness of the west	**Page 502** Students discuss the differences between the eastern and western empires. **Page 503** Students study a map showing invasions of the empire.	Ask students to examine the map on page 503 and notice the many different areas from which the Romans were attacked.
CST 1	**Page 503** Explains the effect on the Roman Empire of the arrival of the Huns in the territory of the Germanic peoples	**Page 503** Students identify reasons for the move of Germanic peoples into the Roman Empire.	Encourage students to learn about the Huns and the effect they had on the people living on the Roman frontier.

The Fall of the Roman Empire

TERMS & NAMES

barbarian

nomad

plunder

Build on What You Know You have learned how the Roman Empire was permanently split in A.D. 395. Now read about the fall of the Western Roman Empire.

The Two Roman Empires

1 ESSENTIAL QUESTION Why did the Western Roman Empire weaken? It had less secure borders, smaller cities, and was farther from trade routes.

When people talk about the fall of the Roman Empire, they mean the Western Roman Empire. You will learn about the growth of the Eastern Roman Empire in Lesson 3.

Wealthy East The Eastern Roman Empire was much stronger than the Western Roman Empire. The Eastern Empire's capital, Constantinople, bustled with traders from Asia, Africa, and Europe. As a result, the Eastern Empire had more wealth. Also, the eastern cities were larger and better fortified. And the Black Sea was a natural barrier that discouraged invasions. (See the map on page 503.)

Weaker West In contrast, cities in the Western Empire were smaller and less prosperous. They were located farther away from the trade routes that provided both goods and wealth.

The cities of the west were more exposed to attack from groups of invaders along the northern border of the Roman Empire. Defense forces were widely scattered. They were often poorly paid, so they had little reason to risk their lives.

Connect to Today

▼ **Istanbul** Today Constantinople is called Istanbul. The Blue Mosque is visible in the foreground of this aerial view of the city.

501

Terms & Names

barbarian someone who is considered to be uncivilized and primitive

nomad a member of a group that moves from place to place

plunder to take possessions by force

❸ Teach

The Two Roman Empires

↖ **7.1.1, 7.1.2**

Talk About It

- **Critical Thinking: Understanding Cause and Effect** What was the effect of the weakness of the western part of the Roman Empire? *(Possible answer: Because it was weak, it became more subject to attack. The attacks caused more people to leave, making it even weaker.)*

California Resources

California Reading Toolkit, L52

California Modified Lesson Plans for English Learners, p. 107

California Daily Standards Practice Transparencies, TT52

California Standards Enrichment Workbook, pp. 111–112

California Online Test Practice

California Test Generator CD-ROM

California Standards Planner and Lesson Plans, L103

California EasyPlanner CD-ROM

California eEdition CD-ROM

LESSON 2 PROGRAM RESOURCES

ON LEVEL

In-Depth Resources: Unit 6
- Reading Skill: Explaining Sequence, p. 41
- Vocabulary Cards, p. 47

Formal Assessment
- Lesson Quiz, p. 262

ENGLISH LEARNERS

In-Depth Resources in Spanish
- Reading Skill: Explaining Sequence, p. 130
- Skillbuilder Practice, p. 135

Modified Lesson Plans for English Learners, p. 107

Reading Study Guide (Spanish), p. 135

Reading Study Guide Audio CD (Spanish)

STRUGGLING READERS

In-Depth Resources: Unit 6
- Reading Skill: Explaining Sequence, p. 41
- Vocabulary Study Guide, p. 46
- Vocabulary Cards, p. 47
- Reteaching Activity, p. 54

Reading Toolkit, L52

Reading Study Guide, pp. 135

Reading Study Guide Audio CD

GIFTED AND TALENTED STUDENTS

Map Transparencies
- MT30 Europe, A.D. 500

INCLUSION

EasyPlanner CD-ROM
- Reading Skills: Explaining Sequence
- Vocabulary Study Guide
- Reteaching Activity

TECHNOLOGY

eEdition CD-ROM

Power Presentations CD-ROM

Humanities Transparencies
- HT30 Gothic Jewelry

Map Transparencies
- MT30 Europe, A.D. 500

Critical Thinking Transparencies
- CT66 Explaining Sequence

Test Generator CD-ROM

ClassZone.com

In-Depth Resources: Unit 6
• Reading Skill: Explaining Sequence, p. 41

Teach

Invading Peoples

7.1.1, 7.1.2

Talk About It

• How did nomadic peoples living along the north and northeast borders of the Roman Empire respond to the growing weakness of the empire? *(They attacked more frequently.)*

• How did the Romans regard the Germanic peoples living on their borders? *(They considered the Germanic peoples barbarians— uncivilized and primitive.)*

• Were the Romans correct to view the Germanic peoples as barbarians? *(Possible answer: The Germanic peoples were not uncivilized—they had a complex culture.)*

• **Critical Thinking: Summarize** What was the position of Germanic groups when Asian nomads began to appear in their territory around A.D. 370? *(They were trapped between the oncoming Asian invaders and the Roman Empire. They began to seek safety in the Roman Empire, which did not like them and took advantage of them.)*

More About . . .

Germanic Peoples
The Roman frontier was populated by a number of Germanic groups, several of which would figure prominently in the downfall of the empire. These groups included the Goths, which were divided into the Ostrogoths and the Visigoths. In addition, the Franks, the Vandals, the Saxons, the Angles, and several other tribes played some role in the history of the Roman Empire's decline.

Invaders Raid Cities The invaders were often looking for goods to take or people to kidnap and sell as slaves. As attacks on cities increased, the inhabitants chose to leave. They were looking for safer surroundings. The less populated the cities became, the more vulnerable they were to attack.

REVIEW In what ways was the Western Empire weaker than the Eastern Empire? *The Western Empire had less wealth. Its cities were harder to defend. There were fewer natural barriers to help protect it from invaders.*

Invading Peoples

2 **ESSENTIAL QUESTION** What groups moved into the Roman Empire? *Germanic nomads, later the Huns*

Defense forces on the north and northeast borders of the Roman Empire grew weaker. **Nomads**—people who move from place to place—took advantage of this weakness and frequently attacked Roman towns and cities. These groups were known as Germanic peoples. The Romans had clashes with Germanic peoples along their northern borders for hundreds of years.

The Germanic Peoples A variety of groups made up the Germanic peoples. They all spoke languages that were part of a language family also called Germanic. The Goths mentioned in the opening story were a Germanic people.

Romans looked down on these groups but also feared them. To the Romans, the Germanic peoples were barbarians. The term **barbarian** originally meant someone who spoke a language the Greeks could not understand. Barbarian came to mean someone who was primitive and uncivilized. The Romans referred to the people who lived along the borders of the empire as barbarians. Later, the Romans applied the term to anyone living outside the empire.

Although the Romans thought the Germanic peoples were barbaric, they had a very complex culture. They were skilled metalworkers and fond of jewelry. Some groups had elected assemblies. War chiefs headed their military organizations. The Germanic peoples were loyal, especially to their chieftains.

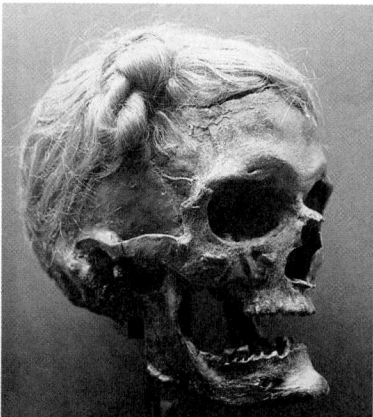

Germanic Skull This skull still has its hair. The knot in the hair is a characteristic style of Germanic people. ▼

DIFFERENTIATING INSTRUCTION

English Learners

Write Descriptions
Ask students to suppose that they have witnessed some of the events that led to the fall of the Roman Empire. Using details from the text, model how to describe an episode illustrating troubles that one might experience.

Have students work with partners to write descriptions of life during the fall of the Roman Empire. Have each pair practice presenting their episode before presenting it to classmates.

Inclusion

Practice Remembering
Point out the heading "Invading Peoples," and have students read the section to themselves. Then have them close their books and tell you everything they can remember about the section. Write the information on the board, leaving room to add more answers.

When students have run out of information to add, have them open their books. They should try to verify the information they have provided and add any details they have left out.

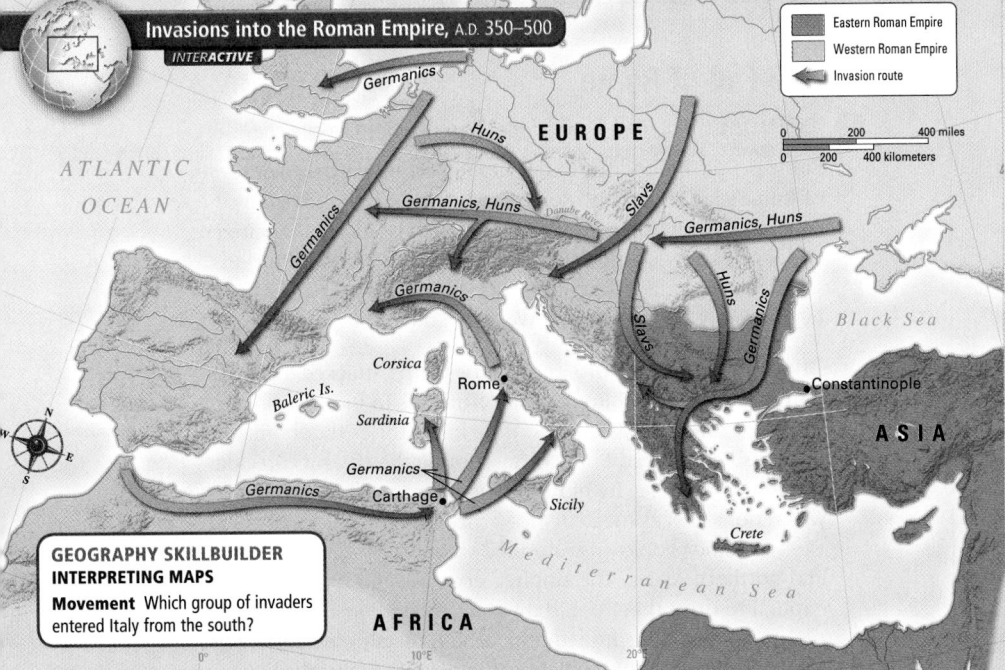

Invasions into the Roman Empire, A.D. 350–500
INTERACTIVE

Eastern Roman Empire
Western Roman Empire
→ Invasion route

ATLANTIC OCEAN

EUROPE

Germanics

Huns

Germanics, Huns

Danube River

Slavs

Germanics, Huns

Black Sea

Germanics

Corsica

Rome

Baleric Is.

Sardinia

Constantinople

ASIA

Germanics

Carthage

Sicily

Crete

Mediterranean Sea

AFRICA

GEOGRAPHY SKILLBUILDER
INTERPRETING MAPS
Movement Which group of invaders entered Italy from the south?

CHAPTER 15 • LESSON 2

The German Migrations In Chapters 2 and 6, you read about nomads. Nomads moved to a new location as their food ran out, or when they were driven out of an area by a stronger force. Nomads often fought for the right to remain in a new place. As Rome began to decline, groups of well-armed nomads posed a huge threat to other nomadic people living along the borders of the empire. The people on those borders would be driven into the Roman Empire by a stronger group of nomads.

Between 370 and 500 A.D., Central Asian nomads were pushing people out of their lands into both the Roman and the Chinese empires. The most important of these nomadic groups was the Huns.

The Huns moved across the grasslands of Asia into Germanic lands. They drove the Germanic peoples west and south into Roman territory. The Germanic peoples were looking for new places to settle and for the protection of the Roman armies. As you learned in the opening story, many Romans did not like the Germanic peoples and took advantage of them.

REVIEW Why did the Germanic peoples move into Roman territory?
The invading Huns forced them west and south.

Rome's Decline and Legacy • 503

DIFFERENTIATING INSTRUCTION

Gifted and Talented Students

Report on the Huns in China
Have students use library and Internet sources to research and report on the invasion of China by the Huns. Students should use the information they gather to create a time line of Hun activities in China and in Europe, as well as a brief report about Hun invasions of the Chinese empire.

Struggling Readers

Shrink the Paragraphs
Have students work in pairs to "shrink the paragraphs" of this section. Each student should take responsibility for one of the subsections under "Invading Peoples," read through the paragraphs, and create a one- or two-sentence summary of each. When students have finished, have them share their summaries with their partners. Then have each pair present their summaries to the rest of the class.

Teach

The Fall of Rome

 7.1.1, 7.1.2, CST 1

Talk About It

- What were some of the causes of Rome's decline? *(Corruption of government officials, indifferent citizens, and a breakdown of society contributed to the decline.)*

- According to historians, what event marked the beginning of Rome's fall? *(the invasion of the city of Rome and the last Roman emperor removed from power)*

- What happened following the Goths' attack on Rome? *(Barbarian groups launched a series of invasions into much of the eastern empire then moved into the western empire.)*

- **Critical Thinking: Making Inferences** What does the text suggest about the quality of the governments that replaced the fallen Western Roman Empire? *(Possible answer: The governments that took power in place of the old empire were not able to achieve the wealth and success of the Roman Empire.)*

Map Transparencies
- MT30 Europe, A.D. 500

History from Visuals

Interpreting Visuals
Have students examine the table on this page. Make sure they recognize that the table compares three sets of features of the Han Empire and the Roman Empire—political, economic, and social.

- In which category was the cause of failure in the Han and Roman empires very different? *(The two empires experienced very different social challenges.)*

The Fall of Rome

③ ESSENTIAL QUESTION How did the Western Roman Empire end?
Breakdown of society, corrupt officials, indifferent citizens, repeated barbarian invasions led to the fall.
Some people believe the barbarian invasions were the cause of Rome's fall. In reality, Rome gradually declined for many reasons. Corruption of government officials, indifferent citizens, and a breakdown of society contributed to the fall. Historians say a barbarian invasion of the city of Rome marked the beginning of the end for the Western Roman Empire.

Invaders Gain Ground In 410, the Goths attacked and plundered the city of Rome. **Plunder** means to loot, or to take things by force. It was the first time in centuries that nomadic invaders had entered Rome. After looting the city for three days, the Goths left. The city of Rome tried to recover and go on, but it was seriously weakened.

Germanic peoples also invaded what is now France, Spain, and northern Africa. The empire's army was no longer strong enough to drive them out. Italy was raided almost constantly.

In 445, the Huns united under the leadership of Attila. First his armies swept into the Eastern Empire. They attacked 70 cities and then moved into the Western Empire. These attacks placed great pressure on the Roman military.

Comparisons Across Cultures

The Decline of Empires: Roman and Han

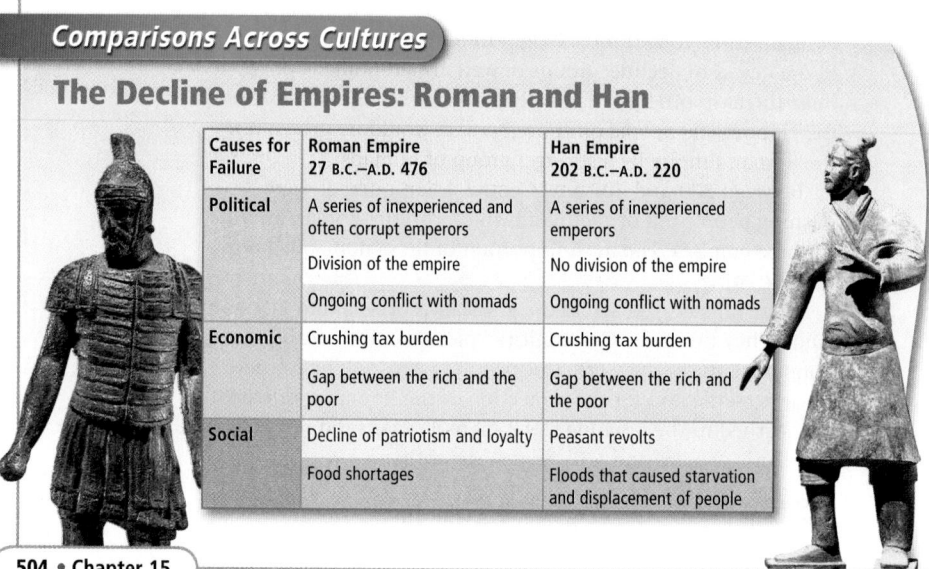

Causes for Failure	Roman Empire 27 B.C.–A.D. 476	Han Empire 202 B.C.–A.D. 220
Political	A series of inexperienced and often corrupt emperors	A series of inexperienced emperors
	Division of the empire	No division of the empire
	Ongoing conflict with nomads	Ongoing conflict with nomads
Economic	Crushing tax burden	Crushing tax burden
	Gap between the rich and the poor	Gap between the rich and the poor
Social	Decline of patriotism and loyalty	Peasant revolts
	Food shortages	Floods that caused starvation and displacement of people

504 • Chapter 15

INTERDISCIPLINARY ACTIVITIES

Language Arts

Report on the Plundering of Rome
Have students assume the role of war correspondents covering the Gothic invasion of the city of Rome. Ask them to write news stories about the events of the attack. The stories should provide standard journalistic information—who, what, where, when, and why. They should also convey the historic significance of the attack.

Language Arts

Profile Attila the Hun
Have students use library and Internet resources to learn about one of the central figures in the decline and fall of Rome—Attila the Hun. Students should write brief biographical sketches of this historical figure, including highlights of his career and especially the effects of his exploits on the Roman Empire.

The Aftermath of Rome's Fall In A.D. 476, the last Roman emperor was removed from power. This date marks the fall of the Western Roman Empire. After Rome's fall, life changed in Western Europe in a number of ways.

- Roads and other public structures fell into disrepair.
- Trade and commerce declined.
- Germanic kingdoms claimed former Roman lands.
- The Roman Catholic Church became a unifying and powerful force.

The Eastern Empire continued for almost another thousand years. You will read about the Eastern Empire in Lesson 3.

REVIEW What caused the continued weakening of the Western Empire? *invasions by Germanic peoples*

Lesson Summary
- The Western Roman Empire was less wealthy and harder to protect from invaders than the East.
- Germanic invaders further weakened the empire.
- In A.D. 476, the Western Roman Empire ceased to exist.

Why It Matters Now . . .
The decline and fall of empires is a repeating pattern of world history. Even large empires eventually break into smaller pieces.

---

2 Lesson Review

Homework Helper
ClassZone.com

Terms & Names

1. Explain the importance of
   barbarian   nomad   plunder

Using Your Notes

Explaining Sequence Use your completed time line to answer the following question:

2. What was the most significant event of the empire's downfall? (7.1.2)

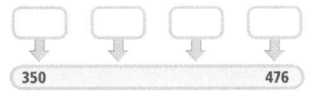
350   476

Main Ideas

3. Why was the Western Empire more likely to be invaded than the Eastern Empire? (7.1.1)

4. What pushed the Germanic peoples south and west into Roman territory? (7.1.2)

5. Why is A.D. 476 considered an important date in Roman history? (CST 1)

Critical Thinking

6. **Recognizing Changing Interpretations of History** How was the movement of the Huns into Europe related to the fall of Rome? Give reasons for your answer. (HI 5)

7. **Making Inferences** Why didn't the Romans make the Germanic peoples their allies? (7.1.2)

Activity **Writing Newspaper Headlines** Write a series of headlines that describe the fall of Rome. Base each headline on a major event or news story. Arrange the headlines in chronological order on a poster. When possible, provide a date for each. (CST 1)

Rome's Decline and Legacy • 505

---

❹ Assess & Reteach

Assess Have pairs of students take turns answering the questions. Ask volunteers to share their completed time lines for question 2.

 Formal Assessment
- Lesson Quiz, p. 262

Reteach Have students work individually. Tell them to read over the bulleted items in the Lesson Summary. For each item, have them review the appropriate section of the text and write an additional sentence or two to expand on and further explain the idea. Have students share their additional summary sentences with the rest of the class.

 In-Depth Resources: Unit 6
- Vocabulary Cards, p. 47
- Reteaching Activity, p. 54

 **Homework Helper**

Visit **ClassZone.com** for a lesson review, a flip-card activity, and links to related Web sites.

---

2 Lesson Review Answers

Terms & Names

1. • barbarian, p. 502
   • nomad, p. 502
   • plunder, p. 504

Using Your Notes

See page 500 for an example of a completed time line.

2. Answers will vary

Main Ideas

3. It was weaker, and it had fewer natural barriers.

4. invasion of their territory by the Huns

5. The last emperor of Rome was removed from power and the fall of the Roman empire.

Critical Thinking

6. Possible answer: The Huns pushed Germanic peoples into the Roman Empire, which further weakened it.

7. Possible answer: The Romans may not have considered the Germanic peoples to be their equals.

Activity Rubric

	Number of Headlines	Accuracy of Presentation
4	many	properly ordered and dated, accurate information
3	several	some events not dated or properly sequenced, accurate information
2	some	several errors of dating, sequence, or accuracy
1	few or none	no accurate sequence, dating, or information

Objectives

- Identify factors related to the fall of Rome.
- Analyze secondary sources to draw conclusions.
- **Language Objective:** Explain the meaning of the word *attitude* in the context of the feature.

❶ Focus & Motivate

Preview Tell students that historical events are not always clearly understood and that historians do not always agree on how and why things happened. For this reason, all students of history must learn skills for drawing their own conclusions on the basis of what they have read.

❷ Teach

Talk About It

- Explain how the facts in example 1 support the conclusion. *(These facts deal with the quality of the government of Rome. Each of the facts—lack of interest and poor quality of officials—logically supports the notion that people did not care as much about government.)*
- What is another conclusion you could draw on the basis of the facts provided in example 1? *(Possible answer: Because of the low level of involvement and the poor quality of officials, the Roman government failed to take proper actions to protect the empire.)*
- How do the facts in example 2 support the conclusion? *(The facts relate to the quality and makeup of the Roman army. It is reasonable to conclude that the poor quality of the army affected the empire.)*
- What is another conclusion you could draw on the basis of the facts provided? *(Possible answer: that the Roman citizenry were unable to protect their land)*

Skillbuilder   Extend Lesson 2

Drawing Conclusions from Sources

CALIFORNIA STANDARDS
REP 4 Students assess the credibility of primary and secondary sources and draw sound conclusions from them.

Goal: To draw conclusions about one of the reasons for the fall of Rome by reading and analyzing a secondary source

Learn the Skill

Drawing conclusions means reading carefully, analyzing what you read, and then forming an opinion based on facts about the subject. Often you must use your own common sense and your experiences to draw a conclusion.

[S] See the Skillbuilder Handbook, page R25.

Practice the Skill

❶ Read the passage at right carefully. Pay attention to the facts, statements that can be proved to be true. A few are labeled for you.

❷ List the facts in a graphic organizer like the one below. It gives two examples of facts and conclusions you can draw from them for the passage you just read. Use your own experiences and common sense to understand how the facts relate to each other.

❸ After reviewing the facts, write down the conclusion you have drawn.

Example:

Facts	Conclusion
Example 1 ❷ People failed to participate in government. ❷ Government officials were not as qualified as they used to be.	❸ People had less interest in good government.
Example 2 ❷ Fewer Romans served in the military. ❷ Foreigners were hired to serve in the Roman military. ❷ Foreigners had little loyalty to Rome.	❸ Rome's army was not as powerful or as dedicated as it once was. These factors may have been some of the causes of the fall of Rome.

DIFFERENTIATING INSTRUCTION

English Learners

Examine Attitudes
Discuss what the word *attitude* means and how attitudes can be perceived as negative or positive. Have students model an example of a positive attitude. Discuss reasons why it is a positive attitude. Follow with an example of a negative attitude and reasons why it is negative. Then have students read the secondary-source passage in the feature and locate examples of attitudes that may have contributed to the fall of the Roman Empire. Have students give reasons for their decisions.

Struggling Readers

Rewrite the Passage
Have students work in teams to create their own versions of the passage, written in their own words. Each team should first go through the passage and identify the key facts and ideas. Then they should create a draft of their version, being careful to include the key facts and details. Have groups share their versions of with one another, and encourage students to offer their opinions about how well other groups paraphrased the passage.

Secondary Source

Historians wonder about the reasons for the decline and fall of the Roman Empire. Most of them agree that there wasn't just one main reason the Roman Empire began to weaken. There were probably many reasons why the empire fell apart. The selection below discusses one of those possible reasons.

The Fall of the Roman Empire

Explaining the decline and fall of Rome is a difficult task for historians. Some historians look at the changes in the social and political attitudes of the Romans to find at least one cause for the weakening of the empire. For example, they believe that the nobles and people in the cities cared more about pleasing themselves than about the well-being of other people.

❶ Historians also know people failed to participate in the government. ❶ Some public officials were not as qualified to perform their jobs as others in the past had been.

The backbone of the Roman Empire was its army. ❶ However, in the later years of the empire fewer men were willing to serve in the military. ❶ This made it necessary to hire foreigners to serve in the Roman army. ❶ Foreigners had little loyalty to Rome. They served because they were being paid to do so, not because they wanted to serve Rome. This lack of dedication weakened the army that was supposed to protect the empire.

▲ **Engraving** A Gothic leader forces the Roman emperor to surrender.

Apply the Skill

Turn to page 380 in Chapter 11. Read the information on Spartan education. Make a chart like the one at left to help you draw conclusions about Spartan culture.

More About . . .

Roman Soldiers
Throughout much of its history, the Roman military was regarded as a premier fighting force. It was a professional army in which soldiers served for 25 years. The soldiers were well trained and well armed and formed a formidable fighting force.

The enormous size of the empire eventually put a strain on the military, as did the ongoing threats from outside—and, over time, within—the empire. The rebellion of the Goths inside the Roman borders severely weakened the empire. Losses elsewhere cut into the empire's income, making it harder for Rome to support the well-paid, well-trained military it had always depended upon.

APPLY THE SKILL

Facts	Conclusion
❷ Spartan boys began military-style training at age seven. ❷ Boys' education focused in part on military skills. ❷ All male citizens served 40 years in the army.	❸ Having a strong army was a very important goal of Spartan society.

❶ Plan & Prepare

Objectives

- Summarize the history of the Byzantine Empire.
- Describe how the Byzantine Empire preserved Roman culture.
- Describe the division of the Christian church into the Roman Catholic and Eastern Orthodox churches.
- **Language Objective:** Compare and contrast details of selected people, characters, events, and ideas.

Quick Look

Lesson 3 explores the history of the Byzantine Empire, the portion of the Roman Empire that survived after the fall of Rome.

❷ Focus & Motivate

Preview Remind students that the end of the last lesson described the collapse of the Western Roman Empire. However, Roman culture carried on in the Eastern Empire, which had as its capital the city of Constantinople, once called Byzantium. This empire is now called the Byzantine Empire.

Introduce the Main Ideas The three main ideas relate to the Big Ideas of economics and government. Help students look for statements related to these Big Ideas as they read the lesson.

Reading Skill: Summarizing Remind students that a summary should be much shorter than the original text and should include only the most important ideas and details.

SAMPLE ANSWERS FOR CHART

Byzantine Empire	Grew out of Eastern Roman Empire
Justinian	Reclaimed lost territories of Roman Empire
Split in Christian church	Led to creation of Roman Catholic and Eastern Orthodox churches
Role of church in government	Differed in Roman Catholic and Eastern Orthodox areas

---

Lesson 3

▶ MAIN IDEAS

❶ **Culture** Roman culture continued in the Byzantine Empire for a thousand years after the fall of Rome.

❷ **Belief Systems** Christianity developed different forms in the western and eastern parts of the former Roman Empire.

❸ **Belief Systems** The Eastern Orthodox Church and the Roman Catholic Church had different relationships with governments.

▶ TAKING NOTES

Reading Skill: Summarizing

Summarizing means restating the main idea and important details about a subject. As you read Lesson 3, make a summary statement about each of the topics listed. Record them on a chart like the one below.

Byzantine Empire	
Justinian	
Split in Christian church	
Role of church in government	

S Skillbuilder Handbook, page R3

▲ **Mosaic of Justinian**
Justinian regained lost lands and briefly reunited the Eastern and Western Roman empires. He is considered one of the Byzantine Empire's most important emperors.

CALIFORNIA STANDARDS

7.1.3 Describe the establishment by Constantine of the new capital in Constantinople and the development of the Byzantine Empire, with an emphasis on the consequences of the development of two distinct European civilizations, Eastern Orthodox and Roman Catholic, and their two distinct views on church-state relations.

HI 1 Students explain the central issues and problems from the past, placing people and events in a matrix of time and place.

HI 3 Students explain the sources of historical continuity and how the combination of ideas and events explains the emergence of new patterns.

Framework In studying each ancient society, students should examine the role of women and the presence or absence of slavery.

HOW TO TEACH THE CALIFORNIA STANDARDS

Standard	Content	Student Question or Activity	Instruction
7.1.3	**Pages 511–512** Traces the development of the Eastern Orthodox and Roman Catholic churches	**Page 513** Students describe differences between the Roman Catholic and Eastern Orthodox churches.	Ask students to study the Venn diagram comparing the Roman Catholic Church and the Eastern Orthodox Church on page 512.
HI 1	**Pages 509–513** Describes the process of rise and fall as it applies to the Byzantine Empire	**Page 513** Students identify a cause of the Byzantine Empire's ultimate collapse.	Have students do additional research on the challenges that faced the Byzantine Empire and on the triumphs it achieved.
HI 3	**Page 510** Explores how the Byzantine Empire retained aspects of Roman culture	**Page 513** explain how Justinian preserved Roman law.	Ask students to think of ways in which the Byzantine Empire took Roman ideas and culture and made them its own.

The Byzantine Empire

Build on What You Know You read in Lesson 1 that Constantine renamed the city of Byzantium Constantinople. That city became the capital of the Eastern Roman Empire. Because of the city's original name, historians call the Eastern Roman Empire the **Byzantine Empire**.

A Continuing Empire

① ESSENTIAL QUESTION How did Justinian restore the Eastern Roman Empire? He reconquered lost territories and rebuilt Constantinople.

The Byzantine Empire continued for about 1,000 years after the fall of the Western Roman Empire. Like the emperors of the Western Roman Empire, the emperor of the Byzantine Empire was its absolute ruler. Also like the Western Roman Empire, the Byzantine emperors struggled to keep Germanic peoples, Huns, and others out of their lands. Despite their efforts, much Byzantine land was lost to invaders.

Justinian One emperor was able to restore control over the former lands of the Eastern Roman Empire. **Justinian** was emperor from A.D. 527 to 565. His armies reconquered lost territories, including Italy, northern Africa, and the southern coast of Spain. (See the map on page 511.)

Hagia Sophia Built by Justinian, Hagia Sophia was the greatest of all churches in Constantinople. Today it is a museum. ▼

509

Terms & Names

Byzantine Empire the Eastern Roman Empire, which lasted for about 1,000 years after the collapse of the west

Justinian a Byzantine emperor

Justinian Code a legal code based on older Roman laws created at the order of Justinian

Roman Catholic Church the Christian church based in Rome and led by the pope

Eastern Orthodox Church the Christian church that developed in the Byzantine Empire

❸ Teach

A Continuing Empire

↘ **7.1.3, HI 1**

Talk About It

- **Critical Thinking: Contrasting** How was the Byzantine Empire different from the Roman Empire? (*It was based in Constantinople, and its people spoke Greek.*)

California Resources

California Reading Toolkit, L53
California Modified Lesson Plans for English Learners, pp. 109
California Daily Standards Practice Transparencies, TT53
California Standards Enrichment Workbook, pp. 111–112
California Online Test Practice
California Test Generator CD-ROM
California Standards Planner and Lesson Plans, L105
California EasyPlanner CD-ROM
California eEdition CD-ROM

LESSON 3 PROGRAM RESOURCES

ON LEVEL

In-Depth Resources: Unit 6
- Reading Skill: Summarizing, p. 42
- Vocabulary Cards, p. 47
- Geography Practice: Constantinople, p. 49

Formal Assessment
- Lesson Quiz, p. 263

ENGLISH LEARNERS

In-Depth Resources in Spanish
- Reading Skill: Summarizing, p. 131
- Geography Practice: Constantinople, p. 137

Modified Lesson Plans for English Learners, p. 109

Reading Study Guide (Spanish), p. 137

Reading Study Guide Audio CD (Spanish)

STRUGGLING READERS

In-Depth Resources: Unit 6
- Reading Skill: Summarizing, p. 42
- Vocabulary Study Guide, p. 46
- Vocabulary Cards, p. 47
- Reteaching Activity, p. 55

Reading Toolkit, L53

Reading Study Guide, p. 137

Reading Study Guide Audio CD

GIFTED AND TALENTED STUDENTS

In-Depth Resources: Unit 6
- Primary Source: A Description by Emperor Constantine Porphyrogenitus, p. 51

Interdisciplinary Projects
- Math, p. 85

INCLUSION

EasyPlanner CD-ROM
- Reading Skill: Summarizing
- Vocabulary Study Guide
- Reteaching Activity

TECHNOLOGY

eEdition CD-ROM

Power Presentations CD-ROM

Critical Thinking Transparencies
- CT67 Summarizing

Test Generator CD-ROM

ClassZone.com

In-Depth Resources: Unit 6
- Reading Skill: Summarizing, p. 42
- Geography Practice: Constantinople, p. 49

More About . . .

The Justinian Code

Before Justinian's rule, Roman law was a hodge podge of rules and customs that had never been collected in one place. Laws enacted by Roman leaders had not always been published and enforced throughout all parts of the old empire. Justinian wanted the various records of Roman law to be pulled together into a single, easy-to-use source. The first step was a 14-month effort to take existing Roman law and convert it into a single code. This was completed in A.D. 529. Later, the code was expanded to provide additional information, including guidance for law students and judges, and to include laws enacted by Justinian's own administration.

History Makers

Theodora

Theodora's father was a bear keeper at the coliseum in Constantinople. She worked as a wool spinner and an actress before her marriage to Justinian. As empress, Theodora became very powerful. She is credited with most of the laws enacted during her lifetime, many of which promoted her social and religious beliefs. Theodora functioned almost as Justinian's coruler, advising him on political affairs and even corresponding with foreign rulers. Justinian was greatly affected by Theodora's death in 548, possibly from cancer. Without Theodora's influence, very little in the way of important legislation was enacted during the remainder of Justinian's rule.

Rebuilding Constantinople Justinian also began to rebuild Constantinople, which had suffered much damage from a revolt. He rebuilt the city walls. He also built schools, hospitals, law courts, and churches. The most famous church was Hagia Sophia (HAY•ee•uh soh•FEE•uh). Constantinople was again a glorious city.

Preserving Roman Culture Justinian appointed a committee to create a uniform code of law based on Roman law. These experts dropped outdated laws and rewrote others to make them clearer. The new code was called the **Justinian Code**. The code included laws on marriage, slavery, property ownership, women's rights, and criminal justice.

Although they spoke Greek, Byzantines thought of themselves as part of the Roman cultural tradition. Byzantine students studied Latin and Greek, and Roman literature and history. In this way, the east preserved Greek and Roman culture. In the former Western Empire, the Germanic peoples blended Roman culture with their own. However, they lost much of the scientific and philosophical knowledge of the Greeks and Romans.

REVIEW How did the Byzantine Empire preserve Roman culture?
Students learned Latin and studied Roman history and literature.

History Makers

Empress Theodora (c. 500–548)

Theodora was an empress of Byzantium—which was unusual, considering her background. Theodora was an actress, and Byzantine society looked down on actresses. Yet Justinian, the heir to the throne, married Theodora in A.D. 525. His choice was a good one.

Justinian and Theodora became emperor and empress in 527. In 532, rioters threatened to overturn the government. Theodora urged Justinian not to flee. She herself refused to leave. Her courage inspired Justinian, and his generals put down the rebellion.

Later, Theodora had laws passed that helped women. Divorced women gained more rights. She founded a home to care for poor girls. She also offered protection to religious minorities.

▲ Theodora's mosaic portrait may still be seen in the Church of San Vitale in Ravenna, Italy.

510 • Chapter 15

DIFFERENTIATING INSTRUCTION

Inclusion

Take Audio Notes
Have students use an audio recorder to take audio notes on this section. Have students work in pairs to read through the section "A Continuing Empire." When they have completed the reading, have them discuss the content. Then have students record notes about the main ideas and supporting details of each paragraph.

Struggling Readers

Create Character Profiles
Point out that pages 509–510 focus on two individuals—Justinian and Theodora. Have each student write these figures' names at the top of a T-chart on a blank sheet of paper. Then have students go through the section, writing down notes about the accomplishments and characteristics of these two leaders of the Byzantine Empire. Have students share their charts with the rest of the class.

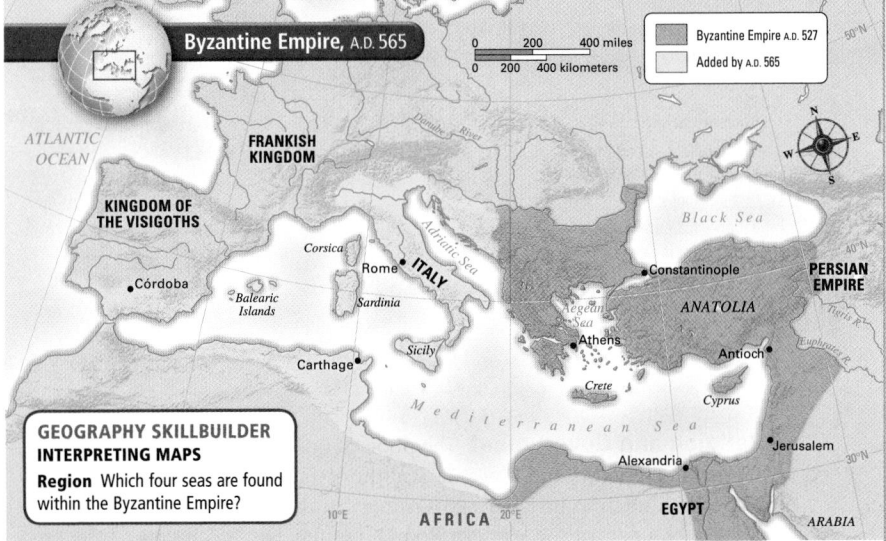

Byzantine Empire, A.D. 565

Byzantine Empire A.D. 527	
Added by A.D. 565	

ATLANTIC OCEAN

FRANKISH KINGDOM

KINGDOM OF THE VISIGOTHS

Córdoba
Balearic Islands
Corsica
Sardinia
Rome ITALY
Sicily
Carthage

Black Sea

Constantinople
PERSIAN EMPIRE

ANATOLIA

Athens
Crete
Cyprus

Antioch

Mediterranean Sea

Alexandria
Jerusalem

AFRICA

EGYPT

ARABIA

GEOGRAPHY SKILLBUILDER
INTERPRETING MAPS
Region Which four seas are found within the Byzantine Empire?

The Church Divides

2 ESSENTIAL QUESTION Why did the Christian church divide?
differences over church practices, especially regarding the roles of the church and state

The division of the empire also affected the Christian church. Religious practices developed differently in the Christian churches of the east and of the west. Cultural practices and limited contact between the two areas caused these differences.

separated the churches in the east and west

The Church Divides Another difference had to do with the authority of the emperor over church matters. In the east, the emperor had authority over the head of the church. In the west, there was no emperor and the pope began assuming more responsibilities in governing the former Western Empire.

Problems between the two churches began to grow. The pope claimed authority over the churches in both eastern and western empires. In A.D. 1054, delegates of the pope attempted to remove the eastern head of the church. The eastern church responded by refusing to recognize the authority of the pope.

Finally, the Christian church split in two. The church in the west became known as the **Roman Catholic Church**. *Catholic* means "universal." The church in the east became the **Eastern Orthodox Church**. *Orthodox* means "holding established beliefs." Over time, the split led to the development of two separate European civilizations. Each had its own view on the relationship between church and state.

Rome's Decline and Legacy • 511

DIFFERENTIATING INSTRUCTION

English Learners

Compare and Contrast
Review the difference between comparing (things alike) and contrasting (things different). Say, "Both the Roman Catholic Church and the Eastern Orthodox Church based their faith on the Gospel of Jesus and the Bible. Roman Catholic services were conducted in Latin, *but* Eastern Orthodox services were conducted in Greek." Have students take turns in using *but* or *both* and make their own comparing and contrasting statements.

Gifted and Talented Students

Create Organizational Charts
Have students use information in the text and from outside resources, if needed, to create organizational charts that show the relationship between the two churches and the nations and empires in which they existed. The charts should show who held authority over political matters and over religious matters. Have students share their findings with the rest of the class.

History from Visuals

Interpreting Maps
Direct students' attention to the map on this page. Be sure they carefully examine the key and understand the meanings of the different colored areas on the map. Suggest that students compare this map with other maps of the Roman Empire they have viewed in this book.

- About how much of the territory of the Western Roman Empire had the Byzantine Empire regained by A.D. 565? *(over half)*

- What other kingdoms or empires appear as potential rivals of the Byzantine Empire on this map? *(Possible answer: those of the Persians, the Franks, and the Visigoths)*

GEOGRAPHY SKILLBUILDER ANSWER
the Mediterranean, Adriatic, Aegean, and Black seas

Teach

The Church Divides

7.1.3, HI 1, HI 3

Talk About It

- According to the text, why did two different major Christian churches emerge in what had been the Roman Empire? *(The split in the empire also affected the church. The east and the west were culturally different.)*

- What were the main areas of difference between the two churches? *(differences in language and religious practices and differences about the authority of the emperors over church matters)*

- **Critical Thinking: Categorize** Briefly describe the differences between the Roman Catholic Church and the Eastern Orthodox Church in terms of leadership. *(Possible answer: In the Roman Catholic Church, the pope was the ultimate authority, even over political leaders. In the Eastern Orthodox Church, the ultimate authority was the emperor.)*

History from Visuals

Interpreting Visuals

Have students examine the Venn diagram on this page. Ask them to explain how this sort of diagram works. *(The two ovals contain features of the two things being compared. The part where the ovals overlap shows common features, and the rest of each oval shows features that are unique to one thing.)*

- Name one unique feature of the Roman Catholic Church. *(Possible answers: Pope is the leader; pope has authority over kings; priests don't marry; Latin is used.)*

- Name one unique feature of the Eastern Orthodox Church. *(Possible answers: Patriarch is the leader; emperor has authority; priests can marry; local languages are used.)*

- Name one feature the churches shared. *(Possible answers: based on Jesus and Bible; led by priests and bishops; aim to convert people)*

Teach

The Byzantine Empire Collapses

7.1.3, HI 1, HI 3

Talk About It

- What made it difficult for the Byzantine Empire to carry on its old traditions? *(The empire faced constant threats from the east and the west.)*

- What were some of the specific threats mentioned in the text? *(Muslim forces, Ottoman Turks, and Serbs)*

- What marked the end of the Byzantine Empire? *(the capture of Constantinople by Ottoman Turks)*

- **Critical Thinking: Understanding Continuity and Change** Judging by what happened to the Roman Catholic Church, what do you think happened to the Eastern Orthodox Church following the fall of the Byzantine Empire? *(Possible answer: It continued to remain an influence in people's lives even after the state that controlled it disappeared.)*

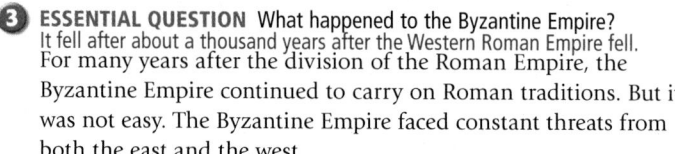

Two Branches of Christianity in the 11th Century

Roman Catholic
- The leader, called the pope, has authority over the bishops.
- Pope has authority over all kings and emperors.
- Priests may not be married.
- Latin is used in services.

Similarities
- Faith is based on Jesus and the Bible.
- Leaders are priests and bishops.
- Both want to convert people to Christianity.

Eastern Orthodox
- The leader, called the patriarch, and the bishops run the church as a group.
- Emperor has authority over officials of the church.
- Priests may be married.
- Local languages such as Greek and Russian are used in services.

Religion and Government The pope claimed authority over Christian emperors and kings. This authority allowed the Roman Catholic Church to influence government in the lands that were once a part of the Western Roman Empire. Disagreements between the church and some kings and emperors of Western Europe would later cause major conflicts in European history.

In the Byzantine Empire, the emperor was the absolute ruler. He had power over the church as well as the government. This meant that the emperor had power over the spiritual head of the Eastern Orthodox Church. Overall, the Byzantine emperor had greater power than the emperors or kings in the west.

REVIEW How did governments and the Christian churches interact?
In the west, the pope had control of the church and advised the rulers. In the east, the emperor controlled both the church and the empire.

The Byzantine Empire Collapses

3 ESSENTIAL QUESTION What happened to the Byzantine Empire?
It fell after about a thousand years after the Western Roman Empire fell.
For many years after the division of the Roman Empire, the Byzantine Empire continued to carry on Roman traditions. But it was not easy. The Byzantine Empire faced constant threats from both the east and the west.

Constantinople Falls In the 600s, a new religion called Islam began in Arabia. Muslim armies arose and attacked nearby territories and Constantinople. Later, civil wars, as well as attacks by Ottoman Turks and Serbs, further weakened the empire. By 1350, all that remained of the Byzantine Empire was a tiny section of the Anatolian peninsula and a strip of land along the Black and Aegean seas.

INTERDISCIPLINARY ACTIVITIES

Math

Create a Graph of Church Members
Have students use library or Internet resources to research the current membership of Christian churches worldwide and to locate separate data for the Roman Catholic Church and the Eastern Orthodox churches. Have each student use his or her findings to create a bar graph. Then have each student write a caption providing an analysis of the figures as they relate to the history of Christianity.

Art

Create a Byzantine Scrapbook
The Byzantine Empire produced some of the world's great artistic and architectural treasures. Have students use library or Internet resources to collect examples of Byzantine art and publish them in a scrapbook. Each illustration should be labeled to tell viewers about the piece and its significance.

Finally in 1453, an army of Ottoman Turks captured Constantinople. The city's conquest marked the end of the Byzantine Empire—a thousand years after the fall of the Western Roman Empire.

REVIEW What was a cause of the fall of the Byzantine Empire?
The Byzantine Empire fell because of constant attacks.

Lesson Summary
- Emperor Justinian regained much of the Roman Empire's land and helped preserve Roman law and culture.
- In 1054, the Christian church divided into the Roman Catholic and Eastern Orthodox churches.
- The pope of the Roman Catholic Church played a greater role in government in the west than the leader of the Eastern Orthodox Church played in the east.

Why It Matters Now . . .
Today millions of people practice their faith as members of the Roman Catholic Church or the Eastern Orthodox Church.

Lion of St. Mark The winged lion stands guard near the Byzantine-style Cathedral of St. Mark located in Venice, Italy. ▼

---

3 Lesson Review

 Homework Helper
ClassZone.com

Terms & Names
1. Explain the importance of

Byzantine Empire	Roman Catholic Church
Justinian	Eastern Orthodox Church
Justinian Code	

Using Your Notes
Summarizing Use your completed chart to answer the following question:
2. In what ways did Justinian restore the Eastern Roman Empire? (7.1.3)

Byzantine Empire	
Justinian	
Split in Christian church	
Role of church in government	

Main Ideas
3. How did Justinian preserve Roman law? (HI 3)
4. On what issue did the church in the east and in the west not agree? (HI 1)
5. In what way did the pope have a greater role in government in the west than the head of the church in the east? (7.1.3)

Critical Thinking
6. **Contrasting** In what ways was the Eastern Roman Empire different from the Western Roman Empire? (HI 1)
7. **Making Inferences** Why did Christian practices develop differently in the eastern and western empires? (HI 3)

Activity **Internet Activity** Use the Internet to research the Hagia Sophia. Plan a virtual field trip of the structure. Include information on its location, construction, and items that are inside the building. (7.1.3)
Internet Keyword: Hagia Sophia

Rome's Decline and Legacy • 513

---

3 Lesson Review Answers

Terms & Names
1. • Byzantine Empire, p. 509
   • Justinian, p. 509
   • Justinian Code, p. 510
   • Roman Catholic Church, p. 511
   • Eastern Orthodox Church, p. 511

Using Your Notes
See page 508 for an example of a completed chart.
2. Possible answer: Justinian reclaimed some lost territories of the Roman Empire.

Main Ideas
3. He appointed a group of experts to collect, examine, and preserve the law through the Justinian Code.
4. the authority of the emperor over church matters
5. The pope had authority over the Roman Catholic Church and over political leaders; the head of the church in the east was subject to the Byzantine emperor.

Critical Thinking
6. Possible answer: In the west, the church was headed by the pope, who had authority over kings and emperors. In the east, the Byzantine emperor controlled both the state and the church.
7. Possible answers: The people were culturally different; the Eastern Orthodox Church developed in a strong state, which limited the power of church officials.

---

4 Assess & Reteach

Assess Organize students into groups of four. Have each group work together to answer questions 3, 4, and 5 in the Lesson Review. Discuss the answers with the class.

 Formal Assessment
• Lesson Quiz, p. 263

Reteach Have students use numbers to indicate their familiarity with the vocabulary terms in this section. Have each student divide a sheet of paper into four parts and write the numbers 0–3 on the parts. Then write the terms on the board. As you point to each term and say it aloud, have students hold up a 0 if they do not understand the term, 1 if they have a vague idea of what it means, 2 if they are fairly sure of the term's meaning, and 3 if they know the term and can use it in a sentence.

 **In-Depth Resources: Unit 6**
• Vocabulary Cards, p. 47
• Reteaching Activity, p. 55

Homework Helper
Visit **ClassZone.com** for a lesson review, a flip-card activity, and links to related Web sites.

Activity Rubric

	Use of Research	Quality of Presentation
4	thorough, accurate information on each required element	interesting and well organized
3	accurate information on each required element	well organized
2	information accurate but not complete	somewhat disorganized
1	little or no information on required elements	very disorganized

❶ Plan & Prepare

Objectives

- Analyze the artistic and cultural legacy of Rome.
- Analyze the technological and architectural legacy of Rome.
- Analyze the legal and religious legacy of Rome.
- **Language Objective:** Skim the text, classifing details by category to make the text more meaningful.

Quick Look

Lesson 4 explores the rich legacy of the Romans in the areas of art, technology, law, religion, and other areas.

❷ Focus & Motivate

Preview Ask students if, in the chapters they have read, they have recognized aspects of Roman culture that are present in the culture of the United States today—for example, words, art forms, or religious institutions. Tell student they will be reading about the many ways our world has been influenced by Roman culture.

Introduce the Main Ideas The three main ideas relate to the Big Ideas of economics, government, and culture. Help students look for statements related to the Big Ideas as they read the lesson.

Reading Skill: Finding Main Ideas Remind students that main ideas are often stated at the beginning of paragraphs and reinforced at the conclusion of the paragraphs.

SAMPLE ANSWERS FOR DIAGRAM

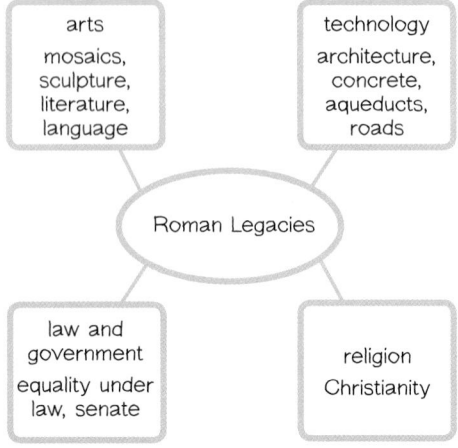

```
     arts                    technology
   mosaics,                architecture,
   sculpture,                concrete,
   literature,              aqueducts,
   language                    roads

           Roman Legacies

   law and
  government                  religion
 equality under            Christianity
  law, senate
```

Lesson 4

▶ MAIN IDEAS

❶ Culture Roman culture was a unique blend of Roman and Greek ideas.

❷ Science and Technology Roman advances in architecture and engineering have influenced builders throughout history.

❸ Culture The spread of Christianity and the Roman system of law left a lasting legacy for the world today.

▶ TAKING NOTES

Reading Skill: Finding Main Ideas

Identifying the main ideas and finding details about those ideas will help you understand the material in Lesson 4. Look for details about Roman legacies, and record the information on a web diagram like the one below.

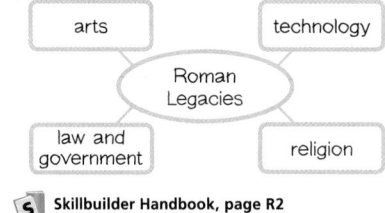

```
   arts              technology
          Roman
          Legacies
   law and
  government          religion
```

Ⓢ **Skillbuilder Handbook, page R2**

▲ **Bas-Relief** The Roman soldiers seen here are examples of bas-relief sculpture, in which the figures stand out from the background.

CALIFORNIA STANDARDS

6.7.8 Discuss the legacies of Roman art and architecture, technology and science, literature, language, and law.

7.1.1 Study the early strengths and lasting contributions of Rome (e.g., significance of Roman citizenship; rights under Roman law; Roman art, architecture, engineering,

and philosophy; preservation and transmission of Christianity) and its ultimate internal weaknesses (e.g., rise of autonomous military powers within the empire, undermining of citizenship by the growth of corruption and slavery, lack of education, and distribution of news).

REP 1 Students frame questions that can be answered by historical study and research.

HOW TO TEACH THE CALIFORNIA STANDARDS

Standard	Content	Student Question or Activity	Instruction
6.7.8	**Pages 515–519** Describes the legacies of Roman art, literature, language, technology, religion, and law	**Pages 516–519** Students discuss the Roman legacies. **Pages 516, 518** Students view illustrations that highlight Roman accomplishments.	Invite students to select one of the areas discussed in this lesson and do outside research on it to learn more about how Romans have influenced the world today in that field.
7.1.1	**Pages 515–519** Describes lasting contributions of Rome including rights under Roman law.	**Page 519** Students explain how Roman law has affected the United States.	Encourage students to research the relationship of Roman legal concepts to the concepts contained in the U.S. Constitution. Have them share their findings.
REP 1	**Page 519** Provides students with an opportunity to frame questions that would aid their study of Roman history	**Page 519** Students formulate questions they would like to explore about the Roman Empire.	Have students research one question they wrote. Have them report back, indicating the answers they found.

The Legacy of Rome

► TERMS & NAMES
- mosaic
- bas-relief
- epic
- oratory
- vault
- aqueduct

Build on What You Know You have already read that Greek and Hellenistic culture came before the Romans. Early in its history, Rome conquered Greece. Some of the Greek culture influenced Roman culture.

Roman Culture

1 ESSENTIAL QUESTION How did Roman culture differ from Greek culture? It was based on strength, loyalty, practicality, and not on idealism.

Roman culture was based on values of strength, loyalty, and practicality. The Romans picked up Greek ideas about the artistic ideal and Greek styles of writing. The result was a culture that blended Roman practicality with elements of Greek idealism and style.

Art Roman artists were especially skillful at creating **mosaics**. A mosaic is a picture made from tiny pieces of colored stone or other material. One famous example shows Alexander the Great in battle (see page 405). This mosaic was found at Pompeii and measures 10 by 19 feet. Many mosaics show scenes of daily life.

◄ **Mosaic** This Roman mosaic was discovered in 2000 by archaeologists working in southeastern Turkey.

515

Terms & Names

mosaic a picture made from tiny pieces of colored stone or other material

bas-relief a type of sculpture in which slightly raised figures stand out against a flat background

epic a long poem about a hero's adventures

oratory the art of public speaking

vault an arch that forms a ceiling or roof

aqueduct a pipe or channel that carries water to a city

❸ Teach

Roman Culture

⚓ **6.7.8, 7.1.1, REP 1**

Talk About It

- **Critical Thinking: Explaining Historical Patterns** How would you describe the process by which the Romance languages developed? *(The Latin language changed and evolved over time into distinct languages, such as Italian, Spanish, and French.)*

LESSON 4 PROGRAM RESOURCES

ON LEVEL

In-Depth Resources: Unit 6
- Reading Skill: Finding Main Ideas, p. 43
- Vocabulary Cards, p. 47

Formal Assessment
- Lesson Quiz, p. 264

ENGLISH LEARNERS

In-Depth Resources in Spanish
- Reading Skill: Finding Main Ideas, p. 132
- Vocabulary Study Guide, p. 136

Modified Lesson Plans for English Learners, p. 111

Reading Study Guide (Spanish), p. 139

Reading Study Guide Audio CD (Spanish)

STRUGGLING READERS

In-Depth Resources: Unit 6
- Reading Skill: Finding Main Ideas, p. 43
- Vocabulary Study Guide, p. 46
- Vocabulary Cards, p. 47
- Reteaching Activity, p. 56

Reading Toolkit, L54

Reading Study Guide, p. 139

Reading Study Guide Audio CD

GIFTED AND TALENTED STUDENTS

In-Depth Resources: Unit 6
- Literature: The Aeneid by Virgil, p. 52

Interdisciplinary Projects
- Science, p. 86
- Language Arts, p. 87

INCLUSION

EasyPlanner CD-ROM
- Reading Skill: Finding Main Ideas
- Vocabulary Study Guide
- Reteaching Activity

TECHNOLOGY

eEdition CD-ROM

Power Presentations CD-ROM

Critical Thinking Transparencies
- CT68 Finding Main Ideas
- CT69 Chapter 15 Visual Summary

Test Generator CD-ROM

ClassZone.com

In-Depth Resources: Unit 6
• Reading Skill: Finding Main Ideas, p. 43

More About . . .

Latin

It is common to hear Latin referred to as a dead language, but that is hardly the case. Although it is no longer spoken by ordinary people, as it was during the Roman Empire, its influence is still widely felt. For hundreds of years after the fall of Rome, Latin was the language in which scholars and scientists shared their knowledge.

Latin has, even in modern times, remained the formal language of the Roman Catholic Church. Until recent years, the Roman Catholic mass was conducted in Latin, and Latin masses are still celebrated in some places.

History from Visuals

Interpreting Visuals

Have students review the table "Latin Origins of Romance Words." Remind students that English is not a Romance language, though English has been greatly influenced by Latin. Therefore, the English words in parentheses appear in the table for reference—as a way of determining what the words in the other languages mean.

Suggest that students read down each column to see how the Latin word compares with the words in the different Romance languages.

• Which English words seem to have been influenced by Latin words? (*Students might notice that* mother, father, *and* night *all resemble the corresponding Latin and Romance-language words.*)

Sculpture Romans learned about sculpture from the Greeks but did not follow the Greek tradition of showing the ideal. Instead, the Romans created sculptures that were realistic portraits of **bas-relief**. In a bas-relief, slightly raised figures stand out against a flat background. See an example of this style on page 514.

Literature The Greeks also influenced Roman literature. Roman writers adopted the form of the **epic**, a long poem about a hero's adventures. The *Aeneid* by Virgil is a well-known Roman epic. Virgil modeled his poem on two Greek epics, the *Odyssey* and the *Iliad*. The *Aeneid* tells the adventures of the hero Aeneas, who survived the Trojan War, sailed to Italy, and founded Rome.

The works of the statesman Cicero provide a picture of Roman life and add to our knowledge of Roman history. Cicero's written works include his speeches. Cicero was a master of **oratory**, the art of public speaking. Oratory was an important means of persuasion for Roman politicians.

Romans also wrote about philosophy. For example, Emperor Marcus Aurelius wrote the *Meditations,* a work expressing the ideas of Stoicism. Stoicism teaches that the world was created by a divine plan. Duty and virtue help people to live by that plan.

Language Latin, the language of Rome, was spoken across the Western Empire. Over time, Latin evolved into a group of languages called the Romance languages. (The word *romance* comes from the word *Roman*.) Today, Romance languages are spoken in countries whose lands were once ruled by Rome. The chart below shows similarities among Romance languages.

REVIEW How did Roman culture influence the languages of Europe?
Latin formed the basis of the Romance languages.

Latin Origins of Romance Words					
Language	**Word**				
Latin	pater ("father")	nox ("night")	bonus ("good")	vita ("life")	mater ("mother")
Spanish	padre	noche	bueno	vida	madre
French	père	nuit	bon	vie	mere
Portuguese	pai	noite	bom	vida	mãe
Italian	padre	notte	buono	vita	madre
Romanian	tatã	noapte	bun	viatã	mamâ

DIFFERENTIATING INSTRUCTION

English Learners

Categorize Details
Explain that categorizing involves grouping similar things together. Tell students they will group the things they read about into the following categories: arts, technology, law and government, and religion. Guide students as they scan the text headings to determine in which of the categories the text material would fit. Next have them take one category and find details about it in the text. Repeat with the other categories.

Inclusion

Read Content Aloud
To help students appreciate the relationships between Latin and the Romance languages, have them read the table "Latin Origins of Romance Words" aloud. Students should read down each column. Encourage students with knowledge of different languages to offer tips on pronunciation. Students may also use Internet dictionaries to help them learn how to pronounce the words.

Technology, Engineering, and Architecture

2 ESSENTIAL QUESTION How did Roman ideas about architecture and engineering influence builders throughout history? Architectural elements such as vaults and domes, and the use of concrete are still a part of construction today.

Greek architecture influenced Roman builders. You've already learned about the Greek building style, with its use of columns, pediments, and graceful proportions. The Romans used these elements but added their own ideas too.

New Styles of Architecture Roman builders were excellent engineers. They found new ways to improve the structure of buildings. These ideas included the use of arches, **vaults**, and domes. A vault is an arch that forms a ceiling or a roof.

Roman developments in building construction made it possible to build larger, taller buildings. Many modern buildings borrow Roman elements of design and structure. The dome of the U.S. Capitol building is a well-known example.

New Building Materials The Romans developed a form of concrete that was both light and strong. They poured the mixture into hollow walls or over curved forms to create strong vaults. Concrete is a common building material today.

Aqueducts The Romans built **aqueducts** to bring water to cities. An aqueduct is a waterway made by people. Aqueducts brought water to public fountains, where people collected water for their homes. Aqueducts also supplied water to public toilets and bathhouses. Eleven major aqueducts brought water to the city of Rome. The longest stretched for 57 miles. Aqueducts can still be found in France and Spain, lands that were once part of the Roman Empire.

Remains of a Roman Aqueduct This aqueduct is near Nîmes, France. It was constructed more than 2,000 years ago. ▼

Rome's Decline and Legacy • 517

INTERDISCIPLINARY ACTIVITIES

Science

Diagram an Aqueduct
Roman aqueducts were engineering marvels that moved large volumes of water over great distances. Have students use library or Internet resources to learn about the technologies Romans used to convey water over long distances. Students should create an illustration that shows the key features of a Roman aqueduct.

Science

Research Concrete
The development of concrete made many great Roman buildings possible. Have students use library or Internet resources to learn about concrete. Students should create a fact sheet that explains how concrete is made, what its properties are, and how it is used in building.

Teach

Technology, Engineering, and Architecture

6.7.8, 7.1.1, REP 1

Talk About It

- Which culture had a strong influence on Roman architecture? *(Greek culture)*

- How did superior Roman engineering affect the kind of architecture Romans were able to produce? *(They were able to build larger, taller buildings, and they incorporated arches, vaults, and domes.)*

- What building material did the Romans develop that we still use widely today? *(concrete)*

- **Critical Thinking: Understanding Cause and Effect** How did the building of Roman roads help the empire survive and thrive? *(Possible answer: The Roman roads made it easier for Roman troops to travel and protect the land. It also enhanced trade, which enriched the empire.)*

Teach

Religion and Law

📞 **6.7.8, 7.1.1, REP 1**

Talk About It

- Which two organizations that grew out of the Roman Empire were largely responsible for the spread of Christianity? *(the Roman Catholic Church and the Eastern Orthodox Church)*

- How far did Christianity spread? *(It spread throughout most of Europe and to parts of western Asia.)*

- How did Rome influence the formation of the U.S. government? *(The structure of the Roman Republic influenced the writers of the U.S. Constitution. Like the Roman Republic, the United States has a senate. Basic rights and principles, such as equality, came from Roman government and law.)*

- **Critical Thinking: Categorizing** What era of Roman history do you think had the greatest influence on the framers of the U.S. Constitution? *(the Roman Republic)*

Roads The Romans are especially famous for the quality of their roads. In 312 B.C., Romans built the first of many roads. It was called the Appian Way, and it ran southeast from Rome. In time, a system of roads extended across much of the empire. Rome was the center of this network.

Many Roman roads were built so that soldiers could move quickly to places in the empire where they were needed. The road system also increased trade because merchants and traders could move their goods more easily. Although the road system helped hold the Roman Empire together, it also made it easier for its enemies to invade.

REVIEW What elements of Roman construction are still in use? concrete, domes, vaults, and arches

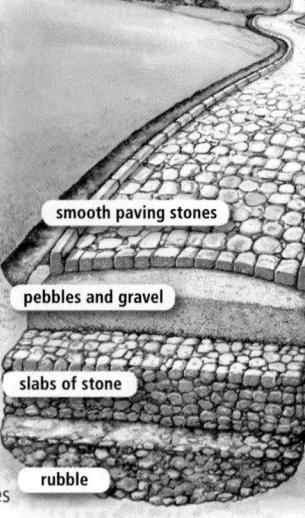

smooth paving stones

pebbles and gravel

slabs of stone

rubble

▲ **Roman Road Construction**
Roman roads were constructed in layers. The average width of a road was 15 to 18 feet.

Religion and Law

③ **ESSENTIAL QUESTION** What religious and legal legacies did Rome leave? Religion——Christianity; Law—law codes, equal treatment under the law

Past civilizations leave their mark through ideas as well as through objects. The western and eastern parts of the Roman Empire had great influence in the areas of religion and law.

Spreading Christianity The Roman Empire played a major role in the spread of Christianity. Christian missionaries converted many within the empire. The Roman Catholic Church became the powerful organization in Western Europe.

The Eastern Orthodox Church, which was the official religion of the Byzantine Empire, also spread Christianity. Many Russians and members of societies on the border of the Byzantine Empire became Eastern Orthodox Christians.

With both the Roman Catholic and Eastern Orthodox churches spreading Christianity, most of Europe and some parts of western Asia became Christian.

Roman Government and Law The structure of the Roman Republic influenced the writers of the U.S. Constitution. Roman senators made up the main political body of the republic. Early

---

DIFFERENTIATING INSTRUCTION

Gifted and Talented Students

Explore Roman Roots in U.S. Government
Have students use library or Internet resources to learn about and report on ways in which the framers of the U.S. Constitution incorporated Roman ideas into the Constitution. Students should present their findings in brief reports, which they can share with the rest of the class.

Struggling Readers

Read the Sections Aloud
Pair students, and have each pair take turns reading the lesson "The Legacy of Rome" aloud to each other. Students may alternate paragraphs or subsections. As students read to each other, encourage them to pause at the end of each section to answer the Review question and review what they have just read.

U.S. citizens followed this example by providing for their own Senate in Article I of the Constitution.

Laws in today's democracies evolved from those of ancient Rome and Byzantine. These laws include the right to own property and to make contracts and write wills.

In the Roman Republic citizens had the right to equal treatment under the law. This principle of equality inspired the creators of democracies in the United States and France.

REVIEW Which elements of Roman law are found in U.S. law?
right to own property, make contracts and wills, and equality under the law

Lesson Summary
- Roman writers and artists were inspired by Greek culture, which they combined with their own ideas.
- Roman builders and engineers developed styles and construction methods that continue to be used.
- Roman laws and government continue to serve as models for modern countries.

Why It Matters Now . . .
Many areas of modern life—from government to architecture to language—still carry the mark of the Roman Empire.

---

4 Lesson Review

 Homework Helper
ClassZone.com

Terms & Names

1. Explain the importance of

mosaic	epic	vault
bas-relief	oratory	aqueduct

Using Your Notes

Finding Main Ideas Use your completed web diagram to answer the following question:

2. What are some examples of Roman technology? (6.7.8)

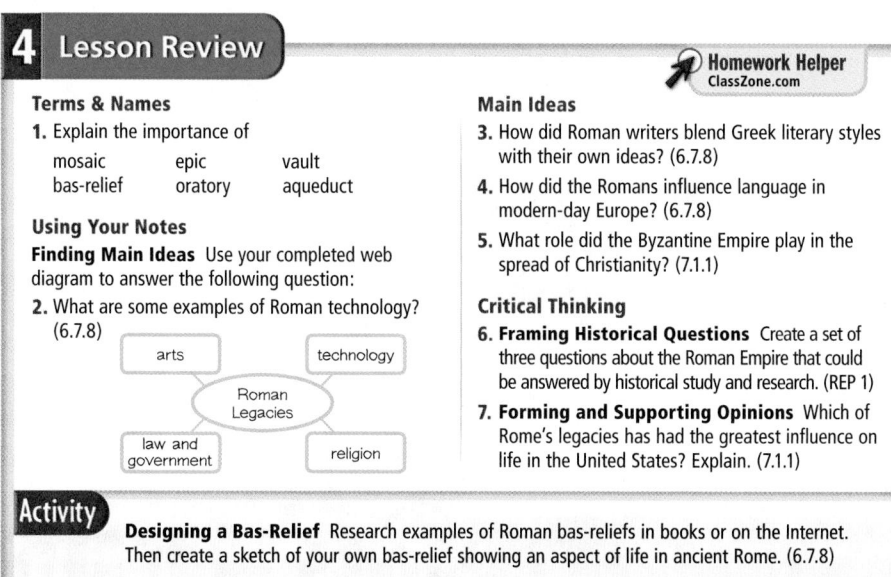

Main Ideas

3. How did Roman writers blend Greek literary styles with their own ideas? (6.7.8)

4. How did the Romans influence language in modern-day Europe? (6.7.8)

5. What role did the Byzantine Empire play in the spread of Christianity? (7.1.1)

Critical Thinking

6. **Framing Historical Questions** Create a set of three questions about the Roman Empire that could be answered by historical study and research. (REP 1)

7. **Forming and Supporting Opinions** Which of Rome's legacies has had the greatest influence on life in the United States? Explain. (7.1.1)

Activity

Designing a Bas-Relief Research examples of Roman bas-reliefs in books or on the Internet. Then create a sketch of your own bas-relief showing an aspect of life in ancient Rome. (6.7.8)

Rome's Decline and Legacy • **519**

---

❹ Assess & Reteach

Assess Have students work on their own to answer the questions, then meet in groups to discuss their answers.

 Formal Assessment
- Lesson Quiz, p. 264

Reteach Pair students. Have each pair take turns "teaching" the content of the sections to each other. Student teachers should highlight key information in the sections and ask review questions of their "students."

 **In-Depth Resources: Unit 6**
- Vocabulary Cards, p. 47
- Reteaching Activity, p. 56

Homework Helper
Visit **ClassZone.com** for a lesson review, a flip-card activity, and links to related Web sites.

---

4 Lesson Review Answers

Terms & Names

1. • mosaic, p. 515
- bas-relief, p. 516
- epic, p. 516
- oratory, p. 516
- vault, p. 517
- aqueduct, p. 517

Using Your Notes

See page 514 for an example of a completed diagram.

2. Possible answers: architectural features such as the vault and dome; concrete; roads and aqueducts

Main Ideas

3. The Romans were influenced by Greek epics but used their own heroes and stories.

4. Latin developed into the Romance languages—Italian, Spanish, French, Portuguese, and Romanian.

5. It made Eastern Orthodoxy the official religion in the east and helped it spread to its borderlands and Russia.

Critical Thinking

6. Questions should reflect topics that have been covered in this chapter but should seek information beyond that presented in the chapter.

7. Students should be able to support their answers with logical points.

Activity Rubric

	Style and Content of Bas-Relief	Quality of Presentation
4	characteristic reproduction, accurately reflects Roman life	clear, clean sketch
3	characteristic reproduction, somewhat reflects Roman life	clear sketch
2	only somewhat characteristic, somewhat reflects Roman life	somewhat unclear
1	not at all characteristic of Roman bas-relief	unclear

Rome's Decline and Legacy • **519**

Objectives

- Describe ways in which legacies of the Roman Empire continue to affect people today.
- Synthesize information in visuals and text and use that information in discussion and writing.
- **Language Objective:** Analyze images and captions that make the text more meaningful.

❶ Focus & Motivate

Preview Briefly discuss how the life of people today is very different from life in the Roman and Byzantine empires. Then tell students that they will be reading about how some features of the modern world come directly from ancient Rome.

❷ Teach

Talk About It

- Which well-known structure in the United States includes a Roman-inspired dome? *(the U.S. Capitol)*

- How does the function of roads in the United States compare with the function of roads in ancient Rome? *(Possible answer: Roads today are not typically built to move military forces, though they can be used for that purpose.)*

- How are Christian worshipers of ancient Rome linked to Christian worshipers of today? *(Many Christians today belong to a church—the Roman Catholic Church—founded in ancient Rome. The Roman Catholic Church is still headquartered where it was in ancient history.)*

- **Critical Thinking: Comparing and Contrasting** In what ways is the United States most similar to ancient Rome? In what ways is it most different? *(Possible answers: the United States is a powerful country with a powerful military and a thriving economy; the United States is not an empire and has a democratic government.)*

Roman Influences Today

CALIFORNIA STANDARDS
6.7.8 Discuss the legacies of Roman art and architecture, technology and science, literature, language, and law.

Purpose: To study the legacies of the Roman Empire that are present in today's life

The United States borrowed some Roman ideas about the structure of government. But the Romans also influenced culture in the United States in other ways. Their ideas about architecture and road-building can be seen in our buildings and our highway systems. The Christian church grew during Roman times. Today, millions of people practice the Christian faith that began in Roman times.

Domes

▶ **Past** Roman architects experimented with using a series of arches in a circle to create a dome. The dome of the Pantheon *(right)* is 142 feet high. The Pantheon was constructed to honor the gods. Later it became a Christian church and, finally, a national shrine in Italy.

▼ **Present** Architects for the U.S. Capitol building *(below right)* used the idea of the Roman dome. The dome of the Capitol is 287 feet high. It is topped by an almost 20-foot-tall statue called the Statue of Freedom.

Dome Strength A dome is strong because pressure at the top of the structure is distributed evenly and travels down the curved sides. This gives the structure strength. A dome and an egg are similar. Although we often think of an egg as fragile, an egg can be very strong because it is shaped like a dome. If you try to crush an egg by pressing down on the top, it will not break.

DIFFERENTIATING INSTRUCTION

Struggling Readers

Make Vocabulary Cards

Have students go through this feature and identify words with which they are unfamiliar. Have them write these words on note cards. Then give students time to look up the words in dictionaries, and have them write the definitions on the opposite side of the cards. Students can use the cards as they read the feature.

Inclusion

Divide and Conquer

Students who have difficulty reading may benefit from the "divide and conquer" technique. Pair students and have each pair read one of the three sections of this feature. Then have the pairs get together for a group discussion in which each pair summarizes what they read and takes notes on what the other pairs report.

Roads

Past The Roman roads were constructed so that military forces could easily move throughout the empire. Under Diocletian, the Roman Empire had 372 main roads covering about 53,000 miles.

▶ **Present** The United States is a nation on the move. There are almost 4 million miles of roads. The interstate system covers 46,467 miles.

Religious Practice

▶ **Past** St. Peter *(right)* was one of Jesus' leading disciples. He became the first bishop of Rome. According to Roman Catholic tradition, the bishop of Rome became the head of the Christian church. Today the bishop of Rome is called the pope and heads the Roman Catholic Church. Rome is the spiritual center of the Church.

▼ **Present** Today the pope lives in a city-state called Vatican City. It is located within Rome. One of the largest Christian churches, St. Peter's Basilica, is located there. Tradition says St. Peter was buried beneath the basilica. In the photograph here the pope greets thousands of believers in St. Peter's Square.

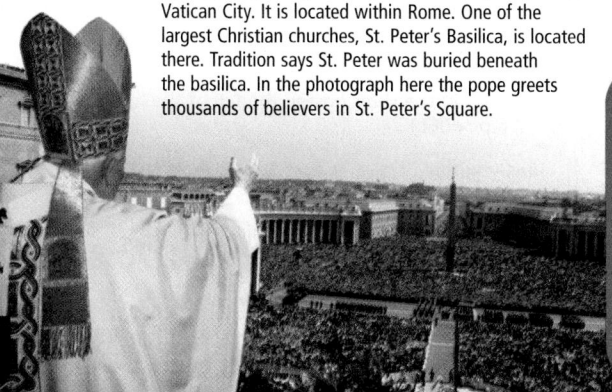

Activities

1. **TALK ABOUT IT** Are there any domed buildings where you live? If so, what activities take place there?

2. **WRITE ABOUT IT** Research information about Roman roads, including how the roads were built and their location in the empire. Write a research report on your findings. (Writing 2.3)

Rome's Decline and Legacy • 521

 **Research Links**

Visit **ClassZone.com** for age-appropriate Web sites related to this topic.

More About . . .

The U.S. Interstate Highway System
The United States does not have to move its troops around the country in the same way that the Roman Empire did. However, the U.S. interstate highway system did get its start in part as a matter of military readiness. The poor state of the nation's network of roads concerned officials in the post–World War II era.

In the 1950s, President Dwight D. Eisenhower recognized that the road system would be unable to handle a major military emergency. Therefore, the U.S. government committed itself to a major highway project that is today referred to as the Dwight D. Eisenhower System of Interstate and Defense Highways.

More About . . .

Vatican City
Vatican City is located within the borders of the city of Rome. Its buildings and squares cover an area of well under one square mile. Since the 1920s, the Vatican has been a politically independent city-state, governed by the pope and the College of Cardinals.

ACTIVITIES ANSWERS

1. **TALK ABOUT IT** Help students identify the functions of domed buildings in your community.

2. **WRITE ABOUT IT** The research report should have a narrowly defined topic; include facts, details, and examples that support the main ideas; draw on several different sources of information and include a bibliography.

2. Writing Rubric

	Content of Report	Number of Errors
4	accurate, detailed	includes no more than one grammatical or spelling
3	accurate	includes two or three grammatical or spelling errors
2	somewhat accurate	includes four or five grammatical or spelling errors
1	not accurate	includes more than five grammatical or spelling errors

Terms & Names

1. **Diocletian** was the absolute ruler who reorganized the Roman Empire.

2. The nomads who lived on the frontiers of the Roman Empire were thought of by the Romans as **barbarians**.

3. The **Eastern Orthodox Church** developed in the Byzantine Empire, while the **Roman Catholic Church** developed in what was once the Western Roman Empire.

4. The **vault** and the **aqueduct** are examples of Roman engineering excellence.

Main Ideas

An Empire in Decline
(pages 494–499)

5. Rome was short of money because people did not pay taxes. Roman citizens felt a loss of loyalty to the empire and a lack of security.

6. He thought it would make the vast empire more manageable.

The Fall of the Roman Empire
(pages 500–507)

7. The Western Empire was more vulnerable to attack from nomadic groups, and its cities were less prosperous and less capable of providing for their defense.

8. They created instability by forcing barbarian groups into the empire and by attacking the empire itself.

The Byzantine Empire
(pages 508–513)

9. It preserved Roman law, and its scholars studied and sought to preserve Roman culture.

10. differences over church practices and the authority of the pope over political leaders, as well as the use of different languages

The Legacy of Rome
(pages 514–521)

11. The Romans learned about sculpture and epic poetry from the Greeks.

12. Roman principles, such as equality, have remained influential, and the Justinian Code has continued to influence some aspects of modern law.

▶ **VISUAL SUMMARY**

Roman Empire

Government (6.7.8)
- Absolute ruler, law codes

Science & Technology (6.7.8)
- Roads, aqueducts, concrete, arches, domes

Belief Systems (7.1.1)
- Spread Christianity

Culture (6.7.8)
- Realism, bas-reliefs, mosaics, epics, oratory

Empire Splits

Western Roman Empire (7.1.2, 7.1.3)
- Roman Catholic
- Germanic migrations/invasions
- Ended A.D. 476

Eastern Roman Empire (7.1.2, 7.1.3)
- Eastern Orthodox
- Germanic/Muslim invasions
- Ended A.D. 1453

▶ **TERMS & NAMES**

Explain why the words in each set below are linked with each other.

1. **Diocletian** and **absolute ruler**
2. **barbarian** and **nomad**
3. **Eastern Orthodox Church** and **Roman Catholic Church**
4. **vault** and **aqueduct**

▶ **MAIN IDEAS**

An Empire in Decline (pages 494–499)
5. What economic and political problems weakened the Roman Empire? (7.1.1)
6. Why did Diocletian believe reorganizing the empire would strengthen Rome? (7.1.2)

The Fall of the Roman Empire (pages 500–507)
7. Why was the Western Roman Empire more likely to fall than the Eastern Roman Empire? (7.1.2)
8. How did the Huns hasten the fall of the empire? (7.1.2)

The Byzantine Empire (pages 508–513)
9. In what ways did the Byzantine Empire preserve the Roman culture? (7.1.3)
10. What caused the Christian church to split in A.D. 1054? (7.1.3)

The Legacy of Rome (pages 514–521)
11. What artistic styles did the Romans borrow from Greek culture? (6.7.8)
12. How has Roman law shaped modern law? (6.7.8)

ALTERNATIVE ASSESSMENT RUBRICS

1. Writing Rubric

	Description of Roman and Gothic Life	Quality of Writing
4	many accurate details	lively, conveys feelings
3	some accurate details	conveys feelings
2	few accurate details	conveys few feelings
1	no accurate details	conveys no feelings

2. Language Arts Rubric

	Number of Words	Clarity of Explanation
4	nine or ten words	accurately illustrates all concepts
3	five to eight words	illustrates all concepts
2	fewer than five words	illustrates some concepts
1	no words	fails to illustrate any concepts

CRITICAL THINKING Big Ideas: Economics

13. UNDERSTANDING CAUSES AND EFFECTS How was economics a cause of Rome's downfall? (7.1.1)

14. ANALYZING ECONOMIC AND POLITICAL ISSUES How are the nomadic attacks on Rome related to Rome's economic problems? (7.1.1)

15. MAKING INFERENCES How did economics play a part in the survival of the Byzantine Empire? (7.1.3)

ALTERNATIVE ASSESSMENT

1. WRITING ACTIVITY Imagine you lived in the city of Rome when the Goths attacked the city in A.D. 410. Write a description of the attack. (Writing 2.1)

2. INTERDISCIPLINARY ACTIVITY— LANGUAGE ARTS Use books and the Internet to research Latin-based words in the English language. Make a list of five to ten terms used in everyday life. Create an illustrated chart listing the Latin word and an image of the concept the word represents. (6.7.8)

3. STARTING WITH A STORY

 Review your speech explaining why the Goths should either seek peace or stand up to the Romans. Now outline a speech that takes the opposite view. (Writing 2.5)

Technology Activity

4. MAKING AN ILLUSTRATED MAP Use the Internet to research the locations of Roman aqueducts. Make an illustrated map of the Roman Empire that shows their locations. (6.7.8)

• Display an image of the aqueduct located at each location.
• Identify the location by city and modern-day country.
• Document your sources.

 **Research Links**
ClassZone.com

Reading a Map Use the map below to answer the questions. (6.7.8)

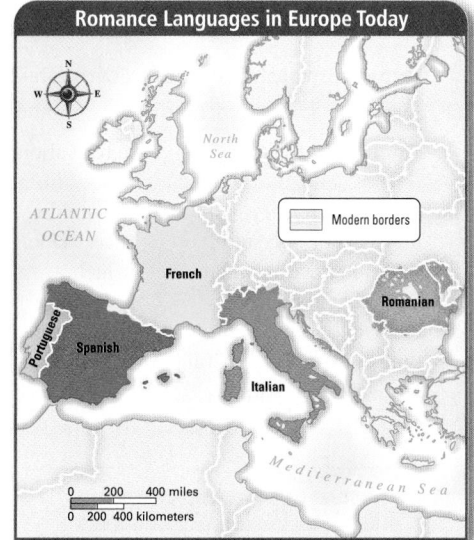

Romance Languages in Europe Today

Modern borders

North Sea

ATLANTIC OCEAN

French

Portuguese

Spanish

Romanian

Italian

Mediterranean Sea

0   200   400 miles
0 200 400 kilometers

1. The Romance languages are concentrated in which part of Europe?

A. north
B. east
C. southwest
D. southeast

2. Which statement best describes the pattern of Romance languages?

A. The pattern of languages is random.
B. The Romance languages are found in the former Roman Empire.
C. The Romance languages are dying out.
D. The Romance languages spread throughout Europe.

 **Test Practice**
ClassZone.com

Additional Test Practice, pp. S1–S33

Rome's Decline and Legacy • 523

Critical Thinking

Big Idea: Economics

13. Rome spent too much money on defense. This left little money for other government services.

14. To defend the empire against attack, Rome had to employ a large army requiring high taxes. The refusal of people to pay the taxes left the empire unable to defend itself.

15. The Byzantine Empire was wealthy because of trade. A lack of money contributed to the decline of the west. One can assume wealth helped the Byzantine Empire survive.

Standards-Based Assessment

1. The correct answer is C. Most of the Romance languages are spoken in southwestern Europe.

2. The correct answer is B. The territory in which Romance languages are spoken is within the old Roman Empire.

 Research Links

Visit **ClassZone.com** for links to Web sites that can be used for research.

 Test Practice

Visit **ClassZone.com** to access strategies and tutorials for taking standardized tests.

 Formal Assessment
• Chapter Test, Forms A, B, and C, pp. 265–279

 Test Generator
• Chapter Tests, Forms A, B, and C (English and Spanish)

ALTERNATIVE ASSESSMENT RUBRICS

3. Starting with a Story Rubric

	Content of Outline
4	clear, compelling, persuasive arguments
3	compelling and persuasive
2	not very persuasive
1	not persuasive, failure to argue opposite position

4. Technology Rubric

	Content Included on Map	Presentation of Map
4	all required elements	clear, neat, complete
3	most required elements	neat, complete
2	some required information	somewhat sloppy or incomplete
1	little or no required information	sloppy or substantially incomplete

Objectives

- Describe problem-solution writing.
- Analyze an example of cultural borrowing to determine whether it created or solved a problem.
- Publish a composition in a class magazine.

❶ Focus & Motivate

Preview Discuss with students how cultures often borrow practices, ideas, technologies, languages, and other cultural features from one another. Ask students to identify foods, customs, and words that they can trace back to other cultures. For example, many foods frequently enjoyed by people in the United States have Spanish or Mexican origins, such as tortillas and tacos. Explain that students will be using their text to examine major examples of cultural borrowing in the past.

❷ Teach

Talk About It

- Which examples of cultural borrowing described in the book might provide a strong basis for this paper? *(Possible answers: the Kush civilization's borrowing religion and hieroglyphs from Egyptian culture; Rome's borrowing gods from Greece; the United States' borrowing its system of government from Rome)*

- What determines whether a cultural borrowing creates or solves a problem? *(its immediate and long-term effects)*

- Why is an outline useful when writing a long paper? *(Following an outline ensures that all major ideas will be covered in the most effective order possible.)*

- **Critical Thinking: Making Generalizations** What is the reason behind many instances of cultural borrowing? *(Possible answer: Cultures doing the borrowing need to solve problems.)*

Writing About History

Writing Model
ClassZone.com

Expository Writing: Problem and Solution
The Interaction of Cultures

CALIFORNIA STANDARDS
Writing 2.2 Write expository compositions.

Purpose: To analyze the impact of cultural borrowing

Audience: Other students in your class and school

Throughout this book, you have read about times when cultures borrowed things from other cultures. How can you measure the impacts of these cultural influences? One way is to analyze whether an influence created a problem or solved one. Writing that explores problems and solutions is a type of expository writing called **problem-and-solution** writing.

Alphabet on Greek ostracon (see page 376.) ▶

Culture	Characters from Alphabet						
Phoenician	⅄	⊄	⅂	Δ	⅃	Ⅎ	
Greek	A	B	Γ	Δ	E		
Modern	A	B	C	D	E	F	G

Organization & Focus

Your assignment is to (1) identify a time when one culture borrowed something important from another and (2) decide whether that borrowing solved a problem or created one. Then you will write a two- to three-page composition for a magazine that your class will publish.

Choosing a Topic Review the visual summaries in all the chapters. Take notes about cultural interactions—what caused them and how they affected the cultures that did the borrowing. If you need to, review the chapters for more information. When you have finished, choose one cultural interaction as the topic of your composition.

Identifying Purpose and Audience Your purpose is to analyze the problem or solution represented by an instance of cultural borrowing. Your readers are other students in your school. Keep their interests in mind as you write.

Analyzing Review your notes about the effects of cultural borrowing. Decide whether the borrowing you chose solved a problem or created a problem. For example, the Greeks' borrowing of the Phoenician alphabet solved their problem of not having a writing system.

524 • Unit 6

DIFFERENTIATING INSTRUCTION

Inclusion

Share Ideas

Have students work in small groups to complete the steps of the assignment. Have each group decide together on which instance of cultural borrowing they will focus. Once they have made their selection, they should identify the reasons for and the effects of the borrowing. Each group should then present its ideas to the class for discussion before collaborating on the outline and the final paper.

Research & Technology

To decide whether the cultural borrowing was a problem or a solution, consider both short-term and long-term effects. Consider whether what was borrowed changed society or influenced even later cultures. Use a library and the Internet to research long-term effects.

Outlining and Drafting Consider how to organize your composition. Your outline might be in this form:

I. Introduction
II. Reasons for cultural borrowing
III. Effects of cultural borrowing
   A. On the receiver
   B. On the giver
IV. Identification as problem or solution
   A. Immediate outcomes
   B. Long-term outcomes
V. Conclusion

Use your completed outline as you draft your composition.

Technology Tip Many word-processing programs offer help with making outlines. Check the instruction manual or the help menu to see if your program will format an outline with the proper indents.

Evaluation & Revision

Many writers read their work several times, each time looking at a different aspect of their writing. The list below shows some aspects to review.

- **Ideas** In good compositions, the ideas are interesting, clearly presented, supported with details, and organized logically.
- **Sentence Variety** Using a variety of sentences makes a composition interesting to read. Good writers vary both the structure and the length of their sentences.
- **Word Choice** Precise words give the reader clear visuals. For example, instead of the word *trouble*, a writer might use the more specific word *riot*.

Self-Check

Does my composition have

☐ an introduction that grabs attention and states a thesis?

☐ an explanation of the effects of an instance of cultural borrowing?

☐ a thorough analysis of how the borrowing solved or created a problem?

☐ evidence to support that analysis?

☐ a strong conclusion?

Publish & Present

Make a neat final copy of your composition. With your classmates, discuss how to arrange the compositions, create a table of contents, and design a magazine cover. Share your magazine with other classes.

525

More About . . .

Revising
Suggest that students use one or all of the following strategies to help them revise and proofread their papers:

- Read your paper aloud. Listen to the way the words sound and watch for errors as you read.

- Read one line at a time, covering the rest with a sheet of blank paper.

- Point to every word as you read. Do not proceed to the next one until you have said the word. Watch for omitted words and duplicates.

ANSWERS

Problem-and-Solution Composition Rubric

	Structure of Composition	Content of Composition	Errors in Mechanics
4	effectively organized and extensively developed	interesting ideas that are clearly expressed in varied sentences	few or none
3	good organization and development	good ideas, some variety of sentence structure and length	some
2	some organization, some development	fairly obvious ideas expressed in mostly complete sentences	many
1	little organization or development	lack of ideas, incomplete sentences	many major

Reference Section

Skillbuilder Handbook

CONTENTS

1.1 Finding Main Ideas

Learn the Skill

The **main idea** is a statement that summarizes the subject of a speech, an article, a section of a book, or a paragraph. Main ideas can be stated or unstated. The main idea of a paragraph is often stated in the first or last sentence. If it is in the first sentence, it is followed by sentences that support that main idea. If it is in the last sentence, the details build up to the main idea. To find an unstated idea, you must use the details of the paragraph as clues.

Practice the Skill

The following paragraph deals with Indian mathematics, science, and technology during the reign of the Guptas. Use the strategies listed below to help you identify the main idea.

How to Find the Main Idea

Strategy ❶ Identify what you think may be the stated main idea. Check the first and last sentences of the paragraph to see if either could be the stated main idea.

Strategy ❷ Identify details that support the main idea. Some details explain that idea. Others give examples of what is stated in the main idea.

> ### ADVANCES UNDER THE GUPTAS
>
> ❶ During the reign of the Guptas, Indians made significant advances in mathematics, science, and technology. ❷ Indian scholars developed the decimal system and the symbol for zero. ❷ They also invented the numeral system we use today. ❷ Meanwhile, Indian doctors made key contributions to Ayurvedic medicine. It is one of the oldest systems of medicine. It promotes health by using diet, exercise, and other methods to maintain energy in the body. ❷ Indian artisans developed advanced methods of working with metal. In Delhi, an iron pillar erected about A.D. 400 towers almost 23 feet over the city.

Make a Chart

Making a chart can help you identify the main idea and details in a passage or paragraph. The chart below identifies the main idea and details in the paragraph you just read.

MAIN IDEA: During the reign of the Guptas, Indians made significant advances in mathematics, science, and technology.			
DETAIL: Indian scholars developed the decimal system and the symbol for zero.	DETAIL: Indian scholars invented the numeral system we use today.	DETAIL: Indian doctors advanced Ayurvedic medicine.	DETAIL: Indian artisans developed advanced methods of working with metal.

Apply the Skill

Turn to Chapter 2, Lesson 3, "The First Communities." Read "Villages Grow More Complex" and create a chart that identifies the main idea and the supporting details.

1.2 Summarizing

Learn the Skill

When you **summarize,** you restate a paragraph, a passage, or a chapter in fewer words. You include only the main ideas and most important details. It is important to use your own words when summarizing.

Practice the Skill

The passage below describes early inventions that aided a group in ancient Mesopotamia known as the Sumerians. Use the strategies listed below to help you summarize the passage.

How to Summarize

Strategy ❶ Look for topic sentences that state the main idea or ideas. These are often at the beginning of a section or paragraph. Briefly restate each main idea in your own words.

Strategy ❷ Include key facts and any names, dates, numbers, amounts, or percentages from the text.

Strategy ❸ Write your summary and review it to see that you have included only the most important details.

> ### EARLY INVENTIONS
>
> ❶ The plow and the wheel helped the Sumerians a great deal in their daily life. ❷ Plows helped to improve agriculture. They broke up hard soil, which made planting easier. In addition, rainfall often flowed deeper into plowed soil. As a result, the roots of plants received more water.
>
> Meanwhile, Sumerians used the wheel in many ways. ❷ They built wheeled wagons, which helped farmers take their crops to market more easily and quickly. ❷ They also built potter's wheels, which enabled them to make pottery more quickly and efficiently.

Write a Summary

You should be able to write your summary in a short paragraph. The paragraph below summarizes the passage you just read.

> ❸ The plow and the wheel helped Sumerians in their daily life. Sumerians used plows to improve farming. They used wheels to construct transport wagons and to build potter's wheels, which helped them make pottery more quickly.

Apply the Skill

Turn to Chapter 1, Lesson 4, "How Historians Study the Past." Read "The Historian's Tools" and write a paragraph summarizing the passage.

1.3 Comparing and Contrasting

Learn the Skill

Comparing means looking at the similarities and differences among two or more things. **Contrasting** means examining only the differences among them. Historians compare and contrast events, personalities, behaviors, beliefs, and situations in order to understand them better.

Practice the Skill

The following passage describes the ancient Assyrian and Persian empires. Use the strategies below to help you compare and contrast these two empires.

How to Compare and Contrast

Strategy ❶ Look for two subjects that can be compared and contrasted. This passage compares the Assyrian and Persian empires.

Strategy ❷ To find similarities, look for clue words indicating that two things are alike. Clue words include *both, together, also,* and *similarly.*

Strategy ❸ To find contrasts, look for clue words that show how two things differ. Clue words include *by contrast, but, on the other hand,* and *yet.*

> ### ASSYRIAN EMPIRE AND PERSIAN EMPIRE
>
> ❶ During ancient times, Assyria and Persia ❷ *both* developed into mighty empires. The Assyrians had a fierce army that conquered many lands. ❷ The Persians *also* had a powerful army. The Assyrians governed their empire by choosing the person to rule each region. ❷ *Similarly,* the Persians set up governors to carry out orders in the various regions of their empire. There were differences between the two empires, including the way in which they treated conquered peoples. The Assyrians were cruel to the groups they defeated. ❸ *By contrast,* the Persians largely respected the people they captured.

Make a Venn Diagram

Making a Venn diagram will help you identify similarities and differences between two things. In the overlapping area, list characteristics shared by both subjects. Then, in the separate ovals, list the characteristics that the two subjects do not share. This Venn diagram compares and contrasts the Assyrian and Persian empires.

ASSYRIAN EMPIRE
-cruel toward conquered peoples

BOTH
-mighty empires
-strong armies
-officials govern regions

PERSIAN EMPIRE
-respected conquered peoples

Apply the Skill

Turn to Chapter 1, Lesson 2, "How Maps Help Us Study History." Read "Different Maps for Different Purposes." Then make a Venn diagram showing similarities and differences between political and physical maps.

1.4 Making Inferences

Learn the Skill

Inferences are ideas that the author has not directly stated. **Making inferences** involves reading between the lines to interpret the information you read. You can make inferences by studying what is stated and using your common sense and previous knowledge.

Practice the Skill

The passage below examines the Kushite civilization in northern Africa. Use the strategies below to help you make inferences from the passage.

How to Make Inferences

Strategy 1 Read to find statements of facts and ideas. Knowing the facts will give you a good basis for making inferences.

Strategy 2 Use your knowledge, logic, and common sense to make inferences that are based on facts. Ask yourself, "What does the author want me to understand?" For example, from the facts about Kushite civilization, you can make the inference that trade was important to the Kushites.

> ### KUSHITE CIVILIZATION
>
> The Kushite kings chose a new capital, Meroë, in about 500 B.C. Meroë was located on the Nile River south of the Egyptian Empire. The city boasted abundant supplies of iron ore. **1** As a result, the Kushite people manufactured iron weapons and tools. **1** Merchants in Meroë traded iron goods for jewelry, fine cotton cloth, and glass bottles. **1** In Kush, royal women held a significant degree of power. In the absence of the king, a queen ruled the country.

Make a Chart

Making a chart will help you organize information and make logical inferences. The chart below organizes information from the passage you just read.

1 STATED FACTS AND IDEAS	**2** INFERENCES
The people of Kush manufactured iron weapons and tools.	The Kushite people possessed strong technological skills.
Merchants from Meroë exchanged iron goods for products from faraway lands.	Trade was an important part of the Kushite empire.
In Kush, royal women sometimes ruled.	In Kush, some women were influential and well respected.

Apply the Skill

Turn to Chapter 6, Lesson 2, "The Kingdom of Aksum." Read "Aksum's Achievements" and use a chart like the one above to make inferences about Aksum's civilization.

1.5 Categorizing

Learn the Skill

To **categorize** is to sort people, objects, ideas, or other information into groups, called categories. Historians categorize information to help them identify and understand patterns in historical events.

Practice the Skill

The following passage discusses the development of villages during ancient times. Use the strategies listed below to help you categorize information in a passage.

How to Categorize

Strategy ❶ First, decide what the passage is about.

Strategy ❷ Then find out what the categories will be. Look for different ways that villages became more complex. These will be your category headings.

Strategy ❸ Once you have chosen the categories, sort information into them. For example, how did the economy grow more complex? How did society grow more complex?

VILLAGES GROW MORE COMPLEX

Advances in agriculture and technology resulted in extra food and supplies. This meant that larger groups of people could live together in one place. ❶ As a result, villages soon grew larger and more complex. With fewer farmers needed, people learned new skills and crafts. ❷ They became carpenters, tool makers, and potters. As a result, a new and more diverse economic system emerged. Social systems also grew more diverse. ❷ As villages grew, social classes with varying wealth, power, and influence emerged. ❷ The growing populations of early villages also led to the creation of more organized political systems. Villagers established a government, or a system of ruling, to provide greater order and leadership.

Make a Chart

Making a chart can help you categorize information. The chart below shows how the information from the passage you just read can be categorized.

VILLAGES GROW MORE COMPLEX		
ECONOMIC	SOCIAL	POLITICAL
specialized workers; new professions	defined classes	creation of government

Apply the Skill

Turn to Chapter 7, Lesson 1, "Geography and Indian Life." Read "Physical Geography of India" and make a chart in which you categorize the physical geography of India.

1.6 Making Decisions

Learn the Skill

Making decisions involves choosing between two or more options, or courses of action. In most cases, decisions have consequences, or results. By understanding how historical figures made decisions, you can learn how to improve your own decision-making skills.

Practice the Skill

The passage below explains a decision Emperor Shi Huangdi faced about governing China. Use the strategies below to analyze his decision.

How to Make Decisions

Strategy ① Identify a decision that needs to be made. Think about what factors make the decision difficult.

Strategy ② Identify possible consequences of the decision. Remember that there can be more than one consequence to a decision.

Strategy ③ Identify the decision.

Strategy ④ Identify actual consequences that resulted from the decision.

> ### HOW TO GOVERN
>
> When Shi Huangdi became emperor in 221 B.C., China suffered from many internal battles between warring states. ① Shi Huangdi had to decide how to govern. ② If he imposed a strong and harsh rule, he could end the internal battles and restore order. However, the Chinese people might react angrily to such a strong government. ② If Shi Huangdi ruled with tolerance, the internal battles might continue. ③ Shi Huangdi decided to rule harshly. ④ Shi Huangdi's strong rule did bring order. ④ However, his harsh rule caused great resentment among the people. After Shi Huangdi's death, the Chinese people rebelled.

Make a Flow Chart

A flow chart can help you identify the steps involved in making a decision. The flow chart below shows the decision-making process in the passage you just read.

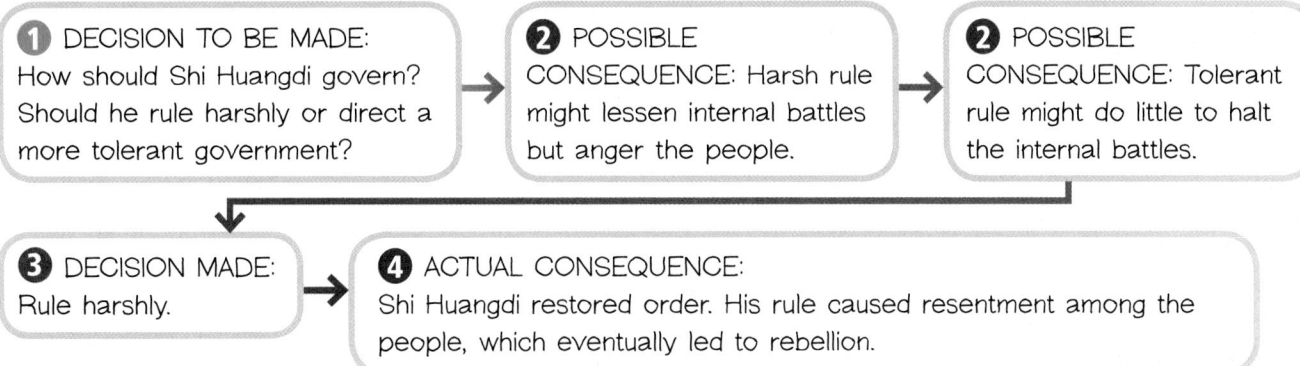

① DECISION TO BE MADE: How should Shi Huangdi govern? Should he rule harshly or direct a more tolerant government?

② POSSIBLE CONSEQUENCE: Harsh rule might lessen internal battles but anger the people.

② POSSIBLE CONSEQUENCE: Tolerant rule might do little to halt the internal battles.

③ DECISION MADE: Rule harshly.

④ ACTUAL CONSEQUENCE: Shi Huangdi restored order. His rule caused resentment among the people, which eventually led to rebellion.

Apply the Skill

Turn to Chapter 4, Lesson 3, "Persia Controls Southwest Asia." Read "Cyrus Founds an Empire" and make a flow chart to identify Cyrus' decision about how to rule his empire.

1.7 Making Generalizations

Learn the Skill

To **make generalizations** means to make broad judgments based on information. When you make generalizations, you should gather information from several sources.

Practice the Skill

The following three passages contain descriptions of Sparta. Use the strategies listed below to make a generalization about Sparta based on these descriptions.

How to Make Generalizations

Strategy ❶ Look for information that the sources have in common. For example, all three sources describe the military might of Sparta.

Strategy ❷ Form a generalization about these descriptions in a way that agrees with all three sources. State your generalization in a sentence.

LIFE IN SPARTA

❶ From the 5th century, the ruling class of Sparta devoted itself to war and diplomacy, deliberately neglecting the arts, philosophy, and literature. . . .
–*Encyclopaedia Britannica*

❶ From the age of seven a Spartan boy was educated and trained by the state to become a soldier.
–*Encyclopedia Americana*

❶ The Spartan people paid a high price for their military supremacy. All forms of individual expression were discouraged.
❶ As a result, Spartans did not value . . . artistic or intellectual pursuits.
–*World History: Patterns of Interaction*

Make a Diagram

Using a diagram can help you make generalizations. The diagram below shows how the information you just read can be used to generalize about Sparta.

❶ Spartan boys were trained from early on to be soldiers.	
❶ Sparta discouraged artistic, intellectual, and other nonmilitary pursuits.	❷ GENERALIZATION Sparta became a powerful military state by stressing military service and training over all other pursuits in society.
❶ The Spartans devoted themselves to war and military training.	

Apply the Skill

Turn to Chapter 8, Lesson 2, "China's Ancient Philosophies." Read "Confucianism," and the primary source on page 261. Also read the History Maker feature about "Confucius" on page 262. Use a chart like the one above to make a generalization about Confucius.

2.1 Reading a Map

Learn the Skill

Maps are representations of features on Earth's surface. Some maps show political features, such as national borders. Other maps show physical features, such as mountains and bodies of water. By learning to use map elements, you can better understand how to read maps.

Practice the Skill

The following map shows the Sumerian city-states. Use the strategies listed below to help you identify the elements common to most maps.

How to Read a Map

**Strategy ① ** Read the title. This identifies the main idea of the map.

**Strategy ② ** Look for the grid of lines that forms a pattern of squares over the map. These numbered lines are the lines of latitude (horizontal) and longitude (vertical). They indicate the location of the area on Earth.

**Strategy ③ ** Read the map key. It is usually in a box. The key will help you interpret the symbols or colors on the map.

**Strategy ④ ** Use the scale and the pointer, or compass rose, to determine distance and direction.

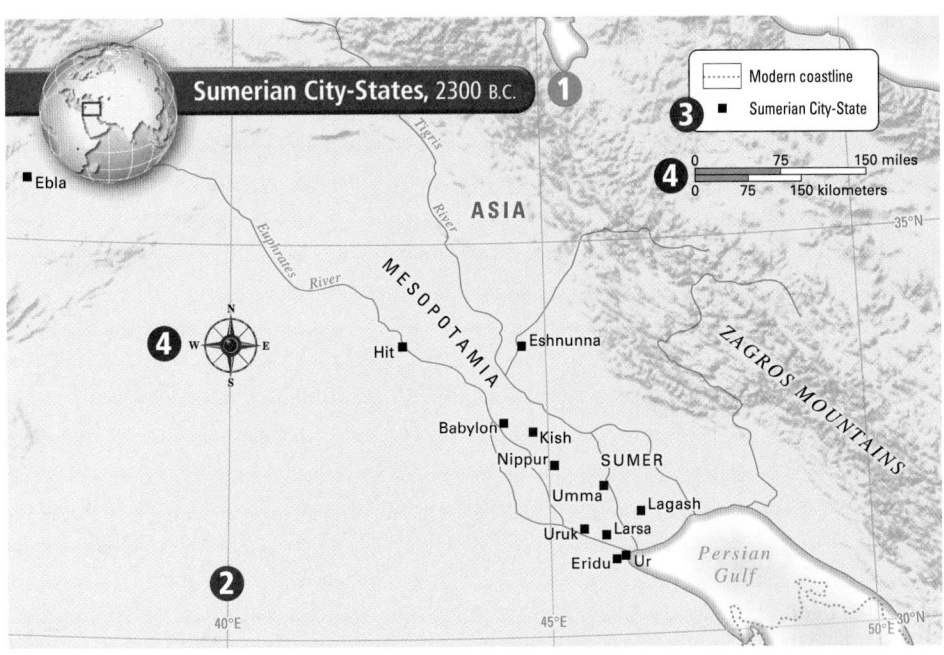

Make a Chart

A chart can help you organize information given on maps. The chart below summarizes information about the map you just studied.

TITLE	Sumerian City-States, 2300 B.C.
LOCATION	"between longitudes 50°E and 40°E and latitudes 30°N and 35°N, except for Ebla which is located between longitude 35°E and 40°E, just north of 35°N"
KEY INFORMATION	square = Sumerian city-state
SUMMARY	Sumerian city-states developed mostly along the southern regions of the Tigris and Euphrates rivers.

2.1 Reading a Map (continued)

Practice the Skill

The following map shows the Aryan invasions into India. Use the strategies listed below to help you identify the elements common to most maps.

How to Read a Map

Strategy ① Read the title. This identifies the main idea of the map.

Strategy ② Look for the grid of lines that forms a pattern of squares over the map. These numbered lines are the lines of latitude (horizontal) and longitude (vertical). They indicate the location of the area on Earth.

Strategy ③ Read the map key. It is usually in a box. The key will help you interpret the symbols or colors on the map.

Strategy ④ Use the pointer, or compass rose, to determine direction.

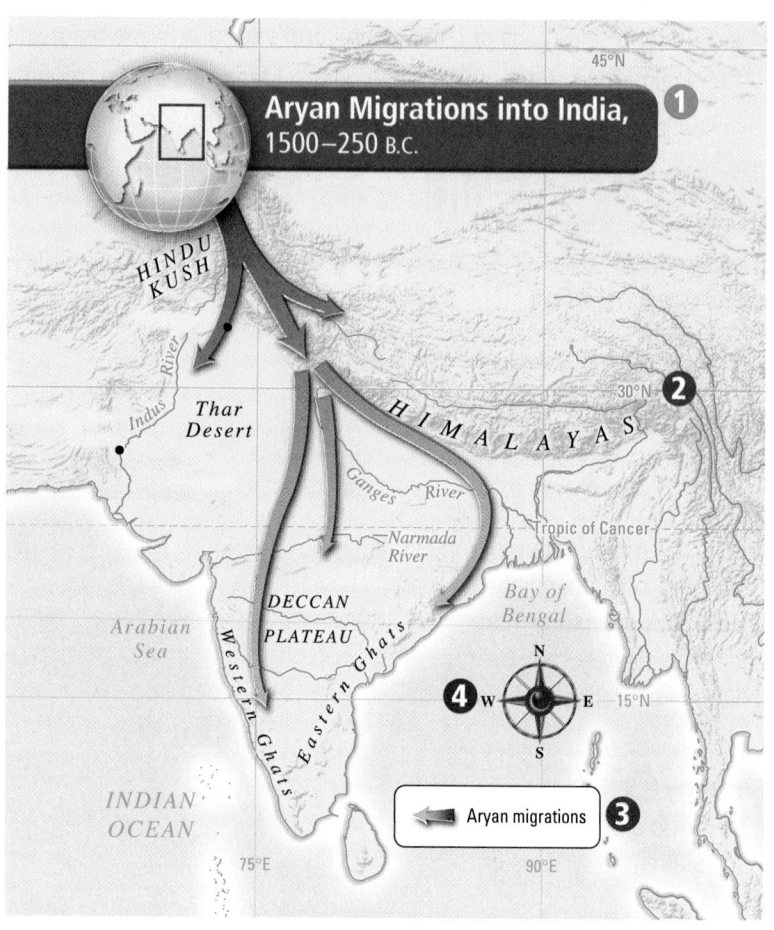

Make a Chart

A chart can help you organize information given on maps. The chart below summarizes information about the map you just studied.

TITLE	Aryan Migrations into India, 1500–250 B.C.
LOCATION	"between longitudes 75°E and 90°E and latitudes 30°N and the equator."
KEY INFORMATION	arrows = paths of Aryan migrations
SUMMARY	Over a roughly 1200-year period, the Aryans migrated south and settled throughout much of India.

Apply the Skill

Turn to Chapter 4, Lesson 2, "Assyria Rules the Fertile Crescent." Read the map entitled "Assyrian Empire, 650 B.C." and make a chart to identify information on the map.

2.2 Creating a Map

Learn the Skill

Creating a map involves representing geographical information. When you draw a map, it is easiest to use an existing map as a guide. On the map you draw, you can show geographical information. You can also show political information such as the area covered by empires, civilizations, and countries. In addition, maps can show data on climates, population, and resources.

Practice the Skill

Below is a map that a student created that shows the furthest extent of the Gupta Empire. Read the strategies listed below to see how the map was created.

How to Create a Map

Strategy 1 Select a title that identifies the geographical area and the map's purpose. Include a date in your title.

Strategy 2 Draw lines of latitude and longitude using short dashes.

Strategy 3 Create a key that shows the colors and symbols.

Strategy 4 Draw the colors and symbols on the map to show information.

Strategy 5 Draw a compass rose and scale.

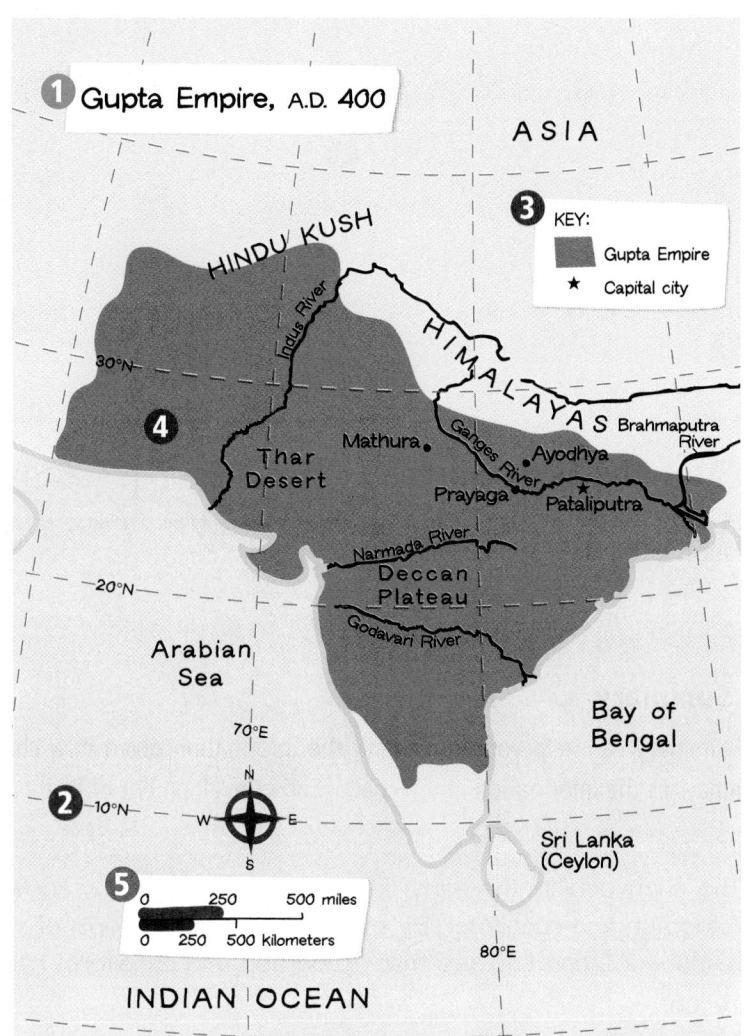

Apply the Skill

Turn to Chapter 8, Lesson 1, "Geography Shapes Life in Ancient China." Read "Isolated by Barriers" under "Geographic Features of China." Use the information in this passage and the strategies mentioned above to create a map of China that shows the approximate areas covered by the Gobi Desert and the Taklimakan Desert. Use the map on pages A6–A7 as a model for your map.

2.3 Interpreting Charts

Learn the Skill

Charts present information in a visual form. Charts are created by simplifying, summarizing, and organizing information. This information is then presented in a format that is easy to understand. Tables and diagrams are examples of commonly used charts.

Practice the Skill

The chart below focuses on the early development of writing. Use the strategies listed below to help interpret the information in the chart.

How to Interpret a Chart

Strategy ① Read the title. It will tell you what the chart is about. Ask yourself what kinds of information the chart shows.

Strategy ② Read the headings to see how the chart is organized. In this chart, information is organized by examples of pictograph and cuneiform.

Strategy ③ Study the data in the chart to understand the facts that the chart was designed to show.

Strategy ④ Summarize the information shown in each part of the chart. Use the title to help you focus on what information the chart is presenting.

① Early Development of Writing

② word	pictograph	cuneiform
③ bird		
cow		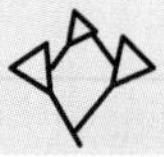
fish		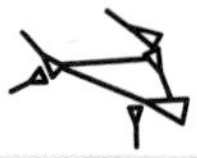
mountain		
water		

Write a Summary

Writing a summary can help you understand the information given in a chart. The paragraph below summarizes the information in the chart "Early Development of Writing."

> **④** The chart depicts the early development of writing by showing examples of pictograph and cuneiform. By examining how each form of writing expressed the same word, one can see that pictograph and cuneiform had similarities and differences.

Apply the Skill

Turn to Chapter 12, Lesson 1, "The Golden Age of Greece." Study the political information presented in the chart entitled "Athenian and U.S. Democracy." Then write a paragraph in which you summarize what you learned from the chart.

2.4 Interpreting Graphs

Learn the Skill

Graphs use pictures and symbols, instead of words, to show information. There are many different kinds of graphs. Bar graphs, line graphs, and pie graphs are the most common. Line graphs show trends or changes over time.

Practice the Skill

The line graph below shows the relationship between the growth of farming (Agricultural Revolution) and the increase in the world population during the past 25,000 years. Use the strategies listed below to help you interpret the graph.

How to Interpret a Graph

Strategy ① Read the title to identify the main idea of the graph.

Strategy ② Read the vertical axis (the one that goes up and down) on the left side of the graph. In this graph, the vertical axis indicates the world population.

Strategy ③ Read the horizontal axis (the one that runs across the bottom of the graph). In this graph, the horizontal axis shows the progression of time.

Strategy ④ Look at any legends that accompany the graph in order to understand what colors and certain marks stand for.

Strategy ⑤ Summarize the information shown in each part of the graph.

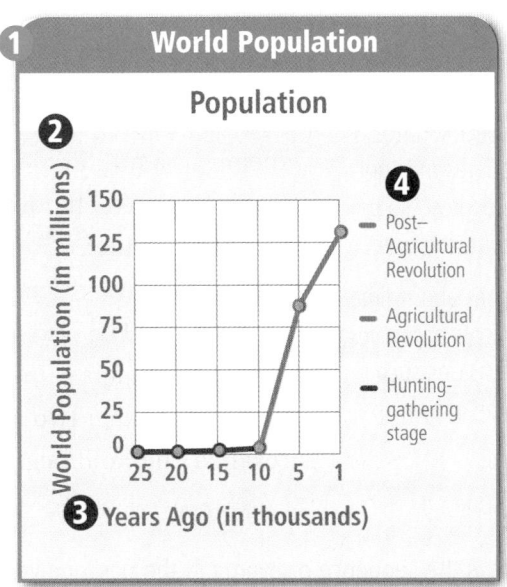

① World Population

Population

② World Population (in millions)

150
125
100
75
50
25
0

④
— Post–Agricultural Revolution
— Agricultural Revolution
— Hunting-gathering stage

25 20 15 10 5 1

③ Years Ago (in thousands)

Source: *A Geography of Population: World Patterns*

Write a Summary

Writing a summary will help you understand the information in the graph. The paragraph below summarizes the information from the line graphs.

> **⑤** As a result of the agricultural revolution, world population grew steadily over a period of 10,000 years.

Apply the Skill

Examine a current news magazine and look for any graphs that might be used to convey information. Write a summary of the information in the graph using the strategies you learned on this page. Share your graph and information with the class.

2.5 Constructing Time Lines

Learn the Skill

A **time line** is a visual list of events and dates shown in the order in which they occurred. Time lines show **sequence,** or the order in which events follow one another. The ability to sequence historical events by constructing a time line enables you to get an accurate sense of the relationship among those events.

Practice the Skill

The following passage shows the sequence of events in Rome's transition from a republic to an empire. Use the strategies listed below to help you construct a time line of the events.

How to Construct a Time Line

Strategy ❶ Look for specific dates provided in the text. The dates may not always read from earliest to latest, so be sure to match an event with the date

Strategy ❷ Look for clues about time that allow you to order events according to sequence. Words and phrases such as *day, week, year,* or *century* may help to sequence the events.

> ### FROM REPUBLIC TO EMPIRE
>
> Beginning in 60 B.C., a group of three leaders ruled Rome. Among them was a military leader named Julius Caesar. ❶ In 46 B.C., Caesar claimed all power for himself. Caesar governed Rome as an absolute ruler. His power made many officials jealous. ❶ In 44 B.C., a group of senators ambushed Caesar and stabbed him to death. ❷ The next *year,* Caesar's adopted son Octavian and two other leaders gained control of Rome. Octavian eventually pushed the other two aside. He took the title of Augustus, or "exalted one" and began his rule as emperor ❶ in 27 B.C.

Make a Time Line

The time line below shows the sequence of events in the passage you just read.

46 B.C.: Caesar becomes sole ruler of Rome.

The next year: Octavian rules Rome with two other leaders.

50 B.C.   25 B.C.

44 B.C.: Group of senators assassinate Caesar.

27 B.C.: Octavian takes the name "Augustus" and begins rule as emperor.

Apply the Skill

Turn to Chapter 4, Lesson 2, "Assyria Rules the Fertile Crescent." Read "Assyria Builds a Huge Empire" and "A New Babylonian Empire." Then make a time line showing the sequence of events in those two passages.

R14 • SKILLBUILDER HANDBOOK

2.6 Explaining Chronological Order and Sequence

Learn the Skill

Explaining chronological order and sequence means identifying the order in which major historical events occur. Major events that follow each other in time are often linked by a series of occurrences.

Practice the Skill

The following passage deals with the captivity of ancient Israel. Use the strategies listed below to help you identify the major events and the series of occurrences that connect them.

How to Explain Chronological Order and Sequence

Strategy ① Look for specific dates provided in the text. The dates may not always read from earliest to latest, so be sure to match an event with the date.

Strategy ② Look for clues about time that allow you to order events according to sequence. Words and phrases such as *day, week, year,* or *century* may help to sequence the events.

> ### THE BABYLONIAN CAPTIVITY
>
> Solomon became the third king of Israel ① in 962 B.C. Soon after Solomon's death in ② in 922 B.C. Israel split into two separate kingdoms—Israel and Judah. Around 586 B.C.., the Babylonians conquered both Israel and Judah. They took thousands of Jews to Babylon as slaves. These Jews spent roughly the ② next 50 years in Babylon. This time is known as the Babylonian Captivity. ① In 539 B.C., Persia conquered Babylonia. ② The next *year*, the Persian king Cyrus freed the Jewish slaves and allowed them to return to their homeland.

Make a Time Line

Making a time line can help you visualize chronological order. The time line below shows the order of events in the passage you just read.

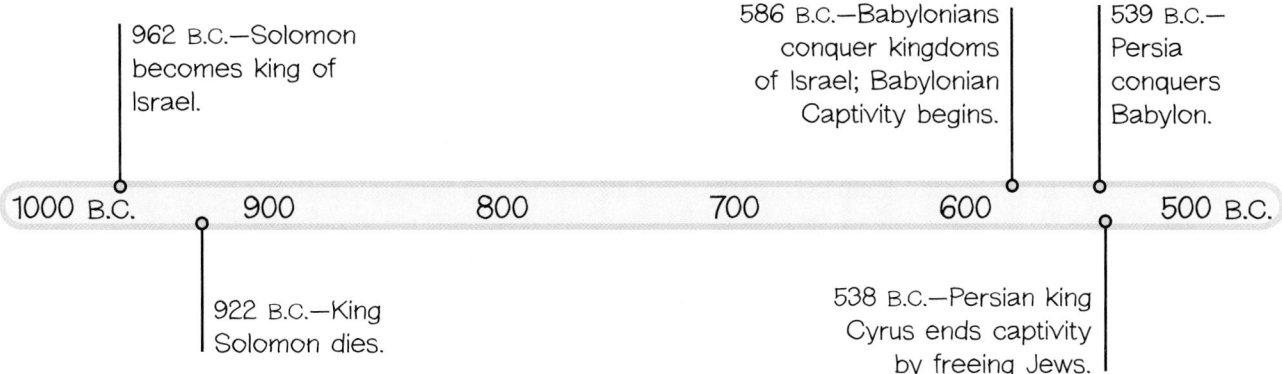

Apply the Skill

Turn to Chapter 10, Lesson 2, "The Fall of the Roman Empire." Read "Invading People" and "The Fall of Rome." Then make a chart that shows the major events and connecting events and summarizes how the major events relate to each other.

2.7 Explaining Geographic Patterns

Learn the Skill

Explaining geographic patterns involves understanding the movement of such things as people, cultures, or ideas across the earth. Geographic patterns include the migration of people, the expansion or decline of empires, the growth of economic systems, and the spread of religion. Some maps show geographic patterns. By studying these maps, you can better understand the development of cultures, ideas, and political systems.

Practice the Skill

The following map deals with the spread of Buddhism. Use the strategies listed below to help you study this map and others that show geographic patterns.

How to Explain Geographic Patterns

Strategy ❶ Locate the title of the map. The title usually identifies the geographic pattern shown on the map.

Strategy ❷ Locate any shaded areas on the map. The shaded areas show important regions of the geographic pattern. On this map, the shaded area shows the region where the Buddhism originated.

Strategy ❸ Identify any graphics on the map, such as arrows. Arrows are often used to show the movement of ideas, goods, or people. Use the compass rose to determine the directions that the arrows point.

Strategy ❹ Using the above strategies, write a summary about the geographic pattern shown on the map.

❶ **Spread of Buddhism** by A.D. 600

■ Core area of Buddhism

❸ ← Spread of Buddhism by A.D. 600

❹ Buddhism began in India and spread southward and eastward. Its influence eventually reached China, Southeast Asia, Korea, Japan, and Sri Lanka.

Apply the Skill

Turn to Chapter 7, Lesson 2, "Western, Central, and Southern Africa." Study the map "Aryan Migrations into India, 1500–250 B.C." on page 228. Using the strategies mentioned above, write a summary of the geographic pattern shown on this map.

2.8 Creating a Model

Learn the Skill

When you **create a model,** you use information and ideas to show an event or a situation in a visual way. A model might be a poster or a diagram that explains how something happened. Or, it might be a three-dimensional model, such as a diorama, that depicts an important scene or situation.

Practice the Skill

The following sketch shows the early stages of a model of the Great Pyramid of Khufu's interior. Use the strategies listed below to help you create your own model.

How to Create a Model

Strategy ❶ Gather the information you need to understand the situation or event. In this case, you need to be able to show parts of the inside of the Great Pyramid of Khufu.

Strategy ❷ Visualize and sketch an idea for your model. Once you have created a picture in your mind, make an actual sketch to plan how the model might look.

Strategy ❸ Think of symbols you may want to use. Since the model should give information in a visual way, think about ways you can use color, pictures, or other visuals to tell the story.

Strategy ❹ Gather the supplies you will need. For example, for this model, you will need pictures of the Great Pyramid of Khufu and diagrams of the inside of this pyramid. You will also need art supplies. Then create the model.

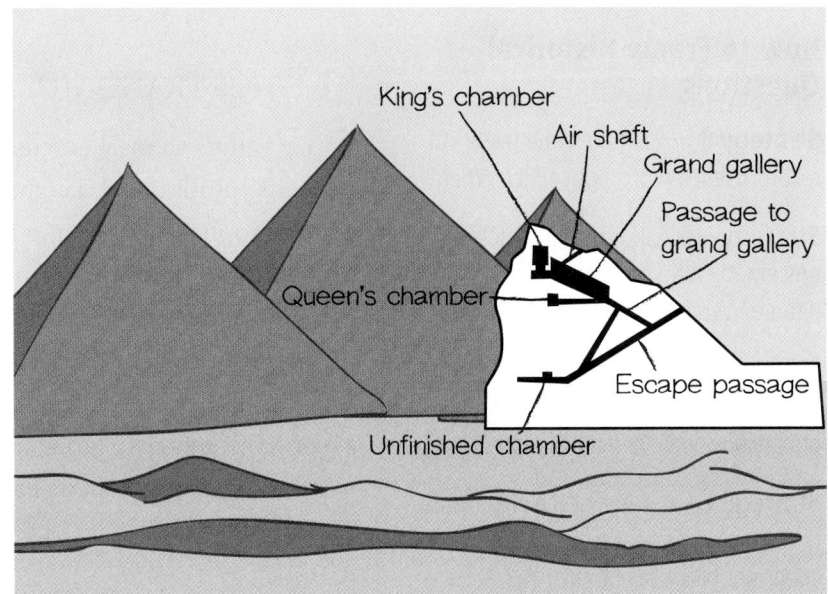

King's chamber
Air shaft
Grand gallery
Passage to grand gallery
Queen's chamber
Escape passage
Unfinished chamber

Apply the Skill

Turn to Chapter 12, Lesson 1, "The Golden Age of Greece" and read "Beautifying Athens." Also read descriptions and study images of the inside of the Parthenon. Then draw a diagram of the inside of the Parthenon. Include labels that identify parts of the Parthenon's interior.

3.1 Framing Historical Questions

Learn the Skill

Framing historical questions is important as you study primary sources—firsthand accounts, documents, letters, and other records of the past. As you analyze a source, ask questions about what it means and why it is significant. This will help you to better understand the information you read.

Practice the Skill

The following passage is an excerpt from a biography of Julius Caesar written by Roman scholar Caius Suetonius Tranquillus. This excerpt describes the assassination of Caesar. It mentions Spurinna, a prophet who had warned that harm would come to Caesar on the ides (15th) of March. Use the strategies listed below to help you frame historical questions.

Skillbuilder Handbook

How to Frame Historical Questions

Strategy ❶ Ask about the historical record itself. Who produced it? When?

Strategy ❷ Ask about the facts presented. Who were the main people? What did they do?

Strategy ❸ Ask about the person who created the record. What judgments or opinions does the author express?

Strategy ❹ Ask about the importance of the record. Does the record convey important historical information?

> ❶ CAIUS TRANQUILLUS, 1ST CENTURY B.C.
>
> ❷ He [Julius Caesar] entered the House [Senate] in defiance of portents [prophecies], laughing at ❷ Spurinna and calling him a false prophet, because the ides of March were come without bringing him harm. . . . As he took his seat, the ❷ conspirators gathered about him [Caesar] as if to pay their respects. . . . He [Caesar] saw that he was beset on every side by drawn daggers. . . . He was stabbed with three and twenty wounds, ❸ uttering not a word, but merely a groan at the first stroke, though some have written that when Marcus Brutus rushed at him, he said in Greek, "You too, my child?" . . . ❹

Make a Chart

Making a chart can help you list and answer questions about a historical source. The chart below lists historical questions and answers based on the passage you just read.

	QUESTIONS	ANSWERS
HISTORICAL RECORD	Who produced it? When?	Caius Suetonius Tranquillus; first century B.C.
FACTS PRESENTED	Who were the main people? What did they do?	Julius Caesar, Spurinna, Marcus Brutus, Conspirators The conspirators killed Caesar.
CREATOR	What were his opinions?	Caesar died without uttering a word.
IMPORTANCE	What is its importance?	Provides insight into the death of a famous historical figure

Apply the Skill

Turn to Chapter 6, Lesson 2, "The Kingdom of Aksum." Read the "Primary Source: King Ezana of Aksum." Use a chart like the one shown here to ask and answer historical questions about this primary source.

3.2 Distinguishing Facts from Opinions

Learn the Skill

Facts are events, dates, statistics, or statements that can be proved to be true. **Opinions** are judgments, beliefs, and feelings. By understanding the difference between facts and opinions, you will be able to think critically when a person is trying to influence your own opinion.

Practice the Skill

The following passage describes the Greek philosopher Aristotle and some of his views on government. Use the strategies listed below to distinguish facts from opinions

How to Distinguish Facts from Opinions

Strategy ❶ Look for specific information that can be proved or checked for accuracy.

Strategy ❷ Look for assertions, claims, and judgments that express opinions. In this case, one speaker's opinion is addressed in quotation marks.

Strategy ❸ Think about whether statements can be checked for accuracy. Then identify the facts and opinions in a chart.

ARISTOTLE'S VIEWS

❶ Artistotle was born in 384 B.C. in Stagira, a small town in northern Greece. At the age of 17, Aristotle entered a school directed by the noted philosopher Plato. ❶ Aristotle quickly became a standout student. Plato referred to him as the "intelligence of the school." Aristotle is considered one of the greatest thinkers in Western culture. He expressed views on a number of significant subjects, including politics and government. ❷ Aristotle believed the middle class was the most suited to rule, calling this group "the steadiest element" of society.

Make a Chart

The chart below analyzes the facts and opinions from the passage above.

❸ STATEMENT	CAN IT BE PROVED	FACT OR OPINION
Aristotle was born in 384 B.C. in the town of Stagira.	Yes, check historical documents.	Fact
Aristotle became a standout philosophy student.	Yes, check Plato's comments; other historical records.	Fact
The middle class is the group most suited to rule.	No, this cannot be proved. It is what one speaker believes.	Opinion

Apply the Skill

Turn to Chapter 9, Lesson 2, "Ancient Andean Civilizations," and read the section entitled "The Nazca Civilization." Make a chart in which you analyze key statements to determine whether they are facts or opinions.

3.3 Detecting Historical Points of View

Learn the Skill

A **historical point of view** is an attitude that a person has about an event in the past. Detecting and analyzing different points of view can help you to better understand a historical figure's thoughts and actions.

Practice the Skill

The following passage describes the political rise of the Roman leader Julius Caesar. Use the strategies below to help you detect and analyze what historical points of view are expressed.

How to Detect Points of View

Strategy ❶ Look for clue words that indicate a person's view on an issue. These include words such as *believe, insist, support,* and *oppose.*

Strategy ❷ Look for reasons why someone has taken a particular point of view.

> **THE RISE OF CAESAR**
>
> Julius Caesar was a brilliant military leader who eventually became dictator of Rome. Although Rome had been a republic in which no single person held all the power, ❶ many people *supported* Caesar's rise to dictator. ❷ In addition to his military skills, Caesar was a good politician with a reputation as a reformer. All of this made him popular with the common people of Rome.
>
> But some people opposed Caesar. One of his opponents was Cicero, a Roman politician. ❶ Cicero *believed* it was wrong for Caesar to have complete control over Rome. ❷ Cicero was a strong supporter of a republic. He opposed the idea of giving all political power to one person.

Make a Chart

Using a chart can help you detect and analyze historical points of view. The chart below analyzes the views in the passage you just read.

PERSON(S)	VIEW	REASONS
Common People	supported Caesar as dictator	military hero; reputation as a reformer
Cicero	opposed Caesar as dictator	favored a republic; distrusted rule by one person

Apply the Skill

Turn to Chapter 8, Lesson 3, "The Qin and the Han." Read "The Qin Unified China" and "The Han Dynasty." Then make a chart like the one above to analyze the different points of view taken by the two dynasties.

3.4 Determining Historical Context

Learn the Skill

Determining historical context means finding out how events and people were influenced by the context of their time. It means judging the past not by current values, but by taking into account the beliefs of the time.

Practice the Skill

The following passage is from the writings of the fourth-century Roman historian Ammianus Marcellinus. In this passage, Marcellinus describes the Huns, one of the groups that eventually invaded Rome and helped bring down the empire.

How to Determine Historical Context

Strategy ❶ Identify the historical figure, the occasion, and the date.

Strategy ❷ Look for clues to the attitudes, customs, and values of people living at the time. In this case, Marcellinus is expressing a view, most likely held by many Romans, that the outside invaders threatening their empire were uncivilized "barbarians."

Strategy ❸ Explain how people's actions and words reflected the attitudes, values, and passions of the era. Here, Marcellinus is issuing a warning of sorts to his fellow Romans that the Huns are wild and fierce fighters that need to be taken seriously.

Strategy ❹ Using the strategies mentioned above, write a conclusion about the historical context of the passage.

> ❶ from *The Chronicle of Events* (fourth century)
> Ammianus Marcellinus
>
> The nation of the Huns . . . ❷ surpasses all other barbarians in wildness of life. . . . And though [the Huns] do just bear the likeness of men (of a very ugly pattern), ❷ they are so little advanced in civilization that they . . . feed upon the . . . half-raw flesh of any sort of animal. . . . ❸ When attacked . . . they fill the air with varied and discordant cries. . . . They fight in no regular order of battle, but by being extremely swift and sudden in their movements, they disperse . . . spread havoc over vast plains, and . . . pillage the camp of their enemy almost before he has become aware of their approach.

> ❹ CONCLUSION
> Like perhaps many Romans, Marcellinus considered the Huns far less civilized than the Romans themselves. As barbaric as the Romans thought they were, however, many probably agreed with Marcellinus that their fierce and chaotic fighting style made them a serious threat to the empire.

Apply the Skill

Turn to Chapter 12, Lesson 2, "Peloponnesian War." Read the Primary Source feature "Pericles' Funeral Oration." Using the above strategies, write a conclusion about the historical context of this passage.

3.5 Forming and Supporting Opinions

Learn the Skill

When you **form opinions**, you interpret and judge the importance of events and people in history. You should always **support your opinions** with facts, examples, and quotations.

Practice the Skill

The following passage describes characteristics of the Egyptian kings, known as pharaohs. Use the strategies listed below to form and support an opinion about these rulers.

How to Form and Support Opinions

Strategy ❶ Look for important information about the subject. Information can include facts, quotations, and examples.

Strategy ❷ Form an opinion about the subject by asking yourself questions about the information. For example, how important was the subject? How does it relate to similar subjects in your own experience?

Strategy ❸ Support your opinions with facts, quotations, and examples.

> ### EGYPTIAN PHARAOHS
>
> ❶ The pharaoh stood at the center of Egypt's religion as well as its government and army. Egyptians believed that the pharaoh bore full responsibility for the kingdom's well being. ❶ Many Egyptians believed it was the pharaoh who caused the sun to rise, the Nile to flood, and the crops to grow. It was the pharaoh's duty to promote truth and justice. Egyptians believed that the pharaoh ruled even in death. ❶ As a result, they built giant pyramids to serve as elaborate resting places for pharaohs who passed away. These pyramids were remarkable engineering achievements that took the work of thousands of people.

Make a Chart

Making a chart can help you organize your opinions and supporting facts. The following chart summarizes one possible opinion about Egyptian pharaohs.

❷ OPINION	Egyptians viewed pharaohs as god-like and worshiped these rulers intensely.
❸ FACTS	Pharaohs served as the center of political and cultural life in Egypt.
	Many Egyptians looked to pharaohs to control nature.
	Thousands of Egyptian citizens worked to build elaborate pyramids to serve as tombs for deceased pharaohs.

Apply the Skill

Turn to Chapter 4, Lesson 2, "Assyria Rules the Fertile Crescent." Read "Assyria Builds a Huge Empire," and form your own opinion about the Assyrian Empire. Make a chart like the one above to summarize your opinion and the supporting facts and examples.

3.6 Evaluating Information

Learn the Skill

To **evaluate** is to make a judgment about something. Historians evaluate information about peoples, cultures, and events by determining what material is essential to the main point and whether or not the information is verifiable.

Practice the Skill

The following passage examines the rule of the Greek leader Solon. Use the strategies listed below to evaluate his rule.

How to Evaluate

Strategy ❶ Determine the major point of a passage. In this case, think about what Solon set out to achieve.

Strategy ❷ Look for statements that convey information relevant and essential to the main point. Think about how Solon achieved his goal.

Strategy ❸ Consider what text does not support the main point.

Strategy ❹ Ask whether most or all of the essential information can be verified in historical texts or other documents.

> ### SOLON RULES ATHENS
>
> Solon was the son of a noble family. ❶ After being elected leader of Athens, he made reforms that helped prevent a revolt by the poor. ❷ First, he freed people who had become slaves because they owed too much money. ❷ He also made a law that no citizen could be enslaved. ❷ In addition, Solon allowed all citizens to serve in the assembly and help elect leaders. Some powerful officials opposed the reform and criticized Solon. ❸ Tired of defending his actions, Solon left on a trip for ten years. He traveled to Egypt and Cyprus among other places. ❹

Make a Diagram

The diagram below shows how to evaluate information and organize the essential material from the passage you just read.

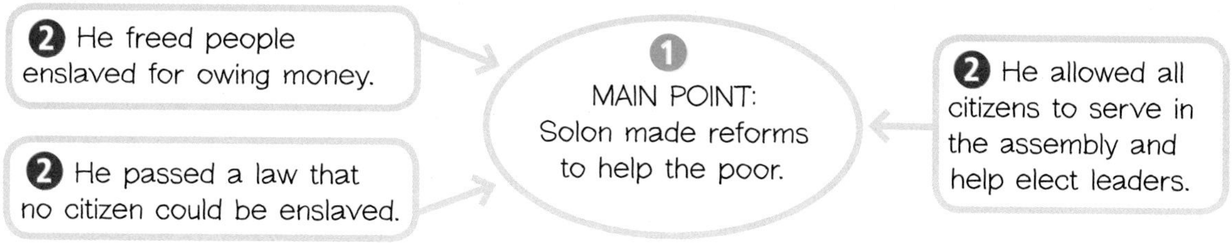

❷ He freed people enslaved for owing money.

❷ He passed a law that no citizen could be enslaved.

❶ MAIN POINT: Solon made reforms to help the poor.

❷ He allowed all citizens to serve in the assembly and help elect leaders.

Apply the Skill

Turn to Chapter 7, Lesson 3, "Buddhism and India's Golden Age." Read "Asoka, the Buddhist King" under "The Maurya Empire," and make a chart in which you decide what information is the most essential about the rule of Asoka.

3.7 Assessing Credibility of Sources

Learn the Skill

Assessing the credibility of sources means determining if the source material accurately portrays events, facts, and people. Primary sources are materials written or made by people who lived during a historical event. They include letters, diaries, articles, and photographs. Secondary sources are written after a historical event by people who were not present at the event. Books that appear long after an event are examples of secondary sources.

Practice the Skill

The following passage describes the Roman ruler Augustus. It includes both primary source and secondary source observations. Use the strategies listed below to help you assess the credibility of the sources.

How to Assess Credibility of Sources

Strategy 1 Determine the thesis, or main point, of the source.

Strategy 2 Check for details that support the thesis.

Strategy 3 Determine the credibility of primary sources. Is the speaker objective or not. Here, Augustus is speaking for himself.

> THE EMPEROR AUGUSTUS
>
> **1** Despite his enormous power, Augustus liked to present himself as an average citizen with simple tastes. **2** He lived in a small house and wore plain clothes. His favorite foods were those of common people—bread, cheese, and olives. **2** In addition, he tried to present himself as a servant of the Roman people. In taking power, **3** Augustus is reported to have said, "What more have I to ask of the immortal gods than that I may retain this same unanimous approval of yours to the very end of my life?"

Make a Chart

Making a chart can help you assess the credibility of sources. The chart below organizes questions to ask about the credibility of sources.

Questions	Answers
What is the main idea?	Augustus portrayed himself as a humble ruler.
What are the supporting details?	He lived in a small house. He dressed and ate simply. He called himself a servant of the people.
Are the sources credible?	Secondary sources—can be verified in historical texts. Primary sources—views may vary; people may or may not trust what historical figures say about themselves.

Apply the Skill

Turn to Chapter 8, Lesson 2, "China's Ancient Philosophies." Read the "History Maker" feature on Confucius and use a chart like the one above to assess the credibility of the sources you encounter.

3.8 Drawing Conclusions from Sources

Learn the Skill

Drawing conclusions from sources means analyzing what you have read and forming an opinion about its meaning. To draw conclusions, look at the facts and then use your own common sense and experience to decide what the facts mean.

Practice the Skill

The following passage presents information about the Persian Empire. Use the strategies listed below to help you draw conclusions about the Persians.

How to Draw Conclusions from Sources

Strategy ❶ Read carefully to understand all the facts or statements.

Strategy ❷ List the facts and review them. Use your own experiences and common sense to understand how the facts relate to each other.

Strategy ❸ After reviewing the facts, write down the conclusions you have drawn about them.

> THE PERSIAN EMPIRE
>
> The Persian Empire stretched some 2,800 miles from east to west. ❶ The Persian king Darius divided the empire into 20 provinces. Each province, had a local government. Darius set up governors called satraps to rule the provinces. ❶ Darius also built the Royal Road, a road for government purposes. The Royal Road was 1,775 miles long. The road greatly improved travel and communication across the empire. In addition, ❶ Darius created standard coins throughout the empire. This made it easier for residents of the far-flung and diverse kingdom to conduct trade and other commercial activities.

Make a Diagram

Making a diagram can help you draw conclusions from sources. The diagram below shows how to organize facts to draw a conclusion about the passages you just read.

❷ FACTS

> Darius divided the empire into 20 provinces and installed governors to rule over each province.

> Darius created the Royal Road, which stretched for 1,775 miles and improved travel and communication throughout the empire.

> Darius created standard coins for use throughout the empire, which helped people conduct trade and commerce more easily.

❸ CONCLUSION

> The Persians were a highly organized people who succeeded in bringing order and stability to their far-reaching empire.

Apply the Skill

Turn to Chapter 6, Lesson 3, "West, Central, and Southern Africa." Read the section titled "Nok Culture" and use the strategies on this page to draw conclusion about the Nok people.

4.1 Understanding Cause and Effect

Learn the Skill

A **cause** is an action in history that makes something happen. An **effect** is the historical event that is the result of the cause. A single event may have several causes. It is also possible for one cause to result in several effects. Historians identify cause-and-effect relationships to help them understand why historical events took place.

Practice the Skill

The following paragraph describes the growth of Christianity in the Roman Empire. Use the strategies below to help you identify the cause-and-effect relationships.

Skillbuilder Handbook

How to Analyze Causes and Recognize Effects

Strategy ① Ask why an action took place. Ask yourself a question about the title or topic sentence, such as, "How did Christianity spread?"

Strategy ② Look for the results (the effect). Ask yourself, What happened?

Strategy ③ Look for the reasons why something happened (the cause). Search for clue words that signal causes, such as *cause* and *led to*.

> ① THE SPREAD OF CHRISTIANITY
>
> In the decades after it developed, Christianity came under attack in the Roman Empire. Roman officials jailed and killed Christians mainly because they refused to worship Roman gods. ② Nonetheless, Christianity grew and spread throughout the Roman Empire. ③ A major *cause* of its spread was the contribution of St. Paul the Apostle. St. Paul was a Jewish leader who converted to Christianity. He traveled throughout the Roman world preaching Christian beliefs and attracting followers. ③ Another factor that *led to* the spread of Christianity was the decision by the Roman emperor Constantine to legalize Christianity and allow Christians to worship freely.

Make a Diagram

Using a diagram can help you understand causes and effects. The diagram below shows causes and an effect for the passage you just read.

CAUSE: Paul promoted Christianity across the empire.

CAUSE: The emperor Constantine legalized Christianity.

→ EFFECT: Christianity grew and spread throughout the empire.

Apply the Skill

Turn to Chapter 6, Lesson 3, "West, Central, and Southern Africa." Read "The Bantu Migrations." Then make a diagram about the causes and effects of the Bantu migrations.

4.2 Explaining Historical Patterns

Learn the Skill

When humans develop new ways of thinking and acting that are repeated by other people over time or in other places, these ways become historical patterns. **Explaining historical patterns** will help you better understand how and why certain ideas influence events and movements at different times in history.

Practice the Skill

The following passage discusses the recurring development of farming throughout the ancient world. Use the strategies listed below to help you explain the historical pattern.

How to Explain Historical Patterns

Strategy ❶ Identify the historical movement or idea being examined.

Strategy ❷ Identify previous or subsequent periods in history during which a similar movement or idea occurred.

> ### THE DEVELOPMENT OF FARMING
>
> About 10,000 years ago, humans began experimenting with planting seeds and growing plants. ❶ This led to the development of farming. The foothills of the Zagros Mountains in northeastern Iraq appear to be a birthplace of agriculture. There, residents established a farming settlement as early as 9,000 years ago. Within a few thousand years, many other regions worldwide turned to farming. ❷ About 7,000 years ago, residents along the Huang River in China cultivated a grain called millet. About 1,000 years later, people began growing rice in the Chang Jiang River delta. ❷ Meanwhile, farmers in Mexico and Central America started growing corn, beans, and squash.

Make a Flow Chart

Making a flow chart can help you visualize historical patterns. The flow chart below helps to explain the historical pattern in the passage you just read.

The residents along the Zagros Mountains in Iraq developed farming 9,000 years ago.	Residents along China's rivers cultivated millet and rice in the centuries that followed.	Farmers in Mexico and Central America began to grow corn, beans and squash.

Apply the Skill

Turn to Chapter 12, Lesson 1, "The Golden Age of Greece." Read "Pericles Leads Athens." Use the information in the text as well as your own knowledge to create a flow chart about the development of democracy.

4.3 Identifying Issues and Problems

Learn the Skill

Identifying issues and problems means finding and understanding the difficulties faced by a particular group of people and the historical factors that contributed to these difficulties. By identifying historical issues and problems, you can learn to identify and understand problems in today's world.

Practice the Skill

The following paragraph describes the problems of floods and droughts in early Mesopotamia. Use the strategies listed below to find and understand these problems.

How to Identify Issues and Problems

Strategy ① Look for the difficulties or problems faced by a group of people.

Strategy ② Look for situations that existed at that time and place, which contributed to these problems.

Strategy ③ Look for the solutions that people or groups employed to deal with the problems.

> FLOOD AND DROUGHT IN MESOPOTAMIA
>
> ① In ancient Mesopotamia, farmers had to deal with both floods and droughts. ② If too much rain fell, the rivers might overflow and wash everything away. Too little rain also created difficulties. ② During a drought, the river levels dropped, making it hard to water crops.
> ③ To combat the lack of rain, farmers in Mesopotamia eventually built canals to carry water from the river to the fields. Such a system is called irrigation. ③ Farmers also built dams to hold back excess water during floods.

Make a Chart

Making a chart will help you identify and organize information about problems. The chart below shows the problem, the factors that contributed to the problem, and solutions to the problem in the passage you just read.

① PROBLEM	② CONTRIBUTING FACTORS	③ SOLUTIONS
Floods and droughts made farming difficult in ancient Mesopotamia.	Too much rain caused floods that washed everything away.	built canals to carry water from the river to the fields
	Drought caused the river level to drop, making it hard to water crops.	built dams to hold back excess water during floods

Apply the Skill

Turn to Chapter 13, Lesson 4, "The Daily Life of Romans." Read "Life in Roman Cities." Using the above chart as a model, identify the urban problems faced by ancient Romans.

4.4 Understanding Continuity and Change

Learn the Skill

Understanding continuity and change means understanding why certain political and social systems continue without major change for many years and why sometimes they undergo significant change. Continuity and change is a process that happens repeatedly throughout history.

Practice the Skill

The following passage describes the Han Dynasty of China. Use the strategies listed below to help you understand the continuity and change of this empire.

How to Understand Continuity and Change

Strategy ❶ Identify the system that is undergoing continuity and change. In this case, it is the Han Dynasty.

Strategy ❷ Identify the elements that contributed to the continuity of this system.

Strategy ❸ Identify the elements that contributed to the change of this system.

> THE HAN DYNASTY
>
> ❶ The Han Dynasty began in China in 202 B.C. ❷ The Han rulers put family members and trusted people in local government positions. They set up a system of tests to find the most educated and ethical people for the imperial bureaucratic state. ❷ Under the Han, China witnessed improvements in education and numerous advances in technology and culture. ❷ Throughout its long reign, the Han Dynasty withstood rebellions, peasant revolts, floods, famine, and economic disasters. ❸ Eventually, however, these episodes of economic and political unrest made the empire weak. By 220, the Han Dynasty had disintegrated into three rival kingdoms.

Make a Chart

A chart can help you understand the main contributors to continuity and change. The chart below shows the possible reasons for the Han's long reign and eventual fall.

HAN DYNASTY FLOURISHES FOR 400 YEARS.	HAN DYNASTY COLLAPSES.
REASONS:	REASONS:
• placed educated, ethical people in charge • promoted cultural and technological advances • withstood numerous challenges and disasters	• could not remain strong amid continuous social and economic unrest

Apply the Skill

Turn to Chapter 2, Lesson 2, "Assyria Rules the Fertile Crescent." Read "Assyria Rules a Huge Empire." Using the above strategies, create a chart highlighting why the Assyrian Empire continued for many years and the changes that led to its decline.

4.5 Analyzing Economic and Political Issues

Learn the Skill

An **issue** is a matter of public concern. Issues in history are often economic or political. **Analyzing economic and political issues** means studying the various components of the issue in order to reach a better understanding of the issue and its impact on a particular event.

Practice the Skill

The following passage describes the growing difficulties that the Roman Empire faced in the centuries before it eventually fell. Use the strategies listed below to help you analyze the economic and political issues involved in Rome's decline.

How to Analyze Economic and Political Issues

Strategy ❶ Identify the discussion of economic and political issues. Look for clue words and phrases such as *pay,* and *sources of wealth.* Then look for clue words and phrases such as *government, politician, ruler,* and *public affairs.*

Strategy ❷ Determine what are the different components of each issue.

Strategy ❸ Write an analysis that summarizes the issues.

> ### INTERNAL WEAKNESSES OF ROME
>
> During the second century, the empire stopped expanding. The end of new conquests meant an end to new ❶ *sources of wealth.* ❷ As a result, it grew harder for the government to *pay* for needed services, especially the army.
>
> Meanwhile, the empire had to deal with other difficulties. ❶ Over time, Roman *politics* grew increasingly corrupt. As a result, ❷ citizens lost their sense of pride in ❶ *government* and their interest in ❶ *public affairs.*

Make a Diagram

Use this diagram to help you pull out the components of various economic and political issues in order to better analyze them.

❸ ECONOMIC ISSUE	❸ POLITICAL ISSUE
Components • The empire stops expanding, which ends new sources of wealth. • Government has fewer funds for needed services.	Components • Politics grows corrupt. • Residents lose civic pride and duty to empire.
Analysis With no new income, the Roman government became unable to pay for key services.	Analysis As the government became more corrupt, Romans lost their sense of civic duty.

Apply the Skill

Turn to Chapter 9, Lesson 4, "The Mayan Civilization." Read "Mayan Life" and "Mayan Culture."
Using the above graphic as a model, analyze the economic and political issues in these passages.

4.6 Recognizing Changing Interpretations of History

Learn the Skill

Recognizing changing interpretations of history means identifying historical viewpoints that have changed over time. Historical interpretations often change when new evidence is found that causes historians to rethink an interpretation. When studying history, you should be able to identify both old and new interpretations of history—and any reasons for the change.

Practice the Skill

The following passage discusses hunter-gatherer societies. Use the strategies listed below to help you identify changing interpretations of history.

How to Recognize Changing Interpretations of History

Strategy ① Identify old interpretations of history.

Strategy ② Identify new interpretations of history.

Strategy ③ Determine what factors led to the new interpretation.

Strategy ④ Recognize any details that attempt to support the new interpretation.

> ### HUNTER–GATHERER SOCIETIES
>
> ① For many years, scholars thought that life for hunter-gatherers was very hard. ② Now, many scholars believe that life for these ancient people was quite good. ③ They have based their new beliefs on studies of hunter-gatherers in the modern world. ④ Scholars now think that the surrounding environment gave hunter-gatherers all the kinds of food they needed. They had a varied diet of meat, fish, fruit, and wild plants. In addition, hunting and gathering did not require too much time and energy. People had time to relax, visit with friends, and play games.

Skillbuilder Handbook

Make a Chart

The chart below addresses changing historical interpretations about hunter-gatherer societies.

OLD INTERPRETATION	NEW INTERPRETATION	REASON	DETAILS
life difficult for hunter-gatherers	life good for hunter-gatherers	closer study of modern hunter-gatherers	healthy and well-balanced diet; didn't have to work too hard for food; had plenty of relaxation time

Apply the Skill

Turn to Chapter 1, Lesson 4, "How Historians Study the Past." Read "How Knowledge of the Past Changes." Using the above chart as a model, identify an old and new historical interpretation about the "mummy's curse."

4.7 Conducting Cost-Benefit Analyses

Learn the Skill

A **cost-benefit analysis** involves determining the economic costs and benefits of an action. Imagine, for example, that you own a lawn-mowing business. Your business would be economically beneficial if, at the end of the summer, the total amount of money you earned was greater than the costs of buying the mower, paying for gas, cleaning and repairing the tools, and so on. The ability to recognize the costs and benefits of an action in history will help you to better understand why people made the decisions they did.

Practice the Skill

The following passage examines the decision to travel the ancient Silk Roads that connected China and Europe. Use the strategies below to analyze the costs and benefits related to this issue.

Skillbuilder Handbook

How to Conduct a Cost-Benefit Analysis

Strategy 1 Identify the historical topic or event that is under consideration.

Strategy 2 Locate the potential costs of the action.

Strategy 3 Identify the potential benefits associated with the action.

Strategy 4 Determine what decision was made based on the cost-benefit analysis.

---

1 THE SILK ROADS

The Silk Roads were a series of trade routes that connected Europe and China. The Silk Roads flourished primarily from the second century B.C. to the 1400s. **2** The routes were not easy to travel. They stretched about 4,000 miles across harsh terrain of mountains and deserts. **2** The journey was long and slow, as traders back then had to rely on horses or other animals to take them to their destination. **2** The trip also could be dangerous. Travelers along the roads had to watch for bandits, who might rob or even kill them.

3 However, the roads offered a way for people from different cultures to spread their ideas. **3** The roads also presented traders with a way to introduce their goods to a new population of buyers. Merchants from China wanted to sell silk, paper, pottery, and other items to Westerners. Meanwhile, Westerners wanted to sell such items as sesame, metals, and precious stones to the people of the East. **4** As a result, many people from both Europe and Asia made the long and difficult journey along the route.

(continued)

Make a Diagram

Making a diagram can help you organize the components of a cost-benefit analysis. The diagram below shows you how to create a cost-benefit analysis from the passage you just read.

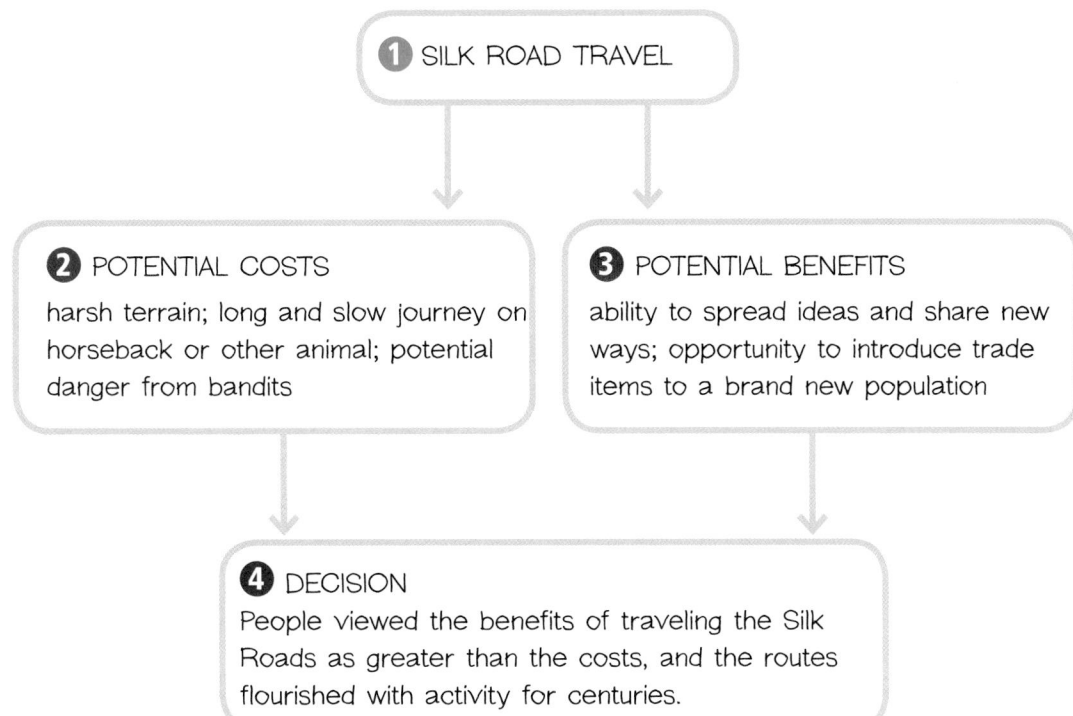

1 SILK ROAD TRAVEL

2 POTENTIAL COSTS
harsh terrain; long and slow journey on horseback or other animal; potential danger from bandits

3 POTENTIAL BENEFITS
ability to spread ideas and share new ways; opportunity to introduce trade items to a brand new population

4 DECISION
People viewed the benefits of traveling the Silk Roads as greater than the costs, and the routes flourished with activity for centuries.

Apply the Skill

Turn to Chapter 3, Lesson 3, "The Pyramid Builders." Read "Khufu's Great Pyramid." Then use the strategies you have learned to conduct a cost-benefit analysis of pyramid building in ancient Egypt.

Primary Source Handbook

CONTENTS

from *Disclosing the Past*

By Mary Leakey

Background: Mary Leakey and her husband, Louis, formed an archaeological partnership that lasted more than 30 years. They made many important discoveries in East Africa. In the following excerpt, Mary Leakey summarizes the importance of a set of prints.

Primary Source

The discovery of the trails was immensely exciting—something so extraordinary that I could hardly take it in or comprehend its implications for some while. It was a quite different feeling from the discovery of a major hominid[1] fossil . . . because that happens to you all at once, and within a short time you know exactly what you have found. The Laetoli hominid trails were something that grew in extent, in detail and in importance over two seasons. But then again, there was an immediate impact in the vastness of our discovery because from a very early stage it was clear that we had before us unique evidence, of an unimpeachable[2] nature, to establish that our hominid ancestors were fully bipedal[3] a little before 3.5 million years ago—the kind of thing anthropologists had argued over for many decades, with no real hope of proving or disproving their views. The Laetolil Beds might not have included any foot bones among the hominid remains they had yielded to our search, but they had given us instead one of the most graphic alternative kinds of evidence for bipedalism one could dream of discovering. The essentially human nature and the modern appearance of the footprints were quite extraordinary.

▲ **Mary Leakey** Mary Leakey on site during excavations at Laetoli, Tanzania, in 1978

1. **hominid:** a human or humanlike creature that walks on two feet.
2. **unimpeachable:** beyond doubt; unquestionable.
3. **bipedal:** walking on two feet.

DOCUMENT–BASED QUESTIONS

1. What sorts of prints did Leakey discover and investigate?

2. What did the prints prove beyond doubt?

Chapter Connection For more about the discoveries made by the Leakeys, see Chapter 1, Lesson 3.

More About . . .

Mary Leakey

Mary Nicols Leakey was born in England in 1913. When she was young, Mary visited an excavation of prehistoric caves in the Dordogne in France. This inspired her to seek a career in geology and archaeology.

Mary was artistic and began her work in archaeology at age 17 as an illustrator of Stone Age artifacts. It was through her work that she met Louis Leakey, who wanted Mary to illustrate one of his books. Louis and Mary were married in 1937 and had three sons.

At Olduvai Gorge, the Leakeys made numerous discoveries that advanced our knowledge of early humans. In 1959, for example, Mary uncovered the 1.75-million-year-old skull of *Australopithecus bosei.* This created a major shift in theories about early hominids. Previously, scientists had placed human development in Asia several hundreds of thousands of years ago. Mary's discovery showed that hominids were in Africa long before that.

After Louis's death in 1972, Mary continued her work. She made several more important discoveries, including the set of footprints discussed here. She died in 1996 at age 83.

Primary Source Handbook

ANSWERS TO DOCUMENT-BASED QUESTIONS

1. hominid prints

2. that hominids were bipedal about 3.5 million years ago

More About . . .

The Copper Age

The Iceman lived during the Copper Age, or Chalcolithic period. The word *chalcolithic* is from the Greek for "copper" and "stone." High levels of copper and arsenic in the Iceman's hair show that he had worked at copper smelting.

The Copper Age was not a distinct phase in Europe but a transitional stage between the Neolithic period and the Bronze Age. It signaled a time when some local cultures began to purposefully work metals. However, not all peoples did. Also, copper tools were not made for hunting or farming. Copper could not be made hard enough to work as well as the flint and stone tools already in use, or the bronze tools that would be made in the future.

However, copper was used to make and decorate personal items, such as the Iceman's copper-bladed ax. These items gave the owner prestige and increased social status.

from *The Man in the Ice*

By Dr. Konrad Spindler

Background: Konrad Spindler led an international team of scientists who investigated the 5,300-year-old body of a man trapped in a glacier in the Alps. *The Man in the Ice* tells a fascinating detective story of how they discovered the identity of the figure they called the Iceman—who he was and where he came from.

Primary Source

Evidently overtaken by a blizzard or sudden fog, or both, the Iceman was in a state of total exhaustion. In a gully in the rock, perhaps familiar to him from previous crossings of the pass, he sought what shelter he could from the bad weather. With his failing strength he settled down for the night. He deposited his axe, bow and backpack on the ledge of the rock. It is possible that he consumed here the last of his food store: a piece of tough dried ibex[1] meat. Two bone splinters had inadvertently been left in the strip of meat as he cut it off: these he chewed off and spat out. Meanwhile it had grown dark. To press on might prove fatal. It was snowing ceaselessly, and in the gale the icy cold penetrated his clothes. A terrible fatigue engulfed his limbs. Between his will to survive and increasing indifference towards his physical danger he once more pulled himself together. He knew that to fall asleep meant death. He reeled forward a few more steps. He dropped his quiver. Below him there was only loose scree.[2] He tripped and fell heavily against a boulder. The container with the hot embers slipped from his hand; his cap fell off. Again pain pierced the

▲ **The Iceman** The frozen mummy of a 5,300-year-old hunter called the Iceman is moved by scientists from its resting place in the Alps.

right side of his chest. He only wanted a short rest, but his need for sleep was stronger than his willpower. . . . He turned on to his left side to dull the pain. He laid his head on the rock. His senses numbed, he no longer noticed the awkward position of his folded ear. His left arm, its muscles relaxed and probably slightly bent at the elbow, lay in front of him. His right arm was almost extended and was hanging down forward. His feet rested one on the other; the left shoe under the right. Soon his clothes froze to the rough ground. He was no longer aware that he was freezing to death. Overnight the body froze stiff.

---

1. **ibex:** wild goat.   2. **scree:** loose rock.

DOCUMENT–BASED QUESTIONS

1. Why might falling asleep have been dangerous for the Iceman?

2. Why might the body of the Iceman have been so well preserved after 5,300 years?

Chapter Connection For more about the Iceman, see Chapter 2, Starting with a Story.

ANSWERS TO DOCUMENT-BASED QUESTIONS

1. because if he falls asleep he will freeze to death
2. the cold, ice, and snow froze and preserved his body

from *The Epic of Gilgamesh*

Translated by N. K. Sandars

Background: *The Epic of Gilgamesh* is one of the oldest surviving works of literature. Like most epics, it is based to some degree on fact. Most scholars think that Gilgamesh was a Sumerian king who ruled over the city of Uruk around 2700 B.C. In the centuries following his death, stories about him grew. Through the oral tradition of storytelling, Gilgamesh developed over time into a legendary figure. In the following excerpt, Enkidu (Gilgamesh's friend) has died, and Gilgamesh experiences for the first time the human emotions of grief and fear.

Primary Source

Bitterly Gilgamesh wept for his friend Enkidu; he wandered over the wilderness as a hunter, he roamed over the plains; in his bitterness he cried, "How can I rest, how can I be at peace? Despair is in my heart. What my brother is now, that shall I be when I am dead. Because I am afraid of death I will go as best I can to find Utnapishtim[1] whom they call the Faraway, for he has entered the assembly of the gods." So Gilgamesh traveled over the wilderness, he wandered over the grasslands, a long journey, in search of Utnapishtim, whom the gods took after the deluge;[2] and they set him to live in the land of Dilmun,[3] in the garden of the sun; and to him alone of men they gave everlasting life.

At night when he came to the mountain passes Gilgamesh prayed: "In these mountain passes long ago I saw lions, I was afraid and I lifted my eyes to the moon; I prayed and my prayers went up to the gods, so now, O moon god Sin, protect me." When he had prayed he lay down to sleep, until he was woken from out of a dream. He saw the lions round him glorying in life; then he took his axe in his hand, he drew his sword from his belt, and he fell upon them like an arrow from the string, and struck and destroyed and scattered them.

▲ **Gilgamesh** Assyrian stone relief of Gilgamesh

1. **Utnapishtim (OOT•nuh•PEESH•tuhm):** Friend of the Sumerian god Ea, he and his wife survive a flood and are the only mortals to be granted the gift of eternal life.
2. **deluge:** an unusually heavy flood.
3. **Dilmun:** a paradise in the world of the gods.

DOCUMENT–BASED QUESTIONS

1. Why is Gilgamesh grieving at the beginning of this excerpt?

2. What danger does Gilgamesh encounter as he begins his journey to find Utnapishtim, and how does he deal with the danger?

Chapter Connection For more about Sumerian civilization, see Chapter 3, Lessons 2 and 3.

More About . . .

The Epic of Gilgamesh

The Sumerian warrior-king Gilgamesh is one of the great heroes of the ancient world. The text of his epic story is based on a collection of 12 incomplete clay tablets, which are written in the Akkadian language, unearthed by archaeologist Hormuzd Rassam in 1853. At the time, Rassam was overseeing excavations by the British Museum in Nineveh, where he discovered the tablets in the remains of the library of Assyrian king Ashurbanipal. The tablets are the longest work of literature in Akkadian.

Gaps in the epic were filled with material found in other parts of Mesopotamia and in Anatolia. These include five poems in Sumerian written around 2000 B.C.

The Akkadian tablets tell of Gilgamesh's search for immortality and include a prologue, the creation of Enkidu by the god Anu, the two friends' encounters with various deities, Enkidu's death, and Gilgamesh's search for Utnapishtim, a proto-Noah figure who survived a mythic flood.

Primary Source Handbook

ANSWERS TO DOCUMENT-BASED QUESTIONS

1. His friend Enkidu has died.

2. lions; he overcomes his fear and vanquishes the lions

More About . . .

King Hammurabi

Hammurabi was the sixth king of the Amorite dynasty of Babylon. When still young, he succeeded his father, Sin-muballit, to the throne.

Hammurabi spent much of his reign amassing territory and struggling to maintain a balance of power in the region. Other difficulties with nearby kingdoms appear to have been based on conflicts over water rights or for control of trade routes. Hammurabi also worked to control the Euphrates River for crop irrigation, although sometimes the river was manipulated to cause drought or flood in the kingdoms of his downstream rivals.

Hammurabi paid personal attention to the details of ruling his empire. This hands-on approach may have caused his failure to set up a system for administering the lands he conquered. This, in turn, led to a loss of territory after his death. However, during his rule he conquered much of southern Mesopotamia, bringing the region once again under a central power.

from the **Code of Hammurabi**
Translated by L. W. King

Background: Hammurabi was a king of the Babylonian Empire who reigned between 1792 and 1750 B.C. Hammurabi's law code listed punishments ranging from fines to death. Often a punishment was based on the social class of the victim. Following are some examples of the laws.

Primary Source

▲ **Pillar of Hammurabi**
Hammurabi receiving the laws from the god Shamash

8. If a man has stolen an ox, a sheep, a pig, or a boat that belonged to a temple or palace, he shall repay thirty times its cost. If it belonged to a private citizen, he shall repay ten times. If the thief cannot pay, he shall be put to death.

142. If a woman hates her husband and says to him "You cannot be with me," the authorities in her district will investigate the case. If she has been chaste and without fault, even though her husband has neglected or belittled her, she will be held innocent and may return to her father's house.

143. If the woman is at fault, she shall be thrown into the river.

196. If a man put out the eye of another man, his eye shall be put out.

198. If he put out the eye of a free man or break the bone of a free man, he shall pay one gold mina.[1]

199. If he put out the eye of a man's slave, or break the bone of a man's slave, he shall pay one-half of its value.

1. **mina:** a unit of money in ancient Asia.

DOCUMENT–BASED QUESTIONS

1. Did the code apply equally to all people? Why or why not?

2. What was the point of making the punishments for crimes known to all?

Chapter Connection For more about Hammurabi's Code, see Chapter 4, Lesson 1, Primary Source.

ANSWERS TO DOCUMENT-BASED QUESTIONS

1. No, when the offender and victim are of equal rank, the offender is punished in the same manner in which the victim was harmed. But when the victim is of lower rank, the offender only pays a fine.

2. Knowing the severity of the punishments might prevent people from breaking the law.

from the *Book of the Dead*

Translated by E. A. Wallis Budge

Background: The Egyptian *Book of the Dead* is a series of texts that assists the soul in the search for happiness in the afterlife. Egyptians believed that after death an individual faced 42 gods and testified about his or her behavior on Earth. That testimony was called the negative confession. Below you will see some of that confession.

Primary Source

Hail, Hept-khet, who comest forth from Kher-aha,
I have not committed robbery with violence.

Hail, Fenti, who comest forth from Khemenu,
I have not stolen.

Hail, Am-khaibit, who comest forth from Qernet,
I have not slain men and women.

Hail, Neha-her, who comest forth from Rasta,
I have not stolen grain.

Hail, Unem-besek, who comest forth from Mabit,
I have not stolen cultivated land.

Hail, Ari-em-ab-f, who comest forth from Tebu,
I have never stopped [the flow of] water.

Illustration This illustration comes from the *Book of the Dead.* ▼

DOCUMENT–BASED QUESTIONS

1. Why might stopping the flow of water have been a serious sin or crime in ancient Egypt?

2. What did Egyptians hope to do by making this confession?

Chapter Connection For more on beliefs about the afterlife in ancient Egypt, see Chapter 5, Lesson 2.

Primary Source Handbook

More About . . .

Shabtis

At various times of the year, ancient Egyptians had to perform free labor on government projects, such as work on public buildings and maintenance of the irrigation system. Wealthy Egyptians could avoid this by getting someone else to do it for them. After death, however, they needed shabtis.

Shabtis were small models of servants. They held tools or carried loads. On their backs was written Chapter 6 of the Book of the Dead. It read, "Oh, Shabti, if the deceased is called upon to do any work required . . . you shall say 'Here I am, I will do it.'" In this way, the dead person's obligatory work would be done.

Originally, there was only one shabti in a tomb. Later, there might be one for every day of the year, along with 36 overseer shabtis to manage them all.

ANSWERS TO DOCUMENT-BASED QUESTIONS

1. because water was critical in a society surrounded by desert that depended on the Nile River for life.

2. They probably hoped to convince the gods that they had led a good life and so deserved happiness in the afterlife.

More About . . .

Piankhi and the 25th Dynasty

Piankhi was the birth name of Kushite ruler and military leader Piye. Once on the Egyptian throne Piye took the name Men-kheper-re, or "The Manifestation of Re Abides." Re was the Egyptian sun god. Although his brother Shabaka, who succeeded him, was the first official ruler of Egypt's 25th Dynasty, many consider Piye to have founded it. This dynasty ruled Egypt from 712 to 657 B.C.

Piye was the son of the Kushite king Kashta, who had made some earlier incursions into Egypt. However, Piye was the first to rule both Kush and Egypt simultaneously.

When he invaded Egypt, Piye made his sister the successor to Shepenupet I, the daughter of the last native king of Egypt. Piye's sister became Amunirdis I, and the divine consort of Amun, the most important Egyptian deity. This helped Piye legitimize his rule—the first by a non-Egyptian for 1,000 years. When he died, Piye was buried in a small, narrow pyramid in El-Kurru, a royal burial ground in Kush.

from **Piankhi's Monument**

Background: Piankhi was a Kushite king who overthrew a dynasty that had ruled Egypt for about 100 years. He gathered a large fleet and army and sailed northward to lay siege to the Egyptian city of Hermopolis. He was victorious and united the Nile valley from the delta in the north to his capital of Napata in the south. After his victory, Piankhi erected a monument in his homeland of Kush. On the monument were inscribed writings that celebrated his victory. The inscriptions contained a catalog of the riches of Egypt. An excerpt from the monument follows.

Primary Source

Hermopolis threw herself upon her belly and pleaded before the king. Messengers came forth and descended bearing everything beautiful to behold; gold, every splendid costly stone, clothing in a chest, and the diadem [crown] which was upon his head; the uraeus[1] which inspireth fear of him, without ceasing during many days. . . .

Then the ships were laden with silver, gold, copper, clothing, and everything of the Northland, every product of Syria and all sweet woods of God's-Land. His Majesty sailed upstream [south], with glad heart, the shores on his either side were jubilating. West and east were jubilating in the presence of his Majesty.

---

1. **uraeus:** a sacred serpent shown as an emblem of sovereignty on the headdress of ancient Egyptian rulers.

▲ **Piankhi's Monument** This black granite slab was discovered in Piankhi's capital of Napata.

DOCUMENT–BASED QUESTIONS

1. What were some of the riches that Piankhi gained in Egypt?

2. In what direction does Piankhi sail with the treasure he has acquired in Egypt?

Chapter Connection For more about Piankhi's monument, see Chapter 6, Lesson 1.

ANSWERS TO DOCUMENT-BASED QUESTIONS

1. silver, gold, copper, gems, clothing, crown
2. He sails south (upstream) to return to his capital of Napata.

from the *Bhagavad Gita*

Translated by Barbara Stoler Miller

Background: The *Bhagavad Gita* is the most beloved and widely translated religious work of India. It begins on the eve of battle, as the warrior-prince Arjuna sees his uncles, cousins, friends, and teachers lined up on the field against him. Overcome with grief at the thought of fighting against, and possibly killing, his relatives, Arjuna refuses to fight. The god Krishna explains to Arjuna that as a warrior he has a sacred duty to fight.

Primary Source

Our bodies are known to end,
but the embodied self[1] is enduring,
indestructible, and immeasurable;
therefore, Arjuna, fight the battle!

He who thinks this self a killer
and he who thinks it killed,
both fail to understand;
it does not kill, nor is it killed.

It is not born,
it does not die;
having been,
it will never not be;
unborn, enduring,
constant, and primordial,[2]
it is not killed
when the body is killed.

Arjuna, when a man knows the self
to be indestructible, enduring, unborn,
unchanging, how does he kill
or cause anyone to kill?

---

1. **embodied self:** soul or spirit.
2. **primordial:** first; original.

War Chariot Arjuna is led into battle by his chariot driver, the god Krishna. ▶

DOCUMENT–BASED QUESTIONS

1. Why does Arjuna not want to fight?

2. What argument does Krishna use to urge Arjuna to fight?

Chapter Connection For more about the *Bhagavad Gita*, see Chapter 7, Lesson 2, Primary Source.

More About . . .

the *Bhagavad Gita*

The *Bhagavad Gita*, or "Song of the Lord," is actually Book VI of a much longer saga, the *Mahabharata*, or "Great Epic of the Bharata Dynasty."

The *Mahabharata* is a collection of myths, legends, and other material associated with major episodes in a great war between two family groups, the Pandavas and Kauravas. Presented in poetic form, the saga contains about 100,000 couplets, making it seven times longer than the *Iliad* and the *Odyssey* combined. The credit for the compilation of the *Mahabharata* is traditionally given to a sage named Vyasa, and it probably came into its present form in about A.D. 400.

An ancient and enduringly popular masterpiece of South Asian literature, the *Mahabharata* is one of the two major epics of India—the other being the *Ramayana*—and presents the *dharma*, or code of conduct proper to various classes of Hindu society, including kings, warriors, and those living in troubled times.

ANSWERS TO DOCUMENT-BASED QUESTIONS

1. He sees friends and relatives waiting to fight him on the opposite side.

2. Krishna argues that death is an illusion; that it is Arjuna's duty as a warrior to fight and that the souls of those killed never die but simply take a new form.

More About . . .

Confucius

K'ung-fu-tzu, or Confucius, was born in the state of Lu on September 28, 551 B.C. He began teaching in his 30s and was the first person in China to want to make education available to all men. He was also central in the development of teaching as a career.

For many years, Confucius held various posts in the government and became an advisor to the king of Lu. However, he later went into self-imposed exile to find a ruler more open to his ideas about proper conduct. By this time, he already had a large following, and his reputation as a visionary thinker was secure.

Confucius returned to Lu when he was 67 and continued writing and teaching. He died in 479 B.C. at age 73. Today, his birthday is still celebrated in much of East Asia and is an official holiday, "Teachers' Day," in Taiwan.

from the *Analects* of Confucius

Translated by Simon Leys

Background: The *Analects* is a collection of about 500 sayings, dialogues, and brief stories. It was put together over many years following the death of Confucius. Confucius was a great Chinese teacher who lived in the sixth century B.C. The *Analects* presents Confucius' teachings on how people should live to create an orderly and just society.

Primary Source

The Master[1] said: "He who rules by virtue is like the polestar,[2] which remains unmoving in its mansion while all the other stars revolve respectfully around it." (2.1)

The Master said: "To study without thinking is futile.[3] To think without studying is dangerous." (2.15)

Lord Ji Kang asked: "What should I do in order to make the people respectful, loyal, and zealous?"[4] The Master said: "Approach them with dignity and they will be respectful. Be yourself a good son and a kind father, and they will be loyal. Raise the good and train the incompetent, and they will be zealous." (2.20)

The Master said: "Set your heart upon the Way;[5] rely upon moral power; follow goodness; enjoy the arts." (7.6)

The Master said: "A gentleman abides by three principles which I am unable to follow: his humanity knows no anxiety; his wisdom knows no hesitation; his courage knows no fear." Zigong[6] said: "Master, you have just drawn your own portrait." (14.28)

◀ **Confucius** Portrait of the Chinese philosopher Confucius

1. **the Master:** Confucius.
2. **polestar:** the North Star, which appears to remain in the same place in the sky as Earth rotates.
3. **futile:** useless.
4. **zealous:** enthusiastic.
5. **Way:** ideal pattern of behavior.
6. **Zigong:** a student.

DOCUMENT–BASED QUESTIONS

1. What kinds of behavior does Confucius talk about in the *Analects*?

2. What kind of person does Confucius seem to have been?

Chapter Connection For more about Confucius, see Chapter 8, Lesson 2.

ANSWERS TO DOCUMENT-BASED QUESTIONS

1. He talks about how a person should view his or her own worth and how a person should relate to others. He emphasizes courtesy, respect, kindness, and courage.

2. His aim is to live a moral and virtuous life and to teach others to live such a life. He looks for the most ethical, courteous, and generous way to respond to each situation. He is humble but also firm in stating his views and ideas.

from the *Dao De Jing*

By Laozi
Translated by Stephen Mitchell

Background: Laozi was a philosopher who lived in China. The teachings of Laozi are called Daoism. Laozi's *Dao De Jing* ("way of power") was written in the sixth century B.C. The book's main message is that a universal force called the Dao ("way") guides all things. In passage 37 from the *Dao De Jing*, Laozi explains the wisdom of the Dao.

Primary Source

The Dao never does anything,
yet through it all things are done.

If powerful men and women
could center themselves in it,
the whole world would be transformed
by itself, in its natural rhythms.
People would be content
with their simple, everyday lives,
in harmony, and free of desire.

When there is no desire,
all things are at peace.

Laozi Portrait of Laozi, the father of Daoism ▶

More About . . .

Laozi

Not much is known about Laozi. The main source for information about his life is China's first history, the *Shih-chi,* or "Historical Records." It says that Laozi held the post of court archivist during the Chou Dynasty and that he was a teacher of Confucius.

Later, Laozi felt that the Chou Dynasty was on the decline, so he went west, leaving China. Nothing was heard of him again. The *Shih-chi* says that Laozi wrote the *Dao De Jing* at the request of a border guard on his way out of the country. Most scholars believe that the *Dao De Jing* is a compilation, rather than the work of one writer, and that it achieved its final form in the 200s B.C.

DOCUMENT–BASED QUESTIONS

1. What does this passage say prevents people from feeling content and at peace?

2. According to Laozi, how should people overcome the obstacle to peace and contentment?

Chapter Connection For more about Laozi, see Chapter 8, Lesson 2.

ANSWERS TO DOCUMENT-BASED QUESTIONS

1. desire
2. If people would follow the Way and center themselves in it, then they would overcome desire and achieve peace and serenity.

Primary Source Handbook

More About . . .

Mayan Cosmology

The Maya had a complex set of beliefs about the universe and how it was structured. For example, they thought that Earth was flat with four corners supported by gods called Bacabs or by four trees of different species. Each corner was in a cardinal direction and had a specific color. East was red, west was black, north was white, and south was yellow. The flat Earth was carried on the back of a giant crocodile that floated in a pool filled with water lilies.

The Maya believed in a heaven made up of 13 layers and an underworld made up of 9. Their pantheon may have included at least 166 different gods.

from the *Popol Vuh*

Translated by Dennis Tedlock

Background: The Maya developed a civilization in southern Mexico and Central America around 400 B.C. The *Popol Vuh* is an important Mayan work. The title means "Council Book." The work tells the Mayan story of the creation of the world. The following excerpt tells how the gods ("Bearers, Begetters") created the animals.

Primary Source

Now they planned the animals of the mountains, all the guardians of the forests, creatures of the mountains: the deer, birds, pumas, jaguars, serpents, rattlesnakes, fer-de-lances,[1] guardians of the bushes.

A Bearer, Begetter speaks:

"Why this pointless humming? Why should there merely be rustling beneath the trees and bushes?"

"Indeed—they had better have guardians," the others replied. As soon as they thought it and said it, deer and birds came forth.

And then they gave out homes to the deer and birds:

"You, the deer: sleep along the rivers, in the canyons. Be here in the meadows, in the thickets, in the forests, multiply yourselves. You will stand and walk on all fours," they were told.

So then they established the nests of the birds, small and great:

"You, precious birds: your nests, your houses are in the trees, in the bushes. Multiply there, scatter there, in the branches of trees, the branches of bushes," the deer and birds were told.

When this deed had been done, all of them had received a place to sleep and a place to stay. So it is that the nests of the animals are on the earth, given by the Bearer, Begetter. Now the arrangement of the deer and birds was complete.

▲ **Mayan Vessel** This ceramic vessel shows a dignitary armed with spear and shield sitting on a throne.

1. **fer-de-lances** (**FEHR**•duhl•**AN**•sihz): poisonous tropical snakes.

DOCUMENT–BASED QUESTIONS

1. What are some of the creatures that populate the Mayan natural world, and which two are the focus of this story?

2. What is the essential role or task of the animals created by the gods?

Chapter Connection For more about the Maya, see Chapter 9, Lesson 4.

R44 • PRIMARY SOURCE HANDBOOK

ANSWERS TO DOCUMENT-BASED QUESTIONS

1. deer, birds, pumas, jaguars, serpents—deer and birds
2. guardians of different aspects of the natural world

from the **Hebrew Bible: The Creation**

Background: The Book of Genesis is the first book in the Torah, or Hebrew Bible. It tells the history of the Hebrew people. According to Genesis, God created the world in six days. The excerpts below tell what God created on the first and sixth days of creation.

Primary Source

THE FIRST DAY

In the beginning God created the heaven and the earth. And the earth was without form, and void; and darkness was upon the face of the deep. And the Spirit of God moved upon the face of the waters. And God said, "Let there be light": and there was light. And God saw the light, that it was good: and God divided the light from the darkness. And God called the light Day, and the darkness he called Night.

And the evening and the morning were the first day.

THE SIXTH DAY

And God said, "Let the earth bring forth the living creature after his kind, cattle, and creeping thing, and beast of the earth after his kind": and it was so. And God made the beast of the earth after his kind, and cattle after their kind, and every thing that creepeth upon the earth after his kind: and God saw that it was good.

And God said, "Let us make man in our image, after our likeness: and let them have dominion[1] over the fish of the sea, and over the fowl of the air, and over the cattle, and over all the earth, and over every creeping thing that creepeth upon the earth." So God created man in his own image, in the image of God created he him; male and female created he them. And

▲ **Sistine Chapel** Detail of Michelangelo's Sistine Chapel ceiling, showing the creation of the stars and planets

God blessed them, and God said unto them, "Be fruitful, and multiply, and replenish[2] the earth, and subdue it: and have dominion over the fish of the sea, and over the fowl of the air, and over every living thing that moveth upon the earth." And God said, "Behold, I have given you every herb bearing seed, which is upon the face of all the earth, and every tree, in the which is the fruit of a tree yielding seed; to you it shall be for meat. And to every beast of the earth, and to every fowl of the air, and to everything that creepeth upon the earth, wherein there is life, I have given every green herb for meat." And it was so. And God saw every thing that he had made, and, behold, it was very good.

And the evening and the morning were the sixth day.

1. **dominion:** authority; control.   2. **replenish:** fill up again.

DOCUMENT–BASED QUESTIONS

1. What does God create on the first day?

2. To whom does God give control over the world's natural resources?

Chapter Connection For more about the ancient Hebrews, see Chapter 10.

Primary Source Handbook

ANSWERS TO DOCUMENT-BASED QUESTIONS

1. He separates the light from the dark and creates day and night.

2. humanity

More About . . .

Mount Ararat

Mount Ararat is a dormant volcanic peak that reaches a height of 16,854 feet (5,137 meters). It is located near the borders of Turkey, Armenia, and Iran.

Tradition says that Mount Ararat was where Noah's Ark landed after the Flood. This idea is based on the interpretation of a Hebrew word in the Torah. The word has been translated as Ararat, but some scholars think it might really be *Urartu*. Urartu was an historical location—a kingdom in the Upper Tigris River area—but it also means "a faraway land" or "a place in the north."

In any case, explorers have searched Mount Ararat for remnants of the Ark for centuries. The mountain is also sacred to the Armenians who believe that they are descendants of the first humans to repopulate Earth after the Flood.

from the **Hebrew Bible: Noah and the Flood**

Background: The story of a devastating flood appears among the legends of ancient peoples throughout the world. In the Hebrew Bible, the hero of the story is Noah, who builds an ark to save God's creatures.

Primary Source

And God said to Noah, "I have determined to make an end of all flesh, for the earth is filled with violence because of them. . . . Make yourself an ark of cypress wood. . . . And of every living thing, of all flesh, you shall bring two of every kind into the ark . . . they shall be male and female." . . .

The rain fell on the earth forty days and forty nights. . . . At the end of forty days Noah opened the window of the ark . . . and . . . sent out the dove . . . and the dove came back . . . and there in its beak was a freshly plucked olive leaf; so Noah knew that the waters had subsided from the earth. . . .

Then God said to Noah, "Go out of the ark. . . . Bring out with you every living thing that is with you. . . . I establish my covenant with you, that . . . never again shall there be a flood to destroy the earth."

Noah's Ark Modern painting (1972) showing Noah's Ark ▶

DOCUMENT–BASED QUESTIONS

1. How does Noah know that the waters of the flood have receded?

2. What promise does God make to humankind?

Chapter Connection For more about the ancient Hebrews, see Chapter 10.

ANSWERS TO DOCUMENT-BASED QUESTIONS

1. He sends forth a dove from the ark which returns with an olive leaf in its beak.
2. God promises that never again will he allow a flood to destroy all of humanity.

from the Hebrew Bible: Daniel in the Lions' Den

Background: The Hebrew Bible contains many stories that can be connected to ancient history. One of the most popular of these stories is that of Daniel in the lions' den. This story is set in the court of the Persian king Darius in the sixth century B.C., at a time when the Persians ruled much of Southwest Asia.

Primary Source

It pleased Darius to set over the kingdom a hundred and twenty princes who were to rule the whole kingdom. And over these were three presidents, and of them Daniel was the first. The princes were to give account to them, so that the king would have no troubles.

Daniel was put over the presidents and princes because of his excellent mind. And the king planned to put him over the whole kingdom. Then the presidents and princes tried to find some fault with Daniel concerning the kingdom, but they could find no fault, because he was faithful and loyal, and there was no error or fault to be found in him. And these men said:

"We shall not find any grounds for complaint against Daniel unless it concerns his worship of his God."

So those presidents and princes assembled together before the king and said to him:

"King Darius, live for ever! All the presidents of the kingdom and the governors and the princes, the counselors and the captains, have consulted together about establishing a royal law, by a firm order, that whoever asks anything of any god or man for thirty days, except of you, O king, shall be cast into a den of lions.

"Now, O king, establish this order, and sign the writing, that it may not be changed, according to the law of the Medes and the Persians, which does not change."

Then King Darius signed his name to the writing.

▲ **Mosaic** Daniel in the lions' den as shown in a mosaic in a monastery church in Greece

When Daniel knew that the law was signed and ratified, he went into his house, and his windows being open in his chamber facing Jerusalem, he kneeled down three times a day and prayed and gave thanks to his God just as he had done before.

Then the men came together and found Daniel praying and entreating God. They hurried to the king and reminded him of his order.

"Did you not sign an order that any man asking a favor of any god or man within thirty days, except yourself, O king, shall be thrown into the den of lions?"

(continued)

More About . . .

Daniel

Not much is known about Daniel beyond what is found in the biblical book he is said to have written. The prophet was born into a noble family belonging to the tribe of Judah. At the age of 14, he was captured and brought to Babylon by King Nebuchadnezzar as part of the Babylonian Captivity of the Jews. The Babylonians educated Daniel so that he might be fit to serve the king.

As an adult, Daniel did become an important advisor to the Babylonian monarch. After Nebuchadnezzar's death, however, Daniel lost his place at court and went into a long retirement. He was probably about 80 years old when the Persians conquered Babylon, and he gained a position in the new court. It was the high favor of King Darius that led Daniel's enemies to trick the king into punishing Daniel by sending him into the lion's den.

(continued)

The king answered and said:

"That is true, according to the law of the Medes and the Persians, which does not change."

Then they answered and said to the king: "That Daniel who is one of the children of the captivity of Judah, does not respect you, O king, nor the decree which you have signed, but makes his request three times a day."

When he heard these words, the king was very much displeased with himself, and he set his heart on saving Daniel. He thought until the setting of the sun about how to save Daniel.

Then the men came before the king and said to him: "Remember, O king, that it is the law of the Medes and the Persians that no order or law which the king lays down can be changed."

Then the king commanded them to take Daniel and throw him into the den of lions. And the king said to Daniel: "Your God whom you serve so faithfully, surely he will save you."

Then the king went to his palace and passed the night in fasting. No musical instruments were brought in to him, and he did not sleep at all.

Very early in the morning the king arose and hurried to the den of lions. When he came to the den, he cried out in a sorrowing voice to Daniel and said to him: "O Daniel, servant of the living God, has your God, whom you serve so faithfully, been able to save you from the lions?"

Then Daniel said to the king: "O king, live for ever. My God has sent his angel and has shut the lions' mouths, so that they have not hurt me, because I was innocent in his sight; and I have done no harm to you either, O king."

Then the king was exceedingly glad for him, and commanded that Daniel should be brought up out of the den. So Daniel was brought up out of the den, and no wound of any kind was found on him, because he believed in his God.

Then the king gave commands, and they brought the men who had accused Daniel, and they cast them into the den of lions, and their children and their wives as well. And the lions broke all their bones into pieces.

Then king Darius wrote to all people and nations, and in all the languages of the earth:

"Peace be multiplied to you! I now command that in every part of my kingdom men tremble and fear before the God of Daniel, for he is the living God, unchanging for ever, and his kingdom shall never be destroyed, and his power shall continue to the end. He rescues and saves, and he works signs and wonders in heaven and on earth, he who has saved Daniel from the power of the lions."

So Daniel prospered in the reign of Darius, and in the reign of Cyrus the Persian.

DOCUMENT–BASED QUESTIONS

1. What is the king's attitude toward Daniel?

2. How does the king feel about Daniel's punishment, and what does he do to Daniel's accusers?

Chapter Connection For more about the ancient Hebrews, see Chapter 10.

ANSWERS TO DOCUMENT-BASED QUESTIONS

1. The king trusts Daniel because of his intelligence and loyalty.

2. The king regrets having to punish Daniel and hopes that his God will save him; when Daniel survives his ordeal, the king attributes it to God protecting Daniel and then he executes his accusers.

from the Hebrew Bible: Proverbs

Background: A proverb is a short saying that expresses a widely held belief. The Book of Proverbs in the Hebrew Bible provides a rich supply of wisdom. It is traditionally attributed to Solomon. Here is an example from Proverbs 6: 6–11.

Primary Source

Go to the ant, O sluggard,[1]
Observe her ways and be wise,
Which, having no chief,
Officer or ruler,
Prepares her food in the summer,
And gathers her provision in the harvest.
How long will you lie down, O sluggard?
When will you arise from your sleep?
"A little sleep, a little slumber,
A little folding of the hands to rest"—
And your poverty will come in like a vagabond,[2]
And your need like an armed man.

---

1. **sluggard:** lazy person.
2. **vagabond:** tramp.

▲ **Solomon** King Solomon reading the Torah as shown in a Hebrew biblical text of the 1200s

Primary Source Handbook

More About . . .

King Solomon

Solomon was the son of King David and his beloved wife Bathsheba. Solomon is considered to be the greatest king of Israel. Although not the eldest son, he was the favorite of his father and ascended the throne at about 18 years of age. His reign lasted for 40 years and was, for the most part, peaceful.

Solomon became famous for his great wisdom and sense of justice, his peaceful relations with neighboring states, and for his building projects. Among the latter were an enormous palace and, his crowning achievement, the Temple in Jerusalem. Solomon also increased the size of the army, oversaw fortifications, and developed a strong trade network.

The peace he engineered during his reign also led to an expansion of intellectual pursuits, including the writing of Proverbs and some 1,005 songs that are attributed to the great poet-king.

DOCUMENT–BASED QUESTIONS

1. What should the sluggard learn by observing the ant?

2. What does the speaker say will happen if the sluggard does not mend his ways?

Chapter Connection For more about the ancient Hebrews, see Chapter 10.

PRIMARY SOURCE HANDBOOK • **R49**

ANSWERS TO DOCUMENT-BASED QUESTIONS

1. how to be productive and busy

2. Poverty and need will come upon the sluggard.

More About . . .

King David

Born in Bethlehem in 1085 B.C., David was the youngest of eight sons in a family of the tribe of Judah. He first appears in the Bible when the prophet Samuel is sent by God to anoint the boy as the next king. David also plays his harp to help raise the spirits of the king, Saul. Later, David slays the giant Goliath.

As an adult, David became a great military leader and gained the throne of Israel after Saul's death in battle. During his 33-year reign, David fought a series of wars that made Israel an independent nation. He also created a royal court, wrote sacred poems and songs, and planned the Temple that his son Solomon would later build. To Jews, David is a great king and prophet. To Christians, he heralds the appearance of his descendant Jesus. He died at age 70 in 1015 B.C.

from the **Hebrew Bible: Psalm 100**

Background: The Book of Psalms in the Hebrew Bible served as a hymn book for the temple in Jerusalem. It contains 150 songs on a wide variety of topics. Many have been attributed to King David, who ruled over Israel around 1000 B.C. They remain a part of both Jewish and Christian worship to this day. Psalm 100 is a joyful expression of religious feeling.

Primary Source

Make a joyful noise unto the Lord, all ye lands.
Serve the Lord with gladness;
Come before his presence with singing.
Know ye that the Lord, he is God;
It is he that hath made us,
 and not we ourselves;
We are his people,
 and the sheep of his pasture.
Enter into his gates with thanksgiving,
And into his courts with praise;
Be thankful unto him,
 and bless his name.
For the Lord is good, his mercy is everlasting,
And his truth endureth to all generations.

David David is depicted as a young shepherd playing his pipe in this French manuscript illumination, c. 1250. ▶

DOCUMENT–BASED QUESTIONS

1. How are the faithful told to come into the presence of the Lord?

2. What are some of the qualities of the Lord that are praised in this psalm?

Chapter Connection For more about the ancient Hebrews, see Chapter 10.

ANSWERS TO DOCUMENT-BASED QUESTIONS

1. with music and singing
2. goodness, mercy, truth

from the *Iliad*

By Homer
Translated by Robert Fagles

Background: Homer has long been recognized as one of the world's greatest poets. It is likely that Homer heard singer-poets narrate tales about the Trojan War, a ten-year war waged by Greeks against the wealthy city of Troy, or Ilium, in Asia Minor. In the late 19th century, archaeologists discovered the ruins of ancient Troy. Most scholars now believe that Greek armies probably did attack Troy sometime in the 1200s B.C. Many scholars think that the *Iliad* was created in the 700s B.C. The Greek warrior Achilles enters the battle when his best friend, Patroclus, has been killed by the Trojan hero Hector. Achilles kills every Trojan in his path until he finally meets Hector in single combat outside the city walls.

Primary Source

Athena[1] luring him [Hector] on with all her immortal cunning—
and now, at last, as the two came closing for the kill
it was tall Hector, helmet flashing, who led off:
"No more running from you in fear, Achilles!
Not as before. Three times I fled around
the great city of Priam—I lacked courage then
to stand your onslaught. Now my spirit stirs me
to meet you face-to-face. Now kill or be killed!
Come, we'll swear to the gods, the highest witnesses—
the gods will oversee our binding pacts. I swear
I will never mutilate you—merciless as you are—
if Zeus[2] allows me to last it out and tear your life away.
But once I've stripped your glorious armor, Achilles,
I will give your body back to your loyal comrades.
Swear you'll do the same."

(continued)

1. **Athena** (uh•THEE•nuh): the goddess of wisdom and warfare; protects the Greeks.
2. **Zeus** (zoos): the king of the gods, father of Athena.

Greek Vase Achilles and Hector duel on this Greek vase, c. 490 B.C. ▶

R51

PRIMARY SOURCE HANDBOOK

More About . . .

The Discovery of Troy

Before German archaeologist Heinrich Schliemann (1822–1890) began his work, most people believed that Troy was only a legend. A lifelong Homeric enthusiast, Schliemann disagreed. In 1871, working from clues in the Iliad, he decided that Troy must have been at Hisarlik, a hill in present-day Turkey. With the help of English archaeologist Frank Calvert, Schliemann began to dig there.

In 1873, several layers within Hisarlik, Schliemann found the remains of ancient city walls and buildings, along with many gold objects. He was convinced that he had found Homer's Troy. Schliemann went on to make other major archaeological discoveries, including those at Mycenae.

Since Schliemann's initial work, ten settlement levels have been found at Hisarlik dating between 3000 B.C. and A.D. 500. Most scholars identify the level called Troy VIIa, which was destroyed by fire, as the war-torn Troy of the Iliad.

▲ **Painting** Achilles in his chariot

(continued)

> A swift dark glance
> and the headstrong runner[3] answered, "Hector, stop!
> You unforgivable, you . . . don't talk to me of pacts.
> There are no binding oaths between men and lions—
> wolves and lambs can enjoy no meeting of the minds—
> they are all bent on hating each other to the death.
> So with you and me. No love between us. No truce
> till one or the other falls and gluts with blood
> Ares[4] who hacks at men behind his rawhide shield.
> Come, call up whatever courage you can muster.
> Life or death—now prove yourself a spearman,
> a daring man of war! No more escape for you—
> Athena will kill you with my spear in just a moment.
> Now you'll pay at a stroke for all my comrades' grief,
> all you killed in the fury of your spear!"

3. **headstrong runner:** Achilles.
4. **Ares (AIR•eez):** the god of war.

DOCUMENT–BASED QUESTIONS

1. What pact does Hector wish to make with Achilles before they fight?

2. Why does Achilles reject the pact?

Chapter Connection For more about Homer and the *Iliad,* see Chapter 11, Lesson 2.

ANSWERS TO DOCUMENT-BASED QUESTIONS

1. Hector wants them to promise that, whoever wins, the victor will not mutilate the loser's body.
2. He says that the mutual hatred between them makes such a pact or agreement impossible.

from Aesop's Fables:
The Wolf in Sheep's Clothing

Background: Aesop (EE•suhp) was a Greek slave who supposedly lived around the sixth century B.C. Aesop's Fables are brief stories that convey lessons about life and conclude with morals that offer useful advice.

▲ **Aesop** A woodcut of Aesop made in Venice in 1492

Primary Source

A certain wolf could not get enough to eat because of the watchfulness of the shepherds. But one night he found a sheep skin that had been cast aside and forgotten. The next day, dressed in the skin, the wolf strolled into the pasture with the sheep. Soon a little lamb was following him about and was quickly led away to slaughter.

That evening the wolf entered the fold with the flock. But it happened that the shepherd took a fancy for mutton[1] broth that very evening and, picking up a knife, went to the fold. There the first he laid hands on and killed was the wolf.

The evildoer often comes to harm through his own deceit.

_____
1. **mutton:** the meat of a fully grown sheep.

Photograph A humorous illustration of the Aesop fable ▼

Primary Source Handbook

DOCUMENT–BASED QUESTIONS

1. What happens to the lamb in this story?

2. What happens to the wolf?

Chapter Connection For more about Aesop, see Chapter 11, Lesson 2.

ANSWERS TO DOCUMENT-BASED QUESTIONS

1. It is killed and eaten by the wolf, who is disguised as a sheep.

2. He is killed by the shepherd who thinks he is butchering a fully grown sheep for soup or broth; thus the wolf is killed by his own deceit.

More About . . .

Daedalus and Icarus

Daedalus, whose name means "skillfully made," was a mythological Athenian architect and inventor. He was said to have received his gifts of creation and invention from the goddess Athena.

Daedalus had to flee Athens when he murdered his apprentice, who was also his nephew, out of jealousy for the youth's invention of the saw. The inventor went to Crete, where he provided King Minos and Queen Pasiphae with many services, the most impressive of which was the designing and building of the labyrinth, the prison of the Minotaur.

Some versions of this myth say that after Icarus fell, Daedalus went on to Sicily, where he continued his work and regained his reputation and great fame. In historic times, the Greeks attributed buildings and statues of unknown origins to the mythic inventor.

Greek Myth: "The Boy Who Flew"

Retold by Anne Rockwell

Background: Many Greek myths focus on individuals who suffer for their prideful or disobedient behavior. Set mainly on the island of Crete in the Aegean Sea, the following story tells the Greek myth of Daedalus (DEHD•uhl•uhs) and Icarus (IHK•uhr•uhs). Daedalus was a brilliant inventor who disobeyed the ruler of Crete; his son, Icarus, disobeyed him. Both suffered for their actions. As this selection opens, Queen Pasiphae (puh•SIHF•uh•EE) of Crete is angry with Daedalus for helping to kill her son, a monster called the Minotaur.

Primary Source

▲ **Painting** The fall of Icarus is shown in this painting on the ceiling of the rotunda of Apollo in the Louvre in Paris.

Queen Pasiphae was very angry because, as its mother, she loved the Minotaur, terrible as it had been. Her husband,[1] in order to soothe her, decided to punish Daedalus. He made Daedalus and his son prisoners.

No captain of any ship that sailed to Crete dared take them away because the king had decreed that the inventor and his son could never leave the island. They lived in an isolated tower, where Daedalus had a simple workshop. They had only the seagulls for company. How Daedalus yearned to show Icarus the world beyond their island prison!

One day as Daedalus was watching the gulls wheeling and circling above the surf, he had an inspiration. He shouted down to his son, who was gathering shells on the lonely beach, "Minos may rule the sea, but he does not rule the air!"

Daedalus had observed how the gulls' wings were shaped, and how they worked. No mortal had ever before figured out how a bird could fly, but Daedalus thought he understood.

He and Icarus began to collect all the gull feathers they could find along the beach. They gathered the large, stiff ones and the tiny, light, downy ones that floated in the breeze. They saved the wax that honeybees made. Then Daedalus made wings of the seagull feathers and the beeswax for himself and Icarus. He worked long and patiently, and Icarus helped him, always doing what his father told him to do.

After they had made two pairs of long, curved wings, Daedalus made two harnesses of leather. He showed Icarus how to place the wings on his shoulders. Then he showed him how to run along the beach until he caught the wind and, like a seagull, flew up into the air.

(continued)

1. **her husband:** King Minos of Crete.

Primary Source Handbook

(continued)

Father and son practiced together until, one day, Daedalus decided it was time for them to leave the island. As they rose into the air and headed away from their island prison toward the sea, Daedalus called out to Icarus, "Follow me! Do not fly too low, or you will lose the air and sink into the waves. But do not fly too high, or the heat from the sun will melt the beeswax."

"Yes, Father," shouted Icarus above the sea noises and the wailing of the seagulls who flew beside him.

Higher and higher they flew. At last, Daedalus said, "We will stay at this level all the way. Remember what I told you—follow me!"

As they flew by, fishermen dropped their nets in wonder and farmers stopped at their plows. They thought they were seeing two gods in flight, for surely only gods could fly.

Icarus began to feel more and more sure of himself. He flew upward, then downward. He swooped and soared like a gull, laughing joyously as he did so. He cried out, "Look at me, Father!" and soared upward.

Daedalus beckoned him down, but Icarus thought, He is old and timid while I am young and strong. Surely I can fly a little better than he. Suddenly the boy disappeared into a cloud and flew up and up and up, higher and higher.

Too late, he saw feathers begin to fall from his wings. As the hot sun melted the wax, more and more feathers dropped away. Frantically, the boy flapped his arms in the air, but he could not fly without the wings. Instead, he dropped down and down until he fell into the sea and drowned.

Daedalus flew up in search of his son, calling as he went, "Icarus! Come down to me!"

Then he saw the telltale feathers drifting past him, and he heard the distant splash as Icarus fell into the sea. The old man cried as he continued on his journey, but he flew to freedom. He never made wings for anyone again.

DOCUMENT–BASED QUESTIONS

1. How do Daedalus and Icarus escape from the island?

2. What happens to Icarus?

Chapter Connection For more about Greek myths, see Chapter 11, Lesson 2.

ANSWERS TO DOCUMENT-BASED QUESTIONS

1. Daedalus makes wings so that they can fly away.

2. He disobeys his father, flies too close to the sun, his wings melt, and he plunges into the sea and drowns.

More About . . .

Thucydides

Not much is known about the ancient Greek historian Thucydides. He probably lived between about 460 and 404 B.C. and was an Athenian whose family had roots in Thrace.

During the Peloponnesian War, Thucydides was given command of a fleet, but he lost the city of Amphipolis to the Spartans. For this, he was sentenced to exile, where he remained for the duration of the war. However, from his position outside of the conflict, he was able to gather the information for his great, unfinished *History of the Peloponnesian War.*

With this work, Thucydides created the first recorded scholarly history. Unlike earlier historians, however, he wrote his work to be read, not recited, and was also extremely careful in the presentation of the facts. He portrayed events as the results of human acts, not as the whims of gods or as the consequences of fate.

from *History of the Peloponnesian War*

By Thucydides
Translated by Rex Warner

Background: Thucydides (thoo•SIHD•ih•DEEZ) was a Greek historian who wrote about the bitter 27-year-long war between Athens and Sparta. He was probably in attendance when Pericles, the greatest Athenian statesman of his time, gave a funeral oration for soldiers killed in the first year of the war. In the following excerpt, Pericles speaks of the special qualities of Athens.

Primary Source

"Our love of what is beautiful does not lead to extravagance; our love of the things of the mind does not make us soft. We regard wealth as something to be properly used, rather than as something to boast about. As for poverty, no one need be ashamed to admit it: the real shame is in not taking practical measures to escape from it. Here each individual is interested not only in his own affairs but in the affairs of the state as well: even those who are mostly occupied with their own business are extremely well-informed on general politics—this is a peculiarity of ours: we do not say that a man who takes no interest in politics is a man who minds his own business; we say that he has no business here at all. We Athenians, in our own persons, take our decisions on policy or submit them to proper discussions: for we do not think that there is an incompatibility[1] between words and deeds; the worst thing is to rush into action before the consequences have been properly debated. And this is another point where we differ from other people. We are capable at the same time of taking risks and of estimating them beforehand. Others are brave out of ignorance; and, when they stop to think, they begin to fear. But the man who can most truly be accounted brave is he who best knows the meaning of what is sweet in life and of what is terrible, and then goes out undeterred[2] to meet what is to come."

▲ **Engraving** Portrait of Pericles, the Athenian statesman

1. **incompatibility:** lack of harmony; conflict.
2. **undeterred:** not discouraged.

DOCUMENT–BASED QUESTIONS

1. Why did the Athenians view public discussion as useful before taking action?

2. What was Pericles' definition of courage?

Chapter Connection For more about Pericles' funeral oration, see Chapter 12, Lesson 2, Primary Source.

ANSWERS TO DOCUMENT-BASED QUESTIONS

1. because power is in the hands of the people
2. taking action knowing the risks involved

from *The Life of Caesar*

By Suetonius
Translated by Robert Graves

Background: Julius Caesar was a member of a noble Roman family. He became a great general and sole ruler of Rome. He was assassinated in 44 B.C. More than a century after his death, a Roman historian named Suetonius wrote a biography of this powerful leader.

Primary Source

Caesar was a most skillful swordsman and horseman, and showed surprising powers of endurance. He always led his army, more often on foot than in the saddle, went bareheaded in sun and rain alike, and could travel for long distances at incredible speed in a gig,[1] taking very little luggage. If he reached an unfordable[2] river he would either swim or propel himself across it on an inflated skin; and often arrived at his destination before the messengers whom he had sent ahead to announce his approach. . . .

Sometimes he fought after careful tactical planning, sometimes on the spur of the moment—at the end of a march, often; or in miserable weather, when he would be least expected to make a move. . . . It was his rule never to let enemy troops rally when he had routed them, and always therefore to assault their camp at once. If the fight were a hard-fought one he used to send the chargers[3] away—his own among the first—as a warning that those who feared to stand their ground need not hope to escape on horseback.

Julius Caesar Bronze statue of Julius Caesar ▼

1. **gig:** a light two-wheeled carriage drawn by one horse.
2. **unfordable:** uncrossable.
3. **chargers:** horses.

DOCUMENT–BASED QUESTIONS

1. What were some of the personal qualities of Caesar?

2. What was probably the attitude of Caesar's soldiers toward him?

Chapter Connection For more about Julius Caesar, see Chapter 13, Lesson 3.

More About . . .

Suetonius

The Roman biographer Suetonius was born in A.D. 69 and died after A.D. 122. His family belonged to the *equites,* the wealthy, non-senatorial class of Roman society. After deciding against a career in law, Suetonius entered imperial service, rising from manager of the libraries to Emperor Hadrian's private secretary. However, Suetonius was fired for lapses in court protocol and dedicated himself thereafter to writing.

Suetonius wrote several historical works, but two stand out. The first is *De viris illustribus,* or *Concerning Illustrious Men,* which covers the lives of famous Roman writers, thinkers, and speakers. Only fragments of this work survive.

The second work is *De vita Caesarum,* or the *Lives of the Caesars.* This nearly complete text is a collection of biographies of the first 11 Roman emperors. Colorful and full of gossip but clear and unpretentious, it has provided modern readers with vivid impressions of the first rulers of imperial Rome.

ANSWERS TO DOCUMENT-BASED QUESTIONS

1. skilled fighter; had endurance; led his troops by example; quick and decisive in his actions; shrewd and intelligent; courageous

2. probably admiration and respect since he seems to have led by example and to have faced the same dangers and hardships they faced

More About . . .

Jesus' Teaching

Jesus was a Jew and a prophet and, to Christians, the Messiah. However, he was also a rabbi, or Jewish religious teacher, and taught using established conventions of the rabbis of his time.

One teaching form that would have been familiar to his audience was the question-and-answer. A person in the audience would ask a particular question that would allow Jesus to make an important point as he answered it.

However, Jesus also often taught through parables. The word *parable* comes from the Greek word *parabole*, which means, roughly, "a comparison." The word was first used in the Jewish translation of the Bible into Greek. The idea was to tell a story with a moral lesson to which people could then compare real situations or behavior. For example, in the "Parable of the Lost Sheep," Jesus is comparing a lost sheep found by his shepherd to a repentant sinner welcomed by God.

from the New Testament: Parable of the Lost Sheep

Background: Jesus often taught in parables—stories that teach morals or lessons. In the following parable, Jesus tells about a lost sheep, but he is really talking about something else.

▲ **Brooch** Roman brooch shows the Lamb of God. The halo symbolizes Jesus.

Primary Source

Among the people who gathered to see Jesus were those who were very religious.

"As a teacher of the Law," said one, "I am very concerned to make sure that this wandering preacher is not leading the people astray with what he says."

"As a Pharisee,"[1] added another, "I am worried that he doesn't teach the importance of a pure and holy life."

They all looked to where Jesus was sitting. On this occasion, he was surrounded by a motley array[2] of beggars, vagrants, and people who were suspected of criminal dealing and terrorism.

Jesus waved them over. They stepped forward but then had to wait as a shepherd led his sheep along the path that lay between them, ambling slowly forward so the animals that straggled behind could catch up.

"Just think about shepherds and how they go about their work," said Jesus when they arrived. "Imagine—a shepherd has one hundred sheep. He is leading them along, but when he turns and counts them, he finds that one is missing. What does he do? He leaves the ninety-nine grazing in the pasture and goes looking for the one that is lost.

"And what does he do when at last he finds it? Does he beat it and punish it till it bleats in terror and pain? Of course not! It is his treasure, and he is delighted to find it. So he picks it up and lays it across his shoulders so he can carry it home.

"Then, when it is safely home, he calls to all his friends, 'Today is my happy day. I found my lost sheep. Let us celebrate together!'

"I tell you," said Jesus, "there is more rejoicing in heaven over one sinner who repents of their ways than over ninety-nine respectable people who do not need to repent."

---

1. **Pharisee:** member of a Jewish sect that emphasized a strict interpretation of the law of Moses.
2. **motley array:** odd collection.

DOCUMENT–BASED QUESTIONS

1. What does the lost sheep stand for?

2. What sort of message about the fate of sinners does the parable convey?

Chapter Connection For more parables of Jesus, see Chapter 14, Literature Connection.

ANSWERS TO DOCUMENT-BASED QUESTIONS

1. a sinner

2. The parable sends an optimistic message because it says that sinners can be saved and that hope for the fallen sinner must never be abandoned.

from the *Annals*

By Tacitus
Translated by Michael Grant

Background: Tacitus was one of the greatest historians of ancient Rome. In the following excerpt, Tacitus tells about a terrible fire that swept Rome in A.D. 64. Many Romans believed that the emperor Nero had ordered the fire set so that he could rebuild Rome according to his own designs.

Primary Source

Of Rome's fourteen districts only four remained intact. Three were leveled to the ground. The other seven were reduced to a few scorched and mangled ruins. To count the mansions, blocks, and temples destroyed would be difficult. They included shrines of remote antiquity, the precious spoils[1] of countless victories, Greek artistic masterpieces, and authentic records of old Roman genius. All the splendor of the rebuilt city did not prevent the older generation from remembering these irreplaceable objects. . . .

But Nero profited by his country's ruin to build a new palace. Its wonders were not so much customary and commonplace luxuries like gold and jewels, but lawns and lakes and faked rusticity[2]—woods here, open spaces and views there. With their cunning, impudent artificialities,[3] Nero's architects and contractors outbid Nature.

▲ **Bust** This marble bust portrays the Emperor Nero.

1. **spoils:** goods or property seized after a conflict.
2. **rusticity:** resemblance to the countryside.
3. **impudent artificialities:** shameless and unnatural designs.

DOCUMENT–BASED QUESTIONS

1. What effect might a public calamity such as a fire have on political stability?

2. How might people at the time have interpreted the event?

Chapter Connection For more about the decline of Rome, see Chapter 15.

More About . . .

Emperor Nero

Nero Claudius Caesar is one of the most notorious Roman emperors. His bad reputation stems largely from the number of friends and family—including his mother and wife—he either had murdered or forced to commit suicide.

He is also often blamed for the Great Fire of Rome in A.D. 64, although he most likely had nothing to do with it. It was the extravagant Domus Aurea, or "Golden House", as his new palace built over the ruined city was called, that set people to speculating.

Along with this callous disregard for the needs of his subjects after such a disaster, Nero began indulging his artistic side by singing publicly on stage. This shocked many of the powerful in Rome. After a failed coup attempt in which the conspirators, including Seneca, were discovered and forced to commit suicide, Nero was finally deposed and committed suicide himself in A.D. 68.

ANSWERS TO DOCUMENT-BASED QUESTIONS

1. In a political capital such as Rome, such an event might result in political turmoil that would threaten the stability of the state.

2. Some probably saw it as a political plot on the part of the emperor to remake Rome in his own image; others probably saw it as a sign of displeasure on the part of God or the gods with Rome's moral failings.

World Religions and Ethical Systems

A Global View

A religion is an organized system of beliefs and practices, often centered on one or more gods. In this book, you have learned about many different religions and their impact on world history. Religions have guided people's beliefs and actions for thousands of years. They have brought people together. But they have also torn them apart.

Religions are powerful forces today as well. They affect everything from what people wear to how they behave. There are thousands of religions in the world. In the following pages, you will learn about five major religions: Buddhism, Christianity, Hinduism, Islam, and Judaism. You will also learn about Confucianism, an ethical system. Like a religion, an ethical system provides guidance on how to live your life. However, unlike religions, ethical systems do not center on the worship of gods. The chart on the opposite page shows what percentages of the world population practice the five major religions. The map shows where these religions are practiced.

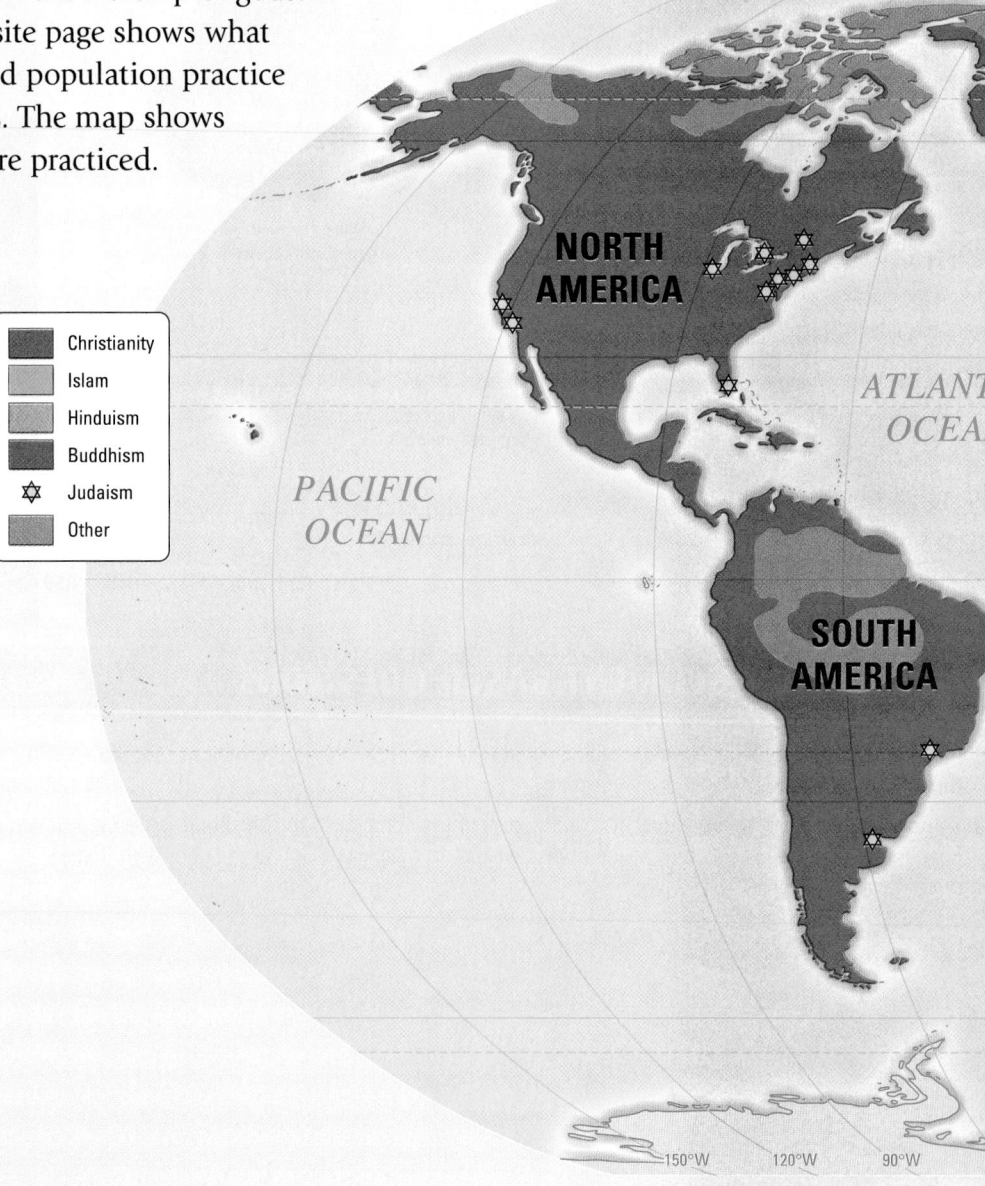

Christianity
Islam
Hinduism
Buddhism
✡ Judaism
Other

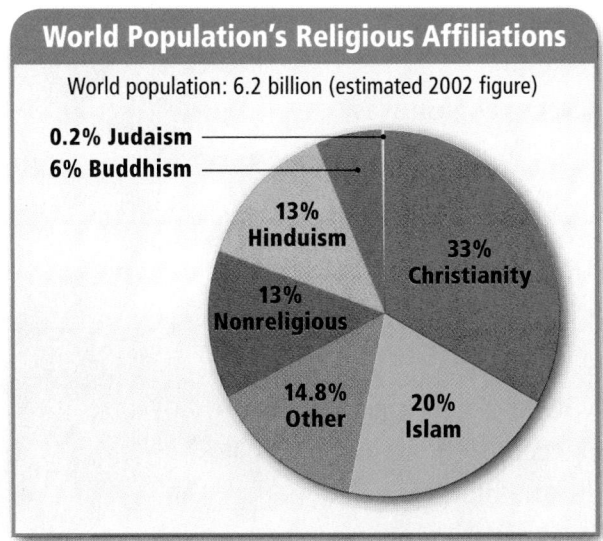

World Population's Religious Affiliations

World population: 6.2 billion (estimated 2002 figure)

- 0.2% Judaism
- 6% Buddhism
- 13% Hinduism
- 13% Nonreligious
- 14.8% Other
- 20% Islam
- 33% Christianity

Source: *World Almanac 2003*

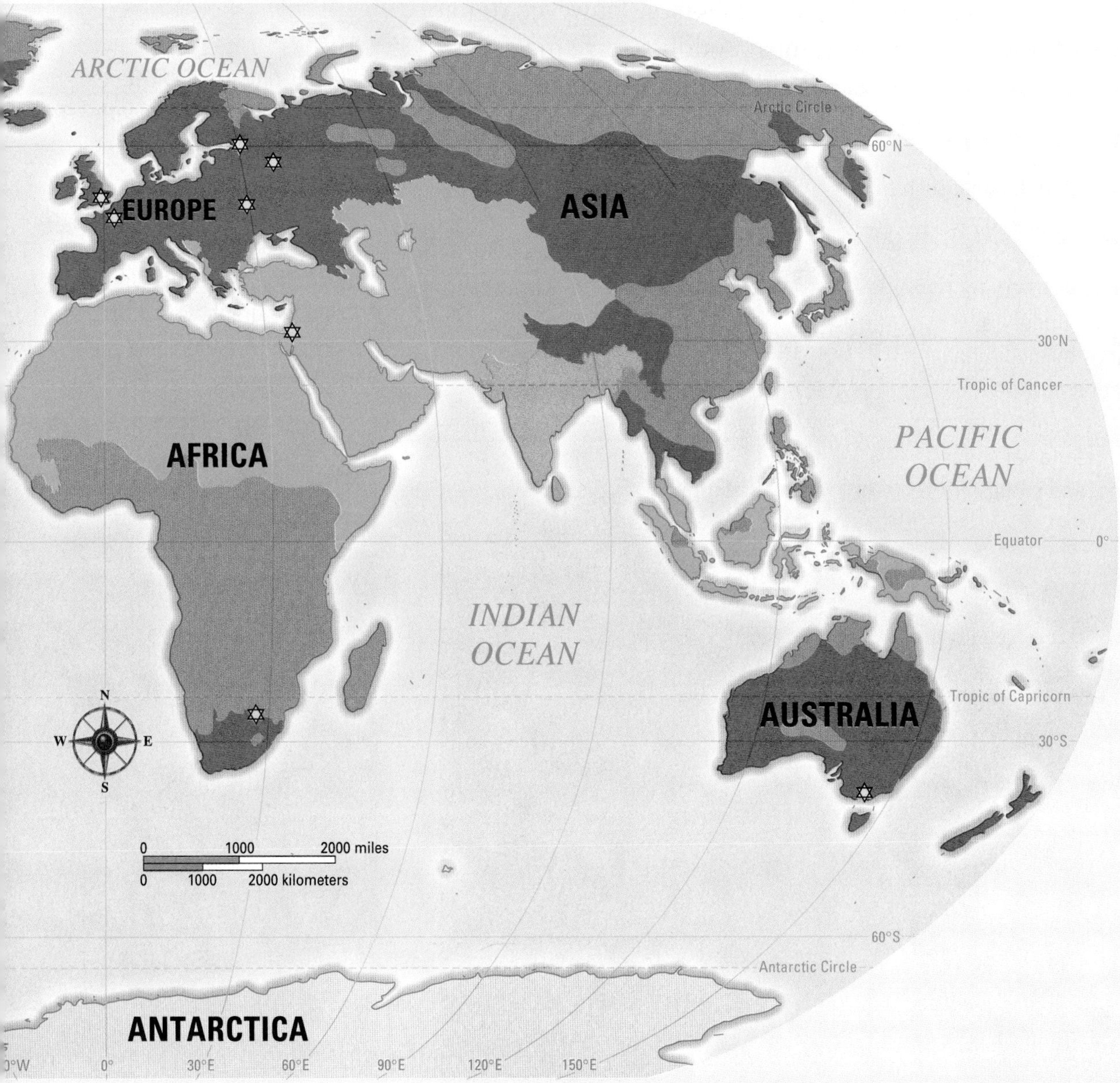

ARCTIC OCEAN

Arctic Circle

60°N

EUROPE

ASIA

30°N

Tropic of Cancer

AFRICA

PACIFIC OCEAN

Equator 0°

INDIAN OCEAN

Tropic of Capricorn

AUSTRALIA

30°S

N W E S

60°S

Antarctic Circle

ANTARCTICA

| 0 | 1000 | 2000 miles |
| 0 | 1000 | 2000 kilometers |

0°W 0° 30°E 60°E 90°E 120°E 150°E

Buddhism

Buddhism began in India in the sixth century **B.C.** The religion was founded by Siddhartha Gautama (sihd•DAHR•tuh GOW•tuh•muh), who came to be known as the Buddha. *Buddha* means "enlightened one." He was born into a noble family but left home to search for enlightenment, or wisdom. The Buddha is said to have achieved enlightenment after long study. According to Buddhist tradition, he taught his followers that the way to end suffering was by practicing the Noble Eightfold Path. This path involved observing the following: right opinions, right desires, right speech, right action, right job, right effort, right concentration, and right meditation.

After the Buddha's death, Buddhism spread in India, Ceylon, and Central Asia. Missionaries spread the faith. Buddhist ideas also traveled along trade routes. The religion, however, did not survive on Indian soil. Today, most Buddhists live in Sri Lanka (formerly Ceylon), East Asia, Southeast Asia, and Japan.

▼ Buddha

Statues of the Buddha, such as this one in Japan, appear in shrines throughout Asia. Buddhists try to follow the Buddha's teachings by meditating, a way of emptying the mind of thought. They also make offerings at shrines, temples, and monasteries.

▼ Monks

Buddhist monks dedicate their entire life to the teachings of the Buddha. They live together in religious communities called monasteries. There, the monks lead a life of poverty, meditation, and study. In this photograph, Buddhist monks in Myanmar hold their begging bowls.

▲ Pilgrimage

For centuries, Buddhists have come to visit places in India and Nepal associated with the Buddha's life. These sites include the Buddha's birthplace and the fig tree where he achieved his enlightenment. Worshipers also visit the site of the Buddha's first sermon, shown here.

Learn More About Buddhism

Symbol The Buddha's teaching, known as the dharma, is often symbolized by a wheel because his teaching was intended to end the cycle of births and deaths. The Buddha is said to have "set in motion the wheel of the dharma" during his first sermon.

Primary Source

The Buddha called his insight into the nature of suffering the Four Noble Truths (see page 234). In the following selection, the Buddha tells his followers how they can end suffering and find enlightenment. The path involves understanding that life on Earth is brief and full of sadness. It also involves giving up selfish desire.

All created things are transitory [short-lived]; those who realize this are freed from suffering. This is the path that leads to pure wisdom.

All created beings are involved in sorrow; those who realize this are freed from suffering. This is the path that leads to pure wisdom.

All states are without self; those who realize this are freed from suffering. This is the path that leads to pure wisdom.

from the Dhammapada
Translated by Eknath Easwaran

Chapter Connection For more about Buddhism, see Chapter 7.

WORLD RELIGIONS AND ETHICAL SYSTEMS • **R63**

Christianity

Christianity is the largest religion in the world, with about 2 billion followers. It is based on the life and teachings of Jesus, as described in the Bible's New Testament. Jesus, a Jew, taught many ideas from the Jewish tradition. Some biblical prophets had spoken of a day when a promised figure would come to save all of humankind. By the end of the first century A.D., many Jews and non-Jews had come to believe that Jesus was the one who would make this happen. Now called "Christians," they spread their faith throughout the Roman Empire.

Christians regard Jesus as the Son of God. They believe that Jesus entered the world and died to save humanity.

▼ Easter and Palm Sunday

On Easter, Christians celebrate their belief in Jesus' resurrection, or his being raised to heavenly life after he was put to death. The Sunday before Easter, Christians observe Palm Sunday. This day celebrates Jesus' triumphal entry into Jerusalem. Palm branches, like those carried here, were spread before him.

▲ **Jesus and the Disciples**
Jesus' followers included 12 disciples, or pupils. Jesus passed on his teachings to his disciples. This painting from the 1400s shows Jesus with his disciples.

▼ **St. Paul**
St. Paul was one of the apostles who spread Christian beliefs throughout the Roman Empire. Paul started churches almost everywhere he went. Many churches today, such as this great cathedral in London, are named for this apostle.

Symbol Jesus was crucified, or put to death on a cross. As a result, the cross became an important symbol of Christianity. It represents the belief that Jesus died to save humanity.

Primary Source

One of Jesus' most famous sermons is the Sermon on the Mount. In this talk, Jesus provided guidance to his followers. His words were written down in the New Testament, the part of the Bible that describes the teaching of Jesus Christ. In the following verses, Jesus explains that people can be saved by opening their hearts to God and by treating others as they would like to be treated.

"Ask, and it will be given you; seek, and you will find; knock, and it will be opened to you. For every one who asks receives, and he who seeks finds, and to him who knocks it will be opened. Or what man of you, if his son asks him for a loaf, will give him a stone? Or if he asks for a fish, will give him a serpent? If you then, who are evil, know how to give good gifts to your children, how much more will your Father who is in heaven give good things to those who ask him? So whatever you wish that men would do to you, do so to them; for this is the law and the prophets."

Matthew 7:7–12

Chapter Connection For more about Christianity, see Chapter 14.

Hinduism

Hinduism is a way of life guided by religious beliefs and practices that developed over thousands of years. Hindus believe that a supreme being called Brahman is the soul of the universe. The same presence, they believe, can also be found within each person. People can be freed from suffering and desires once they understand the nature of Brahman. The religious practices of Hindus include prayer, meditation, selfless acts, and worship of the various Hindu gods.

Today, Hinduism is the major religion of India and Nepal. It also has followers in Indonesia, Africa, Europe, and the Western Hemisphere.

▼ **Festival of Diwali**
Diwali, the Festival of Lights, is the most important festival in India. Diwali may have begun as a harvest festival in ancient India. Today, it marks the beginning of the year for many Hindus. They celebrate the festival by lighting candles and lamps, as shown in this photograph.

▲ Gods

Brahman often takes the form of three gods in Hinduism. Brahma is the creator of the universe. Vishnu is its protector. Shiva is its destroyer. All three gods are represented in this sculpture.

▼ Brahmin Priest

Brahmin priests, like the one shown here, are among Hinduism's religious leaders. These priests take care of the holy images in temples and read from the religion's sacred books.

Learn More About Hinduism

Symbol This symbol represents the word *Om* (or *Aum*), which is used at the beginning and end of prayers. *Om* is the most sacred syllable for Hindus because they believe that it is the basic sound of the world and that it contains all other sounds.

Primary Source

Hinduism has many sacred writings. The Vedas, four collections of prayers, rituals, and other sacred texts, are the oldest Hindu scriptures. They are believed to contain all knowledge, past and future.

The *Bhagavad Gita* is another important Hindu text. In this work, the god Vishnu takes on the personality of a chariot driver named Krishna. Krishna and the warrior Arjuna discuss the meaning of life and religious faith. In this selection, Krishna explains that Brahman cannot be destroyed.

> Weapons do not cut it,
> fire does not burn it,
> waters do not wet it,
> wind does not wither it.
>
> It cannot be cut or burned;
> it cannot be wet or withered;
> it is enduring, all-pervasive,
> fixed, immovable, and timeless.
>
> *Bhagavad Gita* 2:23–24

Chapter Connection For more about Hinduism, see Chapter 7.

Islam

Islam is a religion based on the teachings of the Qur'an, the religion's holy book. Followers of Islam, known as Muslims, believe that God revealed these teachings to the prophet Muhammad through the angel Gabriel around A.D. 610. Islam teaches that there is only one God—the same God that is worshiped in Christianity and Judaism. In Arabic, God is called Allah. Muslims also believe in the prophets of Judaism and Christianity. In fact, Muslims traditionally refer to Christians and Jews as "people of the book." That is because Christians and Jews have received divine revelations from scriptures in the Bible.

Today, Muslims live in southwestern and central Asia and parts of Africa. Islam also has many followers in Southeast Asia. Muslims show their devotion by performing acts of worship known as the Five Pillars of Islam. These include faith, prayer, charity, fasting, and a pilgrimage to Mecca.

▼ The Dome of the Rock
The Dome of the Rock in Jerusalem is one of Islam's holiest sites. The rock on the site is the spot from which Muslims say Muhammad rose to heaven to learn Allah's will. With Allah's blessing, Muhammad returned to Earth to bring God's message to all people.

▲ Muslim Prayer
Five times a day—dawn, noon, mid-afternoon, sunset, and evening—Muslims face toward Mecca to pray. Like the people in this photograph, Muslims stop what they are doing when they hear the call to prayer. Everything comes to a halt—even traffic.

▼ Ramadan

During the holy month of Ramadan, Muslims fast, or do not eat or drink, from dawn to sunset. The family shown here is ending their fast. The most important night of Ramadan is called the Night of Power. This is believed to be the night the angel Gabriel first spoke to Muhammad.

Learn More About Islam

Symbol The crescent moon has become a symbol of Islam. The symbol may be related to the new moon that begins each month in the Islamic lunar calendar.

Primary Source

The Qur'an is the spiritual guide for Muslims. It also contains teachings for Muslim daily life. The following chapter is called the Exordium (introduction). Muslims recite this short chapter as well as other passages from the Qur'an, when they pray.

> *In the Name of God, the Compassionate, the Merciful*
>
> Praise be to God, Lord of the Universe,
> The Compassionate, the Merciful,
> Sovereign of the Day of Judgment!
> You alone we worship, and to You alone
>   we turn for help.
> Guide us to the straight path,
> The path of those whom You have favored,
> Not of those who have incurred Your wrath,
> Nor of those who have gone astray.
>
> Qur'an 1:1–6

WORLD RELIGIONS AND ETHICAL SYSTEMS • **R69**

Judaism

Judaism was the first major monotheistic religion—that is, based on the concept of one God. The basic teachings of Judaism come from the Torah, the first five books of the Hebrew Bible. Judaism teaches that a person serves God by studying the Torah and living by its teachings. The Torah became the basis for the civil and religious laws of Judaism. The followers of Judaism, or Jews, also believe that God set down many moral laws for all of humanity with the Ten Commandments.

Today, there are more than 14 million Jews throughout the world. Many live in Israel, where a Jewish state was created in 1948.

▼ Abraham
According to the Torah, God chose a Hebrew shepherd named Abraham to be the "father" of the Hebrew people. In the 19th century B.C., Abraham led his family to a land that he believed God had promised them. This painting illustrates their journey.

Symbol The Star of David, also called the Shield of David, is a very important symbol of Judaism. The symbol honors King David, who ruled the kingdom of Israel about 1000–962 B.C.

▲ Rabbi

Rabbis are the Jewish people's spiritual leaders and teachers. A rabbi often conducts the services in a synagogue, or Jewish house of worship. Like the rabbi shown here, he or she may also conduct the ceremony that marks Jewish children's entrance into the religious community.

▼ Western Wall

Many Jews make the pilgrimage to the Western Wall, shown here. The sacred wall, also known as the Wailing Wall, formed the western wall of the courtyard of the Second Temple of Jerusalem. The temple was built in the second century B.C. The Romans destroyed it in A.D. 70.

Primary Source

The Book of Genesis is the first book of the Hebrew Bible and of the Torah. Genesis tells the history of the Hebrew people. It focuses on the individuals with whom God had a special relationship. In the following verses, God speaks to Abraham. His words express a promise of land and a special pledge to the Hebrew people.

Now the Lord said to Abram [Abraham], "Go from your country and your kindred and your father's house to the land that I will show you. And I will make of you a great nation, and I will bless you, and make your name great, so that you will be a blessing. I will bless those who bless you, and him who curses you I will curse; and by you all the families of the earth will bless themselves."

Genesis 12:1–3

Chapter Connection For more about Judaism, see Chapter 10.

Confucianism

Confucianism is an ethical system based on the teachings of the Chinese scholar Confucius. It stresses social and civic responsibility. Confucius was born in 551 B.C., during a time of crisis in China. He hoped his ideas and teachings would restore the order of earlier times to his society. But although Confucius was active in politics, he never had enough political power to put his ideas into practice. After his death, Confucius' students spread his teachings. As a result, his ideas became the foundation of Chinese thought for more than 2,000 years.

Today, Confucianism guides the actions of millions of Chinese people and other peoples of the East. It has also greatly influenced people's spiritual beliefs. While East Asians declare themselves to follow a number of religions, many also claim to be Confucians.

▼ **Temple**
Although Confucianism has no clergy or gods to worship, temples, like this one in Taiwan, have been built to honor Confucius. In ancient times, the temples provided schools of higher education. Today, many have been turned into museums.

◀ Confucius

Confucius believed that society should be organized around five basic relationships. These are the relationships between (1) ruler and subject, (2) father and son, (3) husband and wife, (4) elder brother and junior brother, and (5) friend and friend.

▲ Confucius' Birthday

Historians do not know for certain the day when Confucius was born, but people in East Asia celebrate his birthday on September 28. In Taiwan and China, it is an official holiday known as Teachers' Day. The holiday pays tribute to teachers because Confucius himself was a teacher. Here, students in Beijing take part in a ceremony honoring their teachers.

Learn More About Confucianism

Symbol The yin-and-yang symbol represents opposite forces in the world working together. Yin represents all that is cold, dark, soft, and mysterious. Yang represents everything that is warm, bright, hard, and clear. The yin-and-yang symbol represents the harmony that Confucius hoped to restore to society.

Primary Source

Confucius' teachings were collected by his students in a book called the *Analects*. In the following selections from the *Analects*, Confucius (called the Master) instructs his students about living a moral and thoughtful life.

The Master said: "Even in the midst of eating coarse rice and drinking water and using a bent arm for a pillow happiness is surely to be found; riches and honors acquired by unrighteous means are to me like the floating clouds." (7.16)

The Master said: "When I walk with two others, I always receive instruction from them. I select their good qualities and copy them, and improve on their bad qualities." (7.22)

The Master said: "The people may be made to follow something, but may not be made to understand it." (8.9)

from the *Analects*
Translated by Raymond Dawson

Chapter Connection For more about Confucianism, see Chapter 8.

WORLD RELIGIONS AND ETHICAL SYSTEMS • **R73**

Other Important Religions

You have learned about the five major world religions. Now find out about some other important religions: Bahaism, Shinto, Sikhism, and Zoroastrianism. These religions are important both historically and because they have many followers today.

▼ Shinto

Shinto, meaning "way of the gods," is Japan's oldest and only native religion. Shintoists worship many gods, called *kami*. They believe that kami are spirits found in mountains, rivers, rocks, trees, and other parts of nature. Shintoists often worship the kami at shrines in their homes. They also celebrate the gods during special festivals, such as the one shown here. Today, there are about 3 million Shintoists, mostly in Japan.

▲ Bahaism

Bahaism (buh•HAH•IHZ•uhm) is a young religion, with more than 7 million followers throughout the world. It was founded in 1863 in Persia (modern-day Iran) by a man known as Bahaullah, which means "splendor of God" in Arabic. Followers believe that, in time, God will make barriers of race, class, and nation break down. When this happens, people will form a single, united society. All of the Baha'i houses of worship have nine sides and a central dome, symbolizing this unity. The Baha'i house of worship shown here is located in Illinois.

◄ Sikhism

Sikhism (SEEK•IHZ•uhm) was founded in India over 500 years ago by Guru Nanak, a man raised in the Hindu tradition. The religion's 24 million followers, called Sikhs, believe in one God. Like Buddhists and Hindus, Sikhs believe that the soul goes through repeated cycles of life and death. However, Sikhs do not believe that they have to live outside the world to end the cycle. Rather, they can achieve salvation by living a good and simple life. Uncut hair symbolizes this simple life. Many Sikh men cover their long hair with a turban, like the one worn by the man here.

▲ Zoroastrianism

Zoroastrianism (ZAWR•oh•AS•tree•uh•NIHZ•uhm) was founded in ancient Persia around 600 B.C. by a prophet named Zoroaster. This prophet taught that Earth is a battleground where a great struggle is fought between the forces of good and the forces of evil. Each person is expected to take part in this struggle. At death, the Zoroastrian god, called Ahura Mazda (ah•HUR•uh MAZ•duh), will judge the person on how well he or she fought. This stone relief shows Ahura Mazda (*right*) giving the crown to a Persian king. Today, there are about 2.5 million Zoroastrians throughout the world.

WORLD RELIGIONS AND ETHICAL SYSTEMS • **R75**

Comparing World Religions and Ethical Systems

World Religions Handbook

	Buddhism	Christianity	Hinduism	Islam	Judaism	Confucianism
Followers worldwide (estimated 2003 figures)	364 million	2 billion	828 million	1.2 billion	14.5 million	6.3 million
Name of god	no god	God	Brahman	Allah	God	no god
Founder	the Buddha	Jesus Christ	no one founder	no founder but spread by Muhammad	Abraham	Confucius
Holy book	many sacred books, including the Dhammapada	Bible, including Old Testament and New Testament	many sacred books, including the *Bhagavad Gita*	Qur'an	Hebrew Bible, including the Torah	*Analects*
Clergy	Buddhist monks	priests, ministers, monks, and nuns	Brahmin priests, monks, and gurus	no clergy but a scholar class, called the ulama, and imams, who may lead prayers	rabbis	no clergy
Basic beliefs	• Followers can achieve enlightenment by understanding the Four Noble Truths and by following the Noble Eightfold Path of right opinions, right desires, right speech, right action, right jobs, right effort, right concentration, and right meditation.	• There is only one God, who watches over and cares for his people. • Jesus Christ is the Son of God. He died to save humanity. His death and resurrection made eternal life possible for others.	• The soul never dies but is continually reborn until it becomes enlightened. • Persons achieve happiness and enlightenment after they free themselves from their earthly desires. • Freedom from earthly desires comes from many lifetimes of worship, knowledge, and virtuous acts.	• Persons achieve salvation by following the Five Pillars of Islam and living a just life. The pillars are faith, prayer, charity, fasting, and pilgrimage to Mecca.	• There is only one God, who watches over and cares for his people. • God loves and protects his people but also holds people accountable for their sins and shortcomings. • Persons serve God by studying the Torah and living by its teachings.	• Social order, harmony, and good government should be based on strong family relationships. • Respect for parents and elders is important to a well-ordered society. • Education is important for the welfare of both the individual and society.

Source: *World Almanac 2004*

Review

MAIN IDEAS

Buddhism (pages R62–R63)

1. How did the Buddha believe that his followers could end their suffering?
2. How did Buddhism spread?

Christianity (pages R64–R65)

3. Why is Jesus Christ important to the Christian religion?
4. What are some Christian beliefs?

Hinduism (pages R66–R67)

5. What is the importance of Brahman in Hinduism?
6. What three gods does Brahman often take the form of?

Islam (pages R68–R69)

7. How do Muslims believe the teachings of the Qur'an were revealed?
8. Why do Muslims traditionally refer to Christians and Jews as "people of the book"?

Judaism (pages R70–R71)

9. What does it mean to say that Judaism is a monotheistic religion?
10. What are the Ten Commandments?

Confucianism (pages R72–R73)

11. What did Confucius hope to restore?
12. What five relationships are important in Confucianism?

Other Important Religions (pages R74–R75)

13. How does Shinto differ from Bahaism, Sikhism, and Zoroastrianism?
14. How is Sikhism similar to Buddhism and Hinduism?

CRITICAL THINKING

15. **COMPARING** What goal do Buddhists and Hindus have in common?
16. **DRAWING CONCLUSIONS** How does Islam affect the everyday lives of its followers?
17. **SUMMARIZING** Which of the religions you have studied are monotheistic?

Interpreting a Pie Chart The pie chart below shows what percentages of the population of India practice the major religions. Use the pie chart to answer the following questions.

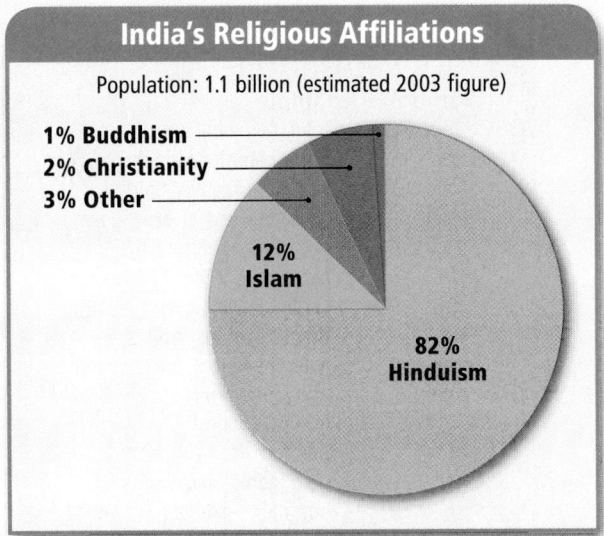

India's Religious Affiliations

Population: 1.1 billion (estimated 2003 figure)

- 1% Buddhism
- 2% Christianity
- 3% Other
- 12% Islam
- 82% Hinduism

Source: *World Almanac 2004*

1. **What percentage of the people in India practice Hinduism?**

   A. 1 percent
   B. 2 percent
   C. 12 percent
   D. 82 percent

2. **Which religion is practiced by 12 percent of the population?**

   A. Christianity
   B. Hinduism
   C. Buddhism
   D. Islam

Test Practice
ClassZone.com

Additional Test Practice, pp. S1–S33

World Religions Handbook

Glossary

The Glossary is an alphabetical listing of many of the key terms from the chapters, along with their meanings. The definitions listed in the Glossary are the ones that apply to the way the words are used in this textbook. The Glossary gives the part of speech of each word. The following abbreviations are used:

adj. adjective   *n.* noun   *v.* verb

Pronunciation Key

Some of the words in this book are followed by respellings that show how the words are pronounced. The following key will help you understand what sounds are represented by the letters used in the respellings.

Symbol	Examples	Symbol	Examples
a	apple [ap•uhl], catch [kach]	oh	road, [rohd], know [noh]
ah	barn [bahrn], pot [paht]	oo	school [skool], glue [gloo]
air	bear [bair], dare [dair]	ow	out [owt], cow [kow]
aw	bought [bawt], horse [hawrs]	oy	coin [koyn], boys [boyz]
ay	ape [ayp], mail [mayl]	p	pig [pihg], top [tahp]
b	bell [behl], table [TAY•buhl]	r	rose [rohz], star [stahr]
ch	chain [chayn], ditch [dihch]	s	soap [sohp], icy [EYE•see]
d	dog [dawg], rained [raynd]	sh	share [shair], nation [NAY•shuhn]
ee	even [EE•vuhn], meal [meel]	t	tired [tyrd], boat [boht]
eh	egg [ehg], ten [tehn]	th	thin [thihn], mother [MUH•thuhr]
eye	iron [EYE•uhrn]	u	pull [pul], look [luk]
f	fall [fawl], laugh [laf]	uh	bump [buhmp], awake [uh•WAYK],
g	gold [gohld], big [bihg]		happen [HAP•uhn], pencil [PEHN•suhl],
h	hot [haht], exhale [ehks•HAYL]		pilot [PY•luht]
hw	white [hwyt]	ur	Earth [urth], bird [burd], worm [wurm]
ih	into [IHN•too], sick [sihk]	v	vase [vays], love [luhv]
j	jar [jahr], badge [baj]	w	web [wehb], twin [twihn]
k	cat [kat], luck [luhk]	y	As a consonant: yard [yahrd], mule [myool]
l	load [lohd], ball [bawl]		As a vowel: ice [ys], tried [tryd], sigh [sy]
m	make [mayk], gem [jehm]	z	zone [zohn], reason [REE•zuhn]
n	night [nyt], win [wihn]	zh	treasure [TREHZH•uhr], garage [guh•RAHZH]
ng	song [sawng], anger [ANG•guhr]		

Syllables that are stressed when the words are spoken appear in CAPITAL LETTERS in the respellings. For example, the respelling of *history* (HIHS•tuh•ree) shows that the first syllable of the word is stressed.

Syllables that appear in SMALL CAPITAL LETTERS are also stressed, but not as strongly as those that appear in capital letters. For example, the respelling of *anthropology* (AN•thruh•PAHL•uh•gee) shows that the third syllable receives the main stress and the first syllable receives a secondary stress.

Abraham *n.* according to the Bible, a shepherd from the city of Ur in Mesopotamia who became the father of the Hebrews. (p. 325)

absolute ruler *n.* a person who has total power and governs alone. (p. 497)

acropolis (uh•KRAHP•uh•lihs) *n.* a fortified high place in an ancient Greek city, which contained important temples, monuments, and buildings. (p. 396)

Adulis (ah•DOO•lihs) *n.* an ancient city on the Red Sea, which served as the main trading port of the kingdom of Aksum. (p. 198)

Aeneas (ih•NEE•uhs) *n.* a hero of the Trojan War. (p. 431)

afterlife *n.* a life believed to follow death. (p. 159)

agriculture *n.* the cultivation of soil to produce useful crops. (p. 60)

ahimsa (uh•HIHM•SAH) *n.* nonviolence. (p. 233)

Aksum (AHK•SOOM) *n.* an ancient African kingdom on the Red Sea, in what is now Ethiopia and Eritrea. It replaced the kingdom of Kush. (p. 197)

Alexander the Great *n.* a king of Macedonia from 336 to 323 B.C., who conquered parts of Asia and Egypt, spreading Greek culture throughout his empire. (p. 407)

Alexandria *n.* a Hellenistic city in Egypt, on the Mediterranean Sea. Founded by Alexander the Great in 332 B.C., it was noted for its extensive ancient library as well as its lighthouse, one of the Seven Wonders of the World. (p. 408)

alphabet *n.* a set of letters used to represent the individual sounds of a language. (p. 358)

Anatolia *n.* the peninsula between the Mediterranean and Black seas that is now occupied by most of Turkey; also called Asia Minor. (p. 131)

animism *n.* the belief that spirits exist in animals, plants, other natural objects, and natural forces. (p. 205)

aqueduct (AK•wih•DUHKT) *n.* a pipe or channel that carries water from a distant source to a city. (pp. 457, 517)

aquifer *n.* an underground layer of sand, gravel, or spongy rock that contains water. (p. 297)

aristocracy (AR•ih•STAHK•ruh•see) *n.* an upper class or nobility. (p. 373)

artifact *n.* a human-made object. (p. 28)

artisan *n.* a person trained in a particular skill or craft. (p. 67)

Aryan (AIR•ee•uhn) *n.* a member of an Indo-European people who crossed into India around 1500 B.C. (p. 228)

Asoka (uh•SOH•kuh) *n.* the greatest Maurya king, whose reign began in 269 B.C. (p. 236)

Athens *n.* a city-state of ancient Greece, which reached its greatest cultural achievements in the fifth century B.C. It is the capital and largest city of modern Greece. (p. 379)

Augustus (aw•GUHS•tuhs) *n.* the first Roman emperor (originally named Octavian), who became emperor in 27 b.c. (p. 446)

B

Babylonian Captivity *n.* a 50-year period in which the Israelites were held in Babylon, away from their homeland of Judah. During this period, the Israelites became known as Jews. (p. 338)

Bantu *n.* a group of West African peoples that gradually migrated eastward and southward, bringing farming and herding to new regions. (p. 206)

barbarian *n.* a person belonging to a group seen as primitive and uncivilized; especially, a person living outside the ancient Roman Empire. (p. 502)

barracks *n.* a group of buildings used to house soldiers. (p. 380)

bas-relief (BAH•rih•LEEF) *n.* a type of sculpture in which slightly raised figures stand out against a flat background. (p. 516)

bishop *n.* a high-ranking local official in some Christian churches. (p. 485)

Brahmanism (BRAH•muh•NIHZ•uhm) *n.* the early religion of the Aryans in ancient India. (p. 229)

bronze *n.* a metal that is a mixture of copper and tin. (p. 101)

Buddhism *n.* a religion that began in India and is based on the teachings of Siddhartha Gautama. (p. 233)

bureaucracy (byu•RAHK•ruh•see) *n.* a system of organized government departments staffed by appointed officials. (p. 269)

Byzantine (BIHZ•uhn•teen) **Empire** *n.* the Eastern Roman Empire, which was ruled from Constantinople and lasted for about a thousand years after the fall of the Western Roman Empire. (p. 509)

C

Caesar, Julius *n.* a Roman general and politician (100–44 B.C.) who received great support from Rome's commoners and was given the right to rule for life in 44 B.C. He was assassinated the same year. (p. 444)

caste *n.* a social class that a person belongs to by birth. (p. 228)

catapult *n.* an ancient military machine for hurling stones or other objects at enemy troops and fortresses. (p. 405)

cataract (KAT•uh•RAKT) *n.* a steep waterfall. (p. 147)

catholic *adj.* universal. (p. 485)

Chavín (chah•VEEN) *n.* a culture that flourished between 900 and 200 B.C. in the Andes of Peru. (p. 295)

Cicero (SIHS•uh•ROH) *n.* a Roman consul and famous orator who opposed Julius Caesar. (p. 445)

Cincinnatus *n.* a dictator of Rome for one day in 458 B.C. (p. 438)

citizen *n.* a person who is loyal to a particular government and entitled to be protected by that government. (p. 374)

city-state *n.* a political unit that includes a city and its nearby farmlands. (p. 91)

civilization *n.* a human society with an advanced level of development in social and political organization and in the arts and sciences. (p. 89)

civil war *n.* an armed conflict between groups within the same country. (p. 444)

climate *n.* the pattern of weather conditions in a certain location over a long period of time. (p. 12)

code of law *n.* a set of written rules for people to obey. (p. 115)

codex *n.* a book of the type used by early Meso-American civilizations to record important historical events. (p. 310)

Colosseum *n.* a large arena in Rome, where the ancient Romans attended entertainments, such as battles of gladiators. (p. 458)

comedy *n.* a form of drama usually having a happy ending and often making fun of politics, people, and ideas of the times. (p. 412)

Confucianism (kuhn•FYOO•shuh•nihz•uhm) *n.* a philosophy based on the teachings of Confucius (551–479 B.C.), as recorded in the collection called the *Analects*. (p. 260)

consul *n.* one of a pair of elected officials who headed ancient Rome's executive branch and commanded the army. (p. 438)

continent *n.* one of the seven large landmasses of Earth—North America, South America, Europe, Asia, Africa, Australia, and Antarctica. (p. 9)

convert *v.* to convince someone to change his or her religion or beliefs. (p. 477)

creed *n.* a statement of religious beliefs. (p. 486)

crucifixion *n.* an execution by hanging on a cross. (p. 470)

cultural diffusion *n.* the spread of ethnic ideas and customs to other areas of the world. (p. 277)

cuneiform (KYOO•nee•uh•fawr m) *n.* an ancient writing system developed by the Sumerians, made up of wedge-shaped markings. (p. 102)

D

Daoism (DOW•IHZ•uhm) *n.* a belief system said to have begun with the sixth-century-B.C. philosopher Laozi. Daoism emphasizes living in harmony with nature. (p. 262)

David *n.* the king of the Israelites who won control of Jerusalem in 1000 B.C. (p. 336)

Delian League *n.* an alliance of Greek city-states formed at the end of the Persian War to protect Athens and its overseas allies. (p. 395)

delta *n.* the area near a river's mouth where the river deposits large amounts of sand and silt. (p. 147)

democracy *n.* a government in which citizens make political decisions, either directly or through elected representatives. (p. 375)

dharma (DAHR•muh) *n.* the collected teachings of Buddha. (p. 235)

Diaspora (dy•AS•puhr•uh) *n.* the scattering of Jewish people after they were forced out of Judea by the Romans in A.D. 70. (p. 345)

Diocletian (DY•uh•KLEE•shuhn) *n.* a Roman leader who became emperor in A.D. 284 and introduced reforms in Rome's administration, army, and economy. (p. 497)

direct democracy *n.* a form of democracy in which citizens participate directly in running the government. (p. 394)

disciple *n.* one of Jesus' 12 closest followers. (p. 468)

domesticate *v.* to raise and tend (a plant or an animal) to be of use to humans. (p. 59)

drama *n.* a story designed to be performed by actors. (p. 411)

drought (drowt) *n.* a period of little rainfall, in which growing crops becomes difficult. (p. 85)

dynastic cycle *n.* the pattern of the rise and fall of dynasties. (p. 256)

dynasty (DY•nuh•stee) *n.* a line of rulers from the same family. (p. 165)

E

Eastern Orthodox Church *n.* a branch of Christianity that developed in the Byzantine Empire and is not under the authority of the pope. (p. 511)

embalm *v.* to preserve a body after death. (p. 160)

emperor *n.* the ruler of an empire. (p. 113)

empire *n.* a group of territories and peoples brought together under one supreme ruler. (p. 113)

epic poem *n.* a long poem that tells a story of heroes. (pp. 364, 516)

Epistle *n.* one of the letters included in the New Testament, written by Jesus' apostles to early Christian churches to instruct them in Christian beliefs and practices. (p. 480)

exile *n.* forced removal from one's homeland. (p. 120)

Exodus (EHK•suh•duhs) *n.* the migration of the Israelites from Egypt, as told in the Torah. (p. 327)

Ezana (AY•zah•nah) *n.* a strong king of Aksum who came to power in a.d. 325, greatly expanded the kingdom, and made Christianity the official religion. (p. 198)

F

fable *n.* a short story that conveys a moral lesson, often by means of animal characters that possess human characteristics. (p. 364)

fertile *adj.* favorable for the growth of crops and other plants. (p. 147)

Fertile Crescent *n.* an area of rich soil in the Middle East, stretching from the Mediterranean Sea through Mesopotamia to the Persian Gulf. (p. 114)

filial piety *n.* respect for one's parents and ancestors—an important teaching of Confucianism. (p. 261)

floodplain *n.* flat land bordering a river. (p. 84)

fossil *n.* a remain of early life that has been preserved in the ground. (p. 28)

G

Gandhi (GAHN•dee), **Mohandas** (MOH•huhn•DAHS) *n.* a leader who used nonviolence to oppose the British rule of India. (p. 242)

Gentile (JEHN•TYL) *n.* a person who is not Jewish. (p. 478)

geography *n.* the study of Earth and its people. (p. 9)

gladiator (GLAD•ee•AY•tuhr) *n.* in ancient Rome, a trained warrior who engaged in combat to the death to entertain the public. (p. 458)

glyph (glihf) *n.* a symbol, usually carved or engraved, that represents a syllable or a whole word. (p. 310)

Gospel *n.* one of the first four books of the New Testament, describing the life and teachings of Jesus. (p. 468)

government *n.* a system for creating order and providing leadership. (p. 67)

griot (gree•OH) *n.* an official storyteller in an ancient African civilization. (p. 205)

H

Hammurabi (HAM•uh•RAH•bee) *n.* the ruler of the Babylonian Empire from 1792 to 1750 B.C., who expanded the empire. (p. 114)

Han Dynasty *n.* a Chinese dynasty begun in 202 B.C. by Liu Bang, which reunified China. (p. 269)

Hanging Gardens of Babylon *n.* an artificial mountain covered with trees and plants, built by Nebuchadnezzar II for his wife. The gardens are one of the Seven Wonders of the World. (p. 122)

Harappan (huh•RAP•uhn) **civilization** *n.* an ancient Indian culture, dating back to 2500 B.C., that included the people of the entire Indus River region. (p. 221)

Hatshepsut (hat•SHEHP•soot) *n.* a female pharaoh of ancient Egypt, who initially ruled with her stepson but declared herself the only ruler in 1472 B.C. (p. 173)

Hellenistic *adj.* relating to the blend of Greek, Persian, Egyptian, and Indian cultures that lasted from the death of Alexander the Great in 323 B.C. until Augustus became emperor of Rome in 27 B.C. (p. 408)

helot *n.* an agricultural slave in ancient Sparta. (p. 379)

hemisphere *n.* a half of Earth's surface. (p. 18)

hieroglyph (HY•uhr•uh•GLIHF) *n.* a picture standing for a word or sound. (p. 158)

Himalayas (HIHM•uh•LAY•uhs) *n.* a high mountain range that extends through northern India, southern Tibet, Nepal, and Bhutan. (p. 220)

Hindu-Arabic numerals *n.* the numerals used in the United States and western Europe, which originated in India. (p. 242)

Hinduism *n.* a religion and philosophy developed in ancient India, characterized by a belief in reincarnation and a supreme being who takes many forms. (p. 229)

Hindu Kush (HIHN•doo KUSH) *n.* a mountain range along the northwestern border of India. (p. 220)

hominid (HAHM•uh•nihd) *n.* a human or humanlike creature that walks on two feet. (p. 29)

Horn of Africa *n.* the easternmost projection of the African continent—the region occupied by the present-day countries of Somalia and Ethiopia. (p. 197)

hunter-gatherer *n.* a human being who hunts animals and gathers plants for food, moving to a different location whenever such food becomes scarce. (p. 51)

I

ideal *n.* a thing in its most perfect form. (p. 412)

irrigation *n.* the watering of crops. (p. 61)

isthmus (IHS•muhs) *n.* a narrow strip of land that connects two larger landmasses. (pp. 289, 355)

J

Jesus *n.* a teacher whose life and teachings serve as the basis of the Christian religion. Christians believe Jesus to be the Son of God. (p. 467)

Judaism *n.* the religion of the Hebrews, based on the Hebrew Scriptures and a belief in one god. (p. 326)

justice *n.* fair treatment of people, in keeping with the law. (p. 115)

Justinian *n.* the emperor of the Eastern Roman Empire from A.D. 527 to 565, who ruled with his wife, Theodora, and reconquered lost territories for the empire. (p. 509)

Justinian Code *n.* a revised code of Roman law—including laws dealing with marriage, slavery, property ownership, women's rights, and criminal justice—prepared at the order of the Byzantine emperor Justinian. (p. 510)

K

karma *n.* in Hindu belief, the sum of a person's actions in this life, which determine his or her fate in the next life. (p. 230)

Khufu (KOO•FOO) *n.* the Egyptian pharaoh who, about 2550 B.C., ordered the construction of the largest pyramid ever built. (p. 167)

king *n.* the highest-ranking leader of a group of people. (p. 95)

Kush *n.* an ancient Nubian kingdom that conquered all of upper and lower Egypt in the 700s b.c. (p. 190)

L

landform *n.* a naturally formed feature of Earth's land surface, such as an island, a mountain, or a plateau. (p. 10)

latitude *n.* a measure of distance north or south of the equator. (p. 16)

legalism *n.* the belief that a ruler should use the legal system to force people to obey laws. (p. 259)

legend *n.* a popular story handed down from earlier times, which may be believed to be true but cannot be proved. (p. 431)

linen *n.* a fabric woven from fibers of the flax plant. (p. 149)

longitude *n.* a measure of distance east or west of the prime meridian. (p. 16)

M

maize (mayz) *n.* a type of corn grown by Native American civilizations. (p. 308)

Mandate of Heaven *n.* an ancient Chinese belief that a good ruler had the gods' approval. (p. 256)

Marathon *n.* a plain in ancient Greece, northeast of Athens. (p. 382)

Maya (MAH•yuh) *n.* a civilization of present-day southern Mexico and northern Central America, which reached its height from A.D. 250 to 900. (p. 307)

mercenary *n.* a soldier hired to serve in an army. (p. 496)

Meroë (MEHR•oh•EE) *n.* the capital of the kingdom of Kush from around 590 B.C., located on the Nile and having access to trade routes as well as gold and iron. (p. 192)

Meso-America *n.* a region that extends southeastward from central Mexico and includes the countries of Guatemala, El Salvador, and Belize and parts of Honduras and Nicaragua. (p. 292)

Mesolithic (MEHZ•uh•LIHTH•ihk) **Age** *n.* the Middle Stone Age—a period that lasted from about 10,000 to 6000 B.C., during which people began to control fire and develop language. (p. 32)

Mesopotamia (MEHS•uh•puh•TAY•mee•uh) *n.* the area of Southwest Asia between the Tigris and Euphrates rivers—home to many early civilizations. (p. 83)

Messiah (mih•SY•uh) *n.* the savior and king foretold by Jewish prophets. (p. 338)

migration *n.* a movement from one region or country to settle in another. (pp. 52, 206)

missionary *n.* a person who travels to a foreign land to spread his or her religious beliefs. (p. 479)

Moche (MOH•chay) *n.* an ancient culture that inhabited what is now the northern coast of Peru between A.D. 100 and 700. (p. 298)

monotheism (MAHN•uh•thee•IHZ•uhm) *n.* the belief that only one god exists. (p. 326)

monsoon *n.* a seasonal wind that produces a wet or dry period in a region, especially in southern Asia. (p. 220)

mosaic (moh•ZAY•ihk) *n.* a picture created from tiny pieces of colored stone or other material. (p. 515)

Moses *n.* according to the Bible, the prophet who led the Israelites from Egypt and was their lawgiver. (p. 327)

mother culture *n.* a culture that shapes and influences the customs and ideas of later cultures. (p. 303)

mummy *n.* the body of a human or animal that has been preserved and dried out to prevent decay. (p. 160)

myth *n.* a story that explains beliefs, practices, or natural phenomena, often featuring gods and goddesses or other supernatural beings. (p. 362)

N

Nazca (NAHZ•kuh) *n.* an ancient culture that arose near what is now the southern coast of Peru and prospered from 200 B.C. to A.D. 600. (p. 296)

Neolithic (NEE•uh•LIHTH•ihk) **Age** *n.* the New Stone Age—a period that lasted from about 8000 to 3000 B.C. and was marked by the beginning of farming and the development of pottery and weaving. (p. 32)

nirvana (neer•VAH•nuh) *n.* in Buddhism and Hinduism, a state of wisdom which breaks the cycle of reincarnation. (p. 234)

Nok *n.* an ancient African civilization in what is now southeastern Nigeria, noted for its manufacture of iron tools. (p. 205)

nomad *n.* a member of a group of people who have no set home but move from place to place. (pp. 52, 502)

Nubia (NOO•bee•uh) *n.* an ancient region of Africa, which extended from the southern border of Egypt through what is now Sudan. (p. 189)

O

obelisk (AHB•uh•lihsk) *n.* a four-sided shaft with a pyramid-shaped top. (p. 174)

oligarchy (AHL•ih•GAHR•kee) *n.* a government that is controlled by the few, with the basis of power often being wealth. (p. 373)

Olmec (AHL•mehk) *n.* the earliest known Meso-American culture, which flourished from 1200 to 400 B.C. and was centered along the Gulf Coast of what is now southern Mexico. (p. 301)

Olympics *n.* an ancient Greek festival in honor of the god Zeus, which took place every four years and featured competitions in athletics and poetry. (p. 363)

Olympus (uh•LIHM•puhs), **Mount** *n.* the highest mountain in Greece—in Greek mythology, the home of the major gods and goddesses. (p. 361)

oracle bone *n.* an animal bone or turtle shell used by the Shang kings of China to communicate with and influence the gods. (p. 255)

oral history *n.* an unwritten verbal account of an event. (p. 41)

oratory *n.* the art of public speaking. (p. 516)

P

Paleolithic (PAY•lee•uh•LIHTH•ihk) **Age** *n.* the Old Stone Age—a period that lasted from about 2.5 million to 8000 B.C. and was marked by the use of simple stone tools by the earliest humans. (p. 32)

papyrus (puh•PY•ruhs) *n.* a paperlike material made from stems of the papyrus plant and used for writing by the ancient Egyptians. (p. 158)

parable *n.* a simple story that conveys a religious or moral lesson. (p. 468)

Parthenon *n.* a temple of the Greek goddess Athena, built in the fifth century B.C. on the acropolis of Athens. (p. 396)

patrician (puh•TRIHSH•uhn) *n.* one of the wealthy landowners who held the highest positions in government in ancient Rome. (p. 437)

Paul *n.* the most important of the apostles who spread Jesus' teachings. (p. 479)

Pax Romana *n.* a long period of stability and peace in the Roman Empire, beginning in the reign of Augustus, during which the empire grew to its greatest size. (p. 447)

Peloponnesian (PEHL•uh•puh•NEE•zhuhn) **War** *n.* a war between Athens and the Peloponnesian League, led by Sparta, which ended with a Spartan victory in 404 B.C. (p. 400)

Peloponnesus (PEHL•uh•puh•NEE•suhs) *n.* a peninsula forming the southern part of Greece. (p. 355)

peninsula *n.* a body of land that is connected to a larger landmass and surrounded on three sides by water. (pp. 355, 433)

Pericles (PEHR•ih•KLEEZ) *n.* a leader of ancient Athens who set out to strengthen democracy and expand the Athenian empire. (p. 393)

persecute *v.* to oppress or harass. (p. 478)

pharaoh (FAIR•oh) *n.* a king of ancient Egypt. (p. 166)

philosophy *n.* an investigation of basic truths about the universe, based on logical reasoning. (pp. 259, 414)

Phoenician (fih•NIHSH•uhn) *n.* a member of a trading people who lived on the coast of the eastern Mediterranean. (p. 358)

physical map *n.* a map showing landforms and bodies of water. (p. 20)

Piankhi (PYANG•kee) *n.* a king of Kush around 750 B.C., who gained control of almost all of Egypt, becoming pharaoh and uniting the two kingdoms. (p. 190)

pictograph *n.* a picture or drawing that represents a word or an idea in an early system of writing. (pp. 101, 255)

plague (playg) *n.* a disease that spreads very easily and usually causes death, affecting a significant portion of a population. (p. 401)

planned city *n.* a city that is built according to a set design. (p. 221)

plebeian (plih•BEE•uhn) *n.* a member of the common people of ancient Rome, who were allowed to vote but not to hold important government positions. (p. 437)

plunder *v.* to take possessions from by force. (p. 504)

polis (POH•lihs) *n.* a Greek city-state, such as Athens or Sparta. (p. 371)

political map *n.* a map showing features people have created, such as cities, states, provinces, territories, and countries. (p. 19)

polytheism (PAHL•ee•thee•IHZ•uhm) *n.* a belief in many gods or goddesses. (p. 93)

pope *n.* the bishop of Rome and head of the Roman Catholic Church. (p. 485)

primary source *n.* something written or created by a person who witnessed a historical event. (p. 40)

prophet *n.* a spiritual leader who conveys the words and wishes of God or a god. (p. 338)

province *n.* a subdivision of an empire or country. (p. 132)

pyramid (PIHR•uh•mihd) *n.* a structure with four triangular sides that meet at a point. (p. 166)

Q

Qin (chihn) *n.* a state of ancient China. (p. 267)

R

rabbi (RAB•eye) *n.* a religious leader and teacher trained in Jewish law, rituals, and tradition. (p. 346)

Ramses (RAM•SEEZ) **II** *n.* a pharaoh who ruled Egypt for 66 years, greatly expanding the Egyptian empire by conquering surrounding territories. (p. 175)

reincarnation *n.* the rebirth of a soul in another body. (p. 230)

religion *n.* the worship of a god, gods, or spirits. (p. 54)

Remus (REE•muhs) *n.* the twin brother of Romulus. (p. 432)

republic *n.* a form of government in which the people elect leaders and representatives. (p. 432)

resurrection *n.* a return to life after death. (p. 470)

Roman Catholic Church *n.* the branch of Christianity that is under the authority of the pope. (p. 511)

Romulus (RAHM•yuh•luhs) *n.* a legendary hero, descended from Aeneas, who is said to have founded Rome. (p. 431)

Royal Road *n.* a road for government use built by the ancient Persian ruler Darius, which helped unite the empire. (p. 132)

S

satrap (SAY•TRAP) *n.* the governor of a province in the ancient Persian Empire. (p. 132)

scribe *n.* a person who specializes in writing and serves as a record keeper. (pp. 102, 155)

secondary source *n.* an account of a historical event written by someone who did not witness the event. (p. 41)

semiarid (SEHM•ee•AR•ihd) *adj.* having little rainfall and warm temperatures. (p. 84)

senate *n.* a governing body of ancient Rome, made up of 300 members who advised Roman leaders. (p. 438)

Shi Huangdi (shee hwahng•dee) *n.* a Chinese ruler who came to power in 221 B.C. and unified and expanded China by ending internal battles and conquering rival states. (p. 267)

Siddhartha Gautama (sihd•DAHR•tuh GAW•tuh•muh) *n.* an Indian prince who founded Buddhism; also known as the Buddha. (p. 233)

Silk Roads *n.* the overland trade routes along which silk and other Chinese goods passed to Mesopotamia and Europe. (p. 277)

silt *n.* fine, fertile soil deposited by a river. (pp. 84, 147)

slash-and-burn *adj.* relating to a type of agriculture in which patches of land are prepared for planting by cutting down and burning the natural vegetation. (pp. 60, 293)

smelting *n.* the heating and melting of certain rocks to separate the metals they contain. (p. 192)

social class *n.* a group of people with similar customs, backgrounds, training, and income. (p. 67)

Solomon *n.* the third king of Israel, under whom it became a powerful nation. (p. 336)

Sparta *n.* an ancient Greek city-state of the Peloponnesus, noted for its militarism. (p. 379)

specialization *n.* a skill in one type of work. (p. 66)

stele (STEE•lee) *n.* a carved stone slab set upright in the ground, usually commemorating a person or event. (p. 309)

step pyramid *n.* a pyramid whose sides rise in a series of giant steps. (p. 167)

stylus *n.* a sharpened reed used to press markings into clay tablets. (p. 102)

subcontinent *n.* a large landmass that is part of a continent but considered a separate landform. (p. 219)

succession *n.* the order in which members of a royal family inherit a throne or title. (p. 165)

Sumer *n.* an ancient region of southern Mesopotamia, in which civilization arose around 3300 B.C. (p. 89)

surplus *n.* an amount produced in excess of what is needed. (pp. 65, 86)

synagogue (SIHN•uh•gahg) *n.* a building for Jewish prayer and worship and instruction in the Jewish faith. (p. 346)

T

technology *n.* people's application of knowledge, tools, and inventions to meet their needs. (p. 53)

Ten Commandments *n.* the basis of the law of the Israelites, given, according to the Torah, by God to Moses. (p. 327)

terrace *n.* a leveled area on a hillside. (p. 200)

textile *n.* a woven or knitted cloth. (p. 296)

thematic map *n.* a map that presents a particular type of information about a place or region. (p. 21)

toleration *n.* the practice of allowing people to keep their customs and beliefs. (p. 131)

tragedy *n.* a form of serious drama that presents the downfall or ruin of the main character or characters. (p. 412)

trans-Eurasian *adj.* involving the continents of Europe and Asia. (p. 277)

tribute *n.* a payment of money or goods by one ruler to another in order to ensure protection. (p. 120)

Trinity *n.* the union of three persons—Father, Son, and Holy Spirit—in one God. (p. 486)

tropical *adj.* having a warm and rainy climate. (p. 290)

truce *n.* a temporary agreement to stop fighting. (p. 401)

tyrant *n.* a ruler who has taken power illegally and rules without restrictions. (p. 373)

V

vault *n.* an arch that forms a ceiling or roof. (p. 517)

vegetation *n.* the plant life of an area. (p. 12)

Y

Yucatán (yoo•kuh•TAN) **Peninsula** *n.* an area of dense jungle in southeastern Mexico, extending into the Gulf of Mexico and the Caribbean Sea. (p. 292)

Z

Zeus (zoos) *n.* the ruler of the gods in Greek mythology. (p. 361)

ziggurat (ZIHG•uh•RAT) *n.* an ancient Sumerian or Babylonian temple that rose in a series of steplike levels. (p. 92)

Spanish Glossary

A

Abraham *s.* según la Biblia, pastor de la ciudad de Ur en la Mesopotamia, que se convirtió en el patriarca de los hebreos. (pág. 325)

absolute ruler [monarca absoluto] *s.* soberano que tiene poder ilimitado y que gobierna solo. (pág. 497)

acropolis [acrópolis] *s.* cima fortificada de las antiguas ciudades griegas, que contenía templos, monumentos y edificios importantes. (pág. 396)

Adulis *s.* antigua ciudad del Mar Rojo, que servía como el principal puerto mercantil del reino de Aksum. (pág. 198)

Aeneas [Eneas] *s.* héroe de la guerra de Troya. (pág. 431)

afterlife [más allá] *s.* vida después de la muerte. (pág. 159)

agriculture [agricultura] *s.* cultivo del suelo para producir cosechas útiles. (pág. 60)

ahimsa *s.* no-violencia. (pág. 233)

Aksum *s.* antiguo reino africano del Mar Rojo, en lo que hoy es Etiopía y Eritrea. Reemplazó al reino de Kush. (pág. 197)

Alexander the Great [Alejandro Magno] *s.* rey de Macedonia desde 336 hasta 323 a.C. que conquistó partes de Asia y Egipto y así propagó la cultura griega por todo su imperio. (pág. 407)

Alexandria [Alejandría] *s.* ciudad helenística de Egipto, en el Mediterráneo. Fue fundada por Alejandro Magno en el año 332 a.C. y se caracterizó por su extensa biblioteca antigua además de su faro, una de las siete maravillas del mundo. (pág. 408)

alphabet [alfabeto] *s.* conjunto de letras utilizadas para representar los sonidos individuales de un idioma. (pág. 358)

Anatolia *s.* península entre el Mediterráneo y el mar Negro actualmente ocupada por casi la totalidad de Turquía. También llamada Asia Menor. (pág. 131)

animism [animismo] *s.* creencia de que los animales, plantas, otros objetos naturales y fuerzas naturales tienen espíritu. (pág. 205)

aqueduct [acueducto] *s.* tubería o canal que transporta agua de una fuente distante a una zona poblada. (págs. 457, 517)

aquifer [acuífero] *s.* capa subterránea de arena, grava o rocas esponjosas que contiene agua. (pág. 297)

aristocracy [aristocracia] *s.* clase alta o nobleza. (pág. 373)

artifact [artefacto] *s.* objeto fabricado por el hombre. (pág. 28)

artisan [artesano] *s.* trabajador especializado en un determinado arte u oficio. (pág. 67)

Aryan [ario] *s.* miembro de un pueblo indoeuropeo que emigró a la India hacia 1500 a.C. (pág. 228)

Asoka *s.* el rey más importante de la dinastía mauria, cuyo reinado comenzó en el año 269 a.C. (pág. 236)

Athens [Atenas] *s.* ciudad estado de la antigua Grecia, que alcanzó su máximo esplendor cultural en el siglo V a.C. Es la capital y ciudad más grande de la Grecia moderna. (pág. 379)

Augustus [Augusto] *s.* primer emperador romano (originalmente llamado Octavio), que se convirtió en emperador en el año 27 a.C. (pág. 446)

B

Babylonian Captivity [cautividad babilónica] *s.* período de 50 años durante el cual los israelitas fueron retenidos en Babilonia, lejos de su patria de Judea. Fue durante ese período que los israelitas comenzaron a ser llamados judíos. (pág. 338)

Bantu [Bantúes] *s.* pueblo de África occidental que gradualmente emigró hacia el oriente y hacia el sur, llevando la agricultura y ganadería hacia nuevas regiones. (pág. 206)

Barbarian [bárbaro] *s.* persona perteneciente a un grupo considerado primitivo e incivilizado, especialmente una persona externa al antiguo imperio romano. (pág. 502)

barracks [barraca] *s.* grupo de edificios utilizados para albergar soldados. (pág. 380)

bas-relief [bajorrelieve] *s.* tipo de escultura en la cual las figuras resaltan un poco de un fondo plano. (pág. 516)

bishop [obispo] *s.* autoridad eclesiástica cristiana que supervisa varias iglesias. (pág. 485)

Brahmanism [brahmanismo] *s.* antigua religión de los arios en la antigua India. (pág. 229)

bronze [bronce] *s.* metal resultante de la mezcla de cobre y estaño. (pág. 101)

Buddhism [budismo] *s.* religión que comenzó en la India y se basa en las enseñanzas de Siddhartha Gautama. (pág. 233)

bureaucracy [burocracia] *s.* sistema en el cual el gobierno se divide en departamentos organizados administrados por funcionarios designados. (pág. 269)

Byzantine Empire [imperio bizantino] *s.* Imperio Romano de Oriente, con capital en Constantinopla, que duró aproximadamente cien años hasta la caída del Imperio Romano de Occidente. (pág. 509)

C

Caesar, Julius [César, Julio] *s.* general y político romano (100–44 a.C.) que obtuvo un gran apoyo de los plebeyos de Roma y recibió el derecho de gobernar de por vida en el año 44 a.C. Fue asesinado al año siguiente. (pág. 444)

caste [casta] *s.* clase social a la cual una persona pertenece desde el nacimiento. (pág. 228)

catapult [catapulta] *s.* antigua máquina militar para arrojar piedras u otros objetos a tropas y fortalezas enemigas. (pág. 405)

cataract [catarata] *s.* cascada grande. (pág. 147)

catholic [católico] *adj.* universal. (pág. 485)

Chavín *s.* cultura que floreció entre los años 900 y 200 a.C. en los Andes peruanos. (pág. 295)

Cicero [Cicerón] *s.* cónsul y famoso orador romano que se opuso a Julio César. (pág. 445)

Cincinnatus [Cincinato] *s.* dictador de Roma por un día en el año 458 a.C. (pág. 438)

citizen [ciudadano] *s.* persona leal a un determinado gobierno y que tiene el derecho de recibir protección por parte de ese gobierno. (pág. 374)

city-state [ciudad estado] *s.* unidad política que comprende una ciudad y sus territorios aledaños. (pág. 91)

civilization [civilización] *s.* sociedad humana con un nivel avanzado de desarrollo en la organización social y política, así como en las artes y ciencias. (pág. 89)

civil war [guerra civil] *s.* conflicto armado entre grupos dentro de un mismo país. (pág. 444)

climate [clima] *s.* conjunto de condiciones atmosféricas en un determinado lugar durante un largo período de tiempo. (pág. 12)

code of law [código de leyes] *s.* conjunto de reglas escritas que los habitantes deben obedecer. (pág. 115)

codex [códice] *s.* libro que utilizaban las primitivas civilizaciones mesoamericanas para registrar acontecimientos históricos importantes. (pág. 310)

Colosseum [Coliseo] *s.* extensa arena de Roma, donde los antiguos romanos presenciaban espectáculos tales como batallas de gladiadores. (pág. 458)

comedy [comedia] *s.* tipo de teatro generalmente con final feliz y que a menudo se burla de la política, las personas y las ideas de la época. (pág. 412)

Confucianism [confucionismo] *s.* filosofía basada en las enseñanzas de Confucio (551–479 a.C.), según se registra en la colección llamada Analects. (pág. 260)

consul [cónsul] *s.* uno de los dos pares de funcionarios electos a cargo del poder ejecutivo de la antigua Roma, que además comandaban el ejército. (pág. 438)

continent [continente] *s.* una de las siete grandes extensiones de tierra del planeta: América del Norte, América del Sur, Europa, Asia, África, Australia y la Antártida. (pág. 9)

convert [convertir] *s.* convencer a alguien de cambiar su religión y sus creencias. (pág. 477)

creed [credo] *s.* declaración de creencias religiosas. (pág. 486)

Crucifixión [crucifixión] *s.* ejecución que consiste en colgar en una cruz. (pág. 470)

cultural diffusion [difusión cultural] *s.* propagación de ideas y costumbres étnicas hacia otras áreas del mundo. (pág. 277)

cuneiform [cuneiforme] *s.* antiguo sistema de escritura desarrollado por los sumerios que consiste en signos con forma de cuña. (pág. 102)

D

Daoism [taoísmo] *s.* sistema de creencias supuestamente iniciado en el siglo VI a.C. por el filósofo Laozi. El taoísmo enfatiza la vida en armonía con la naturaleza. (pág. 262)

David *s.* rey de los israelitas que ganó el control de Jerusalén en el año 1000 a.C. (pág. 336)

Delian League [Liga de Delos] *s.* alianza de ciudades griegas formada al final de la guerra Persa para proteger a Atenas y a sus aliados extranjeros. (pág. 395)

delta *s.* zona cercana a la boca de un río donde el río deposita grandes cantidades de arena y limo. (pág. 147)

democracy [democracia] *s.* gobierno en el cual los ciudadanos toman las decisiones políticas, ya sea en forma directa o mediante representantes elegidos por el pueblo. (pág. 375)

dharma [darma] *s.* enseñanzas del Buda. (pág. 235)

Diaspora [Diáspora] *s.* dispersión del pueblo judío después de ser expulsado de Judea por los romanos en el año70 d.C. (pág. 345)

Diocletian [Diocleciano] *s.* líder romano que se convirtió en emperador en el año 284 d.C. y que introdujo reformas en la administración, el ejército y la economía de Roma. (pág. 497)

direct democracy [democracia directa] *s.* forma de democracia en la cual los ciudadanos gobiernan directamente. (pág. 394)

disciple [discípulo] *s.* uno de los 12 seguidores más cercanos a Jesús. (pág. 468)

domesticate [domesticar] *v.* criar y ocuparse (de una planta o un animal) para que sirva al hombre. (pág. 59)

drama [pieza de teatro] *s.* historia creada para ser representada por actores. (pág. 411)

drought [sequía] *s.* período con poca lluvia, en el cual se hace difícil el cultivo. (pág. 85)

dynastic cycle [ciclo dinástico] *s.* patrón del surgimiento y la caída de las dinastías. (pág. 256)

dynasty [dinastía] *s.* serie de gobernantes de una misma familia. (pág. 165)

E

Eastern Orthodox Church [Iglesia Ortodoxa Oriental] *s.* rama del cristianismo que se desarrolló en el imperio bizantino y no se encuentra bajo la autoridad del papa. (pág. 511)

embalm [embalsamar] *v.* conservar un cuerpo después de la muerte. (pág. 160)

emperor [emperador] *s.* soberano de un imperio. (pág. 113)

empire [imperio] *s.* grupo de territorios y habitantes gobernados por un soberano supremo. (pág. 113)

epic poem [poema épico] *s.* extenso poema que relata una historia de héroes. (págs. 364, 516)

Epistle [Epístola] *s.* una de las cartas incluidas en el Nuevo Testamento, escrita por los apóstoles de Jesús a las primeras iglesias cristianas para transmitirles las creencias y prácticas cristianas. (pág. 480)

exile [exilio] *s.* expulsión forzada de la patria. (pág. 120)

Exodus [Éxodo] *s.* emigración de los israelitas de Egipto, según se relata en el Torah. (pág. 327)

Ezana *s.* poderoso rey de Aksum, que asumió el poder en el año 325 d.C., expandió enormemente el reino y estableció el cristianismo como religión oficial. (pág. 198)

F

fable [fábula] *s.* narración corta que transmite una enseñanza moral, a menudo mediante personajes animales que poseen características humanas. (pág. 364)

fertile [fértil] *adj.* favorable para plantar cultivos y otras plantas. (pág. 147)

Fertile Crescent [Medialuna Fértil] *s.* zona de suelos ricos en el Medio Oriente, que se extiende desde el mar Mediterráneo a través de la Mesopotamia hasta el golfo Pérsico. (pág. 114)

filial piety [amor filial] *s.* respeto de los hijos hacia sus padres y ancestros, enseñanza importante del confucionismo. (pág. 261)

floodplain [llanura de inundación] *s.* superficie de tierra baja adyacente a un río. (pág. 84)

fossil [fósil] *s.* restos de un ser vivo antiguo que se ha preservado en la tierra. (pág. 28)

G

Gandhi, Mohandas [Gandhi, Mahatma] *s.* líder que utilizó la no-violencia para oponerse al gobierno británico en la India. (pág. 242)

Gentile [pagano] *s.* no-judío. (pág. 478)

geography [geografía] *s.* estudio de la Tierra y de sus habitantes. (pág. 9)

gladiator [gladiador] *s.* en la antigua Roma, guerrero entrenado que combatía hasta la muerte para divertir al público. (pág. 458)

glyph [glifo] *s.* símbolo, generalmente esculpido o grabado, que representa una silaba o una palabra entera. (pág. 310)

Gospel [Evangelio] *s.* uno de los cuatro primeros libros del Nuevo Testamento, que describe la vida y enseñanzas de Jesús. (pág. 468)

government [gobierno] *s.* sistema que sirve para crear orden y proporcionar liderazgo. (pág. 67)

griot *s.* narrador oficial en la civilización africana antigua. (pág. 205)

H

Hammurabi *s.* rey del imperio babilónico desde 1792 hasta 1750 a.C., que contribuyó a la expansión de su imperio. (pág. 114)

Han Dynasty [Dinastía Han] *s.* dinastía china comenzada en el año 202 a.C. por Liu Bang, que reunificó la China. (pág. 269)

Hanging Gardens of Babylon [Jardines colgantes de Babilonia] *s.* montaña artificial cubierta por árboles y plantas, construida por Nabuconodosor II para su esposa. Es una de las siete maravillas del mundo. (pág. 122)

Harappan civilization [civilización harappa] *s.* antigua cultura india, que se remonta al año 2500 a.C., y que comprende los pueblos de toda la región del río Indo. (pág. 221)

Hatshepsut *s.* mujer faraón del antiguo Egipto, que al principio reinó junto con su hijastro pero que luego se declaró reina única en el año 1472 a.C. (pág. 173)

Hellenistic [helénico] *adj.* relativo a la mezcla de las culturas griega, persa, egipcia e india que duró desde la muerte de Alejandro Magno en el año 323 a.C. hasta que Augusto se transformó en emperador de Roma, en el año 27 a.C. (pág. 408)

helot [ilota] *s.* esclavo campesino en la antigua Esparta. (pág. 379)

hemisphere [hemisferio] *s.* mitad de la superficie de la Tierra. (pág. 18)

hieroglyph [jeroglífico] *s.* dibujo que representa una palabra o sonido. (pág. 158)

Himalayas [Himalaya] *s.* alta cadena montañosa que se extiende a través del norte de la India, el sur del Tíbet, Nepal y Bhután. (pág. 220)

Hindu-Arabic numerals [números indo-arábigos] *s.* números utilizados en los Estados Unidos y Europa occidental, que tuvieron origen en la India. (pág. 242)

Hinduism [hinduismo] *s.* religión y filosofía desarrollada en la antigua India, caracterizada por una creencia en la reencarnación y en un ser superior que puede tomar distintas formas. (pág. 229)

Hindu Kush *s.* cadena de montañas que se extiende por el límite norte-occidental de la India. (pág. 220)

hominid [homínido] *s.* criatura humana o especie parecida que camina en dos patas. (pág. 29)

Horn of Africa [Cuerno de África] *s.* proyección del extremo oriental del continente africano: región que hoy ocupan los países de Somalia y Etiopía. (pág. 197)

hunter-gatherer [cazador-recolector] *s.* ser humano que caza animales y recolecta platas como alimento, y que cambia de lugar cada vez que su comida escasea. (pág. 51)

I

ideal *s.* que se encuentra en su forma más perfecta. (pág. 412)

irrigation [irrigación] *s.* riego de los cultivos. (pág. 61)

isthmus [istmo] *s.* angosta lengua de tierra que conecta dos extensiones más grandes de tierra. (págs. 289, 355)

J

Jesus [Jesús] *s.* maestro cuya vida y enseñanzas sirvieron como base de la religión cristiana. Los cristianos creen que Jesús es el hijo de Dios. (pág. 467)

Judaism [judaísmo] *s.* religión de los hebreos, basada en las escrituras hebreas y en la creencia de un solo dios. (pág. 326)

justice [justicia] *s.* tratamiento equitativo de las personas, en cumplimiento de la ley. (pág. 115)

Justinian [Justiniano] *s.* emperador del Imperio Romano de Oriente de 527 a 565 d.C., quien reinó con su esposa, Teodora, y reconquistó territorios perdidos para el imperio. (pág. 509)

Justinian Code [Código Justiniano] *s.* código revisado de leyes romanas (incluyendo leyes relativas al matrimonio, esclavitud, posesión de propiedad, derechos de la mujer y justicia criminal) preparado por orden del emperador bizantino Justiniano. (pág. 510)

K

karma *s.* en la creencia hindú, la suma de las acciones de una persona en esta vida, que determina su destino en su próxima vida. (pág. 230)

Khufu *s.* faraón egipcio que, alrededor del año 2550 a.C., ordenó la construcción de la pirámide más grande jamás construida. (pág. 167)

king [rey] *s.* líder de mayor rango de un grupo de personas. (pág. 95)

Kush *s.* antiguo reino nubio que conquistó la totalidad del Alto y el Bajo Egipto en el siglo VIII a.C. (pág. 190)

L

landform [accidente geográfico] *s.* característica natural de la superficie de la tierra, como una isla, montaña o meseta. (pág. 10)

latitude [latitud] *s.* distancia norte-sur con respecto al ecuador. (pág. 16)

legalism [legalismo] *s.* creencia de que un soberano debe utilizar el sistema legal para obligar a las personas a obedecer las leyes. (pág. 259)

legend [leyenda] *s.* narración popular transmitida desde épocas remotas, que puede creerse verdadera pero no puede ser probada. (pág. 431)

linen [lino] *s.* tela tejida con fibras provenientes de la planta de lino. (pág. 149)

longitude [longitud] *s.* distancia este-oeste a partir del primer meridiano. (pág. 16)

M

maize [maíz] *s.* cereal cultivado por las civilizaciones nativas americanas, cuyos granos se encuentran en mazorcas. (pág. 308)

Mandate of Heaven [Mandato del Cielo] *s.* antigua creencia china que postulaba que la autoridad real era producto de la aprobación divina. (pág. 256)

Marathon [Maratón] *s.* llanura en la antigua Grecia, al noreste de Atenas. (pág. 382)

Maya [mayas] *s.* civilización del sur de México y norte de América Central, que alcanzó su máximo esplendor desde el año 250 hasta el año 900 d.C. (pág. 307)

mercenary [mercenario] *s.* soldado contratado para prestar servicio en un ejército. (pág. 496)

Meroë *s.* capital del reino de Kush desde aproximadamente 590 a.C., ubicada en el Nilo y con acceso a las rutas comerciales así como al oro y al hierro. (pág. 192)

Meso-America [Mesoamérica] *s.* región que se extiende hacia el sudeste desde México central y comprende países como Guatemala, El Salvador, Belice y parte de Honduras y Nicaragua. (pág. 292)

Mesolithic Age [Mesolítico] *s.* Edad de Piedra Media: período que duró desde alrededor del año 10.000 hasta el año 6000 a.C., durante el cual el ser humano comenzó a controlar el fuego y a desarrollar el lenguaje. (pág. 32)

Mesopotamia *s.* área del suroeste asiático entre los ríos Tigris y Éufrates, cuna de muchas civilizaciones antiguas. (pág. 83)

Messiah [Mesías] *s.* salvador y rey que predicen los profetas judíos. (pág. 338)

migration [migración] *s.* acción de mudarse de una región o país a otro. (págs. 52, 206)

missionary [misionero] *s.* persona que viaja a otros países para diseminar sus creencias religiosas. (pág. 479)

Moche *s.* antigua cultura que habitó en lo que hoy es la costa norte del Perú entre los años 100 y 700 d.C. (pág. 298)

Monotheism [monoteísmo] *s.* creencia en la existencia de un solo dios. (pág. 326)

monsoon [monzón] *s.* viento de estación que produce un período húmedo o seco en una región, especialmente en el sur asiático. (pág. 220)

mosaic [mosaico] *s.* pintura creada a partir de pequeños trozos coloreados de piedra u otro material. (pág. 515)

Moses [Moisés] *s.* según la Biblia, profeta que condujo a los israelitas fuera de Egipto y les entregó las Tablas de la Ley. (pág. 327)

mother culture [cultura madre] *s.* cultura que modela e influye las costumbres e ideas de culturas más recientes. (pág. 303)

mummy [momia] *s.* cuerpo de un humano o animal que ha sido conservado y disecado para evitar que se descomponga. (pág. 160)

myth [mito] *s.* relato que explica creencias, prácticas o fenómenos naturales, con frecuencia protagonizado por dioses y diosas u otros seres sobrenaturales. (pág. 362)

N

Nazca *s.* antigua cultura que surgió cerca de lo que hoy es la costa sur de Perú y prosperó desde el año 200 a.C. hasta el año 600 d.C. (pág. 296)

Neolithic Age [Neolítico] *s.* Nueva Edad de Piedra: Período que duró desde alrededor del año 8000 hasta el año 3000 a.C. y se caracterizó por el comienzo de la agricultura y el desarrollo de la alfarería y el tejido. (pág. 32)

nirvana *s.* en el budismo y el hinduismo, estado de sabiduría que rompe el ciclo de la reencarnación. (pág. 234)

Nok *s.* antigua civilización africana en lo que hoy es el sudeste de Nigeria, caracterizada por la fabricación de herramientas de hierro. (pág. 205)

nomad [nómada] *s.* miembro de un grupo de personas que no tienen hogar fijo y se mudan de un lugar a otro. (págs. 52, 502)

Nubia *s.* antigua región de África, que se extiende desde la frontera sur de Egipto hasta lo que hoy es Sudán. (pág. 189)

O

obelisk [obelisco] *s.* monumento en forma de pilar de cuatro caras que termina en una punta con forma de pirámide. (pág. 174)

oligarchy [oligarquía] *s.* gobierno controlado por una minoría, para el cual la base del poder es a menudo la riqueza. (pág. 373)

Olmec [olmeca] *s.* la cultura mesoamericana más antigua que se conoce, que floreció entre el año 1200 y el año 400 a.C. y se centró en la costa sur del golfo de México. (pág. 301)

Olympics [Olimpíada] *s.* festival de la antigua Grecia en honor del dios Zeus, que se llevaba a cabo cada cuatro años y presentaba competencias atléticas y poéticas. (pág. 363)

Olympus, Mount [Olimpo, monte] *s.* montaña más alta de Grecia; en la mitología griega, hogar de los dioses y diosas más importantes. (pág. 361)

oracle bone [hueso de oráculo] *s.* hueso de animal o caparazón de tortuga que utilizaban los reyes Shang de China para comunicarse con los dioses e influenciarlos. (pág. 255)

oral history [historia oral] *s.* narración verbal no escrita de un acontecimiento. (pág. 41)

oratory [oratoria] *s.* arte de hablar en público. (pág. 516)

P

Paleolithic Age [Paleolítico] *s.* Antigua Edad de Piedra: período que duró desde el año 2,5 millones hasta el año 8000 a.C. y se caracterizó por el uso de herramientas simples de piedra por parte de los primeros seres humanos. (pág. 32)

papyrus [papiro] *s.* material parecido al papel realizado con hojas de la planta de papiro y que los antiguos egipcios utilizaban para escribir. (pág. 158)

parable [parábola] *s.* narración simple que transmite una enseñanza religiosa o moral. (pág. 468)

Parthenon [Partenón] *s.* templo de la diosa griega Atenea, construido en el siglo V a.C. en la acrópolis de Atenas. (pág. 396)

patrician [patricio] *s.* miembro de una familia adinerada y hacendada que ocupaba los puestos más importantes del gobierno en la antigua Roma. (pág. 437)

Paul [Pablo] *s.* el más importante de los apóstoles que divulgaba las enseñanzas de Jesús. (pág. 479)

Pax Romana *s.* largo período de estabilidad y paz en el Imperio Romano que comenzó con el reinado e Augusto y durante el cual el imperio creció hasta alcanzar su máxima dimensión. (pág. 447)

Peloponnesian War [guerra del Peloponeso] *s.* guerra entre Atenas y la Liga del Peloponeso, liderada por Esparta, que terminó con la victoria de Esparta en el año 404 a.C. (pág. 400)

Peloponnesus [Peloponeso] *s.* península que forma la parte sur de Grecia. (pág. 355)

peninsula [península] *s.* masa de tierra conectada a otra tierra de mayor extensión y rodeada de agua en tres de sus lados. (págs. 355, 433)

Pericles *s.* líder de la antigua Atenas que se propuso reforzar la democracia y expandir el imperio ateniense. (pág. 393)

persecute [perseguir] *v.* oprimir u hostigar. (pág. 478)

pharaoh [faraón] *s.* antiguo rey egipcio. (pág. 166)

philosophy [filosofía] *s.* investigación de las verdades básicas del universo, basada en razonamiento lógico. (págs. 259, 414)

Phoenician [fenicio] *s.* miembro de un pueblo comerciante que vivió en las costas orientales del Mediterráneo. (pág. 358)

physical map [mapa físico] *s.* mapa que muestra relieves y masas de agua. (pág. 20)

Piankhi *s.* rey de Kush alrededor del año 750 a.C., que ganó control de casi todo Egipto, se convirtió en faraón y unificó los dos reinos. (pág. 190)

pictograph [pictografía] *s.* fotografía o dibujo que representa una palabra o una idea en un antiguo sistema de escritura. (págs. 101, 255)

plague [plaga] *s.* enfermedad a menudo mortal que se expande fácilmente y que afecta a una gran parte de la población. (pág. 401)

planned city [ciudad planificada] *s.* ciudad construida según un diseño establecido. (pág. 221)

plebeian [plebeyo] *s.* ciudadano corriente en la antigua Roma, que tenía derecho de voto pero no a ocupar puestos importantes de gobierno. (pág. 437)

plunder [saquear] *v.* tomar posesión de algo por la fuerza. (pág. 504)

polis *s.* ciudad central de una ciudad estado en la antigua Grecia, como por ejemplo Atenas o Esparta. (pág. 371)

political map [mapa político] *s.* mapa que muestra características creadas por el hombre, como ciudades, estados, provincias, territorios y países. (pág. 19)

polytheism [politeísmo] *s.* creencia en muchos dioses o diosas. (pág. 93)

pope [papa] *s.* obispo de Roma y jefe de la Iglesia Católica Romana. (pág. 485)

primary source [fuente primaria] *s.* relato de un acontecimiento histórico narrado por una persona que lo presenció. (pág. 40)

prophet [profeta] *s.* guía espiritual que transmite las palabras y deseos de Dios o de un dios. (pág. 338)

province [provincia] *s.* subdivisión de un imperio o país. (pág. 132)

pyramid [pirámide] *s.* estructura con cuatro lados triangulares que convergen en un punto. (pág. 166)

Q

Qin *s.* estado de la antigua China. (pág. 267)

R

rabbi [rabino] *s.* líder y maestro religioso formado en las leyes, los rituales y las tradiciones judías. (pág. 346)

Ramses II [Ramsés II] *s.* faraón que gobernó Egipto durante 66 años, y que expandió enormemente el imperio egipcio al conquistar territorios vecinos. (pág. 175)

reincarnation [reencarnación] *s.* renacimiento de un alma en otro cuerpo. (pág. 230)

religion [religión] *s.* veneración de un dios, dioses o espíritus. (pág. 54)

Remus [Remo] *s.* hermano gemelo de Rómulo. (pág. 432)

republic [república] *s.* forma de gobierno en la cual los ciudadanos eligen a sus líderes y representantes. (pág. 432)

resurrection [resurrección] *s.* vuelta a la vida después de la muerte. (pág. 470)

Roman Catholic Church [Iglesia Católica Romana] *s.* rama del cristianismo que se encuentra bajo la autoridad del papa. (pág. 511)

Romulus [Rómulo] *s.* héroe legendario, descendiente de Eneas, que fue fundador de Roma. (pág. 431)

Royal Road [Camino Real] *s.* camino para el uso del gobierno construido por el antiguo monarca persa Darío, que ayudó a unificar el imperio. (pág. 132)

S

satrap [sátrapa] *s.* gobernador de una provincia en el antiguo imperio persa. (pág. 132)

scribe [escriba] *s.* persona especializada en escribir y archivar documentos. (págs. 102, 155)

secondary source [fuente secundaria] *s.* relato de un acontecimiento histórico realizado por una persona que no presenció los hechos. (pág. 41)

semiarid [semiárido] *adj.* con poca lluvia y altas temperaturas. (pág. 84)

senate [senado] *s.* cuerpo gubernamental de la antigua Roma, formado por 300 miembros que asesoraban a los líderes romanos. (pág. 438)

Shi Huangdi *s.* soberano chino que asumió el poder en el año 221 a.C. y unificó y expandió la China al acabar con batallas internas y conquistar estados rivales. (pág. 267)

Siddhartha Gautama *s.* príncipe indio fundador del Budismo, también conocido como Buda. (pág. 233)

Silk Roads [Ruta de la seda] *s.* rutas comerciales terrestres por las cuales la seda y otras mercancías chinas pasaban hacia la Mesopotamia y Europa. (pág. 277)

silt [limo] *s.* tierra fina y fértil depositada por un río. (págs. 84, 147)

slash-and-burn [tala y quema] *adj.* tipo de agricultura que consiste en talar y quemar la vegetación natural para obtener parcelas de tierra para el cultivo. (págs. 60, 293)

smelting [fundición] *s.* calentamiento y fundición de ciertas rocas para separar los metales que contienen. (pág. 192)

social class [clase social] *s.* grupo de personas que comparten las mismas costumbres, orígenes, formación y nivel de ingresos. (pág. 67)

Solomon [Salomón] *s.* tercer rey de Israel que transformó su estado en una nación poderosa. (pág. 336)

Sparta [Esparta] *s.* ciudad estado de la antigua Grecia en el Peloponeso, caracterizada por su militarismo. (pág. 379)

specialization [especialización] *s.* habilidad para un tipo de trabajo. (pág. 66)

stele [estela] *s.* losa esculpida de piedra clavada en el suelo, generalmente en conmemoración de una persona o acontecimiento. (pág. 309)

step pyramid [pirámide escalonada] *s.* pirámide cuyos lados se elevan en una serie de escalones gigantes. (pág. 167)

stylus [estilo] *s.* punzón afilado utilizado para hacer marcas en lápidas de barro. (pág. 102)

subcontinent [subcontinente] *s.* gran extensión de tierra que forma parte de un continente pero se considera como un accidente geográfico separado. (pág. 219)

succession [sucesión] *s.* orden en el cual los miembros de una familia real heredan un trono o título. (pág. 165)

Sumer [Sumeria] *s.* antigua región del sur de la Mesopotamia, donde surgieron civilizaciones alrededor del año 3300 a.C. (pág. 89)

surplus [excedente] *s.* cantidad producida en exceso de lo que se necesita. (págs. 65, 86)

synagogue [sinagoga] *s.* edificio de culto y oración de los judíos, donde se enseña la fe judía. (pág. 346)

T

technology [tecnología] *s.* aplicación del conocimiento, herramientas e invenciones del ser humano para satisfacer sus necesidades. (pág. 53)

Ten Commandments [Diez Mandamientos] *s.* base de la ley de los israelitas que, según el Torah, Dios entregó a Moisés. (pág. 327)

terrace [terraza] *s.* zona elevada en la ladera de una colina. (pág. 200)

textile [textil] *s.* tela tramada o tejida. (pág. 296)

thematic map [mapa temático] *s.* mapa que representa un tipo específico de información sobre un lugar o región. (pág. 21)

toleration [tolerancia] *s.* práctica de dejar que los demás vivan según sus costumbres y creencias. (pág. 131)

tragedy [tragedia] *s.* forma de teatro serio que representa la caída o la ruina del personaje o personajes principales. (pág. 412)

trans-Eurasian [trans-euroasiático] *adj.* relativo a los continentes de Europa y Asia. (pág. 277)

tribute [tributo] *s.* pago de dinero o mercancías por parte de un monarca a otro a cambio de protección. (pág. 120)

Trinity [Trinidad] *s.* unión de tres personas (el Padre, el Hijo y el Espíritu Santo) en un solo Dios. (pág. 486)

tropical *adj.* con clima cálido y lluvioso. (pág. 290)

truce [tregua] *s.* acuerdo temporal de detener una pelea. (pág. 401)

tyrant [tirano] *s.* soberano que ha tomado el poder en forma ilegal y que gobierna sin restricciones. (pág. 373)

V

vault [bóveda] *s.* arco que forma un cielorraso o techo. (pág. 517)

vegetation [vegetación] *s.* vida vegetal de un área. (pág. 12)

Y

Yucatán Peninsula [península de Yucatán] *s.* zona de selva densa en el sudeste mexicano, que se extiende hacia el golfo de México y el mar Caribe. (pág. 292)

Z

Zeus *s.* dios supremo en la mitología griega. (pág. 361)

ziggurat [zigurat] *s.* antiguo templo sumerio o babilónico construido en una serie de niveles escalonados. (pág. 92)

Index

An *i* preceding an italic page reference indicates that there is an illustration, and usually text information as well, on that page. An *m* or a *c* preceding an italic page reference indicates a map or chart, as well as text information on that page.

Socrates, *i414*, 415, *i415*
philosophy, 259
Chinese, 259–263, 278
Greek, 414–415
Phoenicians, 358–359
physical map, 20, *i20*
Piankhi (Kushite king), *cl84*, 190–191, *i191*, *c249*
pictographs, 101, *cl07*, 222, 255, *i255*
plague, 401
planned cities, 221
plate movement, 10
plateau, 10
Plato, *i414*, 415
plebeians, 437
plunder, 504
Plutarch, 380
political ideas
direct democracy, 381, 394
of Hammurabi's Code, 115–116
political map, 19, *i19*
political systems. *See also* democracy; government.
democracy, 393, *c395*, 414
direct democracy, 381, 394
republic, 432
polytheism, 93, 160. *See also* monotheism.
pope(s), 485
population(s)
of Africa, *m45*
pottery, 101 *See also* art; sculpture.
of early humans, 66, *i66*
Hungarian, *i58*
invention of, 105, *i105*
Moche, *i298*
Nubian, *i188*
priests
early, 66
Brahmin, R67, *iR67*
Egyptian, 156, *cl56*
primary source, 40, *i41*, 68, *i68*
prime meridian, 18
Prodigal Son, 468, 472, 474–475
Prometheus, 362
Promised Land, 328
prophets, 338
province, 132
Ptolemy, 22, *i23*, 416
Punic Wars, 440, *m440*
pyramids, 166
comparison of, *cl83*
Egyptian, 140–141, *i140–141*, *cl42*, *il43*, 163, *i163*, 165, *i165*, *i167*, *i168*
Mayan, *i307*, 310, *i310*

Q

Qin Dynasty, 266, 267–268, 271, 272–275, 283
Queen Hatshepsut. *See* Hatshepsut.

quetzal bird, *i288*
Qur'an, R68–R69

R

rabbis, 346, R71, *iR71*
Ramayana, *i242*
Ramses II (Ramses the Great), *cl43*, *il43*, 144–145, *i144*, 175–177, *i176*, 182–183
reincarnation, 230
religion, 54, R60–R61. *See also* Buddhism; Christianity; Hinduism; Judaism.
of Aryans, 229
of early humans, 54
Egyptian, 156, 159–160, 175
of India, 229–235, 241
spread of Indian, 241–242
religious beliefs. *See also* religion.
of ancient China, 248
animism, 205
comparison of, *cR76*
Mayan, 309
world population, *cR60–R61*, *mR60–R61*
religious symbolism
of Buddhism, R63, *iR63*
of Confucianism, R73, *iR73*
cross as, *i466*, 484, R65, *iR65*
of Hinduism, R67, *iR67*
of Islam, R69, *iR69*
of Judiasm, R71, *iR71*
Remus, 431
republic, 432
Republic, The (Plato), 415
resurrection, 470
rift valley, 30, *i30*
river valley, 61
roads. *See* Roman Empire, roads in; Royal Road; Silk Roads.
Roman Catholic Church. *See also* church.
beginnings, 485–486
beliefs, 486
and fall of Roman Empire, 511
Roman Empire, 443–449
agriculture, 448
ancient, 424, *m426–427*
aqueducts, 457, 517, *i517*
art and architecture, 456, *i456–457*, 515–516, *i515*, 517, 520, *i520*
Augustus, 446–447, *i447*
beginnings, *c426–427*, 431–432
Christianity in, *c462–463*, *m462–463*, 483–486, 518
cities of, 456–457
civil wars, 497
currency, 449
daily life in, 453–458
decline of, *c490–491*, 495–498, *c504*

Eastern, 497, 501
economy, 448–449
Etruscan influence on, 455
expansion of, 443–449, 450–451, 460–461
fall of, 500–505, *c506*, 506–507, *i507*
family life in, 453
forts, 450, *i450–451*
geographic borders, 427, 448, 490–491
gladiators, 458
gods of, 455, *c455*, *i455*
government of, 496, 515–519
Greek influence on, 455
invasions into, 502, *m503*
Julius Caesar, 428–429, 444–446, *i444*
Latin language in, *c489*, *c516*
legacy of, 439, 441, 514–519, 520–521, 522–523
military force, 447
reasons for expansion of, 426–427, 440–441, 443–449, 450–451, 460–461
reforms in, 443, 446
religion in, 454–455, 518, 521
roads, 518, *i518*, 521, *i521*
silk roads during, 276, 277–279, 280, 281, 282
slavery in, 454
social classes, 454
sports, 458
trade, 448, *m448*
Western, 497, 501
Roman Republic, *c249*, 436–441, 460–461
civil wars, 444
early society, 437
expansion of, 440–441
government of, 428–429, 437–439, *i438*, *c439*
legacy of, 438
social classes, 437
Rome. *See also* Roman Empire; Roman Republic
beginnings, 431
early farming, 434–435
founding of, 432
geography, 431–435
location, 433
Seven Hills of, *m432*
Romulus, 431
Rosetta Stone, 41, *i41*
Royal Road, *ml30*, 132
Ruth, 322–323, 335

S

St. Paul the Apostle, 479–481, *i480*, R65
Epistles, 480
Sahara, *c78*

Index of Skills

Chronological and Spatial Thinking

chronological order/sequence, 172, 177, 188, 193, 243, 334, 339, 421, 442, 466, 471, 500, 505. *See also* Reading and Critical Thinking: chronological order/sequence.

creating charts, graphs, diagrams, 8, 14, 26, 38, 50, 56, 57, 58, 64, 73, 82, 87, 88, 98, 118, 128, 146, 154, 164, 196, 202, 207, 218, 225, 226, 232, 240, 252, 258, 266, 265, 276, 280, 288, 294, 300, 306, 324, 342, 354, 360, 378, 392, 398, 404, 410, 430, 436, 452, 458, 476, 482, 487, 494, 506, 507, 508, 514

creating maps, 23, 55, 133, 193, 209, 271, 281, 293, 329, 359, 397, 449, 481, 523

creating murals, posters, 12, 13, 33, 62, 69, 95, 107, 137, 183, 239, 243, 247, 283, 311, 349, 383, 387, 461, 465

economic/trading systems, 13, 124, 182, 194–195, 224, 246, 280, 386, 426, 460, 490

expansion and disintegration, 13, 133, 200, 296, 449, 450–451, 460, 505

interpreting visuals/graphics, 10, 54, 84, 156, 194–195, 204, 220, 297, 303, 310, 316, 433, 439, 455, 456–457, 461

interpreting/reading maps, 12, 13, 19, 20, 21, 23, 44, 45, 52, 61, 94, 96–97, 120, 130, 148, 169, 174, 190, 194–195, 198, 206, 228, 237, 247, 269, 278–279, 283, 290, 291, 292, 296, 299, 301, 308, 315, 337, 345, 356, 377, 382, 387, 401, 407, 409, 432, 440, 448, 471, 503, 511, 523

migration, 13, 52, 193, 207, 208, 228, 246, 388

relating events, 12, 23, 170, 243, 505

time lines, 96, 172, 177, 188, 193, 334, 339, 340–341, 421, 442, 449, 466, 486, 500, 505

using historical documents, 13, 41, 68, 69, 102, 115, 159, 199, 230, 231, 239, 244–245, 261, 327, 349, 380, 400, 445, 469. See also Research, Evidence and Point of View evaluating information; primary sources; secondary sources.

Research, Evidence and Point of View

context, 397, 417, 471

credibility of sources. See primary sources; secondary sources.

evaluating information, 44, 314, 365

fact vs. opinion, 43. *See also* Reading and Critical Thinking: forming and supporting opinions.

framing historical questions, 43, 44, 45, 224, 519

point of view/perspective, 6–7

primary sources, 41, 43, 44, 68, 102, 115, 159, 199, 224, 230, 231, 239, 244–245, 261, 303, 327, 349, 365, 380, 400, 445, 469, 481, 506–507

secondary sources, 43, 44, 57, 224, 239, 265, 341, 365, 506–507

Historical Interpretation

analyzing political issues, 359, 387, 395, 397, 418–419, 420, 460, 522, 523

causal relationship, 12, 23, 24–25, 243, 365, 366–369, 383, 458, 505. *See also* Reading and Critical Thinking: cause and effect.

cause and effect, 12, 23, 24–25, 58, 62, 72, 86, 95, 106, 107, 118, 123, 151, 161, 183, 207, 209, 224, 246, 257, 280, 283, 304, 311, 314, 324, 329, 354, 359, 383, 387, 402, 404, 409, 420, 435, 436, 441, 449, 481, 486, 494, 523. *See also* Reading and Critical Thinking: cause and effect.

chance and error, 417

correlation, 24–25, 161

cost-benefit analysis, 217

economic performance, 104–105, 151, 208, 418–419, 449, 450–451, 460, 500, 522, 523

geographic patterns/factors, 10, 13, 44, 61, 78, 84, 86, 87, 94, 106, 116, 120, 124–127, 130, 142, 148, 169, 174, 182, 190, 194–195, 198, 202, 204, 206, 207, 208, 220, 225, 228, 237, 246, 252, 257, 269, 278–279, 282, 288, 290, 291, 292, 293, 296, 297, 301, 308, 314, 329, 337, 345, 348, 356, 359, 382, 386, 387, 388, 401, 407, 418–419, 432, 433, 440, 448, 450–451, 460, 488, 503, 511. *See also* Chronological and Spatial Thinking: interpreting maps.

historical continuity/patterns, 11, 24–25, 33, 44, 59, 83, 85, 95, 104–105, 107, 121, 132, 133, 137, 149, 162–163, 167, 178–181, 183, 189, 191, 231, 234, 235, 244–245, 246, 260, 262, 271, 277, 281, 300, 311, 335, 336, 358, 363, 366–369, 387, 393, 394, 409, 417, 418–419, 420, 434, 441, 443, 447, 458, 460, 467, 483, 485, 494, 501, 505, 510, 513, 520–521

interpretation changes with technological changes, 34–37, 43, 44, 55, 72, 103, 105, 106, 151, 193, 208, 280, 282, 284, 293, 314, 505

interpretation, 33, 159, 231

issues and problems (identifying), 33, 86, 116, 128, 131, 133, 182, 200, 208, 299, 304, 305, 348, 417, 420, 460, 471, 513

sequence, 24–25, 172, 177, 188, 193, 243, 334, 339, 421, 442, 466, 471, 500, 505. *See also* Reading and Critical Thinking: chronological order/sequence.

time and place, 31, 70–71, 86, 121, 152–153, 167, 178–181, 191, 234, 262, 312–313, 335, 348, 384–385, 394, 402, 417, 420, 447, 450–451, 471, 485, 510, 513

Reading and Critical Thinking

aloud, 48–49, 144–145

analysis, 80–81, 110–111, 216–217, 250–251, 264–265, 322–323, 330–333, 352–353, 390–391, 428–429, 464–465

anticipation, 284, 388

assessing sources, 231, 239, 365, 481

categorizing, 38, 43, 64, 69, 98, 103, 154, 161, 240, 243, 276, 280, 300, 304, 430, 435

Writing and Speaking

Acknowledgments

This product contains proprietary property of **MAPQUEST.COM**
Unauthorized use, including copying, of this product, is expressly prohibited.

Text Acknowledgments

LITERATURE CONNECTIONS

Chapter 1, page 34: Excerpt from *A Bone from a Dry Sea* by Peter Dickinson. Copyright © 1993 by Peter Dickinson. Used by permission of Dell Publishing, a division of Random House, Inc.

Chapter 8, page 272: Excerpt from *The Emperor's Silent Army* by Jane O'Connor. Copyright © 2002 by Jane O'Connor. Used by permission of Viking Penguin, a division of Penguin Young Readers Group, a member of Penguin Group (USA) Inc., 345 Hudson Street, New York, NY, 10014. All rights reserved.

Chapter 14, page 473: "The Parable of the Good Samaritan" and "The Prodigal Son," from *Everlasting Stories* by Lois Rock. Copyright © 2004 by Lois Rock. Used with permission of Chronicle Books LLC, San Francisco. Visit ChronicleBooks.com.

PRIMARY SOURCE HANDBOOK

Chapter 2, page R36: Excerpt from *The Man in the Ice* by Konrad Spindler, translated by Ewald Osers. Copyright © 1995 by Ewald Osers. Used by permission of Crown Publishers, a division of Random House, Inc.

Chapter 3, page R37: Excerpt from *The Epic of Gilgamesh*, translated by N. K. Sanders. Copyright © 1960, 1964, 1972 by N. K. Sanders. Used by permission of Penguin books, a division of Penguin Group (USA), Inc.

Chapter 7, page R41: Excerpts from *Bhagavad-Gita*, translated by Barbara Stoler Miller. Copyright © 1986 by Barbara Stoler Miller. Used by permission of Bantam Books, a division of Random House, Inc.

Chapter 8, page R42: Excerpts from *The Analects of Confucius*, translated by Simon Leys. Copyright © 1997 by Pierre Ryckmans. Reprinted by permission of W. W. Norton & Company, Inc.

Chapter 8, page R43: Excerpt from *Tao Te Ching: A New English Version with Foreword and Notes* by Stephen Mitchell. Translation copyright © 1988 by Stephen Mitchell. Used by permission of HarperCollins Publishers Inc.

Chapter 8, page R44: Excerpt from *Popul Vuh* by Dennis Tedlock. Copyright © 1985, 1996 by Dennis Tedlock. Reprinted with the permission of Simon & Schuster Adult Publishing Group.

Chapter 10, page R45: Excerpt from *The Bible Designed to Be Read as Living Literature: The Old and the New Testaments in the King James Version* by Ernest Sutherland Bates. Updated scholarship by Loddwick Allison. Copyright © 1936 by Simon & Schuster, Inc. Copyright renewed © 1964 by Simon & Schuster, Inc. Revised text copyright © 1993 by Loddwick Allison. Reprinted with the permission of Simon & Schuster Adult Publishing Group.

Chapter 11, page R51: "The Death of Hector," from *The Iliad* by Homer, translated by Robert Fagles. Copyright © 1990 by Robert Fagles. Used by permission of Viking Penguin, a division of Penguin Group (USA), Inc.

Chapter 11, page R54: "The Boy Who Flew," from *The Robber Baby: Stories from the Greek Myths* by Anne Rockwell. Copyright © 1994 by Anne Rockwell. Used by permission of HarperCollins Publishers Inc.

Chapter 12, page R56: Excerpt from "Pericles' Funeral Oration," from *History of the Peloponnesian War* by Thucydides, translated by Rex Warner. Copyright © 1934 by Rex Warner. Used by permission of Penguin Group (USA), Inc.

Chapter 13, page R57: Excerpt from *The Twelve Caesars*, translated by Robert Graves. Copyright © 1957 by Robert Graves. Used by permission of Carcanet Press Limited.

Chapter 14, page R58: "The Lost Sheep," from *Everlasting Stories* by Lois Rock. Copyright © 2001 by Lois Rock. Used with permission of Chronicle Books LLC, San Francisco. Visit ChronicleBooks.com.

The editors have made every effort to trace the ownership of all copyrighted material found in this book and to make full acknowledgment for its use. Omissions brought to our attention will be corrected in a subsequent edition.

Art and Photography Credits

COVER

Background El Castillo. Chichén Itzá, Yucatán, Mexico. Photo © Warren Marr/Panoramic Images/NGSImages.com; *top* Queen Nefertiti. Photo by Margarete Buesing/Staatliche Museen zu Berlin/Aegyptisches Museum *center left* Head of Buddah. © Christie's Images/Corbis; *center right* Giant Olmec head. © Danny Lehman/Corbis *bottom left* Statue of Athena. © Alinari/Bridgeman Art Library; *bottom center* Kuba mask. Private collection. Photo © Aldo Tutino/Art Resource, New York; *bottom right* Augustus coin. © Mimmo Jodice/Corbis.

FRONT MATTER

ii *top* Lucy skeleton. © Science Photo Library; *bottom* Aboriginal rock painting. © Penny Tweedie/Corbis; **iii** *top to bottom* Sitting woman holding a small vase. Louvre, Paris. Photo © Erich Lessing/Art Resource, New York; Detail of the Ishtar Gate. The Granger Collection, New York; Iranian valley. © Alamy Images; **iv** *top to bottom* Double crown illustration. © Wildlife Art Ltd.; Ngady Amwaash. National Museum, Ghana. Photo © Werner Forman/Art Resource, New York; Pyramids at Giza. © Alamy Images **v** *top to bottom* Shiva sculpture. © Burstein Collection/Corbis; Terracotta soldier on its side. O. Louis Mazzatenta/National Geographic Image Collection; Colossal Olmec head. © Jean-Pierre Courau/Bridgeman Art Library; **vi** *top to bottom* Fortress of Masada. © Nathan Benn/Corbis; Zeus on ceramic pot. © Réunion des Musées Nationaux/Art Resource, New York; Equestrian portrait of Alexander the Great in combat. Museo Archeologico Nazionale, Naples. Photo © Alinari/Art Resource, New York; **vii** *top to bottom* Cameo of Augustus Caesar (63 B.C.–A.D. 14). From the Treasury of Boscoreale near Pompeii. Louvre, Paris. Photo © Erich Lessing/Art Resource, New York; Reliquary cross of Justinian (A.D. 500–600). Museum of the Treasury, St. Peter's Basilica, Vatican State. Photo © Scala/Art Resource, New York; Roman aqueduct (1900–1800 B.C.). Pont du Gard, Nimes. Photo © SEF/Art Resource, New York.

UNIT 1

2-3 Stonehenge. Illustration by Roger Stewart; **3** *top* Paleolithic axe. The Granger Collection, New York; *bottom* Red bull wall painting. © James Mellaart.

Chapter 1

4 *top to bottom* Alfred Wegner. The Granger Collection, New York; Ancient footprint. © John Reader/Science Photo Library/Photo Researchers; Paleolithic hand ax. The Granger Collection, New York; **5** *left to right* Skull. © Science Photo Library/Photo Researchers; Small mask (Neolithic period) from Predionica, Kosovo. Terracotta. Muzej Kosova, Pristina, Serbia and Montenegro. © Erich Lessing/Art Resource, New York; **6** Lascaux bull. The Granger Collection, New York; **6-7** Lascaux cave. Illustration by Frank Ordaz; **8** Earth from space. © Science VU/NASA/Visuals Unlimited; **10** *top to bottom* San Francisco earthquake aftermath. © Bettmann/Corbis; Transform plates. Illustration by Roberta Polfus; **11** Key West Hurricane. AP/Wide World Photos; **13** Kids making geography poster. Photo by Sharon Hoogstraten; **14** Compass. © Science and Society Picture Library, London; **15** Globe with wooden stand. © Comstock Images/Alamy Images; **22** Historical map of early North America. The Granger Collection, New York; **23** Bust of Ptolemy (geographer, astronomer, mathematician) from the choir stalls of Ulm Cathedral (Alexandria, A.D. 100–200). Cathedral, Ulm, Germany. © Erich Lessing/Art Resource, New York; **24** *left to right* Sextant. © DK Images, Dorling Kindersley Ltd.; Ship by stars. The Granger Collection, New York; **25** *top to bottom* Galileo satellite. © Science Photo Library/Photo Researchers; Car with GPS. © Comstock/Alamy Images; Kid with GPS watch. AP/Wide World Photos; **26** Hominid footprint. © John Reader/Science Photo Library/Photo Researchers; **27** Archeological dig. © Richard T. Nowitz/Corbis; **30** Rift valley. Christophe Ratier/NHPA/Photo Researchers; **31** Lucy skeleton. © Science Photo Library/Photo Researchers; **32** *top to bottom* Anthropomorphic figurine (20,000–18,000 B.C.). Maininsk settlement, Siberia. Photo © The State Hermitage Museum; Neolithic idol (3,000–2,000 B.C.). Usvyaty IV settlement, Pskov region. Photo © The State Hermitage Museum; **33** Australopithecine skull. © Gallo Images/Corbis; **34** *foreground* Magnifying glass. © Getty Images; **34-35** *background* Dusting brush, nail, tape measure. Photo by Sharon Hoogstraten; **35** *right* Trowel. © Dr. Michael B. Collins/Texas Archeological Research Laboratory; **36** Hominid fossils. National Museum of Ethiopia © 1999 Tim D. White/Brill Atlanta; **37** Notebook, note card, shovel handle. Photo by Sharon Hoogstraten; **38** Cave paintings. National Geographic Image Collection; **39** Griot Jeli playing the bolon. Kerouane, Guinea. © David C. Conrad; **40** *left to right* Paleolithic ax. The Granger Collection, New York; Neolithic ax. The Granger Collection, New York; Bronze age ax. The Granger Collection, New York; **41** Rosetta Stone. The Granger Collection, New York; **42** Burial chamber of King Tutankhamen. Tomb of Tutankhamen, Valley of the Kings, Thebes, Egypt. © Scala/Art Resource, New York; **44** Icons. Illustrations by Robert Coleman.

Chapter 2

46 Cavemen during the Ice Age (1800-1899), W. Kranz, after a sketch by Professor Klaatsch. Bibliothèque des Arts Decoratifs, Paris. Photo © Archives Charmet/Bridgeman Art Library; **47** *left to right* Glacier. © Photo Researchers, Inc.; Bronze deer. © ARPL/Topham/The Image Works; Agricultural tool. © The British Museum/Topham–HIP/The Image Works; **48** *inset* Discovery of the Ice Man. © Sygma/Corbis; **48-49** Hunters in the Alps. Illustration by Frank Ordaz; **50** *top to bottom* Man using spear thrower. Illustration by Steve Cowden; Paleolithic spear-thrower with the form of a horse, called "au cheval sautant" (14,000–13,000 B.C.). Carved wood, 28 cm long. MAN 82722. Photo: Jean Schormans. © Réunion des Musées Nationaux/Art Resource, New York; **51** African savanna. © Image Bank/Getty Images; **53** *left to right* Mattock (antler digging tool). © Museum of London/Topham–HIP/The Image Works; Three harpoons used for spearing fish (4,000 B.C.). Bone, early Neolithic. Collections of IDAM. Photo © Erich Lessing/Art Resource, New York; Ax. Museum of London/Topkan–HF/The Image Works; **54** *top to bottom* Native American cave painting. Photo © 2004 Doak Heyser; Australian cave painting. Photo © Pam Gardner/Frank Lane Picture Agency/Corbis; **55** Stag antler headdress. Photo © 2000 The British Museum; **57** Rock painting of animals (produced since the Later Stone Age, probably by the ancestors of Sandawe hunter gatherers still living in the region). The animals predicting may be the favoured game of hunters or hallucinations seen during the shamanistic trance dancing known as simbo. Tanzania National Museum, Dar es Salaam, Tanzania. Photo © Werner Forman/Art Resource, New York; **58** God with a sickle and female idol, both seated on throne-like chairs (4,000–3,000 B.C.). Neolithic sculpture. Tizsa culture, from Szigvar-Tuzkoves and Koekenydomb, Hungary. Koszta Josef Museum, Szentes, Hungary. Photo © Erich Lessing/Art Resource, New York; **59** Sheep grazing landscape in Andes. © Dave Wilhelm/Corbis; **63** Girl growing plants. Photo by Sharon Hoogstraten. **64** Brooch. Photo © The Museum of London/Topham–HIP/The Image Works; **65** Atlas mountains farming village. © Ben Mangor/SuperStock, Inc.; **66-67** Pottery jar (1850–1550 B.C.), 12.6 cm high, and necklace (1850–1550 B.C.) made of 31 white and brown biconical beads, quartz, 22 cm long, from the Bethlehem area. Canaanite, Bronze Age. Reuben and Edith Hecht Collection, Haifa University, Haifa, Israel. Photo © Erich Lessing/Art Resource, New York; **68** *top to bottom* Seal. Photo © James Mellaart; Dagger. Photo © James Mellaart; **69** Bull wall painting. Photo © James Mellaart; **70-71** Catal Hyuk. Illustrations by Inklink, Florence/Virgil Pomfret; **72** Icons. Illustrations by Robert Coleman.

UNIT 2

76-77 Ishtar Gate. Illustration by Inklink, Florence/Virgil Pomfret; **77** *top to bottom* Golden helmet from Ur (2450 B.C.). Early dynastic. Iraq Museum, Baghdad, Iraq. Photo © Scala/Art Resource, New York; Orant of Larsa, probably Hammurabi (1792-1750 B.C.), law-giver and sixth king of the Amorite dynasty of Babylon. From Larsa. Bronze, face and hands gold-plated. Louvre, Paris. Photo © Erich Lessing/Art Resource, New York.

Chapter 3

78 *top to bottom* Urn decorated in red (Proto-literate period). Terracotta. From Tell Agrab, Iraq. Iraq Museum, Baghdad, Iraq. Photo © Scala/Art Resource, New York; Sahara desert © Photowood, Inc./Corbis; **79** *top to bottom* Calculation of the surface area of a terrain at Umma, Mesopotamia (Iraq) (2100 B.C.). Clay tablet. Sumerian. Louvre, Paris. Photo © Erich Lessing/Art Resource, New York; Mohenjo Daro. © Paul Springett/Alamy Images; **80** *inset* Wheat. © Creatas/PictureQuest; **80-81** Drought. Illustration by Gino D'Achille/Artist Partners; **82** Bull in a Thicket. © The Art Archive/British Museum; **83** Euphrates River. © Alamy Images; **84** Ancient irrigation systems. Illustration by Peter Bull; **85** Reed house. © Jane Sweeney/Lonely Planet Images; **87** Boy making a diagram. Photo by Sharon Hoogstraten; **88** Two gypsum statuettes with folded hands. Male figure, height: 72 cm, Nr. 19752. Female figure, height: 59 cm, Nr. 19751. Eshnunna (Tel Asmar), from the temple carre of the God Abu. Sumerian. Iraq Museum, Baghdad, Iraq. Photo © Erich Lessing/Art Resource, New York; **89** Ruins of Ur. © David Lees/Corbis; **90** Gudea, King of Lagash (2120 B.C.). Sumerian dolerite sculpture. Louvre, Paris. Photo © Scala/Art Resource, New York; **91** *top to bottom* Golden helmet from Ur (2450 B.C.). Early dynastic. Iraq Museum, Baghdad, Iraq. Photo © Scala/Art Resource, New York; Sumerian bronze sword. © 2000 The British Museum; **92-93** Ziggurat. Illustration by Luigi Galante; **95** Sumerian ring (about 3,000 B.C.). Tello-Lagash, Mesopotamia. Louvre, Paris. Photo © Réunion des Musées Nationaux/Art Resource, New York; **97** Cuneiform. © Araldo de Luca/Corbis; **98** Sumerian woman holding a vase. © Erich Lessing/Art Resource, New York; **99** Standard of Ur (2600–2400 B.C.). © The British Museum. **100** Reconstruction of Sumerian wheel. Deutsches Museum, Munich, Germany. Photo © SEF/Art Resource, New York; **101** *top to bottom* Figure of a god on top of a foundation nail (about 2140 B.C.). Male head, perhaps a member of the family of King Gudea of Lagash. Black diorite. Louvre, Paris. Photo © Erich Lessing/Art Resource, New York; Sumerian cuneiform tablet. © Araldo de Luca/Corbis; **102** Cuneiform tablet. © David Lees/Corbis; **103** Assyrian scribe. The Granger Collection, New York; **104** *top to bottom* Sumerian plowing scene. © Ashmolean Museum, Oxford; Farmer plowing field. © Sylvain Saustier/Corbis; **105** *top, left to right* Royal Game of Ur. © 2000 The British Museum; Checkers. Photo by Sharon Hoogstratten; *bottom, top to bottom* Mitannian pottery jar (about 1370–1270 B.C.). Photo © The British Museum/Topham-HIP/The Image Works; Teen using potters wheel. © Tom Stewart/Corbis; **106** Icons. Illustrations by Robert Coleman.

Chapter 4

108 *left to right* Large circular seal with mythical animal from Mohenjo-Daro. Yellow steatite. National Museum of Pakistan, Karachi, Pakistan. Photo © Borromeo/Art Resource, New York; Diorite bust, called the Head of Hammurabi (about 1800 B.C.). Louvre, Paris. Photo © Chuzeville/Réunion des Musées Nationaux/Art Resource, New York (Inv. SB 95); **109** *left to right* Western Zhou dynasty square ding. Bronze. © Asian Art and Archaeology, Inc./Corbis; Ivory head of a woman, thought to be Mona Lisa (720 B.C.). Assyrian. Iraq Museum, Baghdad, Iraq. Photo © Scala/Art Resource, New York; Urn from Monte Alban. Zapotec culture. Museo Nacional de Antropología, Mexico City, D.F., Mexico. Photo © SEF/Art Resource, New York; **110** *inset* Model of a house (2900–2290 B.C.). Early dynastic. Terracotta. Akkadian. National Museum, Aleppo, Syria. Photo © Erich Lessing/Art Resource, New York; **110-111** Collapsed House. Illustration by Roger Stewart; **112** Male head with beard (Sargon), from Niniveh. Bronze or copper. Akkadian. Height, 36 cm. Inv. IM 11331. Iraq Museum, Baghdad, Iraq. Photo © Erich Lessing/Art Resource, New York; **113** Ruins of Uruk © Nik Wheeler/Corbis; **114** Orantes Larsa, probably Hammurabi, law-giver and sixth king of the Amorite dynasty of Babylon. From Larsa. Bronze, face and hands gold-plated. Louvre, Paris. Photo © Erich Lessing/Art Resource, New York; **115** Upper section of the stele of the law code of Hammurabi (about 1792–1750 B.C.). Diorite, from Babylon (found at Susa). First Babylonian dynasty. Louvre, Paris. Photo © Hervé Lewandowki/Réunion des Musées Nationaux/Art Resource, New York; **117** Boy and girl building a monument. Photo by Sharon Hoogstraten; **118** Tree pendant from Nimrud. © Bill Lyons Photography; **119** Capture of Hamann. © Erich Lessing/Art Resource, New York; **121** Palace of Nimrud. © Dagli Orti/The British Museum/The Art Archive; **122** Ishtar Gate (Processional Way) © Ruggero Vanni/Corbis; **123** Dragon detail of Ishtar Gate. The Granger Collection, New York; **126** Hanging gardens of Babylon. © DK Images. Dorling Kindersley, Ltd.; **128** Gold rhyton decorated with winged lion (400–200 B.C.). Achaemenid. Archaeological Museum, Teheran, Iran. Photo © Scala/Art Resource, New York; **129** Iranian valley. © Alamy Images; **131** Surrender of Lachish. © Dagli Orti/The British Museum/The Art Archive; **132** Ruins of ancient Persepolis. Photo © zefa/TH-Foto; **133** Persian coins. © The British Museum; **134-135** Court of Darius. Illustrations by Inklink, Florence/Virgil Pomfret; **136** Icons. Illustrations by Robert Coleman.

UNIT 3

140-141 Pyramid builders. Illustration by Angus McBride/Linden Artists, Ltd.; **141** *top to bottom* Sphinx. © Photodisc/Getty Images; Nok head (900 B.C.–A.D. 200). Courtesy Entwistle Gallery, London. Photo © Werner Forman/Art Resource, New York.

Chapter 5

142 *left to right* Harrappan elephant seal. The National Museum, Karachi. Photo © Dagli Orti/The Art Archive; The pyramids at Giza. Old Kingdom. Giza, Egypt. Photo © E. Strouhal and Werner Forman/Art Resource, New York; **143** *top counterclock-wise* The Great Sphinx. © Alamy Images; Step pyramid. © Carl and Ann Purcell/Corbis; Queen Hatshepsut's

R112 • ACKNOWLEDGMENTS

temple. © Alamy Images; King Ramses II's temple. © Alamy Images; *bottom* Olmec colossal head (1200–900 B.C.). Photo © Gianni Dagli Orti/Corbis; **144** *inset* Ramses stone head. © Michael Melford/Getty Images; 144-145 Death of Ramses II. Illustration by Bill Cigliano; **146** Lotus pendant. © Araldo de Luca/Archivio White Star; **147** The Nile valley. © G.J. Owen, Cambridge; **148** Nile delta. Photo provided by the SeaWiFS project/NASA/Goddard Space Flight Center and ORBIMAGE; **149** Shaduf. © H. Armstrong Roberts; 150-151 Nebamun Hunting Fowl (1425–1400 B.C.). Photo © Archivo Iconografico, S.A./Corbis; **151** Bracelet from the tomb of Djer (2920–2770 B.C.). Egyptian Museum, Cairo. Photo © Araldo De Luca/ Archivio White Star; 152-153 Nile river ship. Illustration by Inklink Firenze; **154** Egyptian mummified cat (Late period, 664–332 B.C.). Stuccoed and painted. Louvre, Paris. Photo © Art Resource, New York; **155** Temple at Luxor. © Tibor Bognar/Corbis; **156** Egyptian social roles. Illustration by Michael Jaroszko; **158** Seated scribe, 3/4 view (Egypt, Fifth Dynasty). Louvre, Paris. Photo © Chuzeville/Réunion des Musées Nationaux/Art Resource, New York; **159** Hieroglyph carving. © Roger Wood/Corbis; **160** Detail of Judgment of the Dead (1400–1300 B.C.). Photo © Historical Picture Archive/ Corbis; **161** Head of Anubis (1314–1085 B.C.). Louvre, Paris. Photo © Giraudon/Art Resource, New York; **162** Calendar tomb painting. The Metropolitan Museum of Art, Rogers Fund, 1948. Photo © 1979 The Metropolitan Museum of Art (48.105.52); **163** *clockwise from top left* Egyptian surgical instruments. Photo © Art Resource, New York; Laser surgery. © Corbis Images/PictureQuest; Stone pyramids. © Philip Coblentz/Brand X Pictures/PictureQuest; Glass pyramid. © Bill Ross/Corbis; **164** Ankh. © Araldo de Luca/Archivio White Star; **165** Pyramids. © Alamy Images; **166** Crown illustrations. © Wildlife Art Ltd.; **167** *top to bottom* Pyramid. © Corbis; Step pyramid. © Corbis; Khufu (Cheops) (Fourth Dynasty). Egyptian Museum, Cairo. Photo © Dagli Orti/The Art Archive; **168** Great pyramid of Khufu. © Alamy Images; **171** Paper pyramid/hand. Photo by Sharon Hoogstraten; **172** Gold mask of King Tutankhamen (Egypt, Eighteenth Dynasty). Egyptian Museum, Cairo, Egypt. © Scala/Art Resource, New York; **173** Queen Hatshepsut's temple. © Art Kowalsky/Alamy Images; **175** Bust of Nefertiti (thought to be an 1800–1900 copy of sculpture in the Egyptian Museum, Berlin). Museo Archeologico, Florence. Photo © Scala/Art Resource, New York; **176** Abu Simbel © Getty Images; **177** Bust of Cleopatra. © Bettmann/Corbis; **178** *inset* The Voyage to Punt: Sailors rowing (New Kingdom, Eighteenth Dynasty). Colored limestone relief, from the temple of Queen Hatshepsut (Maat Ka-Re) (1495–1475 B.C.), in Deir el-Bahri. Aegyptisches Museum, Staatliche Museen zu Berlin, Berlin, Germany. Photo © Erich Lessing/Art Resource, New York; **179** Portraits of Seninefer and Queen Hatshepsut (Eighteenth Dynasty, about 1479–1458 B.C.). Egypt. Painted plaster. Louvre, Paris. Photo © Scala/Art Resource, New York; 178-181 Water and palm trees. © Corbis; **180** Monkeys (1346–1337 B.C.). Wallpainting in the tomb of Pharaoh Tutankhamun (1346–1337 B.C.). Tomb of Tutankhamen, Valley of the Kings, Thebes, Egypt. Photo © Erich Lessing/Art Resource, New York; **181** Two daggers (1600–1000 B.C.). *Left:* crescent-shaped handle, copper, 31 cm long. Middle Kingdom. E 22895. *Right:* bronze, 28.8 cm long, New Kingdom. Louvre, Paris. Photo © Erich Lessing/Art Resource, New York (N 2113 B); **182** Icons. Illustrations by Robert Coleman.

Chapter 6
184 *left to right* Pericles bust. © The British Museum; Nok head, front view (500 B.C.–A.D. 200). Rafin Kura, Nok. Terra-cotta, 36 cm high. National Museum, Lagos, Nigeria. Photo © Werner Forman/Art Resource, New York; **185** *top to bottom* Sahara desert. © Photowood Inc./Corbis; Rainforest in Gabon. © Gallo Images/Corbis; Savanna with zebras. © Paul Sprin-gett/Alamy Images; Page from an illuminated manuscript, Marici and her followers (Tang Dynasty). Ink on paper, 24 x 22.5 cm. Musée des Arts Asiatiques-Guimet, Paris. Photo © Ravaux/Réunion des Musées Nationaux/Art Resource, New York; **186** *inset* Courtyard and entrance to Ark of the Covenant Temple. Axum, Ethiopia. Photo © Dave Bartruff/Corbis; 186-187 African pilgrimage. Illustration by Frank Ordaz; **188** Kush pottery. Photo © University of Pennsylvania Museum of Archaeology and Anthropology; **189** Cataract on Upper Nile. © Bojan Brecelj/Corbis; **191** The Great Stelae of Piankhi. Photo © Topham/The Image Works; 192-193 Taharqa sphinx. Photo © The British Museum/HIP/The Image Works; **193** Armlet with winged Goddess Mut, from the treasure of Amanishakheto (100–0 B.C.). Meroe, Pyramide N 6. Gold with glass paste inlay, 4.5 cm high. Aegyptisches Museum, Staatliche Museen zu Berlin, Berlin, Germany. © Bildarchiv Pre-ussischer Kulturbesitz/Art Resource, New York (Inv. Mue 2455); **196** The tallest of the still erect stelae at Aksum (A.D. 300–400). Aksumite. Aksum, Ethiopia. Photo © Werner Forman/Art Resource, New York; **197** National Park in Ethiopia. © Robert Preston/Alamy Images; **199** Crown of Aksum. © Sonia Halliday Photographs; **200** Geéz script scroll. Courtesy of BC Galleries, Melbourne; **201** Girl building pillar. Photo by Sharon Hoogstraten. **202** Terracotta sculpture. © Heini Sch-neebeli/The Bridgeman Art Library; **204** The Sahel and Desertification. Illustration by Stephen R. Wagner; **205** Nok Figure. Private Collection. Photo Joshua Nefsky, New York. Courtesy Entwistle, London; **207** Ngady Amwaash, representing Mweel, sister of the founding ancestor Woot. Kuba culture of Central Zaire. National Museum, Ghana. Photo © Werner Forman/Art Resource, New York; **208** Icons. Illustrations by Robert Coleman.

UNIT 4
212-213 The Great Stupa at Sanchi. Illustration by Roger Stewart; **213** *top to bottom* Shiva. © Burstein Collection/Corbis; Vase fanjia (1650–1066 B.C.). From Anyang, China. Bronze, 31 x 14.5 cm. Musée des Arts Asiatiques-Guimet, Paris, France. Inv. MA 6071. Photo © Richard Lambert/Réunion des Musées Nationaux/Art Resource, New York; Mayan pyramid. The Granger Collection, New York.

Chapter 7
214 *left to right* Indus culture necklace. © Archivo Iconografico, S.A./Corbis; Fragment of a statue from the queen's temple at Deir el-Bahari representing Hatshepsut in the form of Osiris (1470–1490). Egyptian Museum, Cairo, Egypt. Photo © Werner Foreman/Art Resource, New York; **215** *left to right* Alexander the Great, so-called Alexander Azara. Copy (200-100 B.C.) of original bust (320 B.C.). Marble, 65 cm high. Louvre, Paris. Photo © Erich Lessing/Art Resource, New York; Horse Sacrifice coin, reign of Samudra Gupta; Lion coin, reign of Kumar Gupta; Chatra and Couchiglia coins, reign of Chandra Gupta (about 500-400 B.C.). National Museum, New Delhi, India. Photo © Borromeo/Art Resource, New York; 216–217

Sarasvati Earthquake. Illustration by Gino D'Achille/Artist Partners; **218** Harappan royal priest. © Jean-Louis Nou/akg-images; **219** Ganges River. © The Image Bank/Getty Images; **220** Summer and winter monsoons. Illustrations by Gary Hincks; **221** Indus valley pictograph seal. The National Museum, Karachi. © Dagli Orti/The Art Archive; **222-223** Mohenjo-Daro ruins. Mohenjo-Daro, Pakistan. Photo © Borromeo/Art Resource, New York; **223** *left to right* Great bath of Mohenjo-Daro. Mohenjo-Daro, Pakistan. Photo © Borromeo/Art Resource, New York; Terracotta pot and lid (1500–1200 B.C.). National Museum, New Delhi, India. © The Bridgeman Art Library; **224** Indus culture bronze tools. © Angelo Hornak/Corbis; **225** Boy making climate graph. Photo by Sharon Hoogstraten; inset Graph paper with bar graph. Photo by Sharon Hoogstraten; **226** Shiva © Burstein Collection/Corbis; **227** Hindu Kush range. © Grant Dixon/Lonely Planet Images; **229** Sweeper with broom (1846). Photo © The British Library/Topham-HIP/The Image Works; **230** Shri Krishna, Indian school. Private collection. Photo © Dinodia Picture Agency, Bombay, India/Bridgeman Art Library; **232** Pillar of Asoka (273–236 B.C.). Maurya Dynasty. Museum, Samath, Uttar Pradesh, India. Photo © Borromeo/Art Resource, New York; **233** Reclining Buddha. © Lindsay Hebberd/Corbis; **234** Siddhartha Gutama. Bodhgaya, Bihar, India. Photo © DPA/SOA/The Image Works; **235** Indian flag. © Royalty Free/Corbis; **236** Vishnu (1750). Photo © Jean-Louis Nou/akg-images; **238** Exterior view of Vishnu temple (500–400 B.C.). Gupta Dynasty. Vishnu temple, Deogarh, Rajasthan, India. Photo © Borromeo/Art Resource, New York; **239** The Iron Pillar and the Quwwat-ul-Islam Masjid. Delhi, India. © The Bridgeman Art Library; **240** Gandhi. © Peter Ruhe/Hulton Archives/Getty Images; **241** Angkor Wat. © The Image Bank/Getty Images; **242** Dance of the Ramayana during a festival in Bangkok. © C. Walker/Topham/The Image Works; **244** *top to bottom* Harappan seal with yoga pose. © Charles and Josette Lenars/Corbis; Modern yoga. © Jose Luis Pelaez, Inc./Corbis; **245** *top, left to right* Ayurvedic herbs and spices. © Botanica; Modern Ayurvedic treatment. © Thinkstock; *bottom, left to right* Sacred bull. © Philadelphia Museum of Art/Corbis; Indian vegetarian food. © Foodpix; **246** Icons. Illustrations by Robert Coleman.

Chapter 8

248 *left to right* Bronze stag figurine. © Royal Ontario Museum/Corbis; Olmec sitting man. © Veintimilla/akg-images; **249** *left to right* Confucious stone engraving. © akg-images; Roman Colloseum. © Royalty Free/Corbis; **250** *inset* Wooden Confucius. © Royalty Free/Corbis; **250-251** Confucius teaching disciples. Illustration by Eric Robson; **252** Vase fanjia (1650–1066 B.C.). Bronze, 31 x 14.5 cm. From Anyang, China. Musée des Arts Asiatiques-Guimet, Paris. Photo © Richard Lambert/Réunion des Musées Nationaux/Art Resource, New York (Inv. MA 6071); **253** Gobi desert. © Keren Su/China Span; **254** Yangtze River. © Alamy Images; **255** Chinese oracle bone (Shang Dynasty, 1766-1122 B.C.). The engraved characters are the earliest known examples of Chinese script. The bones originally used for divination also provide information about rulers battles folk religion and religious rites. British Museum, London. Photo © Werner Forman/Art Resource, New York; **256** Jade dragon. © Royal Ontario Museum/Corbis; **257** Jade pendant in the shape of a dragon (Qing Dynasty, 1644–1911). This pendant, dating to the Quing dynasty was inspired by an example dating to the Zhou dynasty (1050-221 B.C.). British Museum, London. Photo © HIP/Scala/Art Resource, New York; **259** Confucius with his disciples. © Lauros/Giraudon/The Bridgeman Art Library; **260-261** Ceremony honoring Confucius. © Stone/Getty Images; **261** The Analects. © Steve Raymer/National Geographic Image Collection; **262** Drawing of Confucious. © Bettmann/Corbis; **265** *top to bottom* Woodcut of Confucius. © akg-images; Laozi astride a bull, accompanied by a servant (1600-1700). Chinese scroll painting. Bibliotheque Nationale, Paris. Photo © Snark/Art Resource, New York; **266** Jade Funeral Suit. © Alamy Images; **267** Terracotta soldiers. O. Louis Mazzatenta/National Geographic Image Collection; **268** The Great Wall of China. Photo © Hideo Haga/HAGA/The Image Works; **270** Court women (206 B.C.–A.D. 220), François Guénet. Private collection. © François Guénet/akg-images; **271** Flying horse, one leg resting on a swallow (Eastern Han Dynasty). Bronze figure, 34.5 x 45 cm. Excavated 1969 at Wu-Wai, Kansu, China. National Museum, Beijing. Photo © Erich Lessing/Art Resource, New York; **272-273** Terracotta soldier on its side. O. Louis Mazzatenta/National Geographic Image Collection; **274-275** Terracotta army in pit two. O. Louis Mazzatenta/National Geographic Image Collection; **275** Terracotta horses for army. O. Louis Mazzatenta/National Geographic Image Collection; **276** Tang silk tapestry of Buddha. Photo © 2000 The British Museum; **277** Modern silk merchant. © Alamy Images; **278** Silk Road, Afghanistan. © Alamy Images; **281** Girl with notebook and books. Photo by Sharon Hoogstraten; **282** Icons. Illustrations by Robert Coleman.

Chapter 9

284 *top to bottom* Olmec wrestler. © Giraudon/The Bridgeman Art Library; Sphinx with pyramid. © Corbis; **285** *top to bottom* Mayan rain god. © Robert Harding World Imagery/Alamy Images; Chavin art. © Ken Walsh/The Bridgeman Art Library; Nazca lines. © Roman Soumar/Corbis; Emperor Liu Ban. © The Art Archive/British Library; **286** *inset* The jade burial mask of Pacal (Classic Maya, A.D. 600–700) found in the Temple of the Inscriptions at Palenque. Museo Nacional de Antropologia, Mexico City, D.F., Mexico. Photo © Werner Forman/Art Resource, New York; **286-287** King Pacal II and his Sons. Illustration by Philip Howe; **288** Quetzal bird. © Michael Maslan Historic Photographs/Corbis; **289** Amazon with people. © Owen Franken/Corbis; **291** *top to bottom* High region of Andes mountains. © The Image Bank/Getty Images; Andes valley region. © Photofrenetic/Alamy Images; **293** Maize. © Macduff Everton/Corbis; **294** Jaguar pendant. Photo © Dumbarton Oaks; **295** Gargoyle at Chavin de Huantar. Photo © Charles and Josette Lenars/Corbis. **297** *top to bottom* Nazca lines hummingbird. © Stockfolio/Alamy Images; Nazca lines parrot. © David Nunuk/Science Photo Library; **298** Moche jug. © Nathan Benn/Corbis; **299** A yellow, blue and red wollen poncho (A.D. 600–700). Nazca/Huari. From the South coast of Peru. Dallas Museum of Art, Dallas, Texas. Photo © Werner Forman/Art Resource, New York; **300** Olmec jade figure. Justin Kerr/The Brooklyn Museum; **302** *inset* Monolithic Olmec head found near La Venta. La Venta, Mexico. Photo © SEF/Art Resource, New York; **302-303** Colossal Olmec head. © Jean-Pierre Courau/The Bridgeman Art Library; **303** Olmec were-jaguar (900–300 B.C.). Photo © Dumbarton Oaks; **305** Girl and boy making time capsule. Photo by Sharon Hoogstraten; **306** Mosaic mask, a funerary gift from tomb 160. It was laid over the face of the dead dignitary to adorn him during his voyage through the Underworld. Jadeite, diopsite, shells, conch-shells, mother of pearl, 34.5 cm high. Inv. 11082, Maya. Tikal, El Peten, Guatemala. Museo Nacional de Arqueologia, Guatemala City, Guatemala. Photo © Erich Lessing/Art

Resource, New York; **307** Tikal and surrounding jungle. © Giraudon/The Bridgeman Art Library; **309** Stele. © The Granger Collection, New York; **310** *clockwise from top left* Mayan pyramid. © The Granger Collection, New York; Mayan heiroglyphs. © Museo Nacional de Antropologia, Mexico City, Mexico/Giraudon/Bridgeman Art Library; Egyptian heiroglyphs. © Roger Wood/Corbis; Egyptian pyramid. © Giraudon/The Bridgeman Art Library; **311** Maya today. © Danny Lehman/Corbis; **312-313** Illustrations by Inklink, Florence/Virgil Pomfret; **314** Icons. Illustrations by Robert Coleman; **315** Mayan nobleman. © Justin Kerr.

UNIT 5

318-319 Visiting the Temple of Solomon. Illustration by David Bergen; **319** *top to bottom* Hanukkah menorah for the synagogue (1700–1800). Eastern Europe. Brass: cast, cut and engraved. Photo © The Jewish Museum, New York/Art Resource, New York; Apollo of Belvedere, detail of head. Roman copy after Greek original (about 350–320 B.C.). Museo Pio Clementino, Vatican Museums, Vatican State. Photo © Scala/Art Resource, New York; The Parthenon. Photo © Dagli Orti/The Art Archive.

Chapter 10

320 *top to bottom* Russian icon (Abraham and Sarah) (1600–1700). Open Air Museum, Kizhi Island, Russia. Photo © Erich Lessing/Art Resource, New York; Olmec jade head. The Granger Collection, New York; **321** *left to right* Urn from Monte Alban. Zapotec culture. Museo Nacional de Antropologia, Mexico City, D.F. Photo © SEF/Art Resource, New York; Bust of Titus. © Gianni Dagli Orti/Corbis; **322-323** Ruth and Naomi. Illustration by Christian Hook; **324** Torah tik (1919–1925). Iran. The Jewish Museum, New York. Photo © The Jewish Museum, New York/Art Resource, New York; **326** Peregrination of the family of Abraham, Giovanni Benedetto Castiglione. Palazzo Rosso, Genoa, Italy. Photo © Scala/Art Resource, New York; **327** Moses with the Tablets of the Law, Guido Reni. Galleria Borghese, Rome, Italy. Photo © Scala/Art Resource, New York; **328** Deborah. The Granger Collection, New York; **330-331** Moses Parting the Red Sea. Private Collection. Photo © Dagli Orti/The Art Archive; **332** Crossing the Red Sea. The Granger Collection, New York; **333** King in a chariot. Detail from lid of chest of Tutankhamun (Eighteenth dynasty, 1357–1349 B.C.). The king in his chariot hunts desert animals. Stuccoed wood. Egyptian Museum, Cairo, Egypt. © Werner Forman/Art Resource, New York; **334** Mezuzah. © Jewish Museum, London/The Bridgeman Art Library; **335** Sheep in Galilee. © Richard T. Nowitz/Corbis; **336** David (1623-1624), Gian Lorenzo Bernini. Left side, post-restoration. Marble. Galleria Borghese, Rome, Italy. Photo © Scala/Art Resource, New York; **338** Cyrus the Great. The Granger Collection, New York; **339** Pomegranate. Photo © Adar Media/Corbis; **341** King David and King Solomon, detail from "The Resurrection" (1000–1100). Byzantine mosaic. Monastery Church, Hosios Loukas, Greece. Photo © Erich Lessing/Art Resource, New York; **342** Menorah for the synagogue (1700–1800). Brass: cast, cut and engraved. Eastern Europe. The Jewish Museum, New York. Photo © The Jewish Museum, New York/Art Resource, New York; **343** View of ruins (A.D. 150–200). Synagogue, Capernaum, Israel. Photo © Art Resource, New York; **344-345** Masada. © Nathan Benn/Corbis; **346** Boy and rabbi studying the Torah. © Celestial Panoramas/Alamy Images; **347** Girl and boy drawing a fortress. Photo by Sharon Hoogstraten; **348** Icons. Illustrations by Robert Coleman.

Chapter 11

350 *top to bottom* Tiara from Grave III (about 1600–1500 B.C.). Mycenaean. National Archaeological Museum, Athens, Greece. Photo © The Bridgeman Art Library; Olmec sitting man. © Veintimilla/akg-images; **351** *left to right* Gold ring with ornaments (450–400 B.C.). From Ezerovo near Parvomai. Diam. 2.7 cm. Archaeological Museum, Sofia, Bulgaria. Photo © Erich Lessing/Art Resource, New York; Head of a Buddha, from Angkor (Khmer, A.D. 1100–1200). Musée des Arts Asiatiques-Guimet, Paris, France. Photo © Erich Lessing/Art Resource, New York; **352** *inset* Spartan warrior, possibly Leonidas (490–480 B.C.). Archaeological Museum, Sparta, Greece. Photo © Vanni/Art Resource, New York; **352-353** Persian Wars. Illustration by Frank Orday Studio; **354** Fish plate (350–300 B.C.). Red figure vase painting. Louvre, Paris, France. Photo © Réunion des Musées Nationaux/Art Resource, New York; **355** Greek coastline. © Alamy Images; **357** Greek ship. The Granger Collection, New York; **358** Sign language. Seth Perlman/AP/Wide World Photos; **359** Athena/owl coin. The Granger Collection, New York; **360** Heracles leading Alcestris out of the Underworld (about 525–520 B.C.). Black figure amphora, 42.4 cm high. From Vulci. Inv. F 60. Louvre, Paris. Photo © Hervé Lewandowski/Réunion des Musées Nationaux/Art Resource, New York; **361** Mt. Olympus. © Robert Gill; Papilio/Corbis; **362-363** Statue of Zeus (about 500 B.C.). Museo Archeologico Nazionale. Photo © Andrea Baguzzi/akg-images; **363** *clockwise from top* Wheelchair race, Olympic games. AP/Wide World Photos; Apollo of Belvedere, detail of head (about 350–320 B.C.). Roman copy after Greek original. Museo Pio Clementino, Vatican Museums, Vatican State. Photo © Scala/Art Resource, New York; Athena with her owl in flight (about 360 B.C.). *To the right,* Poseidon with the trident. Detail of a a red figure crater. Etruscan vase. Louvre, Paris. Photo © Hervé Lewandowski/Réunion des Musées Nationaux/Art Resource, New York (Inv. CA 7426); Demeter (A.D. 0–100). Carthage, Tunisia. Photo © Jean-Louis Nou/akg-images; **364** "Troy" film still. © Bureau L.A. Collections/Simon Smith-Hutchon/Warner Brothers/Corbis; **365** Cyclops. © Bridgeman Art Library; **366** The Atalanta Lekythos (500–490 B.C.), attributed to Douris. The Cleveland Museum of Art. Leonard C. Hanna, Jr., Fund 1966.114. Photo © The Cleveland Museum of Art 2004; **367** Artemis. The Granger Collection, New York; **368-369** Acropolis at sunset. © Stone/Getty Images; **368** Statue of Atalanta. © C. M. Dixon. **369** Golden apple. © Creatas/PictureQuest; **370** Water timer. Photo © The American School of Classical Studies at Athens. **371** Ruins of Agora. © Dagli Orti/The Art Archive; **372** Athens aerial. © akg-images; **374** Bust of Solon (630–560 B.C.). Greek. Uffizi, Florence, Italy. Photo © Scala/Art Resource, New York; **375** *counter-clockwise from top* Solid ballot. Photo © The American School of Classical Studies at Athens; Hollow ballot. Photo © The American School of Classical Studies at Athens. Ballot box. Photo © The American School of Classical Studies at Athens; **376** Ostrakon. Greek potsherd. Agora Museum, Athens, Greece. Photo © Scala/Art Resource, New York; **377** Girl and boy making vocabulary cards. Photo by Sharon Hoogstraten. **378** Athena wearing crested helmet and peplos (340 B.C.). Archaeological Museum, Piraeus. Photo © Dagli Orti/Archaeological Museum

Piraeus/Art Archive; **379** Attacking warrior (510–500 B.C.). Formerly part of a vessel. Greek bronze, from Dodona, 12.8 cm high. Antikensammlung, Staatlone Museen zu Berlin, Berlin, Germany. Photo © Johannes Laurentius/Bildarchiv Preussischer Kulturbesitz/Art Resource, New York (Inv. Misc 7470); **380** *top to bottom* Barracks. © Anders Ryman/Corbis; Lycurgus Demonstrates the Meaning of Education (1660–1661), Caesar Beotius van Everdingen. Alkmaar. Oil on canvas. Photo © Stedelijk Museum/akg-images; **381** Girls playing knucklebones. The Granger Collection, New York; **384** Fish seller. Illustration by Roger Stewart; **384-385** Life in the Agora. Illustrations by Roger Stewart; **386** Icons. Illustrations by Robert Coleman.

Chapter 12

388 *top to bottom* Oracle at Delphi. © Alamy Images; Parthenon. Todd Gipstein/National Geographic Image Collection; Jerusalem and temple. The Granger Collection, New York; **389** *top to bottom* Lion statues at Delos. © Alamy Images; Portrait statuette of Socrates (about 200 B.C.–A.D. 100). Athenian statesman. Greek. British Museum, London, Great Britian. Photo © HIP/Scala/Art Resource, New York; Olmec artifact. © Veintimilla/akg-images; **390** *inset* Bust of Pericles (about 495–429 B.C.). Museo Pio Clementino, Vatican Museums. Photo © Scala/Art Resource, New York; **390-391** Pericles and others having discussion. Illustration by Ezra Tucker; **392** Caryatids. © Alamy Images; **393** Modern Acropolis aerial. © Digital Vision; **394** Pericles engraving. © akg-images; **396** Parthenon. © Dagli Orti/The Art Archive; **398** Spartan soldier statue. © Alamy Images; **399** Triera, Rafael Monleon y Torres. Watercolor. © Museo Naval Madrid/Dagli Orti/The Art Archive; **400** Pericles, Athens politician (1852), Philipp von Foltz. Photo © akg-images; **403** Boy making a storyboard. Photo by Sharon Hoogstraten; **404** Philip of Macedonia. © Chiaramonti Museum Vatican/Dagli Orti/The Art Archive; **405** Mosaic of the battle between Alexander the Great and Darius III. © Archaeological Museum Naples/Dagli Orti/The Art Archive; inset Alexander the Great mosaic detail. © Archaeological Museum Naples/Dagli Orti/The Art Archive; **406-407** Equestrian portrait of Alexander the Great in combat. Museo Archeologico Nazionale, Naples. © Alinari/Art Resource, New York; **408** Aristotle teaching astronomers (1200–1250). Al-Mubashshir, Mukhtar al-Hikan (The better sentences and most precise dictions). Saljup dynasty. Topkapi Palace Museum, Istanbul, Turkey. Photo © Ms. Ahmet III/Giraudon/Art Resource (3206); **409** Alexandria lighthouse (1800–1899). The Granger Collection, New York; **410** Nike of Samothrace, goddess of victory (about 190 B.C.). Hellenistic. Louvre, Paris. Photo © Erich Lessing/Art Resource, New York; **411** Greek theatre. © Jon Davison/Lonely Planet Images; **412** *top to bottom* Greek comedy mask. © Alfio Garozzo/akg-images; Greek tragedy mask. © akg-images; **413** *clockwise from top* Building in Montpellier, France. Photo © Ric Ergenbright/Corbis; Corinthian column. © Corbis; Doric column. © Alamy Images; Ionic column. © John Hios/akg-images; **414** *left to right* Bust of Plato. Musei Capitolini, Rome. Photo © SEF/Art Resource, New York; Portrait statuette of Socrates (about 200 B.C.–A.D. 100). Athenian statesman. Greek. British Museum, London, Great Britain. Photo © HIP/Scala/Art Resource, New York; **415** *top to bottom* Death of Socrates. © Francis G. Mayer/Corbis; Aristotle. Roman sculpture after Greek original. Galleria Spada, Rome. Photo © Alinari/Art Resource, New York; **417** Archimede's screw. The Granger Collection, New York; **418** *top to bottom* Myron of Athens, Discobolus (500–400 B.C.). Museo Nazionale Romano (Terme di Diocleziano), Rome. Photo © Alinari/Art Resource, New York; Cathy Freeman. © Le Segretian Pascal/Corbis; **419** *clockwise from top left* Temple of Hephaestus (600–500 B.C.). Athens, Greece. © Index/Bridgeman Art Library; Lincoln memorial. © Angelo Hornak/Corbis; Greek allotment machine. © Agora Museum, Athens/Dagli Orti/The Art Archive; Jury. © Bob Daemmrich/The Image Works. **420** Icons. Illustrations by Robert Coleman.

UNIT 6

424 The Roman Colosseum and the Games. Illustration by Frank Ordaz; **425** Colloseum. Photo © ML Sinbaldi/Corbis; Reliquary cross of Justinian (A.D. 500–600). Byzantine. Museum of the Treasury, St. Peter's Basilica, Vatican State. Photo © Scala/Art Resource, New York; Justinian I with crown and sceptre. Mosaic. S. Apollinare in Classe, Ravenna, Italy. Photo © Erich Lessing/Art Resource, New York.

Chapter 13

426 *top to bottom* She-wolf. © Araldo de Luca/Corbis; Greek temple at twilight. © Getty Images; **427** *left to right* Horse (Han dynasty). Funerary terracotta figurine. Museo d'Arte Orientale, Rome. Photo © Scala/Art Resource, New York; Cameo showing the young Emperor Augustus (63 B.C.–A.D. 14). From the Treasury of Boscoreale near Pompeii. Louvre, Paris. Photo © Erich Lessing/Art Resource, New York; **428** Julius Caesar, Roman statesman. Green slate bust, 41 cm high. Antikensammlung, Staatliche Museen zu Berlin, Berlin, Germany. Photo © Juergen Liepe/Bildarchiv Preussischer Kulturbesitz/Art Resource, New York (Inv. SK 342); **428-429** The Assassination of Caesar. Illustration by Eric Robson; **430** Detail of Rome with the Tiber and the Anio Fountain, Giovanni Ceccarini. Photo © John Heseltine/Corbis; **431** Palatine Hill. Photo © Scala/Art Resource, New York; **433** Tiber river. © John and Lisa Merrill/Corbis; **434** Farm. © Gary Braasch/Corbis; **436** Lucius Junuis Brutus. © Araldo de Luca/Corbis; **437** Roman Forum. Dave Bartruff/Corbis; **438** Cicero Denouncing Catalina Before the Senate (1800–1899), Cesare Maccari. Wallpainting. Palazzo Madama, Rome, Italy. Photo © Scala/Art Resource, New York; **441** Laurel wreath. © DK Images. Dorling Kindersley Ltd; **442** Imperial eagle figurine from a horse's harness (A.D. 0–100). Ensign bearer. Bronze. Kunsthistorisches Museum, Vienna, Austria. Photo © Erich Lessing/Art Resource, New York; **443** Colosseum today. © ML Sinbaldi/Corbis; **444** Portrait of Caesar. The Granger Collection, New York; **445** Portrait bust of Cicero. Uffizi, Florence, Italy. Photo © Alinari/Art Resource, New York; **446** Roman coins. The Granger Collection, New York; **447** Augustus in a toga. Roman sculpture. Uffizi, Florence, Italy. © Alinari/Art Resource, New York; **449** SPQR sewer grate. Rome, Italy. Photo © Timothy McCarthy/Art Resource, New York; **450-451** Illustrations by Roger Stewart; **452** Cave canem. Pompeiian mosaic. House of the Tragic Poet, Pompeii, Italy. Photo © Scala/Art Resource, New York; **453** View of Hadrian's Villa. Hadrian's Villa, Tivoli, Italy. Photo © Werner Forman/Art Resource, New York; **454** Portrait of a Young Girl (A.D. 0–100). Museo e Gallerie Nazionali di Capodimonte, Naples, Italy. © Lauros/Giraudon/Bridgeman Art Library; **455** Statue of Jupiter. Photo © Araldo de Luca/Corbis; **456-457** Public baths. Illustration by John James; **459** Boy making a mosaic. Photo by Sharon Hoogstraten; **460** Icons. Illustration by Robert Coleman; **461** Relief from Trajan's Column. Column of Trajan, Rome, Italy. Photo © Alinari/Art Resource, New York;

Chapter 14

462 Deer-headed anthropomorphic figure which could represent a shaman undergoing transformation. Peru (north coast), Mochica culture. British Museum, London, Great Britain. Photo © Werner Forman/Art Resource, New York; **463** *left to right* Flying horse, one leg resting on a swallow (Eastern Han Dynasty). Excavated in 1969 at Wu-Wai, Kansu China. Bronze figure, 34.5 x 45 cm. National Museum, Beijing. Photo © Erich Lessing/Art Resource, New York; Colossal bust of Emperor Constantine the Great and other fragments. Palazzo dei Conservatori, Rome, Italy. © Vanni/Art Resource, New York; **464** *inset* Coin of Nero. © Private Collection/The Bridgeman Art Library; **464-465** The burning of Rome. Illustration by Melvyn Grant; **466** Reliquary cross of Justinian (A.D. 500–599). Byzantine. Museum of the Treasury, St. Peter's Basilica, Vatican State. Photo © Scala/Art Resource, New York; **467** Church of the Nativity in Bethlehem. © Celestial Panoramas, Ltd./Alamy Images; **469** The Sermon on the Mount (1295), La Somme Le Roy. Vellum. Bibliotheque Mazarine, Paris, France. © Bridgeman Art Library; **470** Tomb with rolling stone. © Richard Nowitz Photos; **471** Fish with cross, from the Coptic cemetery at Ermant (A.D. 300–399). Limestone relief. Photo © Erich Lessing/Art Resource, New York (Inv. MA 3034); **472-474** Stained glass. From The Story of the Bible in Stained Glass: Christ Church Windows by W. Robert Johnstone and R. Theodore Lutz. Art by Russell Goodman, C.M., and Goodman-Zissoff Studio. Photography by Grant Rushton. Courtesy of Christ Church. The United Church of Canada. Mississauga, Ontario. **476** Communion cup. The Granger Collection, New York; **477** City of Ephesus. © Michael Nicholson/Corbis; **478** *left to right* Nativity (about 1500), Sandro Botticelli. Canvas. The Granger Collection, New York; Mosaic of St. Paul. Photo © Alamy Images; **479** Cruciform page, frontispiece to the Gospel of St. Matthew (A.D. 800–900). Lambeth Palace Library, London. Photo © Bridgeman Art Library; Colossal bust of Constantine the Great and other fragments. Palazzo dei Conservatori, Rome. Photo © Vanni/Art Resource, New York; **480** Portrait of St. Paul, Pompeo Batoni. Basildon Park, Berkshire, Great Britain. Photo © National Trust/Art Resource, New York; **481** A ship, symbol of life, with lowered sails (A.D. 0–50), Naevoleia Tyche. Relief on the mausoleum of C. Munatius Faustus, built by his wife Naevoleia Tyche. From the west side of Via dei sepolcri, Pompeii. Mausoleum of C. Munatius, Rome. Photo © Erich Lessing/Art Resource, New York; **482** Bronze statue of Valentinian I, called The Colossos (A.D. 364–375). Late Roman. Barletta, Italy. Photo © Scala/Art Resource, New York; **483** Rome with St. Peter's dome. © Dennis Degnan/Corbis; **484** Burial niches with fresco "Christ, ruler of the World" (Pantocrator), as followed in Byzantine pattern of the time (800–600 B.C.). Catacomb of S. Callisto, Rome. Photo © Erich Lessing/Art Resource, New York; **485** Constantine mosaic. © The Bridgeman Art Library; **487** Open book. Photo by Sharon Hoogstraten; **487** Student making a pie graph. Photo by Sharon Hoogstraten; **488** Icons. Illustrations by Robert Coleman.

Chapter 15

490 *left to right* Marcus Aurelius relief, Mino da Fiesole. Marble. Bargello, Florence, Italy. © Bridgeman Art Library; Tallest of the still erect stelae at Axum (A.D. 300–499), Axumite. © Werner Forman/Art Resource, New York; **491** Kublai Khan. The Granger Collection, New York; **491** Mayan temple. The Granger Collection, New York; **492** *inset* Roman soldier on horseback attacking a fallen Barbarian. Bronze figurine from a horse's harness, 12 x 9.5 cm. Kunsthistorisches Museum, Vienna, Austria. Photo © Erich Lessing/Art Resource, New York; **492-493** Arrival of the Visigoths. Illustration by Frank Ordaz; **494** Trajan's Column. © Russell Mountford/Lonely Planet Images; **495** Hadrian's Wall. © Sandro Vannini/Corbis; **496** The Tetrarches (A.D. 476–1453). Porpyry. South Marco, Venice, Italy. Photo © Alinari/Art Resource, New York; **497** Colossal head of Constantine the Great. Musei Capitolini, Rome. Photo © Werner Forman/Art Resource, New York; **499** Three students holding a debate. Photo by Sharon Hoogstraten; **500** Ostrogothic jewelry (A.D. 450–550). Photo © The British Museum/Topham-HIP/The Image Works; **501** Istanbul. © Harvey Lloyd/Taxi/Getty Images; **502** Germanic skull. Photo © Archäologisches Landesmuseum der Christian-Albrechts-Universität, Schloss Gottorf, Schleswig, Germany; **504** *left to right* Figurine of Roman Legionnaire. Bronze. Photo © The British Museum; Striding Infantryman (221–206 B.C.), Qin dynasty. Courtesy of the Cultural Relics Bureau, Beijing and The Metropolitan Museum of Art, New York; **507** End of the Roman Empire. The Granger Collection, New York; **508** Justinian I with crown and sceptre. Mosaic. S. Apollinare in Classe, Ravenna, Italy. Photo © Erich Lessing/Art Resource, New York; **509** Hagia Sophia. © H. Spichtinger/zefa; **510** Empress Theodora. © Dagli Orti/The Art Archive; **512** *left to right* Roman cross (1100–1199). Back of walrus ivory cross from Bury St. Edmunds, England. The Granger Collection, New York; Byzantine cross (A.D. 900–1000). Reliquary of the True cross. Constantinople. Treasury, Cathedral, Limburg an der Lahn, Germany. Photo © Werner Forman/Art Resource, New York; **513** Lion of St. Mark's (A.D. 500–600). Bronze sculpture. S. Marco, Venice, Italy. Photo © Cameraphoto/Art Resource, New York; **514** Praetorian guard bas-relief. © Bridgeman Art Library; **515** Mosaic from Izmir. Getty News Services. (#372147_06); **517** Roman aqueduct. © Miles Ertman/masterfile/zefa; **518** Cross-section of a Roman road. Illustration by Peter Bull; **520** *top to bottom* Pantheon engraving. © Historical Picture Archive/Corbis; U.S. Capitol. © Joseph Sohm/Alamy Images; **521** *clockwise from top left* Roman road photo. © Corbis; Highway interchange aerial. © Kevin Fleming/Corbis; St. Peter catalan (1150). Os de Tremp. Photo © akg-images. Pope John Paul II overlooking St. Peter's square. Photo Arturo Mari/AP/Wide World Photos; **522** Icons. Illustrations by Robert Coleman.

McDougal Littell has made every effort to locate the copyright holders of all copyrighted material in this book and to make full acknowledgment for its use. Omissions brought to our attention will be corrected in a subsequent edition.